S0-BJK-348

THE OLD TESTAMENT

books of poetry from 26 translations

THE OLD TESTAMENT books of poetry from 26 translations

CURTIS VAUGHAN, Th. D.

general editor

ZONDERVAN BIBLE PUBLISHERS

OF THE ZONDERVAN CORPORATION
GRAND RAPIDS, MICHIGAN

The Old Testament Books of Poetry From 26 Translations

Library of Congress Catalog Card Number 67—22689

Printed in the United States of America.

Second Printing—June 1976—5000 copies

CONTENTS

INTRODUCTION

In the prologue of the Paris edition of the 1538 Coverdale diglot (in Latin and English), Miles Coverdale wrote of the value of differing translations of the Scriptures:

> Now for thy part, most gentle reader, take in good worth that I here offer thee with a good will, and let this present translation be no prejudice to the other that out of the Greek have been translated afore, or shall be hereafter. For if thou open thine eyes and consider well the gift of the Holy Ghost therein, thou shalt see that *one translation declareth, openeth and illustrateth another, and that in many cases one is a plain commentary unto another.*

The Old Testament Books of Poetry From 26 Translations is sent forth in the firm belief that this is true.

The Bible which has enjoyed the most widespread and lasting acceptance in the English speaking world is the King James Version. It is marked by simplicity, dignity, and power of statement, and has for centuries been greatly used of God to nurture the faith of His people. But for all the merits of the King James Version the modern Bible reader finds it increasingly difficult to understand its archaic style and diction.

The aim of the present volume is to clarify the meaning of the King James Version by the use of other translations of the biblical text. These serve somewhat as a commentary on the text of the older translation.

The King James Version is the base for this work, and it is the only translation which is quoted in its entirety. Other translations are included only when they differ significantly from the King James. Sometimes only a few words of a given translation of a single passage require quotation. In such instances, omitted material is indicated by ellipses marks (. . .). The text of the King James Version is set in bold face type, while other translations quoted appear under the King James in roman type.

All marks of punctuation in the King James Version are retained, but in other translations the punctuation marks at the end of the quoted phrase or clause are, as a rule, omitted. An exception to this is made whenever the punctuation mark seems to be required for complete understanding of the quotation.

Special styles of print (such as italics and bold face type) used in some of the versions are not reproduced. Because the use of such devices varies so widely, it is felt that these might be a hindrance rather than a help in using this volume. For example, some translations use italics for words which have no equivalent in the original text; others use italics to bring out emphasis. In reading a complete copy of any given version, these are readily understood and are generally quite helpful, but they would not be intelligible in this work. Had they been reproduced here, a special note explaining their significance would be required for each separate entry.

The reader will observe that the translators at times differ sharply in their renderings of the same passage. Often this simply indicates a difference of opinion in their understanding of the meaning of the original text. In other cases, however, the difference may be accounted for by the fact that the translators were not rendering the same text. Monsignor Ronald Knox's version, for example, is based on the Latin Vulgate, and George N. Lamsa has translated the Aramaic text. The Septuagint, of course, is a Greek translation of the Hebrew text, and what has been used in this volume is an English rendering of the Greek.

Wide divergencies of rendering are much more frequently found in the Old Testament than in the New. The reader should remember that at many points the Hebrew Old Testament presents great and ancient textual difficulties. Lacunae in the earliest form of the Septuagint reveal that even the Jewish scholars of Alexandria found some of the text baffling. Where such uncertainty exists, each translator must decide for himself which reading is nearest the original. "A translator of Holy Scripture," wrote Henry Alford, "must be absolutely colorless; ready to sacrifice the choicest text, and the plainest proof of doctrine, if the words are not those of what he is constrained in his conscience to receive as God's testimony."

The General Editor is pleased to acknowledge his indebtedness to Mr. Jack Hamm of Dallas, Texas, and to Dr. William H. Rossell, formerly Professor of Old Testament at Southwestern Baptist Theological Seminary, Fort Worth, Texas. It was Mr. Hamm who conceived the idea of a multi-version Bible, and who in many other ways worked untiringly to make it a reality. Dr. Rossell laid the groundwork for the New Testament volume, and until his untimely death in July, 1964 was the General Editor. It is a source of deep regret that so soon after its initiation the work was deprived of his scholarly insight and linguistic proficiency.

The prayer of all who have shared in the labor of bringing this book to completion is that God may seal it with His approval and be pleased to use it for the honor and glory of His name.

CURTIS VAUGHAN
General Editor

ACKNOWLEDGMENTS

Appreciation is expressed to the publishers for permission to reprint selections from the following translations of the Bible:

Baker Book House. *Young's Literal Translation of the Holy Bible* by Robert Young.

Cambridge University Press. *The Holy Bible: Revised Version.*

Cambridge University Press and E. P. Dutton and Company. *The Bible in Basic English.*

Division of Christian Education, National Council of the Churches of Christ in the United States of America. *The Revised Standard Version of the Bible.* Copyright © 1946, 1952 by the Division of Christian Education of the National Council of the Churches of Christ in the United States of America.

Doubleday and Company, Inc. *The Jerusalem Bible.* Copyright © 1966 by Darton, Longman, and Todd, Ltd. and Doubleday and Company, Inc.

Harper and Row Publishers, inc. and Hodder and Stoughton, Ltd. *A New Translation of the Bible* by James Moffatt. Copyright © 1954 by James Moffatt. Used by permission of Harper and Row, Inc. and Hodder and Stoughton, Ltd.

A. J. Holman Company, a subsidiary of J. B. Lippincott Company. *The Holy Bible From Ancient Eastern Manuscripts* by George M. Lamsa. Copyright © 1940, 1957, 1961 by A. J. Holman Company.

The Jewish Publication Society. *The Holy Scriptures According to the Masoretic Text: A New Translation.* Copyright © 1955 by The Jewish Publication Society of America.

The Jewish Publication Society. *The Torah: The Five Books of Moses.*

P. J. Kenedy and Sons. *The New American Bible.* Copyright © 1970 by the Confraternity of Christian Doctrine, Washington, D. C.

Kregel Publications. *The Emphasized Bible: A New Translation* by J. B. Rotherham.

The MacMillan Company. *Four Prophets: Amos, Hosea, First Isaiah, Micah* by J. B. Phillips. Copyright © 1963 by J. B. Phillips.

Oxford University Press and Cambridge University Press. *The New English Bible.* Copyright © 1961 by The Delegates of the Oxford University Press and The Syndics of the Cambridge University Press. Reprinted by permission.

Sheed and Ward, Inc. and Burns and Oats, Ltd. *The Holy Bible: A Translation From the Latin Vulgate in the Light of the Hebrew and Greek Originals* by Monsignor Ronald Knox. Copyright © 1954 by Sheed and Ward, Inc., New York, with the kind permission of His Eminence, the Cardinal Archbishop of Westminster and Burns and Oates, Ltd.

Tyndale House Publishers. *The Living Bible: Paraphrased* by Kenneth Taylor. Copyright © 1971 by Tyndale House Publishers.

University of Chicago Press. *The Bible: An American Translation* by J. M. Powis Smith and Edgar J. Goodspeed. Copyright © 1935 by the University of Chicago.

Zondervan Publishing House. *The Amplified Bible.* Copyright © 1965 by Zondervan Publishing House.

Zondervan Publishing House. *The Modern Language Bible: The New Berkeley Version in Modern English.* Copyright © 1945, 1959, 1969 by Zondervan Publishing House.

Zondervan Publishing House. *The Psalms for Today: A New Translation From the Hebrew Into Current English* by R. K. Harrison. Included in *Norlie's Simplified New Testament.* Copyright © 1961 by Zondervan Publishing House.

AN EXPLANATION OF ABBREVIATIONS

The complete text of the King James Version appears in boldface type. The abbreviations used here may be identified by the following code:

- AAT — The Bible: An American Translation (J. M. Powis Smith and Edgar J. Goodspeed)
- ABPS — The Holy Bible Containing the Old and New Testaments: An Improved Edition (American Baptist Publication Society)
- ASV — The American Standard Version
- JPS — The Holy Scriptures According to the Masoretic Text: A New Translation (The Jewish Publication Society)
- NAB — The New American Bible
- NEB — The New English Bible
- PBV — From the Psalms in the Book of Common Prayer of the Anglican Church
- RSV — The Revised Standard Version
- RV — The Holy Bible: Revised Version
- YLT — Young's Literal Translation of the Holy Bible (Robert Young)
- Amp — The Amplified Bible
- Bas — The Bible in Basic English
- Ber — The Modern Language Bible: The New Berkeley Version in Modern English
- DeW — Praise-Songs of Israel: A Rendering of the Book of Psalms (John DeWitt)
- Har — The Psalms for Today: A New Translation From the Hebrew Into Current English (R. K. Harrison)
- Jerus — The Jerusalem Bible
- Knox — The Holy Bible: A Translation From the Latin Vulgate in the Light of the Hebrew and Greek Originals (Monsignor Ronald Knox)
- Lam — The Holy Bible From Ancient Eastern Manuscripts (George Lamsa)
- Mof — A New Translation of the Bible (James Moffatt)
- Phi — Four Prophets: Amos, Hosea, First Isaiah, Micah (J. B. Phillips)
- Rhm — The Emphasized Bible: A New Translation (J. B. Rotherham)
- Sept — The Septuagint (Charles Thomson)
- Sprl — A Translation of the Old Testament Scriptures From the Original Hebrew (Helen Spurrell)
- Tay — The Living Bible: Paraphrased (Kenneth Taylor)
- Torah — The Torah: The Five Books of Moses

EDITORS

GENERAL EDITOR

CURTIS VAUGHAN, TH. D.

CONTRIBUTING EDITORS TO THIS VOLUME

E. M. BLAIKLOCK, LITT. D.
Emeritus Professor of Classics,
University of Auckland, Auckland, New Zealand

HENRY R. MOELLER, TH. D.
Central Baptist Theological Seminary
Kansas City, Kansas

CURTIS VAUGHAN, TH. D.
Southwestern Baptist Theological Seminary
Fort Worth, Texas

THE OLD TESTAMENT
books of poetry from 26 translations

THE BOOK OF JOB

CHAPTER 1

1. There was a man in the land of Uz, whose name was Job; and that man was perfect and upright,

. . . and that man was blameless and upright — Rhm

. . . and that man was wholehearted and upright — JPS

. . . a man of integrity and upright — Ber

. . . a man of truth and integrity — Sept

. . . a sound and honest man — Jerus

and one that feared God, and eschewed evil.

and one who revered God and avoided evil — Rhm

and one that feared God and turned away from evil — ASV

and one who feared God and shunned evil — ABPS

just, pious, and who abstained from everything that was evil — Sept

who feared God and set his face against wrongdoing — NEB

2. And there were born unto him seven sons and three daughters.

3. His substance also was seven thousand sheep, and three thousand camels, and five hundred yoke of oxen, and five hundred she asses, and a very great household;

. . . and very many servants — ABPS

. . . and a body of servants exceeding large — Rhm

so that this man was the greatest of all the men of the east.

And this man was great, above all the sons of the East — ABPS

And this man was wealthy above all the sons of the east — Sprl

in all the East none was Job's rival — Knox

This man was indeed a man of mark among all the people of the East — Jerus

He was also a man of illustrious birth, among the people of the east — Sept

He was, in fact, the richest cattleman in that entire area — Tay

4. And his sons went and feasted in their houses, every one his day;

Now his sons went and held a feast, at the house of each, on his day — ABPS

Now his sons were wont to go and make a banquet, at the house of each one upon his day — Rhm

His sons used to go and feast in the house of each on his day [birthday] — Amp

His sons regularly went to one another's houses, and everyone on his day gave a feast — Bas

His sons were accustomed to hold a feast in the house of each in turn — Ber

His sons used to go and feast together, each acting in turn as host for the day — Mof

and sent and called for their three sisters to eat and to drink with them.

and they would send and invite their three sisters to eat and drink with them — RSV

5. And it was so, when the days of their feasting were gone about, that Job sent and sanctified them,

And when they had let the feast days go round, Job sent and purified them — ABPS

And at the end of their days of feasting, Job sent and made them clean — Bas

Each time when the days of their feasting were completed Job would summon and dedicate them — Ber

Then, when a round of feasts was finished, Job sent for his children and sanctified them — NEB

And even when their week of feasting was over, Job would send for them, and have them rid of all defilement — Knox

And when each feast had run its course, Job would send for them and sanctify them — NAB

and rose up early in the morning, and offered burnt offerings according to the number of them all:

and he would rise early in the morning and offer burnt offerings according to the number of them all — RSV

for Job said, It may be that my sons

have sinned, and cursed God in their hearts.
for Job said, It may be that my sons have sinned, and have forsaken God in their hearts — ABPS
. . . It may be that my sons have done wrong and said evil of God . . . — Bas
. . . Perhaps my sons have sinned and renounced God . . . — Ber
. . . Perhaps my children have sinned, And cursed God in their thoughts — AAT
. . . Who knows but they may have slighted God in their secret thoughts? — Knox
. . . Perhaps my children have in their mind conceived evil before God — Sept
. . . Peradventure my sons have transgressed and blessed strange gods in their hearts — Sprl
Thus did Job continually.
This Job did habitually — NAB
This Job did every time — Ber

6. **Now there was a day when the sons of God came to present themselves before the LORD,**
One day, when the heavenly powers stood waiting upon the Lord's presence — Knox
Now one day when the heavenly beings had come to stand in the presence of the LORD — AAT
One day the angels came to present themselves before the Eternal — Mof
The day came when the members of the court of heaven took their places in the presence of the LORD — NEB
and Satan came also among them.
and among them was the Adversary — Mof
so the accuser also entered in their midst — Rhm

7. **And the LORD said unto Satan, whence comest thou? Then Satan answered the LORD, and said,**
"Where have you been?" said the Eternal to the Adversary; and the Adversary answered — Mof
From going to and fro in the earth, and from walking up and down in it.
From going to and fro in the earth, and wandering about therein—Rhm
From wandering this way and that on the earth, and walking about on it — Bas
From roaming the earth and patrolling it — NAB
"Roaming here and there, roving about the earth" — Mof
Having gone round the earth, and roved the whole of it under heaven, I am come here — Sept

8. **And the LORD said unto Satan,**
And Yahweh said unto the accuser — Rhm
Hast thou considered my servant Job, that there is none like him in the earth,
Hast thou observed my servant Job . . . — ABPS
Have you noticed . . . — AAT
Did you notice . . . — Jerus
a perfect and an upright man, one that feareth God, and escheweth evil?
a man of integrity and upright, a man who reveres God and turns away from evil — Ber
a man unblameable, true, pious, abstaining from everything evil—Sept

9. **Then Satan answered the LORD and said, Doth Job fear God for nought?**
. . . Is it for nothing that Job reveres God — Ber
. . . Doth Job worship the LORD for nothing — Sept
"Why shouldn't he when you pay him so well?" Satan scoffed — Tay
Job fears his God, the Enemy answered, and loses nothing by it. — Knox

10. **Hast not thou made an hedge about him, and about his house, and about all that he hath on every side?**
Hast not thou hedged him about, and his house, and all that he has, on every side — ABPS
Have you not put a wall round about him . . . — Bas
Have you not hedged him safely in, his house and all he has — Mof
Have you not surrounded him and his family and all that he has with your protection — NAB
Thou hast rested thy hand of protection upon him and upon his house and upon his children and upon everything that he has everywhere — Lam
Sheltered his life by thy protection,

sheltered his home, his property — Knox

Thou hast blessed the work of his hands, and his substance is increased in the land.

The work of his hands thou hast blessed, and his substance is spread abroad in the earth — ABPS

Thou hast blessed the labor of his hands, and his holdings have increased in the land — Ber

You have blessed all he undertakes, and his flocks throng the countryside — Jerus

you have prospered him in his business, and his flocks are teeming on the land — Mof

thy blessing on all he undertakes; worldly goods that still go on increasing; he loses nothing — Knox

11. But put forth thine hand now, and touch all that he hath, and he will curse thee to thy face.

One little touch of thy hand, assailing all that wealth of his! Then see how he will turn and blaspheme thee — Knox

But, put forth now thy hand and touch all that he has, — if he will not renounce thee, to thy face! — ABPS

However, put forth Thy hand, and lay it on everything he has, and he will deny Thee to Thy face — Ber

But put forth thine hand and touch all that he hath, he will indeed openly renounce thee — Sept

But stretch out your hand and lay a finger on his possessions: I warrant you, he will curse you to your face — Jerus

12. And the LORD said unto Satan, Behold, all that he hath is in thy power; only upon himself put not forth thine hand.

. . . Take note! All that he has is in your power; only do not lay hands on his person — Ber

. . . There! I have all that he has within your power; but lay no hand upon the man himself — Mof

So Satan went forth from the presence of the LORD.

13. And there was a day when his sons and his daughters were eating and drinking wine in their eldest brother's house:

Now it was the day, that his sons and daughters were eating, and drinking wine, in the house of their brother, the first-born — ABPS

And it fell on a day when his sons and his daughters were eating and drinking wine in the eldest brother's house — ASV

14. And there came a messenger unto Job, and said, The oxen were plowing, and the asses feeding beside them:

15. And the Sabeans fell upon them, and took them away; yea, they have slain the servants with the edge of the sword; and I only am escaped alone to tell thee.

And the men of Sheba . . . — Bas

And robbers raided them . . . — Lam

when the Sabeans attacked and captured them . . . — Ber

when the Arabs made a foray . . . — Mof

when the Sabeans swooped down . . . — Rhm

and the plunderers came . . . — Sept

16. While he was yet speaking, there came also another, and said,

While he was still speaking, another messenger arrived and said — NEB

The fire of God is fallen from heaven, and hath burned up the sheep, and the servants, and consumed them;

"Lightning fell from the sky and burned up sheep and goats and shepherds to a cinder — Mof

A fire of God fell out of the heavens, and burned up the sheep and the young men and consumed them — Rhm

God's fire flashed from heaven. It struck the sheep and the shepherds and burnt them up — NEB

and I only am escaped to tell thee.

17. While he was yet speaking, there came also another, and said, The Chaldeans made out three bands, and fell upon the camels, and have carried them away, yea, and slain the servants with the edge of the sword;

The Chaldeans formed three bands, made a raid on the camels and captured them, slaying the servants with the edge of the sword — Ber

The Chaldeans formed three parties for a raid upon the camels . . . — Mof

The Chaldeans sent out three corps; and they rushed forth upon the camels . . . — Sprl

The horsemen, having formed three bands against us, surrounded the camels and have carried them off, and slain thy servants with the sword — Sept

and I only am escaped alone to tell thee.

18. While he was yet speaking, there came also another, and said, Thy sons and thy daughters were eating and drinking wine in their eldest brother's house:

19. And, behold, there came a great wind from the wilderness, and smote the four corners of the house, and it fell upon the young men, and they are dead;

When a great wind came rushing from the waste land against the four sides of the house, and it came down on the young men, and they are dead — Bas

when suddenly a mighty wind came from across the desert . . . — Ber

when suddenly from the wilderness a gale sprang up, and it battered all four corners of the house which fell in on the young people. They are dead — Jerus

when a whirlwind swept across the desert . . . — Mof

a great blast of wind came up suddenly from the wilderness . . . — Sept

and I only am escaped alone to tell thee.

20. Then Job arose, and rent his mantle, and shaved his head, and fell down upon the ground and worshipped,

Then Eyob [Job] rose, tore his tunic, shaved his head, and dropped upon the ground in humble worship — Mof

And Job riseth, and rendeth his robe, and shaveth his head, and falleth to the earth, and doth obeisance — YLT

21. And said, Naked came I out of my mother's womb, and naked shall I return thither:

and said, With nothing I came out of my mother's body, and with nothing I will go back there — Bas

Naked I came, said he, when I left my mother's womb, and whence I came, naked I must go — Knox

the LORD gave, and the LORD hath taken away; blessed be the name of the LORD.

the Lord gave and the Lord has taken away; let the Lord's name be praised — Bas

Yahweh gave, Yahweh has taken back. Blessed be the name of Yahweh! — Jerus

22. In all this Job sinned not, nor charged God foolishly.

In all this Job sinned not, nor uttered folly against God — ABPS

. . . nor charged God with foolishness — RV

. . . nor challenged with human folly God's wisdom — Knox

. . . nor did he give offence to God — Mof

In all these things which befel him, Job transgressed not against the Lord, nor imputed indiscretion to his God — Sept

Notwithstanding all this, Job did not sin; nor did he charge anything unseemly against God — AAT

In all this Job did not sin or charge God with wrong — RSV

In all this Job did no sin, and did not say that God's acts were foolish — Bas

CHAPTER 2

1. Again there was a day when the sons of God came to present themselves before the LORD, and Satan came also among them to present himself before the LORD.

2. And the LORD said unto Satan, From whence comest thou? And Satan answered the LORD, and said, From going to and fro in the earth, and from walking up and down in it.

3. And the LORD said unto Satan, Hast thou considered my servant Job, that there is none like him in the earth, a perfect and an upright man, one that feareth God and escheweth evil?*

and still he holdeth fast his integrity, although thou movedst me against him, to destroy him without cause.

and he still keeps his righteousness, though you have been moving me to

*Compare 2:1-3a with 1:6-8.

send destruction on him without cause — Bas

He still holds fast to his integrity, though you did incite Me against him to consume him without cause — Ber

he still holds to his loyalty: it was idle of you to entice me to undo him — Mof

and still he is holding fast his integrity, although Thou movedst me against him to swallow him up without cause — Rhm

Still he retaineth his innocence; so that thou hast ordered the destruction of his property, without accomplishing thy purpose — Sept

And still he holdest fast his integrity, although thou incited Me against him to destroy him causelessly — Sprl

4. **And Satan answered the LORD, and said, Skin for skin, yea, all that a man hath will he give for his life.**

Nay, answered the Enemy, skin must suffer before skin grieves. Nothing a man owns, but he will part with it to keep his skin whole — Knox

But the Adversary answered, "He has saved his own skin! A man will let all he has go, to preserve his life — Mof

5. **But put forth thine hand now, and touch his bone and his flesh, and he will curse thee to thy face.**

but now stretch forth Thine hand, and afflict his bone and his flesh; will he not curse thee to thy face? — Sprl

6. **And the LORD said unto Satan, Behold, he is in thine hand; but save his life.**

So the Eternal said to the Adversary, "There! he is in your power; only spare his life" — Mof

And Yahweh said unto the accuser, Behold him! in thy hand, only his life preserve thou! — Rhm

7. **So went Satan forth from the presence of the LORD, and smote Job with sore boils from the sole of his foot unto his crown.**

. . . and smote Job with cancer from the sole of his foot to his brain — Lam

. . . with loathsome boils . . . — Ber

. . . with painful ulcers . . . — Mof

. . . with black leprosy . . . — Sprl

And the Satan went out from before the Lord, and sent on Job an evil disease covering his skin from his feet to the top of his head — Bas

8. **And he took him a potsherd to scrape himself withal, and he sat down among the ashes.**

And he took a broken bit of pot, and, seated in the dust, was rubbing himself with the sharp edge of it — Bas

so that he was fain to sit him down on the dung-hill, and scratch himself with a shard where he itched — Knox

So he took broken pottery with which to scrape himself and sat down in the ashes — Ber

so that he took a shell to scrape away the ichor, and sat down in an unclean place without the city — Sept

9. **Then said his wife unto him, Dost thou still retain thine integrity? curse God, and die.**

. . . Are you still keeping your righteousness? . . . — Bas

. . . Do you now still mean to persist in your blamelessness? . . . — Jerus

. . . Are you still trying to be godly when God has done all this to you? Curse him and die — Tay

Little comfort his own wife gave him; What, she said, still maintaining thy innocence? Better thou shouldest renounce God, and have done with living — Knox

Then said his wife to him, Dost thou still hold fast thy integrity? Bless God, and die! — ABPS

10. **But he said unto her, Thou speakest as one of the foolish women speaketh.**

. . . You are talking like an impious fool — Knox

. . . You talk as any wicked fool of a woman might talk — NEB

. . . Thou speakest as one of the ungodly women speaketh — Sprl

. . . You talk like some heathen woman — Tay

As one of the base women speaketh, speakest thou? — Rhm

What? shall we receive good at the hand of God, and shall we not receive evil?

Are we to receive only what is good from God, and are we to receive no misfortune — Ber

If we take happiness from God's hand, must we not take sorrow too—Jerus

11. Now when Job's three friends heard of this evil that was come upon him,

Now three friends of Job heard of all this evil that had come upon him — ABPS

When the three friends of Job heard of all this disaster . . . — AAT

. . . all the tragedy that had befallen him — Tay

they came every one from his own place;

. . . his own home — Mof

. . . his own country — Sept

. . . his own station — Sprl

Eliphaz the Temanite, and Bildad the Shuhite, and Zophar the Naamathite:

Eliphaz from Teman, Bildad from Shuah, and Zophar from Maan — Mof

Eliphaz the king of the Thaimanites, Baldad the sovereign of the Saucheans, and Sophar the king of the Minaians — Sept

for they had made an appointment together to come to mourn with him and to comfort him.

So they came together to a meeting-place, in order that they might go and make clear to Job their grief for him, and give him comfort — Bas

They met by appointment and came to sympathize with him and to comfort him — Ber

they arranged to go and condole with him, to comfort him — Mof

for they had by appointment met together to come to shew sympathy with him and to comfort him—Rhm

12. And when they lifted up their eyes afar off,

But when they caught sight of him from a distance — Ber

and knew him not,

and did not recognize him — Ber

and saw him disfigured beyond recognition — Amp

it did not seem that the man they saw was Job because of the change in him — Bas

they lifted up their voice, and wept;

they began to weep aloud — NAB

and they rent every one his mantle, and sprinkled dust upon their heads toward heaven.

. . . and they cast dust over their heads toward the heavens — AAT

they tore their cloaks and threw dust upon their heads — NAB

13. So they sat down with him upon the ground seven days and seven nights, and none spake a word unto him:

And for seven days and seven nights they sat there on the ground with him, and no word was spoken — Knox

for they saw that his grief was very great.

. . . that his suffering was very great — Ber

. . . that exceeding great was the stinging pain — Rhm

. . . that the stroke was grevious and very great — Sept

. . . how terrible was his anguish — Mof

. . . how greatly the affliction raged — Sprl

here, they saw plainly, was overmastering grief — Knox

CHAPTER 3

1. After this opened Job his mouth, and cursed his day.

In the end it was Job who broke the silence and cursed the day of his birth — Jerus

2. And Job spake, and said,

3. Let the day perish wherein I was born, and the night in which it was said, There is a man child conceived.

And this was his plaint: Blotted out for ever be the day of my birth; that night, too, which gave word that a human life had been conceived in the womb! — Knox

Eyob began:
"Perish the day I was born,
the night that said,
'It is a boy!' — Mof

4. Let that day be darkness:

Plunged be that day in darkness — Knox

Utter darkness may it be — Mof

That day — let it be dark — Bas

let not God regard it from above, neither let the light shine upon it.

Let not God from above seek for it,
Neither let the light shine upon it — ASV
let not God take note of it from on high, and let not the light be shining on it — Bas
may God above not inquire after it, and may no light shine upon it—Ber
may God on high forget it, and grant it never shine of sun — Knox
May God on high ignore it,
till not a ray illumines it! — Mof
May God on high not search for it;
May light not shine upon it — AAT

5. Let darkness and the shadow of death stain it;
Let darkness and the shadow of death claim it for their own — ASV
Let darkness and death-shade reclaim it — ABPS
Let darkness and death-shade buy it back — Rhm
Let gloom and deep darkness claim it — RSV
may blackness sully it, and murk and gloom — NEB
let a cloud dwell upon it;
may black clouds settle upon it — Ber
may dense clouds rest on it — Mof
deep gloom lie heavy on it — Knox
let the blackness of the day terrify it.
Let darkenings of the day affright it — ABPS
Let all that maketh black the day terrify it — ASV
may the eclipse of the sun terrify it — Ber
may all eclipses scare it — Mof
the blackness of night affright it! — NAB

6. As for that night, let darkness seize upon it;
. . . let thick darkness set it on edge — Sprl
. . . may a pitchy darkness sweep it away — Sept
That night — may blackness seize it — AAT
let it not be joined unto the days of the year, let it not come into the number of the months.
Let it not rejoice among the days of the year;
Let it not come . . . — ASV
Be it severed from the days of the year,
kept out of the months' count—Mof
May it be blotted off the calendar, never again to be counted among the days of the month of that year — Tay

7. Lo, let that night be solitary,
. . . barren — ASV
As for that night, let it have no fruit — Bas
But as for that night, may it be sorrow — Sept
Lo! that night — let it be gloomy — YLT
a night doomed to exile — Knox
let no joyful voice come therein.
And no sound of joy enter therein — ABPS
let no joyful outcry greet it! — NAB
Let no joyous shouting enter therein — Rhm
and may there never come upon it gladness or mirth! — Sept
bereft of any joyous cry! — Mof

8. Let them curse it that curse the day, who are ready to raise up their mourning.
. . . Who are ready to rouse up leviathan — ASV
Let them that curse days, curse it;
They that are skilled to rouse up leviathan — ABPS
Let day-cursers denounce it,
Those skilled in rousing the dragon of the sky — Rhm
But let him curse it who curseth the day—him who is to attack the great sea-monster — Sept
Let those execrate it who execrate the day
When they arouse leviathan! — Sprl
Cursed be it by those whose magic binds even the monster of the deep, who are ready to tame Leviathan himself with spells — NEB

9. Let the stars of the twilight thereof be dark;
Let its morning stars be dark — Bas
May the stars of its twilight be darkened — NAB
blacken its starlight — Knox
let it look for light, but have none;
Let it wait for light, and there be none — ABPS
let the morning wait in vain for the light — Ber
let it wait for the morning light, and see it never — Knox
may it look for daylight, but have none — NAB

may it long for light, but never reach it — Sept
may it wait for a dawn that never comes — NEB
neither let it see the dawning of the day:
Neither let it see the eyelashes of the dawn — Rhm
Neither let it behold the eyelids of the morning — ABPS
nor gaze on the eyes of the dawn — NAB
nor see the rising of the morning star — Sept

10. Because it shut not up the doors of my mother's womb, nor hid sorrow from my eyes.
the night that should have closed the doors of the womb against me, shut these eyes forever to sights of woe — Knox
Because it did not keep the doors of my mother's body shut, so that trouble might be veiled from my eyes — Bas
because it shut not up the door of my mother's womb for that would have removed sorrow from mine eyes — Sept
Because it did not shut the doors of my mother's womb,
And so conceal trouble from my eyes — AAT

11. Why died I not from the womb? why did I not give up the ghost when I came out of the belly?
Why did I not die new-born,
not perish as I left the womb? — Jerus
Wherefore did I not die from the womb —
Come forth from the womb, and expire? — ABPS
Why was I not still-born,
why did I not die when I came out of the womb? — NEB
Had but the womb been the tomb of me, had I died at birth — Knox
Why did I not perish at birth,
come forth from the womb and expire? — NAB

12. Why did the knees prevent me? or why the breasts that I should suck?
Wherefore did the knees receive me?
or why did I suck at the breasts? — NAB
Why were knees ready for me,
And why breasts, that I might suck? — ABPS
Why were there knees to welcome me?
why were there breasts to suck? — Mof
Why were there two knees to receive me,
two breasts for me to suck? — Jerus
Why did the midwife let me live? Why did she nurse me at her breasts? — Tay
had no lap ever cherished me, no breast suckled me — Knox

13. For now should I have lain still and been quiet, I should have slept: then had I been at rest.
For then I might have gone to my rest in quiet, and in sleep have been in peace — Bas
all would be rest now, all would be silence. Deeply I would take my repose — Knox
Had there not been, I should now be lying in peace,
wrapped in a restful slumber — Jerus

14. With kings and counsellors of the earth,
With kings and the wise ones of the earth — Bas
with the old kings and senators — Knox
with despots of the earth — Sept
which build desolate places for themselves;
who put up great houses for themselves — Bas
who rebuilt ruins for themselves — Ber
who built where now there are ruins — NAB
who build themselves vast vaults — Jerus
that once restored cities for their whim — Knox
who had built pyramids for themselves — Mof
who gloried in their swords — Sept
Who built sepulchral mansions for themselves — Sprl

15. Or with princes that had gold, who filled their houses with silver:
or with princes who have gold and to spare
and houses crammed with silver — Jerus
the chieftans that had such wealth of gold, houses full of silver — Knox

16. Or as an hidden untimely birth I had

not been; as infants which never saw light.

with babe still-born and babe unborn,
hidden away in the sunless grave — Knox

why was I not buried like an abortion,
like still-born babes that never see daylight? — Mof

Or put away like a still-born child that never came to be,
like unborn babes that never see the light — Jerus

17. **There the wicked cease from troubling; and there the weary be at rest.**

There, the wicked cease from tumult,
And there, the wicked are at rest — ABPS

There the passions of the evil are over, and those whose strength has come to an end have rest — Bas

Down there, bad men bustle no more,
there the weary rest — Jerus

There villains cease to rage,
and their victims are at peace — Mof

There the lawless cease from raging,
and there the toil-worn are at rest — Rhm

18. **There the prisoners rest together; they hear not the voice of the oppressor.**

The prisoners all are at ease;
They hear not the taskmaster's voice — ABPS

untroubled the thrall sleeps, his tyrant's bidding cannot reach him now — Knox

— captives lying quiet together,
deaf to the slave-driver's shout — Mof

19. **The small and great are there; and the servant is free from his master.**

The small and the great are there,
and the slave is free from his master — RSV

Small and great are there the same,
and the servant is free from his master — NAB

20. **Wherefore is light given to him that is in misery, and life unto the bitter in soul;**

Wherefore gives He light to the wretched,
And life to the sorrowful in heart — ABPS

Why should they see the light that groan to see it; why should they live, that must live in bitterness of soul? — Knox

Why does God give sufferers light,
and life to men in bitter despair — Mof

Wherefore is light given to the miserable,
And life to the galled in soul — Sprl

Why give light to a man of grief?
Why give life to those bitter of heart — Jerus

Why is light given to the toilers,
and life to the bitter in spirit — NAB

21. **Which long for death, but it cometh not; and dig for it more than for hid treasures;**

Why should they be like treasure-seekers, longing for the death that still cheats them — Knox

who long for death, and long in vain,
who dig for it more than buried treasure — Mof

who long for a death that never comes,
and hunt for it more than for a buried treasure — Jerus

22. **Which rejoice exceedingly, and are glad, when they can find the grave?**

Who are joyful, even to exulting,
Are glad, when they find the grave — ABPS

Who exult exceedingly, yea, leap for joy,
When they can find the grave — Sprl

They would be glad to see the grave-mound
and shout with joy if they reached the tomb — Jerus

what a blessed relief when at last they die! — Tay

23. **Why is light given to a man whose way is hid, and whom God hath hedged in?**

Why should a man be born to wander blindly,
hedged in by God on every side? — NEB

Why does God give light to a man at his wits' end,
a man he has hemmed in — Mof

To the man whose pathway is broken up,
And whom God has overwhelmed —Sprl

Such men as I, that must tread blindfold in a maze of God's making! —Knox

Why is a man allowed to be born if God is only going to give him a hopeless life of uselessness and frustration — Tay

24. For my sighing cometh before I eat,
For with my food, comes my sighing —ABPS
My only food is sighs — Jerus
I cannot eat for sighing — Tay
For sighing comes more readily to me than food — NAB
and my roarings are poured out like the waters.
And my moans are poured forth as water — ABPS
and cries of sorrow come from me like water — Bas
and my groanings are poured out like water — RSV
and my groans well forth like water — NAB
grief floods over me unrestrained — Knox

25. For the thing which I greatly feared is come upon me, and that which I was afraid of is come unto me.
. . . hath overtaken me — JPS
For what I feared has come upon me, and what I dreaded has struck me — Ber
Must I have nothing left to daunt me? Must each calamity be felt as soon as feared? — Knox
Whatever I fear comes true, whatever I dread befalls me — Jerus

26. I was not in safety, neither had I rest, neither was I quiet; yet trouble came.
I am not at ease, nor am I quiet. I get no rest, but trouble arises — Ber
I have no peace nor ease;
I have no rest, for trouble comes! — NAB
I have no ease, nor quiet;
I have no rest, yet trouble comes — ABPS
For me there is no calm, no peace;
my torments banish rest — Jerus
And still I kept my own counsel, still patient and silent I, till my angry mood overcame me at last — Knox
I get no peace, I get no rest,
I get no ease, only attacks of agony — Mof
I was not careless nor was I secure nor had I settled down, —
When there came — consternation! — Rhm
There is no peace of mind nor quiet for me;
I chafe in torment and have no rest — NEB

CHAPTER 4

1. Then Eliphaz the Temanite answered and said,
Eliphaz of Teman spoke next. He said: — Jerus

2. If we assay to commune with thee, wilt thou be grieved?
Should one venture a word to thee, wilt thou be offended — ABPS
Would you resent it, if we dare to speak — Mof
If someone attempts a word with you, will you mind — NAB
Speak we, it may be thou wilt take our words amiss — Knox
If one attempt a word unto thee wilt thou be impatient — Rhm
If one ventures to speak with you, will you lose patience — NEB
but who can withhold himself from speaking?
But who can forbear speaking — ABPS
yet speech will out — Knox
And to keep in words who is able? — YLT
Yet who can keep silent — Jerus
For who could hold his tongue any longer — NEB

3. Behold, thou hast instructed many, and thou hast strengthened the weak hands.
Lo, thou hast admonished many,
And hast strengthened the feeble hands — ABPS
You have yourself set many right,
and put strength into feeble souls — Mof
Many another, once, you schooled,
giving strength to feeble hands — Jerus
Think how once you encouraged those who faltered — NEB

4. Thy words have upholden him that was falling,
Thy words have confirmed the faltering — ABPS
Your words have often upheld the stumbling — Ber
[Thou knewest how to] give courage to the waverer — Knox
your words have kept men on their feet — Mof

and thou hast strengthened the feeble knees.
support to flagging knees — Knox
the weak-kneed you have nerved — Mof

5. **But now it is come upon thee, and thou faintest; it toucheth thee, and thou art troubled.**
Now the blow has fallen on thyself, and thy strength is gone; the nearer neighbourhood of misfortune unmans thee — Knox
But now that it comes upon you, you lose heart;
It touches you and you are dismayed — AAT
And now your turn has come, and you lose patience too;
and now it touches you, and you are overwhelmed — Jerus
But now that adversity comes upon you, you lose patience;
it touches you, and you are unmanned — NEB

6. **Is not this thy fear, thy confidence, thy hope, and the uprightness of thy ways?**
Is not thy fear of God thy confidence,
And the integrity of thy ways thy hope — ASV
Is not your reverence for God your confidence . . . — Ber
No more we hear now of that fear of God, that life perfectly lived, which once gave thee confidence, gave thee strength to endure! — Knox
Is your religion no comfort to you?
Does your blameless life give you no hope — NEB

7. **Remember, I pray thee, who ever perished, being innocent? or where were the righteous cut off?**
Remember now, who that was guiltless has perished?
And where were the righteous cut off — ABPS
Can you recall a guiltless man that perished,
or have you ever seen good men brought to nothing — Jerus
Think now, what guiltless man has ever perished?
When have the just ever been swept away — Mof
Have you ever seen destruction come to an upright man? or when were the god-fearing ever cut off — Bas
And, sure enough, ruin never fell yet on the innocent; never yet was an upright soul lost to memory — Knox

8. **Even as I have seen, they that plow iniquity, and sow wickedness, reap the same.**
I speak of what I know: those who plough iniquity
and sow the seeds of grief reap a harvest of the same kind — Jerus
Men, as I see it, reap the evil that they plough,
the trouble that they sow — Mof
As I have seen—ploughers of iniquity,
And sowers of misery, reap it! — YLT

9. **By the blast of God they perish, and by the breath of his nostrils are they consumed.**
By the breath of God they perish;
And by the blast of his anger are they consumed — ABPS
one breath, one blast of the divine anger withers them quite, and they are gone — Knox
Through the breath of God they perish,
And through his angered spirit they are destroyed — AAT

10. **The roaring of the lion, and the voice of the fierce lion, and the teeth of the young lions, are broken.**
Roar lion, growl lioness, the fangs of the lion-cubs will yet be scattered — Knox
roaring lions, hoarse with fury,
they have their fierce fangs shattered — Mof
Though the lion roars, though the king of beasts cries out,
yet the teeth of the young lions are broken — NAB
The roar of the lion, the whimpering of his cubs, fall silent;
the teeth of the young lions are broken — NEB
Though they are fierce as young lions, they shall all be broken and destroyed — Tay

11. **The old lion perisheth for lack of prey, and the stout lion's whelps are scattered abroad.**
The old lion comes to his end for need of food, and the young of the she-lion go wandering in all directions — Bas
The lion perishes for lack of prey,

And the cubs of the lioness are scattered — AAT
Like aged, helpless lions they shall starve, and all their children shall be scattered — Tay

12. **Now a thing was secretly brought to me,**
Now a word was stealthily brought to me — ABPS
Now, I have had a secret revelation — Jerus
Once a word came stealing to me — Mof
and mine ear received a little thereof.
And my ear caught the whisper thereof —ABPS
it was but the breath of a whisper overheard — Knox
so that my ear caught just a whisper from it — AAT

13. **In thoughts and visions of the night, when deep sleep falleth on men,**
It was the hour when night-visions breed disquiet, as men lie chained by sleep; — Knox
When men fall into trances in the night,
rapt I lay in my visions — Mof
Amid thoughts from visions of the night,
when deep sleep falls on men —RSV

14. **Fear came upon me, and trembling, which made all my bones to shake.**
a shiver of horror ran through me,
and my bones quaked with fear — Jerus
fear took hold of me, a fit of trembling that thrilled my whole frame — Knox
A palpitation and a tremor seized upon me,
And the multitude of my bones shook together — Sprl
terror and trembling seized me,
till all my limbs shuddered — Mof
I was seized with a horror and trembling, which gave a violent jog to my bones — Sept
Fear fell upon me, and trembling,
And filled all my bones with dread — AAT

15. **Then a spirit passed before my face;**
a spirit glided past my face — Ber
And a breath swept over my face—AAT
A wind brushed my face — NEB
the hair of my flesh stood up:
till my hair was bristling — Mof
The hair of my flesh stood on end — AAT

16. **It stood still, but I could not discern the form thereof: an image was before mine eyes, there was silence, and I heard a voice saying,**
It stood still, but I could not distinguish its appearance. There stood a form before my eyes; there was silence, then I heard a voice — Ber
there it stood, no face I knew, yet I could see the form of it, and catch its voice, light as a rustling breeze — Knox
It paused, but its likeness I could not discern;
a figure was before my eyes,
and I heard a still voice — NAB
It stood; but I could not discern its appearance;
a form was before my eyes;
I heard a gentle voice — AAT
there it stood!
I could not make it out,
this form before my eyes, but in the hush I heard it murmuring — Mof
It stood still but I could not distinguish its appearance,
I looked but there was no form before mine eyes —
A whispering voice I heard — Rhm

17. **Shall mortal man be more just than God? shall a man be more pure than his maker?**
Can man have right on his side, the voice asked, when he is matched with God? Can a mortal creature shew blameless in its Creator's presence — Knox
Can a mortal be righteous before God,
Or a man be pure before his Maker — AAT

18. **Behold, he put no trust in his servants; and his angels he charged with folly:**
Nay, in his own retinue God finds loyalty wanting; angels may err — Knox
Even in his servants he puts no trust,
and his angels he charges with error — RSV
Even on his heavenly servants he cannot rely,
his very angels he convicts of error — Mof
If God cannot trust his own messen-

gers (for even angels make mistakes) — Tay

19. **How much less in them that dwell in houses of clay, whose foundation is in the dust, which are crushed before the moth?**
how much more those who dwell in houses of clay,
whose foundation is in the dust,
who are crushed before the moth — RSV
and what of those in houses made of clay,
with dust for their foundations,
frail as a moth — Mof
How much more those who live in houses of clay, whose foundation is in the dust and who are crushed as easily as moths! — Ber
How much more those living in houses of earth, whose bases are in the dust! They are crushed more quickly than an insect — Bas

20. **They are destroyed from morning to evening:**
Betwixt morning and evening they are destroyed — ASV
one day is enough to grind them to powder — Jerus
they perish for ever without regarding it.
They perish for ever without any regarding it — ASV
... without anyone noticing it — AAT
They vanish for ever, and no one remembers them — Jerus

21. **Doth not their excellency which is in them go away?**
Is not their tent-cord plucked up within them? — ASV
Their tent-peg is snatched from them — Jerus
Is not their tent cord plucked up within them [so that the tent falls]? — Amp
they die, even without wisdom.
and they die for lack of wisdom — Jerus
and the rest of them shall die without wisdom — Lam
they die, and die in ignorance of him — Mof
They die disrobed of wisdom! — Rhm
Do they not die, and that without acquiring wisdom? — Amp

CHAPTER 5

1. **Call now, if there be any that will answer thee;**
Call now; is there anyone who will answer you? — Ber
Make your appeal then. Will you find an answer? — Jerus
Call together a meeting, I entreat, if there be one who will reply for thee — Sprl
and to which of the saints wilt thou turn?
To which of the holy ones will you turn — RSV
Wilt thou turn to one of his angels for redress — Knox

2. **For wrath killeth the foolish man,**
For grief slays the foolish — ABPS
Vexation slays the fool — Ber
Resentment kills the senseless — Jerus
Impatience is a great murderer of fools — Knox
For provocation slayeth the perverse — YLT
The fool is destroyed by his own angry passions — NEB
and envy slayeth the silly one.
and jealousy kills the simple — Ber
and envy killeth the wanderer — Sept
'tis death for a fool to flame out against God — Mof
And passion kills the simpleton — AAT
and indignation slays the simple one — NAB

3. **I have seen the foolish taking root:**
I have seen a fool spreading his roots — NAB
Never have I seen a fool secure in his possessions — Knox
I have seen the wicked prosper — Lam
but suddenly I cursed his habitation.
but his household suddenly decayed — NAB
until a swift curse fell on his House — Jerus
but I prophesied disaster, there and then, for his fair prospects — Knox
but his habitation is suddenly destroyed — Lam
but their sustenance was quickly consumed — Sept
And I mark his habitation straightway — YLT

4. **His children are far from safety, and they are crushed in the gate, neither**

is there any to deliver them.
Now his children have no safe place, and they are crushed before the judges, for no one takes up their cause — Bas
his children are left in peril,
defrauded — none to defend them — Mof
And still would I see his children bereft of hope, ground down by false judgment, and none to bring redress — Knox

5. **Whose harvest the hungry eateth up, and taketh it even out of the thorns, and the robber swalloweth up their substance.**
his harvest is a prey for hungry neighbours, himself for the armed robber, his wealth drunk up by thirsty mouths — Knox
Whose gathered fruits the starving shall eat; Even amongst the prickly thorns they will seize them:
And the thirsty swallow their subsistence — Sprl
His harvest the hungry eat, and take it even [when it grows] among the thorns; the snare opens for [his] wealth — Amp
Whose harvest the hungry devour,
And take it, even from the thorns;
And the snare is gaping for their substance — ABPS
His harvest the hungry eat,
and he takes it even out of thorns;
and the thirsty pant after his wealth — RSV
What they have reaped the hungry shall eat up;
[or God shall take it away by blight;]
and the thirsty shall swallow their substance — NAB

6. **Although affliction cometh not forth of the dust, neither doth trouble spring out of the ground;**
Grief does not grow out of the earth, nor sorrow spring from the ground — Jerus
For sorrow cometh not forth out of the dust, —
Nor out of the ground sprouteth trouble — Rhm
Surely, calamity does not spring from the dust, nor does trouble sprout out of the ground — Ber
Never was ill without a cause; never did mischief spring up self-sown — Knox
Mischief does not grow out of the soil nor trouble spring from the earth — NEB

7. **Yet man is born unto trouble, as the sparks fly upward.**
man brings trouble on himself,
as surely as the sparks fly up — Mof
Mankind heads for sin and misery as predictably as flames shoot upward from a fire — Tay

8. **I would seek unto God, and unto God would I commit my cause:**
If I were as you are, I should appeal to God,
and lay my case before him — Jerus
Wherefore I would address myself to God,
Even my cause unto God the Atoner — Sprl

9. **Which doeth great things and unsearchable; marvellous things without number:**
His magnificent counsels none may fathom, none reckon up his marvellous deeds — Knox
His works are great, past all reckoning, marvels, beyond all counting—Jerus

10. **Who giveth rain upon the earth, and sendeth waters upon the fields:**
His to grant the parched earth rain, watering the countryside — Knox

11. **To set up on high those that be low; that those which mourn may be exalted to safety.**
He sets the humble on high,
And the mourning are raised to prosperity — ABPS
He lifts the lowly up high and He raises the sufferers to positions of safety — Ber
Who setteth on high them who are low, and raiseth up them who have been ruined — Sept

12. **He disappointeth the devices of the crafty, so that their hands cannot perform their enterprise.**
He frustrates the plans of the cunning, so that their hands achieve no success — NAB
he wrecks the plans of the artful, and brings to naught their intrigues — Jerus
he foils the plots of wily men,
till they win no success — Mof

Who doth frustrate the schemes of the crafty,
That their hands cannot achieve abiding success — Rhm

13. **He taketh the wise in their own craftiness:**
He takes the wise in their subtlety — Lam
He snares the wise in their own craftiness — Ber
He traps the crafty in the snare of their own shrewdness — Jerus
and the counsel of the froward is carried headlong.
and the plottings of the wily are frustrated — Ber
and the schemes of the wily are brought to a quick end — RSV
and knavish plots are scattered to the winds — Knox
baffling the schemes of shifty men — Mof
turns subtle counsellors to idiots — Jerus
So that the counsel of schemers is confused — AAT

14. **They meet with darkness in the daytime,**
They handle things in the daytime as though they were in darkness — Lam
In daylight they come against darkness — Jerus
By day they encounter darkness — Rhm
In the daylight they run into darkness — NEB
and grope in the noonday as in the night.
and grope their way as if noon were night — Jerus
they see no better in the daytime than at night — Tay
And as though it were night they grope at high noon — Rhm

15. **But he saveth the poor from the sword, from their mouth, and the hand of the mighty.**
But He saves the fatherless from the sword of their mouth, and the needy from the clutch of the mighty — Ber
So from their slander and their violence, he rescues the poor and the unbefriended — Knox
He rescues the bankrupt from their jaws,
and the poor man from the hands of the violent — Jerus

16. **So the poor hath hope, and iniquity stoppeth her mouth.**
So the lowly gain hope, and injustice shuts her mouth — Ber
Thus to the poor hath come hope, and perversity hath shut her mouth — Rhm
Thus the unfortunate have hope, and iniquity closes her mouth — NAB
Thus the wretched can hope again and wickedness must shut its mouth — Jerus
now, misery, take heart, let malice stand dumb with confusion! — Knox

17. **Behold, happy is the man whom God correcteth:**
. . . reproves — RSV
. . . rebukes — NEB
Blessed indeed, is the man whom God disciplines — Ber
Truly, that man is happy who has training from the hand of God — Bas
therefore despise not thou the chastening of the Almighty:
so do not let your heart be shut to the teaching of the Ruler of all — Bas
Then do not refuse this lesson from Shaddai — Jerus
Spurn not the discipline of the Almighty — Mof

18. **For he maketh sore, and bindeth up: he woundeth, and his hands make whole.**
Wounds he, it is but to heal; the same hand, which smote, shall medicine thee — Knox
he binds up where he wounds,
he hurts and heals — Mof
For he wounds, but he binds up;
he smites, but his hands heal — RSV
For he who wounds is he who soothes the sore,
and the hand that hurts is the hand that heals — Jerus

19. **He shall deliver thee in six troubles: yea, in seven there shall no evil touch thee.**
So in six perils thou shalt go unharmed, and yet find one deliverance more — Knox
He will deliver you again and again — Tay

20. **In famine he shall redeem thee from**

death: and in war from the power of the sword.
hunger shall not starve thee, sword wound thee — Knox
In famine he will ransom thee from death,
And in battle from the power of the sword — Rhm
In famine he will deliver you from death,
and in war from the threat of the sword — NAB

21. **Thou shalt be hid from the scourge of the tongue:**
you will be safe from slander — Tay
When the tongue scourgeth thou art hid — YLT
You shall be safe from the lash of the tongue — Jerus
You will be shielded from the lash of slander — NEB
neither shalt thou be afraid of destruction when it cometh.
and shall not fear approaching ruin — NAB
and when violence comes you need not fear — NEB

22. **At destruction and famine shalt thou laugh:**
rapine and death thou shalt defy — Knox
You will laugh at violence and starvation — NEB
neither shalt thou be afraid of the beasts of the earth.
and you shall not fear the wild beasts — Lam

23. **For thou shalt be in league with the stones of the field: and the beasts of the field shall be at peace with thee.**
friendly soil for thee are the desert rocks, and the wild things are in league with thee — Knox
the very animals shall be your allies, and the wild beasts your friends — Mof

24. **And thou shalt know that thy tabernacle shall be in peace;**
. . . that thy tent is in peace — JPS
. . . that thy family is at peace — Sept
Thou shalt be confident of peace in thy tabernacle — Sprl
You shall find your tent secure—Jerus
and thou shalt visit thy habitation, and shalt not sin.
and shalt visit thy pastures, and miss nothing — ABPS
and thou shalt visit thy fold, and shalt miss nothing — RV
you shall miss nothing when you count your flock — Mof
And superintend thy household, and thou shalt not labour in vain — Sprl

25. **Thou shalt know also that thy seed shall be great, and thine offspring as the grass of the earth.**
You shall know also that your descendants shall be many, and your offspring like the grass of the earth — Lam
you shall find yourself with many children,
offspring in number like the blades of grass — Mof
You shall see your descendants multiply,
your offspring grow like the grass in the field — Jerus

26. **Thou shalt come to thy grave in a full age, like as a shock of corn cometh in in his season.**
Thou shalt come to thy grave in ripe age,
Like as a shock of corn cometh in its season — JPS
when go to the grave thou must, it shall be with strength undiminished, like ripe corn at harvest-home — Knox
You shall come to your grave gently, like a shock of grain in its season — Lam
You shall approach the grave in full vigor,
as a shock of grain comes in at its season — NAB
Thou shalt come yet robust to the grave,
As a stack of sheaves mounteth up in its season — Rhm
In ripe age you shall go to the grave, like a wheatsheaf stacked in due season — Jerus
You shall live a long, good life; like standing grain, you'll not be harvested until it's time! — Tay

27. **Lo this, we have searched it, so it is; hear it, and know thou it for thy good.**
All this we have observed: it is true. Heed it, and do so to your profit — Jerus
Here are thoughts tested and found

true; well for thee if thou wilt heed them, and ponder them in thy heart — Knox
This is the truth we have found to be true;
this we have heard: now, lay it to heart — Mof
I have found from experience that all this is true. For your own good, listen to my counsel — Tay

CHAPTER 6

1. But Job answered and said,
2. O that my grief were throughly weighed,
. . . Oh, that my grief could be fully weighed — ABPS
. . . O that my vexation were weighed — RSV
. . . O that some person would weigh my passion — Sept
. . . O that the grounds for my resentment might be weighed — NEB
. . . Ah, could my anguish but be measured — NAB
and my calamity laid in the balances together!
And my calamity be laid in the balances with it — ABPS
and all my ills put on the scales — Jerus
and poise in the balance against it my calamities — Sept
and my misfortunes set with them on the scales — NEB
3. For now it would be heavier than the sand of the sea:
The sand of the shore of ocean could not match the burden of them — Knox
therefore my words are swallowed up.
For this cause, my words have been rash — ABPS
Because of this I speak without restraint — NAB
That makes my words so wild — Mof
what wonder if my words are wild? — NEB
Therefore my words have been rash — YLT
4. For the arrows of the Almighty are within me,
The arrows of the Almighty find their mark in me — NEB
Deep the Lord's arrows rankle in me — Knox
the poison whereof drinketh up my spirit:
Whose poison my spirit drinks up — ABPS
draining my life — Knox
their poison stings my soul — Mof
my spirit absorbs their poison — Jerus
the terrors of God do set themselves in array against me.
The terrors of God beset me — AAT
God's onslaughts wear me away — NEB
5. Doth the wild ass bray when he hath grass? or loweth the ox over his fodder?
What! will a wild ass bray without cause? Will it do so, except when in search of food? Or will an ox low having fodder in his stall — Sept
Brays the wild ass, be sure he lacks pasture; lows the ox, he stands before an empty crib — Knox
When wild donkeys bray, it is because their grass is gone; oxen do not low when they have food; — Tay
6. Can that which is unsavoury be eaten without salt?
Can that which is tasteless be eaten without salt — ABPS
Can one eat insipid food and saltless — Mof
a man complains when there is no salt in his food — Tay
or is there any taste in the white of an egg?
. . . in the juice of mallows — JPS
. . . in the slime of the purslane — RSV
or is there any relish in vain words — Sept
And is there any relish in the drivel of dreams — Sprl
7. The things that my soul refused to touch are as my sorrowful meat.
The very dishes which I cannot stomach,
these are my diet in my sickness — Jerus
my appetite is gone when I look at it; I gag at the thought of eating it — Tay
I refuse to touch them;
they are loathesome food to me — NAB
My appetite refuses to touch them!

They are like uncleanness in my food — AAT

8. **Oh that I might have my request; and that God would grant me the thing that I long for!**
Oh may my prayer find fulfilment, may God grant me my hope! — Jerus

9. **Even that it would please God to destroy me;**
May it please God to crush me — Jerus
that he would let loose his hand, and cut me off!
to give his hand free play and do away with me! — Jerus
to let his hand snap off my thread of life! — Mof
to die beneath His hand, and be freed from His painful grip — Tay

10. **Then should I yet have comfort;**
This thought, at least, would give me comfort — Jerus
That would be some comfort to me — Mof
For that would bring me relief — NEB
yea, I would harden myself in sorrow: let him not spare;
Yea, I would exult in pain, though He spare not — JPS
Yea I would exult in pain that spares not — ABPS
Yes, I would leap for joy in unsparing pain — Ber
(a thrill of joy in unrelenting pain) — Jerus
For I have not concealed the words of the Holy One.
that I had not denied the Holy One's decrees — Jerus
I have not been false to the words of the Holy One — Bas

11. **What is my strength, that I should hope?**
What strength have I left to hold out — Ber
Have I the strength to wait? — NEB
and what is mine end, that I should prolong my life?
and what will result if I remain patient — Ber
What use is life to me when doomed to certain death — Jerus

12. **Is my strength the strength of stones? or is my flesh of brass?**
Have I the strength of a rock, or is my body of bronze — Ber

13. **Is not my help in me?**
Is there any help at all in me — Rhm
Oh, how shall I find help within myself — NEB
Have I no helper — NAB
Am I not completely helpless — Ber
No, there is no help, none — Mof
Verily, there is no help in me — AAT
and is wisdom driven quite from me?
and has advice deserted me? — NAB
Is not abiding success driven from me? — Rhm
and is not recovery driven from me? — Ber
has not all help deserted me? — Jerus
human aid keeps its distance from me now — Knox
And effective aid is removed far from me — AAT

14. **To him that is afflicted pity should be shewed from his friend; but he forsaketh the fear of the Almighty.**
To him that is ready to faint kindness is due from his friend,
Even to him that forsaketh the fear of the Almighty — JPS
Friends should be kind to a despairing man,
or he will give up faith in the Almighty — Mof
The despairing from his friend should have lovingkindness,
Or the reverence of the Almighty he may forsake — Rhm
Devotion is due from his friends
to one who despairs and loses faith in the Almighty — NEB

15. **My brethren have dealt deceitfully as a brook, and as the stream of brooks they pass away;**
My friends have been false like a stream, like streams in the valleys which come to an end — Bas
My brothers are as unreliable as a brook, as the bed of torrents that rush on — Ber
My brothers have been fickle as a torrent,
as the course of a seasonal stream — Jerus
See how the men that are my brothers have failed me, fickle as the mountain brooks that run headlong down their ravines — Knox
but my friends disappoint me like a stream,

like mountain brooks that overflow their banks — Mof

Mine own brothers have proved treacherous like a torrent,
Like a channel of torrents which disappear — Rhm

My brethren are undependable as a brook,
as watercourses that run dry in the wadies — NAB

16. Which are blackish by reason of the ice, and wherein the snow is hid:

turbid with dirty ice and with snow melting in them — Ber

Ice is the food of their dark waters, they swell with the thawing of the snow — Jerus

Swollen and dark with ice,
with melting snow — Mof

Though they may be black with ice, and with snow heaped upon them — NAB

17. What time they wax warm, they vanish: when it is hot, they are consumed out of their place.

Under the burning of the sun they are cut off, and come to nothing because of the heat — Bas

but in the hot season they dry up, with summer's heat they vanish — Jerus

Yet once they flow, they cease to be; in the heat they disappear from their place — NAB

but vanishing when they are scorched, and disappearing in the summer's glow — Mof

When they diminish, they disappear, and when it is hot, they dry up from their place — Ber

By the time they begin to thaw they are dried up,
As soon as it is warm they have vanished out of their place — Rhm

18. The paths of their way are turned aside; they go to nothing, and perish.

From them caravans divert their route; they enter wastes and are lost — Ber

Caravans leave the trail to find them, go deep into the desert, and are lost — Jerus

caravans turn to them, then turn away, take to the desert and then perish — Mof

19. The troops of Tema looked, the companies of Sheba waited for them.

The caravans of Tema look for them; those of Sheba wait in hope — Ber

The caravans of Tema look to them, and on them Sheba's convoys build their hopes — Jerus

caravans from Tema look to them for water,
traders from Arabia are in hopes — Mof

20. They were confounded because they had hoped;

They are disappointed because they had hoped so confidently — Ber

Their trust proves vain — Jerus

but their hopes are disappointed — Mof

But they are disappointed, for all their confidence — NEB

they came thither, and were ashamed.

they came nearer and found themselves deceived — Ber

they reach them only to be thwarted — Jerus

they reach them only to be balked — NEB

21. For now ye are nothing, ye see my casting down, and are afraid.

It is thus that you have now become for me;
you see a terrifying thing and are afraid — NAB

Such have you now become to me; you notice my dismay, and you, too, are afraid — Ber

So, at this time, do you behave to me: one sight of me, and then you flee in fright — Jerus

Ay, you have come, but finding me so sorely smitten, you dread my company — Knox

And so my hopes in you are dashed — you turn away from me in terror and refuse to help — Tay

22. Did I say, Bring unto me? or, Give a reward for me of your substance?

23. Or, Deliver me from the enemy's hand? or, Redeem me from the hand of the mighty?

Have I said, Give for me;
And of your wealth make a present for me,
And deliver me from an enemy's hand,
And from the hand of the violent set me free? — ABPS

Have I ever said, 'Make me a gift,' and, 'From your abundance offer a bribe for me,' and, 'Save me from the hand of the oppressor,' and, 'Ransom me from brigands'? — Ber

I never bade you diminish your own wealth by bringing gifts for me, never begged your aid to rid me of some enemy that was too strong for me — Knox

Have I said to you, 'Give me this or that,
bribe someone for me at your own cost,
snatch me from the clutches of an enemy,
or ransom me from a tyrant's hand'? — Jerus

24. Teach me, and I will hold my tongue: and cause me to understand wherein I have erred.

Put me right, and I will say no more; shew me where I have been at fault — Jerus

Come, be my instructors; I will hear you out in silence; tell me what is the fault I have committed, all unknowing? — Knox

All I want is a reasonable answer — then will I keep quiet. Tell me, what have I done wrong? — Tay

25. How forcible are right words! but what doth your arguing reprove?

Fair comment can be borne without resentment,
but what is the basis of your strictures — Jerus

How pleasant are the sayings that are right!
But what can a decision from you decide — Rhm

How strong are just arguments;
But where is the demonstration in your reproof — Sprl

How agreeable are honest words;
yet how unconvincing is your argument! — NAB

It is wonderful to speak the truth, but your criticisms are not based on fact — Tay

26. Do ye imagine to reprove words, and the speeches of one that is desperate, which are as wind?

Do you intend to censure a man's word, when the utterances of a desperate man are as wind — Ber

Do you think mere words deserve censure,
desperate speech that the wind blows away — Jerus

Do you consider your words as proof, but the sayings of a desperate man as wind — NAB

Are you going to condemn me just because I impulsively cried out in desperation — Tay

27. Yea, ye overwhelm the fatherless, and ye dig a pit for your friend.

Truly, you are such as would give the child of a dead man to his creditors and would make a profit out of your friend — Bas

You would cast lots over an orphan and strike a bargain over a friend — Ber

Yea, ye would cast lots upon the fatherless,
And make merchandise of your friend — ASV

Soon you will be casting lots for an orphan,
and selling your friend at bargain prices! — Jerus

That would be like injuring a helpless orphan or selling a friend — Tay

28. Now therefore be content, look upon me; for it is evident unto you if I lie.

But now, please, look at me; surely I would not lie to your face — Ber

Come, I beg you, look at me:
as man to man, I will not lie — Jerus

Come, now, give me your attention;
surely I will not lie to your face — NAB

Browbeat me, then, at your pleasure; try if close scrutiny can prove me false — Knox

29. Return, I pray you, let it not be iniquity;

Turn, I pray you, let no wrong be done — RSV

Let your minds be changed, and do not have an evil opinion of me — Bas

Repent, I pray you, and do not become like ungodly men — Lam

Reply, I pray you, let there be no perversity — Rhm

Think again, let me have no more injustice — NEB

Stop assuming my guilt — Tay

yea, return again, my righteousness is in it.

Turn now, my vindication is at stake — RSV

yes, be changed, for my righteousness is still in me — Bas

relent, my case is not yet tried — Jerus

think again, for my integrity is in question — NEB

30. Is there iniquity in my tongue?

Is there insincerity on my tongue — NAB

Is falsehood to be found on my lips — Jerus

Do I ever give voice to injustice — NEB

You will not fasten guilt on any word of mine — Knox

cannot my taste discern perverse things?

or cannot my taste discern falsehood — NAB

cannot my taste discern mischievous things — RV

cannot my palate tell the taste of misfortune — Jerus

is not the cause of my trouble clear to me — Bas

Does my sense not warn me when my words are wild — NEB

Don't I know the difference between right and wrong — Tay

CHAPTER 7

1. Is there not an appointed time to man upon earth? are not his days also like the days of an hireling?

Does not man have to struggle hard on earth, and are not his days like those of a hired man? — Ber

Is not man's life on earth a drudgery? Are not his days those of a hireling — NAB

Is not man's life on earth nothing more than pressed service,
his time no better than hired drudgery — Jerus

2. As a servant earnestly desireth the shadow, and as an hireling looketh for the reward of his work:

Like the slave, sighing for the shade, or the workman with no thought but his wages — Jerus

Like a slave who sighs for the shadow, and like a day laborer who longs for his wages — Ber

He is a slave who longs for the shade, a hireling who waits for his wages — NAB

3. So am I made to possess months of vanity, and wearisome nights are appointed to me.

so I am allotted months of misery, and nights of trouble are apportioned to me — Ber

months of delusion I have assigned to me,
nothing for my own but nights of grief — Jerus

I am allotted months of emptiness, and nights of misery are apportioned to me — RSV

So months of futility are my portion, troubled nights are my lot — NEB

4. When I lie down, I say, When shall I arise, and the night be gone?

Lying in bed I wonder, 'When will it be day?'
Risen I think, 'How slowly evening comes!' — Jerus

Lie I down to sleep, I weary to be up with the day — Knox

When I lie down I say, 'When shall I arise?'
But the night is long — RSV

and I am full of tossings to and fro unto the dawning of the day.

and I am turning from side to side till morning light — Bas

And I am wearied with tossings until the breeze of twilight — Rhm

Restlessly I fret till twilight falls — Jerus

I do nothing but toss till morning twilight — NEB

5. My flesh is clothed with worms and clods of dust;

Vermin cover my flesh, and loathsome scabs — Jerus

my skin is broken, and become loathsome.

my skin is cracked and oozes pus — Jerus

my skin is stiff, and peels off — Sprl

my skin cracks and festers — NAB

6. My days are swifter than a weaver's shuttle, and are spent without hope.

Frail as the weaver's thread my years vanish away, spent without hope — Knox

My life flies by — day after hopeless day — Tay

7. O remember that my life is wind: mine eye shall no more see good.

Remember that my life is a breath; my eye shall not again see good — ABPS

. . . a puff, a breath, a sob . . .— Amp

Bethink thee, Lord, it is but a breath, this life of mine, and I shall look on this fair world but once —Knox

8. The eye of him that hath seen me shall see me no more: thine eyes are upon me, and I am not.

Those who see me shall never again see me;
I shall be gone, under thy very gaze — Mof

The eye that once saw me will look on me no more,
your eyes will turn my way and I shall not be here — Jerus

You see me now, but not for long. Soon you'll look upon me dead — Tay

9. As the cloud is consumed and vanisheth away:

. . . dissolves and disappears — Ber

. . . fades and disappears — Mof

so he that goeth down to the grave shall come up no more.

so he who descends to Sheol . . .—Lam

so he that descendeth to hades . . . — Rhm

10. He shall return no more to his house,

never again the home-coming—Knox

never shall he come home again—Mof

neither shall his place know him any more.

never shall tidings of him reach the haunts he knew — Knox

11. Therefore will I not refrain my mouth; I will speak in the anguish of my spirit; I will complain in the bitterness of my soul.

And should I utter no word? Nay, the crushed spirit will find a voice, the embittered heart will not keep its own counsel — Knox

Ah, let me express my anguish. Let me be free to speak out of the bitterness of my soul — Tay

Also I — I withhold not my mouth — I speak in the distress of my spirit, I talk in the bitterness of my soul — YLT

Well, I will restrain myself no longer; I will speak out, so bitter is my soul — Mof

12. Am I a sea, or a whale, that thou settest a watch over me?

Am I a raging sea, a ravening monster, that thou guardest me so close? — Knox

Am I a crocodile of the waters,
That Thou settest a watch upon me? — Sprl

A sea-monster am I, or a dragon . . . — YLT

O God, am I some monster, that You never let me alone — Tay

13. When I say, My bed shall comfort me, my couch shall ease my complaint;

If I say, 'My bed will comfort me, my couch will soothe my pain' — Jerus

Even when I try to forget my misery in sleep — Tay

14. Then thou scarest me with dreams, and terrifiest me through visions:

what dreams thou sendest to daunt me, what sights of terror to unman me! — Knox

. . . you terrify me with nightmares — Tay

15. So that my soul chooseth strangling, and death rather than my life.

Strangling I would welcome rather, and death itself, than these my sufferings — Jerus

The rope for me! Death only will content this frame — Knox

I would rather die of strangulation than go on like this — Tay

I would rather be choked outright; I would prefer death to all my sufferings — NEB

16. I loathe it: I would not live alway: let me alone; for my days are vanity.

I am tired of it; I would not live always. Leave me alone, for my days are fleeting — Ber

I am in despair, I would not go on living;
leave me alone, for my life is but a vapour — NEB

To despair I yield myself, I will live on no more; loose thy hold of me; this life of mine is but the shadow of a life — Knox

I waste away, my life is not unending; leave me then, for my days are but a breath — Jerus

I waste away: I cannot live forever; let me alone, for my days are but a breath — NAB

17. What is man, that thou shouldest magnify him?

What is man, that you should make so much of him — Jerus

What is a mortal

That thou shouldst nurture him — Rhm

and that thou shouldest set thine heart upon him?

and be so concerned about him — Ber

18. **And that thou shouldest visit him every morning,**

That thou shouldst inspect him morning by morning — Rhm

Must you be his inquisitor every morning — Tay

punishing him every morning — Mof

and try him every moment?

Moment by moment shouldst test him — Rhm

and test him every moment of the day — Tay

19. **How long wilt thou not depart from me, nor let me alone till I swallow down my spittle?**

How long will it be before you look away from me,
and let me alone long enough to swallow my spittle — NAB

Nay, gaze on me no more; leave me, though it were but for a breathing space, to myself — Knox

Why won't You let me alone — even long enough to spit — Tay

20. **I have sinned; what shall I do unto thee, O thou preserver of men?**

If I sin, what do I to thee, thou observer of men — ABPS

Suppose I have sinned, what have I done to you, you tireless watcher of mankind — Jerus

. . . O thou Spy upon mankind — Mof

. . . O keeper of men — Bas

If I have sinned, what harm have I done Thee, O Thou watcher of men — Ber

why hast thou set me as a mark against thee,

Why hast Thou made me Thy target — Ber

Wherefore hast thou set me as thine object of attack — Rhm

why hast thou set me up as thy mark to shoot at? — Sept

Why do you choose me as your target? — Jerus

so that I am a burden to myself?

Or have I become unto thee a burden — Rhm

Why have I become a burden to thee — RSV

Am I indeed a burden to thee — Sept

21. **And why dost thou not pardon my transgression, and take away mine iniquity? for now shall I sleep in the dust; and thou shalt seek me in the morning, but I shall not be.**

Would it cost thee much to forgive sin of mine, pass over fault of mine, when I, so soon, shall be lying in the dust, missing at my post, as thou makest thy rounds at dawn? — Knox

CHAPTER 8

1. **Then answered Bildad the Shuhite, and said,**

Bildad of Shuah spoke next. He said: — Jerus

2. **How long wilt thou speak these things? and how long shall the words of thy mouth be like a strong wind?**

Is there no end to these words of yours, to your long-winded blustering — Jerus

What, still at thy old complaining; blustering still, like a high wind, on and on — Knox

How long will you go on like this, Job, blowing words around like wind — Tay

How long will you say such things, the long-winded ramblings of an old man — NEB

3. **Doth God pervert judgment?**

Will God pervert right — ABPS

Does God give a wrong decision — Bas

Can sentence undeserved come from God — Knox

Can God deflect the course of night — Jerus

Is God partial in judgment — Sprl

Does God twist justice — Tay

or doth the Almighty pervert justice?

or Shaddai falsify justice — Jerus

4. **If thy children have sinned against him, and he have cast them away for their transgression;**

If your sons sinned against him,
they have paid for their sins — Jerus

What if these children of thine committed some fault, and he allowed justice to take its course? — Knox

If thy children have turned aside from Him,

And he hath removed them in the very act of their transgression—Sprl

If your children have sinned against him
and he has left them in the grip of their guilt — NAB

5. If thou wouldest seek unto God betimes, and make thy supplication to the Almighty;

For thyself, thou hast but to keep early tryst with God, and make thy plea to his omnipotence — Knox

If you would seek God
and make supplication to the Almighty — RSV

6. If thou wert pure and upright;

Then, if thou comest before him innocent and upright — Knox

if you are pure and upright — RSV

surely now he would awake for thee,

then he will certainly be moved to take up your cause — Bas

he will give thee audience betimes — Knox

surely then he will rouse himself for you — RSV

then indeed will he watch over you —NEB

and make the habitation of thy righteousness prosperous.

And make thy righteous dwelling secure — ABPS

by building up your house again — Bas

and reward you with a rightful habitation — RSV

and bless you with a happy home — Tay

7. Though thy beginning was small, yet thy latter end should greatly increase.

Then, though thy beginning be small,
Thy end shall be exceeding great — ABPS

Your former state will seem to you as nothing beside your new prosperity — Jerus

A poor thing thy old prosperity will seem, matched with the abundance he gives thee now — Knox

8. For inquire, I pray thee, of the former age, and prepare thyself to the search of their fathers:

Question the generation that is passed, meditate on the experience of its fathers — Jerus

Question men of bygone ages,
attend to what our fathers found — Mof

For inquire, I pray, of the former generation,
And note what their fathers have searched out — ABPS

Read the history books, and see — Tay

9. (For we are but of yesterday, and know nothing, because our days upon earth are a shadow:)

How blind are we, creatures of a day, whose time on earth passes like a shadow! — Knox

(for what know we, mere men of yesterday? —
our days on earth are but a flitting shadow) — Mof

10. Shall not they teach thee, and tell thee, and utter words out of their heart?

will they not tell you what they know, and teach you in their wisdom this — Mof

Will not they speak to you and teach you
and pour out the wisdom of their hearts? — NEB

11. Can the rush grow up without mire?

Does papyrus flourish except in marshes — Jerus

Can the paper-reed grow up without a marsh — Rhm

Can papyrus grow up without ooze — Sprl

Doth a rush rise without mire — YLT

can the flag grow without water?

. . . reed grass . . . — NAB

. . . rushes . . . — Jerus

. . . reeds . . . — RSV

. . . the bulrush . . . — Sprl

12. Whilst it is yet in his greenness, and not cut down, it withereth before any other herb.

Pluck them even at their freshest:
fastest of all plants they wither — Jerus

No, all uncut, all fresh and green,
it withers before any plant — Mof

While it is in its budding — uncropt,
Even before any herb it withereth — YLT

13. So are the paths of all that forget God; and the hypocrite's hope shall perish:

So frail their happiness, who leave God unremembered; so fade the hopes of false hearts — Knox

So end all who care not for God,
so perishes the hope of an ungodly man — Mof

So shall be the latter end of all who forget GOD,
And the hope of the impious shall perish — Rhm

14. Whose hope shall be cut off,
His trust is only a thread — Jerus
Whose confidence is gossamer — JPS
Whose trust shall be contemptible — Rhm
For his confidence breaks — AAT
His confidence breaks in sunder — RSV
Everything he counts on will collapse — Tay

and whose trust shall be a spider's web.
and his trust is a spider's web — RSV
his assurance a spider's web — Jerus
and whose house is a spider's web — Lam
And a spider's web his confidence — Rhm

15. He shall lean upon his house, but it shall not stand: he shall hold it fast, but it shall not endure.
The wicked shall put his trust in his house . . . — Lam
Vain his reliance on the house he has built; vainly he seeks to underpin it — Knox
If he counts on his home for security, it won't last — Tay
He leans against his house but it does not stand;
he clutches at it but it does not hold firm — NEB
He shall rely upon his family, but it shall not last;
he shall cling to it, but it shall not endure — NAB

16. He is green before the sun, and his branch shooteth forth in his garden.
Like some lush plant in the sunlight, he sprouteth his early shoots over the garden; — Jerus
Here is a plant that seems well-watered enough, spreads abroad its early shoots — Knox
He is full of sap before sunrise,
and beyond his garden his shoots go forth — NAB
He is a green plant, growing in the sun,
with shoots all over the garden — Mof
At dawn he seems so strong and virile, like a green plant; his branches spread across the garden — Tay

17. His roots are wrapped about the heap, and seeth the place of stones.
Over a stone-heap are its roots entwined;
It sees the habitation of stones — ABPS
His roots twine about the stoneheap; he lives among the rocks — RSV
wrapped about stones are the roots of it, and stones all its dwelling-place — Knox
with roots twined round the spring, thriving inside the greenhouse—Mof
His roots are in the stream, down among the stones — Tay
but its roots become entangled in a stony patch
and run against a bed of rock — NEB

18. If he destroy him from his place, then it shall deny him, saying, I have not seen thee.
Snatch him from his bed,
and it denies it ever saw him — Jerus
But when he disappears, he isn't even missed! — Tay
Then someone uproots it from its place, which disowns it and says, 'I have never known you' — NEB

19. Behold, this is the joy of his way, and out of the earth shall others grow.
That is how its life withers away,
and other plants spring up from the earth — NEB
There he lies rotting beside the road,
and out of the soil another sprouts — NAB
So brief its pride; they are waiting even now underground, the shoots that will fill its place — Knox
So ends a godless man,
and others rise up in his stead—Mof
That is all he can look forward to! And others spring up from the earth to replace him! — Tay

20. Behold, God will not cast away a perfect man, neither will he help the evil doers:
Behold, God will not cast away the upright;
neither will he take the hand of the wicked — NAB
Trust me, God will not cast off the innocent, will not lend his aid to the malice of their enemies — Knox
Lo, God doth not reject the perfect, nor taketh hold on the hand of evil doers — YLT

21. Till he fill thy mouth with laughing, and thy lips with rejoicing.
Ere long, he will teach those lips to smile, that mouth to sing praise — Knox
While he filleth with laughter thy mouth,
And thy lips with shouting — YLT
At length he shall fill with laughter thy mouth,
And thy lips with a shout of triumph — Rhm

22. They that hate thee shall be clothed with shame;
brief shall be the triumph of thy foes — Knox
Those hating thee shall put on shame — YLT
your enemies shall be wrapped in confusion — NEB
and the dwelling place of the wicked shall come to naught.
and the tent of the wicked shall be no more — ASV
brief the security of the wrongdoer — Knox
But the tent of the lawless shall not be! — Rhm
And the tent of the wicked is not — YLT

CHAPTER 9

1. Then Job answered and said,
Job spoke next. He said: — Jerus
2. I know it is so of a truth: but how should man be just with God?
Indeed I know it is as you say:
how can man be in the right against God — Jerus
No need to teach me that; how should a man win his suit matched against God — Knox
"Sure, I know all that. You're not telling me anything new. But how can a man be truly good in the eyes of God — Tay
3. If he will contend with him, he cannot answer him one of a thousand.
If any were so rash as to challenge him for reasons,
one in a thousand would be more than they could answer — Jerus
Who would go to law, where one plea on this side is arrayed against a thousand on that? — Knox
Even if God chose to argue,
you could not answer one of his thousand questions — Mof
. . . one out of a thousand questions — Bas
If a man chooses to argue with him, God will not answer one question in a thousand — NEB
4. He is wise in heart, and mighty in strength:
His all-knowing mind, his all-conquering arms — Knox
Wise in heart and strong in power — YLT
who hath hardened himself against him, and hath prospered?
who has hardened himself against him, and succeeded — RSV
Who hath hardened toward Him and is at peace — YLT
who then can successfully defy him — Jerus
what man ever throve yet that defied them — Knox
5. Which removeth the mountains, and they know not: which overturneth them in his anger.
He that removes mountains, ere they are aware;
Who overturns them in his anger — ABPS
Who removeth mountains unawares,
Who overturneth them in his anger — Rhm
He moves the mountains, though they do not know it;
he throws them down when he is angry — Jerus
God, the unseen power that can thrust mountains this way and that, uproot them in his anger — Knox
6. Which shaketh the earth out of her place, and the pillars thereof tremble.
He shakes the earth out of its foundations, and its inhabitants tremble — Lam
Who shaketh the earth out of its place, and all the pillars thereof shudder — Rhm
can move earth from its place, and set all its pillars quaking — Knox
7. Which commandeth the sun, and it riseth not; and sealeth up the stars.
The sun, at his command, forbears to rise,

and on the stars he sets a seal — Jerus
can prevent, with a word, the sun's rising, or imprison, under his royal seal, the very stars — Knox
The sun won't rise, the stars won't shine, if he commands it so! — Tay

8. Which alone spreadeth out the heavens, and treadeth upon the waves of the sea.
He and no other stretched out the skies,
and trampled the Sea's tall waves — Jerus
He it was, and no other, that spread out heaven to be his coverage, made ocean a floor under his feet — Knox
Who spreadeth out the heavens by himself alone!
And marches along on the heights of the sea — Rhm

9. Which maketh Arcturus, Orion, and Pleiades, and the chambers of the south.
. . . and the vast starry spaces of the south — Amp
Who made the Bear, the Giant, and the Cluster,
And the chambers of the south — Rhm
. . . the Bear, Orion, and the Pleiades, and the constellations of the southern Zodiac — Tay
He made the Bear and Orion,
the Pleiades and the constellations of the south — NAB

10. Which doeth great things past finding out: yea, and wonders without number.
great wonders he does beyond all our understanding and all our reckoning — Knox
Doing great things till there is no searching,
And wonderful, till there is no numbering — YLT
He does incredible miracles, too many to count — Tay

11. Lo, he goeth by me, and I see him not: he passeth on also, but I perceive him not.
Hidden from my sight, hidden from my thought, he comes and goes — Knox
He passes me — I cannot see him;
he sweeps on — I behold him not — Mof
Should he come near me, I see him not;
should he pass by, I am not aware of him — NAB
He passes by me, and I do not see him;
he moves on his way undiscerned by me — NEB

12. Behold, he taketh away, who can hinder him? who will say unto him, What doest thou?
Were he to snatch a prize, who could prevent him,
or dare to say, 'What are you doing?' — Jerus
he pounces — who can stop him?
Who dare ask him what he means — Mof
Lo, He snatches away, who bringeth it back?
Who saith unto Him, 'What dost Thou?' — YLT
Should he seize me forcibly, who can say him nay?
Who can say to him, "What are you doing?" — NAB

13. If God will not withdraw his anger, the proud helpers do stoop under him.
There is no braving the anger of such a God, when even the Titanic powers obey him — Knox
God never goes back on his anger,
Rahab's minions still lie at his feet — Jerus
He is God and he does not relent;
the helpers of Rahab bow beneath him — NAB
God will not withdraw His anger; the [proud] helpers of Rahab [arrogant monster of the sea] bow under Him — Amp
And God does not abate His anger. The pride of man collapses before him — Tay

14. How much less shall I answer him, and choose out my words to reason with him
How dare I plead my cause, then,
or choose arguments against him — Jerus
and what am I that I should use phrases of studied eloquence for my pleading — Knox
How then could I answer him,
what words could I pick to dispute with him — Mof
And who am I that I should try to

argue with Almighty God, or even reason with him — Tay

15. Whom, though I were righteous, yet would I not answer, but I would make supplication to my judge.

Suppose I am in the right, what use is my defence?
For he whom I must sue is judge as well — Jerus

Though I am innocent, I cannot answer him;
I might appeal for mercy to my accuser — RSV

Even though I were right, I could not answer him,
but should rather beg for what was due me — NAB

16. If I had called, and he had answered me; yet would I not believe that he had hearkened unto my voice.

If he deigned to answer my citation,
could I be sure that he would listen to my voice? — Jerus

And even if my prayers were answered I could scarce believe that he had heard my cry — Tay

If I summoned him and he answered me,
I would not believe that he was listening to my voice — RSV

If I summoned him to court and he responded,
I do not believe that he would listen to my plea — NEB

17. For he breaketh me with a tempest, and multiplieth my wounds without cause.

his storms would overwhelm me, faster than ever the unmerited blows would fall — Knox

For he storms and strikes at me
with many a wanton blow — Mof

For he bears hard upon me for a trifle
and rains blows on me without cause — NEB

Because with a tempest He bruiseth me,
And hath multiplied my wounds for nought — YLT

18. He will not suffer me to take my breath,

he will not let me get my breath — RSV

He permitteth me not to refresh my spirit — YLT

never a breathing-space — Knox

He will not let me breathe — Tay

but filleth me with bitterness.

But fills me with bitter plagues — ABPS

never a draught but of gall — Knox

but fills me with bitter sorrows — Tay

but fills me with bitter thoughts — NEB

19. If I speak of strength, lo, he is strong: and if of judgment, who shall set me a time to plead?

Shall I try force? Look how strong he is!
Or go to court? But who will summon him — Jerus

Nought avails might, when a giant threatens me; nought avails right, when none dares to support my quarrel — Knox

It is a trial of strength? Well there he stands!
Is it a lawsuit? Who then can arraign him — Mof

If it be a question of strength, he is mighty;
And if of judgment, who will call him to account — NAB

20. If I justify myself, mine own mouth shall condemn me: if I say, I am perfect, it shall also prove me perverse.

Would I plead in defence, he turns my own words against me; be I never so upright, he will prove me a hypocrite — Knox

Should I acquit myself, my own mouth will condemn me — Sprl

Though I am innocent, my own mouth would condemn me;
though I am blameless, he would prove me perverse — RSV

21. Though I were perfect, yet would I not know my soul: I would despise my life.

But am I innocent after all? Not even I know that,
and, as for my life, I find it hateful — Jerus

Perfect am I? I know nothing!
My soul would disavow its own being! — Sprl

And innocent I am, but of that I take regard no longer; I am aweary of life itself — Knox

Though I am innocent, I myself cannot know it;
I despise myself — NAB

22. This is one thing, therefore I said it,

He destroyeth the perfect and the wicked.

It is all the same to me; so I say, He puts an end to the sinner and to him who has done me no wrong together — Bas

Still unchanged is the burden of my complaint; innocent and guilty, he sweeps all away — Knox

It is all one, and this I dare to say: innocent and guilty, he destroys all alike — Jerus

Innocent or evil, it is all the same to him. For he destroys both kinds — Tay

23. If the scourge slay suddenly, he will laugh at the trial of the innocent.

When a sudden deadly scourge descends,
he laughs at the plight of the innocent — Jerus

When he is scourging us with sudden death,
he mocks at the despair of innocent men — Mof

When disaster brings sudden death,
he mocks at the calamity of the innocent — RSV

. . . at the foolishness of the innocent — Lam

24. The earth is given into the hand of the wicked: he covereth the faces of the judges thereof;

Earth hath been given
Into the hand of the wicked one.
The face of its judges he covereth — YLT

When a country falls into a tyrant's hands,
it is he who blindfolds the judges — Jerus

if not, where, and who is he?

If not — where, who is he — YLT

Or if not he, who else? — Jerus

If it be not He, then who is it? — JPS

He is answerable for it, who else? — Knox

25. Now my days are swifter than a post: they flee away, they see no good.

My days have been swifter than a runner,
They have fled, they have not seen good — YLT

My days run hurrying by,
seeing no happiness in their flight — Jerus

Swift as a royal courier my days pass, and joyless each one — Knox

My days go quicker than a courier,
they fly without one happy ray — Mof

26. They are passed away as the swift ships: as the eagle that hasteth to the prey.

skimming along like a reed canoe,
or the flight of an eagle after its prey — Jerus

They have passed away with boats of paper-reed,
Like a vulture [which] rusheth upon food — Rhm

They go by like skiffs of reed,
like an eagle swooping on the prey — RSV

27. If I say, I will forget my complaint, I will leave off my heaviness, and comfort myself:

If I resolve to stifle my moans,
change my countenance, and wear a smiling face — Jerus

Though I say, 'I forget my talking,
I forsake my corner, and I brighten up!' — YLT

If I say, I will forget my complaint,
I will put off my sad countenance,
and be of good cheer — ASV

28. I am afraid of all my sorrows,

still would I have pains to daunt me — Knox

I shrink back into all my sorrows — Sprl

I become afraid of all my suffering — RSV

Then he would pour even greater sorrows upon me — Tay

I know that thou wilt not hold me innocent.

for I know that . . .— RSV

for such, I know, is not your treatment of the innocent — Jerus

I have known that thou dost not acquit me — YLT

I know that thou wilt not pronounce me innocent — Rhm

29. If I be wicked, why then labour I in vain?

And if I am guilty,
why should I put myself to useless trouble — Jerus

If I must be accounted guilty,
why then should I strive in vain — NAB

I am wicked: But wherefore strive I in vain — Sprl

I — I am become wicked; why is this?
In vain I labour — YLT
I shall be held guilty, —
Wherefore then in vain should I toil — Rhm
. . . So what's the use of trying — Tay

30. If I wash myself with snow water, and make my hands never so clean;
If I wash me in snow water,
And cleanse my hands in the well — Sprl
If I should wash myself in snow, and clean my hands with lye — AAT
. . . and purify with soap my hands — YLT

31. Yet shalt thou plunge me in the ditch, and mine own clothes shall abhor me.
thy condemnation must roll me in the mire again, till the very clothes I wear shun the touch of me — Knox
Then thou wouldst plunge me into the cesspool
And my clothes would abhor me — AAT
Then in corruption Thou dost dip me . . . YLT

32. For he is not a man, as I am, that I should answer him; and we should come together in judgment.
He is not a man as I am, that I can answer him
or that we can confront one another in court — NEB
Yes, I am a man, and he is not, and so no argument,
no suit between the two of us is possible — Jerus

33. Neither is there any daysman betwixt us,
There is no arbiter between us — ABPS
There is not between us a mediator — Rhm
There is no one to give a decision between us — Bas
Oh for some umpire over both of us — Mof
Would that there were an arbiter between us — NAB
that might lay his hand upon us both.
to claim jurisdiction over both—Knox
that he might silence us both — Lam
who could lay his hand upon us both — NAB

34. Let him take his rod away from me, and let not his fear terrify me:
Let him take his rod away from me, and let not dread of him terrify me — RSV
Let him lay by his rod, let his terrors cease to daunt me — Knox
Oh, let Him stop beating me, so that I need no longer live in terror of his punishment — Tay

35. Then would I speak, and not fear him; but it is not so with me.
Then I would say what is in my mind without fear of him; for there is no cause of fear in myself — Bas
Then I will speak out bravely to his face; it is fear that holds me dumb — Knox
Then I would not be afraid to speak — for inwardly I have no guilty fears — Mof
Then I could speak without fear to him, and tell him boldly that I am not guilty — Tay
Nevertheless, I shall speak, not fearing him:
I do not see myself like that at all — Jerus

CHAPTER 10

1. My soul is weary of my life;
Since I have lost all taste for life — Jerus
Oh, I am weary of life — Knox
I am sick of life, sick of it — Mof
My soul is disgusted with my life — Sept
I will leave my complaint upon myself;
I will give free course to my complaining — ABPS
I will let my sad thoughts go free in words — Bas
I will speak out, come what may — Knox
I will give rein to my complaint of him — Mof
I leave off talking to myself — YLT
I will speak in the bitterness of my soul.
my soul will make a bitter outcry — Bas
I shall let my embittered soul speak out — Jerus
my soul is too embittered for silence — Knox

2. I will say unto God, Do not condemn me; shew me wherefore thou contendest with me.
. . . Do not treat me as guilty, without formulating Thy charge against me — Ber
. . . Do not put me in the wrong! Let me know why you oppose me — NAB
. . . Don't just condemn me — tell me why you are doing it — Tay
I will protest against God's sentence, demand to know why his judgment is so cruel — Knox

3. Is it good unto thee that thou shouldest oppress,
Is it right for you to injure me — Jerus
Is it well done in thee to play the tyrant — Knox
Is it a pleasure for you to oppress — NAB
Does it befit thee to be hard on men — Mof
Does it really seem right to you to oppress — Tay

that thou shouldest despise the work of thine hands,
to spurn me, the creature of thy own hands — Knox
cheapening the work of your own hands — Jerus
and despise me, a man you have made — Tay

and shine upon the counsel of the wicked?
and favor the designs of the wicked — RSV
looking kindly on the design of evil-doers — Bas
and abetting the schemes of the wicked — Jerus
to smile on the ill designs of the godless — Knox

4. Hast thou eyes of flesh? or seest thou as man seeth?
Are those eyes of thine human after all — Knox
Have you got human eyes,
do you see as mankind sees — Jerus
As a mortal dost thou look down? Or as a man looketh dost thou behold? — Sprl

5. Are thy days as the days of man? are thy years as man's days,
Is your life mortal like man's,
do your years pass as men's days pass — Jerus
Is your life so short — Tay

6. That thou inquirest after mine iniquity, and searchest after my sin?
You, who inquire into my faults
and investigate my sins — Jerus
that thou must search for faults in me, labour to convict me of wrong done — Knox
that thou huntest out my guilt
and searchest thus for sin in me — Mof
that thou hast sought out mine iniquity, and diligently traced my sins — Sprl
that you must hound me for sins — Tay

7. Thou knowest that I am not wicked; and there is none that can deliver out of thine hand.
when thou knowest full well that I am innocent, knowest that I am in thy power beyond hope of rescue? — Knox
Even though you know that I am not wicked,
and that none can deliver me out of your hand? — NAB
all the while knowing I am innocent, knowing there is no perfidy in me? — Mof
you know full well I've not committed? Is it because you know no one can save me from your hand — Tay

8. Thine hands have made me and fashioned me together round about;
Thy hands have fashioned me, and made me,
In every part — ABPS
It was thy hand that made me, no part of me but is thy fashioning — Knox
Thine own hands shaped me and made me,
All in unison round about — Rhm
Thine hands have fashioned me and moulded me
Compactly on every side — Sprl

yet thou dost destroy me.
and yet thou dost destroy me! — ABPS
and you turn around and destroy me? Amp
will you then turn and destroy me? — NAB

9. Remember, I beseech thee, that thou has made me as the clay;
Remember now, that thou hast formed me, as with clay — ABPS

Remember, I beseech thee, how thou didst manipulate me as the clay — Sprl
Oh, please remember that I'm made of dust — Tay
and wilt thou bring me into dust again?
will you change me back again to dust so soon — Tay
and must all be ground to dust again — Knox

10. Hast thou not poured me out as milk, and curdled me like cheese?
Milk of thy milking, cheese of thy pressing — Knox
You have already poured me from bottle to bottle like milk, and curdled me like cheese — Tay

11. Thou hast clothed me with skin and flesh, and hast fenced me with bones and sinews.
Thou has clothed me with skin and flesh,
And knit me together with bones and sinews — ASV

12. Thou hast granted me life and favour,
. . . and lovingkindness — ASV
. . . and compassion — Ber
. . . and peace — Lam
. . . and love — Mof
. . . and steadfast love — RSV
. . . and grace — Sept
And then you endowed me with life — Jerus
and thy visitation hath preserved my spirit.
And thy providence has preserved my spirit — ABPS
And thy solicitude has . . . — AAT
and your care has kept my spirit safe — Bas
And thy watchful care preserved my breath — Rhm
watched each breath of mine with tender care — Jerus

13. And these things hast thou hid in thine heart:
Yet, after all, you were dissembling — Jerus
Only in thy heart the memory of this is stored — Knox
And all the while this was thy dark design! — Mof
Yet this was the secret purpose of thy heart — NEB
I know that this is with thee.
I know that this was in thy mind — ABPS
biding your time, I know — Jerus
but I know thou hast not forgotten — Knox
plotting this, well I know it, against me! — Mof
I know that this was thy purpose — RSV

14. If I sin, then thou markest me, and thou wilt not acquit me from mine iniquity.
If I sin, thou observest me,
And wilt not absolve me from my guilt — ABPS
If I indeed have sinned inadvertently, thou hast me in custody, and hast not acquitted me of transgression — Sept
to mark if I should sin
and to let no fault of mine go uncensured — Jerus

15. If I be wicked, woe unto me; and if I be righteous, yet will I not lift up my head.
If I am wicked, woe to me!
If I am righteous, I cannot lift up my head — RSV
. . . still I cannot lift up my head — Lam
Just the slightest wickedness, and I am done for. And if I'm good, that doesn't count — Tay
I am full of confusion; therefore see thou mine affliction;
for I am filled with disgrace
and look upon my affliction — RSV
Being filled with ignominy
And looking upon mine affliction — ASV
I have enough of reproach; I have seen my affliction — Lam
So filled with shame, that I am of downcast countenance — Sprl
I am filled with frustration — Tay

16. For it increaseth. Thou huntest me as a fierce lion:
And if I make a stand, like a lion you hunt me down — Jerus
And if I exalt myself . . . — Lam
And if I lift myself up . . . — RSV
If I start to get up from the ground, you leap upon me like a lion — Tay
If I am proud as a lion, thou dost hunt me down — NEB
and again thou shewest thyself marvellous upon me.

And show again thy wondrous power upon me — ABPS
Then again thou dost shew thyself marvellous against me — Rhm
and then thou dost turn and show thyself gigantic over me — Lam
and again work wonders against me — RSV
repeatedly you show your wondrous power against me — NAB
adding to the tale of your triumphs — Jerus

17. Thou renewest thy witness against me, and increasest thine indignation upon me;

You attack, and attack me again,
with stroke upon stroke of your fury — Jerus
so keen to put me in the wrong,
so eager in thy rising wrath! — Mof
Renewing the examination against me, thou hast exercised against me great wrath — Sept

changes and war are against me.

letting loose new armies on me — Bas
in waves your troops come against me — NAB
relentlessly your fresh troops assail me — Jerus
Host succeeding host against me — JPS

18. Wherefore then hast thou brought me forth out of the womb?

Why then did you even let me be born — Tay

Oh that I had given up the ghost, and no eye had seen me!

Would that I had perished and no eye had seen me! — JPS
Why could I not have died there in the dark? — Mof
Why didn't you let me die at birth? — Tay

19. I should have been as though I had not been; I should have been carried from the womb to the grave.

Then I would have been as though I had never existed; borne from the womb directly to the tomb! — Ber
a being without being, carried from womb to tomb — Knox
Then I should have been spared this miserable existence. I would have gone directly from the womb to the grave — Tay

20. Are not my days few? cease then, and let me alone, that I may take comfort a little,

Are not the days of my life small in number? Let your eyes be turned away from me, so that I may have a little pleasure — Bas
Brief, brief is my span of days; for a little leave me to myself, to find some comfort in my misery — Knox
Are not my days few? — then forbear,
And set me aside that I may brighten up for a little — Rhm

21. Before I go whence I shall not return, even to the land of darkness and the shadow of death;

22. A land of darkness, as darkness itself; and of the shadow of death, without any order, and where the light is as darkness.

Soon I must go to a land whence there is no returning, a land of darkness, death's shadow over it, a land of gloomy night, where death's shadow lies over all, and no peace haunts it, only everlasting dread — Knox
before I go whence I shall not return,
to the land of gloom and deep darkness,
the land of gloom and chaos,
where light is as darkness — RSV
before I leave for the land of darkness and the shadow of death, never to return — A land as dark as midnight, a land of the shadow of death where only confusion reigns, and where the brightest light is dark as midnight — Tay
Before I go, never to return,
To a land of darkness and blackness,
A land of shadow, like gloom,
Of blackness without order,
And when it shines, it is like gloom — AAT
before I go to the place of no return,
the land of murk and deep shadow,
where dimness and disorder hold sway,
and light itself is like the dead of night — Jerus

CHAPTER 11

1. Then answered Zophar the Naamathite, and said,
Zophar of Naamath spoke next. He said: — Jerus

2. Should not the multitude of words be answered?
Are all these words to go unanswered — Bas
Should a deluge of words remain unanswered — Ber
Ready to speak should be ready to listen — Knox
A multitude of words answereth nothing. — Sprl
Shouldn't someone stem this torrent of words? — Tay

and should a man full of talk be justified?
. . . be accounted right — ABPS
. . . be pronounced free from guilt or blame — Amp
Must a glib talker be right — Ber
Is wordiness in man a proof of right — Jerus
glibness will not make an innocent man of thee. — Knox
Else the talkative man would be justified. — Sprl
Is a man proved right by all this talk — Tay

3. Should thy lies make men hold their peace?
Shall thy boastings put men to silence — ABPS
Are your words of pride to make men keep quiet — Bas
Behold, at your words, only the dead can hold their peace; — Lam
Should I remain silent while you boast — Tay

and when thou mockest, shall no man make thee ashamed?
will you jeer with no one to refute you — Jerus
shall none make answer to thy raillery — Knox
are you to talk nonsense and no one rebuke you — NEB

4. For thou hast said, My doctrine is pure and I am clean in thine eyes.
For you have said, 'My teaching is pure,
And I am clean in thy sight' — AAT
. . . My way is clean . . . — Bas
Still thou wilt have it that all thy dealings are upright, that thy heart, as God sees it, is pure — Knox
You claim that your opinions are sound;
you say to God, 'I am spotless in thy sight' — NEB
You claim you are pure in the eyes of God! — Tay

5. But oh that God would speak, and open his lips against thee;
But if God had a mind to speak,
to open his lips and give you answer — Jerus
Oh, that God would speak and tell you what he thinks! — Tay

6. And that he would shew thee the secrets of wisdom,
were he to show you the secrets of wisdom — Jerus
Oh, that he would make you truly see yourself — Tay

that they are double to that which is!
which put all cleverness to shame — Jerus
What mazes there are in transgression! — Sprl
For insight is a wonderful thing — AAT

Know therefore that God exacteth of thee less than thine iniquity deserveth.
You would then see that God holds against you less than your iniquities deserve — Ber
Listen! God is doubtless punishing you far less than you deserve! — Tay

7. Canst thou by searching find out God? canst thou find out the Almighty unto perfection?
Can you claim to grasp the mystery of God,
to understand the perfection of Shaddai — Jerus
Canst thou find out the deep things of God?
Canst thou attain unto the purpose of the Almighty — JPS
Canst thou trace the footsteps of the Lord?
Or hast thou reached the extent of what the Almighty hath done — Sept
Can you find out the limits of God?
Or can you attain unto the boundary of the Almighty — AAT
Can you penetrate the designs of God?

Dare you vie with the perfection of the Almighty — NAB

8. **It is as high as heaven; what canst thou do? deeper than hell; what canst thou know?**

... Deeper than Sheol ... — RSV

... Deeper than the nether-world ... — JPS

High as heaven is that wisdom, and thy reach so small; deep as hell itself, and thy thought so shallow! — Knox

The heaven is high, what then canst thou do
And there are things deeper than the mansion of the dead; what dost thou know — Sept

He is as faultless as heaven is high — but who are you? His mind is fathomless — what can you know in comparison — Tay

9. **The measure thereof is longer than the earth, and broader than the sea.**

Far as earth it stretches, wide as ocean — Knox

Its scope is vaster than the earth, and wider than the sea — Mof

10. **If he cut off, and shut up, or gather together, then who can hinder him?**

When He rushes in and arrests a person, calling the wicked to judgment, who can hinder him — Ber

If he seize and imprison
or call to judgment, who then can say him nay — NAB

If He rushes in, makes an arrest, and calls the court to order, who is going to stop him — Tay

11. **For he knoweth vain men:**

... hollow, wicked and useless men — Amp

For in his eyes men are as nothing — Bas

For he detects the worthlessness in man — Jerus

He knows the false hearts of men — Knox

he seeth wickedness also;

he sees evil — Bas

and he seeth iniquity — YLT

will he not then consider it?

and takes note of it — Bas

and wouldst thou have him overlook it? — Knox

12. **For vain man would be wise, though man be born like a wild ass's colt.**

And so a hollow-minded man will get wisdom, when a young ass of the field gets teaching — Bas

And so the idiot grows wise,
thus a young wild donkey grows tame — Jerus

But an empty man will get understanding,
When a wild ass's colt is born a man — JPS

Mere man is as likely to be wise as a wild donkey's colt is likely to be born a man! — Tay

Can a fool grow wise?
can a wild ass's foal be born a man? — NEB

Poor fools, that would have a mind of their own, and think they were born free as the wild ass! — Knox

13. **If thou prepare thine heart, and stretch out thine hands toward him;**

But if you put your heart right ... — Bas

Come, you must set your heart right ... — Jerus

14. **If iniquity be in thine hand, put it far away,**

Renounce the iniquity which stains your hands — Jerus

and let not wickedness dwell in thy tabernacles.

And let not wrong abide in thy dwellings — ABPS

... perverseness dwell in thy tents — YLT

let no injustice live within your tents — Jerus

let no iniquity make its home with you — NEB

15. **For then shalt thou lift up thy face without spot;**

... with no mark of sin — Bas

... free from blemish — Rhm

Then you may face the world in innocence — Jerus

Then thou mayst lift up thy head again, free from reproach — Knox

yea, thou shalt be stedfast, and shalt not fear:

you may stand firm and unafraid — NAB

unwavering and free from fear — Jerus

waver no more, tremble no more — Knox

a man of iron, knowing no fear — NEB

16. **Because thou shalt forget thy misery, and remember it as waters that pass away:**

you shall forget about your misery,
remembering it no more than floods gone by — Mof
Then you will forget your trouble;
you will remember it only as flood-waters that have passed — NEB

17. **And thine age shall be clearer than the noonday; thou shalt shine forth, thou shalt be as the morning.**
And brighter than noonday, shall life arise;
The darkness shall become as the morning — ABPS
Your life, more radiant than the noonday,
will make a dawn of darkness — Jerus
Radiance of noon shall dispel twilight, dawn shall rise where darkness seemed to envelop thee — Knox

18. **And thou shalt be secure, because there is hope;**
And thou shalt be confident that there is hope — Rhm
Full of hope, you will live secure — Jerus
fresh confidence shall be thine, fresh hope — Knox
And you will have courage because you will have hope — Tay
yea, thou shalt dig about thee,
hidden away in safety — Knox
Yea, thou shalt dig wells — Sept
and thou shalt take thy rest in safety,
thou shalt sleep secure — Knox
you will lie down in confidence — NEB

19. **Also thou shalt lie down, and none shall make thee afraid;**
and that rest of thine, none shall disturb — Knox
You will sleep and no one will alarm you — Ber
For thou shalt rest at ease, and none shall be at war with thee — Sept
and you shall take your rest with none to disturb — Jerus
yea, many shall make suit unto thee.
and many a man will seek your favour — Jerus

20. **But the eyes of the wicked shall fail,**
But the wicked will look around with weary eyes — Jerus
but the wicked looking on shall be consumed with envy — NAB
But evil men shall strain their eyes in vain — Mof
Blindness will fall on the wicked — NEB
and they shall not escape,
and no rescue shall ever reach them — Knox
But safety shall forsake them — Sept
Even flight is denied unto them — Sprl
the ways of escape are closed to them — NEB
and their hope shall be as the giving up of the ghost.
their only hope remaining is to breathe their last — Ber
And their hope vanisheth like a puff of breath — Sprl

CHAPTER 12

1. **And Job answered and said,**
Job spoke next. He said: — Jerus

2. **No doubt but ye are the people, and wisdom shall die with you.**
Strange, that you alone should have the gift of reason, that when you die, wisdom must die too! — Knox
No doubt you are the men who know!
Wisdom will die with you! — Mof
Yes, I realize you know everything!
All wisdom will die with you! — Tay

3. **But I have understanding as well as you; I am not inferior to you:**
I can reflect as deeply as ever you can,
I am no way inferior to you — Jerus
Well, I too have my thoughts; I am yet a match for you — Knox
Well, I know a few things myself — you are no better than I am — Tay
yea, who knoweth not such things as these?
And who, for that matter, has not observed as much? — Jerus
this knowledge you bring me is knowledge common to all — Knox

4. **I am as one mocked of his neighbor, who calleth upon God, and he answereth him: the just upright man is laughed to scorn.**
I am as one that is a laughingstock to his neighbor
I called upon God and he answered:
The just, the perfect man, is a laughingstock — ASV
A man becomes a laughingstock to his friends
if he cries to God and expects an answer.

The blameless innocent incurs only mockery — Jerus

I am a laughingstock to my friends;
I, who called upon God and he answered me,
a just and blameless man, am a laughingstock — RSV

I, the man who begged God for help, and God answered him, have become a laughingstock to my neighbors. Yes, I, a righteous man, am now the man they scoff at — Tay

I have become the sport of my neighbors: "The one whom God answers when he calls upon him, the just, the perfect man," is a laughingstock — NAB

5. He that is ready to slip with his feet is as a lamp despised in the thought of him that is at ease.

In the thought of him who is in comfort there is no respect for one who is in trouble; such is the fate of those whose feet are slipping — Bas

For ruin there is contempt in the thought of the man at ease,
Ready for such as are of faltering feet! — Rhm

In the thought of one who is at ease there is contempt for misfortune;
it is ready for those whose feet slip — RSV

A torch — despised in the thoughts of the secure is prepared for those sliding with the feet — YLT

Those who prosper and live in ease have contempt for those in misfortune, which await those whose feet are ready to slip — Ber

6. The tabernacles of robbers prosper, and they that provoke God are secure; into whose hand God bringeth abundantly.

The tents of robbers are at peace,
and those who provoke God are secure,
who bring their god in their hand — RSV

And yet, the tents of the brigands are left in peace,
and those who challenge God live in safety,
and make a god of their two fists! — Jerus

Meanwhile, see how well the robbers store their houses, braving God's anger, and yet in all things he lets them have their way — Knox

For robbers prosper. Go ahead and provoke God — it makes no difference! He will supply your every need anyway! — Tay

7. But ask now the beasts, and they shall teach thee; and the fowls of the air, and they shall tell thee:

If you would learn more, ask the cattle, seek information from the birds of the air — Jerus

Dost thou doubt it? The very beasts will tell thee, the birds in the air will be thy counsellors — Knox

8. Or speak to the earth, and it shall teach thee: and the fishes of the sea shall declare unto thee.

The creeping things of earth will give you lessons
and the fishes of the sea will tell you all — Jerus

the secret is known in every cranny of the earth; the fish in the sea will make it known to thee — Knox

9. Who knoweth not in all these that the hand of the Lord hath wrought this?

Who among all these does not know that the hand of the LORD has done this — RSV

none doubts, I tell thee, that all this is the Lord's doing — Knox

10. In whose hand is the soul of every living thing, and the breath of all mankind.

all living things that breathe, all the spirits of all mankind, lie in the hollow of his hand — Knox

in whose control lies every living soul, and the whole life of man — Mof

In his hand is the life of every living thing
and the breath of all mankind — RSV

11. Doth not the ear try words? and the mouth taste his meat?

The ear is judge of speeches, is it not, just as the palate can tell one food from another — Jerus

12. With the ancient is wisdom; and in length of days understanding.

Wisdom is found in the old,
and discretion comes with great age — Jerus

Wisdom, you argue, lies with aged men,
a long life means intelligence? — Mof

13. With him is wisdom and strength, he hath counsel and understanding.
Nay, wisdom and authority belong to God;
strength and knowledge are his own — Mof
But true wisdom and power are God's. He alone knows what we should do; He understands — Tay

14. Behold, he breaketh down, and it cannot be built again:
The ruins he makes, none can rebuild — Knox
He breaks down: there is no rebuilding — Mof
And how great is His might! What he destroys can't be rebuilt — Tay
he shutteth up a man, and there can be no opening.
He shuts up a man, and he shall not be free — ABPS
whom he imprisons, none can release — Jerus
his imprisonment none can escape — Knox
imprisons: there is no release — Mof
When he closes in on a man, there is no escape — Tay

15. Behold, he withholdeth the waters, and they dry up:
Is there a drought? He has checked the waters — Jerus
If he holds up waters, there is drought — NEB
He withholds the rain, and the earth becomes a desert — Tay
also he sendeth them out, and they overturn the earth.
And he sends them forth, and they lay waste the earth — ABPS
Do these play havoc with the earth? He has let them loose — Jerus
if he releases them they ruin the land — Lam
He sends the storms, and floods the ground — Tay

16. With him is strength and wisdom:
Yes, he is strong, he is wise — Knox
Powers and providence belong to him — Mof
Strength and success belong to him — NEB
the deceived and the deceiver are his.
The erring and he that causes to err are his — ABPS
reads the knave's heart as easily as the fool's — Knox
The wanderer and the delinquent are His — Sprl

17. He leadeth counsellors away spoiled,
He leads counselors away barefoot — Ber
He makes counsellors behave like idiots — NEB
He robs the country's counsellors of their wits — Jerus
He can thwart the counsellor — Knox
and maketh the judges fools.
turns judges into fools — Jerus
bemuse the judge — Knox
and drives judges mad — NEB

18. He looseth the bond of kings, and girdeth their loins with a girdle.
He looses fetters ordered by kings, and has the waistcloth [of a slave] girded about their own loins — Amp
he dismantles royalty,
and drives off kings in chains — Mof

19. He leadeth princes away spoiled, and overthroweth the mighty.
He makes priests walk barefoot,
and overthrows the powers that are established — Jerus
He leads priests away stripped,
and overthrows the mighty — RSV
he makes priests behave like idiots
and overthrows men long in office — NEB

20. He removeth away the speech of the trusty, and taketh away the understanding of the aged.
He strikes the cleverest speakers dumb,
and robs old men of their discretion — Jerus
He silences the trusted adviser,
and takes discretion from the aged — NAB

21. He poureth contempt upon princes, and weakeneth the strength of the mighty.
. . . and he unnerves the powerful — Mof
. . . and looses the belt of the strong — RSV
. . . and abates the arrogance of nobles — NEB

22. He discovereth deep things out of darkness,
He robs the depths of their darkness — Jerus
He uncovers mysteries deep in obscurity — NEB
dark policies he brings to light — Mof

and bringeth out to light the shadow of death.
and brings to light black gloom — Ber
and into thick darkness he brings light — NEB
and shady mysteries he exposes — Mof

23. **He increaseth the nations, and destroyeth them:**
He gives the nations growth, and he destroys them — ABPS
he will extend a nation to undo it — Mof
He makes nations great, and he destroys them — RSV
he enlargeth the nations, and straighteneth them again.
or makes a people grow and then destroys it — Jerus
he enlarges nations, and leads them away — RSV
he will enlarge a nation, then enslave it — Mof
he spreads peoples abroad and he abandons them — NAB

24. **He taketh away the heart of the chief of the people of the earth,**
The leaders of the people of the land he deprives of understanding — ABPS
he will distract its leading men — Mof
He strips a country's leaders of their judgment — Jerus
and causeth them to wander in a wilderness where there is no way.
and makes them wander in a jungle — Ber
and set them in a pathless waste astray — Mof
and leaves them to wander in a trackless waste — Jerus

25. **They grope in the dark without light,**
where in the dark they grope without a light — Mof
They feel darkness, and not light — YLT
and he maketh them to stagger like a drunken man.
wandering aimless like a drunken wight — Mof
And they stumble like a drunken man — Sprl

CHAPTER 13

1. **Lo, mine eye hath seen all this, mine ear hath heard and understood it.**
I have seen all this with my own eyes, heard with my own ears, and understood — Jerus
Eyes nor ears nor wits are wanting to me — Knox

2. **What ye know, the same do I know also: I am not inferior to you.**
I know all this as well as you, but I am still a match for you — Knox
What you know, I know too,
I am no more fool than you — Mof

3. **Surely I would speak to the Almighty, and I desire to reason with God.**
But my words are intended for Shaddai;
I mean to remonstrate with God — Jerus
Yet I for the Mighty One do speak,
And to argue for God I delight — YLT

4. **But ye are forgers of lies,**
. . . plasterers of lies — JPS
But as for you, you are only charlatans — Jerus
You whitewash everything with lies — Mof
For in truth you do besmear with falsehood — Rhm
But ye are foolish, stringers-up of falsehoods! — Sprl
You are glossing over falsehoods — NAB
ye are all physicians of no value.
you are all quack doctors — Ber
you patch up futile arguments, all of you — Mof
Physicians of nought — YLT
and offering vain remedies, every one of you! — NAB

5. **O that ye would altogether hold your peace!**
O that ye would keep perfectly silent — YLT
If only you would keep quiet — Bas
I wish someone would teach you to be quiet — Jerus
and it should be your wisdom.
and let silence be your wisdom — NEB
it would be a sign of wisdom — Bas
it would serve you for wisdom — Lam
then you might pass for wise men — Mof

6. **Hear now my reasoning, and hearken to the pleadings of my lips.**

Kindly listen to my accusation . . . — Jerus
Listen now to the charge I bring . . . — Mof
Hear, I pray you, my argument,
And to the pleadings of my lips attend — YLT
Hear now the rebuke I shall utter and listen to the reproof from my lips — NAB

7. Will ye speak wickedly for God?
Will you speak unfairly on behalf of God — Ber
Will you plead God's defence with prevarication — Jerus
Do you think God stands in need of your shifts — Knox
Is it for God that you speak falsehood — NAB

and talk deceitfully for him?
his case in terms that ring false — Jerus
Will you tell lies on his behalf — Mof
And do you in his presence utter deceit in a solemn manner — Sept
Is it for him that you utter deceit — NAB

8. Will ye accept his person?
Will you choose His side — Ber
Will you be partial in his favour — Jerus
Are you God's hired partisans — Knox
Will you be sycophants of the Almighty — Mof
Is it for him that you show partiality — NAB

will ye contend for God?
posing as special pleaders for God — Ber
and act as his advocates — Jerus
Do you play advocate on the part of God — NAB
resolve to acquit him — Knox

9. Is it good that he should search you out?
Will it be well when He examines you — Ber
Why then, beware of his own infallible scrutiny — Knox
Ah, it would be well if He strictly searched you — Sprl
Be careful that he doesn't find out what you are doing! — Tay

or as one man mocketh another, do ye so mock him?
Or, as a man is deceived, can ye deceive him — ABPS
think you he will be blinded, as men are blinded, by your sophistries — Knox
When ye trifle with Him, as trifling with a mortal man! — Sprl
Will you quibble with him as you quibble with a man — NEB
Or do you think you can fool God as well as men — Tay

10. He will surely reprove you,
Harsh rebuke you will receive from him — Jerus
Nay, he himself will be the first to blame you — Knox
No, he will punish you — Mof

if ye do secretly accept persons.
if you secretly practice partiality — Ber
if you use lies to help him out — Tay
for wrongful attachment to his cause — Knox

11. Shall not his excellency make you afraid? and his dread fall upon you?
Shall not his majesty make you afraid,
And the dread of him fall upon you — ABPS
Shall not his majesty overwhelm you?
And the dread of him fall upon you — Rhm
your turn, then, to fear every movement of his, to cower before his terrors! — Knox
will not his awful majesty confound you; and the terror of him fall upon you — Sept

12. Your remembrances are like unto ashes,
Your memorable sayings are proverbs of ashes — ASV
Your old maxims are proverbs of ashes — Jerus
Your wise memories will vanish into dust — Knox
Your maxims crumble like mere ashes — Mof
Dusty are your stored-up parables — Sprl
These tremendous statements you have made have about as much value as ashes — Tay
Your pompous talk is dust and ashes — NEB

your bodies to bodies of clay.
Your defences are defences of clay — ASV
your retorts, retorts of clay — Jerus
your pride will prove to be a thing of clay — Knox

your arguments collapse like mounds of clay — Mof
Like miry heaps your swelling words — Sprl
Your defense of God is as fragile as a clay vase! — Tay

13. Hold your peace, let me alone,
Silence! — Jerus
Oh, be ye silent before me — Sprl
that I may speak, and let come on me what will.
Now I will do the talking,
whatever may befall me — Jerus
I must have speech,
whatever happens! — Mof

14. Wherefore do I take my flesh in my teeth,
Do not ask why I set my teeth so firmly — Knox
I will run any risks — Mof
I will put my neck in the noose — NEB
and put my life in mine hand?
hazard my very life! — Mof

15. Though he slay me, yet will I trust in him: but I will maintain mine own ways before him.
Let him kill me if he will; I have no other hope
than to justify my conduct in his eyes — Jerus
He may kill me — what else can I expect? I will maintain my innocence to his face — Mof
Slay me though he might, I will wait for him;
I will maintain my conduct before him — NAB

16. He also shall be my salvation: for an hypocrite shall not come before him.
and spare me he will; let the guilty shun his presence, not I — Knox
This at least will be in my favor, that I am not godless, to be rejected instantly from his presence — Tay
And this shall be my salvation,
that no impious man can come into his presence — NAB
But this will be my deliverance,
That an impious man would not come before him — AAT
This at least assures my success,
that no godless man may appear before him — NEB

17. Hear diligently my speech, and my declaration with your ears.
Listen attentively to what I say, and let my plea enter your ears — Ber
Nay, hear me out; let me open my mind in full — Knox
Hearken, O hearken ye unto my speech;
Yea, my declarations with your ears — Sprl

18. Behold now, I have ordered my cause; I know that I shall be justified.
As I have prepared my defense, I am sure that I shall be vindicated — Ber
You shall see, I will proceed by due form of law,
persuaded, as I am, that I am guiltless — Jerus
This is my case: I know that I am righteous — Tay

19. Who is he that will plead with me? for now, if I hold my tongue, I shall give up the ghost.
Who comes against me with an accusation?
Let him come! I am ready to be silenced and to die — Jerus
Only let me meet my accuser! Why must I die unheard? — Knox
Who can argue with me over this? If you could prove me wrong I would stop defending myself and die — Tay

20. Only do not two things unto me: then will I not hide myself from thee.
Spare me two things . . . — Ber
But grant me these two favours . . . — Jerus
But two rights I claim, if I am to face thee openly — Knox

21. Withdraw thine hand far from me: and let not thy dread make me afraid.
Take your hand away, which lies so heavy on me,
no longer make me cower from your terror — Jerus
lift off thy heavy hand,
scare me not with thy terrors — Mof
Don't abandon me. And don't terrify me with your awesome presence — Tay

22. Then call thou, and I will answer: or let me speak, and answer thou me.
Then arraign me, and I will reply;
or rather, I will speak and you shall answer me — Jerus
then I will answer thy summons —
or, answer thou my summons — Mof

23. How many are mine iniquities and sins? make me to know my transgression and my sin.
Tell me, what are all these transgres-

sions, these faults thou findest in me? — Knox

What are my faults and my sins?
My misdeeds and my sins make known to me! — NAB

24. Wherefore hidest thou thy face, and holdest me for thine enemy?

Why is it that thou turnest thy back on me, and wilt treat me as an enemy — Knox

Why do you hide your face
and look on me as your enemy — Jerus

25. Wilt thou break a leaf driven to and fro?

Will you intimidate a wind-blown leaf — Jerus

Wilt thou tread upon a fallen leaf — Lam

Wilt thou harry a poor fluttering leaf — Mof

A driven leaf wilt thou put in fear — ABPS

and wilt thou pursue the dry stubble?

And pursue the dry chaff — ABPS

or chase the dried-up chaff — Jerus

. . . the dry grass in the air — Lam

. . . a withered straw — Mof

26. For thou writest bitter things against me, and makest me to possess the iniquities of my youth.

you list bitter accusations against me, taxing me with the faults of my youth — Jerus

A bitter sentence thou hast passed on me, that I must pay for errors of my youth! — Mof

For thou writest bitter things against me,
And makest me inherit the sins of my youth — ABPS

27. Thou puttest my feet also in the stocks,

Thou fastenest logs to my feet — Mof

and put my feet in a clog — Sept

and lookest narrowly unto all my paths;

setting bounds to my footsteps — Ber

thou watchest every step I take — Mof

thou settest a print upon the heels of my feet.

measuring my footprints — Jerus

Thou drawest a line about the soles of my feet — AAT

28. And he, as a rotten thing, consumeth,

Though a man comes to nothing like a bit of dead wood — Bas

Though he wears out like a leather bottle — NAB

I am like the severed root of a tree which soon decays — Ber

While my life is crumbling like rotten wood — Jerus

when I am no better than rotting carrion — Knox

Yet a man is like a worn-out waterskin — Lam

Man wastes away like a rotten thing — RSV

I am like a fallen, rotten tree — Tay

as a garment that is moth eaten.

than a garment fretted away by the moth! — Knox

like a moth-eaten coat — Tay

CHAPTER 14

1. Man that is born of a woman is of few days, and full of trouble.

As for man, the son of woman, his days are short . . . — Bas

Man, born of a woman!
His days cut short, and filled with disquietude — Sprl

Man, born of woman,
has a short life yet has his fill of sorrow — Jerus

So frail man's life, woman-born, so full of trouble — Knox

2. He cometh forth like a flower, and is cut down:

He unfolds like a flower and fades — Ber

He blossoms, and he withers, like a flower — Jerus

brief as a flower that blooms and withers — Knox

he fleeth also as a shadow, and continueth not.

he goes in flight like a shade, and is never seen again — Bas

he is fleeting like a shadow and does not remain — Ber

He glideth away indeed like a shadow and can make no stay — Sept

as the shadow of a passing cloud, he quickly disappears — Tay

fugitive as a shadow, changing all the while — Knox

3. **And dost thou open thine eyes upon such an one, and bringest me into judgment with thee?**
Is it on such a one as this that your eyes are fixed, with the purpose of judging him — Bas
And is this what you deign to turn your gaze on,
him that you would bring before you to be judged — Jerus
and is he worth that watchfulness of thine, must thou needs call him to account — Knox
And thou wilt fasten upon such!
Thou wilt bring him to justice — Mof
Must you be so harsh with frail men, and demand an accounting from them — Tay
4. **Who can bring a clean thing out of an unclean? not one.**
Oh, that there were one pure among the impure! But there is none — Ber
How can you demand purity in one born impure? — Tay
5. **Seeing his days are determined, the number of his months are with thee, thou hast appointed his bounds that he cannot pass;**
Since man's days are already determined and the number of his months is wholly in Your control, and he cannot pass the bounds of his allotted time — Amp
Since man's days are measured out, since his tale of months depends on you,
since you assign him bounds he cannot pass — Jerus
Whether the course of his life on earth be one day; or months be numbered out for him, he cometh to the term thou hast set, but cannot pass it — Sept
6. **Turn from him that he may rest, till he shall accomplish, as an hireling, his day.**
then look away from him, and let him rest, so that, like a hired man, he may enjoy his day — Ber
take thine eye off him, let him have some peace,
until his labouring day be done — Mof
look away from him, and desist,
that he may enjoy, like a hireling, his day — RSV
7. **For there is hope of a tree, if it be cut down, that it will sprout again, and that the tender branch thereof will not cease.**
There is always hope for a tree:
when felled it can start its life again,
its shoots continue to sprout — Jerus
8. **Though the root thereof wax old in the earth, and the stock thereof die in the ground;**
Though its roots age in the earth, and its stump dies in the ground — Ber
9. **Yet through the scent of water it will bud,**
but let it scent the water, and it buds — Jerus
but at the breath of water it revives — Knox
Through the vapour of water it will sprout — Sprl
Yet at the first whiff of water it may flourish again — NAB
and bring forth boughs like a plant.
And put forth boughs like a sapling — ABPS
and the leaves come as they came when it first was planted — Knox
10. **But man dieth, and wasteth away:**
But man dieth and lieth low — JPS
But (the brave, strong) man must die and lie prostrate — Amp
But man? He dies, and lifeless he remains — Jerus
But a man dies, and he disappears — NEB
yea, man giveth up the ghost, and where is he?
yes, man breathes his last, and where is he — Amp
Yea the son of earth doth cease to breathe and where is he — Rhm
11. **As the waters fail from the sea, and the flood decayeth and drieth up:**
Like the water of a vanished lake, like a dry, drained river — Mof
As waters evaporate from the lake, and the river drains and dries up — Amp
Where is the sea, when its waters dry up, the river when its bed is empty? — Knox
12. **So man lieth down and riseth not:**
man, once in his resting place, will never rise again — Jerus
so man falls asleep, never to rise again — Knox
till the heavens be no more, they shall not awake, nor be raised out of their sleep.

Till the heavens be no more, they shall not awake,
Nor be roused out of their sleep — ASV

the heavens will wear away before he wakes,
before he rises from his sleep — Jerus

never to waken, though the skies wear out,
never to stir out of his slumber — Mof

13. O that thou wouldest hide me in the grave, that thou wouldest keep me secret, until thy wrath be past, that thou wouldst appoint me a set time, and remember me!

If only you would hide me in Sheol, and shelter me there until your anger is past,
fixing a certain day for calling me to mind — Jerus

Ah, if the grave were only a place of shelter, where thou wouldst hide me away until thy anger was spent, with a time appointed when thou wouldst bethink thyself of me again!—Knox

Oh, that you would hide me with the dead, and forget me there until your anger ends; but mark your calendar to think of me again! — Tay

14. If a man die, shall he live again? all the days of my appointed time will I wait, till my change come.

for once a man is dead can he come back to life?
day after day of my service I would wait
for my relief to come — Jerus

Ah, if the dead might live again! Then I could wait willingly enough, all the time of my campaigning, till I were relieved at my post — Knox

If a man die, shall he live again?
All the days of my warfare would I wait,
Till my release should come — ASV

If only man might die and live again, I could endure my weary post until relief arrived — Mof

15. Thou shalt call, and I will answer thee: thou wilt have a desire to the work of thine hands.

Then you would call, and I should answer,
you would want to see the work of your hands once more — Jerus

thou wouldst summon me at last, and I would answer thy summons, thy creature, safe in thy loving hands! — Knox

Thou wouldst call, and I would answer thee; Thou wouldst yearn after Thy handiwork — Ber

16. For now thou numberest my steps: dost thou not watch over my sin?

But now that Thou art watching my every step and art recording my every sin, — Ber

Now you count every step I take,
but then you would cease to spy on my sins; — Jerus

So jealous a record thou keepest of every step I take, and hast thou never a blind eye for my faults? — Knox

thou would'st not keep account of all I do,
thou would'st not watch for nothing but my faults; — Mof

17. My transgression is sealed up in a bag,

My transgression is sealed up in a package — ABPS

I would that my transgressions were sealed up in a sack — Ber

Instead, must you seal up every wrong-doing of mine, as in a casket—Knox

You bundle them all together as evidence against me — Tay

you would seal up my crime in a bag — Jerus

and thou sewest up mine iniquity.

and you glue up my iniquity [to preserve it in full for the day of reckoning] — Amp

And thou dost plaster over my guilt — AAT

and whiten my fault over — Jerus

embalm the memory of my transgressions? — Knox

Thou dost keep my iniquity under seal — NEB

18. And surely the mountain falling cometh to nought,

But as a mountain, if it falls, crumbles to nothing — Amp

But no! Soon or late the mountain falls — Jerus

Nay there is no help for it; mountain-side or cliff that begins to crumble scales away — Knox

But alas! even mountains crumble — Mof

and the rock is removed out of his place.
and vanishes at last — Knox
rocks are swept aside — Mof

19. **The waters wear the stones:**
the waters wear away the stones — RSV
stones are worn out by water — Mof
as waters wear smooth great stones — Ber
thou washest away the things which grow out of the dust of the earth;
its floods sweep away the dust of the earth — ABPS
The overflowings thereof wash away the dust of the earth — ASV
and as floods wash away the soil of the earth — Amp
the cloudburst erodes the soil — Jerus
and thou destroyest the hope of man.
so You, O Lord, destroy the hope of man — Amp
just so do you destroy man's hope — Jerus
and Thou hast made no less inevitable man's doom — Knox
So every hope of man is worn away — Tay

20. **Thou prevailest for ever against him, and he passeth:**
Thou overpowerest him, and he departs forever — Ber
You crush him once for all, and he is gone — Jerus
Thou art too strong for him, so he has to go — Mof
Always you are against him, and then he passes off the scene — Tay
Thou assailest him continually, and he goes hence — ABPS
thou changest his countenance, and sendeth him away.
You change his appearance [in death], and send him away [from the presence of the living] — Amp
with changed appearance you send him away — NAB
thou alterest his face in death, and he departs — Mof
You make him old and wrinkled, then send him away — Tay

21. **His sons come to honour, and he knoweth it not; and they are brought low, but he perceiveth it not of them.**
His sons achieve honor, but he is unaware of it; or they are humbled, but he does not notice — Ber

22. **But his flesh upon him shall have pain, and his soul within him shall mourn.**
But his body [lamenting its decay in the grave] shall grieve over him, and his soul shall mourn [over the body of clay which it once enlivened] — Amp
He feels only the pain of his own body, and he mourns only for himself — RSV
His flesh upon him becomes black, and his life blood dries up within him — NEB

CHAPTER 15

1. **Then answered Eliphaz the Temanite, and said,**
Eliphaz the Temanite spoke next. He said: — Jerus

2. **Should a wise man utter vain knowledge,**
Should a wise man utter such windy knowledge? — Amp
Should a wise man answer with bombast — Ber
Does a wise man answer with airy reasonings — Jerus
This is not a wise man's way, to answer with windy sophistries — Knox
Would any man of sense argue so wildly — Mof
You are supposed to be a wise man, yet you give us all this foolish talk — Tay
and fill his belly with the east wind?
and fill his chest with a hot, dry wind — Ber
and answer with a bellyful of wind — NEB
as if thou hadst the sirocco in thy blood — Knox
or will he give birth to the east wind — Bas
or make himself a windbag — Mof
You are nothing but a windbag. — Tay

3. **Should he reason with unprofitable talk? or with speeches wherewith he can do no good?**

arguing with pointless talk in speeches that do no good — Ber

Does he defend himself with empty talk
and ineffectual wordiness — Jerus

Would he talk on, to no profit,
with words that serve no purpose — Mof

4. **Yea, thou castest off fear, and restrainest prayer before God.**

Yea, thou doest away with fear,
And hinderest devotion before God — ASV

You destroy reverence, and you hinder prayer before God — Ber

Yea, you are also discarding reverence, and talk too much in the presence of God — Lam

You undermine religion,
with your threatening of God — Mof

Surely thou wouldst make void godly fear,
And suppress devotion before God — Sprl

You in fact do away with piety,
and you lessen devotion toward God — NAB

5. **For thy mouth uttereth thine iniquity, and thou choosest the tongue of the crafty.**

For thine iniquity teacheth thy mouth,
And thou choosest the tongue of the crafty — ASV

For your guilt prompts your mouth what to say, and you choose the language of the shrewd — Ber

Thy tongue takes its instructions from a sinful heart; this is rebel speech — Knox

your iniquity dictates what you say,
and deceit is the language of your choice — NEB

Your sins are telling your mouth what to say! Your words are based on clever deception, not truth — Tay

6. **Thine own mouth condemneth thee, and not I: yea, thine own lips testify against thee.**

Not I, but your mouth convicts you, and your own lips witness against you — Ber

Your own mouth condemns you, not I;
your own lips refute you — NAB

But why should I condemn you? Your own mouth does! — Tay

7. **Art thou the first man that was born? or wast thou made before the hills?**

Are you the first-born of the human race,
brought into the world before the hills — Jerus

Tell me, was thine some primeval birth; wast thou made before the hills — Knox

8. **Hast thou heard the secret of God? and dost thou restrain wisdom to thyself?**

Hast thou listened in the council of God;
And reservest thou wisdom to thyself — ABPS

Did you listen in on the council of God? Do you have a monopoly on wisdom — Ber

Are you a member of God's inner council?
Have you made divine wisdom all your own — Mof

Are you privy to the counsels of God,
And do you restrict wisdom to yourself — NAB

9. **What knowest thou, that we know not? what understandest thou, which is not in us?**

What do you understand which is not equally clear to us — Amp

What insight have you that we lack — Ber

10. **With us are both the gray-headed and very aged men, much elder than thy father.**

A gray-haired man, and an ancient, are of our numbers;
these have seen more summers than your father — Jerus

On our side are aged men much older than your father! — Tay

11. **Are the consolations of God small with thee? is there any secret thing with thee?**

Are the consolations of God too little for thee?
And the word that gently deals with thee — ABPS

. . . too trivial for you? Is there any secret thing which you have not given up — Amp

Do you scorn the comfort that God gives,
and the moderation we have used in speaking — Jerus

It should be of no great matter for God to comfort thee, if thy untimely

speech did not forbid it — Knox
The divine comfort that we bring, you slight,
these words of ours which deal with you so gently? — Mof

12. Why doth thine heart carry thee away?
Why is your heart uncontrolled — Bas
Why let your passions carry you away — Ber
What makes you so bold at heart — NEB
what mean these transports — Knox
and what do thy eyes wink at,
And why twinkle thine eyes? — ABPS
And why do thine eyes flash — ASV
and why allow your eyes to flash — Ber
How evil you look — Jerus
why does that eye roll so wildly? — Knox

13. That thou turnest thy spirit against God, and lettest such words go out of thy mouth?
when you thus loose your anger on God
and utter speeches such as these! — Jerus
What pride is this that would cross God himself, moving thee to rash utterance — Knox
And you turn against God and say all these evil things against him — Tay

14. What is man, that he could be clean? and he which is born of a woman, that he should be righteous?
What is mortal man, that he could be pure; or one born of a woman, that he could be righteous — Ber
It is not in man to live a life all blameless; never a son of woman yet found acquittal — Knox

15. Behold, he putteth no trust in his saints; yea, the heavens are not clean in his sight.
Fickle natures God finds among his very angels; the purity of heaven itself does not suffice him — Knox
If in his holy ones God places no confidence,
and if the heavens are not clean in his sight — NAB
Why, God doesn't even trust His angels! Even the heavens can't be absolutely pure compared with him! — Tay

16. How much more abominable and filthy is man, which drinketh iniquity like water?
How much less one that is abominable and corrupt,
A man that drinketh iniquity like water! — ASV
How much less someone like you, who is corrupt and sinful, drinking in sin as a sponge soaks up water! — Tay
How much less so is the abominable, the corrupt:
man, who drinks in iniquity like water! — NAB

17. I will shew thee, hear me; and that which I have seen I will declare;
Listen to me, I have a lesson for you:
I will tell you of my own experience — Jerus
Listen, and I will answer you from my own experience — Tay

18. Which wise men have told from their fathers, and have not hid it:
what wise men have told, and their fathers have not hidden — RSV
and of the teaching of the sages,
those faithful guardians of the traditions of their fathers — Jerus
a truth that wise men handed down, imparted to them by their fathers — Mof
confirmed by the experience of wise men who have been told this same thing from their fathers — Tay

19. Unto whom alone the earth was given,
to whom alone the land was given — NAB
that dwelt ever in their own land — Knox
who had the land all to themselves — Mof
and no stranger passed among them.
and no stranger intruded among them — Ber
and with never a foreigner to mix with them — Jerus
and held no commerce with strangers — Knox
untainted by a foreigner — Mof

20. The wicked man travaileth with pain all his days,
. . . is tormented with anxiety . . . — Ber
. . . writhes in pain . . . — RSV
All the days of the wicked man he is in pain — ABPS

and the number of years is hidden to the oppressor.
Even the number of years that are laid up for the oppressor — ASV
through all the years that are laid up for the ruthless — RSV
and the number of years stored up for the cruel is small — Bas
the years allotted to the tyrant are numbered — Jerus

21. **A dreadful sound is in his ears:**
Sounds of fear are in his ears — ABPS
A sound of terrors is in his ears — ASV
The danger signal ever echoes . . . — Jerus
terror whispers in his ear — Knox
in prosperity the destroyer shall come upon him.
in the midst of peace the marauder swoops on him — Jerus
danger there is none, but he sees plots everywhere — Knox
some plunderer will break his peace, he fears — Mof

22. **He believeth not that he shall return out of darkness,**
He has no hope of coming safe out of the dark — Bas
He cannot hope to escape from dark death — NEB
He dares not go out into the darkness, lest he be murdered — Tay
and he is waited for of the sword.
And he is destined for the sword — ABPS
and his fate will be the sword — Bas
but knows that he is destined for the sword, — Jerus

23. **He wandereth abroad for bread, saying, Where is it? he knoweth that the day of darkness is ready at his hand.**
He wanders about for food. Where is it? He feels that the day of darkness is upon him — Ber
marked down as meat for the vulture. He knows that his ruin is at hand — Jerus
he is flung out as food for vultures; such a man knows that his destruction is certain — NEB
A wanderer, food for vultures,
he knows that his destruction is imminent — NAB

24. **Trouble and anguish shall make him afraid; they shall prevail against him, as a king ready to the battle.**
trouble and worry threaten him; they overwhelm him as a king ready for assault — Ber
He lives in fear, distress, and anguish. His enemies conquer him as a king defeats his foes — Tay
The hour of darkness makes him terrified;
distress and anguish close in on him, as though some king were mounting an attack — Jerus

25. **For he stretcheth out his hand against God, and strengtheneth himself against the Almighty.**
And all because he chose God for his enemy, matched himself against omnipotence — Knox
For he challenged God,
he matched himself against the Almighty — Mof
he clenches his fist against God, defying the Almighty — Tay
Because he has stretched out his hand against God, and behaveth himself proudly against the Almighty — RV
He raised his hand against God,
he ventured to defy Shaddai—Jerus

26. **He runneth upon him, even on his neck, upon the thick bosses of his bucklers:**
He runneth against him with a stiff neck, with the thick bosses of his bucklers — RV
Running stubbornly against Him with a thickly ornamented shield — Amp
Blindly he bore down on him
from behind his massive shield—Jerus
running stubbornly against him
with a thick-bossed shield — RSV

27. **Because he covereth his face with his fatness, and maketh collops of fat on his flanks.**
. . . And gathered fat upon his loins — ABPS
Because he has blinded himself with his crassness,
padding his loins with fat — NAB
— so swollen in prosperity,
so bloated in his wealth — Mof
Although his face be anointed with oil,
And his loins rubbed with ointment — Sept
This wicked man is fat and rich — Tay

28. **And he dwelleth in desolate cities,**
And he inhabiteth cities cut off — YLT
He has made his resting place in the

towns which have been pulled down — Bas
Now he is like some plant that grows amid deserted streets — Knox
let him therefore lodge in deserted cities — Sept
and has lived in conquered cities, after killing off its citizens — Tay
and in houses which no man inhabiteth, which are ready to become heaps.
in houses which no man should inhabit,
which were destined to become heaps of ruins — RSV
in houses where no man had a right to be, whose fate was to become masses of broken walls — Bas
upon houses uninhabited that lie in ruins — Knox

29. He shall not be rich, neither shall his substance continue,
He shall not be rich, nor shall his wealth endure — ABPS
He does not get wealth for himself, and is unable to keep what he has got — Bas
no root shall he strike into the earth of true wealth or abiding prosperity — Knox
But what he won he cannot keep — Mof
neither shall he prolong the perfection thereof upon the earth.
Nor shall their possession spread abroad in the earth — ABPS
nor will he strike root in the earth — RSV
Neither shall their produce bend to the earth — RV
the heads of his grain are not bent down to the earth — Bas
the harvest of his gain he cannot reap — Mof

30. He shall not depart out of darkness;
never leave the shadows — Knox
he will not escape from darkness — RSV
He turneth not aside from darkness — YLT
the flame shall dry up his branches,
A flame will wither up his tender buds — Jerus
but he is withered up by the heat — Knox
His tender branch doth a flame dry up — YLT
and by the breath of his mouth shall he go away.
And by the breath of God's mouth shall he go away — ASV
the wind will carry off his blossom — Jerus
or carried away by the blast — Knox
and his blossom will be swept away by the wind — RSV
And he turneth aside at the breath of his mouth — YLT

31. Let not him that is deceived trust in vanity:
Let him not trust in vanity, deceiving himself — ASV
Let him not trust in emptiness, deceiving himself — RSV
for vanity shall be his recompence.
For evil shall be his reward — ABPS
for the money he trusts in will be his only reward — Tay
for all his dealings will come to nothing — NEB

32. It shall be accomplished before his time,
It shall be accomplished and paid in full while he still lives — Amp
His boughs will wither before their time — Jerus
his boughs fade all too soon — Mof
fall he must before his time — Knox
Before he dies, all this futility will become evident to him — Tay
and his branch shall not be green.
withered every branch — Knox
before their fronds are green — Mof

33. He shall shake off his unripe grape as the vine, and shall cast off his flower as the olive.
He shall be like a vine that sheds its grapes unripened,
and like an olive tree casting off its bloom — NAB
despoiled the vine with clusters yet unripe, shed the olive's flower — Knox

34. For the congregation of hypocrites shall be desolate,
For the household of the impure is desolate — ABPS
For the company of the godless shall be barren — ASV
For the band of the evil-doers gives no fruit — Bas
For the godless are a barren tribe — Mof

and fire shall consume the tabernacles of bribery.
and the tents of those who give wrong decisions for reward are burned with fire — Bas
the house of the bribe-taker shall burn about his ears — Knox

35. **They conceive mischief, and bring forth vanity,**
They conceive malice and bring forth emptiness — NAB
Conceive mischief, and you breed disaster — Jerus
big with mischief, they bear mischief — Mof
and their belly prepareth deceit.
And their womb matures falsehood — ABPS
and their inmost soul hatches deceit — Amp
and carry in yourself deceitfulness — Jerus
they give birth to failure — NAB

CHAPTER 16

1. **Then Job answered and said,**
Job spoke next. He said: — Jerus

2. **I have heard many such things: miserable comforters are ye all.**
I have heard this sort of thing many times.
Wearisome comforters are you all! — NAB
. . . What sorry comforters you are! — Jerus
Old tales, and cold comfort; you are all alike — Knox

3. **Shall vain words have an end?**
Will your futile words of wind have no end — Amp
Words are but wind; there is no end to them — Knox
Won't you ever stop your flow of foolish words — Tay
or what emboldeneth thee that thou answerest?
What incites you to answer — Ber
Or what so strongly exciteth thee that thou must respond — Rhm
Or what sickness have you that you speak on — NAB
What a plague your need to have the last word is! — Jerus

4. **I also could speak as ye do: if your soul were in my soul's stead,**
I also could speak as you do,
if you were in my place — RSV
It would not be hard for me to say such things if your souls were in my soul's place — Bas
Believe me, I could do as well, were you in my case — Knox
But perhaps I'd sermonize the same as you — if you were I and I were you — Tay
I could heap up words against you,
I could join words together against you — ASV
I could compose words against you — Ber
I too could overwhelm you with sermons — Jerus
talk the language of consolation — Knox
I would spout off my criticisms against you — Tay
and shake mine head at you.
and wag my head at you — NEB
and mock you all the while — Knox
and toss my head in scorn — Mof

5. **But I would strengthen you with my mouth,**
I could strengthen you with talk — NAB
I might encourage you with my mouth — Ber
But no, I would speak words of encouragement — NEB
But no! I would speak in such a way that it would help you — Tay
and the moving of my lips should assure your grief.
And the comfort of my lips should uphold! — ABPS
and bring you comfort with my lips — Ber
and shake my head with silent lips — NAB
my lips should tremble with a show of pity — Knox
I would try to take away your grief — Tay

6. **Though I speak, my grief is not assuaged:**
If I say what is in my mind, my pain becomes no less — Bas
But, while I am speaking, my suffering remains — Jerus

But here is grief words cannot assuage — Knox

and though I forbear, what am I eased?

and if I keep quiet, how much of it goes from me — Bas

if I leave off, it will not depart from me — NAB

nor silence banish — Knox

7. **But now he hath made me weary:**

And now ill-will drives me to distraction — Jerus

Here is God wearing me out, dazing me! — Mof

Surely now God has worn me out — RSV

For God has ground me down — Tay

thou hast made desolate all my company.

He has disbanded my whole family — Ber

and taken away my family — Tay

8. **And thou hast filled me with wrinkles,**

And Thou hast shrivelled me up — JPS

O God, you have turned me to skin and bones — Tay

which is a witness against me:

it [my gauntness] is an open evidence against me! — Mof

it has become a witness! — AAT

as a proof, they say, of my sins — Tay

and my leanness rising up in me beareth witness to my face.

And my leanness riseth up against me, it testifieth to my face — JPS

And so my wasting away hath risen up against me,
In my face it answereth — Rhm

9. **He teareth me in his wrath, who hateth me:**

He has torn me and broken me in his wrath — Lam

God hates me and angrily tears at my flesh — Tay

he gnasheth upon me with his teeth;

he shows his teeth at me — Mof

mine enemy sharpeneth his eyes upon me.

My enemies look sharply at me — Ber

my enemy looks daggers at me — AAT

10. **They have gaped upon me with their mouth;**

their mouths are agape to bite me — NAB

Their mouths are open wide against me — Bas

Mouths that deride me — Knox

These 'comforters' have gaping jaws to swallow me — Tay

they have smitten me upon the cheek reproachfully;

. . . insolently — Amp

Their insults strike like slaps in the face — Jerus

hands that smite me on the cheek in reproof — Knox

they have gathered themselves together against me.

all of them come together in a mass against me — Bas

Together against me they have closed their ranks — Rhm

They are all in league against me — NEB

11. **God hath delivered me to the ungodly, and turned me over into the hands of the wicked.**

God delivers me up to the unrighteous,
And casts me into the hands of the wicked — ABPS

God gives me over to the power of sinners, sending me violently into the hands of evil-doers — Bas

to what ill neighbourhood God has condemned me, what tyrants hold me in their grip! — Knox

GOD doth abandon me to him that is perverse,
And into the hands of the lawless he throweth me headlong — Rhm

12. **I was at ease, but he hath broken me asunder:**

I was at rest, — and he shattered me — ABPS

I was at peace, but he dislodged me — NAB

When I was happy, he, he crushed me — Mof

I was living quietly until he broke me apart — Tay

I was living at ease, but [Satan] crushed me and broke me apart — Amp

he hath also taken me by my neck,

He grabbed me by the neck — Ber

Yea he seized me by my neck — Rhm

and shaken me to pieces,

and dashed me in pieces — Rhm

and broke me down — Ber

and he breaketh me in pieces — YLT

and set me up for his mark.

He set me up for His target — Ber

then hung me up as his target — Tay

13. His archers compass me round about, he cleaveth my reins asunder, and doth not spare; he poureth out my gall upon the ground.
[Satan's] arrows whiz around me; he slashes open my vitals, and does not spare; he pours out my gall on the ground — Amp
They surrounded me with javelins, darting them into my veins — without mercy they poured my gall on the ground — Sept
His arrows are round about me, he shoots at my kidneys and does not spare; he pours out my gall on the ground — Lam
his arrows rain upon me,
piercing my vitals without pity,
till my entrails ooze out on the earth — Mof
His archers surround me, letting fly their arrows, so that the ground is wet from my wounds — Tay

14. He breaketh me with breach upon breach,
He pierces me through with thrust upon thrust — Jerus
I am broken with wound after wound — Bas
Breach upon breach he makes upon my walls — Mof
They shot me, one deadly wound on another — Sept
he runneth upon me like a giant.
He runs upon me like a warrior — ABPS
he storms me with a warrior's rush — Mof

15. I have sewed sackcloth upon my skin,
I have made haircloth the clothing of my skin — Bas
No wonder I go clad in sackcloth — Knox
and defiled my horn in the dust.
and rubbed my brow in the dust — Jerus
and buried my forelock . . . — NEB
and bowed my glory to the dust — Mof
and have laid my strength in the dust — RSV
And I have rolled my turban in the dust — Sprl
disfigured with ashes — Knox

16. My face is foul with weeping,
. . . inflamed . . . — ABPS
. . . red . . . — ASV
. . . flushed . . . — NEB
. . . swollen . . . — Knox
. . . disfigured . . . — Sprl
and on my eyelids is the shadow of death;
and a veil of shadow hangs on my eyelids — Jerus
and black shadows are on my eyelids — AAT

17. Not for any injustice in mine hands:
though my hands are guilty of no violence — Ber
Although there is no violence in my hands — JPS
Such is the reward of a guiltless life — Knox
also my prayer is pure.
and my prayer is undefiled — Jerus
of prayer offered without stain — Knox

18. O earth, cover not thou my blood, and let my cry have no place.
I charge thee, earth, to leave my blood unburied, never to muffle the echoes of my protest — Knox
O earth, do not conceal my blood. Let it protest on my behalf — Tay
O earth, cover not my blood and let my cry for justice find no rest! — NEB

19. Also now, behold, my witness is in heaven,
there is one in high heaven that knows the truth and must bear witness — Knox
Yet even now the Witness to my innocence is there in heaven — Tay
and my record is on high.
And he that voucheth for me is on high — RV
and the supporter of my cause is on high — Bas
and my spokesman . . . — NAB
my Advocate . . . — Ber
and he who hath perfect knowledge of me is on high — Sept

20. My friends scorn me: but mine eye poureth out tears unto God.
My friends deride me,
but my tears turn to God in prayer — Mof
While my friends are my scorners, my eyes turn weepingly to God — Ber
Friends, prate on; these tears of mine issue their challenge to God! — Knox
My friends it is who wrong me;

before God my eyes drop tears — NAB

21. O that one might plead for a man with God,

O that there were one who might plead for a man with God and that he would maintain his right with Him — Amp

If only there were one to arbitrate between man and God — NEB

Let this plead for me as I stand before God — Jerus

Ah, could but a mortal bring God to justice — Knox

as a man pleadeth for his neighbour!

as a man will plead for his fellows — Jerus

as between a man and his neighbour! — NEB

as man impleads man — Knox

22. When a few years are come, then I shall go the way whence I shall not return.

For in a short time I will take the journey from which I will not come back — Bas

Come but a few years more,
and I go, never to return — Mof

For all so soon I must go down that road from which I shall never return — Tay

CHAPTER 17

1. My breath is corrupt,

My breath grows weak — Jerus

My spirit is broken — Amp

My mind is distraught — NEB

My life is ruined — Ber

Broken my will to live — Knox

my days are extinct,

. . . are spent — Amp

. . . are extinguished — Ber

. . . are snuffed out — AAT

. . . are numbered — NEB

the graves are ready for me.

the last resting-place is ready for me — Bas

the grave is yawning for me! — Ber

and the gravediggers are gathering for me — Jerus

2. Are there not mockers with me?

Of a truth, mockeries beset me — ABPS

Truly, those who make sport of me are round about me — Bas

I am the butt of mockers — Jerus

Illusions are indeed my lot — Mof

Wherever I turn, men taunt me — NEB

and doth not mine eye continue in their provocation?

and my eye dwells on their obstinacy, insults and resistance — Amp

and my eyes become dark because of their bitter laughing — Bas

my eye gazes on their contention — Ber

Alas! mine eye penetrateth their provocations! — Sprl

And on their insults mine eye doth rest — Rhm

and my day is darkened by their sneers — NEB

3. Lay down now, put me in a surety with thee;

Give a pledge, I pray thee;
Be thou my surety with thee — ABPS

You yourself must take my own guarantee — Jerus

Give me a pledge that thou thyself will act — Mof

Grant me one to offer you a pledge on my behalf — NAB

Give me a pledge with Yourself [acknowledge my innocence before my death] — Amp

who is he that will strike hands with me?

who is there that will give security for me — Amp

for who else can pledge himself for me — NEB

since no one cares to clap his hand on mine. — Jerus

who else would undertake thy cause against thee — Mof

4. For thou hast hid their heart from understanding:

But their heart [Lord] You have closed to understanding — Amp

But their heart Thou hast closed to reason — Ber

You have kept their hearts from wisdom — Bas

thou hast robbed their hearts of all discernment — Knox

You darken their minds to knowledge — NAB

therefore shalt thou not exalt them.
therefore You will not let them triumph — Amp
for this cause you will not give them honour — Bas
and they shall have no cause for boasting — Knox
therefore they do not understand — NAB

5. **He that speaketh flattery to his friends, even the eyes of his children shall fail.**
Whoso betrays friends for a prey, Even the eyes of his children shall fail — ABPS
He who informs against his friends to get a share of their property, the eyes of his children will fail — RSV
Like a man who invites his friends to share his property while the eyes of his own sons languish, — Jerus
He who denounces his friends for a price, the eyes of his children shall see famine — Ber

6. **He hath made me also a byword of the people;**
. . . a word of shame . . . —Bas
. . . a proverb . . . — Ber
. . . a mockery . . . — Tay
and aforetime I was as a tabret.
And they spit in my face — ASV
And I am become an open abhorring — RV
I have become a mark for their sport — Bas
And one before whom men spit am I become — AAT
and I am become a subject of laughter for them — Sept
a portent for all to see — NEB

7. **Mine eye also is dim by reason of sorrow,**
My eye is bedimmed with grief — ABPS
. . . dim because of anger — Lam
and all my members are as a shadow.
and all my body is wasted to a shade — Bas
and I am but a shadow of my former self — Tay

8. **Upright men shall be astonied at this, and the innocent shall stir up himself against the hypocrite.**
The upright are surprised at this, and he who has done no wrong is troubled because of the evil-doers — Bas
Fair-minded men are appalled at this and the innocent are indignant at the wicked — Ber
At this, honest men are shocked, and the guiltless man rails against the godless — Jerus
Fair-minded men are astonished when they see me. Yet, finally, the innocent shall come out on top, above the godless — Tay

9. **The righteous also shall hold on his way, and he that hath clean hands shall be stronger and stronger.**
just men grow more settled in their ways, those whose hands are clean add strength to strength — Jerus
Nevertheless the upright shall not falter; a stainless soul grows even stronger — Mof
In spite of all, the righteous man maintains his course; and he whose hands are clean grows strong again — NEB

10. **But as for you all, do ye return, and come now:**
But come back, now, all of you, come — Bas
Come, then, all of you: set on me once more! — Jerus
Nay, sirs, return to the charge as often as you will — Knox
As for you — all of you please go away — Tay
for I cannot find one wise man among you.
I shall not find a single sage among you — Jerus

11. **My days are past, my purposes are broken off, even the thoughts of my heart.**
My days are passing; my purposes, my heart's desires are foiled — Ber
My days have passed, far otherwise than I had planned, and every fibre of my heart is broken — Jerus
My days die away like an echo; my heart-strings are snapped — NEB
My good days are in the past. My hopes have disappeared. My heart's desires are broken — Tay
My days are passed away, my plans

are at an end, the cherished purposes of my heart — NAB

12. They change the night into day: the light is short because of darkness.

Night, they say, makes room for day, and light is near at hand to chase the darkness — Jerus

night is a day to me,
and light is darkness — Mof

They say that night is day and day is night; how they pervert the truth! — Tay

They make night into day;
'The light,' they say, 'is near to the darkness' — RSV

Such men change the night into day; where there is darkness they talk of approaching light — NAB

13. If I wait, the grave is mine house: I have made my bed in the darkness.

Lo, I wait my abode in the underworld,
In the darkness have I spread my couch — ABPS

All I look forward to is dwelling in Sheol,
and making my bed in the dark — Jerus

14. I have said to corruption, Thou art my father: to the worm, Thou art my mother, and my sister.

I tell the tomb, 'You are my father,' and call the worm my mother and my sister — Jerus

only from corruption I claim a father's welcome, mother's and sister's greeting the worms shall offer me — Knox

If I must call corruption "my father", and the maggot "my mother" and "my sister" — NAB

15. And where is now my hope?

What hope is this — Knox

Where then have I any ground of hope — Sept

Where then is my hope — NAB

as for my hope, who shall see it?

And, if I have hope, who will see [its fulfillment] — Amp

And my desires! who shall behold them — Sprl

and my prosperity, who shall see — NAB

Wait patiently or impatiently, who cares — Knox

16. They shall go down to the bars of the pit, when our rest together is in the dust.

Will they descend with me into Sheol? Shall we go down together into the dust? — Ber

Unto the cells of the vault they shall be led down;
Together shall we then rest in the dust — Sprl

It will go down to the bars of the underworld,
So soon as there is rest in the dust — ABPS

CHAPTER 18

1. Then answered Bildad the Shuhite, and said,

Bildad of Shuah spoke next. He said: — Jerus

2. How long will it be ere you make an end of words?

How long will ye hunt for words — ASV

How long will ye lay snares for words — RV

Will you never learn to check such words — Jerus

Ah, you word-mongers, you have never had enough! — Knox

Will you keep quiet? — Mof

Who are you trying to fool? — Tay

mark, and afterwards we will speak.

Understand, and afterward let us speak — ABPS

Reflect, and then we can have discussion — NAB

Do some clear thinking, and then we will reply — Amp

First grasp our meaning, and we might argue to some purpose — Knox

silence! and let us speak — Mof

Speak some sense if you want us to answer! — Tay

3. Wherefore are we counted as beasts, and reputed vile in your sight?

Wherefore are we counted as beasts,
And are become unclean in your sight — ASV

Why do you regard us as beasts,
look on us as dumb animals — Jerus

What do you mean by treating us as cattle?

Are we nothing but brute beasts to you — NEB
but no, to men like thee we are worthless as dumb beasts — Knox

4. **He teareth himself in his anger:**
Thou that tearest thyself in thine anger — ASV
Tear yourself to pieces if you will — Jerus
See with what fury he rends his own bosom! — Knox
You are tearing yourself in your rage — Ber
Just because you tear your clothes in anger — Tay
shall the earth be forsaken for thee?
Shall the earth be depopulated for your sake — Ber
shall the earth be neglected on your account — NAB
but the world, for all your rage, will not turn to desert — Jerus
is the world to go to wrack and ruin — Mof
is this going to start an earthquake — Tay
and shall the rock be removed out of his place?
the rocks will not shift from their places. — Jerus

5. **Yea, the light of the wicked shall be put out, and the spark of his fire shall not shine.**
The wicked man's light must certainly be put out,
his brilliant flame cease to shine — Jerus
Truly, the light of the wicked is extinguished;
no flame brightens his hearth — NAB
Verily, the light of the wicked shall burn out;
And the flame of his fire shall not be bright — Sprl

6. **The light shall be dark in his tabernacle, and his candle shall be put out with him.**
The light darkens in his tent,
And the lamp above him goes out — ABPS
In his tent the light is dimmed,
the lamp that shone on him is snuffed — Jerus
The light shall be dark in his tent,
And his lamp above him shall be put out — ASV
The light in his tent darkens, and the wick above it is extinguished — Ber
The light is darkened in his tent;
in spite of him, his lamp goes out — NAB

7. **The steps of his strength shall be straitened,**
The pompous march of his designs shall be straitened — Sprl
His strong steps shall become straitened — ABPS
His manly steps are shortened — Ber
His vigorous stride grows cramped — Jerus
In his iniquity his steps totter — NEB
and his own counsel shall cast him down.
and his disobedience trips him up — NEB
his own design downs him — Ber
his own cunning brings him down — Jerus

8. **For he is cast into a net by his own feet,**
He gets into the net by his own feet — Ber
he entangles himself in a net — Mof
and he walketh upon a snare.
and he walks upon a lattice-covered pit — Amp
and he walks on a pitfall — RSV
and sprawls within its meshes — Mof

9. **The gin shall take him by the heel,**
A trap catches him by the heel — Ber
A spring grips him by the heel — Jerus
and the robber shall prevail against him.
And a snare shall lay hold on him — ASV
the noose grips him tight — NEB
a trap snaps shut, and he is caught — Jerus

10. **The snare is laid for him in the ground,**
A rope is hidden for him . . . — RSV
A noose is hid for him . . . — ASV
Hidden is its cord in the earth — ABPS
and a trap for him in the way.
And its noose upon the pathway — ABPS

11. **Terrors shall make him afraid on every side,**
Terrors attack him . . . — Jerus
fears attend him everywhere — Knox
Terrors surround and startle him — Mof

On every side, terrors affright him — ABPS
and shall drive him to his feet.
And pursue him, at his footsteps — ABPS
And shall chase him at his heels — ASV
hounding him at his heels — Ber
and follow behind him step for step — Jerus

12. **His strength shall be hunger-bitten,**
His strength is made feeble for need of food — Bas
Calamity is hungry for him — Ber
Hunger becomes his companion — Jerus
His trouble shall be ravenous — JPS
Ruin is ravenous for him — Mof
and destruction shall be ready at his side.
And calamity shall be ready for his halting — RV
and ruin stands ready for his stumbling — Ber
by his side Disaster stands — Jerus
disaster only waits for him to stumble — Mof

13. **It shall devour the strength of his skin:**
The members of his body shall be devoured — ASV
By disease his skin is eaten up — Ber
Disease devours his flesh — Jerus
even the firstborn of death shall devour his strength.
Death's eldest child devours his limbs — NEB
and his body is food for the worst of diseases — Bas
deadly disease eats away his limbs — Mof

14. **His confidence shall be rooted out of his tabernacle,**
He shall be rooted out of his tent wherein he trusteth — ASV
He is pulled out of the tent where he was safe — Bas
He is torn from the shelter of his tent — Jerus
Gone the security of his home—Knox
and it shall bring him to the king of terrors.
and dragged before the King of Terrors — Jerus
now its master lies under the heels of tyrant death — Knox

15. **It shall dwell in his tabernacle, because it is none of his:**
There shall dwell in his tent that which is none of his — ASV
brimstone shall be scattered upon his habitation.
sulphur . . . — Amp
while people scatter brimstone on his holding — Jerus

16. **His roots shall be dried up beneath, and above shall his branch be cut off.**
Under the earth his roots are dry, and over it his branch is cut off — Bas
He shall die from the roots up, and all his branches will be lopped off — Tay

17. **His remembrance shall perish from the earth, and he shall have no name in the street.**
His memory is gone from the earth, and in the open country there is no knowledge of his name — Bas
His memory fades from the land,
his name is forgotten in his homeland — Jerus
Gone the fame of him, gone the name of him, from street and countryside, — Knox

18. **He shall be driven from light into darkness, and chased out of the world.**
Driven from light into darkness,
he is an exile from the earth — Jerus
eclipsed in utter darkness, lost to the world — Knox

19. **He shall neither have son nor nephew among his people,**
. . . son nor grandson . . . — Amp
. . . offspring nor descendant . . . — Ber
nor any remaining in his dwellings.
and in his living-place is no one of his name — Bas
nor any survivor in his old home — Ber

20. **They that come after him shall be astonied at his day, as they that went before were affrighted.**
At his fate those of the west are shocked, and those of the east are overcome with fear — Bas
At his fate men of sunset years are appalled, and they of sunrise years are filled with horror — Ber
His tragic end appalls the West,
and fills the East with terror—Jerus
in the west men hear of his doom and are appalled;

in the east they shudder with horror — NEB

21. **Surely such are the dwellings of the wicked, and this is the place of him that knoweth not God.**

A fate like his awaits every sinful house,
the home of every man who knows not God — Jerus

Here (they will say) was a home of wrong-doing; he who lived here, lived a stranger to God — Knox

Surely such are the dwellings of the impious and such is the place of him who does not acknowledge God — Ber

CHAPTER 19

1. **Then Job answered and said,**

Job spoke next. He said: — Jerus

2. **How long will ye vex my soul,**

How long will ye make my soul sorrowful — Sprl

. . . make my life bitter — Bas

. . . exhaust me — NEB

. . . harrow my soul — Mof

Will you never stop tormenting me — Jerus

What, will you torment me still — Knox

and break me in pieces with words?

and pulverize me with words — NEB

and crush me with words — Ber

and shattering me with speeches — Jerus

Every word of yours a fresh weight to crush me — Knox

You are indeed destroying me with words. — Sept

3. **These ten times have ye reproached me:**

These ten times you have derided me — Ber

Ten times now you have made sport of me — Bas

Ten times, no less, you have insulted me — Jerus

Time and again you have taunted me — Mof

ye are not ashamed that ye make yourselves strange to me.

ye blush not.
Ye make yourselves strange to me — YLT

Ye are not ashamed that ye deal hardly with me — ASV

feeling no shame about wronging me — Ber

and ill-treating me without a trace of shame — Jerus

Without shame, ye stun me — ABPS

Shameless, ye wrong me — Rhm

4. **And be it indeed that I have erred, mine error remaineth with myself.**

. . . would remain with me [I would be conscious of it] — Amp

. . . the effect of my error is only on myself — Bas

. . . it concerns none but myself — Knox

Supposing I have sinned,
does my sin concern you? — Mof

5. **If indeed ye will magnify yourselves against me, and plead against me my reproach:**

If you would assume a superior attitude toward me and reproach me for my misery — Ber

not for you to claim authority over me, bring home to me my disgrace! — Knox

If indeed you magnify yourselves against me,
and make my humiliation an argument against me — RSV

6. **Know now that God hath overthrown me,**

Know now, that God turned me upside down — YLT

Know then that God has dealt unfairly with me — NAB

God, you must know, is my oppressor — Jerus

Understand, it is God who has undone me — Mof

The fact of the matter is that God has overthrown me — Tay

and hath compassed me with his net.

and his is the net that closes round me — Jerus

and with his net enclosed me — Rhm

and caught me in His net — Tay

and raised his bulwark against me — Sept

caught me in his toils! — Knox

7. **Behold, I cry out of wrong, but I am not heard:**

Note this: I cry out because of violence, . . . — Ber

Behold, I cry out, Violence! . . . — Amp
I cry out 'Murder'! — there is no reply — Mof
Behold, I exclaim against the wrong, but He answereth not — Sprl
I scream for help and no one hears me — Tay
I cry aloud, but there is no judgment.
I call aloud, and there is no justice — ABPS
I shriek for help, but I receive no justice — Ber
I shriek, but get no justice — Tay
I cry for help but there is no redress — NAB

8. He hath fenced up my way that I cannot pass,
. . . walled up . . . — ASV
. . . blocked up my road . . . — Mof
My path He has fenced in so that I cannot advance — Ber
. . . so that there is no escape — Knox
and he hath set darkness in my paths.
And over my goings hath He fixed darkness — Sprl
and darkened my path — Mof
and covered my way with darkness — Jerus
my direction lost, and I benighted — Knox

9. He hath stripped me of my glory,
He has robbed me of my honor — Ber
He has stolen my honour away — Jerus
By him discredited — Knox
and taken the crown from my head.
And upset the diadem from off my head — Sprl
discrowned — Knox
and degraded me — Mof

10. He hath destroyed me on every side, and I am gone:
He hath broken me down . . . — ASV
He broke me on every side and I fled — Sept
On every side he breaks through my defences, and I succumb — Jerus
by him left defenceless on every side, I go my ways — Knox
and mine hope hath he removed like a tree.
My hope he uproots like the tree — ABPS
And my hope hath he plucked up like a tree — ASV
As a man a shrub, so he uproots my hope — Jerus

11. He hath also kindled his wrath against me,
His anger flares against me — Jerus
he has flamed in wrath at me — Mof
and he counteth me unto him as one of his enemies.
and considers me His enemy — Ber
treating me as a foe — Mof

12. His troops come together, and raise up their way against me,
His troops come together, and cast up their way and siegeworks against me — Amp
Unitedly all His troops come on and build their road against me — Ber
against whom he musters all his forces, to ride over me — Knox
Together enter his troops
And have cast up against me their mound — Rhm
With one consent his troops fell upon me . . . — Sept
His troops advance as one man; they build up their road and attack me — NAB
and encamp round about my tabernacle.
And have encamped all around my tent — Rhm
laid siege to my tent — Jerus
to beleaguer my dwelling place — Knox

13. He hath put my brethren far from me,
My brothers stand aloof from me — Jerus
Sundered am I from my brethren — Knox
My clansmen have abandoned me — Mof
and mine acquaintance are verily estranged from me.
And they that know me are wholly estranged from me — ABPS
a stranger to all that knew me — Knox
they acknowledged strangers rather than me — Sept

14. My kinsfolk have failed,
My kinsmen stand aloof — ABPS
My relatives stay away — Ber
My relatives have disappeared — AAT
forsaken by my kindred — Knox
and my familiar friends have forgotten me.
And mine intimate acquaintances have forgotten me — Rhm

and the guests in my house have forgotten me — Jerus
and my guests ignore me — Mof
and those who knew my name forgot me — Sept

15. They that dwell in mine house, and my maids, count me for a stranger:
Guests that dwell in my house, ay, and the very serving-women, stare at me — Knox
As for my domesticks and maid servants, in their view I was a stranger — Sept
The serving maids look on me as a stranger — Jerus
I am an alien in their sight.
and seem to them as one from another country — Bas
I am like a foreigner to them — Tay

16. I called my servant, and he gave me no answer; I intreated him with my mouth.
I summon my servant, and he does not answer; humbly I must entreat him — Ber
I call my servant, but he doesn't come; I even beg him! — Tay
My servant does not answer when I call him,
I am reduced to entreating him — Jerus

17. My breath is strange to my wife,
I am repulsive to my wife — RSV
My breath is obnoxious . . . — Ber
To my wife my breath is unbearable — Jerus
though I intreated for the children's sake of mine own body.
Although I affectionately implored because of the offspring of my own loins — Sprl
loathesome to the sons of my own mother — RSV
and my body loathsome to my brothers — Ber

18. Yea, young children despised me;
Even urchins despise me — JPS
Even young children have no respect for me — Bas
Even the young slaves spurn me — Sprl
I arose, and they spake against me.
ever ready with a gibe when I appear — Jerus
When I stand to speak, they mock — Tay

19. All my inward friends abhorred me:
All my familiar friends abhor me — ABPS
All my intimate friends avoid me — Ber
All my dearest friends recoil from me in horror — Jerus
All the men of mine intimate circle abhor me — Rhm
no counsellor so trusted but he is weary of me — Knox
and they whom I loved are turned against me.
and they whom I loved rose up against me — Sept
no friend so loved but he abandons me now — Knox

20. My bone cleaveth to my skin and to my flesh, and I am escaped with the skin of my teeth.
Beneath my skin, my flesh begins to rot,
and my bones stick out like teeth — Jerus
And I so wasted! Skin clinging to bone, save where the lips cover my teeth — Knox
My bones stand out through my skin and my flesh,
And on the gum am I denuded of teeth — Sprl
I am skin and bones and have escaped death by the skin of my teeth — Tay
My skin is clinging to my bones,
my teeth are falling out — Mof

21. Have pity upon me, have pity upon me, O ye my friends;
Pity me! Pity me! ye my friends — Rhm
Friends, friends, do you at least have pity — Knox
for the hand of God hath touched me.
for the hand of God has struck me — Jerus
For the hand of God hath stricken against me — YLT

22. Why do ye persecute me as God,
Why do you hound me down like God — Jerus
Why do you hound me as though you were divine — NAB
Would you take part in God's hue and cry against me — Knox
and are not satisfied with my flesh?
and you are not satisfied with the hurt of my flesh — Lam

slander me to your heart's content — Knox
will you never have enough of my flesh — Jerus
and insatiably prey upon me — NAB

23. Oh that my words were now written!
Oh then that my words could be written,
Oh that in a record they could be inscribed — Rhm
oh that they were printed in a book!
Ah, would that these words of mine were written down,
inscribed on some monument — Jerus
Oh that my defence were written,
oh that my case could be presented in writing — Mof

24. That they were graven with an iron pen and lead in the rock for ever!
That with an iron pen and [molten] lead they were graven in the rock for ever! — Amp
That with a stylus of iron and [with] lead
For all time — in the rock they could be graven! — Rhm
Oh, that with an iron pen they were engraved on a rock, and sealed with lead forever — Ber
O that my words were written and recorded in a book forever! That they were engraven with a graver of iron on lead, or on rocks — Sept

25. For I know that my redeemer liveth,
This I know: that my Avenger lives — Jerus
This at least I know, that one lives on who will vindicate me — Knox
But as for me, I know that my Vindicator lives — AAT
But in my heart I know that my vindicator lives — NEB
and that he shall stand at the latter day upon the earth:
and that he shall stand up at the last upon the earth — RV
and at the end he will reveal himself on earth — Lam
and he, the Last, will take his stand on earth — Jerus
And as the next-of-kin he will stand upon my dust — AAT
and that he will rise at last to speak in Court — NEB
rising up from the dust when the last day comes — Knox

26. And though after my skin worms destroy this body, yet in my flesh shall I see God:
And after this my skin is destroyed,
And without my flesh, I shall see God — ABPS
Once more my skin shall clothe me, and in my flesh I shall have sight of God — Knox
This body may break up, but even then my life shall have a sight of God — Mof
and after my skin has been thus destroyed,
then from my flesh I shall see God — RSV
and after my skin has thus been destroyed, then, out of my flesh I shall see God — Ber

27. Whom I shall see for myself, and mine eyes shall behold, and not another;
Whom I, even I, shall see, on my side,
And mine eyes shall behold, and not as a stranger — ASV
Then he will be on my side! Yes, I shall see him, not as a stranger, but as a friend! — Tay
though my reins be consumed within me.
My heart is broken with desire — Bas
Deep in my heart is this hope reposed — Knox
Exhausted are my deepest desires in my bosom! — Rhm
My heart faints within me! — RSV
My emotions are spent within me! — — AAT

28. But ye should say, Why persecute we him, seeing the root of the matter is found in me?
If you say, How cruel we will be to him! because the root of sin is clearly in him — Bas
If you say, 'How we will pursue him!' and, 'The root of the matter is found in him' — RSV
You that would raise the hue and cry, finding matter of complaint against me — Knox

29. Be ye afraid of the sword: for wrath bringeth the punishments of the sword, that ye may know there is a judgment.
should rather take flight yourselves, the sword at your heels; the sword that avenges wrong, proof to you that justice shall be done — Knox

beware of your false charges!
Such slanders call for God's own sword,
to teach you impious men what the Almighty is — Mof

Tremble for yourselves before the sword;
for such things are crimes deserving the sword,
That you may know that there is judgment — AAT

Be ye afraid — on your part — of the sword
Because wrath [bringeth] the punishments of the sword,
To the end that ye may know the Almighty — Rhm

CHAPTER 20

1. Then answered Zophar the Naamathite, and said,

Zophar of Naamath spoke next. He said: — Jerus

2. Therefore do my thoughts cause me to answer, and for this I make haste.

For this cause my thoughts are troubling me and driving me on — Bas

Therefore, my thoughts answer me;
And because of the agitation within me — AAT

Now this does rouse my soul,
my heart is stirred — Mof

Whither will my agitated thoughts drive me,
And my perturbations transport me? — Sprl

My thoughts urge me to reply; I am stirred up — Ber

3. I have heard the check of my reproach,

I have heard the reproof which putteth me to shame — ASV

I have heard your presumptuous warning to censure you no more — Ber

I hear the censure which insults me — RSV

You have tried to make me feel ashamed of myself for calling you a sinner — Tay

and the spirit of my understanding causeth me to answer.

and from my understanding a spirit gives me a reply — NAB

but my spirit whispers to me how to answer them — Jerus

but my spirit won't let me stop — Tay

4. Knowest thou not this of old, since man was placed upon earth,

Do you not know, that since time began
and man was set on the earth—Jerus

Surely you know that this has been so since time began,
since man was first set on the earth — NEB

5. That the triumphing of the wicked is short,

[that] the sinner never sings for long — Mof

That the joy-shout of the lawless is short — Rhm

that the exulting of the wicked is short — RSV

But the mirth of the wicked is sudden ruin — Sept

and the joy of the hypocrite but for a moment?

And the joy of the impure for a moment — ABPS

and the sinner's gladness has never lasted long — Jerus

and godless men have short-lived joy — Mof

and the joy of transgressors, destruction — Sept

And the rejoicing of the impious for a moment — Rhm

6. Though his excellency mount up to the heavens, and his head reach unto the clouds;

Though his [proud] height . . . — Amp

Towering to the sky he may have been, with head touching the clouds — Jerus

though his gifts mount up to heaven, and his sacrifices reach the clouds — Sept

Though the godless be proud as the heavens and walk with his nose in the air — Tay

7. Yet he shall perish for ever like his own dung: they which have seen him shall say, Where is he?

Like the waste from his body he comes to an end for ever: those who have seen him say, Where is he — Bas

he is for the dunghill at last; none knows what has become of him — Knox

he shall be swept away like his own dung,

til those who knew him ask, 'Where is he?' — Mof

Yet he shall perish forever, cast away like his own dung. Those who knew him will wonder where he is gone — Tay

8. He shall fly away as a dream, and shall not be found: yea, he shall be chased away as a vision of the night.

Vanished and gone like a dream, the phantom of yesternight — Knox

He disappears like a dream — no trace of him —
he vanishes like a vision of the night — Mof

Like a dream which is gone, he cannot be found. He is vanished, like a spectre of the night — Sept

9. The eye also which saw him shall see him no more; neither shall his place any more behold him.

unmarked by human eyes, lost to the scenes he knew! — Knox

The eye had a glimpse of him, but it shall not again;
Neither shall his abode behold him more — Sprl

10. His children shall seek to please the poor, and his hands shall restore their goods.

His children will curry the favor of the poor, and his own hands will give back his wealth — Ber

His sons must recoup his victims,
and his children pay back his riches — Jerus

His children shall seek charity — beggars!
And his branches shall be implicated in his iniquity — Sprl

Crushing poverty shall be his children's lot; his acts shall yield their own harvest of shame — Knox

His children shall beg from the poor, their hard labor shall repay his debts — Tay

11. His bones are full of the sin of his youth, which shall lie down with him in the dust.

While his bones still enjoy youthful vigor, they lie down with him in the dust — Ber

With the vigor of youth his bones were filled,
now it lies in the dust with him — Jerus

all the lusty vigour of his frame doomed, like himself, to silence and the dust — Knox

when manly vigour fills his frame,
he and his manly vigour go to dust — Mof

12. Though wickedness be sweet in his mouth, though he hide it under his tongue;

Sweet in the mouth is the taste of evil-doing; how the tongue cherishes it! — Knox

Though sin is a sweet morsel in his mouth,
though he rolls it under his tongue — Mof

He enjoyed the taste of wickedness, letting it melt in his mouth — Tay

13. Though he spare it, and forsake it not; but keep it still within his mouth:

Although he tenderly guard it, and will not forsake it;
But retaineth it under his palate — Sprl

Though he is loath to let it go, but keeps it still within his mouth — Amp

How he treasures it, loath to lose the secret pleasure of his palate!—Knox

Sipping it slowly, lest it disappear — Tay

14. Yet his meat in his bowels is turned,

Yet his food turns [to poison] in his stomach — Amp

it is the gall of asps within him.

working inside him like the poison of a viper — Jerus

The bitterness of asps is in his heart — YLT

15. He hath swallowed down riches, and he shall vomit them up again:

He must bring up all the wealth which he has swallowed — Jerus

Riches collected unrighteously shall be vomited up — Sept

God shall cast them out of his belly.

God makes him disgorge it — Jerus

16. He shall suck the poison of asps: the viper's tongue shall slay him.

poisonous as the asp's head or the viper's tongue were those juices he sucked — Knox

May he suck the venom of dragons! and may the tongue of the viper slay him! — Sept

He shall suck the poison of asps; the tongue of an adder shall slay him — Lam

17. He shall not see the rivers, the floods, the brooks of honey and butter.

. . . the flowing streams of honey and curd — JPS

He shall not feed on milk from the meadows, on honey or on butter from the pastures — Mof

Never shall he gaze upon rich meadows, upon valleys of honey and curds — AAT

18. That which he laboured for shall he restore, and shall not swallow it down:

Endlessly he shall pay for the wrong he did — Knox

He will give back the fruit of his toil, and will not swallow it down — RSV

He hath wearied himself for emptiness and vanity — for riches, of which he shall not have a taste — Sept

He gives back the product of toil and cannot consume it — AAT

according to his substance shall the restitution be, and he shall not rejoice therein.

plagued in the measure of his own false dealings — Knox

Like wealth to be restored in which he cannot exalt — Rhm

from the profit of his trading he will get no enjoyment — RSV

He does not rejoice in proportion to the wealth he gains by trade — AAT

19. Because he hath oppressed and hath forsaken the poor; because he hath violently taken away an house which he builded not;

Because he oppressed, abandoned the weak,
The house he has plundered he shall not build up — ABPS

Since he once destroyed the huts of poor men,
and stole other men's houses when he should have built his own — Jerus

Because he oppressed and forsook the poor;
Plundered the house, instead of building it up — Sprl

As he was hard upon the poor,
and seized on houses that he never built — Mof

20. Surely he shall not feel quietness in his belly, he shall not save of that which he desired.

Because he knew no rest in his bosom,
Of all his delights he shall save nothing — ABPS

Surely he hath known no peace in his inmost mind, —
With his dearest thing he shall not get away — Rhm

Because his greed knew no rest,
he shall not save anything in which he delights — RSV

Because he knew no quietness within him, he shall not save aught of that wherein he delighteth — RV

Though he has known no quiet in his greed,
his treasures shall not save him — NAB

21. There shall none of his meat be left; therefore shall no man look for his goods.

He has won enough for his desire; for this cause his well-being will quickly come to an end — Bas

As nothing is left after he has eaten, his prosperity will not last — Ber

he, that never had a crust to spare, will be stripped now of all his goods — Knox

There was nothing left after he had eaten;
therefore his prosperity will not endure — RSV

22. In the fulness of his sufficiency he shall be in straits:

When his abundance is gone he shall be in straits — Rhm

Even when his wealth is great, he is full of care — Bas

with every need satisfied his troubles begin — NEB

Once so full fed, now he goes in need — Knox

every hand of the wicked shall come upon him.

The hand of every one that is in misery shall come upon him — ASV

All the power of distress shall come upon him — Rhm

And the force of misery . . . — RSV

All the weight of trouble . . . — AAT

Every hand shall bring trouble — Sprl

23. When he is about to fill his belly,

When he is about to gorge himself — Ber

It cometh to pass, at the filling of his belly — YLT

God shall cast the fury of his wrath upon him,

God shall cast the fierceness of his wrath . . . — RV

He sendeth forth against him the fierceness of his anger — YLT

and shall rain it upon him while he is eating.

raining down all its weapons — Knox

and rain it upon him as his food — RSV

24. He shall flee from the iron weapon, and the bow of steel shall strike him through.

No use to run away from the iron armoury,
for the bow of bronze will shoot him through — Jerus

shuns he the steel, to the bow of bronze he falls a prey — Knox

He will be chased and struck down — Tay

Should he escape the iron weapon,
the bow of bronze shall pierce him through — NAB

25. It is drawn, and cometh out of the body;

He plucks it out; it comes forth from his body — ABPS

out at his back the point comes — NEB

yea, the glittering sword cometh out of his gall: terrors are upon him.

Yea, the glittering point . . . — ASV

Yea, the flashing arrow-head . . . — Rhm

and its shining point comes out of his side — Bas

the gleaming tip from his gall-bladder — NEB

26. All darkness shall be hid in his secret places:

Utter darkness settles on his treasures — Ber

He hides away where thick darkness broods over him — Knox

Every misfortune is laid up for his treasures — Rhm

Darkness unrelieved awaits him — NEB

a fire not blown shall consume him;

a fire that needs no fanning will consume him — NEB

A fire unlit by man devours him — Jerus

straightway a fire no human hand has kindled threatens to devour him — Knox

it shall go ill with him that is left in his tabernacle.

woe betide any that would take refuge in that dwelling — Knox

It shall destroy what remaineth in his tent — Rhm

27. The heaven shall reveal his iniquity;

The heavens make clear his sin — Bas

The heavens will disclose his guilt — AAT

and the earth shall rise up against him.

and the earth gives witness against him — Bas

28. The increase of his house shall depart, and his goods shall flow away in the day of his wrath.

All that was accumulated in his house is moved out in the day of his wrath — Ber

his well-stored house is swept to ruin, accursed in the day of wrath divine — Mof

The possessions of his house will be carried away,
dragged off in the day of God's wrath — RSV

The increase of his house will go into exile,
Like things melting away on the day of his wrath — AAT

The flood shall sweep away his house with the waters that run off in the day of God's anger — NAB

29. This is the portion of a wicked man from God, and the heritage appointed unto him by God.

Such is the lot God sends to the wicked, such their divinely appointed doom — Knox

This is what God bestows upon a sinner,
this is what God awards a godless man — Mof

This is what awaits the wicked man, for God prepares it for him — Tay

This is the wicked man's lot from God and the legacy alloted him of God — Ber

CHAPTER 21

1. But Job answered and said,

Job spoke next. He said: — Jerus

2. Hear diligently my speech,

Hear ye attentively my speech — ABPS

Listen closely to what I say — Ber

Listen carefully to my words — RSV

Listen, only listen to my words — Jerus

Hearkening hearken ye unto my words — Sprl

and let this be your consolations.
this is the consolation you can offer me — Jerus
And let this draw forth your sympathy — Sprl

3. **Suffer me that I may speak;**
Suffer me when I speak — Sprl
Let me have my say — Jerus
Bear with me, and I speak — YLT
and after that I have spoken, mock on.
And after I have spoken, you may jeer — AAT
And after my speaking — ye may deride — YLT

4. **As for me, is my complaint to man?**
As for me, is my outcry against man — Bas
What! is my pleading with man — Sept
Ah me! Wherefore make I my complaint to man — Sprl
I am complaining about God, not man. — Tay
and if it were so, why should not my spirit be troubled?
Or wherefore should I not be impatient — ABPS
I have better reason than that to be indignant — Knox
Or, why shall I not be inflamed with indignation — Sept
no wonder my spirit is troubled — Tay

5. **Mark me, and be astonished, and lay your hand upon your mouth.**
Hear what I have to say, and you will be dumbfounded,
will place your hands over your mouths — Jerus
See here! let this astound you,
awe you into silence — Mof
Look at me, and be appalled,
and lay your hand upon your mouth — RSV
Mark my complaint well, and you shall be astonished, hold your breath in amazement — Knox

6. **Even when I remember I am afraid, and trembling taketh hold on my flesh.**
Even I am frightened when I see myself. Horror takes hold upon me and I shudder — Tay
I myself am appalled at the very thought,
and my flesh begins to shudder — Jerus
as I too tremble with dismay at the thought of it — Knox
For at the bare recollection I shudder:
and tortures rack my flesh — Sept
When I think of it I am dismayed,
and shuddering seizes my flesh — RSV
When I stop to think, I am filled with horror,
and my whole body is convulsed — NEB

7. **Wherefore do the wicked live, become old, yea, are mighty in power?**
Why do the wicked live on, become old and even increase in strength — Ber
Why do the wicked still live on, their power increasing with their age — Jerus
Why do the wicked live and grow old, abounding in wealth — Sept

8. **Their seed is established in their sight with them,**
Their children are ever with them — Bas
They see their posterity ensured — Jerus
They live to see their children settled — NEB
and their offspring before their eyes.
kinsmen and grandsons thronging all around — Knox

9. **Their houses are safe from fear,**
The peace of their houses has nothing to fear — Jerus
their families are secure and safe — NEB
neither is the rod of God upon them.
the rod that God wields is not for them — Jerus
God's scourge passes them by — Knox

10. **Their bull gendereth, and faileth not; their cow calveth, and casteth not her calf.**
Their bulls breed unfailingly;
their cows calve and do not miscarry — Ber
No mishap with their bulls at breeding-time,
nor miscarriage with their cows at calving — Jerus

11. **They send forth their little ones like a flock, and their children dance.**
. . . skip about — Amp
. . . hop around — Ber
blithe as lambs the little children go out to play — Knox

12. They take the timbrel and harp,
. . . the tambourines and the lyre — Amp
They take up the psaltery and kithara — Sept
They shout, with tabret and harp — ABPS
everywhere is tambour and harp-playing — Knox
and rejoice at the sound of the organ.
And rejoice, to the sound of the pipe — ABPS
. . . of the flute — Ber
And merrily trip to the sound of the bag-pipe — Sprl

13. They spend their days in wealth, and in a moment go down to the grave.
They end their lives in happiness and go down in peace to Sheol — Jerus
and having spent their lives in festivity, they are composed to rest in the peaceful grave — Sept
They live out their days in prosperity, and tranquilly go down to the nether world — NAB

14. Therefore they say unto God, Depart from us; for we desire not the knowledge of thy ways.
Yet these were the ones who said to God, 'Go away!
We do not choose to learn your ways — Jerus
And these are the men who bade God keep his distance from them, refused to learn his will — Knox
All this despite the fact that they ordered God away and wanted no part of him and his ways — Tay

15. What is the Almighty, that we should serve him? and what profit should we have, if we pray unto him?
What is the point of our serving Shaddai?
What profit should we get from praying to him?' — Jerus
what right had he, the Omnipotent, to their obedience, what advantage would they gain by offering prayer to him — Knox
'Who is Almighty God?' they scoff; 'Why should we obey him? What good will it do us?' — Tay

16. Lo, their good is not in their hand: the counsel of the wicked is far from me.
But notice, [you say] the prosperity of the wicked is not in their power; the mystery [of God's dealings] with the ungodly is far from my comprehension — Amp
Note this: Men are not the architects of their own fortune; the planning of the wicked is far from me — Ber
Is it not true, they held their fortune in their own two hands,
and in their counsels, left no room for God? — Jerus
Are they not masters of their fortunes? Does God concern himself with what they scheme? — Mof
Look, everything the wicked touch has turned to gold!
But I refuse even to deal with people like that — Tay

17. How oft is the candle of the wicked put out!
How often is it that the wicked are left without an heir — Lam
How oft is it that the lamp of the wicked is put out? — RV
Do we often see a wicked man's light put out? — Jerus
Tell me, how often in very deed are the hopes of the wicked extinguished? — Knox
Yet the wicked get away with it every time — Tay
and how oft cometh their destruction upon them!
that their calamity cometh upon them? — RV
They never have trouble — Tay
God distributeth sorrows in his anger.
that God distributeth sorrows in his anger? — RV
Does God's vengeance often deal out misfortune to them? — Knox
God skips them when he distributes his sorrows and anger — Tay

18. They are as stubble before the wind, and as chaff that the storm carrieth away.
How often they are like the straw before the wind, like chaff which the whirlwind sweeps away! — Ber
How often do we see him harrassed like a straw before the wind,
or swept off like chaff before a gale? — Jerus
sweeping them away like chaff before the wind, ashes beneath the storm? — Knox

Are they driven before the wind like straw?
Are they carried away by the storm? Not at all! — Tay

Let them be like straw before the wind,
and like chaff which the storm snatches away! — NAB

19. **God layeth up his iniquity for his children:**

But 'God,' you say, 'stores up their iniquity for their children' — Ber

'God,' you say, 'punishes the children for it'? — Mof

he rewardeth him, and he shall know it.

Let Him recompense it to the man himself that he may know and feel it — Amp

Better he made themselves feel punishment! — Mof

But I say that God should punish the man who sins, not his children! Let him feel the penalty himself — Tay

20. **His eyes shall see his destruction, and he shall drink of the wrath of the Almighty.**

Let his own eyes see his destruction, and let him drink of the wrath of the Almighty — Amp

Let their own eyes see their calamity, and let them drink of the indignation of the Almighty! — Ber

The evil man should witness his own ruin,
and drink the Almighty's anger for himself — Mof

21. **For what pleasure hath he in his house after him,**

For of what interest is his family to a man who is dead — Ber

When he is gone, how can the fortunes of his House affect him — Jerus

Little he cares what befalls his posterity after he is gone — Knox

when the number of his months is cut off in the midst?

When the number of his months is cut in twain — Rhm

though halved be the time of its continuance — Knox

once his own span of life is snapped? — Mof

22. **Shall any teach God knowledge? seeing he judgeth those that are high.**

But who can give lessons in wisdom to God,
to him who is judge of those on high? — Jerus

The God that passes judgment on his angels needs none to instruct him — Knox

But who can rebuke God, the supreme Judge? — Tay

23. **One dieth in his full strength, being wholly at ease and quiet.**

One dies in his full prosperity;
He is wholly at ease, and secure — ABPS

And again: one man dies in the fulness of his strength, in all possible happiness and ease — Jerus

. . . sound of body, being wholly confident and at ease — Lam

This man dieth in the very perfection of his prosperity, Wholly tranquil and secure — Rhm

. . . wholly at ease and content — NAB

One man, I tell you, dies crowned with success,
lapped in security and comfort — NEB

24. **His breasts are full of milk, and his bones are moistened with marrow.**

His pails are full of milk,
And the marrow of his bones is moistened — ASV

His buckets are full of milk, and there is no loss of strength in his bones — Bas

His sides are full of fat,
And the marrow of his bones is moistened — ABPS

his sides filled out with fat, and the marrow of his bones still fresh — Ber

His veins are filled with nourishment,
And the marrow of his bones is fresh — Rhm

his body full of fat,
and the marrow of his bones moist — RSV

his loins full of vigour
and the marrow juicy in his bones — NEB

25. **And another dieth in the bitterness of his soul,**

Another dies with bitterness in his heart — Jerus

. . . in a mood of bitterness — AAT

. . . with a bitter soul — YLT

. . . broken-hearted — Mof

and never eateth with pleasure.

And hath never tasted good fortune — Rhm
never having tasted happiness — Jerus
and never gets the good of life — Mof

26. They shall lie down alike in the dust, and the worms shall cover them.
But they are both composed alike underground, and putrefaction hath covered them — Sept
Both are alike buried in the same dust, both eaten by the same worms — Tay

27. Behold, I know your thoughts, and the devices which ye wrongfully imagine against me.
I know, indeed, your deliberations and your schemes to do me wrong — Ber
I know well what is in your mind, the spiteful thoughts you entertain against me — Jerus
I know well what you are thinking and the arguments you are marshalling against me — NEB
I know what you are going to say — Tay

28. For ye say, Where is the house of the prince?
'What has become of the great lord's house,' you say — Jerus
What becomes of the tyrant's palace — Knox
and where are the dwelling places of the wicked?
And where are the fixed habitations of the wicked? — Sprl
'where is the tent where the wicked lived?' — Jerus

29. Have ye not asked them that go by the way? and do ye not know their tokens,
Have you not asked those that travel this way, and do you not accept their testimony and evidences — Amp
Have you not put the question to the travellers, and do you not take note of their experience — Bas
Have you never asked those that have travelled,
or have you misunderstood the tale they told — Jerus
Well, talk to travellers,
learn what they have to tell: — Mof
But I reply, Ask anyone who has been around and he can tell you the truth. — Tay

30. That the wicked is reserved to the day of destruction?
'The wicked man is spared for the day of disaster — Jerus
that the evil man is spared in the day of calamity — Ber
of how an evil man is spared calamity — Mof
That the evil man is usually spared in the day of calamity — Tay
they shall be brought forth to the day of wrath.
and that in the day of wrath he is allowed to escape? — Ber
he is being slowly drawn on to his doom — Knox
how he goes scatheless from the wrath of God — Mof
and allowed to escape — Tay

31. Who shall declare his way to his face?
Who rebukes a man to his face — Ber
But who is there then to accuse him to his face for his deeds — Jerus
Fools, how can anyone bring home his guilt to him now — Knox
Who ever tells him what he is — Mof
No one rebukes him openly. — Tay
and who shall repay him what he hath done?
and who repays him for his behavior — Ber
Who ever punishes him for his misdeeds — Mof
No one repays him for what he has done. — Tay

32. Yet shall he be brought to the grave, and shall remain in the tomb.

33. The clods of the valley shall be sweet unto him, and every man shall draw after him, as there are innumerable before him.
When he is borne to the grave, a watch is kept over his tomb. Softly the clods of the valley cover him, and all men follow him, while countless numbers are ahead of him — Ber
Yet he to the graves is borne,
And over the tomb one keepeth watch;
Pleasant to him are the mounds of the torrent-bed, —
And after him doth every man march,
As before him there were without number — Rhm
He is being slowly drawn on to his

tomb, where he shall wait on in the ranks of the dead; made welcome in the dark valley, whither all men shall follow, as numberless that went before him — Knox

When he is borne to the grave,
watch is kept over his tomb.
The clods of the valley are sweet to him;
all men follow after him,
and those who go before him are innumerable — RSV

When he is carried to the grave,
all the world escorts him, before and behind;
the dust of the earth is sweet to him,
and thousands keep watch at his tomb — NEB

34. How then comfort ye me in vain, seeing in your answers there remaineth falsehood?

How then can you comfort me with empty and futile words, since in your replies there lurks falsehood — Amp

Vain is all your consolation, while the answer you give me matches so ill with truth. — Knox

How then will you comfort me with empty nothings?
There is nothing left of your answers but falsehood. — RSV

How can you comfort me when your whole premise is so wrong — Tay

Why then do you give me comfort with words in which there is no profit, when you see that there is nothing in your answers but deceit — Bas

CHAPTER 22

1. Then Eliphaz the Temanite answered and said,

Eliphaz of Teman spoke next. He said: — Jerus

2. Can a man be profitable unto God, as he that is wise may be profitable unto himself?

Can a man be of any use to God,
when even the wise man's wisdom is of use only to himself — Jerus

A man cannot hope to implead God, even a man of perfect wisdom — Knox

Can even a great man obtain profit for God,
As the wise may obtain profit for himself — Sprl

3. Is it any pleasure to the Almighty, that thou art righteous?

Just though thou be, how is God the better for knowing thou art just — Knox

Has the Almighty any interest in your goodness — Mof

Is it an asset to the Almighty if you are righteous — NEB

or is it gain to him, that thou makest thy ways perfect?

Can stainless life of thine advantage him — Knox

Does he gain by your blameless life — Mof

or any profit that thou shouldst keep a straight course — Sept

4. Will he reprove thee for fear of thee? will he enter with thee into judgment?

Would he punish you for your piety,
and hale you off to judgment — Jerus

Why should he punish you for your religion,
and pass sentence on you — Mof

Is it for your fear of him that he reproves you,
and enters into judgment with you — RSV

Is it for thy reverence that he
will accuse thee?
will enter with thee into judgment — Rhm

5. Is not thy wickedness great? and thine iniquities infinite?

. . . There is no end to your iniquities. — Amp

No, rather for your manifold wickednesses,
for your unending iniquities! — Jerus

Not at all! It is because of your wickedness! Your sins are endless! — Tay

No: it is because you are a very wicked man,
and your depravity passes all bounds — NEB

6. For thou hast taken a pledge from thy brother for nought, and stripped the naked of their clothing.

You have exacted needless pledges from your brothers,

and men go naked now through your despoiling — Jerus
You have fleeced your fellows selfishly, and stripped your debtors to the skin — Mof
For instance, you must have refused to loan money to needy friends unless they gave you all their clothing as a pledge — yes, you must have stripped them to the bone — Tay

7. **Thou hast not given water to the weary to drink,**
you have grudged water to the thirsty man — Jerus
You must have refused water . . . — Tay
and thou hast withholden bread from the hungry.
and refused bread to the hungry — Jerus
but hast robbed the hungry of their morsel — Sept

8. **But as for the mighty man, he had the earth; and the honourable man dwelt in it.**
But [you, Job] the man with power possessed the land, and the favored and accepted man dwelt in it — Amp
The man with power possessed the land,
and the favored man dwelt in it — RSV
But no doubt you gave men of importance anything they wanted, and let the wealthy live wherever they chose — Tay
As to the man of arm — he hath the earth,
And the accepted of face — he dwelleth in it — YLT
Is the earth, then, the preserve of the strong
and a domain for the favoured few? — NEB

9. **Thou hast sent widows away empty,**
you have sent widows away empty-handed — Mof
. . . without helping them — Tay
and the arms of the fatherless have been broken.
And the arms of the fatherless are bruised — YLT
you have been oppressing orphans — Mof
and done injustice to orphans — Sept
and the resources of orphans you have destroyed — NAB

10. **Therefore snares are round about thee,**
That is why you are now surrounded by traps — Tay
No wonder that there are pitfalls in your path — NEB
and sudden fear troubleth thee;
and sudden panic confounds you — Ber
and dread startleth thee suddenly — Rhm

11. **Or darkness, that thou canst not see;**
therefore has your light turned to darkness — Mof
and abundance of waters cover thee.
and the flood of waters covers thee — ABPS

12. **Is not God in the height of heaven?**
. . . high in heaven — Mof
and behold the height of the stars, how high they are!
Observe the farthest stars . . . — Ber
Does he not look down on the topmost star? — Mof
And see the summit of the stars, that they are high — YLT

13. **And thou sayest, How doth God know? can he judge through the dark cloud?**
Because he is far above, you said, 'What does God know?
Can he peer through the shadowed darkness?' — Jerus
And yet you say, 'God never notices!
Can he rule through the darkness dense? — Mof
But you reply, 'That is why He can't see what I am doing! How can He judge through the thick darkness? — Tay

14. **Thick clouds are a covering to him, that he seeth not;**
The clouds to him are an impenetrable veil — Jerus
he cannot see us for the clouds that veil him' — Mof
Thick clouds enwrap him so that he does not see — RSV
and he walketh in the circuit of heaven.
And he walks upon the vault of heaven — ABPS
and he prowls on the rim of the heavens — Jerus

15. **Hast thou marked the old way which wicked men have trodden?**

Will you keep the old way by which evil men went — Bas
Is that the line you choose, the line that evil men took long ago — Mof

16. Which were cut down out of time,
Who have been cut down unexpectedly — YLT
who were untimely snatched away — Ber
They came to an untimely end — Mof
whose foundation was overflown with a flood:
. . . was poured out like a river — AAT
their foothold washed out by a deluge — Ber
with rivers swamping their foundations — Jerus
a flood engulfed the solid ground beneath them — Knox
The flood poured forth over their habitations — Sprl

17. Which said unto God, Depart from us: and what can the Almighty do for them?
. . . 'Leave us alone' . . . — Ber
. . . 'Go away!' . . . — Jerus

18. Yet he filled their houses with good things:
to him who fills them with prosperity! — Mof
He, who had indeed filled their houses with good things — Sept
but the counsel of the wicked is far from me.
Not for nothing do I shun their counsels! — Knox
Far be such impious thoughts from me! — Mof
though the counsel of the wicked is far from him — Sept
(God forbid that I should say a thing like that) — Tay

19. The righteous see it, and are glad: and the innocent laugh them to scorn.
Here is a sight to make the just triumphant, and make innocent folk laugh aloud in scorn — Knox
The righteous see their fate and exult, the innocent make game of them — NEB

20. Whereas our substance is not cut down, but the remnant of them the fire consumeth.
'See how their greatness is brought to nothing!
See how their wealth has perished in the flames!' — Jerus
to see how their proud hopes vanished, and all that was left of them perished in the flames — Knox
saying, 'Surely our adversaries are cut off,
and what they left the fire has consumed' — RSV
for their riches are swept away,
and the profusion of their wealth is destroyed by fire — NEB

21. Acquaint now thyself with him, and be at peace:
Agree with God . . . — RSV
Well then! Make peace with him, be reconciled — Jerus
Shew thyself to be one with him — I pray thee — and prosper — Rhm
Come to terms with God and you will prosper — NEB
thereby good shall come unto thee.
Thereby shall there come on thee blessing — Rhm
Thereby thine increase is good — YLT
and all your happiness will be restored to you — Jerus
that is the way to mend your fortune — NEB

22. Receive, I pray thee, the law from his mouth,
Receive, I pray thee, from his mouth, the terms of deliverance — Sept
Welcome the teaching from his lips — Jerus
Let his lips be thy oracle — Knox
and lay up his words in thine heart.
and keep his words close to your heart — Jerus
his words written on thy heart—Knox

23. If thou return to the Almighty, thou shalt be built up,
If thou wilt return and humble thyself before the Lord, thou shalt be placed on a mount — Sept
If you return to the Almighty, you will be restored — NAB
Turn back to the Almighty for thy healing — Knox
thou shalt put away iniquity far from thy tabernacles.
and put right all the wrong in your home — Tay
and rid thy dwelling place of guilt — Knox
If you put injustice far from your tent — AAT

24. Then shalt thou lay up gold as dust, and the gold of Ophir as the stones of the brooks.
if you reckon gold as dust,
and Ophir as pebbles of the torrent — Jerus
Firm rock thou shalt have for shifting dust, and for firm rock streams of gold — Knox
And lay gold in the dust,
and gold of Ophir among the stones of the brooks — AAT
If you give up your lust for money,
and throw your gold away — Tay

25. Yea, the Almighty shall be thy defence, and thou shalt have plenty of silver.
And the Almighty shall be thy treasure,
and precious silver unto thee — RV
For the Almighty will be thy precious ores,
And silver, sought with toil, for thee — ABPS
and make the Almighty your gold nuggets and your silver ore — Ber
then you will find Shaddai worth bars of gold
or silver piled in heaps — Jerus
The Almighty will be your gold,
And your shining silver — AAT

26. For then shalt thou have thy delight in the Almighty, and shalt lift up thy face unto God.
In those omnipotent arms thou shalt rest content, thy face upturned toward God himself — Knox
Then Shaddai will be all your delight,
and you will lift your face to God — Jerus
then the Almighty shall be a joy to you,
and you can raise your eyes to God — Mof
Then indeed thou shalt have confidence before the Lord; and mayst look up to heaven with cheerfulness — Sept

27. Thou shalt make thy prayer unto him, and he shall hear thee, and thou shalt pay thy vows.
thy prayer heard as soon as offered,
thy vows paid as soon as due — Knox

28. Thou shalt also decree a thing, and it shall be established unto thee:
For thou wilt purpose a thing, and it shall stand — ABPS
Whatever you undertake will go well — Jerus
all thy desire thou shalt have — Knox
and the light shall shine upon thy ways.
and all thy paths will be sunshine — Knox
and you shall live in sunshine — Mof
and the light of heaven will shine upon the road ahead of you — Tay

29. When men are cast down, then thou shalt say,
When they cast thee down . . . — JPS
When men cast themselves down then thou shalt say — Rhm
There is lifting up;
Up! — Rhm
'Lift up.' — YLT
and he shall save the humble person.
the downcast eye shall win deliverance — Knox
and he helps the lowly — Mof
And him that is of downcast eyes shall he save — Rhm
And the bowed down of eyes he saveth — YLT

30. He shall deliver the island of the innocent:
He will deliver even him that is not innocent — ASV
He delivers the innocent man — RSV
He makes safe the man who is free from sin — Bas
If a man is innocent he will bring him freedom — Jerus
and it is delivered by the pureness of thine hands.
and if your hands are clean, salvation shall be yours — Bas
and freedom for you if your hands are kept unstained — Jerus
in a pair of clean hands shall be safety ever — Knox

CHAPTER 23

1. Then Job answered and said,
Job spoke next. He said: — Jerus

2. Even today is my complaint bitter:
. . . defiant — AAT
Today again my complaint becomes rebellious — Ber
My thoughts today are resentful — NEB

And still I repine as bitterly as ever — Knox
my stroke is heavier than my groaning.
his hand is hard on my sorrow — Bas
for God's hand is heavy on me in my trouble — NEB
that heavy hand of his drags groans from me — Jerus
my punishment far more severe than my fault deserves — Tay

3. Oh that I knew where I might find him! that I might come even to his seat!
Oh, that I knew where I might find Him, that I might approach His tribunal — Ber
If only I knew how to reach him, or how to travel to his dwelling! — Jerus
Ah, if I could but find my way to God, reach his very throne — Knox

4. I would order my cause before him,
. . . present my case . . . — Ber
. . . set out my case . . . — Jerus
. . . plead my suit before him — Knox
and fill my mouth with arguments.
my mouth would not want for arguments — Jerus
in reproachful accents — Knox

5. I would know the words which he would answer me,
I would learn the words with which he would answer — NAB
Then I could learn his defence, every word of it — Jerus
Fain would I learn what his reply would be — Mof
and understand what he would say unto me.
taking note of everything he said to me — Jerus

6. Will he plead against me with his great power?
Would he exert his great power to browbeat me? — NEB
No; but he would put strength in me.
No! he surely would give heed to me — ABPS
No, he would listen with sympathy — Tay
No; God himself would never bring a charge against me — NEB

7. There the righteous might dispute with him;
There, the upright might reason with him — ABPS
He would see that he was contending with an honest man — Jerus
The justice of my cause once made known to him — Knox
there I might argue with him as one innocent — Mof
There the upright are vindicated before him — NEB
so should I be delivered for ever from my judge.
so I should be acquitted by my Judge for ever — Amp
I should triumph at last — Knox
And triumphantly should I come forth from my Judge — Sprl
and have my judge acquit me for all time — Mof

8. Behold, I go forward, but he is not there; and backward, but I cannot perceive him:
Lo, I go toward the east, but he is not there,
And toward the west, but I perceive him not — ABPS
But I search in vain. I seek Him here, I seek Him there, and cannot find him — Tay

9. On the left hand, where he doth work, but I cannot behold him:
Toward the north where he works, but I behold him not — ABPS
I seek him in his workshop in the North . . . — Tay
he hideth himself on the right hand, that I cannot see him:
He covers himself in the south, and I see him not — ABPS
nor can I find him in the south; there, too, he hides himself — Tay

10. But he knoweth the way that I take:
And he, all the while, keeps watch over my doings — Knox
Yet he knows how I live — Mof
But he knows every detail of what is happening to me — Tay
when he hath tried me, I shall come forth as gold.
Let him test me in the crucible . . . — Jerus
when he tests me, I shall prove sterling gold — Mof

11. My foot hath held his steps,
My feet have stayed steady in His path — Ber
I have kept closely to his footsteps — Mof

My feet have kept to the path he has set me — NEB
his way have I kept, and not declined.
I have kept His way and have never swerved aside — Ber
never swerving from his path — Mof

12. **Neither have I gone back from the commandment of his lips;**
Nor have I strayed from the orders of His lips — Ber
I have not refused his commandments — Tay
I have esteemed the words of his mouth more than my necessary food.
cherishing the words from his mouth in my breast — Jerus
but have enjoyed them more than my daily food — Tay
Above my allotted portion have I laid up the sayings of His mouth — YLT

13. **But he is in one mind, and who can turn him?**
But his purpose is fixed and there is no changing it — Bas
But He remains true to Himself, and who can turn Him? — Ber
But once he has decided, who can change his mind? — Jerus
and what his soul desireth, even that he doeth.
and he gives effect to the desire of his soul — Bas
Whatever he plans, he carries out — Jerus

14. **For he performeth the thing that is appointed for me:**
For he will complete what he appoints for me — RSV
He will carry out what He has planned for me — Ber
and many such things are with him.
and his mind is full of such designs — Bas
and there is more ahead — Tay

15. **Therefore am I troubled at his presence:**
. . . awed . . . — Ber
. . . cowed . . . — Mof
. . . terrified . . . — Tay
. . . dismayed . . . — NAB
Therefore do I tremble before him — ABPS
Therefore I am fearful of meeting him — NEB
when I consider, I am afraid of him.
my thoughts of him overcome me — Bas
and the more I think, the greater grows my dread of him — Jerus
the thought of him dismays me — Mof

16. **For God maketh my heart soft,**
. . . faint, timid, and broken — Amp
It is God who makes me faint-hearted — NEB
Indeed God has made my courage fail — NAB
and the Almighty troubleth me:
. . . has terrified me — Amp
. . . has dismayed me — Ber
and the Almighty who fills me with fear — NEB

17. **Because I was not cut off before the darkness, neither hath he covered the darkness from my face.**
For I am overcome by the dark, and by the black night which is covering my face — Bas
I am hemmed in by the darkness, thick darkness covers my face — Ber
For darkness hides me from him, and the gloom veils his presence from me — Jerus
I am appalled at his dark mystery, and its black shadow has bewildered me — Mof
Why cannot I draw darkness over my face
And cover my face with the thick gloom? — Sprl

CHAPTER 24

1. **Why, seeing times are not hidden from the Almighty, do they that know him not see his days?**
Why are not times appointed by the Almighty,
And why do not they that know him see his days — ABPS
Why has not Shaddai his own store of times,
and why do his faithful never see his Days — Jerus
Since he, who is omnipotent, determines every event, how is it that those who know him wait in vain for his doom to fall — Knox

Why has not the Almighty sessions of set justice?
Why do his followers never see him intervening — Mof

But why have set times escaped the notice of the Lord; and the wicked transgressed all bounds — Sept

Why doesn't God open the court and listen to my case? Why must the godly wait for him in vain — Tay

The day of reckoning is no secret to the Almighty,
though those who know him have no hint of its date — NEB

2. **Some remove the landmarks; they violently take away flocks, and feed thereof.**

Here are men that alter their neighbour's landmark, drive stolen cattle to pasture — Knox

The wicked move boundary-marks away,
they carry off flock and shepherd — Jerus

3. **They drive away the ass of the fatherless, they take the widow's ox for a pledge.**

. . . the orphan's donkey . . . for security — Jerus

4. **They turn the needy out of the way:**

They crowd the poor and needy off the roads — Amp

Beggars, now, avoid the roads — Jerus

shoulder the poor aside — Knox

evicting poor folk — Mof

They thrust the poor off the road — RSV

They have turned the weak out of the right way — Sept

the poor of the earth hide themselves together.

the destitute huddle together, hiding from them — NEB

All the oppressed of the land are made to hide themselves — ABPS

and conspire to oppress the friendless — Knox

till these humble souls must hide and huddle away — Mof

5. **Behold, as wild asses in the desert, go they forth to their work;**

Like wild donkeys in the desert, they go out — Jerus

leave others to make their living as best they may, like the wild ass in the desert — Knox

rising betimes for a prey:

seeking diligently for food — ASV

waking betimes to scrape food — Knox

the wilderness yieldeth food for them and for their children.

driven by the hunger of their children — Jerus

for hungry mouths at home — Knox

6. **They reap every one his corn in the field:**

They cut their provender in the field — ASV

They must do the harvesting in the scoundrel's field — Jerus

They cut hay in a field which is not theirs — Lam

They have to steal corn from the fields by night — Mof

They reap a field not their own — Sprl

and they gather the vintage of the wicked.

and they take away the late fruit from the vines of those who have wealth — Bas

and they gather grapes from the vineyard of the wicked — Lam

and rob the vineyards of the rich — Mof

And wickedly gather the vintage — Sprl

7. **They cause the naked to lodge without clothing, that they have no covering in the cold.**

Naked they pass the night, without clothing,
And with no shelter in the cold — ABPS

They lie all night naked without clothing, and have no covering in the cold — RV

8. **They are wet with the showers of the mountains,**

They are wet with the mountain storm — ABPS

drenched by downpour from the hills — Mof

and embrace the rock for want of a shelter.

and get into the cracks of the rock for cover — Bas

shelterless, they hug the rocks — Jerus

9. **They pluck the fatherless from the breast, and take a pledge of the poor.**

Fatherless children are robbed of their lands,
and poor men have their cloaks seized as security — Jerus

They snatch the orphan from the breast,
And they take the infant of the poor as security — AAT
They tear the fatherless from the breast,
And take the garment of the poor in pledge — Sprl

10. They cause him to go naked without clothing, and they take away the sheaf from the hungry;
Naked they go about, without clothing;
And hungry they bear the sheaves — ABPS
So that they go about naked without clothing, and being an-hungered they carry the sheaves — RV
They have by injustice caused some to be naked; and robbed the hungry of their morsel — Sept

11. Which make oil within their walls, and tread their winepresses, and suffer thirst.
They are forced to press out the olive oil without tasting it, and to tread out the grapejuice as they suffer from thirst — Tay
they press the oil in the shade where two walls meet,
they tread the winepress but themselves go thirsty — NEB

12. Men groan from out of the city,
For anguish do the dying groan — ABPS
From the town come sounds of pain — Bas
From the towns come the groans of the dying — Jerus
A cry goes up from the city streets — Knox
The groan of victims rises from the town — Mof
and the soul of the wounded crieth out:
and the gasp of wounded men crying for help — Jerus
where wounded men lie groaning — Knox
yet God layeth not folly to them.
And God heeds not the prayer — ABPS
yet God pays no attention to their prayer — RSV
Yet God regardeth not the folly — ASV

13. They are of those that rebel against the light; they know not the ways thereof, nor abide in the paths thereof.
Others evade the daylight,
caring not for the ways of God,
refusing to pursue his paths — Mof
They are enemies of the light;
They do not know its ways;
Nor do they dwell in its paths — AAT

14. The murderer rising with the light
At the dawn, the murderer rises up — ABPS
The murderer must be stirring before daylight — Knox
The murderer rises in the dark — RSV
killeth the poor and needy,
to catch his helpless prey — Knox
He cutteth off the afflicted and distressed — Sprl
that he may kill the poor and needy — RSV
and in the night is as a thief.
or prowl, as the thieves prowl, at night — Knox

15. The eye also of the adulterer waiteth for the twilight,
For darkness, too, must the adulterer wait — Knox
saying, No eye shall see me: and disguiseth his face.
'No one will see me,' he mutters
as he masks his face — Jerus

16. In the dark they dig through houses,
. . . he makes holes in the walls of houses — Bas
under cover of darkness he will break into the house — Knox
which they had marked for themselves in the daytime:
to keep the tryst made yesterday — Knox
by day they shut themselves up — RSV
they know not the light.
these folk who have no love for the light — Jerus
no daylight for him — Knox

17. For the morning is to them even as the shadow of death:
For the middle of the night is as morning to them — Bas
For all of them, morning is their darkest hour — Jerus
To him the first flush of dawn is death's shadow — Knox
For deep darkness is morning to all of them — RSV
if one know them, they are in the terrors of the shadow of death.
they are not troubled by the fear of the dark — Bas
deep gloom is the sunshine he walks by — Knox

for they are friends with the terrors of deep darkness — RSV

18. He is swift as the waters;

Swiftly they pass away on the face of the waters — ASV

They go quickly on the face of the waters — Bas

Headlong he flees from the daylight — Jerus

Such men are scum on the surface of the water — NEB

You say, 'They are swiftly carried away upon the face of the waters — RSV

But how quickly they disappear from the face of the earth — Tay

their portion is cursed in the earth:

their fields have a bad name throughout the land — NEB

Speedily vanished their share in the land — Rhm

Everything they own is cursed — Tay

he beholdeth not the way of the vineyards.

not for him the vineyard's sunny slope — Knox

grape treaders turn no more to their vineyards — Ber

and no labourers will go near their vineyards — NEB

19. Drought and heat consume the snow waters: so doth the grave those which have sinned.

Swift as snow melts under the noonday heat, let his guilty soul pass to the grave — Knox

Death consumes sinners like drought and heat consume snow — Tay

20. The womb shall forget him;

The womb that shaped him forgets him — Jerus

unpitied — Knox

Maternal love shall forget him — Rhm

Even the sinner's own mother shall forget him — Tay

The squares of the town forget them — RSV

The streets of his native place forget him — Mof

the worm shall feed sweetly on him;

The worm shall feed daintily upon him — Sprl

with worms for his boon-companions — Knox

the worm shall find him sweet — Rhm

he shall be no more remembered;

forgotten — Knox

their name is no longer remembered — RSV

and wickedness shall be broken as a tree.

Thus wickedness is blasted as a tree is struck — Jerus

overthrown like an unfruited tree! — Knox

21. He evil entreateth the barren that beareth not:

He devoureth the barren that beareth not — ASV

The childless woman was his prey — Knox

They feed on the barren childless woman — RSV

Because he did not treat the barren with tenderness — Sept

and doeth not good to the widow.

in vain the widow looked to him for mercy — Knox

and had no compassion for a poor weak woman — Sept

22. He draweth also the mighty with his power: he riseth up, and no man is sure of life.

And he removes the strong by his might;
He rises up, and no one is sure of life — ABPS

Yet God preserveth the mighty by his power:
He riseth up that hath no assurance of life — ASV

Yet [God] prolongs the life of the [wicked] mighty by His power; they rise up when they had despaired of life — Amp

Yet God lets them remain alive and strong;
they rise, though they despaired of life — Mof

Yet sometimes it seems as though God preserves the rich by his power, and restores them to life when anyone else would die — Tay

But he who lays mighty hold on tyrants
rises up to take away that life which seemed so secure — Jerus

now, surely, God has pulled the tyrant down; firm he has stood, but now he despairs of life itself — Knox

The wealth of a man of power is sustained by his own strength; he does not depend on divine guidance — Lam

23. Though it be given him to be in safety, whereon he resteth;
He grants to them safety, and they are at rest — ABPS
God giveth them to be in security, and they rest thereon — ASV
Time for repentance God gave him . . . — Knox
He lets them rest in safety — Mof
God gives them confidence and strength — Tay
He let him build his hopes on false security — Jerus
He lulls them into security with confidence — NEB
yet his eyes are upon their ways.
but kept his eyes on every step he took — Jerus
he watches over them! — Mof
and helps them in many ways — Tay
but his eyes are fixed on their ways — NEB

24. They are exalted for a little while, but are gone and brought low;
The man had his time of glory, now he vanishes — Jerus
Have patience! they will soon be gone, brought low — Mof
But though they are very great now, yet in a moment they shall be gone like all others — Tay
High they were for a little, and they are not — YLT
they are taken out of the way as all other,
and bundled off like all the rest — Mof
drooping like a mallow plucked from its bed — Jerus
they wither and fade like the mallow — RSV
and cut off as the tops of the ears of corn.
and withering like an ear of corn — Jerus
lopped like the ears of corn — Mof
they are cut off like the heads of grain — RSV
they wither and are shaken out like the heads of grain — Lam

25. And if it be not so now, who will make me a liar,
And if it be not so, who then will prove me false — ABPS
Can anyone claim otherwise? — Tay
and make my speech nothing worth?
And make my words of no effect? — ABPS
or show that my words have no substance — Jerus

CHAPTER 25

1. Then answered Bildad the Shuhite, and said,
Bildad of Shuah spoke next. He said: — Jerus

2. Dominion and fear are with him, he maketh peace in his high places.
Dominion and fear are with God; he makes peace in his high heaven — RSV
What sovereignty, what awe, is his who keeps the peace in his heights! — Jerus
Ay, but what power, ay, but what terror he wields, who reigns peacefully, there in high heaven! — Knox
He wields a dread authority, he keeps the peace within high heaven — Mof
God is powerful and dreadful. He enforces peace in heaven — Tay
What! Is there any apology or fear with him who made the universe and is supreme? — Sept

3. Is there any number of his armies? and upon whom doth not his light arise?
Can anyone number his armies, or boast of having escaped his ambushes — Jerus
He, the lord of countless armies, he, whose light dazzles every eye! — Knox
Who can number his hosts of angels? And his light shines down on all the earth — Tay
His squadrons are without number; at whom will they not spring from ambush — NEB

4. How then can man be justified with God?
Can any man ever think of himself as innocent, when confronted with God — Jerus
. . . win his suit, prove his innocence, when he is matched with God — Knox
How can a mere man stand before God and claim to be righteous — Tay

or how can he be clean that is born of a woman?
Born of woman, how could he ever be clean — Jerus
Who in all the earth can boast that he is clean — Tay

5. **Behold even to the moon, and it shineth not; yea, the stars are not pure in his sight.**
The very moon lacks brightness,
and the stars are unclean as he sees them — Jerus
Dim shews the moon, tarnished the stars, under his eye — Knox
To him the very moon is not unsullied, the very stars are stained! — Mof

6. **How much less man, that is a worm? and the son of man, which is a worm?**
. . . a grub . . . — YLT
What then of man, maggot that he is, the son of man, a worm — Jerus
and what is man but waste and worm in his presence — Knox

CHAPTER 26

1. **But Job answered and said,**
2. **How hast thou helped him that is without power? how savest thou the arm that hath no strength?**
What help you give to the powerless, what strength to the feeble arm! — NAB
To one so weak, what a help you are, for the arm that is powerless, what a rescuer! — Jerus
Bravely spoken, for a cause that so much needed it! That arm of thine ever upheld the weak. — Knox
What a help you are to poor God!
What a support to his failing powers! — Mof
What wonderful helpers you all are! And how you have encouraged me in my great need! — Tay

3. **How hast thou counselled him that hath no wisdom? and how hast thou plentifully declared the thing as it is?**
What excellent advice you give the unlearned,
never at a loss for a helpful suggestion! — Jerus
How thou hast counseled the unwise;
And understanding thou hast taught abundantly! — ABPS
How you have enlightened my stupidity! What wise things you have said! — Tay

4. **To whom hast thou uttered words? and whose spirit came from thee?**
With whose assistance have you uttered these words? And whose spirit [inspired what] came forth from you — Amp
But who are they aimed at, these speeches of yours,
and what spirit is this that comes out of you — Jerus
A fine lesson thou hast read him, the God who gave thee breath! — Knox
Who helped you to such eloquence?
Who was it that inspired you — Mof

5. **Dead things are formed from under the waters, and the inhabitants thereof.**
The Shades tremble beneath the earth;
the waters and their denizens are afraid — Jerus
The shades beneath writhe in terror, the waters and their inhabitants — NAB
Sure enough, there is none but trembles before him; even the old heroes and those who share their dwelling-place under the lower depths — Knox
Before him the primaeval giants writhe,
under the ocean in their prison — Mof

6. **Hell is naked before him, and destruction hath no covering.**
Sheol is naked before God,
And Abaddon hath no covering — ASV
The underworld is uncovered before him, and Destruction has no veil — Bas
bare to his eyes lies the place of shadows, oblivion lies revealed — Knox
The dead stand naked, trembling before God in the place where they go — Tay

7. **He stretcheth out the north over the empty place,**
He stretched out the north over empty space — ABPS
By his hand the north is stretched out in space — Bas

It was he who spread the North above the void — Jerus
He it was spread out the northern skies over emptiness — Knox
God spreads the canopy of the sky over chaos — NEB
and hangeth the earth upon nothing.
and poised the earth on nothingness — Jerus
and suspends earth in the void — NEB
He hanged the earth upon nothing — ABPS

8. **He bindeth up the waters in his thick clouds; and the cloud is not rent under them.**
He fastens up the waters in his clouds —
and the mists do not tear apart under their weight — Jerus
cloud-bound he holds the rain, that else would spill on earth all at once — Knox
He wraps the rain in his thick clouds, and the clouds are not split by the weight — Tay

9. **He holdeth back the face of his throne, and spreadeth his cloud upon it.**
He covers the face of the moon at the full,
his mist he spreads over it — Jerus
He holds back the appearance of the full moon
by spreading his clouds before it — NAB
He shrouds his throne with his clouds — Tay

10. **He hath compassed the waters with bounds, until the day and night come to an end.**
By him a circle is marked out on the face of the waters, to the limits of the light and the dark — Bas
He has traced a ring on the surface of the waters,
at the boundary between light and dark — Jerus
While day and night last, the waters keep the bounds he has decreed for them — Knox
The dome of heaven he arched over the deep,
bounding the darkness from the light — Mof
He has fixed the horizon on the surface of the waters
at the farthest limit of light and darkness — NEB

11. **The pillars of heaven tremble and are astonished at his reproof.**
then swayed the pillars of the sky, appalled at the thunder of his rebuke — Mof
The pillars of heaven flutter and are struck with consternation at his rebuke — Sept
The pillars of the heavens tottered,
And were dazed at his rebuke — AAT
the very pillars of heaven tremble awe-struck at his will — Knox
The pillars of heaven quake
and are aghast at his rebuke — NEB

12. **He divideth the sea with his power,**
By his power he quells the sea — ABPS
By his power he stilled the sea — RSV
By his power the sea grows calm—Tay
and by his understanding he smiteth through the proud.
And by his wisdom he smites down pride — ABPS
And by his skill hath he shattered the Crocodile — Rhm
And by his skill he smote through Rahab — AAT
and by his might he crushes Rahab — NAB
He is skilled at crushing its pride! — Tay

13. **By his spirit he hath garnished the heavens;**
By his spirit hath he arched the heavens — Rhm
By his spirit are the heavens adorned — ABPS
By his wind the heavens become bright — Bas
His breath made the heavens luminous — Jerus
by his breath the skies were cleared — Mof
With his angry breath he scatters the waters — NAB
his hand hath formed the crooked serpent.
His hand pierced the fleeing Serpent — ABPS
his hand transfixed the Fleeing Serpent — Jerus
and his hand maimed the swift cloud-monster — Mof
and his hand breaks the twisting sea-serpent — NEB

14. **Lo, these are parts of his ways:**

Lo, these are the borders of His way — YLT
Lo, these are but the outskirts of his ways — ASV
All this but skirts the ways he treads — Jerus
Here is but a small part of his doings — Knox
And all this is the mere fringe of his force — Mof
Lo, these are but the outlines of his ways — NAB

but how little a portion is heard of him?
And how small a whisper do we hear of him! — ASV
a whispered echo is all we hear of him — Jerus

but the thunder of his power who can understand?
But the thunder of his acts of power is outside all knowledge. — Bas
who dares to contemplate the thunder of his full magnificence — Knox

CHAPTER 27

1. Moreover Job continued his parable, and said,
And Job again took up his discourse, and said: — RSV
. . . continued his solemn discourse. He said: — Jerus
. . . resumed his grave argument, and he said: — Sprl

2. As God liveth, who hath taken away my judgment; and the Almighty, who hath vexed my soul;
I swear by the living God who denies me justice,
by Shaddai who has turned my life sour — Jerus

3. All the while my breath is in me, and the spirit of God is in my nostrils;
So long as my breath is in me,
And the spirit of God is in my nostrils — ABPS
so long as there is any life left in me and God's breath is in my nostrils — NEB
That as long as I live, while I have breath from God — Tay

4. My lips shall not speak wickedness, nor my tongue utter deceit.
my lips shall never speak untruth,
nor any lie be found on my tongue — Jerus
I swear I speak the truth,
no lie upon my lips — Mof

5. God forbid that I should justify you: till I die I will not remove mine integrity from me.
Far from ever admitting you to be in the right:
I will maintain my innocence to my dying day — Jerus
Gain your point with me you shall not; I will die sooner than abandon my plea of innocence — Knox
when I maintain (by God!) that you are wrong,
when I assert that I am innocent! — Mof
I will never, never agree that you are right; until I die I will vow my innocence — Tay
Pollution to me — if I justify you,
Till I expire I turn not aside mine integrity from me — YLT

6. My righteousness I hold fast, and will not let it go:
My justice I maintain and I will not relinquish it — NAB
I take my stand on my integrity, I will not stir — Jerus
And for asserting my righteousness I make no apology — Sept
I am not a sinner — I repeat it again and again — Tay

my heart shall not reproach me so long as I live.
My heart reproaches none of my days — ABPS
not one act in all my life bids conscience reproach me — Knox
My conscience is clear for as long as I live — Tay

7. Let mine enemy be as the wicked, and he that riseth up against me as the unrighteous.
May my enemy meet a criminal's end,
and my opponent suffer with the guilty — Jerus
Count him a knave that is my enemy, every detractor of mine a friend of wrong! — Knox

Those who declare otherwise are my wicked enemies. They are evil men — Tay

8. **For what is the hope of the hypocrite, though he hath gained, when God taketh away his soul?**

For what hope, after all, has the godless when he prays
and raises his soul to God — Jerus

What is the sinner's hope worth after all his greedy getting, when God takes the life away from him — Knox

For though he has accumulated riches, what is the hope of the godless at the time when God takes away his life — Lam

For what hope has a godless man
when God demands his soul — Mof

For what shall be the hope of the impious though he graspeth with greed,
When God shall draw forth his soul — Rhm

9. **Will God hear his cry when trouble cometh upon him?**

In that hour of need, his cry for reprieve will go unheard — Knox

Will God attend unto his supplication
When anguish cometh upon him — Sprl

10. **Will he delight himself in the Almighty? will he always call upon God?**

he cannot go on for ever basking in the Almighty's favour, calling God to his aid — Knox

No, unless he delight himself in the Almighty
And pray unto God at all times — Sprl

Will he trust himself to the Almighty and call upon God at all times — NEB

11. **I will teach you by the hand of God: that which is with the Almighty will I not conceal.**

I will teach you concerning God's hand;
What is with the Almighty I will not conceal — ABPS

Now be God's hand laid bare, now let me acknowledge openly the counsels of omnipotence! — Knox

I can show you how God's power works,
I will disclose the dealings of the Almighty — Mof

I will teach you what is in God's power,
I will not conceal the purpose of the Almighty — NEB

I will teach you about God . . . — Tay

12. **Behold, all ye yourselves have seen it;**

And if you all had understood them for yourselves — Jerus

Not one of you but knows the truth of it already — Knox

But really, I don't need to, for you yourselves know as much about him as I do — Tay

why then are ye thus altogether vain?

And why then speak ye what is utterly vain? — ABPS

you would not have wasted your breath on empty words — Jerus

Yet you are saying all these useless things to me — Tay

13. **This is the portion of a wicked man with God, and the heritage of oppressors, which they shall receive of the Almighty.**

Here is the fate that God has in store for the wicked,
and the inheritance with which Shaddai endows the man of violence — Jerus

What spoil after all does God grant to the wicked? From his almighty hand, what abiding possession does the man of violence receive — Knox

Here is what God awards an evil man, what the Almighty bestows upon a tyrant — Mof

14. **If his children be multiplied, it is for the sword: and his offspring shall not be satisfied with bread.**

A sword awaits his sons, however many they may be,
and their children after these will go unfed — Jerus

If his children grow up, some fall by the sword,
some starve — Mof

15. **Those that remain of him shall be buried in death:**

Plague will bury those he leaves behind him — Jerus

Those who survive him the pestilence buries — RSV

His remains shall be buried unembalmed — Sprl

and his widows shall not weep.

and their widows will have no chance to mourn them — Jerus

and there will be no widows to weep — AAT

And no mourning women shall make lamentation — Sprl
with no one to mourn them, not even their wives — Tay

16. Though he heap up silver as the dust, and prepare raiment as the clay;

17. He may prepare it, but the just shall put it on, and the innocent shall divide the silver.

He may collect silver like dust,
and gather fine clothes like clay.
Let him gather! Some good man will wear them,
while his silver is shared among the innocent — Jerus

What avails it, to heap up silver like the sand, buy fine clothes, too, and think such treasures cheap as dirt, if more upright men than he, more innocent than he, must have the wearing of those clothes, share out that silver at last? — Knox

The evil man may accumulate money like dust, with closets jammed full of clothing — yes, he may order them made by his tailor, but the innocent shall wear that clothing, and shall divide his silver among them — Tay

18. He buildeth his house as a moth,

His house has no more strength than a spider's thread — Bas
He has built himself a spider's web — Jerus
For the wicked has built his house upon a spider's web — Lam
The house he builds is flimsy as a bird's nest — NEB

and as a booth that the keeper maketh.

And as a booth, which the watchman makes — ABPS
made himself a watchman's shack — Jerus
Or as a shed constructed by a watchman — Sprl

19. The rich man shall lie down, but he shall not be gathered: he openeth his eyes, and he is not.

He goes to bed a rich man but never again:
he wakes to find not a penny left — Jerus

He goes to bed rich, but will do so no more;
he opens his eyes, and his wealth is gone — RSV

He lies down a rich man, one last time;
he opens his eyes and nothing remains to him — NAB

20. Terrors take hold on him as waters,

Terrors overtake him like waters — ASV
Fears overtake him like rushing waters — Bas
Terrors attack him in broad daylight — Jerus
Disaster overtakes him like a flood — NEB

a tempest stealeth him away in the night.

A storm snatches him away in the night — AAT
and at night a whirlwind sweeps him off — Jerus
driven in darkness by the storm — Knox

21. The east wind carrieth him away, and he departeth:

The east wind lifts him up and he is gone — RSV
The sirocco picks him up and he goes — AAT
The storm wind seizes him and he disappears — NAB

and as a storm hurleth him out of his place.

And it whirls him away from his place — AAT
It sweeps him into eternity — Tay

22. For God shall cast upon him, and not spare:

God sends his arrows against him without mercy — Bas
He is routed before the pitiless onslaught — Knox
For God shall cast him out without pity — Lam
God pelts him without pity — Mof

he would fain flee out of his hand.

He longs to flee from God — Tay

23. Men shall clap their hands at him, and shall hiss him out of his place.

His downfall is greeted with applause,
and hissing meets him on every side — Jerus

hands clapped in triumph, tongues hissing in derision as he goes — Knox

God openly derides him,
and hisses scorn at him from heaven — Mof

Men clench their fists at him,
and hiss him from his place — AAT

Everyone shall cheer at his death, and boo him into eternity — Tay

CHAPTER 28

1. **Surely there is a vein for the silver,**
Surely there is a mine for silver — ASV
Silver has its mines — Jerus
and a place for gold where they fine it.
And a place for the gold, which they refine — ABPS
and a place where gold is washed out — Bas
and gold a place for refining — Jerus

2. **Iron is taken out of the earth, and brass is molten out of the stone.**
Iron is taken out of the dust,
And stone is fused into copper — ABPS
Iron is extracted from the earth,
the smelted rocks yield copper — Jerus

3. **He setteth an end to darkness, and searcheth out all perfection: the stones of darkness, and the shadow of death.**
Man puts an end to the dark, searching out to the farthest limit the stones of the deep places of the dark — Bas
See how man has done away with darkness, has pierced into the very heart of things, into caves underground, black as death's shadow! — Knox
Men put an end to darkness,
and search out to the farthest bound
the ore in gloom and deep darkness — RSV
The miner delveth into darkness,
And searcheth to the utmost limit
The stones of darkness, and of death-shade — Sprl

4. **The flood breaketh out from the inhabitant: even the waters forgotten of the foot: they are dried up, they are gone away from men.**
He makes a deep mine far away from those living in the light of day; when they go about on the earth, they have no knowledge of those who are under them, who are hanging far from men, twisting from side to side on a cord — Bas
He breaketh open a shaft away from where men sojourn; they are forgotten of the foot that passeth by; they hang afar from men, they swing to and fro — RV
Mines the lamp-folk dig
in places where there is no foothold,
and hang suspended far from mankind — Jerus
They open shafts in a valley away from where men live;
they are forgotten by travelers,
they hang afar from men, they swing to and fro — RSV

5. **As for the earth, out of it cometh bread: and under it is turned up as it were fire.**
The earth from which bread comes
is ravaged underground by fire — Jerus
That earth, from whose surface our bread comes to us, must be probed by fire beneath — Knox
The earth — bread comes forth from it,
But underneath it is turned into what looks like fire — AAT
While corn is springing from the earth above,
what lies beneath is raked over like a fire — NEB

6. **The stones of it are the place of sapphires: and it hath dust of gold.**
Down there, the rocks are set with sapphires,
full of spangles of gold — Jerus
till the rocks yield sapphires, and the clods gold — Knox
Its stones are the source of sapphires,
And it has dust of gold — AAT
and out of its rocks come lapis lazuli,
dusted with flecks of gold — NEB

7. **There is a path which no fowl knoweth, and which the vulture's eye hath not seen:**
That path no bird of prey knoweth, neither hath the falcon's eye seen it — RV
Here are passages no bird discovers in its flight, no vulture's eye has seen — Knox

8. **The lion's whelps have not trodden it,**
a path not trodden by lordly beasts,
where no lion ever walked — Jerus
The beasts of prey have not trodden it,
Nor has the lion passed over it — AAT

9. **He putteth forth his hand upon the rock;**
Man puts out his hand on the hard rock — Bas

Man attacks its flinty sides — Jerus
Boldly man matches himself against the flint — Knox
The miner puts forth his hand upon the hard rock to break it — Lam
he overturneth the mountains by the roots.
uproots the mountain — Knox
he overturns the mountains from their foundations — Lam
He turns the mountains upside down — AAT
and lays bare the roots of the mountains — NEB

10. He cutteth out rivers among the rocks;
In the rocks he cleaves out rivers — ABPS
driving tunnels through the rocks — Jerus
cuts channels through the rock — Knox
They drill tunnels in the rocks — Tay
and his eye seeth every precious thing.
and gems of every kind meet his eye — NEB
on the watch for anything precious — Jerus
where things of price have dazzled his eye — Knox
and lay bare precious stones — Tay

11. He bindeth the floods from overflowing;
He bindeth the streams that they trickle not — ASV
He keeps back the streams from flowing — Bas
They dam up streams of water — Tay
and the thing that is hid bringeth he forth to light.
and brings to daylight secrets that are hidden — Jerus
and pan the gold — Tay

12. But where shall wisdom be found and where is the place of understanding?
But tell me, where does wisdom come from?
Where is understanding to be found — Jerus

13. Man knoweth not the price thereof;
Man knows nothing to equal it — NAB
The road to it is still unknown to man — Jerus
Man knows not the way of it — AAT
neither is it found in the land of the living.
nor hath it indeed been found out by men — Sept
in fact, it is not to be found among the living — Tay

14. The depth saith, It is not in me: and the sea saith, It is not with me.
'It is not in me' says the Abyss;
'Nor here' replies the Sea — Jerus
'It's not here,' the oceans say; and the seas reply, 'Nor is it here' — Tay

15. It cannot be gotten for gold, neither shall silver be weighed for the price thereof.
Pure gold cannot be given for it,
Nor can silver be weighed out as its price — AAT

16. It cannot be valued with the gold of Ophir, with the precious onyx, or the sapphire.
It cannot be bought with gold of Ophir,
With precious onyx and sapphires — AAT
She is not to be compared with the ingot of Ophir,
With the precious [onyx], or the sapphire — Sprl

17. The gold and the crystal cannot equal it:
No gold, no glass can match it in value — Jerus
and the exchange of it shall not be for jewels of fine gold.
Nor is its exchange a vessel of fine gold — YLT
nor for a fine gold vase can it be bartered — Jerus
Nor can articles of fine gold be exchanged for it — AAT

18. No mention shall be made of coral, or of pearls: for the price of wisdom is above rubies.
Nor is there need to mention coral, nor crystal;
beside wisdom pearls are not worth the fishing — Jerus
As to corals and pearls they shall not be thought of,
For the attraction of wisdom is beyond opals — Sprl

19. The topaz of Ethiopia shall not equal it, neither shall it be valued with pure gold.
Topaz from Cush is worthless in comparison,
and gold, even refined, is valueless — Jerus

20. Whence then cometh wisdom? and where is the place of understanding?

. . . where is discernment to be found — Knox

21. **Seeing it is hid from the eyes of all living, and kept close from the fowls of the air.**

It is outside the knowledge of every living thing,
hidden from the birds of the sky — Jerus

For it is hid from the eyes of all mankind. Even the sharp-eyed birds in the sky cannot discover it — Tay

No creature on earth can see it,
and it is hidden from the birds of the air — NEB

22. **Destruction and death say, We have heard the fame thereof with our ears.**

Perdition and Death can only say,
'We have heard reports of it' — Jerus

Abaddon and Death say,
"Only by rumor have we heard of it" — NAB

23. **God understandeth the way thereof, and he knoweth the place thereof.**

God alone has traced its path
and found out where it lives — Jerus

God surely knows where it is to be found — Tay

24. **For he looketh to the ends of the earth, and seeth under the whole heaven;**

25. **To make the weight for the winds; and he weigheth the waters by measure.**

(For he sees to the ends of the earth, and observes all that lies under heaven.)
When he willed to give weight to the wind
and measured out the waters with a gauge — Jerus

26. **When he made a decree for the rain,**

when he made the laws and rules for the rain — Jerus

when he laid down a limit for the rain — NEB

and a way for the lightning of the thunder:

And a track for the thunder's flash — ABPS

and mapped a route for thunderclaps to follow — Jerus

27. **Then did he see it, and declare it; he prepared it, yea, and searched it out.**

Then did he see it and declare it;
He established it and investigated it — AAT

then he had it in sight, and cast its worth,
assessed it, fathomed it — Jerus

even then he saw wisdom and took stock of it,
he considered it and fathomed its depths — NEB

28. **And unto man he said, Behold the fear of the Lord, that is wisdom; and to depart from evil is understanding.**

And he said to men,
'Wisdom? It is fear of the Lord.
Understanding? — avoidance of evil — Jerus

And to man he said, Behold, the reverence of God, that is wisdom; and to depart . . . — Lam

CHAPTER 29

1. **Moreover Job continued his parable, and said,**

And Job continued his solemn discourse. He said: — Jerus

2. **Oh that I were as in months past, as in the days when God preserved me;**

Oh that I were as in the months of old,
As in the days when God watched over me — ASV

. . . when God was my guardian — Jerus

Oh, for the years gone by when God took care of me — Tay

3. **When his candle shined upon my head, and when by his light I walked through darkness;**

when his lamp shone over my head,
and his light was my guide in the darkness — Jerus

When he lighted the way before me and I walked safely through the darkness — Tay

4. **As I was in the days of my youth, when the secret of God was upon my tabernacle;**

As I was in my autumn days,
When the favor of God was over my dwelling — ABPS

As I was in the ripeness of my days,
When the friendship of God was upon my tent — ASV

As I was in my flowering years, when

my tent was covered by the hand of God — Bas
Days of ripe manhood, when God was my home's familiar guest — Knox
As I was in the days of my prime,
When the intimacy of God was over my tent — Rhm

5. When the Almighty was yet with me, when my children were about me;
he, the Almighty, at my side! I had my children still about me — Knox

6. When I washed my steps with butter, and the rock poured me out rivers of oil;
When my steps [through rich pasturage] were washed with butter . . . — Amp
the milk frothed in pools at my feet, no rock so hard but my olives bathed it in oil — Knox
when my ways abounded in butter, and my mountain flowed with milk — Sept

7. When I went out to the gate through the city, when I prepared my seat in the street!
When I went out to the gate of the city, when I prepared my seat in the street — the broad place [for the council at the city's gate] — Amp
Those were the days when I went out to the city gate and took my place among the honored elders — Tay

8. The young men saw me, and hid themselves:
as soon as I appeared, the young men stepped aside — Jerus
young men saw me and kept out of sight — NEB
and the aged arose, and stood up.
rose the aged to do me honour — Knox
and even the aged arose and stood up in respect at my coming — Tay

9. The princes refrained talking, and laid their hand on their mouth.
Men of note interrupted their speeches, and put their fingers on their lips — Jerus
men in authority broke off their talk and put their hand to their lips—NEB

10. The nobles held their peace, and their tongue cleaved to the roof of their mouth.
the voices of rulers were silenced,
and their tongues stayed still in their mouths — Jerus
The highest officials in the city stood in quietness — Tay

11. When the ear heard me, then it blessed me; and when the eye saw me, it gave witness to me:
My praises echoed in every ear
and never an eye but smiled on me — Jerus
None heard the fame of me then, but called me a happy man; none watched my doings then, but spoke in my praise — Knox
All rejoiced in what I said. All who saw me spoke well of me — Tay
Whoever heard of me spoke in my favour,
and those who saw me bore witness to my merit — NEB

12. Because I delivered the poor that cried, and the fatherless, and him that had none to help him.
because I freed the poor man when he called
and the orphan who had no one to help him — Jerus

13. The blessing of him that was ready to perish came upon me: and I caused the widow's heart to sing for joy.
When men were dying, I it was who had their blessing;
if widows' hearts rejoiced, that was my doing — Jerus
The man threatened with ruin blessed me,
and I made the widow's heart sing for joy — NEB

14. I put on righteousness, and it clothed me: my judgment was as a robe and a diadem.
I put on righteousness as a garment and it clothed me;
justice, like a cloak or a turban, wrapped me round — NEB
I put on righteousness; and it clothed itself with me;
As a mantle and a turban was my rectitude — ABPS
I wore my honesty like a garment;
justice was my robe and my turban — NAB

15. I was eyes to the blind, and feet was I to the lame.
in me, the blind found sight, the lame strength — Knox

16. I was a father to the poor: and the

cause which I knew not I searched out.
Who but I was father of the poor?
The stranger's case had a hearing from me — Jerus
I was as a father to the poor, and saw to it that even strangers received a fair trial — Tay
17. **And I brake the jaws of the wicked,**
And I broke the fangs of the wicked — ABPS
. . . the talons . . . — AAT
Also the grinders of the unjust I shivered to pieces — Sprl
And I shivered the fangs of the perverse — Rhm
I knocked out the fangs of the godless oppressors — Tay
and plucked the spoil out of his teeth.
And out of his teeth I tore the prey — Rhm
And from his teeth I dashed the prey — ABPS
and made them drop their victims — Tay
18. **Then I said, I shall die in my nest, and I shall multiply my days as the sand.**
. . . I will come to my end with my children round me, my days will be as the sand in number — Bas
. . . I shall die with my nestlings,
And make my days as many as the sand — AAT
I thought, Surely I shall die quietly in my nest after a long, good life — Tay
I thought, I shall die with my powers unimpaired
and my days uncounted as the grains of sand — NEB
19. **My root was spread out by the waters, and the dew lay all night upon my branch.**
My roots thrust out to the water,
my leaves freshened by the falling dew at night — Jerus
For everything I did prospered; the dew lay all night upon my fields and watered them — Tay
20. **My glory was fresh in me,**
My reputation will never fade — Jerus
Fresh honors were constantly given me — Tay
and my bow was renewed in my hand.
and my bow will be readily bent in my hand — Bas
21. **Unto me men gave ear, and waited, and kept silence at my counsel.**
. . . And kept silence for my counsel — ASV
They waited anxiously to hear me,
and listened in silence to what I had to say — Jerus
Everyone listened to me and valued my advice, and were silent until I spoke — Tay
22. **After my words they spake not again; and my speech dropped upon them.**
When I paused, there was no rejoinder,
and my words dropped on them, one by one — Jerus
And after I spoke, they spoke no more, for my counsel satisfied them — Tay
When I had spoken, no one spoke again;
my words fell gently on them — NEB
Once I spoke, they said no more,
but received my pronouncement drop by drop — NAB
23. **And they waited for me as for the rain; and they opened their mouth wide as for the latter rain.**
Yea, they craved after me, as for a shower;
And they opened wide their mouth, as if for the latter rain — Sprl
They longed for me to speak as those in drought-time long for rain. They waited eagerly with open mouths — Tay
They waited for me, as men wait for rain,
open-mouthed, as if to catch the year's last showers — Jerus
24. **If I laughed on them, they believed it not;**
If I smiled at them, it was too good to be true — Jerus
I smiled on them when they had no confidence — ASV
When I smiled on them, they took heart — NEB
When I smiled on them they were reassured — NAB
Were they faint-hearted, they found me smiling still — Knox
If I ridiculed them, they did not take offense — Lam
and the light of my countenance they cast not down.
they watched my face for the least sign of favour — Jerus
and the encouragement of my glance

never failed them — Knox
when my face lit up, they lost their gloomy looks — NEB

25. **I chose out their way, and sat chief, and dwelt as a king in the army, as one that comforteth the mourners.**
I took my place as a chief, guiding them on their way and I was as a king among his army — Bas
In a lordly style, I told them which course to take,
and like a king amid his armies,
I led them where I chose — Jerus
Deigned I to be their leader, the first place was mine; yet ever when I sat like a king, with his retinue about him, I would comfort the mourner's tears — Knox

CHAPTER 30

1. **But now they that are younger than I have me in derision, whose fathers I would have disdained to have set with the dogs of my flock.**
And now I am a laughing-stock
of my juniors, the young people,
whose fathers I did not consider fit to put with the dogs that looked after my flock — Jerus
And now? Now I am a laughing-stock, even to younger men, a flock of such base breed as theirs sheep-dog of mine never tended! — Knox

2. **Yea, whereto might the strength of their hands profit me, in whom old age was perished?**
The strength of their hands would have been useless to me,
enfeebled as they were — Jerus
So profitless their puny strength, I would have let them die before ever they came to maturity — Knox
The strength of their hands, too — of what use is it to me?
Among them manly vigor has perished — AAT
What could I gain from the strength of their hands,
men whose vigor is gone — RSV

3. **For want and famine they were solitary; fleeing into the wilderness in former time desolate and waste.**
They are gaunt with want and famine;
They gnaw the dry ground, in the gloom of wasteness and desolation — ASV
Through want and hard hunger
they gnaw the dry and desolate ground — RSV

4. **Who cut up mallows by the bushes, and juniper roots for their meat.**
Who pluck the salt-plant by the bushes,
And broom-roots are their food — ABPS
Plucking off the heliums from amongst the bushes,
With the root of the genista for their food — Sprl
they pick mallow and the leaves of bushes,
and to warm themselves the roots of the broom — RSV
They plucked saltwort and shrubs;
the roots of the broom plant were their food — NAB

5. **They were driven forth from among men, (they cried after them as after a thief;)**
Outlawed from the society of men,
who, as against thieves, raised hue and cry against them — Jerus

6. **To dwell in the cliffs of the valleys, in caves of the earth, and in the rocks.**
To dwell in gloomy gorges,
In holes of the earth and rocks — ABPS
In the gullies of the torrents they must dwell,
in holes of the earth and of the rocks — RSV

7. **Among the bushes they brayed; under the nettles they were gathered together.**
You could hear them wailing from the bushes,
as they huddled together in the thistles — Jerus
They sound like animals among the bushes, huddling together for shelter beneath the nettles — Tay
They bray among the bushes;
Stretch themselves beneath the brambles — ABPS

8. **They were children of fools, yea, children of base men: they were viler than the earth.**
Their children are as worthless a brood as they are,
nameless people, outcasts of society — Jerus

A senseless and nameless breed, earth is well rid of them — Knox
Irresponsible, nameless men,
they were driven out of the land — NAB
Sons of the foolish, yea, sons of infamy!
They are beaten out of the land — ABPS
A race of fools and despicable wretches, whose name and honour are extinguished from the earth — Sept

9. **And now am I their song, yea, I am their byword.**
. . . a word of shame to them — Bas
And these are the ones that now sing ballads about me,
and make me the talk of the town! — Jerus
And now I have become the subject of their ribald song! I am a joke among them! — Tay

10. **They abhor me, they flee far from me,**
I am disgusting to them, they keep away from me — Bas
They despise me and won't come near me — Tay
and spare not to spit in my face.
do not scruple to . . . — Jerus
and don't mind spitting in my face — Tay

11. **Because he hath loosed my cord, and afflicted me,**
For he hath loosed his cord, and afflicted me — ASV
. . . made loose the cord of my bow . . . — Bas
. . . unbent my bow . . . — Jerus
For, He having loosed my bowstring and having humbled me — Ber
they have also let loose the bridle before me.
And they have cast off the bridle before me — ASV
they have cast off all restraint before me — Ber
They have cast off restraint in my presence — AAT

12. **Upon my right hand rise the youth;**
. . . rise the rabble — ASV
On the right they rise up in swarms — AAT
they push away my feet,
they have tripped me up — Lam
they drive me forth — RSV
and they raise up against me the ways of their destruction.
and they take threatening strides towards me — Jerus
They strew hindrances before me in the highways in their insolence — Sprl

13. **They mar my path,**
They break up my path — ABPS
They tear up my pathway — Sprl
They block my road — Tay
they set forward my calamity,
. . . promote . . . — RSV
they rejoice for what has befallen me — Lam
They help on my ruin — AAT
and do everything they can to hasten my calamity — Tay
they have no helper.
There is no helper against them! — ABPS
and no one restrains them — RSV
knowing full well that I have no one to help me — Tay

14. **They came upon me as a wide breaking in of waters:**
As through a wide breach they come — ASV
As through a wide broken place in the wall they come on — Bas
They move in, as though through a wide breach — Jerus
As a mighty breaker advance they — Sprl
They come at me from all directions — Tay
in the desolation they rolled themselves upon me.
I am overturned by the shock of their attack — Bas
in the midst of the ruin they roll themselves upon me — RV
and I am crushed beneath the rubble — Jerus
They rush upon me when I am down — Tay

15. **Terrors are turned upon me:**
Terrors turn to meet me — Jerus
Terror upon terror overwhelms me — NEB
I live in terror now — Tay
they pursue my soul as the wind:
They chase away, like the wind, my princely state — ABPS
They chase mine honor as the wind — ASV

it sweeps away my resolution like the wind — NEB
and my welfare passeth away as a cloud.
And my prosperity has passed like the cloud — ABPS
and my prosperity has vanished as a cloud before a strong wind — Tay
and my hope of victory vanishes like a cloud — NEB

16. And now my soul is poured out upon me;
And now my soul is weary — Lam
And now the life in me trickles away — Jerus
my heart is dead within me — Knox
My heart is broken — Tay
So now my soul is in turmoil within me — NEB
the days of affliction have taken hold upon me.
days of grief have gripped me — Jerus
a prey to long despairs — Knox
and misery has me daily in its grip — NEB
The days of my trouble lay hold of me — AAT
Depression haunts my days — Tay

17. My bones are pierced in me in the night season:
At night-time sickness saps my bones — Jerus
By night pain pierces my very bones — NEB
My weary nights are filled with pain as though something were relentlessly gnawing at my bones — Tay
and my sinews take no rest.
And the pains that gnaw me take no rest — ASV
and there is ceaseless throbbing in my veins — NEB
I am gnawed by wounds that never sleep — Jerus
sleepless the cares which consume me — Knox

18. By the great force of my disease is my garment changed: it bindeth me about as the collar of my coat.
With great force he takes a grip of my clothing, pulling me by the neck of my coat — Bas
With immense power it has caught me by the clothes,
clutching at the collar of my coat — Jerus
their poison seems to eat away the very garments I wear, clings fast about me like the collar of my coat — Knox
All night long I toss and turn, and my garments bind about me — Tay
my garments are all bespattered with my phlegm,
which chokes me like the collar of a shirt — NEB

19. He hath cast me into the mire,
It has thrown me into the mud — Jerus
No better I than mud in the streets — Knox
and I am become like dust and ashes.
where I am no better than dust and ashes — Jerus
little thought of as dust or ashes — Knox

20. I cry unto thee, and thou dost not hear me:
I cry to thee, and thou answerest me not — ABPS
unheard I cry to thee — Knox
I stand up, and thou regardest me not.
I stand before you, but you take no notice — Jerus
unregarded I stand in thy presence — Knox

21. Thou art become cruel to me:
You have grown cruel in your dealings with me — Jerus
with thy strong hand thou opposest thyself against me.
With thy strong hand thou liest in wait for me — ABPS
your hand lies on me, heavy and hostile — Jerus

22. Thou liftest me up to the wind;
You carry me up to ride the wind — Jerus
Didst thou exalt me — Knox
You throw me into the whirlwind — Tay
thou causest me to ride upon it,
and let me be borne away — ABPS
lift me so high in air — Knox
and dissolvest my substance.
And thou dissolvest me in the storm — ASV
only to hurl me down in ruin? — Knox
and dissolve me in the storm — Tay

23. For I know that thou wilt bring me to death, and to the house appointed for all living.
I know it is to death that you are taking me,

the common meeting place of all that lives — Jerus

For I know that thou wilt turn me over to Death,
And to the house of assembly for all living — AAT

24. Howbeit he will not stretch out his hand to the grave, though they cry in his destruction.

Howbeit doth not one stretch out the hand in his fall?
Or in his calamity therefore cry for help? — ASV

Yet does not one in a heap of ruins stretch out his hand,
and in his disaster cry for help? —

I expected my fall to be broken, just as one who falls stretches out his hand or cries for help in his calamity — Tay

but surely thou dost not exert thy power only to destroy, surely thou hast mercy on the fallen? — Knox

Yet should not a hand be held out to help a wretched man in his calamity? — NAB

25. Did not I weep for him that was in trouble? was not my soul grieved for the poor?

Verily, I have wept for him whose lot is hard,
And my soul has sorrowed for the needy. — ABPS

I myself know what it is to pity the afflicted, to shed tears over human need! — Knox

26. When I looked for good, then evil came unto me:

I hoped for happiness, but sorrow came — Jerus

But no, hope I for better things, I hope in vain — Knox

I therefore looked for good to come. Evil came instead — Tay

and when I waited for light, there came darkness.

even deeper the darkness shews to eyes straining for the light — Knox

I looked for light, but there was darkness — Jerus

27. My bowels boiled, and rested not:

My bowels are in ferment and know no peace — NEB

My stomach seethes, is never still — Jerus

My heart is troubled and resteth not — ASV

My feelings are strongly moved and give me no rest — Bas

the days of affliction prevented me.

The days of trouble have overtaken me — ABPS

for every day brings further suffering — Jerus

28. I went mourning without the sun:

I go blackened, but not with sunheat — ABPS

I go about in dark clothing, uncomforted — Bas

I go about dejected and friendless — NEB

I stood up, and I cried in the congregation.

I stand up in the assembly and cry for help — ASV

and if I rise in the council, I rise to weep — Jerus

29. I am a brother to dragons, and a companion to owls.

I am become a brother to Jackals,
And a companion to the Ostrich-brood — ABPS

as if I had jackals for my brothers, ostriches for my company — Knox

A brother became I to the brutes that howl,
And a companion to the birds that screech — Rhm

The wolf is now my brother,
the owls of the desert have become my companions — NEB

30. My skin is black upon me,

My skin blackens and falls from me — ABPS

And all the while, fever to discolour this flesh — Knox

and my bones are burned with heat.

. . . with fever — Jerus

to shrivel this frame! — Knox

31. My harp also is turned to mourning,

My harp is tuned to funeral wails — Jerus

Thus is attuned to mourning — my lyre — Rhm

and my organ into the voice of them that weep.

And my pipe to sounds of the weeping ABPS

And my flute to the noise of them that weep — Rhm

CHAPTER 31

1. I made a covenant with mine eyes;
I made a pact with my eyes — Jerus
I made a vow with my eyes — Lam
I have come to terms with my eyes — NEB
I imposed a rule on my eyes — AAT
And this was a man who bound his eyes over by covenant — Knox
why then should I think upon a maid?
How then could I gaze upon a virgin — Rhm
never should even his fancy dwell upon the thought of a maid. — Knox
that I would never lust after a virgin. — Lam
never to take notice of a girl. — NEB

2. For what portion of God is there from above? and what inheritance of the Almighty from on high?

3. Is not destruction to the wicked? and a strange punishment to the workers of iniquity?
For what portion should I have from God above [if I were lewd], and what heritage from the Almighty on high?
Does not calamity [justly] befall the unrighteous, and disaster the workers of iniquity — Amp
For what could I expect from God as recompense; or what heritage from the Almighty on high? Should not calamity befall the wrongdoer and disaster the workers of iniquity — Ber
What would the Almighty send on me for that? What but the suffering that falls to sinners, the ruin that rewards the vicious — Mof
Now, what shares does God deal out on high, what lots does Shaddai assign from heaven, if not disaster for the wicked,
and calamities for the iniquitous — Jerus

4. Doth not he see my ways,
Does not He observe my path — Ber
But surely he sees how I behave — Jerus
He sees everything I do — Tay
and count all my steps?
does he not count all my steps — Jerus
trace my footsteps one by one — Knox
and every step I take. — Tay

5. If I have walked with vanity, or if my foot hath hasted to deceit;
Have I been a fellow traveller with falsehood
or hastened my steps towards deceit? — Jerus

6. Let me be weighed in an even balance, that God may know mine integrity.
He will weigh me in scales of justice, Yea, God will know my innocence — ABPS
If he weighs me on honest scales, being God, he cannot fail to see my innocence — Jerus
he can weigh my offence with true scales; let God himself bear witness to my innocence! — Knox

7. If my step hath turned out of the way,
If my feet have wandered from the rightful path — Jerus
Or if I have stepped off God's pathway — Tay
and mine heart walked after mine eyes,
or my thoughts have followed my eyes — Ber
or if my eyes have led my heart astray — Jerus
or if my heart has lusted for what my eyes have seen — Tay
and if any blot hath cleaved to mine hands;
and if any spot has stained my hands with guilt — Amp
or if with my hand I have touched bribes — Sept

8. Then let me sow, and let another eat;
Then let another man enjoy the harvest I have sowed — Knox
yea, let my offspring be rooted out.
Yea, let the produce of my field be rooted out — ASV
and let my young shoots all be rooted out — Jerus
then let my race be doomed to extinction — Knox

9. If mine heart have been deceived by a woman,
If my heart has been enticed towards a woman — ABPS
If I ever lost my heart to any woman — Jerus
or if I have laid wait at my neighbour's door;

... under my neighbour's window — Knox
Or if I have longed for another man's wife — Tay

10. Then let my wife grind unto another,
may my own wife be a slave to strangers — Mof
Then may I die, and may my wife be in another man's home — Tay
and let others bow down upon her.
And let others lie with her — ABPS
and someone else become her husband — Tay

11. For this is an heinous crime;
That were sin in me — Knox
Adultery would be an infamous offense — Mof
For that would be a premeditated crime — Sprl
For lust is a shameful sin — Tay
yea, it is an iniquity to be punished by the judges.
and foul wrong done — Knox
a crime that calls for punishment — Mof
a crime that should be punished — Tay

12. For it is a fire that consumeth to destruction,
it is a fire that burns life to a cinder — Mof
that fire, once lighted, will rage till all is consumed — Knox
For passion is a fire that consumes to destruction — Lam
and would root out all mine increase.
never a crop shall escape it — Knox
it would burn up whatever I possess — Mof
and it would burn to the root all mine increase — RSV

13. If I did despise the cause of my manservant or of my maidservant,
Did I refuse justice to ... — Knox
If I have rejected the cause ... — RSV
If I have ever rejected the plea of my slave
or of my slave girl — NEB
when they contended with me;
when they went to law with me — Bas
when they had a claim against me — Ber
when they brought a complaint against me — RSV

14. What then shall I do when God riseth up?
What then shall I do when God rises up [to judge] — Amp
what shall I do if God appears — NEB
How could I face God — Tay
and when he visiteth, what shall I answer him?
And when He remembereth ... — JPS
When he makes inquiry ... — RSV
What shall I say, when he holds his assize — Jerus
What could I say when he questioned me about it — Tay

15. Did not he that made me in the womb make him? and did not one fashion us in the womb?
They, no less than I, were created in the womb
by the one same God who shaped us all within our mothers — Jerus
Did not my Maker make my servant too,
and form us both alike within the womb — Mof
For God made me, and made my servant too. He created us both — Tay

16. If I have withheld the poor from their desire,
... withheld aught that the poor desired — JPS
... denied the poor what he petitioned — Ber
Have I been insensible to poor men's needs — Jerus
Did I deny some poor man the alms he craved — Knox
I never grudged a poor man anything — Mof
or have caused the eyes of the widow to fail;
... to weep — Sprl
... to look in vain (for relief) — Amp
or let a widow's eyes grow dim? — Jerus
keep the widow waiting for her pittance — Knox
I never let a widow pine in want — Mof

17. Or have eaten my morsel myself alone,
If I kept my food for myself — Bas
sit over my meal alone — Knox
I never ate my bite of food alone — Mof
and the fatherless hath not eaten thereof;

not giving a share to the orphan? — Jerus
and never an orphan-boy to share it? — Knox

18. (For from my youth he was brought up with me, as with a father, and I have guided her from my mother's womb;)
I, whom God has fostered father-like, from childhood,
and guided since I left my mother's womb — Jerus
For, like a father, God has brought me up,
caring for me since ever I was born — Mof
(Rather from my youth have I nurtured him like a father)
And guided her from my mother's womb — Sprl
(But we have always cared for orphans in our home, treating them as our own children) — Tay

19. If I have seen any perish for want of clothing, or any poor without covering;

20. If his loins have not blessed me, and if he were not warmed with the fleece of my sheep;
Have I ever seen a wretch in need of clothing,
or a beggar going naked,
without his having cause to bless me from his heart,
as he felt the warmth of the fleece from my lambs? — Jerus

21. If I have lifted up my hand against the fatherless, when I saw my help in the gate:
Have I raised my hand against the guiltless,
presuming on my credit at the gate — Jerus
If I shook my fist at the orphan,
Because I saw my help in the gate — AAT
If my hand has been lifted up against him who had done no wrong, when I saw that I was supported by the judges — Bas
Or if I have taken advantage of an orphan because I thought I could get away with it — Tay
if I have raised my hand against the innocent,
knowing that men would side with me in court — NEB

22. Then let mine arm fall from my shoulder blade, and mine arm be broken from the bone.
May my arm be pulled from my body, and be broken from its base — Bas
Then may my shoulder drop from its socket,
my arm snap from the collar-bone! — Mof

23. For destruction from God was a terror to me,
For to me, destruction from God is a terror — ABPS
For the fear of God kept me back — Bas
No, I feared suffering at the hands of God — Mof
For the fear of the Lord restrained me — Sept
and by reason of his highness I could not endure.
And before his majesty I am powerless — ABPS
how could I hold my ground before his majesty? — Jerus
I could not do it, in my dread of him — Mof
and the burden of that I could not endure — Sept

24. If I have made gold my hope, or have said to the fine gold, Thou art my confidence;
Have I put all my trust in gold,
from finest gold sought my security? — Jerus
If I have put my trust in money — Tay

25. If I rejoiced because my wealth was great, and because mine hand had gotten much;
Have I ever gloated over my great wealth,
or the riches that my hands have won? — Jerus
doted I upon my great riches, upon all my toil had earned? — Knox
If my happiness depends on wealth — Tay

26. If I beheld the sun when it shined, or the moon walking in brightness;

27. And my heart hath been secretly enticed, or my mouth hath kissed my hand:
Or has the sight of the sun in its glory,

or the glow of the moon as it walked the sky,
stolen my heart, so that my hand blew them a secret kiss? —Jerus
Or if I have looked at the sun shining in the skies, or the moon walking down her silver pathway,
And my heart has been secretly enticed, and I have worshipped them by kissing my hand to them — Tay
if I looked on the shining sun
or on the moon that moved in splendour,
and let my heart go out to them, wafting a kiss to them — Mof

28. **This also were an iniquity to be punished by the judge: for I should have denied the God that is above.**
This too were a crime to be judged;
For I should have been false to God on high — ABPS
This, too, must be punished by the judges. For if I had done such things, it would mean that I denied the God of heaven — Tay
This too would be a crime for condemnation,
for I should have denied God above — NAB

29. **If I rejoiced at the destruction of him that hated me,**
If I have felt happy at the calamity of him who hated me — Ber
Did I triumph over a fallen foe — Knox
or lifted up myself when evil found him:
or exulted when misfortune hit him — Ber
And triumphed when evil befell him — ABPS
rejoice at his ruin — Knox
and my heart hath said, Aha! — Sept

30. **Neither have I suffered my mouth to sin by wishing a curse to his soul.**
I who allowed my tongue to do no wrong,
by cursing them or vowing them to death? — Jerus
(Rather, never have I permitted my mouth to transgress by desiring a curse upon his soul); — Sprl
(But actually I have never cursed anyone nor asked for revenge) — Tay
(Yea, I suffered not my mouth to sin,
To ask, with cursing for his life); — ABPS

31. **If the men of my tabernacle said not, Oh, that we had of his flesh! we cannot be satisfied.**
The people of my tent, did they not say,
'Is there a man he has not filled with meat?' — Jerus
My friends said, Oh this man would give us even of his own flesh! but we are not satisfied — Lam
If the men of my tent have not said,
Where is one, that with his meat has not been filled! — ABPS
Have the men of my household never said,
'Let none of us speak ill of him! — NEB

32. **The stranger did not lodge in the street:**
No stranger ever had to sleep outside — Jerus
(Actually I have never turned away even a stranger — Tay
but I opened my doors to the traveller.
My doors I opened to the roadside —JPS
but have opened my doors to all) — Tay

33. **If I covered my transgressions as Adam, by hiding mine iniquity in my bosom:**
If I have covered up my sins like some men, or if I have hid my guilt in secret places — Lam
if I have concealed my transgressions from men, by hiding my iniquity in my bosom — RSV
Have I ever concealed my misdeeds as men do, keeping my guilt to myself — NEB
Had I, out of human weakness, hidden my sins and buried my guilt in my bosom — NAB

34. **Did I fear a great multitude, or did the contempt of families terrify me, that I kept silence, and went not out of the door?**
Then let me dread the great assembly,
And let the contempt of the tribes confound me,
And let me hold my peace, and not go forth at the door. — ABPS
Have I ever stood so in fear of common gossip,
or so dreaded my family's contempt,

that I have been reduced to silence, not venturing out of doors — Jerus

Was I daunted by fear of the throng, of my neighbours' contemptuous looks? Did I hold my tongue and keep within doors — Jerus

if ever I kept quiet within doors, afraid of what the crowd would say, dreading public opinion — Mof

Because I feared the noisy multitude and the scorn of the tribes terrified me —
then I should have remained silent, and not come out of doors! — NAB

35. Oh that one would hear me! behold, my desire is, that the Almighty would answer me, and that mine adversary had written a book.

Oh that I had one to hear me!
(Lo; here is my signature, let the Almighty answer me)
And that I had the indictment which mine adversary hath written! — ASV

Oh, for a hearing! O, for an answer from the Almighty, and that my adversary would write out His indictment [and put his vague accusations in a tangible form] in a book! — Amp

Oh, that there were someone who would listen to me and try to see my side of this argument. Look, I will sign my signature to my defense; now let the Almighty show me that I am wrong; let him approve the indictments made against me by my enemies — Tay

If only God would give ear to me, and the Ruler of all would give me an answer! or if what he has against me had been put in writing! — Bas

Who can get me a hearing from God?
I have had my say from A to Z;
Now let Shaddai answer me.
When my adversary has drafted his writ against me — Jerus

36. Surely I would take it upon my shoulder, and bind it as a crown to me.

I shall wear it on my shoulder,
and bind it round my head like a royal turban — Jerus

Surely I would [proudly] bear it on my shoulder, and wind the scroll about my head as a diadem — Amp

I would treasure it like a crown — Tay

37. I would declare unto him the number of my steps; as a prince would I go near unto him.

I will give him an account of every step in my life,
and go as boldly as a prince to meet him — Jerus

Then I would tell him exactly what I have done and why, presenting my defence as one he listens to — Tay

38. If my land cry against me, or that the furrows likewise thereof complain;

If my land calls down vengeance on my head and every furrow runs with tears — Jerus

Can these lands of mine bear testimony against me, Can their furrows tell a sad tale — Knox

If my land cries out against me,
And all its furrows weep — ABPS

39. If I have eaten the fruits thereof without money, or have caused the owners thereof to lose their life:

If without payment I have eaten fruit grown on it
or given those who toiled there cause to groan — Jerus

of harvests enjoyed, and no price paid for them, of labourers cruelly treated? — Knox

40. Let thistles grow instead of wheat, and cockle instead of barley.

Let thorns come forth, in place of wheat,
And weeds, in place of barley — ABPS

let nettles . . . and bramble bushes . . . — Sept

The words of Job are ended.

Job's speeches are finished — NEB

CHAPTER 32

1. So these three men ceased to answer Job, because he was righteous in his own eyes.

. . . because he seemed to himself to be right — Bas

. . . because he was convinced of his innocence — Jerus

. . . because he kept insisting on his innocence — Tay

2. Then was kindled the wrath of Elihu

the son of Barachel the Buzite, of the kindred of Ram: against Job was his wrath kindled:

And Elihu . . . was angry, burning with wrath against Job — Bas

But another man was infuriated — Elihu son of Barachel the Buzite, of the clan of Ram. He fumed with rage against Job — Jerus

because he justified himself rather than God.

because he accounted himself more just than God — ABPS

for thinking that he was right and God was wrong — Jerus

because Job refused to admit that he had sinned and to acknowledge that God had just cause for punishing him — Tay

3. **Also against his three friends was his wrath kindled, because they had found no answer, and yet had condemned Job.**

. . . and yet they had pronounced Job wrong — Ber

. . . and had not made Job's sin clear — Bas

4. **Now Elihu had waited till Job had spoken, because they were elder than he.**

Now Elihu had waited to speak to Job because they were older than he — RSV

5. **When Elihu saw that there was no answer in the mouth of these three men, then his wrath was kindled.**

. . . that the three men had not another word to say in answer, his anger burst out — Jerus

. . . his anger flared up — Ber

. . . he could contain himself no longer — Knox

6. **And Elihu the son of Barachel the Buzite answered and said, I am young and ye are very old; wherefore I was afraid, and durst not shew you mine opinion.**

. . . therefore I hesitated and dared not shew you my views — Ber

. . . so I was shy, afraid,
to tell you what I know — Jerus

. . . so I held back and did not dare to tell you what I think — Tay

7. **I said, Days should speak, and multitude of years should teach wisdom.**

. . . 'Let age speak, and added years announce wisdom' — Ber

I felt the word lay with a long life, and years entitled men to instruct wisely — Mof

For those who are older are said to be wiser — Tay

8. **But there is a spirit in man: and the inspiration of the Almighty giveth them understanding.**

But there is [a vital force] a spirit [of intelligence] in man, and the breath of the Almighty gives men understanding — Amp

But I see now that man speaks by inspiration; only the breath of the most High can grant discernment — Knox

But now I know that it is a breath in man,
the spirit of Shaddai, that gives discernment — Jerus

Yet God inspires a man,
'tis the Almighty that breathes knowledge into him — Mof

However, it is a spirit in man,
And the breath of the Almighty, that makes him intelligent — AAT

But the spirit of God himself is in man,
and the breath of the Almighty gives him understanding — NEB

9. **Great men are not always wise: neither do the aged understand judgment.**

long life does not make men wise, it is not always the aged that give true award — Knox

They need not be great, that they may be wise;
Neither old, to understand judgment — Sprl

It is not the aged who are wise, nor the elders who understand what is justice — Ber

10. **Therefore I said, Hearken to me; I also will shew my opinion.**

So I ask you for a hearing . . . — Jerus

So listen to me awhile . . . — Tay

11. **Behold, I waited for your words;**

You see, I waited . . . — Amp

I gave ear to your reasons,

with ears opened for your reasoned remarks — Ber

I listened to your arguments — Mof

whilst ye searched out what to say.
while you searched about for reasons — Knox

12. Yea, I attended unto you,
I gave you my undivided attention — Ber
Yea, I pondered your testimonies — Sprl
and, behold, there was none of you that convinced Job, or that answered his words:
And lo, Job has none that confutes him,
None of you that answers his words — ABPS
But lo! there was, for Job, nothing to convince,
Nor could one of you answer his speeches — Rhm

13. Lest ye should say, We have found out wisdom: God thrusteth him down, not man.
So do not dare to say that you have found wisdom,
or that your teaching is from God not man — Jerus
Do not flatter yourselves that you have tracked down the truth; God must put him down, not man — Knox
Say not, 'We have found him too clever for us;
It must be God, not man, who puts him down!' — Mof
Lest you say, 'We have met with wisdom;
God may rout him, not man' — AAT
And don't give me that line about 'only God can convince the sinner of his sins' — Tay
Do not say, 'We have found wisdom; God only, and not men, can put him down' — Ber

14. Now he hath not directed his words against me: neither will I answer him with your speeches.
He has not met me yet;
and I will not meet him with your replies — Mof
I am not going to follow the same line of argument;
my reply to Job will be couched in different terms — Jerus
If Job had been arguing with me, I would not answer with that kind of logic! — Tay
I will not string words together like you
or answer him as you have done — NEB

15. They were amazed, they answered no more, they left off speaking.
Dismayed they stand, having no further answer. Their verbosity has gone; they are silent — Ber
What, all abashed, these wise men, no answer ready, the words driven from their lips? — Knox
You sit there baffled, with no further replies — Tay

16. When I had waited, (for they spoke not, but stood still, and answered no more;)
And am I to go on waiting while they have nothing to say? — Bas
I have been waiting. Since they are silent,
and have abandoned all efforts to reply, — Jerus
I have had enough of waiting for them to speak, and seeing them stand dumb — Knox
But am I to wait because they will not speak,
because they stand in silence? — Mof

17. I said, I will answer also my part, I will also shew mine opinion.
now I will have my say,
my turn has come to say what I know — Jerus
I will take my turn at pleading, tell out my thoughts — Knox
I, too, have a furrow to plough;
I will express my opinion — NEB

18. For I am full of matter, the spirit within me constraineth me.
For I am filled with words,
choked by the rush of them within me — Jerus
For I am full of words, I am unable to keep in my breath any longer — Bas
For I am full of things to say,
and my mind urges me to speech — Mof
for I am bursting with words,
a bellyful of wind gripes me — NEB

19. Behold, my belly is as wine which hath no vent; it is ready to burst like new bottles.

I have a feeling in my heart like new wine seeking a vent,
and bursting a brand-new wineskin — Jerus
My mind is like wine bottled up,
ready to burst out, like new bottles — Mof
Lo! my bosom is like wine not opened,
Like new wine-skins it will burst — Rhm
I am like a vessel full of new wine, in fermentation, without vent; or like the labouring bellows of a smith — Sept
My stomach is distended as if with wine,
bulging like a blacksmith's bellows — NEB

20. I will speak, that I may be refreshed:
I will speak, and be relieved — ABPS
Nothing will bring relief but speech — Jerus
I will speak, that I may freely breathe — Rhm
I will open my lips and answer.
unburden my lips of their answer — Knox

21. Let me not, I pray you, accept any man's person,
Let me not regard the person of man — ABPS
I shall not show any partiality towards anyone — Jerus
neither let me give flattering titles unto man.
nor heap on any fulsome flatteries — Jerus

22. For I know not to give flattering titles;
For I know not how to flatter — ABPS
Indeed, I can not flatter — Ber
I have not skill in flattery — Jerus
Let me be frank — Tay
in so doing my maker would soon take me away.
lest my Maker should put an end to me — Ber
my creator would soon silence me otherwise — Jerus
lest God should strike me dead — Tay

CHAPTER 33

1. Wherefore, Job, I pray thee, hear my speeches, and hearken to all my words
Now, Job, be kind enough to listen to my words,
and attend to all I have to say — Jerus
Listen, then, Job, to my remonstrances . . . — Knox

2. Behold, now I have opened my mouth, my tongue hath spoken in my mouth.
Now as I open my mouth,
and my tongue shapes words against my palate — Jerus
flows my speech free, tongue and throat are loosed — Knox
Look, I am ready to answer;
the words are on the tip of my tongue — NEB

3. My words shall be of the uprightness of my heart:
My words declare the uprightness of my heart — RSV
my heart shall utter sayings full of wisdom — Jerus
here be plain words — Knox
Mine utterances come straight from mine own heart — Rhm
My words shall proceed from a pure heart — Sept
I will state directly what is in my mind — NAB
and my lips shall utter knowledge clearly.
And that which my lips know they shall speak sincerely — ASV
and my lips speak the honest truth — Jerus
uttered in all honesty — Knox

4. The Spirit of God hath made me, and the breath of the Almighty hath given me life.
A creature I; God's spirit made me, the breath of omnipotence woke me to life — Knox

5. If thou canst answer me, set thy words in order before me, stand up.
If thou are able, answer me;
Array thyself against me, take thy stand — ABPS
If you can, answer me;
Draw up before me; take your position — AAT
Answer me if you can,
marshal your arguments and confront me — NEB

6. Behold, I am according to thy wish in

God's stead: I also am formed out of clay.
See, I am the same as you are in the eyes of God; I was cut off from the same bit of wet earth — Bas
See, I am your fellow man, not a god; like you, I was fashioned out of clay — Jerus
Behold, I am just like you with God; From clay I too was nipped off — AAT

7. Behold, my terror shall not make thee afraid, neither shall my hand be heavy upon thee.
here are no terrors to daunt thee, no threats to overbear thee — Knox
No fear of me need scare you; I will not be hard on you — Mof
Fear of me need not abash you, nor any pressure from me overawe you — NEB

8. Surely thou hast spoken in my hearing, and I have heard the voice of thy words, saying,
How could you say in my hearing — for the sound of your words did not escape me — Jerus
You argued, in my hearing, for I heard your claim — Mof

9. I am clean without transgression, I am innocent; neither is there iniquity in me.
Innocent though I be of all wrong, free from the stain of guilt — Knox

10. Behold, he findeth occasions against me,
Lo, he devises quarrels against me — ABPS
Yet he is inventing grievances against me — Jerus
Yet he invents pretexts against me — NAB
God has picked a quarrel with me — Knox
he counteth me for his enemy,
and imagining me his enemy — Jerus

11. He putteth my feet in the stocks,
He puts chains on my feet — Bas
he fastens logs to my feet — Mof
he marketh all my paths.
and watches me wherever I go — Knox
and watches every move I make — Tay

12. Behold, in this thou art not just: I will answer thee, that God is greater than man.
In saying so, I tell you, you are wrong: God does not fit man's measure — Jerus
All right, here is my reply: In this very thing, you have sinned by speaking of God that way, for God is greater than man — Tay

13. Why dost thou strive against him? for he giveth not account of any of his matters.
Why do you put forward your cause against him, saying, He gives no answer to any of my words? — Bas
Why do you rail at him for not replying to you, word for word? — Jerus
Why do you make accusations against him, That 'he answers none of my arguments'? — AAT

14. For God speaketh once, yea twice, yet man perceiveth it not.
For once does God speak, Yea twice — when one heeds it not — ABPS
God speaks first in one way, then in another, but no one notices — Jerus
God has one mode of speech; yes, and if man heeds it not, another — Mof
Indeed, once God has spoken he does not speak a second time to confirm it — NEB

15. In a dream, in a vision of the night, when deep sleep falleth upon men, in slumberings upon the bed;
He speaks by dreams, and visions that come in the night, when slumber comes on mankind, and men are all asleep in bed — Jerus
In a dream for instance, or in a nightly vision: As when a dread horror falleth upon men, during their slumbers on a bed — Sept

16. Then he openeth the ears of men,
Then he makes his secrets clear to men — Bas
Then it is he whispers in the ear of man — Jerus
he speaks words of revelation — Knox
and sealeth their instruction.
and affirms the warnings directed to them — Ber
to teach them the lesson they need — Knox

and humbles them according to their rebelliousness — Lam
and terrifies them with warnings — RSV

17. That he may withdraw man from his purpose, and hide pride from man.
to turn him away from evil-doing, and make an end of his pride — Jerus
This is one means by which he will turn a man away from his designs, purge him of his pride — Knox
to withdraw man from his purpose and to make him give up his pride — Ber
To turn a man from reckless conduct, to check the pride of mortal man — NEB

18. He keepeth back his soul from the pit, and his life from perishing by the sword.
to save his soul from the pit and his life from the pathway to Sheol — Jerus
and so the grave is disappointed, the sword misses its prey — Knox
at the edge of the pit he holds him back alive
and stops him from crossing the river of death — NEB

19. He is chastened also with pain upon his bed, and the multitude of his bones with strong pain:
With suffering, too, he corrects man on his sick-bed,
when his bones keep trembling with palsy — Jerus
Or, God sends sickness and pain, even though no bone is broken — Tay

20. So that his life abhorreth bread,
And his spirit abhors bread — ABPS
his stomach abhors food — Ber
when his whole self is revolted by food — Jerus
So that a man loses all taste and appetite for food — Tay
and his soul dainty meat.
and his appetite spurns dainties — Jerus
and doesn't care for even the daintiest dessert — Tay

21. His flesh is consumed away, that it cannot be seen;
His flesh becomes so wasted that it cannot be seen — Ber
when his flesh rots as you watch it — Jerus
He becomes thin, mere skin and bones — Tay
and his bones that were not seen stick out.
but his bones, not seen before, protrude into view — Ber
and his bare bones begin to show — Jerus
and his bones corrode to unsightliness — JPS

22. Yea, his soul draweth near unto the grave, and his life to the destroyers.
. . . to the angels of death — Bas
his life is on the verge of death,
near the destroying angels — Mof
His soul draws near the Pit,
and his life to those who bring death — RSV

23. If there be a messenger with him,
If now there may be an angel sent to him — Bas
If a man have an angel — Lam
If there had been near him a messenger — Rhm
But if a messenger from heaven is there — Tay
an interpreter, one among a thousand,
one of the thousands which there are, to be between him and God — Bas
a Mediator, chosen out of thousands — Jerus
to whom one would listen once in a thousand times — Lam
who could interpret — Rhm
to intercede for him as a friend — Tay
to shew unto man his uprightness:
and to make clear to man what is right for him — Bas
to remind a man where his duty lies — Jerus
To vouch for a man's uprightness — JPS
the angel would show him the way of uprightness — Lam
To declare to the son of earth His uprightness — Rhm
to show him what is right — Tay

24. Then he is gracious unto him, and saith,
and the word of mercy will be spoken — Knox
And be gracious to him and say — Lam
then God pities him and says — Tay
Deliver him from going down to the pit:

Let be, the grave is not for him — Knox
Set him free. Do not make him die — Tay
I have found a ransom.
I have given the price for his life — Bas
I have received an atonement — Sprl
for I have found a substitute — Tay

25. His flesh shall be fresher than a child's: he shall return to the days of his youth:
his flesh recovers the bloom of its youth,
he lives again as he did when he was young — Jerus
Then his body will become as healthy as a child's, firm and youthful again — Tay

26. He shall pray unto God, and he will be favourable unto him: and he shall see his face with joy: for he will render unto man his righteousness.
So, God's pardon wooed and won, the sick man stands in his presence once more, all thankfulness, restored to favour — Knox
he prays to God and wins his favour, he worships in his presence joyfully; he tells men how God saved him — Mof
He made supplication unto God, who hath accepted him,
And he hath beheld his face with a shout of triumph.
Thus hath he given back to man his righteousness — Rhm
He prays to God, and He accepts him; he beholds God's face and is joyful; the man is restored to his normal living — Ber

27. He looketh upon men, and if any say, I have sinned,
he tells others how God has saved him; he sings with joy and says, 'I have sinned — Ber
He cometh before men and saith: 'I have sinned — JPS
He turns to the bystanders and makes acknowledgement, A sinner I — Knox
and perverted that which was right,
and twisted what was straight — Ber
and it profited me not;
but He requited me not according to my iniquity — Ber
but he has not punished me — Mof
and it was not requited to me — RSV

28. He will deliver his soul from going into the pit, and his life shall see the light.
Now God has reprieved me from death's exile, I am to live still, and see the light — Knox

29. Lo, all these things worketh God oftentimes with man,

30. To bring back his soul from the pit,
All this God does
again and yet again for man,
rescuing his soul from the pit — Jerus
to be enlightened with the light of the living.
and letting the light of life shine bright on him — Jerus
rekindling the lamp of life for him — Knox

31. Mark well, O Job, hearken unto me: hold thy peace, and I will speak.
. . . I have more to say — Jerus

32. If thou hast any thing to say, answer me:
make answer to me, if answer you can — Knox
speak, for I desire to justify thee.
for it is my desire that you may be judged free from sin — Bas
speak out, for I would gladly recognize your innocence — Jerus

33. If not, hearken unto me: hold thy peace, and I shall teach thee wisdom.
. . . listen to me in silence while I unfold the truth — Knox

CHAPTER 34

1. Furthermore Elihu answered and said,

2. Hear my words, O ye wise men; and give ear unto me, ye that have knowledge.
. . . give ear to me, you who have [so much] knowledge — Amp
. . . lend me your ears, you learned men — Jerus
And Elihu spoke on: A word for the wise; listen, you that are the world's sages — Knox

3. For the ear trieth words, as the mouth tasteth meat.

For words are tested by the ear, as food is tasted by the mouth — Bas

The ear is a judge of speeches, just as the palate can tell one food from another — Jerus

for food, the discerning palate, for wisdom, the discerning ear — Knox

We can choose the sounds we want to listen to; we can choose the taste we want in food — Tay

4. Let us choose to us judgment:

Let us examine for ourselves the right — ABPS

Let us choose for us that which is right — ASV

Let us make the decision for ourselves as to what is right — Bas

Let us discover together where justice lies — Jerus

and we should choose to follow what is right — Tay

let us know among ourselves what is good.

let us determine among us what is good — Ber

and settle among us what is best — — Jerus

5. For Job hath said, I am righteous: and God hath taken away my judgment.

. . . and God refuses to grant me justice — Jerus

Here is Job telling us that he is innocent, that God denies him his rights — Knox

For Job has claimed that he is innocent; that God has taken away his right — Ber

6. Should I lie against my right?

Concerning my own right shall I tell a falsehood — Rhm

that, in spite of being right, he seems to be a liar; — Ber

in spite of my right I am counted a liar; — RSV

judges him falsely, — Knox

'Though I am right,' he says, 'God makes me out a liar, — Mof

my wound is incurable without transgression.

My arrow is fatal, without transgression — ABPS

in my wound the arrow rankles, sinless though I am — NAB

my state is desperate, yet I have done no wrong' — NEB

and plies him with punishment undeserved — Knox

that his wound is incurable, though he is without transgression — Ber

he wounds me fatally, though I am faultless' — Mof

7. What man is like Job, who drinketh up scorning like water?

What man is like Job, a man who freely makes sport of God — Bas

. . . who drinks down blasphemy like water — Ber

Are there many men like Job, who drink scurrility like water — Jerus

Are there many such, many that thirst so greedily for the opportunity to cavil? — Knox

Was there ever a man like Job with his thirst for irreverent talk? — NEB

8. Which goeth in company with the workers of iniquity, and walketh with wicked men.

Who is a companion and friend of the workers of iniquity, and walks with wicked men — Lam

who keep company with evil-doers, and march in step with the wicked? — Jerus

What is this but to take part with wrong-doers, range himself among the impious — Knox

He must have spent much time with evil men — Tay

9. For he hath said, It profiteth a man nothing that he should delight himself with God,

. . . that he should be in accord with God — JPS

Did he not say it was useless for man to try to please God? — Jerus

when he complains that there is no pleasing God, however ready a man is to do his will? — Knox

For he says, 'A man gains nothing By being on good terms with God' — AAT

10. Therefore hearken unto me, ye men of understanding:

. . . you men of discernment — Ber

Listen then to me, like intelligent men — Jerus

Now then, you wise, take note — Bas
far be it from God, that he should do wickedness; and from the Almighty, that he should commit iniquity.
Far be it from God that He should work ungodliness, and from the Almighty that He should do wrong — Ber
So far is God removed from wickedness,
and Shaddai from injustice — Jerus
Surely everyone knows that God doesn't sin! — Tay

11. For the work of a man shall he render unto him,
For according to the deeds of a man God will proportion his pay — Amp
For according to the deeds of a man will He requite him — Ber
that he requites a man for what he does — Jerus
he treats men only as they deserve — Knox
He makes man answer for his deeds — Mof
and cause every man to find according to his ways.
and he sees that he gets the fruit of his ways — Bas
and as by his behavior he deserves — Ber
treating each one as his way of life deserves — Jerus
giving due reward to each — Knox
and fare exactly as he may deserve — Mof

12. Yea, surely God will not do wickedly,
God never does wrong, do not doubt that! — Jerus
But dost thou think that the Lord will do improper things? — Sept
Of a surety then God does not falsify — AAT
There is no truer statement than this: God is never wicked — Tay
neither will the Almighty pervert judgment.
. . . justice — ABPS
and the Ruler of all is not a false judge — Bas
And the Almighty does not distort the right — AAT

13. Who hath given him a charge over the earth?
Who put the earth into his care — Bas
Who gave him government over the earth — NAB
It is not as if someone else had given him the earth in trust — Jerus
he is no viceroy lording it on earth! — Mof
or who hath disposed the whole world?
And who founded the whole habitable world — ABPS
or made him responsible for the world — Bas
or confided the whole universe to his care. — Jerus

14. If he set his heart upon man, if he gather unto himself his spirit and his breath;
If God were to withdraw His spirit and gather to Himself His spirit and His breath — Ber
Were he to recall his breath
to draw his breathing back into himself — Jerus
He has but to turn his thought towards men, reclaiming the spirit he once breathed into them — Knox

15. All flesh shall perish together, and man shall turn again unto dust.
things of flesh would perish all together,
and man would return to dust — Jerus
and all life would fail everywhere; mankind would return to its dust — Knox
the human race would perish in a moment,
man would return to dust — Mof
All flesh together would cease to breathe,
And the earth-born unto dust would return — Rhm

16. If now thou hast understanding, hear this: hearken to the voice of my words.
If you have any intelligence, listen to this,
and lend your ear to what I have to say — Jerus

17. Shall even he that hateth right govern?
Can he indeed bear rule that hates right — ABPS
Could an enemy of justice ever govern — Jerus
Could God govern if he hated justice — Tay
What! shall he who hateth right govern — Sprl

and wilt thou condemn him that is most just?
And wilt thou condemn Him Who is eminently just — Sprl
Or wilt thou condemn the Just, the Mighty — ABPS
Are you going to condemn the Almighty Judge — Tay

18. Is it fit to say to a king, Thou art wicked? and to princes, ye are ungodly?
Shall one say to a king, O Worthless! O wicked! to princes — ABPS
who can tell kings that they are good for nothing,
and treat noblemen like criminals — Jerus
Who says to a king, "You are worthless!"
and to nobles "You are wicked!" — NAB

19. How much less to him that accepteth not the persons of princes, nor regardeth the rich more than the poor? for they all are the work of his hands.
Who has no respect for rulers, and who gives no more attention to those who have wealth than to the poor, for they are all the work of his hands — Bas
who shows no partiality to princes
and makes no distinction between the rich and the poor,
all alike being made by his own hands? — Jerus
Nothing cares he for royal dignity, nor takes the oppressor's part against the friendless; are not all alike his creatures? — Knox

20. In a moment shall they die,
Suddenly they come to an end — Bas
In a moment they die — RV
and the people shall be troubled at midnight, and pass away:
At midnight the people are smitten and pass away — ABPS
even at midnight; the people are shaken and pass away — RV
great though they are, they perish in the dead of night — Jerus
there is a stir among the people at midnight, and they pass by — Knox
and the mighty shall be taken away without hand.
and the strong are taken away without the hand of man — Bas
it costs him no effort to remove a tyrant — Jerus
to see the tyrant carried out, and yet no hand laid on him! — Knox
the mighty disappear mysteriously — Mof
The mighty are removed by an unseen hand — AAT

21. For his eyes are upon the ways of man, and he seeth all his goings.
His eyes, you see, keep watch on all men's ways,
and he observes their every step — Jerus
for God's eye is on human life,
he watches every step that man makes — Mof
For God carefully watches the goings on of all mankind; he sees them all — Tay

22. There is no darkness, nor shadow of death, where the workers of iniquity may hide themselves.
There is no darkness, nor thick gloom,
Where the workers of iniquity may hide themselves — ASV
darkness is none, though it were the shadow of death itself, that can hide the wrong-doer — Knox
there is nowhere so dark, so deep in shadow,
that wrongdoers may hide from him — NEB
There is no dark place and no thick cloud, in which the workers of evil may take cover — Bas

23. For he will not lay upon man more than right; that he should enter into judgment with God.
[God] sets before man no appointed time that he should appear before [Him] in judgment — Amp
For he does not give man a fixed time to come before him to be judged — Bas
He serves no writ on men
summoning them to appear before God's court — Jerus
God has not to fix sessions,
in order to bring men to justice — Mof
For he has not appointed a time for any man
to go before God in judgment — RSV

24. He shall break in pieces mighty men without number,
He breaketh in pieces mighty men in ways past finding out — ASV
He sends the strong to destruction without searching out their cause — Bas
he smashes great men's power without enquiry — Jerus
. . . without investigation — AAT
Without making a federal case of it, God simply shatters the greatest of men — Tay
and set others in their stead.
and puts others in their place — Bas

25. Therefore he knoweth their works, and he overturneth them in the night, so that they are destroyed.
Knowing well their works, He overthrows them in the night and crushes them — Ber
He knows well enough what they are about,
and one fine night he throws them down for men to trample on — Jerus
Weary of their ill deeds, he bids darkness fall, and there is an end of them — Knox

26. He striketh them as wicked men in the open sight of others;
As the wicked does he smite them,
In the place where men look on — ABPS
he puts his hand on them by force before the eyes of all onlookers — Bas
In some place where many triumph at the sight, he beats down the rebels — Knox
He shatters the wicked;
He smites them in the sight of the public — AAT

27. Because they turned back from him, and would not consider any of his ways:
because they turned aside from following Him and showed no regard for any of His ways — Ber
that hitherto of set purpose defied him, recked nothing of his commandments — Knox
because they swerved from following his lead,
reckless of all his rules — Mof

28. So that they cause the cry of the poor to come unto him,
So that the lament of the lowly reached up to Him — Ber
till wails reached him from the oppressed — Mof
and he heareth the cry of the afflicted.
and the wailing of the humble has assailed his ears — Jerus
and cries from the forlorn came to his ears — Mof

29. When he giveth quietness, who then can make trouble? and when he hideth his face, who then can behold him? whether it be done against a nation, or against a man only:
When he giveth quietness, who then can condemn?
And when he hideth his face, who then can behold him?
Alike whether it be done unto a nation, or unto a man — ASV
If He remains quiet, who can condemn Him? If he hides His face, who can catch a glimpse of Him? He watches alike over nations and over individuals — Ber
If he did nothing, who would dare denounce him?
Were he indifferent, who dare blame him?
— though he does watch over men and nations — Mof

30. That the hypocrite reign not, lest the people be ensnared.
That the godless man reign not, that there be none to ensnare the people —RV
that none may reign who would beguile the people — Mof
Again he may prevent a vile man from ruling, thus saving a nation from ruin — Tay

31. Surely it is meet to be said unto God, I have borne chastisement, I will not offend any more.

32. That which I see not teach thou me; if I have done iniquity, I will do no more.
It is well to confess to God, 'I have felt discipline; now I will offend no more'; and to ask God to explain to him what he has done amiss and cannot understand — Ber
For hath any said unto God:
'I have borne chastisement, though I offend not;
That which I see not teach Thou me;

If I have done iniquity, I will do it no more'? — JPS
No, tell God: 'Now that I have suffered,
I will offend me no more;
teach me what I am blind to,
and, if I sinned, I will not sin again' — Mof

33. **Should it be according to thy mind? he will recompense it, whether thou refuse, or whether thou choose; and not I:**
Then He will repay you as you deserve. Will you reject it? You yourself must choose, not I — Ber
in such a case, do you think he ought to punish him,
you who reject his decisions?
Since it is you who make his choice, not I, — Jerus
Leave him to deal with you, as he may please;
are you to choose the terms, not God? — Mof
Will he then make requital to suit you, because you reject it?
For you must choose, and not I — RSV
Must God tailor His justice to your demands? Must he change the order of the universe to suit your whims? — Tay
therefore speak what thou knowest.
Whatever you know, that declare — Ber
let us all share our knowledge! — Jerus
Say what you like — Mof
The answer must be obvious even to you! — Tay

34. **Let men of understanding tell me, and let a wise man hearken unto me.**
Men of understanding will say unto me, yea, every wise man that heareth me: — RV
But this is what all sensible folk will say,
and any wise man among my hearers, — Jerus
but thinking men will say with me,
any wise man who hears me will agree, — Mof

35. **Job hath spoken without knowledge,**
Job does not speak intelligently — Ber
This Job has spoken as fools do — Knox
and his words were without wisdom.
and there is no sense in what he says — NEB

36. **My desire is that Job may be tried unto the end because of his answers for wicked men.**
My desire is, that Job may be tried to the end,
For answers in the manner of evil men — ABPS
May Job be tested to the end, because his answers have been like those of evil men — Bas
Put him unsparingly to the proof
since his retorts are the same as those which the wicked make — Jerus
let Job be tried still, tried to the uttermost; have no patience with a man so perverse — Knox

37. **For he addeth rebellion unto his sin,**
that sets a crown on his sins by blasphemy! — Knox
He is a sinner and a rebel as well — NEB
he clappeth his hands among us,
before our eyes he makes sport of God — Bas
calling justice into question in our midst — Jerus
He clenches his fists at us — AAT
and multiplieth his words against God.
and heaping abuse on God — Jerus

CHAPTER 35

1. **Elihu spake moreover, and said,**
Elihu continued his speech. He said: — Jerus

2. **Thinkest thou this to be right, that thou saidst, My righteousness is more than God's?**
Do you think it is right to claim that you are more righteous than God — Ber
Do not presume to maintain that you are in the right,
to insist on your innocence before God, — Jerus

3. **For thou saidst, What advantage will it be unto Thee? and, What profit shall I have, if I be cleansed from my sin?**
And to ask, 'What profit is there in being good; in what respect have I

gained advantage above sinners?' — Ber
even to ask him, 'How does it affect you,
what harm has it done you if I have sinned?' — Jerus
For thou sayest, What will it profit thee;
What shall I gain more than by my sin — ABPS

4. I will answer thee, and thy companions with thee.
Well then, this is how I will answer you,
and your friends as well — Jerus

5. Look unto the heavens, and see;
Look up at the sky and then consider — NEB
Look up at the skies, look at them well — Jerus
and behold the clouds which are higher than thou.
gaze at the clouds high above you! — Ber
and see how high the clouds are above you — Jerus
and mark how the skies tower above thee — Knox

6. If thou sinnest, what dost thou against him? or if thy transgressions be multiplied, what doest thou unto him?
If you sin, what do you achieve against him?
If you heap up crimes, what is the injury you do him — Jerus
If you sin, what injury do you do to God?
Even if your offenses are many, how do you hurt him? — NAB
If you have sinned, how does that affect Him? and if your transgressions are repeated, what have you done to Him? — Ber

7. If thou be righteous, what givest thou him? or what receiveth he of thine hand?
If you do right, what good do you bring him,
or what does he gain from you? — NEB
be honest as the day, no gift thou makest him, he is none the richer for thy pains. — Knox

8. Thy wickedness may hurt a man as thou art; and thy righteousness may profit the son of man.
But your wickedness affects your own self and your righteousness a human being — Ber
Your fellow men are the ones to suffer from your crimes,
humanity is the gainer if you are good — Jerus
Your wickedness can affect only a man like yourself;
and your justice only a fellow human being — NAB

9. By reason of the multitude of oppressions they make the oppressed to cry:
At often repeated oppressions men cry out — Ber
When people groan under the weight of oppression — Jerus
Cries and groans there are in plenty when oppression abounds — Knox
The oppressed may shriek beneath their wrongs — Tay
they cry out by reason of the arm of the mighty.
they cry for help because of the violence of the mighty — Amp
or cry out under the tyranny of the mighty — Jerus
and groan beneath the power of the rich — Tay

10. But none saith, Where is God my maker, who giveth songs in the night;
no one thinks to ask, 'Where is God, my maker,
who makes glad songs ring out at dead of night — Jerus
yet none of them cry to God, asking 'Where is God my Maker who gives songs in the night — Tay
And none says, Where is God my Maker, who gives counsel in the night — Lam

11. Who teacheth us more than the beasts of the earth, and maketh us wiser than the fowls of heaven?
He makes us more intelligent than the earth's animals and grants us greater wisdom than the birds of the air — Ber

12. There they cry, but none giveth answer, because of the pride of evil men.
These [men] make outcry and he answereth not,
Because of the arrogance of evildoers — Rhm

So, when they cry out, he does not answer,
because they are self-willed and proud — NEB
But when anyone does cry out this question to him, he never replies by instant punishment of the tyrants — Tay

13. **Surely God will not hear vanity, neither will the Almighty regard it.**
Surely God will not hear an empty cry,
Neither will the Almighty regard it — ASV
Because God does not hear the empty pride of evildoers, nor does he praise it — Lam
But God will not hear falsehood,
Nor will the Almighty look upon it — AAT
How idle to maintain that God is deaf, that Shaddai notices nothing! — Jerus
But it is false to say he doesn't hear those cries; and it is even more false to say that he doesn't see what is going on — Tay

14. **Although thou sayest thou shalt not see him, yet judgment is before him; therefore trust thou in him.**
How much less in your case, when you admit you do not see Him, and, though you wait for Him, your cause is not considered — Ber
You even claim, 'He does not see me; my cause is exposed before him, and yet I wait and wait' — Jerus
Nay, when he seems to take no heed, submit thyself to his judgment and wait his hour — Knox
He does bring about justice at last, if you will only wait — Tay

15. **But now, because it is not so, he hath visited in his anger; yet he knoweth it not in great extremity:**
And now, because God has not visited you in His anger and does not attend to your transgression — Ber
But now, because he hath not visited in his anger, neither doth he greatly regard arrogance — RV
Or even, 'His anger never punishes, he does not seem to know of men's rebellion' — Jerus
thy present sufferings do not betoken his anger, he is not taking vengeance to the full — Knox
But now that you have done otherwise, God's anger punishes,
nor does he show concern that a man will die. — NAB

16. **Therefore doth Job open his mouth in vain; he multiplieth words without knowledge.**
And Job's mouth is open wide to give out what is of no profit, increasing words without knowledge — Bas
Job uselessly opens his mouth and indulges in unreasonable verbiage — Ber
See, then, how all Job's utterance misses the mark; glib words with no tincture of knowledge — Knox
Hence when Job opens his mouth, it is for idle talk:
his spate of words comes out of ignorance — Jerus
Job gives vent to windy nonsense
and makes a parade of empty words — NEB

CHAPTER 36

1. **Elihu also proceeded, and said,**
And Elihu continued and said: — RSV

2. **Suffer me a little,**
"Bear with me a little longer — Ber
"Let me go on — Tay
and I will shew thee that I have yet to speak on God's behalf.
and I will make it clear to you; for I have still something to say for God — Bas

3. **I will fetch my knowledge from afar,**
I will fetch my knowledge from the past — Sprl
I will range far afield for my arguments — Jerus
From a deep source I will draw my reasons — Knox
from a wide survey of the truth—Mof
and will ascribe righteousness to my Maker.
to prove my Maker just — Jerus
I will now justify my Creator — Mof

4. **For truly my words shall not be false;**
What I say contains no fallacies, I assure you — Jerus
here is no delusive eloquence — Knox

I am telling you the honest truth — Tay
There are no flaws in my reasoning — NEB
he that is perfect in knowledge is with thee.
one who has all knowledge is talking with you — Bas
you see before you an enlightened man — Jerus
One that is upright in mind is with thee — JPS
the full truth shall be made known to thee — Knox
for I am a man of well-rounded knowledge — Tay
before you stands one whose conclusions are sound — NEB

5. Behold, God is mighty, and despiseth not any:
Behold! God is mighty, and yet despises no one, nor regards anything as trivial — Amp
He, the all-powerful, does not grudge men power — Knox
he is mighty in strength and wisdom.
. . . in power of understanding — Ber
. . . in vigour of mind — Rhm

6. He preserveth not the life of the wicked:
it is only to the wicked he denies his aid — Knox
He will not keep alive one who is lawless — Rhm
but giveth right to the poor.
but He will give the wronged one his right — Ber
the friendless shall have redress — Knox

7. He withdraweth not his eyes from the righteous: but with kings are they on the throne; yea, he doth establish them for ever, and they are exalted.
His eyes are ever on the upright, and he gives to the crushed their right — Bas
Never from the just is his favour withdrawn; a royal throne is theirs for ever, so high he exalts them — Knox
He does not ignore good men but honors them by placing them upon eternal kingly thrones — Tay

8. And if they be bound in fetters, and be holden in cords of affliction;
And if they have been prisoned in chains, and taken in cords of trouble — Bas
If he should leave them in chains, caught in the toils of sore need — Knox
Next you may see them loaded with fetters,
held fast in captives' chains — NEB

9. Then he sheweth them their work, and their transgressions that they have exceeded.
Then he makes clear to them what they have done, even their evil works in which they have taken pride — Bas
it is but to apprise them of their own ill deeds, their own tyrannous deeds — Knox
he lets them see what they have done, so proudly, so rebelliously — Mof
Then sheweth them their work, and their transgressions, that they have behaved themselves proudly — RV
he denounces their conduct to them, showing how insolence and tyranny was their offence — NEB

10. He openeth also their ear to discipline, and commandeth that they return from iniquity.
He openeth also their ear to instruction, and commandeth that they return from iniquity — RV
Their ear is open to his teaching, and he gives them orders so that their hearts may be turned from evil — Bas
He also opens their ears for admonition and bids them to renounce iniquity — Ber
he makes them listen to sense then, bidding them turn from sin — Mof
his warnings sound in their ears
and summon them to turn back from evil courses — NEB
He opens their ear to correction
and exhorts them to turn back from evil — NAB

11. If they obey and serve him, they shall spend their days in prosperity, and their years in pleasures.
If they listen and do as he says,
their days end in happiness,
and their closing years are full of ease — Jerus

12. But if they obey not, they shall perish

by the sword, and they shall die without knowledge.

If not, then a thunderbolt destroys them,
and death comes on them unawares — Jerus

if hear they will not, it is the sword's point for them, to their last gasp fools still — Knox

But if not, then they die a violent death,
perishing in their folly — Mof

If they won't listen to Him, they shall perish in battle and die because of their lack of good sense — Tay

but if they give no heed, then they perish by the sword, to die in ignorance — Ber

But, if they do not listen, they die, their lesson unlearnt — NEB

13. **But the hypocrites in heart heap up wrath:**

But they that are godless in heart lay up anger — ASV

But those who have no fear of God keep wrath stored up in their hearts — Bas

Proud men rage against him — NEB

But those pretending in heart harvest anger — Ber

But the godless reap his anger — Tay

they cry not when he bindeth them.

they give no cry for help when they are made prisoners —Bas

from them no cry comes when the chains close round them — Knox

They do not even return to him when he punishes them — Tay

14. **They die in youth, and their life is among the unclean.**

. . . their life ends in shame — RSV

. . . their lives end in dissipation — Ber

they die young after lives of dissipation and depravity — Tay

so they die in their prime, like male prostitutes, worn out — NEB

15. **He delivereth the poor in his affliction,**

It is the friendless he rescues in their need — Knox

God saves the sufferer by suffering — Mof

Those who suffer he rescues through suffering — NEB

and openeth their ears in oppression.

opening their ears by their trouble — Bas

he uses distress to open their eyes — Jerus

And he openeth their ear by tribulation — JPS

and by adversity gets them to listen — Mof

and teaches them by the discipline of affliction — NEB

16. **Even so would he have removed thee out of the strait into a broad place, where there is no straitness:**

Yea, he would have led thee away out of distress into a broad place — RV

. . . into a broad place where there was no cramping — RSV

Yes, He would still allure you out of distress into a broad place, where there is no restraint — Ber

From the pit's mouth, where the ground seems lost under thy feet, he will bring thee out into full freedom — Knox

and that which should be set on thy table should be full of fatness.

and what was set on your table was full of fatness — RSV

thou shalt take thy ease at a table loaded with dainties — Knox

17. **But thou hast fulfilled the judgment of the wicked: judgment and justice take hold on thee.**

But you fully deserve the judgment that befalls the wicked; judgment and justice have caught up with you — Ber

But thou art full of the judgement of the wicked: judgement and justice take hold on thee — RV

18. **Because there is wrath, beware lest he take thee away with his stroke:**

Because there is wrath, beware lest thou be led away by thy sufficiency — RV

For beware, lest anger stir thee up against chastisement — ABPS

For let not wrath entice you into scorning chastisements — Amp

In future beware of being led astray by riches — Jerus

Let not his chastening make you rage at him — Mof

then a great ransom cannot deliver thee.

or corrupted by fat bribes — Jerus

let not the cost of discipline deter you — Mof
Then let not a great ransom mislead thee — Rhm

19. Will he esteem thy riches? no, not gold, nor all the forces of strength.
Will he value thy riches?
Nay not precious ore,
Nor all the forces of strength — Rhm
Would your wealth have saved you without suffering, or would all your resources have given you back your strength? — Ber
Will thy riches suffice, that thou be not in distress, or all the forces of thy strength? — RV
What will that wealth of yours, however great, avail you,
or all the resources of your high position? — NEB

20. Desire not the night, when people are cut off in their place.
Do not pant for the night,
When peoples disappear from their place — Rhm
Do not desire the nighttime with its opportunities for crime — Tay

21. Take heed, regard not iniquity:
Take heed, turn not to iniquity — ABPS
Take care not to be turned to sin — Bas
Do not yield to the rebellious mood — Knox
Beware, banish all evil thoughts — Mof
for this hast thou chosen rather than affliction.
for this you were tested by suffering — Ber
thou hast cherished since affliction came upon thee — Knox
you prefer sin to suffering! — Mof

22. Behold, God exalteth by his power:
Lo, God shows himself great in his power — ABPS
Behold, God is sublime in his power — NAB
Look, by reason of his power God is supreme — Jerus
Look, God is all-powerful — Tay
God towers in majesty above us — NEB
who teacheth like him?
what teacher can be compared with him — Jerus
who wields such sovereign power as he — NEB

23. Who hath enjoined him his way? or who can say, Thou hast wrought iniquity?
Who ever gave orders to him, or said to him, You have done wrong — Bas
Who has prescribed his course for him?
Who has said to him, 'Thou hast done wrong' — NEB

24. Remember that thou magnify his work, which men behold.
Remember that thou magnify his work,
Whereof men have sung — ASV
See that you give praise to his work, about which men make songs — Bas
Remember to extol his work,
of which men have sung — RSV
Remember then to sing the praises of his work,
as men have always sung them — NEB

25. Every man may see it; man may behold it afar off.
All men look on it, but a mortal sees it only from afar — Ber

26. Behold, God is great, and we know him not,
Truly, God is great, greater than all our knowledge — Bas
Lo, God is great beyond our knowledge — NAB
Truly there is no measuring God's greatness — Knox
Consider; God is so great that we cannot know him — NEB
neither can the number of his years be searched out.
the number of His years is incalculable — Ber
no reckoning his length of days — Knox
No one can begin to understand eternity — Tay

27. For he maketh small the drops of water:
For he draws up the water-drops — ABPS
For he takes up the drops from the sea — Bas

He holds in check the waterdrops — NAB
He draws up the water vapor — Tay
they pour down rain according to the vapour thereof:
Which distil in rain from his vapor — ASV
he sends them through his mist as rain — Bas
They trickle as rain through his mist — Rhm
he distils his mist in rain — RSV
and then distills it into rain — Tay

28. Which the clouds do drop and distil upon man abundantly.
which the clouds pour down, dropping in showers on man — Ber
which the skies pour down,
and drop upon man abundantly — RSV

29. Also can any understand the spreadings of the clouds, or the noise of his tabernacle?
Yea, can one comprehend the bursting of the cloud,
The crash of his pavilion — ABPS
And who has knowledge of how the clouds are stretched out, or of the thunders of his tent — Bas
Can any man read the secret of the sailing clouds,
spread like a carpet under his pavilion — NEB
Lo, he spreads the clouds in layers
as the carpeting of his tent — NAB

30. Behold, he spreadeth his light upon it, and covereth the bottom of the sea.
Lo, around him he spreads his light, and covers over with ocean depths — ABPS
See, he is stretching out his mist, covering the tops of the mountains with it — Bas
Behold, he scatters his lightning about him,
and covers the roots of the sea — RSV
See how he unrolls the mist across the waters,
and its streamers cover the sea — NEB

31. For by them judgeth he the people; he giveth meat in abundance.
Thus he sustains the nations
and gives them food in plenty — NEB
Has he not a whole world to rule, a whole race of mortals to supply with food — Knox

32. With clouds he covereth the light; and commandeth it not to shine by the cloud that cometh betwixt.
He covereth his hands with the lightning,
And giveth it a charge that it strike the mark — ASV
He fills his hands with lightning bolts.
He hurls each at its target — Tay
He charges the thunderbolts with flame
and launches them straight at the mark — NEB

33. The noise thereof sheweth concerning it, the cattle also concerning the vapour.
The noise thereof telleth concerning him, the cattle also concerning the storm that cometh up — RV
His thunder announces His presence; the cattle feel warned of the storm — Ber
His thunder tells of him;
To the herds, even of Him who is on high — ABPS
Its crashing declares concerning him, who is jealous with anger against iniquity — RSV
We feel his presence in the thunder.
May all sinners be warned — Tay

CHAPTER 37

1. At this also my heart trembleth,
At this my own heart quakes — Jerus
. . . man's heart trembles — Lam
on account of this my heart was troubled — Sept
Does it not make you tremble? — Mof
and is moved out of his place.
And starts up from its place — ABPS
and palpitates in its dwelling-place — Sprl
does it not make your heart leap to your mouth? — Mof

2. Hear attentively the noise of his voice, and the sound that goeth out of his mouth.
Listen to the rolling of His voice, the

thunder that comes out of His mouth — Ber

Listen, oh listen, to the blast of his voice
and the sound that blares from his mouth — Jerus

Hear! oh hear! the raging of his voice,
A growling sound also out of his mouth goeth forth — Rhm

3. He directeth it under the whole heaven,

He sendeth it forth under the whole heaven — ASV

He lets it loose under the whole heaven — Ber

He sends the sound pealing across the sky — Mof

and his lightning unto the ends of the earth.

And his light over the margins of the earth — ABPS

it strikes to the very ends of the earth — Jerus

he sends his flash to the fringes of earth — Mof

4. After it a voice roareth: he thundereth with the voice of his excellency; and he will not stay them when his voice is heard.

After it comes the roar of his voice
the peal of God's majestic thunder.
He does not check his thunderbolts
until his voice resounds no more — Jerus

Then what a crash resounds, the magnificent peal of his thunder; a voice heard, and none can tell whence it comes! — Knox

After it his voice roars; he thunders with his majestic voice and he does not restrain the lightnings when his voice is heard — RSV

5. God thundereth marvellously with his voice; great things doeth he, which we cannot comprehend.

No doubt of it, but God reveals wonders,
and does great deeds that we cannot understand — Jerus

God's voice in the thunder, a marvel worthy of him, whose deeds are so great and unsearchable — Knox

His voice is glorious in the thunder.
We cannot comprehend the greatness of his power — Tay

God thundereth with His voice marvellously;
He worketh mightily beyond our ken — Sprl

6. For he saith to the snow, Be thou on the earth;

He it is that bids the snow fall over the earth — Knox

For to the snow he says, 'Fall on the earth' — RSV

likewise to the small rain, and to the great rain of his strength.

And to the pouring rain, even the pouring of his mighty rains — ABPS

likewise He speaks to the showers, and to the downpour of his mighty rain — Amp

likewise to the gentle rain and to the heavy rain — Lam

and to the shower and the rain, 'Be strong' — RSV

7. He sealeth up the hand of every man; that all men may know his work.

he brings all men's strivings to a standstill
so that each must acknowledge his hand at work — Jerus

He limits the power of every man, that all men may know his work — Lam

Man's work stops at such a time, so that all men everywhere may recognize his power — Tay

On the hand of every man he setteth a seal,
That all men may take note of his doing — Rhm

8. Then the beasts go into dens, and remain in their places.

And beasts go into the lair,
And in their dens abide — ABPS

the beasts retire into their dens,
and lurk inside their lairs — Mof

The wild animals hide in the rocks or in the dens — Tay

9. Out of the south cometh the whirlwind:

Out of its place comes the stormwind — Bas

From its chamber comes the whirlwind — RSV

Out of the dark thick clouds issueth the whirlwind — Sprl

The hurricane bursts from its prison — NEB

and cold out of the north.

and the north winds usher in the cold — Jerus

and the rain winds bring bitter cold — NEB

and cold from the scattering winds — RSV
And from condensed air, ice — Sprl

10. By the breath of God frost is given:
By the breath of God there is ice — ABPS
God breathes, and the ice is there — Jerus
At God's breath the frost binds fast — Knox
By the strong wind the frost congealeth — Sprl
and the breadth of the waters is straitened.
and the surface of the waters freezes over — Jerus
and freezes the broad waters hard — Mof
and the broad waters are frozen fast — RSV
and even the widest torrents freeze — Tay

11. Also by watering he wearieth the thick cloud: he scattereth his bright cloud:
Yea, with moisture he loads the thick cloud,
He spreads his lightning-cloud abroad — ABPS
He loads the clouds with moisture and they send forth His lightning — Tay
He weighs the clouds down with moisture,
and the storm clouds radiate his lightning — Jerus
With hail, also, the clouds are laden, as they scatter their flashes of light — NAB

12. And it is turned round about by his counsels:
And it turns with his guidance every way — ABPS
Under His control they circle about — Ber
He himself guides their wheeling motion
directing all their seasonal changes — Jerus
They turn round and round by his guidance — RSV
that they may do whatsoever he commandeth them upon the face of the world in the earth.
That they may do all he commands,
Over the face of the habitable earth — ABPS
. . . on the face of the world of men — Bas
they carry out his orders to the letter all over his inhabited world — Jerus

13. He causeth it to come, whether for correction, or for his land, or for mercy.
Whether as a scourge, for his land,
Or as a kindness he allots it — ABPS
whether sent on the earth for correction or as acts of mercy, He directs it to its goal — Ber

14. Hearken unto this, O Job: stand still, and consider the wondrous works of God.
Hear this, O Job:
stop and consider the wondrous works of God — RSV
Listen to all this Job: no backsliding now!
Meditate on God's wonders — Jerus
Matter enough, Job, for thy heeding! Halt where thou standest, and consider the marvellous acts of God — Knox

15. Dost thou know when God disposed them, and caused the light of his cloud to shine?
Dost thou know, when God sets his thoughts upon them,
And the light of his cloud blazes forth — ABPS
Can you tell how God controls them or how his clouds make the lightning flash — Jerus
Do you know how God controls all nature, and causes the lightning to flash forth from his clouds — Tay

16. Dost thou know the balancings of the clouds, the wondrous works of him which is perfect in knowledge?
Do you know how the clouds are balanced [and poised in the heavens], the wonderful works of Him Who is perfect in knowledge — Amp
Can you tell how he holds the clouds in balance:
a miracle of consummate skill — Jerus
Dost thou understand the balancings of the clouds?
Marvels! the perfections of wisdom! — Sprl

17. How thy garments are warm, when he quieteth the earth by the south wind?

When your clothes are hot to your body
and the earth lies still under the south wind, — Jerus
See if thy garments do not cling warm about thee when the south wind cheers the earth! — Knox
Do you know why your garments get hot when the earth changes its position after the equinox — Lam
Do you have any idea why your clothes are hot when the earth is stilled, awaiting a hot wind — Ber

18. Hast thou with him spread out the sky, which is strong, and as a molten looking glass?
can you help him to spread the vault of heaven,
or temper that mirror of cast metal — Jerus
And was it with help of thine God fashioned the heavens, firm as cast bronze — Knox
Can you, like him, roll out the sky, solid, as any molten mirror — Mof
Can you beat out with him the skies, Hard as a molten mirror — AAT
Can you spread out the gigantic mirror of the skies as he does — Tay
Dost thou with him spread out the skies,
Firm as the molten mirror — ABPS

19. Teach us what we shall say unto him;
Tell us [Job] with what words of man we may address such a Being — Amp
You who think you know so much, teach the rest of us how we should approach God — Tay
for we cannot order our speech by reason of darkness.
we cannot state our case because we are in the dark — Amp
How can we argue, with our darkened minds? — Mof
We cannot do justice because of our ignorance — Sprl
For we are too dull to know — Tay

20. Shall it be told that I speak? if a man speak, surely he shall be swallowed up.
Shall it be told him that I would speak?
Did a man ever wish that he would be swallowed up? — RSV
Can my words carry weight with him?
Do man's commands reach his ears? — Jerus
What! man to cavil at his word?
Man to charge him with confusion? — Mof
Can any man dictate to God when he is to speak?
or command him to make proclamation? — NEB
Will he be told about it when I speak, or when a man says he is being destroyed? — NAB

21. And now men see not the bright light which is in the clouds: but the wind passeth, and cleanseth them.
For now, they look not on the light,
When it is shining in the skies,
And the wind has passed over and cleared them — ABPS
There are times when the light vanishes
behind darkening clouds;
then comes the wind, sweeping them away — Jerus
Light fails men's eyes; all of a sudden, the air is thick with clouds; then a breath of passing wind has driven them away! — Knox
We cannot even now gaze upon the light of the sun
When it shineth forth in the heavens;
And the wind passing along hath cleared the skies — Sprl

22. Fair weather cometh out of the north: with God is terrible majesty.
Out of the north cometh golden splendor:
God hath upon him terrible majesty — ASV
and brightness spreads from the north.
God is clothed in fearful splendour — Jerus
now radiant light streams from the northern sky;
and the Splendour of God is awful — Mof

23. Touching the Almighty, we cannot find him out: he is excellent in power, and in judgment, and in plenty of justice: he will not afflict.
The Almighty we cannot understand.
He excells in power and in fairness.
He who is great in righteousness will not pervert justice — Ber
the Almighty is beyond our minds.
Supreme in power and rich in justice,

he violates no right — Mof
The Almighty! we cannot comprehend Him!
Magnificent in might and in judgment!
So exceedingly just, none can gainsay — Sprl
We cannot imagine the power of the Almighty, and yet he is so just and merciful that he does not destroy us — Tay
The Almighty, we cannot find him out,
Great in power and rectitude.
And in fulness of justice, he will not oppress — ABPS

he, Shaddai, is far beyond our reach.
Supreme in power, in equity,
excelling in justice, yet no oppressor — Jerus

24. **Men do therefore fear him: he respecteth not any that are wise of heart.**
Therefore men revere Him; but He will not respect anyone who is conceited — Ber
— no wonder that men fear him,
and thoughtful men hold him in awe — Jerus
For this men do him reverence,
and thoughtful men revere him — Mof

CHAPTER 38

1. **Then the LORD answered Job out of the whirlwind, and said,**
Then from the heart of the tempest Yahweh gave Job his answer. He said: — Jerus

2. **Who is this that darkeneth counsel by words without knowledge?**
Who is this obscuring my designs
with his empty-headed words — Jerus
Here is one that must ever be clouding the truth of things with words ill-considered! — Knox
Who darkens my design
with a cloud of thoughtless words — Mof
Who is this whose ignorant words cloud my design in darkness — NEB
Why are you using your ignorance to deny my providence — Tay

3. **Gird up now thy loins like a man; for I will demand of thee, and answer thou me.**
Brace yourself like a fighter;
now it is my turn to ask questions and yours to inform me — Jerus
Confront me like a man;
come, answer these my questions — Mof
Now get ready to fight, for I am going to demand some answers from you, and you must reply — Tay

4. **Where wast thou when I laid the foundations of the earth?**
From what vantage-point wast thou watching when I laid the foundations of the earth — Knox
declare, if thou hast understanding.
Tell me, since you are so well-informed! — Jerus
Answer me that, if you have wit to know — Mof

5. **Who hath laid the measures thereof, if thou knowest? or who hath stretched the line upon it?**
Who determined its measurements? You surely know! Or who stretched the builder's line upon it — Ber
Tell me, since thou art so wise, was it thou or I designed earth's plan, measuring it out with the line — Knox
Do you know how its dimensions were determined, and who did the surveying — Tay

6. **Whereupon are the foundations thereof fastened?**
Whereon were its foundations sunken — ABPS
On what were its bases sunk — RSV
What supports its pillars at their bases — Jerus
How came its base to stand so firm — Knox
What were its pedestals placed on — Mof
or who laid the corner stone thereof:
or who put down its angle-stone — Bas
Or who laid her key-stone — Sprl
Who set its cornerstone in place — NEB

7. **When the morning stars sang together, and all the sons of God shouted for joy?**

when all the stars of the morning were singing with joy,
and the Sons of God in chorus were chanting praise — Jerus
as the morning stars sang together and all the angels shouted for joy — Tay

8. Or who shut up the sea with doors, when it brake forth, as if it had issued out of the womb?
Who fixed the boundaries of the sea, when it burst forth from the womb — Ber
who pent up the sea behind closed doors
when it leaped tumultuous out of the womb — Jerus
Who watched over the birth of the sea, when it burst in flood from the womb — NEB

9. When I made the cloud the garment thereof, and thick darkness a swaddlingband for it,
when I wrapped it in a robe of mist
and made black clouds its swaddling bands — Jerus
when I swathed it in mists,
and swaddled it in clouds of darkness — Mof
when I wrapped it in a blanket of cloud
and cradled it in fog — NEB

10. And brake up for it my decreed place,
And appointed it my bound — ABPS
Ordering a fixed limit for it — Bas
set it within bounds of my own choosing — Knox
when I fixed its boundaries — Mof
When I imposed upon it my decree — AAT
and set bars and doors,
with locks and doors — Bas
and made it fast with a bolted gate — Jerus
made fast with bolt and bar — Knox
barred and bolted it — Mof
and fixed a bar and double doors — Rhm
And established its barrier and doors — AAT

11. And said, Hitherto shalt thou come, but no further:
Come thus far, I said, and no further — Jerus
and here shall thy proud waves be stayed?
here your proud waves shall break. — Jerus
here let thy swelling waves spend their force. — Knox
And here appoint I the boundary of your tossing wave. — Sprl
And a command is placed
On the pride of thy billows. — YLT

12. Hast thou commanded the morning since thy days; and caused the dayspring to know his place;
Hast thou commanded the morning since thy days began,
And caused the dayspring to know its place — ASV
Have you ever in your life given orders to the morning
or sent the dawn to its post — Jerus
Have you ever roused the morning, given directions to the dawn — Mof
In all your life have you ever called up the dawn
or shown the morning its place — NEB

13. That it might take hold of the ends of the earth, that the wicked might be shaken out of it?
So that [light] may get hold of the corners of the earth and shake the wickedness [of night] out of it — Amp
telling it to grasp the earth by its edges
and shake the wicked out of it — Jerus
to catch earth by the corners
and shake out the wicked — Mof
Have you taught it to grasp the fringes of the earth
and shake the Dog-star from its place — NEB

14. It is turned as clay to the seal; and they stand as a garment.
It is changed as clay into which a seal is pressed, and things stand out like a many-colored garment — Amp
The dawn, that stamps its image on the clay of earth; stands there, flung over it like a garment, — Knox
earth stands out clear like clay stamped by a seal,
in all its colours like a robe — Mof
It transformeth itself like the clay of a seal,
So that things stand forth like one arrayed — Rhm

Have you ever robed the dawn in red, — Tay

15. And from the wicked their light is withholden, and the high arm shall be broken.

taking away from ill-doers the darkness that is their light, so that all their power goes for nothing — Knox

The light of sinners shall be withheld, and the arm of the arrogant shall be broken — Lam

while wicked men are robbed of their dark hours,
and their uplifted arms are broken — Mof

and disturbed the haunts of wicked men and stopped the arm raised to strike? — Tay

16. Hast thou entered into the springs of the sea? or hast thou walked in the search of the depth?

Have you journeyed all the way to the sources of the sea,
or walked where the Abyss is deepest — Jerus

Didst thou ever make thy way into the sea's depths, walk at thy ease through its hidden caverns — Knox

Have you explored the springs from which the seas come, or walked in the sources of their depths — Tay

Have you descended to the springs of the sea
or walked in the unfathomable deep — NEB

Hast thou come to the springs of the sea,
And walked in the recesses of the deep — ABPS

17. Have the gates of death been opened unto thee? or hast thou seen the doors of the shadow of death?

Have the gates of death been shown to you, and have you stood before the doors of deep darkness — Ber

Have the gates of death been rolled aside for thee,
And the gates of death-shade that thou mightest see — Sprl

Have the gates of death been revealed to you?
Have you ever seen the door-keepers of the palace of darkness — NEB

18. Hast thou perceived the breadth of the earth? declare if thou knowest it all.

Have you an inkling of the extent of the earth?
Tell me about it if you have! — Jerus

Nay, hast thou viewed the whole surface of the earth itself? Tell me, if such knowledge is thine, all its secrets — Knox

Have you comprehended the vast expanse of the world?
Come, tell me all this, if you know — NEB

19. Where is the way where light dwelleth? and as for darkness, where is the place thereof,

Which is the way to the home of the light,
and where does darkness live? — Jerus

What path leads to the home of Light,
and where does darkness dwell? — Mof

There is a region where light dwelleth: where is that?
And an abiding-place for darkness: where is that? — Sprl

Where does the light come from, and how do you get there? Or tell me about the darkness. Where does it come from? — Tay

20. That thou shouldest take it to the bound thereof, and that thou shouldest know the paths to the house thereof?

That you may conduct it to its home, and may know the paths to its house — Amp

You could then show them the way to their proper places,
or put them on the path to where they live! — Jerus

hast thou followed either of these to the end of its journey, tracked it to its lair? — Knox

Do you know its borders and the path to its house? — Lam

Can you conduct them to their fields, and lead them home again — Mof

21. Knowest thou it, because thou wast then born? or because the number of thy days is great?

If you know all this, you must have been born with them,
you must be very old by now! — Jerus

Didst thou forsee the time of thy own birth,

couldst thou foretell the years of life that lay before thee — Knox

Do you remember when you were born, and do you know if you will live many days — Lam

You must know, since you were born then? Or because you are so extremely old! — Amp

Doubtless you know all this; for you were born already,
so long is the span of your life! — NEB

22. Hast thou entered into the treasures of the snow? or hast thou seen the treasures of the hail,

. . . the treasuries . . . — ASV

. . . the storehouse . . . — NAB

Have you ever visited the place where the snow is kept,
or seen where the hail is stored up — Jerus

23. Which I have reserved against the time of trouble, against the day of battle and war?

which I keep for times of stress,
for days of battle and war? — Jerus

my armoury against the times of stress, when there are wars to be fought, battles to be won? — Knox

the hail I keep for stormy days,
for battery and assault? — Mof

24. By what way is the light parted, which scattereth the east wind upon the earth?

Which is the way to the place where the wind is measured out, and the east wind sent out over the earth? — Bas

From which direction does the lightning fork
when it scatters sparks over the earth? — Jerus

Or in what manner is light distributed, and whence the wind comes forth upon the earth? — Lam

How are the mists marshalled,
that scatter fresh water on earth? — Mof

25. Who hath divided a watercourse for the overflowing of waters, or a way for the lightning of thunder;

Who divided channels for the rain,
And a track for the thunder's crash? — ABPS

Who has dug gullies for the torrents of rain, or a path for the thunderbolts — Ber

Who carves a channel for the downpour,
and hacks a way for the rolling thunder — Jerus

26. To cause it to rain on the earth, where no man is; on the wilderness, wherein there is no man;

that they should fall on some lonely desert where the foot of man never trod — Knox

27. To satisfy the desolate and waste ground; and to cause the bud of the tender herb to spring forth?

giving drink to the lonely wastes
and making grass spring where everything was dry — Jerus

to gladden lonely wastes,
and clothe the dry land with green sward — Mof

To satisfy wilds and wastes,
And cause the springing grass to grow — ABPS

To enrich the waste and desolate land
till the desert blooms with verdure — NAB

28. Hath the rain a father? or who hath begotten the drops of dew?

What sire gendered the rain, or the drops of dew — Knox

Have showers a human sire?
Who was the father of the dew — Mof

29. Out of whose womb came the ice? and the hoary frost of heaven, who hath gendered it?

30. The waters are hid as with a stone, and the face of the deep is frozen.

what mother's womb bore the ice, the frost that comes from heaven to make water hard as stone, [to] imprison the depths beneath its surface? — Knox

From whose womb did the ice come forth?
And who gave birth to the hoarfrost of the skies,
When the waters congeal like a stone,
And the surface of the deep is frozen solid? — AAT

31. Canst thou bind the sweet influences of Pleiades, or loose the bands of Orion?

Canst thou bind the cluster of the Pleiades,
Or loose the bands of Orion — ASV
Can you fasten the harness of the Pleiades,
or untie Orion's bands — Jerus
Is it at thy command the glittering bright Pleiads cluster so close, and Orion's circlet spreads so wide? — Knox

32. **Canst thou bring forth Mazzaroth in his season?**
Dost thou lead forth the Signs in their season — ABPS
Can you lead forth the signs of the Zodiac in their season — Amp
Can you guide the morning star season by season — Jerus
or canst thou guide Arcturus with his sons?
And the Bear and her young — ABPS
Or can you guide [the stars of] the Bear with her young — Amp

33. **Knowest thou the ordinances of heaven? canst thou set the dominion thereof in the earth?**
Have you grasped the celestial laws? Could you make their writ run on earth — Jerus
Is it thine to understand the motions of the heavens, and rule earth by their influence — Knox
Can you control the skies?
Can you prescribe their sway over the earth — Mof
Do you know the laws of the heavens? or do you appoint the arrangements of the earth — AAT
Do you know the laws of the universe and how the heavens influence the earth — Tay

34. **Canst thou lift up thy voice to the clouds, that abundance of waters may cover thee?**
Can your voice carry as far as the clouds
and make the pent-up waters do your bidding — Jerus
Can you send orders to the clouds
for water in abundance to be yours — Mof
Can you shout to the clouds and make it rain — Tay

35. **Canst thou send lightnings, that they may go, and say unto thee, Here we are?**
Will lightning flashes come at your command
and answer, 'Here we are' — Jerus
Can you send out the lightning on its mission?
Does it say humbly to you, 'Here am I' — Mof

36. **Who hath put wisdom in the inward parts? or who hath given understanding to the heart?**
Who has imparted wisdom in the inner self, or who has given the heart understanding — Ber
Who gave the ibis wisdom
and endowed the cock with foreknowledge — Jerus
What power gives either man's heart prescience, or the cock its sure instinct — Knox
Who has put wisdom in the clouds, or given understanding to the mists — RSV
Who gives intuition and instinct — Tay

37. **Who can number the clouds in wisdom? or who can stay the bottles of heaven,**
Whose skill details every cloud
and tilts the flash of heaven — Jerus
Who has the skill to mass the clouds, or tilt the pitcher of the sky — Mof
Who is wise enough to number all the clouds? Who can tilt the water jars of heaven — Tay
Who is wise enough to marshal the rain-clouds
and empty the cisterns of heaven — NEB

38. **When the dust groweth into hardness, and the clods cleave fast together?**
When the earth becomes hard as metal, and is joined together in masses — Bas
causing the dust to form lumps and the clods to stick together like mud — Ber
when the dust runs into a mass
and the clods cleave fast together — RSV

39. **Wilt thou hunt the prey for the lion? or fill the appetite of the young lions,**

Is it thou or I that finds the lioness her prey, to satisfy those hungry whelps of hers — Knox

Can you stalk prey like a lioness, to satisfy the young lions' appetites — Tay

40. When they couch in their dens, and abide in the covert to lie in wait?

where they lie in rocky caves, their lurking-places — Knox

When they crouch in dens,
Or lie in wait in the thicket — AAT

41. Who provideth for the raven his food? when his young ones cry unto God, they wander for lack of meat.

who makes provision for the raven
when his squabs cry out to God
and crane their necks in hunger? — Jerus

Which of us feeds the ravens? Is it not to God their nestlings cry so shrilly, homeless for want of food? — Knox

CHAPTER 39

1. Knowest thou the time when the wild goats of the rock bring forth? or canst thou mark when the hinds do calve?

Not thine to know when the wild goats give birth on their high crags, to watch the hinds in their throes — Knox

Do you know when the mountain goats deliver, or have you watched the travail of the does? — Ber

Knowest thou the time when the wild goats of the rock bring forth?
Keepest thou an entry of when the hinds calve? — Sprl

2. Canst thou number the months that they fulfil? or knowest thou the time when they bring forth?

How many months do they carry their young?
At what time do they give birth? — Jerus

Can you number the months they fulfil, and do you know the time of their gestation? — Ber

3. They bow themselves, they bring forth their young ones, they cast out their sorrows.

They crouch to drop their young,
and let their burdens fall in the open desert — Jerus

And do you know when they kneel and bring forth their young ones? — Lam

. . . and carry their burden no longer? — Tay

They kneel down, their young they bring forth,
Their pains they throw off — Rhm

4. Their young ones are in good liking, they grow up with corn; they go forth, and return not unto them.

Their young mature, grow up in the field,
Go forth, and return not to them — ABPS

Their young are strong, they grow up in the open field;
they run off and do not go back to them — Ber

5. Who hath sent out the wild ass free? or hath loosed the bands of the wild ass?

Who gave the wild donkey his freedom,
and untied the rope from his proud neck — Jerus

Who has left the wild ass to be free, and made him to escape the yoke — Lam

6. Whose house I have made the wilderness, and the barren land his dwellings.

For he has made the plain his house, and the salt land his dwelling place — Lam

7. He scorneth the multitude of the city, neither regardeth he the crying of the driver.

He mocks at the clamor of the city;
The driver's shouts he hears not —ABPS

He scorns the noisy town,
he hears no driver's shout — Mof

For they hate the noise of the city and want no drivers shouting at them! — Tay

He scorns the tumult of the city, and hears not the shoutings of the taskmaster — Amp

8. The range of the mountains is his pasture, and he searcheth after every green thing.

He explores the mountains for pasture, searching after every green thing — Ber

The tops of mountains are his pasture, and he treads over every green thing — Lam

The mountain ranges are their pasture-land; there they search for every blade of grass — Tay

9. Will the unicorn be willing to serve thee, or abide by thy crib?

Will the wild-ox be willing to serve thee,
Or abide at thy crib — ABPS

Will the wild ox be content to slave for you?
Will he stay in your stable — Mof

10. Canst thou bind the unicorn with his band in the furrow? or will he harrow the valley after thee?

[Canst thou] bind him to the plough with thongs and lead him out to break clods in the valley — Knox

Can you rope him to your plough? Will he harrow the furrows for you — Mof

Can you use a wild ox to plow with? Will he pull the harrow for you — Tay

11. Wilt thou trust him, because his strength is great? or wilt thou leave thy labour to him?

Can you rely on his massive strength and leave him to do your heavy work — Jerus

Will you trust to his tremendous strength,
and let him do your field work — Mof

Do you trust him because his strength is great?
And do you leave your hard-won gains to him — AAT

Because he is so strong, will you trust him? Will you let him decide where to work — Tay

12. Wilt thou believe him, that he will bring home thy seed, and gather it into thy barn?

Would you rely on him to bring your grain home and gather it onto your threshing floor — Ber

Can you rely on him to thresh out your grain
and gather in the yield of your threshing floor — NAB

13. Gavest thou the goodly wings unto the peacocks? or wings and feathers unto the ostrich?

The wings of the ostrich wave proudly;
But are they the pinions and plumage of love — ASV

The wing of the ostrich rejoiceth; but are her pinions and feathers kindly — RV

The wing of the ostrich beateth joyously;
But are her pinions and feathers the kindly stork's — JPS

The ostrich flaps her wings grandly, but has no true motherly love — Tay

14. Which leaveth her eggs in the earth, and warmeth them in dust,

She lays her eggs on top of the earth, to warm them in the dust — Tay

She leaves her eggs upon the earth to warm and hatch out in the dust — Mof

15. And forgetteth that the foot may crush them, or that the wild beast may break them.

Heedless, though foot of man should trample or wild beast devour them — Knox

She forgets that someone may step on them and crush them, or the wild animals destroy them — Tay

16. She is hardened against her young ones, as though they were not hers: her labour is in vain without fear;

she steels herself to pity as if the brood was none of hers; throws away all her hopes in causeless alarm — Knox

She ignores her young as though they weren't her own, and is unconcerned though they die — Tay

She treats her young cruelly, as if they were not hers, quite unconcerned that her labor may have been in vain — Ber

17. Because God hath deprived her of wisdom, neither hath he imparted to her understanding.

God, you see, has made her unwise, and given her no share of common sense — Jerus

For God has denied her wisdom and has imparted to her no intelligence — Ber

18. What time she lifted her herself on high, she scorneth the horse and his rider.

When she flaps her wings to flee, she mocks the horse and his rider — Ber

Yet, if she bestirs herself to use her height,
she can make fools of horse and rider too — Jerus

When she rouses herself to flee,
she laughs at the horse and his rider — RSV

But whenever she jumps up to run,
she passes the swiftest horse with its rider — Tay

19. Hast thou given the horse strength? hast thou clothed his neck with thunder?

Are you the one who makes the horse so brave
and covers his neck with flowing hair — Jerus

Ay, and what of the horse? Is it of thy gift his great strength comes, was it thou didst caparison him with terrors — Knox

Do you supply the war-horse with his strength,
or cover his neck with the tossing mane — Mof

20. Canst thou make him afraid as a grasshopper? the glory of his nostrils is terrible.

Dost thou make him bound like the locust?
His proud snorting is terrible! — ABPS

Thou wilt not scare him away like a locust; fiercely he breathes — Knox

Do you make him leap forward like a locust,
snorting bravely, furiously — Mof

Have you made him able to leap forward like a locust? His majestic snorting is something to hear! —Tay

Do you make him quiver like a locust's wings,
when his shrill neighing strikes terror? — NEB

21. He paweth in the valley, and rejoiceth in his strength: he goeth on to meet the armed men.

Exultantly he paws the soil of the valley,
and prances eagerly to meet the clash of arms — Jerus

deeply he paws the ground, bravely he prances, as he goes out to meet the shock of battle — Knox

22. He mocketh at fear, and is not affrighted; neither turneth he back from the sword.

Fear cannot daunt him, nor the sword drive him back — Knox

he is unafraid and does not run away — Tay

He laughs at fear; he is afraid of nothing,
he recoils before no sword — Jerus

23. The quiver rattleth against him, the glittering spear and the shield.

On his back the quiver rattles,
the flashing spear and javelin — Jerus

The quiver rattleth against him,
The flashing spear and the javelin — ASV

The quiver rattles at his side,
the spear and sabre flash — NEB

24. He swalloweth the ground with fierceness and rage: neither believeth he that it is the sound of the trumpet.

Quivering and excited he eats up the ground, no longer willing to stand still, having heard the sound of the trumpet — Ber

He gallops with rage that makes the ground to tremble, nor does he fear the sound of the trumpet — Lam

Trembling with eagerness, he devours the ground
and cannot be held in when he hears the horn — NEB

Quivering with impatience, he eats up the miles;
when the trumpet sounds, there is no holding him — Jerus

25. He saith among the trumpets, Ha, ha; and he smelleth the battle afar off, the thunder of the captains, and the shouting.

At each trumpet blast he shouts 'Hurrah!'
He scents the battle from afar,
hearing the thundering of chiefs, the shouting — Jerus

26. Doth the hawk fly by thy wisdom, and stretch her wings toward the south?

Is it of thy devising the hawk grows full-fledged, in time to spread her wings for the southward journey — Knox

Is it by your wisdom that the hawk was created and wings his way toward the south — Lam

Hath the hawk by thy wisdom poised herself aloft with wings expanded, unmoved, surveying the regions of the south — Sept

Is it by your wisdom that the hawk soars,
and spreads his wings toward the south — RSV

27. **Doth the eagle mount up at thy command, and make her nest on high?**

Or does the vulture fly high at your command,
When he sets his nest aloft — AAT

Does your word make the eagle mount to nest aloft among the hills — Mof

28. **She dwelleth and abideth on the rock, upon the crag of the rock, and the strong place.**

On the cliff she dwelleth, and maketh her home,
Upon the point of the cliff, and the stronghold — ASV

On the rock he dwells and makes his home
in the fastness of the rocky crag — RSV

29. **From thence she seeketh the prey, and her eyes behold afar off.**

from which she watches for prey,
fixing it with her far-ranging eye — Jerus

From thence she spieth out with her eyes for food;
Her eyes detect the prey afar off — Sprl

30. **Her young ones also suck up blood: and where the slain are, there is she.**

She feeds her young on blood:
wherever men fall dying, there she is — Jerus

Blood-thirsty her brood, and where the carcass waits, waits she — Knox

His brood gorge themselves with blood,
And wherever the slain are, there are they" — AAT

CHAPTER 40

1. **Moreover the LORD answered Job, and said,**

Then Yahweh turned to Job, and he said: — Jerus

2. **Shall he that contendeth with the Almighty instruct him? he that reproveth God, let him answer it.**

Will the faultfinder contend with the Almighty? He, who would reprove God, let him answer — Ber

"Shall a faultfinder contend with the Almighty?
He who argues with God, let him answer it — RSV

Is Shaddai's opponent willing to give in?
Has God's critic thought up an answer? — Jerus

Do you still want to argue with the Almighty? Or will you yield? Do you — God's critic — have the answers? — Tay

3. **Then Job answered the LORD and said,**

Job replied to Yahweh: — Jerus

4. **Behold, I am vile; what shall I answer thee? I will lay mine hand upon my mouth.**

Behold, I am of small account: what shall I answer thee?
I lay my hand upon my mouth — ASV

Behold, I am insignificant; what can I answer thee?
I put my hand over my mouth — AAT

I am nothing — how could I ever find the answers? I lay my hand upon my mouth in silence — Tay

My words have been frivolous: what can I reply?
I had better lay my fingers on my lips — Jerus

5. **Once have I spoken; but I will not answer: yea, twice; but I will proceed no further.**

I have spoken once . . . I will not speak again;
more than once . . . I will add nothing — Jerus

I have spoken once, and I will not reply;
Yea, twice; but not again — AAT

I have said too much already — Tay

6. **Then answered the LORD unto Job out of the whirlwind, and said,**

Yahweh gave Job his answer from the heart of the tempest. He said: — Jerus

And once more, from the midst of a whirlwind, the Lord gave Job his answer: — Knox

7. **Gird up thy loins now like a man:**

I will demand of thee, and declare thou unto me.
Brace yourself like a fighter,
now it is my turn to ask questions and yours to inform me — Jerus
Stand up like a man and brace yourself for battle. Let me ask you a question, and give me the answer — Tay

8. **Wilt thou also disannul my judgment? wilt thou condemn me, that thou mayest be righteous?**
Will you discredit My justice? Will you condemn Me and claim that you are righteous — Ber
Do you really want to reverse my judgement,
and put me in the wrong to put yourself in the right — Jerus
Will you even make my right of no value? will you say that I am wrong in order to make clear that you are right — Bas
Dare you deny that I am just
or put me in the wrong that you may be right — NEB

9. **Hast thou an arm like God? or canst thou thunder with a voice like him?**
Has your arm the strength of God's, can your voice thunder as loud — Jerus
why then, let us see thee shew strength like the strength of God, let us hear thee thunder as God thunders. — Knox
Are you as strong as God, and can you shout as loudly as he — Tay

10. **Deck thyself now with majesty and excellency; and array thyself with glory and beauty.**
Deck thyself now with grandeur, and majesty,
And array thyself in splendor and beauty — ABPS
Put on the ornaments of your pride; be clothed with glory and pride — Bas
All right then, put on your robes of state, your majesty and splendor — Tay

11. **Cast abroad the rage of thy wrath: and behold every one that is proud, and abase him.**
Send out the floods of thy wrath;
And behold all that is high, and abase it — ABPS
Pour forth the overflowings of thine anger: and look upon every one that is proud, and abase him — RV
Scatter the proud in that indignation of thine, with thy frown abase the tyrant — Knox
Pour out thy transports of anger,
And look on everyone who is high, and lay him low — Rhm
Let the spate of your anger flow free; humiliate the haughty at a glance! — Jerus

12. **Look on everyone that is proud, and bring him low; and tread down the wicked in their place.**
Look at everything that is haughty, and throw it down; crush the wicked where they stand — Ber
here is an oppressor for thee to thwart; here is one that defies thee, crush him! — Knox
lay all the lofty low,
and crush the wicked on the spot — Mof
Regard every haughty one, and lay him low,
And stamp the wicked to pieces under foot — Sprl

13. **Hide them in the dust together; and bind their faces in secret.**
Bury the lot of them in the ground,
shut them, silent-faced, in the dungeon — Jerus
Knock them into the dust, stone-faced in death — Tay
Hide them in the dust together;
Bind their faces in the hidden place — ASV
Hide them all in the dust together; bind their faces in the world below — RSV
Hide them in the dust together;
Bandage their faces for the sepulchre — Sprl

14. **Then will I also confess unto thee that thine own right hand can save thee.**
I myself will be the first to acknowledge
that your own right hand can assure your triumph — Jerus
then I will acknowledge thee for one whose strength can bring him victory — Knox

15. **Behold now behemoth, which I made with thee; he eateth grass as an ox.**

Behold now the river-ox, which I have made with thee;
He eats grass like the herd — ABPS
Look at the hippopotamus. I made him, as I made you; he eats grass like cattle — Ber
Here is Behemoth, my creature as thou art, fed on the same grass the oxen eat — Knox
Now think of Behemoth;
he eats greenstuff like the ox — Jerus
Consider the chief of beasts, the crocodile,
who devours cattle as if they were grass — NEB

16. Lo now, his strength is in his loins, and his force is in the navel of his belly.
yet what strength in his loins, what lustihood in the navel of his belly! — Knox
Look at the strength of his thighs,
and the stout muscles of his belly — Mof
Look at the strength in his loins and his force in the muscles of his body — Ber
But what strength he has in his loins,
what power in his stomach muscles! — Jerus
See now, his strength is in his loins,
And his virility in the navel of his belly — Sprl

17. He moveth his tail like a cedar: the sinews of his stones are wrapped together.
His tail is as stiff as a cedar,
the sinews of his thighs are tightly knit — Jerus
He bends his tail like a cedar;
The sinews of his thighs are knit together — ABPS
He moves his tail like a cedar tree;
the tendons of his thighs are twisted together [like a rope] — Amp
He carries his tail like a cedar;
the sinews of his thighs are like cables — NAB

18. His bones are as strong pieces of brass; his bones are like bars of iron.
His bones are pipes of bronze;
His bones are as bars of iron — ABPS
His bones are barrels of bronze,
His frame is like hammered bars of iron — Rhm
His vertebrae are bronze tubing,
his bones as hard as hammered iron — Jerus
bones like pipes of bronze, gristle like plates of steel! — Knox
His bones are tubes of bronze,
his ribs like iron bars — Mof

19. He is the chief of the ways of God: he that made him can make his sword to approach unto him.
He is the masterpiece of all God's work,
but his Maker threatened him with the sword — Jerus
[The hippopotamus] is the first [in magnitude and power] of the works of God [in animal life]; only He Who made him provides him with his [sword-like tusks, or God Who made him, alone can bring near His sword to master him] — Amp
How ferocious he is among all God's creation, so let whoever hopes to master him bring a sharp sword! — Tay
He is the chief of God's works,
made to be tyrant over his peers — NEB

20. Surely the mountains bring him forth food, where all the beasts of the field play.
forbidding him the mountain regions where all the wild beasts have their playground — Jerus
The rivers furnish him with food;
wild animals are all amazed at him — Mof
The mountains offer their best food to him — the other wild animals on which he preys — Tay
for he takes the cattle of the hills for his prey
and in his jaws he crushes all wild beasts — NEB

21. He lieth under the shady trees, in the covert of the reed, and ferns.
He takes his rest under the trees of the river and in the pool, under the shade of the water-plants — Bas
Under the lotus plants he lies,
in the covert of the reeds and in the marsh — RSV
They go to rest under trees of every sort, by the papyrus, the reed and the bulrush — Sept

22. The shady trees cover him with their

shadow; the willows of the brook compass him about.

The leaves of the lotus give him shade, the willows by the stream shelter him — Jerus

23. **Behold, he drinketh up a river, and hasteth not: he trusteth that he can draw up Jordan into his mouth.**

Lo the stream swells, he startles not; Is fearless, though Jordan rush forth to his mouth — ABPS

Behold if a river is violent and overflows, he does not tremble, he is confident though a Jordan swells and rushes against his mouth — Amp

Should the river overflow on him, why should he worry?
A Jordan could pour down his throat without his caring — Jerus

The flooded river he drinks unconcerned; Jordan itself would have no terrors for that gaping mouth — Knox

He is not disturbed by raging rivers, not even when the swelling Jordan rushes down upon him — Tay

24. **He taketh it with his eyes: his nose pierceth through snares.**

Shall any take him when he is on the watch, or pierce through his nose with a snare? — ASV

Can one seize him by his eyes?
Can one pierce his nose with traps? — AAT

No one can catch him off guard or put a ring in his nose and lead him away — Tay

CHAPTER 41

1. **Canst thou draw out leviathan with a hook? or his tongue with a cord which thou lettest down?**

Wilt thou draw out the crocodile with a hook,
And press down his tongue with a cord — ABPS

Or Leviathan, wilt thou find a hook that will draw him to land, a line that will hold his tongue fast — Knox

Can you draw up the crocodile with a fish-hook,
Or can you press down his tongue with a cord — AAT

Leviathan, too! Can you catch him with a fish-hook
or run a line round his tongue — Jerus

Canst thou draw out Dragon with a hook, or put a bandage round his nostrils — Sept

2. **Canst thou put an hook into his nose?**

Wilt thou put a rush-cord in his nose — ABPS

Can you put a rush line through his gills — Ber

Can you put a ring through his nose — Jerus

Canst thou ring him — Knox

Or canst thou fasten a ring in his snout — Sept

or bore his jaw through with a thorn?

Or pierce his jaw through with a hook? — ASV

or pierce his jaw with a clasp? — Knox

or bore his lip for a jewel? — Sept

Or puncture his cheek through with the barb? — Sprl

3. **Will he make many supplications unto thee? will he speak soft words unto thee?**

Will he plead and plead with you,
will he coax you with smooth words — Jerus

Will he importune thee with entreaties, or cajole thee with blandishments — Knox

Will he beg you to desist or try to flatter you from your intentions — Tay

Will he make repeated requests of you? Will he use friendly words in addressing you? — Ber

Will he make many supplications to you? Or will he speak flattering words to you? — Lam

4. **Will he make a covenant with thee? wilt thou take him for a servant for ever?**

Will he make a bargain with you, that you should take him as your servant for life — Ber

Will he come to terms with you,
always be at your service — Mof

Will he agree to let you make him

your slave for life — Tay

Will he make a covenant with you? Or will you count him as a servant for ever — Lam

5. **Wilt thou play with him as with a bird? or wilt thou bind him for thy maidens?**

Will you make a pet of him, like a bird, keep him on a lead to amuse your maids — Jerus

Wilt thou make a plaything of him, as if he were a tame bird, chain him up to make sport for thy maid-servants — Knox

Can you make a pet of him like a bird, or give him to your little girls to play with — Tay

6. **Shall the companions make a banquet of him? shall they part him among the merchants?**

Will the bands of fisherman make traffic of him?
Will they part him among the merchants — ASV

Is he to be sold by the fishing-guild and then retailed by merchants — Jerus

Will fishermen make a meal of him?
Will traders cut him up — Mof

will fishermen traders bargain over him, apportioning him among the merchants — Ber

7. **Canst thou fill his skin with barbed irons? or his head with fish spears?**

Wilt thou fill his skin with darts,
And his head with fish spears — ABPS

Can you fill his skin with harpoons?
Or his head with fishing spears — Amp

Riddle his hide with darts?
Prod his head with a harpoon? — Jerus

8. **Lay thine hand upon him, remember the battle, do no more.**

Only put your hand on him and see what a fight you will have; you will not do it again! — Bas

You have only to lay a finger on him never to forget the struggle or risk it again! — Jerus

Just lay a hand on him!—just once!—you will not forget the fray! — Mof

Lay thy hand upon him!
Of battle thou shalt think no more — ABPS

9. **Behold, the hope of him is in vain: shall not one be cast down even at the sight of him?**

Truly, the hope of his attacker is false; he is overcome even on seeing him! — Bas

The man who hopes to master him will be disillusioned; at the sight of him a person is paralyzed! — Ber

All hopes of seizing him are vain;
the very sight of him dismays — Mof

Behold, the expectation of snaring him would be in vain;
Doth not even the sight of him dispel it? — Sprl

No, it's useless to try to capture him. It is frightening even to think about it! — Tay

10. **None is so fierce that dare stir him up: who then is able to stand before me?**

No one is foolhardy enough to stir him up; who then is he who can stand before Me — Ber

When roused, he grows ferocious,
no one can face him in a fight. — Jerus

No one is bold enough to stir him up;
what man could face him — Mof

None are so courageous that they dare stir him up:
Who then is he that would array himself against Me? — Sprl

11. **Who hath prevented me, that I should repay him? Whatsoever is under the whole heaven is mine.**

Who has first given unto me that I should repay him?
Whatsoever is under the whole heaven is mine — ASV

Who could attack him with success?
None, none beneath the sky — Mof

nor can any deserve my thanks by lending me the aid I lacked; nothing on earth but is at my disposal — Knox

12. **I will not conceal his parts, nor his power, nor his comely proportion.**

I will not be silent concerning his limbs, his mighty strength, and his artistic portions — Ber

Next I will talk of his limbs
and describe his matchless strength — Jerus

I will not keep silence concerning his limbs,
or his mighty strength, or his goodly frame — RSV

13. Who can discover the face of his garment? or who can come to him with his double bridle?
Who has uncovered the face of his garment?
His double jaws, who enters in — ABPS
Who can strip off his outer garment? Who shall come within his jaws — ASV
Who has ever stripped off his thick coat of mail, or pierced his impenetrable scales — Ber
Who can strip off his outer garment? Who can penetrate his double coat of mail — RSV

14. Who can open the doors of his face? his teeth are terrible round about.
Who can open the doors of his face? round about his teeth is terror — RV
Who dare open the gates of his mouth? Terror dwells in those rows of teeth! — Jerus

15. His scales are his pride, shut up together as with a close seal.
His back is shingled with scales, as closely fitted together as a tight seal — Ber
His back is like a row of shields, sealed with a seal of stone — Jerus
The body of him is like shields of cast metal, scale pressing on scale — Knox

16. One is so near to another, that no air can come between them.
touching each other so close
that not a breath could pass between — Jerus
so close to one another as to leave no vent between — Knox

17. They are joined one to another, they stick together, that they cannot be sundered.
They clasp one another, joined so closely that they cannot be separated — Ber
sticking to one another
to make an indivisible whole — Jerus
so well joined that nothing will part them — Knox

18. By his neesings a light doth shine, and his eyes are like the eyelids of the morning.
His sneezings flash forth light,
And his eyes are like the eyelids of the morning — ASV
Let him but sneeze, the fire flashes out; let him open his eyes, it is like the glimmer of dawn — Knox
His sneezings sparkle light; his eyes are like the rays of morning — Ber
His sneezing sends out sprays of light, and his eyes gleam like the shimmer of dawn — NEB

19. Out of his mouth go burning lamps, and sparks of fire leap out.
From his mouth go flames,
And sparks of fire escape — ABPS
flames come from his jaws, bright as a burning torch, — Knox

20. Out of his nostrils goeth smoke, as out of a seething pot or caldron.
From his nostrils goes forth smoke,
Like a kettle with kindled reeds — ABPS
His nostrils belch smoke
like a cauldron boiling on the fire — Jerus
smoke from his nostrils, thick as the fumes of a seething pot; — Knox
Out of his mouth go forth firebrands; sparks of fire leap forth — NAB

21. His breath kindleth coals, and a flame goeth out of his mouth.
his very breath will set coals aflame, such fire issues from that mouth — Knox

22. In his neck remaineth strength, and sorrow is turned into joy before him.
Such strength dwells in his neck that panic moves before him — Ber
In his neck abides strength,
And terror dances before him — ABPS
Strength has made a home in his neck, fear leaps before him as he goes — Jerus

23. The flakes of his flesh are joined together: they are firm in themselves; they cannot be moved.
The folds of his flesh close in on each other, firmly and immovably cast upon him — Ber
Firm-set are the folds of his flesh, unyielding though a thunder-bolt should strike them — Knox
The dewlaps of his flesh cleave together,
Hardened upon him they cannot be moved — Rhm

24. His heart is as firm as a stone: yea, as hard as a piece of the nether millstone.

His heart is as hard as a rock; solid as a nether millstone — Ber

firm-set, too, is the heart of him, firm as ever stone was, or smith's anvil — Knox

His heart is as hard as a rock
unyielding as a millstone — Jerus

25. When he raiseth up himself, the mighty are afraid: by reason of breakings they purify themselves.

When he stands up, the waves themselves take fright,
the billows of the sea retreat — Jerus

Rises he up, angels themselves are afraid and take sanctuary in their dread — Knox

When he comes up, strong men are terrified,
scared by the swirl in the water — Mof

When he raises himself, strong men take fright,
bewildered at the lashings of his tail — NEB

At his rising up the mighty are afraid;
They lose themselves for terror — ABPS

When he raises himself up, the mighty are afraid;
beside themselves with panic — Ber

When he raises himself up the mighty are afraid;
at the crashing they are beside themselves — RSV

26. The sword of him that layeth at him cannot hold: the spear, the dart, nor the habergeon.

If one assail him with the sword, it shall not hold;
The spear, the dart, and the mail — ABPS

To hit him with a sword is useless; so with a spear, a dart or javelin — Ber

no sword avails against him,
no spear, no dart, no shaft — Mof

As for him that assaileth him, the sword availeth not,
Spear, dart or coat of mail — Rhm

27. He esteemeth iron as straw, and brass as rotten wood.

Iron means no more to him than straw,
nor bronze than rotting wood — Jerus

he treats a harpoon like a straw,
a bronze lance is like rotten wood — Mof

28. The arrow cannot make him flee: slingstones are turned with him into stubble.

The arrow cannot make him flee;
To him, sling-stones are turned to chaff — ABPS

Arrows cannot make him flee. Slingstones are as ineffective as straw — Tay

29. Darts are counted as stubble: he laugheth at the shaking of a spear.

Clubs are counted as stubble:
He laugheth at the rustling of the javelin — ASV

bludgeons are mere bulrushes, and whizzing javelins he derides — Mof

The bludgeon is reckoned as but chaff,
And he laughs at the whiz of the lance — AAT

to him a club is a mere reed,
and he laughs at the swish of the sabre — NEB

30. Sharp stones are under him: he spreadeth sharp pointed things upon the mire.

His underparts are like sharp pieces of broken pottery; he spreads [grooves like] a threshing sledge upon the mire — Amp

He has sharp potsherds underneath,
and moves across the slime like a harrow — Jerus

His lower parts are like sharp potsherds;
He prints a threshing-sledge upon the mud — AAT

31. He maketh the deep to boil like a pot: he maketh the sea like a pot of ointment.

He churns the depths into a seething cauldron,
he makes the sea fume like a scent burner — Jerus

He makes the water boil and foam,
churning the deep like unguents in a pot — Mof

He makes the deep water boil like a cauldron,
he whips up the lake like ointment in a mixing bowl — NEB

32. He maketh a path to shine after him: one would think the deep to be hoary.

Behind him he makes a glistening path;

One would think the deep hoar with age — ABPS

Behind him he leaves a glittering wake —
a white fleece seems to float on the deeps — Jerus

He leaves a shining wake of froth behind him. One would think the sea were made of frost! — Tay

33. Upon earth there is not his like, who is made without fear.

On earth there is not his equal, a creature devoid of fear! — Ber

34. He beholdeth all high things:

He looks all mighty [beasts of prey] in the face [without terror] — Amp

He looks the haughtiest in the eye — Jerus

he is a king over all the children of pride.

He is king over all the proud beasts — JPS

Over all the pride of earth he reigns supreme — Knox

Of all the beasts, he is the proudest — monarch of all he sees — Tay

CHAPTER 42

1. Then Job answered the LORD, and said,

This was the answer Job gave to Yahweh: — Jerus

2. I know that thou canst do every thing, and that no thought can be withholden from thee.

I know that thou canst do all things,
And that no purpose of thine can be restrained — ASV

I know that you are all-powerful:
what you conceive, you can perform — Jerus

I admit thou canst do anything,
that nothing is too hard for thee — Mof

I know that you can do anything and that no one can stop you — Tay

3. Who is he that hideth counsel without knowledge? therefore have I uttered that I understood not; things too wonderful for me, which I knew not.

I am the man who obscured your designs with my empty-headed words.
I have been holding forth on matters I cannot understand,
on marvels beyond me and my knowledge — Jerus

Here indeed is one that clouds over the truth with his ignorance! I have spoken as fools speak, of things far beyond my ken — Knox

I thoughtlessly obscured the issues;
I spoke without intelligence,
of wonders beyond my ken — Mof

You ask who it is who has so foolishly denied your providence. It is I. I was talking about things I knew nothing about and did not understand — Tay

4. Hear, I beseech thee, and I will speak: I will demand of thee, and declare thou unto me.

(Listen, I have more to say,
now it is my turn to ask questions and yours to inform me.) — Jerus

Henceforth it is my turn to speak, thine to listen; my turn to ask questions, thine to impart knowledge! — Knox

[You said,] 'Listen and I will speak! Let me put the question to you! See if you can answer them!' — Tay

5. I have heard of thee by the hearing of the ear: but now mine eye seeth thee.

6. Wherefore I abhor myself, and repent in dust and ashes.

. . . and in sorrow I take my seat in the dust — Bas

. . . Wherefore I abhor my words, and repent, seeing I am dust and ashes — JPS

I knew you then only by hearsay;
but now having seen you with my eyes,
I retract all I have said,
and in dust and ashes I repent — Jerus

[But now I say,] 'I had heard about you before, but now I have seen you, and I loathe myself and repent in dust and ashes.' — Tay

7. And it was so, that after the LORD had spoken these words unto Job, the LORD said to Eliphaz the Temanite, My wrath is kindled against thee, and against thy two friends: for ye have not spoken of me the thing that is right, as my servant Job hath.

My indignation is kindled against you and against your two friends; for you have not, as My servant Job, spoken the truth about Me — Ber
You have earned my displeasure, thou and these two friends of thine, by speaking amiss of me as my servant Job never did — Knox

8. **Therefore take unto you now seven bullocks and seven rams, and go to my servant Job, and offer up for yourselves a burnt offering; and my servant Job shall pray for you:**
for him will I accept: lest I deal with you after your folly, in that ye have not spoken of me the thing which is right, like my servant Job.
for I will accept his plea that I deal not with you according to your misdemeanor; for you have not spoken the truth about Me, as My servant Job has — Ber
and for his sake your folly shall be pardoned, that spoke amiss of me when he spoke the truth — Knox
out of regard for him, I will not wreak destruction upon you for your impiety — Mof

9. **So Eliphaz the Temanite and Bildad the Shuhite and Zophar the Naamathite went, and did according as the LORD commanded them: the LORD also accepted Job.**
. . . and the Lord had regard for Job — Ber
. . . and Yahweh listened to Job with favour — Jerus
. . . For Job's sake the Lord pardoned them — Knox

10. **And the LORD turned the captivity of Job, when he prayed for his friends: also the LORD gave Job twice as much as he had before.**
And the Lord made up to Job for all his losses after he had made prayer for his friends . . . — Bas
The Lord gave a turn to the fortune of Job when he interceded for his friends . . . — Ber
Yahweh restored Job's fortunes, because he had prayed for his friends. More than that, Yahweh gave him double what he had before — Jerus
and, as he prayed for these friends of his, the Lord relented at the sight of his penitence. So he gave back to Job twice over all that he had lost — Knox

11. **Then came there unto him all his brethren, and all his sisters, and all they that had been of his acquaintance before, and did eat bread with him in his house: and they bemoaned him, and comforted him over all the evil that the LORD had brought upon him:**
And all his brothers and all his sisters and all his friends of former times came to see him and sat down at table with him. They showed him every sympathy, and comforted him for all the evils Yahweh had inflicted on him — Jerus
. . . and sat down as guests in his house, and made great ado bemoaning all the afflictions the Lord had sent him — Knox
every man also gave him a piece of money, and every one an earring of gold.
And everyone presented him with a lamb and a quarter of a drachm of gold bullion — Sept
Each of them gave him a silver coin, and each a gold ring — Jerus

12. **So the LORD blessed the latter end of Job more than his beginning: for he had fourteen thousand sheep, and six thousand camels, and a thousand yoke of oxen, and a thousand she asses.**
Yahweh blessed Job's new fortune even more than his first one. He came to own . . . — Jerus
A richer man the Lord made Job now than ever he had been in the old days . . . — Knox

13. **He had also seven sons and three daughters.**

14. **And he called the name of the first, Jemima; and the name of the second, Kezia; and the name of the third, Kerenhappuch.**
his first daughter he called 'Turtledove', the second 'Cassia', and the third 'Mascara' — Jerus
. . . Ringdove, Cassia, and Applescent — Mof
the first he called Fair as the Day, and the second Sweet as Cassia, and the third Dark Eyelids — Knox

15. **And in all the land were no women found so fair as the daughters of Job:**

throughout the land there were no women as beautiful as the daughters of Job — Jerus

and their father gave them inheritance among their brethren.

. . . had them inherit on a par with their brothers — Ber

. . . gave them inheritance rights like their brothers — Jerus

. . . put them into his will along with their brothers — Tay

16. After this lived Job an hundred and forty years, and saw his sons, and his sons' sons, even four generations.

17. So Job died, being old and full of days.

Job died, an old man, after a full life — Ber

so he died at last as old men die, that have taken their full toll of the years — Knox

So Job died old and satisfied with days — Rhm

PSALMS
BOOK I

PSALM 1

1. Blessed is the man that walketh not in the counsel of the ungodly,
Happy the man who never goes by the advice of the ungodly — Mof
How happy the man
Who hath not walked in the counsel of the lawless — Rhm
O the blessedness of the man,
Who walketh not in the counsel of the wicked — DeW
Oh, the joys of the man who walks not after the advice of the wicked — Ber
Happy is the man
who does not take the wicked for his guide — NEB
nor standeth in the way of sinners,
who does not loiter in the way taken by sinners — Har
nor walk the road that sinners tread — NEB
nor sitteth in the seat of the scornful.
Nor sits in the seat of scoffers — ABPS
nor joins the company of scoffers — Mof
nor sits in the company of mockers — Lam
nor sits in the company of the insolent — NAB
2. But his delight is in the law of the LORD;
But his delight is in the law of Jehovah — ASV
but finds his joy in the Eternal's law — Mof
but finds his pleasure in the Law of Yahweh — Jerus
But whose greatest pleasure is in the law of the Lord — Har
and in his law doth he meditate day and night.
And in his law doth he talk with himself day and night — Rhm
so that day and night he recites this law to himself — Har
And in his law does he study day and night — AAT
poring over it day and night — Mof
3. And he shall be like a tree planted by the rivers of water,
So he becometh
Like a tree planted by the water-courses — DeW
He stands firm as a tree planted by running water — Knox
that bringeth forth his fruit in his season;
Which shall produce its fruit at the proper season — Sprl
and its fruit shall not fall untimely — Sept
his leaf also shall not wither;
and its leaf withereth not — DeW
and whose leaves never fade — NAB
and whatsoever he doeth shall prosper.
And whatever it bears comes to maturity — AAT
and whatsoever he begins he accomplishes — Lam
success attends all he does — Jerus
In all that he does, he prospers — RSV
and he will do well in all his undertakings — Bas
4. The ungodly are not so:
Not so the ungodly! — Mof
Not so the lawless — Rhm
Not so are the wicked — ABPS
It is nothing like this with the wicked, nothing like this! — Jerus
but are like the chaff which the wind driveth away.
But they are like chaff, which the wind scattereth — DeW
No, they are like chaff swept away by the wind — Mof
But they are like the chaff [worthless, dead, without substance] which the wind drives away — Amp
5. Therefore the ungodly shall not stand in the judgment,
For this cause shall the lawless not stand in the judgment — Rhm
So then the wicked will have no permanent status when judgment is meted out — Har
when judgments come, the ungodly shall not stand — Mof
nor sinners in the congregation of the righteous.
Nor sinners in the assembly of the righteous — Rhm
nor shall the sinful last in the community of the just — Mof
sinners will have no part in the reunion of the just — Knox

and the evil-doers will have no place among the upright — Bas
there will be no sinners where the righteous assemble — Har
6. **For the LORD knoweth the way of the righteous:**
For Jehovah knoweth . . . — ASV
For Yahweh doth acknowledge . . . — Rhm
For the LORD regardeth . . . — JPS
The Eternal cares for the life of the just — Mof
For the Lord watches over the way of the just — NAB
They walk, the just, under the Lord's protection — Knox
but the way of the ungodly shall perish.
But the way of the lawless shall vanish — Rhm
but the way of the wicked vanishes — NAB
the path of the wicked, how soon is it lost to the sight! — Knox
but the way of the wicked is doomed — Jerus
but the way of the ungodly shall end in ruin — Ber

PSALM 2

1. **Why do the heathen rage,**
Why do the nations rage — ASV
Why do the Gentiles rage — Lam
Why are the heathen in tumult — DeW
Wherefore have nations assembled in tumult — Rhm
Why are the nations in an uproar — JPS
Why are the nations in turmoil — NEB
What means this turmoil among the nations — Knox
Why this uproar among the nations — Jerus
Why do the nations conspire — RSV
and the people imagine a vain thing?
And the peoples plot in vain — AAT
and the peoples devise an empty scheme — Ber
and the peoples utter folly — NAB
Why do the peoples cherish vain dreams — Knox
Why do the peoples hatch their futile plots — NEB
Why this impotent muttering of pagans — Jerus
2. **The kings of the earth set themselves,**
Kings of the earth take their stand — DeW
The kings of the earth stand ready — NEB
See how the kings of the earth stand in array — Knox
The kings of the earth rise up — NAB
kings on earth rising in revolt — Jerus
and the rulers take counsel together,
And grave men have met by appointment together — Rhm
and the princes conspire together — NAB
princes plotting — Jerus
against the LORD, and against his anointed, saying,
Against Yahweh
And against his Anointed One [saying] — Rhm
against Yahweh and his Anointed — Jerus
against the Eternal and his chosen one,
crying — Mof
Against JEHOVAH, and against His Messiah, saying — Sprl
against the Lord, and against the King he has anointed, crying — Knox
against the Lord, and against the king of his selection, saying — Bas
3. **Let us break their bands asunder,**
Let us burst their fetters — DeW
Let us break away from their bondage — Knox
Let us tear their restraining bands apart — Ber
Now let us break their fetters! — Jerus
and cast away their cords from us.
And cast from us their bonds! — DeW
and fling off their control — Mof
and fling off their restraints — Har
and let us cast their shackles from us — Ber
and cast their cords [of control] from us — Amp
now let us throw off their yoke! — Jerus
4. **He that sitteth in the heavens shall laugh:**
He who dwelleth in heaven will laugh them to scorn — Sept
He who dwells in heaven is laughing at their threats — Knox

The Enthroned in high heaven laughs — DeW
The One whose throne is in heaven sits laughing — Jerus
the LORD shall have them in derision.
the Lord will treat them with derision — Sept
My Lord will mock at them — Rhm
The Lord makes sport of them — AAT

5. Then shall he speak unto them in his wrath,
and at last, in his displeasure, he will speak out — Knox
Then angrily he addresses them — Jerus
Then He speaks to them in His indignation — Ber
then he rebukes them in anger — NEB
and vex them in his sore displeasure.
And will confound them in his hot displeasure — ABPS
in a rage he strikes them with panic — Jerus
And in His fury will terrify them, saying — Sprl

6. Yet have I set my king upon my holy hill of Zion.
Yet I have installed my king, — On Zion my holy mountain — Rhm
Yet it is I that have annointed my king, On Zion, my holy mount — ABPS
Truly it is I that have established My king
Upon Zion, My holy mountain — JPS
Of me he says, 'I have enthroned my king
on Zion my holy mountain' — NEB
Here, on mount Sion, my sanctuary, I enthrone a king of my own choice — Knox

7. I will declare the decree:
I will tell of the decree of the LORD — RSV
I will repeat the LORD's decree — NEB
Let me tell the Eternal's message — Mof
Let me proclaim Yahweh's decree — Jerus
the LORD hath said unto me, Thou art my Son;
Jehovah said unto me, Thou art my son — ASV
He said to me, "You are my son — RSV
You are now my son — Mof
this day have I begotten thee.
this day am I your father — Mof
today I have become your father — Jerus

8. Ask of me, and I shall give thee the heathen for thine inheritance,
Ask of me what you will:
I will give you nations as your inheritance — NEB
ask, and I make you master of pagans — Mof
and the uttermost parts of the earth for thy possession.
and the remote places of the earth for Your property — Har
the very ends of the world for thy domain — Knox
lord over all to the ends of the earth — Mof

9. Thou shalt break them with a rod of iron;
You will shatter them with an iron shaft — Har
Thou shalt shepherd them with a sceptre of iron — Rhm
Thou shalt herd them like sheep with a crook of iron — Knox
Thou shalt rule them with a rod of iron — Sept
thou shalt dash them in pieces like a potter's vessel.
As a potter's vessel shalt thou shatter them! — DeW
you shall shatter them like a clay pot' — NEB
and toss them aside like potters' earthenware — Har

10. Be wise now therefore, O ye kings:
Now therefore, O kings, act wisely — Ber
Now therefore ye kings shew your prudence — Rhm
Be cautious, therefore, O kings — AAT
And now, O kings, give heed — NAB
be instructed, ye judges of the earth.
Be admonished ye judges of earth — Rhm
Be warned, ye judges of the earth — ABPS
Take warning, O rulers of the earth — AAT
learn your lesson, ye that rule the world — Knox
follow this advice, those of you who rule on earth — Har

11. Serve the LORD with fear,
Serve Jehovah with fear — ASV

Serve Yahweh with reverence — Rhm
worship the Eternal reverently — Mof
and rejoice with trembling.
And exult with trembling awe — Sprl
rejoice and be in high spirits, with trembling [lest you displease him] — Amp
and rejoice before him; with trembling — NAB[1]

12. Kiss the Son, lest he be angry, and ye perish from the way,
Kiss the chosen one,
Lest he be angry and you perish in the way — AAT
do homage to him truly, lest he be angry and you end in ruin — Mof
Kiss the rod, do not brave his anger and go astray from the sure path — Knox
Bow to the ground before Him
lest He become angry and you perish through your indiscretions — Har
pay homage to him,
Lest he be angry and you perish from the way — NAB

when his wrath is kindled but a little.
when his anger blazes suddenly — NAB
For his wrath will soon be kindled — ASV
For quickly will his anger burn — ABPS
for his anger quickly flames — Mof
for His displeasure is quickly provoked — Har
When the fire of his vengeance blazes out suddenly[2] — Knox

Blessed are all they that put their trust in him.
O the blessedness of all that take refuge in Him! — DeW
How happy are all who seek refuge in him! — Rhm
happy are they who find their refuge in him — Knox
But, oh, the joy of all who take refuge in Him! — Ber

PSALM 3

A Psalm of David, when he fled from Absalom his son.

1. LORD, how are they increased that trouble me!
Jehovah, how are mine adversaries increased — ASV
LORD, how my enemies have multiplied — NEB
Jehovah, how many are my foes — ABPS
Yahweh, more and more are turning against me — Jerus

many are they that rise up against me.
Multitudes are rising against me — Rhm
How many are rising against me! — DeW
there are many rising to challenge me — Har
more and more rebelling against me — Jerus

2. Many there be which say of my soul,
Many say respecting my life — Sept
How many are saying of my soul — DeW
People without number are saying of me — Har
more and more saying about me — Jerus

There is no help for him in God.
There is no help for him in his God — PBV
There is no salvation for him in God — ABPS
In this God of his he hath no safety — Sept
His God cannot save him now — Knox
God can do nothing to help him — Har
God will not bring him victory — NEB

Selah.
(Pause.) — ABPS
Selah [pause, and calmly think of that]! Amp

3. But thou, O LORD, art a shield for me;
But thou, O Jehovah, art a shield about me — ASV
But thou, O Lord, art my protector — Sept
But thou, O LORD, art my defender — PBV
Yet, Lord, thou art my champion — Knox

---

[1]NAB connects "with trembling" with verse 12. The Hebrew of verses 11b and 12a is uncertain.

[2]Knox begins a new sentence with these words and construes them with the words that follow.

Ah, but thou shieldest me, O thou Eternal — Mof
But your strength, O Lord, is round me — Bas
my glory, and the lifter up of mine head.
my glory, my sustainer — Har
my glory, and my only hope. You alone can lift my head, now bowed in shame — Tay
thou art my glory, and thou dost raise my head high — NEB

4. I cried unto the LORD with my voice,
I cry unto Jehovah with my voice — ASV
I have but to cry out to the Lord — Knox
Loudly I cry to Yahweh — Jerus
and he heard me out of his holy hill. Selah.
And he answereth me . . . — ASV
And he hears me from his holy mount. (Pause.) — ABPS
and my voice reaches his mountain sanctuary, and there finds hearing — Knox

5. I laid me down and slept;
I lie down and sleep — AAT
Now I can lie down and go to sleep — Jerus
When I lie down in sleep — NAB
Safe in God's hand I lay down, and slept — Knox
I awaked; for the LORD sustained me.
I awoke,
Surely Yahweh sustaineth me! — Rhm
I awoke in safety,
for JEHOVAH sustained me — Sprl
I wake again, for the Lord sustains me — NAB
again, I awake, for the Lord upholds me — Har
and then awake, for Yahweh has hold of me — Jerus
I awoke. Because the Lord will protect me[3] — Sept

6. I will not be afraid of ten thousands of people,
I will not be afraid of myriads of people — Rhm
that have set themselves against me round about.
Who have arrayed themselves . . . — ABPS
That assail me on every side — DeW
who have resisted me from all sides — Har
posted against me wherever I turn — Jerus

7. Arise, O LORD; save me, O my God:
Arise, O LORD!
Deliver me, O my God! — RSV
Arise, O Jehovah! Help me, O my God — DeW
Arise, O JEHOVAH! rescue me, O my God! — Sprl
Bestir thyself, Lord; my God, save me — Knox
Up, O Eternal, to the rescue! — Mof
for thou hast smitten all mine enemies upon the cheek bone;
Thou dost strike all my foes across the face — NEB
Surely Thou hast smitten all mine enemies with a jaw-bone — Sprl
My enemies thou wilt all disable — Mof
Deal my enemies a decisive blow — Har
thou hast broken the teeth of the ungodly.
The teeth of the lawless hast thou broken — Rhm
Thou wilt break the teeth of the wicked — AAT
and the ungodly thou wilt crush — Mof
the teeth of the wicked you break — NAB
and destroy the rapacious evildoer — Har

8. Salvation belongeth unto the LORD:
With Jehovah there is salvation! — DeW
'Tis for the Eternal to bring help — Mof
From the Lord all deliverance comes — Knox
Thine is the victory, O LORD — NEB
thy blessing is upon thy people.
Thy blessing be upon thy people — ASV
and may thy blessing rest upon thy people — NEB
What joys He gives to all His people — Tay
Selah.
(Pause.) — ABPS

[3]Sept construes "Because the Lord will protect me" with verse 6.

PSALM 4

To the chief Musician on Neginoth, A Psalm of David.
For the Chief Musician; on stringed instruments . . . — RV
To the Chief Musician: with stringed instruments. A Melody of David — Rhm
To the director: with harps . . . — AAT
From the Choirmaster's collection. To a string accompaniment . . . — Mof

1. Hear me when I call, O God of my righteousness:
When I call, answer thou me, my righteous God! — ABPS
Answer me when I call, O God, maintainer of my right — NEB
O God, my champion, answer my appeal — Mof
thou hast enlarged me when I was in distress;
Thou hast set me at large when I was in distress — ASV
Thou who didst set me free when I was in distress — JPS
In my distress Thou gavest me relief — DeW
when I am in trouble, you come to my relief — Jerus
have mercy upon me, and hear my prayer.
Be gracious to me and hear my prayer — ABPS
Pity me now, and hear my prayer! — DeW
Shew me favour and hear my prayer — Rhm

2. O ye sons of men, how long will ye turn my glory into shame?
. . . how long shall my glory be turned into dishonour — RV
. . . how long will ye blaspheme mine honour — PBV
. . . how long shall my glory be put to shame — JPS
Men, how long will you obscure my glory — Lam
How long, mortal men, shall my honor be defamed — Har
Men of rank, how long will you be dull of heart — NAB
Great ones of the world, will your hearts always be hardened — Knox
how long will ye love vanity, and seek after leasing?
. . . and seek after falsehood — RV
How long will you love futility and pursue falsehood — Ber
How long will you love vain words, and seek after lies — RSV
how long will you give your love to foolish things, going after what is false — Bas
will you never cease setting your heart on shadows, following a lie — Knox
or set your heart on trifles and run after lies — NEB
In that ye love vanity, and seek after falsehood — JPS
Selah.
Selah [pause, and calmly think of that]! — Amp

3. But know that the LORD hath set apart him that is godly for himself:
But know that the LORD hath set apart the godly man as His own — JPS
But know that the Lord has set apart the redeemed for Himself — Ber
But know that Jehovah has set apart his Beloved — ABPS
Know ye then that Yahweh hath set apart the man of lovingkindness for himself — Rhm
Know that the Lord does wonders for his faithful one — NAB
To the souls he loves, be sure the Lord shews wondrous favour — Knox
Know this, Yahweh works wonders for those he loves — Jerus
the Lord will hear when I call unto him.
Jehovah will hear when I call unto him. — ASV
The Eternal listens when I call to him — Mof

4. Stand in awe, and sin not:
Tremble ye and sin not! — DeW
Be deeply moved but do not sin — Rhm
Be agitated, but do not sin — Ber
Be angry, but sin not — RSV
Let this challenge you, and stop sinning — Har
Stand before the Lord in awe, and do not sin against Him — Tay
Let there be fear in your hearts, and do no sin — Bas
Be afraid lest ye should sin — Sprl
commune with your own heart upon your bed, and be still.
Ponder in your own heart upon your bed and be silent — Rhm
reflect, upon your beds, in silence — NAB

take thought, as you lie awake, in the silence of your hearts — Knox
spend your night in quiet meditation — Jerus
Lie quietly upon your bed in silent meditation — Tay
Selah.
5. **Offer the sacrifices of righteousness,**
Offer righteous sacrifices — AAT
offer true sacrifice — Mof
Offer sacrifice in a right spirit — Jerus
and put your trust in the LORD.
and confide ye in JEHOVAH — Sprl
and trust the Eternal — Mof
6. **There be many that say, Who will shew us any good?**
There are many that say,
Who will show us where good may be found — DeW
There are many who say, O that we might see some good! — AAT
Many are saying, Who will cause us to see good — ABPS
Many say, Oh, that we might see better times! — NAB
Multitudes are saying
Who will shew us prosperity — Rhm
Many long for a sight of prosperous days — Mof
Many say that God will never help us — Tay
LORD, lift thou up the light of thy countenance upon us.
Lift upon us, O Jehovah!
The light of thy presence — DeW
do thou, then, Lord, shew us the sunshine of thy favour — Knox
Bestow Your good will upon us, Lord — Har
Prove them wrong, O Lord, by letting the light of your face shine upon us — Tay
But the light of thy presence has fled from us, O LORD — NEB
7. **Thou hast put gladness in my heart, more than in the time that their corn and their wine increased.**
Yet in my heart thou hast put more happiness than they enjoyed when there was corn and wine in plenty — NEB
Yes, the gladness you have given me is far greater than their joys at harvest time as they gaze at their bountiful crops — Tay
You put gladness into my heart, more than when grain and wine abound — NAB
Never did rich harvests of corn and wine bring gladness like the gladness thou puttest into my heart — Knox
Yahweh, you have given more joy to my heart
than others ever knew, for all their corn and wine — Jerus
8. **I will both lay me down in peace, and sleep:**
In peace will I both lay me down and sleep — RV
In peace I will lay me down,
And at once will sleep — DeW
As soon as I lie down, I fall peacefully asleep — NAB
Even as I lie down, sleep comes, and with sleep tranquility — Knox
So quietly I lay me down to sleep — Mof
for thou, LORD, only makest me dwell in safety.
For Thou alone, O JEHOVAH, wilt cause me to abide in safety — Sprl
for you alone, O LORD,
bring security to my dwelling — NAB
for You, Lord, alone afford me a secure existence — Har
what need, Lord, of aught but thyself to bring me confidence — Knox
For THOU, O Jehovah! when I am alone
Makest me to dwell securely — DeW
for even alone, thanks to thee, I am secure — Mof

PSALM 5

To the chief Musician upon Nehiloth, A Psalm of David.
For the Chief Musician; with the Nehiloth ... — RV
To the chief Musician. To the music of wind-instruments ... — ABPS
To the director: for the flutes ... — AAT

1. **Give ear to my words, O LORD,**
... O Jehovah — ASV
Ponder my words, O LORD — PBV
consider my meditation.
Consider my complaining — ABPS

Heed Thou my moaning — DeW
give heed to my groaning — RSV
Understand thou my softly murmured prayer — Rhm
Attend to my sighing — AAT
and hear the murmur of my soul — Mof
give thought to my heart-searchings —Bas

2. Hearken unto the voice of my cry, my King, and my God:
Hearken to my cry for help,
My King and my God! — DeW

for unto thee will I pray.
For unto thee do I pray — Rhm
for it is to You that I am appealing — Har

3. My voice shalt thou hear in the morning, O LORD;
Jehovah, at morning Thou hearest my voice — YLT
O LORD, in the morning thou dost hear my voice — RSV
oh hear my morning prayer — Mof

in the morning will I direct my prayer unto thee, and will look up.
In the morning will I order my prayer unto thee, and will keep watch — ASV
in the morning I prepare a sacrifice for thee, and watch — RSV
in the morning I prepare for You and expect You — Har
In the morning I will lay it before thee and wait — AAT
at dawn I bring my plea expectantly before you — NAB
early in the morning I lay my petition before thee and await thy pleasure — Knox
and at dawn I hold myself in readiness for you,
I watch for you — Jerus

4. For thou art not a God that hath pleasure in wickedness:
. . . a God who welcomes wickedness — NEB
For not a God finding pleasure in lawlessness art thou — Rhm
Because thou art not a God pleased with iniquity — Sept
Thou art no God to take delight in vice — Mof

neither shall evil dwell with thee.
evil shall not sojourn with thee — RV
evil has no place in Your activities — Har
And wrong can be no guest of thine — Rhm
therefore he who is wicked cannot dwell near thee — Sept
and cannot tolerate the slightest sin — Tay

5. The foolish shall not stand in thy sight:
The arrogant . . . — RV
The proud . . . — ABPS
Boasters shall not station themselves before thine eyes — Rhm
There is no place for arrogance before thee — NEB
no arrogance can look thee in the face — Mof
boasters collapse
under your scrutiny — Jerus
Therefore proud sinners will not survive your searching gaze — Tay

thou hatest all workers of iniquity.
Thou hatest the wrongdoer — Knox
Thou hatest all who practice the wrong — Ber
You abhor all evildoers — Amp

6. Thou shalt destroy them that speak leasing:
Thou shalt destroy them that speak lies — PBV
thou makest an end of all liars — NEB

the Lord will abhor the bloody and deceitful man.
the LORD abhorreth the blood-thirsty and deceitful man — RV
blood-thirsty and treacherous men the Lord holds in abhorrence — Knox
The LORD detests traitors and men of blood — NEB
murderers and frauds
Yahweh detests — Jerus
Bloodshed and fraud, Jehovah abhorreth — DeW

7. But as for me, I will come into thy house in the multitude of thy mercy:
But as for me, in the abundance of thy lovingkindness will I come into thy house — ASV
But as for me, by the greatness of Thy unfailing love
I will enter Thy house — Ber
As for me, I through thine abundant mercy, will go to thy house — Sept
But I through the abundance of thy steadfast love
will enter thy house — RSV
but I have access to thy house, by thy great generosity — Mof

I, then, encompassed by thy mercy, will betake myself to thy house — Knox

and in thy fear will I worship toward thy holy temple.

I will bow down towards thy holy temple in reverence of thee — Rhm

at Thy holy temple I will worship in reverence of Thee — Ber

I can bow reverently before thy sacred shrine — Mof

8. Lead me, O LORD, in thy righteousness because of mine enemies;

O Yahweh! lead me in thy righteousness because of mine adversaries — Rhm

O JEHOVAH, lead me into Thy righteousness,
Because of my watchful enemies — Sprl

because of my enemies, guide me in your justice — NAB

make thy way straight before my face.

make thy way plain before my face — RV

make thy path smooth before me — Mof

Make Your way level (straight and right) before my face — Amp

give me a straight path to follow — NEB

Tell me clearly what to do, which way to turn — Tay

9. For there is no faithfulness in their mouth;

For there is no sincerity in their mouth — JPS

For there is no justice in their mouth — Lam

For there is no stability in their mouth — YLT

For there is nothing certain in their mouth — ABPS

For there is nothing in their speech upon which one can rely — Ber

because there is no truth in their mouth — Sept

For no faith may be put in their words — Bas

Not a word from their lips can be trusted — Jerus

their inward part is very wickedness;

Their inward purpose is engulphing ruin — Rhm

Their inward part is a yawning gulf — JPS

Their inward part is corruption — ABPS

their inner part is nothing but evil — Bas

Their heart is false — Sept

their hearts are deep with mischief — Mof

their heart teems with treacheries — NAB

their heart is treacherous — AAT

their hearts are all treachery — Knox

their heart is a destructive chasm — Ber

their heart is destruction — RSV

their motives are destruction — Har

deep within them lies ruin — Jerus

Their hearts are filled to the brim with wickedness — Tay

they are nothing but wind — NEB

their throat is an open sepulchre;

An open grave is their throat — YLT

their mouths gaping tombs — Knox

their throats are yawning graves — Jerus

Their suggestions are full of the stench of sin and death — Tay

they flatter with their tongue.

with their tongues they practised deceit — Sept

smooth-tongued deceivers! — Mof

smooth talk runs off their tongues — NEB

they make their tongues so smooth! — Jerus

10. Destroy thou them, O God;

Hold them guilty, O God — RV

Declare them guilty O God — Rhm

Judge them, O God — Sept

Bring ruin on them, O God — NEB

let them fall by their own counsels;

They shall fall by their own counsels — ABPS

let them perish through their own imaginations — PBV

let them fall for their devices — Sept

let their own plots end them — Mof

let them fall foul of their own schemes — Har

make their intrigues their own downfall! — Jerus

cast them out in the multitude of their transgressions;

Into the throng of their own transgressions thrust them down — Rhm

for the mass of their transgressions thrust them away — Ber

according to the multitude of their crimes cast them out — Sept

Down with them, for their many crimes — Mof
Banish them for their repeated transgressions — Har
Hound them for their countless crimes — Jerus
for they have rebelled against thee.
have they not defied thee? — Knox
11. **But let all those that put their trust in thee rejoice:**
But let all those that take refuge in thee rejoice — ASV
May all these who come to You for shelter be happy — Har
let them ever shout for joy, because thou defendest them:
They shall ever shout for joy, and thou wilt defend them — ABPS
They shall exult forever, and thou wilt dwell among them — Sept
For ever let them sing for joy!
And do Thou shelter them — DeW
let them ever sing for joy;
and do thou defend them — RSV
let them also that love thy name be joyful in thee.
And they may leap for joy in thee who are lovers of thy Name — Rhm
and all who love thy name will glory in thee — Sept
lovers of thy name ever exult in thee — Mof
all they that love thy name shall be strengthened by thee — Lam
that those who love thy name may exult in thee — RSV
that those who cherish Your name may rejoice in You — Har

12. **For thou, LORD, wilt bless the righteous;**
with favour wilt thou compass him as with a shield.
Thou dost surround him with favor as with a shield. — AAT
as with an all-covering shield — with good pleasure wilt thou encompass him — Rhm
Thou, O Lord, hast covered us with armour of favour — Sept
thou dost throw thy loving-kindness about us like a shield — Knox
you surround him with the shield of your good will — NAB
you protect him with your shield of love — Tay

PSALM 6

To the chief Musician on Neginoth upon Sheminith, A Psalm of David.
For the Chief Musician; on stringed instruments, set to the Sheminith . . . — RV
To the Chief Musician, with stringed Instruments upon the eighth. A Melody of David — Rhm
A Psalm of David's to the Eternal Victor, upon a harp of eight strings — Sprl
To the choir-master. On stringed instruments. Over the octave. A psalm. Of David — Knox
For the choirmaster. For strings, for the octachord . . . — Jerus
the Choirmaster's collection. To a string accompaniment. For bass voices . . . — Mof

1. **O LORD, rebuke me not in thine anger,**
O Yahweh! do not in thine anger correct me — Rhm
Lord, when thou dost reprove me, let it not be in anger — Knox
neither chasten me in thy hot displeasure.
And do not in thy hot displeasure correct me — ABPS
Neither chasten me in Thy burning indignation — Sprl
do not send punishment on me in the heat of your passion — Bas
when thou dost chastise me, let it not be in displeasure — Knox
2. **Have mercy upon me, O LORD; for I am weak:**
Have mercy upon me, O Jehovah: for I am withered away — ASV
Be gracious to me, Jehovah, for I waste away — ABPS
O LORD, heal me; for my bones are vexed.
O Jehovah, heal me; for my bones are troubled — ASV
Heal me, O Jehovah! for my bones are trembling — DeW
Heal me, O LORD, for my bones are affrighted — JPS
Assuage my pain, O JEHOVAH, for my bones ache — Sprl
make me well, for even my bones are troubled — Bas
cure me, Lord, for my bones are racked with terror — Har
heal me, my bones are in torment — Jerus
heal me, my very bones are shaken — NEB

3. My soul is also sore vexed:
My soul also is sore troubled — ASV
Yea my soul is dismayed greatly — Rhm
And my soul is sorely shaken — ABPS
My soul, too, is utterly terrified — NAB
my soul is in utter torment — Jerus
my spirits are altogether broken — Knox
I am greatly distraught — Har
My [inner] self [as well as my body] is also exceedingly disturbed and troubled — Amp
but thou, O LORD, how long?
but, LORD, how long wilt thou punish me — PBV
Lord, wilt thou never be content — Knox
Why do You linger so, Lord — Har
But You, O Lord, how long [until You return and speak peace to me] — Amp
4. Return, O LORD, deliver my soul:
Return, O Jehovah! rescue my soul! — DeW
Come back, Yahweh, rescue my soul — Jerus
O thou Eternal, save my life once more — Mof
Change Your attitude and rescue me, Lord — Har
oh save me for thy mercies' sake.
Save me for the sake of thy lovingkindness — Rhm
. . . for the sake of Thy covenant love — Ber
. . . in Your loving compassion — Har
. . . if you love me — Jerus
for thy love's sake, succour me — Mof
deliver me for the sake of thy steadfast love — RSV
5. For in death there is no remembrance of thee:
For in death none can make mention of thee — Sept
for in death's realm there is no thought of thee — Mof
For in death there are no memorials made to Thee — Ber
None talk of thee among the dead — NEB
in the grave who shall give thee thanks?
In Sheol who shall give thee thanks — ASV
In the underworld who will give thee thanks — ABPS
In the world unseen, who shall give Thee praise — DeW
none can praise thee in the tomb — Knox
6. I am weary with my groaning;
I am weary with my sighing — Rhm
I faint with moaning — Mof
I am worn out with moaning — AAT
I am spent with sighing — Knox
all the night make I my bed to swim;
every night my bed is drenched with tears — Mof
every night I lie weeping on my bed — Knox
all night long my pillow is wet with tears — NEB
I water my couch with tears.
I soak my bed with weeping — NEB
With my tears I cause my bed to dissolve — Rhm
7. Mine eye is consumed because of grief;
Mine eye wasteth away because of grief — RV
My beauty is gone for very trouble — PBV
My face is all sunken with sorrow — Rhm
Shrivelled with grief is mine eye — DeW
trouble wears away my strength — Mof
Grief has dimmed my eyes — Knox
it waxeth old because of all mine enemies.
they are worn out with all my woes — NEB
I age under outrages from my foes — Mof
I have grown old with enemies all round me — Jerus
8. Depart from me, all ye workers of iniquity;
. . . all you that traffic in iniquity — Knox
Begone, all of you, evildoers! — Mof
for the LORD hath heard the voice of my weeping.
For the LORD has heard the sound of my weeping — AAT
For Jehovah heareth my weeping — DeW
The Eternal listens to my wail — Mof
the Lord has heard my cry of distress — Knox

9. The LORD hath heard my supplication:
The LORD has heard my entreaty — AAT
The LORD hath heard my petition — PBV
the LORD will receive my prayer,
the LORD will accept my prayer — NEB
10. Let all mine enemies be ashamed and sore vexed:
Let all my enemies be ashamed and defeated — Lam
Let all my foes turn pale and be greatly dismayed — Rhm
All my foes shall be ashamed and greatly terrified — AAT
My foes shall all be utterly dismayed — Mof
My enemies will all burn with shame, and be horrified — Har
All my enemies shall be put to shame in utter terror— NAB
let them return and be ashamed suddenly.
Again let them turn pale in a moment — Rhm
they shall be turned back, and put to shame suddenly — PBV
They shall retreat, and in a moment be put to the blush — Sprl
once again they will experience sudden humiliation — Har
they shall fall back in sudden shame — NAB
they shall turn away in sudden confusion — NEB

PSALM 7

Shiggaion of David, which he sang unto the LORD, concerning the words of Cush the Benjamite.
An Ode of David: which he sang unto Yahweh, on account of the words of Cush the Benjamite — Rhm
A plaintive song of David, which he sang to Jehovah concerning the words of Cush, a Benjamite — ABPS
A dithyramb of David, sung to the Eternal, about the taunts of Cush the Benjamite — Mof
Lamentation Of David, who sang it to Yahweh about Cush the Benjaminite — Jerus
An Ode of David, [probably] in a wild, irregular, enthusiastic strain, which he sang to the Lord, concerning the words of Cush, a Benjamite — Amp

1. O LORD my God, in thee do I put my trust:
O Jehovah my God, in thee do I take refuge — ASV
I have taken shelter in thee, O LORD, my God — AAT
save me from all them that persecute me, and deliver me:
save me from all them that pursue me, and deliver me — RV
from all who hound me, save me, rescue me — Jerus
2. Lest he tear my soul like a lion,
Lest they tear my soul like a lion — ASV
rending it in pieces, while there is none to deliver.
Rending in pieces, and there be no deliverer! — ABPS
dragging me away, with none to rescue — RSV
3. O LORD my God, if I have done this;
O JEHOVAH my God, if I have acted thus — Sprl
O LORD, my God, if I am at fault in this — NAB
O LORD my God, if I have done any of these things — NEB
if there be iniquity in my hands;
If there hath been perversity in my hands — Rhm
If iniquity cling to my hands — DeW
if I have stained my hands with guilt — NEB
If there is guilt on my hands — AAT
if there is injustice on my hands — Ber
4. If I have rewarded evil unto him that was at peace with me;
If I have requited my friend with wrong — Rhm
If I have requited evil to him who sought my welfare — Sprl
If I have paid back with evil him who was at peace with me — Amp
(yea, I have delivered him that without cause is mine enemy:)
Or have oppressed mine adversary without need — Rhm
if I made havoc of my foe for no cause — Mof
or plundered my enemy without cause — RSV
or caused my opponents needless loss — Har
or set free an enemy who attacked me without cause — NEB

I who spared those who without cause were my foes — NAB
I, that would rescue my causeless foe — DeW

5. Let the enemy persecute my soul, and take it;
Then let the enemy pursue my soul, and overtake it — ABPS
then let the foe chase me,
then let the foe catch me — Mof
may the enemy hunt me down until he overtakes me — Har

yea, let him tread down my life upon the earth,
may he trample my very life to the ground — Har
let him stamp my life into the ground — Jerus

and lay mine honour in the dust.
and lay my glory in the dust — RV
let him lay me low in the dust! — Mof
and lay my soul in the dust — RSV
and level my pride with the dust! — Knox
and leave my entrails lying in the dust! — Jerus

Selah.
(Pause.) — ABPS

6. Arise, O LORD, in thine anger,
Bestir thyself in anger, O Eternal — Mof

lift up thyself because of the rage of mine enemies:
Lift thyself up because of the haughty outbursts of mine adversaries — Rhm
Lift Thyself against the wrath of my foes! — DeW
lift thyself up against the fury of my enemies — RSV
lift up thyself over the neck of mine enemies — Lam
rouse thyself in wrath against my foes — NEB
stir up opposition to my violent enemies — Har

and awake for me to the judgment that thou hast commanded.
and awake for me; thou hast commanded judgement — RV
Awake, my God who hast ordered that justice be done — NEB
Yea, arouse Thee in my behalf,
Thou that hast justice at Thy command — DeW
Stir up for me the justice thou hast commanded — Rhm
awake, O my God; thou hast appointed a judgment — RSV
awake for me, Thou who has ordained judgment — Ber
bestir thyself, O Lord my God, in defence of the laws thou thyself hast given us — Knox
awake to aid us, to maintain the right — Mof
Wake up; demand justice for me — Har

7. So shall the congregation of the people compass thee about:
Let the nations muster around you in a body — Jerus
let the peoples assemble around thee — NEB
Let an assembly of nations surround Thee — DeW
Summon all nations before thee — Mof
Gather all peoples before you — Tay
When the assembly of peoples gather round thee — Rhm

for their sakes therefore return thou on high.
Then above it — on high do thou return — Rhm
And to Thy throne high above them, return! — DeW
be seated on thy lofty throne — Mof
take your seat, then, over them, on high — Bas
and over it take thy seat on high — RSV
preside over them from the regions above — Har

8. The LORD shall judge the people:
JEHOVAH will plead the cause of His people — Sprl
The Lord will plead my cause with the people — Har
Jehovah will judge the nations — ABPS
Jehovah ruleth the nations — DeW
May the LORD judge the people — Ber
Yahweh is arbiter of nations — Jerus
O LORD, thou who dost pass sentence on the nations — NEB

judge me, O LORD, according to my righteousness, and according to mine integrity that is in me.
judge me, O Lord, according to my righteousness: and according to mine innocence be for me — Sept
do me justice, O LORD,
In accordance with my righteousness and my integrity — AAT
Do me justice, O LORD, because I am just,

and because of the innocence that is mine — NAB

Give judgement for me, Yahweh: as my virtue and my integrity deserve — Jerus

Vindicate me, O LORD, according to my righteousness
and according to the integrity that is upon me — Ber

O LORD, judge me as my righteousness deserves,
for I am clearly innocent — NEB

But justify me publicly; establish my honor and truth before them all — Tay

9. Oh let the wickedness of the wicked come to an end; but establish the just:

Let the wrong of the lawless I pray thee come to an end,
And establish thou him that is righteous — Rhm

Let, I pray Thee, the wickedness of the wicked be brought to nought,
And do Thou establish the Righteous One — Sprl

Let the malice of the wicked come to an end,
but sustain the just — NAB

Let the wicked men do no more harm, establish the reign of righteousness — NEB

for the righteous God trieth the hearts and reins.

For the righteous God trieth the minds and hearts — ASV

For Thou triest the depths of the heart, O righteous God — DeW

for Thou, who triest hearts and emotions, art a righteous God — Ber

The God of justice reads the inmost heart — Mof

10. My defence is of God, which saveth the upright in heart.

My shield is with God,
Who saveth the upright in heart — ASV

My shield is held by God,
Who is ready to save the upright in heart — Rhm

It is God who beareth my shield,
He that helpeth the upright in heart — DeW

My help cometh of God, who preserveth them that are true of heart — PBV

From the Lord, refuge of true hearts, my protection comes — Knox

God is the shield that protects me,
he preserves upright hearts — Jerus

11. God judgeth the righteous, and God is angry with the wicked every day.

God is a righteous Judge, strong, and patient; and God is provoked every day — PBV

God is a righteous judge, yea, a God that hath indignations every day — RV

God is a righteous judge;
And God is angry every day — ABPS

God, who is a righteous Judge,
And a wrathful Power every day — DeW

God judges ever true; day by day his indignation mounts up — Knox

God is a just judge,
every day he requites the raging enemy — NEB

God is an equitable judge,
a God who is daily pronouncing sentence — Har

A just judge is God,
a God who punishes day by day — NAB

12. If he turn not, he will whet his sword; he hath bent his bow, and made it ready.

If a man turn not, he will whet his sword;
He hath bent his bow, and made it ready — ASV

If one repent not, He whetteth His sword;
His bow, He hath bent and aimeth — DeW

There he is, whetting his sword again!
His bow is strung and stretched — Mof

He sharpens his sword,
strings his bow and makes it ready — NEB

13. He hath also prepared for him the instruments of death; he ordaineth his arrows against the persecutors.

. . . He maketh his arrows fiery shafts — ASV

He hath also prepared for him the weapons of death,
Yea, His arrows which He made sharp — JPS

His deadly darts are ready,
his arrows are fire-tipped — Mof

deadly are the weapons he is preparing for them; he has barbed his arrows with fire — Knox

14. Behold, he travaileth with iniquity, and hath conceived mischief, and brought forth falsehood.
Lo! He gendereth trouble,
And conceiveth mischief
But giveth birth to a disappointment — Rhm
But the enemy is in labour with iniquity;
he conceives mischief and his brood is lies — NEB
See how the wicked man travails with iniquity
and is pregnant with malice,
bringing forth falsehood — Har
Behold, the wicked man conceives evil,
and is pregnant with mischief,
and brings forth lies — RSV
the scoundrel is alive with malice,
hatching mischief and deception — Mof
The wicked man conceives an evil plot, labors with its dark details, and brings to birth his treachery and lies — Tay

15. He made a pit, and digged it, and is fallen into the ditch which he made.
He digged a pit, and hollowed it out,
And fell into the ditch he made — ABPS
He dug a pit, hollowed it out,
only to fall into his own trap! — Jerus

16. His mischief shall return upon his own head, and his violent dealing shall come down upon his own pate.
His mischief will return upon his own head,
And upon his crown will his violence descend — ABPS
His malice rebounds on his own head;
his violence descends on himself alone — Har
His spite recoils on his own head,
his brutality falls back on his own skull — Jerus

17. I will praise the LORD according to his righteousness: and will sing praise to the name of the LORD most high.
I will give thanks unto Jehovah according to his righteousness,
And will sing praise to the name of Jehovah Most High — ASV
I will give to the LORD the thanks due to his righteousness,
and I will sing praise to the name of the LORD, the Most High — RSV
I will commend the Lord for his justice;
I will sing praise to the name of the Lord Most High — Har
I shall praise the Lord for his loving kindness. I shall sing to the name of the Lord Most High — Sept
I will ever thank the Lord for his just retribution, singing praises to the name of the Lord, the most High — Knox

PSALM 8

To the chief Musician upon Gittith, A Psalm of David.
For the Chief Musician; set to the Gittith . . . — RV
To the Chief Musician On "the Gittith". A Melody of David — Rhm
From the Choirmaster's collection. Set to a vintage melody. A song of David. — Mof

1. O LORD our Lord, how excellent is thy name in all the earth! who hast set thy glory above the heavens.
O LORD our Governor, how excellent is thy Name in all the world; thou hast set thy glory above the heavens! — PBV
O LORD our sovereign,
how glorious is thy name in all the earth!
Thy majesty is praised high as the heavens — NEB
O Yahweh our Lord!
How majestic is thy Name in all the earth,
Who hast set thy splendour upon the heavens — Rhm
O LORD, our Lord, how thy name ought to be admired in all the earth, since thine excellence is exalted above the heavens! — Sept
O LORD, our Lord,
how majestic is thy name in all the earth!
Thou whose glory above the heavens is chanted[4] — RSV
O LORD, our Master, how the majesty of thy name fills all the earth! Thy greatness is high above heaven itself — Knox

[4]RSV construes the last clause with verse 2.

O Jehovah, our LORD, how glorious is Thy name in all the earth!
Thou hast displayed thy majesty above the heavens — Ber

Lord God, how renowned is Your name in all the earth,
for You have established Your majesty in the heavens — Har

O Lord our God, the majesty and glory of your name fills all the earth and overflows the heavens — Tay

2. Out of the mouth of babes and sucklings hast thou ordained strength because of thine enemies, that thou mightest still the enemy and the avenger.

by the mouth of babes and infants,
thou hast founded a bulwark because of thy foes,
to still the enemy and the avenger — RSV

Thou hast made the lips of children, of infants at the breast, vocal with praise, to confound thy enemies; to silence malicious and revengeful tongues — Knox

Out of the mouths of babes, of infants at the breast,
thou hast rebuked the mighty,
silencing enmity and vengeance to teach thy foes a lesson — NEB

You have taught the little children to praise you perfectly. May their example shame and silence your enemies! — Tay

3. When I consider thy heavens, the work of thy fingers, the moon and the stars, which thou hast ordained;

When I look at thy heavens, the work of thy fingers,
the moon and the stars which thou hast established — RSV

When I contemplate Your handiwork in the skies,
the moon and the stars which You have set in position — Har

4. What is man, that thou art mindful of him? and the son of man, that thou visitest him?

What was weak man that thou shouldst make mention of him?
Or the son of the earthborn that thou shouldst set him in charge — Rhm

I exclaim: What is mean man, that Thou art mindful of him?
And the son of man, that Thou shouldst notice him — Sprl

What is man that thou shouldst think of him,
And the son of man that thou shouldst care for him — AAT

5. For thou hast made him a little lower than the angels, and hast crowned him with glory and honour.

Yet Thou hast made him little less than heavenly beings,
and Thou dost crown him with glory and honor — Ber

For thou hast made him but little lower than God, and crownest him with glory and honour — RV

Thou hast made him little less than Divine,
And with glory and honour hast crowned him! — DeW

Yet thou hast made him little less than a god,
crowning him with glory and honour — NEB

In comparison with Deity You made him inferior,
yet graced him with glory and dignity — Har

6. Thou madest him to have dominion over the works of thy hands; thou hast put all things under his feet:

You gave him authority over Your creation,
making everything subservient to him — Har

7. All sheep and oxen, yea, and the beasts of the field;

Sheep and oxen, all of them;
Yea, and the beasts of the field — ABPS

the sheep and the cattle, and the wild beasts besides — Knox

8. The fowl of the air, and the fish of the sea, and whatsoever passeth through the paths of the seas.

birds of the air and fish of the sea —
all that swims on the wet sea paths! — Mof

the birds in the air and the fish in the sea,
and all that moves along the paths of ocean — NEB

9. O LORD our Lord, how excellent is thy name in all the earth![5]

[5]See verse 1.

PSALM 9

To the chief Musician upon Muthlabben, A Psalm of David.

For the Chief Musician; set to Muthlabben . . . — RV

To the chief Musician. After [the melody] Death of the Son . . . — ABPS

To the Eternal Victor. A Psalm of David upon the death of his son — Sprl

From the Choirmaster's collection. For a soprano boys' choir. A song of David — Mof

1. I will praise thee, O LORD, with my whole heart; I will shew forth all thy marvellous works.

I will praise Yahweh with all my heart,
I will recount all thy wonderful doings — Rhm

I thank you, Yahweh, with all my heart;
I recite your marvels one by one — Jerus

2. I will be glad and rejoice in thee: I will sing praise to thy name, O thou most High.

I will be glad and exult in thee: . . . — RV

I thrill and triumph in thee,
singing praise to thee . . . — Mof

I am happy and jubilant because of You, loudly proclaiming Your name, Most High — Har

3. When mine enemies are turned back, they shall fall and perish at thy presence.

When mine enemies turn back,
They stumble and perish at thy presence — ASV

For mine enemies turn back;
They stumble . . . — DeW

For my foes are routed,
stumbling to their ruin at thy frown — Mof

See how my enemies turn back, how they faint and melt away at the sight of thee! — Knox

My enemies are in retreat,
stumbling, perishing as you confront them — Jerus

4. For thou hast maintained my right and my cause; thou satest in the throne judging right.

For thou hast maintained my right and my cause; thou art set in the throne that judgest right — PBV

. . . Thou sittest on the throne, a righteous Judge — DeW

For thou hast executed my right and my cause,
Thou hast sat on the throne judging righteously — Rhm

you have upheld the justice of my cause
from the throne where you sit as righteous judge — Jerus

5. Thou hast rebuked the heathen, thou hast destroyed the wicked, thou hast put out their name for ever and ever.

Thou hast rebuked the nations, thou hast destroyed the wicked, thou hast blotted out their name for ever and ever — RV

You have reprimanded pagan nations and dispersed the wicked,
obliterating their name for ever — Har

6. O thou enemy, destructions are come to a perpetual end: and thou hast destroyed cities; their memorial is perished with them.

The enemy are come to an end, they are desolate for ever; and the cities which thou hast overthrown, their very memorial is perished — RV

The foe — they are destroyed;
Perpetual ruins are the cities which thou hast rooted up;
The very memory of them has perished — AAT

The enemy have vanished in everlasting ruins;
their cities thou hast rooted out;
the very memory of them has perished — RSV

Spent is the enemy's power, doomed to everlasting ruin; the memory of them has died with the fall of their cities — Knox

7. But the LORD shall endure for ever: he hath prepared his throne for judgment.

But the LORD sitteth as king for ever . . . — RV

But the LORD is enthroned for ever;
He hath established His throne for judgment — JPS

But the Lord is enthroned for ever;
He has established His seat for government — Har

The LORD thunders, he sits enthroned for ever:
he has set up his throne, his judgment-seat — NEB

8. And he shall judge the world in righteousness, he shall minister judgment to the people in uprightness.
HE judgeth the world in righteousness;
HE ruleth the nations justly — DeW
he governs all the world with justice,
ruling its folk with equity — Mof
He will judge mankind with equity,
and will impose just punishments on the peoples — Har

9. The LORD also will be a refuge for the oppressed, a refuge in times of trouble.
Jehovah also will be a high tower for the oppressed,
A high tower in times of trouble — ASV
The LORD is a stronghold for the oppressed,
a stronghold in times of trouble — RSV
The Lord will be a refuge for the oppressed;
a safe retreat in times of emergency — Har
And JEHOVAH, He will be a refuge for the poor,
a high fortress in times of distress — Sprl
Jehovah is a tower for the crushed;
A tower for their times of sore pressure — DeW
So the downtrodden are safe with the Eternal,
he is a refuge in desperate hours — Mof
Thus be Yahweh a refuge for the crushed one,
A refuge for times of destitution — Rhm
So let Jehovah be a refuge for the oppressed,
A refuge in times of distress — ABPS
So may the LORD be a tower of strength for the oppressed,
a tower of strength in time of need — NEB

10. And they that know thy name will put their trust in thee: for thou, LORD, hast not forsaken them that seek thee.
And they that know thy Name will put their trust in thee; for thou, LORD, hast never failed them that seek thee — PBV
Thus let them who know thy Name put confidence in thee,
That thou hast not forsaken the searchers for thee O Yahweh — Rhm
those who know what thou art can trust in thee,
for never wilt thou abandon those those who seek thee — Mof
Those who acknowledge your name can rely on you,
you never desert those who seek you, Yahweh — Jerus

11. Sing praises to the LORD, which dwelleth in Zion: declare among the people his doings.
Sing praise to Jehovah, who dwells in Zion;
Make known his deeds among the peoples — ABPS
Strike the harp to Jehovah, enthroned in Zion;
Tell among the nations His doings — DeW
Sing, then, to the Lord, who dwells in Sion, tell the Gentiles of his great deeds — Knox
To Yahweh, with his home in Zion, sing praise,
tell the nations of his mighty actions — Jerus
Oh, sing out your praises to the God who lives in Jerusalem. Tell the world about his unforgettable deeds — Tay

12. When he maketh inquisition for blood, he remembereth them: he forgetteth not the cry of the humble.
For he that maketh inquisition for blood remembereth them: he forgetteth not the cry of the poor — RV
how he, the avenger of blood, cares for the afflicted, does not forget them when they cry to him — Knox
how he bears you in mind, this Avenger of bloodshed,
how he never forgets the wail of the weak — Mof
That he who makes inquisition for blood has remembered them,
Has not forgotten the cry of the suffering — ABPS
For the Avenger of blood remembereth —
He forgetteth not the cry of the suffering — DeW
For he who avenges blood is mindful of them;
he does not forget the cry of the afflicted — RSV
He who avenges murder has an open ear to those who cry to him for

justice. He does not ignore the prayers of men in trouble when they call to him for help — Tay

13. Have mercy upon me O LORD; consider my trouble which I suffer of them that hate me, thou that liftest me up from the gates of death:

Shew me favour O Yahweh!
Behold my humiliation due to them who hate me,
Lift me on high out of the gates of death — Rhm

Pity me, O Jehovah!
See how I suffer from my foes;
Thou who hast raised me from the gates of death — DeW

Be kind to me, Lord:
see what I endure from those who despise me,
for You have drawn me away from the brink of death — Har

The Eternal has seen what I suffer, and pitied me,
lifting me from the very gates of death — Mof

14. That I may shew forth all thy praise in the gates of the daughter of Zion: I will rejoice in thy salvation.

That I may recount all thy praises,
In the gates of the daughter of Zion may exult in thy salvation — Rhm

that I may recount all thy praises,
that in the gates of the daughter of Zion
I may rejoice in thy deliverance — RSV

That I may proclaim all Thy praise!
In the gates of the daughter of Zion,
I will rejoice in Thy salvation! — DeW

that in the gates of the daughter of Zion
I may recite your praises one by one,
rejoicing that you have saved me — Jerus

15. The heathen are sunk down in the pit that they made: in the net which they hid is their own foot taken.

The nations are sunk in the pit they have made;
in the snare they set, their foot is caught — NAB

The nations have sunk into a pit of their own making,
they are caught by the feet in the snare they set themselves — Jerus

16. The LORD is known by the judgment which he executeth: the wicked is snared in the work of his own hands.

The LORD is known to execute judgment; the ungodly is trapped in the work of his own hands — PBV

Jehovah hath made himself known, he hath executed judgment:
The wicked is snared in the work of his own hands — ASV

Known is Jehovah! He dealeth out justice:
In the work of his own hands
Is the wicked ensnared — DeW

The Eternal has shown what he is, by a sentence of doom,
as his hands have trapped the ungodly — Mof

The Lord has manifested himself by executing judgment;
the wicked are trapped by their own schemes — Har

Higgaion. Selah.

Resounding music. Selah — Rhm
Muted music Pause — Jerus
(Music Pause.) — ABPS
Meditation. Selah — YLT
O meditate thereon. Selah — Sprl

17. The wicked shall be turned into hell, and all the nations that forget God.

The wicked shall be turned back unto Sheol,
Even all the nations that forget God — ASV

The lawless shall return to hades,
All nations forgetful of God — Rhm

The wicked shall turn back to the underworld,
All the nations that forget God — ABPS

The ungodly must go back to death,
all pagans who are forgetful of God — Mof

To the place of death the wicked must return, heathens that have no thought of God — Knox

May the iniquitous return to the realms of the dead,
with all the nations who disregard God — Har

18. For the needy shall not alway be forgotten: the expectation of the poor shall not perish for ever.

For not always shall the needy be forgotten, —
Nor the hope of the oppressed perish for ever — Rhm

For the needy shall not always be forgotten;
The hope of the humble shall not perish forever — ABPS
But the poor shall not always be unheeded
nor the hope of the destitute be always in vain — NEB
for one day the needy will be remembered,
the hopes of the downtrodden will not always be disappointed — Mof

19. Arise, O LORD: let not man prevail: let the heathen be judged in thy sight.
Up LORD, and let not man have the upper hand; let the heathen be judged in thy sight — PBV
Take action, O Eternal, let not man have the upper hand;
let pagans get their doom from thee! — Mof
Arise, Lord,
do not allow mortal man to triumph;
may the peoples be judged according to Your purpose — Har

20. Put them in fear, O LORD: that the nations may know themselves to be but men.
Put them in fear, O Jehovah:
Let the nations know themselves to be but men — ASV
Strike them with terror, O Eternal,
let pagans know that they are only men! — Mof

Selah.
(Pause.) — ABPS

PSALM 10

1. Why standest thou afar off, O LORD? why hidest thou thyself in times of trouble?
Why standest thou so far off, O LORD, and hidest thy face in the needful time of trouble — PBV
Wherefore, O JEHOVAH, tarriest Thou in the far-off distance?
wilt Thou hide Thyself in times of trouble — Sprl
Why do You remain aloof, Lord,
and conceal Yourself in times of emergency — Har
Lord, why are you standing aloof and far away? Why do you hide when I need you the most — Tay

2. The wicked in his pride doth persecute the poor: let them be taken in the devices that they have imagined.
In the pride of the wicked the poor is hotly pursued;
Let them be taken in the devices that they have conceived — ASV
The wicked in his pride persecutes the lowly;
Let them be taken in the devices which they contrived — ABPS
The ungodly are haughty and harry the downtrodden —
may they be snared in their own schemes! — Mof
In arrogance the wicked hotly pursue the poor;
let them be caught in the schemes which they have devised — RSV
The wicked man in his pride hunts down the poor:
may his crafty schemes be his own undoing — NEB

3. For the wicked boasteth of his heart's desire, and blesseth the covetous, whom the LORD abhorreth.
For the lawless one hath boasted over the longing of his soul,
And the robber hath blasphemed Yahweh — Rhm
The wicked sings the praises of his own desires,
And the robber curses, and rejects God — AAT
For the wicked boasts of the desires of his heart,
and the man greedy for gain curses and renounces the LORD — RSV
For the wicked boasts of his heart's desire;
the greedy one curses and spurns the LORD — Ber
For the wicked man glories in his covetous desires;
the defrauder reviles and rejects the Lord — Har
The wicked man is obsessed with his own desires . . . — NEB

4. The wicked, through the pride of his countenance, will not seek after God: God is not in all his thoughts.
The ungodly is so proud, that he careth not for God, neither is God in all his thoughts — PBV

The lawless one in the loftiness of his countenance will not enquire,
God is not in any of his plots — Rhm

The wicked, in the pride of his countenance, saith, He will not require it. All his thoughts are, There is no God — RV

he thinks, in his insolence, God never punishes;
his thoughts amount to this, "There is no God at all" — Mof

5. His ways are always grievous; thy judgments are far above out of his sight: as for all his enemies, he puffeth at them.

His doings are always grievous. Thy judgments are far beyond his notice;
He is violent against every one of his opponents — Sprl

His ways are always devious;
thy judgements are beyond his grasp,
and he scoffs at all restraint — NEB

His ways are sure at all times:
Thy judgments are far above, out of his sight;
As for all his adversaries, he scoffs at them — ABPS

His ways prosper at all times;
thy judgments are on high, out of his sight;
as for all his foes, he puffs at them — RSV

His affairs progress smoothly at all times;
Your decrees are completely above and beyond him.
He disdains all his opponents — Har

His ways are secure at all times;
your judgments are far from his mind;
all his foes he scorns — NAB

as he goes on prospering, he banishes thy laws from his mind, and makes light of his enemies — Knox

at every moment his course is assured,
your rulings are too lofty for his notice;
his rivals? He sneers at them all — Jerus

Yet there is success in everything they do, and their enemies fall before them. They do not see your punishment awaiting them — Tay

6. He hath said in his heart, I shall not be moved: for I shall never be in adversity.

For he hath said in his heart, Tush, I shall never be cast down, there shall no harm happen unto me — PBV

He saith in his heart: I shall by no means be moved:
Because from generation to generation I shall proceed without adversity — Sprl

He saith in his heart,
I shall not be overthrown
From age to age no ill shall befall me! — DeW

He says to himself, 'I shall never be shaken;
no misfortune can check my course' — NEB

7. His mouth is full of cursing and deceit and fraud: under his tongue is mischief and vanity.

His mouth is full of cursing and deceit and oppression: under his tongue is mischief and iniquity — RV

His speech is full of deceit and oppression;
mischief and iniquity lurk in his remarks — Har

Fraud and oppression fill his mouth, spite and iniquity are under his tongue — Jerus

8. He sitteth in the lurking places of the villages: in the secret places doth he murder the innocent: his eyes are privily set against the poor.

He abideth in the lurking-place of villages
In the hiding-places he murdereth the innocent, —
His eyes for the unfortunate are on the watch — Rhm

He abideth in ambush within the brushwood;
In lurking-places he murdereth the innocent:
His eye secretly observes the defenceless — Sprl

He sits in ambush by the villages;
On the secret places he slays the innocent;
His eyes lurk for the wretched — ABPS

He sits in ambush in the villages;
in hiding places he murders the innocent.
His eyes stealthily watch for the hapless — RSV

9. He lieth in wait secretly as a lion in his den: he lieth in wait to catch the

poor: he doth catch the poor, when he draweth him into his net.

Like a lion in his lair he lurks in his dwelling;
he lies in wait to rob the defenceless,
and plunders him when he draws him into his trap — Har

10. He croucheth, and humbleth himself, that the poor may fall by his strong ones.

He croucheth he lieth down,
Then falleth he with his strong claws upon the unfortunate — Rhm

Then he will crouch, he will stoop downwards;
That the defenceless might fall through his greater strength — Sprl

He croucheth, he boweth down,
And the helpless fall into his mighty claws — JPS

The hapless is crushed, sinks down, and falls by his might — RSV

The victim is crushed,
he sinks down and succumbs to his superior strength — Har

11. He hath said in his heart, God hath forgotten: he hideth his face; he will never see it.

He hath said in his heart, Tush, God hath forgotten; he hideth away his face, and he will never see it — PBV

He says in his heart, God has no memory of me: his face is turned away; he will never see it — Bas

Why not? he thinks to himself, God has forgotten about it; God still turns his face away, and sees nothing — Knox

"God isn't watching," they say to themselves; "he'll never know!" — Tay

12. Arise, O LORD; O God, lift up thine hand: forget not the humble.

O God, JEHOVAH, rise up!
Lift up Thine hand. Can God forget the defenceless? — Sprl

Take action, O Eternal, lift thy hand;
O God, forget not the afflicted — Mof

O Lord God, bestir thyself, lift up thy hand; do not forget the helpless — Knox

Rise up, Lord;
manifest Your power, my God.
Do not neglect the oppressed — Har

13. Wherefore doth the wicked contemn God? he hath said in his heart, Thou wilt not require it.

Wherefore should the wicked blaspheme God, while he doth say in his heart, Tush, thou God carest not for it? — PBV

Wherefore hath the lawless one blasphemed God?
He hath said in his heart
Thou wilt not require [it]! — Rhm

Wherefore should the wicked blaspheme God, saying in his heart:
Thou wilt not require redress? — Sprl

Why do the wicked despise God,
Saying in their heart Thou avengest not? — DeW

How dare ungodly men scorn God, thinking that thou wilt never punish? — Mof

Why does the wicked renounce God, and say in his heart, "Thou wilt not call to account"? —RSV

Why is the sinner allowed to defy God, to think he will never exact punishment? — Knox

Why does the wicked man spurn God, assuring himself, 'He will not make me pay'? — Jerus

14. Thou hast seen it: for thou beholdest mischief and spite, to requite it with thy hand: the poor committeth himself unto thee; thou art the helper of the fatherless.

Surely thou hast seen it; for thou beholdest ungodliness and wrong, that thou mayest take the matter into thy hand.
The poor committeth himself unto thee; for thou art the helper of the friendless — PBV

Thou hast seen; for thou dost look upon trouble and sorrow,
To set them on thy hand.
To thee the wretched will commit it;
The orphan's helper hast thou been — ABPS

Thou hast seen it, surely Thou beholdest mischief and provocation,
To requite with Thine hand:
O Thou, who hast been the Defender of the fatherless;
Unto Thee do the defenceless commit their cause — Sprl

But thou hast seen this misery and mischief;
thou markest it, to punish it thyself!

The hapless can leave their plight to thee,
thou Helper of the forlorn — Mof
But in truth thou seest it; thou hast eyes for misery and distress, and wilt take them into thy keeping. The destitute are cast on no care but thine; to thee only the orphan looks for redress — Knox

15. Break thou the arm of the wicked and the evil man: seek out his wickedness till thou find none.
Break the power of wickedness and wrong;
hunt out all wickedness until thou canst find no more — NEB
Break the power of the guilty and wicked;
punish his iniquity till You have completely obliterated it — Har
Break the strength of the wicked and of the evildoers;
punish their wickedness; let them not survive — NAB

16. The LORD is King for ever and ever: the heathen are perished out of his land.
JEHOVAH remaineth for ever and ever!
The heathen shall perish from off His earth — Sprl
Jehovah is King for ever and ever:
The nations are perished out of his land — ASV

17. LORD, thou hast heard the desire of the humble: thou wilt prepare their heart, thou wilt cause thine ear to hear:
The longing of the patient thou hast heard of, Yahweh,
Thou wilt establish their heart
Thou wilt make attentive thy ear — Rhm
The desire of the lowly thou hast heard, O Jehovah;
Thou wilt confirm their heart, thou wilt incline thine ear — ABPS
O LORD, thou wilt hear the desire of the meek;
thou wilt strengthen their heart, thou wilt incline thine ear — RSV
Yahweh, you listen to the wants of the humble,
you bring strength to their hearts,
you grant them a hearing — Jerus

18. To judge the fatherless and the oppressed, that the man of the earth may no more oppress.
To judge the fatherless and the oppressed,
That man who is of the earth may be terrible no more — ASV
To vindicate the fatherless and the crushed,
A man of the earth shall no further cause terror! — Mof
bringing justice to the orphan and the downtrodden
that fear may never drive men from their homes again — NEB

PSALM 11

To the chief Musician, A Psalm of David.
From the Choirmaster's collection. A song of David — Mof
For the choirmaster Of David — Jerus

1. In the LORD put I my trust: how say ye to my soul, Flee as a bird to your mountain?
In Jehovah do I take refuge:
How say ye to my soul,
Flee as a bird to your mountain; — ASV
In the LORD I have found my refuge;
why do you say to me,
'Flee to the mountains like a bird;' — NEB
How dare you tell me, "Flee to the mountains for safety," when I am trusting in the Lord — Tay

2. For, lo, the wicked bend their bow, they make ready their arrow upon the string, that they may privily shoot at the upright in heart.
for lo, the wicked bend the bow,
they have fitted their arrow to the string,
to shoot in the dark at the upright in heart — RSV

3. If the foundations be destroyed, what can the righteous do?
When the foundations are destroyed,
What hath the righteous wrought — JPS
For when the foundations are broken down,
what can the righteous man accomplish — Har
The pillars of the State are falling:
what can a just man do — Mof

"Law and order have collapsed," we are told. "What can the righteous do but flee?" — Tay

4. The LORD is in his holy temple, the LORD'S throne is in heaven: his eyes behold, his eyelids try, the children of men.

JEHOVAH is in His holy temple, JEHOVAH, Whose throne is in the heavens!
His eyes contemplate, His eyelids prove the children of men — Sprl

The Lord is in His holy shrine;
the Lord is enthroned in the heavens.
He observes and surveys all mankind — Har

Ah, but the Eternal is within his sacred palace,
the Eternal is enthroned in heaven,
his searching glance is upon mortal men — Mof

The LORD is in his holy temple,
the LORD's throne is in heaven.
His eye is upon mankind, he takes their measure at a glance — NEB

But the Lord is still in his holy temple; He still rules from heaven. He closely watches everything that happens here on earth — Tay

5. The LORD trieth the righteous: but the wicked and him that loveth violence his soul hateth.

The LORD tests the righteous and the wicked,
And he hates the lover of violence — AAT

The Lord scrutinizes the virtuous and wicked alike,
and He detests the men who love violence — Har

The LORD weighs just and unjust
and hates with all his soul the lover of violence — NEB

6. Upon the wicked he shall rain snares, fire and brimstone, and an horrible tempest: this shall be the portion of their cup.

Upon the ungodly he shall rain snares, fire and brimstone, storm and tempest: this shall be their portion to drink — PBV

Upon the wicked he will rain snares; Fire and brimstone and burning wind shall be the portion of their cup — ASV

He will shower blazing embers and sulphur on evildoers;
a furious storm will mark their end — Har

He rains coals of fire and brimstone on the wicked,
he serves them a scorching wind to swallow down — Jerus

7. For the righteous LORD loveth righteousness; his countenance doth behold the upright.

For Jehovah is righteous; he loveth righteousness:
The upright shall behold his face — ASV

For the LORD is just and loves just dealing;
his face is turned towards the upright man — NEB

The Lord is essentially righteous, and loves justice.
For this reason the upright will finally see Him — Har

PSALM 12

To the chief Musician upon Sheminith, A Psalm of David.

For the Chief Musician; set to the Sheminith . . . — RV

To the Chief Musician. On the Octave. A Melody of David — Rhm

From the Choirmaster's collection. For bass voices. A song of David — Mof

For the choirmaster For the octachord Psalm Of David — Jerus

To the Chief Musician; set [possibly] an octave below . . . — Amp

1. Help, LORD; for the godly man ceaseth; for the faithful fail from among the children of men.

Help me, LORD, for there is not one godly man left; for the faithful are minished from among the children of men — PBV

O save Yahweh
For the man of lovingkindness is no more,
For the faithful have vanished from among the sons of men — Rhm

Help, O Eternal, goodness is no more, fidelity has vanished from mankind! — Mof

Save us, Yahweh! There are no devout men left,

fidelity has vanished from mankind — Jerus

Help, LORD, for loyalty is no more; good faith between man and man is over — NEB

Lord! Help! Godly men are fast disappearing. Where in all the world can dependable men be found? — Tay

2. They speak vanity every one with his neighbour: with flattering lips and with a double heart do they speak.

Everyone tells lies to his neighbor; their speech is flattering, their mind deceitful — Har

Everyone deceives and flatters and lies. There is no sincerity left — Tay

3. The LORD shall cut off all flattering lips, and the tongue that speaketh proud things:

JEHOVAH will cut off all flattering lips,
The tongue that speaketh arrogantly — Sprl

May Yahweh cut off
All the lips that utter smooth things,—
The tongue that speaketh swelling words — Rhm

May the Lord silence beguiling lips, and the tongue that boasts of great exploits — Har

May Yahweh slice off every flattering lip,
each tongue so glib with boasts — Jerus

4. Who have said, With our tongue will we prevail; our lips are our own: who is lord over us?

They have said, With our tongues will we overcome; our lips are ours: who is lord over us — Bas

Those who say: Our lips are our own!
With our tongues we are strong;
Who is lord over us — DeW

men who declare, "We give rein to our tongues;
our lips are our own: who calls us to account?" — Mof

Those who say, "We will make ourselves great by our tongue.
Our lips are with us; who is our master?" — AAT

those who say, 'In our tongue lies our strength,
our lips have the advantage; who can master us?' — Jerus

Those who say, "We are heroes with our tongues;
our lips are our own; who is lord over us?" — NAB

They said, 'Our tongue can win the day.
Words are our ally; who can master us?' — NEB

5. For the oppression of the poor, for the sighing of the needy, now will I arise, saith the LORD; I will set him in safety from him that puffeth at him.

Because of the oppression of the poor, because of the sighing of the needy,
Now will I arise, saith Jehovah;
I will set him in the safety he panteth for — ASV

Because of the oppression of the poor; because of the groans of the needy; now will I arise, saith the Lord; I will set in safety and speak boldly — Sept

'For the plundered poor, for the needy who groan,
now will I act' says Yahweh.
'I will grant them the safety they sigh for' — Jerus

"Because the poor are exploited, because the needy groan,
I will now arise," says the LORD;
"I will place him in the safety for which he longs" — AAT

6. The words of the LORD are pure words: as silver tried in a furnace of earth, purified seven times.

The sayings of Jehovah are pure sayings;
Silver tried in a furnace of earth,
Seven times refined — ABPS

The words of Yahweh are without alloy,
nature's silver coming from the earth
seven times refined — Jerus

And what the Eternal promises is true,
sterling as silver seven times purified — Mof

The promises of the LORD are promises that are pure,
silver refined in a furnace on the ground,
purified seven times — RSV

The promises of the LORD are sure,
like tried silver, freed from dross,
sevenfold refined — NAB

7. Thou shalt keep them, O LORD, thou

shalt preserve them from this generation for ever.

Yes, Lord, thou wilt watch over us, and keep us ever safe from these evil days — Knox

Do thou protect us, O LORD; Guard us from this generation forever — AAT

Do thou, LORD, protect us and guard us from a profligate and evil generation — NEB

8. The wicked walk on every side, when the vilest men are exalted.

The wicked walk on every side, when vileness is exalted among the sons of men — RV

On every side the lawless march about, — When worthlessness is exalted by the sons of men — Rhm

The wicked parade to and fro, When baseness is exalted among the sons of men — AAT

On every side the wicked prowl, as vileness is exalted among the sons of men — RSV

The wicked parade about when vileness is exalted among humanity — Har

The wicked flaunt themselves on every side, while profligacy stands high among mankind — NEB

While about us the wicked strut and in high place are the basest of men — NAB

where all around us the ungodly strut, and where base creatures rise to power — Mof

PSALM 13

To the chief Musician, A Psalm of David.

1. How long wilt thou forget me, O LORD? for ever? how long wilt thou hide thy face from me?

How long, O Jehovah? Wilt thou forget me for ever? How long wilt thou hide thy face from me — ASV

Eternal One, how long wilt thou forget me? How long wilt thou withhold thy favour from me — Mof

How long will you forget me, Lord? Forever? How long will you look the other way when I am in need — Tay

2. How long shall I take counsel in my soul, having sorrow in my heart daily? how long shall mine enemy be exalted over me?

How long must I bear pain in my soul, and have sorrow in my heart all the day? How long shall my enemy be exalted over me — RSV

How long shall I lay up cares within my soul Sorrow in my heart day by day? How long shall mine enemy lift himself up over me — Rhm

How long must I cherish a daily grief? How long is my foe to triumph over me — Mof

How long am I to lay cares upon myself, And trouble in my heart daily? How long shall my enemy triumph over me — AAT

How long must I keep my worries to myself, and carry grief in my mind daily? How long are my enemies to be my superiors — Har

Each day brings a fresh load of care, fresh misery to my heart; must I be ever the sport of my enemies — Knox

3. Consider and hear me, O LORD my God: lighten mine eyes, lest I sleep the sleep of death;

Look! answer me, O Jehovah, my God! Give light to mine eyes, lest I sleep in death — DeW

Look upon me, O Lord my God, and listen to me; give light to these eyes, before they close in death — Knox

Take notice of me and answer me, my Lord God; refresh me, otherwise I shall die — Har

4. Lest mine enemy say, I have prevailed against him; and those that trouble me rejoice when I am moved.

Lest mine enemy say I have prevailed over him! And mine adversaries exult that I totter — Rhm

Lest my enemy say, I have prevailed over him;
Lest my foes exult when I am ready to fall — ABPS

lest my foe claim, I have mastered him, lest my enemies exult over my downfall — Mof

Then my enemy will boast,
I have overcome him,
and my opponents will rejoice at my collapse — Har

5. But I have trusted in thy mercy; my heart shall rejoice in thy salvation.

But I have trusted in thy steadfast love . . . — RSV

But my trust is in thy mercy, and my heart is joyful in thy salvation — PBV

But I in thy lovingkindness have put my trust
My heart shall exult in thy salvation — Rhm

But on thy kindness I indeed rely;
let me exult over thy saving aid — Mof

But I have trusted in Thine unfailing love:
my heart rejoices in Thy deliverance — Ber

I cast myself on thy mercy; soon may this heart boast of redress granted — Knox

But for my part I trust in thy true love.
My heart shall rejoice, for thou hast set me free — NEB

6. I will sing unto the LORD, because he hath dealt bountifully with me.

I do sing to Jehovah,
For He hath conferred benefits upon me! — YLT

Let me sing to the LORD
because He has dealt generously with me — Ber

I will sing to the LORD, who has granted all my desire — NEB

I will sing to the Lord because he has blessed me so richly — Tay

PSALM 14[6]

To the chief Musician, A Psalm of David[7]

1. The fool hath said in his heart, There is no God.

Profane men think,
"There is no God!" — Mof

There is no God above us, is the fond thought of reckless hearts — Knox

That man is a fool who says to himself,
"There is no God!" — Tay

They are corrupt, they have done abominable works, there is none that doeth good.

They have corrupted their behavior and made it abominable.
There is none who does right — Ber

Hence their depraved, their impious acts:
Not one of them performeth that which is right — Sprl

They are corrupt,
They are vile in their wickedness;
There is none that doeth good! — DeW

Depraved their lives are and detestable, not one of them does right — Mof

How vile men are, how depraved and loathesome;
not one does anything good! — NEB

Anyone who talkes like that is warped and evil and cannot really be a good person at all — Tay

2. The LORD looked down from heaven upon the children of men, to see if there were any that did understand, and seek God.

Yahweh out of the heavens looked down over the sons of men, —
To see whether there was one that shewed wisdom,
Enquiring after God — Rhm

The LORD looks down from heaven upon the children of men,
to see if there are any that act wisely,
that seek after God — RSV

From the heavens the Lord surveys humanity,
to see if any are sufficiently discerning
to search for God — Har

The Lord looks down from heaven at the race of men, to find one soul that reflects, and makes God its aim — Knox

Yahweh is looking down from heaven at the sons of men,

---

[6]Compare Psalm 53.
[7]See Psalm 11.

to see if a single one is wise,
if a single one is seeking God — Jerus

The Eternal looks from heaven upon mankind,
to see if any have the sense to care for God — Mof

3. They are all gone aside, they are all together become filthy: there is none that doeth good, no, not one.

They have all turned aside; together they are corrupted;
There is none that does good, not even one — ABPS

But all are faithless,
one and all are tainted;
not one does right,
no, not a single one — Mof

But all are disloyal, all are rotten to the core;
not one does anything good,
no, not even one — NEB

4. Have all the workers of iniquity no knowledge? who eat up my people as they eat bread, and call not upon the LORD.

Have they no knowledge, all the evildoers
who eat up my people as they eat bread,
and do not call upon the LORD? — RSV

Will all these evildoers never learn,
they who eat up my people just as they eat bread?
They have not called upon the LORD — NAB

Shall they not rue it,
all evildoers who devour my people as men devour bread,
and never call upon the LORD? — NEB

5. There were they in great fear: for God is in the generation of the righteous.

They were seized with terror, where there was no fear; because God was among a righteous generation — Sept

Then were they in great fear: for God is in the generation of the upright — Bas

What wonder if fear unmans them, when the Lord takes the part of the innocent? — Knox

In that very situation they became desperately alarmed,
because God appeared on the side of the righteous — Har

There they were in dire alarm;
for God was in the brotherhood of the godly — NEB

Ha! there they are in a panic,
for God is indeed with the godly! — Mof

6. Ye have shamed the counsel of the poor, because the LORD is his refuge.

The purpose of the poor ye would put to shame,
Because Yahweh is his refuge — Rhm

Have you despised the counsel of the poor; because his trust is in the Lord? — Sept

You would baffle these weak folk?
But the Eternal is their resource — Mof

You would put to shame the plans of the poor;
But the LORD is his refuge — AAT

You would confound the plans of the poor,
but the LORD is his refuge — RSV

Though one might thwart the plans of the poor,
the Lord is their refuge — Har

deride as you may the poor man's hopes,
Yahweh is his shelter — Jerus

He is the refuge of the poor and humble when evildoers are oppressing them — Tay

7. Oh that the salvation of Israel were come out of Zion!

O that he would for Sion's sake send deliverance to Israel — Sept

Oh, that it might dawn over Sion, Israel's deliverance — Knox

who bestows deliverance upon Israel from Zion — Har[8]

when the LORD bringeth back the captivity of his people, Jacob shall rejoice, and Israel shall be glad.

When Jehovah turns the captivity of his people,
Jacob will exult, Israel will rejoice — ABPS

[8]Har construes this phrase with the preceding verse.

When the Lord hath brought back the captives of his people: Let Jacob rejoice and let Israel be glad — Sept

When the Eternal restores the fortunes of his people,
how Jacob will exult,
how glad will Israel be! — Mof

When Yahweh brings his people home,
what joy for Jacob, what happiness for Israel! — Jerus

PSALM 15

A Psalm of David.
A Melody of David — Rhm

1. LORD, who shall abide in thy tabernacle? who shall dwell in thy holy hill?

O Yahweh!
Who shall be a guest in thy tent?
Who shall abide in thy holy mountain — Rhm

Who is it, Lord, that will make his home in thy tabernacle, rest on the mountain where thy sanctuary is — Knox

Yahweh, who has the right to enter your tent,
or to live on your holy mountain — Jerus

2. He that walketh uprightly, and worketh righteousness, and speaketh the truth in his heart.

Even he that leadeth an uncorrupt life, and doeth the thing which is right and speaketh the truth from his heart — PBV

He that walketh without blame
And doeth what is right,
And speaketh truth with his heart — Rhm

3. He that backbiteth not with his tongue, nor doeth evil to his neighbour, nor taketh up a reproach against his neighbour.

He that slandereth not with his tongue, nor doeth evil to his friend, nor taketh up a reproach against his neighbour — RV

He is not hasty with his tongue.
He does no wrong to his fellows;
Nor does he take blame upon himself because of his neighbor — AAT

who utters no treacherous word, never defrauds a friend, or slanders a neighbour — Knox

4. In whose eyes a vile person is contemned; but he honoureth them that fear the LORD.

in whose eyes a reprobate is despised,
but who honors those who fear the LORD — RSV

the man who shows his scorn for the worthless
and honours all who fear the LORD — NEB

He that sweareth to his own hurt, and changeth not.

If he has sworn to his harm, he does not change — ABPS

he keeps to his oath, though he may lose by it — Mof

and is true, come what may, to his pledged word — Knox

One who will keep a promise, even to his own detriment,
and will not retract — Har

who stands by his pledge at any cost — Jerus

5. He that putteth not out his money to usury, nor taketh reward against the innocent.

His silver hath he not put out on interest
Nor a bribe against the innocent hath he taken — Rhm

he takes no interest on a loan;
he is not to be bribed against the innocent — Mof

He that doeth these things shall never be moved.

Whoso doeth these things shall never fail — PBV

He who doeth these things shall never be overthrown — Sprl

If a man does all this, nothing can ever shake him — Jerus

He who does these things shall never be brought low — NEB

He who so lives will stand firm for ever — Knox

PSALM 16

Michtam of David.
A Precious Psalm of David — Rhm
Memorial [Psalm] of David — ABPS
A secret Treasure of David — YLT
A golden ode of David — Mof
A Poem of David [probably] intended to record memorable thoughts — Amp

1. Preserve me, O God: for in thee do I put my trust.
Keep me safe, Lord; I put my trust in thee — Knox
Preserve me, O God; for in thee do I take refuge — ASV
Guard me, O God, for I have taken shelter in Thee — Sprl
Keep me, O God, for in thee have I found refuge — NEB

2. O my soul, thou hast said unto the LORD, Thou art my Lord:
O my soul, thou hast said unto Jehovah, Thou art my Lord — ASV
my goodness extendeth not to thee;
I have no good but in thee — JPS
I have no good apart from thee — RSV
my goodness cometh from thee — Lam
thou hast no need of my goods — Sept
My charitable gifts are naught to Thee — Sprl
my welfare rests on thee alone — Mof
my wellbeing depends entirely on You — Har
I have no other help but yours — Tay

3. But to the saints that are in the earth, and to the excellent, in whom is all my delight.
All my delight is upon the saints that are in the earth, and upon such as excel in virtue — PBV
As for the saints that are in the earth,
They are the excellent in whom is all my delight — ASV
As for the holy that are in the earth,
They are the excellent in whom is all my delight — JPS
in the saints of the land, thy noble followers,
is all my delight — Mof
As for the godly that are in the land, they are the glorious in whom is all my delight — Ber
There are faithful souls in this land of his; wondrous delight he gives me in their companionship — Knox
As to the gods who are in the land
And the lofty ones, I have no pleasure in them — AAT
The gods whom earth holds sacred are all worthless,
and cursed are all who make them their delight — NEB

4. Their sorrows shall be multiplied that hasten after another god:
Their sorrows shall be multiplied that give gifts for another god — ASV
Their griefs shall be multiplied who follow after another god — Sprl
The sorrows of those who choose otherwise shall be multiplied — Ber
But they that run after another god shall have great trouble — PBV
those who run after them find trouble without end — NEB[9]
their drink offerings of blood will I not offer, nor take up their names into my lips.
Their drink-offerings of blood will I not offer,
Nor take their names upon my lips — ASV
their bloody libations I will never pour,
their names I will never mention — Mof
I will not offer them libations of blood nor take their names upon my lips — NEB

5. The LORD is the portion of mine inheritance and of my cup: thou maintainest my lot.
The Lord is my heritage and the wine of my cup; you are the supporter of my right — Bas
O Jehovah! Mine allotted portion and my cup!
Thou Thyself art my sure domain — DeW
Thou art what I obtain from life, O thou Eternal,
thou thyself art my share — Mof
The Lord is my allotted part, my share and my fate;
You are the Master of my destiny — Har
No, it is the Lord I claim for my prize, the Lord who fills my cup; thou, and no other, wilt assure my inheritance to me — Knox
The Lord himself is my inheritance, my prize. He is my food and drink,

[9]Connect with NEB rendering of verse 3.

my highest joy! He guards all that is mine — Tay

6. The lines are fallen unto me in pleasant places; yea, I have a goodly heritage.

the lines fall for me in pleasant places, indeed I am well content with my inheritance — NEB

The lines have fallen to me in the best places: for this inheritance of mine is the best for me — Sept

the measuring line marks out delightful places for me,
for me the heritage is superb indeed — Jerus

The lots have fallen unto me in sweet possessions:
Yea, a beauteous inheritance is mine — Sprl

I have been given a prosperous inheritance;
my assigned portion is indeed pleasant to me — Har

He sees that I am given pleasant brooks and meadows as my share! What a wonderful inheritance! — Tay

7. I will bless the LORD, who hath given me counsel: my reins also instruct me in the night seasons.

I will thank the LORD for giving me warning; my reins also chasten me in the night season — PBV

I will bless Jehovah, who hath given me counsel;
Yea, my heart instructeth me in the night seasons — ASV

I will bless Yahweh who hath counselled me,
Surely by night shall mine impulses admonish me — Rhm

I will bless the Eternal for his counsel, for teaching me during the very night — Mof

Blessed be the Lord, who schools me; late into the night my inmost thoughts chasten me — Knox

I will bless the Lord for His counsel; even for the nights when my conscience rebuked me — Har

8. I have set the LORD always before me: because he is at my right hand, I shall not be moved.

I set Jehovah before me alway;
With Him at my right hand,
I shall not be overthrown — DeW

I keep the Eternal at all times before me;
with him so close, I cannot fail — Mof

Always I can keep the Lord within sight; always he is at my right hand, to make me stand firm — Knox

I have kept the Lord in mind continually;
with Him beside me I cannot be disturbed — Har

I keep Yahweh before me always,
for with him at my right hand nothing can shake me — Jerus

9. Therefore my heart is glad, and my glory rejoiceth: my flesh also shall rest in hope.

. . . My flesh also shall dwell in safety — ASV

So my heart is glad, my spirit exulteth;
My flesh, too, abideth securely — DeW

Therefore my heart is glad, and my soul rejoices;
my body also dwells secure — RSV

And so my heart and soul rejoice,
my body rests secure — Mof

10. For thou wilt not leave my soul in hell; neither wilt thou suffer thine Holy One to see corruption.

For thou wilt not leave my soul to Sheol;
Neither wilt thou suffer thy holy one to see corruption — ASV

For thou wilt not abandon my soul to the underworld;
Thou wilt not suffer thy Holy One to see corruption — ABPS

For Thou wilt not abandon my soul to Sheol,
Nor let waste in the grave Thy beloved — DeW

For thou dost not give me up to Sheol, or let thy godly one see the Pit — RSV

for thou wilt not abandon me to Sheol nor suffer thy faithful servant to see the pit — NEB

For You will not abandon me to Sheol [the place of the dead], neither will You suffer Your holy one to see corruption — Amp

11. Thou wilt shew me the path of life: in thy presence is fulness of joy; at thy right hand there are pleasures for evermore.

. . . in thy right hand are pleasures for evermore — RV

thou wilt reveal the path to life,

to the full joy of thy presence,
to the bliss of being close to thee for ever — Mof

Thou wilt shew me the way of life, make me full of gladness in thy presence; at thy right hand are delights that will endure for ever — Knox

you will reveal the path of life to me, give me unbounded joy in your presence,
and at your right hand everlasting pleasures — Jerus

PSALM 17

A Prayer of David.

1. Hear the right, O LORD, attend unto my cry, give ear unto my prayer, that goeth not out of feigned lips.

Hear O Yahweh the right
Attend to my loud cry
Give ear unto my prayer,
On lips that would not deceive — Rhm

Hear, LORD, my plea for justice, give my cry a hearing,
for it is innocent of all deceit — NEB

2. Let my sentence come forth from thy presence;

from thee let my vindication come! — RSV

let thine eyes behold the things that are equal.

Let thy eyes see the right! — RSV

for You will see that justice is done — Har

your eyes behold what is right — NAB

3. Thou hast proved mine heart; thou hast visited me in the night; thou hast tried me, and shalt find nothing; I am purposed that my mouth shall not transgress.

If thou triest my heart, if thou visitest me by night,
if thou testest me, thou wilt find no wickedness in me;
my mouth does not transgress — RSV

Thou hast tested my heart
Hast made inspection by night
Hast refined me until thou couldst find nothing,
Had I devised evil my mouth should not have transgressed — Rhm

Thou hast tested my heart and watched me all night long;
thou hast assayed me and found in me no mind to evil — NEB

You have examined my motives, You have tried me secretly
and have tested me severely,
without discovering any improper conduct:
I do not even give offence in speech as worldly men do — Har

Though you test my heart, searching it in the night,
though you try me with fire, you shall find no malice in me.
My mouth has not transgressed after the manner of man;[10] — NAB

4. Concerning the works of men, by the word of thy lips I have kept me from the paths of the destroyer.

As for the doings of men,
By the word of Thy lips
I have shunned the paths of oppressors — DeW

With regard to the works of men,
by the word of thy lips
I have avoided the ways of the violent — RSV

Through Your solemn decrees
I have avoided lawless behavior — Har

according to the words of your lips I have kept the ways of the law — NAB

5. Hold up my goings in thy paths, that my footsteps slip not.

My steps have held fast to thy paths,
My feet have not slipped — ASV

My steps have held fast thy ways;
My feet have not wavered — ABPS

My steps hold firm to Thy footprints;
My tread wavereth not — DeW

My steps have held fast to thy tracks;
My footsteps have not faltered — AAT

6. I have called upon thee, for thou wilt hear me, O God: incline thine ear unto me, and hear my speech.

I call Thee, for Thou wilt answer me, O GOD!
Incline Thine ear to me; hear Thou my plea — DeW

[10]Connect with NAB rendering of verse 4.

Therefore I entreat You, for You will answer me, my God;
give me audience, hear what I have to say — Har

7. **Shew thy marvellous lovingkindness, O thou that savest by thy right hand them which put their trust in thee from those that rise up against them.**
Show thy marvellous loving-kindness, thou that art the Saviour of them which put their trust in thee, from such as resist thy right hand — PBV
Show thy marvellous lovingkindness,
O thou that savest by thy right hand them that take refuge in thee
From those that rise up against them — ASV
Strong saviour, in thy kindness interpose,
for those who shelter with thee from their foes — Mof
Show thy wonderful kindness, O savior of those who seek shelter
From their adversaries at thy right hand — AAT
Make clear the wonder of your mercy, O saviour of those who put their faith in your right hand, from those who come out against them — Bas
Show Your compassionate love
by rescuing those who look to Your power
for liberation from their enemies — Har
Show your wondrous kindness,
O savior of those who flee from their foes to refuge at your right hand — NAB
Show me how marvellous thy true love can be,
who with thy hand dost save
all who seek sanctuary from their enemies — NEB

8. **Keep me as the apple of the eye, hide me under the shadow of thy wings.**
Guard me as the pupil of the eye, —
Under the shadow of thy wings wilt thou hide me — Rhm
Protect me as the pupil of the eye;
Under thy shadowing wings let me hide — DeW
Protect me like the delicate pupil of the eye,
shelter me within Your shielding power — Har

9. **From the wicked that oppress me, from my deadly enemies, who compass me about.**
From the wicked that would destroy me,
My deadly foes that compass me about — DeW
from the wicked who despoil me,
my deadly enemies who surround me — RSV

10. **They are enclosed in their own fat: with their mouth they speak proudly.**
Their own fat [heart] have they shut up,
With their mouth have they spoken proudly — Rhm
They are fortified in their own esteem:
With their mouths speak they arrogantly — Sprl
They have stifled all compassion;
their mouths are full of pride — NEB
Their gross hearts they have closed,
And with their mouth they speak proudly — DeW
Their hearts are closed to pity,
their words are insolent — Mof
They are enclosed in their own prosperity and have shut up their heart to pity; with their mouth they make exorbitant claims and proudly and arrogantly speak — Amp

11. **They have now compassed us in our steps: they have set their eyes bowing down to the earth;**
They lie waiting in our way on every side, watching to cast us down to the ground — PBV
They have made a circle round our steps: their eyes are fixed on us, forcing us down to the earth — Bas
at every step they dog us,
alert to pull us down — Mof
They track me down; now they surround me;
they set their eyes to cast me to the ground — RSV
Wherever we go, they have surrounded us;
they fix their eyes to cast us to the ground — Ber

12. **Like as a lion that is greedy of his prey, and as it were a young lion lurking in secret places.**
They are like a lion eager to tear,
as a young lion lurking in ambush — RSV
like lions hungry to devour,

like lions lurking for their prey — Mof

13. Arise, O LORD, disappoint him, cast him down: deliver my soul from the wicked, which is thy sword:

Up, LORD, disappoint him, and cast him down; deliver my soul from the ungodly, by thine own sword — PBV

Arise, O Jehovah,
Confront him, cast him down:
Deliver my soul from the wicked by thy sword — ASV

Arise, LORD, meet him face to face and bring him down.
Save my life from the wicked;
make an end of them with thy sword — NEB

Up, O Eternal, face them, crush them; let thy sword save us from ungodly men! — Mof

14. From men which are thy hand, O LORD, from men of the world, which have their portion in this life, and whose belly thou fillest with thy hid treasure: they are full of children, and leave the rest of their substance to their babes.

from men by thy hand, O LORD,
from men whose portion in life is of the world.
May their belly be filled with what thou hast stored up for them;
may their children have more than enough;
may they leave something over to their babes — RSV

with your hand, Yahweh, rescue me from men,
from the sort of men whose lot is here and now.
Cram their bellies from your stores,
give them all the sons that they could wish for,
let them have a surplus to leave their children! — Jerus

by your hand, O LORD, from mortal men:
From mortal men whose portion in life is in this world,
where with your treasures you fill their bellies.
Their sons are enriched
and bequeath their abundance to their little ones — NAB

With thy hand, O LORD, make an end of them;
thrust them out of this world in the prime of their life,
gorged as they are with good things,
blest with many sons
and leaving their children wealth in plenty — NEB

15. As for me, I will behold thy face in righteousness: I shall be satisfied, when I awake, with thy likeness.

As for me, I shall behold thy face in righteousness;
I shall be satisfied, when I awake, with beholding thy form — ASV

But as for me, let me appear righteous before thee; let me be satisfied with a display of thy glory — Sept

But as for me, in righteousness
I shall have vision of Thy face;
I will be satisfied, when I awake,
And Thou wilt appear unto me — DeW

For me the reward of virtue is to see your face,
and, on waking, to gaze my fill on your likeness — Jerus

But my plea is just: I shall see thy face, and be blest with a vision of thee when I awake — NEB

But as for me, my contentment is not in wealth but in seeing you and knowing all is well between us. And when I awake in heaven, I will be fully satisfied, for I will see you face to face — Tay

PSALM 18

To the chief Musician, A Psalm of David, the servant of the LORD, who spake unto the LORD the words of this song in the day that the LORD delivered him from the hand of all his enemies, and from the hand of Saul: And he said,

To the choirmaster. A Psalm of David the servant of the LORD, who addressed the words of this song to the LORD on the day when the LORD delivered him from the hand of all his enemies, and from the hand of Saul. He said: — RSV

1. I will love thee, O LORD, my strength.

I love thee, O Jehovah, my strength — ASV

2. The LORD is my rock, and my fortress, and my deliverer; my God, my strength, in whom I will trust; my buckler, and the horn of my salvation, and my high tower.

The LORD is my rock, and my fortress,

and my deliverer,
my God, my rock, in whom I take refuge,
my shield, and the horn of my salvation, my stronghold — RSV

The Lord is my firm foundation, my fort and my liberator;
my God, my trustworthy defense,
my protector, my strong deliverer and my place of retreat — Har

3. **I will call upon the LORD, who is worthy to be praised: so shall I be saved from mine enemies.**

All I need to do is cry to him — oh, praise the Lord — and I am saved from all my enemies! — Tay

4. **The sorrows of death compassed me, and the floods of ungodly men made me afraid.**

The cords of death compassed me,
And the floods of ungodliness made me afraid — ASV

The meshes of death encompassed me,
The torrents of perdition made me afraid — Rhm

Around me were the snares of Death,
And the floods of Destruction affrighted me — DeW

The breakers of death engulfed me,
Torrents of ruin terrified me — AAT

The travail of death swept over me,
torrents of destruction flooded upon me — Har

For waves of death broke round me,
floods of destruction burst on me — Mof

When the bonds of death held me fast,
destructive torrents overtook me — NEB

5. **The sorrows of hell compassed me about: the snares of death prevented me.**

The cords of Sheol were round about me;
The snares of death came upon me — ASV

The bands of the underworld surrounded me,
The snares of death confronted me — ABPS

The clutches of the grave laid hold of me;
the snares of death twined around me — Har

The cords of Sheol [the place of the dead] surrounded me; the snares of death confronted and came upon me — Amp

the bonds of Sheol tightened round me,
the snares of death were set to catch me — NEB

6. **In my distress I called upon the LORD, and cried unto my God:**

In my distress I called on Jehovah,
Unto my God I cried for help — DeW

then in anguish of heart I cried to the LORD;
I called for help to my God — NEB

he heard my voice out of his temple, and my cry came before him, even into his ears.

He heard out of his temple my voice,
And my outcry for help came before him — entered into his ears! — Rhm

From his temple he heard my voice,
and my cry to him reached his ears — RSV

7. **Then the earth shook and trembled; the foundations also of the hills moved and were shaken, because he was wroth.**

Then the earth shook and trembled;
The foundations also of the mountains quaked
And were shaken, because he was wroth — ASV

Then the earth reeled and rocked;
the foundations also of the mountains trembled
and quaked, because he was angry — RSV

8. **There went up a smoke out of his nostrils, and fire out of his mouth devoured: coals were kindled by it.**

Smoke went up from his nostrils,
and devouring fire from his mouth;
glowing coals flamed forth from him — RSV

His fury mounted visibly, and fire from His presence raged;
blazing embers flashed out from it — Har

9. **He bowed the heavens also, and came down: and darkness was under his feet.**

Then he stretched out the heavens, and came down, —
And thick gloom was under his feet — Rhm

He straddled the sky and came down;
intense darkness formed under Him — Har

He swept the skies aside as he descended,
thick darkness lay under his feet — NEB

10. And he rode upon a cherub, and did fly: yea, he did fly upon the wings of the wind.

. . . Yea, he soared upon the wings of the wind — ASV

. . . Yea, He did swoop down upon the wings of the wind — JPS

He rode on a cherub, he flew through the air;
he swooped on the wings of the wind — NEB

11. He made darkness his secret place; his pavilion round about him were dark waters and thick clouds of the skies.

He made darkness his covering,
His pavilion round about him;
Dark waters, thick clouds of the skies — ABPS

He shrouded Himself with darkness as His covering;
the recesses of the clouds, black with water, concealed Him — Har

He made darkness around him his hiding-place
and dense vapour his canopy — NEB

12. At the brightness that was before him his thick clouds passed, hail stones and coals of fire.

At the flash of the lightning before him, the clouds burst. Hail stones and coals of fire! — Sept

From the splendour of His presence the dark clouds passed away
Into hail stones and coals of fire — Sprl

Out of the brightness before Him,
There passed through His dense clouds
Hailstones and flames of fire — DeW

Thick clouds came out of the radiance before him,
hailstones and glowing coals — NEB

From the brightness before Him
the clouds poured out hail and blazing embers — Har

Suddenly the brilliance of his presence broke through the clouds with lightning and a mighty storm of hail — Tay

From the brightness of his presence
coals were kindled to flame — NAB

13. The LORD also thundered in the heavens, and the Highest gave his voice; hail stones and coals of fire.

Jehovah also thundered in the heavens,
And the Most High uttered his voice,
Hailstones and coals of fire — ASV

Then Jehovah thundered in the heavens;
The Most High uttered His voice,
With hailstones and flames of fire! — DeW

14. Yea, he sent out his arrows, and scattered them; and he shot out lightnings, and discomfited them.

He sent forth his bolts and scattered them: he multiplied his lightnings and confounded them — Sept

He sent forth His arrows and scattered them;
Lightnings He shot forth and routed them — DeW

And he sent forth his arrows and scattered them,
Yea lightnings he shot out, and confused them — Rhm

He discharged lightning and dispersed them;
He hurled down great thunderbolts and routed them — Har

He loosed his arrows, he sped them far and wide,
he shot forth lightning shafts and sent them echoing — NEB

15. Then the channels of water were seen, and the foundations of the world were discovered at thy rebuke, O LORD, at the blast of the breath of thy nostrils.

And the bed of the sea was seen,
The foundations of the world were laid bare,
At Thy rebuke, O Jehovah!
At the blast of the breath of Thy nostrils — DeW

The bed of the sea became visible;
the foundations of the earth were uncovered
at Your rebuke, Lord,
at the fierce blast of Your anger — Har

Then the bed of the sea appeared,
and the foundations of the world were laid bare,
At the rebuke of the LORD,
at the blast of the wind of his breath — NAB

16. He sent from above, he took me, he drew me out of many waters.

He sent down from on high to fetch me, and took me out of many waters — PBV

He sent from on high and took me — he took me to himself from many waters — Sept

He reached from on high; He grasped me:
He drew me out of the great waters — DeW

He reached down from above and took me:
He drew me up from the raging waters — Har

17. He delivered me from my strong enemy, and from them which hated me: for they were too strong for me.

he frees me from my foe so strong,
from haters far too strong for me — Mof

he rescued me from my enemies, strong as they were,
from my foes when they grew too powerful for me — NEB

18. They prevented me in the day of my calamity: but the LORD was my stay.

They surprised me in the day of my distress; but the Lord was my firm support — Sept

They came upon me in the day of my trouble; but the LORD was my upholder — PBV

They confronted me in the day of my calamity;
And Jehovah became a stay for me — ABPS

When calamity overtook me they set upon me,
but the Lord was my support — Har

19. He brought me forth also into a large place; he delivered me, because he delighted in me.

He brought me forth also into a place of liberty; he brought me forth, even because he had a favour unto me — PBV

He brought me forth into an open place;
He delivered me, for He delighted in me — DeW

He led me forth into a broad place;
He set me free, for he was pleased with me — AAT

He set me free in the open,
and rescued me, because he loves me — NAB

20. The LORD rewarded me according to my righteousness; according to the cleanness of my hands hath he recompensed me.

Yahweh rewarded me according to my righteousness,
According to the cleanness of my hands he repaid me — Rhm

The Lord repaid me for my virtue;
He rewarded me for my upright conduct — Har

The LORD rewarded me as my righteousness deserved;
my hands were clean, and he requited me — NEB

21. For I have kept the ways of the LORD, and have not wickedly departed from my God.

For I had kept the ways of Yahweh,
And not broken away from my God — Rhm

For I have kept the ways of Jehovah,
And have not by sin forsaken my God — DeW

For I have observed the requirements of the Lord,
and I have not strayed wantonly from my God — Har

22. For all his judgments were before me, and I did not put away his statutes from me.

For all his regulations were before me,
And his statutes did I not put from me — Rhm

For all his ordinances were before me,
and his statutes I did not put away from me — RSV

For I have an eye unto all his laws, and will not cast out his commandments from me — PBV

his rules are all before my mind,
I never set aside his orders — Mof

23. I was also upright before him, and I kept myself from mine iniquity.

So became I blameless with him,
And kept myself from mine iniquity — Rhm

And I was single-hearted with Him,
And I kept myself from mine iniquity — JPS

I was blameless before him,
and I kept myself from guilt — RSV

I have lived morally before Him,
and guarded myself against sin — Har

24. Therefore hath the LORD recompensed me according to my righteousness.

So Jehovah rendereth to me
According to my righteousness — DeW

So the Eternal has rewarded me for my integrity — Mof
Therefore has the Lord recompensed me according to my righteousness [my uprightness and right standing with Him] — Amp
according to the cleanness of my hands in his eyesight.
According to the pureness of my hands before his eyes — Rhm

25. With the merciful thou wilt shew thyself merciful; with an upright man thou wilt shew thyself upright;
With the merciful thou wilt show thyself merciful;
With the perfect man thou wilt show thyself perfect — ASV
With the loving thou didst shew thyself loving, —
With the blameless man thou didst shew thyself blameless — Rhm
With the gracious thou wilt show thyself gracious;
With an upright man thou wilt show thyself upright — ABPS
To the loyal You show Yourself full of love,
manifesting Your integrity to the upright — Har

26. With the pure thou wilt shew thyself pure; and with the froward thou wilt shew thyself froward.
With the pure thou didst shew thyself pure,
But with the perverse thou didst shew thyself ready to contend — Rhm
With the pure Thou dost show Thyself pure;
And with the crooked Thou dost show Thyself subtle — JPS
Toward the pure thou dost act purely;
And toward the crooked thou dost act craftily — AAT
Toward the sincere you are sincere,
but toward the crooked you are astute — NAB
with the pure Thou showest Thyself pure;
and with the perverse Thou showest Thyself opposed — Ber

27. For thou wilt save the afflicted people; but wilt bring down high looks.
For thou shalt save the people that are in adversity, and shalt bring down the high looks of the proud — PBV
For thou wilt save the afflicted people;
but the haughty eyes thou wilt bring down — RV
For thou wilt save an afflicted people,
And lofty eyes thou wilt bring low — ABPS
For you are the saviour of those who are in trouble; but eyes full of pride will be made low — Bas
The humble thou wilt raise,
but the haughty thou wilt abase — Mof
Thou deliverest humble folk,
and bringest proud looks down to earth — NEB

28. For thou wilt light my candle: the LORD my God will enlighten my darkness.
Thou also shalt light my candle; the LORD my God shall make my darkness to be light — PBV
It is thou, Lord, that keepest the lamp of my hopes still burning; shinest on the darkness about me, O my God — Knox
You indeed, O LORD, give light to my lamp;
O my God, you brighten the darkness about me — NAB
Yahweh, you yourself are my lamp,
my God lights up my darkness — Jerus

29. For by thee I have run through a troop: and by my God have I leaped over a wall.
For in thee I shall discomfit an host of men, and with the help of my God I shall leap over the wall — PBV
For through thee I have pursued a band of robbers; and through my God have I leaped over a fence — Lam
For by Thee I can attack a troop,
and by my God I can leap a wall — Ber
by thy help I can face a troop,
by God's help I can leap a wall — Mof
Yea, by thee I can crush a troop;
and by my God I can leap over a wall — RSV
In thy strength I will engage a host of the enemy, in my God's strength I shall leap over all their defences — Knox

30. As for God, his way is perfect: the word of the LORD is tried:
As for GOD blameless is his way,

The speech of Yahweh hath been proved — Rhm
The way of God is an undefiled way: the word of the LORD also is tried in the fire — PBV
The way of God is blameless,
The speech of the LORD is sincere — AAT
The way of God is perfect,
the LORD's word has stood the test — NEB
God is unerring in his ways,
the Eternal's promises are tried and true — Mof
This God — his way is perfect;
the promise of the LORD proves true — RSV
Such is my God, unsullied in his dealings; his promises are like metal tested in the fire — Knox
What a God he is! How perfect in every way! All his promises prove true — Tay

he is a buckler to all those that trust in him.
he is the defender of all them that put their trust in him — PBV
He is a shield unto all them that take refuge in him — ASV
he is the protector of all who trust in him — Sept
he is the sure defence of all who trust in him — Knox

31. For who is God save the LORD?
For who is God, save Jehovah — ASV
What god is there but the LORD — NEB

or who is a rock save our God?
or who hath any strength, except our God — PBV
and there is no one who is mighty like our God. — Lam
What other refuge can there be, except our God — Knox
And who is a secure foundation apart from our God — Har

32. It is God that girdeth me with strength, and maketh my way perfect.
It is GOD that girdeth me with strength,
And that prospereth me in my way — DeW
The God that girdeth me with strength, and maketh my way perfect — RV
The God that girdeth me with strength,
And maketh my way straight — JPS
— the God who girdles me with strength,
and clears the path for me — Mof
— the God who girded me with strength,
and made my way safe — RSV
— the God who invests me with strength,
and makes my progress easy — Har
It is he that girds me with strength, bids me go on my way untroubled — Knox

33. He maketh my feet like hinds' feet, and setteth me upon my high places.
who makest my feet like those of a hind, and who steadiest me on high places — Sept
who makes me swift as a hind
and sets me secure on the mountains — NEB
He makes me nimble as a deer
and sets me on the height — Mof
He makes me sure-footed as the deer, and gives me the freedom of the hills — Knox
He gives me the surefootedness of a mountain goat upon the crags. He leads me safely along the top of the cliffs — Tay

34. He teacheth my hands to war, so that a bow of steel is broken by mine arms.
He teacheth mine hands to fight, and mine arms shall break even a bow of steel — PBV
Teaching my hands to war,
And a bow of bronze is bent by my arms — ABPS
who instructest my hands for battle, and hast made my arms like a bow of steel — Sept
He makes my hands expert in war, so that a bow of brass is bent by my arms — Bas
these hands, through him, are skilled in battle, these arms are a match for any bow of bronze — Knox

35. Thou hast also given me the shield of thy salvation:
Thou hast given me the defence of thy salvation — PBV
Thou hast shielded me with thine aid — Mof
And Thou givest me Thy saving shield — DeW
You have afforded me Your saving protection — Har
Thy saving power, Lord, is my defence — Knox

and thy right hand hath holden me up.

And thy right hand sustained me — Rhm
And Thy right hand doth support me — YLT
And Your might sustains me — Har
and thy gentleness hath made me great.
and thy discipline hath made me great — Lam
and thy loving correction shall make me great — PBV
And thy condescension will make me great — ABPS
And thy help makes me great — AAT
thy providence makes me great — NEB
and you have stooped to make me great — NAB
thine answers to prayer have raised me — Mof

36. Thou hast enlarged my steps under me, that my feet did not slip.
Thou hast enlarged my steps under me, And my feet have not slipped — ASV
Thou didst widen my stepping-places under me,
So that mine ankles faltered not — Rhm
Thou dost enlarge the range of my steps, And my ankles do not give way — AAT
You have enlarged the scope of my activities,
and I do not become fatigued — Har
Through thee, my steps are untrammelled as I go, my tread never falters — Knox
Thou hast given me room to move, and a foothold sure! — Mof

37. I have pursued mine enemies, and overtaken them:
I will pursue mine enemies, and overtake them — RV
I pursue my enemies and overtake them — Jerus
neither did I turn again till they were consumed.
neither will I turn again till I have destroyed them — PBV
nor will I withdraw until they are completely destroyed — Har
nor turn back till an end is made of them — Jerus

38. I have wounded them that they were not able to rise:
I crushed them, and they were unable to rise — Rhm
I will smite them, that they shall not be able to stand — PBV
I will smite them through, so that they shall not be able to rise — ASV
I strike them down, and they cannot rise — Jerus
they are fallen under my feet.
They shall fall under my feet — ASV
they fall, they are under my feet — Jerus

39. For thou hast girded me with strength unto the battle:
For thou hast girded me with strength for the battle — ABPS
You will give me strength for the conflict — Har
Thou girdest me about with a warrior's strength — Knox
thou hast subdued under me those that rose up against me.
thou shalt throw down mine enemies under me — PBV
Thou wilt make them crouch under me that rise up against me — ABPS
You will make my opponents subservient to me — Har
whatever power challenges me, thou dost subdue before me — Knox

40. Thou hast also given me the necks of mine enemies;
Thou hast made mine enemies also to turn their backs upon me — PBV
Through Thee I seize on my fleeing foe — DeW
You put my enemies to flight — Har
that I might destroy them that hate me.
That I might cut off them that hate me — ASV
And those that hate me I utterly destroy — DeW

41. They cried, but there was none to save them:
They will cry, and there is no deliverer — ABPS
They shall cry, but there shall be none to help them — PBV
They cry out,
but there is no one to rescue them — Har
They cried for help, but there was none to save — RSV
even unto the LORD, but he answered them not.
yea, even unto the LORD shall they cry, but he shall not hear them — PBV

Even unto Jehovah, but he answered them not — ASV
they appeal to the Lord, but He does not answer them — Har

42. **Then did I beat them small as the dust before the wind:**
Then did I beat them in pieces like dust on the face of the wind — Rhm
I beat them fine as dust before the wind — RSV
I did cast them out as the dirt in the streets.
I did cast them out as the mire of the streets — RV
As mire of the streets I will pour them out — ABPS
Like the dirt of the streets I scatter them — DeW

43. **Thou hast delivered me from the strivings of the people;**
Thus didst thou rescue me from the contentions of a people — Rhm
Thou dost deliver me from the clamour of the people — NEB
You are the one to rescue me from the onslaught of the heathen — Har
and thou hast made me the head of the heathen:
thou hast made me the head of the nations — RV
you place me at the head of the nations — Jerus
and makest me master of the nations — NEB
You establish me as victor over the nations — Har
a people whom I have not known shall serve me.
people whom I had not known served me — RSV
People whom I do not know are my vassals — Har
A people I never knew shall be my subjects — NEB

44. **As soon as they hear of me, they shall obey me:**
no sooner do they hear of me, than they obey me — Jerus
As soon as they hear of me, they submit to me — AAT
the strangers shall submit themselves unto me.
The foreigners shall submit themselves unto me — ASV
The sons of the foreigner came cringing unto me — Rhm
Aliens come cringing to me — DeW
foreigners cower before me — Har
outsiders fawn on me — Mof

45. **The strangers shall fade away, and be afraid out of their close places.**
The foreigners shall fade away, And shall come trembling out of their close places — ASV
The strangers shall fail, and come trembling out of their strongholds — PBV
Aliens wither, And come trembling out of their strongholds — DeW
Aliens languish, and steal from their fortresses trembling — Har
The sons of the foreigner lost heart, And came quaking out of their fortresses — Rhm

46. **The LORD liveth; and blessed be my rock;**
The LORD liveth; and blessed be my strong helper — PBV
The Lord lives; praised be my sure foundation — Har
and let the God of my salvation be exalted.
and praised be the God of my salvation — PBV
Yea, exalted be God that saveth me — DeW
Extolled be God my savior — NAB
high above all is God who saves me — NEB

47. **It is God that avengeth me.**
Even the God that executeth vengeance for me — RV
The Mighty, who avenges me — ABPS
The Mighty One, that giveth me revenge — DeW
The God who exacts retribution for me — Har
and subdueth the people under me.
And subdueth nations under me — DeW
and makes nations subject to me — Har

48. **He delivereth me from mine enemies:**
He rescueth me from mine enemies — ASV
yea, thou liftest me up above those that rise up against me:
yea, thou didst exalt me above my adversaries — RSV
thou hast delivered me from the violent man.
thou didst deliver me from men of violence — RSV

49. Therefore will I give thanks unto thee, O LORD, among the heathen, and sing praises unto thy name.
Therefore I will give thanks unto thee,
O Jehovah, among the nations,
And will sing praises unto thy name — ASV
For this cause will I praise thee among the nations O Yahweh,
And to thy Name will I sweep the strings — Rhm
So then I will glorify You, Lord, among the nations,
and loudly proclaim Your name — Har

50. Great deliverance giveth he to his king;
Who giveth great victories to His king — DeW
Who hath made great the victories of his King — Rhm
Great triumphs he gives to his king — RSV
He bestows glorious conquests on His king — Har
and sheweth mercy to his anointed.
And shewn lovingkindness to his Anointed One — Rhm
and shows steadfast love to his anointed — RSV
and in all his acts keeps faith with his anointed king — NEB
to David, and to his seed for evermore.
To David and to his Seed,
Unto times age-abiding — Rhm
To David and his descendants for ever — RSV
to David, and David's line for ever — Knox

PSALM 19

To the chief Musician, A Psalm of David.
To the choirmaster . . . — RSV

1. The heavens declare the glory of God;
The heavens are telling the glory of GOD — Rhm
The heavens are recounting the honour of God — YLT
The heavens proclaim God's splendour — Mof
The heavens tell out the glory of God — NEB
See how the skies proclaim God's glory — Knox
and the firmament sheweth his handiwork.
And the work of his hands the expanse is declaring — Rhm
And the expanse proclaims his handiwork — ABPS
The skies show forth the work of His hands — DeW
the arch of the sky makes clear the work of his hands — Bas
the vault of the sky proclaims what He has done — Har

2. Day unto day uttereth speech, and night unto night sheweth knowledge.
Day unto day doth pour forth speech,
and night unto night doth breathe out knowledge — Rhm
Day after day they speak,
and night after night reveal knowledge — Har
Each day echoes its secret to the next,
each night passes on to the next its revelation of knowledge — Knox
day discourses of it to day,
night to night hands on the knowledge — Jerus
One day speaks to another,
night with night shares its knowledge — NEB
Day and night they keep on telling about God — Tay

3. There is no speech nor language, where their voice is not heard.
There is no speech nor language; their voice cannot be heard — RV
There is no speech, and there are no words, —
Unheard is their voice! — Rhm
There is no speech, nor are there words;
their voice is not heard — RSV
No utterance at all, no speech,
no sound that anyone can hear — Jerus
and this without speech or language
or sound of any voice — NEB

4. Their line is gone out through all the earth, and their words to the end of the world.
Their range extends throughout the earth,
and their message to the ends of the world — Har
[yet] through all the earth hath gone forth their voice, —

And to the end of the world their sayings — Rhm
yet their voice goes out through all the earth,
and their words to the end of the world — RSV
Their music goes out through all the earth,
their words reach to the end of the world — NEB
In them hath he set a tabernacle for the sun,
In them he has set a tent for the sun — RSV
He has made among them a dwelling for the sun — Har
High above, he pitched a tent for the sun — Jerus
5. **Which is as a bridegroom coming out of his chamber,**
which cometh forth as a bridegroom out of his chamber — PBV
Who is like a newly married man coming from his bride-tent — Bas
Like a radiant bridegroom it arises from its covering horizon — Har
and rejoiceth as a strong man to run a race.
and rejoiceth as a giant to run his course — PBV
and is glad like a strong runner starting on his way — Bas
and is jubilant like a warrior, in running its course — Har
and exults like some great runner who sees the track before him — Knox
exulting like a hero to run his race — Jerus
6. **His going forth is from the end of the heaven, and his circuit unto the ends of it:**
It goeth forth from the uttermost part of the heaven, and runneth about unto the end of it again — PBV
From the horizon of the heavens marcheth he forth,
And makes his circuit unto the horizon again — Sprl
he sets out from one end of heaven, and round he passes to the other — Mof
From one end of the sky it arises
and moves around to the other — Har
He has his rising on the edge of heaven, the end of his course is its furthest edge — Jerus
and there is nothing hid from the heat thereof.
And nothing is hid from his glowing heat — Rhm
nothing escapes its heat — NAB
7. **The law of the LORD is perfect,**
The law of the LORD is an undefiled law — PBV
The law of Jehovah is perfect — ASV
The law of Yahweh is complete — Rhm
converting the soul:
restoring the soul — RV
restoring the [whole] person — Amp
refreshing the soul — NAB
reviving the soul — RSV
reviving life — Mof
renewing the life — AAT
promoting spiritual vigor — Har
the testimony of the LORD is sure,
The testimony of the Lord is faithful — Sept
The decree of the LORD is trustworthy — AAT
The decrees of the Lord are reliable — Har
The LORD's instruction never fails — NEB
making wise the simple.
making wise the foolish — Sprl
making the ignorant wise — Har
8. **The statutes of the LORD are right, rejoicing the heart:**
The precepts of Jehovah are right, rejoicing the heart — ASV
the Eternal's orders are just,
a joy to the heart — Mof
The teachings of the Lord are true, making one happy — Har
the commandment of the LORD is pure, enlightening the eyes.
The commandment of Jehovah is pure, enlightening the eyes — ASV
the Eternal's command is clear,
a light to the mind — Mof
The commandment of the Lord is intelligible,
enlightening the mind — Har
The commandment of the LORD shines clear
and gives light to the eyes — NEB
9. **The fear of the LORD is clean, enduring for ever:**
The reverence of Yahweh is clean,
Enduring evermore — Rhm
Reverence for the Lord is a pure and lasting way of life — Har

the judgments of the LORD are true and righteous altogether.
The ordinances of Jehovah are true, and righteous altogether — ASV
The decisions of Yahweh are faithful, They are righteous altogether — Rhm
The ordinances of Jehovah are true, And righteous, all of them — DeW
the Eternal's rulings are upright, and altogether just — Mof
the ordinances of the Lord are genuine and perfectly just — Har

10. More to be desired are they than gold, yea, than much fine gold:
They are more to be desired than gold, or many precious stones — Sept
They are more to be coveted than gold, yea, before most solid gold — Sprl
more to be prized than gold, than plenty of rare gold — Mof
All these are more precious than gold, than a hoard of pure gold — Knox
more desirable than gold, even than the finest gold — Jerus
They are more precious than gold, than a heap of purest gold — NAB

sweeter also than honey and the honeycomb.
Sweeter also than honey and the droppings of the honeycomb — ASV
And sweeter than honey, As it droppeth from the combs — DeW
and sweeter than honey, even when dripping from the honeycomb — Har

11. Moreover by them is thy servant warned:
Moreover, by them is thy servant taught — PBV
Also by them is Thy servant enlightened — Sprl

and in keeping of them there is great reward.
in following them there is rich profit — Mof

12. Who can understand his errors?
Who can discern his errors — RV
Errors, who can understand! — ABPS
yet who can detect failings — NAB
But who can detect his own failings — Jerus
And yet, who knows his own frailties — Knox
Who is aware of his sins — Ber
Who is aware of his unwitting sins — NEB

cleanse thou me from secret faults.
Clear thou me from hidden faults — ASV
From things that are hidden acquit me — Rhm
From hidden faults do Thou pronounce me clear — DeW
Cleanse me from inadvertent sins — Har
If I have sinned unwittingly, do thou absolve me — Knox

13. Keep back thy servant also from presumptuous sins;
As well, from bolder sins restrain Thy servant — DeW
And hold thy servant back from wilful sins — Mof
From wanton sin especially, restrain your servant — NAB

let them not have dominion over me:
lest they get the dominion over me — PBV
Let them not rule over me — DeW
may such never again gain control over me — Har

then shall I be upright, and I shall be innocent from the great transgression.
so shall I be undefiled, and innocent from the great offence — PBV
Then shall I be upright, And I shall be clear from great transgression — ASV
Then shall I be blameless; I shall be free from great transgression — DeW

14. Let the words of my mouth, and the meditation of my heart, be acceptable in thy sight,
The words of my mouth And the soft utterance of my heart Shall come with acceptance before thee — Rhm
Let the words of my mouth and the thought of my heart find favor before you — NAB
May all that I say and think be acceptable to thee — NEB

O LORD, my strength, and my redeemer.
O Jehovah, my rock, and my redeemer — ASV
O Lord, my defender, my redeemer! — Knox
Lord, my powerful protector — Har

PSALM 20

To the chief Musician, A Psalm of David.
To the choirmaster . . . — RSV

1. **The LORD hear thee in the day of trouble;**
Yahweh answer thee in the day of distress — Rhm
May the Lord answer you in times of calamity — Har
The Lord listen to thee in thy time of need — Knox
the name of the God of Jacob defend thee;
the name of the God of Jacob set thee up on high — RV
The Name of the God of Jacob give thee safety — Rhm
the power of Jacob's God be thy protection! — Knox
The name of Jacob's God be your tower of strength — NEB

2. **Send thee help from the sanctuary, and strengthen thee out of Zion;**
May he send you help from the sanctuary,
and give you support from Zion! — RSV
May he send thee aid from his holy place, watch over thee, there on Mount Sion — Knox
May he send you help from the sanctuary,
from Zion may he sustain you — NAB

3. **Remember all thy offerings, and accept thy burnt sacrifice;**
May he remember all your offerings,
and regard with favor your burnt sacrifices! — RSV
Selah.
Selah [pause, and think of that]! — Amp

4. **Grant thee according to thine own heart, and fulfil all thy counsel.**
May he grant you your heart's desire,
and fulfil all your plans! — RSV
may he grant you your heart's desire, and crown all your plans with success — Jerus

5. **We will rejoice in thy salvation, and in the name of our God we will set up our banners: the LORD fulfil all thy petitions.**
May we shout for joy over your victory,
and in the name of our God set up our banners!
May the LORD fulfil all your petitions! — RSV
so that we can rejoice at your success,
and hoist our banners in the name of our God.
May the Lord fulfil all your resolves — Har
We will shout for joy over your victory,
exulting in our God;
our cry, "May the Eternal fulfil all your petitions!" — Mof
We shout for joy in Thy salvation;
In the Name of our God we display our banner —
JEHOVAH FULFILLETH ALL THY REQUESTS! — DeW
May there be shouts of joy when we hear the news of your victory, flags flying with praise to God for all that he has done for you. May he answer all your prayers! — Tay

6. **Now know I that the LORD saveth his anointed;**
Now do I know that Yahweh hath saved his Anointed One — Rhm
Now I know that the LORD will help his anointed — RSV
Now am I sure the Eternal grants victory to his chosen king — Mof
he will hear him from his holy heaven with the saving strength of his right hand.
he will answer him from his holy heaven
with mighty victories by his right hand — RSV
He will answer him from His sacred abode with a
powerful display of saving strength — Har

7. **Some trust in chariots, and some in horses: but we will remember the name of the LORD our God.**
Some boast of chariots, and some of horses;
but we boast of the name of the LORD our God — RSV
These by chariots
And those by horses,
But we by the Name of Yahweh our God
Will prevail — Rhm

Some depend in the chariot, and some upon horses:
But we will invoke the Name of JEHOVAH our God — Sprl
Let others talk of horses and chariots; our refuge is in the name of the Lord our God — Knox
Some are strong in chariots; some, in horses;
but we are strong in the name of the LORD, our God — NAB

8. They are brought down and fallen: but we are risen, and stand upright.
They will collapse and fall;
but we shall rise and stand upright — RSV
They will falter and collapse,
but we shall arise and stand erect — Har
They totter and fall,
but we rise up and are full of courage — NEB

9. Save, LORD: let the king hear us when we call.
Save, LORD; and hear us, O King of heaven, when we call upon thee — PBV
Save, Jehovah:
Let the King answer us when we call — ASV
Yahweh hath saved the king.
Answer us then on the day when we call — Rhm
Grant victory to the king, O thou Eternal,
and answer our appeal this day — Mof
Grant victory to our king, O Lord; oh, hear our prayer — Tay

PSALM 21

To the chief Musician, A Psalm of David.
To the choirmaster . . . — RSV

1. The king shall joy in thy strength, O LORD; and in thy salvation how greatly shall he rejoice!
Jehovah, in thy strength shall the king rejoice;
And in thy salvation how greatly shall he exult! — ABPS
The king rejoices in thy might, O LORD:
well may he exult in thy victory — NEB

2. Thou hast given him his heart's desire, and hast not withholden the request of his lips.
for thou hast given him his heart's desire
and hast not refused him what he asked — NEB
Thou hast given him his heart's desire, and hast not denied him the request of his lips — PBV
The longing of his heart hast thou given him,
And the request of his lips hast thou not withheld — Rhm
Never a wish in his heart hast thou disappointed, never a prayer on his lips denied — Knox
Selah.
(Pause.) — ABPS
Selah [pause, and think of that]! — Amp

3. For thou preventest him with the blessings of goodness:
For thou meetest him with the blessings of goodness — ASV
For Thou meetest him with rich blessings — DeW
For Thou meetest him with choicest blessings — JPS
For thou dost anticipate him with blessings of goodness — ABPS
For Thou puttest before him blessings of goodness — YLT
For You precede him with abundant blessings — Har
For you go before him with the blessings of good things — Bas
thou settest a crown of pure gold on his head.

4. He asked life of thee, and thou gavest it him, even length of days for ever and ever.

5. His glory is great in thy salvation: honour and majesty hast thou laid upon him.
Great is his glory through Thy helping power,
Renown and majesty hast Thou laid on him — DeW
Great his glory through your saving help,
you have loaded him with splendour and majesty — Jerus
His fame is great because of Your help;

You confer honor and majesty upon him — Har

6. For thou hast made him most blessed for ever:

For thou makest him a blessing for-ever — ABPS

For thou wilt appoint him blessings evermore — Rhm

You have endowed him with eternal happiness — Tay

thou hast made him exceeding glad with thy countenance.

Thou makest him glad with joy in thy presence — ASV

Thou makest him glad with the joy of Thy presence — DeW

You have given him the unquenchable joy of your presence — Tay

You gladden him by Your radiant presence — Har

7. For the king trusteth in the LORD, and through the mercy of the most High he shall not be moved.

And why? because the King putteth his trust in the LORD; and in the mercy of the Most Highest he shall not miscarry — PBV

For the king trusteth in Jehovah;
And through the lovingkindness of the Most High he shall not be moved — ASV

For the king trusts in the LORD;
and through the steadfast love of the Most High he shall not be moved — RSV

The king places his trust in the Lord,
and through the loving favor of the Most High
he shall not be overthrown — Har

The king puts his trust in the LORD;
the loving care of the Most High holds him unshaken — NEB

8. Thine hand shall find out all thine enemies: thy right hand shall find out those that hate thee.

All thine enemies shall feel thine hand;
thy right hand shall find out them that hate thee — PBV

You will uncover all Your enemies;
Your great power will ferret out those who hate You — Har

9. Thou shalt make them as a fiery oven in the time of thine anger:

Thou wilt make them as a fiery furnace in the time of thine anger — ASV

Thou wilt make them like a furnace of fire at the time of thy presence — Rhm

you will burn them like a blazing furnace,
when you arrive in anger — Mof

at your coming you will plunge them into a fiery furnace — NEB

the LORD shall swallow them up in his wrath, and the fire shall devour them.

the Eternal will consume them in his wrath,
devouring them in flames of rage — Mof

the LORD in his anger will strike them down,
and fire shall consume them — NEB

10. Their fruit shalt thou destroy from the earth, and their seed from among the children of men.

You will destroy their offspring from the earth,
and their children from among the sons of men — RSV

You will wipe out their offspring from the earth,
and their descendants from among human society — Har

11. For they intended evil against thee: they imagined a mischievous device, which they are not able to perform.

For they have held out against thee a wicked thing,
They have devised a scheme they cannot accomplish — Rhm

For their thoughts were bitter against you: they had an evil design in their minds, which they were not able to put into effect — Bas

If they plan evil against you,
if they devise mischief, they will not succeed — RSV

For when they plan evil against You
and hatch crafty schemes,
they shall not succeed — Har

Plot though they do to harm you
and weave their plan as they may,
they cannot win — Jerus

12. Therefore shalt thou make them turn their back, when thou shalt make ready thine arrows upon thy strings against the face of them.

For you will put them to flight;
you will aim at their faces with your bows — RSV

because You will disperse them;
You will take aim at them with

Your weapons — Har
They will turn and flee when they see your arrows aimed straight at them — Tay

13. **Be thou exalted, LORD, in thine own strength:**
Exalt thyself, Jehovah, in thy strength — ABPS
Rise up, O thou Eternal, in thy power — Mof
Stand high above us, Lord, in thy protecting strength — Knox
so will we sing and praise thy power.
We will sing, chant the praise of your might — NAB
We will sing and strike the harp to Thy power! — DeW
With song and with string will we sound forth thy power — Rhm
that we may sing and praise Your power — Har

PSALM 22

To the chief Musician upon Aijeleth Shahar, A Psalm of David.
To the Choirmaster: according to The Hind of the Dawn. A Psalm of David — RSV
To the Chief Musician. On "the Hind of the Dawn." A Melody of David — Rhm
From the Choirmaster's collection. To the tune, "Deer of the Dawn." A song of David — Mof

1. **My God, my God, why hast thou forsaken me?**
My God, my God, why have You abandoned me — Har
why art thou so far from helping me, and from the words of my roaring?
and art so far from saving me, from heeding my groans — NEB
Why do you refuse to help me or even to listen to my groans — Tay
Why art Thou afar from helping me, Afar from my suffering cry — DeW
How far from saving me, the words I groan! — Jerus
Why do my cries of anguish bring no help — Mof

2. **O my God, I cry in the daytime, but thou hearest not; and in the night season, and am not silent.**
My God! I keep crying —
By day and thou dost not answer, and
By night and there is no rest for me — Rhm
O my God! I call thee through the day,
But Thou answerest not:
And in the night season,
But there is no relief for me — DeW

3. **But thou art holy, O thou that inhabitest the praises of Israel.**
And thou continuest holy, O thou Worship of Israel — PBV
Yet art Thou HOLY,
Enthroned amid the praises of Israel — DeW
Yet Thou art holy,
O Thou that art enthroned upon the praises of Israel — JPS
And yet thou art enthroned in holiness,
thou art he whose praises Israel sings — NEB
Nevertheless You are enthroned as the Holy One,
the praise of Israel — Har

4. **Our fathers trusted in thee: they trusted, and thou didst deliver them.**
Our fathers trusted in thee,
They cried unto thee and were delivered — ABPS
On thee our fathers did rely,
relied, and thou didst rescue them — Mof
Our forebears put their trust in You;
they believed, and You delivered them — Har

5. **They cried unto thee, and were delivered: they trusted in thee, and were not confounded.**
To thee they cried, and were saved;
in thee they trusted, and were not disappointed — RSV
Unto Thee they cried and were set free;
In Thee they trusted and were not put to shame — DeW

6. **But I am a worm, and no man; a reproach of men, and despised of the people.**
But as for me, I am a worm, and no man; a very scorn of men, and the outcast of the people — PBV
But I am a worm, and not a man;
Reviled by men, despised by the people — DeW
But I am a worm and not a man,
A shame to mankind, and despised of the people — AAT

For my part I am a worm, and not a human being;
insulted by men, despised by society — Har

But I, poor worm, have no manhood left; I am a by-word to all, the laughing-stock of the rabble — Knox

Yet here am I, now more worm than man,
scorn of mankind, jest of the people — Jerus

7. All they that see me laugh me to scorn:

All who see me mock at me — RSV

. . . jeer at me — NEB

they shoot out the lip, they shake the head, saying,

They open wide the mouth,
They shake the head: — Rhm

they toss their heads and sneer, — Mof

they gape at me and shake their heads: — Har

they mock me with parted lips,
they wag their heads: — NAB

make mouths at me and wag their heads: — NEB

8. He trusted on the LORD that he would deliver him: let him deliver him, seeing he delighted in him.

Commit thyself unto Jehovah; let him deliver him:
Let him rescue him, seeing he delighteth in him — ASV

Commit it to Jehovah, he will deliver him;
He will rescue him, for he delights in him — ABPS

Roll Thy care on JEHOVAH, let Him deliver Him,
Let Him save Him, if He delighteth in Him! — Sprl

"He left it to the Eternal! let him come to the rescue;
if the Eternal cares for him, let him come to the rescue!" — Mof

"He committed his cause to the LORD; let him deliver him,
let him rescue him, for he delights in him!" — RSV

"He relied on the LORD; let him deliver him,
let him rescue him, if he loves him" — NAB

'He threw himself on the LORD for rescue;
let the LORD deliver him, for he holds him dear!' — NEB

9. But thou art he that took me out of the womb: thou didst make me hope when I was upon my mother's breasts.

But thou art he that took me out of my mother's womb; thou wast my hope, when I hanged yet upon my mother's breasts — PBV

But thou art he that took me out of the womb: thou didst make me trust when I was upon my mother's breasts — RV

Yet thou didst bring me forth from the womb;
Thou didst give me security on my mother's breast — AAT

You have been my guide since I was first formed,
my security at my mother's breast — NAB

Yet you drew me out of the womb,
you entrusted me to my mother's breasts — Jerus

'Twas thou indeed didst take me from the womb,
didst lay me on my mother's breast — Mof

10. I was cast upon thee from the womb: thou art my God from my mother's belly.

I was cast upon thee from the womb;
Thou art my God since my mother bare me — ASV

Upon Thee I was cast from my birth;
From my earliest breath, Thou art my God! — DeW

From the hour of my birth, thou art my guardian; since I left my mother's womb, thou art my God! — Knox

placed on your lap from my birth,
from my mother's womb you have been my God — Jerus

I was thrown on Your care from birth;
from my conception You have been my God — Har

11. Be not far from me; for trouble is near; for there is none to help.

O go not from me; for trouble is hard at hand, and there is none to help me — PBV

O stand not at a distance from me; for trouble is near — for there is no helper — Sept

Do not leave me now, when trouble is close at hand; stand near, when

I have none to help me — Knox

12. Many bulls have compassed me: strong bulls of Bashan have beset me round.

Many oxen are come about me; fat bulls of Bashan close me in on every side — PBV

Many bulls have surrounded me;
The strong of Bashan encircle me — DeW

A brutal horde besets me,
fierce bulls of Bashan hem me in — Mof

My enemies ring me round, packed close as a herd of oxen, strong as bulls from Basan — Knox

I am surrounded by fearful enemies, strong as the giant bulls from Bashan — Tay

13. They gaped upon me with their mouths as a ravening and a roaring lion.

They have opened wide against me their mouth,
A lion rending and roaring — Rhm

panting for me open-mouthed,
like lions roaring as they rend — Mof

They have opened their mouths at me like a voracious, roaring lion — Har

14. I am poured out like water, and all my bones are out of joint:

I am poured out like water,
And all my bones are parted — ABPS

I am poured out like water, and all my bones are torn asunder — Sept

I am weak like water,
And all My bones are disjointed — Sprl

I am spent as spilt water, all my bones out of joint — Knox

my strength is weak as water,
all my limbs give way — Mof

My energy drains away from me like water,
and all my bones are dislocated — Har

I am like water draining away,
my bones are all disjointed — Jerus

my heart is like wax; it is melted in the midst of my bowels.

my heart also in the midst of my body is even like melting wax — PBV

My heart is like wax;
It is melted within me — ASV

My heart hath become like wax;
It is melted within my breast — DeW

My heart has become like wax
melting away within my bosom — NAB

my heart turned to molten wax within me — Knox

15. My strength is dried up like a potsherd;

Dried up as an earthen vessel is my power — YLT

My strength is dried up like baked earthenware — Har

my throat is as dry as a potsherd — Mof

My throat is dry like a broken vessel — Bas

My throat is dried up like baked clay — NAB

parched is my throat, like clay in the baking — Knox

and my tongue cleaveth to my jaws;

and my tongue sticks to my palate — Har

and my tongue is stuck to my jaw — Jerus

and thou hast brought me into the dust of death.

And in the dust of death wilt thou lay me — Rhm

and I am laid low in the dust of death — Mof

You are laying me in my last resting-place — Har

thou hast laid me in the dust, to die — Knox

16. For dogs have compassed me: the assembly of the wicked have enclosed me:

For dogs have surrounded me, —
An assembly of evil doers have encircled me — Rhm

A pack of dogs surrounds me,
a mob of ruffians encircles me — Har

The huntsmen are all about me;
a band of ruffians rings me round — NEB

The enemy, this gang of evil men, circles me like a pack of dogs — Tay

they pierced my hands and feet.

like a lion they mangle my hands and feet — Har

and they have hacked off my hands and my feet — NEB

17. I may tell all my bones: they look and stare upon me.

I may tell all my bones: they stand staring and looking upon me — PBV
As if they would number all My bones, They gaze at Me, they stare at Me — Sprl
I can count all my bones, But mine enemies gloat over me — DeW
I can count my bones one by one; and they stand there watching me, gazing at me in triumph — Knox
I can count all my bones; [the evildoers] gaze at me — Amp
I tell my tale of misery, while they look on and gloat — NEB

18. They part my garments among them, and cast lots upon my vesture.
They distribute my garments among them, And over my robe they cast lots — AAT
they divide my garments among them, and for my clothing do they cast lots — Ber
They divide my clothes among themselves by a toss of the dice — Tay

19. But be not thou far from me, O LORD: O my strength, haste thee to help me.
But be not thou far off, O Jehovah: O thou my succor, haste thee to help me — ASV
Do not remain aloof, Lord; hurry to my assistance, for You are my sustainer — Har

20. Deliver my soul from the sword;
Rescue from the sword my life — Rhm
Snatch away from the sword my life — DeW
Rescue me from the sword — Mof
my darling from the power of the dog.
From the power of the dog my solitary self — Rhm
My life from the power of the dog — ABPS
my dear life from the paw of the dog — Jerus
My only life from the power of the dog — DeW
Mine only one from the power of the dog — JPS
my only one from the hand of the vicious — Lam
spare my precious life from all these evil men — Tay
save my solitary soul from these powerful beasts — Har
save my life from these curs — Mof

21. Save me from the lion's mouth:
pluck me from the lion's jaws — Mof
Rescue me from the jaws of the lion — Har
for thou hast heard me from the horns of the unicorns.
Yea, from the horns of the wild-oxen thou hast answered me — ASV
Yea from the horns of wild beasts hast thou delivered me — Rhm
And from the horns of wild cattle — THOU HAST ANSWERED ME! — DeW
And my afflicted self from the horns of the wild ox — AAT
and my poor body from the horns of the wild ox — NEB

22. I will declare thy name unto my brethren: in the midst of the congregation will I praise thee.
I will declare thy name unto my brethren: In the midst of the assembly will I praise thee — ASV
Then shall I tell my fellows of thy fame, and praise thee in our gathering — Mof
I will tell my brothers of Your power, and sing Your praises in the great assembly — Har

23. Ye that fear the LORD, praise him; all ye the seed of Jacob, glorify him; and fear him, all ye the seed of Israel.
You who fear the LORD, praise him! all you sons of Jacob, glorify him, and stand in awe of him, all you sons of Israel! — RSV

24. For he hath not despised nor abhorred the affliction of the afflicted;
For He despised not, nor spurned the sufferer's pain — DeW
For He neither spurned nor loathed the afflictions of the oppressed — Har
For he has not despised or disdained the poor man in his poverty — Jerus
He has not scorned or slighted the appeal of the friendless — Knox
For he has not scorned the downtrodden, nor shrunk in loathing from his plight — NEB
For he has not been unmoved by the pain of him who is troubled — Bas
neither hath he hid his face from him;

but when he cried unto him, he heard.
and he has not hid his face from him, but has heard, when he cried to him — RSV
nor has He concealed His presence from them,
but has listened when they appealed to Him for help — Har

25. My praise shall be of thee in the great congregation:
From thee comes my praise in the great congregation — RSV
From Thee is my praise in the great assembly — DeW
Therefore do I praise him in our great gathering — Mof
Thou dost inspire my praise in the full assembly — NEB
I will praise You in the assembly — Har

I will pay my vows before them that fear him.
I pay my vows before his worshippers — Mof
I will pay my vows before those who revere Him — Ber
I will discharge my vows in the presence of His worshippers — Har
I will pay to Him my vows [made in the time of trouble] before them who fear — revere and worship — Him — Amp

26. The meek shall eat and be satisfied: they shall praise the LORD that seek him: your heart shall live for ever.
The afflicted shall eat and be satisfied; those who seek him shall praise the LORD!
May your hearts live for ever! — RSV
The lowly in spirit shall eat and be filled;
They that seek Jehovah shall praise Him:
May your heart find life for ever! — DeW
The lowly shall eat their fill;
they who seek the LORD shall praise him:
"May your hearts be ever merry!" — NAB
Let the humble eat and be satisfied.
Let those who seek the LORD praise him
and be in good heart for ever — NEB

27. All the ends of the world shall remember and turn unto the LORD:
The furthest dwellers on earth will bethink themselves of the Lord, and come back to him — Knox
The extremities of the earth will bear it in mind, and turn to the Lord — Har
The whole earth, from end to end, will remember and come back to Yahweh — Jerus
Let all the ends of the earth remember and turn again to the LORD — NEB

and all the kindreds of the nations shall worship before thee.
Yea all the families of the nations will bow themselves down before thee — Rhm
let all the families of the nations bow down before him — NEB
All the clans of the nations will worship before him — AAT
the entire human family will worship in His presence — Har
the people of every nation shall worship him — Tay

28. For the kingdom is the LORD's: and he is the governor among the nations.
For the kingdom is Jehovah's:
And he is the ruler over the nations — ASV
for the Eternal reigns, lord of all nations — Mof
For dominion belongs to the LORD, and he rules over the nations — RSV
to the Lord royalty belongs, the whole world's homage is his due — Knox
For Yahweh reigns, the ruler of nations! — Jerus

29. All they that be fat upon earth shall eat and worship: all they that go down to the dust shall bow before him: and none can keep alive his own soul.
All the fat ones of the earth shall eat and worship:
All they that go down to the dust shall bow before him,
Even he that cannot keep his soul alive — ASV
They eat and worship, all the rich of the earth;
Before him shall bow all that go down to the dust,
And he that can not keep his soul alive — ABPS

Yea, to him shall all the proud of the earth bow down;
before him shall bow all who go down to the dust,
and he who cannot keep himself alive — RSV
prosperous peoples sacrifice to him and worship,
dying peoples bow before him,
folk who cannot keep themselves alive — Mof
All the mighty ones upon earth shall eat [in thanksgiving] and worship; all they that go down to the dust shall bow before Him, even he who cannot keep himself alive — Amp
Prosperous men have become sated and corrupt;
yet all who are dying shall acknowledge His supremacy,
for no one preserves his soul alive — Har
To him alone shall bow down
all who sleep in the earth;
Before him shall bend
all who go down into the dust.
And to him my soul shall live; — NAB

30. **A seed shall serve him; it shall be accounted to the Lord for a generation.**
A seed shall serve him; it shall be told of the Lord unto the next generation — RV
my descendants shall serve him.
Let the coming generation be told of the LORD — NAB
Posterity shall serve him;
men shall tell of the LORD to the coming generation — RSV
Posterity will serve Him,
and tell of the Lord to future generations — Har
Our children too shall serve him, for they shall hear from us about the wonders of the Lord — Tay

31. **They shall come, and shall declare his righteousness unto a people that shall be born, that he hath done this.**
and they will proclaim his saving mercy to a people that shall be born, whom the Lord made — Sept
his saving deeds shall be declared
to generations yet unborn — Mof
And may they tell of his righteousness to the people that shall be born,
That he has wrought it — AAT
and proclaim his deliverance to a people yet unborn,
that he has wrought it — RSV
that they may proclaim to a people yet to be born
the justice he has shown — NAB
Generations yet unborn shall hear of all the miracles He did for us — Tay

PSALM 23

A Psalm of David.

1. **The LORD is my shepherd; I shall not want.**
The Lord is my shepherd; therefore can I lack nothing — PBV
The Lord shepherds me,
I shall never be in need — Har
Yahweh is my shepherd,
I lack nothing — Jerus
The Lord is my shepherd [to feed, guide and shield me]; I shall not lack — Amp
The Lord takes care of me as his sheep; I will not be without any good thing — Bas
Because the Lord is my shepherd, I have everything I need! — Tay

2. **He maketh me to lie down in green pastures: he leadeth me beside the still waters.**
He shall feed me in a green pasture, and lead me forth beside the waters of comfort — PBV
In pastures of tender grass he maketh me lie down,
Unto restful waters he leadeth me — Rhm
In a verdant pasture he hath fixed my abode. He hath fed me by gently flowing water — Sept
He maketh me to repose in verdant pastures;
Beside the tranquil waters He will gently guide me — Sprl
he makes me lie in meadows green,
he leads me to refreshing streams — Mof
He makes a resting-place for me in the green fields: he is my guide by the quiet waters — Bas

3. **He restoreth my soul: he leadeth me**

in the paths of righteousness for his name's sake.

He gives new life to my soul: he is my guide in the ways of righteousness because of his name — Bas

He gives me renewed life,
He guides me along a virtuous course
in accordance with His nature — Har

there he revives my soul.
He guides me by paths of virtue for the sake of his name — Jerus

he renews life within me,
and for his name's sake guides me in the right path — NEB

. . . as in honour pledged, by sure paths he leads me — Knox

He restores my failing health. He helps me do what honors him the most — Tay

4. Yea, though I walk through the valley of the shadow of death, I will fear no evil: for thou art with me;

Yea though I walk through a valley death-shadowed
I will fear no harm for thou art with me — Rhm

For though I walk amidst the shades of death: I will fear no ills, because thou art with me — Sept

My road may run through a glen of gloom,
but I fear no harm, for thou art beside me — Mof

Even though I walk in the darkest valley,
I fear no harm; for thou art with me — AAT

Even though I walk through a valley dark as death
I fear no evil, for thou art with me — NEB

thy rod and thy staff they comfort me.

thy rod and thy staff have been my comfort — Sept

thy club, thy staff — they give me courage — Mof

thy rod, thy crook are my comfort — Knox

Your rod [to protect] and Your staff [to guide], they comfort me — Amp

Your strength and support are indeed my comfort — Har

5. Thou preparest a table before me in the presence of mine enemies:

Thou shalt prepare a table before me in the presence of them that trouble me — PBV

Thou art my host, spreading a feast for me
while my foes have to look on! — Mof

Envious my foes watch, while thou dost spread a banquet for me — Knox

thou anointest my head with oil; my cup runneth over.

thou hast anointed my head with oil, and my cup shall be full — PBV

Thou hast anointed with oil my head, my cup hath run over — Rhm

Thou hast anointed with oil my head, My cup is full! — YLT

Thou hast anointed my head with oil. Ah! my cup overfloweth — Sprl

Thou hast poured oil upon my head, my cup is brimming over — Mof

You anoint my head with oil,
my fortunes prosper greatly — Har

You have welcomed me as your guest; blessings overflow! — Tay

6. Surely goodness and mercy shall follow me all the days of my life:

Surely thy loving-kindness and mercy shall follow me all the days of my life — PBV

Surely goodness and lovingkindness will pursue me all the days of my life — Rhm

Goodness and love alone will accompany me through life — Har

Surely, goodness and unfailing love shall follow me all the days of my life — Ber

and I will dwell in the house of the LORD for ever.

Through the long years the Lord's house shall be my dwelling-place — Knox

and I shall live in the house of the Lord all my days — Har

my home, the house of Yahweh,
as long as I live! — Jerus

PSALM 24

A Psalm of David.

1. The earth is the LORD's, and the fulness thereof;
The earth is the LORD's, and all that therein is — PBV
The earth belongs to the Eternal, and all earth holds — Mof
The earth is the Lord's, with all its wealth — Bas
the world, and they that dwell therein.
the world and all the people living in it — Bas
the world and all its inhabitants — Sept

2. For he hath founded it upon the seas, and established it upon the floods.
For it is He that founded it upon the seas,
That made it firm upon the floods — DeW
For he founded it upon the seas,
And established it upon the ocean-currents — AAT
for he has founded it upon the seas, and established it upon the rivers — RSV
For it was he who founded it upon the seas
and planted it firm upon the waters beneath — NEB

3. Who shall ascend into the hill of the LORD? or who shall stand in his holy place?
Who dares climb the mountain of the Lord, and appear in his sanctuary — Knox
Who has the right to climb the mountain of Yahweh,
who the right to stand in his holy place — Jerus

4. He that hath clean hands, and a pure heart;
The clean of hands
And pure of heart — Rhm
The guiltless in act, the pure in heart — Knox
The man of impeccable behavior and pure motives — Har
who hath not lifted up his soul unto vanity, nor sworn deceitfully.
Who hath not lifted up his soul unto falsehood,
And hath not sworn deceitfully — ASV
who does not lift up his soul to what is false,
and does not swear deceitfully — RSV
Whoso hath not lifted up his heart unto an idol,
Neither sworn intending to deceive — Sprl
whose soul does not pay homage to worthless things
and who never swears to a lie — Jerus
who never sets his mind on what is false,
who never breaks his word — Mof
who desires not what is vain,
nor swears deceitfully to his neighbor — NAB

5. He shall receive the blessing from the LORD, and righteousness from the God of his salvation.
He shall receive a blessing from Jehovah,
And righteousness from the God of his salvation — ASV
He will receive a blessing from the LORD,
And justification from the God of his deliverance — AAT
He will receive blessing from the LORD,
and vindication from the God of his salvation — RSV

6. This is the generation of them that seek him, that seek thy face, O Jacob.
This is the generation of them that seek after him, that seek thy face, O God of Jacob — RV
Such is the generation of those who seek him,
who seek the face of the God of Jacob — RSV
Of such a kind are those who resort to Him,
looking for the presence of Jacob's God — Har
These are the ones who are allowed to stand before the Lord and worship the God of Jacob — Tay
Such is the fortune of those who seek him,
who seek the face of the God of Jacob — NEB
Selah.
(Pause.) — ABPS

7. **Lift up your heads, O ye gates; and be ye lift up, ye everlasting doors;**
Lift up your heads, O gates!
and be lifted up, O ancient doors! — RSV
Gates, raise your arches,
rise, you ancient doors — Jerus
and the King of glory shall come in.
That the king of glory may come in — Rhm
Welcome the glorious King! — Mof
to let the King enter in triumph! — Knox
let the king of glory in! — Jerus
8. **Who is this King of glory?**
Who, then, is the King of Glory — DeW
The LORD strong and mighty, the LORD mighty in battle.
Jehovah strong and mighty,
Jehovah mighty in battle — ASV
The Lord, strong and mighty, invincible in battle — Tay
9. **Lift up your heads, O ye gates; even lift them up, ye everlasting doors:**
Gates, raise your arches,
rise, you ancient doors — Jerus
and the King of glory shall come in.
that the glorious King may enter — Har
10. **Who is this King of glory?**
Who is this glorious King — Har
The LORD of hosts, he is the King of glory.
Jehovah of hosts,
He is the King of glory — ASV
The Lord of armies, he is the King of glory — Bas
He is Yahweh Sabaoth,
King of glory, he! — Jerus
The Commander of all of heaven's armies! — Tay
Selah.
(Pause.) — ABPS

PSALM 25

A Psalm of David.

1. **Unto thee, O LORD, do I lift up my soul.**
On thee, Eternal One, I set my heart — Mof
To you, O Lord, I pray — Tay
2. **O my God, I trust in thee: let me not be ashamed, let not mine enemies triumph over me.**
Let me not be put to shame,
Let not my foe exult over me — Rhm
do not let me be disappointed:
do not allow my rivals to triumph over me — Har
Don't let my enemies succeed. Don't give them victory over me — Tay
3. **Yea, let none that wait on thee be ashamed: let them be ashamed which transgress without cause.**
Yea, let none that wait for thee be put to shame;
let them be ashamed who are wantonly treacherous — RSV
Surely no one who trusts in You will be disgraced.
May those who behave deceitfully for no reason be humiliated — Har
No, those who hope in you are never shamed,
shame awaits disappointed traitors — Jerus
No man who hopes in thee is put to shame;
but shame comes to all who break faith without cause — NEB
4. **Shew me thy ways, O LORD; teach me thy paths.**
Make known Your plans to me, Lord;
inform me of Your intentions — Har
5. **Lead me in thy truth, and teach me:**
Guide me by Your truth and instruct me — Har
Set me in the way of your truth, and teach me — Jerus
Make me to tread along in Thy truth, and teach me — Sprl
for thou art the God of my salvation; on thee do I wait all the day.
for thou art the God of my salvation;
in thee hath been my hope all the day long — PBV
For thou art my delivering God,
For thee have I waited all the day — Rhm
For thou art the God of my help;
For thee do I long continually — AAT
6. **Remember, O LORD, thy tender mercies and thy lovingkindnesses; for they have been ever of old.**
Be mindful of thy mercy, O LORD. and of thy steadfast love,

for they have been from of old — RSV
Remember thy compassions O Yahweh and thy lovingkindnesses,
For from age-past times have they been — Rhm
Remember Your sympathy and mercy, Lord,
for they are eternal — Har
Remember your kindness, Yahweh, your love that you showed long ago — Jerus

7. Remember not the sins of my youth, nor my transgressions:
Do not recall my youthful sins and offences — Har
Overlook my youthful sins, O Lord! — Tay
according to thy mercy remember thou me for thy goodness' sake, O LORD.
according to thy steadfast love remember me,
for thy goodness' sake, O LORD! — RSV
but according to thy mercy think thou upon me, O LORD, for thy goodness — PBV
but think of me in terms of Your unfailing love,
because You are the essence of goodness — Har

8. Good and upright is the LORD: therefore will he teach sinners in the way.
Gracious and righteous is the LORD; therefore will he teach sinners in the way — PBV
Good and upright is Yahweh,
For this cause will he direct sinners into the way — Rhm
Kind and upright is the Eternal,
he teaches any who go astray — Mof

9. The meek will he guide in judgment: and the meek will he teach his way.
The meek will he guide in justice;
And the meek will he teach his way — ASV
May he guide patient wronged-ones to be righted,
And teach such oppressed-ones his way — Rhm
He gives proper direction to the humble, and reveals His plans to the lowly — Har
He will be an upright guide to the poor in spirit: he will make his way clear to them — Bas

10. All the paths of the LORD are mercy and truth unto such as keep his covenant and his testimonies.
All the paths of the LORD are steadfast love and faithfulness,
for those who keep his covenant and his testimonies — RSV
All the paths of Jehovah are lovingkindness and truth
Unto such as keep his covenant and his testimonies — ASV
kindly and faithfully he ever deals with those who keep his compact and commands — Mof
The Lord is the essence of mercy and truth
for those who observe His covenant and His decrees — Har
All the ways of the LORD are loving and sure
to men who keep his covenant and his charge — NEB
And when we obey him, every path he guides us on is fragrant with his lovingkindness and his truth — Tay

11. For thy name's sake, O LORD, pardon mine iniquity; for it is great.
For thy name's sake, O LORD,
pardon my guilt, for it is great — RSV
Because of what You are, Lord,
pardon my sin, despite its extent — Har
But Lord, my sins! How many they are. Oh, pardon them for the honor of your name — Tay

12. What man is he that feareth the LORD?
Who then is the man that revereth Yahweh — Rhm
If there is any man who fears the LORD, — NEB
him shall he teach in the way that he shall choose.
He will point out to him the direction which he should take — Har
he shall be shown the path that he should choose — NEB

13. His soul shall dwell at ease; and his seed shall inherit the earth.
He abides in prosperity,
and his descendants inherit the land — NAB
He himself shall abide in prosperity,
and his children shall possess the land — RSV

14. The secret of the LORD is with them that fear him; and he will shew them his covenant.
The secret of the Lord is with those

in whose hearts is the fear of him; he will make his agreement clear to them — Bas

The close secret of Yahweh belongs to them who fear him, his covenant also, to bring them knowledge — Jerus

The LORD confides his purposes to those who fear him, and his covenant is theirs to know — NEB

Friendship with God is reserved for those who reverence him. With them alone he shares the secrets of his promises — Tay

Intimate communion with the Lord is the prerogative of those who revere Him; to them only He reveals His covenant — Har

15. Mine eyes are ever toward the LORD, for he shall pluck my feet out of the net.

On the Lord I fix my eyes continually, trusting him to save my feet from the snare — Knox

My eyes are ever looking to the Lord for help, for he alone can rescue me — Tay

16. Turn thee unto me, and have mercy upon me;

Turn thou unto me, and shew me favour — Rhm

for I am desolate and afflicted.

for I am desolate, and in misery — PBV

For alone and oppressed I am — Rhm

For I am lonely and suffering — DeW

17. The troubles of my heart are enlarged: O bring thou me out of my distresses.

the troubles of my heart are multiplied: O deliver me from these my distresses — Sept

The sorrows of my heart are enlarged: O bring thou me out of my troubles — PBV

The distresses of my heart hath he relieved, — And out of my straits brought me forth — Rhm

Relieve the oppression of my heart, And bring me out of my distresses — DeW

relieve the anguish of my heart, free me from all this pressure — Mof

Give me respite from trouble, and rid me of my afflictions — Har

18. Look upon mine affliction and my pain; and forgive all my sins.

Consider my affliction and my trouble, and forgive all my sins — RSV

Behold my humiliation and my pain, And take away all my sins — Rhm

Take stock of my misery and wretchedness, and forgive all my sins — Har

19. Consider mine enemies; for they are many; and they hate me with cruel hatred.

Consider how many are my foes, and with what violent hatred they hate me — RSV

20. O keep my soul, and deliver me: let me not be ashamed; for I put my trust in thee.

Oh keep my soul, and deliver me: Let me not be put to shame, for I take refuge in thee — ASV

Protect me and rescue me; do not let me be discredited, for I have put my faith in You — Har

Save me from them! Deliver my life from their power! Oh, let it never be said that I trusted you in vain! — Tay

21. Let integrity and uprightness preserve me; for I wait on thee.

Let blamelessness and uprightness watch over me, Because I have waited for thee — Rhm

Uprightness and purity be my shield, as I wait patiently, Lord, for thy help — Knox

Let innocence and integrity be my protection, since my hope is in you, Yahweh — Jerus

Assign me Godliness and Integrity as my bodyguards, for I expect you to protect me — Tay

22. Redeem Israel, O God, out of all his troubles.

Redeem Israel O God, — Out of all his distresses — Rhm

PSALM 26

A Psalm of David.

1. Judge me, O LORD; for I have walked in mine integrity:
Vindicate me, O LORD,
for I have walked in my integrity — RSV
Do me justice O Yahweh
For I in my blamelessness have walked — Rhm
Do what is right by me, Lord,
for I have conducted myself blamelessly — Har
I have trusted also in the LORD; therefore I shall not slide.
my trust hath been also in the LORD,
therefore shall I not fall — PBV
And in JEHOVAH have I put my trust;
I shall not falter — Sprl
I have trusted also in Jehovah without wavering — ASV
my trust in the Eternal never wavers — Mof
and I have placed unswerving faith in the Lord — Har

2. Examine me, O LORD, and prove me; try my reins and my heart.
Examine me, O Jehovah, and prove me;
Try my heart and my mind — ASV
Examine me, O JEHOVAH, and prove me;
Purify my inner self, and my heart — Sprl
Search me, O Jehovah! and try me;
Cleanse from evil mine inmost heart! — DeW
Try me, Lord, and test me;
examine my motives and my mind — Har
Test me, Lord, put me to the proof;
assay my inmost desires and thoughts — Knox
Search me, O Lord, and try me;
test my soul and my heart — NAB

3. For thy lovingkindness is before mine eyes: and I have walked in thy truth.
For thy lovingkindness hath been before mine eyes,
And I have walked to and fro in thy faithfulness — Rhm
For Thy kindness is before mine eyes,
And I have walked habitually in Thy truth — YLT
For thy steadfast love is before my eyes,
and I walk in faithfulness to thee — RSV
For Your gracious love is at the forefront of my mind,
and I have lived by your principles of truth — Har
For I have taken your lovingkindness
and your truth as my ideals — Tay

4. I have not sat with vain persons, neither will I go in with dissemblers.
I have not dwelt with vain persons;
neither will I have fellowship with the deceitful — PBV
I have not sat with men of falsehood;
Neither will I go in with dissemblers — ASV
I do not sit with false men,
nor do I consort with dissemblers — RSV
I never mix with deceitful people,
nor do I associate with hypocrites — Har
I have not associated with deceptive men,
nor do I fellowship with pretenders — Ber

5. I have hated the congregation of evildoers; and will not sit with the wicked.
I have hated the convocation of evildoers,
And with lawless men would I not sit — Rhm
I hate the company of evildoers,
And with reprobates I will not sit down — AAT
I detest the company of criminals,
and I refuse to mingle with the wicked — Har
I hate the sinners' hangouts and refuse to enter them — Tay

6. I will wash mine hands in innocency: so will I compass thine altar, O LORD:
I will bathe in pureness my hands, —
So will I go in procession around thine altar O Yahweh — Rhm
I wash my hands in innocence
and join the procession round your altar — Jerus

7. That I may publish with the voice of thanksgiving, and tell of all thy wondrous works.
That I may make the voice of thanksgiving to be heard, and tell of all thy wondrous works — RV
To sound aloud a song,

And to recount all thy wonderful doings — Rhm
singing aloud a song of thanksgiving, and telling all thy wondrous deeds — RSV
Giving voice to my thanks, and recounting all your wondrous deeds — NAB

8. LORD, I have loved the habitation of thy house, and the place where thine honour dwelleth.

Jehovah, I love the habitation of thy house,
And the place where thy glory dwelleth — ASV
O Yahweh I have loved the asylum of thy house,
Even the place of the habitation of thy glory! — Rhm
I adore the shrine where You dwell, Lord,
and the place where Your glory resides — Har
O LORD, I love the house in which you dwell,
the tenting-place of your glory — NAB
Lord, I love your home, this shrine where the brilliant, dazzling splendor of your presence lives — Tay

9. Gather not my soul with sinners, nor my life with bloody men:

Sweep me not away with sinners, nor my life with bloodthirsty men — RSV
Sweep me not away with sinful men, slay me not with the bloodthirsty — Mof
Do not let my soul share the fate of sinners,
or my life the doom of men of blood — Jerus

10. In whose hands is mischief, and their right hand is full of bribes.

men in whose hands are evil devices, and whose right hands are full of bribes — RSV
In whose hands there is crime,
And their right hands are full of bribes! — DeW
whose hands are stained with outrage, their right hands full of bribes — Mof
whose hands are soiled with villainy, their right hands overflowing with bribes — Har
hands ever stained with guilt, palms ever itching for a bribe! — Knox
men with guilt on their hands,
whose right hands are heavy with bribes — Jerus

11. But as for me, I will walk in mine integrity: redeem me, and be merciful unto me.

For my part I will continue in my integrity;
deliver me and act graciously towards me — Har

12. My foot standeth in an even place: in the congregations will I bless the LORD.

My foot standeth in an even place;
In the assemblies I bless Jehovah! — DeW
My foot stands on level ground;
in the great congregation I will bless the LORD — RSV
On sure ground my feet are set;
where his people gather I will join in blessing the Lord's name — Knox
I have a safe resting-place for my feet; I will give praise to the Lord in the meetings of the people — Bas

PSALM 27

A Psalm of David.

1. The LORD is my light and my salvation; whom shall I fear? the LORD is the strength of my life; of whom shall I be afraid?

Yahweh is the refuge of my life
Of whom shall I be in dread — Rhm
Jehovah is the stronghold of my life;
Of whom shall I be in dread — ABPS
The Lord is the defender of my life.
Of whom shall I be afraid — Sept
Yahweh is the fortress of my life,
of whom should I be afraid — Jerus

2. When the wicked, even mine enemies and my foes, came upon me to eat up my flesh, they stumbled and fell.

When evil men assail me
with their slanders,
'tis they, my enemies and foes,
who stumble to their fall — Mof
When deadly enemies assailed me,
to devour me completely,

it was those very opponents and enemies of mine
who stumbled and fell — Har
Vainly the malicious close about me, as if they would tear me in pieces, vainly my enemies threaten me; all at once they stumble and fall — Knox

3. **Though an host should encamp against me, my heart shall not fear:**
Even though an army were arrayed against me,
my heart would have no fear — Mof
Though a whole host were arrayed against me, my heart would be undaunted — Knox
though war should rise against me, in this will I be confident.
Should war rise against me,
Even then will I be trustful — DeW
if war was made on me, my faith would not be moved — Bas
though war were waged against me, my trust would still be firm — Jerus

4. **One thing have I desired of the LORD, that will I seek after;**
One thing only I request of the Lord — something which I earnestly desire — Har
One favour I have asked of the Lord; and this I will earnestly seek — Sept
that I may dwell in the house of the LORD all the days of my life, to behold the beauty of the LORD, and to inquire in his temple.
That I may dwell in the house of Yahweh all the days of my life,
To view the delightfulness of Yahweh
And to contemplate in his temple — Rhm
That I may dwell in the house of Jehovah
All the days of my life,
To enjoy the graciousness of Jehovah,
And to delight in His temple — DeW
to dwell in the Lord's house my whole life long, resting content in the Lord's goodness, gazing at his temple — Knox
to live in the house of Yahweh
all the days of my life,
to enjoy the sweetness of Yahweh
and to consult him in his Temple — Jerus
To dwell in the house of the LORD
all the days of my life,
That I may gaze on the loveliness of the LORD
and contemplate his temple — NAB

5. **For in the time of trouble he shall hide me in his pavilion:**
For he will hide me in his shelter in the day of trouble — RSV
For in the time of my misfortune He will shelter me in His house — Har
For in the time of trouble he will keep me safe in his tent — Bas
in the secret of his tabernacle shall he hide me; he shall set me upon a rock.
He will conceal me in the secrecy of his tent,
Within a rock will he set me on high — Rhm
He will hide me in His haven of refuge, and establish me upon a firm foundation — Har
he will hide me under the cover of his tent;
he will raise me beyond the reach of distress — NEB

6. **And now shall mine head be lifted up above mine enemies round about me:**
And now shall my head be high above my enemies round about me — ABPS
Then shall my head be set on high,
Above mine enemies around me — DeW
Now I can raise my head high
above the enemy all about me — NEB
And now I am elevated above my foes who hem me in — Har
Even now my head is held high
above my enemies on every side — NAB
therefore will I offer in his tabernacle sacrifices of joy; I will sing, yea, I will sing praises unto the LORD.
and I will offer in his tent
sacrifices with shouts of joy;
I will sing and make melody to the LORD — RSV
at this time I will offer joyous sacrifices in His shrine;
I will sing and proclaim the praises of the Lord — Har
And I will sacrifice in his tent the sacrifices of triumphant joy,
I will sing and touch the strings to Yahweh — Rhm
And I will offer in his tabernacle
Sacrifices with a trumpet sound:

I will sing and strike the harp to Jehovah — DeW

7. **Hear, O LORD, when I cry with my voice: have mercy also upon me, and answer me.**

Hear O Yahweh, With my voice do I cry,
Oh then shew me favour and answer me — Rhm

Hear my voice, O Jehovah! when I call;
Deal kindly with me, and answer me — DeW

O JEHOVAH! listen to my voice when I cry aloud;
And be compassionate unto me, and answer me — Sprl

Yahweh, hear my voice as I cry!
Pity me! Answer me! — Jerus

8. **When thou saidst, Seek ye my face; my heart said unto thee, Thy face, LORD, will I seek.**

Thou hast said, "Seek ye my face."
My heart says to thee,
"Thy face, LORD, do I seek" — RSV

My heart has said of you,
'Seek his face.'
Yahweh, I do seek your face — Jerus

My heart has heard you say, "Come and talk with me, O my people."
And my heart responds, "Lord, I am coming" — Tay

9. **Hide not thy face far from me; put not thy servant away in anger: thou hast been my help;**

Hide not thy face from me.
Turn not thy servant away in anger,
thou who hast been my help — RSV

leave me not, neither forsake me, O God of my salvation.

cast me not off, neither forsake me,
O God of my salvation — RV

Do not send me away nor forsake me
O my saving God! — Rhm

Never leave me, never desert me,
God, my saviour! — Jerus

10. **When my father and my mother forsake me, then the LORD will take me up.**

For my father and my mother have forsaken me,
but the LORD will take me up — RSV

When my own father and mother had forsaken me
Then Yahweh took me up! — Rhm

Even if my father and mother were to forsake me,
the Lord would adopt me — Har

Father and mother may neglect me,
but the Lord takes me into his care — Knox

If my father and mother desert me,
Yahweh will care for me still — Jerus

11. **Teach me thy way, O LORD, and lead me in a plain path, because of mine enemies.**

Point out to me O Yahweh, thy way, —
And guide me in a level path,
Because of mine adversaries — Rhm

Teach me what is thy way, O thou Eternal,
and lead me by a level road;
let not my foes thwart me — Mof

Reveal Your designs to me, Lord,
and give me direct guidance on account of my enemies — Har

Tell me what to do, O Lord, and make it plain because I am surrounded by waiting enemies — Tay

12. **Deliver me not over unto the will of mine enemies:**

Do not give me up unto the desire of mine adversaries — Rhm

Deliver me not up to the will of them who are afflicting me — Sept

Do not abandon me to the schemes of my rivals — Har

for false witnesses are risen up against me, and such as breathe out cruelty.

For false witnesses rise against me,
That pant after cruelty — DeW

for false witnesses have risen against me,
and they breathe out violence — RSV

for men of bad faith have risen against me,
fuming violently — Har

13. **I had fainted, unless I had believed to see the goodness of the LORD in the land of the living.**

What if I had not believed to see the LORD's goodness
in the land of the living! — Ber

I believe that I shall see the goodness of the LORD
in the land of the living! — RSV

However, I am confident
that I shall see the goodness of the Lord
in this present life — Har

I am expecting the Lord to rescue me again, so that once again I will see his goodness to me here in the land of the living — Tay

14. Wait on the LORD: be of good courage, and he shall strengthen thine heart:

Wait for the LORD with courage; be stouthearted — NAB

Wait for Jehovah: Be strong, and let thy heart take courage — ASV

Wait thou for Yahweh, — Be strong and let thy heart be bold — Rhm

Wait patiently for the Lord to help thee; be brave, and let thy heart take comfort — Knox

wait, I say, on the LORD.

Yea, wait thou for Jehovah — ASV

put your hope in Yahweh — Jerus

Trust in the Lord — Har

PSALM 28

A Psalm of David.

1. Unto thee will I cry, O LORD my rock; be not silent to me:

Unto thee will I cry, O LORD. my strength: think no scorn of me — PBV

Unto thee Yahweh do I cry O my Rock! do not turn in silence from me — Rhm

Unto Thee, O Jehovah! I call; O my Rock! be not deaf to me — DeW

I am calling to You, Lord; do not be indifferent to me, my strong defense — Har

lest, if thou be silent to me, I become like them that go down into the pit.

lest, if thou art deaf, I droop like a dying man — Mof

for if You pay no attention to me I shall become like those who have been buried — Har

listen to me, or I am no better than a dead man, sinking to the grave — Knox

If you refuse to answer me, I might as well give up and die — Tay

2. Hear the voice of my supplications, when I cry unto thee,

Hear the voice of my supplications when I cry to thee for help — ABPS

when I lift up my hands toward thy holy oracle.

when I hold up my hands towards the mercy-seat of thy holy temple — PBV

When I lift up my hands toward thy holy shrine — Rhm

as I lift up my hands toward thy most holy sanctuary — RSV

as I raise my hands in prayer towards thy holy temple — Knox

3. Draw me not away with the wicked, and with the workers of iniquity, which speak peace to their neighbours, but mischief is in their hearts.

Do not drag me away — With the lawless Or with the workers of iniquity, — Who speak peaceably with their neighbours, But wrong is in their heart — Rhm

Snatch me not away with the wicked, and with those who do wrong, Who offer friendly greetings to their neighbors, while evil is in their hearts — AAT

4. Give them according to their deeds, and according to the wickedness of their endeavours:

Reward them according to their works; And according to the wickedness of their doings — Sprl

Repay them for their deeds, for the evil of their doings — NAB

give them after the work of their hands; render to them their desert.

Recompense them after the work of their hands; pay them that they have deserved — PBV

For the work of their hands repay them; give them their deserts — NAB

as they did, be it done to them, in their own coin repaid — Knox

5. Because they regard not the works of the LORD, nor the operation of his hands, he shall destroy them, and not build them up.

Because they do not regard the works of the Lord, or the work of his hands, he will break them down and build them up no more — RSV

For they have no respect for what the Lord has done,
nor for the manifestations of His power.
(May He demolish them: May He not establish them.) — Har

Of the Lord's acts, the Lord's ways, they took no heed; ruin be theirs, ruin irreparable — Knox

How blind they are to the works of Yahweh,
to his own handiwork!
May he pull them down and not rebuild them! — Jerus

They care nothing for God or what he has done or what he has made; therefore God will dismantle them like old buildings, never to be rebuilt again — Tay

6. Blessed be the LORD, because he hath heard the voice of my supplications.

Praised be the LORD; for he hath heard the voice of my humble petitions — PBV

Blessed be the Eternal, who has listened to my voice of pleading! — Mof

May the Lord be praised
for listening to my imploring voice — Har

Blessed be the LORD,
for he has heard my cry for mercy — NEB

7. The LORD is my strength and my shield;

The Lord is my strength and my protection — Har

The LORD is my defense and my shield — Ber

my heart trusted in him, and I am helped: therefore my heart greatly rejoiceth; and with my song will I praise him.

my heart hath trusted in him, and I am helped; therefore my heart danceth for joy, and in song will I praise him — PBV

Trusting in him, I found redress; there is triumph in my heart, on my lips the song of praise — Knox

I trusted in him, and he helped me! Joy rises in my heart until I burst out in songs of praise to him — Tay

8. The LORD is their strength, and he is the saving strength of his anointed.

Jehovah is their strength,
And he is a stronghold of salvation to his anointed — ASV

Yahweh is strength to his people, —
And the all-saving refuge of his Anointed One is he! — Rhm

The LORD is the strength of his people and a refuge;
the help of his anointed is he — AAT

The Lord is the strength of His people,
a safe refuge for His anointed — Har

The LORD is their protection;
He is the saving defence of His anointed — Ber

Yahweh is the strength of his people,
a saving fortress for his anointed — Jerus

The Lord defends his own people, protects the kind he has anointed — Knox

The Lord is their [unyielding] strength, and He is the stronghold of salvation to [me] His Anointed — Amp

9. Save thy people, and bless thine inheritance:

Give victory to thy people,
and bless thine inheritance — AAT

Be a saviour to your people, and send a blessing on your heritage — Bas

Lord, save thy people, bless thine own chosen race — Knox

feed them also, and lift them up for ever.

Be their shepherd also, and bear them up for ever — ASV

be thou their shepherd, and carry them for ever — RSV

shepherd them and support them for ever — Har

be their shepherd, evermore in thy arms upholding them — Knox

Lead them like a shepherd and carry them forever in your arms — Tay

PSALM 29

A Psalm of David.

1. Give unto the LORD, O ye mighty, give unto the LORD glory and strength.

Ascribe unto the LORD, O ye mighty, ascribe unto the LORD worship and strength — PBV

Ascribe to the LORD, O heavenly beings, ascribe to the LORD glory and strength — RSV

Praise the Lord, you angels of his; praise his glory and his strength — Tay

2. Give unto the LORD the glory due unto his name; worship the LORD in the beauty of holiness.

Ascribe unto the LORD the honour due unto his Name; worship the LORD with holy worship — PBV

Ascribe unto Jehovah the glory due unto his name;
Worship Jehovah in holy array — ASV

Give to Yahweh the glory of his Name,
Bow down to Yahweh in the adornment of holiness — Rhm

Give to Jehovah the glory of His name,
Worship Jehovah in holy attire! — DeW

Praise the Eternal for his open glory, worship the Eternal in festal attire! — Mof

Ascribe to the Lord the renown due to him;
worship the Lord in seemly attire — Har

3. The voice of the LORD is upon the waters: the God of glory thundereth; the LORD is upon many waters.

The voice of the LORD is upon the waters;
the God of glory thunders,
the LORD, upon many waters — RSV

The voice of the Eternal peals across the waters —
it is the God of glory thundering,
the Eternal pealing over the mighty waters — Mof

The Lord fulminates across the waters;
the glorious God is thundering.
The Lord roars out over the vast deeps — Har

The voice of the LORD is upon the waters; it is the glorious God that maketh the thunder. It is the LORD that ruleth the sea — PBV

4. The voice of the LORD is powerful; the voice of the LORD is full of majesty.

The voice of the LORD is mighty in operation; the voice of the LORD is a glorious voice — PBV

The voice of Yahweh is with power,
The voice of Yahweh is with majesty — Rhm

The thunder of the Lord is resplendent with power;
the thunder of the Lord is majestic — Har

The voice of Yahweh in power!
The voice of Yahweh in splendour! — Jerus

5. The voice of the LORD breaketh the cedars; yea, the LORD breaketh the cedars of Lebanon.

The voice of Jehovah breaketh the cedars;
Yea, Jehovah breaketh in pieces the cedars of Lebanon — ASV

His thunder shatters the cedars;
the Lord uproots the cedars of Lebanon — Har

6. He maketh them also to skip like a calf; Lebanon and Sirion like a young unicorn.

And hath made them leap like a calf,
Lebanon and Sirion like the bull-calf of wild oxen — Rhm

And He maketh them spring like a calf,
Lebanon and Sirion like a young antelope — DeW

He makes Lebanon jump like a calf,
and Sirion like a young buffalo — Har

making Lebanon leap like a calf,
Sirion like a young wild bull — Jerus

7. The voice of the LORD divideth the flames of fire.

The voice of the LORD flashes forth flames of fire — RSV

The thunder of the Lord
carves out tongues of flame — Har

The Lord's voice kindles flashing fire — Knox

The voice of Yahweh sharpens lightning shafts! — Jerus

8. The voice of the LORD shaketh the wilderness; the LORD shaketh the wilderness of Kadesh.

The voice of Yahweh bringeth birth-pains upon the wilderness;
Yahweh bringeth birth-pains upon the wilderness of Kadesh! — Rhm

the voice of the LORD makes the wilderness writhe in travail;
the LORD makes the wilderness of Kadesh writhe — NEB

the voice of the Eternal whirls the sand,
the Eternal whirls the desert of Kadesh — Mof

The voice of the LORD makes the desert whirl;
The LORD whirls the desert of Kadesh — AAT

the thunder of the Lord stirs up the desert.
The Lord makes the wilderness of Kadesh tremble — Har

9. The voice of the LORD maketh the hinds to calve, and discovereth the forests:

The voice of the LORD maketh the hinds to bring forth young, and strippeth bare the forests — PBV

The voice of Yahweh causeth the gazelles to bring forth
And hath stript forests — Rhm

The voice of the LORD makes the hinds calve
and brings kids early to birth — NEB

The voice of the LORD makes the oaks to whirl,
and strips the forests bare — RSV

JEHOVAH's voice causeth the oaks to whither,
And denudeth the trees of the woods — Sprl

The voice of the Eternal twists the trees,
the voice of the Eternal strips the forest — Mof

The thunder of the Lord smashes down the oak trees,
and strips the forest bare — Har

and in his temple doth every one speak of his glory.

and in his temple all cry, "Glory!" — RSV

while in his palace all are chanting, "Glory!" — Mof

Meanwhile, in his sanctuary, there is no sound but tells of his glory — Knox

Surely through this His universal temple
Everything speaks of His glory — Sprl

10. The LORD sitteth upon the flood; yea, the LORD sitteth King for ever.

The LORD sits enthroned over the flood;
the LORD sits enthroned as king for ever — RSV

The Lord dwells above the flood;
the Lord is enthroned as King for ever — Har

Out of a raging flood, the Lord makes a dwelling-place; the Lord sits enthroned as a king for ever — Knox

Jehovah sat as King at the Flood;
Yea, Jehovah sitteth as King for ever — ASV

At the Flood, the Lord showed his control of all creation. Now he continues to unveil his power — Tay

11. The LORD will give strength unto his people; the LORD will bless his people with peace.

Yahweh will give strength to his people, —
Yahweh will bless his people with prosperity — Rhm

May the LORD give strength to his people!
May the LORD bless his people with peace! — RSV

PSALM 30

A Psalm and Song at the dedication of the house of David.

A Melody. A Song for the Dedication of the House. David's — Rhm

A Psalm of David. A Song at the dedication of the Temple — RSV

1. I will extol thee, O LORD; for thou hast lifted me up, and hast not made my foes to rejoice over me.

I will magnify thee, O LORD; for thou hast set me up, and not made my foes to triumph over me — PBV

I will praise You, Lord
because You have elevated me,
and have prevented my enemies from rejoicing over me — Har

2. O LORD my God, I cried unto thee, and thou hast healed me.

O Yahweh my God,
I cried for help unto thee,
And thou hast healed me — Rhm

3. O LORD, thou hast brought up my soul from the grave:

O Jehovah, thou hast brought up my soul from Sheol — ASV

You, Lord, have snatched me from death — Har

thou hast kept me alive, that I should not go down to the pit.

Thou hast revived me, that I descend not to the grave — DeW

You have revived me, and have not allowed me to die — Har

4. Sing unto the LORD, O ye saints of his, and give thanks at the remembrance of his holiness.

Sweep the strings to Yahweh
Ye his men of lovingkindness,
And give ye praise at the mention of his holiness — Rhm

Strike the harp to Jehovah, O ye whom He loveth!
And praise ye His holy memorial Name — DeW

Play music in Yahweh's honour, you devout,
remember his holiness, and praise him — Jerus

5. For his anger endureth but a moment; in his favour is life:

For his wrath endureth but the twinkling of an eye, and in his pleasure is life — PBV

For his anger is but for a moment;
His favor is for a life-time — ASV

In his anger is disquiet, in his favour there is life — NEB

weeping may endure for a night, but joy cometh in the morning.

In the evening cometh Weeping to lodge
But by the morning 'tis a Shout of Triumph! — Rhm

At evening, weeping cometh in to lodge;
In the morning, there is a song of joy! — DeW

tears may visit us at night,
but in the morning there are shouts of joy — Mof

sorrow is but the guest of a night, and joy comes in the morning — Knox

6. And in my prosperity I said, I shall never be moved.

As for me, I said in my prosperity, I shall never be moved — RV

But I said in my tranquillity,
I shall not be shaken to times age-abiding! — Rhm

But as for me, I said in my security,
I shall not be overthrown for ever — DeW

When I was enjoying prosperity, I said,
"I shall never be dispossessed" — Har

Once, in my security, I said,
"I shall never be disturbed" — NAB

In my prosperity, I used to say,
'Nothing can ever shake me!' — Jerus

7. LORD, by thy favour thou hast made my mountain to stand strong:

By thy favor, O LORD,
thou hadst established me as a strong mountain — RSV

for You, Lord, had established me by Your favor
as it were on an impregnable mountain — Har

O LORD, in your good will you had endowed me with majesty and strength — NAB

But, LORD, it was thy will to shake my mountain refuge — NEB

thou didst hide thy face, and I was troubled.

thou didst hide thy face, and I was struck with dismay — NEB

Thou didst hide thy face — I was dismayed! — Rhm

Thou didst hide Thy face; I was affrighted — JPS

You concealed Yourself; I became alarmed — Har

Thou didst hide Thy face; I felt disaster — Ber

Then thou didst turn thy face away from me, and I was at peace no more — Knox

but when thy favour was withdrawn,
I fell into dismay — Mof

but when you hid your face I was terrified — NAB

8. I cried to thee, O LORD; and unto the LORD I made supplication.

Then cried I unto thee, O LORD; and gat me to my LORD right humbly — PBV

To you, O LORD, I cried out;
with the LORD I pleaded: — NAB

9. What profit is there in my blood, when I go down to the pit?

"What profit would my death be,
if I went down to the grave — Mof

"What profit is there in my death,
if I go down to the Pit — RSV

"What will have been gained by my death when I am buried — Har

How will it profit thee to take my life?

I can but go down into the grave — Knox

"What gain would there be from my lifeblood,
from my going down into the grave — NAB

Shall the dust praise thee? shall it declare thy truth?

Can dust praise thee?
Can it declare thy faithfulness — Rhm

10. Hear, O LORD, and have mercy upon me: LORD, be thou my helper.

Hear O Yahweh and shew me favour,
O Yahweh! become thou a helper unto me — Rhm

Hear, O Jehovah! and pity me!
O Jehovah! come and help me! — DeW

11. Thou hast turned for me my mourning into dancing:

Thou hast turned my heaviness into joy — PBV

Thou hast turned my lamenting for me into a processional — Ber

thou hast put off my sackcloth, and girded me with gladness;

you have stripped off my sackcloth
and decked me with joy — Har

12. To the end that my glory may sing praise to thee, and not be silent.

that my soul may praise thee and not be silent — RSV

That my spirit may sing to Thee, and not be silent — DeW

that my soul might sing thy praises without ceasing — Mof

In order that I may sing praises to thee and not be silent — AAT

So may this heart never tire of singing praises — Knox

O LORD my God, I will give thanks unto thee for ever.

O Jehovah, my God! for ever will I praise thee! — DeW

PSALM 31

To the chief Musician, a Psalm of David.

1. In thee, O LORD, do I put my trust; let me never be ashamed: deliver me in thy righteousness.

In Thee, O Jehovah! I take refuge:
Let me never come to shame;
In Thy righteousness deliver me — DeW

With thee, O thou Eternal, I take shelter,
never let me be disappointed;
oh rescue me, as thou art faithful — Mof

To thee, O Lord, I look for refuge,
never let me be ashamed of my trust;
in thy faithful care, deliver me — Knox

Lord, I trust in you alone. Don't let my enemies defeat me. Rescue me because you are the God who always does what is right — Tay

2. Bow down thine ear to me; deliver me speedily:

Incline thy ear to me,
rescue me speedily! — RSV

Incline Thine ear to me,
Haste Thee to my rescue — DeW

Pay attention to my needs, rescue me quickly — Har

be thou my strong rock, for an house of defence to save me.

Be thou to me a strong rock,
A house of defence to save me — ASV

Become to me a Rock of refuge,
a Place of security,
For saving me — Rhm

Let me find thee a rock-built fortress;
A castle where I may dwell in safety — DeW

Be a sheltering rock for me,
a walled fortress to save me! — Jerus

Be my rock of refuge,
a stronghold to give me safety — NAB

be my sure protection, a stronghold for my safety — Har

3. For thou art my rock and my fortress;

For thou art my strong rock, and my castle — PBV

Because my mountain crag and my stronghold thou art — Rhm

for thou art my crag and castle — Mof

For you are my defense and my fortress — Har

therefore for thy name's sake lead me, and guide me.

lead me and guide me for the honour of thy name — NEB

lead me and direct me in accordance with Your nature — Har

honor your name by leading me out of this peril — Tay

4. **Pull me out of the net that they have laid privily for me:**
take me out of the net which is hidden for me — RSV
Draw me out of the snare which they have put down for me — Har
for thou art my strength.
For thou art my stronghold — ASV
For thou art my refuge — Rhm
For thou art my defense — ABPS
Because Thou art my saving power — DeW
for You are my protector — Har

5. **Into thine hand I commit my spirit: thou hast redeemed me, O LORD God of truth.**
Into thy hand I commit my spirit;
thou hast redeemed me, O LORD, faithful God — RSV

6. **I have hated them that regard lying vanities: but I trust in the LORD.**
I hate those that wait on vain idols,
And I put my trust in Jehovah — DeW
Thou hatest those who pay regard to vain idols;
but I trust in the LORD — RSV
Thou hatest, O JEHOVAH, those who worship false gods,
But as for me, in JEHOVAH put I my trust — Sprl

7. **I will be glad and rejoice in thy mercy:**
I will rejoice and be glad for thy steadfast love — RSV
. . . in thy unfailing love — NEB
I will indeed exult and rejoice in thy lovingkindness — Rhm
for thou hast considered my trouble; thou hast known my soul in adversities;
Because Thou hast considered mine affliction,
Thou hast befriended my soul in distress — Sprl
because thou hast seen my affliction,
thou hast taken heed of my adversities — RSV
In that thou hast looked upon my humiliation,
Thou hast taken note that in distresses was my life — Rhm
For thou hast seen my affliction,
Hast known the troubles of my soul — ABPS
. . . and hast cared for me in my distress — NEB

8. **And hast not shut me up into the hand of the enemy:**
and hast not delivered me into the hand of the enemy — RSV
You have not surrendered me to the power of the foe — Har
thou hast set my feet in a large room.
Thou hast given standing in a roomy place unto my feet — Rhm
Thou hast made my feet stand in a place of liberty — Sprl
you have given my feet space and to spare — Jerus
but hast set me free to range at will — NEB

9. **Have mercy upon me, O LORD, for I am in trouble:**
Be gracious to me, O LORD, for I am in distress — RSV
Pity me, O Jehovah! for I am in distress — DeW
Have pity on me, Eternal One; I am in misery — Mof
mine eye is consumed with grief, yea, my soul and my belly.
Mine eye languisheth with grief,
Yea, my soul and mine inmost being — DeW
my eye is wasted from grief,
my soul and my body also — RSV
Mine eye, my soul, and my body
Have become old by provocation — YLT
my sight is failing through sorrow.
Soul and body are weakened — Har
my health is wasting under my woe — Mof

10. **For my life is spent with grief, and my years with sighing:**
For my life is waxen old with heaviness, and my years with mourning — PBV
For my life is consumed in sorrow,
and my years in groaning — AAT
For my life passeth away in sorrow,
And my years in sighing — DeW
For my life is worn out with sorrow,
my years with sighs — Jerus
My life is all grief, my years are but sighs — Knox
my strength faileth because of mine iniquity, and my bones are consumed.
my strength fails because of my misery,

and my bones waste away — RSV

My strength hath staggered with my humiliation,
And my bones are without marrow — Rhm

My strength has failed because of my sin,
Even my bones have languished — Ber

strong as I am, I stumble under my load of misery;
there is disease in all my bones — NEB

11. **I was a reproach among all mine enemies, but especially among my neighbours, and a fear to mine acquaintance:**

I am the scorn of all my adversaries,
a horror to my neighbors,
an object of dread to my acquaintances — RSV

To every one of my oppressors
I am contemptible,
loathsome to my neighbours,
to my friends a thing of fear — Jerus

I have such enemies that all men scorn me;
my neighbours find me a burden,
my friends shudder at me — NEB

they that did see me without fled from me.

When they saw me in the street they fled from me — ABPS

those who see me in the street flee from me — RSV

Those who see me in the street
hurry past me — Jerus

They dread meeting me and look the other way when I go by — Tay

12. **I am forgotten as a dead man out of mind: I am like a broken vessel.**

I have been forgotten like one dead — out of mind,
I have been as a missing vessel — Rhm

I am forgotten, like a dead man out of mind;
I have come to be like something lost — NEB

I am forgotten as a dead man out of mind;
I have become like a thing that perisheth — DeW

I am forgotten like a buried corpse,
flung aside like a discarded pot — Mof

I am forgotten like the unremembered dead;
I am like a dish that is broken — NAB

13. **For I have heard the slander of many: fear was on every side: while they took counsel together against me, they devised to take away my life.**

Yea, I hear the whispering of many — terror on every side! —
as they scheme together against me,
as they plot to take my life — RSV

For I hear many slandering;
hostility surrounds me.
Every one of them plots against me,
scheming to take my life — Har

I hear their endless slanders,
threats from every quarter,
as they combine against me,
plotting to take my life — Jerus

14. **But I trusted in thee, O LORD: I said, Thou art my God.**

But I have complete confidence in You, Lord;
I have said, "You are my God" — Har

15. **My times are in thy hand: deliver me from the hand of mine enemies, and from them that persecute me.**

My destiny is under Your control:
rescue me from the power of my pursuing enemies — Har

16. **Make thy face to shine upon thy servant: save me for thy mercies' sake.**

Let thy face shine on thy servant;
save me in thy steadfast love! — RSV

Make thy face shine upon thy servant;
save me in thy unfailing love — NEB

Cause thy face to shine upon thy servant,
Save me in thy lovingkindness — Rhm

Let Your presence radiate around Your servant;
save me because of Your loving favor — Har

17. **Let me not be ashamed, O LORD; for I have called upon thee:**

O Jehovah! let me not come to shame,
For on Thee I call — DeW

On thee have I called, O Eternal,
disappoint me not — Mof

Do not let me be humiliated, Lord,
for I have entreated You — Har

let the wicked be ashamed, and let them be silent in the grave.

let the wicked be put to shame,

let them go dumbfounded to Sheol — RSV
Let the wicked be disgraced;
let them languish in the grave — Har
disappoint the wicked, send them to the silent grave! — Mof

18. Let the lying lips be put to silence; which speak grievous things proudly and contemptuously against the righteous.
Let the lying lips be dumb,
which speak insolently against the righteous
in pride and contempt — RSV
Strike dumb these lying lips,
so insolent in pride and scorn against the just! — Mof

19. Oh how great is thy goodness, which thou hast laid up for them that fear thee;
How great is thy goodness which thou hast hidden away for them who revere thee — Rhm
How great is Thy goodness
Which Thou hast treasured up for such as reverence Thee — Sprl
What wealth of kindness thou hast laid up for thy worshipers — Mof
which thou hast wrought for them that trust in thee before the sons of men!
and wrought for those who take refuge in thee,
in the sight of the sons of men! — RSV
made manifest before the eyes of men
for all who turn to thee for shelter — NEB

20. Thou shalt hide them in the secret of thy presence from the pride of man:
In the covert of thy presence shalt thou hide them from the plottings of man — RV
Thou wilt conceal them in the secrecy of thine own presence from the conspiracies of men — Rhm
Safe in your presence you hide them
far from the wiles of men — Jerus
thou shalt keep them secretly in a pavilion from the strife of tongues.
Thou concealest them in a pavilion
From the contention of tongues — DeW
thou holdest them safe under thy shelter
from the strife of tongues — RSV
thou keepest them beneath thy roof,
safe from contentious men — NEB
thou shelterest them from the scourge of slander! — Mof

21. Blessed be the LORD: for he hath shewed me his marvellous kindness in a strong city.
Blessed be Yahweh,
For he hath made wonderful his lovingkindness for me, in a fortified city — Rhm
Blessed be Jehovah!
For he hath treated me with wondrous love,
In a city that hath walls — DeW
Blessed be the LORD!
For he showed me his wonderful kindness in a besieged city — AAT
Blessed be the LORD,
for he has wondrously shown his steadfast love to me
when I was beset as in a besieged city — RSV
Blessed be the Eternal,
for wondrous favour shown me in desperate plight — Mof
May the Lord be blessed,
for He has shown me wonderful kindness
in a time of emergency — Har
Blessed be Yahweh, who performs
marvels of love for me
(in a fortress-city)! — Jerus
Blessed is the Lord, for he has shown me that his never-failing love protects me like the walls of a fort! — Tay
Blessed be the LORD,
who worked a miracle of unfailing love for me
when I was in sore straits — NEB

22. For I said in my haste, I am cut off from before thine eyes:
but I had said in mine alarm
I am cut off from before thine eyes — Rhm
In my distraction I cried out,
"I am cast out of thy sight!" — Mof
I had said in my alarm,
"I am driven far from thy sight" — RSV
For I had said in my alarm,
"I am denied access to Your presence" — Har
nevertheless thou heardest the voice of my supplications when I cried unto thee.

But thou didst hear the voice of my supplications,
When I cried to thee for help — ABPS

Nevertheless You heard my imploring voice
when I cried to You for help — Har

Yet you heard the sound of my pleading
when I cried out to you — NAB

23. O love the LORD, all ye his saints:

Love Yahweh all ye his men of lovingkindness — Rhm

O love the LORD, all ye His godly ones — JPS

Oh, love the Lord all you who are his people — Tay

for the LORD preserveth the faithful, and plentifully rewardeth the proud doer.

Faithfulness doth Yahweh observe,
But repayeth abundantly him that worketh proudly — Rhm

Jehovah preserveth the faithful,
But repayeth the proud in full measure — DeW

The LORD preserves the faithful,
but abundantly requites him who acts haughtily — RSV

The Lord safeguards the faithful,
but fully recompenses arrogant behavior — Har

Yahweh, protector of the faithful,
will repay the arrogant with interest — Jerus

24. Be of good courage, and he shall strengthen your heart, all ye that hope in the LORD.

Be strong, and let your heart take courage,
All ye that hope in Jehovah — ASV

Be strong and let your heart be bold,
All ye who are waiting for Yahweh — Rhm

Take courage and be stouthearted,
all you who hope in the LORD — NAB

So cheer up! Take courage if you are depending on the Lord! — Tay

PSALM 32

A Psalm of David, Maschil.

David's. An Instructive Psalm — Rhm

[A Psalm of David,] A skillful song, or a didactic or reflective poem — Amp

1. Blessed is he whose transgression is forgiven, whose sin is covered.

How happy is he
Whose transgression is forgiven!
Whose sin is pardoned! — Rhm

O the blessedness of him,
Whose transgression is taken away,
Whose sin is covered! — DeW

Blessed — happy, fortunate [to be envied] — is he who has forgiveness of his transgression continually exercised upon him, whose sin is covered — Amp

2. Blessed is the man unto whom the LORD imputeth not iniquity, and in whose spirit there is no guile.

O the blessedness of the man,
To whom Jehovah imputeth no guilt,
And in whose spirit there is no deceit! — DeW

Oh the bliss of him whom the Eternal has absolved,
whose spirit has made full confession! — Mof

Happy indeed is the man
to whom the Lord doth not ascribe guilt,
and in whose mind there lurks no deceit — Har

3. When I kept silence, my bones waxed old through my roaring all the day long.

For whilst I held my tongue, my bones consumed away through my daily complaining — PBV

When I kept silence my bones became worn out,
Through my groaning all the day — Rhm

When I kept silence, my bones wasted away
Through my groaning all the day long — ABPS

So long as I refused to own my guilt,
I moaned unceasingly, life ebbed away — Mof

When I declared not my sin, my body wasted away
through my groaning all day long — RSV

4. For day and night thy hand was heavy upon me: my moisture is turned into the drought of summer.

For day and night heavy upon me was thy hand, —
Changed was my life-sap into the drought of summer — Rhm
for thy hand crushed me night and day, my body dried up, as in summer heat — Mof
For day and night thy hand was heavy upon me;
my strength was dried up as by the heat of summer — RSV
For your punishment lay heavily upon me day and night;
my strength was sapped like moisture in summer heat — Har
Selah.
(Pause.) — ABPS
Selah [pause, and calmly think of that]! — Amp

5. **I acknowledged my sin unto thee, and mine iniquity have I not hid.**
I made known to thee my sins, and my iniquity I have not covered — ABPS
Then I acknowledged my sin to Thee, And my guilt I ceased to conceal — DeW
At last I admitted to you I had sinned; no longer concealing my guilt — Jerus
I said, I will confess my transgressions unto the LORD;
I said, 'I will go to Yahweh
and confess my fault' — Jerus
and thou forgavest the iniquity of my sin.
And Thou didst bear away the guilt of my sin — Sprl
And you, you have forgiven the wrong I did,
have pardoned my sin — Jerus
Selah.
Selah [pause, and calmly think of that]! — Amp

6. **For this shall every one that is godly pray unto thee in a time when thou mayest be found: surely in the floods of great waters they shall not come nigh unto him.**
For this [forgiveness] let every one who is godly pray; pray to You in a time when You may be found; surely when the great waters [of trial] overflow they shall not reach [the spirit in] him — Amp
So let each loyal heart in trouble pray to thee:
the floods may roar,
but they will never reach him — Mof
Therefore let every godly man pray to thee,
That in the time of distress, in the rush of great waters,
They may not reach him — AAT
That is why each of your servants prays to you
in time of trouble; even if floods come rushing down,
they will never reach him — Jerus

7. **Thou art my hiding place; thou shalt preserve me from trouble;**
Thou art a hiding-place for me
From distress wilt thou preserve me — Rhm
Thou art my hiding-place; Thou wilt preserve me from the adversary — JPS
You are my haven of refuge,
preserving me in my peril — Har
Thou art a refuge for me from distress
so that it cannot touch me — NEB
thou shalt compass me about with songs of deliverance.
With shouts of deliverance wilt thou compass me about — Rhm
Thou dost surround me with deliverances — AAT
with glad cries of freedom you will ring me round — NAB
thou dost guard me and enfold me in salvation[11]
beyond all reach of harm — NEB
Selah.

8. **I will instruct thee and teach thee in the way which thou shalt go:**
I will make thee discreet
I will point out to thee the way which thou must go — Rhm
I will guide thee with mine eye.
I will fix upon thee mine eye — Rhm
I will counsel thee with mine eye upon thee — ASV
I will watch over you and be your adviser — Jerus
I will keep you under my eye — NEB

9. **Be ye not as the horse, or as the mule, which have no understanding:**
Do not behave like a horse or a mule, neither of which possess understanding — Har
whose mouth must be held in with

[11]NEB transposes from the end of verse 9 the words that follow the reference mark.

bit and bridle, lest they come near unto thee.
whose mouths must be held with bit and bridle, else they will not obey thee — PBV
with bit and bridle their temper must be curbed,
else they will not come near you — NAB
whose course must be checked with bit and bridle — NEB

10. **Many sorrows shall be to the wicked: but he that trusteth in the LORD, mercy shall compass him about.**
The torments of the wicked are many, but he who trusts in the Lord is surrounded by His favor — Har
Many are the pangs of the wicked; but steadfast love surrounds him who trusts in the LORD — RSV
Great plagues remain for the ungodly; but whoso putteth his trust in the LORD, mercy embraceth him on every side — PBV
Many are the torments of the ungodly; but unfailing love enfolds him who trusts in the LORD — NEB
Again and again the sinner must feel the lash; he who trusts in the Lord finds nothing but mercy all around him — Knox

11. **Be glad in the LORD, and rejoice, ye righteous: and shout for joy, all ye that are upright in heart.**

PSALM 33

1. **Rejoice in the LORD, O ye righteous: for praise is comely for the upright.**
Rejoice in the LORD, O ye righteous; for it becometh well the just to be thankful — PBV
Shout for joy ye righteous in Yahweh, To the upright seemly is praise — Rhm
Rejoice in Jehovah, ye righteous; Praise is becoming to the upright — ABPS
Rejoice in the Lord, you upright. It is fitting for the virtuous to be joyful — Har

2. **Praise the LORD with harp: sing unto him with the psaltery and an instrument of ten strings.**
Give ye thanks unto Yahweh with the lyre, With a harp of ten strings make ye music unto him — Rhm
Give praise to Jehovah with the harp; With a ten-stringed lute sing praise to him — ABPS

3. **Sing unto him a new song; play skilfully with a loud noise.**
Sing to him a new song, play skilfully on the strings, with loud shouts — RSV
Sing unto Him a new song; Play skilfully amid shouts of joy — JPS
Sing ye unto Him a new song; Strike the lute tunefully with a shout of triumph — Sprl
Sing unto the Lord a new song; sing praises lustily unto him with a good courage — PBV
Sing unto him a song that is new, With skill sweep the strings with loud noise — Rhm

4. **For the word of the LORD is right; and all his works are done in truth.**
For the word of Jehovah is right; And all his work is done in faithfulness — ASV
For the promises of the Lord are reliable, and all that He does is trustworthy — Har
The word of the LORD holds true, and all his work endures — NEB

5. **He loveth righteousness and judgment: the earth is full of the goodness of the LORD.**
He loveth righteousness and justice; The earth is full of the lovingkindness of Jehovah — DeW
He cherishes righteousness and justice; the earth is full of divine blessing — Har
He loves righteousness and justice; the earth is full of the steadfast love of the LORD — RSV
he loves virtue and justice, Yahweh's love fills the earth — Jerus

6. **By the word of the LORD were the heavens made; and all the host of them by the breath of his mouth.**
At the bidding of the Lord the heavens were formed,
and all their company at his decree — Har

By the word of Yahweh the heavens were made,
their whole array by the breath of his mouth — Jerus

7. He gathereth the waters of the sea together as an heap: he layeth up the deep in storehouses.

He gathereth the waters of the sea together, as it were upon an heap; and layeth up the deep, as in a treasure-house — PBV

Who gathereth as into a skin-bottle the waters of the sea,
Delivering into treasuries the roaring deeps — Rhm

he holds the seas as in a waterskin,
and stores up the abysses of the deep — Mof

He gathered the waters of the sea as in a bottle;
he put the deeps in storehouses — RSV

8. Let all the earth fear the LORD: let all the inhabitants of the world stand in awe of him.

Let all the earth reverence JEHOVAH:
Let all the inhabitants of the world stand in awe before Him — Sprl

9. For he spake, and it was done; he commanded, and it stood fast.

For he spoke, and it came to be;
he commanded, and it stood forth — RSV

for he it was who spoke — and earth existed,
'twas at his bidding it appeared — Mof

He spoke, and it was created;
he commanded, and there it stood — Jerus

10. The LORD bringeth the counsel of the heathen to nought:

Jehovah bringeth the counsel of the nations to nought — ASV

Yahweh hath frustrated the counsel of nations — Rhm

The Eternal wrecks the purposes of pagans — Mof

The Lord frustrates the schemes of pagan nations — Har

The LORD brought to nought the counsel of the Gentiles — Ber

he maketh the devices of the people of none effect.

he maketh the thoughts of the peoples to be of none effect — RV

he brings to nothing what the nations plan — Mof

he frustrates the plans of the people — RSV

11. The counsel of the LORD standeth for ever, the thoughts of his heart to all generations.

The counsel of Jehovah standeth fast for ever,
The thoughts of his heart to all generations — ASV

But Jehovah's counsel standeth for ever,
The thoughts of His heart to the farthest age — DeW

but the Eternal's purpose stands for ever,
and what he plans will last from age to age — Mof

12. Blessed is the nation whose God is the LORD; and the people whom he hath chosen for his own inheritance.

How happy the nation whose God is Yahweh,
The people he hath chosen as his own inheritance! — Rhm

Happy the nation whose God is Jehovah,
The people He hath chosen for His possession — DeW

13. The LORD looketh from heaven; he beholdeth all the sons of men.

The Lord surveys the scene from heaven;
He observes all human society — Har

Yahweh looks down from heaven,
he sees the whole human race — Jerus

14. From the place of his habitation he looketh upon all the inhabitants of the earth.

Out of his settled place of abode hath he fixed his gaze
On all the inhabitants of the earth — Rhm

From the place of His habitation He looketh intently
Upon all the inhabitants of the earth — JPS

from where he sits enthroned he looks forth
on all the inhabitants of the earth — RSV

15. He fashioneth their hearts alike; he considereth all their works.

He that fashioneth the hearts of them

all, that considereth all their works — RV

He who fashioned the heart of each, he who knows all their works — NAB

he who moulds every heart
and takes note of all men do — Jerus

For He fashioned their minds;
so He takes notice of all their doings — Har

16. There is no king saved by the multitude of an host: a mighty man is not delivered by much strength.

Not a king can be saved by greatness of force,
Nor hero deliver himself by greatness of strength — Rhm

A king is not saved by a vast army,
Nor a warrior rescued by great power — DeW

17. An horse is a vain thing for safety: neither shall he deliver any by his great strength.

A horse is a vain hope for victory;
Even by his great strength he cannot deliver — DeW

The war horse is a vain hope for victory,
and by its great might it cannot save — RSV

A man cannot trust his horse to save him,
nor can it deliver him for all its strength — NEB

18. Behold, the eye of the LORD is upon them that fear him, upon them that hope in his mercy;

Lo! the eye of Yahweh is toward them who revere him,
Unto such as are waiting for his lovingkindness — Rhm

The LORD's eyes are turned towards those who fear him,
towards those who hope for his unfailing love — NEB

No, the Eternal's eye rests on his worshippers,
who rest their hopes upon his kindness — Mof

But see, the eyes of the LORD are upon those who fear him,
upon those who hope for his kindness — NAB

19. To deliver their soul from death, and to keep them alive in famine.

20. Our soul waiteth for the LORD: he is our help and our shield.

Our own soul hath waited for Yahweh,
Our help and our shield is he! — Rhm

We trust in the Lord,
for He is our help and protection — Har

21. For our heart shall rejoice in him, because we have trusted in his holy name.

22. Let thy mercy, O LORD, be upon us, according as we hope in thee.

Let thy lovingkindness, O Jehovah, be upon us,
According as we have hoped in thee — ASV

Let thy steadfast love, O LORD, be upon us,
even as we hope in thee — RSV

Yahweh, let your love rest on us
as our hope has rested in you — Jerus

PSALM 34

A Psalm of David, when he changed his behaviour before Abimelech; who drove him away, and he departed.

BY DAVID WHEN HE FEIGNED MADNESS BEFORE ABIMELECH . . . — DeW

[A Psalm] of David, when he pretended to be insane before Abimelech, who drove him out, and he went away — Amp

1. I will bless the LORD at all times: his praise shall continually be in my mouth.

2. My soul shall make her boast in the LORD; the humble shall hear thereof, and be glad.

My soul makes its boast in the LORD;
let the afflicted hear and be glad — RSV

In Jehovah my soul gloryeth;
Let the suffering hear and rejoice! — DeW

I will boast of all his kindness to me.
Let all who are discouraged take heart — Tay

3. O magnify the LORD with me, and let us exalt his name together.

Ascribe ye greatness unto Yahweh with me,
And let us exalt his Name together — Rhm

Proclaim with me the greatness of Yahweh,
together let us extol his name — Jerus

4. I sought the LORD, and he heard me, and delivered me from all my fears.
I besought the Eternal and he answered me,
he rescued me from all my terrors — Mof

5. They looked unto him, and were lightened: and their faces were not ashamed.
They looked unto him and were radiant,
And as for their faces let them not be abashed — Rhm
They that look unto Him are illumined;
And let not their faces be ashamed — DeW
Every face turned to him grows brighter
and is never ashamed — Jerus
look to him, and you shall beam with joy,
you shall never be abashed — Mof
Look to him, and be radiant;
so your faces shall never be ashamed — RSV

6. This poor man cried, and the LORD heard him, and saved him out of all his troubles.
This sufferer called, and Jehovah heard . . . — ABPS
This oppressed one cried, and Yahweh heard, —
And out of all his distresses saved him — Rhm
Here is a poor man whose cry the Eternal heard,
and helped him out of all his troubles — Mof
Friendless folk may still call upon the Lord and gain his ear, and be rescued from all their afflictions — Knox

7. The angel of the LORD encampeth round about them that fear him, and delivereth them.
The messenger of Yahweh encampeth around them who revere him,
Thus hath he delivered them — Rhm
The Angel of Jehovah keepeth guard,
Around those that fear Him.
And He delivereth them — DeW

8. O taste and see that the LORD is good: blessed is the man that trusteth in him.
O taste and see that good is Yahweh —
How happy the man who seeketh refuge in him! — Rhm
Try the Eternal; you will find him kind;
happy the man who takes shelter with him! — Mof

9. O fear the LORD, ye his saints: for there is no want to them that fear him.
O fear the LORD, ye that are his saints;
for they that fear him lack nothing — PBV
Revere Yahweh ye his holy ones,
For there is no want to them who revere him — Rhm

10. The young lions do lack, and suffer hunger: but they that seek the LORD shall not want any good thing.
Rich men have become poor and hungry: but they who seek the Lord shall not want any good thing — Sept
The great grow poor and hungry;
but those who seek the LORD want for no good thing — NAB
The renegade may be in need, and go hungry;
but those who search for the Lord shall not be short of anything good — Har
apostates may be famishing and starving,
but those who turn to the Eternal lack no good — Mof
Unbelievers suffer want and grow hungry,
but those who seek the LORD lack no good thing — NEB

11. Come, ye children, hearken unto me: I will teach you the fear of the LORD.
Come ye children! hearken unto me,
The reverence of Yahweh will I teach you — Rhm
Come, listen to me, my sons,
I will teach you true religion — Mof

12. What man is he that desireth life, and loveth many days, that he may see good?
Who is the man that desireth long life,
That loveth to see days of prosperity — DeW

'Tis your desire to live,
to live long and be happy? — Mof

13. Keep thy tongue from evil, and thy lips from speaking guile.

Keep thy tongue from wickedness,
And thy lips from speaking deceit — Rhm

Then keep your tongue from evil
and your lips from uttering lies — NEB

14. Depart from evil, and do good; seek peace, and pursue it.

Depart from wickedness and do good,
Aim at well-being and pursue it — Rhm

you must forsake evil and do good;
desire peace, and then safeguard it — Har

15. The eyes of the LORD are upon the righteous, and his ears are open unto their cry.

The eyes of the LORD are over the righteous, and his ears are open unto their prayers — PBV

The eyes of Jehovah are upon the righteous,
His ears are open to their cry for help — DeW

16. The face of the LORD is against them that do evil, to cut off the remembrance of them from the earth.

The countenance of the LORD is against them that do evil, to root out the remembrance of them from the earth — PBV

But the Lord opposes those who do evil,
that He may eradicate their memory from the earth — Har

17. The righteous cry, and the LORD heareth, and delivereth them out of all their troubles.

The righteous cry, and Jehovah heareth,
And delivereth them out of all their distresses — DeW

When the righteous cry for help, the LORD hears,
and delivers them out of all their troubles — RSV

18. The LORD is nigh unto them that are of a broken heart; and saveth such as be of a contrite spirit.

Jehovah is near to the broken in heart;
He saveth the crushed in spirit — DeW

The LORD is close to those whose courage is broken
and he saves those whose spirit is crushed — NEB

The Eternal is near the broken-hearted,
and for crushed spirits he has help — Mof

19. Many are the afflictions of the righteous: but the LORD delivereth him out of them all.

Many are the misfortunes of the righteous,
But out of them all doth Yahweh rescue him — Rhm

the good man may have many a mishap,
but from them all the Eternal rescues him — Mof

20. He keepeth all his bones: not one of them is broken.

He guards every bone of him;
not one is broken — Mof

God even protects him from accidents — Tay

21. Evil shall slay the wicked: and they that hate the righteous shall be desolate.

Their own misdeeds are death to the wicked,
and those who hate the righteous are brought to ruin — NEB

But misfortune shall slay the ungodly;
and they that hate the righteous shall be desolate — PBV

Misfortune shall be the death of the lawless one,
and the haters of the righteous man shall be held guilty — Rhm

22. The LORD redeemeth the soul of his servants: and none of them that trust in him shall be desolate.

Jehovah redeemeth the soul of his servants;
And none of them that take refuge in him shall be condemned — ASV

Jehovah redeems the soul of his servants,
And none shall be held guilty that trust in him — ABPS

The LORD ransoms the lives of his servants,
and none who seek refuge in him are brought to ruin — NEB

PSALM 35

A Psalm of David.

1. Plead my cause, O LORD, with them that strive with me: fight against them that fight against me.
Contend O Yahweh with them who contend with me,
Make war upon them who make war upon me — Rhm
Stir up opposition to my rivals, Lord;
fight those who attack me — Har

2. Take hold of shield and buckler, and stand up for mine help.
Grasp the shield and the buckler,
And arise in my defence — DeW
seize thy shield and buckler,
stand up as my champion — Mof

3. Draw out also the spear, and stop the way against them that persecute me:
Draw the spear and javelin
against my pursuers! — RSV
Draw thy spear and battle-axe,
to cope with my pursuers — Mof
Then draw the spear and close up against my pursuers — Rhm
Uncover the spear and bar the way against my pursuers — NEB
Draw out the spear and shut off my pursuers — DeW
say unto my soul, I am thy salvation.
Say to my soul,
"I am your deliverance!" — RSV
Say unto my soul, I will save thee — DeW
say to me, O Eternal,
"I am your safety" — Mof
Let me hear thee declare,
'I am your salvation' — NEB

4. Let them be confounded and put to shame that seek after my soul:
Let them be put to shame and brought to dishonor that seek after my soul — ASV
Let them be put to shame and dishonor
who seek after my life! — RSV
May those who wish to kill me be dishonored and humiliated — Har
let them be turned back and brought to confusion that devise my hurt.
Let them be turned back in dishonour,
That intend me evil — DeW
May they be routed and confounded who aim to injure me! — Mof
may those who plan evil against me be routed and disgraced — Har

5. Let them be as chaff before the wind: and let the angel of the LORD chase them.
Let them be as chaff before the wind,
The Angel of Jehovah thrusting them on — DeW
Let them be like chaff before the wind,
with the angel of the LORD driving them on! — RSV

6. Let their way be dark and slippery: and let the angel of the LORD persecute them.
May their way be dark and dangerous,
with the Angel of the Lord pursuing them — Har

7. For without cause have they hid for me their net in a pit, which without cause they have digged for my soul.
For without any provocation
they hid a snare for me;
without any cause
they have dug a trap for me — Har

8. Let destruction come upon him at unawares;
Let ruin come upon them unawares! — RSV
May destruction overtake each of them unexpectedly — Har
and let his net that he hath hid catch himself: into that very destruction let him fall.
And let the net which they hid ensnare them;
let them fall therein to ruin! — RSV

9. And my soul shall be joyful in the LORD: it shall rejoice in his salvation.
Then my soul will rejoice in Yahweh,
exult that he has saved me — Jerus
Then my soul shall rejoice in the LORD,
exulting in his deliverance — RSV
Then shall my soul exult in Jehovah;
It shall rejoice in his saving power — DeW

10. All my bones shall say, LORD, who is like unto thee, which deliverest the poor from him that is too strong for him, yea, the poor and the needy from him that spoileth him?
My whole being will say,
"Who is like you, Lord, for delivering the feeble from
the one who is too powerful for him;
the wretched and needy from those

who would plunder them?" — Har
All my bones will exclaim, 'Yahweh,
who can compare with you
in rescuing the poor man from the stronger,
the needy from the man who exploits him?' — Jerus
All my being shall say,
"O LORD, who is like you,
The rescuer of the afflicted man from those too strong for him,
of the afflicted and the needy from their despoilers?" — NAB
this be the cry of my whole being,
There is none like thee, Lord; who else rescues the afflicted from the hand of tyranny, the poor, the destitute, from his oppressors — Knox
My very bones cry out,
'LORD, who is like thee? —
thou saviour of the poor from those too strong for them,
the poor and wretched from those who prey on them' — NEB

11. False witnesses did rise up; they laid to my charge things that I knew not.
Slanderous accusers rise against me,
Who ask me of that which I know not — DeW
Malevolent witnesses have stood up,
questioning me about matters of which I knew nothing — Har

12. They rewarded me evil for good to the spoiling of my soul.
They rewarded me evil for good, to the great discomfort of my soul — PBV
They repay me evil for good
Bereaving my soul — Rhm
They requite me evil for good;
my soul is forlorn — RSV
They return me evil for good,
lying in wait to take my life — NEB

13. But as for me, when they were sick, my clothing was sackcloth: I humbled my soul with fasting;
For my own part, I put on sackcloth when they were ill,
and disciplined myself with fasting — Har
But I, when they were sick —
I wore sackcloth,
I afflicted myself with fasting — RSV
and my prayer returned into mine own bosom.
I prayed for them
with my head bent down on my chest — Har
And my prayer — let it return into my own bosom! — DeW
When my prayer came back unanswered — NEB

14. I behaved myself as though he had been my friend or brother:
I walked with head bowed in grief
as if for a brother — NEB
I bowed down heavily, as one that mourneth for his mother.
as one in sorrow for his mother I lay prostrate in mourning — NEB
I bowed in mourning like a man would in grieving for his mother — Har
As when one mourneth for a mother,
In garments of woe I bowed down — DeW

15. But in mine adversity they rejoiced, and gathered themselves together:
But in mine overthrow have they rejoiced
And gathered themselves together — Rhm
But when I was staggering
they rejoiced and gathered together — Har
But at my stumbling they gathered in glee,
they gathered together against me — RSV
yea, the abjects gathered themselves together against me, and I knew it not; they did tear me, and ceased not:
malicious wretches whom I did not know
banded together against me,
tearing my reputation to shreds incessantly — Har
nameless ruffians jeered at me
and nothing would stop them — NEB
cripples whom I knew not
slandered me without ceasing — RSV

16. With hypocritical mockers in feasts, they gnashed upon me with their teeth.
Like the most profane mockers of a sacred feast,
they ground their teeth against me — Har

they impiously mocked more and more,
gnashing at me with their teeth — RSV
When I slipped, brutes who would mock even a hunchback
ground their teeth at me — NEB

17. Lord, how long wilt thou look on? Rescue my soul from their destructions, my darling from the lions.
How much longer, Lord, will you look on?
Rescue my soul from their onslaughts,
my dear life from these lions — Jerus
How long will you merely be an onlooker, Lord?
rescue me from their destructive designs:
save my distraught soul from these ravaging lions — Har
O Lord, how long wilt thou look on?
Draw me back from the roaring ones,
My solitary self from the young lions — AAT
Lord, how long will you stand there, doing nothing? Act now and rescue me, for I have but one life and these young lions are out to get it — Tay

18. I will give thee thanks in the great congregation: I will praise thee among much people.
I will thank thee in the midst of a great convocation, —
In the midst of a mighty people will I praise thee — Rhm
I will give You thanks in the great assembly; I will praise You among a mighty throng — Amp

19. Let not them that are mine enemies wrongfully rejoice over me: neither let them wink with the eye that hate me without a cause.
Let not my foes rejoice over me wrongfully,
let not my wanton haters wink maliciously! — Mof
Do not let my lying enemies
gloat over me,
do not let those who hate me for no reason
exchange sly glances — Jerus

20. For they speak not peace: but they devise deceitful matters against them that are quiet in the land.
For they do not discuss peace,
but instead they devise treachery against those who are peaceably inclined — Har

21. Yea, they opened their mouth wide against me, and said, Aha, aha, our eye hath seen it.
They gaped upon me with their mouths,
and said, Fie on thee, fie on thee, we saw it with our eyes — PBV
wide-mouthed, they are taunting me,
shouting, "Aha! aha! we see his plight!" — Mof
They shout that they have seen me doing wrong! "Aha!" they say. "With our own eyes we saw him do it" — Tay

22. This thou hast seen, O LORD: keep not silence: O Lord be not far from me.
Thou hast seen it, O Jehovah; keep not silence:
O Lord, be not far from me — ASV
Lord you know all about it. Don't stay silent! Don't desert me now! — Tay

23. Stir up thyself, and awake to my judgment, even unto my cause, my God and my Lord.
Awake, and stand up to judge my quarrel; avenge thou my cause, my God and my Lord — PBV
Arouse Yourself and exact justice for me,
my God and my Lord.
Champion my cause — Har

24. Judge me, O LORD my God, according to thy righteousness; and let them not rejoice over me.
Vindicate me according to thy righteousness O Yahweh my God!
And let them not rejoice over me — Rhm
Yahweh my God, you are righteous, so give verdict for me,
and do not let them gloat over me — Jerus

25. Let them not say in their hearts, Ah, so would we have it:
Let them not say to themselves,
"Aha, we have our heart's desire!" — RSV
let them not say, We have swallowed him up.
neither let them say, We have devoured him — PBV
Do not let them say, 'Now we have

got him down!' — Jerus
Do not let them say to themselves, 'Hurrah!
We have swallowed him up at one gulp' — NEB

26. Let them be ashamed and brought to confusion together that rejoice at mine hurt:
Let them be put to shame and confusion altogether
who rejoice at my calamity! — RSV
let them be clothed with shame and dishonour that magnify themselves against me.
may those who exalt themselves above me
be covered with shame and disgrace — Har

27. Let them shout for joy, and be glad, that favour my righteous cause:
Let them shout in triumph and rejoice
Who are desiring my justification — Rhm
Let those who desire my vindication
shout for joy and be glad — RSV
yea, let them say continually, Let the LORD be magnified, which hath pleasure in the prosperity of his servant.
and say evermore,
"Great is the LORD,
who delights in the welfare of his servant!" — RSV

28. And my tongue shall speak of thy righteousness and of thy praise all the day long.
Mine own tongue also shall softly utter thy righteousness, —
All the day long — thy praise! — Rhm
Then all day long my tongue shall talk
of thy justice and thy praise — Mof
Then my tongue will shout your goodness,
and sing your praises all day long — Jerus

PSALM 36

To the chief Musician, A Psalm of David the servant of the LORD.

1. The transgression of the wicked saith within my heart, that there is no fear of God before his eyes.
The wicked man's oracle is Sin
in the depths of his heart;
there is no fear of God
before his eyes — Jerus
Deep in his heart, sin whispers to the wicked man
who cherishes no fear of God — NEB
Sin appeals to the wicked deep in his heart;
no dread of God is present before his eyes — Ber
Rebellion is delightful to the wicked within his heart;
There is no dread of God before his eyes — AAT
Rebellion flares up stubbornly in the mind of the wicked;
reverence for God has no place in such an outlook — Har
The unjust conceives wickedness within his heart, for there is fear of God before his eyes — Lam
Sin lurks deep in the hearts of the wicked, forever urging them on to evil deeds. They have no fear of God to hold them back — Tay

2. For he flattereth himself in his own eyes, until his iniquity be found to be hateful.
For he flattereth himself in his own eyes, that his iniquity shall not be found out and be hated — RV
For he flatters himself continually
that his sin cannot be exposed and denounced — Har
He sees himself with too flattering an eye to detect and detest his guilt — Jerus
For he takes comfort in the thought that his sin will not be uncovered and hated — Bas
Instead, in their conceit, they think they can hide their evil deeds and not get caught — Tay
For he flatters himself in his own opinion
and, when he is found out, he does not mend his ways — NEB

3. The words of his mouth are iniquity and deceit: he hath left off to be wise, and to do good.
The words of his mouth are falsehood and deceit;

He has ceased to do wisely, to do well — ABPS

The words of his mouth are mischief and falsehood;
He hath forsaken wisdom and virtue — DeW

All that he says is mischievous and false;
he has turned his back on wisdom — NEB

4. **He deviseth mischief upon his bed; he setteth himself in a way that is not good; he abhorreth not evil.**

in his bed he plots how best to do mischief.
So set is he on his wrong courses that he rejects nothing evil — NEB

He plots mischief while on his bed;
he sets himself in a way that is not good;
he spurns not evil — RSV

5. **Thy mercy, O LORD, is in the heavens; and thy faithfulness reacheth unto the clouds.**

Thy lovingkindness, O Jehovah, is in the heavens;
Thy faithfulness reacheth unto the skies — ASV

Thy steadfast love, O LORD, extends to the heavens,
thy faithfulness to the clouds — RSV

6. **Thy righteousness is like the great mountains;**

Thy righteousness standeth like the strong mountains — PBV

Thy righteousness is like the mountains of God — RV

Your justice is like the mountains of God — NAB

Your justice is as solid as God's mountains — Tay

thy justice is like mighty mountains — Mof

thy judgments are a great deep;

thy judgments are like the great deep — PBV

And thy just decrees are a great resounding deep — Rhm

thy judgments are like the deep sea — Mof

Your justice is like a mighty ocean — Har

O LORD, thou preservest man and beast.

Thou, O Jehovah! hast care over man and beast — DeW

You are concerned for men and animals alike — Tay

Thy providence is over man and beast — Mof

7. **How excellent is thy lovingkindness, O God!**

How precious is thy lovingkindness, O God — RV

. . . thy steadfast love . . . — RSV

. . . thy unfailing love — NEB

therefore the children of men put their trust under the shadow of thy wings.

and the children of men take refuge under the shadow of thy wings — RV

for this reason mankind desires to shelter
within Your protecting power — Har

8. **They shall be abundantly satisfied with the fatness of thy house;**

They shall be satisfied with the plenteousness of thy house — PBV

They shall be fully satisfied with the abundance of thy house — ABPS

They feast on the abundance of thy house — RSV

They will be satisfied abundantly from Your vast reserves — Har

and thou shalt make them drink of the river of thy pleasures.

and thou shalt give them drink of thy pleasures, as out of the river — PBV

And from Thine Eden river Thou refreshest them — DeW

and thou givest them drink from the river of thy delights — RSV

from your delightful stream you give them to drink — NAB

9. **For with thee is the fountain of life: in thy light shall we see light.**

for life's own fountain is within thy presence,
and in thy smile we have the light of life — Mof

for with thee is the fountain of life,
and in thy light we are bathed with light — NEB

In thee is the source of all life; thy brightness breaks on our eyes like dawn — Knox

For the source of life itself springs from You;
we shall increase in wisdom as You enlighten us — Har

10. O continue thy lovingkindness unto them that know thee; and thy righteousness to the upright in heart.
Stretch forth Thy tender mercy to those who know Thee;
And Thy righteousness to the upright of heart — Sprl
Maintain thy love unfailing over those who know thee,
and thy justice toward men of honest heart — NEB
O continue thy steadfast love to those who know thee,
and thy salvation to the upright of heart! — RSV

11. Let not the foot of pride come against me, and let not the hand of the wicked remove me.
Let not the foot of pride reach me,
Nor the hand of the lawless scare me away — Rhm
Let not the foot of pride overtake me,
Nor the hand of the wicked drive me away! — DeW
Do not allow any arrogant foot to trample me down;
do not let an evil power expel me — Har

12. There are the workers of iniquity fallen:
There the evildoers lie prostrate — RSV
See how the evildoers have fallen — NAB
The evil men have fallen, there they lie — Jerus
they are cast down, and shall not be able to rise.
They are thrust down, and are not able to rise! — DeW
They are overthrown and are not able to rise — AAT

PSALM 37

A Psalm of David.

1. Fret not thyself because of evildoers,
Burn not with vexation because of evil-doers — Rhm
Be not enraged at evil doers — DeW
Do not show annoyance because of the wicked — Har
Do not worry about the wicked — Jerus
neither be thou envious against the workers of iniquity.
neither be thou envious against them that work unrighteousness — RV
Nor jealous against the unrighteous — DeW
do not become excited over evildoers — Har

2. For they shall soon be cut down like the grass, and wither as the green herb.
For they shall soon wither like the grass,
And fade as the green herb — JPS
For like grass they soon wither,
and fade like the green of spring — NEB

3. Trust in the LORD, and do good; so shalt thou dwell in the land, and verily thou shalt be fed.
Trust in Jehovah, and do good;
Dwell in the land, and feed on his faithfulness — ASV
Trust in Jehovah and do good;
Dwell in the land, and feed securely — ABPS
Trust in the LORD, and do good;
so you will dwell in the land, and enjoy security — RSV

4. Delight thyself also in the LORD; and he shall give thee the desires of thine heart.
Yea rest thy delight on Yahweh,
that he may give thee the requests of thy heart — Rhm
Seek thy pleasure in Jehovah,
And He will give thee thy heart's desire — DeW
make Yahweh your only joy
and he will give you what your heart desires — Jerus

5. Commit thy way unto the LORD; trust also in him; and he shall bring it to pass.
Roll on Yahweh thy way,
Trust also in him and he will effectually work — Rhm
Commit your enterprise to the Lord, and trust Him to accomplish it — Har
Commit your life to the LORD;
trust in him and he will act — NEB

6. And he shall bring forth thy righteousness as the light, and thy judgment as the noonday.
So will he bring forth as the light thy righteousness,

And thy vindication as the noonday — Rhm
He will make your vindication as clear as the day,
and your just cause like high noon — Har
he will bring your innocence to light, and make the justice of your cause clear as noonday — Mof

7. Rest in the LORD, and wait patiently for him:
Be still before the LORD, and wait patiently for him — RSV
Be silent before Jehovah, and wait for him — ABPS
Stay thee in Jehovah, and hold to Him firmly — DeW
Resign thyself unto the LORD,
and wait patiently for Him — JPS
Leave it to the LORD,
and wait for him — NAB

fret not thyself because of him who prospereth in his way, because of the man who bringeth wicked devices to pass.
fret not yourself over him who prospers in his way,
over the man who carries out evil devices! — RSV
Burn not with vexation
At him who prospereth in his way, —
At the man who doeth wickedness — Rhm
Rage not against him who prospereth in his way,
The man that succeedeth in his evil devices — DeW
Be not vexed at the successful path
of the man who does malicious deeds — NAB
be not envious of him who prospers in his way;
of the man who carries out wicked plans — Ber
do not strive to outdo the successful
nor envy him who gains his ends — NEB

8. Cease from anger, and forsake wrath:
Refrain from anger, and forsake wrath! — RSV
Desist from anger, abandon bitterness — Har

fret not thyself in any wise to do evil.
fret not thyself, else shalt thou be moved to do evil — PBV
Burn not with vexation — [it would be] only to do evil — Rhm
be not vexed, it will only harm you — NAB
Fret not thyself; it tends only to evil — RSV
do not show annoyance;
it brings nothing but harm — Har

9. For evildoers shall be cut off:
Wicked doers shall be rooted out — PBV

but those that wait upon the LORD, they shall inherit the earth.
But those that wait for Jehovah shall possess the land — DeW
but those who trust in the Lord
shall obtain their promised blessings — Har

10. For yet a little while, and the wicked shall not be:
Yet a little while, and the ungodly shall be clean gone — PBV
Yet a little while, and the wicked will be no more — RSV

yea, thou shalt diligently consider his place, and it shall not be.
Yea thou shalt look about over his place —
And he shall have vanished! — Rhm
though you look carefully for the place where he was,
it will have disappeared — Har

11. But the meek shall inherit the earth;
But the patient oppressed-ones shall inherit the earth — Rhm
But the humble shall inherit the land — ABPS
But the gentle . . . — Ber
But the lowly in spirit shall possess the land — DeW
But the humble will come into their true inheritance — Har

and shall delight themselves in the abundance of peace.
And shall delight themselves over the abundance of prosperity — Rhm
And delight in abundant blessing — DeW
and be happy amidst great prosperity — Har
and enjoy untold prosperity — NEB

12. The wicked plotteth against the just, and gnasheth upon him with his teeth.
The wicked man plots against the virtuous,
and grinds his teeth at him — Jerus

13. The Lord shall laugh at him: for he seeth that his day is coming.
but the Eternal laughs at him,
knowing his doom is near — Mof

14. The wicked have drawn out the sword, and have bent their bow, to cast down the poor and needy, and to slay such as be of upright conversation.

. . . to cast down the poor and needy,
to slay such as be upright in the way — RV

The wicked draw the sword, and bend the bow,
To bring down the suffering and needy,
And to slay those whose way is upright — DeW

The wicked draw the sword and bend their bows,
to bring down the poor and needy,
to slay those who walk uprightly — RSV

15. Their sword shall enter into their own heart, and their bows shall be broken.

Their sword shall pierce their own hearts,
and their bow shall be smashed — Har

16. A little that a righteous man hath is better than the riches of many wicked.

The shortage which the righteous man experiences
is better than the abundant wealth of the wicked — Har

Better is the little that the righteous have,
than the riches of many evil-doers — Ber

The little that a good man has
is better than a godless man's wealth — Mof

17. For the arms of the wicked shall be broken: but the LORD upholdeth the righteous.

For the arms of the wicked shall be shattered,
But Jehovah upholdeth the righteous — DeW

For the strength of the wrongdoers shall be destroyed,
but the Lord will sustain the righteous — Har

18. The LORD knoweth the days of the upright: and their inheritance shall be for ever.

Jehovah careth for the days of the upright;
And their inheritance shall endure for ever — DeW

The LORD watches over the lives of the wholehearted;
their inheritance lasts forever — NAB

The LORD knows each day of the good man's life,
and his inheritance shall last for ever — NEB

19. They shall not be shamed in the evil time: and in the days of famine they shall be satisfied.

They shall not come to shame in the time of evil,
And in the days of famine they shall be filled — DeW

they are not put to shame in evil times,
in the days of famine they have abundance — RSV

They shall not be put to shame in time of trouble;
even in days of famine they shall be satisfied — Ber

20. But the wicked shall perish,

But the wicked perish — RSV

and the enemies of the LORD shall be as the fat of lambs: they shall consume; into smoke shall they consume away.

the enemies of the LORD are like the glory of the pastures,
they vanish — like smoke they vanish away — RSV

the enemies of the Lord will waste away like the glory of the meadows, and vanish in smoke — Har

21. The wicked borroweth, and payeth not again:

The wicked borrows, and cannot pay back — RSV

The wicked man borrows without meaning to repay — Jerus

but the righteous sheweth mercy, and giveth.

but the righteous is merciful and liberal — PBV

But the righteous dealeth graciously, and giveth — ASV

but a virtuous man is generous and open-handed — Jerus

22. For such as be blessed of him shall inherit the earth;

for those blessed by the LORD shall possess the land — RSV

and they that be cursed of him shall be cut off.

but those whom He curses will be obliterated — Har

23. The steps of a good man are ordered by the LORD: and he delighteth in his way.

A man's goings are established of Jehovah;
And he delighteth in his way — ASV
By the LORD are the steps of a man made firm,
and he approves his way — NAB
The steps of a man are from the LORD, and he establishes him in whose way he delights — RSV
A man's progress comes from the Lord; He establishes him, and is pleased with his conduct — Har
It is the LORD who directs a man's steps,
he holds him firm and watches over his path — NEB
When a man's life pleases the Eternal, he gives him a sure footing — Mof

24. Though he fall, he shall not be utterly cast down:
He may stumble, but he will not fall headlong — Har
he may fall, but never fatally — Jerus
Though he fall, he shall not lie prostrate — AAT
for the LORD upholdeth him with his hand.
For Yahweh is holding his hand — Rhm
for the hand of the LORD sustains him — NAB
for the Lord is a support to which he can cling — Har

25. I have been young, and now am old;
Once I was young, and now I am aged — Har
yet have I not seen the righteous forsaken, nor his seed begging bread.
Yet have I not seen the righteous forsaken,
nor his offspring begging for bread — DeW
I never saw a virtuous man deserted, or his descendants forced to beg their bread — Jerus

26. He is ever merciful, and lendeth; and his seed is blessed.
He is continually lending, ever generous,
and his descendants become a blessing — Har
they always have something to give away,
something wherewith to bless their families — Mof
All the day long he showeth kindness and lendeth,
And his offspring are blessed — DeW
he is always compassionate, always lending:
his children will be blessed — Jerus

27. Depart from evil, and do good; and dwell for evermore.
Depart from evil, and do good;
so shall you abide for ever — RSV
Forsake evil, and do what is good,
and you will continue for ever — Har

28. For the LORD loveth judgment, and forsaketh not his saints;
For the LORD loves justice;
he will not forsake his saints — RSV
For Yahweh loveth justice
And will not forsake his men of lovingkindness — Rhm
For JEHOVAH loveth justice;
And will not forsake His devoted people — Sprl
For Jehovah delighteth in justice,
And He forsaketh not His beloved — DeW
for Yahweh loves what is right,
and never deserts the devout — Jerus
For the Lord loves justice;
He will not abandon His faithful followers — Har
they are preserved for ever: but the seed of the wicked shall be cut off.
For ever they shall be preserved:
But the offspring of the wicked shall be cut off — DeW

29. The righteous shall inherit the land, and dwell therein for ever.
The upright will have the earth for their heritage, and will go on living there for ever — Bas
The virtuous will receive their promised heritage,
and enjoy it continually — Har

30. The mouth of the righteous speaketh wisdom, and his tongue talketh of judgment.
The mouth of a righteous man softly uttereth wisdom,
And his tongue speaketh justice — Rhm
The mouth of the righteous utters wisdom,
and his tongue speaks what is right — Ber

31. The law of his God is in his heart; none of his steps shall slide.
The law of his God is in his heart,
His steps shall not swerve — Rhm

The law of his God is in his heart;
And his footsteps falter not — DeW

The law of his God is in his heart; he will never make a false step — Bas

his steps never falter, because the law of God rules in his heart — Knox

32. The wicked watcheth the righteous, and seeketh to slay him.

The wicked lies in wait for the righteous
and seeks to put him to death — Ber

The wicked man spies on the just, and seeks to slay him — NAB

33. The LORD will not leave him in his hand, nor condemn him when he is judged.

The LORD will not abandon him to his power,
or let him be condemned when he is brought to trial — RSV

34. Wait on the LORD, and keep his way, and he shall exalt thee to inherit the land:

Wait for the LORD,
and keep his way;
He will promote you to ownership of the land — NAB

Trust in the Lord, and observe His requirements,
and He will promote you so that you emerge triumphant — Har

when the wicked are cut off, thou shalt see it.

when the wicked are destroyed, you shall look on — NAB

you yourself will witness the extinction of the wicked — Har

35. I have seen the wicked in great power, and spreading himself like a green bay tree.

I have seen the wicked in great power, and spreading himself like a green tree in its native soil — RV

I have watched a wicked man at his work,
rank as a spreading tree in its native soil — NEB

I saw a wicked man, fierce,
and stalwart as a flourishing, age-old tree — NAB

I saw a godless man once on a time, a terror —
towering like any cedar of Lebanon — Mof

I have seen the wicked in his triumph towering like a cedar of Lebanon — Jerus

36. Yet he passed away, and, lo, he was not:

Again I passed by, and, lo, he was no more — RSV

I passed by one day, and he was gone — NEB

But he passed on, and, lo, he was gone — DeW

Yet he disappeared; he vanished completely — Har

yea, I sought him, but he could not be found.

though I sought him, he could not be found — RSV

37. Mark the perfect man, and behold the upright:

Mark the man of integrity, and behold the upright — JPS

Cling to integrity, hold fast to uprightness — Har

Keep innocency, and take heed unto the thing that is right — PBV

for the end of that man is peace.

for that shall bring a man peace at the last — PBV

For there is a happy end to the man of peace — ASV

for there is a future for the man who loves peace — Har

For there is a hereafter for the man of peace — Rhm

For there is a posterity for the man of peace — AAT

38. But the transgressors shall be destroyed together:

But the transgressors shall all be cut off — DeW

Sinners shall all alike be destroyed — NAB

But sinners shall be wiped out at a blow — Mof

But wrongdoers shall perish completely — Har

the end of the wicked shall be cut off.

The future of the wicked is destroyed — DeW

the remnants of the wicked shall be rooted out — Sept

the posterity of the wicked shall be cut off — RSV

39. But the salvation of the righteous is of the LORD:

But the deliverance of the righteous is from Yahweh — Rhm

Help comes from the Eternal to good men — Mof

he is their strength in the time of trouble.
Their refuge in a time of distress — Rhm
and he is their protector in time of trouble — Sept
He is their shelter in time of trouble — Har
their fortress in a time of trouble — Ber

40. **And the LORD shall help them, and deliver them:**
The LORD helps them and delivers them — RSV
And the Lord shall stand by them, and save them — PBV
And Jehovah helpeth them, and rescueth them — ASV
he shall deliver them from the wicked, and save them, because they trust in him.
He will deliver them from the lawless and will save them,
Because they have sought refuge in him — Rhm
he rescueth them from the wicked, and saveth them, because they have taken refuge in him — RV

PSALM 38

A Psalm of David, to bring to remembrance.
Psalm Of David In commemoration — Jerus

1. **O LORD, rebuke me not in thy wrath: neither chasten me in thy hot displeasure.**
O Yahweh do not in thine anger correct me,
Nor in thy wrath chastise me — Rhm
O Jehovah! punish me not in Thy wrath,
Nor correct me in Thy hot displeasure — DeW

2. **For thine arrows stick fast in me, and thy hand presseth me sore.**
For thine arrows have sunk down into me,
And thy hand presseth heavily upon me — Rhm
For Your missiles have pierced me deeply,
And Your punishment lies heavily upon me — Har
Your arrows have struck deep; your blows are crushing me — Tay

3. **There is no soundness in my flesh because of thine anger; neither is there any rest in my bones because of my sin.**
There is no soundness in my flesh
By reason of thine indignation,
There is no peace in my bones,
By reason of my sin — Rhm
There is no soundness in my flesh because of thine indignation; neither is there any health in my bones because of my sin — RV
Thy indignation has left no part of my body unscarred;
there is no health in my whole frame because of my sin — NEB

4. **For mine iniquities are gone over mine head: as an heavy burden they are too heavy for me.**
For my wickednesses are gone over my head, and are like a sore burden, too heavy for me to bear — PBV
For my iniquities have overwhelmed me;
they are like a heavy burden, beyond my strength — NAB
They are like a flood, higher than my head; they are a burden too heavy to bear — Tay

5. **My wounds stink and are corrupt because of my foolishness.**
My wounds are of bad odour — they have festered,
By reason of my folly — Rhm
My stripes are putrid, and running,
Because of my foolishness — ABPS
My stripes have become loathsome and corrupt,
Because of my foolishness — DeW
my wounds fester and rankle, with my own folly to blame — Knox

6. **I am troubled; I am bowed down greatly; I go mourning all the day long.**
I am brought into so great trouble and misery, that I go mourning all the day long — PBV
I writhe; I am depressed exceedingly;
I go mourning all the day long — DeW
bowed down, bent double, overcome,
I go mourning all the day — Jerus
I am bowed down and utterly prostrate.
All day long I go about as if in mourning — NEB
Because of my sins I am bent and

racked with pain. My days are filled with anguish — Tay

7. For my loins are filled with a loathsome disease: and there is no soundness in my flesh.

For my loins are filled with inflamation,
And there is no soundness in my flesh — Rhm

For my loins are filled with burning pains;
There is no health in my flesh — NAB

for my thighs are full of fever,
there is no soundness in my body — Mof

My loins are burnt up with fever,
there is no soundness in my flesh — Jerus

My body is full of a feverish disease, and there is no health in my flesh — Har

my whole frame afire, my whole body diseased — Knox

8. I am feeble and sore broken: I have roared by reason of the disquietness of my heart.

I am benumbed and crushed exceedingly, —
I have cried aloud because of the groaning of my heart — Rhm

I am numbed and severely crushed;
I roar with anguish of heart — NAB

I am utterly spent and crushed;
I groan because of the tumult of my heart — RSV

numbed and crushed and overcome,
my heart groans, I moan aloud — Jerus

My strength is spent; I am badly crushed.
I lament in agony of soul — Har

All battered and benumbed,
I groan aloud in my heart's longing — NEB

9. Lord, all my desire is before thee; and my groaning is not hid from thee.

Lord, thou knowest all my desire . . . — PBV

Lord, before Thee is all my longing,
And my sighs are not hid from Thee! — DeW

Lord, all my longing is wellknown to thee,
thou art no stranger to my sighs — Mof

Lord, all that I long for is known to you,
my sighing is no secret from you — Jerus

Lord, you know how I long for my health once more. You hear my every sigh — Tay

10. My heart panteth, my strength faileth me: as for the light of mine eyes, it also is gone from me.

My heart throbs, my strength fails me;
and the light of my eyes — it also has gone from me — RSV

My heart fluttereth, my strength forsaketh me;
The light of mine eyes — even this hath left me — DeW

My heart beats wildly, my strength fails, and I am going blind — Tay

11. My lovers and my friends stand aloof from my sore;

My friends and companions stand aloof from my plague — RSV

My friends and my companions stand back because of my affliction — NAB

My friends and my companions shun me in my sickness — NEB

and my kinsmen stand afar off.

And my neighbors stand afar off — ABPS

and my relatives stand at a distance — Har

even the dearest of them keep their distance — Jerus

12. They also that seek after my life lay snares for me:

Those who desire my death set traps — Har

and they that seek my hurt speak mischievous things, and imagine deceits all the day long.

those who seek my hurt speak of ruin, and meditate treachery all the day long — RSV

Bent on my ruin, they speak deadly words:
They utter falsehoods all the day long — DeW

those who mean to injure me spread cruel gossip
and mutter slanders all day long — NEB

13. But I, as a deaf man, heard not; and I was as a dumb man that openeth not his mouth.

But I, as a deaf man, will hear nothing;
I will be like a dumb man, that openeth not his mouth — DeW

But I am like a deaf man, I do not hear,
like a dumb man who does not open his mouth — RSV

14. Thus I was as a man that heareth not, and in whose mouth are no reproofs.

Yea, I have become as one that heareth not,
And in whose mouth there are no replies — DeW

I am just like a person deprived of hearing,
and as one who has no argument at his command — Har

I behave like a man who cannot hear
and whose tongue offers no defence — NEB

15. For in thee, O LORD, do I hope: thou wilt hear, O Lord my God.

But for thee, O LORD, do I wait;
it is thou, O LORD my God, who wilt answer — RSV

For I put my trust in you, Yahweh,
and leave you to answer for me, Lord my God — Jerus

16. For I said, Hear me, lest otherwise they should rejoice over me: when my foot slippeth, they magnify themselves against me.

For I have prayed: Let them not rejoice over me;
When my foot faltereth,
Let them not swell proudly against me — DeW

For I pray, "Only let them not rejoice over me,
who boast against me when my foot slips!" — RSV

Put an end to their arrogance, these who gloat when I am cast down! — Tay

17. For I am ready to halt, and my sorrow is continually before me.

For I am on the verge of a collapse;
my plight is ever present to my mind — Mof

For I am ready to fall,
and my pain is ever with me — RSV

I am indeed prone to stumble,
and suffering is never far away — NEB

18. For I will declare mine iniquity; I will be sorry for my sin.

For I will declare my iniquity,
Will be anxious for my sin — ABPS

For I do declare mine iniquity;
I am full of care because of my sin — JPS

Yea, I confess mine iniquity;
I am troubled because of my sin — DeW

I confess my guilt,
and repent of my sin — Har

19. But mine enemies are lively, and they are strong:

But as for mine enemies they live and are stronger than I — Sept

Those who are my foes without cause are mighty — RSV

Those who are my enemies without provocation are numerous — Har

But mine enemies are strong and alert — Lam

and they that hate me wrongfully are multiplied.

Yea, many are they that hate me wrongfully — DeW

20. They also that render evil for good are mine adversaries; because I follow the thing that good is.

They repay good with evil;
They set themselves against me
Because I press onward in good — DeW

Those who repay good with evil
oppose me because my purpose is good — NEB

21. Forsake me not, O LORD: O my God, be not far from me.

Do not forsake me, Lord:
Do not desert me, my God — Har

22. Make haste to help me, O Lord my salvation.

Hasten to my assistance,
my Lord, my deliverer — Har

PSALM 39

To the chief Musician, even to Jeduthun, a Psalm of David.

To the Chief Musician. For Jeduthun. A Melody of David — Rhm

To the choirmaster: to Jeduthun. A Psalm of David — RSV

From the Choirmaster Jeduthun's collection. A song of David — Mof

1. I said, I will take heed to my ways, that I sin not with my tongue:

I said: I will keep close watch over myself
that all I say may be free from sin — NEB

I said, I will be careful what I do,
lest I sin with my tongue — Mof
I vowed that I would be circumspect in my behavior,
committing no sin in what I said — Har
I said, 'I will watch how I behave,
and not let my tongue lead me into sin — Jerus
I said to myself, I'm going to quit complaining! — Tay
I will keep my mouth with a bridle, while the wicked is before me.
I will put a muzzle on my mouth,
As long as the wicked is before me — AAT
I will keep a muzzle on my mouth,
so long as wicked men confront me — NEB
that I would muzzle myself
as long as the wicked were in my company — Har

2. I was dumb with silence, I held my peace, even from good;
I held my tongue, and spake nothing:
I kept silence, yea, even from good words — PBV
I became dumb, saying not a word:
I was silent, holding off from relief — DeW
I was dumb with silence; I held my peace, had no comfort — JPS
I was dumb and silent,
I held my peace to no avail — RSV
I became dumb with silence;
I was quiet from a good motive — Har
and my sorrow was stirred.
but it was pain and grief to me — PBV
and my grief was renewed — Sept
Yet this only stirred my grief — Mof
my distress grew worse — RSV
but my unhappiness increased — Har
the turmoil within me grew to the bursting point — Tay

3. My heart was hot within me, while I was musing the fire burned:
My heart was hot within me: and while I was thus musing the fire kindled — PBV
Thus my heart became hot within me,
And in my grieving a fire kindled — DeW
My heart within me inflamed with earnest musings;
The fire within me burst into flame! — Sprl
The more I mused, the hotter the fires inside — Tay
then spake I with my tongue,
then spake I with my tongue: — RV
and I prayed aloud: — Mof
and at the last I spake with my tongue: — PBV
Then at last I spoke, and pled with God: — Tay

4. LORD, make me to know mine end, and the measure of my days, what it is; that I may know how frail I am.
LORD, let me know mine end, and the number of my days; that I may be certified how long I have to live — PBV
Teach me, O Jehovah! mine end,
And what is the measure of my days:
For I would know how frail I am — DeW
'Tell me, Yahweh, when my end will be,
how many days are allowed me,
show me how frail I am — Jerus
Make me to know, O LORD, my end,
and the length of my days, what it is.
Let me know how transient I am — Ber

5. Behold, thou hast made my days as a handbreadth;
Behold, thou hast made my days as it were a span long — PBV
Behold, thou hast made my days as handbreadths — RV
See how You have fixed my life at a few spans of the hand — Har
My life is no longer than my hand! — Tay
and mine age is as nothing before thee:
and my lifetime is as nothing in thy sight — RSV
My whole lifetime is but a moment to you — Tay
verily every man at his best state is altogether vanity.
Only a breath is all mankind,
Even when firmly standing — DeW
Surely every man stands as a mere breath! — RSV
each man that stands on earth is only a puff of wind — Jerus
Man, though he stands upright, is but a puff of wind — NEB
Proud man! Frail as breath! A shadow! — Tay
Selah.

6. Surely every man walketh in a vain shew:
Surely as a shadow doth every man wander — Rhm
Truly man walks the world like a shadow — Knox
Man walks about like a shadowy image — Har
he moves like a phantom — NEB
surely they are disquieted in vain:
Surely in vain is their busy tumult! — Sprl
Surely in vain do they bustle about — Rhm
and all his fuss is in vain — Har
And all his busy rushing ends in nothing — Tay
he heapeth up riches, and knoweth not who shall gather them.
He heapeth things up, and knoweth not who shall gather them in — Rhm
He heaps up treasures, and knows not who will gather them — ABPS
He gathereth, but knoweth not who shall enjoy — DeW
He heaps up riches for someone else to spend — Tay

7. And now, Lord, what wait I for? my hope is in thee.
And now, JEHOVAH, what is my hope?
In Thyself is my hope — Sprl
For what, then, do I wait, O Lord!
My expectation is from Thee — DeW
So tell me, Lord, what can I expect?
My hope is in you — Jerus

8. Deliver me from all my transgressions: make me not the reproach of the foolish.
From all my transgressions deliver me;
Make me not the scorn of the profane — DeW
Rid me of all my wilful sins:
do not make me the scorn of the foolish — Har
From all my sins deliver me;
a fool's taunt let me not suffer — NAB
Save me from being overpowered by my sins, for even fools will mock me then — Tay
Deliver me from all who do me wrong, make me no longer the butt of fools — NEB

9. I was dumb, I opened not my mouth; because thou didst it.
I am dumb; I open not my mouth;
Because it is Thou that doest it — DeW
I am speechless,
I do not open my mouth,
for it is Your doing — Har
Lord, I am speechless before you. I will not open my mouth to speak one word of complaint, for my punishment is from you — Tay

10. Remove thy stroke away from me:
Remove thy plague from me — AAT
Take away your scourge from me — NAB
Lord, don't hit me anymore — Tay
I am consumed by the blow of thine hand.
By the blow of Thy hand I perish — DeW
at the blow of your hand I wasted away — NAB
I am worn out with the blows you deal me — Jerus
I am exhausted beneath your hand — Tay

11. When thou with rebukes dost correct man for iniquity, thou makest his beauty to consume away like a moth:
When You punish and correct a man for his iniquity,
You cause his attractiveness to deteriorate
as though motheaten — Har
When by rebukes for iniquity thou hast corrected a man
Then hast thou consumed as a moth all that was delightful within him — Rhm
With rebukes for guilt thou dost chastise a man,
And thou dost wipe out his desire like a cobweb — AAT
When thou dost chasten man
with rebukes for sin,
thou dost consume like a moth
what is dear to him — RSV
When you punish a man for his sins,
he is destroyed; he is as fragile as a moth-infested cloth — Tay
When thou dost rebuke a man to punish his sin,
all his charm festers and drains away — NEB
surely every man is vanity.
Surely every man is but a vapour! — Sprl
indeed man is only a puff of wind — NEB

yes, man is frail as breath — Tay
indeed, every man is as nothing — Har
Selah.
Selah [pause, and think calmly of that]! — Amp

12. Hear my prayer, O LORD, and give ear unto my cry;
Hear my prayer, O Jehovah,
And give ear to my cry for help — ABPS
hold not thy peace at my tears:
At my tears do not be silent — Rhm
At my weeping be not silent — DeW
to my weeping be not deaf! — NAB
Do not remain unmoved at my tears — Har
for I am a stranger with thee, and a sojourner, as all my fathers were.
For I am a guest with Thee,
A sojourner as all my fathers were — DeW
For I am but a wayfarer before you,
a pilgrim like all my fathers — NAB
For I am thy passing guest,
a sojourner, like all my fathers — RSV
For I am your guest! I am a traveler passing through the earth, as all my fathers were! — Tay

13. O spare me, that I may recover strength, before I go hence, and be no more.
Look away from me, and let me cheer up,
Before I go hence, and be no more — ABPS
Turn from me Thine anger and disperse my gloom,
Before I go hence and be no more! — DeW
Turn your gaze from me, that I may find respite
ere I depart and be no more — NAB
Frown on me no more and let me smile again,
before I go away and cease to be — NEB
Spare me, Lord! Let me recover and be filled with happiness again before my death — Tay

PSALM 40

To the chief Musician, A Psalm of David.

1. I waited patiently for the LORD; and he inclined unto me, and heard my cry.
I waited patiently for Jehovah,
And he inclined to me and heard my cry for help — ABPS
I waited and waited for the LORD;
then He bent over to me and heard my cry — Ber
I waited patiently and expectantly for the Lord, and He inclined to me and heard my cry — Amp

2. He brought me up also out of an horrible pit, out of the miry clay,
He drew me up from the yawning chasm,
out of the muddy swamp — Har
He lifted me out of the pit of destruction,
Out of the miry clay — DeW
He drew me up from the desolate pit,
out of the miry bog — RSV
He lifted me out of the pit of despair,
out from the bog and the mire — Tay
and set my feet upon a rock, and established my goings.
and set my feet on a rock and directed my steps — Sept
He placed my feet on a solid foundation,
making my steps firm — Har
he set my foot on a rock and steadied my steps — Mof

3. And he hath put a new song in my mouth, even praise unto our God:
And He put into my mouth a new song,
A hymn of praise to our God — DeW
He gave me a new song to sing,
one of praise to our God — Har
many shall see it, and fear, and shall trust in the LORD.
Many shall see and revere,
And shall trust in Yahweh — Rhm
Many will see and be struck with awe,
and trust in the Lord — Sept
Many shall look on in awe
and trust in the LORD — NAB
Many will take notice of it, and become alarmed,
and will trust in the Lord — Har
dread will seize many at the sight,
and they will put their trust in Yahweh — Jerus

4. Blessed is that man that maketh the LORD his trust,
How happy the man
Who hath made Yahweh his confidence — Rhm
Happy the man
Who has made Jehovah his trust — ABPS
O the blessedness of the man
Who maketh Jehovah his trust — DeW
and respecteth not the proud, nor such as turn aside to lies.
Who hath not turned unto the haughty
Nor gone aside unto falsehood — Rhm
and who hath not looked to vanities and lying fooleries — Sept
And who resorteth not to the proud,
Nor to lying apostates! — DeW
who turns not to idolatry
or to those who stray after falsehood — NAB
who does not turn to the proud,
to those who go astray after false gods! — RSV

5. Many, O LORD my God, are thy wonderful works which thou hast done, and thy thoughts which are to us-ward: they cannot be reckoned up in order unto thee:
Thou hast multiplied, O LORD my God,
thy wondrous deeds and thy thoughts toward us;
none can compare with thee! — RSV
Many, Jehovah, my God! are the wonders Thou hast wrought,
And many are Thy thoughts for us:
O Thou with whom none can compare! — DeW
How numerous have you made, O LORD, my God, your wondrous deeds!
And in your plans for us
there is none to equal you — NAB
How many wonders you have done for us,
Yahweh, my God!
How many plans you have made for us;
you have no equal! — Jerus
Great things thou hast done,
O LORD my God;
thy wonderful purposes are all for our good;
none can compare with thee — NEB
if I would declare and speak of them, they are more than can be numbered.
If I should declare them, and speak of them, they should be more than I am able to express — PBV
I would declare and speak them,
But they are more than can be told! — DeW
I want to proclaim them, again and again,
but they are more than I can count — Jerus

6. Sacrifice and offering thou didst not desire;
Thou carest not for sacrifice and offering — Mof
It isn't sacrifices and offerings which you really want from your people — Tay
mine ears hast thou opened:
Ears didst thou pierce for me — Rhm
but thou hast given me an open ear — RSV
but You bestowed on me an attentive ear — Har
but ears open to obedience you gave me — NAB
but preparedst for me a body — Sept
burnt offering and sin offering hast thou not required.
Burnt animals bring no special joy to your heart — Tay

7. Then said I, Lo, I come: in the volume of the book it is written of me,
Then said I, Lo, I am come; in the roll of the book it is written of me — RV

8. I delight to do thy will, O my God: yea, thy law is within my heart.
To do thy good-pleasure O my God is my delight,
And thy law is in the midst of mine inward parts — Rhm
To do Thy pleasure is my delight,
And Thy law is in my inmost heart — DeW

9. I have preached righteousness in the great congregation:
I have proclaimed glad tidings of righteousness in the great assembly — ASV
I have told the good-tidings of righteousness in a great convocation — Rhm
lo, I have not refrained my lips, O LORD, thou knowest.
Lo! my lips I did not close,
Thou, O Jehovah! knowest — DeW
I did not restrain my lips, as you, O LORD, know — NAB

I exercise no restraint over my testimony,
as you, Lord, know very well — Har
I have not been timid about it, as you well know, O Lord — Tay

10. I have not hid thy righteousness within my heart; I have declared thy faithfulness and thy salvation:
Thy righteousness I hid not in my heart,
But Thy faithful, saving power I proclaimed — DeW
I have not hid thy saving help within my heart,
I have spoken of thy faithfulness and thy salvation — RSV
I have not kept Your righteousness concealed in my mind;
I have spoken openly of Your fidelity and Your deliverance — Har
I have never kept your righteousness to myself,
but have spoken of your faithfulness and saving help — Jerus
I have not concealed thy lovingkindness and thy truth from the great congregation.
I have not concealed thy lovingkindness and thy truthfulness from the great convocation — Rhm
I have made no secret of your kindness and your truth
in the vast assembly — NAB
I have not concealed thy steadfast love and thy faithfulness
from the great congregation — RSV

11. Withhold not thou thy tender mercies from me, O LORD:
Withhold not, O LORD, your compassion from me — NAB
For You, Lord, will not hold back Your sympathy from me — Har
let thy lovingkindness and thy truth continually preserve me.
Thy lovingkindness and thy truthfulness shall continually watch over me — Rhm
Let Thy lovingkindness and Thy truth ever guard me — DeW
let thy steadfast love and thy faithfulness
ever preserve me! — RSV
may Your grace and Your faithfulness continue to be my protection — Har
My only hope is your love and faithfulness — Tay

12. For innumerable evils have compassed me about:
For there have closed in upon me misfortunes beyond number — Rhm
For countless sorrows have beset me — Har
mine iniquities have taken hold upon me, so that I am not able to look up;
My iniquities have overtaken me,
and I can not behold them! — ABPS
and my sins have overwhelmed me, so that I cannot see — Har
my sins close in on me
until I can hardly see — Jerus
they are more than the hairs of mine head: therefore my heart faileth me.
They have become more than the hairs of my head,
And my courage hath forsaken me! — Rhm
They are more numerous than the hairs of my head;
my morale is completely shattered — Har

13. Be pleased, O LORD, to deliver me: O LORD, make haste to help me.
Take pleasure, Lord, in rescuing me;
hurry to my assistance, Lord — Har
Oh come and rescue me, Yahweh,
Yahweh come quickly and help me! — Jerus

14. Let them be ashamed and confounded together that seek after my soul to destroy it;
Let them turn pale and then at once blush
Who are seeking my life to snatch it away — Rhm
Let them be put to shame and confusion altogether
who seek to snatch away my life — RSV
let them be driven backward and put to shame that wish me evil.
Let them draw back and be confounded,
Who are taking pleasure in my calamity — Rhm
Let them be turned backward and put to shame
That delight in my harm — ABPS
let them be turned back and brought to dishonor
who desire my hurt! — RSV
May they be driven back and routed who desire my ruin! — AAT

15. Let them be desolate for a reward of

their shame that say unto me, Aha, aha.

Let them be desolate, and rewarded with shame, that say unto me, Fie upon thee! fie upon thee! — PBV

Let them be astonished on account of their own shame,
who are saying of me Aha! Aha! — Rhm

Let those be struck dumb through their shame,
That say to me Aha! Aha! — DeW

Let them be appalled because of their shame
who say to me, "Aha, Aha!" — RSV

let those who cry 'Hurrah!' at my downfall
be horrified at their reward of shame — NEB

16. Let all those that seek thee rejoice and be glad in thee:

But may all who seek thee
rejoice and be glad in thee — RSV

let such as love thy salvation say continually, The LORD be magnified.

may those who love thy salvation say continually, "Great is the LORD!" — RSV

and let those who long for thy saving help ever cry,
'All glory to the LORD!' — NEB

17. But I am poor and needy; yet the Lord thinketh upon me:

As for me, I am poor and needy; but the Lord careth for me — PBV

As for me, I am weak and wretched; yet the Eternal will take thought for me — Mof

thou art my help and my deliverer; make no tarrying, O my God.

Thou art my helper and redeemer; make no long tarrying, O my God — PBV

My helper, my saviour, my God,
come and do not delay — JPS

Thou art my help and my deliverer;
O my God, delay not! — DeW

Thou art my champion and my refuge; do not linger, my God, do not linger on the way — Knox

PSALM 41

To the chief Musician, A Psalm of David.
To the choirmaster . . . — RSV

1. Blessed is he that considereth the poor: the LORD will deliver him in time of trouble.

How happy is he that is attentive to the poor,
In the day of calamity will Yahweh deliver him — Rhm

How blest is he that taketh thought for the feeble;
Jehovah deliver him in the evil day — DeW

Happy the man who has a concern for the helpless!
The LORD will save him in time of trouble — NEB

Happy the man who cares for the poor and the weak:
if disaster strikes, Yahweh will come to his help — Jerus

God blesses those who are kind to the poor. He helps them out of their troubles — Tay

2. The LORD will preserve him, and keep him alive;

Jehovah guard him, and let him live — DeW

The LORD protects him and keeps him alive — AAT

The Lord will protect and sustain him — Har

and he shall be blessed upon the earth:

That he may be happy in the earth — DeW

He shall be prospered in the land — ABPS

the Lord will let him be a blessing on the earth — Bas

And he shall be pronounced happy in the land — Rhm

and thou wilt not deliver him unto the will of his enemies.

Do not then give him up at the desire of his enemies! — Rhm

You will not abandon him to the schemes of his enemies — Har

3. The LORD will strengthen him upon the bed of languishing:

The LORD comfort him when he lieth sick upon his bed — PBV

Yahweh will sustain him upon the bed of sickness — Rhm

He nurses him on his sick-bed — NEB

thou wilt make all his bed in his sickness.

His bed of sickness Thou wilt wholly transform — DeW
most carefully you make his bed when he is sick — Jerus
he turns his bed when he is ill — NEB
in his illness thou healest all his infirmities — RSV
by you will all his grief be turned to strength — Bas

4. I said, LORD, be merciful unto me:
As for me, I said, Jehovah, be gracious to me — ABPS
As for me, I said: O Jehovah, pity me! DeW
heal my soul; for I have sinned against thee.
Heal me, though I have sinned against Thee — DeW
restore me, for I have sinned against You — Har

5. Mine enemies speak evil of me, When shall he die, and his name perish?
Mine enemies say of me in malice:
When will he die and his name perish — DeW
My enemies speak maliciously of me:
When will he die, and his reputation fade — Har

6. And if he come to see me, he speaketh vanity: his heart gathereth iniquity to itself; when he goeth abroad, he telleth it.
And if he come to see, he speaks falsehood;
In his heart he gathers up to himself mischief,
He goes forth, he tells it abroad — ABPS
If one come to see me, he speaketh falsehood;
His heart gathereth a slander;
When he goeth abroad he telleth it — DeW
When one comes to see me, he speaks without sincerity;
his heart stores up malice;
when he leaves he gives voice to it outside — NAB
When any of them visits me,
his heart is false;
he gathers matter for his malice,
then goes away to spread the tale — Mof
And when one comes to see me, he utters empty words,
while his heart gathers mischief;
when he goes out, he tells it abroad — RSV
They visit me, their hearts full of spite,
they offer hollow comfort, and go out to spread the news — Jerus
All who visit me speak from an empty heart,
alert to gather bad news;
then they go out to spread it abroad — NEB

7. All that hate me whisper together against me:
against me do they devise my hurt.
They lay charges against me of evil — DeW
they imagine the worst for me — RSV
and love to make the worst of everything — NEB
they predict misfortune for me — Har
they plan harm against me — Ber

8. An evil disease, say they, cleaveth fast unto him: and now that he lieth he shall rise up no more.
A base deed is visited upon him:
He hath lain down, and will never arise — DeW
Here is a foul plague loosed on him;
he will leave his bed no more — Knox
They say, "A deadly thing has fastened upon him;
he will not rise again from where he lies" — RSV
"It's fatal, whatever it is," they say.
"He'll never get out of that bed!" — Tay

9. Yea, mine own familiar friend, in whom I trusted, which did eat of my bread, hath lifted up his heel against me.
Even the man whom I used to salute
In whom I put confidence,
Who used to eat my bread, —
Hath magnified his heel against me! — Rhm
Yea, my trusted friend, who hath eaten my bread,
Hath lifted his heel against me — DeW
Even my friend in whom I trusted,
He who ate my bread, has acted deceitfully against me — AAT
Even my bosom friend in whom I trusted,
who ate of my bread, has lifted his heel against me — RSV

Even my friend in whom I confided,
who dined at my table, has behaved contemptuously towards me — Har
Even my closest and most trusted friend,
who shared my table, rebels against me — Jerus
Even the friend whom I trusted, who ate at my table,
exults over my misfortune — NEB

10. **But thou, O LORD, be merciful unto me, and raise me up,**
But Thou, O Jehovah! pity and restore me — DeW
that I may requite them.
That I may render them their desert — DeW

11. **By this I know that thou favourest me, because mine enemy doth not triumph over me.**
Hereby do I know that thou delightest in me,
In that mine enemy shall not raise a shout over me — Rhm
Then I shall know that thou delightest in me
and that my enemy will not triumph over me — NEB

12. **And as for me, thou upholdest me in mine integrity,**
And as for me, Thou upholdest me because of mine integrity — JPS
But as for me
In my blamelessness hast thou held me fast — Rhm
You have preserved me because I was honest — Tay
and settest me before thy face for ever.
and established me before thee forever — Sept
nevermore wilt thou banish me from thy presence — Knox
thou keepest me for ever in thy sight — NEB

13. **Blessed be the LORD God of Israel from everlasting, and to everlasting.**
Blessed be the LORD God of Israel, world without end — PBV
Blessed is Jehovah, God of Israel,
From the age — and unto the age — YLT
Blessed be Yahweh the God of Israel,
From the age that is past even unto the age yet to come — Rhm
BLESSED BE JEHOVAH, THE GOD OF ISRAEL,
TO THE FARTHEST AGES — TIME BEYOND TIME! — DeW
Amen, and Amen.
So be it. So be it — Bas

BOOK II

PSALM 42

To the chief Musician, Maschil, for the sons of Korah.
To the Chief Musician. An Instructive Psalm for the Sons of Korah — Rhm
To the Chief Musician. A skillful song, or a didactic or reflective poem of the sons of Korah — Amp
From the Choirmaster's collection. An ode of the Korahites — Mof

1. **As the hart panteth after the water brooks, so panteth my soul after thee, O God.**
As a deer longs for the water-courses,
So my whole being longs for thee, O God — AAT
As a hind longs for the running streams,
so do I long for thee, O God — NEB

2. **My soul thirsteth for God, for the living God:**
My soul is athirst for God, yea, even for the living God — PBV
My being thirsts for God,
for the living God — Har
My soul is dry for need of God, the living God — Bas
My soul thirsts for God,
the God of life — Jerus
when shall I come and appear before God?
O when shall I come and appear in the presence of God — Sprl
When shall I enter in, and see the face of God — Rhm

3. **My tears have been my meat day and night,**
My tears have been my food day and night — ASV
I have no food but tears,
day and night — Jerus
while they continually say unto me, Where is thy God?

while men say to me continually,
"Where is your God?" — RSV
and all the while my enemies taunt me. "Where is this God of yours?" they scoff — Tay

4. **When I remember these things, I pour out my soul in me:**
These things will I call to mind,
And pour out my heart within me — ABPS
These things I remember,
as I pour out my soul — RSV
I recall these things as my soul overflows with sorrow — Har
These things I ponder upon and pour out my very self — AAT
My soul is melting with secret sorrow, for well I remember it all — Mof
As I pour out my soul in distress, I call to mind — NEB
for I had gone with the multitude, I went with them to the house of God, with the voice of joy and praise, with a multitude that kept holyday.
how I led the throng once to the house of God,
chanting, praising, pacing in full festival — Mof
how I went with the throng,
and led them in procession to the house of God,
with glad shouts and songs of thanksgiving,
a multitude keeping festival — RSV
how I used to go with the crowd,
leading them joyfully to the temple of God
with jubilant shouts and thanksgiving;
a multitude celebrating a festival — Har
how I marched in the ranks of the great to the house of God,
among exultant shouts of praise,
the clamour of the pilgrims — NEB

5. **Why art thou cast down, O my soul? and why art thou disquieted in me?**
Why art thou so full of heaviness, O my soul? and why art thou so disquieted within me — PBV
Why shouldst thou be cast down O my soul?
And [why] shouldst thou moan over me — Rhm
Why art thou cast down, O my soul?
And why moanest thou within me — JPS
Why art thou downcast, O my soul?
Why so despairing — Mof
Why are you so despondent, my soul,
and why are you so agitated — Har
Why then be downcast? Why be discouraged and sad — Tay
How deep I am sunk in misery,
groaning in my distress: — NEB
hope thou in God: for I shall yet praise him for the help of his countenance.
Hope in God; for I shall again praise him,
my help and my God — RSV
Wait patiently upon God: for I shall yet give Him thanks;
My present Salvation, and my God — Sprl
yet I will wait for God;
I will praise him continually,
my deliverer, my God — NEB

6. **O my God, my soul is cast down within me:**
O my God! my soul boweth down within me — DeW
My spirit is downcast within me — AAT
I am depressed — Har
I am sunk in misery — NEB
therefore will I remember thee from the land of Jordan, and of the Hermonites, from the hill Mizar.
Therefore will I remember Thee from Jordan's land;
Amongst the Hermons, even from this insignificant hill — Sprl
therefore I remember thee
from the land of Jordan and of Hermon,
from Mount Mizar — RSV
so I remember thee
in this far land of Jordan and of Hermon,
at Mount Mizar — Mof

7. **Deep calleth unto deep at the noise of thy waterspouts:**
where deep echoes to deep in the roaring cataract — Har
Deep is sounding to deep at the noise of your waterfalls — Bas
Deep calls to deep
at the thunder of thy cataracts — RSV
floods of sorrow pour upon me like a thundering cataract — Tay
all thy waves and thy billows are gone over me.

All Thy breakers and thy billows passed over me — YLT
all Your waves and breakers have swamped me — Har

8. **Yet the LORD will command his lovingkindness in the daytime,**
By day the LORD will confirm His lovingkindness — Ber
By day the LORD commands his steadfast love — RSV
By day the LORD bestows his grace — NAB
and in the night his song shall be with me, and my prayer unto the God of my life.
and in the night season will I sing of him, and make my prayer unto the God of my life — PBV
and at night I sing a song to Him,
a prayer to my living God — Har
and through the night I sing his songs and pray to God who gives me life — Tay

9. **I will say unto God my rock,**
I will say unto God my refuge —DeW
I will say unto the God of my strength — PBV
I sing to God, my rock: — NAB
Why hast thou forgotten me? why go I mourning because of the oppression of the enemy?
Wherefore hast thou forgotten me?
Wherefore in gloom should I go because of oppression by the enemy — Rhm
"Why do you forget me?
Why must I go about in mourning, with the enemy oppressing me? — NAB
"Why have You overlooked me? Why must I live in sorrow under the oppression of my enemy?" — Har

10. **As with a sword in my bones, mine enemies reproach me;**
The reproach of my enemies is like a murderous weapon in my bones — Sprl
As if crushing my bones, mine enemies scoff at me — DeW
It crushes my bones that my foes mock me — NAB
Their taunts pierce me like a fatal wound — Tay
My enemies taunt me, jeering at my misfortunes — NEB
while they say daily unto me, Where is thy God?
Whilst they enquire of me throughout the day: Where is thy God — Sprl
again and again they scoff, "Where is that God of yours?" — Tay

11. **Why art thou cast down, O my soul? and why art thou disquieted within me? hope thou in God: for I shall yet praise him, who is the health of my countenance, and my God.**[12]
But O my soul, don't be discouraged. Don't be upset. Expect God to act! For I know that I shall again have plenty of reason to praise him for all that he will do. He is my help! He is my God! — Tay

PSALM 43

1. **Judge me, O God, and plead my cause against an ungodly nation:**
Vindicate me O God and plead my cause
Against a nation without lovingkindness — Rhm
Give me justice, O God!
Defend my right from a cruel nation — DeW
Treat me justly, O God, and plead my cause against a merciless people — Ber
O deliver me from the deceitful and unjust man.
from deceitful and unjust men deliver me! — RSV

2. **For thou art the God of my strength:**
For thou art my defending God — Rhm
For thou art my protecting God — DeW
why dost thou cast me off?
Wherefore hast thou rejected me — Rhm
Why, then, have You abandoned me — Har
why go I mourning because of the oppression of the enemy?
Must I go mourning, with enemies pressing me hard — Knox

3. **O send out thy light and thy truth:**

[12] See verse 5.

Send forth thy light and thy faithfulness — Rhm
Send out Your radiance and Your truth — Har
let them lead me;
that they may lead me — PBV
They shall guide me — ABPS
let them bring me unto thy holy hill, and to thy tabernacles.
Let them bring me into thy holy mountain and into thy habitations — Rhm
They shall bring me to thy holy mount,
And to thy tabernacles — ABPS
Let them lead me to your Temple on your holy mountain, Zion — Tay
4. Then will I go unto the altar of God, unto God my exceeding joy:
Then will I approach the altar of God,
unto God my ecstatic joy — Sprl
That I may go in unto the altar of God
Unto God mine exultant joy — Rhm
That I may come to the altar of God,
Unto God my joy of joys — DeW
Let me come to the altar of God,
to God my joy and delight — Mof
May I go to the altar of God, to God my highest joy — AAT
There I will go up to the altar of God, the giver of triumphant happiness — Knox
yea, upon the harp will I praise thee, O God my God.
That I may praise thee with the lyre
O God — mine own God! — Rhm
5. Why art thou cast down, O my soul? and why art thou disquieted within me? hope in God: for I shall yet praise him, who is the health of my countenance, and my God.[13]

PSALM 44

To the chief Musician for the sons of Korah, Maschil.
To the Chief Musician. For the Sons of Korah. An Instructive Psalm — Rhm

1. We have heard with our ears, O God, our fathers have told us, what work thou didst in their days, in the times of old.
O God, we have heard with our ears,
Our fathers have related unto us
The wonders which Thou didst perform in their days,
Even in the days of antiquity — Sprl
2. How thou didst drive out the heathen with thy hand, and plantedst them;
By Thine own hand the heathen were dispossessed,
And themselves were planted—DeW
How thou didst destroy the Gentiles with thy hand, and established thy people — Lam
By Your power You dispossessed pagan nations,
that they might take root — Har
Uprooting the nations with your hand, and planting our fathers in their place — Bas
how you drove the heathen nations from this land and gave it all to us — Tay
how thou didst afflict the people, and cast them out.
how thou hast destroyed the nations,
and made thy people to flourish — PBV
By Thee the nations were broken up,
But their own borders were enlarged — DeW
You smashed the peoples, but for them you made room — NAB
cutting down the nations, but increasing the growth of your people — Bas
3. For they got not the land in possession by their own sword, neither did their own arm save them:
for not by their own sword did they win the land,
nor did their own arm give them victory — RSV
but thy right hand, and thine arm, and the light of thy countenance, because thou hadst a favour unto them.
But Thy right hand, and Thine arm, and the light of Thy presence;
For Thou didst take pleasure in them — DeW
but it was Your mighty power,
Your strength and Your radiant Presence,
through showing favor to them — Har
it was your right hand, your arm
and the light of your face — because

[13]See 42:5 and 11.

you loved them — Jerus
but by your mighty power and because you smiled upon them and favored them — Tay

4. Thou art my King, O God: command deliverances for Jacob.
Thou art my King, O God; send help unto Jacob — PBV
Thou thyself art my king O God,
Command thou the victories of Jacob — Rhm
Thou art my King and my God,
who ordainest victories for Jacob — RSV
You it was, my King, my God,
who won those victories for Jacob — Jerus

5. Through thee will we push down our enemies:
In Thee alone shall we overcome our adversaries — Sprl
through thy name will we tread them under that rise up against us.
In thy Name will we tread down our assailants — Rhm

6. For I will not trust in my bow, neither shall my sword save me.
For not in my bow will I trust,
Nor shall my sword give me victory — Rhm

7. But thou hast saved us from our enemies, and hast put them to shame that hated us.
But you saved us from our foes,
and those who hated us you put to shame — NAB
You are the One to rescue us from our enemies,
and humiliate those who detest us — Har

8. In God we boast all the day long, and praise thy name for ever.
In God we have boasted continually,
and we will give thanks to thy name for ever — RSV
In God we gloried day by day;
your name we praised always — NAB
Selah.
(Pause.) — ABPS

9. But thou hast cast off, and put us to shame; and goest not forth with our armies.
Yet Thou hast cast us off in dishonour,
And Thou goest not forth with our hosts — DeW
Yet now you have cast us off and put us in disgrace,
and you go not forth with our armies — NAB
And yet for a time, O Lord, you have tossed us aside in dishonor, and have not helped us in our battles — Tay

10. Thou makest us to turn back from the enemy:
Thou makest us retreat before our oppressors — Sprl
You have let us be driven back by our foes — NAB
Thou hast hurled us back before the enemy — NEB
and they which hate us spoil for themselves.
so that they which hate us spoil our goods — PBV
And they who hate us have plundered at will — Rhm

11. Thou hast given us like sheep appointed for meat;
Thou lettest us be eaten up like sheep — PBV
Thou hast surrendered us as slaughter-sheep — Ber
Thou hast given us up to be butchered like sheep — NEB
and hast scattered us among the heathen.
And among the nations Thou hast scattered us — DeW

12. Thou sellest thy people for nought, and dost not increase thy wealth by their price.
Thou sellest thy people for nought, and takest no money for them — PBV
You have bartered Your people for a mere trifle,
making no profit from their sale — Har
Thou hast sold thy people for next to nothing
and had no profit from the sale — NEB
You sold us for a pittance. You valued us at nothing at all — Tay

13. Thou makest us a reproach to our neighbours, a scorn and a derision to them that are round about us.
Thou makest us a taunt to our neighbors,
A scorn and a derision to those around us — AAT
Thou dost make us a scorn to our neighbours,
A scoff and a jeer to those around us — DeW

Thou hast exposed us to the taunts of our neighbours,
to the mockery and contempt of all around — NEB

14. Thou makest us a byword among the heathen, a shaking of the head among the people.

Thou dost make us a byword among the heathen;
The Gentiles toss their head in contempt — DeW

Thou hast made us a byword among the nations,
a laughingstock among the peoples — RSV

Through You we have become notorious in the world,
so that nations shake their heads over us — Har

15. My confusion is continually before me, and the shame of my face hath covered me,

Throughout the day my confusion is present to me,
And the shame of my face hath veiled me — Sprl

All day long my disgrace is before me,
and shame has covered my face — RSV

All day long I brood on this disgrace,
my face covered in shame — Jerus

16. For the voice of him that reproacheth and blasphemeth; by reason of the enemy and avenger.

at the words of the taunters and revilers,
at the sight of the enemy and the avenger — RSV

at the shouts of those who taunt and abuse me
as the enemy takes his revenge — NEB

17. All this is come upon us;

All this has befallen us — NEB

yet have we not forgotten thee, neither have we dealt falsely in thy covenant.

though we have not forgotten thee,
or been false to thy covenant — RSV

yet never have we forgotten thee,
never proved false to thy bond — Mof

18. Our heart is not turned back, neither have our steps declined from thy way;

Our purpose has never faltered,
nor have our steps swerved from Your path — Har

19. Though thou hast sore broken us in the place of dragons,

That thou shouldst have crushed us down in the place of wild dogs — Rhm

that thou shouldst have broken us in the place of jackals — RSV

even when You crumpled us up in the place where jackals prowl — Har

yet you crushed us in the place where the jackals live — Jerus

Yet thou hast crushed us as the sea-serpent was crushed — NEB

and covered us with the shadow of death.

and covered us with the darkness of death — NEB

and covered us with deep darkness — RSV

And covered us over with a deadly shadow — Rhm

covering us over with deadly gloom — Har

and threw the shadow of death over us — Jerus

20. If we have forgotten the name of our God,

If we had forgotten the name of our God — RSV

or stretched out our hands to a strange god;

or have stretched out our hands to a pagan deity — Har

And spread forth our hands to an alien Power — DeW

21. Shall not God search this out?

would not God discover this — RSV

Would not God have searched into this — Rhm

would not he know of it — Knox

for he knoweth the secrets of the heart.

For He knows the secrets of the mind — Har

22. Yea, for thy sake are we killed all the day long;

No, it is for thy sake that we face death at every moment — Knox

Yet for your sake we are being slain all the day — NAB

Because of thee we are done to death all day long — NEB

But that is not our case. For we are facing death threats constantly because of serving you! — Tay

we are counted as sheep for the slaughter.

we are looked upon as sheep to be slaughtered — NAB
We are like sheep awaiting slaughter — Tay

23. Awake, why sleepest thou, O Lord?
Bestir thyself, Lord, why dost thou sleep on — Knox
Up, Lord, why sleepest thou — PBV
arise, cast us not off for ever.
Bestir thee! do not reject us altogether! — Rhm
Arouse Thee! spurn us not for ever! — DeW

24. Wherefore hidest thou thy face, and forgettest our affliction and our oppression?
Why do You conceal Yourself, ignoring our hardship and misery — Har
How canst thou turn thy face away, without a thought for our need and our affliction — Knox

25. For our soul is bowed down to the dust:
For our soul is brought low, even unto the dust — PBV
Our pride is bowed in the dust — Knox
For we have collapsed in the dust — Har
our belly cleaveth unto the earth.
Our body clingeth to the earth! — Sprl
our bodies are pressed to the earth — NAB
we are lying flat on the ground — Har
our bodies crushed to the ground — Jerus

26. Arise for our help, and redeem us for thy mercies' sake.
Arise for our complete deliverance;
And oh redeem us for Thy tender mercy's sake! — Sprl
Arise to our help,
And ransom us because of thine own lovingkindness — Rhm
Oh arise! become a help for us!
Redeem us for Thy lovingkindness' sake! — DeW
Rise up, come to our help!
Deliver us for the sake of thy steadfast love! — RSV

PSALM 45

To the chief Musician upon Shoshannim, for the sons of Korah, Maschil, A Song of loves.
To the Chief Musician. After [the melody] Lilies. Didactic [Psalm] of the Sons of Korah. A Song of Delights — ABPS
From the Choirmaster's collection of Korahite songs. To the tune of "The Lilies". An ode or love-song — Mof

1. My heart is inditing a good matter:
My heart overfloweth with a good matter — PBV
My heart overfloweth with a glorious oracle — Sprl
Overflowed hath my heart with an excellent theme — Rhm
My heart is overflowing with a beautiful thought! — Tay
My heart is stirred by a noble theme — NEB
My heart boileth over with goodly words — DeW
I speak of the things which I have made touching the king:
I will recite my poem concerning the king — Rhm
I address my verses to the king — RSV
my tongue is the pen of a ready writer.
My tongue resembles the pen of an accomplished scribe — Sprl
My tongue is the pen of a swift writer — DeW
may my tongue be like the pen of a gifted writer — Har

2. Thou art fairer than the children of men:
You are fairer than all mortals — Mof
You are the fairest of humanity — Har
grace is poured into thy lips:
full of grace are thy lips — PBV
Graciousness hath been poured forth by thy lips — Rhm
charm flows through your lips — Har
thy lips overflow with gracious utterance — Knox
therefore God hath blessed thee for ever.
Therefore God will bless thee for ever! — DeW
so you are blessed by God for ever — NEB

3. Gird thy sword upon thy thigh, O most mighty, with thy glory and thy majesty.
Gird your sword upon your thigh, O mighty one,
in your glory and majesty! — RSV

Gird thy sword upon thy thigh O Champion!
With thy renown and thy splendour! — DeW

Gird thy sword upon thy thigh O mighty one,
['Tis] thine honour and thy majesty — Rhm

Arm yourself, O Mighty One,
So glorious, so majestic! — Tay

4. And in thy majesty ride prosperously because of truth and meekness and righteousness;

And in this Thy magnificence ride prosperously
In the cause of truth, and of meekness, and of righteousness — Sprl

And [in] thy majesty be successful! ride forth!
On behalf of faithfulness and humility — righteousness — Rhm

In thy splendour ride on to victory,
In behalf of truth, and piety, and right — DeW

In your majesty ride forth victoriously for the cause of truth and to defend the right — RSV

and thy right hand shall teach thee terrible things.

Surely Thy right hand shall perform wonderful things! — Sprl

And thy right hand will teach thee fearful deeds — ABPS

let your right hand teach you dread deeds! — RSV

let your strength lead you to perform wonderful exploits — Har

Your right hand shall show you a scene of terror — NEB

5. Thine arrows are sharp in the heart of the king's enemies; whereby the people fall under thee.

Sharp shall be Thine arrows
When they pierce the heart of the King's enemies.
Nations shall prostrate themselves before Thee — Sprl

Thine arrows are sharp — nations fall under thee —
Thine arrows are in the heart of the king's foes! — DeW

your sharp arrows flying, nations beneath your feet,
the courage of the king's foes melting away — NEB

6. Thy throne, O God, is for ever and ever: the sceptre of thy kingdom is a right sceptre.

Thy throne, O God! is for ever and ever;
A sceptre of justice is Thy sceptre of rule — DeW

Your divine throne endures for ever and ever.
Your royal scepter is a scepter of equity — RSV

Your throne is like God's throne, eternal,
your royal sceptre a sceptre of righteousness — NEB

May your throne, established by God, endure permanently;
may a scepter of equity be your sovereign emblem — Har

7. Thou lovest righteousness, and hatest wickedness:

Thou hast loved righteousness and hated lawlessness — Rhm

therefore God, thy God, hath anointed thee with the oil of gladness above thy fellows.

so God, your God, crowns you with bliss
above your fellow-kings — Mof

Therefore the Lord your God has anointed you
in preference to your associates,
with sweet-smelling oil — Har

8. All thy garments smell of myrrh, and aloes, and cassia, out of the ivory palaces, whereby they have made thee glad.

your robes are all fragrant with myrrh and aloes and cassia.
From ivory palaces stringed instruments make you glad — RSV

9. Kings' daughters were among thy honourable women:

Kings' daughters were amongst Thy precious jewels — Sprl

Daughters of kings are among thy precious ones — ABPS

Daughters of kings are among thy treasures — DeW

daughters of kings are among your ladies of honor — RSV

upon thy right hand did stand the queen in gold of Ophir.

The consort was enthroned on Thy right hand,
Adorned in purest gold of Ophir — Sprl

At thy right hand stands the queen, in gold of Ophir — ABPS

10. Hearken, O daughter, and consider, and incline thine ear;

Hear, O daughter! and see; yea, incline thine ear — DeW

Listen, daughter, and take notice; pay attention to me — Har

forget also thine own people, and thy father's house;

"Forget your own people and your family home — Har

11. So shall the king greatly desire thy beauty: for he is thy Lord; and worship thou him.

So will the king desire thy beauty;
For he is thy lord; and reverence thou him — ASV

and the king will desire your beauty. Since he is your lord, bow to him — RSV

then the king will fall in love with your beauty.
He is your master now, bow down to him — Jerus

And let the king desire thy beauty;
For he is thy lord, and do thou do him homage — ABPS

"When the king desires your beauty, submit to him, for he is your lord" — Har

12. And the daughter of Tyre shall be there with a gift; even the rich among the people shall entreat thy favour.

And the daughter of Tyre with a gift shall court thy favor,
The rich ones of the people — ABPS

And the daughter of Tyre shall bring gifts;
the richest among the people shall win thy favour — DeW

And the city of Tyre is here with gifts; the rich among the people seek your favor — NAB

The people of Tyre, the richest people of our day, will shower you with gifts and entreat your favors — Tay

13. The king's daughter is all glorious within: her clothing is of wrought gold.

The king's daughter within the palace is all glorious: her clothing is inwrought with gold — RV

The princess is decked in her chamber with gold-woven robes — RSV

Inside the palace, the princess is magnificently dressed;
her robes are embroidered with gold — Har

14. She shall be brought unto the king in raiment of needlework:

In gayly wrought garments she shall be conducted to the king — ABPS

On broidered tapestries she is led forth to the king — DeW

In clothes of rich hue she is led to the king — Har

the virgins her companions that follow her shall be brought unto thee.

The virgins in her train shall be introduced to the king — Sept

with her companions, a maiden escort, brought by her — Har

15. With gladness and rejoicing shall they be brought: they shall enter into the king's palace.

They shall be conducted with gladness and rejoicing;
They shall enter in to the palace of the king — ABPS

With joy and gladness they are led along
as they enter the palace of the king — RSV

16. Instead of thy fathers shall be thy children, whom thou mayest make princes in all the earth.

Your sons shall step into your father's place,
and rise to be princes over all the land — Mof

Your sons will some day be kings like their father. They shall sit on thrones around the world! — Tay

17. I will make thy name to be remembered in all generations: therefore shall the people praise thee for ever and ever.

I will make thy Name to be remembered from one generation to another; therefore shall the people give thanks unto thee, world without end — PBV

I will make your name a memory for successive generations,
that nations may praise you for ever — Har

carrying your name on from age to age,
till nations praise you evermore — Mof

PSALM 46

To the chief Musician for the sons of Korah, A Song upon Alamoth.

To the Chief Musician. To [voices of] Maidens. A song of the Sons of Korah — ABPS

To the Chief Musician. [A Psalm] of the sons of Korah, set to treble voices. A song — Amp

From the Choirmaster's collection of Korahite songs. For soprano voices — Mof

For the leader. A song of the sons of Korah; according to "Virgins" — NAB

1. **God is our refuge and strength, a very present help in trouble.**

God is our shelter and strength:
An exceedingly ready help in the time of distress — Sprl

God — for us is a refuge and strength,
A help in distresses, soon found — Rhm

God is to us a refuge and strength;
A help in troubles, most surely found — ABPS

God is on our side, a refuge and fortress;
A help in distress, to be found without fail — DeW

God is our protection and strength;
a reliable help when trouble occurs — Har

God is for us a refuge and a fortress;
found to be a mighty help in troubles — Ber

2. **Therefore will not we fear, though the earth be removed, and though the mountains be carried into the midst of the sea;**

Therefore will we not fear, though the earth change its position;
And although the mountains slide away into the bosom of the sea — Sprl

Therefore we do not fear though the earth is displaced,
though the mountains reel into the midst of the sea — Ber

So then we will not be afraid
though the earth itself is transformed,
and the mountains collapse into the deep oceans — Har

And so we need not fear even if the world blows up, and the mountains crumble into the sea — Tay

3. **Though the waters thereof roar and be troubled, though the mountains shake with the swelling thereof.**

Let the waters thereof roar and foam;
Let the mountains quake with their swelling! — DeW

though its waters roar and foam,
though the mountains tremble with its tumult — RSV

Selah.

(Pause.) — ABPS

4. **There is a river, the streams whereof shall make glad the city of God,**

There is a river whose streams make glad the city of God — RSV

There is a river
whose tributaries bring joy to the divine city — Har

the holy place of the tabernacles of the most High.

The holy dwellings of the Most High! — DeW

which the Most High has made his holy dwelling — NEB

5. **God is in the midst of her; she shall not be moved:**

God is within her; she will not be overthrown — Har

God is in her midst; she shall not totter — Ber

God himself is living in that City; therefore it stands unmoved despite the turmoil everywhere — Tay

God shall help her, and that right early.

God will help her, at the turning of the morning — ABPS

God will help her at the morning dawn — DeW

6. **The heathen raged, the kingdoms were moved:**

The nations rage, the kingdoms totter — RSV

The nations roared, kingdoms were overthrown — DeW

Nations may be in turmoil, and thrones totter — Knox

he uttered his voice, the earth melted.

he utters his voice, the earth melts — RSV

When He uttered His voice, the earth melted — DeW

when he thunders, the earth surges like the sea — NEB

thunder crashes out, the earth disintegrates — Har

7. **The LORD of hosts is with us;**

Yahweh of hosts is with us — Rhm

The Lord, the God of armies, is with us — Har

the God of Jacob is our refuge.
. . . our secure abode — Sprl
. . . our defence — DeW
. . . our fortress — Mof
. . . our high tower — JPS
Selah.

8. **Come, behold the works of the LORD, what desolations he hath made in the earth.**
Come, behold the works of the LORD, how he has wrought desolations in the earth — RSV
Come! view the doings of Yahweh,— Who hath set desolations in the earth — Rhm
Come and view the doings of the Lord, and see the amazing things He has achieved on earth — Har
Come, think of Yahweh's marvels, the astounding things he has done in the world — Jerus

9. **He maketh wars to cease unto the end of the earth;**
from end to end of the earth he stamps out war — NEB
He puts an end to war throughout the world — Har
he breaketh the bow, and cutteth the spear in sunder;
The bow he shivereth, And breaketh in pieces the spear — Rhm
He smashes the bow and snaps the spear — Har
he burneth the chariot in the fire.
War-chariots burneth he up with fire — Rhm
burning vehicles of war with fire — Har

10. **Be still, and know that I am God:**
Stop your striving, and recognize that I am God — Har
Pause a while and know that I am God — Jerus
Let be! and know that I am God — Rhm
Desist! and confess that I am God — NAB
I will be exalted among the heathen, I will be exalted in the earth.
I am exalted among the nations, I am exalted in the earth! — RSV
exalted among the nations, exalted upon the earth — NAB

11. **The LORD of hosts is with us; the God of Jacob is our refuge.**[14]
The Commander of the heavenly armies is here among us! He, the God of Jacob, has come to rescue us! — Tay
Selah.

PSALM 47

To the chief Musician, A Psalm for the sons of Korah.

1. **O clap your hands, all ye people; shout unto God with the voice of triumph.**
Clap your hands, all peoples! Shout to God with loud songs of joy! — RSV
All ye peoples, clap the hand, Shout to God with a voice of singing — YLT
Come everyone, and clap for joy! Shout triumphant praises to the Lord! — Tay

2. **For the LORD most high is terrible;**
For the LORD Most High is awe-inspiring — Ber
For Jehovah, the Most High, is to be feared — DeW
For Yahweh — as Most High is to be revered — Rhm
he is a great King over all the earth.

3. **He shall subdue the people under us, and the nations under our feet.**
He will subjugate Peoples under us, and Tribes of men beneath our feet — Rhm
He makes pagan nations our vassals, bringing peoples under our authority — Har

4. **He shall choose our inheritance for us, the excellency of Jacob whom he loved.**
He will choose for us our inheritance, The pride of Jacob, whom he loved — ABPS
he chose our heritage for us, our land, the jewel of his beloved Jacob — Mof
Selah.

5. **God is gone up with a shout, the LORD with the sound of a trumpet.**
God has gone up with shouting, Jehovah with sound of trumpet — ABPS
God ascended among triumphal shouts;

[14] See also verse 7.

amid the blare of trumpets the Lord went up — Har
God has gone up with shouts of acclamation,
the LORD has gone up with a fanfare of trumpets — NEB

6. Sing praises to God, sing praises: sing praises unto our King, sing praises.
Strike the harp unto God, strike the harp!
Strike the harp to our King, strike the harp! — DeW
A psalm, a psalm for our God, a psalm, a psalm for our King! — Knox

7. For God is the King of all the earth: sing ye praises with understanding.
For God is king of all the earth;
Sing praise, in instructive song — ABPS
For God is King over all the earth;
Strike the harp with a song of praise! — DeW
For God is king over all the earth;
celebrate His praises skillfully — Har

8. God reigneth over the heathen: God sitteth upon the throne of his holiness.
God reigns over the nations;
God sits on his holy throne — ABPS

9. The princes of the people are gathered together, even the people of the God of Abraham:
The willing-hearted of the peoples have gathered themselves together
The people of the God of Abraham — Rhm
The nobles of the nations are assembled,
To be the people of Abraham's God — DeW
The princes of the peoples gather as the people of the God of Abraham — RSV
The nobles from pagan peoples assemble,
to be one with the people of the God of Abraham — Har
for the shields of the earth belong unto God: he is greatly exalted.
for God, which is very high exalted, doth defend the earth, as it were with a shield — PBV
Surely the shields of the earth belong unto God.
How exceedingly is He exalted! — Sprl
For unto God belong the shields of the earth;
He is supremely exalted! — DeW
For the princes of the earth belong to God,
who is highly exalted — Har

PSALM 48

A Song and Psalm for the sons of Korah.
A Melodious Song. For the Sons of Korah — Rhm

1. Great is the LORD, and greatly to be praised in the city of our God, in the mountain of his holiness.
Great is Jehovah, most worthy to be praised,
In the city of our God, in His holy mountain — DeW
Great is the LORD and greatly to be praised
in the city of our God!
His holy mountain — RSV

2. Beautiful for situation, the joy of the whole earth, is mount Zion, on the sides of the north, the city of the great King.
The hill of Sion is a fair place, and the joy of the whole earth; upon the north side lieth the city of the great King — PBV
A beautiful height, a joy to the whole earth,
Is Mount Zion at the farthest north,
The city of the great king — DeW
beautiful in elevation,
is the joy of all the earth,
Mount Zion, in the far north,
the city of the great King — RSV
What a glorious sight! See Mount Zion rising north of the city high above the plains for all to see — Mount Zion, joy of all the earth, the residence of the great King — Tay

3. God is known in her palaces for a refuge.
God is well known in her palaces as a sure refuge — PBV
God is acknowledged in her palaces as a high fortress — Sprl
God hath made himself known in her palaces for a refuge — RV

within those walls, God has proved himself a sure defence — Knox

God has revealed Himself in her palaces
as a trustworthy shelter — Har

In her palaces God is known for a tower of strength — NEB

4. For, lo, the kings were assembled, they passed by together.

For lo, the kings were assembled,
They passed along together — ABPS

See how the kings all gather round her,
marching on in company — NEB

The kings of the earth have arrived together to inspect the city — Tay

5. They saw it, and so they marvelled; they were troubled, and hasted away.

When they saw, they were at once amazed —
Were terrified — were put to flight — DeW

they looked, they were amazed,
they panicked, they ran! — Jerus

As soon as they saw it, they were astounded,
they were in panic, they took to flight — RSV

6. Fear took hold upon them there, and pain, as of a woman in travail.

Trembling seized them there,
Writhing, as of one in travail — DeW

Trembling seized them on that very spot,
and throes like those of childbirth — Har

There they shuddered and writhed
like women in labour — Jerus

they are seized with trembling,
they toss in pain like a woman in labour — NEB

7. Thou breakest the ships of Tarshish with an east wind.

By the east wind thou didst shatter the ships of Tarshish — RSV

For God destroys the mightiest warships with a breath of wind! — Tay

like the ships of Tarshish
when an east wind wrecks them — NEB

8. As we have heard, so have we seen in the city of the LORD of hosts, in the city of our God: God will establish it for ever.

Just as we have heard,
so we have seen in the city of the Lord, the God of armies;
in our divine city,
which God will establish for ever — Har

What once we heard of, now our eyes have seen
within the city of the Lord of hosts;
God does preserve it evermore,
the city of our God — Mof

Selah.

9. We have thought of thy lovingkindness, O God, in the midst of thy temple.

We wait for thy loving-kindness, O God, in the midst of thy temple — PBV

We have thought on thy steadfast love,
O God, in the midst of thy temple — RSV

10. According to thy name, O God, so is thy praise unto the ends of the earth:

Let Your renown, Lord,
extend like Your glory to the ends of the earth — Har

thy fame shall echo, like thy name,
to the very ends of earth — Mof

As Thy Name, O God! so Thy praise
Extendeth to the bounds of the earth — DeW

thy right hand is full of righteousness.

Thy right hand is filled with victory — RSV

Of justice your right hand is full — NAB

for You are completely righteous — Har

11. Let mount Zion rejoice, let the daughters of Judah be glad, because of thy judgments.

Let Mount Zion rejoice,
Let the daughters of Judah exult,
Because of thy judgments — ABPS

Let Mount Zion rejoice, let the daughters of Judah leap for joy,
because of Thy just decisions — Ber

Mount Zion is jubilant,
the towns of Judah are joyful
because You have meted out justice — Har

Let Sion hill rejoice,
let the towns of Judah joy,
over thy saving deeds — Mof

12. Walk about Zion, and go round about her: tell the towers thereof.

Walk about Zion, and go round about her;
Number the towers thereof — ASV

Walk about Zion and encompass her;

Number her pinnacles — DeW
Go on a tour of Zion;
travel around and count her turrets — Har
Go, inspect the city! Walk around and count her many towers! — Tay

13. Mark ye well her bulwarks, consider her palaces;
Mark well her rampart,
Go through her palaces — ABPS
Mark ye well her rampart;
Note thoughtfully her fortresses — DeW
Examine her defenses, survey her fortresses — Har
that ye may tell it to the generation following.
that you may tell the next generation — RSV

14. For this God is our God for ever and ever:
that this is God,
our God for ever and ever — RSV
that such is God,
Our God forever and ever — NAB
he will be our guide even unto death.
He will guide us to the very end — Har

PSALM 49

To the chief Musician, A Psalm for the sons of Korah.

1. Hear this, all ye people; give ear, all ye inhabitants of the world:
2. Both low and high, rich and poor, together.
of lowly birth or high degree, rich and poor alike — NAB
3. My mouth shall speak of wisdom; and the meditation of my heart shall be of understanding.
My mouth speaketh wisdom;
The utterance of my heart is discernment — DeW
My mouth shall speak wisdom;
prudence shall be the utterance of my heart — NAB
My lips have wisdom to utter,
my heart whispers sound sense — Jerus
My mouth speaks wisdom,
And my heart's meditation is insight — AAT
for the words that I speak are wise,
my thoughtful heart is full of understanding — NEB
4. I will incline mine ear to a parable:
I will clothe my thoughts in proverbial form — Har
I will set my ear to catch the moral of the story — NEB
I will open my dark saying upon the harp.
My enigma will I expound upon the harp — Sprl
I disclose my hidden thought upon the harp — DeW
I will solve my riddle to the music of the lyre — RSV
With the twang of a harp I will solve my problem — Har
and tell on the harp how I read the riddle — NEB
5. Wherefore should I fear in the days of evil, when the iniquity of my heels shall compass me about?
Wherefore should I fear in the days of calamity,
Though the iniquity of them who lie in wait for me should enclose me — Rhm
Why should I fear in times of trouble,
when the iniquity of my persecutors surrounds me — RSV
6. They that trust in their wealth, and boast themselves in the multitude of their riches;
As for them who are trusting in their wealth, —
And in the abundance of their riches do boast themselves — Rhm
men who trust in their wealth
and boast of the abundance of their riches? — RSV
7. None of them can by any means redeem his brother, nor give to God a ransom for him:
Truly no man can ransom himself,
or give to God the price of his life — RSV
Alas! no man can ever ransom himself
nor pay God the price of that release — NEB
8. (For the redemption of their soul is precious, and it ceaseth for ever:)
9. That he should still live for ever, and not see corruption.
for the ransom of his life is costly,

and can never suffice,
that he should continue to live on for ever,
and never see the Pit — RSV

For the redemption of the soul is too costly;
so that he must abandon the idea completely
that he will live for ever,
and not experience death — Har

For a soul is far too precious to be ransomed by mere earthly wealth. There is not enough of it in all the earth to buy eternal life for just one soul, to keep it out of hell — Tay

For the ransom of their life is too costly, and [the price they can pay] can never suffice,
So that he should live on for ever and never see the pit [the grave] and corruption — Amp

10. For he seeth that wise men die, likewise the fool and the brutish person perish, and leave their wealth to others.

Indeed, he notices that wise men die;
that foolish and ignorant perish alike,
leaving their wealth to others — Har

Yea, he shall see that even the wise die,
the fool and the stupid alike must perish
and leave their wealth to others — RSV

11. Their inward thought is, that their houses shall continue for ever, and their dwelling places to all generations; they call their lands after their own names.

And yet they think that their house shall continue for ever, and that their dwelling-places shall endure from one generation to another; and call the lands after their own names — PBV

But their graves shall be their houses forever — their dwelling places to all generations. On these parcels of earth, they have put their names — Sept

Their graves are their homes for ever,
their dwelling places to all generations,
though they named lands their own — RSV

Their graves are their perpetual abodes,
their resting places through the ages,
even though they named their lands after themselves — Har

12. Nevertheless man being in honour abideth not: he is like the beasts that perish.

But a son of earth though wealthy cannot tarry,
He hath made himself a by-word —
Beasts they resemble! — Rhm

But man abideth not in honour; he is like the beasts that perish — RV

Man cannot abide in his pomp,
he is like the beasts that perish — RSV

Man in his splendor has no stability:
he is like the animals which perish — Har

But man with all his pomp must die like any animal — Tay

13. This their way is their folly: yet their posterity approve their sayings.

This is their way, to whom folly belongs;
And they that come after them will delight in their sayings — ABPS

This their way is a folly to them,
And yet their followers with their mouth approve — Rhm

In this their way they have confidence;
And those that follow applaud their sayings — DeW

This is the way of them that are foolish,
And of those who after them approve their sayings — JPS

This is the fate of those who have foolish confidence,
the end of those who are pleased with their portion — RSV

Such is the fate of the self-satisfied,
the end of all whose faith is in themselves — Mof

Such is the folly of these men, though after they die they will be quoted as having great wisdom. — Tay

Selah.

Selah [pause, and calmly think of that]! — Amp

14. Like sheep they are laid in the grave; death shall feed on them;

They lie in the grave like sheep; death is their shepherd — PBV

They are herded like sheep to the grave;
death urges them on — Har

Like sheep they are appointed for Sheol;
Death shall be their shepherd — RSV

Like sheep they are herded into the nether world;
death is their shepherd — NAB

and the upright shall have dominion over them in the morning; and their beauty shall consume in the grave from their dwelling.

And the upright shall have dominion over them in the morning
Even their form is to decay
Hades is all that remaineth of a habitation for him — Rhm

and upright rule over them.
Quickly their form is consumed; the nether world is their palace — NAB

The virtuous will be superior to them in the tomb;
their form will waste away,
and the abode of the dead will be their home — Har

straight to the grave they descend,
and their form shall waste away;
Sheol shall be their home — RSV

15. **But God will redeem my soul from the power of the grave: for he shall receive me.**

But God will certainly redeem me from the clutches of the grave,
when it lays hold upon me — Har

But God will redeem my life
from the grasp of Sheol, and will receive me — Jerus

But God will redeem me from the power of Sheol [the place of the dead], for He will receive me — Amp

Selah.

16. **Be not thou afraid when one is made rich, when the glory of his house is increased;**

Fear not when a man grows rich,
when the wealth of his house becomes great — NAB

Be not afraid when some one grows rich,
when the splendor of his house increases — Ber

So do not be dismayed when evil men grow rich and build their lovely homes — Tay

Do not envy a man when he grows rich,
when the wealth of his family increases — NEB

Do not be disturbed, then, when a man grows rich, and there is no end to his household's magnificence — Knox

17. **For when he dieth he shall carry nothing away: his glory shall not descend after him.**

For he shall carry nothing away with him when he dieth, neither shall his pomp follow him — PBV

For when he dieth he shall carry nothing away;
His wealth shall not descend after him — JPS

he cannot take all that with him when he dies, magnificence will not follow him to the grave — Knox

For when they die they carry nothing with them! Their honors will not follow them — Tay

18. **Though while he lived he blessed his soul: and men will praise thee, when thou doest well to thyself.**

19. **He shall go to the generation of his fathers; they shall never see light.**

Though, while he lives, he counts himself happy,
and though a man gets praise when he does well for himself,
he will go to the generation of his fathers,
who will never more see the light — RSV

Though while he lived he blessed his soul,
(And men praise thee, when thou doest well to thyself,)
He shall go to the generation of his fathers;
They shall never see the light — ASV

In life he flatters himself on his fortune,
praising himself for his prosperity;
but down he goes to where his fathers dwell,
who see no light to all eternity — Mof

20. **Man that is in honour, and understandeth not, is like the beasts that perish.**

A great man with magnificence and without understanding,
Is comparable to the perishable beasts! — Sprl

Man, for all his splendor, if he have not prudence,
resembles the beasts that perish — NAB

Man cannot abide in his pomp,
he is like the beasts that perish — RSV

PSALM 50

A Psalm of Asaph.
A Melody of Asaph — Rhm

1. The mighty God, even the LORD, hath spoken, and called the earth from the rising of the sun unto the going down thereof.
El Elohim Yahweh hath spoken and called the earth,
From the rising of the sun unto the going in thereof — Rhm
God, the Mighty God, Jehovah,
Speaketh and calleth the earth,
From the rising to the setting of the sun — DeW
The Eternal speaks! — from east to west
earth falls a-trembling — Mof
The Lord, the supreme God, has spoken;
He summons the earth from the east to the west — Har
It is the Lord God that speaks; his message goes out to all the earth, from the sun's rise to its setting — Knox

2. Out of Zion, the perfection of beauty, God hath shined.
From Zion, the perfection of beauty,
God shines gloriously — Har
From Sion, perfect in beauty,
God shines forth — NAB
From Sion, so peerless in beauty,
the God of gods is flashing! — Mof
From Zion, most beautiful of places,
God has sent out his light — Bas

3. Our God shall come, and shall not keep silence:
Our God will come, and will not be inactive — Har
Let our God come and let him not keep silence! — Rhm
Let our God come, and be silent no more! — Jerus
May our God come and not be deaf to us! — NAB

a fire shall devour before him, and it shall be very tempestuous round about him.
before him is a devouring fire,
round about him a mighty tempest — RSV
Before him is a devouring fire;
around him is a raging storm — NAB
A fire devoureth before Him,
And round about Him it stormeth mightily — JPS
Fire devours before him;
And round about him the storm rages terribly — AAT

4. He shall call to the heavens from above, and to the earth, that he may judge his people.
He calleth to the heavens above,
And to the earth, that he may judge his people — ASV
He summoneth the heavens on high,
And the earth, to the judgment of His people — DeW

5. Gather my saints together unto me; those that have made a covenant with me by sacrifice.
Gather yourselves unto me — ye my men of lovingkindness,
Who have solemnised my covenant over sacrifice — Rhm
Gather unto me My favoured ones,
That have covenanted with Me by sacrifice! — DeW
Gather to Me My holy ones,
who made a covenant with Me by sacrifice — Ber
"Gather to me my faithful ones,
who made a covenant with me by sacrifice!" — RSV

6. And the heavens shall declare his righteousness: for God is judge himself.
Now have the heavens declared his righteousness,
Because God is about to judge — Rhm
And the heavens proclaim his justice;
For God himself is the judge — NAB

Selah.
Selah [pause, and calmly think of that]! — Amp

7. Hear, O my people, and I will speak; O Israel, and I will testify against thee: I am God, even thy God.
O Israel, I will testify against you.
I am God, your God — RSV
O Israel, I will testify against thee —
I, that am God, thine own God! — DeW

8. I will not reprove thee for thy sacrifices or thy burnt offerings, to have been continually before me.

I do not reprove you for your sacrifices;
your burnt offerings are continually before me — RSV

9. I will take no bullock out of thy house, nor he goats out of thy folds.
I will accept no bull from your house, nor he-goat from your folds — RSV
I will not accept any bullock from your household,
not even a ram from your sheep-pen — Har
I need no bullock from your farms, no goat out of your herds — Mof
But it isn't sacrificial bullocks and goats that I really want from you. — Tay

10. For every beast of the forest is mine, and the cattle upon a thousand hills.
I own already every wild beast in the forest, the hills are mine, and the herds that people them — Knox
I have all the animals of the forest; the cattle upon a thousand hillsides — Har

11. I know all the fowls of the mountains: and the wild beasts of the field are mine.
I know all the birds of the air,
and all that moves in the field is mine — RSV
There is no bird flies in heaven, no life stirs in the country-side, but I know of it — Knox

12. If I were hungry, I would not tell thee: for the world is mine, and the fulness thereof.

13. Will I eat the flesh of bulls, or drink the blood of goats?
Do I eat the flesh of bulls,
Or drink the blood of goats — JPS
No, I don't need your sacrifices of flesh and blood. — Tay

14. Offer unto God thanksgiving; and pay thy vows unto the most High:
But sacrifice unto God thanksgiving,
And pay unto the Highest thy vows — DeW
Offer to God praise as your sacrifice and fulfill your vows to the Most High — NAB
What I want from you is your true thanks; I want your promises fulfilled — Tay

15. And call upon me in the day of trouble:
And in the day of distress call upon Me — Sprl
I want you to trust me in your times of trouble — Tay
I will deliver thee, and thou shalt glorify me.
I will deliver thee that thou mayest glorify me — Rhm
I will come to your rescue, and you shall honour me — NEB
so I can rescue you and you can give me glory — Tay

16. But unto the wicked God saith, What hast thou to do to declare my statutes, or that thou shouldest take my covenant in thy mouth?
But unto the ungodly saith God, Why dost thou preach my laws, and takest my covenant in thy mouth — PBV
And to the wicked God says,
What right hast thou to declare my statutes,
And take my covenant in thy mouth — ABPS
But to the wicked God saith:
What! is it for thee to tell My statutes,
And to take My covenant in thy mouth — DeW

17. Seeing thou hatest instruction, and castest my words behind thee.
Seeing that thou hast hated correction,
And hast cast my words behind thee — Rhm
For you hate discipline,
and you cast my words behind you — RSV
Thou, that hast hated instruction,
And hast cast My words behind thee — DeW

18. When thou sawest a thief, then thou consentedst with him, and hast been partaker with adulterers.
If thou sawest a thief then didst thou run with him, —
And with adulterers hath been thy chosen life — Rhm
When thou seest a thief, thou hast pleasure in him,
And art in fellowship with adulterers — DeW
When you see a thief, you keep pace with him,
and with adulterers you throw in your lot — NAB
You are a friend to any thief you see,

you ally yourselves with adulterers — Mof

You make friends with a thief as soon as you see one,
you feel at home with adulterers — Jerus

19. Thou givest thy mouth to evil, and thy tongue frameth deceit.

Thy mouth hath abounded in wickedness, and thy tongue hath framed deceits — Sept

You open your mouth freely with malicious intent;
your tongue formulates deceit — Har

You curse and lie, and vile language streams from your mouths — Tay

20. Thou sittest and speakest against thy brother; thou slanderest thine own mother's son.

You sit speaking against your brother,
against your mother's son you spread rumors — NAB

You are for ever talking against your brother,
stabbing your own mother's son in the back — NEB

21. These things hast thou done, and I kept silence; thou thoughtest that I was altogether such an one as thyself:

These things you have done and I have been silent;
you thought that I was one like yourself — RSV

you have been doing such things,
and because I was silent you thought that I was such another as yourself — Har

You do this, and expect me to say nothing?
Do you really think I am like you? — Jerus

When you do these things, shall I be deaf to it?
Or think you that I am like yourself? — NAB

but I will reprove thee, and set them in order before thine eyes.

I will correct you in this, and prove it to you clearly — Har

I will censure you and put the case in order before your eyes — Ber

But now I rebuke you, and lay the charge before you — RSV

but I will reprove you, and correct these sins before your eyes — Lam

but point by point I will rebuke you to your face — NEB

22. Now consider this, ye that forget God, lest I tear you in pieces, and there be none to deliver.

Mark this, then, you who forget God, lest I rend, and there be none to deliver! — RSV

Think well on this, you who forget God,
or I will tear you in pieces and no one shall save you — NEB

You are leaving God out of account; take care!
Or I will tear you to pieces where no one can rescue you! — Jerus

23. Whoso offereth praise glorifieth me:

He who brings thanksgiving as his sacrifice honors me — RSV

and to him that ordereth his conversation aright will I shew the salvation of God.

and to him who follows my way
I will show the salvation of God — NEB

to him who orders the course of his life properly
I will extend divine deliverance — Har

to the upright man I will show how God can save — Jerus

PSALM 51

To the chief Musician, A Psalm of David, when Nathan the prophet came unto him, after he had gone in to Bath-sheba.

1. Have mercy upon me, O God, according to thy lovingkindness:

. . . according to thy steadfast love — RSV

Be gracious to me, O God, according to thy loving-kindness — ABPS

Take pity on me, my God, in your divine sympathy — Har

according unto the multitude of thy tender mercies blot out my transgressions.

According to the multitude of Thy compassions,
Obliterate my transgressions — Sprl

in the greatness of your compassion wipe out my offense — NAB

2. Wash me throughly from mine in-

iquity, and cleanse me from my sin.
Wash me thoroughly from my guilt,
And cleanse me from my sin — AAT

3. **For I acknowledge my transgressions: and my sin is ever before me.**
For my transgressions I know,
And my sin is before me continually — ABPS
Well do I know my offences;
my sin is never out of mind — Mof
For I am fully aware of my failings;
my wrongdoing confronts me continually — Har

4. **Against thee, thee only, have I sinned, and done this evil in thy sight:**
Thee only my sins have offended; it is thy will I have disobeyed — Knox
It is against you and you alone I sinned, and did this terrible thing — Tay
that thou mightest be justified when thou speakest, and be clear when thou judgest.
so that thou mayest be proved right in thy charge
and just in passing sentence — NEB
That you may be justified in your sentence,
vindicated when you condemn — NAB
So then You are acting justly when You pronounce sentence;
You are behaving impartially in Your judgments — Har
so that thou art justified in thy sentence
and blameless in thy judgment — RSV
Yes, thou art just in thy charge,
justified in thy sentence — Mof

5. **Behold, I was shapen in iniquity, and in sin did my mother conceive me.**
Behold, in iniquity was I brought forth,
And in sin did my mother conceive me — ABPS
Ah! 'twas in guilt that I was born,
'twas in sin that my mother conceived me — Mof
See how I was brought to birth in guilt;
my mother conceived me in iniquity — Har
You know I was born guilty,
a sinner from the moment of conception — Jerus
Behold, in sinful state I was born
and in sin did my mother conceive me — Ber
But I was born a sinner, yes, from the moment my mother conceived me — Tay

6. **Behold, thou desirest truth in the inward parts: and in the hidden part thou shalt make me to know wisdom.**
Behold, you are pleased with sincerity of heart,
and in my inmost being you teach me wisdom — NAB
Behold, Thou desirest truth in the inward parts;
Make me, therefore, to know wisdom in mine inmost heart — JPS
Behold, thou desirest truth in the inward being;
therefore teach me wisdom in my secret heart — RSV
Surely, Thou desirest truth in the inner self,
and Thou makest me to understand hidden wisdom — Ber
You take a delight in truth;
You have initiated me into the hidden depths of wisdom — Har

7. **Purge me with hyssop, and I shall be clean: wash me, and I shall be whiter than snow.**
Wilt thou cleanse me from sin with hyssop
That I may be pure?
Wilt thou wash me,
That I may be whiter than snow? — Rhm
Purify me with hyssop until I am clean;
wash me until I am whiter than snow — Jerus

8. **Make me to hear joy and gladness; that the bones which thou hast broken may rejoice.**
Thou wilt make me hear joy and gladness;
The bones thou hast broken shall exult — ABPS
fill me with gladness and rejoicing,
that the life thou hast crushed may thrill with joy — Mof
let me hear the sounds of joy and gladness,
let the bones dance which thou hast broken — NEB

9. **Hide thy face from my sins, and blot out all mine iniquities.**
. . . And wipe out all my guilt — AAT

10. Create in me a clean heart, O God; and renew a right spirit within me.
. . . and put a new and right spirit within me — RSV
A pure heart create for me, O God! A steadfast spirit renew within me — DeW
Produce in me a purified heart, my God;
a new, unwavering attitude of mind — Har
Create in me a new, clean heart, O God, filled with clean thoughts and right desires — Tay

11. Cast me not away from thy presence; and take not thy holy spirit from me.
Cast me not away from Thy presence, And Thy Holy Spirit take not from me — DeW
banish me not from thy presence, deprive me not of thy sacred Spirit — Mof

12. Restore unto me the joy of thy salvation; and uphold me with thy free spirit.
O give me the comfort of thy help again, and stablish me with thy free Spirit — PBV
Restore unto me the joy of Thy salvation,
And with a willing spirit uphold me — DeW
gladden me with thy saving aid again, and give me a willing spirit as my strength — Mof
Restore to me the joy found in Your salvation,
and give me a charitable disposition to assist me — Har
Restore to me again the joy of your salvation, and make me willing to obey you — Tay

13. Then will I teach transgressors thy ways; and sinners shall be converted unto thee.
I will teach transgressors thy ways, And sinners shall return to thee — ABPS
I will teach transgressors the ways that lead to thee
and sinners shall return to thee again — NEB

14. Deliver me from bloodguiltiness, O God, thou God of my salvation:
Deliver me from the guilt of murder, O God, thou God of my salvation — Sprl
My God, my divine Deliverer, save me from the guilt of bloodshed! — Knox
Be my saviour from violent death, O God, the God of my salvation — Bas
Rescue me from death, my saving God — Har

and my tongue shall sing aloud of thy righteousness.
That my tongue may exult in Thy righteousness — DeW
then my tongue shall revel in your justice — NAB
and my tongue shall praise thy faithfulness aloud — Mof
and my tongue will sing aloud of thy deliverance — RSV
This tongue shall boast of thy mercies — Knox
and my tongue will acclaim your righteousness — Jerus

15. O Lord, open thou my lips; and my mouth shall shew forth thy praise.
O Lord, thou wilt open my lips,
And my mouth shall declare thy praise — ABPS
O thou Eternal, open thou my lips, till my mouth makes thy praises known — Mof
Open my lips, Lord,
that my mouth may proclaim Your praise — Har

16. For thou desirest not sacrifice; else would I give it: thou delightest not in burnt offering.
For thou hast no delight in sacrifice;
were I to give a burnt offering, thou wouldst not be pleased — RSV
You do not desire sacrifice;
nor would You be gratified, even if I gave You a burnt-offering — Har
Thou hast no delight in sacrifice;
if I brought thee an offering, thou wouldst not accept it — NEB

17. The sacrifices of God are a broken spirit:
The sacrifice of God is a troubled spirit — PBV
The sacrifice for God is a contrite spirit — Sept
The sacrifice acceptable to God is a broken spirit — RSV
here, O God, is my sacrifice, a broken spirit — Knox
My sacrifice, my God, is a shattered spirit — Har

God's sacrifice is a soul with its evil crushed — Mof

a broken and a contrite heart, O God, thou wilt not despise.

A heart — broken and crushed O God thou wilt not despise — Rhm

a wounded heart, O God, thou wilt not despise — NEB

a heart contrite and humbled, O God, you will not spurn — NAB

a broken and sorrowing heart, O God, you will not put from you — Bas

You will not scorn a broken and penitent heart, my God — Har

you will not scorn this crushed and broken heart — Jerus

18. Do good in thy good pleasure unto Zion:

O be favourable and gracious unto Sion — PBV

Be bountiful, O LORD, to Zion in your kindness — NAB

Lord, in thy great love send prosperity to Sion — Knox

In Your divine mercy show favor to Zion — Har

Show your favour graciously to Zion — Jerus

And Lord, don't punish Israel for my sins — Tay

build thou the walls of Jerusalem.

Thou wilt build the walls of Jerusalem — ABPS

by rebuilding the walls of Jerusalem — NAB

so that the walls of Jerusalem may rise again — Knox

19. Then shalt thou be pleased with the sacrifices of righteousness, with burnt offering and whole burnt offering:

then wilt thou delight in right sacrifices,
in burnt offerings and whole burnt offerings — RSV

Then only shalt thou delight in the appointed sacrifices — NEB

then shall they offer bullocks upon thine altar.

PSALM 52

To the chief Musician, Maschil, A Psalm of David, when Doeg the Edomite came and told Saul, and said unto him, David is come to the house of Ahimelech.

To the Chief Musician. A Psalm of Instruction, of David . . . — Rhm

1. Why boastest thou thyself in mischief, O mighty man?

Why do you glory in evil,
you champion of infamy — NAB

Why do you boast of evil, you wicked tyrant — Har

Why do you boast, O mighty man,
of mischief done against the godly — RSV

the goodness of God endureth continually.

The lovingkindness of GOD [lasteth] all the day — Rhm

The lovingkindness of the Almighty shall endure through all time — DeW

All the day you are plotting destruction — RSV

2. Thy tongue deviseth mischiefs; like a sharp razor, working deceitfully.

Thy tongue imagineth wickedness, and with lies thou cuttest like a sharp razor — PBV

Engulfing ruin doth thy tongue devise,
Like a whetted razor working deceit — Rhm

Thy tongue deviseth plans of destruction;
It is like a whetted razor, O worker of guile! — DeW

Your tongue is like a sharp razor,
you worker of treachery — RSV

3. Thou lovest evil more than good; and lying rather than to speak righteousness.

Thou hast loved unrighteousness more than goodness, and falsehood more than righteousness — PBV

Thou lovest injury rather than kindness,
Falsehood more than righteous speaking — DeW

You love the bad better than the good,
You would rather lie than tell the truth — AAT

Selah.

Selah [pause, and calmly think of that]! — Amp

4. Thou lovest all devouring words, O thou deceitful tongue.

Thou lovest every destructive word, O rebellious tongue! — Sprl

You love all that means ruin,
you of the deceitful tongue! — NAB

you revel in deadly speech,

you and your sly tongue! — Mof
You love injurious words
and treacherous speech — Har
cruel gossip you love and slanderous talk — NEB

5. God shall likewise destroy thee for ever, he shall take thee away, and pluck thee out of thy dwelling place, and root thee out of the land of the living.

GOD also will break thee down utterly, —
He will snatch thee up and tear thee away tentless,
And uproot thee out of the land of the living — Rhm

The Almighty will likewise destroy thee for ever;
He will seize thee and pluck thee from thy tent,
And uproot thee from the land of the living — DeW

But God will crush you forever;
He will seize you and pluck you out of your tent,
And uproot you from the land of the living — AAT

May God destroy you for ever;
may He snatch you up and pluck you out of your dwelling,
and uproot you from the midst of human life — Har

So may God pull you down to the ground,
sweep you away, leave you ruined and homeless,
uprooted from the land of the living — NEB

Selah.

6. The righteous also shall see, and fear, and shall laugh at him:

The upright will observe it, and become awed;
they will laugh at him, saying — Har

The followers of God will see it happen. They will watch in awe. They will laugh and say — Tay

7. Lo, this is the man that made not God his strength; but trusted in the abundance of his riches, and strengthened himself in his wickedness.

Lo, there is the man that made not God his refuge;
But trusted in his abundant wealth,
And was strong in his wickedness! — DeW

Lo! the man who made not God his refuge, —
But trusted in the abundance of his riches,
Emboldened himself in his wealth! — Rhm

Lo, this is the man who trusted not in God; but trusted in the abundance of his riches, and boasted in his possessions — Lam

"Look at the man who refused to take shelter in God,
but trusted in the accumulation of his wealth, and flourished in his wickedness" — Har

8. But I am like a green olive tree in the house of God: I trust in the mercy of God for ever and ever.

As for me, I am like a green olive-tree in the house of God; my trust is in the tender mercy of God for ever and ever — PBV

But I am like a flourishing olive-tree in the house of God,
I have put confidence in the lovingkindness of God for times age-abiding and beyond — Rhm

But I am like a sheltered olive tree protected by the Lord himself. I trust in the mercy of God forever and ever — Tay

9. I will praise thee for ever, because thou hast done it: and I will wait on thy name; for it is good before thy saints.

I will alway give thanks unto thee for that thou hast done; and I will hope in thy Name, for thy saints like it well — PBV

I will praise thee to times age-abiding
Because thou didst effectually work, —
And I will wait on thy Name
Because it is good,
In the presence of thy men of lovingkindness — Rhm

I will thank thee for ever,
because thou hast done it.
I will proclaim thy name, for it is good,
in the presence of the godly — RSV

I will praise You for ever for what You have done,
and in company with Your saints
I will proclaim the goodness of Your nature — Har

PSALM 53

To the chief Musician upon Mahalath, Maschil, A Psalm of David.
To the chief Musician. Of [moral] disease. Didactic [Psalm] of David — ABPS
To the Chief Musician; in a mournful strain. A skillful song, or didactic or reflective poem of David — Amp

1. **The fool hath said in his heart, There is no God.**
The impious hath said in his heart
There is no God! — Rhm
The impious fool says in his heart, 'There is no God' — NEB
There is no God above us, is the fond thought of reckless hearts — Knox
Profane men say to themselves, "There is no God" — Har
Only a fool would say to himself, "There is no God" — Tay
Corrupt are they, and have done abominable iniquity: there is none that doeth good.
They have acted corruptly
They have wrought abominable perversity,
There is none that doeth good — Rhm

2. **God looked down from heaven upon the children of men, to see if there were any that did understand, that did seek God.**
God looks down from heaven
upon mankind,
to see if any have the sense
to care for God — Mof
God looks down from heaven at the race of men, to find one soul that reflects, and goes in search of him — Knox
From Heaven the Lord surveys humanity,
to see if there are any sufficiently discerning
to search for God — Har

3. **Every one of them is gone back: they are altogether become filthy; there is none that doeth good, no, not one.**
They all have turned back
Together have they become tainted, —
There is none that doeth good,
Not so much as one! — Rhm
They have all fallen away;
they are all alike depraved;
there is none that does good,
no, not one — RSV
But all are unfaithful, all are rotten to the core;
not one does anything good,
no, not even one — NEB

4. **Have the workers of iniquity no knowledge? who eat up my people as they eat bread: they have not called upon God.**
Have the workers of iniquity no knowledge,
Who eat up my people as they eat bread,
And call not upon God? — ASV
Will all these evildoers never learn,
they who eat up my people just as they eat bread,
who call not upon God? — NAB
Are those miscreants devoid of sense,
devouring God's people like bread,
without consideration for the Lord? — Har

5. **There were they in great fear, where no fear was:**
There they are, in great terror,
in terror such as has not been! — RSV
Ha! here they are in a panic! — Mof
for God hath scattered the bones of him that encampeth against thee: thou hast put them to shame, because God hath despised them.
For God will scatter the bones of the ungodly;
they will be put to shame, for God has rejected them — RSV
For God hath scattered the bones of my besiegers;
Thou hast put them to shame;
Yea, God hath rejected them — DeW
God scatters them;
their evil plan is defeated,
for God spurns them — Mof

6. **Oh that the salvation of Israel were come out of Zion!**
Oh that there might come out of Zion
Salvation for Israel! — DeW
O that the deliverance of Israel would come from Zion! — AAT
Oh, that God would come from Zion now and save Israel! — Tay
When God bringeth back the captivity of his people, Jacob shall rejoice, and Israel shall be glad.

When Jehovah returneth to His captive people,
Jacob shall be glad, Israel shall rejoice! — DeW

When God restores the well-being of his people,
then shall Jacob exult and Israel be glad — NAB

When the Lord reverses the fortunes of His people,
Jacob will be jubilant; Israel will be joyful — Har

When God brings his people home,
what joy for Jacob, what happiness for Israel! — Jerus

PSALM 54

To the chief Musician on Neginoth, Maschil, A Psalm of David, when the Ziphims came and said to Saul, Doth not David hide himself with us?

To the Chief Musician: with Stringed Instruments. A Psalm of Instruction, of David. When the Ziphites came and said unto Saul, Is not David hiding himself with us — Rhm

1. **Save me, O God, by thy name, and judge me by thy strength.**

Save me, O God, for thy Name's sake,
and avenge me in thy strength — PBV

O God, save me for Thy Name's sake;
And in Thy might plead my cause — Sprl

O God! by Thy Name save me,
And in Thy power defend me — DeW

Save me, O God, by thy name,
and vindicate me by thy might — RSV

2. **Hear my prayer, O God; give ear to the words of my mouth.**

3. **For strangers are risen up against me, and oppressors seek after my soul:**

For insolent men have risen against me,
ruthless men seek my life — RSV

For aliens have risen up against me
And men of violence have sought my life — Rhm

they have not set God before them.

They have no regard for God — Har

Selah.

Selah [pause, and calmly think of that]! — Amp

4. **Behold, God is mine helper: the Lord is with them that uphold my soul.**

Lo, God hath become my helper;
The Lord sustaineth me in life — DeW

Behold, God is my helper;
the Lord is the upholder of my life — RSV

But God is my helper,
the Lord the mainstay of my life — NEB

5. **He shall reward evil unto mine enemies: cut them off in thy truth.**

He will requite the evil unto mine enemies:
Destroy thou them in thy truth — ASV

He will return the evil to my enemies;
In thy faithfulness cut them off — ABPS

Let him turn back the mischief upon mine adversaries,
In thy faithfulness destroy them! — Rhm

He will requite my enemies with evil;
in thy faithfulness put an end to them — RSV

6. **I will freely sacrifice unto thee: I will praise thy name, O LORD; for it is good.**

An offering of a free heart will I give thee, and praise thy Name, O LORD; because it is so comfortable — PBV

With a free-will offering will I sacrifice to thee;
I will praise thy name, Jehovah, for it is good — ABPS

I will offer thee a willing sacrifice
and praise thy name, for that is good — NEB

7. **For he hath delivered me out of all trouble: and mine eye hath seen his desire upon mine enemies.**

For out of all distress has he delivered me,
And my eye has seen its desire on my enemies — ABPS

Because from all distress you have rescued me,
and my eyes look down upon my enemies — NAB

He has rescued me from all my troubles,
and let me see my enemies defeated — Jerus

when You have rescued me from every affliction,
and my eye has feasted in delight on my enemies — Har

PSALM 55

To the chief Musician on Neginoth, Maschil, A Psalm of David.

To the Chief Musician: with stringed Instruments. A Psalm of Instruction, of David. — Rhm

1. Give ear to my prayer, O God; and hide not thyself from my supplication.

Hearken, O God, to my prayer;
turn not away from my pleading — NAB

Give audience to my prayer, O God;
do not spurn this plea of mine — Knox

Listen to my prayer, O God; don't hide yourself when I cry to you — Tay

2. Attend unto me, and hear me:

Oh, listen to me, and answer me — Sprl

I mourn in my complaint, and make a noise;

I am restless in my complaining, and disquieted — ABPS

I rock with grief, and am troubled — NAB

I am overcome by my trouble.
I am distraught — RSV

3. Because of the voice of the enemy, because of the oppression of the wicked:

by the noise of the enemy,
because of the oppression of the wicked — RSV

at the voice of the enemy and the clamor of the wicked — NAB

for they cast iniquity upon me, and in wrath they hate me.

For they would let trouble drop upon me,
And in anger would they entrap me — Rhm

For they cause mischief to impend over me,
And in anger lay a snare for me — ABPS

For they threaten me with evil,
And angrily assail me — DeW

for they burden me with affliction
and violently assail me — Har

4. My heart is sore pained within me: and the terrors of death are fallen upon me.

My heart quakes within me,
And terrors of death have fallen upon me — ABPS

My heart is disquieted within me, and the fear of death is fallen upon me — PBV

My heart is throbbing in my breast,
and deadly anguish overpowers me — Mof

My mind is awhirl inside me;
deadly terror has engulfed me — Har

My heart aches in my breast,
Death's terrors assail me — Jerus

5. Fearfulness and trembling are come upon me, and horror hath overwhelmed me.

Fear and trembling came against me;
and a dark gloom overwhelmed me — Sept

Fear and trembling enter into me,
And horror overwhelms me — ABPS

Fear and trembling overtake me,
and shivering seizes me — Har

Fear and trembling overwhelm me
and I shudder from head to foot — NEB

6. And I said, Oh that I had wings like a dove! for then would I fly away, and be at rest.

so that I say, "If only I were given wings like a dove,
I would fly away, and live in peace — Har

7. Lo, then would I wander far off, and remain in the wilderness.

I would go wandering far away, living in the waste land — Bas

I would wander far away,
and make my home in the wilderness — Har

Yes, then I would wander far away,
and lodge in the desert — Ber

Selah.

Selah [pause, and calmly think of that]! — Amp

8. I would hasten my escape from the windy storm and tempest.

I would haste me to a shelter from the stormy wind and the tempest — RV
I would hasten to find shelter from the violent storm and the tempest — NAB
I would haste to find me a shelter from the raging wind and tempest — RSV
I would haste to my shelter Faster than the stormy wind and the tempest — AAT

9. Destroy, O Lord, and divide their tongues:
Confuse, O Lord, and divide their tongues! — AAT
Destroy, O LORD, and render useless their tongues — Lam
Destroy their plans, O Lord, confuse their tongues — RSV
Destroy them, Lord; confuse their plans — Har

for I have seen violence and strife in the city.
for I see violence and strife in the city — RSV
I can see how violence and discord fill the city; — Jerus

10. Day and night they go about it upon the walls thereof:
day and night they prowl about upon its walls — NAB
day and night they stalk together along the city walls — Jerus
Day and night they patrol her walls — Har
Though they patrol their walls night and day against invaders — Tay

mischief also and sorrow are in the midst of it.
And trouble and misery are in her midst — Rhm
while within her rage distress and tumult — Har
Sorrow and Misery live inside — Jerus
their real problem is internal — wickedness and dishonesty are entrenched in the heart of the city — Tay

11. Wickedness is in the midst thereof: deceit and guile depart not from her streets.
Engulfing ruin is in her midst. And there depart not from her broadway oppression and deceit — Rhm
Corruption is within her, And from her market-place depart not extortion and deceit — ABPS
Ruin is within her; Oppression and fraud do not depart from her market-place — AAT
Wickedness is rampant; oppression and fraud are for ever in her streets — Har
Ruin is an inmate; tyranny and treachery are never absent from its central square — Jerus
There is murder and robbery there, and cheating in the markets and everywhere you look — Tay

12. For it was not an enemy that reproached me; then I could have borne it: neither was it he that hated me that did magnify himself against me; then I would have hid myself from him:
It is not an enemy who taunts me — then I could bear it; it is not an adversary who deals insolently with me — then I could hide from him. — RSV

13. But it was thou, a man mine equal, my guide, and mine acquaintance.
But it was even thou, my companion, my guide, and mine own familiar friend — PBV
But it was you, my valued companion, my bosom friend — Har
No, you are an equal of my own, my close companion and my trusted friend! — Mof
It was you, a man of my own sort, my comrade, my own dear friend — NEB

14. We took sweet counsel together, and walked unto the house of God in company.
We used to hold sweet converse together; within God's house we walked in fellowship — RSV
We were together in sweet fellowship, And went to God's house with the festal throng — DeW
You, whose comradeship I enjoyed; at whose side I walked in procession in the house of God! — NAB

15. Let death seize upon them, and let them go down quick into hell:
Let death come hastily upon them, and let them go down alive into the pit — PBV
Death will seize them in a moment; They shall descend alive unto Hades! — Sprl
Desolations are upon them; they shall

go down alive to the underworld — ABPS
Desolations on them!
Let them go down into hades alive — Rhm
Let death come upon them suddenly;
Let them go down into Sheol alive — DeW
May destruction fall upon them;
let them be buried alive — Har
for wickedness is in their dwellings, and among them.
for wickedness is deeply entrenched in their dwelling — Har
For wicked doings are at home within them — Rhm
for their homes are haunts of evil! — NEB

16. As for me, I will call upon God; and the LORD shall save me.
I unto God will cry, —
And Yahweh will save me — Rhm
For my part I will call to God,
and the Lord will rescue me — Har

17. Evening, and morning, and at noon, will I pray, and cry aloud: and he shall hear my voice.
At evening and morning and high noon have I been wont to lament and complain,
And he hath heard my voice! — Rhm
Evening, morning, and noon, I grieve and moan;
And He will hear my voice — DeW
Evening and morning and at noon
I nurse my woes, and groan.
He has heard my cry — NEB
Morning, noon and night I will voice my complaint and lament,
and He will hear me — Har

18. He hath delivered my soul in peace from the battle that was against me: for there were many with me.
He will deliver my soul in peace,
So that none can approach me;
For many, many come against me — DeW
He will deliver my soul in safety
from the battle that I wage,
for many are arrayed against me — RSV
He will deliver me safely from my foes,
Though many there be against me — AAT
he rescued me and gave me back my peace,
when they beset me like archers, massing against me — NEB

19. God shall hear, and afflict them, even he that abideth of old.
Yes, even God, that endureth for ever, shall hear me, and bring them down — PBV
The Almighty will hear and answer them,
He that sitteth King from of old — DeW
God will give ear, and humble them,
he who is enthroned from of old — RSV
GOD will hear
Yea He will humble them who aforetime sat [enthroned] — Rhm
Selah.
Because they have no changes, therefore they fear not God.
Because in them there has been no change
and they do not revere God — Ber
because they keep no law,
and do not fear God — RSV
For improvement is not in them,
nor do they fear God — NAB
With Him there is no change,
yet they do not revere Him as God — Har

20. He hath put forth his hands against such as be at peace with him: he hath broken his covenant.
My companion stretched out his hand against his friends,
he violated his covenant — RSV
He used his power against his friends;
he violated his agreement — Har
This friend of mine betrayed me — I who was at peace with him. He broke his promises — Tay

21. The words of his mouth were smoother than butter, but war was in his heart:
His mouth was smoother than butter,
While war was in his heart — AAT
Smoother than curds were [the words of] his mouth
But war was [in] his heart — Rhm
his words were softer than oil, yet were they drawn swords.
his words may soothe more than oil,
but they are naked swords — Jerus
their words are slippery as oil
but sharp as drawn swords — NEB

22. Cast thy burden upon the LORD, and he shall sustain thee:

O cast thy burden upon the LORD, and he shall nourish thee — PBV

Cast thy care on the Lord, and he will sustain thee — Sept

Cast the burden of thy cares upon the Lord, and he will sustain thee — Knox

Commit your problems to the Lord and He will uphold you — Har

Unload your burden on to Yahweh, and he will support you — Jerus

he shall never suffer the righteous to be moved.

He will never suffer the righteous to be overthrown — DeW

never will he permit the just man to be disturbed — NAB

He will never let the righteous totter — AAT

23. But thou, O God, shalt bring them down into the pit of destruction:

But thou, O God, wilt cast them down into the lowest pit — RSV

You will hurl them down into the engulfing grave, Lord — Har

bloody and deceitful men shall not live out half their days;

Bloodthirsty and deceitful men shall not live out half their days — ASV

men of blood and treachery
shall not live out half their days — RSV

You will not allow murderers and deceivers
to enjoy even half their allotted time — Har

but I will trust in thee.

But as for me, I will trust in thee — ABPS

PSALM 56

To the chief Musician upon Jonath-elem-rechokim, Michtam of David, when the Philistines took him in Gath.

To the Chief Musician. Upon "The Dove of God from the distant Sea." David's. A precious Psalm. When the Philistines seized him in Gath — Rhm

To the chief Musician. After the [melody] "The mute dove in far-off lands." Memorial [Psalm] of David, when the Philistines seized him in Gath — ABPS

1. Be merciful unto me, O God: for man would swallow me up;

Shew me favour O God,
For weak man hath panted for me — Rhm

Have pity on me, O God, for men trample upon me — NAB

he fighting daily oppresseth me.

he is daily fighting, and troubling me — PBV

All the day long he fiercely presseth me — DeW

all the day they press their attack against me — NAB

2. Mine enemies would daily swallow me up:

Mine enemies pant for me all the day long — DeW

my enemies trample upon me all day long — RSV

for they be many that fight against me, O thou most High.

For many are fighting with me loftily — Rhm

For many are they that fight against me proudly — ABPS

for many of them are fighting me bitterly — Har

3. What time I am afraid, I will trust in thee.

In the day that I am afraid,
I will put my trust in Thee — JPS

When I am afraid,
I put my trust in thee — RSV

O Most High, when I begin to fear,
in you will I trust — NAB

4. In God I will praise his word, in God I have put my trust; I will not fear what flesh can do unto me.

In God (I will praise his word),
In God have I put my trust, I will not be afraid;
What can flesh do unto me? — ASV

In God, whose word I praise,
in God I trust without a fear.
What can flesh do to me? — RSV

In God, whose promises I extol,
in God I have placed unwavering trust.
What can mortal man do to me? — Har

5. Every day they wrest my words: all their thoughts are against me for evil.

All the day they molest me in my efforts;
their every thought is of evil against me — NAB

All day long they seek to injure my cause;
all their thoughts are against me for evil — RSV
They are perpetually thwarting my plans;
all their scheming is directed to a bad end — Har
All day long they twist what I say,
all they think of is how to harm me — Jerus

6. They gather themselves together, they hide themselves, they mark my steps, when they wait for my soul.
They gather in bands; they lie in ambush;
They are close at my heels upon the watch,
For they are waiting for my life — DeW
they conspire, lurk, spy on my movements,
determined to take my life — Jerus

7. Shall they escape by iniquity? in thine anger cast down the people, O God.
By their iniquity shall they escape?
In anger cast down the heathen, O God! — DeW
For their crimes recompense them;
In wrath cast down the peoples, O God! — AAT

8. Thou tellest my wanderings:
Thou numberest my wanderings — ASV
Thou hast kept count of my tossings — RSV
Thou hast noted my wandering steps — DeW
Thou countest up my sleepless hours — Mof
put thou my tears into thy bottle: are they not in thy book?
Put thou my tears in thy bottle,
Are they not in thy record — Rhm
Put thou my tears in thy bottle;
Are they not in thy reckoning — ABPS
my tears are stored in your flask;
are they not recorded in your book — NAB

9. When I cry unto thee, then shall mine enemies turn back:
Whensoever I call upon thee, then shall mine enemies be put to flight — PBV
Then shall mine enemies turn back in the day that I call — ASV
Then shall my enemies fall back in the day of my crying out — Ber
Then my enemies will have to fall back as soon as I call for help — Jerus
One cry raised to thee, and my enemies are driven back — Knox
this I know; for God is for me.
this I know; for God is on my side — PBV
This I know, that God is for me — JPS
now I know that God is with me — NAB

10. In God will I praise his word: in the LORD will I praise his word.

11. In God have I put my trust: I will not be afraid what man can do unto me.
In God will I praise the word;
In Jehovah will I praise the word.
In God do I trust, I will not fear;
What can man do to me? — ABPS
In God will I praise with good cause;
In Yahweh will I praise with good cause;
In God have I trusted, I will not fear,
What can a son of earth do unto me? — Rhm
In God (I will praise his word),
In Jehovah (I will praise his word),
In God have I put my trust, I will not be afraid;
What can man do unto me? — ASV
In God, whose word I praise,
in the LORD, whose word I praise,
in God I trust without a fear.
What can man do to me? — RSV
In God, whose promises I commend,
in the Lord, whose assurances I praise,
in God I have placed unwavering trust.
What can mortal man do to me? — Har

12. Thy vows are upon me, O God: I will render praises unto thee.
My vows to thee I must perform, O God;
I will render thank offerings to thee — RSV
I have bound myself with vows to thee, O God,
and will redeem them with due thank-offerings — NEB
I will surely do what I promised, Lord,
and thank you for your help — Tay

13. For thou hast delivered my soul from death: wilt not thou deliver my feet from falling,
For thou hast rescued my soul from death

Wilt thou not [rescue] my feet from stumbling? — Rhm

For thou hast delivered my soul from death,
yea, my feet from falling — RSV

hast thou not saved my life from every peril, my feet from every slip? — Knox

that I may walk before God in the light of the living?

That I may walk before God,
In the light of life — ABPS

that I might live, ever mindful of God,
in the sunshine of life — Mof

So now I may conduct myself in the Divine Presence
with brightness and vigor — Har

PSALM 57

To the chief Musician, Al-taschith, Michtum of David, when he fled from Saul in the cave.

To the Chief Musician: set to the tune, Do Not Destroy. A record of memorable thoughts of David, when he fled from Saul in the cave. — Amp

1. **Be merciful unto me, O God, be merciful unto me:**
for my soul trusteth in thee:

For in thee has my soul sought refuge — ABPS

For in Thee my soul takes refuge — Sprl

For in Thee, O God! my soul hideth — DeW

for I am looking to You for shelter — Har

yea, in the shadow of thy wings will I make my refuge, until these calamities be overpast.

And in the shadow of thy wings will I seek refuge
Until the storm of ruin pass by — Rhm

in the shadow of thy wings I shelter,
till the deadly danger passes — Mof

in the shadow of thy wings I will take refuge,
till the storms of destruction pass by — RSV

2. **I will cry unto God most high; unto God that performeth all things for me.**

I will call upon the Most High God;
Unto my accomplishing God! — Sprl

I will cry out to the most high God, the God who has ever befriended me — Knox

I cry to God Most High,
to God who fulfils his purpose for me — RSV

3. **He shall send from heaven, and save me from the reproach of him that would swallow me up.**

He will send from heaven and save me,
From the revilers that pant for my life — DeW

May he send from heaven and save me;
may he make those a reproach who trample upon me — NAB

He will send from heaven and save me,
he will put to shame those who trample upon me — RSV

Selah.

Selah [pause, and calmly think of that]! — Amp

God shall send forth his mercy and his truth.

God will send out his lovingkindness and his faithfulness — Rhm

God will send forth his steadfast love and his faithfulness! — RSV

God will demonstrate His loving mercy and His fidelity — Har

He will send his truth and his love that never fails — NEB

4. **My soul is among lions: and I lie even among them that are set on fire, even the sons of men, whose teeth are spears and arrows, and their tongues a sharp sword.**

My soul is in the midst of lions;
I will lie down with them that breathe out flames,
Sons of men whose teeth are spears and arrows,
And their tongue a sharp sword — ABPS

I have to live among lions,
who prey upon men;
their teeth are spears and arrows,
their tongue is a sharp sword — Mof

Fallen among lions I, that hungrily eat men's flesh; here are envious teeth that bite deeper than spear or arrow, tongues sharp as any sword — Knox

I lie in the midst of lions
that greedily devour the sons of men;
their teeth are spears and arrows,
their tongues sharp swords — RSV

I am among lions indeed;
I have to deal with angry people

whose teeth are javelins and arrows, and their tongue a whetted sword — Har

I am surrounded by fierce lions — hotheads whose teeth are sharp as spears and arrows. Their tongues are like swords — Tay

5. Be thou exalted, O God, above the heavens; let thy glory be above all the earth.

Show thyself, O God, high above the heavens;
let thy glory shine over all the earth — NEB

6. They have prepared a net for my steps; my soul is bowed down:

They have set a snare for my feet;
my mind is burdened with trouble — Har

they have digged a pit before me, into the midst whereof they are fallen themselves.

They dug a pit in my way,
but they have fallen into it themselves — RSV

Selah.

7. My heart is fixed, O God, my heart is fixed:

My heart is confident, O God!
My heart is confident — Sprl

My heart is stedfast, O God, my heart is stedfast — JPS

My heart is ready, God,
my heart is ready — Jerus

O God, my heart is quiet and confident — Tay

I will sing and give praise.

I will sing and touch the strings — Rhm

I will sing, and strike the chords — DeW

I will sing and make melody! — RSV

No wonder I can sing your praises! — Tay

8. Awake up, my glory; awake, psaltery and harp:

Awake mine honour
Awake harp and lyre — Rhm

Awake, my soul!
Awake, O harp and lyre! — RSV

Let me wake up;
make the lute and harp vibrate — Har

I myself will awake early.

I will awaken the dawn — Rhm

I mean to wake the Dawn! — Jerus

Let us greet the dawn with song! — Tay

9. I will praise thee, O Lord, among the people: I will sing unto thee among the nations.

I will give thanks unto thee, O Lord, among the peoples: I will sing praises unto thee among the nations — RV

I will confess thee, O Lord, among the peoples,
among the nations I will raise a psalm to thee — NEB

10. For thy mercy is great unto the heavens, and thy truth unto the clouds.

For Thy tender mercy reacheth unto the heavens,
And Thy truthfulness unto the skies — Sprl

For Thy great lovingkindness is high as the heavens;
And Thy truth reacheth unto the skies — DeW

For thy steadfast love is great to the heavens,
thy faithfulness to the clouds — RSV

for thy unfailing love is wide as the heavens
and thy truth reacheth to the skies — NEB

11. Be thou exalted, O God, above the heavens: let thy glory be above all the earth.[15]

PSALM 58

To the chief Musician, Al-taschith, Michtam of David.[16]

1. Do ye indeed speak righteousness, O congregation?

Are ye verily tongue-tied,
Ye that should vindicate the right — DeW

Do you indeed decree what is right, you gods — RSV

Do you indeed decree justice, you sovereign rulers — Har

Answer, you rulers: are your judgements just — NEB

Justice? You high and mighty politicians don't even know the meaning of the word! — Tay

[15]See verse 5.
[16]See Psalm 57.

do ye judge uprightly, O ye sons of men?
With equity do ye judge, ye sons of men — ABPS
Do you judge the sons of men uprightly — RSV
Do you judge mankind fairly — Har
Do you decide impartially between man and man — NEB

2. Yea, in heart ye work wickedness; ye weigh the violence of your hands in the earth.
Nay, in your hearts you devise wrongs; your hands deal out violence on earth — RSV
Behold you all speak evil on earth, and your hands are soiled with injustice — Lam
No; in your minds you devise injustice; by your actions you promote violence on earth — Har
On the contrary, in your hearts you meditate oppression, with your hands you dole out tyranny on earth — Jerus

3. The wicked are estranged from the womb: they go astray as soon as they be born, speaking lies.
The wicked are aliens from the womb; They go astray from their birth, speaking lies — DeW
The wicked are estranged from the womb; The speakers of lies go astray as soon as they are born — JPS
These men are born sinners, lying from their earliest words! — Tay

4. Their poison is like the poison of a serpent: they are like the deaf adder that stoppeth her ear;

5. Which will not hearken to the voice of charmers, charming never so wisely.
They are as venomous as the poison of a serpent, even like the deaf adder, that stoppeth her ears; Which refuseth to hear the voice of the charmer, charm he never so wisely — PBV
They have a venom like that of a serpent — like that of a deaf adder which stoppeth its ears; which will not hearken to the voice of charmers; nor to the charm administered by the wise — Sept
Their venom is like the venom of a serpent; They are like the deaf asp that stoppeth her ear; Which hearkeneth not to the voice of charmers, Or of the most cunning binder of spells — JPS
Theirs is poison like a serpent's, like that of a stubborn snake that stops its ears, That it may not hear the voice of enchanters casting cunning spells — NAB
their poison is the poison of the snake, they are deaf as the adder that blocks its ears so as not to hear the magician's music and the clever snake-charmer's spells — Jerus

6. Break their teeth, O God, in their mouth: break out the great teeth of the young lions, O LORD.
O God, break the teeth in their mouths; tear out the fangs of the young lions, O LORD! — RSV
O God! tear their teeth from their mouth; Crush the grinders of these lions, O Jehovah! — DeW
My God, break their cruel fangs; Lord, shatter their jaws, strong as the jaws of lions — Knox
God, break their teeth in their mouths, Yahweh, wrench out the fangs of these savage lions! — Jerus

7. Let them melt away as waters which run continually:
Let them vanish like water that runs away — RSV
Let them disappear like water draining away — Har
May they melt, may they vanish like water — NEB

when he bendeth his bow to shoot his arrows, let them be as cut in pieces.
When he aimeth his arrows, let them be as though they were cut off — ASV
When one bendeth the bow, let his arrows be blunt — DeW
when they draw the bow, let their arrows be headless shafts — NAB
Make their weapons useless in their hands — Tay
let them come to an end like the discharging of an arrow — Har

like grass let them be trodden down and wither — RSV
may they wither like trodden grass — NEB

8. As a snail which melteth, let every one of them pass away:
Let them be like the snail which dissolves into slime — RSV
like the untimely birth of a woman, that they may not see the sun.
As the abortive birth of a woman, which seeth not the sun — Sprl
like the untimely birth that never sees the sun — RSV
and as those who die at birth, who never see the sun — Tay

9. Before your pots can feel the thorns, he shall take them away as with a whirlwind, both living, and in his wrath.
Before your pots can feel the thorns, he shall take them away with a whirlwind,
the green and the burning alike — RV
Sooner than your pots can feel the heat of thorns,
whether green or ablaze, may he sweep them away! — RSV
God will sweep away both old and young. He will destroy them more quickly than a cooking pot can feel the blazing fire of thorns beneath it — Tay
Before your pots can feel the thorns [that are placed under them for fuel], He will take them away as with a whirlwind, the green and the burning ones alike — Amp
Unexpectedly, like a thorn-bush,
or like thistles, let the whirlwind carry them away — NAB
All unawares, may they be rooted up like a thorn-bush,
like weeds which a man angrily clears away! — NEB

10. The righteous shall rejoice when he seeth the vengeance: he shall wash his feet in the blood of the wicked.
The righteous will rejoice that he has seen vengeance;
His steps he will bathe in the blood of the wicked — ABPS
Let the righteous be glad,
For he hath vision of vengeance;
In the blood of the wicked he shall bathe his steps — DeW
The upright will be glad to witness his revenge;
he will wade in the streaming blood of the wicked — Har

11. So that a man shall say, Verily there is a reward for the righteous: verily he is a God that judgeth in the earth.
Men shall say: Truly there is fruit for the righteous;
Truly there is a God that judgeth in the earth — DeW
"Yes," men shall say, "the good do get their due;
yes, a God rules on earth indeed!" — Mof
Then at last everyone will know that good is rewarded, and that there is a God who judges justly here on earth — Tay

PSALM 59

To the chief Musician, Al-taschith, Michtam of David; when Saul sent, and they watched the house to kill him.[17]

1. Deliver me from mine enemies, O my God: defend me from them that rise up against me.
Deliver me from my enemies, O my God,
protect me from those who rise up against me — RSV
Deliver me from my foes, O my God!
Set me on high from my assailants — DeW
Rescue me from my enemies, O my God,
be my tower of strength against all who assail me — NEB

2. Deliver me from the workers of iniquity, and save me from bloody men.
Rescue me from the workers of iniquity,
And from the men of bloodshed save me — Rhm
Deliver me from the iniquitous;
Oh save me from bloodthirsty men — DeW
Rescue me from evildoers,
and keep me secure from murderers — Har

3. For, lo, they lie in wait for my soul:

[17]See Psalm 57.

For, lo, they are in ambush for my life — DeW
the mighty are gathered against me;
fierce men band themselves against me — RSV
not for my transgression, nor for my sin, O LORD.
though not for any wrongdoing or sin of mine, Lord God — Har

4. They run and prepare themselves without my fault:
Without iniquity on my part, they hurry and formidably array themselves — Sprl
Without guilt of mine, they run and prepare — DeW
for no guilt of mine they hurry to take up arms — NAB
Though I am innocent
they make hurried preparations — Har
awake to help me, and behold.
Rouse thyself to meet me and see — Rhm
Rouse yourself to see it, and aid me — NAB
Rouse thyself, come to my help, and see! — RSV

5. Thou therefore, O LORD God of hosts, the God of Israel, awake to visit all the heathen:
Lord God of armies, God of Israel, awake, and punish all the heathen — Har
be not merciful to any wicked transgressors.
Do not shew favour to any iniquitous traitors — Rhm
have no pity on any worthless traitors — NAB
show no mercy to these villains and traitors! — Jerus
spare none of those who treacherously plot evil — RSV
spare not one vile traitor — Mof
Selah.
Selah [pause, and calmly think of that]! — Amp

6. They return at evening: they make a noise like a dog, and go round about the city.
They return at evening
They growl like a dog,
And go round the city — Rhm
They return at evening; they snarl like dogs,
And go the rounds of the city — DeW
Each evening they come back,
howling like dogs
and prowling about the city — RSV
See how they come back at nightfall, like yelping dogs, to prowl about the city! — Knox

7. Behold, they belch out with their mouth: swords are in their lips: for who, say they, doth hear?
There they are, bellowing with their mouths,
and snarling with their lips —
for "Who," they think, "will hear us?" — RSV
See how they slaver at the mouth,
with swords between their teeth,
'There is no one listening' — Jerus
See them foaming at the mouth,
with whetted fangs within their lips.
"Who can hear us?" they say — Har
From their mouths comes a stream of nonsense;
'But who will hear?' they murmur — NEB

8. But thou, O LORD, shalt laugh at them; thou shalt have all the heathen in derision.
But thou, Jehovah, wilt laugh at them;
Thou wilt mock at all the nations — ABPS
and all the while thou, Lord, makest light of them, thou, in whose esteem all the nations are as nothing — Knox
But You, Lord, simply laugh at them;
You ridicule all the pagan nations — Har
Yahweh, you laugh at them,
you make fun of these pagans — Jerus

9. Because of his strength will I wait upon thee: for God is my defence.
O my Strength! for Thee will I watch;
For it is God that setteth me on high — DeW
O my Strength unto thee will I make melody,
For God is my high tower — Rhm
O my strength, to thee I turn in the night-watches;
for thou, O God, art my strong tower — NEB
O my Strength, I will sing praises to thee;

for thou, O God, art my fortress — RSV
O God my Strength! I will sing your praise, for you are my place of safety — Tay
10. The God of my mercy shall prevent me:
My God, my mercy, will go before me — Sprl
My compassionate God will precede me — Har
My gracious God will go before me — AAT
My God of lovingkindness will come to meet me — Rhm
My God in lovingkindness meeteth me — DeW
My God in his steadfast love will meet me — RSV
My God, in his true love, shall be my champion — NEB
God shall let me see my desire upon mine enemies.
God giveth me joy over my foes — DeW
my God will let me look in triumph on my enemies — RSV
God will let me gloat over my enemies — Har
with God's help, I shall gloat over my watchful foes — NEB
11. Slay them not, lest my people forget:
Don't kill them — for my people soon forget such lessons — Tay
Put them not to death, for so my people will keep the memory of them — Bas
O God, slay them, lest they beguile my people — NAB
Pity them not, lest my people forget — Mof
scatter them by thy power; and bring them down, O Lord our shield.
Make them reel by thy might, and bring them down,
Our shield, O Lord! — ABPS
rout them, ruin them, by thy might,
O Lord who art shielding me — Mof
make them totter by thy power, and bring them down,
O Lord, our shield! — RSV
12. For the sin of their mouth and the words of their lips let them even be taken in their pride: and for cursing and lying which they speak.
13. Consume them in wrath, consume them, that they may not be: and let them know that God ruleth in Jacob unto the ends of the earth.
For the sin of their mouth, for the words of their lips,
Let them be ensnared in their pride;
For their cursing, and the lies which they speak.
Consume them in wrath;
Consume them that they be no more;
And teach them that God who ruleth in Jacob,
Ruleth to the bounds of the earth — DeW
Let them be trapped
by their sinful speech and their utterances;
by their proud curses, and the lies which they tell.
Devour them in anger; ruin them that they may exist no longer.
Then it will be realized to the ends of the earth
that God rules over Jacob — Har
For the sin of their mouths, the words of their lips,
let them be trapped in their pride.
For the cursing and lies which they utter,
consume them in wrath,
consume them till they are no more,
that men may know that God rules over Jacob
to the ends of the earth — RSV
Selah.
Selah [pause, and calmly think of that]! — Amp
14. And at evening let them return; and let them make a noise like a dog, and go round about the city.[18]
When they return at evening,
They will snarl like dogs,
And go the rounds of the city — DeW
Each evening they return, they snarl like dogs
and prowl about the city — NAB
Each evening they come back,
howling like dogs
and prowling about the city — RSV
At night they return, whining like dogs,
and slink about the city — Har
Back they come at nightfall,
snarling like curs,
prowling through the town — Jerus
15. Let them wander up and down for

[18]Compare verse 6.

meat, and grudge if they be not satisfied.
They roam about for food,
and growl if they do not get their fill — RSV

16. **But I will sing of thy power;**
But as for me, I will sing of thy might — ABPS
yea, I will sing aloud of thy mercy in the morning:
And will sing aloud of thy lovingkindness in the morning — ABPS
I will sing aloud of thy steadfast love in the morning — RSV
for thou hast been my defence and refuge in the day of my trouble.
For thou hast been to me a fortress and a refuge in the day of my distress — RSV
you have always been my citadel, a shelter when I am in trouble — Jerus
for thou hast been my strong tower and a sure retreat in days of trouble — NEB

17. **Unto thee, O my strength, will I sing:**
O my Strength unto thee will I make melody — Rhm
Unto Thee, O my strength! I strike the harp — DeW
for God is my defence, and the God of my mercy.
for thou, O God, art my fortress,
the God who shows me steadfast love — RSV
For God who is my tower, is God who loveth me — DeW
For God is my high tower, the God of my mercy — ASV
for you, O God, are my stronghold,
my gracious God! — NAB

PSALM 60

To the chief Musician upon Shushan-eduth, Michtam of David, to teach; when he strove with Aram-naharaim and with Aram-zobah, when Joab returned, and smote of Edom in the valley of salt twelve thousand.
To the Chief Musician; set to the tune of The Lily of Testimony. A poem intended by David to record memorable thoughts; to teach; when he had striven with the Arameans of Mesopotamia and the Arameans of Zobah, and Joab returned and smote twelve thousand Edomites in the Valley of Salt — Amp

1. **O God, thou hast cast us off, thou hast scattered us, thou hast been displeased; O turn thyself to us again.**
O God, thou hast cast us off, thou hast broken us down; thou hast been angry; O restore us again — RV
O God, thou hast rejected us, broken our defenses;
thou hast been angry; oh, restore us — RSV
Thou hast discarded us,
crushed us in anger, O God;
restore us to power — Mof

2. **Thou hast made the earth to tremble; thou hast broken it: heal the breaches thereof; for it shaketh.**
Thou hast convulsed the land, Thou hast riven it asunder;
Rebuild the breaches thereof, for it falleth into ruin — DeW
Thou hast made the land to quake, thou hast rent it open;
repair its breaches, for it totters — RSV
Thou hast made the earth quake, thou hast rent it;
Heal its wounds; for it staggers — AAT

3. **Thou hast shewed thy people hard things:**
Thou hast afflicted Thy people with hardship — DeW
Heavy the burden thou didst lay on us — Knox
thou hast made us to drink the wine of astonishment.
thou hast given us a drink of deadly wine — PBV
Thou hast let them drink the wine of confusion — Rhm
Thou hast made us to drink the wine of staggering — ASV
you have given us stupefying wine — NAB
thou hast given us wine to drink that made us reel — RSV
such a draught thou didst brew for us as made our senses reel — Knox

4. **Thou hast given a banner to them that fear thee, that it may be displayed because of the truth.**
Thou hast set up a banner for those who fear thee,
to rally to it from the bow — RSV

You have set up a standard for those who fear You,
which they can rally around when hostile arms approach — Har
But thou hast given a warning to those who fear thee,
to make their escape before the sentence falls — NEB
Selah.

5. That thy beloved may be delivered; save with thy right hand, and hear me.
That thy beloved may be delivered,
give victory by thy right hand and answer us! — RSV
To bring rescue to those you love,
save with your right hand and answer us! — Jerus
To the rescue of thy dear folk!
Save by thy right hand, answer our entreaty — Mof

6. God hath spoken in his holiness;
God gave his sacred promise: — Mof
God has spoken in his sanctuary: — RSV
I will rejoice, I will divide Shechem, and mete out the valley of Succoth.
that I shall triumph!
That Sechem shall become my portion;
And the Valley of Succoth shall be measured out to me — Sprl
Therefore I will exult!
I will portion out Shechem,
And will measure the valley of Succoth — DeW
"With exultation I will divide up Shechem
and portion out the Vale of Succoth — RSV
"I will divide Shechem in triumph,
and apportion the valley of Succoth — Har

7. Gilead is mine, and Manasseh is mine; Ephraim also is the strength of mine head; Judah is my lawgiver;
Mine is Gilead, and mine is Manasseh;
And Ephraim is the defence of my head;
As for Judah, he is my royal staff — DeW
Gilead is mine; Manasseh is mine;
Ephraim is my helmet;
Judah is my scepter — RSV
Gilead is Mine, and Manasseh also.
Ephraim is My principal stronghold;
Judah is My emblem of authority — Har

8. Moab is my washpot; over Edom will I cast out my shoe: Philistia, triumph thou because of me.
Moab is my wash-bowl
Upon Edom will I throw my shoe,
Over Philistia! raise a shout of triumph — Rhm
Moab is my washpot; over Edom I extend my sway;
Concerning me, O Philistia, cry aloud! — DeW
Moab is my washbasin;
upon Edom I cast my shoe;
over Philistia I shout in triumph" — RSV
Moab is My washpot [reduced to vilest servitude]; upon Edom I cast My shoe in triumph; over Philistia I raise the shout of victory — Amp

9. Who will bring me into the strong city? who will lead me into Edom?
Who will conduct me to a fortified city?
Who will lead me as far as Edom! — Rhm
Who will bring me [David] into the strong city [of Petra]? Who will lead me into Edom — Amp

10. Wilt not thou, O God, which hadst cast us off? and thou, O God, which didst not go out with our armies?
Is it not thou O God? — thou hast rejected us!
And wilt thou not go forth O God with our hosts — Rhm
Hast thou not rejected us, O God?
Thou dost not go forth, O God, with our armies. — RSV
Have not you, O God, rejected us,
so that you go not forth, O God, with our armies — NAB
God will! He who cast us off! He who abandoned us to our foes! — Tay
Ah! Thou, O God, hast not rejected us!
For hast not Thou, O God, marched along with our hosts? — Sprl

11. Give us help from trouble: for vain is the help of man.
Oh give us help against the adversary!
For futile is the help of man — Sprl
Grant us help out of distress,
For vain is the deliverance of man — Rhm
Give us aid against the foe,
for worthless is the help of men — NAB
Help us in this hour of crisis,

the help that man can give is worthless — Jerus
Grant us help against the enemy,
for deliverance by man is a vain hope — NEB

12. Through God we shall do valiantly:
Through God will we do great acts — PBV
Through God we can exert power — Sept
In God we do mightily — YLT
Through God we shall perform brave deeds — Har
Only through God can we fight victoriously — Knox
With God among us we shall fight like heroes — Jerus
for he it is that shall tread down our enemies.
only he can trample our oppressors in the dust — Knox
He Himself will trample down our enemies — Har

PSALM 61

To the chief Musician upon Neginah, a Psalm of David.
To the Chief Musician. Upon a Stringed Instrument. David's — Rhm

1. Hear my cry, O God;
Hear O God my loud cry — Rhm
God, hear my cry for help — Jerus
attend unto my prayer.
listen to my prayer — RSV
2. From the end of the earth will I cry unto thee, when my heart is overwhelmed:
From the ends of the earth will I call upon thee, when my heart is in heaviness — PBV
from the end of the earth I call to thee, when my heart is faint — RSV
I will call to You from the borders of the earth
in my weariness of spirit — Har
From the end of the earth I call to you, with sinking heart — Jerus
lead me to the rock that is higher than I.
O set me up upon the rock that is higher than I — PBV
Lead me to the rock that is high above me — DeW
Be my guide;
set me up on a towering crag — Har
3. For thou hast been a shelter for me,
for thou hast been my hope — PBV
For thou hast been a refuge for me — ABPS
For Thou hast become my refuge — DeW
For You are my shelter — Har
and a strong tower from the enemy.
A tower of strength, from before the enemy — ABPS
A Tower of Strength from the face of the foe — Rhm
A tower of strength, away from the foe — DeW
a strong fortress against the enemy — Har
a tower for refuge from the enemy — NEB
4. I will abide in thy tabernacle for ever:
I would be a guest in thy tent to the ages — Rhm
Let me abide in Thy Tent for eternities — DeW
Oh, that I might lodge in your tent forever — NAB
I will trust in the covert of thy wings.
and my trust shall be under the covering of thy wings — PBV
I would seek refuge in the concealment of thy wings — Rhm
Let me hide under cover of Thy wings — DeW
oh to be sheltered underneath thy wings! — Mof
let me find security within Your protecting power — Har
Selah.
Selah [pause, and calmly think of that]! — Amp
5. For thou, O God, hast heard my vows:
For You, my God, have heard my solemn promises — Har
thou hast given me the heritage of those that fear thy name.
Thou hast granted a possession unto them who revere thy Name — Rhm
Thou hast granted the wish of those who fear thy name — AAT
You have restored the prosperity of those who revere Your name — Har
6. Thou wilt prolong the king's life:
Thou wilt add days to the days of the king — ABPS
Prolong the life of the king — RSV

Let the king live on and on — Jerus
and his years as many generations.
His years shall be as many generations — ASV
may his years endure to all generations! — RSV
while generations come and go, may his life still last — Knox
7. **He shall abide before God for ever:**
May he be enthroned for ever before God — RSV
O prepare mercy and truth, which may preserve him.
O prepare thy loving mercy and faithfulness, that they may preserve him — PBV
Appoint that lovingkindness and faithfulness may watch over him! — Rhm
Cause that mercy and faithfulness preserve him — ABPS
bid steadfast love and faithfulness watch over him! — RSV
8. **So will I sing praise unto thy name for ever, that I may daily perform my vows.**
Thus will I harp to Thy Name for ever, While daily performing my vows — DeW
So I will sing praise to Your name continually,
and discharge my vows daily — Har

PSALM 62

To the chief Musician, to Jeduthun, A Psalm of David.
For the Chief Musician; according to Jeduthun. . . . — Ber
From the Choirmaster's collection. To Jeduthun's tune. A song of David — Mof
1. **Truly my soul waiteth upon God:**
My soul waiteth in silence for God only — ASV
To God alone is my spirit resigned — AAT
To God alone I commit myself silently — Har
Truly my soul looks in stillness to God — Ber
Only in God is my soul quieted — ABPS
Only in God is my soul at rest — NAB
In God alone there is rest for my soul — Jerus
Leave it all quietly to God, my soul — Mof
from him cometh my salvation.
my rescue comes from him alone — Mof
From him is my deliverance — AAT
From him comes my safety — Jerus
2. **He only is my rock and my salvation; he is my defence; I shall not be greatly moved.**
He only is my sure foundation and my help:
He is my refuge,
I shall not be dispossessed — Har
He alone is my rock and my health, my fortress; I shall not be greatly shaken — Ber
In truth he is my rock of deliverance, my tower of strength, so that I stand unshaken — NEB
rock, rescue, refuge, he is all to me, never shall I be overthrown — Mof
with him alone for my rock, my safety, my fortress, I can never fall — Jerus
3. **How long will ye imagine mischief against a man? ye shall be slain all of you: as a bowing wall shall ye be, and as a tottering fence.**
How long will ye shout at a man?
Ye shall be crushed all of you, —
Like a wall that bulgeth, — a fence pushed in! — Rhm
How long will ye set upon a man,
That ye may slay him, all of you,
Like a leaning wall, like a tottering fence? — ASV
How long will you people continue to assail a person,
striking him down as though he were a leaning fence,
or a tottering wall — Har
4. **They only consult to cast him down from his excellency:**
They only consult to thrust him down from his dignity — ASV
To thrust him forth from his dignity is their only thought — DeW
They plot with the sole intention
of removing him from his eminent position — Har
they delight in lies:
They take pleasure in falsehood — RSV
they bless with their mouth, but they curse inwardly.
they give good words with their mouth, but curse with their heart — PBV
Selah.

Selah [pause, and calmly think of that]! — Amp

5. My soul, wait thou only upon God;

My soul, wait thou in silence for God only — ASV

Leave it all quietly to God, my soul — Mof

For God alone my soul waits in silence — RSV

To God alone I commit myself silently — Har

for my expectation is from him.

for my hope is in him — PBV

For from him comes my hope — NAB

6. He only is my rock and my salvation: he is my defence; I shall not be moved.[19]

7. In God is my salvation and my glory:

In God have I safety and glory — DeW

On God rests my deliverance and my honor — RSV

Upon God [depend] my salvation and mine honour — Rhm

the rock of my strength, and my refuge, is in God.

my mighty rock, my refuge is God — RSV

my God is my shelter,
my powerful defense — Har

8. Trust in him at all times; ye people, pour out your heart before him:

Always rely on him, my followers,
pour out your prayers to him — Mof

Trust Him continually, all you nations;
disclose the depths of your minds to Him — Har

O my people, trust him all the time. Pour out your longings before him — Tay

God is a refuge for us.

for God is our hope — PBV

God is a shelter for us — Sprl

for he can help! — Tay

Selah.

9. Surely men of low degree are vanity, and men of high degree are a lie:

Men of low estate are but a breath,
men of high estate are a delusion — RSV

Ordinary men are only a puff of wind,
important men delusion — Jerus

In very truth men are a puff of wind,
all men are faithless — NEB

Humanity as such is worthless;
the offspring of man is unreliable — Har

to be laid in the balance, they are altogether lighter than vanity.

In the balances they go up;
They are alike lighter than breath! — DeW

put them in the balance and they can only rise,
all of them lighter than wind — NEB

weigh them, they prove to be lighter and slighter than a breath of air — Mof

put both in the scales and up they go,
lighter than a puff of wind — Jerus

10. Trust not in oppression, and become not vain in robbery:

Put no confidence in extortion,
set no vain hopes on robbery — RSV

Rely not on extortion,
pride not yourselves on robbery — Mof

Have no faith in rewards of evildoing,
or in profits wrongly made — Bas

Put no trust in extortion,
do not be proud of stolen goods — NEB

if riches increase, set not your heart upon them.

though riches may increase, keep your heart detached — Jerus

11. God hath spoken once; twice have I heard this; that power belongeth unto God.

There is one thing God has said;
ay, twice have I heard him say it:
that power belongs to God — Mof

Not once, but twice I have heard God's voice of warning; all power is God's — Knox

One thing God has spoken,
two things have I learnt: 'Power belongs to God' — NEB

12. Also unto thee, O Lord, belongeth mercy:

and that to thee, O Lord, belongs steadfast love — RSV

and that merciful favor is part of Your nature — Har

And that in Thee, O God! there is lovingkindness — DeW

and 'True love, O Lord, is thine' — NEB

for thou renderest to every man according to his work.

For thou dost requite a man
according to his work — RSV

for You repay a person according to his doings — Har

[19]Compare verse 2.

PSALM 63

A Psalm of David, when he was in the wilderness of Judah.

1. O God, thou art my God; early will I seek thee:
. . . earnestly will I seek thee — ASV
. . . I yearn for thee — Mof
God, you are my God:
I am searching for You — Har
my soul thirsteth for thee, my flesh longeth for thee in a dry and thirsty land, where no water is;
my soul thirsts for thee;
my flesh faints for thee,
as in a dry and weary land where no water is — RSV
for you my flesh pines and my soul thirsts
like the earth, parched, lifeless and without water — NAB
I long for You earnestly,
with my whole being I yearn for You,
as in a parched and arid land, where there is no water — Har
with a heart that thirsts for thee
and a body wasted with longing for thee
like a dry and thirsty land that has no water — NEB

2. To see thy power and thy glory, so as I have seen thee in the sanctuary.
Thus have I looked for thee in the sanctuary, that I might behold thy power and glory — PBV
Thus have I gazed toward you in the sanctuary
to see your power and your glory — NAB
I long to gaze on you in the Sanctuary,
and to see your power and glory — Jerus
So longing, I come before thee in the sanctuary
to look upon thy power and glory — NEB
How I wish I could go into your sanctuary to see your strength and glory — Tay

3. Because thy lovingkindness is better than life, my lips shall praise thee.
Surely Thy loving-kindness is preferable to life!
My lips would adore Thee! — Sprl
For your kindness is a greater good than life;
my lips shall glorify you — NAB
because Your merciful love is preferable to life itself,
I will praise You — Har

4. Thus will I bless thee while I live: I will lift up my hands in thy name.
So I will bless thee as long as I live;
I will lift up my hands and call on thy name — RSV
. . . lifting my hands in prayer to thee — Mof

5. My soul shall be satisfied as with marrow and fatness;
As with fatness and richness shall my soul be satisfied — Rhm
As with the riches of a banquet shall my soul be satisfied — NAB
I am satisfied as with a rich and sumptuous feast — NEB
My longing will be satisfied as with succulent fat meat — Har
My whole being shall be satisfied as with marrow and fatness — Amp
and my mouth shall praise thee with joyful lips:
And with joyfully shouting lips shall my mouth utter praise — Rhm

6. When I remember thee upon my bed, and meditate on thee in the night watches.
when I think of thee upon my bed,
and meditate on thee in the watches of the night — RSV
when I remember You in my bed,
and commune with You throughout the night — Har
I will remember you upon my couch,
and through the night-watches I will meditate on you — NAB

7. Because thou hast been my help, therefore in the shadow of thy wings will I rejoice.
For thou hast become a help unto me, —
And in the shadow of thy wings will I shout for joy — Rhm
For since Thou hast become my helper,
Overshadowed by Thy wings, I sing for joy — DeW
For You have been of assistance to me,
and under Your mighty protection I shout for joy — Har
That you are my help,
and in the shadow of your wings I shout for joy — NAB

8. My soul followeth hard after thee: thy

right hand upholdeth me.

My soul hangeth upon thee; thy right hand hath upholden me — PBV

My soul cleaveth close in following Thee,
Held fast by Thine own right hand — DeW

I have clung close to thee;
Thy right hand has sustained me — AAT

I have clung fast to You;
You have supported me by Your great power — Har

9. But those that seek my soul, to destroy it, shall go into the lower parts of the earth.

But those who seek to destroy my life shall go down into the depths of the earth — RSV

But they shall be destroyed who seek my life,
they shall go into the depths of the earth — NAB

But they, to their ruin, seek after my life;
They go down into the depths of the earth — DeW

10. They shall fall by the sword: they shall be a portion for foxes.

Let them fall upon the edge of the sword, that they may be a portion for foxes — PBV

They shall be given over to the power of the sword;
They shall become a prey for jackals — DeW

They are doomed to die by the sword, to become the food of jackals — Tay

11. But the king shall rejoice in God; every one that sweareth by him shall glory:

all who swear allegiance to Him will praise Him — Har

All who swear by Him shall triumph — Sprl

but the mouth of them that speak lies shall be stopped.

for the mouths of liars will be stopped — RSV

silence shall fall on the lips that muttered treason — Knox

PSALM 64

To the chief Musician, A Psalm of David.

1. Hear my voice, O God, in my prayer:

Hear, O God, my voice, in my meditation — YLT

Hear, O God, my voice in my complaint — ABPS

Hear my voice, O God! in my lamentation — DeW

God, hear me as I make my plea — Jerus

preserve my life from fear of the enemy.

From dread peril by the foe wilt thou guard my life — Rhm

keep me safe from the threats of the enemy — NEB

2. Hide me from the secret counsel of the wicked;

Wilt thou hide me
From the conclave of evil-doers — Rhm

Conceal me from the secret plots of the wicked — Sprl

from the insurrection of the workers of iniquity:

From the tumultuous throng of workers of iniquity — ABPS

From the crowd of the iniquitous — DeW

from the scheming of evildoers — RSV

3. Who whet their tongue like a sword, and bend their bows to shoot their arrows, even bitter words:

Who have whet their tongue like a sword,
And have aimed their arrows, even bitter words — ASV

who whet their tongues like swords, who aim bitter words like arrows — RSV

4. That they may shoot in secret at the perfect:

shooting from ambush at the blameless — RSV

to shoot from ambush at the innocent — Har

suddenly do they shoot at him, and fear not.

shooting at him suddenly and without fear — RSV

They let fly boldly without warning — Har

5. They encourage themselves in an evil matter:

They encourage themselves in an evil purpose — ASV

They hold fast to their evil purpose — RSV
They confirm themselves in an evil purpose — DeW
They confirm their intent by an evil plan — Har
they commune of laying snares privily;
They talk of laying snares secretly — RSV
they discuss the setting of traps in secret — Har
they say, Who shall see them?
thinking, "Who can see us?" — RSV
saying, "Who will notice them?" — Har
'Who is going to see us?' they say — Jerus

6. They search out iniquities; they accomplish a diligent search: both the inward thought of every one of them, and the heart, is deep.
"Who can search out our crimes?
We have thought out a cunningly conceived plot."
For the inward mind and heart of a man are deep! — RSV
They go over the plot thoroughly:
"We have discovered a cleverly devised scheme,"
for the human heart and mind is indeed cunning — Har
Who? He who probes the inmost mind and the depths of the heart — Jerus

7. But God shall shoot at them with an arrow; suddenly shall they be wounded.
God will shoot them with his own arrow, wound them without warning — Jerus

8. So they shall make their own tongue to fall upon themselves: all that see them shall flee away.
Yea, their own tongues shall make them fall; insomuch that whoso seeth them shall laugh them to scorn — PBV
Because of their tongue he will bring them to ruin;
all who see them will wag their heads — RSV
They will come to ruin through their malicious speech;
all who behold them will shake their heads — Har
he trips them up in their own plot,
till all who see them recoil in horror — Mof

9. And all men shall fear, and shall declare the work of God;
And all men that see it shall say, This hath God done — PBV
Then all men will fear;
they will tell what God has wrought — RSV
Everyone will then be awestruck,
and proclaim what God has done — Har
for they shall wisely consider of his doing.
and ponder what he has done — RSV

10. The righteous shall be glad in the LORD, and shall trust in him;
The righteous shall be glad in Jehovah,
and shall take refuge in him — ASV
Let the righteous rejoice in the LORD,
and take refuge in him! — RSV
and all the upright in heart shall glory.
and all they that are true of heart shall be glad — PBV
right-minded men will all exult — Mof
Let all the upright in heart glory! — RSV

PSALM 65

To the chief Musician, A Psalm and Song of David.

1. Praise waiteth for thee, O God, in Sion:
Praise is due to thee,
O God, in Zion — RSV
and unto thee shall the vow be performed.

2. O thou that hearest prayer, unto thee shall all flesh come.
And to thee shall the vow be paid.
Thou that hearest prayer,
To thee shall all flesh come — ABPS
and to thee shall vows be performed,
O thou who hearest prayer!
To thee shall all flesh come — RSV
and vows will be discharged to You in Jerusalem.
All mankind will approach You,
because You listen to prayer — Har

3. Iniquities prevail against me: as for our transgressions, thou shalt purge them away.
Mine iniquities overpower me;
But THOU wilt cover our transgressions — DeW

Guilty deeds overwhelm me,
yet You forgive our wrongdoing — Har
our sins are too heavy for us;
only thou canst blot them out — NEB

4. Blessed is the man whom thou choosest, and causest to approach unto thee, that he may dwell in thy courts:
Blessed is he whom thou dost choose and bring near,
to dwell in thy courts! — RSV
Happy indeed is he whom You choose, and allow to reside in your dwelling — Har

we shall be satisfied with the goodness of thy house, even of thy holy temple.
We shall be satisfied with
The blessing of thy house,
The holiness of thy temple — Rhm
We shall be satisfied with the riches of thy house,
Thy holy temple — ABPS
May we be satisfied with the goodness of Thy house,
The holy place of Thy temple! — JPS
let us enjoy the blessing of thy house,
thy holy temple — NEB

5. By terrible things in righteousness wilt thou answer us, O God of our salvation;
By dread deeds thou dost answer us with deliverance,
O God of our salvation — RSV
You will reply to us with wonderful deeds of vindication,
our delivering God — Har
Thou shalt show us wonderful things in thy righteousness, O God of our salvation — PBV

who art the confidence of all the ends of the earth, and of them that are afar off upon the sea:
thou that art the hope of all the ends of the earth, and of them that remain in the broad sea — PBV

6. Which by his strength setteth fast the mountains; being girded with power:
who by thy strength hast established the mountains,
being girded with might — RSV
He who has set mountains in position by His might
is surrounded with power — Har
thou art girded with strength,
and by thy might dost fix the mountains in their place — NEB
What power girds thee about! In thy strength the mountains stand firm — Knox

7. Which stilleth the noise of the seas, the noise of their waves, and the tumult of the people.
Who stilleth
The noise of the seas
The noise of their rolling waves, and
The tumult of races of men? — Rhm
You still the roaring of the seas,
the roaring of their waves and the tumult of the peoples — NAB
He soothes alike raging oceans with roaring waves,
and turbulent humanity — Har
thou dost calm the raging of the sea, raging sea-billows, ay, and the turmoil of angry nations — Knox
He quiets the raging oceans and all the world's clamor — Tay

8. They also that dwell in the uttermost parts are afraid at thy tokens:
so that the inhabitants of distant lands become awed at Your portents — Har
so that those who dwell at earth's farthest bounds
are afraid at thy signs — RSV
And the dwellers at the earth's ends are in fear at your marvels — NAB
In the farthest corners of the earth the glorious acts of God shall startle everyone — Tay

thou makest the outgoings of the morning and evening to rejoice.
The goings forth of morning and evening thou causest to shout for joy — Rhm
the farthest east and west you make resound with joy — NAB
You can give occasion for rejoicing at dawn and sunset — Har
Thou makest the morning dawn and the evening sunset to shout for joy — Ber

9. Thou visitest the earth, and waterest it: thou greatly enrichest it with the river of God, which is full of water: thou preparest them corn, when thou hast so provided for it.
Thou visitest the earth and waterest it,
thou greatly enrichest it;
the river of God is full of water;
thou providest their grain,
for so thou hast prepared it — RSV

You have shown consideration for the land
in watering it abundantly.
You have enriched it greatly.
You have prepared the sacred river, filling it with water for their grain.
In this way You have made provision — Har

He waters the earth to make it fertile.
The rivers of God will not run dry!
He prepares the earth for his people and sends them rich harvests of grain — Tay

10. Thou waterest the ridges thereof abundantly: thou settlest the furrows thereof:

You make the ploughed lands full of water; you make smooth the slopes — Bas

This is how you provide it:
by drenching its furrows, by levelling its ridges — Jerus

thou makest it soft with showers: thou blessest the springing thereof.

by softening it with showers, by blessing the firstfruits — Jerus

moistening it with showers,
and blessing its young growth — Har

you make the earth soft with showers, sending your blessings on its growth — Bas

11. Thou crownest the year with thy goodness; and thy paths drop fatness.

Thou crownest the year with Thy goodness,
And Thy footsteps are dropping with riches — DeW

You have crowned the year with your bounty,
and your paths overflow with a rich harvest — NAB

You crown the year with your bounty, abundance flows wherever you pass — Jerus

Thy bounty it is that crowns the year; where thy feet have passed, the stream of plenty flows — Knox

The year is crowned with the good you give; life-giving rain is dropping from your footsteps — Bas

12. They drop upon the pastures of the wilderness: and the little hills rejoice on every side.

On the wilderness pastures they are dropping;
And the hills are girdled with joy — DeW

The luxuriant pastures in the uncultivated country drip [with moisture], and the hills gird themselves with joy — Amp

The untilled meadows overflow with it, and rejoicing clothes the hills — NAB

13. The pastures are clothed with flocks; the valleys also are covered over with corn; they shout for joy, they also sing.

The pastures are decked with flocks of sheep,
And the valleys shall be arrayed with a mantle of corn;
They shall wave with delight; yea, they shall sing — Sprl

The pastures are clothed with flocks,
And the valleys are robed with grain;
They shout together, yea they sing — ABPS

the meadows clothe themselves with flocks,
the valleys deck themselves with grain,
they shout and sing together for joy — RSV

The pastures are filled with flocks of sheep, and the valleys are carpeted with grain. All the world shouts with joy, and sings — Tay

PSALM 66

To the chief Musician, A Song or Psalm.
. . . A Melodious Song — Rhm

1. Make a joyful noise unto God, all ye lands:

Raise ye a joyous shout unto God, all the earth! — Sprl

Send up a glad cry to God, all the earth — Bas

2. Sing forth the honour of his name: make his praise glorious.

Sing ye glory to His name!
Sing the glory of His praise! — Sprl

Praise ye in song the glory of his Name,
Celebrate the glory of his praise — Rhm

Strike the harp to His glorious Name;
Give Him glory in a song of praise — DeW

sing the glory of his name;
give to him glorious praise! — RSV

Sing of his glorious name! Tell the world how wonderful he is — Tay

3. **Say unto God, How terrible art thou in thy works!**

Say to God, How fearful are thy doings — ABPS

Say unto God: How tremendous is Thy work — JPS

Say to God, How greatly to be feared are your works — Bas

Cry out to God, What dread, Lord, thy acts inspire — Knox

saying to God,
"How awesome are Your doings!"— Har

Say to God, How awesome and fearfully glorious are Your works — Amp

through the greatness of thy power shall thine enemies submit themselves unto thee.

Through the abounding of thy power shall thy foes come cringing unto thee — Rhm

Through the greatness of Thy power shall Thine enemies dwindle away before Thee — JPS

Thy foes cower through the greatness of thy strength — NEB

4. **All the earth shall worship thee, and shall sing unto thee; they shall sing to thy name.**

For all the world shall worship thee, sing of thee, and praise thy Name — PBV

Let all the earth worship and harp to Thee;
Let them make melody to Thy Name — DeW

All the earth shall bow themselves down to thee
And sing praises unto thee,
Shall praise in song thy name — Rhm

All men on earth fall prostrate in thy presence,
and sing to thee, sing psalms in honour of thy name — NEB

Selah.

Selah [pause, and calmly think of that]! — Amp

5. **Come and see the works of God: he is terrible in his doing toward the children of men.**

O come hither, and behold the works of God; how wonderful he is in his doing toward the children of men — PBV

Come and see what God hath accomplished;
How fearful His deeds toward the sons of men! — DeW

Come and see the works of God,
his tremendous deeds among men — NAB

Come and observe the works of God;
he is awe-inspiring in His activity among men — Har

Come and see what marvels God has done,
so much to be feared for his deeds among mankind — Jerus

Come, see the glorious things God has done. What marvelous miracles happen to his people! — Tay

6. **He turned the sea into dry land: they went through the flood on foot: there did we rejoice in him.**

He has changed the sea into dry land;
through the river they passed on foot;
therefore let us rejoice in him — NAB

7. **He ruleth by his power for ever; his eyes behold the nations: let not the rebellious exalt themselves.**

In that power of his he reigns for ever, and has eyes for what the Gentiles do; let rebellious souls tame their pride — Knox

who rules for ever by his power:
his eyes keep watch on the nations,
let no rebel raise his head! — Jerus

Because of his great power he rules forever. He watches every movement of the nations. O rebel lands, he will deflate your pride — Tay

Selah.

8. **O bless our God, ye people, and make the voice of his praise to be heard:**

You nations, bless our God
and make his praise resound — Jerus

9. **Which holdeth our soul in life, and suffereth not our feet to be moved.**

He preserveth our lives among the living,
And suffereth not our feet to slip — Sprl

For He preserveth our soul in life,
And suffereth not our feet to stumble — DeW

He it is who hath kept my soul alive;
and hath not given my feet to the briny deep — Sept

for He has sustained us in the world,
and has not allowed our steps to falter — Har

10. For thou, O God, hast proved us: thou hast tried us, as silver is tried.

For Thou hast tested us, O God,
Thou hast smelted us as silver is smelted — Sprl

For thou hast tested us, O God;
Thou hast refined us as silver is refined — AAT

You have purified us with fire, O Lord,
like silver in a crucible — Tay

11. Thou broughtest us into the net; thou laidst affliction upon our loins.

Thou broughtest us into the hunter's net;
Thou laidst heavy burdens upon our loins — DeW

you let us fall into the net,
you laid heavy burdens on our backs — Jerus

You have made us enter prison,
You put chains about our waists — Har

You let us be put in prison; chains were put on our legs — Bas

12. Thou hast caused men to ride over our heads;

You allowed men to be placed over us — Har

we went through fire and through water: but thou broughtest us out into a wealthy place.

we went through fire and through water;
yet thou has brought us forth to a spacious place — RSV

We went into fire and into water,
But thou didst bring us forth into freedom — Rhm

we have passed through fire and water.
But thou hast brought us to a place of rest — Sept

we went through fire and water,
but you have led us out to refreshment — NAB

though we had to pass through fire and water,
yet thou hast granted us a rich relief,
setting us free in liberty — Mof

we endured torments of fire and water,
yet You brought us out to abundant prosperity — Har

we went through fire and through water,
and Thou hast brought us to an overflowing abundance — Ber

13. I will go into thy house with burnt offerings: I will pay thee my vows,

14. Which my lips have uttered, and my mouth hath spoken, when I was in trouble.

Those which my lips have uttered,
And my mouth hath spoken in my distress — DeW

15. I will offer unto thee burnt sacrifices of fatlings, with the incense of rams;

I will offer You burnt-offerings of fatlings
with the fragrant smoke of rams — Har

I will offer bullocks with goats.

I will make an offering of bulls and goats — RSV

Selah.

16. Come and hear, all ye that fear God,

Come, listen, all you who reverence God — Har

Come, all ye worshippers of God — Mof

and I will declare what he hath done for my soul.

and I will tell what he has done for me — RSV

17. I cried unto him with my mouth, and he was extolled with my tongue.

To him I cried with my mouth;
And praise is beneath my tongue — ABPS

I cried loudly to Him,
and praised Him in my speech — Har

18. If I regard iniquity in my heart, the Lord will not hear me:

If I had cherished iniquity in my heart,
the Lord would not have listened — RSV

If my heart had delighted in evil;
The Lord would not hear me — DeW

Were I to cherish wickedness in my heart,
the Lord would not hear — NAB

Had I been thinking secretly of sin,
the Lord would never have listened — Mof

Had I nursed evil in my mind,
the Lord would not have listened — Har

19. But verily God hath heard me; he

hath attended to the voice of my prayer.
But God did hear,
and paid attention to my prayerful appeal — Har

20. **Blessed be God, which hath not turned away my prayer, nor his mercy from me.**
Blessed be God,
Who hath not turned away my prayer
Nor his own lovingkindness from me — Rhm

May God be blessed,
for He did not reject my petition,
and did not withdraw His loving mercy from me — Har

PSALM 67

To the chief Musician on Neginoth, A Psalm or Song.
To the Chief Musician. With stringed Instruments. A Melody, a Song — Rhm

1. **God be merciful unto us, and bless us;**
May God be gracious to us and bless us — RSV
God be favourable to us and bless us — Rhm
and cause his face to shine upon us;
And let His presence shine upon us! — DeW
may He radiate His presence upon us — Har
may thy face smile on us — Mof
Selah.
Selah [pause, and calmly think of that]! — Amp

2. **That thy way may be known upon earth, thy saving health among all nations.**
That thy way may be known throughout the earth,
Throughout all nations thy saving help! — Rhm
That thy way may be known in the earth,
Thy salvation among all the nations — ABPS
that so thy purpose may be plain to men,
thy saving power to every nation — Mof
that mortal men may know Your intentions,
and every nation recognize Your ability to save — Har
For then the earth will acknowledge your ways
and all the nations will know of your power to save — Jerus

3. **Let the people praise thee, O God; let all the people praise thee.**
Let the nations praise you, O God,
let all the nations praise you! — Jerus
O God, may the whole world praise thee,
may all races praise thee — Mof

4. **O let the nations be glad and sing for joy:**
Let the nations be glad and shout for joy — ABPS
Races of men will be glad and shout for joy — Rhm
The nations will rejoice and be jubilant — Har
for thou shalt judge the people righteously, and govern the nations upon earth.
Because thou wilt judge peoples with equity,
And races of men throughout the earth thou wilt lead — Rhm
For thou wilt judge the peoples righteously,
And the nations in the earth, thou wilt guide them — ABPS
because You judge mankind equitably,
and guide the races of the earth — Har
Selah.

5. **Let the people praise thee, O God; let all the people praise thee.**[20]

6. **Then shall the earth yield her increase;**
Earth will have given her increase — Rhm
The land has yielded her harvest — Mof
The soil has given its harvest — Jerus
and God, even our own God, shall bless us.
God, our God, has blessed us — RSV

7. **God shall bless us; and all the ends of the earth shall fear him.**
May God bless us;

[20]See verse 3.

And let all the ends of the earth fear Him — JPS
bless us, O God, bless us,
till men revere thee to the world's far end — Mof
God grant us his blessing,
that all the ends of the earth may fear him — NEB
God has blessed us;
let all the ends of the earth fear him! — RSV
God has bestowed His blessing upon us:
let every corner of the earth revere Him — Har

PSALM 68

To the chief Musician, A Psalm or Song of David.

1. **Let God arise, let his enemies be scattered:**
God ariseth, His enemies scatter — DeW
When God arises,
His enemies are dispersed — Har
let them also that hate him flee before him.
Those that hate Him flee before Him — DeW
and those who hate Him flee from His presence — Har

2. **As smoke is driven away, so drive them away:**
As smoke is driven about
Let them be driven about — Rhm
As smoke is driven away,
Thou drivest them away — DeW
as wax melteth before the fire, so let the wicked perish at the presence of God.
As wax is melted before a fire
Let the lawless perish before God — Rhm
As wax melteth before the fire,
The wicked perish before God — DeW

3. **But let the righteous be glad; let them rejoice before God: yea, let them exceedingly rejoice.**
But let the righteous be glad, and rejoice before God; let them also be merry and joyful — PBV
But let the righteous be joyful;
let them exult before God;
let them be jubilant with joy! — RSV
But let them who are righteous rejoice — let them shout for joy at the presence of God — let them be transported with gladness — Sept
But the virtuous will be happy;
they will be joyful in the Divine presence,
and radiant with contentment — Har
But the righteous are glad — they rejoice before God;
Yea, they exult in their gladness — DeW

4. **Sing unto God, sing praises to his name:**
Sing to Yahweh, play music to his name — Jerus
Sing ye to God
Make music of his Name — Rhm
Sing ye to God! strike the harp to His Name! — DeW
Sing to God; celebrate his name in songs — Sept
Sing, then, in God's honour, praise his name with a psalm — Knox
extol him that rideth upon the heavens by his name JAH, and rejoice before him.
magnify him that rideth upon the heavens; praise him in his Name, JAH, and rejoice before him — PBV
Lift up (a song) to him that rideth through the waste plains, —
Since Yah is his name exult ye before him — Rhm
lift up a song to him who rides upon the clouds;
his name is the LORD, exult before him! — RSV
give glory to Him who rides upon the storm clouds,
His name is Jehovah;
be joyful in His presence — Har
Make a highway for the rider through deserts!
I AM is His Name; oh, exult ye before Him — DeW
Cast up a highway for him that rideth through the deserts;
His name is Jehovah; and exult ye before him — ASV
build a road for the Rider of the Clouds,

rejoice in Yahweh, exult at his coming! — Jerus

5. **A father of the fatherless, and a judge of the widows, is God in his holy habitation.**
Father of the fatherless and protector of widows
is God in his holy habitation — RSV
He is a Father of the fatherless, and defendeth the cause of the widows; even God in his holy habitation — PBV
The Father of the orphan, and the Advocate of the widow,
Is God in His holy habitation — Sprl
Father of orphans, and Defender of widows,
Is God in His holy dwelling — DeW
Father of orphans, Protector of widows,
such is the Lord in His holy abode — Har

6. **God setteth the solitary in families:**
God gives the desolate a home to dwell in — RSV
God brings the disconsolate back home — Har
God gives the lonely a permanent home — Jerus
God gives a home to the forsaken — NAB
This is the God who makes a home for the outcast — Knox
Those who are without friends, God puts in families — Bas
he bringeth out those which are bound with chains:
he leads out the prisoners to prosperity — RSV
He leads the imprisoned out to success — Har
He bringeth out the prisoners into abundance — DeW
but the rebellious dwell in a dry land.
but letteth the runagates continue in scarceness — PBV
But the rebellious have made their habitation in a sunburnt land — Rhm
But rebels inhabit a parched land — ABPS
but rebels must live in the scorching desert — NEB

7. **O God, when thou wentest forth before thy people, when thou didst march through the wilderness;**
God, when you set out at the head of your people,
and marched across the desert — Jerus
When You went out, Lord, among Your people,
when You tramped through the desert — Har
Selah:
Selah [pause, and calmly think of that]! — Amp

8. **The earth shook, the heavens also dropped at the presence of God:**
the earth quaked, the heavens poured down rain,
at the presence of God — RSV
The earth trembled;
Yea, the heavens dissolved in drops before God — DeW
the earth quaked,
the skies rained torrents at the Divine presence — Har
the earth rocked,
the heavens deluged at God's coming — Jerus
even Sinai itself was moved at the presence of God, the God of Israel.
yon Sinai quaked at the presence of God,
the God of Israel — RSV
even Mount Sinai trembled
at the sacred presence of the God of Israel — Har

9. **Thou, O God, didst send a plentiful rain, whereby thou didst confirm thine inheritance, when it was weary.**
Rain in abundance, O God, thou didst shed abroad;
thou didst restore thy heritage as it languished — RSV
A copious rain didst thou pour down, O God;
Thine exhausted and worn-out land thou didst re-establish — AAT
God, you rained a downpour of blessings,
when your heritage was faint and you gave it strength — Jerus

10. **Thy congregation hath dwelt therein:**
For therein Thy living ones were dwelling — DeW
thy flock found a dwelling in it — RSV
thy household were settled there — Mof
Your people inhabited it — Har
your family found a home — Jerus

thou, O God, hast prepared of thy goodness for the poor.
Thou dost provide in thy bounty for the humbled one — O God! — Rhm
In Thy goodness, O God! Thou carest for the poor — DeW
in thy goodness thou didst provide for the distressed — Sept
You provided for the destitute in Your goodness, Lord — Har

11. The Lord gave the word:
The Lord gives the command — RSV
great was the company of those that published it.
great is the host of those who bore the tidings: those who proclaimed it were a mighty company — Har
The herald bands will be a mighty host — Rhm
The women that published the tidings are a great host — ASV
women bear the glad tidings, a vast army: — NAB
The women at home cry out the happy news! — Tay

12. Kings of armies did flee apace: and she that tarried at home divided the spoil.
"The kings of the armies, they flee, they flee!"
The women at home divide the spoil — RSV
"The armies that came to destroy us have fled!" Now all the women of Israel are dividing the booty — Tay
Routed the kings, routed their armies; they have left their spoils for house-wives to carry away — Knox

13. Though ye have lain among the pots, yet shall ye be as the wings of a dove covered with silver, and her feathers with yellow gold.
though they stay among the sheep-folds —
the wings of a dove covered with silver,
its pinions with green gold — RSV
never shone silver so bright on a dove's feathers, never gold so fair on a dove's wings; and you, all the while, resting quiet among the sheep-folds! — Knox
Though you rested among the sheep-folds,
the wings of the dove shone with silver,
and her pinions with a golden hue — NAB
Though you [the slackers] may lie among the sheepfolds [in slothful ease], yet for Israel the wings of a dove covered with silver, its pinions excessively green with gold [are trophies taken from the enemy] — Amp
See them sparkle with jewels of silver and gold, covered all over as wings cover doves! — Tay

14. When the Almighty scattered kings in it, it was white as snow in Salmon.
When the Almighty scattered kings therein,
It was snow-white on Salmon — ABPS
When the Almighty scattered kings there,
snow fell on Zalmon — RSV
When the kings were routed in the field,
'twas like snow falling on Mount Zalmon — Mof
God scattered their armies like snow-flakes melting in the forests of Zalmon — Tay

15. The hill of God is as the hill of Bashan; an high hill as the hill of Bashan.
A mountain of God is the mountain of Bashan;
A high mountain is the mountain of Bashan — ASV
A mighty mountain is the mountain of Bashan,
A mountain of peaks is the mountain of Bashan! — Rhm
O mighty mountain, mountain of Bashan;
O many-peaked mountain, mountain of Bashan! — RSV
A mountain of God is the mountain of Bashan;
a mountain studded with peaks is the Bashan range — Ber
That peak of Bashan, a mountain of God?
Rather, a mountain of pride, that peak of Bashan! — Jerus

16. Why leap ye, ye high hills? this is the hill which God desireth to dwell in; yea, the LORD will dwell in it for ever.
Why look you with envy, O many-peaked mountain,

at the mount which God desired for his abode,
yea, where the LORD will dwell for ever? — RSV
Peaks of pride, have you the right to look down on
a mountain where God has chosen to live,
where Yahweh is going to live for ever? — Jerus
Why do you look enviously, you many-crested hills,
at the mountain which God has chosen for His dwelling?
There the Lord will abide perpetually — Har
Why look you jealously, you rugged mountains,
at the mountain God has chosen for his throne,
where the LORD himself will dwell forever? — NAB
Why look you with grudging and envy, you many-peaked mountains, at the mountain [of the city called Zion] which God has desired for His dwellingplace? Yes, the Lord will dwell in it for ever — Amp

17. The chariots of God are twenty thousand, even thousands of angels: the Lord is among them, as in Sinai, in the holy place.
With mighty chariotry, twice ten thousand,
thousands upon thousands,
the Lord came from Sinai into the holy place — RSV
The chariots of God are myriad, thousands on thousands;
the Lord advances from Sinai to the sanctuary — NAB
The chariots of God are myriads, even thousands upon thousands;
The Lord is among them, as in Sinai, in holiness — JPS

18. Thou hast ascended on high, thou hast led captivity captive: thou hast received gifts for men;
Thou didst ascend the high mount,
leading captives in thy train,
and receiving gifts among men — RSV
You have emerged victorious,
carrying off captives and receiving tribute from men — Har
Thou hast ascended on high
Thou hast led in procession a body of captives
Thou hast received gifts consisting of men — Rhm
You have ascended on high, taken captives,
received men as gifts — NAB
yea, for the rebellious also, that the LORD God might dwell among them.
Yea even the rebellious,
That Yah Elohim might settle down to rest — Rhm
Yea, with the rebellious there is a dwelling for Jehovah God! — DeW
even among the rebellious, that the LORD God may dwell there — RSV
even from rebels,
that the Lord might dwell there — Har
— even rebels; the LORD God enters his dwelling — NAB

19. Blessed be the Lord, who daily loadeth us with benefits, even the God of our salvation.
Blessed be the Lord, who daily beareth our burden, even the God who is our salvation — RV
Blessed be God, who daily beareth our burden,
The Mighty One who is our salvation! — DeW
Blessed be the Lord,
who daily bears us up;
God is our salvation — RSV
May the Lord be blessed for sustaining us daily,
the God who is our deliverance — Har
Blessed be the LORD; day by day He carries us,
the God of our salvation — Ber
Blessed be the Lord day after day,
the God who saves us and bears our burdens! — Jerus
What a glorious Lord! He who daily bears our burdens also gives us our salvation — Tay
Blessed be the Lord now and ever, the God who bears our burdens, and wins us the victory — Knox
Selah.

20. He that is our God is the God of salvation;
The God we have is a God of saving deeds — Rhm
Our God is a God of rescuings — Ber

Our God is a God of deliverance — Knox
God is for us a God of victories — Mof
God is to us a God for deliverances — ABPS
This God of ours is a God who saves — Jerus

and unto GOD the Lord belong the issues from death.

GOD is the Lord, by whom we escape death — PBV
Through Jehovah, our Lord, are the escapes from death — DeW
the LORD, my Lord, controls the passageways of death — NAB
and to GOD, the Lord, belongs escape from death — RSV
to the Lord Yahweh belong the ways of escape from death — Jerus

21. But God shall wound the head of his enemies, and the hairy scalp of such an one as goeth on still in his trespasses.

Yea God himself will smite through the head of his foes, —
The hairy crown of him that is marching on in his guilty deeds — Rhm
Surely God will crush the head of his enemies,
The hairy crown of him that goes on in his trespasses — ABPS
But God will shatter the heads of his enemies,
the hairy crown of him who walks in his guilty ways — RSV
God himself will smite the head of his enemies,
those proud sinners with their flowing locks — NEB
yes, God will shatter the head of his foes,
each long-haired sinner who defies him — Mof
but God will smash the heads of his enemies,
the hairy skull of the man who parades his guilt — Jerus
God will indeed crush the power of His enemies,
and the stubborn will of him who persists in guilty conduct — Har
God will surely crush the head of his foes,
The skull of Seir who goes on in his guilt — AAT

22. The Lord said, I will bring again from Bashan, I will bring my people again from the depths of the sea:

The Lord said, From Bashan will I bring thee back,
I will bring thee back out of the depths of the sea — DeW
The Lord has promised, 'I will bring them back from Bashan,
I will bring them back from the bottom of the sea' — Jerus
The Lord said, I will bring back [your enemies] from Bashan, I will bring them back from the depths of the [Red] Sea — Amp

23. That thy foot may be dipped in the blood of thine enemies, and the tongue of thy dogs in the same.

"that you may bathe your feet in blood.
that the tongues of your dogs may have their portion from the foe" — RSV
"in order that your feet may wade in blood,
and the tongue of your dogs have a share of your enemies" — Har

24. They have seen thy goings, O God; even the goings of my God, my King, in the sanctuary.

Thy solemn processions are seen, O God,
the processions of my God, my King, into the sanctuary — RSV
Your triumphal processions have been seen:
the processions of my God and King in the holy place — Har

25. The singers went before, the players on instruments followed after; among them were the damsels playing with timbrels.

In front are the singers
Behind are the harpers,
In the midst of damsels playing on timbrels: — Rhm
the singers in front, the minstrels last, between them maidens playing timbrels: — RSV
The singers precede, the musicians follow;
between them are maidens playing on tambourines: — Har
singers in front, musicians behind, between them girls with tambourines, — Mof

26. Bless ye God in the congregations,

even the Lord, from the fountain of Israel.

singing, "Bless the Lord God in your choirs,
O Israel's offspring!" — Mof

"Bless God in the great congregation,
the LORD, O you who are Israel's fountain!" — RSV

Bless God in your choirs,
bless the Lord, you who spring from Israel! — Jerus

27. There is little Benjamin with their ruler, the princes of Judah and their council, the princes of Zebulun, and the princes of Naphtali.

There is Benjamin the Diminutive — ruling them
The princes of Judah — their throng,
The princes of Zebulun,
The princes of Naphtali — Rhm

There is Benjamin, the least of them, in the lead,
the princes of Judah in their throng,
the princes of Zebulun, the princes of Naphtali — RSV

In front the Benjamites, so few,
the chiefs of Judah, a great company,
the chiefs of Zebulun and Naphtali! — Mof

There is little Benjamin in the lead [in the procession], the princes of Judah and their company, the princes of Zebulun, and the princes of Naphtali — Amp

The little tribe of Benjamin leads the way. The princes and elders of Judah, and the princes of Zebulun and Naphtali are right behind — Tay

28. Thy God hath commanded thy strength: strengthen, O God, that which thou hast wrought for us.

Summon thy might, O God;
show thy strength, O God, thou who hast wrought for us — RSV

Muster Your resources, Lord;
display Your power, my God, since You have worked on our behalf — Har

29. Because of thy temple at Jerusalem shall kings bring presents unto thee.

30. Rebuke the company of spearmen, the multitude of the bulls, with the calves of the people, till every one submit himself with pieces of silver: scatter thou the people that delight in war.

Rebuke the beasts that dwell among the reeds,
the herd of bulls with the calves of the peoples.
Trample under foot those who lust after tribute;
scatter the peoples who delight in war — RSV

Rebuke the wild beasts of the reeds,
The herds of strong cattle, with the steers of the nations,
That come crouching with bars of silver;
He hath scattered the nations that have pleasure in war — DeW

Rebuke the Beasts of the Reeds,
that herd of bulls, those calves, that people,
until, humbled, they bring gold and silver.
Scatter those warmongering pagans! — Jerus

Rebuke that beast which inhabits the papyrus reeds,
the conclave of princes which dominates the offspring of the people;
trample down those who crave for tribute,
and rout the nations who delight in fighting — Har

Check that Brute of a Nile-power,
the bullocks and steers of pagans;
trample down crafty policy,
rout all the races that rejoice in war — Mof

Rebuke the wild beasts dwelling among the reeds [in Egypt], the herd of bulls [the leaders], with the calves of the peoples; trample under foot those who lust for tribute money; scatter the peoples who delight in war — Amp

31. Princes shall come out of Egypt; Ethiopia shall soon stretch out her hands unto God.

Coming on are the magnates from Egypt;
With gift-laden hands Ethiopia hasteth unto God — DeW

Let nobles come from Egypt;
let Ethiopia extend its hands to God — NAB

till even Egypt sends ambassadors,
and Ethiopia hurries to submit to God — Mof

Let bronze be brought from Egypt; let Ethiopia hasten to stretch out her hands to God — RSV

Rich tribute will come from Egypt; Ethiopia will eagerly extend her hands to God — Har

Ambassadors will come from Egypt, Ethiopia will stretch out her hands to God — Jerus

32. **Sing unto God, ye kingdoms of the earth; O sing praises unto the Lord;**

Sing unto God, ye kingdoms of the earth;
Make melody upon the harp to the Lord — DeW

Selah:

Selah [pause, and calmly think of that]! — Amp

33. **To him that rideth upon the heavens of heavens, which were of old;**

to him who rides in the heavens, the ancient heavens — RSV

To him who rides upon the most ancient heavens — AAT

to Him who soars in the ancient heavens — Har

lo, he doth send out his voice, and that a mighty voice.

Behold, He will send forth His voice in mighty sound — Sprl

Lo, He uttereth His voice — it is a voice of strength! — DeW

Listen to him shouting, to his thundering — Jerus

See how He thunders out a crashing roar — Har

34. **Ascribe ye strength unto God: his excellency is over Israel, and his strength is in the clouds.**

Give glory to God,
majestic over Israel,
mighty in the skies — Har

Ascribe power to God,
whose majesty is over Israel,
and his power is in the skies — RSV

Ascribe all might to God, Israel's High God,
Israel's pride and might throned in the skies — NEB

35. **O God, thou art terrible out of thy holy places: the God of Israel is he that giveth strength and power unto his people.**

Terrible art thou, O God out of thy holy places,
Mighty One of Israel;
He that gives strength and peace to the people — ABPS

O God, wonderful art thou in thy holy places: even the God of Israel, he will give strength and power unto his people — PBV

Awe-inspiring art Thou, O God, from Thy sanctuary;
the God of Israel,
who bestows strength and fulness of might to His people — Ber

Awesome in his sanctuary is God,
the God of Israel;
he gives power and strength to his people — NAB

Blessed be God.

PSALM 69

To the chief Musician upon Shoshannim, A Psalm of David.

To the Chief Musician, set to the tune of Lilies . . . — Amp

1. **Save me, O God; for the waters are come in unto my soul.**

Save me, O God!
For the waters have come up to my neck — RSV

Save me, O God,
for the waters are threatening my life — Mof

2. **I sink in deep mire, where there is no standing:**

I have sunk in a deep swamp
where there is no place to stand — Rhm

I am sunk down into deep mire, and there is no support beneath — Sept

I am like one who sticks fast in deep mire, with no ground under his feet — Knox

I am come into deep waters, where the floods overflow me.

I am come into the depth of the sea, and a tempest hath overwhelmed me — Sept

I have come into deep water,
and the current is sweeping me away — Har

I have stepped into deep water
and the waves are washing over me — Jerus

3. **I am weary of my crying: my throat is dried:**

I am worn out from crying;

my throat is parched — Har
I have cried until I am exhausted — Ber
mine eyes fail while I wait for my God.
Mine eyes have become dim, through waiting for my God — Rhm
my eyes are strained, looking for my God — Jerus
my eyes are swollen with weeping, waiting for my God to act — Tay

4. They that hate me without a cause are more than the hairs of mine head:
I have more men who hate me wantonly
than hairs upon my head — Mof
Countless as the hairs on my head are my wanton enemies — Knox
they that would destroy me, being mine enemies wrongfully, are mighty:
Firmer than my bones
Are they who are my foes for false cause — Rhm
mighty are those who would destroy me,
those who attack me with lies — RSV
Those who wish to destroy me are powerful;
they are my enemies wrongfully — Ber
then I restored that which I took not away.
they force me to repay
what I never extorted — Mof
Should I restore that which I took not away? — JPS
Must I restore what I did not steal? — NAB
How can I make restitution for that which I did not steal? — Har
(They ask me to give back what I never took.) — Jerus
They demand that I be punished for what I didn't do — Tay

5. O God, thou knowest my foolishness; and my sins are not hid from thee.
O God, thou hast known my folly,
And my wrong-doings from thee have not been hid — Rhm
O God, thou knowest my rash doings, no fault of mine is hidden from thy sight — Knox
O God, thou knowest my foolishness;
and my guilt is not hidden from thee — AAT
Thou knowest my blundering;
my guilt is evident to Thee — Ber
O God, you know so well how stupid I am, and you know all my sins — Tay

6. Let not them that wait on thee, O Lord GOD of hosts, be ashamed for my sake:
Let not them that wait for thee be put to shame through me, O Lord Jehovah of hosts — ASV
may naught befall me that would disconcert
those who wait for thee, O Lord God of hosts — Mof
Let not those who hope in thee be put to shame through me,
O Lord GOD of hosts — RSV
Lord God of armies,
do not let those who trust in You be discredited on my account — Har
O Lord God of the armies of heaven, don't let me be a stumbling block to those who trust in you — Tay
let not those that seek thee be confounded for my sake, O God of Israel.
Let not those that seek thee be brought to dishonor through me, O God of Israel — ASV
may naught befall me that would disappoint
thy worshippers, O God of Israel — Mof

7. Because for thy sake I have borne reproach; shame hath covered my face.
And why? for thy sake have I suffered reproof; shame hath covered my face — PBV
But for Thy sake I bear reviling,
And disgrace covereth my face — DeW
'Tis for thy sake that I have suffered taunts,
had insults cover me with shame — Mof
For Your sake I have endured abuse;
shame has spread over my face — Har
Because I have been humiliated for Thy sake,
confusion has covered my face — Ber

8. I am become a stranger unto my brethren, and an alien unto my mother's children.

I have become estranged from my brethren;
Yea, I am an alien to my mother's sons — DeW

I have become an outcast to my brothers,
a stranger to my mother's sons — NAB

9. For the zeal of thine house hath eaten me up;

Because zeal for Thine house hath consumed me — DeW

'Tis zeal for thy house that wears me away — Mof

Was it not jealousy for the honour of thy house that consumed me? — Knox

I am on fire with passion for your house — Bas

Enthusiasm for Your house has devoured me — Har

My zeal for God and his work burns hot within me — Tay

and the reproaches of them that reproached thee are fallen upon me.

The reviling of those that reviled Thee, hath fallen upon me — DeW

And the abuse of them that abuse thee has fallen on me — AAT

and taunts against thee fall on me — Mof

and the insults of those who insult thee have fallen on me — RSV

was it not uttered against thee, the reproach I bore? — Knox

And because I advocate your cause, your enemies insult me even as they insult you — Tay

10. When I wept, and chastened my soul with fasting, that was to my reproach.

I wept, and chastened myself with fasting, and that was turned to my reproof — PBV

When I have humbled my soul with fasting
Then hath it turned to my reproach — Rhm

When I bowed down my soul with fasting; it furnished occasion for reproaching me — Sept

When I fasted, and wept away my soul,
I brought upon me their sharp reproach — DeW

When I chastened my soul with fasting,
men jeered at me — Mof

My bitter weeping, and my going without food, were turned to my shame — Bas

What more could I do? I humbled myself before them by fasting; and that, too, was matter for finding fault — Knox

If I mortify myself with fasting,
they make this a pretext for insulting me — Jerus

How they scoff and mock me when I mourn and fast before the Lord! — Tay

11. I made sackcloth also my garment; and I became a proverb to them.

I put on sackcloth also, and they jested upon me — PBV

When I made sackcloth my clothing,
I became a byword unto them — ASV

When I put on sackcloth for my clothing,
I became a laughingstock to them — Ber

If I assume sackcloth as my clothing,
I become a joke to them — AAT

When I put on the clothing of grief,
they said evil of me — Bas

12. They that sit in the gate speak against me;

Those that sit in the market-places whisper of me — DeW

Idlers in the market-place taunt me — Knox

They who sit at the gate gossip about me — NAB

Those in positions of authority criticize me — Har

and I was the song of the drunkards.

and the drunkards make songs about me — RSV

and the drunkards make me the butt of their songs — NAB

13. But as for me, my prayer is unto thee, O LORD, in an acceptable time: O God, in the multitude of thy mercy hear me, in the truth of thy salvation.

14. Deliver me out of the mire, and let me not sink: let me be delivered from them that hate me, and out of the deep waters.

But as for me, my prayer is to thee, O Jehovah;
At a time of acceptance, O God in abundance of thy mercy,

Answer me in the faithfulness of thy salvation.
Rescue me out of the mire, and let me not sink;
Let me be rescued from them that hate me,
And from the depths of waters — ABPS

But I — O Jehovah! my prayer is unto Thee,
In a time of favour, O God! through Thine abundant lovingkindness:
Answer me in Thy faithful, saving power.
Snatch me out of the mire, and let me not sink;
Let me escape from my foes, and out of the deep waters — DeW

But as for me, I pray to thee;
in thy great generosity, O God, do thou accept me;
answer me with thy loyal aid,
save me from sinking in the mud,
from the deep waters of hatred — Mof

But as for me, my prayer is to thee, O LORD.
At an acceptable time, O God,
in the abundance of thy steadfast love answer me.
With thy faithful help rescue me from sinking in the mire;
let me be delivered from my enemies and from the deep waters — RSV

For my part, I am praying to You, Lord God;
answer me, my God, in Your abundant mercy,
when the time is ripe.
Rescue me from the swamp by Your saving truth,
so that I do not become submerged;
let me be delivered from those who hate me,
and from the deep waters — Har

But I lift up this prayer to thee, O LORD:
accept me now in thy great love,
answer me with thy sure deliverance, O God.
Rescue me from the mire, do not let me sink;
let me be rescued from the muddy depths — NEB

15. Let not the waterflood overflow me, neither let the deep swallow me up, and let not the pit shut her mouth upon me.

Let not the flood of waters overwhelm me,
Nor the abyss swallow me up;
And let not the grave close upon me its mouth — DeW

let not the flood sweep over me,
let not the depths drown me;
let not death close over me — Mof

Do not let the current sweep me away;
do not allow the deep to engulf me,
nor the grave to close over me — Har

so that no flood may carry me away,
no abyss swallow me up,
no deep close over me — NEB

16. Hear me, O LORD; for thy lovingkindness is good:

. . . for Thy grace is good — Ber

. . . for thy steadfast love is good — RSV

Answer me, Lord God, for Your mercy is gratifying — Har

Hear and answer me, O Lord; for Your loving-kindness is sweet and comforting — Amp

Answer me, O LORD, in the goodness of thy unfailing love — NEB

turn unto me according to the multitude of thy tender mercies.

According to the abounding of thy compassions turn thou towards me — Rhm

In Thine abundant mercies turn unto me — DeW

in thy vast pity turn to me — Mof

in your great tenderness turn to me — Jerus

turn towards me in thy great affection — NEB

17. And hide not thy face from thy servant; for I am in trouble: hear me speedily.

Hide not thy face from thy servant;
for I am in distress, make haste to answer me — RSV

do not hide your face from your servant,
quick, I am in trouble, answer me — Jerus

18. Draw nigh unto my soul, and redeem it:

come to me, rescue my life — Mof

Fight for me and deliver me — AAT

Draw near in my distress, and grant deliverance — Knox

Come to me, and rescue me — Har

deliver me because of mine enemies.
set me free because of my enemies! — RSV
as an answer for my enemies, redeem me — NAB
free me from my foes — Ber
ransom me, for I have many enemies — NEB

19. Thou hast known my reproach, and my shame, and my dishonour: mine adversaries are all before thee.
Thou knowest my reviling, my shame, and my disgrace;
Mine adversaries are all before Thee — DeW
Thou knowest my abuse,
And my shame and disgrace;
All my foes are before thee — AAT
Thou knowest my reproach,
and my shame and my dishonor;
my foes are all known to thee — RSV
Thou knowest how I am taunted, shamed, dishonoured,
my foes are plain to thee — Mof
You are aware how I am affronted, disgraced and insulted;
my opponents are well-known to you — Har

20. Reproach hath broken my heart; and I am full of heaviness:
Reproach hath broken my heart and I am weak — Rhm
Their reviling hath broken my heart; I am sick — DeW
Insults have broken my heart,
so that I am in despair — RSV
Abuse has broken my spirit, and I am ill — Har
Reproach has broken my heart and I feel depressed — Ber

and I looked for some to take pity, but there was none;
And I looked for pity, but there was none — ABPS
And I looked for some to show compassion, but there was none — JPS
And I look for sympathy, but there is none — AAT
I had hoped for sympathy, but in vain — Jerus

and for comforters, but I found none.

21. They gave me also gall for my meat;
They gave me also gall for my food — ASV
But they put in my food — poison! — Rhm
They gave me poison for food — RSV

and in my thirst they gave me vinegar to drink.
and gave me sour wine to drink when I was thirsty — Har
and bitter wine for my drink — Bas

22. Let their table become a snare before them:
Let their table before them become a snare — Rhm
May the table they spread be their own ruin — Mof
May their own tables cause their downfall — Har
May their own table prove a trap for them — Jerus

and that which should have been for their welfare, let it become a trap.
And when they are in peace, let it become a trap — ASV
When they are in security, let it become a trap — DeW
let their sacrificial feasts be a trap — RSV
let their feasts become a net to take them — Bas
and their thank-offerings become a trap — Har
and their plentiful supplies, a snare! — Jerus
and their sacred feasts lure them to their ruin — NEB

23. Let their eyes be darkened, that they see not;
Let their eyes become too dim to see — Rhm
may their eyes be blurred and blind — Mof
May their eyesight fail, so that they cannot see — Har

and make their loins continually to shake.
and bow down their neck continually — Sept
And let their loins tremble continually — DeW
may their thighs be all a-quiver! — Mof
make their bodies tremble incessantly — Har
strike their loins with chronic palsy! — Jerus
and make their backs continually to bend — Lam
and keep their backs always feeble — NAB

24. Pour out thine indignation upon them,

and let thy wrathful anger take hold of them.

Pour out thine indignation upon them, and let the fierceness of thine anger overtake them — RV

Pour out over them thine indignation, And let the glow of thine anger overtake them — Rhm

Pour out thy anger upon them, let them be overtaken by the tide of thy vengeance — Knox

Flood them with Your anger, and let Your violent fury engulf them — Har

Vent thine anger on them, may thy burning fury seize them — Mof

25. **Let their habitation be desolate; and let none dwell in their tents.**

Let their encampment become desolate, In their tents be there none to dwell — Rhm

let their dwelling-place be deserted, their tents for ever uninhabited — Knox

may their camp be reduced to ruin, and their tents left unoccupied — Jerus

26. **For they persecute him whom thou hast smitten; and they talk to the grief of those whom thou hast wounded.**

For they persecute the one whom You have afflicted, and increase the agony of those whom You have injured — Har

For they pursue and persecute him whom You have smitten, and they gossip about those whom You have wounded, [adding] to their grief and pain — Amp

27. **Add iniquity unto their iniquity: and let them not come into thy righteousness.**

Add guilt to their guilt, And let them not enter into thy justification — AAT

Let them fall from one wickedness to another, and not come into thy righteousness — PBV

Lay punishment on their iniquity, And let them not enter into thy righteousness — Rhm

Punish them according to their iniquity; And let them not come into Thy righteousness — DeW

Punish them for their crime, exclude them from thy favours — Mof

Add to them punishment upon punishment; may they have no acquittal from thee — RSV

Pile their sins high and do not overlook them — Tay

28. **Let them be blotted out of the book of the living, and not be written with the righteous.**

Let them be blotted from the book of life, And with the righteous let them not be written — ABPS

blot them from the Book of life, blot their name from the list of the upright! — Mof

Let them be obliterated from the record of the living, and not enrolled with the virtuous — Har

29. **But I am poor and sorrowful: let thy salvation, O God, set me up on high.**

As for me, when I am poor and in heaviness, thy help, O God, shall lift me up — PBV

But as for me, O God! in suffering and sorrow, Let Thy saving power set me on high — DeW

But I am afflicted and in pain; let thy salvation, O God, set me on high! — RSV

But though I am afflicted and in distress, Your deliverance, my God, will restore me — Har

But by thy saving power, O God, lift me high above my pain and my distress — NEB

30. **I will praise the name of God with a song, and will magnify him with thanksgiving.**

then I will praise God's name in song and glorify him with thanksgiving — NEB

31. **This also shall please the LORD better than an ox or bullock that hath horns and hoofs.**

And it will please Jehovah better than an ox, Or a bullock that hath horns and hoofs — ASV

'twill please the Eternal more than any bull,
or any bullock that has horns and hoofs — Mof

32. The humble shall see this, and be glad: and your heart shall live that seek God.

The humble shall consider this, and be glad: seek ye after God, and your souls shall live — PBV

The meek have seen it, and are glad: Ye that seek after God, let your heart live — ASV

The suffering will see, and be glad; Ye that seek after God, let your heart revive! — DeW

Mark all this and be glad, O folk forlorn,
take heart, O worshippers of God — Mof

Let the oppressed see it and be glad; you who seek God, let your hearts revive — RSV

May the humble see it and rejoice; let those who are searching for God be revived in spirit — Har

33. For the LORD heareth the poor, and despiseth not his prisoners.

For a Hearkener to the needy is Yahweh,
And his prisoners hath he not despised — Rhm

For the ears of the Lord are open to the poor, and he takes thought for his prisoners — Bas

For the LORD hears the needy,
and does not despise his own that are in bonds — RSV

For the LORD hears the poor,
and his own who are in bonds he spurns not — NAB

Yahweh will always hear those who are in need,
will never scorn his captive people — Jerus

34. Let the heaven and earth praise him, the seas, and every thing that moveth therein.

The heavens and the earth will praise him,
The sea and all that stirs therein — AAT

Let heaven and earth acclaim him, the oceans and all that moves in them! — Jerus

35. For God will save Zion, and will build the cities of Judah:

Because God delivers Zion,
And rebuilds the cities of Judah — AAT

that they may dwell there, and have it in possession.

that people may dwell there and occupy it — Har

So shall men dwell there and possess it — Rhm

and his servants shall dwell there and possess it — RSV

36. The seed also of his servants shall inherit it: and they that love his name shall dwell therein.

and the descendants of his servants shall inherit it,
and those who love his name shall inhabit it — NAB

The children of His followers shall inherit it,
and those who cherish His name shall live there — Har

PSALM 70

To the chief Musician, A Psalm of David, to bring to remembrance.

1. Make haste, O God, to deliver me;

[Be pleased] O God to rescue me — Rhm

O God, — to my rescue — ABPS

Rescue me, my God — Har

make haste to help me, O LORD.

O Yahweh, to help me — make haste — Rhm

2. Let them be ashamed and confounded that seek after my soul:

Let them turn pale and then at once blush
Who are seeking my life — Rhm

Let those who desire to kill me be shamed and disgraced — Har

let them be turned backward, and put to confusion, that desire my hurt.

Let them draw back and be confounded,
Who are taking pleasure in my misfortune — Rhm

Let them be turned back and brought to dishonor
who desire my hurt! — RSV

may those who wish me adversity be routed and dishonored — Har

Down with them! Disgrace on those who enjoy my misfortune! — Jerus

3. **Let them be turned back for a reward of their shame that say, Aha, aha.**

Let them for their reward be soon brought to shame, that cry over me, There! there! — PBV

Let them who say to me, Ha! Ha! be turned back suddenly, covered with shame — Sept

Thwarted and appalled be they who taunt and scoff! — Mof

May they be aghast with shame,
those who say to me, 'Aha! Aha!' — Jerus

4. **Let all those that seek thee rejoice and be glad in thee:**

but let all who seek thee
be jubilant and rejoice in thee — NEB

But fill the followers of God with joy! — Tay

and let such as love thy salvation say continually, Let God be magnified.

May those who love thy saving help have ever cause to say,
"All hail to God!" — Mof

May those who love thy salvation
say evermore, "God is great!" — RSV

To all who love your saving power give constant cause to say, 'God is great!' — Jerus

and let those who long for thy saving help ever cry,
'All glory to God!' — NEB

Let those who love your salvation exclaim, "What a wonderful God he is!" — Tay

5. **But I am poor and needy: make haste unto me, O God:**

And I — suffering and needy —
O God, make haste to me! — DeW

To me, poor wretch,
come quickly, God! — Jerus

But I am in deep trouble. Rush to my aid — Tay

thou art my help and my deliverer; O LORD, make no tarrying.

My help and my deliverer art thou;
O Jehovah, do not delay — ABPS

Thou art my champion and my deliverer; Lord, do not delay thy coming — Knox

My helper, my saviour, Yahweh,
come without delay! — Jerus

PSALM 71

1. **In thee, O LORD, do I put my trust: let me never be put to confusion.**

To thee, O God, I turn for succour; may I never be disappointed! — Knox

In thee, O LORD, do I take refuge;
let me never be put to shame! — RSV

In you, Yahweh, I take shelter;
never let me be disgraced — Jerus

2. **Deliver me in thy righteousness, and cause me to escape:**

Deliver me in thy righteousness, and rescue me — ASV

incline thine ear unto me, and save me.

3. **Be thou my strong habitation, whereunto I may continually resort: thou hast given commandment to save me;**

Become to me a rock-dwelling for continual resort,
Thou that hast commanded that I be saved! — DeW

Be thou to me a protecting God, and a place of strength to save me — Sept

Let me find in thee a rock-fastness, a citadel of defence — Knox

Be thou to me a rock of refuge,
a strong fortress, to save me — RSV

Be a sheltering rock for me,
a walled fortress to save me! — Jerus

Be my rock of refuge, a stronghold to give me safety — NAB

for thou art my rock and my fortress.

for thou art my house of defence, and my castle — PBV

For my mountain crag and my stronghold thou art — Rhm

You are my refuge and my fortress — Har

4. **Deliver me, O my God, out of the hand of the wicked, out of the hand of the unrighteous and cruel man.**

Oh my God deliver me
From the hand of the lawless one,
From the clutch of the perverse and ruthless one — Rhm

O my God, rescue me out of the hand of the wicked,
Out of the grasp of the unrighteous

and ruthless man — JPS

5. For thou art my hope, O Lord GOD: thou art my trust from my youth.

For thou, O Lord GOD, art the thing that I long for: thou art my hope, even from my youth — PBV

For thou art my hope, O Lord Jehovah:
Thou art my trust from my youth — ASV

6. By thee have I been holden up from the womb: thou art he that took me out of my mother's bowels: my praise shall be continually of thee.

On thee have I been sustained from the womb;
Thou art he that took me from the bowels of my mother.
Of thee is my praise continually — ABPS

upon thee I have leaned from the womb: from my birth thou art my protector; thou art the constant subject of my song — Sept

Upon Thee have I been stayed from my birth;
Through Thy help my mother bare me:
My praise is continually of Thee — DeW

Upon thee I have leaned from my birth;
Thou art he who took me from my mother's womb.
My praise is continually of thee — RSV

I have relied on you since I was born,
you have been my portion from my mother's womb,
and the constant theme of my praise — Jerus

7. I am as a wonder unto many; but thou art my strong refuge.

Through thee, my strength and shelter,
I am a marvel to many — Mof

Men stare at me now as a strange portent, so signal the protection thou hast given me — Knox

To many I have seemed an enigma,
but you are my firm refuge — Jerus

My success — at which so many stand amazed — is because you are my mighty protector — Tay

8. Let my mouth be filled with thy praise and with thy honour all the day.

My mouth shall be filled with thy praise,
With thy majesty, all the day — ABPS

Let my mouth be filled with praise, that I may celebrate thy glory — thy majesty, all the day long — Sept

my lips shall be full of thy praise,
singing thy glory all the day long — Mof

My speech will be full of Your praise,
and Your magnificence all day long — Har

My mouth is full of your praises,
filled with your splendor all day long — Jerus

9. Cast me not off in the time of old age; forsake me not when my strength faileth.

Thou wilt not cast me off when oppressed with years.
When my strength is consumed Thou wilt not forsake me — Sprl

Do not give me up when I am old;
be my help even when my strength is gone — Bas

Do not reject me now I am old,
nor desert me now my strength is failing — Jerus

10. For mine enemies speak against me; and they that lay wait for my soul take counsel together,

For my enemies malign me,
and those who lie in ambush for me deliberate together — Har

for murderous foes are plotting,
my enemies say of me — Mof

11. Saying, God hath forsaken him: persecute and take him; for there is none to deliver him.

saying, "God hath forsaken him; pursue and take him, for he hath no deliverer" — Sept

They say, "God has forsaken him;
pursue and seize him,
for there is no one to rescue him" — NAB

and whisper, God has abandoned him; now is the time to overtake and seize him; no one can bring him rescue now — Knox

12. O God, be not far from me: O my God, make haste for my help.

13. Let them be confounded and consumed that are adversaries to my soul;

May my accusers be put to shame and consumed — RSV

Let those come to shame and perish,
That assail my life — DeW

Let all my rivals be shamed and destroyed — Har

let them be covered with reproach and dishonour that seek my hurt.

Let those be covered with scorn and disgrace,
That would fain destroy me — DeW

may insults and dishonour cover all who would injure me! — Mof

May they be covered with abuse and shame who seek to injure me — AAT

may those who are anxious to injure me
have contempt and disgrace poured upon them — Har

14. But I will hope continually, and will yet praise thee more and more.

But as for me, I will hope continually,
And will praise Thee yet more and more — JPS

As for me, I hope on and on,
I praise thee more than ever — Mof

15. My mouth shall shew forth thy righteousness and thy salvation all the day;

My mouth recounteth Thy righteous deeds,
And all the day long Thy deliverances — DeW

My mouth will tell of thy righteous acts,
of thy deeds of salvation all the day — RSV

My mouth shall declare your justice,
day by day your salvation — NAB

all day long thy righteousness,
thy saving acts, shall be upon my lips — NEB

for I know not the numbers thereof.

for their number is past my knowledge — RSV

though never can I tell it to the full — Mof

though I know not their extent — NAB

16. I will go in the strength of the Lord GOD: I will make mention of thy righteousness, even of thine only.

I will enter into the mighty doings of My Lord — Yahweh,
I will make mention of thy righteousness — thine alone — Rhm

I will come with the mighty acts of the Lord Jehovah:
I will make mention of thy righteousness, even of thine only — ASV

I will recite the great deeds of the Lord,
and praise thy faithful aid — and only thine — Mof

I will treat of the mighty works of the Lord;
O GOD, I will tell of your singular justice — NAB

I will go in the strength of the LORD God; I will make mention of Thy righteousness, Thine alone — Ber

I will come in the power of Yahweh to commemorate your righteousness, yours alone — Jerus

Though I should attain to great age, Lord God,
I could only continue to acknowledge Your righteousness — Har

17. O God, thou hast taught me from my youth: and hitherto have I declared thy wondrous works.

Thou hast been teaching it from my youth, O God,
and I have ever told thy wondrous deeds — Mof

18. Now also when I am old and grayheaded, O God, forsake me not;

And now that I am old and gray,
O God, forsake me not — NAB

So then, even in old age,
and when I am grey-headed, my God,
do not renounce me — Har

until I have shewed thy strength unto this generation, and thy power, to every one that is to come.

that I may tell the rising generation of thy strength and thy might — Mof

So that I may tell of thy mighty arm to the generations,
To all that are to come — AAT

till I proclaim thy might
to all the generations to come — RSV

19. Thy righteousness also, O God, is very high, who hast done great things: O God, who is like unto thee!

Thy power[21] and thy righteousness, O God
reach the high heavens.
Thou who hast done great things,
O God, who is like thee? — RSV

Thy faithful aid is high as heaven, O God,
for great things thou hast done;
who is like thee, O God? — Mof

For Your righteousness, my God, ex-

[21]"Thy power" is read with verse 19 in RSV.

tends to the heavens above;
You have performed great deeds.
Who is Your equal? — Har

20. Thou, which hast shewed me great and sore troubles, shalt quicken me again, and shalt bring me up again from the depths of the earth.

Thou who hast let us see many distresses and misfortunes
Wilt again bring us to life,
And out of the resounding depths of the earth wilt again raise us up — Rhm

Thou that hast shown us distresses, many and grievous,
Wilt restore us unto life;
Yea, out of the depths of the earth,
Thou wilt bring us up again — DeW

O thou who hast made us see many dangers and disasters,
Do thou quicken us again,
And from the depths of the earth bring us up again — AAT

O what afflictions many and sore hast thou shewn me! But thou has returned and quickened me; and brought me up again from the depths of the earth — Sept

21. Thou shalt increase my greatness, and comfort me on every side.

Thou wilt increase My happiness, and encompass Me with consolation — Sprl

thou wilt add to our honour,
and comfort us once more — Mof

Increase Thou my greatness,
And return to comfort me — DeW

prolong my old age, and once more comfort me — Jerus

You will give me greater honor than before, and turn again and comfort me — Tay

22. I will also praise thee with the psaltery, even thy truth, O my God:

I will give praise to you with instruments of music, O my God, for you are true — Bas

So shall I praise thee on the lute for loyalty to me, my God — Mof

I will also praise thee with the harp for thy faithfulness, O my God — RSV

I promise I will thank you on the lyre,
my ever-faithful God — Jerus

unto thee will I sing with the harp, O thou Holy One of Israel.

I make melody to Thee with the harp,
Thou Holy One of Israel — DeW

I will make music unto thee with a lyre,
Thou holy one of Israel — Rhm

I will play the harp in your honour,
Holy One of Israel — Jerus

23. My lips shall greatly rejoice when I sing unto thee;

My lips shall make a joyful noise
When I make music unto thee — Rhm

My lips sing with joy while I harp to Thee — DeW

My lips shall ring with joy and praise — Mof

and my soul, which thou hast redeemed.

and so will my soul, which You have redeemed — Har

24. My tongue also shall talk of thy righteousness all the day long:

And my tongue will talk of thy righteous help
all the day long — RSV

Day in, day out, I will repeat the story of thy faithfulness — Knox

and my tongue day by day shall discourse on your justice — NAB

Even my tongue all the day shall softly utter thy righteousness — Rhm

for they are confounded, for they are brought unto shame, that seek my hurt.

For they have turned pale — for they have blushed
Who were seeking my hurt — Rhm

what shame fell, what confusion, on the men who sought to wrong me — Knox

for they have been put to shame and disgraced
who sought to do me hurt — RSV

How shamed and how disgraced are those who sought to harm me! — NAB

PSALM 72

A Psalm for Solomon.
A Psalm of Solomon — RSV

1. Give the king thy judgments, O God, and thy righteousness unto the king's son.
O God! thy justice give unto the king,
And thy righteousness unto the son of a king — Rhm
Give Thy judgments, O God! unto the king;
Thy righteousness to him of royal birth — DeW
Inspire the king, O God, with thine own justice,
endow his majesty with thine own equity — Mof
Endow the king with Your authority, Lord,
and the royal son with Your fairness — Har
O God, help the king to judge as you would, and help his son to walk in godliness — Tay

2. He shall judge thy people with righteousness, and thy poor with judgment.
May he judge
Thy people with righteousness;
And thine oppressed ones with justice — Rhm
Let him rule Thy people in uprightness,
And Thy sufferers with equity — DeW
that he may judge Your people impartially,
dispensing justice to the afflicted — Har

3. The mountains shall bring peace to the people, and the little hills, by righteousness.
May the mountains bring peace to the people,
And the hills [be laden] with righteousness — Rhm
Let the mountains bear blessing to the people;
And the hills be fruitful in righteousness — DeW
The mountains shall bring peace to the people,
and the hills, through [the general establishment of] righteousness — Amp
May the mountains and hills flourish in prosperity because of his good reign — Tay
May hills and mountains afford thy people
peace and prosperity in righteousness — NEB
may justice bring welfare to the people,
from the very hills and mountains! — Mof

4. He shall judge the poor of the people, he shall save the children of the needy, and shall break in pieces the oppressor.
He shall plead for the oppressed of the people;
He shall save the children of the needy;
And He shall crush the oppressor — Sprl
May he Vindicate the oppressed of the people
Bring deliverance to the children of the needy, and
Crush the oppressor — Rhm
May he prove the champion of the weak,
may he deliver the forlorn,
and crush oppressors! — Mof

5. They shall fear thee as long as the sun and moon endure, throughout all generations.
They shall revere thee as long as the sun and moon endure, throughout all generations — Lam
May he endure as long as the sun lasts,
and while the moon shines — for all time — Har
He shall live as long as the sun endures,
long as the moon, age after age — NEB

6. He shall come down like rain upon the mown grass: as showers that water the earth.
Let him come down
Like rain on fields to be mown,
Like myriad drops on land to be reaped — Rhm
Let him come down as rain upon the meadow,
As showers that water the earth — DeW
May his rule be like rainfall on the meadows,
like showers that water the land! — Mof

May the reign of this son of mine be as gentle and fruitful as the springtime rains upon the grass — like showers that water the earth! — Tay

7. In his days shall the righteous flourish; and abundance of peace so long as the moon endureth.

May righteousness in his days blossom forth,
And abundance of peace till there be no moon — Rhm

In his days, let the righteous flourish;
And peace abound till the moon faileth — DeW

May fairness abound in his time,
and peace flourish, till the moon shall exist no longer — Har

Justice shall flower in his days,
and profound peace, till the moon be no more — NAB

8. He shall have dominion also from sea to sea, and from the river unto the ends of the earth.

So let him have dominion
From sea to sea,
And from the River ["Euphrates"] unto the ends of the earth — Rhm

From sea to sea may his domain extend,
from the Euphrates to the earth's far end! — Mof

9. They that dwell in the wilderness shall bow before him; and his enemies shall lick the dust.

They of the desert shall crouch before him,
And his enemies shall lick the dust — ABPS

Before him let the men of the desert kneel,
But as for his foes the dust let them lick — Rhm

May his foes bow down before him,
and his enemies lick the dust! — RSV

May his enemies bow before him;
may his rivals grovel in the dust — Har

10. The kings of Tarshish and of the isles shall bring presents: the kings of Sheba and Seba shall offer gifts.

Let the kings of Tarshish and the isles pay tribute;
The kings of Sheba and Seba bring gifts — DeW

May kings of the west and the seaboard
pay tribute to him,
may kings of the south and of Arabia
offer him presents — Mof

11. Yea, all kings shall fall down before him: all nations shall serve him.

Yea, all kings shall prostrate themselves before him . . . — JPS

All kings shall pay him homage . . . — NAB

Yea, let all kings bow down to him;
Let all the nations serve him — DeW

May all monarchs pay homage to him,
and all nations be his vassals — Har

12. For he shall deliver the needy when he crieth; the poor also, and him that hath no helper.

For he will rescue the needy, crying for help,
The poor, and him that has no helper — ABPS

For he will deliver the needy that crieth,
The sufferer, and him that hath none to aid — DeW

For he shall rescue the poor man when he cries out,
and the afflicted when he has no one to help him — NAB

For he shall rescue the needy from their rich oppressors,
the distressed who have no protector — NEB

For he saves the forlorn who cry to him,
the weak and helpless — Mof

13. He shall spare the poor and needy, and shall save the souls of the needy.

He will have pity on the weak and needy,
And will save the souls of the needy — ABPS

He will pity the wretched and needy,
And the lives of the needy will he save — DeW

He is sympathetic towards the frail and needy,
and saves the life of the poor — Har

14. He shall redeem their soul from deceit and violence: and precious shall their blood be in his sight.

From extortion and from violence he will redeem their soul;
And precious is their blood in his eyes — ABPS

rescuing them from outrage and oppression —

they are not cheap to him — Mof
He delivers them from wrong and violence,
for they are valuable in his estimation — Har
he will redeem their lives from exploitation and outrage,
their lives will be precious in his sight — Jerus

15. And he shall live, and to him shall be given of the gold of Sheba: prayer also shall be made for him continually; and daily shall he be praised.
Let him live then!
And be there given unto him of the gold of Sheba, —
let prayer also be offered for him continually,
All the day let him be blessed — Rhm
and he shall live, and to him shall be given of the gold of Arabia; and prayer shall be made for him continually: and he will be blessed all the day long — Sept
Long may he live,
to receive gold from Arabia!
For him may ceaseless prayer be made,
and all day long may he be blessed! — Mof
Long life shall be his, and gold from Arabia shall be given him; men will pray for him continually, bless his name evermore — Knox

16. There shall be an handful of corn in the earth upon the top of the mountains; the fruit thereof shall shake like Lebanon: and they of the city shall flourish like grass of the earth.
There shall be abundance of grain in the land;
On the top of the mountains its fruit shall wave like Lebanon;
And they shall bloom forth from the city like the herb of the earth — ABPS
May there be an abundance of corn in the earth in the top of the mountains, —
Let the fruit thereof wave like Lebanon,
And they of the city bloom like the fresh shoots of the earth — Rhm
Let grain be abundant in the land,
Even upon the mountain top;
In its growth, let it wave like Lebanon,
And overflowing from the city,
Let the people flourish,
Like the grass of the earth — DeW
May the land be rich in waving corn,
right up to the top of the hills!
May the folk flourish like trees in Lebanon,
may citizens flower like grass in the field! — Mof

17. His name shall endure for ever: his name shall be continued as long as the sun: and men shall be blessed in him: all nations shall call him blessed.
Let his name endure for ever;
While the sun shineth, let his name increase;
And let men find blessing in him;
Let all nations call him blessed — DeW
May his name endure for ever,
his fame continue as long as the sun!
May men bless themselves by him,
all nations call him blessed! — RSV
May his name endure for ever:
may his reputation thrive while the sun lasts.
May mankind be prospered through him,
and all the nations call him blessed — Har

18. Blessed be the LORD God, the God of Israel, who only doeth wondrous things.
Blessed be Jehovah God, the God of Israel,
Who alone doeth wonders — ABPS
Blessed be Yahweh, the God of Israel,
who alone performs these marvels! — Jerus
Blessed be the Lord God of Israel, who does wonderful deeds as none else — Knox
Praise be to the Lord God, the God of Israel, the only doer of wonders — Bas

19. And blessed be his glorious name for ever: and let the whole earth be filled with his glory;
Let His glorious name be blessed eternally;
may the entire earth be replete with His majesty — Har
Amen, and Amen.
So be it, So be it — Bas

20. The prayers of David the son of Jesse are ended.
Here end the prayers of David the son of Jesse — Sprl
An intermission of the Hymns of David son of Jessai — Sept
(This ends the psalms of David, son of Jesse.) — Tay

BOOK III

PSALM 73

A Psalm of Asaph.

1. Truly God is good to Israel, even to such as are of a clean heart.
How good God is to the upright;
the LORD, to those who are clean of heart! — NAB
Truly God is good to the upright,
to those who are pure in heart — RSV

2. But as for me, my feet were almost gone; my steps had well nigh slipped.
But I — my feet had nearly given way;
In a moment, my steps would have failed — DeW
But as for me, I came so close to the edge of the cliff! My feet were slipping and I was almost gone — Tay

3. For I was envious at the foolish, when I saw the prosperity of the wicked.
For I was envious of the arrogant
When I saw the prosperity of the wicked — Sprl
For I was incensed at the boastful;
I beheld the prosperity of the wicked — DeW
And why? I was grieved at the wicked:
I do also see the ungodly in such prosperity — PBV
envying the arrogant as I did,
and watching the wicked get rich — Jerus

4. For there are no bands in their death: but their strength is firm.
For they are in no peril of death; but are lusty and strong — PBV
For there are no painful diseases for them;
Their strength is sound and firm — Sprl
For they have no pangs in their death,
And vigorous is their body — Rhm
For they have no pangs;
their bodies are sound and sleek — RSV

5. They are not in trouble as other men; neither are they plagued like other men.
They come in no misfortune like other folk; neither are they plagued like other men — PBV
They are free from the burdens of mortals,
and are not afflicted like the rest of men — NAB
no part have they in human cares,
no blows like other men — Mof

6. Therefore pride compasseth them about as a chain; violence covereth them as a garment.
Therefore pride is as a chain about their neck; violence covereth them as a garment — RV
Therefore pride hath enchained them:
And a robe of violence enwrappeth them — Sprl
For this cause doth arrogance deck them as a neck-chain,
And a garment of wrong is their attire — Rhm
In consequence they flaunt their pride like a necklace;
violence wraps around them like clothing — Har
So pride is their chain of honour,
violence the garment that covers them — Jerus

7. Their eyes stand out with fatness: they have more than heart could wish.
Their eyes swell out with fatness,
their hearts overflow with follies — RSV
Their imagination exceeds the best that can be provided;
their thoughts emerge from deep inside them — Har
their spite oozes like fat,
their hearts drip with slyness — Jerus
From those pampered hearts what malice proceeds, what vile schemes are hatched! — Knox
vice oozes from their very soul,

their minds are rank and riotous — Mof

These fat cats have everything their hearts could ever wish for! — Tay

Their iniquity comes through like grease; they do according to the evil dictates of the heart — Lam

8. They are corrupt, and speak wickedly concerning oppression: they speak loftily.

They scoff and speak wickedly;
They utter blasphemy against the Most High — Sprl

They scoff, and in wickedness utter oppression:
They speak loftily — ASV

They talk wickedly of oppression;
They speak as from on high — DeW

They scoff and speak with malice;
loftily they threaten oppression — RSV

their talk is mocking and malicious,
and haughtily they lay their plots — Mof

They scoff, and in wickedness utter oppression;
They speak as if there were none on high — JPS

9. They set their mouth against the heavens, and their tongue walketh through the earth.

They set their mouths against the heavens,
and their tongue struts through the earth — RSV

They boast against the very heavens, and their words strut through the earth — Tay

For they stretch forth their mouth unto the heaven, and their tongue goeth through the world — PBV

They set their mouthings in place of heaven,
and their pronouncements roam the earth — NAB

They have assigned authority to their words in heaven,
and what they say traverses the earth — Har

they think their mouth is heaven
and their tongue can dictate on earth — Jerus

They set their mouth against and speak down from heaven, and their tongue swaggers through the earth [invading even heaven with blasphemy and smearing earth with slanders] — Amp

10. Therefore his people return hither: and waters of a full cup are wrung out to them.

Therefore fall the people unto them, and thereout suck they no small advantage — PBV

Therefore God's people turn away after them,
And enjoy the waters of a full stream — DeW

Enviously the men of my own race look on, to see them draining life's cup to the full — Knox

For this reason people resort to them, and greedily gulp down their pronouncements — Har

And so God's people are dismayed and confused, and drink it all in — Tay

Therefore the people turn and praise them;
and find no fault in them — RSV

11. And they say, How doth God know? and is there knowledge in the most High?

Tush, say they, how should God perceive it? is there knowledge in the Most High — PBV

They also say,
"How can God know?" and,
"Is the Most High aware of this?" — Har

asking, 'How will God find out?
Does the Most High know everything?' — Jerus

12. Behold, these are the ungodly, who prosper in the world; they increase in riches.

Lo! these are the lawless,
Who are secure for an age
They have attained unto wealth — Rhm

Behold, these are the wicked;
And, being alway at ease, they increase in riches — ASV

Behold, these are the wicked;
And secure for ever, they increase in power — DeW

Such, then are the wicked;
always carefree, while they increase in wealth — NAB

Look at them: these are the wicked, well-off and still getting richer! — Jerus

Look at these men of arrogance; they never have to lift a finger — theirs is a life of ease; and all the time their riches multiply — Tay

13. Verily I have cleansed my heart in vain, and washed my hands in innocency.

'Tis all in vain I kept my heart from stain,
kept my life clean — Mof

Have I been wasting my time? Why take the trouble to be pure? — Tay

14. For all the day long have I been plagued, and chastened every morning.

All the day long have I been punished, and chastened every morning — PBV

when all day long blows fell on me,
and every dawn brought me some chastening! — Mof

All I get out of it is trouble and woe — every day and all day long! — Tay

15. If I say, I will speak thus: behold, I should offend against the generation of thy children.

Had I thought, "I will speak as they do,"
I had been false to the fellowship of your children — NAB

If I had really said that, I would have been a traitor to your people — Tay

Had I spoken thus [and given expression to my feelings], I would have been untrue and have dealt treacherously against the generation of your children — Amp

16. When I thought to know this, it was too painful for me;

17. Until I went into the sanctuary of God; then understood I their end.

But when I thought how to understand this,
it seemed to me a wearisome task,
until I went into the sanctuary of God;
then I perceived their end — RSV

I set myself to read the riddle, but it proved a hard search, until I betook myself to God's sanctuary, and considered, there, what becomes of such men at last — Knox

Though I tried to understand this
it seemed to me too difficult,
Till I entered the sanctuary of God
and considered their final destiny — NAB

Yet it is so hard to explain it — this prosperity of those who hate the Lord. Then one day I went into God's sanctuary to meditate, and thought about the future of these evil men — Tay

18. Surely thou didst set them in slippery places: thou castedst them down into destruction.

Surely Thou settest them in slippery places;
Thou hurlest them down to utter ruin — JPS

The truth is, thou art making a slippery path for their feet, ready to plunge them in ruin — Knox

You have placed them in a precarious position;
You overthrow them and destroy them — Har

How often thou dost set them on slippery ground
and drive them headlong into ruin! — NEB

19. How are they brought into desolation, as in a moment! they are utterly consumed with terrors.

How they are destroyed in a moment, swept away utterly by terrors! — RSV

O how suddenly do they consume, perish, and come to a fearful end! — PBV

Now have they become desolate as in a moment!
They have ceased — come to an end by reason of calamities — Rhm

How they become a desolation as in a moment,
Are swept away, are destroyed through horrors! — AAT

Then in a moment how dreadful their end,
cut off root and branch by death with all its terrors — NEB

20. As a dream when one awaketh; so, O Lord, when thou wakest, thou shalt despise their image.

They are like a nightmare when one awakens, Lord;
one despises their ghostly forms when fully roused — Har

As a dream when one awakes, O Lord,
So, when thou dost bestir thyself, thou wilt set at naught their fancies — AAT

As a dream when one is awake, they are ended; they are like an image gone out of mind when sleep is over — Bas

When you wake up, Lord, you shrug them off
like the phantoms of a morning dream — Jerus

And thou, Lord, dost rise up and brush aside all their imaginings as a waking man his dream — Knox

As a dream [which seems real] until one awakens, so, O Lord, when You arouse Yourself [to take note of the wicked] You will despise their outward show — Amp

21. Thus my heart was grieved, and I was pricked in my reins.

22. So foolish was I, and ignorant: I was as a beast before thee.

For my soul was grieved,
And I was pricked in my heart:
So brutish was I, and ignorant;
I was as a beast before thee — ASV

When my heart became bitter,
And I was so deeply pained;
Then was I a brute, and knew nothing;
I had become as a beast before Thee — DeW

When my heart was stirred up,
And my feelings were aroused,
Then I was stupid and knew nothing;
A brute was I toward thee! — AAT

When I was worried,
and emotionally disturbed,
then I was stupid and thoughtless,
behaving just like an animal towards You — Har

When I saw this, what turmoil filled my heart! I saw myself so stupid and so ignorant; I must seem like an animal to you, O God — Tay

Because my heart was embittered
and my soul was pierced,
I was stupid and understood not;
I was like a brute beast in your presence — NAB

23. Nevertheless I am continually with thee: thou hast holden me by my right hand.

Nevertheless, I am always in Your presence;
You have grasped me by my right hand — Har

24. Thou shalt guide me with thy counsel, and afterward receive me to glory.

Your wisdom will be my guide, and later you will put me in a place of honour — Bas

You will direct me by your advice,
and afterwards receive me to an honored position — Har

now guide me with advice
and in the end receive me into glory — Jerus

25. Whom have I in heaven but thee? and there is none upon earth that I desire beside thee.

Whom have I in heaven but Thee?
And having Thee, I delight not in the earth — DeW

Whom have I in the heavens but thee?
And having thee, I wish nought else on earth — AAT

What else does heaven hold for me, but thyself? What charm for me has earth, here at thy side? — Knox

I look to no one else in heaven,
I delight in nothing else on earth — Jerus

Whom else have I in heaven?
And when I am with you, the earth delights me not — NAB

26. My flesh and my heart faileth: but God is the strength of my heart, and my portion for ever.

My strength and my heart fail;
The rock of my heart and my portion is God forevermore — ABPS

Body and soul may fail,
but God my strength is mine, my own for evermore — Mof

My flesh and my heart are wasting away: but God is the Rock of my heart and my eternal heritage — Bas

Though my body and my spirit may droop,
God is the source of my stability,
and my eternal choice — Har

Though heart and body fail,
yet God is my possession for ever — NEB

27. For, lo, they that are far from thee shall perish: thou hast destroyed all them that go a whoring from thee.

For, lo, they that are far from thee shall perish:
Thou hast destroyed all them that play the harlot, departing from thee — ASV

For lo, they that forsake thee shall perish; thou hast destroyed all them that are unfaithful unto thee — PBV

So then: those who abandon you are doomed,

you destroy the adulterous deserter — Jerus

28. But it is good for me to draw near to God: I have put my trust in the Lord GOD, that I may declare all thy works.

But it is my happiness to draw near to God;
In JEHOVAH my Lord have I taken up my shelter;
That I may recount all Thy marvellous works — Sprl

But as for me the drawing near of God is my blessedness, —
I have made of My Lord Yahweh my refuge, —
That I may recount all thy works — Rhm

But as for me, my joy is my nearness to God;
In Thee, Lord Jehovah! I take refuge,
That I may tell of all that Thou hast done — DeW

But as for me, the nearness of God is my good;
I have made the Lord GOD my refuge,
That I may tell of all Thy works — JPS

PSALM 74

Maschil of Asaph.
An instructive Psalm. Asaph's — Rhm

1. O God, why hast thou cast us off for ever? why doth thine anger smoke against the sheep of thy pasture?

O God, wherefore art thou absent from us so long? why is thy wrath so hot against the sheep of thy pasture — PBV

Why, O God! dost Thou spurn us for ever?
Why ascendeth the smoke of Thine anger
Over the flock of Thy shepherd care — DeW

Why are You forever rejecting us, Lord?
Why does Your anger fume against Your grazing flock — Har

God, have you finally rejected us,
raging at the flock you used to pasture — Jerus

2. Remember thy congregation, which thou hast purchased of old; the rod of thine inheritance, which thou hast redeemed; this mount Zion, wherein thou hast dwelt.

Bethink thee of the company thou hast gathered, long ago; of the tribe thou hast chosen to be thy domain; of mount Sion, where thou hast thy dwelling-place — Knox

Remember Your community which you acquired long ago;
the tribe which You ransomed formerly as Your inheritance.
Call to mind Mount Zion, which You have inhabited — Har

Remember the people you long since made your own,
your hereditary tribe whom you redeemed,
and this Mount Zion where you came to live — Jerus

Keep in mind your band of worshippers, for whom you gave payment in the days which are past, whom you took for yourself as the people of your heritage; even this mountain of Zion, which has been your resting-place — Bas

3. Lift up thy feet unto the perpetual desolations; even all that the enemy hath done wickedly in the sanctuary.

Lift up Thy steps because of the perpetual ruins,
Even all the evil that the enemy hath done in the sanctuary — JPS

Let Thy footsteps pass up to the perpetual ruins,
Unto all that the enemy hath destroyed in the sanctuary — DeW

Direct thy steps to the perpetual ruins;
the enemy has destroyed everything in the sanctuary! — RSV

Go in the direction of the leveled ruins;
the enemy has devestated Your entire shrine — Har

Walk through the awful ruins of the city, and see what the enemy has done to your sanctuary — Tay

4. Thine enemies roar in the midst of thy congregations; they set up their ensigns for signs.

Thine adversaries roared in the midst of Thy place of assembly;

They set up their own symbols for the symbols of God — DeW
Your foes roar triumphantly in your shrine;
they have set up their tokens of victory — NAB
The shouts of thy enemies filled the holy place,
they planted their standards there as tokens of victory — NEB
Your foes behave rowdily in the center of Your sanctuary;
they have replaced our symbols with their own banners — Har

5. A man was famous according as he had lifted up axes upon the thick trees.
They seemed like men with axes uplifted,
Assaulting the thick growing trees — DeW
they smashed the doors down with their axes,
like woodmen felling trees — Mof
They hew down at the upper entrance
The wooden trellis work with axes — AAT
Everything lies in shambles like a forest chopped to the ground — Tay

6. But now they break down the carved work thereof at once with axes and hammers.
They came with their axes and sledgehammers and smashed and chopped the carved paneling — Tay
they ripped the carvings clean out,
they smashed them with hatchet and pick — NEB

7. They have cast fire into thy sanctuary, they have defiled by casting down the dwelling place of thy name to the ground.
They have set thy sanctuary on fire;
They have profaned the dwelling-place of thy name by casting it to the ground — ASV
They set your sanctuary on fire;
the place where your name abides they have razed and profaned — NAB

8. They said in their hearts, Let us destroy them together: they have burned up all the synagogues of God in the land.
They said in their heart,
"We will crush them at once;"
They have burned all the houses of God in the land — DeW
They said to themselves, "Let us root them out!"
so all the synagogues in the land they burned — Mof
They said in their hearts, "Let us destroy them;
burn all the shrines of God in the land" — NAB
They said to themselves,
"We will desolate them completely."
They burned down all the places for divine assembly in the land — Har
Determined to destroy us once and for all,
they burned down every shrine of God in the country — Jerus

9. We see not our signs: there is no more any prophet: neither is there among us any that knoweth how long.
not an emblem of ours is to be seen.
No prophet now — none knows when this will end! — Mof
Our own emblems are nowhere to be seen; there are no prophets left now, none can tell how long we must endure — Knox
We no longer see our symbols:
the prophet has ceased to exist,
and there is no one among us who knows how long it will last — Har
Deprived of signs, with no prophets left,
who can say how long this will last? — Jerus
There is nothing left to show that we are your people. The prophets are gone, and who can say when it all will end? — Tay

10. O God, how long shall the adversary reproach? shall the enemy blaspheme thy name for ever?
How long, O God! shall the oppressor revile?
Shall the enemy scoff at Thy Name for ever? — DeW
How much longer, God, is the oppressor to blaspheme,
is the enemy to insult your name for ever? — Jerus
How long, O God, will you allow our enemies to dishonor your name?
Will you let them get away with this forever? — Tay

11. Why withdrawest thou thy hand, even thy right hand? pluck it out of thy bosom.
Why withdrawest thou thy hand? why

pluckest thou not thy right hand out of thy bosom to consume the enemy? — PBV

Why dost thou hold back thy hand, why dost thou keep thy right hand in thy bosom? — RSV

Why hold back thy hand, O God? Stretch out thy right hand and strike —Mof

Why do You restrain Your great power?
Release Your might from its confines
and annihilate them — Har

12. For God is my King of old, working salvation in the midst of the earth.

For God is my King of old; the help that is done upon earth, he doeth it himself — PBV

And God is my king of old,
Working deliverances in the earth — ABPS

God is my king from of old,
Who wrought victory in the midst of the earth — AAT

You, my God, have been my King for many years,
working deeds of deliverance amongst humanity — Har

But thou, O God, thou king from of old,
thou mighty conqueror all the world over — NEB

13. Thou didst divide the sea by thy strength: thou brakest the heads of the dragons in the waters.

Thou hast, by Thy power, disparted the sea!
Thou hast shattered the heads of the crocodiles in the water! — Sprl

Thou didst divide the sea by thy strength:
Thou brakest the heads of the sea-monsters in the waters — ASV

by your power you split the sea in two,
and smashed the heads of monsters on the waters — Jerus

You did divide the [Red] Sea by Your might; You broke the heads of the [Egyptian] dragons on the waters — Amp

14. Thou brakest the heads of leviathan in pieces, and gavest him to be meat to the people inhabiting the wilderness.

Thou didst crush the heads of the Sea-Monster.
Thou didst give him to be food for the people of the deserts — Rhm

You crushed the heads of Leviathan [Egypt]; You did give him as food for the creatures inhabiting the wilderness — Amp

You crushed the heads of Leviathan, and made food of him for the dolphins — NAB

You crushed the power of Leviathan; You divided him up as food for the sharks — Har

The heads of the great snake were crushed by you; you gave them as food to the fishes of the sea — Bas

15. Thou didst cleave the fountain and the flood: thou driedst up mighty rivers.

Thou broughtest out fountains and waters out of the hard rocks; thou driedst up mighty waters — PBV

Thou didst cleave the rock, whence a fountain and a river!
Thou hast dried the mighty torrents — Sprl

Thou didst break open the fountain and brook;
Thou didst dry up ever-flowing streams — ABPS

At your command the springs burst forth to give your people water; and then you dried a path for them across the ever-flowing Jordan — Tay

16. The day is thine, the night also is thine: thou hast prepared the light and the sun.

Thine is the day, Thine also the night;
Thou hast established luminary and sun — JPS

Thine is the day and the night is thine: it is thou who preparedst the sun and moon — Sept

thine is the day and thine the night,
thou hast provided sun and starlight — Mof

Both day and night belong to You:
You set the sun and moon in position — Har

17. Thou hast set all the borders of the earth: thou hast made summer and winter.

thou hast arranged the earth in its due order,
thou hast made summer and winter — Mof

You fixed all the boundaries of the earth;
it was You who made both summer and winter — Har

18. Remember this, that the enemy hath reproached, O LORD, and that the foolish people have blasphemed thy name.

Remember this; O Jehovah!
How the enemy hath reviled Thee,
And a foolish people have blasphemed Thy Name — DeW

Remember this, O LORD, how the enemy scoffs,
and an impious people reviles thy name — RSV

19. O deliver not the soul of thy turtledove unto the multitude of the wicked: forget not the congregation of thy poor for ever.

Leave not thy Dove Israel to a brutal power;
forget not thy poor people for all time — Mof

Do not deliver the soul of thy dove to the wild beasts;
do not forget the life of thy poor for ever — RSV

Cast not to the beasts the soul that confesses thee;
forget not for ever the sufferings of thy servants — NEB

20. Have respect unto the covenant: for the dark places of the earth are full of the habitations of cruelty.

Have respect unto the covenant;
For the dark regions of the earth are filled with homes of violence — DeW

Respect the covenant,
for the far reaches of the land are full of disturbances — Har

Respect the covenant! We can bear no more —
every cave in the country is the scene of violence! — Jerus

Remember your promise! For the land is full of darkness and cruel men — Tay

21. O let not the oppressed return ashamed: let the poor and needy praise thy name.

Let not the oppressed turn back in dishonour;
Let the suffering and the needy praise Thy Name — DeW

Let not the downtrodden turn from thee disappointed,
but may the weak and wretched have good cause to praise thee! — Mof

Do not let the hard-pressed retreat in confusion,
give the poor and needy cause to praise your name — Jerus

22. Arise, O God, plead thine own cause: remember how the foolish man reproacheth thee daily.

Up, O God, to vindicate the cause that is thine own!
Remember how the impious scoff at thee all day long — Mof

Rise, God, say something on your own behalf,
do not forget the madman's day-long blaspheming — Jerus

23. Forget not the voice of thine enemies: the tumult of those that rise up against thee increaseth continually.

Forget not the voice of thine enemies:
the presumption of them that hate thee increaseth ever more and more — PBV

Forget not the noise of Thine adversaries,
The uproar of Thy foes that ascendeth continually — DeW

forget not the loud clamour of thy foes,
the endless din that rises from thine enemies — Mof

do not overlook them, the triumphant shouts of thy enemies, the ever growing clamour that here defies thee — Knox

Be not unmindful of the voice of your foes;
the uproar of those who rebel against you is unceasing — NAB

Ignore no longer the cries of thy assailants,
the mounting clamour of those who defy thee — NEB

PSALM 75

To the chief Musician, Al-taschith, A Psalm or Song of Asaph.

To the chief Musician. "Do not Destroy." A Melody of Asaph, a Song — Rhm

1. Unto thee, O God, do we give thanks, unto thee do we give thanks: for that thy name is near thy wondrous works declare.

We give thanks to thee, O God, we give thanks;
And that thy name is near, thy wonders have told — ABPS

We give thee thanks, O God, we give thee thanks;
thy name is brought very near to us in the story of thy wonderful deeds — NEB

We give thanks unto thee, O God; we give thanks, for thy name is near: men tell of thy wondrous works — RV

We offer thanks to thee, O God, we offer thanks to thee,
telling of all thy wondrous deeds — Mof

We give thanks to thee, O God; we give thanks;
we call on thy name and recount thy wondrous deeds — RSV

2. When I shall receive the congregation I will judge uprightly.

When I shall find the set time, I will judge uprightly — RV

When the time is ripe, I will judge strictly — Knox

When the time is ripe,
I will judge in fairness — Har

When the proper time is come [for executing My judgments] I will judge uprightly [says the Lord] — Amp

"Yes", the Lord replies, "And when I am ready, I will punish the wicked!" — Tay

3. The earth and all the inhabitants thereof are dissolved: I bear up the pillars of it.

The earth and all that dwell in it are dissolving;
I, I bear up its pillars — ABPS

When the earth dissolveth, and all that dwell in it,
It is I that adjust the pillars thereof — DeW

when men in any panic melt away,
I still uphold the order of the world — Mof

When the earth totters, and all its inhabitants,
it is I who keep steady its pillars — RSV

Selah.

Selah [pause, and calmly think of that]! — Amp

4. I said unto the fools, Deal not foolishly: and to the wicked, Lift not up the horn:

I tell the boastful, 'Do not boast,'
I tell the impious, 'Never flaunt your power' — Mof

I said to the arrogant and boastful, Deal not arrogantly — do not boast; and to the wicked, Lift not up the horn [of personal aggrandizement] — Amp

5. Lift not up your horn on high: speak not with a stiff neck.

Lift not up your horn on high,
Nor speak insolently — DeW

No, never flaunt your power thus proudly,
defy not God thus loudly — Mof

"Do not flaunt your power,
nor speak with wanton presumption" — Har

how dare you raise your horn like that,
how dare you speak so boldly! — Jerus

6. For promotion cometh neither from the east, nor from the west, nor from the south.

For the east availeth not, nor the west,
Nor the wilderness of mountains — DeW

rely not upon east or west, on the south desert or the northern hills — Mof

For not from the east or from the west
and not from the wilderness comes lifting up — RSV

No power from the east nor from the west,
no power from the wilderness, can raise a man up — NEB

Look east, look west, it will avail you nothing; no help comes from the desert, or the high hills — Knox

7. But God is the judge: he putteth down one, and setteth up another.

And why? God is the Judge; he putteth down one, and setteth up another — PBV

'tis God who rules o'er men,
this one he lowers, this one he lifts — Mof

But God is the judge!
He humbles one and exalts another — AAT

God himself is the Judge:
He deposes one and promotes another — Har

8. For in the hand of the LORD there is a cup, and the wine is red; it is full of mixture;

For in the hand of the LORD there is a cup,
with foaming wine, well mixed — RSV

Within the Lord's dispensing power is a cup of destiny,
with fermenting wine, well mixed — Har

For in the hand of the Lord there is a cup [of His wrath], and the wine foams and is red, well mixed — Amp

and he poureth out of the same: but the dregs thereof, all the wicked of the earth shall wring them out, and drink them.

and he will pour a draught from it,
and all the wicked of the earth
shall drain it down to the dregs — RSV

9. But I will declare for ever; I will sing praises to the God of Jacob.

But as for me, I will exult,
I will sing praises to the God of Jacob — Sprl

But I will rejoice for ever,
I will sing praises to the God of Jacob — RSV

But I will never stop proclaiming the God of Jacob
or playing in his honour — Jerus

10. All the horns of the wicked also will I cut off; but the horns of the righteous shall be exalted.

I will shatter the strength of the wicked,
but the power of the virtuous will be increased — Har

for lopping the power of evil men,
and rallying the power of the upright — Mof

PSALM 76

To the chief Musician on Neginoth, a Psalm or Song of Asaph.

To the Chief Musician. With Stringed Instruments. A Melody of Asaph, a Song — Rhm

1. In Judah is God known: his name is great in Israel.

In Judah God is renowned,
his fame is high in Israel — Mof

God has revealed Himself in Judah:
His name is renowned in Israel — Har

God's reputation is very great in Judah and in Israel — Tay

2. In Salem also is his tabernacle, and his dwelling place in Zion.

In Salem is His retreat;
His resting place in Zion — DeW

His abode has been established in Salem,
his dwelling place in Zion — RSV

His home is in Jerusalem. He lives upon Mount Zion — Tay

3. There brake he the arrows of the bow, the shield, and the sword, and the battle.

There He scattered the flashing bolts of the bow;
The shield, and the sword, and the battle — DeW

There he broke the flashing arrows,
the shield, the sword, and the weapons of war — RSV

he has destroyed all flashing arrows,
shields and swords and martial weapons — Mof

Selah.

Selah. [pause, and calmly think of that]! — Amp

4. Thou art more glorious and excellent than the mountains of prey.

Terrible art thou, mightier than a devouring lion — AAT

Enveloped in light thou art more majestic than the mountains of prey — Rhm

Glorious art Thou, and lordly,
Descending from the mountains of prey — DeW

Glorious art thou, more majestic
than the everlasting mountains — RSV

The everlasting mountains cannot compare with you in glory! — Tay

5. The stout-hearted are spoiled, they have slept their sleep:

The stouthearted were stripped of their spoil;
they sank into sleep — RSV

the valiant fell a prey to thee and slept their last — Mof

The brave were plundered,
they passed into oblivion — Har

men that lust for plunder stand aghast,
the boldest swoon away — NEB

and none of the men of might have found their hands.

the veterans — not a man of them could move a finger — Mof

All the men of war
were unable to use their hands — RSV

all the powerful warriors were thwarted — Har
and the strongest cannot lift a hand — NEB

6. At thy rebuke, O God of Jacob, both the chariot and horse are cast into a deep sleep.
At thy rebuke, O God of Jacob,
both rider and horse lay stunned — RSV
At Your command, God of Jacob,
both rider and horse fell unconscious — Har

7. Thou, even thou, art to be feared:
Thou, even Thou, art terrible — JPS
But thou, terrible art thou! — RSV
You the Terrible! — Jerus
and who may stand in thy sight when once thou art angry?
Who can stand before thee
when once thy anger is roused — RSV
Who can oppose you
and your furious onslaught — Jerus
who can stand thy full weight of wrath — Mof

8. Thou didst cause judgment to be heard from heaven; the earth feared, and was still,
The earth was hushed in terror when thy sentence fell from heaven — Mof
You dispensed judgment from heaven;
earth became fearful and was silent — Har
When your verdicts thunder from heaven,
earth stays silent with dread — Jerus

9. When God arose to judgment, to save all the meek of the earth.
when God arose to act on earth, in succor of the afflicted — Mof
when God arose to administer justice,
and save all the oppressed upon earth — Har
Selah.

10. Surely the wrath of man shall praise thee: the remainder of wrath shalt thou restrain.
For the multitude of mankind shall give thanks unto thee,
The remainder of the multitude shall keep holy festival unto thee — Rhm
All pagans shall give praise to thee;
the rest of us shall keep thy festival — Mof
Even man in his fury will praise You;
You will adorn Yourself with the remnant of their anger — Har
Man's wrath only adds to your glory;
the survivors of your wrath you will draw like a girdle around you — Jerus
Man's futile wrath will bring you glory!
You will use it as an ornament — Tay

11. Vow, and pay unto the LORD your God:
Make your vows to the LORD your God,
and perform them — RSV
fulfill the promises you make to Yahweh your God — Jerus
let all that be round about him bring presents unto him that ought to be feared.
to his dread majesty let all around pay tribute — Mof
let all neighboring tribes bring gifts
to Him who inspires reverence — Har
make offerings to the Terrible, you who surround him — Jerus

12. He shall cut off the spirit of princes: he is terrible to the kings of the earth.
He will restrain the spirit of princes;
He will be reverenced by the kings of the earth — Sprl
who humbles the spirit of powerful leaders,
and who is a source of terror to earthly monarchs — Har
he snuffs out the lives of princes,
he is terrible to the kings of the earth — Jerus
For he cuts down princes and does awesome things to the kings of the earth — Tay

PSALM 77

To the chief Musician, to Jeduthun, A Psalm of Asaph.
To the Chief Musician. On "Jeduthun." Asaph's, a Melody — Rhm

1. I cried unto God with my voice, even unto God with my voice, and he gave ear unto me.
I will raise my voice to God and cry aloud;
I will raise my voice to God, that he may hear me — AAT

2. In the day of my trouble I sought the Lord: my sore ran in the night, and ceased not:
In the day of my trouble I seek the Lord;
in the night my hand is stretched out without wearying — RSV
When trouble overtook me, I sought the Lord;
my hands were extended in the night tirelessly — Har
my soul refused to be comforted.
My mind refused consolation — AAT
There can be no joy for me until he acts — Tay
3. I remembered God, and was troubled; I complained, and my spirit was overwhelmed.
I remember God, and am disquieted:
I complain, and my spirit is overwhelmed — ASV
When I remember God, I must moan;
I must utter my grief, when my spirit languisheth — DeW
I call God to mind, and sigh;
I lament, and my spirit faints — ABPS
I think of God and moan, overwhelmed with longing for his help — Tay
Selah.
4. Thou holdest mine eyes waking:
Thou holdest mine eyes upon the watch — DeW
all night I never close my eyes — Mof
Thou dost hold my eyelids from closing — RSV
You keep me awake — Har
I am so troubled that I cannot speak.
I was driven to and fro and could not speak — Rhm
I toss about, and am speechless — DeW
I was dazed and I could not speak — NEB
5. I have considered the days of old, the years of ancient times.
I have considered the days of old, and the years that are past — PBV
I think of the days of old —
Of the years of far off times — DeW
I think over former days;
I recall years long past — Har
6. I call to remembrance my song in the night: I commune with mine own heart: and my spirit made diligent search.
I commune with my heart in the night;
I meditate and search my spirit: — RSV
Snatches of music come to me in the night;
I turn things over in my mind, and ponder
in a spirit of enquiry: — Har
I spent all night meditating in my heart,
I pondered and my spirit asked this question: — Jerus
7. Will the Lord cast off for ever? and will he be favourable no more?
"Will the Lord for ever discard us,
will he never be kind again — Mof
"Will the Lord spurn for ever,
and never again be favorable — RSV
"Will the Lord abandon me for ever?
Will He never again display kindness — Har
8. Is his mercy clean gone for ever? Doth his promise fail for evermore?
Hath his lovingkindness come to a perpetual end?
Hath his word failed to generation after generation — Rhm
Has his steadfast love for ever ceased?
Are his promises at an end for all time — RSV
Has his merciful love completely disappeared?
Have His decrees ceased for all time — Har
Is his love over for good
and the promise void for all time — Jerus
Has his unfailing love now failed us utterly,
must his promise time and again be unfulfilled — NEB
9. Hath God forgotten to be gracious? hath he in anger shut up his tender mercies?
Hath God forgotten to show favour?
Or hath he shut up in anger his compassions — Rhm
Can God forget to be gracious, can anger move him to withhold his mercy — Knox
Selah.
10. And I said, This is my infirmity: but I will remember the years of the right hand of the most High.
And I said: This is my misery,
That the right hand of the Most High is changed — DeW
For me, I tell myself, this sorrow was reserved; the most High has altered

the fashion of his dealings with men — Knox

I also said,
"It is my misfortune that the power of the Most High
seems altered nowadays." — Har

And I said: This is my fate, that the blessings of God have changed to hate — Tay

And I say, This [apparent desertion of Israel by God] is my appointed lot and trial, but I will recall the years of the right hand of the Most High [in loving-kindness extended toward us] for this is my grief, that the right hand of the Most High changes — Amp

11. I will remember the works of the LORD: surely I will remember thy wonders of old.

I will make mention of the deeds of Jehovah;
For I will remember thy wonders of old — ASV

But then, O LORD, I call to mind thy deeds;
I recall thy wonderful acts in times gone by — NEB

12. I will meditate also of all thy work, and talk of thy doings.

I will meditate on all thy work,
and muse on thy mighty deeds — RSV

13. Thy way, O God, is in the sanctuary:

Thy way, O God, is holy — RSV

Your ways are sublime, my God — Har

who is so great a God as our God?

Who is a great GOD like Elohim — Rhm

What god is great like our God — RSV

14. Thou art the God that doest wonders: thou hast declared thy strength among the people.

Thou art the God who workest wonders, who hast manifested thy might among the peoples — RSV

Thou art the Mighty One that doest wonders;
Thou hast shown Thy strength among the nations — DeW

Thou wast a God of wonders,
thou didst show the world thy strength — Mof

You are the God who did marvellous things
and forced nations to acknowledge your power — Jerus

You are the God of miracles and wonders! You still demonstrate your awesome power — Tay

15. Thou hast with thine arm redeemed thy people, the sons of Jacob and Joseph.

By Your power You ransomed Your people,
the offspring of Jacob and Joseph — Har

Selah.

Selah. [pause, and calmly think of that]! — Amp

16. The waters saw thee, O God, the waters saw thee; they were afraid: the depths also were troubled.

When the waters saw thee, O God,
when the waters saw thee, they were afraid,
yea, the deep trembled — RSV

When the waters [at the Red Sea and the Jordan] saw You, O God, they were afraid; the deep shuddered also, for [all] the waters saw You — Amp

17. The clouds poured out water: the skies sent out a sound: thine arrows also went abroad.

The clouds poured down waters
The skies uttered a voice,
Yea thine arrows flew hither and thither — Rhm

The clouds poured down torrents,
the skies thundered out.
Your lightning flashed to and fro — Har

18. The voice of thy thunder was in the heaven: the lightnings lightened the world: the earth trembled and shook.

The crash of thy thunder was in the whirlwind;
thy lightnings lighted up the world;
the earth trembled and shook — RSV

Your thunder sounded in the hurricane;
lightning illuminated the earth.
The ground shuddered and trembled — Har

19. Thy way is in the sea, and thy path in the great waters, and thy footsteps are not known.

Your way led through the sea;
Your path traversed deep waters,
but Your tracks remained concealed — Har

Thy ways are in the sea, Thy paths in the great waters;
Thy footprints are untraceable — Ber

You strode across the sea,
you marched across the ocean,

but your steps could not be seen — Jerus
Your way [in delivering Your people] was through the sea, and Your paths through the great waters; yet Your footsteps were not traceable, but were obliterated — Amp
Your road led by a pathway through the sea — a pathway no one knew was there! — Tay

20. Thou leddest thy people like a flock by the hand of Moses and Aaron.
Thou didst guide thy people like a flock,
By the hand of Moses and Aaron — ABPS

PSALM 78

Maschil of Asaph.
An Instructive Psalm. Asaph's — Rhm

1. Give ear, O my people, to my law:
Give ear, O my people, to my teaching — RSV
incline your ears to the words of my mouth.
Bend your ear to the sayings of my mouth — Rhm
pay attention to what I am saying — Har

2. I will open my mouth in a parable: I will utter dark sayings of old:
I will open my mouth with a parable;
I will utter dark sayings concerning days of old — JPS
I am going to speak to you in parable and expound the mysteries of our past — Jerus
I will open my mouth in a parable;
I will utter riddles from of old — AAT
I will narrate a parable,
and tell of ancient lore — Har
Opening my mouth I will give out a story, even the dark sayings of old times — Bas
I will open my mouth in a parable — in instruction by [numerous] examples; I will utter dark sayings of old [that hide important truth] — Amp

3. Which we have heard and known, and our fathers have told us.
— such as we have heard and known, which our fathers have related to us — Sept

4. We will not hide them from their children, shewing to the generation to come the praises of the LORD, and his strength, and his wonderful works that he hath done.
We will not hide them from their children,
but tell to the coming generation
the glorious deeds of the LORD, and his might,
and the wonders which he has wrought — RSV
From their sons we will not hide
the praises of the LORD and his might
nor the wonderful acts he has performed — NEB
I will reveal these truths to you so that you can describe these glorious deeds of Jehovah to your children, and tell them about the mighty miracles he did — Tay

5. For he established a testimony in Jacob, and appointed a law in Israel, which he commanded our fathers, that they should make them known to their children:
He established a covenant with Jacob,
and instituted a law in Israel,
which He commanded our forefathers to impart to their children — Har
He set it up as a decree in Jacob,
and established it as a law in Israel,
That what he commanded our fathers they should make known to their sons — NAB

6. That the generation to come might know them, even the children which should be born; who should arise and declare them to their children:
that a succeeding generation might be acquainted with them;
that children yet unborn might grow up to instruct their offspring — Har

7. That they might set their hope in God, and not forget the works of God, but keep his commandments:
to place their trust in God,
and not to forget the Divine workings,
but to observe His commandments — Har
so that they should set their hope in God,
and not forget the works of God,
but keep his commandments — RSV

8. And might not be as their fathers, a stubborn and rebellious generation;

So that they would not be like their predecessors,
a stubborn and refractory generation — Har

a generation that set not their heart aright, and whose spirit was not stedfast with God.

a generation whose heart was not steadfast,
whose spirit was not faithful to God — RSV

a generation with no sincerity of heart,
in spirit unfaithful to God — Jerus

a wavering race —
no loyal hearts for God — Mof

A generation that kept not its heart steadfast
nor its spirit faithful toward God — NAB

9. The children of Ephraim, being armed, and carrying bows, turned back in the day of battle.

The sons of Ephraim, armed bowmen,
Turned back in the day of conflict — ABPS

The Ephraimites, armed with bows,
retreated in the time of battle — Har

The Ephraimites were like a disappointing bow,
that fails upon the day of battle — Mof

10. They kept not the covenant of God, and refused to walk in his law;

They were false to God's covenant,
refused to follow his law — Knox

they would not hold to their compact with God,
they would not follow his directions — Mof

11. And forgat his works, and his wonders that he had shewed them.

They forgot what he had done,
and the miracles that he had shown them — RSV

12. Marvellous things did he in the sight of their fathers, in the land of Egypt, in the field of Zoan.

In the sight of their fathers he wrought wonders,
In the land of Egypt, the plain of Zoan — ABPS

He wrought miracles in the presence of their fathers,
in the land of Egypt, in the locality of Zoan — Har

13. He divided the sea, and caused them to pass through; and he made the waters to stand as an heap.

He parted the sea and let them pass through,
and made the water stand up like a mound — Har

he divided the sea and took them through it,
making the water stand up like banks on either side — NEB

14. In the daytime also he led them with a cloud, and all the night with a light of fire.

he led them with a cloud by day,
and all night with a blazing fire — Mof

In the daytime he led them with a cloud,
and all the night with a fiery light — RSV

By day He guided them with a cloud
and all night with a burning light — Ber

leading them with a cloud by day
and with a fiery glow at night — Jerus

15. He clave the rocks in the wilderness, and gave them drink as out of the great depths.

he split rocks in the wilderness,
to give them a flow of drink in the desert — Mof

He split rocks in the desert
and provided abundant water for them,
as from the great depths — Har

16. He brought streams also out of the rock, and caused waters to run down like rivers.

He brought waters out of the stony rock, so that it gushed out like the rivers — PBV

He made streams come out of the rock,
and caused waters to flow down like rivers — RSV

17. And they sinned yet more against him by provoking the most High in the wilderness.

And they continued still to sin against him,
To rebel against the Most High in the desert — ABPS

But they sinned still more against Him
by showing disobedience
to the Most High in the wilderness — Ber

They only sinned against him more than ever,
defying the Most High in the desert — Jerus

18. And they tempted God in their heart by asking meat for their lust.

Yea, they tempted God in their hearts,
By desiring flesh to please their taste — Sprl

And they tempted God in their heart
By asking food according to their desire — ASV

They tested God in their heart
by demanding the food they craved — RSV

deliberately challenging God
by demanding their favourite food — Jerus

19. Yea, they spake against God; they said, Can God furnish a table in the wilderness?

They disparaged God by saying, "Is it possible for God to set a table in the desert?" — Har

They blasphemed against God,
'Is it likely' they said 'that God could give a banquet in the wilderness?' — Jerus

20. Behold, he smote the rock, that the waters gushed out, and the streams overflowed; can he give bread also? can he provide flesh for his people?

'Admittedly, when he struck the rock,
waters gushed, torrents streamed out,
but bread now, can he give us that,
can he provide meat for his people?' — Jerus

21. Therefore the LORD heard this, and was wroth:

Therefore, when the LORD heard, he was full of wrath — RSV

Then the LORD heard and was enraged — NAB

so a fire was kindled against Jacob, and anger also came up against Israel;

and fire blazed up against Jacob,
and anger rose against Israel — NAB

22. Because they believed not in God, and trusted not in his salvation:

because they had no faith in God,
and did not trust his saving power — RSV

23. Though he had commanded the clouds from above, and opened the doors of heaven,

Yet he commanded the skies above,
and opened the doors of heaven — RSV

Then He commanded the sky above,
and opened the floodgates of heaven — Har

24. And had rained down manna upon them to eat, and had given them of the corn of heaven.

And rained upon them manna for food,
And grain of heaven he gave them — ABPS

He rained manna upon them for food
and gave them heavenly bread — NAB

25. Man did eat angels' food: he sent them meat to the full.

The bread of the mighty was eaten by men;
even a surfeit of provisions he sent them — NAB

26. He caused an east wind to blow in the heaven:

He caused the east wind to blow in the heavens — ASV

He let loose an east wind from the heavens — Rhm

and by his power he brought in the south wind.

And by his power he guided the south wind — ASV

27. He rained flesh also upon them as dust, and feathered fowls like as the sand of the sea:

raining down meat on them thick as dust, birds on the wing, plentiful as the sea-sand — Knox

he rained flesh upon them like dust,
winged birds like the sand of the seas — RSV

28. And he let it fall in the midst of their camp, round about their habitations.

Which fell in the midst of their camp
round about their tents — NAB

He let them fall in the middle of their camp,
around their dwellings — Har

29. So they did eat, and were well filled:

So they ate and were fully satisfied — Ber

for he gave them their own desire;

for He sent them what they had craved — Ber

30. They were not estranged from their lust. But while their meat was yet in their mouths,

But before they had sated their craving,

while the food was still in their mouths,
Yet they did not abandon their complaints
even while the food was in their mouths — NEB

31. The wrath of God came upon them, and slew the fattest of them, and smote down the chosen men of Israel.
the anger of God rose against them
and he slew the strongest of them, and laid low the picked men of Israel — RSV
the fierce anger of God came upon them,
and He made havoc of their well-fed company,
striking down the flower of Israelite youth — Har
God's anger against them reached its height, and slew their lordliest, brought them low, all the flower of Israel — Knox
Then the anger of God blazed up against them;
he spread death among their stoutest men
and brought the young men of Israel to the ground — NEB

32. For all this they sinned still and believed not for his wondrous works.
For all this, they still sinned,
And believed not in his wonders — ABPS
Despite all this, they sinned still more, and did not believe in His great works — Har
Despite all this they went on sinning, and put no faith in his marvels — Jerus

33. Therefore their days did he consume in vanity, and their years in trouble.
So he ended in a breath their days,
And their years, in a sudden terror! — Rhm
And He made their days vanish as a breath;
Their years in sudden terror — DeW
So he made their days brief as a breath, and the end of their life sudden death — Mof

34. When he slew them, then they sought him:
When he slew them, then they inquired after him — ASV
When He devastated them, they resorted to Him — Har
and they returned and inquired early after God.
they repented and sought God earnestly — RSV

35. And they remembered that God was their rock, and the high God their redeemer.
And remembered that Elohim was their rock,
Yea El Most High their redeemer — Rhm
They remembered that God was their Rock,
The Mighty God, the Most High, their Redeemer — DeW
They recalled that God was their sure foundation,
and that the Most High was their Redeemer — Har
remembering God was their strength,
And God Most High their preserver — Mof

36. Nevertheless they did flatter him with their mouth, and they lied unto him with their tongues.
But it was smooth words and no more, their promises to him were false — Mof
But it was only with their words they followed him, not with their hearts — Tay

37. For their heart was not right with him, neither were they stedfast in his covenant.
in their hearts they were not true to him,
they were unfaithful to his covenant — Jerus
they had a wavering mind,
they were not loyal to his compact — Mof
And their hearts were not right with him, and they did not keep their agreement with him — Bas

38. But he, being full of compassion, forgave their iniquity, and destroyed them not:
But he, the compassionate, covers iniquity, and destroys not — ABPS
But He, the merciful One, forgave their sin and did not destroy them — Ber
Compassionately, however,
he forgave their guilt instead of killing them — Jerus
yea, many a time turned he his anger

away, and did not stir up all his wrath.

And many times he turned away his anger,
And would not rouse up all his wrath — ABPS

often he restrained his wrath
and did not rouse his anger to its height — NEB

39. For he remembered that they were but flesh;

For he remembered that they were only human — Har

a wind that passeth away, and cometh not again.

A breath that passeth away, and returneth not — DeW

a passing breath that returns not — NAB

their life no better than a passing breeze — Mof

a puff of wind which passes and does not return — Har

who pass by like a wind and never return — NEB

40. How oft did they provoke him in the wilderness, and grieve him in the desert!

How oft they rebelled against him in the wilderness,
Grieved him in the desert! — ABPS

How frequently did they go against him in the waste land, and give him cause for grief in the dry places — Bas

41. Yea, they turned back and tempted God, and limited the Holy One of Israel.

And they tempted God anew,
And offended the Holy One of Israel — ABPS

They tested him again and again,
and provoked the Holy One of Israel — RSV

Again and again they tried God's patience
and provoked the Holy One of Israel — NEB

42. They remembered not his hand, nor the day when he delivered them from the enemy.

They remembered not his power,
nor the day he saved them from the foe — Mof

43. How he had wrought his signs in Egypt, and his wonders in the field of Zoan:

when he wrought his signs in Egypt,
and his miracles in the fields of Zoan — RSV

What signs He had wrought in Egypt;
What wonders in the field of Zoan — DeW

44. And had turned their rivers into blood; and their floods, that they could not drink.

And turned their rivers into blood, and their streams, that they could not drink — RV

He turned their rivers to blood,
so that they could not drink of their streams — RSV

45. He sent divers sorts of flies among them, which devoured them;

He sent among them swarms of flies, which devoured them — RV

and frogs, which destroyed them.

and frogs which brought devastation — NEB

46. He gave also their increase unto the caterpillar, and their labour unto the locust.

He gave their increase to the grasshopper,
And their labour to the locust — DeW

He gave their harvest to the caterpillar,
the fruits of their toil to the locust — NAB

47. He destroyed their vines with hail, and their sycamore trees with frost.

He destroyed their vines with hailstones, and their mulberry-trees with frost — PBV

With hail He broke down their vines
and with sleet their sycamores — Ber

48. He gave up their cattle also to the hail, and their flocks to hot thunderbolts.

He gave over their cattle to the hail,
And their flocks to the lightnings — DeW

And how he gave their cattle over to the plague,
And their flocks to the pestilence — AAT

He abandoned their cattle to the hail,
and their flocks to the plague — Har

49. He cast upon them the fierceness of his anger, wrath, and indignation, and trouble, by sending evil angels among them.

He let loose on them his fierce anger,
wrath, indignation, and distress,

a company of destroying angels — RSV
He sent among them the heat of his anger
Wrath and indignation and distress, —
A mission of messengers of misfortune — Rhm
He let loose upon them His burning anger;
Wrath, and indignation, and distress,
An embassy of messengers of evil — DeW
He sent upon them his fierce anger,
Wrath and fury and trouble,
An embassy of messengers of woe — AAT
In His fierce anger he sent upon them fury,
wrath and distress;
a flood of destructive powers — Har

50. He made a way to his anger;
He made a path for his anger — ASV
He leveled a path for his anger — ABPS
He blazed a trail for His anger — Har
he spared not their soul from death, but gave their life over to pestilence;
he did not spare them from death,
but gave their lives over to the plague — RSV

51. And smote all the firstborn in Egypt;
He smote all the firstborn of Egypt — DeW
the chief of their strength in the tabernacles of Ham:
the first issue of their strength in the tents of Ham — RSV
the first fruits of manhood in the tents of Ham — NAB
the flower of their manhood in the tents of Ham — NEB
the male first-fruit in the tents of Ham — Har
the first-fruits of their virility in the tents of Ham — Jerus

52. But made his own people to go forth like sheep, and guided them in the wilderness like a flock.
But as for his own people, he led them forth like sheep, and carried them in the wilderness like a flock — PBV
Then he led forth his people like sheep, and guided them in the wilderness like a flock — RSV
He led His people out like a flock,
guiding them like a herd in the desert — Har

53. And he led them in safety, so that they feared not:
He led them in safety, so that they were not afraid — RSV
but the sea overwhelmed their enemies.
and their enemies the sea did cover — Rhm

54. And he brought them to the border of his sanctuary, even to this mountain, which his right hand had purchased.
And he brought them to his holy land, to the mountain which his right hand had won — RSV
He brought them to His sacred land, to the mountain which His great power had acquired — Har

55. He cast out the heathen also before them,
He drove out the nations also before them — RSV
and divided them an inheritance by line,
and allotted them an inheritance by measure — Lam
and allotted them a measured inheritance — Ber
and allotted tracts of land — Har
he allotted their lands to Israel as a possession — NEB
and made the tribes of Israel to dwell in their tents.
and settled the tribes of Israel in their tents — RSV

56. Yet they tempted and provoked the most high God, and kept not his testimonies:
But they tested and resisted God Most High,
And his testimonies did not observe — Rhm
Still they tempted and provoked God Most High,
and did not observe His precepts — Har
Even so, they went on challenging God the Most High,
rebelliously disregarding his decrees — Jerus

57. But turned back, and dealt unfaithfully like their fathers:
but turned away and acted treacherously like their fathers — RSV
They turned back and were faithless like their fathers — NAB
they were turned aside like a deceitful bow.
they twisted like a deceitful bow — RSV

deceiving like an unreliable bow—Har
treacherous as a bow with a warp — Jerus

58. For they provoked him to anger with their high places,
They irritated Him with their sanctuaries — Har
For they grieved him with their hill-altars — PBV
and moved him to jealousy with their graven images.
and provoked him to displeasure with their images — PBV
and with their idols roused his jealousy — NAB

59. When God heard this, he was wroth, and greatly abhorred Israel:
When God heard, he was full of wrath, and he utterly rejected Israel — RSV
God observed this, and became angry; He thoroughly detested Israel—Har
God heard of it, and he was furious — he was done with Israel! — Mof

60. So that he forsook the tabernacle of Shiloh, the tent which he placed among men;
He forsook his dwelling at Shiloh, the tent where he dwelt among men — RSV

61. And delivered his strength into captivity, and his glory into the enemy's hand.
He allowed His emblem of strength to be taken as booty, delivering His glory into enemy keeping — Har
Yes, He delivered His ark into captivity and its glory into the hand of the foe — Ber
And delivered His strength and power [the ark of the covenant] into captivity, and His glory to the hand of [the Philistines] the foe — Amp

62. He gave his people over also unto the sword; and was wroth with his inheritance.
He gave his people over to the sword, and vented his wrath on his heritage — RSV
He abandoned his people to the sword and was enraged against his inheritance — NAB

63. The fire consumed their young men; and their maidens were not given to marriage.
His young men were devoured by fire, And his virgins were not praised in song — Rhm
The fire devoured their chosen men; And their virgins were not given in marriage — Sprl
whose young men were then burnt to death — no brides left to hear the wedding song — Jerus
Their young men were killed by fire and their girls died before they were old enough to sing their wedding songs — Tay
The fire [of war] devoured their young men, and their bereaved virgins were not praised in a wedding song — Amp

64. Their priests fell by the sword; and their widows made no lamentation.
Their priests fell by the sword, and their widows sang no dirges — NAB
The priests were slaughtered and their widows died before they could even begin their lament — Tay
Their priests [Hophni and Phinehas] fell by the sword, and their widows made no lamentation [for the bodies came not back from the scene of battle, and the widow of Phinehas also died that day] — Amp

65. Then the Lord awaked as one out of sleep, and like a mighty man that shouteth by reason of wine.
So the Lord awaked as one out of sleep, and like a giant refreshed with wine — PBV
And the Lord awaked, as one that slept; As a mighty man jubilant with wine — ABPS
Then the Lord awaked as out of sleep, Like a warrior shouting from wine — DeW
Then the Lord started up, as from a sleep, and, like a hero wild with wine — Mof
Then, like a sleeper, like a hero fighting-mad with wine, the Lord woke up — Jerus

66. And he smote his enemies in the hinder parts:
So he smote his adversaries in the rear — Rhm
And he put his foes to flight — NAB
And He smote His adversaries in the back [as they fled] — Amp

he put them to a perpetual reproach.
He laid upon them eternal reproach — ABPS
defeating and disgracing them for ever — Mof
And he inflicted upon them a perpetual disgrace — AAT
he put them to everlasting shame — RSV

67. Moreover he refused the tabernacle of Joseph, and chose not the tribe of Ephraim:
He disowned the house of Joseph,
and did not select the tribe of Ephraim — Har
Moreover He rejected the tent of Joseph and chose not the tribe of Ephraim [in which the tabernacle had been accustomed to stand] — Amp
But he rejected Joseph's family, the tribe of Ephraim — Tay

68. But chose the tribe of Judah, the mount Zion which he loved.
But he chose the tribe of Judah [as Israel's leader], Mount Zion which He loves [to replace Shiloh as His capitol] — Amp

69. And he built his sanctuary like high places,
And he built his sanctuary like the heights — RV
He built His sanctuary like the lofty hills — Har
He built his sanctuary like the high heavens — RSV
And He built His sanctuary [exalted] like the heights [of the heavens] — Amp
And he made his holy place like the high heaven — Bas
And he built his sanctuary on a high place — Lam

like the earth which he hath established for ever.
firm as the earth he has founded for ever — Mof
and enduring like the earth which He has established — Ber

70. He chose David also his servant, and took him from the sheepfolds:

71. From following the ewes great with young he brought him to feed Jacob his people, and Israel his inheritance.
From following the suckling ewes he took him,
To be shepherd over Jacob his people,
And over Israel his inheritance — ABPS
from tending the ewes that had young he brought him
to be the shepherd of Jacob his people, of Israel his inheritance — RSV
From looking after the sheep which were giving milk, he took him to give food to Jacob his people, and to Israel his heritage — Bas

72. So he fed them according to the integrity of his heart;
So he fed them with a faithful and true heart — PBV
So he did shepherd them according to the singleness of his heart — Rhm
With upright heart he tended them — RSV
He shepherded them in sincerity — Har
and guided them by the skilfulness of his hands.
and ruled them prudently with all his power — PBV
and with skillful hands he guided them — NAB
and led them with a sensitive hand — Jerus

PSALM 79

A Psalm of Asaph.

1. O God, the heathen are come into thine inheritance;
O God, the nations are come into thine inheritance — ASV
O God, the pagans have invaded thy preserve — Mof
O God, your land has been conquered by the heathen nations — Tay
thy holy temple have they defiled;
they have profaned Thy holy temple — Ber
they have made your holy Temple unclean — Bas
they have laid Jerusalem on heaps.
Jerusalem have they laid in ruins — Sprl
and have made Jerusalem a ruined heap — Har
they have reduced Jerusalem to a pile of ruins — Jerus

2. The dead bodies of thy servants have

they given to be meat unto the fowls of the heaven,
They have made the dead bodies of thy servants
Food for the birds of heaven — ABPS
the flesh of thy saints unto the beasts of the earth.
The flesh of thy saints for the beasts of the earth — ABPS
The flesh of Thy beloved to the wild beasts of the earth — DeW
the flesh of thy followers to wild beasts — Mof
the flesh of Thy worshipers to the beasts of the earth — Ber
they have made thy loyal servants carrion for wild beasts — NEB

3. Their blood have they shed like water round about Jerusalem;
They have poured out their blood like water
round about Jerusalem — RSV
and there was none to bury them.
and there they lie unburied — NEB
not a gravedigger left! — Jerus

4. We are become a reproach to our neighbours,
we have become a taunt to our neighbors — RSV
We have become contemptible to our neighbors — Har
What a triumph was this for the nations that dwell around us — Knox
we are now insulted by our neighbours — Jerus
[Because of such humiliation] we have become a taunt and reproach to our neighbors — Amp
a scorn and derision to them that are round about us.
A derision and a sneer unto those surrounding us — Sprl
We are a scoff and a jest to those around us — DeW
mocked and ridiculed by those around us — Har

5. How long, LORD? wilt thou be angry for ever? shall thy jealousy burn like fire?
Lord, must we always taste thy vengeance, must thy jealous anger still burn unquenched — Knox
How much longer, Lord God?
Will You continue to be angry indefinitely?
Will Your resentment flare up like fire — Har
How much longer will you be angry, Yahweh? For ever?
Is your jealousy to go on smouldering like a fire — Jerus

6. Pour out thy wrath upon the heathen that have not known thee,
Pour out thy wrath upon the nations that know thee not — ASV
Pour out thy wrath upon the nations who do not acknowledge thee — AAT
and upon the kingdoms that have not called upon thy name.

7. For they have devoured Jacob, and laid waste his dwelling place.
see how they have made Jacob their prey, and left his dwelling-place in ruins! — Knox
For they have destroyed your people Israel, invading every home — Tay

8. O remember not against us former iniquities:
O remember not our old sins — PBV
remember not against us the iniquities of our forefathers — RV
Remember not against us the guilt of our fathers — DeW
Do not hold our ancestors' crimes against us — Jerus
let thy tender mercies speedily prevent us:
Let thy tender mercies speedily meet us — ASV
but have mercy upon us, and that soon — PBV
Haste, let thy compassions meet us — ABPS
Let Your sympathy overtake us quickly — Har
in tenderness quickly intervene — Jerus
and haste in mercy to our side — Knox
for we are brought very low.
for we are come to great misery — PBV
never was need so sore as this — Knox
for we are greatly weakened — Ber
we can hardly be crushed lower — Jerus
for our need is most urgent — Har

9. Help us, O God of our salvation, for the glory of thy name:
Help us, O God of our salvation,
On account of the honor of thy name — ABPS
Help us, O God our saviour,
for the sake of thine own honour — Mof
and deliver us, and purge away our sins, for thy name's sake.

Rescue us then and put a propitiatory-covering over our sins,
For the sake of thy Name — Rhm
rescue us, and pardon our sins for Your name's sake — Har
take us out of danger and give us forgiveness for our sins, because of your name — Bas

10. Wherefore should the heathen say, Where is their God?
Wherefore should the nations say, Where is their God — ASV
Shall the heathen ask, what has become of their God — Knox
Why should the heathen nations be allowed to scoff, "Where is their God?" — Tay

let him be known among the heathen in our sight by the revenging of the blood of thy servants which is shed.
let the revenging of the blood of thy servants which is shed be known among the heathen in our sight — RV
Let the avenging of the outpoured blood of thy servants
be known among the nations before our eyes! — RSV
May we soon see the pagans learning what vengeance
you exact for your servants' blood shed here! — Jerus

11. Let the sighing of the prisoner come before thee;
Let the groaning of the prisoner come before Thee — JPS
May the groans of the captive reach you — Jerus
Oh may the moan of the prisoners reach thee — Mof

according to the greatness of thy power preserve thou those that are appointed to die;
according to thy great power preserve those doomed to die! — RSV
and by thy mighty power
release those who are doomed to die — Mof

12. And render unto our neighbours sevenfold into their bosom their reproach, wherewith they have reproached thee, O Lord.
Return sevenfold into the bosom of our neighbors
the taunts with which they have taunted thee, O Lord! — RSV
Pour out seven-fold retribution into the laps of our neighbours, for all the insults, Lord, which they have put upon thee — Knox
Repay our neighbors seven times over for their mockery
with which they have flouted You, Lord — Har
As for the contempt our neighbours pour on thee, O Lord,
turn it back sevenfold on their own heads — NEB

13. So we thy people and sheep of thy pasture will give thee thanks for ever:
So we, Thy people, and the flock of Thy shepherd care,
Will give Thee thanks for ever — DeW

we will shew forth thy praise to all generations.
From generation to generation will we recount Thy praise — Sprl

PSALM 80

To the chief Musician upon Shoshannim-Eduth, A Psalm of Asaph.
To the Chief Musician. For "the Lilies of Testimony." Asaph's. A Melody — Rhm
From the Choirmaster's collection. To the tune of "Lilies of the Law." An Asaphite song — Mof

1. Give ear, O Shepherd of Israel, thou that leadest Joseph like a flock;
Give audience, thou that art the guide of Israel, that leadest Joseph with a shepherd's care — Knox
O shepherd of Israel, hearken,
O guide of the flock of Joseph! — NAB

thou that dwellest between the cherubims, shine forth.

2. Before Ephraim and Benjamin and Manasseh stir up thy strength, and come and save us.

Thou who art enthroned upon the cherubim, shine forth
before Ephraim and Benjamin and Manasseh!
Stir up thy might,
and come to save us! — RSV
Thou who art enthroned above the cherubim, shine forth!

Before Ephraim, Benjamin, and Manasseh,
arouse Thy strength and come to our rescue — Ber

Thou who art throned on the cherubim, appear!
Before Ephraim and Benjamin and Manasseh stir up thy strength,
And come
to our salvation — Rhm

3. **Turn us again, O God, and cause thy face to shine; and we shall be saved.**

O God bring us back,
And light up thy face
That we may be saved — Rhm

Restore us, O God;
let thy face shine, that we may be saved — RSV

O God, restore us to our own; smile upon us, and we shall find deliverance — Knox

4. **O LORD God of hosts, how long wilt thou be angry against the prayer of thy people?**

O LORD of hosts, how long will you burn with anger
while your people pray — NAB

Lord God of armies,
how long will You be angry with Your praying people — Har

O Lord of hosts, how long will thine anger fume,
though thy people are praying — Mof

O LORD God of Hosts,
how long wilt thou resist thy people's prayer — NEB

5. **Thou feedest them with the bread of tears;**

Thou hast made tears our daily bread — Mof

and givest them tears to drink in great measure.

And hast caused them to drink the water of weeping in threefold abundance — Rhm

and tears on tears our drink — Mof

6. **Thou makest us a strife unto our neighbours:**

Thou dost make us the scorn of our neighbors — RSV

You have made us the ridicule of our neighbors — Har

Thou dost make us an object of contention to our neighbors — Rhm

you now let our neighbours quarrel over us — Jerus

You have left us to be fought over by our neighbors — NAB

Thou hast humbled us before our neighbours — NEB

and our enemies laugh among themselves.

and our enemies laugh us to scorn — PBV

and our enemies mock us — NAB

7. **Turn us again, O God of hosts, and cause thy face to shine; and we shall be saved.**[22]

Restore us, God of armies . . . — Har

O God of hosts, restore us to power . . . — Mof

8. **Thou hast brought a vine out of Egypt:**

You brought a vine [Israel] out of Egypt — Amp

You brought us from Egypt as though we were a tender vine — Tay

thou hast cast out the heathen, and planted it.

You uprooted nations, and planted it — Har

thou didst drive out the nations and plant it — RSV

You drove out the (heathen) nations and planted it [in Canaan] — Amp

9. **Thou preparedst room before it, and didst cause it to take deep root, and it filled the land.**

Thou didst make a clear space before it,
So it rooted well its roots and filled up the land — Rhm

You made ready a place for it, so that it might take deep root, and it sent out its branches over all the land — Bas

10. **The hills were covered with the shadow of it, and the boughs thereof were like the goodly cedars.**

The mountains were covered with its shade,
the mighty cedars with its branches — RSV

11. **She sent out her boughs unto the sea, and her branches unto the river.**

[Israel] sent out its boughs to the [Mediterranean] Sea, and its branches to the [Euphrates] River — Amp

12. **Why hast thou then broken down her hedges, so that all they which pass by the way do pluck her?**

---

[22]See also verse 3.

Why is it that in these days thou hast levelled its wall, for every passer-by to rob it of its fruit — Knox

Why, then, have You broken down its fences,
so that all who pass by pluck off its fruit — Har

But now you have broken down our walls, leaving us without protection — Tay

13. The boar out of the wood doth waste it, and the wild beast of the field doth devour it.

The boar from the forest ravages it,
and all that move in the field feed on it — RSV

The wild hog gnaws at it,
and the animals of the field feed upon it — Har

14. Return, we beseech thee, O God of hosts:

Return, God of armies — Har

O God of hosts, restore us — AAT

look down from heaven, and behold, and visit this vine;

15. And the vineyard which thy right hand hath planted, and the branch that thou madest strong for thyself.

Look down from heaven, and see;
have regard for this vine,
the stock which thy right hand planted — RSV

look from heaven and observe and visit this vine.
Protect what Thy right hand has planted,
the son whom Thou hast raised for Thyself — Ber

Look down from heaven and see our plight and care for this your vine! — Tay

16. It is burned with fire, it is cut down: they perish at the rebuke of thy countenance.

they have burned it with fire, they have cut it down;
may they perish at the rebuke of thy countenance! — RSV

Let those who would burn it with fire or cut it down
perish before you at your rebuke — NAB

For we are chopped and burned by our enemies. May they perish at your frown — Tay

17. Let thy hand be upon the man of thy right hand, upon the son of man whom thou madest strong for thyself.

May your help be with the man of your right hand,
with the son of man whom you yourself made strong — NAB

Bestow Your power upon man,
Your sovereign might upon the offspring which You have raised up for Yourself — Har

May your hand protect the man at your right,
the son of man who has been authorized by you — Jerus

Do thou protect thy chosen folk,
those thou hast nurtured for thyself — Mof

18. So will not we go back from thee:

Then we will never turn back from thee — RSV

Then we will never stray from You — Har

quicken us, and we will call upon thy name.

O let us live, and we shall call upon thy Name — PBV

give us life, and we will call on thy name! — RSV

19. Turn us again, O LORD God of hosts, cause thy face to shine; and we shall be saved.[23]

Restore us, O LORD God of hosts!
let thy face shine, that we may be saved! — RSV

Lord God of armies, restore us:
bestow Your favor upon us, that we may be saved — Har

O Yahweh God of hosts! bring us back,
Light up thy face,
That we may be saved — Rhm

PSALM 81

To the chief Musician upon Gittith, A Psalm of Asaph.

To the Chief Musician. On "The Gittith." Asaph's — Rhm

From the Choirmaster's collection. Set to a vintage melody. An Asaphite song — Mof

To the Chief Musician; set to Philistine lute, or [possibly] a particular Gittite tune. [A Psalm] of Asaph — Amp

1. Sing aloud unto God our strength:

[23]Compare verses 3 and 7.

Sing we merrily unto God our strength — PBV
Shout ye for joy unto God our strength — Rhm
Sing joyfully of our mighty God — Har
Sing out in praise of God our refuge — NEB

make a joyful noise unto the God of Jacob.

shout for joy to the God of Jacob! — RSV
Sound the note of triumph to the God of Jacob — Rhm
cry out with gladness to the God of Jacob — Knox
acclaim the God of Jacob — NEB

2. Take a psalm, and bring hither the timbrel, the pleasant harp with the psaltery.

Raise a song, sound the timbrel,
the sweet lyre with the harp — RSV
Let the music crescendo;
beat the tambourine,
play the soothing harp and the lyre — Har
Start the music, sound the drum,
the melodious lyre and the harp — Jerus
Raise the chant and beat the drum,
Both the pleasant harp and the lute — AAT
raise the chorus, sound the drum,
sound the sweet lyre and the lute — Mof

3. Blow up the trumpet in the new moon, in the time appointed, on our solemn feast day.

Blow the trumpet at the new moon,
At the full moon, on our feast day — ASV
Sound the trumpet at the new moon, and at the day of our festival, when the moon is full — Har
Sound the trumpet! Come to the joyous celebrations at full moon, new moon and all the other holidays — Tay

4. For this was a statute for Israel, and a law of the God of Jacob.

For it is a statute for Israel, an ordinance of the God of Jacob — RV
For it is a statute for Israel — a rite established by the God of Jacob — Sept
This is a custom in Israel,
a decree of the God of Jacob — Har
For God has given us these times of joy; they are scheduled in the laws of Israel — Tay

5. This he ordained in Joseph for a testimony, when he went out through the land of Egypt:

He made it a decree in Joseph,
when he went out over the land of Egypt — RSV
He made it a law for Joseph,
when He marched against the land of Egypt — Har
laid as a solemn charge on Joseph
when he came out of Egypt — NEB

where I heard a language that I understood not.

6. I removed his shoulder from the burden: his hands were delivered from the pots.

I hear a voice I had not known:
"I relieved your shoulder of the burden;
your hands were freed from the basket — RSV
I heard an unfamiliar voice saying,
"I have removed the burden from his shoulder;
his hands were released from carrying the heavy basket — Har
I heard one whom I knew not, saying:
"I freed your shoulder from the load,
your hands from the heavy hod — Mof
In a tongue unknown the message came to me; I have eased his shoulder of the burden, freed his hands from the slavery of the hod! — Knox

7. Thou calledst in trouble, and I delivered thee;

In distress thou didst cry and I delivered thee — Rhm
at your cry of distress I rescued you — Mof

I answered thee in the secret place of thunder:

I answered you from thunderclouds — Mof
I answered you from the recesses of the thundercloud — Har

I proved thee at the waters of Meribah.

I tested you at the waters of Meribah — Mof

Selah.

Selah. [pause, and calmly think of that]! — Amp

8. Hear, O my people, and I will testify unto thee:

Hear, O my people, while I admonish you! — RSV
Give heed, my people, to this warning of mine — Knox
O Israel, if thou wilt hearken unto me;
9. There shall no strange god be in thee; neither shalt thou worship any strange god.
O Israel, if you would but listen to me!
There shall be no strange god among you;
you shall not bow down to a foreign god — RSV
if only you will pay attention to Me, people of Israel,
there will not be one foreign deity among you,
nor will you be subservient to pagan gods — Har
10. I am the LORD thy God, which brought thee out of the land of Egypt:
I am Jehovah thy God,
Who brought thee up out of the land of Egypt — ASV
I Yahweh am thy God
Who brought thee up out of the land of Egypt — Rhm
open thy mouth wide, and I will fill it.
make your requests without limit,
and I will accede to them all — Har
you have only to open your mouth for me to fill it — Jerus
11. But my people would not hearken to my voice; and Israel would none of me.
But my people would not hear my voice; and Israel would not obey me — PBV
But my people did not listen to my voice;
Israel would have none of me — RSV
But My people paid no attention to what I said;
Israel declined My offer — Har
12. So I gave them up unto their own hearts' lust: and they walked in their own counsels.
And I gave them up to the stubbornness of their hearts;
They go on in their own counsels — ABPS
So I have abandoned them to their obstinacy;
they have followed their own inclinations — Har
so I left them to their own self-will,
to follow their own devices — Mof
so I left them to their stubborn selves
to do whatever they pleased — Jerus
13. Oh that my people had hearkened unto me, and Israel had walked in my ways!
14. I should soon have subdued their enemies, and turned my hand against their adversaries.
O that my people would listen to me,
that Israel would walk in my ways!
I would soon subdue their enemies,
and turn my hand against their foes — RSV
If only My people would listen to Me;
if Israel would only follow My directions,
I would subdue their enemies quickly,
and focus My power on their opponents — Har
If only my people would listen,
if Israel would follow my ways,
at one blow I would defeat their enemies
and strike at all who attack them — Jerus
15. The haters of the LORD should have submitted themselves unto him: but their time should have endured for ever.
Those who hate the LORD would cringe toward him,
and their fate would last for ever — RSV
Those who hate the Lord God would cower before him,
and their destiny would be fixed forever — Har
The haters of the Lord would be broken, and their destruction would be eternal — Bas
Then those who hate Yahweh would cringe,
their doom being sealed for ever — Jerus
[Had Israel listened to Me in Egypt, then] those who hated the Lord would have come cringing before Him, and their defeat would have lasted forever — Amp
16. He should have fed them also with the finest of the wheat: and with honey out of the rock should I have satisfied thee.
I would feed you with the finest of the wheat,
and with honey from the rock I would satisfy you" — RSV
He would feed them with the best wheat,

and nourish them with honey gathered from the rocks" — Har
while I would feed you on pure wheat and satisfy you with the wild rock honey' — Jerus

Israel should have full ears of wheat to nourish them, and honey dropping from the rock to their heart's content — Knox

PSALM 82

A Psalm of Asaph.

1. God standeth in the congregation of the mighty; he judgeth among the gods.
God has taken his place in the divine council;
in the midst of the gods he holds judgment: — RSV
God standeth in the congregation of God;
In the midst of the judges He judgeth: — JPS
God stands up in the divine assembly:
in the midst of the judges He gives judgment, — Har
God stands up to open heaven's court.
He pronounces judgment on the judges — Tay

2. How long will ye judge unjustly, and accept the persons of the wicked?
"How long will you judge unjustly,
And show partiality toward the wicked — AAT
'No more mockery of justice,
no more favouring the wicked! — Jerus
Selah.

3. Defend the poor and fatherless: do justice to the afflicted and needy.
"Dispense justice to the needy and orphaned;
uphold the rights of the oppressed and destitute — Har
Let the weak and the orphan have justice,
be fair to the wretched and destitute — Jerus

4. Deliver the poor and needy: rid them out of the hand of the wicked.
Deliver the wretched and needy;
Out of the hand of the wicked rescue them — DeW
rescue the weak and needy,
save them from the clutches of the wicked! — Jerus

5. They know not, neither will they understand;
They have neither knowledge nor understanding — RSV
The magistrates and judges know not, neither will they understand — Amp
they walk on in darkness: all the foundations of the earth are out of course.
they walk about in darkness;
all the foundations of the earth are shaken — RSV
they walk about in bewilderment.
All the foundations of the earth tremble — Har
Ignorant and senseless, they carry on blindly,
undermining the very basis of earthly society — Jerus
they walk on in the darkness [of complacent satisfaction]; all the foundations of the earth [the fundamental principles upon which rests the administration of justice] are shaking — Amp

6. I have said, Ye are gods; and all of you are children of the most High.
I was the one to say that you should be as God:
all of you the kin of the Most High — Har
I once said, 'You too are gods,
sons of the Most High, all of you' — Jerus
I said, You are gods [since you judge on My behalf, as My representatives]; indeed, all of you are children of the Most High — Amp
This is my sentence: Gods you may be,
sons all of you of a high god — NEB

7. But ye shall die like men, and fall like one of the princes.
nevertheless, you shall die like men,
and fall like any prince — RSV
But you shall die like mortal men,
and succumb like any other noble person — Har
but all the same, you shall die like other men;

as one man, princes, you shall fall — Jerus
yet you shall die as men die; princes fall, every one of them, and so shall you — NEB
But in death you are mere men. You will fall as any prince — for all must die — Tay

8. Arise, O God, judge the earth:
Stand up, Lord God, to dispense justice on earth — Har
for thou shalt inherit all nations.
for to thee belong all the nations! — RSV
since no nation is excluded from your ownership — Jerus

PSALM 83

A Song or Psalm of Asaph.

1. Keep not thou silence, O God:
Do not remain silent, Lord God — Har
hold not thy peace, and be not still, O God.
do not show indifference, or refrain from activity — Har
do not be unmoved, O God, or unresponsive! — Jerus
2. For, lo, thine enemies make a tumult:
For lo, thine enemies rage — ABPS
and they that hate thee have lifted up the head.
those who hate You have become haughty — Har
see how those who hate you rear their heads — Jerus
3. They have taken crafty counsel against thy people, and consulted against thy hidden ones.
They lay crafty plans against thy people;
they consult together against thy protected ones — RSV
They have made ingenious plans against Your people,
and they plot together against those whom You protect — Hat
They devise cunning schemes against thy people
and conspire against those thou hast made thy treasure — NEB
4. They have said, Come, and let us cut them off from being a nation;
They say, "Come, let us wipe them out as a nation — RSV
that the name of Israel may be no more in remembrance.
let the name of Israel be remembered no more!" — RSV
so that the very name of Israel will be remembered no more — Knox
5. For they have consulted together with one consent:
Yea, they conspire with one accord — RSV
they are confederate against thee:
against thee they make a covenant — RSV
and form an alliance against You — Har
6. The tabernacles of Edom, and the Ishmaelites; of Moab, and the Hagarenes;
7. Gebal, and Ammon, and Amalek; the Philistines with the inhabitants of Tyre;
— the tents of Edom and the Ishmaelites,
Moab and the Hagrites,
Gebal and Ammon and Amalek,
Philistia with the inhabitants of Tyre — RSV
the families of Edom, the Ishmaelites, Moabites . . . — NEB
8. Assur also is joined with them:
Assyria also has joined them — RSV
Assyria also is in league with them — Har
they have holpen the children of Lot.
They have helped the children of Lot — ASV
. . . the children of Lot [the Ammonites and the Moabites] — Amp
they are the strong arm of the children of Lot — RSV
they constitute the military backing of Lot's descendants — Har
Selah.
9. Do unto them as unto the Midianites;
Do to them as thou didst to Midian — RSV
as to Sisera, as to Jabin, at the brook of Kison:
As to Sisera, as to Jabin, at the river Kishon — ASV
10. Which perished at En-dor:
who were destroyed at En-dor — RSV
they became as dung for the earth.

who became dung for the ground — RSV
becoming corpses on the ground — Har
who became as manure for the earth — Amp
and were spread on the battlefield like dung — NEB

11. Make their nobles like Oreb, and like Zeeb: yea, all their princes as Zebah, and as Zalmunna:

12. Who said, Let us take to ourselves the houses of God in possession.

Who have said, Let us take possession for ourselves
Of the dwelling-places of God — ABPS
who said, "Let us take possession for ourselves
of the pastures of God" — RSV

13. O my God, make them like a wheel;

O my God, make them like the whirling dust — RSV
Make them, my God, like the blown chaff — Har
My God, bowl them along like tumbleweed — Jerus
O my God, make them like leaves in a whirlwind — NAB
My God, send them whirling this way and that, like leaves — Knox

as the stubble before the wind.

like straws before the wind — Knox
like chaff at the mercy of the wind — Jerus

14. As the fire burneth a wood, and as the flame setteth the mountains on fire;

As fire consumes the forest,
as the flame sets the mountains ablaze — RSV

15. So persecute them with thy tempest, and make them afraid with thy storm.

so do thou pursue them with thy tempest
and terrify them with thy hurricane! — RSV
follow them relentlessly by Your storm,
and terrify them by Your tornado — Har

16. Fill their faces with shame; that they may seek thy name. O LORD.

Fill thou their faces with dishonour,
That men may seek thy Name O Yahweh — Rhm
Fill their faces with confusion,
That they may seek thy name, O Jehovah — ASV
Make them thoroughly shamefaced, that they may search You out, Lord — Har
Let their faces be full of shame; so that they may give honour to your name, O Lord — Bas
Darken their faces with disgrace,
that men may seek your name, O LORD — NAB
Let their cheeks blush crimson with shame, Lord, till they come to sue for thy favour — Knox

17. Let them be confounded and troubled for ever;

Let them be ashamed and dismayed for ever — RV
Let them be disgraced
and live in continual terror — Har

yea, let them be put to shame, and perish:

let them perish in disgrace — RSV
Yea let them blush and perish — Rhm

18. That men may know that thou, whose name alone is JEHOVAH, art the most high over all the earth.

That men may know that thou
Whose Name alone is Yahweh
Art Most High over all the earth — Rhm
till they, too, know the meaning of the divine name, acknowledge thee as the most high God, the Overlord of the earth — Knox
So let them learn that thou alone art LORD,
God Most High over all the earth — NEB

PSALM 84

To the chief Musician upon Gittith[24], A Psalm for the sons of Korah.

1. How amiable are thy tabernacles, O LORD of hosts!

How dear are your tents, O Lord of armies — Bas
How I love your palace,
Yahweh Sabaoth — Jerus
How lovely Your dwelling is,
Lord God of armies — Har

---

[24]See Psalm 81.

2. My soul longeth, yea, even fainteth for the courts of the LORD:
My soul longeth — yea even languisheth — for the courts of Yahweh — Rhm
My soul longs and yearns for the shrines of the Lord — Har
my soul longeth, it panteth for the courts of the Lord — Sept
I pine, I faint with longing
for the courts of the LORD's temple — NEB
my heart and my flesh crieth out for the living God.
my mind and body shout for joy to the living God — Har
The living God! at his name my heart, my whole being thrills with joy — Knox

3. Yea, the sparrow hath found an house, and the swallow a nest for herself, where she may lay her young,
Even the sparrow finds a home,
and the swallow a nest for herself,
where she may lay her young — RSV
The sparrow has found its home at last,
the swallow a nest for its young — Jerus
even thine altars, O LORD of hosts, my King, and my God.
at thy altars, O LORD of hosts,
my King and my God — RSV
namely, at Your altars, Lord God of armies,
my King and God — Har
where she rears her brood beside thy altars,
O LORD of Hosts, my King and my God — NEB

4. Blessed are they that dwell in thy house: they will be still praising thee.
O their blessedness that dwell in Thy house!
They shall still be praising Thee — DeW
Happy they who dwell in thy house;
Continually do they praise thee — ABPS
Blessed are those who dwell in thy house,
ever singing thy praise! — RSV
All who live in Your dwelling are happy indeed,
singing Your praises continually — Har
Happy those who live in your house
and can praise you all day long — Jerus
Selah.
Selah [pause, and calmly think of that]! — Amp

5. Blessed is the man whose strength is in thee; in whose heart are the ways of them.
Blessed is the man whose strength is in thee; in whose heart are thy ways — PBV
O the blessedness of the men
Whose strength is in Thee,
In whose heart are the highways to Zion! — DeW
How happy the men whose strength is in thee,
Festive processions are in their heart — Rhm
Happy the man who has his strength in thee,
In their heart the pilgrim-ways — ABPS
Happy the men whose refuge is in thee, whose hearts are set on the pilgrim ways! — NEB
Happy are they who, nerved by thee, set out on pilgrimage! — Mof

6. Who passing through the valley of Baca make it a well; the rain also filleth the pools.
Who going through the vale of misery use it for a well; and the pools are filled with water — PBV
Passing through the valley of Weeping they make it a place of springs; yea, the early rain covereth it with blessings — RV
As they pass through the valley of weeping,
they transform it into a region of springs — Har
When they pass through Weary-glen,
fountains flow for their refreshing,
blessing rain upon them — Mof
As they pass through the thirsty valley
they find water from a spring
and the LORD provides even men who lose their way
with pools to quench their thirst — NEB
When they pass through the arid valley,
they make a spring of it;
the early rain clothes it with generous growth — NAB

7. They go from strength to strength,

every one of them in Zion appeareth before God.
they are the stronger as they go,
till God at last reveals himself in Sion — Mof
They go from strength to strength;
the God of gods will be seen in Zion — RSV
So, at each stage refreshed, they will reach Sion, and have sight there of the God who is above all gods — Knox
Thence they make their way from height,
soon to be seen before God on Zion — Jerus

8. O LORD God of hosts, hear my prayer: give ear, O God of Jacob.
O Jehovah God of hosts, hear my prayer;
Give ear, O God of Jacob — ASV
Lord God of armies, hear my prayer;
pay attention, God of Jacob — Har
Selah.

9. Behold, O God our shield, and look upon the face of thine anointed.
Behold, O God our defender, and look upon the face of thine anointed — PBV
God, our protector, look on us,
welcome thy chosen to thy presence — Mof
Behold our shield, O God;
look upon the face of thine anointed! — RSV
Behold our shield [the king as Your agent], O God, and look upon the face of Your anointed! — Amp
God, ever our protector, do not disregard us now; look favourably upon him whom thou hast anointed! — Knox

10. For a day in thy courts is better than a thousand.
For better is one day in thy courts than a thousand elsewhere — AAT
I had rather be a doorkeeper in the house of my God, than to dwell in the tents of wickedness.
I choose rather to stand at the threshold in the house of my God,
Than to dwell in the tents of lawlessness — Rhm
I would rather sit at the threshold of God's house
than live inside the tents of worldly men — Mof
merely to stand on the steps of God's house
is better than living with the wicked — Jerus

11. For the LORD God is a sun and shield: the LORD will give grace and glory: no good thing will he withhold from them that walk uprightly.
For Jehovah God is a sun and a shield:
Jehovah will give grace and glory;
No good thing will he withhold from them that walk uprightly — ASV
Sun to enlighten, shield to protect us, the Lord God has favour, has honour to bestow. To innocent lives he will never refuse his bounty — Knox
For the Lord God is a towering protection;
He bestows goodness and honor.
He does not withhold prosperity from those who live blamelessly — Har

12. O LORD of hosts, blessed is the man that trusteth in thee.
O Yahweh of hosts!
How happy the man who trusteth in thee! — Rhm
Lord God of armies,
how happy is the one who trusts in You — Har
Jehovah of Hosts! O the happiness of a man trusting in Thee — YLT

PSALM 85

To the chief Musician, A Psalm for the sons of Korah.

1. LORD, thou hast been favourable unto thy land: thou hast brought back the captivity of Jacob.
Thou hast shown favour, O Jehovah! unto Thy land:
Thou hast returned to the captives of Jacob — DeW
LORD, thou wast favorable to thy land;
thou didst restore the fortunes of Jacob — RSV
Yahweh, you favour your own country,
you bring back the captives of Jacob — Jerus
LORD, You have [at last] been favorable and have dealt graciously with

Your land [of Canaan]. You have brought back [from Babylon] the captives of Jacob — Amp

2. Thou hast forgiven the iniquity of thy people, thou hast covered all their sin.

Thou hast taken away the iniquity of thy people,
Thou hast covered all their sin — Rhm

Thou hast lifted off the guilt of Thy people; Thou hast covered all their sin — DeW

You have forgiven the wrongdoing of Your people,
and have pardoned all their sin — Har

Selah.

3. Thou hast taken away all thy wrath:

Thou hast withdrawn all thine indignation — Rhm

thou hast turned thyself from the fierceness of thine anger.

Thou hast ceased from the glow of thine anger — Rhm

you have revoked your burning anger — NAB

4. Turn us, O God of our salvation, and cause thine anger toward us to cease.

Turn us then, O God our Saviour, and let thine anger cease from us — PBV

Restore us O God of our salvation,
And take away thy vexation towards us — Rhm

Return unto us, O God of our salvation!
And cause Thine indignation toward us to cease — DeW

Turn back to us, O God our saviour, and cancel thy displeasure — NEB

And now, God of our deliverance, do thou restore us; no longer let us see thy frown — Knox

5. Wilt thou be angry with us for ever?

Do you mean to be angry with us for ever — Jerus

wilt thou draw out thine anger to all generations?

and wilt thou stretch out thy wrath from one generation to another — PBV

Wilt thou prolong thine anger from generation to generation — Rhm

Must thy resentment smoulder on, age after age — Knox

Will You prolong Your fury indefinitely — Har

6. Wilt thou not revive us again: that thy people may rejoice in thee?

Wilt thou not turn again, and quicken us, that thy people may rejoice in thee — PBV

Wilt not thou thyself again give us life,
That thy people may rejoice in thee — Rhm

Wilt not THOU give back to us our life,
That Thy people may rejoice in Thee — DeW

Will You not rather revive us once more,
that Your people may behave gratefully towards You — Har

7. Shew us thy mercy, O LORD, and grant us thy salvation.

Show us thy lovingkindness, O Jehovah,
And grant us thy salvation — ASV

Show us thy steadfast love, O LORD, and grant us thy salvation — RSV

Show us Your loving concern, Lord, and favor us with speedy release — Har

8. I will hear what God the LORD will speak:

I will hear what God Jehovah will speak — ASV

Let me hear what God the LORD will speak — RSV

for he will speak peace unto his people, and to his saints: but let them not turn again to folly.

for He will speak peace to His people and to His worshipers;
but let them not turn again to folly — Ber

For he will bespeak prosperity to his people
And to his men of lovingkindness,
And to them who return with their heart unto him — Rhm

For He speaketh peace to His people whom He loveth;
But let them not return unto folly — DeW

surely He will assure His people and His saints of peace,
if only they do not return to foolishness — Har

What God is saying means peace
for his people, for his friends,
if only they renounce their folly — Jerus

9. Surely his salvation is nigh them that

fear him; that glory may dwell in our land.

For his salvation is close to them that fear him,
That honor may dwell in our land — AAT

Surely near unto them who revere him is his salvation,
That the Glory may settle down in our land — Rhm

soon shall his worshippers behold his saving aid,
till his Great Presence dwells within our land — Mof

For us, his worshippers, deliverance is close at hand; in this land of ours, the divine glory is to find a home — Knox

His deliverance is near indeed to those who revere Him;
renown will make her abode in our country — Har

10. **Mercy and truth are met together;**

Steadfast love and faithfulness will meet — RSV

Lovingkindness and faithfulness have met together — Rhm

Kindness and faithfulness unite — Mof

righteousness and peace have kissed each other.

Righteousness and prosperity have kissed each other — Rhm

victory and peace embrace — Mof

justice and peace join hands — NEB

11. **Truth shall spring out of the earth; and righteousness shall look down from heaven.**

Truth shall spring out of the earth,
and justice shall look down from heaven — NAB

Faithfulness will spring up from the ground,
and righteousness will look down from the sky — RSV

Truth rises from the earth and righteousness smiles down from heaven —Tay

12. **Yea, the LORD shall give that which is good; and our land shall yield her increase.**

Yea, Jehovah will bestow blessing,
And our land shall yield its increase — DeW

The Lord, now, will grant us his blessing, to make our land yield its harvest — Knox

Yea, the Lord pours down his blessings on the land and it yields its bountiful crops — Tay

13. **Righteousness shall go before him; and shall set us in the way of his steps.**

Righteousness will precede it,
marking the way with its tracks — Har

justice will go on before him, deliverance follow where his feet tread — Knox

Justice shall go in front of him
and the path before his feet shall be peace — NEB

PSALM 86

A Prayer of David.

1. **Bow down thine ear, O LORD, hear me: for I am poor and needy.**

Bow down thine ear, O LORD, and hear me; for I am poor, and in misery — PBV

Incline Thine ear, O JEHOVAH:
Answer me, for I am poor and destitute — Sprl

Bow down O Yahweh thine ear — answer me,
For oppressed and needy am I — Rhm

2. **Preserve my soul; for I am holy:**

Preserve my life, for I am godly — RSV

Keep my soul, for I am a devoted man — Sprl

Keep me secure, for I am a godly person — Har

O guard my life
For a man of lovingkindness am I — Rhm

Preserve Thou my soul; for I am one whom Thou lovest — DeW

O thou my God, save thy servant that trusteth in thee.

3. **Be merciful unto me, O Lord; for I cry unto thee daily.**

Thou art my God; be gracious to me, O Lord,
for to thee do I cry all the day — RSV

4. Rejoice the soul of thy servant;
Gladden the heart of thy servant — AAT
Bring gladness into the life of Your servant — Har
for unto thee, O Lord, do I lift up my soul.
for I dedicate myself to You, Lord — Har
5. For thou, Lord, art good, and ready to forgive; and plenteous in mercy unto all them that call upon thee.
For thou, O Lord, art good and forgiving,
abounding in steadfast love to all who call on thee — RSV
For thou O My Lord art good and forgiving
And abundant in lovingkindness to all who call upon thee — Rhm
Who is so kind and forgiving, Lord, as thou art, who so rich in mercy to all who invoke him? — Knox
6. Give ear, O LORD, unto my prayer; and attend to the voice of my supplications.
O Thou Eternal, listen to my prayer, and hear my pleading cry — Mof
Pay attention, Lord, to my prayer, and listen to my imploring voice — Har
7. In the day of my trouble I will call upon thee: for thou wilt answer me.
In the day of my distress I will call upon Thee,
For thou wilt answer me — Sprl
8. Among the gods there is none like unto thee, O Lord; neither are there any works like unto thy works.
There is none like thee among the gods, O Lord,
And no works like thine — ABPS
There is no god like thee, O Lord, there are no deeds like thine — Mof
Among the deities there is none like You, Lord;
there is nothing to compare with Your mighty deeds — Har
Where among the heathen gods is there a God like you? Where are their miracles? — Tay
9. All nations whom thou hast made shall come and worship before thee, O Lord;
All nations, which thou hast made,
Shall come and bow down before thee, O Lord — ABPS
and shall glorify thy name.
And shall give glory to thy name — ABPS
and will honor Your name — Har
10. For thou art great, and doest wondrous things: thou art God alone.
for thou art great, thou workest wonders,
thou, only thou, art God — Mof
since you alone are great, you perform marvels,
you God, you alone — Jerus
11. Teach me thy way, O LORD: I will walk in thy truth: unite my heart to fear thy name.
Direct me, O JEHOVAH, in Thy way,
That I may walk according to Thy truth:
Dispose my heart to reverence Thy Name — Sprl
Point out to me O Yahweh thy way
I will walk steadfastly in thy truth,
My heart will rejoice to revere thy Name — Rhm
Teach me thy way, O LORD,
That I may walk in fidelity to thee,
That my heart may rejoice in the fear of thy name — AAT
Give me insight into Your ways, Lord,
I will behave loyally toward You.
May my life be centered upon reverence to Your name — Har
Yahweh, teach me your way,
how to walk beside you faithfully,
make me single-hearted in fearing your name — Jerus
Tell me where you want me to go and I will go there. May every fiber of my being unite in reverence to your name — Tay
12. I will praise thee, O Lord my God, with all my heart: and I will glorify thy name for evermore.
I will praise You, my Lord and God, with my whole being,
and I will honor Your name for ever — Har
I will give thanks Adonay my God with all my heart,
And will glorify thy name unto times age-abiding — Rhm
13. For great is thy mercy toward me:
For great is thy steadfast love toward me — RSV
For great is thy lovingkindness toward me — ASV
For the loving sympathy which You

have shown me is immense — Har
and thou hast delivered my soul from the lowest hell.
And thou hast rescued my soul from Hades beneath — Rhm
And thou hast delivered my soul from the lowest Sheol — ASV
And thou hast rescued my soul from the underworld beneath — ABPS
You have liberated me from the recesses of the world beyond — Har
and You have delivered me from the depths of Sheol [from exceeding depth of affliction] — Amp

14. **O God, the proud are risen against me, and the assemblies of violent men have sought after my soul; and have not set thee before them.**
O God, insolent men have risen up against me;
a band of ruthless men seek my life, and they do not set thee before them — RSV
Now arrogant men, God, are attacking me,
a brutal gang hounding me to death: people to whom you mean nothing — Jerus

15. **But thou, O Lord, art a God full of compassion, and gracious, longsuffering, and plenteous in mercy and truth.**
But thou, O Lord, art a God merciful and gracious,
Slow to anger, and abundant in lovingkindness and truth — ASV
But thou, O Lord, art a God merciful and gracious,
slow to anger and abounding in steadfast love and faithfulness — RSV
But thou, Lord, art a Lord of mercy and pity, patient, full of compassion, true to thy promise — Knox

16. **O turn unto me, and have mercy upon me;**
Turn thou unto me and shew me favour — Rhm
Turn toward me, and be gracious to me — ABPS
give thy strength unto thy servant, and save the son of thine handmaid.
Give me your strength, your saving help,
me your servant, this son of a pious mother — Jerus
give your strength to your servant, and your salvation to the son of her who is your servant — Bas

17. **Shew me a token for good;**
Grant me a proof of your favor — NAB
Show me a heartening sign — Har
give me one proof of your goodness — Jerus
that they which hate me may see it, and be ashamed: because thou, LORD, hast holpen me, and comforted me.
that those who hate me may see and be put to shame
because thou, LORD, hast helped me and comforted me — RSV
that my enemies may see, to their confusion,
that you, O LORD, have helped and comforted me — NAB
Yahweh, make my opponents ashamed, show them that you are my help and consolation — Jerus

PSALM 87

A Psalm or Song for the sons of Korah.

1. **His foundation is in the holy mountains.**
He hath founded His city
Upon the holy mountains — DeW
On the holy mount stands the city he founded — RSV

2. **The LORD loveth the gates of Zion more than all the dwellings of Jacob.**
dearer to the Lord are Sion walls than any other home in Israel — Knox

3. **Glorious things are spoken of thee, O city of God.**
Dear city of God, he utters thy glories: — Mof
Glorious things he speaks of you,
O city of God — AAT
Marvelous things have been said in praise of you,
city of God — Har
Selah.
Selah [pause, and calmly think of that]! — Amp

4. **I will make mention of Rahab and Babylon to them that know me: behold Philistia, and Tyre, with Ethiopia; this man was born there.**

I may mention Rahab and Babylon
on account of their famous men,
Philistia, Tyre, and also Ethiopia;
"Such a one was born there!" — AAT

Among those who know me I mention
Rahab and Babylon;
behold, Philistia and Tyre, with
Ethiopia" —
"This one was born there," they say
— RSV

I will make mention of Rahab [the poetic name for Egypt] and Babylon as among those who know [the city of God]; behold, Philistia and Tyre, with Ethiopia (Cush), say, This man was born there — Amp

Nowadays when I mention among my friends the names of Egypt and Babylonia, Philistia and Tyre, or even distant Ethiopia, someone boasts that he was born in one or another of those countries — Tay

5. And of Zion it shall be said, This and that man was born in her: and the highest himself shall establish her.

But of Zion it will be said,
"This one and that one were born
in her!"
And that will place her in the highest
rank — AAT

And of Zion it shall be said,
"This one and that one were born
in her";
for the Most High himself will establish her — RSV

But someday the highest honor will be to be a native of Jerusalem! For the God above all gods will personally bless this city — Tay

6. The LORD shall count, when he writeth up the people, that this man was born there.

The LORD, when he lists the nations,
will record,
"Such a one was born there" — AAT

The LORD records as he registers the
peoples,
"This one was born there" — RSV

When he registers her citizens he will place a checkmark beside the names of those who were born here — Tay

Selah.

7. As well the singers as the players on instruments shall be there: all my springs are in thee.

Singers and dancers alike say,
"All my springs are in you" — RSV

And all shall sing, in their festive
dance:
"My home is within you" — NAB

And in the festivals they'll sing, "All my heart is in Jerusalem" — Tay

As well the singers as the players of instruments shall say, All my springs — my sources of life and joy — are in you [city of our God] — Amp

PSALM 88

A Song or Psalm for the sons of Korah, to the chief Musician upon Mahalath Leannoth, Maschil of Heman the Ezrahite.

A Song, a Melody. For the Sons of Korah. To the Chief Musician. On "Mahalath." For alternate Song. An Instructive Psalm. By Heman the Ezrahite — Rhm

A Korahite song for music from the Choirmaster's collection. To the tune of "Suffering sore." An ode of Heman the Ezrahite — Mof

1. O LORD God of my salvation, I have cried day and night before thee:

O Jehovah, the God of my salvation, I have cried day and night before thee — ASV

O LORD, my God, I call for help by
day;
I cry out in the night before thee
— RSV

LORD, God of my salvation, by day I
cry for help;
at night I am in Thy presence — Ber

Yahweh my God, I call for help all day,
I weep to you all night — Jerus

O thou Eternal, I cry for help in the
day-time,
and at night I moan before thee —
Mof

2. Let my prayer come before thee: incline thine ear unto my cry;

Let my prayer come into thy presence,
Bow down thine ear to my loud cry
— Rhm

Let my prayer come into Thy presence;
Incline Thine ear unto my wailing
— DeW

may my prayer reach you
hear my cries for help — Jerus

3. For my soul is full of troubles:

For my soul is sated with misfortunes
— Rhm

For my soul is full of suffering — DeW

For I am surfeited with troubles — AAT

and my life draweth nigh unto the grave.
And my soul draweth nigh unto Sheol — ASV
And my life draws near to the underworld — ABPS
And my life — unto Hades hath drawn near — Rhm
and my life draweth near to the mansion of the dead — Sept
my life is on the verge of death — Mof
My life sinks ever closer to the grave — Knox
and I am on the verge of the world beyond — Har

4. **I am counted with them that go down into the pit:**
I am numbered with those who go down to the abyss — NEB
I am already reckoned among the departed — Mof
I am included among those destined for the grave — Har

I am as a man that hath no strength:
I am as a man that hath no help — ASV
I have become like a man whose strength is gone — DeW
I became like a man who is past recovery — Sept

5. **Free among the dead, like the slain that lie in the grave, whom thou rememberest no more: and they are cut off from thy hand.**
like one forsaken among the dead,
like the slain that lie in the grave,
like those whom thou dost remember no more,
for they are cut off from thy hand — RSV
a man alone, down among the dead,
among the slaughtered in their graves,
among those you have forgotten,
those deprived of your protecting hand — Jerus

6. **Thou hast laid me in the lowest pit, in darkness, in the deeps.**
Thou hast put me in the depths of the Pit,
in the regions dark and deep — RSV
You have plunged me into the bottom of the pit,
into the dark abyss — NAB
You have plunged me to the bottom of the Pit,
to its darkest, deepest place — Jerus

7. **Thy wrath lieth hard upon me, and thou hast afflicted me with all thy waves.**
Thine indignation lieth hard upon me, and thou hast vexed me with all thy storms — PBV
heavily thy anger weighs down on me, and thou dost overwhelm me with its full flood — Knox
thy wrath lies heavy upon me,
thy waves all overwhelm me — Mof
Your wrath lies heavy on me; wave after wave engulfs me — Tay

Selah.
Selah [pause, and calmly think of that]! — Amp

8. **Thou hast put away mine acquaintance far from me; thou hast made me an abomination unto them:**
Thou hast caused my companions to shun me;
thou hast made me a thing of horror to them — RSV
You have caused my friends to shun me;
You have made me revolting to them — Har
You have turned my friends against me
and made me repulsive to them — Jerus

I am shut up, and I cannot come forth.

9. **Mine eye mourneth by reason of affliction: LORD I have called daily upon thee, I have stretched out my hands unto thee.**
I am shut in so that I cannot escape;
my eye grows dim through sorrow.
Every day I call upon thee, O Lord
I spread out my hands to thee — RSV
I am hemmed in so that I cannot escape.
My sight is degenerating through sorrow;
I have entreated You daily, Lord,
and stretched out my hands to You — Har
I cannot escape from my prison,
and my health pines away under my trouble.
Daily I call to thee, O thou Eternal,
I stretch out my hands to thee — Mof

10. **Wilt thou shew wonders to the dead?**

Dost thou work wonders for the dead — RSV
Will you perform miracles for the dead — Har
are your marvels meant for the dead — Jerus
Soon it will be too late! Of what use are your miracles when I am in the grave — Tay
shall the dead arise and praise thee?
Can ghosts arise to praise thee — Mof
How can I praise you then — Tay
Selah.

11. **Shall thy lovingkindness be declared in the grave?**
Will thy loving-kindness be told in the grave — ABPS
Can any in the grave declare thy kindness — Sept
Is Your divine grace talked of in the grave — Har
Who talks of your love in the grave — Jerus
or thy faithfulness in destruction?
or thy faithfulness in Abaddon — RSV
Or Your faithfulness in the world beyond — Har
of your faithfulness in the place of perdition — Jerus

12. **Shall thy wonders be known in the dark? and thy righteousness in the land of forgetfulness?**
Shall any wonder of thine be known in the dark?
Or thy righteousness in the land of forgetfulness — Rhm
Are Your wonders acknowledged in regions of darkness?
Or Your righteousness in the land of oblivion — Har
Do they hear about your marvels in the dark,
about your righteousness in the land of oblivion — Jerus
Can thy wonders be known in the darkness of death,
thy saving help in the land of oblivion — Mof

13. **But unto thee have I cried, O LORD;**
And I to thee, Jehovah, have cried for help — ABPS
and in the morning shall my prayer prevent thee.
and early shall my prayer come before thee — PBV
And in the morning shall my prayer come before thee — ASV
And in the morning my prayer will confront thee! — Rhm

14. **LORD, why castest thou off my soul?**
Wherefore, O Jehovah, dost thou cast off my soul — ABPS
Why do you spurn me, Lord — Har
why hidest thou thy face from me?
Why dost thou reject my plea, Lord, and turn thy face away from me — Knox

15. **I am afflicted and ready to die from my youth up: while I suffer thy terrors I am distracted.**
I am afflicted, and ready to expire, from my youth;
I have borne thy terrors; am in despair — ABPS
I am in misery, and like unto him that is at the point to die; even from my youth up, thy terrors have I suffered with a troubled mind — PBV
Ever since youth, misery and mortal sickness have been my lot; wearily I have borne thy visitations — Knox
I am afflicted and in agony from my youth;
I am dazed with the burden of your dread — NAB
Afflicted and close to death from my youth up,
I suffer thy terrors; I am helpless — RSV
Ever since I was young I have been oppressed, and at the point of death.
I have endured Your terrors; I am benumbed — Har
Wretched, slowly dying since my youth,
I bore your terrors — now I am exhausted — Jerus
I have suffered from boyhood and come near to death;
I have borne thy terrors, I cower beneath thy blows — NEB
From my youth I have been sickly and ready to die. I stand helpless before your terrors — Tay

16. **Thy fierce wrath goeth over me; thy terrors have cut me off.**
Thy wrathful displeasure goeth over me, and the fear of thee hath undone me — PBV
Over me have passed thy bursts of burning anger,
The alarms of thee have put an end to me — Rhm

Thy wrath has swept over me;
thy dread assaults destroy me — RSV
Your fiery anger has swept over me;
your horrors have left me stunned — Har

17. **They came round about me daily like water; they compassed me about together.**
They surround me like a flood all day long;
they close in upon me together — RSV
They encompass me like water all the day;
on all sides they close in upon me — NAB

18. **Lover and friend hast thou put far from me, and mine acquaintance into darkness.**
Thou hast put far every friend,
and darkness is my one companion — Mof
Friends and neighbours gone, a world of shadows is all my company — Knox
Companion and neighbor you have taken away from me:
my only friend is darkness — NAB
You have made admirer and friend alike stand aloof from me;
obscurity is my only companion — Har
You have turned my friends and neighbours against me,
now darkness is my one companion left — Jerus
Lover, friend, acquaintance — all are gone. There is only darkness everywhere — Tay

PSALM 89

Maschil of Ethan the Ezrahite.
An Instructive Psalm, by Ethan the Ezrahite — Rhm

1. **I will sing of the mercies of the LORD for ever:**
I will sing of the lovingkindness of Jehovah for ever — ASV
with my mouth will I make known thy faithfulness to all generations.
with my mouth will I ever be showing thy truth from one generation to another — PBV
age after age my words shall proclaim your faithfulness — Jerus

2. **For I have said, Mercy shall be built up for ever: thy faithfulness shalt thou establish in the very heavens.**
For I know that lovingkindness is built up for ever,
Thou wilt establish Thy faithfulness in the heavens — DeW
For you have said, "My kindness is established forever";
in heaven you have confirmed your faithfulness — NAB
For I say, "Kindness will be renewed forever;
In the heavens thou dost establish thy faithfulness" — AAT
for I claim that love is built to last for ever
and your faithfulness founded firmly in the heavens — Jerus
For I have said,
"Your loving mercy is established forever
Your loyalty is as reliable as the very heavens" — Har
For thy steadfast love was established for ever,
thy faithfulness is firm as the heavens — RSV

3. **I have made a covenant with my chosen, I have sworn unto David my servant.**
[You have said] I have made a covenant with My chosen one, I have sworn to David My servant, — Amp
I entered into an agreement with My chosen one:
I swore solemnly to David My servant, — Har
Thou hast said, "I have made a covenant with my chosen one,
I have sworn to David my servant: — RSV

4. **Thy seed will I establish for ever, and build up thy throne to all generations.**
I will make your seed go on for ever,
your kingdom will be strong through all generations — Bas
"I will establish your posterity forever;
And I will build your throne throughout the ages" — AAT
"I will establish your descendants for all time,

and build up your dynasty for all ages" — Har

Selah.

Selah [pause, and calmly think of that]! — Amp

5. And the heavens shall praise thy wonders, O LORD:

Let the heavens praise thy wonders, O LORD — RSV

Let heaven [the angels] praise Your wonders, O Lord — Amp

thy faithfulness also in the congregation of the saints.

Your faithfulness also in the assembly of the holy ones [the holy angels] — Amp

6. For who in the heaven can be compared unto the LORD?

For who in the skies can be compared to Jehovah — ABPS

who among the sons of the mighty can be likened unto the LORD?

Who among the heavenly beings is like the LORD — RSV

Who is like the Lord among the deities — Har

7. God is greatly to be feared in the assembly of the saints, and to be had in reverence of all them that are about him.

A God feared in the council of the holy ones,
great and terrible above all that are round about him? — RSV

8. O LORD God of hosts, who is a strong LORD like unto thee?

O Jehovah God of hosts,
Who is a mighty one, like unto thee, O Jehovah — ASV

O Yahweh God of hosts!
Who like thee is mighty O Yah — Rhm

Lord God of armies,
who is as powerful as You, Lord — Har

or to thy faithfulness round about thee?

And thy faithfulness is round about thee — ASV

With thy faithfulness round about thee — Rhm

9. Thou rulest the raging of the sea: when the waves thereof arise, thou stillest them.

Thou rulest over the swelling of the sea,
When the rolling waves thereof lift themselves
Thou dost bid them be still — Rhm

10. Thou hast broken Rahab in pieces, as one that is slain; thou hast scattered thine enemies with thy strong arm.

Thou didst crush Rahab like a carcass,
thou didst scatter thy enemies with thy mighty arm — RSV

You have crushed Rahab with a mortal blow;
with your strong arm you have scattered your enemies — NAB

You have broken Rahab (Egypt) in pieces; with Your mighty arm You have scattered Your enemies — Amp

You have cut haughty Egypt to pieces. Your enemies are scattered by your awesome power — Tay

11. The heavens are thine, the earth also is thine: as for the world and the fulness thereof, thou hast founded them.

Thine are the heavens, yea, Thine is the earth;
The world with its produce: Thou hast founded them — Sprl

The heavens are thine, the earth is thine,
twas thou didst found the world and all it holds — Mof

Yours are the heavens, and yours is the earth;
the world and its fulness you have founded — NAB

12. The north and the south thou hast created them: Tabor and Hermon shall rejoice in thy name.

North and South, thou didst create them;
Tabor and Hermon triumph in thy name — ABPS

you created north and south;
Tabor and Hermon hail your name with joy — Jerus

The north and the south, You have created them; Mount Tabor and Mount Hermon joyously praise Your name — Amp

13. Thou hast a mighty arm; strong is thy hand, and high is thy right hand.

Thine is an arm with might,
Strong is thy hand, High is thy right hand — Rhm

You are possessed with formidable strength:
Your activity is vigorous, Your resources immense — Har

14. Justice and judgment are the habitation of thy throne: mercy and truth shall go before thy face.

Righteousness and justice are the foundation of thy throne:
Lovingkindness and truth go before thy face — ASV

Righteousness and justice are the basis of Your sovereignty.
Divine mercy and truth precede You — Har

Righteousness and Justice support your throne,
Love and Faithfulness are your attendants — Jerus

15. Blessed is the people that know the joyful sound:

Blessed are the people who know the festal shout — RSV

How happy are the people who know the joyful sound! — Rhm

Happy the people who learn to acclaim you! — Jerus

Blessed — happy, fortunate [to be envied] — are the people who know the joyful sound [who understand and appreciate the spiritual blessings symbolized by the feasts] — Amp

they shall walk, O Lord, in the light of thy countenance.

They shall proceed under the smile of Thy face, O Jehovah — Sprl

O Yahweh! in the light of thy countenance shall they firmly march along — Rhm

who walk, O LORD, in the light of thy countenance — RSV

who go about radiant with Your presence — Har

16. In thy name shall they rejoice all the day: and in thy righteousness shall they be exalted.

Their delight shall be daily in thy Name; and in thy righteousness shall they make their boast — PBV

At your name they rejoice all the day, and through your justice they are exalted — NAB

Evermore they take pride in thy name, rejoice over thy just dealings — Knox

who exult in thy name all the day, and extol thy righteousness — RSV

They rejoice in Your name daily, and are exalted through Your righteousness — Har

17. For thou art the glory of their strength: and in thy favour our horn shall be exalted.

For You are their glorious strength; and by Your favor our power is increased — Har

Thou art thyself the strength in which they glory; through thy favour we hold our heads high — NEB

For thou art our pride, thou our strength,
and, thanks to thy favour, our honour is high — Mof

18. For the LORD is our defence; and the Holy One of Israel is our king.

For to Yahweh belongeth our Shield,
And to the Holy One of Israel belongeth our King — Rhm

For our shield belongeth unto Jehovah;
And our king to the Holy One of Israel — ASV

we are defended by the Eternal,
by our King, the Majestic One of Israel — Mof

Yes, our protection is from the Lord himself and he, the Holy One of Israel, has given us our king — Tay

19. Then thou spakest in vision to thy holy one, and saidst, I have laid help upon one that is mighty; I have exalted one chosen out of the people.

Once thou didst speak in vision to thy faithful one,
And didst say, "I have placed a diadem upon a warrior;
I have raised up a chosen one from the people — AAT

You once addressed Your devoted servant in a vision, saying,
"I have placed a youth above the mighty man;
I have raised up a young man over the people" — Har

Once you spoke in vision
and said to your friends
"I have conferred the crown on a hero,
and promoted one chosen from my people — Jerus

Once you spoke in a vision,
and to your faithful ones you said:

"On a champion I have placed a crown;
over the people I have set a youth — NAB

20. I have found David my servant; with my holy oil have I anointed him:

21. With whom my hand shall be established: mine arm also shall strengthen him.

I have found David, my servant;
with my holy oil I have anointed him;
so that my hand shall ever abide with him,
my arm also shall strengthen him — RSV

I have chosen David as My servant,
and have anointed him with holy oil.
My power will sustain him,
My might will strengthem him — Har

He is my servant David! I have anointed him with my holy oil. I will steady him and make him strong — Tay

22. The enemy shall not exact upon him; nor the son of wickedness afflict him.

The enemy shall not be able to do him violence; the son of wickedness shall not hurt him — PBV

No foe shall make exactions on him,
Nor shall a son of perversity humiliate him — Rhm

The enemy shall not outwit him,
the wicked shall not humble him — RSV

23. And I will beat down his foes before his face, and plague them that hate him.

But I will crush his foes before him and those who hate him I will smite — NAB

I will shatter his foes before him
and vanquish those who hate him — NEB

24. But my faithfulness and my mercy shall be with him: and in my name shall his horn be exalted.

My faithfulness and mercy shall go with him; by my favour he shall rise to preeminence — Knox

My fidelity and loving mercy shall accompany him,
and through My name his prestige shall increase — Har

my loyalty and love shall be with him,
and I will lift him high in honour — Mof

25. I will set his hand also in the sea, and his right hand in the rivers.

I will put the sea on one hand,
and the river on the other — Har

I will extend his power to the sea,
and his authority far as the Euphrates — Mof

I will give him control of the sea,
complete control of the rivers — Jerus

I will set his hand in control also on the [Mediterranean] Sea and his right hand on the rivers [Euphrates with its tributaries] — Amp

26. He shall cry unto me, Thou art my father, my God, and the rock of my salvation.

he shall say, 'Thou art my Father,
my God, my saving strength!' — Mof

And he will entreat me,
You are my Father, my God, my sure deliverance — Har

He will invoke me, "My father,
my God and rock of my safety" — Jerus

27. Also I will make him my firstborn, higher than the kings of the earth.

I also will make him my firstborn, the highest of the kings of the earth — RV

Yea I will appoint him firstborn,
Most High to the kings of the earth! — Rhm

and I will acknowledge him as my first-born, overlord to all the kings of the earth — Knox

I will treat him as my firstborn son, and make him the mightiest king in all the earth — Tay

28. My mercy will I keep for him for evermore, and my covenant shall stand fast with him.

My lovingkindness . . . — ASV

I will always keep my word to him,
my compact with him stands secure — Mof

I will keep my mercy for him for ever;
my agreement with him will not be changed — Bas

29. His seed also will I make to endure for ever, and his throne as the days of heaven.

I make his dynasty eternal,

his throne unending as the heavens — Mof
I will give him a posterity that never fails, a throne enduring as heaven itself — Knox
I will establish his succession forever; his dynasty will be as stable as heaven — Har

30. If his children forsake my law, and walk not in my judgments;

31. If they break my statutes, and keep not my commandments;

If his sons forsake my law,
And in my regulations do not walk;
If my statutes they profane,
And my commandments do not keep — Rhm
If his sons renounce My law,
and do not follow My decisions:
if they violate My enactments,
and do not observe My injunctions — Har

32. Then will I visit their transgression with the rod, and their iniquity with stripes.

Then they shall feel the rod for their transgressions, I will scourge them for their sin — Knox

33. Nevertheless my lovingkindness will I not utterly take from him, nor suffer my faithfulness to fail.

but I will not cancel my gracious promise to him; never will I be guilty of unfaithfulness — Knox
but I will not remove from him my steadfast love,
or be false to my faithfulness — RSV
But I will not withdraw My loving compassion,
nor be false to My assurances — Har

34. My covenant will I not break, nor alter the thing that is gone out of my lips.

I will be true to my agreement; the things which have gone out of my lips will not be changed — Bas
my compact I will never violate,
my spoken word I will not change — Mof

35. Once have I sworn by my holiness that I will not lie unto David.

I have sworn by my holiness, once for all,
and cannot turn liar to David — Jerus
Pledged stands my inviolable word, I will never be false to David — Knox

36. His seed shall endure for ever, and his throne as the sun before me.

His line shall endure for ever,
his throne as long as the sun before me — RSV
his posterity shall continue for ever, his royalty, too, shall last on in my presence like the sun — Knox

37. It shall be established for ever as the moon, and as a faithful witness in heaven.

Like the moon it shall be established for ever;
it shall stand firm while the skies endure — RSV

Selah.

Selah [pause, and calmly think of that]! — Amp

38. But thou hast cast off and abhorred, thou hast been wroth with thine anointed.

And yet thou hast scorned, discarded, stormed against thy chosen! — Mof
Yet you have rejected and spurned and been enraged at your anointed — NAB

39. Thou hast made void the covenant of thy servant:

Thou hast renounced the covenant with thy servant — RSV
you have repudiated the covenant with your servant — Jerus
You have made your agreement with your servant of no effect — Bas

thou hast profaned his crown by casting it to the ground.

and flung his crown dishonoured to the ground — Jerus
and have defiled his crown in the dust — Har

40. Thou hast broken down all his hedges;

You have broken down all his defences — Har
thou hast demolished all his walls — Mof

thou hast brought his strong holds to ruin.

and laid his fortifications in ruins — Har
Thou hast laid his fortresses in ruins — Rhm

41. All that pass by the way spoil him:

All who pass by rob him — Har

They plunder him, all that pass by the way — ABPS

he is a reproach to his neighbours.

He has become the scorn of his neighbors — ABPS

He has become a jest to his neighbors — AAT

he is the joke of the neighborhood — Har

42. Thou hast set up the right hand of his adversaries;

You have increased the power of his assailants — Har

You have let his opponents get the upper hand — Jerus

thou hast made all his enemies to rejoice.

Thou hast gladdened all his enemies — Rhm

and given his rivals cause for rejoicing — Har

43. Thou hast also turned the edge of his sword, and hast not made him to stand in the battle.

You have turned back his sharp sword
and have not sustained him in battle — NAB

You have blunted the edge of his sword,
and have not supported him in battle — Har

44. Thou hast made his glory to cease,

Thou hast brought to an end his splendour — Rhm

You have deprived him of his luster — NAB

You have terminated his regal splendor — Har

Thou hast removed the scepter from his hand — RSV

and cast his throne down to the ground.

and hurled his throne to the ground — NAB

45. The days of his youth hast thou shortened:

you have aged him before his time — Jerus

thou hast covered him with shame.

and have covered him with disgrace — Har

Selah.

46. How long, LORD? wilt thou hide thyself for ever? shall thy wrath burn like fire?

Yahweh, how much longer will you hide? For ever?
How much longer must your anger smoulder like a fire — Jerus

47. Remember how short my time is: wherefore hast thou made all men in vain?

Remember, O Lord, what the measure of life is,
for what vanity thou hast created all the sons of men! — RSV

Remember how short my life is;
how frail you created all the children of men! — NAB

48. What is he that liveth, and shall not see death?

What man can live and never see death — RSV

shall he deliver his soul from the hand of the grave?

Who can deliver his soul from the power of Sheol — RSV

who can escape the grave — Mof

and that can rescue his soul from the clutches of the world beyond — Har

Selah.

49. Lord, where are thy former lovingkindnesses, which thou swarest unto David in thy truth?

Lord, where is thy steadfast love of old,
which by thy faithfulness thou didst swear to David — RSV

Where are Your former deeds of mercy, Lord,
which in Your fidelity You solemnly promised to David — Har

Where are thy former lovingkindnesses, O My Lord?
Thou did swear unto David, in thy faithfulness! — Rhm

Lord, where are those earlier signs of your love?
You swore your oath to David on your faithfulness! — Jerus

50. Remember, Lord, the reproach of thy servants;

Remember, O Lord, how thy servant is scorned — RSV

Remember, Lord, the disgrace of Your servant — Har

Lord, do not forget how your servant was insulted — Jerus

how I do bear in my bosom the reproach of all the mighty people;

51. Wherewith thine enemies have re-

proached, O LORD: wherewith they have reproached the footsteps of thine anointed.
how I bear in my bosom the insults of the peoples,
with which thy enemies taunt, O LORD,
with which they mock the footsteps of thy anointed — RSV
and how I bear within myself the abuse of many nations,
which Your enemies hurl, Lord,
and with which they revile Your anointed one at every step — Har

52. **Blessed be the LORD for evermore.**
Blessed be Jehovah for evermore — ASV

Amen, and Amen.
So be it, So be it — Bas

BOOK IV

PSALM 90

A Prayer of Moses the man of God.

1. **Lord, thou hast been our dwelling place in all generations.**
Lord, thou hast been our refuge, from one generation to another — PBV
Lord, You have been our shelter
in all ages — Har
Age after age, Lord, thou hast been our home — Mof
O Lord, thou hast been a refuge for us, from one generation to another — Sept

2. **Before the mountains were brought forth, or ever thou hadst formed the earth and the world, even from everlasting to everlasting, thou art God.**
Before the mountains were formed,
or the earth and the universe were created,
You existed as God eternal — Har
Before the mountains were born,
before the earth or the world came to birth,
you were God from all eternity and for ever — Jerus

3. **Thou turnest man to destruction; and sayest, Return, ye children of men.**
You bring mankind to a state of contrition, saying,
"Repent, offspring of man" — Har
Thou turnest man back to the dust,
and sayest, "Turn back, O children of men!" — RSV
You can turn man back into dust
by saying, 'Back to what you were, you sons of men!' — Jerus
You speak, and man turns back to dust — Tay

4. **For a thousand years in thy sight are but as yesterday when it is past, and as a watch in the night.**
In thy sight, a thousand years are but as yesterday, that has come and gone, or as one of the night watches — Knox
A thousand years are only as the passing of yesterday with You;
a mere period of the night — Har
To you, a thousand years are a single day,
a yesterday now over, an hour of the night — Jerus

5. **Thou carriest them away as with a flood; they are as a sleep: in the morning they are like grass which groweth up.**
Thou dost sweep men away; they are like a dream,
like grass which is renewed in the morning — RSV
You engulf them;
they are like a dream at dawn,
like grass in its development — Har
You carry away [these disobedient people, doomed to die within forty years] as with a flood; they are as a sleep [vague and forgotten as soon as gone]. In the morning they are like grass which grows up, — Amp
We glide along the tides of time as swiftly as a racing river, and vanish as quickly as a dream. We are like grass — Tay

6. **In the morning it flourisheth, and groweth up; in the evening it is cut down, and withereth.**
In the morning it sprouteth and shooteth up,
By the evening it is cut down and withered — Rhm

in the morning it flourishes and is renewed;
in the evening it fades and withers — RSV
In the morning it flourishes and grows;
by evening it has faded and shriveled — Har
sprouting and flowering in the morning,
withered and dry before dusk — Jerus
that is green in the morning but mowed down and withered before the evening shadows fall — Tay

7. For we are consumed by thine anger, and by thy wrath are we troubled.
For we are consumed in thine anger,
And in thy wrath are we dismayed — Rhm
For we are swamped by Your fury,
and ruined by Your anger — Har
We too are burnt up by your anger
and terrified by your fury — Jerus
So we are brought to an end by thy anger
and silenced by thy wrath — NEB
For we [the Israelites in the wilderness] are consumed by Your anger, and by Your wrath are we troubled, overwhelmed and frightened away — Amp

8. Thou hast set our iniquities before thee, our secret sins in the light of thy countenance.
You bear our wrongdoing in mind,
in Your searching presence appear the things we would hide — Har
Thou dost lay bare our iniquities before thee
and our lusts in the full light of thy presence — NEB

9. For all our days are passed away in thy wrath: we spend our years as a tale that is told.
For all our days pass away under thy wrath,
our years come to an end like a sigh — RSV
All our days go by under the shadow of thy wrath;
our years die away like a murmur — NEB
our days all droop under thy displeasure,
our life is over like a sigh — Mof
For all our days vanish in thy wrath;
We come to an end; our years are like a cobweb wiped away — AAT
Day after day vanishes, and still thy anger lasts; swift as a breath our lives pass away — Knox
For all our days [out here in this wilderness, says Moses] are passed away in Your wrath; we spend our years as a tale that is told [for we adults know we are doomed to die soon, without reaching Canaan] — Amp

10. The days of our years are threescore years and ten; and if by reason of strength they be fourscore years, yet is their strength labour and sorrow; for it is soon cut off, and we fly away.
The years of our life are threescore and ten,
or even by reason of strength fourscore;
yet their span is but toil and trouble;
they are soon gone, and we fly away — RSV
The length of life is seventy years;
perhaps eighty, given good health.
Even so, their vigor is but travail and trouble;
they pass quickly, and we disappear — Har
— our life lasts for seventy years,
eighty with good health,
but they all add up to anxiety and trouble —
over in a trice, and then we are gone — Jerus
Seventy is the sum of our years,
or eighty, if we are strong,
And most of them are fruitless toil
for they pass quickly and we drift away — NAB

11. Who knoweth the power of thine anger? even according to thy fear, so is thy wrath.
Who knows the fury of your anger
or your indignation toward those who should fear you? — NAB
Who is aware of the violence of Your fury?
Who stands in reverent awe of Your anger? — Har
Who yet has felt the full force of your fury,
or learnt to fear the violence of your rage? — Jerus
Who feels the power of thy anger,

who feels thy wrath like those that fear thee? — NEB
Who can realize the terrors of your anger? Which of us can fear you as he should? — Tay

12. So teach us to number our days, that we may apply our hearts unto wisdom.
So teach us to number our days,
That we may get us a heart of wisdom — ASV
Teach us to count every passing day, till our hearts find wisdom — Knox
Teach us, then, how to interpret our existence,
so that we may acquire a discerning mind — Har
Teach us to order our days rightly, that we may enter the gate of wisdom — NEB

13. Return, O LORD, how long? and let it repent thee concerning thy servants.
Return Yahweh oh how long?
And have compassion upon thy servants — Rhm
Return O Jehovah; how long!
And have pity on thy servants — ABPS
Change Your attitude, Lord;
how long will it be before You take pity on Your servants? — Har
Relent, Yahweh! How much longer do we have?
Take pity on your servants! — Jerus

14. O satisfy us early with thy mercy; that we may rejoice and be glad all our days.
O satisfy us with thy mercy, and that soon: so shall we rejoice and be glad all the days of our life — PBV
Oh satisfy us in the morning with thy lovingkindness,
That we may rejoice and be glad all our days — ASV
Fill us at daybreak with your kindness, that we may shout for joy and gladness all our days — NAB
Let us wake in the morning filled with your love
and sing and be happy all our days — Jerus

15. Make us glad according to the days wherein thou hast afflicted us, and the years wherein we have seen evil.
Make us glad as many days as thou hast afflicted us,
and as many years as we have seen evil — RSV
make our future as happy as our past was sad,
those years when you were punishing us — Jerus

16. Let thy work appear unto thy servants, and thy glory unto their children.
Let thy work appear to thy servants,
And thy majesty upon their sons — ABPS
Let thy work be manifest to thy servants,
and thy glorious power to their children — RSV
Let your servants see what you can do for them,
let their children see your glory — Jerus
May Your work be evident to all Your servants,
and Your majesty to their children — Har

17. And let the beauty of the LORD our God be upon us:
And let the favor of the Lord our God be upon us — ASV
And let the delightfulness of Adonay our God be upon us — Rhm
Let the graciousness of Jehovah our God be upon us — DeW
May the sweetness of the Lord be on us! — Jerus
And may the gracious care of the LORD our God be ours — NAB
And let the splendor of the Lord our God be over us — Sept
and establish thou the work of our hands upon us; yea, the work of our hands establish thou it.
Make all we do succeed — Jerus
and prosper all the work we undertake — Mof
and do thou direct for us the works of our hands — Sept
O Lord, give strength to the work of our hands — Bas

PSALM 91

1. He that dwelleth in the secret place of the Most High, shall abide under the shadow of the Almighty.
Whoso dwelleth under the defence of the Most High, shall abide under the shadow of the Almighty — PBV

He who dwelleth under the protection of the Most High shall lodge in the shelter of the God of heaven — Sept
He who lives in the secret shelter of the Most High lodges in the shadow of the Almighty — Ber
He who lives as a ward of the Most High
shall repose under the protection of the Almighty — Har
He who dwells in the secret place of the Most High shall remain stable and fixed under the shadow of the Almighty [Whose power no foe can withstand] — Amp
He who dwells under the shelter of the Most High,
Who abides under the shadow of the Almighty, — AAT

2. I will say of the LORD, He is my refuge and my fortress: my God; in him will I trust.
I will say to Jehovah, O my refuge and fortress,
Thou art my God, in whom I will trust — DeW
Says of the LORD, "My refuge and my fortress,
My God, in whom I trust" — AAT
I will say of the Lord,
"You are my sheltering haven; my God whom I trust" — Har

3. Surely he shall deliver thee from the snare of the fowler,
He it is will rescue thee from every treacherous lure — Knox
Certainly it is He who rescues you from the hunter's trap — Ber
and from the noisome pestilence.
And from the deadly pestilence — ASV
. . . destructive pestilence — Rhm
. . . deadly epidemic — Har
and keep you safe from wasting disease — Bas

4. He shall cover thee with his feathers, and under his wings shalt thou trust:
He shall cover thee with his pinions, and under his wings shalt thou take refuge — RV
He will safeguard you with His strength, and you will find shelter within His protecting power — Har
his truth shall be thy shield and buckler.
. . . a shield and armor — Ber
His truth will encompass thee with armour — Sept
His faithfulness is a shield and buckler — AAT
His fidelity is your assurance of security — Har
His faithful promises are your armor — Tay

5. Thou shalt not be afraid for the terror by night; nor for the arrow that flieth by day;
Thou shalt not be afraid
Of the dread of the night,
Of the arrow that flieth by day — Rhm
You need not fear the terrors of the night,
nor arrows flying in the day — Mof
You will not need to be afraid of any nocturnal terror,
nor of any danger that is abroad in daylight — Har

6. Nor for the pestilence that walketh in darkness; nor for the destruction that wasteth at noonday.
Of the pestilence that in darkness doth walk,
Of the plague that layeth waste at noonday — Rhm
you need not fear plague stalking in the dark,
nor sudden death at noon — Mof
neither the plague that stalks at dead of night,
nor the epidemic which devastates at midday — Har
nor the plague that lurks in the darkness,
nor the calamity that spreads havoc at noontime — Ber

7. A thousand shall fall at thy side, and ten thousand at thy right hand; but it shall not come nigh thee.
hundreds may fall beside you,
thousands at your right hand,
but the plague will never reach you — Mof
Though a thousand fall at your side,
ten thousand at your right hand,
you yourself will remain unscathed — Jerus

8. Only with thine eyes shalt thou behold and see the reward of the wicked.
You have only to look on and see
how evil men are punished — Mof
You will but gaze upon with your eyes

And see the reward of the wicked — AAT

You will need only to take careful notice,
to see how the wicked are punished — Har

You will merely see it with your eyes and witness the sinners' reward — Ber

rather, thy eyes shall look about thee, and see the reward of sinners — Knox

Only a spectator shall you be [yourself inaccessible in the secret place of the Most High] as you witness the reward of the wicked — Amp

9. **Because thou hast made the LORD, which is my refuge, even the most High, thy habitation;**

10. **There shall no evil befall thee, neither shall any plague come nigh thy dwelling.**

Because thou hast made Yahweh my refuge, —
The Most High thou hast made thy dwelling-place
There shall not be sent unto thee misfortune,
Nor shall plague come near into thy tent — Rhm

Because you have made the LORD your refuge,
the Most High your habitation,
no evil shall befall you,
no scourge come near your tent — RSV

Because you have made the LORD your refuge,
And the Most High your habitation,
No disaster will befall you,
Nor calamity come near your tent — AAT

Because you have made the Lord your shelter,
and the Most High your protection,
no evil will overwhelm you;
no plague shall approach your dwelling — Har

For THOU, O Jehovah! art my refuge!
Hast thou made the Most High thy habitation?
Then no evil shall befall thee,
Nor any plague come nigh thy tent — DeW

11. **For he shall give his angels charge over thee, to keep thee in all thy ways.**

For his messengers will he charge concerning thee,
To keep thee in all thy ways — Rhm

For he puts you under his angels' charge,
to guard you wherever you go — Mof

For He gives His angels orders regarding you,
to protect you wherever you go — Ber

12. **They shall bear thee up in their hands, lest thou dash thy foot against a stone.**

They shall bear thee in their hands, that thou hurt not thy foot against a stone — PBV

By their power they will uphold you, lest you should even injure your foot on a stone — Har

13. **Thou shalt tread upon the lion and adder: the young lion and the dragon shalt thou trample under feet.**

On the lion and adder shalt thou tread,
Shalt trample on young lion and crocodile — Rhm

Thou shalt tread upon the lion and asp;
The young lion and the serpent shalt thou trample under feet — JPS

you can walk over reptiles and cobras, trampling on lions and on dragons — Mof

You shall tread upon the asp and the viper;
you shall trample down the lion and the dragon — NAB

14. **Because he hath set his love upon me, therefore will I deliver him:**

Because he cleaves to me in love,
I will deliver him — RSV

Because he has anchored his love in Me,
I will deliver him — Ber

Because he clings to me, I will deliver him — NAB

I rescue all who cling to me — Jerus

I will set him on high, because he hath known my name.

I will lift him beyond danger, for he knows me by my name — NEB

I will protect him, because he knows my name — RSV

he acknowledges my name, from me he shall have protection — Knox

15. **He shall call upon me, and I will answer him:**

When he calls to me, I will answer him — RSV

I will be with him in trouble; I will deliver him, and honour him.

I will be with him in hardship,
I will deliver him and honor him — Har

in affliction I am at his side, to bring him safety and honour — Knox

16. With long life will I satisfy him, and shew him my salvation.

I will satisfy him with long life,
and let him see my saving care — Mof

He will have the satisfaction of a long life,
and I shall let him participate in My salvation — Har

I give them life, long and full,
and show them how I can save — Jerus

PSALM 92

A Psalm or Song for the sabbath day.

1. It is a good thing to give thanks unto the LORD, and to sing praises unto thy name, O most High:

It is good to give thanks to Jehovah,
And to make melody to Thy Name, O Most High! — DeW

It is a joy to give thanks to the Eternal,
to sing thy praise, O thou Most High — Mof

It is appropriate to give thanks to the Lord,
and to praise Your name in song, Most High — Har

Sweet it is to praise the Lord, to sing, most high God, in honour of thy name — Knox

It is a good and delightful thing to give thanks to the Lord, to sing praises [with musical accompaniment] to Your name, O Most High — Amp

2. To shew forth thy lovingkindness in the morning, and thy faithfulness every night,

To tell of thy loving-kindness early in the morning, and of thy truth in the night season — PBV

to proclaim thy goodness in the morning
and thy faithfulness at night — Mof

To proclaim your kindness at dawn
and your faithfulness throughout the night — NAB

3. Upon an instrument of ten strings, and upon the psaltery; upon the harp with a solemn sound.

Upon an instrument of ten strings and upon a harp,
With resounding music on the lyre — Rhm

To a ten-stringed instrument, and to the lute,
To the murmuring sound on the harp — ABPS

to the sound of a ten-stringed lute,
to the sweet music of the lyre — Mof

to the music of the lute and the harp,
to the melody of the lyre — RSV

to the music of the zither and lyre,
to the rippling of the harp — Jerus

Here is a theme for ten-stringed harp and viol, for music of voice and zither — Knox

4. For thou, LORD, hast made me glad through thy work:

For thou hast gladdened me, Jehovah,
by thy work — ABPS

For you make me glad, O LORD, by your deeds — NAB

For You have given me cause for rejoicing
through what You have done — Har

I will triumph in the works of thy hands.

In the works of thy hands will I shout for joy — Rhm

I sing for joy at all that thou hast done — Mof

I burst into song
because of your handiwork — Har

5. O LORD, how great are thy works! and thy thoughts are very deep.

O LORD, how glorious are thy works!
thy thoughts are very deep — PBV

How magnificent are Thy works, O JEHOVAH!
How incomprehensibly great Thy thoughts! — Sprl

How great have grown thy works Yahweh,
[How] very deep are laid thy plans! — Rhm

How majestic Your deeds are, Lord;
how profound are Your designs — Har

How magnificent is thy creation, Lord, how unfathomable are thy purposes! — Knox

6. **A brutish man knoweth not; neither doth a fool understand this.**

A man that is brutish cannot know,
And a dullard cannot discern this — Rhm

A stupid man cannot know,
A senseless one cannot understand this — AAT

The dull man cannot know,
the stupid cannot understand this: — RSV

The stupid person is unable to appreciate it;
the dullard cannot comprehend this fact, — Har

7. **When the wicked spring as the grass, and when all the workers of iniquity do flourish; it is that they shall be destroyed for ever:**

8. **But thou, LORD, art most high for evermore.**

that, though the wicked sprout like grass
and all evildoers flourish,
they are doomed to destruction for ever,
but thou, O LORD, art on high for ever — RSV

that when the wicked spring up like grass,
and all the wrongdoers blossom forth,
they are destined for ultimate destruction.
Whereas You, Lord, remain supreme forever — Har

9. **For, lo, thine enemies, O LORD, for, lo, thine enemies shall perish; all the workers of iniquity shall be scattered.**

Look at Your enemies, Lord God —
those who are Your opponents will be destroyed;
all the wicked will be dispersed — Har

10. **But my horn shalt thou exalt like the horn of an unicorn: I shall be anointed with fresh oil.**

But my horn thou wilt exalt as of the wild-ox;
I am anointed with fresh oil — ABPS

But You have promoted me, so that I am like a powerful buffalo;
I am anointed with fresh oil — Har

But thou dost raise me high to honour, thou dost revive my failing strength — Mof

But my horn [emblem of excessive strength and stately grace] you have exalted like that of a wild ox; I am anointed with fresh oil — Amp

But you have made me as strong as a wild bull. How refreshed I am by your blessings! — Tay

11. **Mine eye also shall see my desire on mine enemies, and mine ears shall hear my desire of the wicked that rise up against me.**

And my eye had its desire on them that lie in wait for me,
And my ear on evil-doers that rise up against me — ABPS

My eyes have seen the downfall of my enemies,
my ears have heard the doom of my evil assailants — RSV

I feast mine eyes on my defeated foes,
I hear with joy my enemies' doom Mof

12. **The righteous shall flourish like the palm tree: he shall grow like a cedar in Lebanon.**

The innocent man will flourish as the palm-tree flourishes; he will grow to greatness as the cedars grow on Lebanon — Knox

The upright man will flourish like the palm tree,
and will grow tall like the cedar in Lebanon — Har

13. **Those that be planted in the house of the LORD shall flourish in the courts of our God.**

They are planted in the house of Jehovah;
They shall flourish in the courts of our God — ASV

14. **They shall still bring forth fruit in old age; they shall be fat and flourishing;**

They shall still bring forth fruit in old age;
They shall be full of sap and green — ASV

They shall bear fruit even in old age; vigorous and sturdy shall they be — NAB

15. **To shew that the LORD is upright: he is my rock, and there is no unrighteousness in him.**

eager to declare that the LORD is just, the LORD my rock, in whom there is no unrighteousness — NEB

PSALM 93

1. **The LORD reigneth, he is clothed with majesty;**
The LORD reigns; he is robed in majesty — RSV
The LORD is King, and hath put on glorious apparel — PBV
The LORD is king, in splendor robed — NAB
the LORD is clothed with strength, wherewith he hath girded himself:
the LORD is robed, he is girded with strength — RSV
Jehovah is clothed with strength; he hath girded himself therewith — ASV
Yahweh is robed in power,
he wears it like a belt — Jerus
the world also is stablished, that it cannot be moved.
He hath made the round world so sure, that it cannot be moved — PBV
So the world standeth fast; it cannot be overthrown — DeW
The universe has been established immovably — Har
2. **Thy throne is established of old: thou art from everlasting.**
Firm stood thy throne ere ever the world began; from all eternity, thou art — Knox
Your sovereignty has been founded from old time;
You have existed eternally — Har
3. **The floods have lifted up, O LORD, the floods have lifted up their voice; the floods lift up their waves.**
The floods have lifted up, O God!
The floods have lifted up their voice;
The floods lift up their roaring — DeW
The floods may storm, O thou Eternal,
the floods may storm aloud,
the floods may storm and thunder — Mof
The rivers are swollen, Lord God;
the torrents have increased their thundering;
the floods have piled up their breakers — Har
Loud the rivers echo, Lord, loud the rivers echo, crashing down in flood — Knox
4. **The LORD on high is mightier than the noise of many waters, yea, than the mighty waves of the sea.**
but high above the roaring billows,
high above the ocean breakers,
the Eternal stands supreme — Mof
Mightier than the thunders of many waters,
mightier than the waves of the sea,
the LORD on high is mighty! — RSV
Above the roar of mighty waters,
more majestic than the ocean billows,
is the Lord, gloriously supreme — Har
greater than the voice of ocean,
transcending the waves of the sea,
Yahweh reigns transcendent in the heights — Jerus
5. **Thy testimonies are very sure: holiness becometh thine house, O LORD, for ever.**
Thy decrees are very sure;
holiness befits thy house,
O LORD, for evermore — RSV
Your decrees are firmly established.
It is proper for Your shrine to be eternally sacred, Lord — Har
Thy testimonies are so trustworthy;
holiness is the mark of Thy house,
O LORD, forevermore — Ber
Your decrees will never alter;
holiness will distinguish your house,
Yahweh, for ever and ever — Jerus

PSALM 94

1. **O LORD God, to whom vengeance belongeth; O God, to whom vengeance belongeth, shew thyself.**
O Jehovah, thou God to whom vengeance belongeth,
Thou God to whom vengeance belongeth, shine forth — ASV
God of vengeance — Jehovah!
God of vengeance, shine forth — YLT
In thy divine vengeance, Lord, in thy divine vengeance stand revealed! — Knox
Yahweh, God of revenge,
God of revenge, appear! — Jerus
2. **Lift up thyself, thou judge of the**

earth: render a reward to the proud.
Rise up, O judge of the earth;
render to the proud their deserts! — RSV
Judge of the world, mount thy throne, and give the proud their deserts! — Knox
Stand up, Judge of the world;
mete out retribution to the haughty — Har

3. **LORD, how long shall the wicked, how long shall the wicked triumph?**
How long shall the lawless O Yahweh,
How long shall the lawless exult — Rhm
How long is it to last, O thou Eternal, this exultation of ungodly men — Mof

4. **How long shall they utter and speak hard things? and all the workers of iniquity boast themselves?**
How long shall all wicked doers speak so disdainfully, and make such proud boasting — PBV
They prate, they speak arrogantly:
All the workers of iniquity boast themselves — ASV
They blurt out arrogant words;
all the wrongdoers are boastful — Har

5. **They break in pieces thy people, O LORD, and afflict thine heritage.**
They crush thy people, O LORD,
and afflict thy heritage — RSV
They grind thy people, O Jehovah, and thy heritage they oppress — ABPS
they beat down thy people, O LORD,
and oppress thy chosen nation — NEB

6. **They slay the widow and the stranger, and murder the fatherless.**
They slay the widow and the sojourner,
And murder the fatherless — ASV
They murder widows, immigrants, and orphans — Tay

7. **Yet they say, the LORD shall not see, neither shall the God of Jacob regard it.**
And yet they say, Tush, the LORD shall not see, neither shall the God of Jacob regard it — PBV
Yet have they said —
Yah doth not see,
The God of Jacob doth not understand — Rhm
And they think, the Lord will never see it, the God of Israel pays no heed — Knox
for "The Lord isn't looking," they say, "and besides, he doesn't care" — Tay

8. **Understand, ye brutish among the people: and ye fools, when will ye be wise?**
Understand, O dullest of the people!
Fools, when will you be wise — RSV
Ponder on this, you dull-witted people:
when will you become wise, you dolts? — Har
You most stupid of men, you fools,
think this over and learn some sense — Jerus

9. **He that planted the ear, shall he not hear? he that formed the eye, shall he not see?**
Is he deaf, the God who implanted hearing in us; is he blind, the God who gave us eyes to see — Knox
Is He who formed the hearing deaf?
Is He who constructed the eye blind — Har
Is the inventor of the ear unable to hear?
The creator of the eye unable to see — Jerus

10. **He that chastiseth the heathen, shall not he correct? he that teacheth man knowledge, shall not he know?**

11. **The LORD knoweth the thoughts of man, that they are vanity.**
He who chastens the nations, does he not chastise?
He who teaches men knowledge,
the LORD, knows the thoughts of man,
that they are but a breath — RSV
He that correcteth nations shall he not reprove?
He that teacheth man knowledge!
Yahweh knoweth the plans of men,
That they are a breath! — Rhm
He who disciplines the nations, shall He not correct?
Is He not the One who teaches man all he knows?
The LORD discerns the thoughts of man
that they are futile — Ber
The punisher of the pagans unable to punish?
Yahweh the teacher of mankind
knows exactly how men think,
how their thoughts are a puff of wind — Jerus

He who gives nations their schooling, who taught man all that man knows, will he not call you to account? The Lord looks into men's hearts, and finds there illusion — Knox

12. Blessed is the man whom thou chastenest, O LORD, and teachest him out of thy law;

How happy the man whom thou correctest O Yah!
And whom out of thy law thou instructest! — Rhm

O the blessedness of the man
Whom Thou chastenest, O Jehovah!
And whom Thou teachest out of Thy law — DeW

Blessed is the man whom Thou dost discipline,
whom Thou dost instruct from Thy Law, O LORD — Ber

Blessed — happy, fortunate [to be envied] — is the man whom You discipline and instruct, O Lord, and teach out of Your law — Amp

13. That thou mayest give him rest from the days of adversity, until the pit be digged for the wicked.

to give him respite from days of trouble,
until a pit is dug for the wicked — RSV

that he may enjoy security during the days of distress,
till a pit be dug for the wicked — Ber

his mind is at peace though times are bad,
while a pit is being dug for the wicked — Jerus

So that you may give him rest from the days of evil, till a hole is made ready for the destruction of the sinners — Bas

That You may give him power to hold himself calm in the days of adversity, until the [inevitable] pit of corruption is dug for the wicked — Amp

For him, thou wilt lighten the time of adversity, digging a pit all the while to entrap the sinner — Knox

14. For the LORD will not cast off his people, neither will he forsake his inheritance.

For Yahweh will not abandon his people,
And his inheritance will he not forsake — Rhm

For the Eternal will not leave his people,
never will he forsake his own — Mof

For the LORD will not spurn his people,
Nor abandon his heritage — AAT

The LORD will not abandon his people
nor forsake his chosen nation — NEB

15. But judgment shall return unto righteousness: and all the upright in heart shall follow it.

for justice will return to the righteous,
and all the upright in heart will follow it — RSV

The righteous will receive justice,
and the virtuous will succeed to it — Har

But justice will be applied to the righteous,
and all whose hearts are right will subscribe to it — Ber

no, goodness shall have justice done to it —
the future is with men of upright mind — Mof

16. Who will rise up for me against the evildoers? or who will stand up for me against the workers of iniquity?

Who will protect me from the wicked?
Who will be my shield — Tay

Who is my champion against the ungodly?
Who sides with me against the evildoers — Mof

17. Unless the LORD had been my help, my soul had almost dwelt in silence.

If the LORD had not been my help,
my soul would soon have dwelt in the land of silence — RSV

without Yahweh's help, I should, long ago,
have gone to the Home of Silence — Jerus

If the Lord had not assisted me,
I would have succumbed to death quickly — Har

18. When I said, My foot slippeth; thy mercy, O LORD, held me up.

When I said, My foot slippeth;
Thy lovingkindness, O Jehovah, held me up — ASV

Still, when my foothold seems lost, thy mercy, Lord, holds me up — Knox

If I say, My foot is slipping; your mercy, O Lord, is my support — Bas

19. In the multitude of my thoughts within me thy comforts delight my soul.
. . . Thy comforts soothe my spirits — ABPS
In the multitude of the sorrows that I had in my heart, thy comforts have refreshed my soul — PBV
In the multitude of my inward perplexities,
Thy consolations shall delight my soul — Sprl
when doubts crowd into my mind,
thy comforts cheer me — Mof
In the multitude of distractions within me,
Thy comforts delight my soul — DeW
In the multitude of my cares within me
Thy consolations delight my soul — Rhm
When my cares are many within me,
thy comforts delight my soul — JPS
When the cares of my heart are many,
thy consolations cheer my soul — RSV
amid all the thronging cares that fill my heart, my soul finds comfort in thy consolation — Knox
When cares abound within me,
your comfort gladdens my soul — NAB
When my mind is burdened with worry,
Your comforting encourages me — Har

20. Shall the throne of iniquity have fellowship with thee, which frameth mischief by a law?
Can wicked rulers be allied with thee,
who frame mischief by statute — RSV
What part have these unjust judges with thee, that make mischief in the name of law — Knox

21. They gather themselves together against the soul of the righteous, and condemn the innocent blood.
They band themselves against the life of the righteous,
and condemn the innocent to death — RSV

22. But the LORD is my defence; and my God is the rock of my refuge.
But Yahweh hath become for me a high tower,
And my God my rock of refuge — Rhm

23. And he shall bring upon them their own iniquity, and shall cut them off in their own wickedness; yea, the LORD our God shall cut them off.
He will bring back on them their iniquity
and wipe them out for their wickedness;
the LORD our God will wipe them out — RSV
He has made them pay for their crime,
and He will destroy them in their sin;
the LORD our God will make an end to them — Ber
Who will repay them for their sin,
and destroy them for their iniquity?
The Lord our God will obliterate them — Har

PSALM 95

1. O come, let us sing unto the LORD: let us make a joyful noise to the rock of our salvation.
O come, let us sing unto the LORD; let us heartily rejoice in the strength of our salvation — PBV
Come let us make a joyful noise to Yahweh,
Let us shout in triumph to the rock of our salvation! — Rhm
Come, let us sing joyously to the Lord;
let us shout for joy to our saving defense — Har
Come, let us praise Yahweh joyfully,
acclaiming the Rock of our safety — Jerus
Come, let us sing to the LORD:
let us cheer in honor of the Rock of our salvation — Ber
Come, let us sing unto the LORD;
Let us raise joyful shouts to the rock of our deliverance! — AAT

2. Let us come before his presence with thanksgiving, and make a joyful noise unto him with psalms.
Let us come before his presence with thanksgiving; and show ourselves glad in him with psalms — PBV
O let us come before his face with thanksgiving,
With the sounds of strings let us shout aloud to him — Rhm
Let us come before his face with thanksgiving,

And shout to him in songs — ABPS
Let us approach Him with praise,
and sing jubilantly with hymns of thanks — Har
let us come into his presence with thanksgiving,
acclaiming him with music — Jerus

3. For the LORD is a great God, and a great King above all gods.
For Jehovah is a great God,
And a great King above all gods — ASV
For a great GOD is Yahweh,
And a great king above all gods — Rhm
For the Lord is a majestic Deity;
a King supreme over all gods — Har

4. In his hand are the deep places of the earth: the strength of the hills is his also.
In his hand are the depths of the earth;
the heights of the mountains are his also — RSV
Under His control are the recesses of the earth,
and the towering mountains belong to Him — Har
from depths of earth to mountain top
everything comes under his rule — Jerus

5. The sea is his, and he made it: and his hands formed the dry land.
The sea is His, for he formed it;
His power molded the dry land — Har
the sea belongs to him, he made it,
so does the land, he shaped this too — Jerus

6. O come, let us worship and bow down: let us kneel before the LORD our maker.
O come, let us worship, and fall prostrate;
Let us bend the knee in the presence of JEHOVAH our Creator — Sprl
Come, let us bow down in worship;
let us kneel before the LORD who made us — NAB
Come! Let us throw ourselves at his feet in homage,
let us kneel before the LORD who made us — NEB

7. For he is our God; and we are the people of his pasture, and the sheep of his hand.
For he is our God,
and we are the people he shepherds,
the flock he guides — NAB
To-day if ye will hear his voice,

8. Harden not your heart, as in the provocation, and as in the day of temptation in the wilderness:
O that today you would hearken to his voice!
Harden not your hearts, as at Meribah,
as on the day at Massah in the wilderness — RSV
Oh, if you would only listen to His voice today!
Do not stiffen your heart as at Meribah,
at the time of testing in the wilderness — Ber

9. When your fathers tempted me, proved me, and saw my work.
when your forefathers doubted me,
and tested me, though they had felt my power — Mof
when your fathers tested me,
and put me to the proof, though they had seen my work — RSV
when your ancestors challenged me, tested me,
although they had seen what I could do — Jerus

10. Forty years long was I grieved with this generation, and said, It is a people that do err in their heart, and they have not known my ways:
Forty years did I loathe the generation;
And I said, They are a people that err in heart,
And they know not my ways — ABPS
For forty years I loathed that generation;
I said, "They are a senseless people, who care not for my ways" — Mof

11. Unto whom I sware in my wrath that they should not enter into my rest.
And I sware in mine anger, —
Verily they shall not enter into my rest — Rhm
So I swore solemnly in My anger,
that they should not enter My land of rest — Har

PSALM 96

1. O sing unto the LORD a new song: sing unto the LORD, all the earth.

Oh sing unto Jehovah a new song:
Sing unto Jehovah, all the earth — ASV

Sing the Lord a new song; in the Lord's honour, let the whole earth make melody! — Knox

Sing a new song to the Lord! Sing it everywhere around the world! — Tay

2. Sing unto the LORD, bless his name; shew forth his salvation from day to day.

Sing to Yahweh bless ye his Name, —
Tell the tidings from day to day of his salvation — Rhm

sing to the Eternal, praise him,
day after day tell of his saving aid — Mof

Sing to the Lord, and bless his name; never cease to bear record of his power to save — Knox

3. Declare his glory among the heathen, his wonders among all people.

Declare his glory among the nations, his marvelous works among all the peoples! — RSV

Publish his glory among the heathen; his wonderful acts for all the world to hear — Knox

Tell among the nations His glory,
In all the kingdoms His wonders — DeW

let the heathen hear his glory,
let every nation know his wondrous deeds — Mof

4. For the LORD is great, and greatly to be praised: he is to be feared above all gods.

For the LORD is great, and cannot worthily be praised; he is more to be feared than all gods — PBV

For great is Yahweh and worthy to be mightily praised,
To be revered is he above all gods — Rhm

For great is the LORD and highly to be praised;
awesome is he, beyond all gods — NAB

For the Lord is majestic, and most praiseworthy;
He is to be feared above all deities — Har

Yahweh is great, loud must be his praise,
he is to be feared beyond all gods — Jerus

5. For all the gods of the nations are idols: but the LORD made the heavens.

For all the gods of the peoples are nothings;
And Jehovah made the heavens — ABPS

For all the gods of the peoples are nonentities,
While the LORD made the heavens — AAT

6. Honour and majesty are before him: strength and beauty are in his sanctuary.

Praise and majesty . . . — Rhm

grandeur and majesty attend him,
splendour and power are in his sanctuary — Mof

His presence is one of splendor and majesty;
praise and glory are found in his shrine — Har

Honour and beauty are his escort; worship and magnificence the attendants of his shrine — Knox

7. Give unto the LORD, O ye kindreds of the people, give unto the Lord glory and strength.

Ascribe unto Jehovah, ye kindreds of the peoples,
Ascribe unto Jehovah glory and strength — ASV

Praise the Eternal, O families of the nations,
praise the Eternal for his glory and his might! — Mof

O nations of the world, confess that God alone is glorious and strong — Tay

8. Give unto the LORD the glory due unto his name: bring an offering, and come into his courts.

9. O worship the LORD in the beauty of holiness: fear before him, all the earth.

O worship the LORD in the beauty of holiness: let the whole earth stand in awe of him — PBV

O worship JEHOVAH in the beauty of holiness;

Let the whole earth tremble at His presence — Sprl

Oh worship Jehovah in holy array:
Tremble before him, all the earth — ASV

kneel before God in sacred vestments, tremble before him, all the earth — Mof

Bow down to Yahweh in the adornment of holiness,
Be in anguish at his presence all the earth! — Rhm

worship the Lord in holy array. Before the Lord's presence let the whole earth bow in reverence — Knox

Worship the Lord with a sanctified spirit;
let all the earth stand in awe of Him — Har

10. Say among the heathen that the LORD reigneth: the world also shall be established that it shall not be moved: he shall judge the people righteously.

Tell it out among the heathen, that the LORD is King, and that it is he who hath made the round world so fast that it cannot be moved; and how that he shall judge the peoples righteously — PBV

Say among the nations, Jehovah reigneth:
The world also is established that it cannot be moved:
He will judge the peoples with equity — ASV

Say among the nations, Jehovah reigns;
Yea, the world shall stand fast, it shall not be moved;
He will judge the peoples in rectitude — ABPS

Proclaim to pagans that the Eternal reigns;
he has steadied and settled the world, he will rule the nations justly — Mof

Say among the nations, the Lord is King; yes, the world is ordered so that it may not be moved; he will be an upright judge of the peoples — Bas

11. Let the heavens rejoice, and let the earth be glad; let the sea roar, and the fulness thereof.

Let the skies be glad, let earth rejoice, let the sea and all within it thunder praise — Mof

Let the heavens rejoice, let earth be exultant;
let the sea and all its contents roar — Har

Rejoice, heaven, and let earth be glad; let the sea, and all the sea contains, give thunderous applause — Knox

12. Let the field be joyful, and all that is therein:

Let the field leap for joy and all that is therein — Rhm

let the land and all it holds exult — Mof

then shall all the trees of the wood rejoice

13. Before the LORD: for he cometh, for he cometh to judge the earth:

Then shall all the trees of the forest shout in triumph
Before Yahweh for he is coming
For he is coming to judge the earth — Rhm

Then shall all the trees of the wood sing for joy
Before Jehovah; for he cometh,
For he cometh to judge the earth — ASV

then all the trees in the forest will shout aloud
in the presence of the Lord,
as He comes to dispense justice on earth — Har

he shall judge the world with righteousness, and the people with his truth.

He will judge the world in righteousness,
And the peoples in his faithfulness — ABPS

He will judge the world with justice, and the peoples impartially — Har

He will judge the world with justice, the nations with His faithfulness — Ber

PSALM 97

1. The LORD reigneth; let the earth rejoice;

Yahweh hath become King
Let the earth exult — Rhm

Yahweh is king! Let earth rejoice — Jerus

let the multitude of isles be glad thereof.

Let the multitude of coastlands rejoice — Rhm
let the distant shores be glad — Har

2. Clouds and darkness are round about him:
Clouds and thick darkness are round about him — Rhm
Cloud and mist enfold him — NEB
righteousness and judgment are the habitation of his throne.
Righteousness and justice are the foundations of his throne — ASV
righteousness and justice are the basis of His sovereignty — Har

3. A fire goeth before him, and burneth up his enemies round about.
Fire goes before him,
And blazes around his steps — AAT

4. His lightnings enlightened the world: the earth saw, and trembled.
His lightnings illuminated the world;
The earth beheld it, and trembled — Har
his lightning lights up the world,
earth observes and quakes — Jerus

5. The hills melted like wax at the presence of the LORD, at the presence of the Lord of the whole earth.
The mountains melted like wax at the presence of Jehovah,
At the presence of the Lord of the whole earth — ASV
The mountains melt like wax as the LORD approaches,
the Lord of all the earth — NEB

6. The heavens declare his righteousness, and all the people see his glory.
The heavens declared his saving goodness: and all the peoples saw his glory — Sept
the heavens proclaim his high authority,
all nations see his majesty — Mof
The heavens proclaim His justice,
and all nations can see His glory — Har

7. Confounded be all they that serve graven images, that boast themselves of idols: worship him, all ye gods.
Let all who worship images, who vaunt their idols,
be put to shame;
bow down, all gods, before him — NEB
All worshipers of images are put to shame,
who make their boast in worthless idols;
all gods bow down before him — RSV
All who worship graven things are put to shame,
who glory in the things of naught;
all gods are prostrate before him — NAB
All who serve wrought images are put to shame,
They who prided themselves on their nonentities.
Worship him, all you gods! — AAT

8. Zion heard, and was glad; and the daughters of Judah rejoiced because of thy judgments, O LORD.
Zion hath heard and rejoiced
And the daughters of Judah have exulted,
Because of thy righteous decisions O Yahweh — Rhm
Sion heard it and rejoiced,
the towns of Judah were in joy
at thy saving deeds, O thou Eternal — Mof
Zion has heard, and is delighted;
the towns of Judah rejoice at Your decrees, Lord — Har
Zion heard and was glad; the cities of Judah rejoiced
because of Thy justice, O LORD — Ber

9. For thou, LORD, art high above all the earth: thou art exalted far above all gods.
For thou, Jehovah, art most high above all the earth:
Thou art exalted far above all gods — ASV
For you are Yahweh
Most High over the world,
far transcending all other gods — Jerus

10. Ye that love the LORD, hate evil: he preserveth the souls of his saints: he delivereth them out of the hand of the wicked.
Hate evil, you who love the Lord;
for He preserves the lives of His saints,
rescuing them from the clutches of the wicked — Har
The LORD loves those who hate evil;
he preserves the lives of his saints;
he delivers them from the hand of the wicked — RSV
Yahweh loves those who repudiate evil,

he guards the souls of the devout, rescuing them from the clutches of the wicked — Jerus

11. Light is sown for the righteous, and gladness for the upright in heart.
There is sprung up a light for the righteous, and joyful gladness for such as are true-hearted — PBV
Light dawns for the righteous, and joy for the upright in heart — RSV
A harvest of light is sown for the righteous, and joy for all good men — NEB
Light is scattered abroad by the Righteous One, And joy for the upright of heart — Sprl

12. Rejoice in the LORD, ye righteous; and give thanks at the remembrance of his holiness.
Be glad in Jehovah, ye righteous; And give thanks to his holy memorial name — ASV
Rejoice in the LORD, O righteous, And praise his holy name — AAT
You who are righteous, rejoice in the LORD; be thankful for the consciousness of His holiness — Ber
Rejoice in Yahweh, you virtuous, remember his holiness, and praise him! — Jerus

PSALM 98

A Psalm.

1. O sing unto the LORD a new song; for he hath done marvellous things:
Sing ye to Jehovah a new song, For wonders He hath done — YLT
his right hand, and his holy arm, hath gotten him the victory.
His right hand and his holy arm have wrought salvation for him — ABPS
His right hand and his holy arm have brought him victory — AAT
His great power and supreme strength have achieved victory for Him — Har
his own right hand, his holy arm, gives him the power to save — Jerus
For he has won a mighty victory by his power and holiness — Tay

2. The LORD hath made known his salvation:
The LORD has made known his victory — RSV
The Lord has proclaimed His triumph — Har
Yahweh has displayed his power — Jerus
He has announced this victory — Tay
his righteousness hath he openly shewed in the sight of the heathen.
he has revealed his vindication in the sight of the nations — RSV
Before the eyes of the nations has he revealed his righteousness — ABPS
and revealed it to every nation — Tay

3. He hath remembered his mercy and his truth toward the house of Israel:
He has remembered his steadfast love and faithfulness to the house of Israel — RSV
He hath remembered his lovingkindness and his faithfulness toward the house of Israel — ASV
He has remembered His lovingkindness and His faithfulness to Israel's descendants — Ber
by fulfilling his promise to be kind to Israel — Tay
all the ends of the earth have seen the salvation of our God.
All the ends of the earth have seen the victory of our God — RSV
The most distant parts of the earth have seen the saving power of our God — Jerus
no corner of the world but has witnessed how our God can save — Knox
from end to end the world has seen the victory of our God — Mof
The whole earth has seen God's salvation of his people — Tay

4. Make a joyful noise unto the LORD, all the earth:
Let all the earth shout for joy to the Lord — Har
Show yourselves joyful unto the LORD, all ye lands — PBV
Acclaim Yahweh, all the earth — Jerus
make a loud noise, and rejoice, and sing praise.

Break forth and make a joyful noise and sweep the strings — Rhm
Break forth, sing for joy, and strike the chords — DeW
sing, rejoice, and give thanks — PBV
rejoice, be exultant, and sing praises — Har
break forth in joyful song; yes, sing praises! — Ber

5. Sing unto the LORD with the harp; with the harp, and the voice of a psalm.
Sweep the strings to Yahweh
With the lyre,
With the lyre and the voice of melody — Rhm
Sing praises to the Lord with the lyre, with the harp, and with melodious music — Har
Make music on a harp for the LORD, with the harp and melodious song — Ber
Sing to Yahweh, sing to the music of harps,
and to the sound of many instruments — Jerus

6. With trumpets and sound of cornet make a joyful noise before the LORD, the King.
With trumpets also, and shawms: O shew yourselves joyful before the LORD, the king — PBV
With trumpets and the sound of a horn
Shout aloud before the king — Yahweh — Rhm
With spiral trumpets and the sounding cornet, raise a shout of triumph for the Lord, before the king — Sept
With a fanfare of trumpets and horns, shout aloud in the presence of the Lord and King — Har
With trumpet and echoing horn acclaim the presence of the LORD our king — NEB
to the sound of trumpet and horn acclaim Yahweh the King! — Jerus

7. Let the sea roar, and the fulness thereof; the world, and they that dwell therein.
Let the sea in its vastness roar in praise,
the world and its inhabitants! — Ber

8. Let the floods clap their hands:
Let the rivers unite in applauses — Sept
Let the rivers join in the applause — Har
let the hills be joyful together

9. Before the LORD;
let the hills sing for joy together before the LORD — RSV
let the mountains also rejoice in the presence of the Lord — Har
and the mountains shout for joy,
at the presence of Yahweh — Jerus
for he cometh to judge the earth:
for he comes to rule the earth — NAB
with righteousness shall he judge the world, and the people with equity.
He will rule the world with justice
and the peoples with equity — NAB
He will judge the world righteously
and the nations impartially — Har
He will judge the world with justice,
the peoples with unfaltering fairness — Ber

PSALM 99

1. The LORD reigneth; let the people tremble:
The Lord is sovereign; let pagan nations tremble — Har
The LORD is king; the peoples tremble — NAB
The LORD is King, be the people never so impatient — PBV
The Lord is King; let the peoples be in fear — Bas
he sitteth between the cherubims; let the earth be moved.
he sitteth between the Cherubim, be the earth never so unquiet — PBV
He is enthroned between the cherubim; stagger, O earth! — Sprl
He is enthroned on the cherubim
Let the earth shake — Rhm
He is throned above the cherubim,
Let the earth quake — DeW
He is enthroned in heaven; let the earth quake — Har

2. The LORD is great in Zion; and he is high above all the people.
Jehovah in Zion is great;
And He is high above all the nations — DeW
Great is the Lord who dwells in Sion,

sovereign ruler of all peoples! — Knox
The Lord is majestic in Zion,
and supreme over all races — Har

3. Let them praise thy great and terrible name; for it is holy.
They shall give thanks unto thy Name, which is great, wonderful and holy — PBV
Let them thank his Name — great and reverend,
Holy is he! — Rhm
Let them praise Your pre-eminent and venerable name, saying,
"He is holy" — Har

4. The king's strength also loveth judgment; thou dost establish equity, thou executest judgment and righteousness in Jacob.
Mighty King, lover of justice,
thou hast established equity;
thou hast executed justice
and righteousness in Jacob — RSV
The King's energy is keenly set on justice;
Thou dost establish equity;
Thou dost guarantee justice and truth in Jacob — Ber
You are a king who loves justice,
insisting on honesty, justice, virtue,
as you have done for Jacob — Jerus
This mighty King is determined to give justice. Fairness is the touchstone of everything he does. He gives justice throughout Israel — Tay

5. Exalt ye the LORD our God, and worship at his footstool; for he is holy.
Exalt the LORD, our God; bow in worship at His footstool; He is holy! — Ber

6. Moses and Aaron among his priests, and Samuel among them that call upon his name; they called upon the LORD, and he answered them.
Moses and Aaron were among his priests,
Samuel also was among those who called on his name.
They cried to the LORD, and he answered them — RSV

7. He spake unto them in the cloudy pillar:
In the pillar of cloud he spoke to them — ABPS
He used to converse with them from the column of cloud — Har
they kept his testimonies, and the ordinance that he gave them.
They kept his testimonies, and the statutes he gave them — ABPS
They kept his decrees and the law which he gave them — AAT
they followed his teaching and kept the law he gave them — NEB

8. Thou answeredst them, O LORD our God:
It was You, our Lord and God, who answered them — Har
thou wast a God that forgavest them, though thou tookest vengeance of their inventions.
thou wast a forgiving God to them,
but an avenger of their wrongdoings — RSV
Thou wast a forgiving God to them
although Thou didst make them pay for their evil practices — Ber

9. Exalt the LORD our God, and worship at his holy hill;
Exalt Yahweh our God
And bow down towards his holy mountain — Rhm
for the LORD our God is holy.
For JEHOVAH our God is holy — Sprl
For holy is Yahweh our God — Rhm[25]

PSALM 100

A Psalm of praise.

1. Make a joyful noise unto the LORD, all ye lands.
Shout to Jehovah, all the earth — ABPS
Shout triumphantly for the Lord, all ye of the land — Sept
Hail the LORD joyously, all the earth! — AAT
Let the whole earth keep holiday in God's honour — Knox
Let all the earth shout for joy to the Lord — Har

2. Serve the LORD with gladness: come before his presence with singing.
Serve Yahweh with rejoicing,
Enter before him, with shouts of triumph — Rhm
pay to the Lord the homage of your rejoicing, appear in his presence

[25]Compare verses 3 and 5.

with glad hearts — Knox
serve Yahweh gladly,
come into his presence with songs of joy! — Jerus
worship the LORD in gladness,
enter his presence with songs of exultation — NEB

3. Know ye that the LORD he is God: it is he that hath made us, and not we ourselves;
Know ye that Jehovah, he is God:
It is he that hath made us, and we are his — ASV
Acknowledge the Lord as God:
He has made us, we are His — Har
Learn that it is the Lord, no other, who is God, his we are, he it was that made us — Knox

we are his people, and the sheep of his pasture.
we are his people, the flock that he pastures — Jerus
his people, the flock he tends — NAB
. . . the flock which he shepherds — NEB

4. Enter into his gates with thanksgiving, and into his courts with praise:
Enter His gates with rejoicing,
and His precincts with praise — Har

be thankful unto him, and bless his name.
Give thanks unto him, and bless his name — ASV

5. For the LORD is good; his mercy is everlasting; and his truth endureth to all generations.
For Jehovah is good; his lovingkindness endureth for ever,
And his faithfulness unto all generations — ASV
Yes, Yahweh is good,
his love is everlasting,
his faithfulness endures from age to age — Jerus

PSALM 101

A Psalm of David

1. I will sing of mercy and judgment: unto thee, O LORD, will I sing.
I will sing of loyalty and of justice; to thee, O LORD, I will sing — RSV
I will sing of lovingkindness and justice:
Unto thee, O Jehovah, will I sing praises — ASV
Of lovingkindness and of justice will I sing!
Unto thee O Yahweh will I touch the strings! —Rhm

2. I will behave myself wisely in a perfect way.
I will behave myself wisely in a blameless way — Rhm
I will give heed to the way that is blameless — RSV
I will give heed unto the way of integrity — JPS
I will carefully observe the path of the perfect — Ber

O when wilt thou come unto me?
Ah, when wilt thou grant me thy presence — Knox

I will walk within my house with a perfect heart.
I will walk with integrity of heart within my house — RSV
I will walk to and fro in the blamelessness of my heart, — in the midst of my house — Rhm
I will live an exemplary life in my own home — Har

3. I will set no wicked thing before mine eyes: I hate the work of them that turn aside; it shall not cleave to me.
I will take no wicked thing in hand; I hate the sins of unfaithfulness; there shall no such cleave unto me — PBV
I would not suffer a lawless deed in my presence.
The work of transgressors I hate; it shall not cleave to me — Sprl
I will set no base thing before mine eyes;
For I hate faithless dealing;
It shall not cleave unto me — DeW
I will set before myself no sordid aim;
I will hate disloyalty, I will have none of it — NEB
I will not have anything unworthy in my presence:
dissolute behavior is odious to me;
it shall not gain a hold on me — Har
I will not allow a base thought to attract my attention.
I despise crooked practices;
They shall not gain hold on me — Ber

4. A froward heart shall depart from me: I will not know a wicked person.

A perverse heart shall depart from me,
A maker of mischief will I not acknowledge — Rhm

Perverseness of heart shall be far from me;
I will know nothing of evil — RSV

An evil mind will be a thing utterly remote from me;
I shall have no dealings with wrongdoing — Har

5. Whoso privily slandereth his neighbour, him will I cut off:

He that uttereth slander in secret against his friend
Him will I root out — Rhm

I will destroy
the man who maligns his friend secretly — Har

him that hath an high look and a proud heart will not I suffer.

Whoso is haughty of eye and proud of heart, him will I not suffer — JPS

The man of haughty looks and arrogant heart
I will not endure — RSV

I cannot tolerate
the supercilious and haughty person — Har

I will not tolerate one who is conceited and arrogant — Ber

6. Mine eyes shall be upon the faithful of the land, that they may dwell with me:

I will look with favor on the faithful in the land,
that they may dwell with me — RSV

I will concentrate my attention on the faithful in the land,
that they may remain my allies — Har

I look to the trustworthy in the land to be my associates — Ber

he that walketh in a perfect way, he shall serve me.

He that walketh in the way of uprightness —
It is he that shall serve me — DeW

He that walketh in a way of integrity,
he shall minister unto me — JPS

he who walks in the way that is blameless
shall minister to me — RSV

my servants shall be such as follow the path of innocence — Knox

7. He that worketh deceit shall not dwell within my house; he that telleth lies shall not tarry in my sight.

No man who practices deceit
shall dwell in my house;
no man who utters lies
shall continue in my presence — RSV

There is no room in my house
for any hypocrite;
no liar keeps his post
where I can see him — Jerus

No scandal-monger shall live in my household;
no liar shall set himself up where I can see him — NEB

8. I will early destroy all the wicked of the land; that I may cut off all wicked doers from the city of the LORD.

Morning by morning I will destroy all the wicked in the land,
cutting off all the evildoers
from the city of the LORD — RSV

Morning by morning will I uproot
All the lawless ones of the land,
That I may cut off out of the city of Yahweh —
All the workers of iniquity — Rhm

Morning after morning I will do away with all criminals within the country
that I may eliminate from the city of the LORD all those who practice sin — Ber

My daily task will be to ferret out criminals and free the city of God from their grip — Tay

PSALM 102

A Prayer of the afflicted, when he is overwhelmed, and poureth out his complaint before the LORD.

A Prayer for the Humbled One when he is about to faint, and before Yahweh poureth out his grief — Rhm

1. Hear my prayer, O LORD, and let my cry come unto thee.

O Yahweh, hear thou my prayer,
And let my cry for help unto thee enter in — Rhm

Listen to my prayer, O thou Eternal,
let my cry for help reach thee — Mof

2. Hide not thy face from me in the day when I am in trouble;
Do not hide thy face from me
in the day of my distress! — RSV
incline thine ear unto me: in the day when I call answer me speedily.
incline thine ear unto me when I call;
O hear me, and that right soon — PBV
give me Your full attention,
and answer me quickly at the time when I call — Har
3. For my days are consumed like smoke, and my bones are burned as an hearth.
For my days have vanished in smoke,
And my bones are burned up as by fire — DeW
My days are vanishing like smoke;
my limbs are fevered like a fire — Mof
For my days pass away like smoke,
and my bones burn like a furnace — RSV
For my days vanish like smoke,
and my bones are charred like a burnt stick — Har
for my days go up in smoke;
my bones are inflamed as a bonfire — Ber
4. My heart is smitten, and withered like grass; so that I forget to eat my bread.
My heart is smitten like grass, and withered;
For in my sorrow I forget to eat my bread — DeW
My mind is dulled and withered like grass;
I am wasted away too much even to eat my food — Har
my health is blighted, withering like grass —
I forget to take my food — Mof
5. By reason of the voice of my groaning my bones cleave to my skin.
By reason of my loud outcries,
My bone cleaveth to my flesh — DeW
my skin is stretched tight on the bone,
so bitterly I moan — Mof
I am spent with sighing, till my skin clings to my bones — Knox
Because of my insistent sighing
I am reduced to skin and bone — NAB
Because of my prolonged grieving
I have become skin and bone — Har
whenever I heave a sigh,
my bones stick through my skin — Jerus
6. I am like a pelican of the wilderness: I am like an owl of the desert.
I am like a vulture of the wilderness,
like an owl of the waste places — RSV
I am like the pelican of the desert,
I have become as an owl among ruins — Rhm
I live in a desert like the pelican,
in a ruin like the screech owl — Jerus
I am like a vulture in a far-off wilderness, or like an owl alone in the desert — Tay
7. I watch, and am as a sparrow alone upon the house top.
I have passed sleepless nights; and been like a solitary bird on a house top — Sept
I cannot sleep, I mourn
like a lonely bird on the roof — Mof
I keep mournful watch, lonely as a single sparrow on the house top — Knox
8. Mine enemies reproach me all the day; and they that are mad against me are sworn against me.
All day long my foes insult me;
Those who deride me curse by me — AAT
All the day my enemies taunt me,
those who deride me use my name for a curse — RSV
Still my enemies taunt me, in their mad rage make a by-word of me — Knox
My enemies insult me incessantly;
those who ridicule me use my name in oaths — Har
All the day long mine enemies revile me,
Raving at me as "the accursed" in their oaths — DeW
all day long my foes are taunting me,
those who mock me call me "The accursed" — Mof
9. For I have eaten ashes like bread, and mingled my drink with weeping,
For I eat ashes like bread,
and mingle tears with my drink — RSV
I eat ashes with my food,
tears fall into my drink — Mof
I eat ashes instead of bread. My tears

run down into my drink — Tay

10. Because of thine indignation and thy wrath: for thou hast lifted me up, and cast me down.

And that, because of thine indignation and wrath; for thou hast taken me up, and cast me down — PBV

On account of Thy wrath and indignation.
Surely Thou didst elevate me, then didst cast me down — Sprl

because of thy indignation and anger; for thou hast taken me up and thrown me away — RSV

Because of your fury and your wrath; for you lifted me up only to cast me down — NAB

on account of Your furious anger, for You lifted me up, and then tossed me away — Har

11. My days are like a shadow that declineth; and I am withered like grass.

My days are gone like a shadow, and I am withered like grass — PBV

My days have flitted away like a shadow; and I am withered like mown grass — Sept

My days are like a lengthened shadow,
And I am withering like the grass — DeW

My days are brief as any evening shadow,
and I am withering away like grass — Mof

Like a tapering shadow my days dwindle, wasting away, like grass in the sun! — Knox

12. But thou, O LORD, shalt endure for ever;

But thou, O Jehovah, wilt abide for ever — ASV

But thou, O LORD, art enthroned for ever — RSV

But You, Lord, exist eternally — Har

and thy remembrance unto all generations.

And thy memorial name unto all generations — ASV

from age to age thy fame endures — Mof

thy name endures to all generations — RSV

Your renown endures throughout the ages — Har

and the fame of Your name endures to all generations — Amp

and your name will never come to an end — Bas

13. Thou shalt arise, and have mercy upon Zion: for the time to favour her, yea, the set time, is come.

Thou wilt arise and have pity on Zion;
it is the time to favor her;
the appointed time has come — RSV

14. For thy servants take pleasure in her stones, and favour the dust thereof.

And why? thy servants think upon her stones, and it pitieth them to see her in the dust — PBV

When Thy servants take delight in her very stones:
and have an affection for her very rubbish! — Sprl

For Thy servants take pleasure in her stones,
And love her dust — JPS

her scattered stones are dear to thy servants,
and they are distressed at the dust of her ruins — Mof

For her stones are dear to your servants, and her dust moves them to pity — NAB

15. So the heathen shall fear the name of the LORD, and all the kings of the earth thy glory.

Surely the nations shall reverence the Name of JEHOVAH;
And all the kings of the earth Thy glory — Sprl

The nations will revere the name of the Lord,
and all the earthly monarchs will acknowledge His glory — Har

16. When the LORD shall build up Zion, he shall appear in his glory.

For Jehovah hath built up Zion;
He hath appeared in his glory — ASV

For the LORD will build up Zion,
he will appear in his glory — RSV

When the Lord has rebuilt Zion,
He will manifest Himself in His splendor — Har

when the LORD builds up Zion again and shows himself in his glory — NEB

17. He will regard the prayer of the destitute, and not despise their prayer.

He will respond to the entreaty of the destitute,
and will not spurn their prayer — Har

he will answer the prayer of the abandoned,
he will not scorn their petitions — Jerus
He will listen to the prayers of the destitute, for he is never too busy to heed their requests — Tay

18. **This shall be written for the generation to come: and the people which shall be created shall praise the LORD.**

19. **For he hath looked down from the height of his sanctuary; from heaven did the LORD behold the earth;**

20. **To hear the groaning of the prisoner; to loose those that are appointed to death;**

21. **To declare the name of the LORD in Zion, and his praise in Jerusalem;**

22. **When the people are gathered together, and the kingdoms, to serve the LORD.**

Let this be recorded for a generation to come,
so that a people yet unborn may praise the LORD:
that he looked down from his holy height,
from heaven the LORD looked at the earth,
to hear the groans of the prisoners,
to set free those who were doomed to die;
that men may declare in Zion the name of the LORD,
and in Jerusalem his praise,
when peoples gather together,
and kingdoms, to worship the LORD — RSV

Let this be recorded for future ages,
that a people yet unborn may praise the Lord.
For He looked down from His sacred elevation;
from the heavens the Lord gazed down to earth,
to hear the groans of the imprisoned,
to set free those doomed to die,
that the name of the Lord might be proclaimed in Zion,
and His praise in Jerusalem,
when peoples and kingdoms assemble there
to serve the Lord — Har

This shall be recorded for a generation to come;
a people yet to be born shall praise the LORD.
For He has kept watch from the height of His sanctuary;
from heaven the LORD kept vigil over the earth,
to detect the groaning of the prisoners,
to release those who are destined to die;
that the name of the LORD may be proclaimed in Zion, His praise throughout Jerusalem,
when the nations, even the kingdoms, are brought together
for the purpose of serving the LORD — Ber

23. **He weakened my strength in the way; he shortened my days.**

He has broken my strength in midcourse;
he has shortened my days — RSV
He has sapped my developing strength, and diminished my days — Har
He has afflicted and weakened my strength, humbling and bringing me low [with sorrow] in the way; He has shortened my days [aging me prematurely] — Amp
He has cut me down in middle life, shortening my days — Tay
My strength is broken in mid course;
the time allotted me is short — NEB

24. **I said, O my God, take me not away in the midst of my days: thy years are throughout all generations.**

I plead, "O my God, take me not away in middle age;
O Thou whose years endure through all generations!" — Ber
But I cried to him, "O God, you live forever and forever! Don't let me die half through my years! — Tay

25. **Of old hast thou laid the foundation of the earth: and the heavens are the work of thy hands.**

26. **They shall perish, but thou shalt endure:**

Though they perish, You will remain — Har

yea, all of them shall wax old like a garment;

they will all deteriorate like a garment — Har
And they all like a garment shall fall in pieces — Rhm
they will all wear out like a garment — RSV

as a vesture shalt thou change them, and they shall be changed:
As a vesture wilt thou change them and they shall vanish — Rhm
and like a mantle thou wilt fold them up and they shall be changed — Sept
Thou changest them like raiment, and they pass away — RSV
You will change them like clothing, and they will be discarded — Har
like clothes that need changing you will change them — Jerus
thou shalt cast them off like a cloak, and they shall vanish — NEB

27. **But thou art the same, and thy years shall have no end.**
but thou art still the same, O thou Eternal,
thy years shall never end — Mof
But thou art always the same,
And thy years have no end — AAT
thou art unchanging, thy years can never fail — Knox
But you yourself never grow old. You are forever, and your years never end — Tay

28. **The children of thy servants shall continue, and their seed shall be established before thee.**
The sons of thy servants shall dwell [in the land],
And their seed shall be established before Thee — ABPS
The children of Thy servants shall dwell in peace;
And their offspring shall be established before Thee — Sprl
The posterity of thy servants shall yet hold their lands in peace, their race shall live on in thy keeping — Knox
The children of your servants will have a safe resting-place, and their seed will be ever before you — Bas

PSALM 103

A Psalm of David.

1. **Bless the LORD, O my soul: and all that is within me, bless his holy name.**
Praise the LORD, O my soul; and all that is within me, praise his holy Name — PBV
Bless the Eternal, O my soul,
let all my being bless his sacred name — Mof
Bless the Lord, my soul;
let my innermost being praise His holy name — Har

2. **Bless the LORD, O my soul, and forget not all his benefits:**
Bless the Lord, my soul, remembering all he has done for thee — Knox
Bless Yahweh, my soul,
and remember all his kindnesses — Jerus

3. **Who forgiveth all thine iniquities; who healeth all thy diseases;**
how he pardons all thy sins, heals all thy mortal ills — Knox
Who forgives all my guilt,
Who heals all my sicknesses — AAT
in forgiving all your offences,
in curing all your diseases — Jerus

4. **Who redeemeth thy life from destruction; who crowneth thee with lovingkindness and tender mercies;**
. . . compassion — Rhm
Who redeemeth thy life from the pit;
Who encompasseth thee with lovingkindness and tender mercies — JPS
he saves your life from death,
he crowns you with his love and pity — Mof
who redeems your life from the grave,
who crowns you with loving-kindness and mercy — Ber

5. **Who satisfieth thy mouth with good things; so that thy youth is renewed like the eagle's.**
Who satisfieth thy desire with good things,
So that thy youth is renewed like the eagle — ASV
who satisfies you with good as long as you live
so that your youth is renewed like the eagle's — RSV

6. **The LORD executeth righteousness and judgment for all that are oppressed.**
Yahweh is one who executeth righteousness,
Yea vindication for all the oppressed — Rhm
The LORD works vindication
and justice for all who are oppressed — RSV
Yahweh, who does what is right,
is always on the side of the oppressed — Jerus

7. He made known his ways unto Moses, his acts unto the children of Israel.
he revealed his intentions to Moses,
his prowess to the sons of Israel — Jerus
He taught Moses to know his way
and showed the Israelites what he could do — NEB

8. The LORD is merciful and gracious, slow to anger, and plenteous in mercy.
JEHOVAH is tenderly kind and compassionate,
Long-suffering, and bounteous in mercy — Sprl
The LORD is full of compassion and mercy, long-suffering, and of great goodness — PBV
Compassionate and gracious is Yahweh, —
Slow to anger and abundant in lovingkindness — Rhm
The LORD is merciful and gracious,
slow to anger and abounding in steadfast love — RSV
The LORD is merciful and gracious,
patiently considerate and abounding in mercy — Ber
The Lord is kind and full of pity, not quickly made angry, but ever ready to have mercy — Bas
How pitying and gracious the Lord is, how patient, how rich in mercy! — Knox

9. He will not always chide: neither will he keep his anger for ever.
He will not always be finding fault,
his frown does not last forever — Knox
He will not reprimand continually,
nor harbor resentment forever — Har
his indignation does not last for ever,
his resentment exists a short time only — Jerus
He never bears a grudge, nor remains angry forever — Tay

10. He hath not dealt with us after our sins; nor rewarded us according to our iniquities.
He has not dealt with us to the measure of our sins,
nor rewarded us as our iniquities deserve — Ber
he never treats us, never punishes us,
as our guilt and our sins deserve — Jerus

11. For as the heaven is high above the earth, so great is his mercy toward them that fear him.
For look how high the heaven is in comparison of the earth; so great is his mercy also toward them that fear him — PBV
For as the heavens are exalted over the earth
His lovingkindness hath prevailed over them who revere him — Rhm
but, high as heaven is over earth,
so vast his love is to his worshippers — Mof
For his mercy toward those who fear and honor him is as great as the height of the heavens above the earth — Tay

12. As far as the east is from the west, so far hath he removed our transgressions from us.
Look how wide also the east is from the west; so far hath he set our sins from us — PBV
Far as east is from west,
so far has he put our offences away from us — NEB

13. Like as a father pitieth his children, so the LORD pitieth them that fear him.
Like the compassion of a father for his children
Is the compassion of Yahweh for them who revere him — Rhm
As a father has compassion on his children,
Jehovah has compassion on them that fear him — ABPS
As a father has compassion for his children,
so the LORD tenderly sympathizes with those who revere Him — Ber
As tenderly as a father treats his children,
so Yahweh treats those who fear him — Jerus
For his own worshippers, the Lord has a father's pity — Knox

14. For he knoweth our frame; he remembereth that we are dust.
For He knows what we are made of;
He keeps in mind that we are dust — Ber
does he not know the stuff of which we are made, can he forget that we are only dust? — Knox

15. As for man, his days are as grass: as a flower of the field, so he flourisheth.
Frail man! his days are like the grass:

As the flower of the field, so he flourisheth — Sprl

Poor man! — his days are like the grass,
he blooms like a flower in the meadow — Mof

Man's life is like the grass, he blooms and dies like a flower in the fields — Knox

Man lasts no longer than grass,
no longer than a wild flower he lives — Jerus

16. For the wind passeth over it, and it is gone; and the place thereof shall know it no more.

at the breath of a breeze it is gone,
and its place never sees it again — Mof

once the hot wind has passed over, it has gone, forgotten by the place where it grew — Knox

the wind blows over it, and it is gone,
with not a sign that it has ever been there — Ber

one gust of wind, and he is gone,
never to be seen there again — Jerus

17. But the mercy of the LORD is from everlasting to everlasting upon them that fear him, and his righteousness unto children's children;

But the merciful goodness of the LORD endureth for ever and ever upon them that fear him; and his righteousness upon children's children — PBV

but the lovingkindness of Yahweh is from one age even to another
Upon them who revere him,
And his righteousness to children's children — Rhm

But the Lord's worshippers know no beginning or end of his mercy; he will keep faith with their children's children — Knox

But the loving mercy of the Lord
is eternally present to those who revere Him,
and His equity avails for future generations — Har

But the LORD's love never fails those who fear him;
his righteousness never fails their sons and their grandsons — NEB

18. To such as keep his covenant, and to those that remember his commandments to do them.

If they keep his agreement, and have his laws in mind to do them — Bas

do they but hold fast by his covenant, and live mindful of his law — Knox

as long as they keep covenant
and remember to obey his precepts — Jerus

19. The LORD hath prepared his throne in the heavens; and his kingdom ruleth over all.

In heaven has the Eternal fixed his throne,
and his dominion covers all the world — Mof

The Lord has set up his throne in heaven, rules with universal sway — Knox

20. Bless the LORD ye his angels, that excel in strength, that do his commandments, hearkening unto the voice of his word.

Bless the LORD, O you his angels,
you mighty ones who do his word,
hearkening to the voice of his word! — RSV

Bless the LORD, all you his angels,
you mighty in strength, who do his bidding,
obeying his spoken word — NAB

Bless the Lord, you who are His angels;
powerful beings, who execute His commands,
and listen to His utterances — Har

Bless Yahweh, all his angels,
heroes mighty to enforce his word,
attentive to his word of command — Jerus

Bless the Lord, you mighty angels of his who carry out his orders, listening for each of his commands — Tay

21. Bless ye the LORD, all ye his hosts; ye ministers of his, that do his pleasure.

Bless the Eternal, all his hosts,
ye servants who carry out his will! — Mof

Bless the Lord, you who constitute His armies,
to attend on Him to perform His will — Har

Bless the LORD, all you His armies,
you His servants who continually do what pleases Him! — Ber

22. Bless the LORD, all his works in all places of his dominion:

bless the Lord, all you creatures of his,

in every corner of his dominion — Knox
May all His works bless the Lord
in every place where His sway extends — Har
Let everything everywhere bless the Lord — Tay

bless the LORD, O my soul.
praise thou the LORD, O my soul — PBV
Bless Jehovah, O my soul — ASV
And how I bless him too! — Tay

PSALM 104

1. **Bless the LORD, O my soul.**
Praise the LORD, O my soul — PBV
O LORD my God, thou art very great;
You are most majestic, my Lord and God — Har
O Lord my God, what magnificence is thine! — Knox
thou art clothed with honour and majesty.
In glory and majesty art Thou arrayed — Sprl
You are adorned with honor and splendor — Har
Glory and beauty are thy clothing — Knox

2. **Who coverest thyself with light as with a garment: who stretchest out the heavens like a curtain:**
Putting on light as a robe,
Stretching out the heavens as a curtain — Rhm
covering Yourself with a robe of light,
and stretching out the skies like a tent covering — Har
Thou wrappest thyself in a robe of light,
thou spreadest the sky like a tent — Mof
The light is a garment thou dost wrap about thee, the heavens a curtain thy hand unfolds — Knox

3. **Who layeth the beams of his chambers in the waters: who maketh the clouds his chariot: who walketh upon the wings of the wind:**
He has laid the foundation of His dwelling on the waters;
He makes the clouds His chariot,
and soars on wings of wind — Har
The waters of heaven are thy antechamber, the clouds thy chariot; on the wings of the wind thou dost come and go — Knox
Who frames his chambers in the waters;
Who makes the clouds his chariot;
Who goes on the wings of the wind — ABPS

4. **Who maketh his angels spirits; his ministers a flaming fire:**
Making His messengers winds,
His attendants a flaming fire — Rhm
Who maketh the winds His messengers,
The flaming thunderbolts His ministers — DeW
who makest the winds thy messengers,
fire and flame thy ministers — RSV
making the spirits His messengers,
flames of fire His servants — Ber
you use the winds as messengers
and fiery flames as servants — Jerus

5. **Who laid the foundations of the earth, that it should not be removed for ever.**
He founded the earth on its bases,
That it should not be moved forever and ever — ABPS
He laid the foundations of the earth,
That it should not be overthrown for ever — DeW

6. **Thou coveredst it with the deep as with a garment: the waters stood above the mountains.**
The deep once covered it, like a cloak; the waters stood high above the mountains — Knox
You covered it with the garment of the ocean;
the waters towered above the mountains — Har
you wrapped it with the deep as with a robe,
the waters overtopping the mountains — Jerus

7. **At thy rebuke they fled; at the voice of thy thunder they hasted away.**

8. **They go up by the mountains; they go down by the valleys unto the place which thou hast founded for them.**

9. **Thou hast set a bound that they may not pass over; that they turn not again to cover the earth.**

At thy rebuke they fled;
at the sound of thy thunder they took to flight.
The mountains rose, the valleys sank down
to the place which thou didst appoint for them.
Thou didst set a bound which they should not pass,
so that they might not again cover the earth — RSV

then [the deep] cowered before thy rebuking word, fled away at thy voice of thunder, leaving the mountain heights to rise, the valleys to sink into their appointed place! And to these waters thou hast given a frontier they may not pass; never must they flow back, and cover the earth again — Knox

At your reproof the waters took to flight,
they fled at the sound of your thunder,
cascading over the mountains, into the valleys,
down to the reservoir you made for them;
you imposed the limits they must never cross again,
or they would once more flood the land — Jerus

You spoke, and at the sound of your shout the water collected into its vast ocean beds, and mountains rose and valleys sank to the levels you decreed. And then you set a boundary for the seas, so that they would never again cover the earth — Tay

10. He sendeth the springs into the valleys, which run among the hills.

He sends out springs in the valleys;
they run among the mountains — ABPS

Thou makest springs gush forth in the valleys;
they flow between the hills — RSV

You sent springs gushing in ravines, running down between the mountains — Jerus

11. They give drink to every beast of the field: the wild asses quench their thirst.

They provide water for all the animals of the countryside;
and wild asses slake their thirst in them — Har

12. By them shall the fowls of the heaven have their habitation, which sing among the branches.

By them the birds of the heavens have their habitation;
They sing among the branches — ASV

The birds of heaven, too, will roost beside them; vocal is every bough with their music — Knox

Beside them the birds of heaven dwell;
from among the branches they send forth their song — NAB

Near them live the birds of the sky;
they trill their notes from among the branches — Har

13. He watereth the hills from his chambers: the earth is satisfied with the fruit of thy works.

From thy lofty abode thou waterest the mountains;
the earth is satisfied with the fruit of thy work — RSV

From thy high dwelling-place thou dost send rain upon the hills; thy hand gives earth all her plenty — Knox

He sends rain upon the mountains and fills the earth with fruit — Tay

14. He causeth the grass to grow for the cattle, and herb for the service of man:

Thou dost cause the grass to grow for the cattle,
and plants for man to cultivate — RSV

you make fresh grass grow for cattle and those plants made use of by man — Jerus

You raise grass for the cattle,
and vegetation for men's use — NAB

Thou makest grass grow for the cattle and green things for those who toil for man — NEB

that he may bring forth food out of the earth;

15. And wine that maketh glad the heart of man, and oil to make his face to shine, and bread which strengtheneth man's heart.

that man may produce sustenance from the earth,
and wine to cheer the human spirit,
making his face gleam more brightly than oil;
with bread also, to refresh the human body — Har

that he may derive sustenance from the land,

wine to elate the spirit of man,
oil to brighten his facial appearance,
and bread to improve man's health — Ber

for them to get food from the soil:
wine to make them cheerful,
oil to make them happy
and bread to make them strong — Jerus

16. The trees of the LORD are full of sap; the cedars of Lebanon, which he hath planted;

The trees of Jehovah are filled with moisture;
The cedars of Lebanon, which he hath planted — ASV

The trees of the LORD are watered abundantly . . . — RSV

17. Where the birds make their nests: as for the stork, the fir trees are her house.

In them the birds build their nests;
the stork has her home in the fir trees — RSV

18. The high hills are a refuge for the wild goats; and the rocks for the conies.

The high mountains are for the wild goats;
the rocks are refuge for the badgers — RSV

He made the mountain heights for the wild goats,
the rocky crags for the rock-badger's refuge — Ber

19. He appointed the moon for seasons: the sun knoweth his going down.

Thou hast made the moon to mark the seasons;
the sun knows its time for setting — RSV

He marks the seasons by the moon,
he tells the sun when it must set — Mof

He assigned the moon to mark the months, and the sun to mark the days — Tay

20. Thou makest darkness, and it is night: wherein all the beasts of the forest do creep forth.

Thou dost decree darkness, and the night falls; in the night all the forest is astir with prowling beasts — Knox

Thou makest darkness settle down, so that during the night
all forest animals may roam about — Ber

21. The young lions roar after their prey, and seek their meat from God.

The young lions roar after their prey,
And seek their food from God — ASV

Then the young lions roar for their food; but they are dependent on the Lord — Tay

22. The sun ariseth, they gather themselves together, and lay them down in their dens.

The sun arises, they retire,
And couch down in their dens — ABPS

Then the sun rises, and they slink away to lie down in their dens — Knox

23. Man goeth forth unto his work and to his labour until the evening.

while man goes abroad to toil and drudge till the evening — Knox

But man then starts out to his work
and remains at his task until evening — Ber

24. O LORD, how manifold are thy works! in wisdom hast thou made them all: the earth is full of thy riches.

How manifold are Thy works, O Jehovah!
In wisdom hast Thou wrought them all:
The earth is full of Thy creatures — DeW

What diversity, Lord, in thy creatures!
What wisdom has designed them all!
There is nothing on earth but gives proof of thy creative power — Knox

Yahweh, what variety you have created.
arranging everything so wisely!
Earth is completely full of things you have made — Jerus

25. So is this great and wide sea, wherein are things creeping innumerable, both small and great beasts.

Yonder is the sea, great and wide, wherein are things creeping innumerable, both small and great beasts — RV

There lies the vast ocean, stretching wide on every hand; this, too, is peopled with living things past number, great creatures and small — Knox

26. There go the ships: there is that leviathan, whom thou hast made to play therein.

the ships pass them on their course.
Leviathan himself is among them;

him, too, thou hast created to roam there at pleasure — Knox

There the ships sail,
and Leviathan, which You have made to frolic in it — Har

There go the ships; there is that great beast, which you have made as a plaything — Bas

with the ships going to and fro
and Leviathan whom you made to amuse you — Jerus

27. These wait all upon thee; that thou mayest give them their meat in due season.

These all look to thee,
to give them their food in due season — RSV

All creatures depend on you
to feed them throughout the year — Jerus

28. That thou givest them they gather: thou openest thine hand, they are filled with good.

Thou givest unto them, they gather;
Thou openest thy hand, they are satisfied with good — ASV

what thou givest, that they gather,
feasting from thine open hand — Mof

you provide the food they eat,
with generous hand you satisfy their hunger — Jerus

29. Thou hidest thy face, they are troubled: thou takest away their breath, they die, and return to their dust.

If you hide your face, they are dismayed;
if you take away their breath, they perish
and return to their dust — NAB

30. Thou sendest forth thy spirit, they are created: and thou renewest the face of the earth.

Then thou sendest forth thy spirit, and there is fresh creation; thou dost repeople the face of the earth — Knox

Thou sendest Thy Spirit and more are created,
and Thou dost replenish the surface of the earth — Ber

You give breath, fresh life begins,
you keep renewing the world — Jerus

31. The glory of the LORD shall endure for ever: the LORD shall rejoice in his works.

The glorious majesty of the LORD shall endure for ever; the LORD shall rejoice in his works — PBV

Let the glory of Jehovah be forever;
Let him rejoice in the works of his hands — ABPS

May the glory of the LORD remain forever;
may the LORD be pleased with His works — Ber

32. He looketh on the earth, and it trembleth: he toucheth the hills, and they smoke.

One glance from him makes earth tremble; at his touch, the mountains are wreathed in smoke — Knox

When He contemplates the earth, it quakes;
when He touches the mountains, they belch forth smoke — Har

The earth trembles at his glance; the mountains burst into flame at his touch — Tay

33. I will sing unto the LORD as long as I live: I will sing praise to my God while I have my being.

I will sing to Yahweh as long as I live!
Yea I will touch the strings to my God while I continue — Rhm

34. My meditation of him shall be sweet: I will be glad in the LORD.

oh, may this prayer with him find acceptance, in whom is all my content! — Knox

Let my meditation be sweet unto him:
I will rejoice in Jehovah — ASV

May these my thoughts please him —
I find my joy in the Eternal! — Mof

May he be pleased by all these thoughts about him, for he is the source of all my joy — Tay

35. Let the sinners be consumed out of the earth, and let the wicked be no more.

May sinners be swept off the earth,
and the wicked disappear forever — Har

May sinners vanish from the earth
and the wicked exist no more! — Jerus

Sinners shall be consumed out of the earth
And the lawless no more shall exist — Rhm

Bless thou the LORD, O my soul.

But thou, my soul, bless the Lord — Knox

Bless Jehovah, O my soul — ABPS

Praise thou the LORD, O my soul — PBV

Praise ye the LORD.
Praise ye Jah — ABPS
Praise ye Jehovah — ASV
Hallelujah — Sprl

PSALM 105

1. **O give thanks unto the LORD; call upon his name: make known his deeds among the people.**
Oh give thanks unto Jehovah, call upon his name;
Make known among the peoples his doings — ASV
Praise the Lord, and call upon his name; tell the story of his doings for all the nations to hear — Knox

2. **Sing unto him, sing psalms unto him: talk ye of all his wondrous works.**
O let your songs be of him, and praise him; and let your talking be of his wondrous works — PBV
greet him with song and psalm, recount his acts of miracle — Knox
Sing unto Him, make melody unto Him; Meditate upon all His wonders — DeW
Sing to him, play to him,
tell over all his marvels! — Jerus

3. **Glory ye in his holy name: let the heart of them rejoice that seek the LORD.**
Exult in his hallowed name;
let those who seek the LORD be joyful in heart — NEB
Triumph in that holy name; let every heart that longs for the Lord rejoice — Knox
Boast yourselves in His Holy Name,
the heart of those seeking Jehovah rejoiceth — YLT
Glory in the Lord; O worshipers of God, rejoice — Tay

4. **Seek the LORD, and his strength: seek his face evermore.**
Search out Yahweh and his strength,
Seek diligently his face at all times — Rhm
Worship the Eternal and be strengthened, worship in his presence evermore — Mof
Inquire of the LORD and his might!
Seek his face continually! — AAT
Search out the Lord and His power;
look for His presence continually — Har

5. **Remember his marvellous works that he hath done; his wonders, and the judgments of his mouth;**
Remember the wonders that He has performed;
His miracles and His spoken decrees — Har
Keep in mind the great works which he has done; his wonders and the decisions of his mouth — Bas

6. **O ye seed of Abraham his servant, ye children of Jacob his chosen.**
O offspring of Abraham his servant,
sons of Jacob, his chosen ones! — RSV

7. **He is the LORD our God: his judgments are in all the earth.**
Yahweh himself is our God,
Through all the land are his just decisions — Rhm
He is the Lord our God;
His decrees are universal — Har
He is Yahweh our God,
his authority is over all the earth — Jerus

8. **He hath remembered his covenant for ever, the word which he commanded to a thousand generations.**
He never forgets his compact,
the pledge given for a thousand generations — Bas
He is mindful of his covenant for ever,
of the word that he commanded, for a thousand generations — RSV
He keeps in everlasting memory that covenant of his, that promise which a thousand ages might not cancel — Knox

9. **Which covenant he made with Abraham, and his oath unto Isaac;**
the compact made with Abraham,
the oath he swore to Isaac — Mof
The agreement which he made with Abraham, and his oath to Isaac — Bas
Which He covenanted with Abraham,
the solemn promise which was sworn also to Isaac — Har

10. **And confirmed the same unto Jacob for a law, and to Israel for an everlasting covenant:**
which he confirmed to Jacob as a statute,
to Israel as an everlasting covenant — RSV
He confirmed this to Jacob as a statute,

and unto Israel as a permanent agreement — Har

11. Saying, Unto thee will I give the land of Canaan, the lot of your inheritance:

saying, "To you I will give the land of Canaan
as your portion for an inheritance" — RSV

Saying, To thee will I give the land of Canaan,
As your inherited portion — Rhm

12. When they were but a few men in number; yea, very few, and strangers in it.

13. When they went from one nation to another, from one kingdom to another people;

14. He suffered no man to do them wrong: yea, he reproved kings for their sakes;

15. Saying, Touch not mine anointed, and do my prophets no harm.

At this time they were only few in number,
of very minor importance, and strange to the country.
When they wandered from nation to nation,
from one kingdom to another,
He allowed no one to oppress them;
He even reprimanded kings on their account:
"Leave my anointed ones alone;
do not harm my prophets" — Har

When they were few in number,
of little account, and sojourners in it,
wandering from nation to nation,
from one kingdom to another people,
he allowed no one to oppress them;
he rebuked kings on their account,
saying, "Touch not my anointed ones,
do my prophets no harm!" — RSV

16. Moreover he called for a famine upon the land: he brake the whole staff of bread.

17. He sent a man before them, even Joseph, who was sold for a servant:

18. Whose feet they hurt with fetters: he was laid in iron:

19. Until the time that his word came: the word of the LORD tried him.

When he summoned a famine on the land,
and broke every staff of bread,
he had sent a man ahead of them,
Joseph, who was sold as a slave.
His feet were hurt with fetters,
his neck was put in a collar of iron;
until what he had said came to pass
the word of the LORD tested him — RSV

He sent famine upon the land,
He broke the very staff of life.
He dispatched a man ahead of them,
Joseph, who was sold into slavery.
They forced his feet into fetters;
his body was put in irons.
Until the time that his utterances were actually fulfilled,
the promise of the Lord tested him severely — Har

20. The king sent and loosed him; even the ruler of the people, and let him go free.

The king sent and released him;
the overlord of nations let him go free — Har

21. He made him lord of his house, and ruler of all his substance:

He appointed him supervisor of his household,
and ruler over all his possessions — Har

22. To bind his princes at his pleasure; and teach his senators wisdom.

At his pleasure he could imprison the king's aides and teach the king's advisors — Tay

that he might give orders to his officers at will,
and offer advice to his elders — Har

23. Israel also came into Egypt; and Jacob sojourned in the land of Ham.

So Israel came into Egypt,
And Jacob sojourned in the land of Ham — Rhm

So it was that Israel came into Egypt,
that Jacob dwelt as an alien in the country of Cham — Knox

24. And he increased his people greatly; and made them stronger than their enemies.

And he made his people exceeding fruitful, —
And caused them to become stronger than their adversaries — Rhm

And he made his people very prolific,
And made them more numerous than their foes — AAT

25. He turned their heart to hate his people, to deal subtilly with his servants.

He turned their heart to hate his people,
To plot against his servants — ABPS

He changed their heart so that they hated his people,

So that they dealt treacherously with his servants — AAT

26. He sent Moses his servant; and Aaron whom he had chosen.

And now he sent his servant Moses, and Aaron, the man of his choice — Knox

27. They shewed his signs among them, and wonders in the land of Ham.

They performed His signs among them, Yea, they performed miracles in the land of Ham — Sprl

They showed His signs among them, wonders and miracles in the land of Ham [Egypt] — Amp

28. He sent darkness, and made it dark; and they rebelled not against his word.

He sent [thick] darkness, and made the land dark, and they [God's two servants] rebelled not against His word — Amp

He sent darkness and made it dark, But they rebelled against his words — Rhm

He sent darkness, and made it dark; and yet they rebelled against his word — Lam

He ordered darkness, and it grew black; and they did not disobey His command — Ber

29. He turned their waters into blood, and slew their fish.

He turned [Egypt's] waters into blood, and caused their fish to die — Amp

30. Their land brought forth frogs in abundance, in the chambers of their kings.

Their land swarmed with frogs, even in the chambers of their kings — RSV

31. He spake, and there came divers sorts of flies, and lice in all their coasts.

He spake, and there came swarms of flies, and lice in all their borders — RV

He spake and there came in the gad-fly, Gnats in all their bounds — Rhm

He spoke and a swarm of flies came, Mosquitoes throughout their country — AAT

32. He gave them hail for rain, and flaming fire in their land.

Instead of rain He gave them hail, With flaming fire in their land — DeW

He gave them hail for rain, and lightning that flashed through their land — RSV

He changed their rain into hail and flashed fire over their country — NEB

33. He smote their vines also and their fig trees; and brake the trees of their coasts.

He smote their vines and fig trees, and shattered the trees of their country — RSV

34. He spake, and the locusts came, and caterpillars, and that without number,

He spake, and the locust came in, And grasshoppers without number — DeW

He spoke, and the locusts came, and young locusts without number — RSV

35. And did eat up all the herbs in their land, and devoured the fruit of their ground.

They devoured all the plants in their land; They devoured the fruit of their ground — DeW

36. He smote also all the firstborn in their land, the chief of all their strength.

he struck down all the firstborn in their land, each oldest male child — Mof

Then he struck every first-born throughout their land, the first fruits of all their manhood — NAB

37. He brought them forth also with silver and gold: and there was not one feeble person among their tribes.

Then he led out his clansmen, carrying spoil of gold and silver, not a weary man among them — Mof

Then he sent them forth with silver and gold, And there was no straggler in their ranks — AAT

And he led them forth laden with silver and gold, with not a weakling among their tribes — NAB

38. Egypt was glad when they departed: for the fear of them fell upon them.

Egypt rejoiced at their exodus; For their dread had fallen upon them — Sprl

Egypt was relieved when they left, for apprehension had overtaken them — Har

Egypt was glad to see them go,
they had filled her with alarm — Jerus

39. He spread a cloud for a covering; and fire to give light in the night.
He spread a cloud for a screen;
And fire to give light in the night — JPS
He spread out a cloud to screen them,
and fire to illuminate the night — Har

40. The people asked, and he brought quails, and satisfied them with the bread of heaven.
he sent them quails, at their demand,
and bread of heaven in plenty — Mof
He brought them quails at their request,
and fed them with bread from the heavens — Har

41. He opened the rock, and the waters gushed out; they ran in the dry places like a river.
He opened a rock and waters gushed out,
They flowed through the wastes like a river — DeW
He opened the rock, and water gushed forth;
it flowed through the desert like a river — RSV

42. For he remembered his holy promise, and Abraham his servant.
For he remembered his own sacred pledge
to Abraham his servant — Mof

43. And he brought forth his people with joy, and his chosen with gladness:
So He brought forth His people with joy —
Yea, His chosen with exultant shoutings — Sprl
Thus brought he forth his people with gladness, —
With shouts of triumph his chosen ones — Rhm
and He brought forth His people rejoicing;
His chosen ones were singing with joy — Har

44. And gave them the lands of the heathen: and they inherited the labour of the people;
he gave them the lands of the nations,
and they possessed the fruit of others' toils — Mof

45. That they might observe his statutes, and keep his laws.
that they might be faithful to His statutes
and diligently keep His laws — Ber
Praise ye the LORD.
Bless ye Jah — ABPS
Praise ye Jehovah — ASV
Hallelujah! — Ber

PSALM 106

1. Praise ye the LORD.
Praise ye Jehovah — ASV
Bless ye Jah — ABPS
Hallelujah! — Ber
O give thanks unto the LORD; for he is good: for his mercy endureth for ever.
For his lovingkindness endureth for ever — ASV
for his steadfast love endures for ever! — RSV

2. Who can utter the mighty acts of the LORD? who can shew forth all his praise?
Who can express the noble acts of the LORD, or show forth all his praise — PBV
Who shall utter the mighty deeds of Jehovah;
Shall cause all his praise to be heard — ABPS
Who can proclaim the Eternal's mighty deeds,
or do full justice to his praise — Mof
Who can count all Yahweh's triumphs?
Who can praise him enough — Jerus

3. Blessed are they that keep judgment, and he that doeth righteousness at all times.
Blessed are they who observe justice,
who do righteousness at all times! — RSV
Happy indeed are those who cherish equity,
who live virtuously all the time — Har

4. Remember me, O LORD, with the favour that thou bearest unto thy people:
Remember me, O LORD, when thou showest favor to thy people — RSV
O visit me with thy salvation;

help me when thou deliverest them — RSV

5. **That I may see the good of thy chosen, that I may rejoice in the gladness of thy nation, that I may glory with thine inheritance.**

That I may look upon the welfare of thy chosen ones
That I may rejoice in the joy of thy nation,
That I may glory with thine inheritance — Rhm

that I may see the prosperity of thy chosen,
rejoice in thy nation's joy and exult with thy own people — NEB

6. **We have sinned with our fathers, we have committed iniquity, we have done wickedly.**

We have sinned as have our fathers,
We have become guilty, we have done wickedly — DeW

7. **Our fathers understood not thy wonders in Egypt;**

Our fathers, when they were in Egypt, did not consider thy wonderful works — RSV

When our fathers were in Egypt, they disregarded Your wonders — Har

Our fathers did not appreciate Thy miracles in Egypt — Ber

they remembered not the multitude of thy mercies;

They remembered not the multitude of thy lovingkindnesses — ASV

they did not remember the abundance of thy steadfast love — RSV

they did not remember thy many acts of faithful love — NEB

but provoked him at the sea, even at the Red sea.

but rebelled against the Most High at the Red Sea — RSV

8. **Nevertheless he saved them for his name's sake, that he might make his mighty power to be known.**

Yet he saved them for his own sake,
to display his power — Mof

Yet, for his own honour, to make known his power, he delivered them — Knox

Yet He saved them for the sake of His reputation,
that He might reveal His mighty power — Har

9. **He rebuked the Red sea also, and it was dried up: so he led them through the depths, as through the wilderness.**

He rebuked the Red Sea, and it was dried up,
and he led them through the deep as through a desert — NAB

10. **And he saved them from the hand of him that hated them, and redeemed them from the hand of the enemy.**

He saved them out of the hand of the foe,
He redeemed them from the power of the enemy — DeW

11. **And the waters covered their enemies: there was not one of them left.**

For the waters engulfed their enemies;
not one of them survived — Har

12. **Then believed they his words; they sang his praise.**

Then they believed his promise,
and they sang his praise — Mof

Then, having faith in his promises,
they immediately sang his praises — Jerus

13. **They soon forgat his works; they waited not for his counsel:**

But soon they forgot what he had done,
they would not be patient with his purposes — Mof

But they soon forgot his deeds;
They waited not for his advice — AAT

14. **But lusted exceedingly in the wilderness, and tempted God in the desert.**

They had greedy longings in the wilderness,
And they tempted God in the desert — ABPS

They gave way to their evil desires in the waste land, and put God to the test in the dry places — Bas

their desires overcame them in the desert,
they challenged God in the wilds — Jerus

15. **And he gave them their request; but sent leanness into their soul.**

he let them have what they desired,
then — made them loathe it! — Mof

And he granted their request,
But sent disease upon them — AAT

he gave them what they asked,
but sent a wasting disease among them — RSV

16. **They envied Moses also in the camp, and Aaron the saint of the LORD.**

17. **The earth opened and swallowed up Dathan, and covered the company of Abiram.**

They were incensed at Moses in the camp,
Against Aaron the consecrated of Jehovah.
The earth opened and swallowed up Dathan,
And covered the company of Abiram — DeW

When men in the camp were jealous of Moses
and Aaron, the holy one of the LORD,
the earth opened and swallowed up Dathan,
and covered the company of Abiram — RSV

18. And a fire was kindled in their company; the flame burned up the wicked.

Fire also broke out in their company;
the flame burned up the wicked — RSV

fire flamed out against their faction,
the renegades went up in flames — Jerus

19. They made a calf in Horeb, and worshipped the molten image.

20. Thus they changed their glory into the similitude of an ox that eateth grass.

And they exchanged their Glory
For the likeness of an ox that eateth grass — DeW

They exchanged the glory of God
for the image of an ox that eats grass — RSV

They exchanged their glorious Deity
for the image of an ox that feeds on fodder — Har

21. They forgat God their saviour, which had done great things in Egypt;

They forgot God their deliverer,
who had performed miracles in Egypt — Har

They forgot the God who had saved them
by performing such feats in Egypt — Jerus

22. Wondrous works in the land of Ham, and terrible things by the Red sea.

23. Therefore he said that he would destroy them, had not Moses his chosen stood before him in the breach, to turn away his wrath, lest he should destroy them.

24. Yea, they despised the pleasant land, they believed not his word:

After this, they regarded the pleasant land with contempt,
and had no confidence in His promise — Har

25. But murmured in their tents, and hearkened not unto the voice of the LORD.

They complained while in their tents
and would not listen to the voice of the LORD — Ber

they stayed in their camp and grumbled,
they would not listen to Yahweh's voice — Jerus

26. Therefore he lifted up his hand against them, to overthrow them in the wilderness:

27. To overthrow their seed also among the nations, and to scatter them in the lands.

Therefore he sware unto them,
That he would overthrow them in the wilderness,
And that he would overthrow their seed among the nations,
And scatter them in the lands — ASV

Therefore he raised his hand and swore to them
that he would make them fall in the wilderness,
and would disperse their descendants among the nations,
scattering them over the lands — RSV

28. They joined themselves also unto Baal-peor, and ate the sacrifices of the dead.

They allied themselves with the Baal of Peor,
And ate sacrifices offered to the dead — AAT

They joined themselves also to the [idol] Baal of Peor, and ate sacrifices [offered] to the lifeless [gods] — Amp

29. Thus they provoked him to anger with their inventions:

they provoked the LORD to anger with their doings — RSV

and the plague brake in upon them.

and a plague broke out among them — RSV

and he sent disease on them — Bas

30. Then stood up Phinehas, and executed judgment: and so the plague was stayed.

Then Phineas stood up and intervened,
and the epidemic was checked — Har

31. And that was counted unto him for righteousness unto all generations for evermore.

And that has been reckoned to him as righteousness

from generation to generation for ever — RSV
For this he has been esteemed as righteous
unto all generations for ever — Har
hence his reputation for virtue
through successive generations for ever — Jerus

32. They angered him also at the waters of strife, so that it went ill with Moses for their sakes:
Next, they annoyed Him at the waters of Meribah,
and Moses suffered embarrassment on their account — Har
At Meribah, too, Israel angered God, causing Moses serious trouble — Tay

33. Because they provoked his spirit, so that he spake unadvisedly with his lips.
For they embittered his spirit,
And he spake rashly with his lips — Rhm

34. They did not destroy the nations, concerning whom the LORD commanded them:
They did not destroy the peoples,
As Jehovah commanded them — ASV

35. But were mingled among the heathen, and learned their works.
but they mingled with the nations
and learned to do as they did — RSV

36. And they served their idols: which were a snare unto them.
They worshiped their idols,
and these became their undoing — Har

37. Yea, they sacrificed their sons and their daughters unto devils,
Yea, they sacrificed their sons and their daughters unto demons — ASV

38. And shed innocent blood, even the blood of their sons and of their daughters, whom they sacrificed unto the idols of Canaan: and the land was polluted with blood.

39. Thus were they defiled with their own works, and went a whoring with their own inventions.
Thus were they defiled with their works,
And played the harlot in their doings — ASV
And they became unclean by their works,
And became unchaste in their doings — Rhm
They defiled themselves by such actions,
Their behaviour was that of a whore — Jerus
Thus they became impure through their practices,
and immoral in their behavior — Har
Thus were they defiled by their own works, and played the harlot and practiced idolatry with their own deeds [of idolatrous rites] — Amp

40. Therefore was the wrath of the LORD kindled against his people, insomuch that he abhorred his own inheritance.
Then was kindled the anger of Yahweh with his people,
And he abhorred his own inheritance — Rhm
So the Eternal's anger blazed against his people,
he loathed his heritage — Mof
Then God's anger blazed up against his people, his chosen race became abominable to him — Knox

41. And he gave them into the hand of the heathen; and they that hated them ruled over them.
He delivered them into the power of the nations,
so that those who hated them were their overlords — Har
He handed them over to pagans,
those who hated them became their masters — Jerus

42. Their enemies also oppressed them, and they were brought into subjection under their hand.
And their enemies oppressed them;
And they were humbled under their power — Sprl
Their enemies oppressed them,
and they were subservient to their authority — Har
their enemies tyrannised over them, crushing them under their rule — Jerus

43. Many times did he deliver them;
Time and again he rescued them — Jerus
but they provoked him with their counsel,
but they were rebellious in their purposes — RSV
but they went on defying him deliberately — Jerus
but they were obstinate in their opinions — Har
and were brought low for their iniquity.
And sank low in their iniquity — Rhm

till evildoing wasted them away — Mof
becoming demoralized by their wickedness — Har
and plunging deeper into wickedness — Jerus

44. **Nevertheless he regarded their affliction, when he heard their cry:**
even so, he took pity on their distress each time he heard them calling — Jerus

45. **And he remembered for them his covenant,**
And kept in mind his agreement with them — Bas
he remembered for their sake his compact — Mof
and repented according to the multitude of his mercies.
And was moved to pity according to the abounding of his lovingkindnesses — Rhm
and relented according to the abundance of his steadfast love — RSV
and in infinite kindness He relented — Har

46. **He made them also to be pitied of all those that carried them captives.**
And granted them compassion before all their captors — Rhm
And made them objects of compassion, In presence of all that carried them captive — ABPS
and excited compassion for them among all those who had captivated them — Sept

47. **Save us, O LORD our God, and gather us from among the heathen, to give thanks unto thy holy name, and to triumph in thy praise.**
Save us O Yahweh our God
And gather us from among the nations, —
That we may give thanks unto thy holy Name,
That we may triumph aloud in thy praise — Rhm
Yahweh our God and saviour,
gather us from among the pagans,
to give thanks to your holy name
and to find our happiness in praising you — Jerus
Deliver us, O LORD our God,
and gather us in from among the nations
that we may give thanks to thy holy name
and make thy praise our pride — NEB

48. **Blessed be the LORD God of Israel from everlasting to everlasting:**
BLESSED BE JEHOVAH, THE GOD OF ISRAEL, FROM AGE TO AGE TIME BEYOND TIME! — DeW
Blessed be the Lord, the God of Israel, for all eternity — Har
and let all the people say, Amen.
and let all the people say, So be it — Bas
Praise ye the LORD.
Praise ye Yah! — Rhm
Hallelujah! — Ber

BOOK V

PSALM 107

1. **O give thanks unto the LORD, for he is good: for his mercy endureth for ever.**
. . . for his steadfast love endures for ever! — RSV
. . . For his lovingkindness endureth for ever — ASV
. . . his kindness never fails! — Mof

2. **Let the redeemed of the LORD say so, whom he hath redeemed from the hand of the enemy;**

3. **And gathered them out of the lands, from the east, and from the west, from the north, and from the south.**
Let this be the declaration of the ransomed,
whom the Lord has rescued from hostile clutches,
and assembled from various lands, from east and west, from north and south — Har
let these be the words of Yahweh's redeemed,
those he has redeemed from the oppressor's clutches,
by bringing them home from foreign countries,
from east and west, from north and south — Jerus

4. **They wandered in the wilderness in a**

solitary way; they found no city to dwell in.
They roved the wilderness in desert ways;
They found not a city to dwell in — DeW
They wandered about in the wilderness in a trackless desert;
They could not discover the way to a habitable city — Sprl
Some wandered in desert wastes,
finding no way to a city to dwell in — RSV

5. Hungry and thirsty, their soul fainted in them.
They were hungry and thirsty,
Their courage collapsed within them — AAT
Hungry and thirsty,
their life was wasting away within them — NAB
Hungry and thirsty,
their spirits sank — Har

6. Then they cried unto the LORD in their trouble, and he delivered them out of their distresses.
Then made they outcry to Yahweh in their peril,
Out of their distresses he rescued them — Rhm
Then in their distress they implored the Lord,
and He rescued them from their misfortune — Har

7. And he led them forth by the right way, that they might go to a city of habitation.
he led them by a straight way,
till they reached a city to dwell in — RSV

8. Oh that men would praise the LORD for his goodness, and for his wonderful works to the children of men!
Let them give thanks to Yahweh
for his lovingkindness, and
for his wonderful dealings with the sons of men — Rhm
Let them thank the LORD for his steadfast love,
for his wonderful works to the sons of men — RSV
Let them thank the LORD for his enduring love
and for the marvellous things he has done for men — NEB

9. For he satisfieth the longing soul, and filleth the hungry soul with goodness.
For he satisfies him who is thirsty,
and the hungry he fills with good things — RSV

10. Such as sit in darkness and in the shadow of death, being bound in affliction and iron;
Some sat in darkness and in gloom,
prisoners in affliction and in irons[26] — RSV
There were those who were living in darkness and deep gloom;
prisoners in the irons of oppression — Har

11. Because they rebelled against the words of God, and contemned the counsel of the most High:
Because they rebelled against the words of the Almighty,
And despised the counsel of the Most High — DeW
for they had rebelled against the words of God,
and spurned the counsel of the Most High — RSV
because they rebelled against the Divine injunctions,
and rejected the advice of the Most High — Har

12. Therefore he brought down their heart with labour; they fell down, and there was none to help.
And he bowed down their heart with trouble,
They stumbled, and there was none to help — ABPS
Their spirit was subdued by hard labour;
they stumbled and fell with none to help them — NEB
And he humbled their hearts with trouble;
when they stumbled, there was no one to help them — NAB
He, therefore, brought them low in trouble and sorrow
and they stumbled from weakness with none to help — Ber

13. Then they cried unto the LORD in their trouble, and he saved them out of their distresses.[27]
Then made they outcry to Yahweh in their peril,
Out of their distresses he saved them — Rhm

[26]Compare RSV rendering of verses 4, 17 and 23.
[27]Compare verse 6.

Then they called to Yahweh in their trouble
and he rescued them from their sufferings — Jerus

14. He brought them out of darkness and the shadow of death, and brake their bands in sunder.

He brought them forth out of darkness and death-shade,
And their fetters he tare off — Rhm

He brought them out of darkness and gloom,
and broke their bonds asunder — RSV

He brought them out of darkness and deepest gloom,
and broke their fetters in pieces — Har

15. Oh that men would praise the LORD for his goodness, and for his wonderful works to the children of men![28]

16. For he hath broken the gates of brass, and cut the bars of iron in sunder.

he has shattered doors of bronze,
bars of iron he has snapped in two — NEB

For he broke down their prison gates of brass and cut apart their iron bars — Tay

17. Fools because of their transgression, and because of their iniquities, are afflicted.

18. Their soul abhorreth all manner of meat; and they draw near unto the gates of death.

Stricken because of their wicked ways
and afflicted because of their sins,
They loathed all manner of food,
so that they were near the gates of death — NAB

Some were sick through their sinful ways,
and because of their iniquities suffered affliction;
they loathed any kind of food,
and they drew near to the gates of death — RSV

Some, driven frantic by their sins,
made miserable by their own guilt
and finding all food repugnant,
were nearly at death's door — Jerus

19. Then they cry unto the LORD in their trouble, and he saveth them out of their distresses.[29]

Then make they outcry to Yahweh in their peril,
And out of their distresses he saveth them — Rhm

20. He sent his word, and healed them, and delivered them from their destructions.

He sendeth His word, and healeth them,
And delivereth them from their dangers — DeW

He sent forth his word to heal them
and to snatch them from destruction — NAB

He sent out His word to heal them
and to save their lives from the grave — Ber

21. Oh that men would praise the LORD for his goodness, and for his wonderful works to the children of men![30]

22. And let them sacrifice the sacrifices of thanksgiving, and declare his works with rejoicing.

And let them offer sacrifices of thanksgiving,
and tell of his deeds in songs of joy! — RSV

Let them make thank offerings
and declare his works with shouts of joy — NAB

Let them offer grateful sacrifices,
and recount His deeds in joyful song — Har

23. They that go down to the sea in ships, that do business in great waters;

Some went down to the sea in ships,
doing business on the great waters — RSV

And then there are the sailors sailing the seven seas, plying the trade routes of the world — Tay

24. These see the works of the LORD, and his wonders in the deep,

they too saw what Yahweh could do,
what marvels on the deep! — Jerus

They, too, observe the power of God in action — Tay

25. For he commandeth, and raiseth the stormy wind, which lifteth up the waves thereof.

At his word the stormy wind rose,
churning up its waves — Knox

26. They mount up to the heaven, they go down again to the depths: their soul is melted because of trouble.

They towered to the sky, they sank down to the very depths;

---

[28]Compare verse 8.

[29]Compare verses 6 and 13.

[30]Compare verses 8 and 15.

in their danger their courage melted away — Har

Flung to the sky, then plunged to the depths,
they lost their nerve in the ordeal — Jerus

Their ships are tossed to the heavens and sink again to the depths; the sailors cringe in terror — Tay

27. They reel to and fro, and stagger like a drunken man, and are at their wit's end.

They reel and stagger like a drunken man,
And all their wisdom is engulfed — Rhm

They reel and stagger like a drunken man,
And all their wisdom comes to naught — ABPS

they reel and stagger like one drunk, and all their skill is swallowed up — Sept

see them reeling and staggering to and fro as a drunkard does, all their seamanship forgotten! — Knox

28. Then they cry unto the LORD in their trouble, and he bringeth them out of their distresses.[31]

Then make they outcry to Yahweh in their peril,
And out of their distresses he bringeth them forth — Rhm

29. He maketh the storm a calm, so that the waves thereof are still.

He calmeth the storm to a whisper,
And silent are their rolling waves — Rhm

He hushes the storm to silence,
And the waves thereof are still — ABPS

He hushed the storm to a gentle breeze, and the billows of the sea were stilled — NAB

30. Then are they glad because they be quiet; so he bringeth them unto their desired haven.

Then were they thankful for the abatement,
and He guided them to their desired harbor — Har

31. Oh that men would praise the LORD for his goodness, and for his wonderful works to the children of men![32]

32. Let them exalt him also in the congregation of the people, and praise him in the assembly of the elders.

let them extol his name, where the people gather, glorify him where the elders sit in council — Knox

33. He turneth rivers into a wilderness, and the watersprings into dry ground;

34. A fruitful land into barrenness, for the wickedness of them that dwell therein.

He turns streams into a desert,
and fountains into dry land;
he turns an oasis into a salt waste,
to punish people for their sins — Mof

He transforms rivers into waste land,
and flowing rivers into arid ground.
A productive area becomes a salt marsh,
because of the wickedness of its inhabitants — Har

Sometimes he turned rivers into desert,
springs of water into arid ground,
or a fertile country into salt-flats,
because the people living there were wicked — Jerus

35. He turneth the wilderness into a standing water, and dry ground into watersprings.

He turns a desert into pools of water,
a parched land into springs of water — RSV

Or again, he turned a desert into sheets of water,
and an arid country into flowing springs — Jerus

36. And there he maketh the hungry to dwell, that they may prepare a city for habitation;

There He settles the hungry,
and they establish an inhabited city — Har

37. And sow the fields, and plant vineyards, which may yield fruits of increase.

they sow fields, and plant vineyards,
and get a fruitful yield — RSV

38. He blesseth them also, so that they are multiplied greatly; and suffereth not their cattle to decrease.

Thus hath he blessed them and they have multiplied greatly,
And their cattle he maketh not few — Rhm

By his blessing they multiply greatly;
and he does not let their cattle decrease — RSV

by his blessing they increase,

[31]Compare verses 6, 13, and 19.

[32]Compare verses 8, 15, and 21.

and their herds never diminish — Mof

39. Again, they are minished and brought low through oppression, affliction, and sorrow.

40. He poureth contempt upon princes, and causeth them to wander in the wilderness, where there is no way.

When they are diminished and brought low
through oppression, trouble, and sorrow,
he pours contempt upon princes
and makes them wander in trackless wastes — RSV

When they themselves dwindled in numbers,
and were hard hit by oppression, misfortune and sorrow,
He poured contempt upon the nobility,
making them vagabonds in trackless wastes — Har

He pours contempt on lords,
and sets them in a pathless waste astray,
till they grow few and faint
under the weight of misery — Mof

41. Yet setteth he the poor on high from affliction, and maketh him families like a flock.

but he raises up the needy out of affliction,
and makes their families like flocks — RSV

The poor, however, He lifts out of their afflictions and miseries
and makes their families like a fruitful flock — Ber

but he rescues the poor who are godly
and gives them many children and much prosperity — Tay

42. The righteous shall see it, and rejoice: and all iniquity shall stop her mouth.

Good men rejoice to see this,
wrongdoers are silenced — Mof

Honest men will rejoice to witness it,
and malice will stand dumb with confusion — Knox

The virtuous notice these things, and rejoice;
and all wickedness shall be silenced — Har

The upright see it and are glad,
while evildoers are filled with disgust — NEB

43. Whoso is wise, and will observe these things, even they shall understand the lovingkindness of the LORD.

Whoso is wise will give heed to these things;
And they will consider the lovingkindnesses of Jehovah — ASV

Whoever is wise, let him give heed to these things;
let men consider the steadfast love of the LORD — RSV

Who is wise? then let him observe these things!
And diligently consider the lovingkindness of Yahweh — Rhm

If you are wise, study these things
and realize how Yahweh shows his love — Jerus

PSALM 108

A Song or Psalm of David.

1. O God, my heart is fixed; I will sing and give praise, even with my glory.[33]

My heart is steadfast, O God,
my heart is steadfast!
I will sing and make melody!
Awake, my soul! — RSV

My mind is resolute, my God;
I will sing and play music.
Awake, my soul — Har

2. Awake, psaltery and harp: I myself will awake early.

Awake O harp and lyre,
I will awaken the dawn! — Rhm

3. I will praise thee, O LORD, among the people: and I will sing praises unto thee among the nations.

I will give thanks unto thee, O Jehovah, among the peoples;
And I will sing praises unto thee among the nations — ASV

4. For thy mercy is great above the heavens: and thy truth reacheth unto the clouds.

For thy lovingkindness is great above the heavens;
And thy truth reacheth unto the skies — ASV

For great above the heavens is thy mercy,
And to the clouds thy faithfulness — ABPS

[33]Compare verses 1-5 with Psalm 57:7-11.

5. Be thou exalted, O God, above the heavens: and thy glory above all the earth;

6. That thy beloved may be delivered: save with thy right hand, and answer me.[34]

Be exalted, O God, above the heavens!
Let thy glory be over all the earth!
That thy beloved may be delivered,
give help by thy right hand, and answer me! — RSV

May You be praised, my God, to the heavens;
may Your glory cover the whole earth,
in order that Your loved ones may be liberated:
give us victory by Your power, and respond to us — Har

7. God hath spoken in his holiness; I will rejoice, I will divide Shechem, and mete out the valley of Succoth.

God has promised in his sanctuary:
"With exultation I will divide up Shechem,
and portion out the Vale of Succoth — RSV

God gave his sacred promise:
"I will divide up Shechem in triumph,
and parcel out the vale of Sukkoth — Mof

8. Gilead is mine; Manasseh is mine; Ephraim also is the strength of mine head;

But Ephraim is the defence of my head — Rhm

Ephraim is my helmet — RSV

Judah is my lawgiver;

Judah is my commander's staff — Rhm

Judah is my ruler's staff — ABPS

As for Judah, he is my royal staff — DeW

Judah is my sceptre — ASV

Judah is my sovereign emblem — Har

Judah, my marshal's baton — Jerus

9. Moab is my washpot;

Moab shall serve as my washbowl — NAB

over Edom will I cast out my shoe;

Over Edom I extend my sway — DeW

Over Idumea I shall extend my march — Sept

Edom I claim as subject — Mof

upon Edom [My slave] My shoe I cast [to be cleaned] — Amp

I fling my shoes at Edom — NEB

over Philistia will I triumph.

over Philistia I shout in triumph." — RSV

10. Who will bring me into the strong city? who will lead me into Edom?

Who but God can give me strength to conquer these fortified cities? Who else can lead me into Edom? — Tay

Who will bring me [David] into the strong, fortified city [of Petra]? Who will lead me into Edom? — Amp

11. Wilt not thou, O God, who hast cast us off? and wilt not thou, O God, go forth with our hosts?

Hast thou not rejected us, O God?
Thou dost not go forth, O God, with our armies — RSV

Had not You dispensed with us, my God?
At all events, You did not accompany our forces — Har

God, can you really have rejected us?
You no longer march with our armies — Jerus

12. Give us help from trouble: for vain is the help of man.

Grant us help out of distress,
For vain is the deliverance of man — Rhm

Give us assistance against the enemy;
human help is useless — Har

Help us in this hour of crisis,
the help that man can give is worthless — Jerus

13. Through God we shall do valiantly:

In God we do mightily — YLT

With God we shall do bravely — Mof

Through God we shall perform brave deeds — Har

With God among us, we shall fight like heroes — Jerus

With God we will do great things — Bas

for he it is that shall tread down our enemies.

only he can trample our oppressors in the dust — Knox

[34]Compare verses 6-13 with Psalm 60:5-12.

PSALM 109

To the chief Musician, A Psalm of David.

1. Hold not thy peace, O God of my praise;
God whom I praise, be not silent! — AAT
God that guardest my renown, do not leave me unbefriended — Knox
Do not remain mute, my praiseworthy God — Har

2. For the mouth of the wicked and the mouth of the deceitful are opened against me:
For wicked and deceitful mouths are opened against me — RSV
they have spoken against me with a lying tongue.

3. They compassed me about also with words of hatred; and fought against me without a cause.
They have assailed me with hateful words;
they attack me without provocation — Har

4. For my love they are my adversaries: but I give myself unto prayer.
In return for my love they accuse me, even as I make prayer for them — RSV
They repay my love with enmity;
for my part I pray for them — Har
In return for my friendship, they denounce me,
though all I had done was pray for them — Jerus

5. And they have rewarded me evil for good, and hatred for my love.
kindness is repaid with injury, love with ill will — Knox

6. Set thou a wicked man over him: and let Satan stand at his right hand.
Appoint a wicked man against him;
let an accuser bring him to trial — RSV
Set a wicked judge over him, I pray, and let a perverse accuser stand at his right hand! — Ber

7. When he shall be judged, let him be condemned: and let his prayer become sin.
When he is tried, let him come forth guilty;
let his prayer be counted as sin! — RSV
let him be tried and found guilty,
let his prayer be construed as a crime! — Jerus
let him leave the court of judgement a doomed man, pleading with heaven in vain — Knox
When he is to be judged, let him be condemned;
let his defence incriminate him — Har
When the wicked shall be judged, let him be condemned, and let his prayer [for leniency] be turned into a sin — Amp

8. Let his days be few; and let another take his office.
Let his days become few,
His overseership let another take — Rhm
May his days be few;
may another seize his goods! — RSV
May his days be few;
may his hoarded wealth fall to another! — NEB
Let his days be few in number;
let another take over his functions — Har

9. Let his children be fatherless, and his wife a widow.

10. Let his children be continually vagabonds, and beg: let them seek their bread also out of their desolate places.
Let his sons wander about, and beg,
And seek alms away from their ruined homes — DeW
Let his children wander about and beg,
Let them be driven out of their ruins — Rhm
Let his sons be vagabonds and beg: let them be cast out from their dwellings — Sept
May his children wander about and beg;
And may they be expelled from their hovels! — AAT
May his children wander about and beg;
may they be driven out of the ruins they inhabit! — RSV

11. Let the extortioner catch all that he hath; and let the strangers spoil his labour.
Let the creditor take aim at all that he hath,
And let strangers prey on the fruit of his toil — Rhm
may the creditor seize his possessions and foreigners swallow his profits! — Jerus

12. Let there be none to extend mercy

unto him: neither let there be any to favour his fatherless children.
May not a soul be kind to him,
may no one pity his fatherless children! — Mof
Let no one show him kindness
or even pity his fatherless little ones! — Ber

13. **Let his posterity be cut off; and in the generation following let their name be blotted out.**
May his posterity be rooted out,
and his name blotted out in a single generation! — Mof
Instead, let his sons be cut off
and his name be blotted out
in the following generation! — Ber
May his line be doomed to extinction,
may their name be wiped out within a generation! — NEB

14. **Let the iniquity of his fathers be remembered with the LORD; and let not the sin of his mother be blotted out.**
May the wickedness of his forebears be remembered by the Lord;
let his mother's guilt remain unforgiven — Har
May the evil deeds of his father be remembered before the LORD
and the sins of his mother never once be forgotten! — Ber
May the crimes of his fathers be held against him
and his mother's sin never be effaced — Jerus

15. **Let them be before the LORD continually, that he may cut off the memory of them from the earth.**
Let them be before Yahweh continually,
And let the memory of them be cut off out of the earth — Rhm
may Yahweh bear these constantly in mind,
to wipe their memory off the earth! — Jerus

16. **Because that he remembered not to shew mercy, but persecuted the poor and needy man, that he might even slay the broken in heart.**
Because he remembered not to show kindness;
But pursued the suffering, and needy, and broken-hearted unto death — DeW
Did he himself keep mercy in mind, when he persecuted the helpless, the destitute, the grief-stricken, and marked them down for death? — Knox
Let it be recalled that it never occurred to him to show kindness;
instead, he persecuted the poor, the needy,
and the brokenhearted even unto death — Ber
That wretch never thought of being kind,
but hounded the poor, the needy
and the broken-hearted to death — Jerus

17. **As he loved cursing, so let it come unto him:**
He loved to curse; let curses come on him! — RSV
He loved to curse others; now you curse him — Tay
as he delighted not in blessing, so let it be far from him.
He did not like blessing; may it be far from him! — RSV
He never blessed others; now don't you bless him — Tay

18. **As he clothed himself with cursing like as with his garment, so let it come into his bowels like water, and like oil into his bones.**
He used to wrap curses round him like a cloak,
let them soak right into him like water,
deep into his bones like oil — Jerus
And may he be clothed with cursing as with a robe;
may it penetrate into his entrails like water
and like oil into his bones — NAB

19. **Let it be unto him as the garment which covereth him, and for a girdle wherewith he is girded continually.**
May it be like a garment which he wraps round him,
like a belt with which he daily girds himself! — RSV
Let it be the garb he wears, cling to him like a girdle he can never take off — Knox
May they now envelop him like a gown,
be tied round his waist for ever! — Jerus

20. **Let this be the reward of mine adversaries from the LORD, and of them that speak evil against my soul.**
May this be the way in which the Lord will reward my accusers,

and those who malign me — Har
So, in their own coin, may the Lord repay them, my accusers that defame me so cruelly — Knox

21. But do thou for me, O GOD the Lord, for thy name's sake:
But thou Yahweh Adonay deal effectually with me for the sake of thy Name — Rhm
For Your part, Lord God,
work on my behalf for the sake of Your reputation — Har
But do you, O GOD, my Lord, deal kindly with me for your name's sake — NAB
But THOU, O Jehovah, the Lord!
Become my helper for Thy Name's sake — DeW

because thy mercy is good, deliver thou me.
Because Thy lovingkindness is good, deliver me — DeW
rescue me, since your love is generous! — Jerus
rescue me in Your gracious kindness — Har

22. For I am poor and needy, and my heart is wounded within me.
For I am afflicted and needy,
And my heart is pierced within me — ABPS
for I am destitute and needy,
and my spirits are flagging — Har
Reduced to weakness and poverty,
my heart is sorely tormented — Jerus

23. I am gone like the shadow when it declineth:
I am gone, like a shadow at evening — RSV
Like the shadow, as it lengthens, I am passing away — ABPS
my days are brief as any evening shadow — Mof
I am fading away like an evening shadow — Har

I am tossed up and down as the locust.
they have brushed me off like a locust — Jerus
I am shaken off from life as easily as a man brushes a grasshopper from his arm — Tay

24. My knees are weak through fasting;
My knees wobble from fasting — Har
My knees are weak for lack of food — Jerus

and my flesh faileth of fatness.
and my flesh is wasted of its substance — NAB
And my flesh is lean, and hath no fatness — JPS
my flesh is thin and shrivelled — Mof
my body has become gaunt — RSV
and I am skin and bones — Tay

25. I became also a reproach unto them: when they looked upon me they shaked their heads.
I am an object of scorn to my accusers; when they see me, they wag their heads — RSV
They make a laughing-stock of me, toss their heads in derision as they pass by — Knox
I am a symbol of failure to all mankind; when they see me they shake their heads — Tay

26. Help me, O LORD my God: O save me according to thy mercy:
Help me, O Jehovah my God;
Oh save me according to thy lovingkindness — ASV
Help me, Yahweh my God,
save me since you love me — Jerus

27. That they may know that this is thy hand; that thou, LORD, hast done it.
Let them know that this is thy hand;
thou, O LORD, hast done it! — RSV
prove to them that my woes are a visitation from thee, sent by no hand but thine — Knox
Do it publicly, so all will see that you yourself have done it — Tay

28. Let them curse, but bless thou:
When they curse, do Thou bless — DeW
Counter their curses with your blessing — Jerus

when they arise, let them be ashamed; but let thy servant rejoice.
Let my assailants be put to shame;
may thy servant be glad! — RSV
disappoint my adversaries, and grant thy servant relief — Knox

29. Let mine adversaries be clothed with shame, and let them cover themselves with their own confusion, as with a mantle.
May my accusers be clothed with dishonor;
may they be wrapped in their own shame as in a mantle! — RSV

30. I will greatly praise the LORD with my mouth; yea, I will praise him among the multitude.
I will give the Lord great praise,

and honor him in the presence of large crowds — Har

31. **For he shall stand at the right hand of the poor, to save him from those that condemn his soul.**

For he shall stand at the right hand of the poor, to save his soul from unrighteous judges — PBV

For he stands at the poor man's right side
to save him from his adversaries — NEB

PSALM 110

A Psalm of David.

1. **The LORD said unto my Lord, Sit thou at my right hand, until I make thine enemies thy footstool.**

The declaration of Yahweh to my Lord —
Sit thou at my right hand,
Until I make thy foes thy footstool — Rhm

The Lord said to my Lord,
"Sit on My right, until I subdue your enemies completely." — Har

The LORD said to my lord,
'You shall sit at my right hand
when I make your enemies the footstool under your feet' — NEB

2. **The LORD shall send the rod of thy strength out of Zion:**

Thy sceptre of strength will Yahweh extend out of Zion — Rhm

Thy sceptre of power,
Jehovah sendeth forth out of Zion — DeW

The LORD sends forth from Zion
your mighty scepter — RSV

When the LORD from Zion hands you the sceptre, the symbol of your power — NEB

rule thou in the midst of thine enemies.

Rule in the midst of your foes! — RSV

exercise sovereignty with it among your enemies — Har

march forth through the ranks of your enemies — NEB

3. **Thy people shall be willing in the day of thy power, in the beauties of holiness from the womb of the morning: thou hast the dew of thy youth.**

Your people will offer themselves freely
on the day you lead your host
upon the holy mountains.
From the womb of the morning
like dew your youth will come to you — RSV

The people will proffer their assistance willingly
on the day when you muster your army in holy array at early dawn;
the flower of your young manhood is at your disposal — Har

At birth you were endowed with princely gifts
and resplendent in holiness.
You have shone with the dew of youth
since your mother bore you — NEB

4. **The LORD hath sworn, and will not repent.**

The LORD has sworn
and will not change his mind — RSV

Yahweh has sworn an oath which he never will retract — Jerus

Thou art a priest for ever after the order of Melchizedek.

you are a priest forever like Melchizedek — Tay

'You are a priest for ever,
in the succession of Melchizedek' — NEB

5. **The Lord at thy right hand shall strike through kings in the day of his wrath.**

The Lord is at your right hand.
He has shattered kings on the day of his wrath — AAT

The Lord is at your right hand;
He will crush kings when His anger burns — Har

6. **He shall judge among the heathen, he shall fill the places with dead bodies; he shall wound the heads over many countries.**

He will execute judgment among the nations,
filling them with corpses;
he will shatter chiefs
over the wide earth — RSV

he will pass sentence on the nations,
heap high the bodies, scatter far and wide the heads of the slain — Knox

He will be judge among the nations,
the valleys will be full of dead bodies;
the head over a great country will be wounded by him — Bas

he gives the nations their deserts,
smashing their skulls, he heaps the wide world with corpses — Jerus

7. He shall drink of the brook in the way: therefore shall he lift up the head.
he drinks from any stream he has to cross,
then charges forward triumphing — Mof

Drinking from the stream as he goes,
he can hold his head high in victory — Jerus

But he himself shall be refreshed from springs along the way — Tay

PSALM 111

1. Praise ye the LORD.
Hallelujah! — Ber
Praise ye Jah — ABPS
Praise ye Yah! — Rhm

I will praise the LORD with my whole heart, in the assembly of the upright, and in the congregation.

2. The works of the LORD are great, sought out of all them that have pleasure therein.
Great are the works of the LORD, studied by all who have pleasure in them — RSV

The doings of the Lord are renowned;
they are worthy of consideration by all who delight in them — Har

The works of Yahweh are sublime,
those who delight in them are right to fix their eyes on them — Jerus

Great are the doings of the LORD:
all men study them for their delight — NEB

3. His work is honourable and glorious: and his righteousness endureth for ever.
His work is worthy to be praised and had in honour, and his righteousness endureth for ever — PBV

Every work that he does is full of glory and majesty,
and his righteousness can never change — Jerus

His acts are full of majesty and splendour;
righteousness is his for ever — NEB

4. He hath made his wonderful works to be remembered:
He has won renown for his wondrous deeds — NAB

He allows us to commemorate his marvels — Jerus

He has established a memorial for Himself
on account of His wonderful deeds — Har

the LORD is gracious and full of compassion.
Gracious and compassionate is Jehovah — ABPS
. . . Yahweh — Rhm

5. He hath given meat unto them that fear him:
Food hath he given to them who revere him — Rhm

he will ever be mindful of his covenant.
he will keep his agreement in mind for ever — Bas
he never forgets his covenant — Jerus

6. He hath shewed his people the power of his works, that he may give them the heritage of the heathen.
He hath showed his people the power of his works,
In giving them the heritage of the nations — ASV

He has displayed His powerful works to His people
in giving them nations for an inheritance — Har

He showed his people what his strength could do,
bestowing on them the lands of other nations — NEB

7. The works of his hands are verity and judgment;
The works of his hands are truth and justice — ASV

The works of his hands are faithful and just — RSV

All that he does is done in faithfulness and justice — Jerus

all his commandments are sure.
all His enactments are reliable — Har
all his precepts are trustworthy — RSV

8. They shall stand fast for ever and ever, and are done in truth and uprightness.
They are steadfast always and for ever,
They are made in truth and uprightness — DeW

his orders are enacted for all time,
issued in faithfulness and justice — Mof

9. He sent redemption unto his people: he hath commanded his covenant for ever.
he has sent his people freedom,

fixing his compact with them for all time — Mof
He has sent deliverance to his people; he has ratified his covenant forever — NAB
He sent and redeemed his people; he decreed that his covenant should always endure — NEB

holy and reverend is his name.

Holy and fearful is his name — ABPS
Holy and to be feared is His Name — DeW
holy and awesome is his name — NAB
His name is sacred and august — Har

10. The fear of the LORD is the beginning of wisdom:

Wisdom begins with reverence for the Lord — Har

a good understanding have all they that do his commandments:

All who practise it possess commendable discernment — Har
prudent are all who live by it — NAB
and they who live by it grow in understanding — NEB

his praise endureth for ever.

Let the praise of him endure forever — Sept
His praises will be sung for ever — Jerus

PSALM 112

1. Praise ye the LORD.

Praise ye Yah! — Rhm
Praise ye Jah! — YLT
Hallelujah! — Ber

Blessed is the man that feareth the LORD, that delighteth greatly in his commandments.

How happy is the man who revereth Yahweh,
In his commandments delighteth he greatly — Rhm
O the blessedness of the man,
That feareth Jehovah;
That delighteth greatly in His commandments! — DeW
Happy the man who fears Yahweh
by joyfully keeping his commandments — Jerus

2. His seed shall be mighty upon earth: the generation of the upright shall be blessed.

Children of such a man will be powers on earth,
descendants of the upright will always be blessed — Jerus
His children shall be honored everywhere, for good men's sons have a special heritage — Tay

3. Wealth and riches shall be in his house: and his righteousness endureth for ever.

There will be riches and wealth for his family,
and his righteousness can never change — Jerus
Wealth and riches shall be in his house;
his generosity shall endure forever — NAB
Wealth and riches are in his house;
his good fortune is unfailing — Har

4. Unto the upright there ariseth light in the darkness: he is gracious, and full of compassion, and righteous.

For the upright he shines like a lamp in the dark,
he is merciful, tenderhearted, virtuous — Jerus
To the virtuous he shines like a light in the darkness,
gracious, sympathetic and righteous — Har
He is gracious, compassionate, good,
a beacon in darkness for honest men — NEB
When darkness overtakes him, light will come bursting in. He is kind and merciful — Tay
Light rises in the darkness for the upright;
the LORD is gracious, merciful, and righteous — RSV

5. A good man sheweth favour, and lendeth: he will guide his affairs with discretion.

All goes well with the generous, openhanded,
who will act fairly — Mof
It is well with him who is generous and ready to lend,
the man who conducts his business with fairness — Ber
It is well with the man who is a gracious lender,
Who conducts his business with justice — AAT

It is right for a man to be gracious in his lending,
to order his affairs with judgement — NEB

6. Surely he shall not be moved for ever: the righteous shall be in everlasting remembrance.
never shall that man come to grief;
the good man's memory never fades — Mof
Such a man will never be laid low,
for the just shall be held in remembrance for ever — Ber

7. He shall not be afraid of evil tidings: his heart is fixed, trusting in the LORD.
He will not be alarmed by disquieting news;
his mind is trusting resolutely in the Lord — Har
with constant heart, and confidence in Yahweh,
he need never fear bad news — Jerus

8. His heart is established, he shall not be afraid, until he see his desire upon his enemies.
his heart is firm and fearless,
certain that he will see his foes collapse — Mof
His spirits are firmly upheld;
he will be fearless, until the time comes when he will gloat over his enemies — Har

9. He hath dispersed, he hath given to the poor;
He has distributed freely, he has given to the poor — RSV
Lavishly he gives to the poor — NAB
Quick to be generous, he gives to the poor — Jerus
his righteousness endureth for ever;
his generosity shall endure forever — NAB
and so good fortune never fails him — Mof
his prosperity is unfailing — Har
his horn shall be exalted with honour.
he rises to high power and honour — Mof
His power will be augmented with honor — Har
in honour he carries his head high — NEB

10. The wicked shall see it, and be grieved;
The lawless one shall see it and be indignant — Rhm
The wicked man will observe this, and become irritated — Har
he shall gnash with his teeth, and melt away:
he shall gnash his teeth and pine away — NAB
He will grind his teeth and be eaten up with jealousy — Har
the desire of the wicked shall perish.
The craving of the lawless shall vanish — Rhm
the ungodly's hope will come to nothing — Mof
the expectation of the wicked will be frustrated — Har

PSALM 113

1. Praise ye the LORD.
Praise ye Yah! — Rhm
Praise ye Jah! — YLT
Hallelujah! — Ber
Praise, O ye servants of the LORD, praise the name of the LORD.

2. Blessed be the name of the LORD from this time forth and for evermore.

3. From the rising of the sun unto the going down of the same the LORD'S name is to be praised.
From east to west,
praised be the name of Yahweh! — Jerus

4. The LORD is high above all nations, and his glory above the heavens.
High above all nations is Jehovah;
Above the heavens is his glory — ABPS
The Lord is supreme over all nations;
His glory transcends the skies — Har

5. Who is like unto the LORD our God, who dwelleth on high,

6. Who humbleth himself to behold the things that are in heaven, and in the earth!
Who is like the LORD our God,
who is seated on high,
who looks far down
upon the heavens and the earth? — RSV
Who is the equal of the Lord our God,
enthroned above,
yet directing His gaze downwards
on heaven and earth alike? — Har
Who is like Yahweh our God? —
enthroned so high, he needs to stoop
to see the sky and earth! — Jerus

There is none like the LORD our God
in heaven or on earth,
who sets his throne so high
but deigns to look down so low — NEB

7. **He raiseth up the poor out of the dust, and lifteth the needy out of the dunghill;**
He raises up the poor from the dust, and lifts the destitute from utter degradation — Har
He takes the poor man out of the dust, lifting him up from his low position — Bas

8. **That he may set him with princes, even with the princes of his people.**
To make him sit with nobles,
With the nobles of his people — ABPS

9. **He maketh the barren woman to keep house, and to be a joyful mother of children.**
He gives the barren woman a home, making her the joyous mother of children — RSV
He gives the unfertile woman a family, making her a happy mother of children — Bas
He enthrones the barren woman in her house
by making her the happy mother of sons — Jerus
Praise ye the LORD.
Praise ye Yah — Rhm
praise ye Jah! — YLT
Hallelujah — JPS

PSALM 114

1. **When Israel went out of Egypt, the house of Jacob from a people of strange language;**
When Israel went from Egypt,
and Jacob's household from a foreign folk — Mof
When Israel came out of Egypt, and the sons of Jacob heard no more a strange language — Knox

2. **Judah was his sanctuary, and Israel his dominion.**
Judah became his sanctuary,
Israel his realm — Rhm
Judah became His holy nation,
and Israel His dominion — Har
Judah he took to be his own,
and Israel for his domain — Mof

3. **The sea saw it, and fled: Jordan was driven back.**
The seas fled at the sight they witnessed, backward flowed the stream of Jordan — Knox
The [Red] Sea looked and fled; the Jordan [River] was turned back — Amp

4. **The mountains skipped like rams, and the little hills like lambs.**

5. **What ailed thee, O thou sea, that thou fleddest? thou Jordan, that thou wast driven back?**
Whatever made you recede, sea?
Why did you turn back, Jordan? — Har

6. **Ye mountains, that ye skipped like rams; and ye little hills, like lambs?**
Why, mountains, did you skip like rams? Why, little hills, like lambs? — Tay

7. **Tremble, thou earth, at the presence of the Lord, at the presence of the God of Jacob;**

8. **Which turned the rock into standing water, the flint into a fountain of waters.**
Who transformed rock into a pool of water;
the flint rock into a gushing stream — Har

PSALM 115

1. **Not unto us, O LORD, not unto us, but unto thy name give glory,**
Not by us, Yahweh, not by us,
by you alone is glory deserved — Jerus
Do not give us credit, Lord;
enhance Your own reputation instead — Har
for thy mercy, and for thy truth's sake.
For thy lovingkindness, and for thy truth's sake — ASV
because of Your loving mercy and faithfulness — Har

2. **Wherefore should the heathen say, Where is now their God?**
Why should pagan nations say,
"Where is their God now?" — Har

3. **But our God is in the heavens: he**

hath done whatsoever he hath pleased.
Our God is in heaven;
whatever he wills, he does — NAB

4. **Their idols are silver and gold, the work of men's hands.**
Their idols are of silver and gold,
the product of human design — Har

5. **They have mouths, but they speak not: eyes have they, but they see not:**
They have mouths that cannot speak,
and eyes that cannot see — NEB

6. **They have ears, but they hear not: noses have they, but they smell not:**

7. **They have hands, but they handle not: feet have they, but they walk not:**
They have hands, but they do not feel,
and feet, but they cannot walk — Har
neither speak they through their throat.
neither do they produce any sound in
their throats — Ber
and no sound comes from their throats
— NEB

8. **They that make them are like unto them; so is every one that trusteth in them.**
They that make them, become like unto
them,
With every one that trusteth in them
— DeW
Their makers will end up like them,
and so will anyone who relies on
them — Jerus
Their makers grow to be like them,
and so do all who trust in them —
NEB

9. **O Israel, trust thou in the LORD:**
But Israel trusts in the LORD — NEB
he is their help and their shield.
he is their helper and defender — PBV
He is their help and protection — Har

10. **O house of Aaron, trust in the LORD:**
The house of Aaron trusts in the LORD
— NEB
he is their help and their shield.

11. **Ye that fear the LORD, trust in the LORD:**
Ye that revere Yahweh! trust in Yahweh — Rhm
Those who fear the LORD trust in the
LORD — NEB
he is their help and their shield.

12. **The LORD hath been mindful of us: he will bless us;**
The Eternal remembers us, and he will
bless us — Mof
he will bless the house of Israel; he will bless the house of Aaron.

13. **He will bless them that fear the LORD, both small and great.**
He will bless those who revere the Lord,
insignificant and prominent alike —
Har

14. **The LORD shall increase you more and more, you and your children.**
May the LORD give you increase,
Both you and your children — AAT
May the Lord give you continual
prosperity,
both for you and your children — Har

15. **Ye are blessed of the LORD which made heaven and earth.**
Blessed be ye by Jehovah,
The Maker of heaven and earth! —
DeW
May you be blessed by the Lord
who formed heaven and earth — Har

16. **The heaven, even the heavens, are the LORD'S: but the earth hath he given to the children of men.**
the heavens are the heavens of Jehovah;
But the earth hath he given to the
children of men — ASV
The heavens are the Lord's own,
but He has allotted the earth for
human society — Har

17. **The dead praise not the LORD, neither any that go down into silence.**
The dead cannot praise thee, O Lord;
nor any who go down to the mansion
of the dead — Sept
The dead cannot praise the Eternal,
nor any who sink to the silent land
— Mof
It is not the dead who praise the Lord,
nor all those who pass away into
oblivion — Har
The dead cannot sing praises to Jehovah here on earth — Tay

18. **But we will bless the LORD from this time forth and for evermore.**
but we bless the Lord, we, the living,
from this day to all eternity — Knox
but we, the living, bless the LORD,
now and for evermore — NEB
Praise the LORD.
Praise ye Yah — Rhm
Praise ye Jah! — YLT
Hallelujah — JPS

PSALM 116

1. I love the LORD, because he hath heard my voice and my supplications.
I love the Lord because he hears my prayers and answers them — Tay

2. Because he hath inclined his ear unto me, therefore will I call upon him as long as I live.
He pays attention to me;
therefore I will entreat Him while life lasts — Har
for he has given me a hearing
whenever I have cried to him — NEB

3. The sorrows of death compassed me, and the pains of hell gat hold upon me: I found trouble and sorrow.
The snares of death encompassed me;
the pangs of Sheol laid hold on me;
I suffered distress and anguish — RSV
The cords of death encompassed me,
The tortures of Sheol seized on me;
I came into anguish and sorrow — DeW
The cords of death entwined around me,
the agonies of hell came upon me.
I was distressed and anguished — Har
The cords of death were around me;
the terrors of the grave had laid hold of me;
I suffered anguish and grief — Ber
The cords and sorrows of death were around me, and the terrors of Sheol [the place of the dead] had laid hold of me; I suffered anguish and grief — trouble and sorrow — Amp
Death's noose about me, caught in the snares of the grave, ever I found distress and grief at my side — Knox
Death stared me in the face — I was frightened and sad — Tay

4. Then called I upon the name of the LORD; O LORD, I beseech thee, deliver my soul.
Then I called on the name of the LORD: "O LORD, I beseech thee, save my life!" — RSV
Then in the name of the Lord I cried,
"I beg of You to deliver me, Lord" — Har

5. Gracious is the LORD, and righteous; yea, our God is merciful.
Gracious is Yahweh and righteous,
And our God is full of compassion — Rhm
How kind he is! How good he is! So merciful, this God of ours! — Tay

6. The LORD preserveth the simple:
The Lord protects the innocent — Har
The LORD takes care of the helpless — Ber
The Lord preserveth the sincere — Sept
I was brought low, and he helped me.
I was brought low, and he saved me — RV
When I was languishing, He rescued me — Har
when I am helpless, he is my saving help — Mof
and to me, when I lay humbled, he brought deliverance — Knox

7. Return unto thy rest, O my soul; for the LORD hath dealt bountifully with thee.
Return to your rest, O my spirit,
For the LORD has dealt well with you — AAT
Return, O my soul, to your tranquillity,
for the LORD has been good to you — NAB
Regain your composure, my soul,
for the Lord has treated you kindly — Har
Now I can relax. For the Lord has done this wonderful miracle for me — Tay

8. For thou hast delivered my soul from death, mine eyes from tears, and my feet from falling.
For thou hast rescued my soul from death, —
mine eyes from tears,
my feet from stumbling — Rhm
You have liberated me from death,
my eyes from weeping, my feet from tottering — Har
he has saved my life from peril, banished my tears, kept my feet from falling — Knox

9. I will walk before the LORD in the land of the living.
I will walk to and fro before Yahweh,
in the lands of life — Rhm
I will live mindful of thee now
in the land of the living — Mof
I will conduct myself in a godly manner
in the midst of human society — Har
I shall live! Yes, in his presence — here on earth! — Tay

10. I believed, therefore have I spoken: I was greatly afflicted:
I kept my faith, even when I said,

"I am greatly afflicted" — RSV
I clung to my faith, even when I said,
"I am sorely afflicted" — Ber
I trusted, even when most I bewailed my unhappy lot — Knox

11. I said in my haste, All men are liars.
I said in my consternation,
"Men are all a vain hope" — RSV
I said in my alarm,
"Men are all deceitful" — Ber
. . . "No man is dependable" — NAB
I said in my bewilderment,
"Everyone is unreliable" — Har
In panic I cried,
'How faithless all men are!' — NEB

12. What shall I render unto the LORD for all his benefits toward me?
How shall I give back to Yahweh,
All his benefits unto me — Rhm
What can I offer to the Lord
in payment for all his kindness to me — Har

13. I will take the cup of salvation, and call upon the name of the LORD.
The cup of salvation will I lift,
And on the Name of Yahweh will I call — Rhm
I will offer a libation for my rescue,
and proclaim the Eternal aloud — Mof
I will bring him an offering of wine and praise his name for saving me — Tay

14. I will pay my vows unto the LORD now in the presence of all his people.
I pay my vows unto Jehovah,
Oh let me, in the presence of all His people — DeW
I will pay what I vowed to the Eternal,
in the presence of all his people — Mof
(I will pay what I vowed to Yahweh;
may his whole nation be present!) — Jerus
I will publicly bring him the sacrifice I vowed I would — Tay

15. Precious in the sight of the LORD is the death of his saints.
Costly in the eyes of Yahweh
Is death for his men of lovingkindness — Rhm
The death of His faithful servants
is an important consideration with the Lord — Har
His loved ones are very precious to him and he does not lightly let them die — Tay

16. O LORD, truly I am thy servant; I am thy servant, and the son of thine handmaid:
I am Your follower, Lord,
Your servant, Your true offspring — Har
Yahweh, I am your servant,
your servant, son of a pious mother — Jerus
thou hast loosed my bonds.
Thou hast burst my bonds asunder — Sept.
Thou hast broken the chains that bound me — Knox
thou hast delivered me — Mof

17. I will offer to thee the sacrifice of thanksgiving, and will call upon the name of the LORD.
I will make a sacrificial thank-offering to You;
I will pray in the name of the Lord — Har

18. I will pay my vows unto the LORD now in the presence of all his people,

19. In the courts of the LORD'S house, in the midst of thee, O Jerusalem.
in the precincts of the Divine abode,
in your midst, Jerusalem — Har
Praise ye the LORD.
Praise ye Yah! — Rhm
praise ye Jah! — YLT
Hallelujah — JPS

PSALM 117

1. O praise the LORD, all ye nations: praise him, all ye people.
Praise Yahweh all ye nations,
Laud him all ye tribes of men — Rhm
Praise Jehovah, all ye nations,
Give Him glory, all ye kingdoms — DeW

2. For his merciful kindness is great toward us:
For his lovingkindness is great toward us — ASV
For his lovingkindness hath prevailed over us — Rhm
For His divine mercy to us has been limitless — Har
for his kind love to us is vast — Mof
and the truth of the LORD endureth for ever.

And the faithfulness of the LORD is everlasting — AAT
Praise ye the LORD.
Praise ye Yah! — Rhm
Praise ye Jah! — YLT
Hallelujah — JPS

PSALM 118

1. **O give thanks unto the LORD; for he is good:**
O give thanks unto the LORD, for he is gracious — PBV
because his mercy endureth for ever.
For his lovingkindness endureth for ever — ASV
His love is everlasting! — Jerus
his steadfast love endures for ever! — RSV
his kindness never fails — Mof
2. **Let Israel now say, that his mercy endureth for ever.**
Let Israel say,
"His steadfast love endures for ever" — RSV
Let Israel declare
that His mercy is eternal — Har
3. **Let the house of Aaron now say, that his mercy endureth for ever.**
Let the house of Aaron say,
"His steadfast love endures for ever" — RSV
And let the priests of Aaron chant, "His lovingkindness is forever" — Tay
4. **Let them now that fear the LORD say, that his mercy endureth for ever.**
Let those who revere the Lord affirm
that His mercy is eternal — Har
Let the Gentile converts chant, "His lovingkindness is forever" — Tay
5. **I called upon the LORD in distress: the LORD answered me, and set me in a large place.**
Out of my distress I called on the LORD;
the LORD answered me and set me free — RSV
6. **The LORD is on my side; I will not fear: what can man do unto me?**
With the LORD on my side I do not fear.
What can man do to me? — RSV
7. **The LORD taketh my part with them that help me:**
The LORD is on my side to help me — RSV
I have the Eternal as my Helper — Mof
therefore shall I see my desire upon them that hate me.
I therefore shall gaze upon them who hate me — Rhm
I shall look in triumph on those who hate me — RSV
I shall witness the downfall of those who hate me — Har
And I shall see the defeat of my foes — DeW
Let those who hate me beware — Tay
8. **It is better to trust in the LORD than to put confidence in man.**
It is better to take refuge in Jehovah
Than to put confidence in man — ASV
9. **It is better to trust in the LORD than to put confidence in princes.**
It is better to seek refuge in Yahweh
Than to put confidence in nobles — Rhm
10. **All nations compassed me about: but in the name of the LORD will I destroy them.**
All nations have compassed me about,
In the Name of Yahweh surely I will make them be circumcised — Rhm
All the nations compass me about;
In the name of Jehovah I will surely cut them off — ABPS
The pagans were swarming round me,
in the name of Yahweh I cut them down — Jerus
11. **They compassed me about; yea, they compassed me about: but in the name of the LORD I will destroy them.**
They surrounded me, surrounded me on every side;
in the name of the LORD I cut them off! — RSV
12. **They compassed me about like bees;**
They swarmed around me like bees — Har
they are quenched as the fire of thorns:
They have blazed up like the fire of thorns — Rhm
they blazed up like a fire among thorns — Har
they attack me, as fire attacks brushwood — NEB
for in the name of the LORD I will destroy them.
in the name of the LORD I cut them off! — RSV
13. **Thou hast thrust sore at me that I might fall: but the LORD helped me.**

You [my adversary] thrust sorely at me that I might fall, but the Lord helped me — Amp

I was hard pressed, and on the point of collapse,
but the Lord assisted me — Har

I reeled under the blow, and had well-nigh fallen, but still the Lord was there to aid me — Knox

14. The LORD is my strength and song, and is become my salvation.

The Lord is my strength and my song, and He has become my rescuer — Har

He is my strength and song in the heat of battle, and now he has given me the victory — Tay

15. The voice of rejoicing and salvation is in the tabernacles of the righteous: the right hand of the LORD doeth valiantly.

16. The right hand of the LORD is exalted: the right hand of the LORD doeth valiantly.

Listen to the joyful shout of victory
where the upright are living.
The power of the Lord has brought success.
The might of the Lord is greatly praised;
the resources of the Lord have ushered in victory — Har

Hark, glad songs of victory
in the tents of the righteous:
"The right hand of the LORD does valiantly,
the right hand of the LORD is exalted,
the right hand of the LORD does valiantly!" — RSV

Hark, the joyful shout of triumph
in the tents of the just! —
"The Eternal's right hand carries the day,"
"The Eternal's right hand triumphs,"
"The Eternal's right hand carries the day!" — Mof

17. I shall not die, but live, and declare the works of the LORD.

I shall not die but live,
That I may recount the doings of Yah — Rhm

I shall not die,
but will survive to tell of the Lord's doings — Har

18. The LORD hath chastened me sore: but he hath not given me over unto death.

The Lord has corrected me sternly,
but He has not abandoned me to destruction — Har

19. Open to me the gates of righteousness: I will go into them, and I will praise the LORD:

Open for me the gates of victory,
That I may enter through them to give thanks to the LORD — AAT

Open me the gates where right dwells;
let me go in and thank the Lord! — Knox

Open the gates of the Temple — I will go in and give him my thanks — Tay

Open to me the [temple] gates of righteousness; I will enter through them, and I will confess and praise the Lord — Amp

20. This gate of the LORD, into which the righteous shall enter.

This is the gate of Jehovah;
The righteous shall enter into it — ASV

Those gates are the way into the presence of the Lord, and the godly enter there — Tay

21. I will praise thee: for thou hast heard me, and art become my salvation.

I thank thee that thou hast answered me
and hast become my salvation — RSV

I am thanking You because You have answered me,
and have become my liberator — Har

22. The stone which the builders refused is become the head stone of the corner.

The stone which the builders rejected
Is become the chief corner-stone — JPS

The stone which the builders deemed unsuitable
has become the cornerstone — Har

It was the stone rejected by the builders
that proved to be the keystone — Jerus

The stone the builders cast aside is now the building's strength and pride — Mof

23. This is the LORD'S doing; it is marvellous in our eyes.

This has been done by the Lord;
in our judgment it is a marvelous thing — Har

this is Yahweh's doing
and it is wonderful to see — Jerus

24. This is the day which the LORD hath

made; we will rejoice and be glad in it.
This is the day which the LORD has made;
let us rejoice and be glad in it — RSV
This is the day which the Lord has brought about; we will rejoice and be glad in it — Amp
This is a day we owe to the Eternal; let us be glad and rejoice in it — Mof

25. Save now, I beseech thee, O LORD: O LORD, I beseech thee, send now prosperity.
Save us, we beseech thee, O LORD! O LORD, we beseech thee, give us success! — RSV
Ah now Yahweh do save we beseech thee,
Ah now Yahweh, do send success we beseech thee! — Rhm

26. Blessed be he that cometh in the name of the LORD: we have blessed you out of the house of the LORD.
Blessed be he that cometh in the Name of the LORD: we have wished you good luck, we that are of the house of the LORD — PBV
He who approaches in the name of the LORD is blessed;
we invoke favor on you from the divine abode — Har

27. God is the LORD, which hath shewed us light:
Jehovah is God, and he hath given us light — ASV
The Lord is God; his light shines out to welcome us — Knox
bind the sacrifice with cords, even unto the horns of the altar.
Bind ye the festal sacrifice with cords,
Up to the horns of the altar — Rhm
Bind the festal sacrifice with cords,
Even to the horns of the altar — ABPS
Bind the festal procession with branches,
up to the horns of the altar! — RSV
Join in procession with leafy boughs
up to the horns of the altar — NAB
With branches in your hands draw up in procession
as far as the horns of the altar — Jerus

28. Thou art my God, and I will praise thee: thou art my God, I will exalt thee.

29. O give thanks unto the LORD; for he is good: for his mercy endureth for ever.[35]

PSALM 119

ALEPH

1. Blessed are the undefiled in the way, who walk in the law of the LORD.
O the blessedness of those whose way is blameless,
Who walk in the law of Jehovah! — DeW
How happy the men of blameless life,
Who walk in the law of Yahweh — Rhm
Happy the upright in their way,
Who walk in the law of Jehovah — ABPS
Happy are those whose conduct is beyond reproach,
who are living according to the law of the Lord — Har

2. Blessed are they that keep his testimonies, and that seek him with the whole heart.
Happy are they who follow his injunctions, giving him undivided hearts — Mof
Happy are they who observe his decrees,
who seek him with all their heart — NAB

3. They also do no iniquity: they walk in his ways.
Truly such shall not commit deeds of oppression,
Whilst walking in His ways — Sprl
Yea, they have not wrought perversity,
In his ways they have walked — Rhm
who also do no wrong,
but walk in his ways! — RSV
Who in addition commit no injustices,
but live according to the divine pattern — Har

4. Thou hast commanded us to keep thy precepts diligently.
You Yourself have commanded us
to observe Your injunctions rigidly — Har

[35] See verse 1.

5. O that my ways were directed to keep thy statutes!

Oh would that my ways might be settled!
That I might keep thy statutes — Rhm

Oh, may my behaviour be constant in keeping your statutes — Jerus

oh that my life were set on thine obedience! — Mof

6. Then shall I not be ashamed, when I have respect unto all thy commandments.

Then I would not endure humiliation because I have attended to all Your statutes — Har

Then I will not be disgraced, for I will have a clean record — Tay

Then shall I not be put to shame [by failing to inherit Your promises], when I have respect to all Your commandments — Amp

If I concentrate on your every commandment,
I can never be put to shame — Jerus

7. I will praise thee with uprightness of heart, when I shall have learned thy righteous judgments.

I will thank thee with uprightness of heart,
When I have learned thy righteous regulations — Rhm

I will thank You with a sincere heart when I learn Your equitable laws — Har

I will praise thee in sincerity of heart as I learn thy just decrees — NEB

After you have corrected me I will thank you by living as I should! — Tay

8. I will keep thy statutes: O forsake me not utterly.

I will keep Thy statutes; oh, do not forsake me completely! — Ber

I mean to observe your statutes;
never abandon me — Jerus

I will obey! Oh, don't forsake me and let me slip back into sin again — Tay

BETH

9. Wherewithal shall a young man cleanse his way? by taking heed thereto according to thy word.

How can a young man keep life clean?
By keeping to thy word — Mof

How can a young man keep his way pure?
By guarding it according to thy word — RSV

Wherewithal shall a young man cleanse his way? even by ruling himself after thy word — PBV

How can a young man live a clean life?
Only by paying attention to what You say — Har

How can a youth remain pure?
By behaving as your word prescribes — Jerus

10. With my whole heart have I sought thee: O let me not wander from thy commandments.

I give thee an undivided heart; oh never may I stray from thy control! — Mof

With my whole heart have I sought You, inquiring for and of You, and yearning for You; O let me not wander or step aside [either in ignorance or willfully] from Your commandments — Amp

11. Thy word have I hid in mine heart, that I might not sin against thee.

In my heart have I treasured what thou hast said,
To the end I may not sin against thee — Rhm

Thy word have I laid up in my heart,
That I might not sin against thee — ASV

I have treasured your promises in my heart,
since I have no wish to sin against you — Jerus

12. Blessed art thou, O LORD: teach me thy statutes.

13. With my lips have I declared all the judgments of thy mouth.

With my lips have I recounted
All the regulations of thy mouth — Rhm

With my lips have I declared
All the ordinances of thy mouth — ASV

I have talked forthrightly
of all Your spoken judgments — Har

I say them over, one by one,
the decrees that thou hast proclaimed — NEB

14. I have rejoiced in the way of thy testimonies, as much as in all riches.
I find more joy in thine injunctions than in any wealth — Mof
I am happier in following Your injunctions
than in every possible form of wealth — Har
In the way of your decrees lies my joy,
a joy beyond all wealth — Jerus

15. I will meditate in thy precepts, and have respect unto thy ways.
I will meditate on thy precepts
and keep thy paths ever before my eyes — NEB
In thy precepts will I meditate,
That I may discern thy paths — Rhm
I will meditate on Your teachings,
and give attention to Your purposes — Har

16. I will delight myself in thy statutes: I will not forget thy word.
In thy statutes I find continual delight . . . — NEB
I find my delight in your statutes,
I do not forget your word — Jerus
I find happiness in Your statutes;
I will not forget what You have enjoined — Har

GIMEL

17. Deal bountifully with thy servant, that I may live, and keep thy word.
Deal generously with thy servant, that I may live,
And I will keep thy word — AAT
Bestow thy bounties upon thy servant — let me live,
That I may observe thy word — Rhm
Deal kindly with thy servant, till I live to do thy bidding — Mof
Grant this to me, thy servant: let me live
and, living, keep thy word — NEB

18. Open thou mine eyes, that I may behold wondrous things out of thy law.
Unveil thou mine eyes that I may discern
Wondrous things out of thy law — Rhm
Take the veil from my eyes, that I may see
the marvels that spring from thy law — NEB
Give me discernment,
that I may notice wonderful things in Your law — Har
Open my eyes: I shall concentrate
on the marvels of your Law — Jerus

19. I am a stranger in the earth: hide not thy commandments from me.
I am but a guest in the land;
hide not your commands from me — NAB
I am but a pilgrim here on earth: how I need a map — and your commands are my chart and guide — Tay

20. My soul breaketh for the longing that it hath unto thy judgments at all times.
My soul breaketh out for the very fervent desire that it hath alway unto thy judgments — PBV
My soul wasteth away in pining desire
After Thy judgments at all times — Sprl
My soul is crushed with longing
For thy just decisions at all times — Rhm
I yearn desperately
for Your ordinances at all times — Har
My soul is overcome
with an incessant longing for your rulings — Jerus

21. Thou hast rebuked the proud that are cursed, which do err from thy commandments.
Thou hast rebuked the proud as accursed,
Who stray from thy commandments — Rhm
Thou hast rebuked the haughty; cursed are they who turn aside from thy commands — Sept
Thou dost rebuke the insolent, accursed ones,
who wander from thy commandments — RSV
You rebuke the overbearing;
those who wander from Your decrees are accursed — Har

22. Remove from me reproach and contempt; for I have kept thy testimonies.
relieve me from their insults and

contempt, for I follow thine injunctions — Mof

Take away from me disgrace and scorn,
For I have kept thy decrees — AAT

Don't let them scorn me for obeying you — Tay

23. Princes also did sit and speak against me: but thy servant did meditate on thy statutes.

Yea, though princes conspire against me,
Thy servant doth meditate on Thy statutes — DeW

Even though princes sit plotting against me,
thy servant will meditate on thy statutes — RSV

24. Thy testimonies also are my delight and my counsellors.

my advisers are thine own injunctions — I delight in them — Mof

since your decrees are my delight, your statutes are my counsellors — Jerus

Your unchanging word is my delight, and the guide of my footsteps — Bas

DALETH

25. My soul cleaveth unto the dust: quicken thou me according to thy word.

My soul cleaveth to the dust,
Give me life according to thy word — Rhm

My soul is bowed to the dust: revive me, even as thou hast promised — Mof

My spirit clings to the dust;
Revive me according to thy word — AAT

I am completely discouraged — I lie in the dust. Revive me by your Word — Tay

26. I have declared my ways, and thou heardest me: teach me thy statutes.

I have described my plight to You, and You answered me;
teach me Your statutes — Har

I confessed my ways, and Thou hast answered me; teach me Thy statutes — Ber

I admitted my behaviour, you answered me,
now teach me your statutes — Jerus

I put the record of my ways before you, and you gave me an answer: O give me knowledge of your rules — Bas

27. Make me to understand the way of thy precepts: so shall I talk of thy wondrous works.

The way of thy precepts cause thou me to understand,
And I will indeed meditate in thy wonders — Rhm

Help me to discern the inner meaning of Your teachings,
and I will meditate upon Your wonders — Har

Make me understand what you want; for then I shall see your miracles — Tay

28. My soul melteth for heaviness: strengthen thou me according unto thy word.

My soul weepeth itself away for grief,
Confirm thou me according to thy word — Rhm

My soul melts away with sorrow;
Raise me up, according to thy word — ABPS

My soul is melting under trouble: nerve me, as thou hast promised — Mof

I am sleepless with grief:
raise me as your word has guaranteed — Jerus

29. Remove from me the way of lying: and grant me thy law graciously.

Take from me the way of lying, and cause thou me to make much of thy law — PBV

Put false ways far from me;
and graciously teach me thy law! — RSV

Remove from me the way of falsehood and unfaithfulness [to You], and graciously impart Your law to me — Amp

Take from me every false way; and in mercy give me your law — Bas

Keep falsehood far from me
and grant me the grace of living by the law — NEB

30. I have chosen the way of truth: thy judgments have I laid before me.

I have chosen the way of trustworthiness,
Thine ordinances I crave — AAT

I have taken the way of faith: I have kept your decisions before me — Bas

The way of faithfulness have I chosen,
Thy regulations have I deemed right — Rhm
A faithful life is what I choose, thy demands are my desire — Mof

31. I have stuck unto thy testimonies: O LORD, put me not to shame.
I have kept close to thy testimonies
O Yahweh! do not put me to shame — Rhm
I cling to Your ordinances, Lord;
do not let me be disgraced — Har
I cling to your decrees:
Yahweh, do not disappoint me — Jerus

32. I will run the way of thy commandments, when thou shalt enlarge my heart.
I will obey thee eagerly, as thou dost open up my life — Mof
I will run in the way of thy commandments
when thou enlargest my understanding! — RSV
I will follow Your pattern for living,
for You give me increasing discernment — Har
I will run the course set out in thy commandments,
for they gladden my heart — NEB

HE

33. Teach me, O LORD, the way of thy statutes; and I shall keep it unto the end.
Point out to me O Yahweh the way of thy statutes
That I may observe it unto the end — Rhm
Teach me, Eternal, how thine orders run, and I will follow them step by step — Mof
Instruct me, O LORD, in the way of your statutes,
that I may exactly observe them — NAB
Instruct me in the meaning of Your statutes, Lord,
that I may observe them continually — Har

34. Give me understanding, and I shall keep thy law; yea, I shall observe it with my whole heart.
Give me discernment, that I may observe your law
and keep it with all my heart — NAB
Give me the insight to obey thy law
and to keep it with all my heart — NEB

35. Make me to go in the path of thy commandments; for therein do I delight.
Guide me in the path of thy commandments,
For therein do I find pleasure — Rhm
Guide me along by Your commandments,
for in this way I find happiness — Har
make me walk in the path of thy commandments,
for that is my desire — NEB

36. Incline my heart unto thy testimonies, and not to covetousness.
Incline my heart unto thy testimonies
And not unto unjust gain — Rhm
Turn my mind in the direction of Your injunctions,
and not towards money-making — Har
Help me to prefer obedience to making money! — Tay

37. Turn away mine eyes from beholding vanity; and quicken thou me in thy way.
turn away my eyes from all that is vile,
grant me life by thy word — NEB
Avert my eyes from unreality;
uphold me in Your true principles — Har
Turn away my eyes from looking at futilities, and revive me in Thy ways — Ber
Turn away my eyes from beholding vanity [idols and idolatry]; and restore me to vigorous life and health in Your ways — Amp

38. Stablish thy word unto thy servant, who is devoted to thy fear.
Confirm unto thy servant thy word,
Which is in order unto the fear of thee — ASV
Confirm to thy servant thy promise,
which is for those who fear thee — RSV
Confirm Your promise to Your servant, which is given to all who revere You — Har
Fulfill for your servant
your promise to those who fear you — NAB

Keep your promise to your servant,
so that others in turn may fear you — Jerus

39. Turn away my reproach which I fear: for thy judgments are good.

Turn away the reviling whereof I am afraid;
For Thine ordinances are good — DeW

Turn away from me the disgrace which I fear;
For thine ordinances are good — AAT

How I dread being mocked for obeying, for your laws are right and good — Tay

40. Behold, I have longed after thy precepts: quicken me in thy righteousness.

Behold I have longed for thy precepts;
quicken me by thy saving goodness — Sept

Lo, I have longed for thy precepts;
Revive me through thy righteousness — AAT

Behold, I long for your precepts;
in your justice give me life — NAB

Behold, I long for Your precepts; in Your righteousness give me renewed life — Amp

VAU

41. Let thy mercies come also unto me, O LORD, even thy salvation, according to thy word.

Let thy lovingkindnesses also come unto me, O Jehovah,
Even thy salvation, according to thy word — ASV

May thy gracious deeds come to me, O LORD,
Thy deliverance according to thy promises — AAT

Let thy love come to my rescue, even as thou hast promised — Mof

42. So shall I have wherewith to answer him that reproacheth me: for I trust in thy word.

So shall I make answer unto my blasphemers; for my trust is in thy word — PBV

then I can face my revilers, relying on thy promise — Mof

43. And take not the word of truth utterly out of my mouth; for I have hoped in thy judgments.

And do not snatch away from my mouth the word of truth in any wise,
Because for thy regulation have I waited — Rhm

Do not silence my witness to the truth completely,
for I have implicit trust in Your decisions — Har

Do not deprive me of that faithful word,
since my hope has always lain in your rulings — Jerus

May I never forget your words; for they are my only hope — Tay

44. So shall I keep thy law continually for ever and ever.

I will keep Your law
continually, eternally — Har

Let me observe your Law unfailingly
for ever and ever — Jerus

45. And I will walk at liberty: for I seek thy precepts.

So, having sought your precepts,
I shall walk in all freedom — Jerus

46. I will speak of thy testimonies also before kings, and will not be ashamed.

I shall proclaim your decrees to kings
without fear of disgrace — Jerus

I will speak to kings about their value, and they will listen with interest and respect — Tay

47. And I will delight myself in thy commandments, which I have loved.

for I find my happiness in Your commandments,
and I cherish them — Har

Your commandments fill me with delight,
I love them deeply — Jerus

48. My hands also will I lift up unto thy commandments, which I have loved; and I will meditate in thy statutes.

I will raise my hands in reverence for Your statutes which I treasure, and I will meditate on Your laws — Har

My hands also will I lift up (in fervent supplication) to Your commandments, which I love, and I will meditate on Your statutes — Amp

I revere thy commandments, which I love,
and I will meditate on thy statutes — RSV

ZAIN

49. Remember the word unto thy servant, upon which thou hast caused me to hope.
Remember the promise which You made to Your servant,
upon which I am placing my trust — Har
Remember the word spoken to me, thy servant,
on which thou hast taught me to fix my hope — NEB
Never forget your promises to me your servant; for they are my only hope — Tay

50. This is my comfort in my affliction: for thy word hath quickened me.
This is my comfort in my suffering,
That Thy word giveth me life — DeW
My comfort in my affliction is that your promise gives me life — NAB
They give me strength in all my troubles; how they refresh and revive me! — Tay

51. The proud have had me greatly in derision: yet have I not declined from thy law.
The proud have exceedingly derided me,
Yet have I not swerved from Thy law — Sprl
Insolent men have derided me exceedingly,
From thy law have I not swerved — Rhm
The arrogant have scoffed at me bitterly,
But I have not turned away from thy law — AAT

52. I remembered thy judgments of old, O LORD; and have comforted myself.
When I think of thy ordinances from of old,
I take comfort, O LORD — RSV
I have kept the memory of your decisions from times past, O Lord; and they have been my comfort — Bas

53. Horror hath taken hold upon me because of the wicked that forsake thy law.
A raging heat hath seized me by reason of the lawless,
Who forsake thy law — Rhm
Hot indignation hath taken hold upon me, because of the wicked that forsake thy law — RV
Fury grips me when I see the wicked abandoning your Law — Jerus
I am very angry with those who spurn your commands — Tay

54. Thy statutes have been my songs in the house of my pilgrimage.
Your statutes are the theme of my song in the place of my exile — NAB
Your rules have been melodies to me, while I have been living in strange lands — Bas
Thy statutes are my songs, as I wander through the world — Mof
For these laws of yours have been my source of joy and singing through all these years of my earthly pilgrimage — Tay
Thy statutes are the theme of my song wherever I make my home — NEB

55. I have remembered thy name, O LORD, in the night, and have kept thy law.
I obey them even at night and keep my thoughts, O Lord, on you — Tay

56. This I had, because I kept thy precepts.
This is my consolation,
That I have kept Thy statutes — Sprl
This blessing has fallen to me,
that I have kept thy precepts — RSV
this is my blessed lot, to carry out thy behests — Mof
What a blessing this has been to me — to constantly obey — Tay

HETH

57. Thou art my portion, O LORD: I have said that I would keep thy words.
O JEHOVAH, my portion!
I have determined to observe Thy commands — Sprl
The LORD is my inheritance; I promised that I would keep Thy words — Ber
The Lord is my heritage: I have said that I would be ruled by your words — Bas
Thou, LORD, art all I have;
I have promised to keep thy word — NEB

58. I entreated thy favour with my whole heart: be merciful unto me according to thy word.

I have sought the smile of thy face with all my heart,
Shew me favour according to thy word — Rhm
With all my heart I have tried to please thee;
fulfil thy promise and be gracious to me — NEB

59. I thought on my ways, and turned my feet unto thy testimonies.
I have considered my ways,
And turned my feet toward thy decrees — AAT
I have pondered on my behavior,
and moved in the direction of Your commandments — Har
When I think of thy ways,
I turn my feet to thy testimonies — RSV

60. I made haste, and delayed not to keep thy commandments.
I was prompt and did not hesitate in keeping your commands — NAB

61. The bands of the wicked have robbed me: but I have not forgotten thy law.
The cords of the wicked were around me;
Thy law I have not forgotten — ABPS
The cords of sinners entangled me;
but I did not forget thy law — Sept
Though the cords of the wicked ensnare me,
I do not forget thy law — RSV
The meshes of the lawless have surrounded me,
Thy law have I not forgotten — Rhm
Though the noose of the wicked tighten round me,
I do not forget your Law — Jerus
Evil men have tried to drag me into sin, but I am firmly anchored to your laws — Tay

62. At midnight I will rise to give thanks unto thee because of thy righteous judgments.
At dead of night I rise to thank You,
because of Your impartial judgments — Har
I get up at midnight to thank you
for the righteousness of your rulings — Jerus

63. I am a companion of all them that fear thee, and of them that keep thy precepts.
Companion am I to all who revere thee,
And to them who keep thy precepts — Rhm
I keep company with all thy worshippers who carry out thy will — Mof
I am a friend to all who fear you
and observe your precepts — Jerus
Anyone is my brother who fears and trusts the Lord and obeys him — Tay

64. The earth, O LORD, is full of thy mercy: teach me thy statutes.
The earth, O Jehovah, is full of thy lovingkindness:
Teach me thy statutes — ASV
The earth, O LORD, is full of thy steadfast love;
teach me thy statutes! — RSV
Of thy lovingkindness O Yahweh the earth is full
Thy statutes teach thou me — Rhm

TETH

65. Thou hast dealt well with thy servant, O LORD, according unto thy word.
Thou hast acted graciously unto Thy servant, O JEHOVAH!
According unto Thy word of promise — Sprl
O Lord, thou hast dealt kindly with thy servant; according to thy word — Sept
In accordance with your word, Yahweh,
you have been good to your servant — Jerus

66. Teach me good judgment and knowledge: for I have believed thy commandments.
Teach me good judgment and knowledge,
For I have confidence in Thy commandments — DeW
Teach me good sense and knowledge,
for I rely on your commandments — Jerus
Now teach me good judgment as well as knowledge. For your laws are my guide — Tay

67. Before I was afflicted I went astray: but now have I kept thy word.
Until affliction came, I went astray;
but now I observe Your sayings — Har

In earlier days I had to suffer, I used to stray,
but now I remember your promise — Jerus
I used to wander off until you punished me; now I closely follow all you say — Tay

68. Thou art good, and doest good; teach me thy statutes.
Thou, O Lord, art good; in thy goodness teach me thy statutes — Sept
You are good and bountiful;
teach me your statutes — NAB
You are good and beneficent;
teach me Your statutes — Har

69. The proud have forged a lie against me: but I will keep thy precepts with my whole heart.
Insolent men have plastered falsehood over me,
I with a whole heart will observe thy precepts — Rhm
proud men bespatter me with lies, but I carry out thy behests — Mof
Though the arrogant tell foul lies about me,
I wholeheartedly respect your precepts — Jerus

70. Their heart is as fat as grease; but I delight in thy law.
Thick, as with fat, is their heart:
As for me, in thy law do I delight — ABPS
Their heart is unfeeling as grease;
but I delight in Thy law — Ber
Their heart was curdled like milk: but I meditated on thy law — Sept
their minds are gross and dull, but I thrill to thy law — Mof
Their minds are stupid and impenitent, but I find joy indeed in Your law — Har
Their minds are dull and stupid, but I have sense enough to follow you — Tay

71. It is good for me that I have been afflicted; that I might learn thy statutes.
It is good for me that thou hast humbled me: that I might learn thy rules of rectitude — Sept
It was good for me to have to suffer, the better to learn your statutes — Jerus
The punishment you gave me was the best thing that could have happened to me, for it taught me to pay attention to your laws — Tay

72. The law of thy mouth is better unto me than thousands of gold and silver.
The law of thy mouth is worth more to me
Than thousands in gold and silver — AAT
The law of your mouth is to me more precious
than thousands of gold and silver pieces — NAB
Your decrees are more valuable to me
than gold and silver in abundance — Har
thy law means more to me than piles of gold and silver — Mof
I put the Law you have given
before all the gold and silver in the world — Jerus

YOD

73. Thy hands have made me and fashioned me: give me understanding, that I may learn thy commandments.
Your power has moulded me and established me;
give me understanding, that I may learn Your precepts — Har
You made my body, Lord; now give me sense to heed your laws — Tay

74. They that fear thee will be glad when they see me; because I have hoped in thy word.
They who revere thee shall see me and rejoice
That for thy word I waited — Rhm
Let those who revere You see me and rejoice,
because I had confidence in Your promise — Har
may thy worshippers rejoice to see me waiting on thy word! — Mof
All those who fear and trust in you will welcome me because I too am trusting in your Word — Tay

75. I know, O LORD, that thy judgments are right, and that thou in faithfulness hast afflicted me.
I know O Yahweh that righteous are thy regulations,
And in faithfulness didst thou afflict me — Rhm
I realize, Lord, that Your judgments are fair,

and that You have afflicted me with the best intentions — Har

I know, O LORD, that thy decrees are just
and even in punishing thou keepest faith with me — NEB

76. Let, I pray thee, thy merciful kindness be for my comfort, according to thy word unto thy servant.

O let thy merciful kindness be my comfort, according to thy word unto thy servant — PBV

Oh let Thy tender love now be my consolation,
According unto Thy word of promise unto Thy servant — Sprl

Now, please let your love comfort me, as you have promised your servant — Jerus

But now let Your mercy console me, according to what You promised Your servant — Har

77. Let thy tender mercies come unto me, that I may live: for thy law is my delight.

Let thy compassions reach me that I may live,
For thy law is my dear delight — Rhm

Show some sympathy towards me, that I may survive,
for Your law is my happiness — Har

78. Let the proud be ashamed; for they dealt perversely with me without a cause: but I will meditate in thy precepts.

Let insolent men be ashamed because by means of falsehood they have dealt with me perversely,
I will meditate in thy precepts — Rhm

Let the proud be put to shame, for they have distorted my cause with falsehood;
But I will meditate in Thy precepts — JPS

Let the proud be put to shame for oppressing me unjustly;
I will meditate on your precepts — NAB

79. Let those that fear thee turn unto me, and those that have known thy testimonies.

Let them who revere thee turn unto me,
Even they who know thy testimonies — Rhm

Let those who fear thee turn to me, that they may know thy testimonies — RSV

May those who fear you rally to me, all those familiar with your decrees! — Jerus

Let all others join me, who trust and fear you, and we will discuss your laws — Tay

80. Let my heart be sound in thy statutes; that I be not ashamed.

Let my heart be thorough in thy statutes,
that I may not be ashamed — Rhm

Let my heart be perfect in thy statutes,
That I be not put to shame — ASV

Let my heart be blameless in Thy statutes,
That I be not put to shame — DeW

Let my heart be undivided in Thy statutes,
In order that I may not be put to shame — JPS

let my obedience to thee be perfect, that I may not be disgraced — Har

Help me to love your every wish; then I will never have to be ashamed of myself — Tay

KAPH

81. My soul fainteth for thy salvation: but I hope in thy word.

My soul hath longed for thy salvation, and I have good hope because of thy word — PBV

My soul hath languished for thy salvation,
For thy word have I hoped — Rhm

My soul pines for thy saving aid, I am waiting for thy promise — Mof

I pine for thy deliverance;
I wait for thy word — AAT

Keeping my hope in your word,
I have worn myself out waiting for you to save me — Jerus

I faint for your salvation; but I expect your help, for you have promised it — Tay

82. Mine eyes fail for thy word, saying, When wilt thou comfort me?

I pine with looking for thy promises; when wilt thou comfort me? — Mof

My eyes fail with watching for thy promise;

I ask, "When wilt thou comfort me?" — RSV

My eyes strain after your promise; when will you comfort me? — NAB

My eyes are straining to see your promises come true. When will you comfort me with your help? — Tay

83. For I am become like a bottle in the smoke; yet do I not forget thy statutes.

Though I have been like a wine-skin in the smoke
Thy statutes have I not forgotten — Rhm

Though I became like a leathern bag in frost; I did not forget thy statutes — Sept

Though shrivelled like a wineskin in the smoke, I never forget thine orders — Mof

84. How many are the days of thy servant? when wilt thou execute judgment on them that persecute me?

How few are the days of thy servant!
When wilt thou execute sentence on my persecutors? — Rhm

How long must thy servant endure?
When wilt thou judge those who persecute me? — RSV

85. The proud have digged pits for me, which are not after thy law.

Insolent men digged for me pits,
Men who are not according to thy law — Rhm

The proud have digged pits for me,
Which is not according to Thy law — JPS

The arrogant have dug pitfalls for me in defiance of your Law — Jerus

The overbearing, who violate Your law,
have set traps for me — Har

86. All thy commandments are faithful: they persecute me wrongfully; help thou me.

All thy commandments are sure;
they persecute me with falsehood; help me! — RSV

All your commands are steadfast;
they persecute me wrongfully; help me! — NAB

Your commandments epitomise faithfulness;
when liars hound me you must help me — Jerus

87. They had almost consumed me upon earth; but I forsook not thy precepts.

They nearly made an end of me, but I would not give up thy laws — Mof

They had almost finished me off, yet I refused to yield and disobey your laws — Tay

88. Quicken me after thy lovingkindness; so shall I keep the testimony of thy mouth.

According to thy lovingkindness give thou me life,
So will I keep the testimonies of thy mouth — Rhm

According to thy mercy revive me,
And I will keep the testimony of thy mouth — ABPS

In thy steadfast love spare my life,
that I may keep the testimonies of thy mouth — RSV

Lovingly intervene, give me life,
and I will observe your decrees — Jerus

LAMED

89. For ever, O LORD, thy word is settled in heaven.

For ever, O Jehovah,
Thy word standeth firm in the heavens — DeW

For ever, O LORD, thy word
is firmly fixed in the heavens — RSV

Your word, O LORD, endures forever;
it is firm as the heavens — NAB

90. Thy faithfulness is unto all generations: thou hast established the earth, and it abideth.

Thy faithfulness endures to all generations;
thou hast established the earth, and it stands fast — RSV

your faithfulness lasts age after age;
you founded the earth to endure — Jerus

Your faithfulness extends to every generation, like the earth you created — Tay

Thy promise endures for all time,
stable as the earth which thou hast fixed — NEB

91. They continue this day according to thine ordinances: for all are thy servants.

By thy regulations do they stand today . . . — Rhm

By thy appointment they stand this day;
for all things are thy servants — RSV

To this day things are placed under the control of Your laws,
for everything is subservient to You — Har

This day, as ever, thy decrees stand fast;
for all things serve thee — NEB

Creation is maintained by your rulings, since all things are your servants — Jerus

92. Unless thy law had been my delights, I should then have perished in mine affliction.

Unless thy law had been my comfort, I would have died in my misery — Mof

If Your law had not been my source of happiness,
I should long ago have been engulfed by my miseries — Har

93. I will never forget thy precepts: for with them thou hast quickened me.

Unto times age-abiding will I not forget thy precepts,
For by them has thou given me life — Rhm

I will never forget Your principles, for through them You have kept me alive — Har

I will never lay aside your laws, for you have used them to restore my joy and health — Tay

94. I am thine, save me; for I have sought thy precepts.

I belong to You; rescue me,
for I have looked carefully for Your commands — Har

95. The wicked have waited for me to destroy me: but I will consider thy testimonies.

Though the wicked hide along the way to kill me, I will quietly keep my mind upon your promises — Tay

96. I have seen an end of all perfection: but thy commandment is exceeding broad.

I have observed that perfection has its limits,
but Your law is boundless — Har

I have seen limits to all things, however perfect; but Thy commandment is exceedingly broad — Ber

I see a limit to all things, but thy law has a boundless range — Mof

Look where I may, all good things must end; only thy law is wide beyond measure — Knox

Nothing is perfect except your words — Tay

MEM

97. O how love I thy law! it is my meditation all the day.

Lord, what love have I unto thy law! all the day long is my study in it — PBV

Meditating all day on your Law,
how I have come to love it! — Jerus

98. Thou through thy commandments hast made me wiser than mine enemies: for they are ever with me.

Your commandment makes me wiser than my enemies;
for it is with me continually — Har

They make me wiser than my enemies, because they are my constant guide — Tay

99. I have more understanding than all my teachers: for thy testimonies are my meditation.

I have more understanding than all my teachers
when your decrees are my meditation — NAB

I am more discerning than all my instructors,
for I meditate on Your injunctions — Har

I have deeper insight than all my instructors, because Thy testimonies are my meditation — Ber

100. I understand more than the ancients, because I keep thy precepts.

I am wiser than the aged; because I keep thy commandments — PBV

I have a better grasp on truth than have the elders, because I have kept Thy precepts — Ber

101. I have refrained my feet from every evil way, that I might keep thy word.

I have withdrawn from every evil course of action,
so as to observe Your commands — Har

102. I have not departed from thy judgments: for thou hast taught me.

From thy regulations have I not turned aside,
For thou hast directed me — Rhm
From thy judgments I have not departed,
For thou thyself dost guide me — ABPS

103. How sweet are thy words unto my taste! yea, sweeter than honey to my mouth!
How sweet to my palate are thy sayings;
More than honey to my mouth! — ABPS
How sweet are thy promises to my palate,
Sweeter than honey to my mouth! — AAT

104. Through thy precepts I get understanding: therefore I hate every false way.
Made wise by thy law, I shun every path of evil-doing — Knox
Your precepts endow me with perception;
I hate all deceptive paths — Jerus

NUN

105. Thy word is a lamp unto my feet, and a light unto my path.

106. I have sworn, and I will perform it, that I will keep thy righteous judgments.
I have sworn, and am stedfastly purposed, to keep thy righteous judgments — PBV
I have sworn and have fulfilled it,
To observe thy righteous judgments — ABPS
I have sworn, and have confirmed it, that I will observe thy righteous judgements — RV
I have sworn an oath and confirmed it,
to observe thy righteous ordinances — RSV
I have bound myself by oath and solemn vow
to keep thy just decrees — NEB

107. I am afflicted very much: quicken me, O LORD, according unto thy word.
I have been afflicted exceedingly, — O Yahweh give me life according to thy word — Rhm
I am close to death at the hands of my enemies; oh, give me back my life again, just as you promised me — Tay

108. Accept, I beseech thee, the freewill offerings of my mouth, O LORD, and teach me thy judgments.
Accept my offerings of praise, O LORD, and teach me thy ordinances — RSV
Accept, O LORD, the willing tribute of my lips
and teach me thy decrees — NEB

109. My soul is continually in my hand: yet do I not forget thy law.
I carry my life in my hand continually,
But I have not forgotten thy law — AAT
My life is continually in danger,
yet I do not forget Thy Law — Ber

110. The wicked have laid a snare for me: yet I erred not from thy precepts.
The wicked set a trap for me,
But I have not strayed from thy precepts — AAT

111. Thy testimonies have I taken as an heritage for ever: for they are the rejoicing of my heart.
Thy testimonies have I claimed as mine heritage for ever; and why? they are the very joy of my heart — PBV
Your laws are my joyous treasure forever — Tay

112. I have inclined mine heart to perform thy statutes alway, even unto the end.
I intend in my heart to fulfill your statutes
always, to the letter — NAB
I have set myself to perform Your statutes continually,
from this time on — Har
I am resolved to fulfil thy statutes;
they are a reward that never fails — NEB

SAMECH

113. I hate vain thoughts: but thy law do I love.
Half-hearted ones do I hate,
But thy law do I love — Rhm
The double-minded I hate,
And thy law I love — ABPS
I detest people of uncertain allegiance,
but I cherish Your law — Har

114. Thou art my hiding place and my shield: I hope in thy word.
Thou art my refuge and my shield;

Expectantly hope I for Thy word of promise — Sprl
Thou art my shield and hiding-place; I hope for the fulfilment of thy word — NEB
You are my shelter and my protection; I have complete confidence in Your promise — Har

115. Depart from me, ye evildoers: for I will keep the commandments of my God.
Depart from me, ye evil doers, And let me keep the commandments of my God — DeW

116. Uphold me according unto thy word, that I may live:
Sustain me according to thy promise that I may live — AAT
and let me not be ashamed of my hope.
And do not shame me out of my hope! — Rhm
and let me not be put to shame in my hope! — RSV
disappoint not my hope — Mof
do not let me be disappointed in my trust — Har

117. Hold thou me up, and I shall be safe: and I will have respect unto thy statutes continually.
Sustain me that I may be saved, and may find dear delight in thy statutes continually — Rhm
Strengthen me that I may be delivered; And let me constantly contemplate thy statutes — AAT
Help me, that I may be safe and ever delight in your statutes — NAB

118. Thou has trodden down all them that err from thy statutes: for their deceit is falsehood.
All who swerve from thy will, thou spurnest; their notions end in nothing — Mof
Thou dost spurn all who go astray from thy statutes; yea, their cunning is in vain — RSV
You regard with contempt all who deviate from Your commandments, for their cunning is of no avail — Har
But you have rejected all who reject your laws. They are only fooling themselves — Tay

119. Thou puttest away all the wicked of the earth like dross: therefore I love thy testimonies.
Like dross, thou puttest an end to all the wicked of the earth; Therefore I love thy decrees — AAT
You cast aside all the wicked on earth like rubbish; for this reason I cherish Your decrees — Har
The wicked are the scum you skim off and throw away; no wonder I love to obey your laws — Tay

120. My flesh trembleth for fear of thee; and I am afraid of thy judgments.
My flesh bristled up from dread of thee, And of thy regulations stand I in fear — Rhm
My flesh shudders from dread of thee, And of thy judgments I am afraid — ABPS
My flesh creeps for fear of You, and I am awed by Your judgments — Har
My whole being trembles before you, your rulings fill me with fear — Jerus

AYIN

121. I have done judgment and justice: leave me not to mine oppressors.
I have done justice and righteousness, — Do not leave me to mine oppressors — Rhm
I have done what is just and right; thou wilt not abandon me to my oppressors — NEB

122. Be surety for thy servant for good: let not the proud oppress me.
Pledge me thy word for good; Let not the arrogant oppress me — AAT
Give your servant comforting assurance; do not let the overbearing tyrannize me — Har
Guarantor of your servant's well-being, forbid the arrogant to oppress me! — Jerus
pledge thy word to succour me, let not the arrogant oppress me — Mof

123. Mine eyes fail for thy salvation, and for the word of thy righteousness.

Mine eyes are wasted away with looking for thy health, and for the word of thy righteousness — PBV
Pining away, I look for thy saving help, the faithful keeping of thy promises — Knox
My eyes fail with longing for thy deliverance,
And for thy righteous promise — AAT
My eyes grow dim with longing for you to fulfill your wonderful promise to rescue me — Tay

124. **Deal with thy servant according unto thy mercy, and teach me thy statutes.**
Deal with thy servant according unto thy lovingkindness,
And teach me thy statutes — ASV

125. **I am thy servant; give me understanding that I may know thy testimonies.**

126. **It is time for thee, LORD, to work: for they have made void thy law.**
It is time that Yahweh should work,
They have frustrated thy law! — Rhm
It is time that Jehovah should work;
They have broken thy law — ABPS
It is time for the LORD to act,
for thy law has been broken — RSV

127. **Therefore I love thy commandments above gold; yea, above fine gold.**
Truly I love thy commandments
more than the finest gold — NEB

128. **Therefore I esteem all thy precepts concerning all things to be right; and I hate every false way.**
For this cause all thy precepts concerning all things I deem right,
Every way of falsehood I hate — Rhm
Therefore I direct my steps by all thy precepts;
I hate every false way — RSV
Yes, I rule myself by all your precepts;
I hate all deceptive paths — Jerus
So I avow that all Your precepts are good;
I detest dishonest ways — Har

PE

129. **Thy testimonies are wonderful: therefore doth my soul keep them.**
Wonderful are your decrees;
therefore I observe them — NAB
Thy instruction is wonderful;
therefore I gladly keep it — NEB
Your decrees are so wonderful
my soul cannot but respect them — Jerus

130. **The entrance of thy words giveth light; it giveth understanding unto the simple.**
When thy word goeth forth, it giveth light and understanding unto the simple — PBV
The unfolding of thy words gives light,
Making the simple understand — ABPS
As your word unfolds, it gives light,
and the simple understand — Jerus
As your plan unfolds, even the simple can understand it — Tay
Thy word is revealed, and all is light; it gives understanding even to the untaught — NEB

131. **I opened my mouth, and panted: for I longed for thy commandments.**
My mouth was open wide, waiting with great desire for your teachings — Bas
With open mouth I pant,
because I long for thy commandments — RSV
I gasp with open mouth
in my yearning for your commands — NAB

132. **Look thou upon me, and be merciful unto me,**
Turn thyself unto me and shew me favour — Rhm
as thou usest to do unto those that love thy name.
As is befitting to the lovers of thy Name — Rhm
as is thy wont toward those who love thy name — RSV
as is your way with those who love you — Tay

133. **Order my steps in thy word; and let not any iniquity have dominion over me.**
Establish my footsteps in Thy word,
And let not any iniquity have dominion over me — DeW
Establish my footsteps by thy saying,
And let no wrong have power over me — AAT
Make my step firm according to thy promise,
and let no wrong have the mastery over me — NEB

134. Deliver me from the oppression of man: so will I keep thy precepts.
Redeem me from the oppression of man;
And I will observe thy precepts — ABPS
Rescue me from human oppression, that I may observe Your precepts — Har

135. Make thy face to shine upon thy servant; and teach me thy statutes.
Show the light of thy countenance upon thy servant, and teach me thy statutes — PBV
Restore to thy servant the smile of thy loving favour, and teach him to know thy will — Knox

136. Rivers of waters run down mine eyes, because they keep not thy law.
Mine eyes gush out with water, because men keep not thy law — PBV
My eyes shed streams of tears, because men do not keep thy law — RSV
With streams of water my eyes run down,
Over those who have not kept thy law — AAT

TZADDI

137. Righteous art thou, O LORD, and upright are thy judgments.
Righteous art thou O Yahweh, —
And equitable are thy regulations — Rhm
Thou art righteous, O LORD, and Thy judgments are fair — Ber
How just thou art, O LORD!
How straight and true are thy decrees! — NEB

138. Thy testimonies that thou hast commanded are righteous and very faithful.
Thou hast righteously commanded thy testimonies,
Yea in great faithfulness — Rhm
Strict justice and utter faithfulness inspire all thy decrees — Knox
How just is the instruction thou givest!
It is fixed firm and sure — NEB

139. My zeal hath consumed me, because mine enemies have forgotten thy words.
My zeal hath put an end to me,
For mine adversaries have forgotten thy words — Rhm
My enthusiasm devours me,
because my enemies forget Your injunctions — Har
I am indignant and angry because of the way my enemies have disregarded your laws — Tay

140. Thy word is very pure: therefore thy servant loveth it.
Refined is thy word to the uttermost,
And thy servant loveth it — Rhm
Thy promise has been tried to the utmost,
And thy servant loves it — AAT
Thy promise is well tried,
and thy servant loves it — RSV
I have thoroughly tested your promises and that is why I love them so much — Tay

141. I am small and despised: yet do not I forget thy precepts.
I am lowly, and regarded with contempt;
yet I have not forgotten Your precepts — Har
I am insignificant and despised, yet I do not forget Thy precepts — Ber
Puny and despised as I am,
I do not forget your precepts — Jerus

142. Thy righteousness is an everlasting righteousness, and thy law is the truth.
Thy righteousness is right for ever,
And Thy law is truth — DeW

143. Trouble and anguish have taken hold on me:
Trouble and anguish have overtaken me — JPS
Though distress and anguish have come upon me — NAB
Though distress and anguish grip me — Jerus
yet thy commandments are my delights.
yet I find joy in Your commandments — Har
thy commandments are my continual delight — NEB

144. The righteousness of thy testimonies is everlasting:
Thy testimonies are righteous for ever — RSV
Your laws are always fair — Tay
give me understanding, and I shall live.

Give me understanding, that I may live — DeW
give me discernment and I shall survive — Har

KOPH

145. I cried with my whole heart; hear me, O LORD:
With my whole heart I cry;
answer me, O LORD! — RSV
I have cried out with all my heart,
answer me, O Yahweh — Rhm
I will keep thy statutes.
146. I cried unto thee; save me, and I shall keep thy testimonies.
I implore You to save me,
that I may keep Your enactments — Har
147. I prevented the dawning of the morning, and cried:
I rise at dawn to beg Your assistance — Har
I rise before dawn and cry for help — RSV
I am up before the dawn that I may cry for help — DeW
I hoped in thy word.
I am trusting in Your promises — Har
I hope for the fulfilment of thy word — NEB
148. Mine eyes prevent the night watches, that I may meditate in thy word.
My eyes anticipate the nightwatches,
To meditate on thy sayings — ABPS
My eyes are awake before the watches of the night,
that I may meditate upon thy promise — RSV
I keep awake all through the night,
so as to meditate on your utterances — Har
I lie awake throughout the night,
to meditate on your promise — Jerus
149. Hear my voice according unto thy lovingkindness:
In Your mercy pay attention to my entreaty — Har
O LORD, quicken me according to thy judgment.
O Jehovah, according to thy judgments revive me — ABPS
O LORD, in thy justice preserve my life — RSV
150. They draw nigh that follow after mischief: they are far from thy law.
I am attacked by malicious persecutors
who are far from your law — NAB
My malicious persecutors are near me:
they are far removed from Your law — Har
My cruel persecutors are closing in,
how remote they are from your Law! — Jerus
151. Thou art near, O LORD; and all thy commandments are truth.
But Thou art near, O Jehovah!
And all Thy commandments are truth — DeW
152. Concerning thy testimonies, I have known of old that thou hast founded them for ever.
Long have I known from thy testimonies
that thou hast founded them for ever — RSV
Taught long since by thy decrees, I know well thou hast ordained them everlastingly — Knox
I have long seen that thy decrees are valid for all time — Mof

RESH

153. Consider mine affliction, and deliver me: for I do not forget thy law.
See my affliction, and rescue me;
For thy law I have not forgotten — ABPS
154. Plead my cause, and deliver me:
Plead thou my cause, and redeem me — ASV
Be thou my advocate and win release for me — NEB
quicken me according to thy word.
By thy word give me life — Rhm
give me life according to thy promise! — RSV
155. Salvation is far from the wicked: for they seek not thy statutes.
Such deliverance is beyond the reach of wicked men,
because they do not ponder thy statutes — NEB
156. Great are thy tender mercies, O LORD:
Thy compassions are great O Yahweh — Rhm
quicken me according to thy judgments.
According to thy regulations give me life — Rhm

give me life according to thy justice — RSV
grant me life by thy decree — NEB

157. Many are my persecutors and mine enemies; yet do I not decline from thy testimonies.
Yet have I not swerved from thy testimonies — ASV

158. I beheld the transgressors, and was grieved; because they kept not thy word.
I have seen traitors and felt loathing, Because thy word they kept not — Rhm
I look at the faithless with disgust, because they do not keep thy commands — RSV

159. Consider how I love thy precepts:
See how I love thy precepts — ABPS
quicken me, O LORD, according to thy lovingkindness.
O Yahweh according to thy lovingkindness give me life — Rhm
O Jehovah, according to thy mercy revive me — ABPS
Preserve my life according to thy steadfast love — RSV

160. Thy word is true from the beginning:
The sum of thy word is truth — Rhm
Your sayings are supremely true — Har
and every one of thy righteous judgments endureth for ever.
And every one of thy righteous ordinances endureth for ever — ASV
and your upright decision is unchanging for ever — Bas

SHIN

161. Princes have persecuted me without a cause:
Rulers have persecuted me without cause — Rhm
The powers that be persecute me without cause — NEB
but my heart standeth in awe of thy word.
But because of Thy word my heart vibrated with joy — Sprl
yet my heart thrills at thy word — NEB

162. I rejoice at thy word, as one that findeth great spoil.
Joyful am I over thy word, Like the finder of spoil in abundance — Rhm
I am overjoyed at Your promise, like one who discovers a hoard of treasures — Har
I rejoice in your promise, like someone on finding a vast treasure — Jerus

163. I hate and abhor lying: but thy law do I love.
Falsehood I hate and abhor; Thy law do I love — ABPS

164. Seven times a day do I praise thee because of thy righteous judgments.
Seven times in the day have I praised thee, for thy righteous regulations — Rhm
Seven times a day do I give you praise, because of your upright decisions — Bas

165. Great peace have they which love thy law: and nothing shall offend them.
Blessing in abundance have the lovers of thy law, And nothing to make them stumble — Rhm
Peace is the reward of those who love thy law; no pitfalls beset their path — NEB

166. LORD, I have hoped for thy salvation, and done thy commandments.

167. My soul hath kept thy testimonies; and I love them exceedingly.
I have kept Your enactments; I cherish them dearly — Har
Gladly I heed thy instruction and love it greatly — NEB

168. I have kept thy precepts and thy testimonies: for all my ways are before thee.
Vigilantly I observe precept and bidding of thine, living always as in thy sight — Knox
I observe Your principles and Your injunctions, for all my behavior is evident to You — Har
I heed thy precepts and thy instruction, for all my life lies open before thee — NEB

TAU

169. Let my cry come near before thee, O LORD:
Let my shouting come near before thee O Yahweh — Rhm

Let my entreaty reach You, Lord — Har
O Lord, listen to my prayers — Tay
give me understanding according to thy word.
enlighten me as thou hast promised — Mof
let your word endow me with perception! — Jerus
give me the common sense you promised — Tay

170. Let my supplication come before thee:
May my entreaty reach your presence — Jerus
deliver me according to thy word.
rescue me, as You have promised — Har

171. My lips shall utter praise, when thou hast taught me thy statutes.
My lips shall pour forth praise;
For thou wilt teach me thy statutes — ABPS
My lips pour forth a song of praise,
That Thou teachest me Thy statutes — DeW
I praise you for letting me learn your laws — Tay

172. My tongue shall speak of thy word: for all thy commandments are righteousness.
My tongue will sing of thy word, for all thy commandments are right — RSV

173. Let thine hand help me; for I have chosen thy precepts.
Let Thy hand be ready to help me;
For I have chosen Thy precepts — JPS

174. I have longed for thy salvation, O LORD;
I long for thy deliverance, O LORD — NEB
and thy law is my delight.
Your law is my joy — Har

175. Let my soul live, and it shall praise thee;
If you will let me live, I will praise you — Tay
May I live to praise You — Har
Long may my soul live to praise you — Jerus
and let thy judgments help me.
let thy decrees be my support — NEB
So shall thy regulation help me — Rhm
and may Your enactments uphold me — Har
long be your rulings my help! — Jerus

176. I have gone astray like a lost sheep; seek thy servant;
When I go astray like a lost sheep,
seek Thy servant — DeW
for I do not forget thy commandments.
for I have not turned away from your commandments — Tay

PSALM 120

A Song of Degrees.
A Song of Ascents — Rhm
A Song of the going up — Bas
Pilgrim Song — ABPS
A SONG FOR THE PILGRIMAGES — DeW

1. In my distress I cried unto the LORD, and he heard me.
When I am in trouble, I call to Yahweh, and he answers me — Jerus
In my distress I cry to the LORD,
that he may answer me — RSV

2. Deliver my soul, O LORD, from lying lips, and from a deceitful tongue,
"Deliver me, O LORD,
from lying lips,
from a deceitful tongue" — RSV

3. What shall be given unto thee? or what shall be done unto thee, thou false tongue?
What will you get from Him, O crafty tongue, what punishment in full? — Mof
O lying tongue, what shall be your fate — Tay

4. Sharp arrows of the mighty, with coals of juniper.
The arrows of the hero sharpened,
With burning coals of broom — Rhm
Arrows of the mighty, sharpened,
together with coals of broomwood — DeW
He will inflict sharpened arrows of the warrior,
with glowing embers of the broom tree — Har

You shall be pierced with sharp arrows and burned with glowing coals — Tay

5. Woe is me, that I sojourn in Mesech, that I dwell in the tents of Kedar!

Alas for me, that I sojourn in Mesech,
That I dwell with the tents of Kedar — ABPS

Woe is me, that I sojourn with Meshech, that I dwell beside the tents of Kedar [as if among notoriously barbarous people] — Amp

Hard is my lot, exiled in Meshech,
dwelling by the tents of Kedar — NEB

6. My soul hath long dwelt with him that hateth peace.

Too long have I had my dwelling
among those who hate peace — RSV

7. I am for peace: but when I speak, they are for war.

I myself uphold peace;
but when I say anything, they are anxious for war — Har

PSALM 121

A Song of degrees.[36]

1. I will lift up mine eyes unto the hills, from whence cometh my help.

I lift mine eyes to the mountains; ah, where is help to come from? — Mof

I will lift up my eyes to the hills [around Jerusalem, to sacred Mount Zion and Mount Moriah]. From whence shall my help come? — Amp

Shall I lift up mine eyes unto the hills?
Cometh my help from thence? — Sprl

Shall I look to the mountain gods for help? — Tay

2. My help cometh from the LORD, which made heaven and earth.

No! My help is from Jehovah who made the mountains! And the heavens too! — Tay

Help comes only from the LORD,
maker of heaven and earth — NEB

3. He will not suffer thy foot to be moved: he that keepeth thee will not slumber.

May he not suffer thy foot to slip,
May thy keeper not slumber — Rhm

Never will he let you slip; he who guards you never sleeps — Mof

4. Behold, he that keepeth Israel shall neither slumber nor sleep.

He who guards Israel
neither dozes nor sleeps — Har

The guardian of Israel
never slumbers, never sleeps — NEB

5. The LORD is thy keeper: the LORD is thy shade upon thy right hand.

The LORD himself is thy keeper; the LORD is thy defence upon thy right hand — PBV

The LORD is your guardian; the LORD is your shade;
he is beside you at your right hand — NAB

JEHOVAH is thy Preserver;
JEHOVAH is thy Protector: He is on thy right hand — Sprl

The Lord will keep thee! The Lord at thy right hand will be thy shelter — Sept

The Lord is your protection;
the Lord is a ready shelter — Har

6. The sun shall not smite thee by day, nor the moon by night.

So that the sun shall not burn thee by day, neither the moon by night — PBV

The sun shall not harm you by day,
nor the moon by night — NAB

7. The LORD shall preserve thee from all evil: he shall preserve thy soul.

Yahweh will keep thee from all harm,
He will keep thy life — Rhm

The Lord will guard you from all evil;
He will protect your life — Har

8. The LORD shall preserve thy going out and thy coming in from this time forth, and even for evermore.

The LORD will guard your goings and comings
henceforth and forever — AAT

The Lord will keep you secure as you come and go,
now and forever — Har

he will protect you as you come and go, now and for evermore — Mof

[36]See Psalm 120.

PSALM 122

A Song of degrees of David.
A Song of Ascents. David's — Rhm
A pilgrim song, by David — Mof

1. **I was glad when they said unto me, Let us go into the house of the LORD.**
I was glad when they said to me,
"Let us go to the house of the LORD!" — RSV
I rejoiced when they said . . . — JPS
2. **Our feet shall stand within thy gates, O Jerusalem.**
Our feet have come to stand
Within thy gates, O Jerusalem! — DeW
And now we have set foot
within your gates, O Jerusalem — NAB
3. **Jerusalem is builded as a city that is compact together:**
4. **Whither the tribes go up, the tribes of the LORD, unto the testimony of Israel, to give thanks unto the name of the LORD.**
Jerusalem built as a city
which is bound firmly together,
to which the tribes go up,
the tribes of the LORD,
as was decreed for Israel,
to give thanks to the name of the LORD — RSV
Jerusalem restored! The city,
one united whole!
Here the tribes come up,
the tribes of Yahweh,
they come to praise Yahweh's name,
as he ordered Israel — Jerus
Jerusalem that is now rebuilt, a city solid and unbroken.
Thither go the clans on pilgrimage, the Eternal's clans,
to offer the Eternal praise, as he prescribed for Israel — Mof
Jerusalem that is built to be a city
where people come together in unity;
to which the tribes resort, the tribes of the LORD,
to give thanks to the LORD himself,
the bounden duty of Israel — NEB
5. **For there are set thrones of judgment, the thrones of the house of David.**
For there are set —
Thrones for justice,
Thrones for the house of David — Rhm
For there were located seats of judgment,
the thrones of the Davidic house — Har
For there seats for the judges were placed, even the rulers' seats of the line of David — Bas
For in her are set the thrones of justice,
the thrones of the house of David — NEB
6. **Pray for the peace of Jerusalem: they shall prosper that love thee.**
7. **Peace be within thy walls, and prosperity within thy palaces.**
Pray for the welfare of Jerusalem,
"May all thy homes be safe,
may all go well within thy walls,
within thy palaces!" — Mof
Pray for the peace of Jerusalem!
"May they prosper who love you!
Peace be within your walls,
and security within your towers!" — RSV
Pray for the peace of Jerusalem!
May those who love you prosper!
May peace be within your walls,
prosperity in your buildings — NAB
8. **For my brethren and companions' sakes, I will now say, Peace be within thee.**
For the sake of my friends and fellows
I pray, "May all be well with thee!" — Mof
9. **Because of the house of the LORD our God I will seek thy good.**
For the sake of the house of our God the Eternal, I would have thee prosper — Mof

PSALM 123

A Song of degrees.[37]

1. **Unto thee lift I up mine eyes, O thou that dwellest in the heavens.**
To thee I lift up my eyes,
O thou who art enthroned in the heavens! — RSV
2. **Behold, as the eyes of servants look**

[37] See Psalm 120.

unto the hand of their masters, and as the eyes of a maiden unto the hand of her mistress;

As the eyes of a slave follow his master's hand
or the eyes of a slave-girl her mistress — NEB

so our eyes wait upon the LORD our God, until that he have mercy upon us.

so our eyes look to the LORD our God, till he have mercy upon us — RSV
so our eyes are turned to the LORD our God
waiting for kindness from him — NEB

3. Have mercy upon us, O LORD, have mercy upon us: for we are exceedingly filled with contempt.

. . . for we have had more than enough of contempt — RSV
. . . for we are swamped with contempt — Har
. . . we have had more than our share of scorn — Jerus

4. Our soul is exceedingly filled with the scorning of those that are at ease, and with the contempt of the proud.

Filled to the full is our soul
With the derision of the arrogant,
With the contempt of the proud — DeW
too long have we had to suffer
the insults of the wealthy,
the scorn of proud men — NEB

PSALM 124

A Song of degrees of David.[38]

1. If it had not been the LORD who was on our side, now may Israel say;

2. If it had not been the LORD who was on our side, when men rose up against us:

If Yahweh had not been on our side
— let Israel repeat it —
if Yahweh had not been on our side
when they attacked us — Jerus

3. Then they had swallowed us up quick, when their wrath was kindled against us:

they would have swallowed us alive,
so fierce their anger flamed — Mof

4. Then the waters had overwhelmed us, the stream had gone over our soul:

then the flood would have swept us away,
the torrent would have gone over us — RSV
The waters would have closed over us,
the torrent have swept us away — Jerus

5. Then the proud waters had gone over our soul.

then over us would have gone the raging waters — RSV

6. Blessed be the LORD, who hath not given us as a prey to their teeth.

But, blessed be the Eternal!
he did not leave us for their teeth to tear — Mof
May the Lord be blessed,
for not abandoning us as prey for them to devour — Har

7. Our soul is escaped as a bird out of the snare of the fowlers:

We have escaped with our lives as a bird from a hunter's snare — Tay

the snare is broken, and we are escaped.

the net is broken, and we are free — Bas

8. Our help is in the name of the LORD, who made heaven and earth.

Our help lies in the Eternal,
who made heaven and earth! — Mof
We are helped by the power of the Lord,
who made heaven and earth — Har

PSALM 125

A Song of degrees.[39]

1. They that trust in the LORD shall be as mount Zion, which cannot be removed, but abideth for ever.

Those who trust in Yahweh are like Mount Zion,
unshakeable, standing for ever — Jerus

2. As the mountains are round about Jerusalem, so the LORD is round

[38] See Psalm 122.

[39] See Psalm 120.

about his people from henceforth even for ever.
As the hills enfold Jerusalem,
so the LORD enfolds his people, now and evermore — NEB
The hills protect Jerusalem; so the Lord protects his people, now and for ever — Knox

3. For the rod of the wicked shall not rest upon the lot of the righteous;
For the sceptre of lawlessness shall not remain over the allotment of the righteous — Rhm
For the scepter of wickedness shall not rest
upon the land allotted to the righteous — RSV
No evil power will be allowed to hold sway
over the land allotted to the virtuous — Har

lest the righteous put forth their hands unto iniquity.
lest the righteous put forth
their hands to do wrong — RSV
so that the upright will not hanker after evil — Har
lest the godly be forced to do wrong — Tay
or else just men themselves might take to evil — Mof

4. Do good, O LORD, unto those that be good, and to them that are upright in their hearts.
Deal kindly, Lord, with the kindly, with the true-hearted — Knox
Prosper those who are good, Lord;
the ones who are morally upright — Har

5. As for such as turn aside unto their crooked ways, the LORD shall lead them forth with the workers of iniquity:
But those that turn aside in their crooked ways —
Jehovah will put them away
With the workers of iniquity — DeW
But those who turn aside into crooked ways,
may the LORD destroy them, as he destroys all evildoers! — NEB
As for those who become attracted to dishonest enterprises,
the Lord will lead them away along with the evildoers — Har

but peace shall be upon Israel.
Peace be upon Israel! — ABPS
Prosperity on Israel! — Rhm

PSALM 126

A Song of degrees.[40]

1. When the LORD turned again the captivity of Zion, we were like them that dream.
When Yahweh brought Zion's captives home,
at first it seemed like a dream — Jerus
When the Lord brought back the captives who returned to Zion, we were like those who dream [it seemed so unreal] — Amp
When the Lord restores the fortunes of captive Zion,
it will be like being in a dream — Har

2. Then was our mouth filled with laughter, and our tongue with singing:
Then was our mouth filled with laughter,
And our tongue with a shout of triumph — Rhm
in every mouth was laughter, joy was on every tongue — Knox
Our mouths will be full of laughter,
and our tongues with exclamations of joy — Har

then said they among the heathen, the LORD hath done great things for them.
Among the heathen themselves it was said, What favour the Lord has shewn them! — Knox
Then word went round among the nations,
'The LORD has done great things for them' — NEB
Even the pagans started talking
about the marvels Yahweh had done for us! — Jerus

3. The LORD hath done great things for us; whereof we are glad.
Yahweh hath done great things with us
We are full of joy! — Rhm
Yes, great things he had done for us, and we rejoiced at it — Mof

[40]See Psalm 120.

What marvels indeed he did for us,
and how overjoyed we were! — Jerus

4. Turn again our captivity, O LORD, as the streams in the south.

Restore our fortunes, O LORD, like the watercourses in the Negeb! — RSV

O thou Eternal, bring back now the rest of our exiles,
to fill us up, like streams in the dry south — Mof

Deliver us, Lord, from our bondage; our withered hopes, Lord, like some desert water-course renew! — Knox

5. They that sow in tears shall reap in joy.

They who are sowing with tears
With shouting shall reap — Rhm

Let them who sow with tears reap with rapture — Sept

May those who sow in tears
Reap with shouts of joy! — AAT

6. He that goeth forth and weepeth, bearing precious seed, shall doubtless come again with rejoicing, bringing his sheaves with him.

They went step by step and wept sowing their seed; but let them come tripping with joy, carrying their sheaves — Sept

They went away, went away weeping,
carrying the seed;
they come back, come back singing,
carrying their sheaves — Jerus

Although they go forth weeping,
carrying the seed to be sown,
They shall come back rejoicing,
carrying their sheaves — NAB

He who goes forth bearing seed and weeps [at needing his precious supply of grain for sowing], shall doubtless come again with rejoicing, bringing his sheaves with him — Amp

A man may go out weeping,
carrying his bag of seed;
but he will come back with songs of joy,
carrying home his sheaves — NEB

PSALM 127

A Song of degrees for Solomon.
Pilgrim Song of Solomon — ABPS
A pilgrim song, by Solomon — Mof

1. Except the LORD build the house, they labour in vain that build it:

If JEHOVAH buildeth not up the house,
The builders thereof labour fruitlessly — Sprl

Unless the Lord builds a house, the builders' work is useless — Tay

If the Lord is not helping the builders, then the building of a house is to no purpose — Bas

except the LORD keep the city, the watchman waketh but in vain.

If Yahweh watch not the city
In vain hath the watchmen kept awake — Rhm

If Jehovah keep not the city,
The keeper watches in vain — ABPS

unless the Eternal guards the town,
sentries are on guard in vain — Mof

vainly the guard keeps watch, if the city has not the Lord for its guardian — Knox

2. It is vain for you to rise up early, to sit up late, to eat the bread of sorrows:

Vain for you —
To be early in rising
To be late in lying down
To be eating the bread of wearisome toil — Rhm

Vain is it to rise early for your work,
and keep at work so late,
gaining your bread with anxious toil! —Mof

It is a waste of time for you to get up early,
and to go to bed late at night,
and eat hard-earned bread — Har

In vain you get up earlier,
and put off going to bed,
sweating to make a living — Jerus

It is senseless for you to work so hard from early morning until late at night, fearing you will starve to death — Tay

for so he giveth his beloved sleep.

For in their sleep, even thus He giveth to His beloved — DeW

since he provides for his beloved as they sleep — Jerus

for He gives [blessings] to His beloved in sleep — Amp

he supplies the need of those he loves — NEB

for God wants his loved ones to get their proper rest — Tay

3. Lo, children are an heritage of the

LORD: and the fruit of the womb is his reward.

Lo, sons are a heritage from Jehovah;
The fruit of the womb is a reward — ABPS

Behold, children are a legacy from the LORD;
the fruit of the womb is His reward — Ber

Sons are a gift of the Eternal,
and children are a boon from him — Mof

Fatherhood itself is the Lord's gift, the fruitful womb is a reward that comes from him — Knox

4. **As arrows are in the hand of a mighty man; so are children of the youth.**

As arrows in the hand of a warrior,
So are the children of young men — Rhm

As arrows in the hand of a mighty man,
So are the children of one's youth — JPS

Strong sons, born when one is young,
are like arrows in an archer's hand — Mof

like the arrows in a hero's hand are the sons you father when young — Jerus

5. **Happy is the man that hath his quiver full of them:**

How happy the man who hath filled his quiver with them! — Rhm

O the blessedness of the man,
That hath filled his quiver with them! — DeW

Happy the man who has filled his quiver
with arrows of this sort — Jerus

they shall not be ashamed, but they shall speak with the enemies in the gate.

They shall not come to shame,
When they speak with enemies in the gate — DeW

they will not feel humiliated when they dispute with their enemies in court — Har

in dispute with his enemies at the gate,
he will not be worsted — Jerus

such men shall not be put to shame
when they confront their enemies in court — NEB

PSALM 128

A Song of degrees.[41]

1. **Blessed is every one that feareth the LORD; that walketh in his ways.**

How happy is every one that revereth Yahweh,
Who walketh in his ways! — Rhm

Happy indeed is everyone who reveres the Lord,
and conducts himself according to His stipulations — Har

2. **For thou shalt eat the labour of thine hands: happy shalt thou be, and it shall be well with thee.**

Of the toil of your hands you shall eat;
Happy and prosperous shall you be! — AAT

You will eat what your hands have worked for,
happiness and prosperity will be yours — Jerus

3. **Thy wife shall be as a fruitful vine by the sides of thine house: thy children like olive plants round about thy table.**

Your wife will be like a fruitful vine within your house;
your children will be like olive shoots around your table — RSV

Thy wife shall be fruitful as a vine, in the heart of thy home, the children round thy table sturdy as olive-branches — Knox

Your wife shall be like a prolific vine
in the recesses of your dwelling;
your children around your table
like olive-shoots — Har

4. **Behold, that thus shall the man be blessed that feareth the LORD.**

This is the sort of blessing
which comes to the man who reverences the Lord — Har

5. **The LORD shall bless thee out of Zion: and thou shalt see the good of Jerusalem all the days of thy life.**

The LORD bless you from Zion!
And may you look upon the welfare of Jerusalem
All the days of your life! — AAT

May the Lord who dwells in Sion bless thee; mayest thou see Jerusalem in prosperity all thy life long — Knox

May the LORD bless you from Zion;
may you share the prosperity of Jerusalem

[41] See Psalm 120.

all the days of your life — NEB

6. Yea, thou shalt see thy children's children, and peace upon Israel.

Mayest thou live to see thy children's children, and peace resting upon Israel — Knox

May you live to see your grandchildren.
Let peace rest upon Israel — Har

PSALM 129

A Song of degrees.[42]

1. Many a time have they afflicted me from my youth, may Israel now say:

2. Many a time have they afflicted me from my youth: yet they have not prevailed against me.

Many a time have they harrassed me from my youth,
Well may Israel say:
Many a time have they harrassed me from youth,
Yet have they not prevailed against me — Rhm

"They have oppressed me dreadfully from my early days,"
Israel may well say;
"They have oppressed me dreadfully from my early days,
yet they have not overcome me — Har

Hard as they have harried me since I was young
— let Israel repeat it —
hard as they have harried me since I was young,
they have not overcome me — Jerus

3. The plowers plowed upon my back: they made long their furrows.

Upon my back the wicked hammered, they prolonged their iniquity — Sept

I bent my back to the oppressor, and long was the furrow ere the plow turned — Knox

They have plowed over my prostrate form,
making long furrows like plowmen — Har

They scored my back with scourges,
like ploughmen driving long furrows — NEB

4. The LORD is righteous: he hath cut asunder the cords of the wicked.

but the Lord proved faithful, and cut the bonds of tyranny asunder — Knox

but now Yahweh the Righteous has shattered
the yoke of the wicked — Jerus

Yet the LORD in his justice
has cut me loose from the bonds of the wicked — NEB

5. Let them all be confounded and turned back that hate Zion.

Let all who hate Zion be ashamed and shrink back — Rhm

May all who hate Zion
be disgraced and dispersed — Har

May they all be thrown into confusion, be routed,
who have hated Zion — Jerus

6. Let them be as the grass upon the housetops, which withereth afore it groweth up:

Let them become like grass upon the housetops,
That withereth before it is full grown — DeW

Let them be as the grass upon the house tops, which pulls out and withers when the wind strikes it — Lam

be blasted by winds from the east like grass
sprouting on the roof! — Jerus

7. Wherewith the mower filleth not his hand; nor he that bindeth sheaves his bosom.

Wherewith no reaper hath filled his hand
Nor binder his bosom — Rhm

8. Neither do they which go by say, The blessing of the LORD be upon you: we bless you in the name of the LORD.

Neither have the passers-by ever said
The blessing of Yahweh be unto you, —
We have blessed you in the Name of Yahweh — Rhm

so that passers-by will never say to them,
'The blessing of the LORD be upon you!
We bless you in the name of the LORD' — NEB

[42] See Psalm 120.

PSALM 130

A Song of degrees.[43]

1. **Out of the depths have I cried unto thee, O LORD.**
Out of the depths I cry to thee, O LORD! — RSV

2. **Lord, hear my voice: let thine ears be attentive to the voice of my supplications.**

3. **If thou, LORD, shouldest mark iniquities, O Lord, who shall stand?**
If thou, Jehovah, shouldest mark iniquities,
O Lord, who could stand? — ASV
If thou didst keep strict tally of sins,
O Lord, who could live on — Mof
If You, Lord, were to record sin,
who could possibly survive, Lord? — Har

4. **But there is forgiveness with thee, that thou mayest be feared.**
But forgiveness is part of Your nature,
in order that You may be reverenced — Har
Ah, but with thee there is forgiveness;
be thy name ever revered — Knox
But in thee is forgiveness,
and therefore thou art revered — NEB

5. **I wait for the LORD, my soul doth wait, and in his word do I hope.**
I am trusting in the Lord;
my whole being is confident.
I have faith in His promise — Har

6. **My soul waiteth for the Lord more than they that watch for the morning: I say, more than they that watch for the morning.**
My soul fleeth unto the Lord before the morning watch; I say, before the morning watch — PBV
my soul relies on the Lord
more than a watchman on the coming of dawn — Jerus

7. **Let Israel hope in the LORD:**
O Israel, hope in Jehovah — ASV
Wait O Israel for Yahweh — Rhm
for with the LORD there is mercy, and with him is plenteous redemption.
For with Jehovah there is lovingkindness,
And with him is plenteous redemption — ASV
for with the Eternal there is love,
there is a wealth of saving power — Mof
For in the LORD is love unfailing,
and great is his power to set men free — NEB
for with the Lord is mercy and full salvation — Bas

8. **And he shall redeem Israel from all his iniquities.**
And he, he will redeem Israel,
From all his iniquities — ABPS
He alone will set Israel free
from all their sins — NEB
For he will redeem Israel
From all its guilt — AAT

PSALM 131

A Song of degrees of David.[44]

1. **LORD, my heart is not haughty, nor mine eyes lofty:**
I am not arrogant in disposition, Lord;
my attitude is not that of pride — Har
Yahweh, my heart has no lofty ambitions,
my eyes do not look too high — Jerus
neither do I exercise myself in great matters, or in things too high for me.
neither do I exercise myself in great matters, or in things too wonderful for me — RV
Nor do I concern myself with things too great,
And with things too difficult for me — ABPS
I never meddle with high schemes,
with matters far beyond me — Mof
my mind does not dwell on high things,
on marvels that are beyond my reach — Knox
I busy not myself with great things,
nor with things too sublime for me — NAB
I am not concerned with great affairs
or marvels beyond my scope — Jerus

[43] See Psalm 120.
[44] See Psalm 122.

2. Surely I have behaved and quieted myself, as a child that is weaned of his mother: my soul is even as a weaned child.

But I have calmed and quieted my spirit,
As a weaned child on its mother;
As the weaned child is my spirit within me — ABPS

But I have calmed and quieted my soul, like a child quieted at its mother's breast;
like a child that is quieted is my soul — RSV

No, I have soothed and stilled my soul, as a mother calms her weaned child;
my soul is like a weaned child — Mof

Surely I have calmed and quieted my soul, like a weaned child with his mother; like a weaned child is my soul within me [ceased from fretting] — Amp

3. Let Israel hope in the LORD from henceforth and for ever.

O Israel, hope in Jehovah
From this time forth and for evermore — ASV

Israel, rely on Yahweh,
now and for always! — Jerus

PSALM 132

A Song of degrees.[45]

1. LORD, remember David, and all his afflictions:

Remember, O LORD, for David
all his anxious care — NAB

Remember, O LORD, for David's sake,
All his affliction — AAT

Remember, O LORD, in David's favor,
all the hardships he endured — RSV

O LORD, remember David
in the time of his adversity — NEB

Yahweh, remember David
and all the hardships he suffered — Jerus

2. How he sware unto the LORD, and vowed unto the mighty God of Jacob;

3. Surely I will not come into the tabernacle of my house, nor go up into my bed;

4. I will not give sleep to mine eyes, or slumber to mine eyelids,

5. Until I find out a place for the LORD, an habitation for the mighty God of Jacob.

how he swore to the LORD
and vowed to the Mighty One of Jacob,
"I will not enter my house
or get into my bed;
I will not give sleep to my eyes
or slumber to my eyelids,
until I find a place for the LORD,
a dwelling place for the Mighty One of Jacob" — RSV

and the oath he swore to Yahweh,
his vow to the Mighty One of Jacob:
not to enter tent or house,
not to climb into bed,
not to allow himself to sleep,
not even to close his eyes,
until he had found a place for Yahweh,
a home for the Mighty One of Jacob! — Jerus

6. Lo, we heard of it at Ephratah: we found it in the fields of the wood.

Lo, we heard that it was in Ephrathah;
We found it in the fields of Jaar — AAT

We heard of one in Ephrathah;
we discovered it on the property of Jaar — Har

Lo at Ephratah we [first] heard of [the discovered ark]; we found it in the fields of the wood — at [Kiriath-] Jearim — Amp

First the Ark was in Ephrathah, then in the distant countryside of Jaar — Tay

7. We will go into his tabernacles: we will worship at his footstool.

Let us enter His tabernacles,
Let us worship at His footstool — DeW

But now it will be settled in the Temple, in God's permanent home here on earth. That is where we will go to worship him — Tay

8. Arise, O LORD, into thy rest; thou, and the ark of thy strength.

Arise, O Lord, to Your resting place,
You and the ark [the symbol] of Your strength — Amp

Arise, Lord, and enter Your shrine,
You and Your mighty ark — Har

[45] See Psalm 120.

9. Let thy priests be clothed with righteousness; and let thy saints shout for joy.
Let Thy priests array themselves in righteousness,
And Thy beloved shout aloud for joy — DeW
May your priests be clothed with justice;
let your faithful ones shout merrily for joy — NAB
Let Your priests be clothed with righteousness [right living and right standing with God], and let Your saints shout for joy! — Amp

10. For thy servant David's sake turn not away the face of thine anointed.
For the sake of Your servant David,
do not reject Your anointed one — Har
Do not reject your servant David —
the king you chose for your people — Tay

11. The LORD hath sworn in truth unto David; he will not turn from it; Of the fruit of thy body will I set upon thy throne.

12. If thy children will keep my covenant and my testimony that I shall teach them, their children shall also sit upon thy throne for evermore.
The Lord swore to David a sure oath
from which he will not turn back:
"One of the sons of your body
I will set on your throne.
If your sons keep my covenant
and my testimonies which I shall teach them,
their sons also for ever
shall sit upon your throne" — RSV

13. For the Lord hath chosen Zion; he hath desired it for his habitation.
For Yahweh hath chosen Zion, —
He hath desired it as a dwelling for himself: — Rhm

14. This is my rest for ever: here will I dwell; for I have desired it.
This is my resting-place for ever:
Here will I dwell; for I have desired it — ASV
"Zion is my resting place forever;
in her will I dwell, for I prefer her — NAB

15. I will abundantly bless her provision: I will satisfy her poor with bread.
I will enrich her food-supplies, and satisfy her poor with bread — Mof
I will bless her with abundant provision,
her poor I will fill with bread — NAB
I will richly bless its produce,
and give bread in abundance to its poor — Har

16. I will also clothe her priests with salvation: and her saints shall shout aloud for joy.
With salvation will I clothe her priests;
her loyal servants shall shout for joy — NEB
I will robe her priests in triumph, and make her worshippers shout for joy — Mof

17. There will I make the horn of David to bud:
I will make the power of David flourish in that place — Har
There will I make David's dynasty flourish — Mof
There will I renew the line of David's house — NEB

I have ordained a lamp for mine anointed.
I have prepared a lamp for mine Anointed One — Rhm
I have prepared great authority for My anointed one — Har
I have ordained and prepared a lamp for My anointed [fulfilling the promises of old] — Amp
and my chosen king shine prosperously — Mof
and light a lamp for my anointed king — NEB

18. His enemies will I clothe with shame: but upon himself shall his crown flourish.
His enemies will I clothe with shame,
But upon himself shall his crown be resplendent — Rhm
his foes I shroud with dark disgrace,
but his own crown shall sparkle — Mof
His enemies I will clothe with shame,
but upon himself his crown will shed its luster — RSV
I will cover his enemies with confusion; on his brow the crown I gave shall shine untarnished — Knox
I will cover his enemies with shame,
but his diadem will bring him renown — Har
I'll clothe his enemies with shame, but he shall be a glorious king — Tay

PSALM 133

A Song of degrees of David.[46]

1. **Behold, how good and how pleasant it is for brethren to dwell together in unity!**
Behold how delightful and how sweet it is
For brethren to dwell together in unity — Sprl
What a wonderful thing it is
when brothers live together in harmony — Har

2. **It is like the precious ointment upon the head, that ran down upon the beard, even Aaron's beard: that went down to the skirts of his garments;**
It is like the precious oil upon the head,
running down upon the beard,
upon the beard of Aaron,
running down on the collar of his robes! — RSV
It is fragrant as oil poured upon the head
and falling over the beard,
Aaron's beard, when the oil runs down
over the collar of his vestments — NEB

3. **As the dew of Hermon, and as the dew that descended upon the mountains of Zion:**
It is like the dew of Hermon,
which falls on the mountains of Zion! — RSV
Harmony is as refreshing as the dew on Mount Hermon, on the mountain of Israel — Tay
for there the LORD commanded the blessing, even life for evermore.
There the LORD bestows his blessing,
life for evermore — NEB
where Yahweh confers his blessing,
everlasting life — Jerus

PSALM 134

A Song of degrees.[47]

1. **Behold, bless ye the LORD, all ye servants of the LORD, which by night stand in the house of the LORD.**
Bless the Lord,
all you who are servants of the Lord;
who at night take your appointed places in the house of the Lord — Har
Come, bless the LORD,
all you servants of the LORD,
who stand night after night
in the house of the LORD — NEB

2. **Lift up your hands in the sanctuary, and bless the LORD.**
Lift up your hands to the holy place,
and bless the LORD! — RSV
Lift up your hands in holiness,
And bless Yahweh — Rhm

3. **The LORD that made heaven and earth bless thee out of Zion.**
May Yahweh bless thee out of Zion,
Even he that made heaven and earth — Rhm

PSALM 135

1. **Praise ye the LORD.**
Praise ye Yah — Rhm
Praise ye Jah! — YLT
Hallelujah — Mof
Praise ye the name of the LORD; praise him, O ye servants of the LORD.

2. **Ye that stand in the house of the LORD, in the courts of the house of our God,**
Praise ye the name of Jehovah;
Praise him, O ye servants of Jehovah,
Ye that stand in the house of Jehovah,
In the courts of the house of our God — ASV

3. **Praise the LORD; for the LORD is good: sing praises unto his name; for it is pleasant.**
Praise ye Yah
For good is Yahweh,
Sing praises to his Name,
For it is full of delight — Rhm
Hallelujah; for JEHOVAH is good;

---

[46] See Psalm 122.

[47] See Psalm 120.

Sing praises unto His Name, for it is delightful — Sprl

Praise the LORD, for that is good; honour his name with psalms, for that is pleasant — NEB

May God be praised.
The Lord is good; sing praise to His name,
for to do so is appropriate — Har

4. For the LORD hath chosen Jacob unto himself, and Israel for his peculiar treasure.

For why? the LORD hath chosen Jacob unto himself, and Israel for his own possession — PBV

The LORD has chosen Jacob to be his own
and Israel as his special treasure — NEB

5. For I know that the LORD is great, and that our Lord is above all gods.

Truly I am convinced that JEHOVAH is great,
And that our Lord is above all gods — Sprl

Doubt it never, the Lord is great; he, our master, is higher than all the gods — Knox

I have learnt for myself that Yahweh is great,
that our Lord surpasses all other gods — Jerus

6. Whatsoever the LORD pleased, that did he in heaven, and in earth, in the seas, and all deep places.

Whatever the LORD pleases he does,
in heaven and on earth,
in the seas and all deeps — RSV

In heaven and on earth, in the sea and in the deep waters beneath us, the Lord accomplishes his will — Knox

In the heavens, on the earth,
in the ocean, in the depths,
Yahweh's will is sovereign — Jerus

7. He causeth the vapours to ascend from the ends of the earth; he maketh lightnings for the rain; he bringeth the wind out of his treasuries.

He raises up clouds from the boundaries of the earth,
makes the lightning flash for the downpour
and brings the wind out of his storehouse — Jerus

He makes clouds rise from remote places on earth:
He causes lightning to flash amongst the rain clouds,
and produces the wind from its place of origin — Har

8. Who smote the firstborn of Egypt, both of man and beast.

He it was who smote the first-born of Egypt,
both of man and of beast — RSV

9. Who sent tokens and wonders into the midst of thee, O Egypt, upon Pharaoh, and upon all his servants.

who in thy midst, O Egypt,
sent signs and wonders
against Pharaoh and all his servants — RSV

10. Who smote great nations, and slew mighty kings;

He it was that smote nation after nation, and slew the kings in their pride — Knox

He struck the pagans down in droves,
he slaughtered mighty kings — Jerus

He battered powerful nations,
and destroyed mighty monarchs — Har

11. Sihon king of the Amorites, and Og king of Bashan, and all the kingdoms of Canaan:

12. And gave their land for an heritage, an heritage unto Israel his people.

. . . He apportioned their land as an inheritance;
it became a heritage for His people Israel — Har

. . . he gave their lands as a legacy,
a legacy to his people Israel — Jerus

13. Thy name, O LORD, endureth for ever; and thy memorial, O LORD, throughout all generations.

Your name is eternal, Lord;
Your renown, Lord, will exist through the ages — Har

Your name, O LORD, endures forever,
LORD is your title through all generations — NAB

Yahweh, your name endures for ever!
Yahweh, your memory is always fresh! — Jerus

14. For the LORD will judge his people, and he will repent himself concerning his servants.

For the LORD will vindicate his people,
and have compassion on his servants — RSV

The LORD will give his people justice

and have compassion on his servants — NEB

Since Yahweh vindicates his people, and cares for those who serve him — Jerus

15. The idols of the heathen are silver and gold, the work of men's hands.

The images of pagan nations are only silver and gold things, the product of human design — Har

16. They have mouths, but they speak not; eyes have they, but they see not;

17. They have ears, but they hear not; neither is there any breath in their mouths.

They have a mouth, but make no sound;
they have eyes, but they cannot see.
They possess ears, but they are deaf, nor have they any breath in their mouths — Har

18. They that make them are like unto them: so is every one that trusteth in them.

Those that make them become like unto them,
Yea, every one that trusteth in them — DeW

Their makers will end up like them and so will everyone who relies on them — Jerus

19. Bless the LORD, O house of Israel: bless the LORD, O house of Aaron:

20. Bless the LORD, O house of Levi: ye that fear the LORD, bless the LORD.

21. Blessed be the LORD out of Zion, which dwelleth at Jerusalem. Praise ye the LORD.

. . . Praise ye Yah! — Rhm

. . . Hallelujah! — Ber

PSALM 136

1. O give thanks unto the LORD; for he is good:

Oh give thanks unto Jehovah; for he is good — ASV

Give ye thanks to Yahweh
For he is good — Rhm

for his mercy endureth for ever.

For his lovingkindness endureth for ever — ASV

for his steadfast love endures for ever — RSV

for His covenant love is everlasting — Ber

He is eternally constant — Har

his love is everlasting! — Jerus

his kindness never fails — Mof

2. O give thanks unto the God of gods:

Give thanks to the supreme god — Har

for his mercy endureth for ever.*

3. O give thanks to the Lord of lords:

Give thanks to the supreme Lord — Har

for his mercy endureth for ever.*

4. To him who alone doeth great wonders:

He alone performs great marvels — Jerus

for his mercy endureth for ever.*

5. To him that by wisdom made the heavens:

To Him who skillfully fashioned the heavens — Har

for his mercy endureth for ever.*

6. To him that stretched out the earth above the waters:

He laid the earth upon the waters — NEB

for his mercy endureth for ever.*

7. To him that made great lights:

To Him who formed the great luminaries — Har

for his mercy endureth for ever:*

8. The sun to rule by day:

The sun to control the day — Har

for his mercy endureth for ever:*

9. The moon and stars to rule by night: for his mercy endureth for ever.*

10. To him that smote Egypt in their firstborn:

To Him who destroyed the firstborn of Egypt — Har

for his mercy endureth for ever:*

11. And brought out Israel from among them:

and brought forth Israel out of their midst — Rhm

for his mercy endureth for ever:*

12. With a strong hand, and with a stretched out arm:

With great might and protecting power — Har

*See verse 1.

for his mercy endureth for ever.*

13. To him which divided the Red sea into parts:

To Him who parted the Red Sea — Har

for his mercy endureth for ever:*

14. And made Israel to pass through the midst of it:

And conducted Israel across — Har

for his mercy endureth for ever:*

15. But overthrew Pharaoh and his host in the Red sea:

But tossed Pharaoh and his army into the Red Sea — Har

for his mercy endureth for ever.*

16. To him which led his people through the wilderness:

Who guided His people through the desert — Har

for his mercy endureth for ever.*

17. To him which smote great kings: for his mercy endureth for ever:*

18. And slew famous kings:

And slew majestic kings — Rhm

for his mercy endureth for ever:*

19. Sihon king of the Amorites: for his mercy endureth for ever:*

20. And Og the king of Bashan: for his mercy endureth for ever:*

21. And gave their land for an heritage:

He gave their lands as a legacy — Jerus

for his mercy endureth for ever:*

22. Even an heritage unto Israel his servant:

A possession to His servant Israel — Har

A legacy to his servant Israel — Jerus

for his mercy endureth for ever.*

23. Who remembered us in our low estate:

Who remembered us when we were humiliated — Har

Who remembered us when we were in trouble — PBV

for his mercy endureth for ever:*

24. And hath redeemed us from our enemies:

And freed us with force from our adversaries — Rhm

And rescued us from our adversaries — DeW

And has released us from our oppressors — Har

And snatched us from our oppressors — Jerus

for his mercy endureth for ever.*

25. Who giveth food to all flesh:

Who provides food for everyone — Har

for his mercy endureth for ever.*

26. O give thanks unto the God of heaven: for his mercy endureth for ever.*

PSALM 137

1. By the rivers of Babylon, there we sat down, yea, we wept, when we remembered Zion.

Beside the streams of Babylon
we sat and wept
at the memory of Zion — Jerus

By the streams of Babylon,
There we sat, and wept,
When we remembered Zion — ABPS

2. We hanged our harps upon the willows in the midst thereof.

We hung our harps there,
on the willow trees — Har

3. For there they that carried us away captive required of us a song; and they that wasted us required of us mirth, saying, Sing us one of the songs of Zion.

For there our captors asked of us songs,
Our tormentors asked of us gladness:
Sing for us one of the songs of Zion — DeW

For there our captors
required of us songs,
and our tormentors, mirth, saying,
"Sing us one of the songs of Zion!" — RSV

4. How shall we sing the LORD'S song in a strange land?

How shall we sing Jehovah's song
In a foreign land — ASV

How shall we sing the song of Yahweh,
on a foreign soil — Rhm

5. If I forget thee, O Jerusalem, let my right hand forget her cunning.

If I forget thee, O Jerusalem!
Let my right hand forget its power — DeW

If I forget you, O Jerusalem,
let my right hand wither! — RSV

6. If I do not remember thee, let my tongue cleave to the roof of my mouth; if I prefer not Jerusalem above my chief joy.

7. Remember, O LORD, the children of Edom in the day of Jerusalem; who said, Rase it, rase it, even to the foundation thereof.

---

*See verse 1.

Remember, Lord, how the sons of Edom triumphed when Jerusalem fell; O'erthrow it, they cried, o'erthrow it, till the very foundation is left bare — Knox

Remember, Lord, to the disadvantage of the Edomites,
the day when Jerusalem fell;
when they said,
"Strip it bare; raze it to its very foundations" —Har

Remember, O LORD, against the people of Edom
the day of Jerusalem's fall,
when they said, 'Down with it, down with it,
down to its very foundations!' — NEB

8. **O daughter of Babylon, who art to be destroyed; happy shall he be, that rewardeth thee as thou hast served us.**

O ruined daughter of Babylon, —
How happy the man who shall repay thee
Thy dealing wherewith thou didst deal with us! — Rhm

O daughter of Babylon, you destroyer, happy the man who shall repay you the evil you have done us! — NAB

Babylon, pitiless queen, blessed be the man who deals out to thee the measure thou hast dealt to us — Knox

9. **Happy shall he be, that taketh and dasheth thy little ones against the stones.**

How happy the man who shall snatch away
And dash thy children against the crag! — Rhm

A blessing on him who snatches your babes
and dashes them down on the rocks! — Mof

PSALM 138

A Psalm of David.

1. **I will praise thee with my whole heart: before the gods will I sing praise unto thee.**

I will give thanks with all my heart,
Before the messengers of God will I praise thee in song — Rhm

I will adore thee, O Lord, with my whole heart. And with instrumental musick sing to thee before angels — Sept

I will give Thee thanks with my whole heart,
In the presence of the mighty will I sing praises unto Thee — JPS

2. **I will worship toward thy holy temple, and praise thy name for thy lovingkindness and for thy truth:**

I bow down toward thy holy temple and give thanks to thy name for thy steadfast love and thy faithfulness — RSV

for thou hast magnified thy word above all thy name.

for thou hast magnified thy Name, and thy word, above all things — PBV

for thou hast exalted above everything thy name and thy word — RSV

for you have made great above all things
your name and your promise — NAB

your promise is even greater than your fame — Jerus

for your promises are backed by all the honor of your name — Tay

3. **In the day when I cried thou answeredst me, and strengthenedst me with strength in my soul.**

In the day I cried unto thee
Then didst thou answer me,
And didst excite me in my soul mightily — Rhm

In the day when I called, then thou didst answer me
Didst embolden me with strength in my soul — ABPS

On the occasion when I called
You answered me,
and bolstered my morale greatly — Har

When I called to thee thou didst answer me
and make me bold and valiant-hearted — NEB

4. **All the kings of the earth shall praise thee, O LORD, when they hear the words of thy mouth.**

All the monarchs of the earth will praise you, Lord,
when they have heard Your spoken promises — Har

5. Yea, they shall sing in the ways of the LORD: for great is the glory of the LORD.
Yea, they shall sing of the ways of Jehovah;
For great is the glory of Jehovah — ASV
And they shall sing of the ways of the LORD:
"Great is the glory of the LORD" — NAB

6. Though the LORD be high, yet hath he respect unto the lowly: but the proud he knoweth afar off.
For though Jehovah is high, yet hath he respect unto the lowly;
But the haughty he knoweth from afar — ASV
From far above, Yahweh sees the humble,
from far away he marks down the arrogant — Jerus
For the LORD, high as he is, cares for the lowly,
and from afar he humbles the proud — NEB

7. Though I walk in the midst of trouble, thou wilt revive me:
Though I walk in the midst of distress thou wilt give me life — Rhm
Though I am living in an antagonistic society,
You are safeguarding my life — Har
Though I must pass through the thick of trouble, thou wilt preserve me — Mof
thou shalt stretch forth thine hand against the wrath of mine enemies, and thy right hand shall save me.
Because of the anger of my foes thou wilt thrust forth thy hand,
And thy right hand will save me — Rhm
Against the wrath of my foes; thou dost stretch forth thy hand,
And thy right hand delivers me — AAT
You exert Your strength against my violent enemies,
and Your power saves me — Har

8. The LORD will perfect that which concerneth me: thy mercy, O LORD, endureth for ever:
Yahweh will carry through my cause, —
O Yahweh! thy lovingkindness is age-abiding — Rhm
The LORD will fulfil his purpose for me;
thy steadfast love, O LORD, endures for ever — RSV
forsake not the works of thine own hands.
do not abandon us whom you have made — Jerus
leave not thy work unfinished — NEB

PSALM 139

To the chief Musician, A Psalm of David.
From the Choirmaster's collection A song of David — Mof
To the choirmaster. A Psalm of David — RSV

1. O LORD, thou hast searched me, and known me.
O Yahweh! thou hast searched me and observed — Rhm
Jehovah, thou hast searched me, and thou knowest — ABPS

2. Thou knowest my downsitting and mine uprising, thou understandest my thought afar off.
Thou knowest when I sit down and when I rise up;
thou discernest my thoughts from afar — RSV
You know when I sit down and when I rise;
You are aware of my thoughts when scarcely formulated — Har

3. Thou compassest my path and my lying down, and art acquainted with all my ways.
My path and my couch hast thou examined,
And all my ways thou well knowest — Rhm
Walk I or sleep I, thou canst tell; no movement of mine but thou art watching it — Knox
You have analyzed my habits of business and relaxation alike;
you are familiar with my entire behavior — Har

4. For there is not a word in my tongue, but, lo, O LORD, thou knowest it altogether.
Surely there hath not been a word on my tongue, [But] behold! O Yah-

weh thou hast observed it on every side — Rhm

Even before a word is on my tongue, behold, O LORD, you know the whole of it — NAB

ere ever a word comes to my tongue, O thou Eternal, 'tis well known to thee — Mof

Before ever the words are framed on lips, all my thought is known to thee — Knox

5. Thou hast beset me behind and before, and laid thine hand upon me.

Behind and before hast thou shut me in,
And hast laid upon me thy hand — Rhm

Thou hast hemmed me in behind and before,
And laid Thy hand upon me — JPS

close behind and close in front you fence me round,
shielding me with your hand — Jerus

You have provided for every possible contingency,
sustaining me by Your power — Har

6 Such knowledge is too wonderful for me; it is high, I cannot attain unto it.

Knowledge too wonderful for me!
It is high, I do not comprehend it — ABPS

Knowledge too wonderful for me!
It is too high! I cannot reach it! — DeW

Such knowledge is beyond my understanding,
a height to which my mind cannot attain — Jerus

7. Whither shall I go from thy spirit? or whither shall I flee from thy presence?

Whither shall I go from thy Spirit?
Or whither shall I flee from thy presence? — ASV

To what place shall I withdraw from Your influence?
Where shall I retreat from Your presence? — Har

8. If I ascend up into heaven, thou art there: if I make my bed in hell, behold, thou art there.

If I make my bed in Sheol, behold, thou art there — ASV

If I make the underworld my bed, lo thou art there — ABPS

if I go down to the place of the dead, you are there — Tay

9. If I take the wings of the morning, and dwell in the uttermost parts of the sea;

If I take my flight to the frontiers of the morning
or dwell at the limit of the western sea — NEB

If I flew to the point of sunrise,
or westward across the sea — Jerus

10. Even there shall thy hand lead me, and thy right hand shall hold me.

Your power would guide me even there;
Your strength would uphold me — Har

even there thy hand will meet me
and thy right hand will hold me fast — NEB

11. If I say, Surely the darkness shall cover me; even the night shall be light about me.

12. Yea, the darkness hideth not from thee; but the night shineth as the day: the darkness and the light are both alike to thee.

If I say, Only let me be covered by the dark, and the light about me be night;
Even the dark is not dark to you; the night is as bright as the day: for dark and light are the same to you — Bas

If I asked darkness to cover me,
and light to become night around me,
that darkness would not be dark to you,
night would be as light as day — Jerus

13. For thou hast possessed my reins:

For Thou didst create my inmost being — DeW

For thou didst form my inward parts — ASV

thou hast covered me in my mother's womb.

Thou didst weave me together in the womb of my mother — Rhm

Thou didst fashion me in my mother's womb — AAT

and put me together in my mother's womb — Jerus

14. I will praise thee; for I am fearfully and wonderfully made: marvellous are thy works;

I praise thee for the awful wonder of my birth;
thy work is wonderful — Mof

I will give you praise, for I am strangely and delicately formed; your works are great wonders — Bas
I will praise thee, for thou dost fill me with awe;
wonderful thou art, and wonderful thy works — NEB
I praise thee, for thou art fearful and wonderful.
Wonderful are thy works! — RSV
Thank you for making me so wonderfully complex! It is amazing to think about. Your workmanship is marvelous — Tay

and that my soul knoweth right well.
I am well aware of it — Har
and how well I know it — Tay
Thou knowest me right well — RSV
Thou knowest me through and through — NEB
My soul also you knew full well — NAB

15. **My substance was not hid from thee, when I was made in secret, and curiously wrought in the lowest parts of the earth.**
My frame was not hidden from thee,
When I was made in secret,
Was curiously wrought [as] in the depths of the earth — ABPS
My frame was not hid from Thee,
When I was made in secret,
Skilfully wrought in the depths of the earth — DeW
My bones were not hidden from Thee
when I was made in secrecy
and intricately fashioned in utter seclusion — Ber
my body was no mystery to thee,
as I was being moulded secretly
and put together in the world below — Mof

16. **Thine eyes did see my substance, yet being unperfect; and in thy book all my members were written, which in continuance were fashioned, when as yet there was none of them.**
Your eyes saw my unformed substance;
in your book all my days were recorded, even those which were purposed before they had come into being — Bas
You perceived my shapeless substance;
in Your record were assessed the days that were intended for me,
before they ever existed — Har
Thou didst see my limbs unformed in the womb,
and in thy book they are all recorded;
day by day they were fashioned,
not one of them was late in growing — NEB
Thine eyes saw the sum total of my days,
And in thy book they were all written;
They were formed, when there was not one among them — AAT
You saw me before I was born and scheduled each day of my life before I began to breathe. Every day was recorded in your Book! — Tay
Your eyes have seen my actions;
in your book they are all written;
my days were limited before one of them existed — NAB

17. **How precious also are thy thoughts unto me, O God!**
To me then how precious have thy desires become O God! — Rhm
How weighty are your designs, O God — NAB
How immeasurable Your concepts are, my God — Har
God, how hard it is to grasp your thoughts! — Jerus
How deep I find thy thoughts, O God — NEB

how great is the sum of them!
How vast is the sum of them! — RSV
How impossible to count them! — Jerus
how inexhaustible their themes! — NEB

18. **If I should count them, they are more in number than the sand: when I awake, I am still with thee.**
I could no more count them than I could the sand,
and suppose I could, you would still be with me — Jerus
Were I to enumerate them,
they would outnumber the sands;
if I came to the end, I would still be with You — Har
Can I count them? They outnumber the grains of sand;
to finish the count, my years must equal thine — NEB

19. **Surely thou wilt slay the wicked, O God: depart from me therefore, ye bloody men.**
Wilt thou not slay the wicked, O God?
Depart from me, ye blood-thirsty men — PBV
O that thou wouldst slay the wicked, O God,

and that men of blood would depart from me — RSV
If only You would slaughter the wicked, my God,
and rid me of the murderers — Har
If Thou, O God, wouldst slay the ungodly,
then would bloodguilty men depart from me! — Ber
God, If only you would kill the wicked!
Men of blood, away from me! — Jerus

20. For they speak against thee wickedly, and thine enemies take thy name in vain.
Wickedly they invoke your name;
your foes swear faithless oaths — NAB
men who maliciously defy thee,
who lift themselves up against thee for evil! — RSV
Those who speak of Thee with crafty malice, they exalt themselves as Thy foes to no avail — Ber
They talk blasphemously about you, regard your thoughts as nothing — Jerus

21. Do not I hate them, O LORD, that hate thee?
How I hate them, O LORD, that hate thee! — NEB
and am not I grieved with those that rise up against thee?
And do I not loathe them that rise up against thee — RSV
I am cut to the quick when they oppose thee; — NEB

22. I hate them with perfect hatred: I count them mine enemies.
. . . utmost hatred . . . — JPS
With completeness of hatred I hate them,
As enemies have they become to me — Rhm
I abhor them with deep detestation;
I regard them as my enemies — Har
I hate them with a total hatred,
I regard them as my own enemies — Jerus

23. Search me, O God, and know my heart: try me, and know my thoughts:
God, examine me and know my heart,
probe me and know my thoughts — Jerus
Examine me, O God, and know my thoughts;
test me, and understand my misgivings — NEB

24. And see if there be any wicked way in me, and lead me in the way everlasting.
See whether there is any baneful motive within me,
and lead me on the everlasting way! — Ber
And see if there be any idol-way in me,
And lead me in a way age-abiding — Rhm
See if on any false paths my heart is set, and thyself lead me in the ways of old — Knox
Watch lest I follow any path that grieves thee;
guide me in the ancient ways — NEB

PSALM 140

To the chief Musician, A Psalm of David.[48]

1. Deliver me, O LORD, from the evil man: preserve me from the violent man;
Rescue me O Yahweh from the men of mischief,
From the men of violence wilt thou preserve me — Rhm

2. Which imagine mischiefs in their heart; continually are they gathered together for war.
who plan evil things in their heart,
and stir up wars continually — RSV
who scheme evil in their minds,
and are continually stirring up strife — Har

3. They have sharpened their tongues like a serpent; adders' poison is under their lips.
They make their tongue sharp as a serpent's,
and under their lips is the poison of vipers — RSV
Selah.
Selah [pause, and calmly think of that] — Amp

4. Keep me, O LORD, from the hands of the wicked; preserve me from the violent man; who have purposed to overthrow my goings.

[48]See Psalm 139.

Guard me O LORD, from the hands of the wicked;
preserve me from violent men,
who have planned to trip up my feet — RSV

5. The proud have hid a snare for me, and cords; they have spread a net by the wayside; they have set gins for me.

Arrogant men have hidden a trap for me,
and with cords they have spread a net,
by the wayside they have set snares for me — RSV

Selah.

Selah [pause, and calmly think of that] — Amp

6. I said unto the LORD, Thou art my God: hear the voice of my supplications, O LORD.

7. O GOD the Lord, the strength of my salvation, thou hast covered my head in the day of battle.

O JEHOVAH my Lord! O my Almighty Saviour!
Thou hast covered my head in the day of the clashing of arms — Sprl

O Yahweh My Lord my saving strength,
Thou hast screened my head in the day of battle — Rhm

O GOD the Lord, my strong deliverer,
Thou hast covered my head on the day of battle — AAT

O GOD, my Lord, my strength and my salvation;
you are my helmet in the day of battle! — NAB

Lord God, my powerful deliverer,
You have afforded me protection in time of conflict — Har

8. Grant not, O LORD, the desires of the wicked: further not his wicked device; lest they exalt themselves.

Grant not, O LORD, the desires of the wicked;
do not further his evil plot! — RSV

Do not allow the desires of the wicked to be realized, Lord;
do not let their plans succeed — Har

Selah.

Selah [pause, and calmly think of that] — Amp

9. As for the head of those that compass me about, let the mischief of their own lips cover them.

Those who surround me lift up their head,
let the mischief of their lips overwhelm them! — RSV

Those who surround me lift up their heads;
may the mischief which they threaten overwhelm them — NAB

Those who surround me are haughty in demeanor;
may their own malicious speech engulf them — Har

If any of those at my table rise against me,
let their own conspiracies be their undoing — NEB

10. Let burning coals fall upon them: let them be cast into the fire; into deep pits, that they rise not up again.

Let burning coals fall upon them!
Let them be cast into pits, no more to rise! — RSV

Let burning embers fall upon them:
may they be cast into deep graves from which they cannot emerge — Har

may red-hot embers rain down on them,
may they be flung into the abyss for good — Jerus

11. Let not an evil speaker be established in the earth; evil shall hunt the violent man to overthrow him.

As for the slanderer let him not be established in the earth, —
As for the man of wrongful violence let misfortune hunt him with thrust upon thrust — Rhm

The slanderer shall not be established in the earth;
The cruel man — evil hunteth him to headlong ruin — DeW

Let not the slanderer be established in the land;
let evil hunt down the violent man speedily! — RSV

12. I know that the LORD will maintain the cause of the afflicted, and the right of the poor.

I know that Yahweh will execute
The right of the oppressed one,
The vindication of the needy — Rhm

They shall find the Eternal champions the rights of the forlorn and feeble — Mof
I know that the LORD will give their due to the needy
and justice to the downtrodden — NEB
13. Surely the righteous shall give thanks unto thy name: the upright shall dwell in thy presence.

PSALM 141

A Psalm of David.
1. LORD, I cry unto thee: make haste unto me; give ear unto my voice when I cry unto thee.
I am calling to You, Lord, Hurry to my assistance;
pay attention to my request when I entreat You — Har
2. Let my prayer be set forth before thee as incense; and the lifting up of my hands as the evening sacrifice.
Let my prayer be counted as incense before thee,
and the lifting up of my hands as an evening sacrifice! — RSV
3. Set a watch, O LORD, before my mouth; keep the door of my lips.
Set a guard over my mouth, O LORD, keep watch over the door of my lips! — RSV
4. Incline not my heart to any evil thing, to practise wicked works with men that work iniquity:
Do not let my mind hanker after evil, to engage in wrongdoing with the wicked — Har
Let me feel no impulse to do wrong, to share the godlessness of evil-doers — Jerus
and let me not eat of their dainties.
neither let me eat of such things as please them — PBV
do not permit me to sample their pleasures — Har
5. Let the righteous smite me; it shall be a kindness: and let him reprove me; it shall be an excellent oil, which shall not break my head:
Let a good man strike or rebuke me in kindness,
but let the oil of the wicked never anoint my head — RSV
Let the virtuous man strike me and rebuke me as a kindness;
it will be like oil for my head.
May I never be too proud to accept it — Har
Let a righteous man smite me; it is kindness.
Let him reprove me; it is oil for my head, which my head shall not refuse — Ber
for yet my prayer also shall be in their calamities.
for my prayer is continually against their wicked deeds — RSV
for I am praying continually for them in their misfortune — Har
for I will still pray in the face of their wickedness — Ber
Daily I counter their malice with prayer — Jerus
6. When their judges are overthrown in stony places, they shall hear my words; for they are sweet.
When they are given over to those who shall condemn them,
then they shall learn that the word of the LORD is true — RSV
When their judges are flung on jagged rock,
they will learn how mild my words have been — Jerus
When their rulers are overthrown in stony places, [their followers] shall hear my words, that they are sweet — pleasant, mild, and just — Amp
When their rulers are hurled down by the sides of the cliff,
They will hear my words, which are gracious — DeW
Their rulers have been tossed into the grave;
they will learn that the promise of the Lord is reliable — Har
They will be hurled into the hands of their chieftains,
And they will learn that the word of the LORD is true — AAT
They shall founder on the rock of justice
and shall learn how acceptable my words are — NEB
7. Our bones are scattered at the grave's mouth, as when one cutteth and cleaveth wood upon the earth.
As when one ploweth and cleaveth the earth,

Our bones are scattered at the mouth of Sheol — ASV
Just as one penetrates and plows the ground,
so our bones lie scattered at the open grave — Har
Their bones shall be scattered at the mouth of Sheol,
like splinters of wood or stone on the ground — NEB

8. **But mine eyes are unto thee, O GOD the Lord: on thee is my trust; leave not my soul destitute.**
For mine eyes are unto thee, O Jehovah the Lord:
In thee do I take refuge; leave not my soul destitute — ASV
But my gaze is directed to You, Lord God;
I am looking to You for shelter; do not expose me to danger — Har

9. **Keep me from the snares which they have laid for me,**
Keep me from the trap which they have laid for me — RSV
and the gins of the workers of iniquity.
and from the snares of evildoers! — RSV

10. **Let the wicked fall into their own nets, whilst that I withal escape.**
Let the wicked fall into their own net,
While I altogether escape — DeW
May the wicked stumble into their own trap,
while I pass by unscathed — Har

PSALM 142

Maschil of David; A Prayer when he was in the cave.
An Instructive Psalm of David. When he was in the Cave. A Prayer — Rhm

1. **I cried unto the LORD with my voice; with my voice unto the LORD did I make my supplication.**
I cry with my voice to the LORD,
with my voice I make supplication to the LORD — RSV

2. **I poured out my complaint before him; I shewed before him my trouble.**
I empty myself of grief in His presence,
and tell Him of my trouble — Har
My complaint I pour out before him;
before him I lay bare my distress — Jerus

3. **When my spirit was overwhelmed within me, then thou knewest my path.**
When my spirit faints,
Thou knowest my way — AAT
When my spirit is faint within me,
thou art there to watch over my steps — NEB
In the way wherein I walked have they privily laid a snare for me.
In the path where I walk
they have hidden a trap for me — RSV
In the path where I must walk,
They lay a snare for me — AAT

4. **I looked on my right hand, and beheld, but there was no man that would know me:**
I look to the right and watch,
but there is none who takes notice of me — RSV
I look to the right and I watch.
There is no one who cares about me.
— Ber
Look on my right hand, and see;
For there is no man that knoweth me — ASV
Look at me, and take notice that I have no acquaintance — Har
Look on my right and see,
there is no one to befriend me — Jerus
refuge failed me; no man cared for my soul.
all hope of escape is cut off from me,
none is concerned for my safety — Knox
I have lost all means of escape;
there is no one who cares for my life — NAB
all help has failed me,
none cares for my life — Mof

5. **I cried unto thee, O LORD: I said, Thou art my refuge and my portion in the land of the living.**
Eternal One, I cry unto thee;
I say, "Thou art my help,
I have thee as my very own, in the land of the living — Mof
To thee, Lord, I cry, claiming thee for my only refuge, all that is left me in this world of living men — Knox
I cry to thee, O LORD,
and say, 'Thou art my refuge;
thou art all I have
in the land of the living — NEB

6. **Attend unto my cry; for I am brought very low:**
Pay attention to my cry, for I am in

desperate straits — Har

Listen to my cries for help,
I can hardly be crushed lower — Jerus

deliver me from my persecutors; for they are stronger than I.

rescue me from my persecutors, for they are too powerful for me — Har

7. Bring my soul out of prison, that I may praise thy name:

Bring me out of prison,
that I may give thanks to thy name! — RSV

the righteous shall compass me about; for thou shalt deal bountifully with me.

the virtuous will flock round me when You reward me — Har

May the righteous throng around me,
because Thou dealest kindly with me — Ber

PSALM 143

A Psalm of David.

1. Hear my prayer, O LORD, give ear to my supplications:

O Yahweh hear my prayer
Give ear to my supplications — Rhm

in thy faithfulness answer me, and in thy righteousness.

Answer me because of Your fidelity and equity — Har

Be true to thyself, and listen to my pleading — NEB

2. And enter not into judgment with thy servant: for in thy sight shall no man living be justified.

put not thy servant on his trial,
for before thee no living soul can be acquitted — Mof

do not put your servant on trial,
no one is virtuous by your standards —Jerus

Do not call thy servant to account; what man is there living that can stand guiltless in thy presence? — Knox

Do not summon Your servant for sentence,
for no man alive is righteous in Your estimation — Har

3. For the enemy hath persecuted my soul; he hath smitten my life down to the ground; he hath made me to dwell in darkness, as those that have been long dead.

For the enemy has pursued me;
he has crushed my life to the ground;
he has made me sit in darkness like those long dead — RSV

4. Therefore is my spirit overwhelmed within me; my heart within me is desolate.

And my spirit faints within me;
My heart within me is appalled — AAT

My spirits are crushed within me, my heart is cowed — Knox

so that my spirit fails me
and my heart is dazed with despair — NEB

In consequence my spirits have flagged,
I am full of apprehension — Har

My spirit is losing hope;
my heart within me is numbed with dismay — Ber

5. I remember the days of old; I meditate on all thy works; I muse on the work of thy hands.

And my mind goes back to past days;
I think of all thou didst once, dwell on proofs thou gavest of thy power —Knox

I dwell upon the years long past,
upon the memory of all thou hast done;
the wonders of thy creation fill my mind — NEB

6. I stretch forth my hands unto thee: my soul thirsteth after thee, as a thirsty land.

I stretch out my hands to thee;
my soul thirsts for thee like a parched land — RSV

I stretch out my hands,
like thirsty ground I yearn for you — Jerus

Selah.

Selah [pause, and calmly think of that]! — Amp

7. Hear me speedily, O LORD: my spirit faileth:

Answer me quickly, Lord, for my courage falters — Har

hide not thy face from me, lest I be like unto them that go down into the pit.

Do not conceal Yourself from me,
otherwise I shall be like those who

have been buried — Har
if you hide your face much longer,
I shall go down to the Pit like the rest — Jerus

8. Cause me to hear thy lovingkindness in the morning; for in thee do I trust:
Let me hear in the morning of thy steadfast love,
for in thee I put my trust — RSV
In the morning let me know thy true love;
I have put my trust in thee — NEB
Let dawn bring proof of your love,
for one who relies on you — Jerus
cause me to know the way wherein I should walk; for I lift up my soul unto thee.
Teach me the way I should go,
for to thee I lift up my soul — RSV
show me the direction which I should take,
for I commit myself to You — Har

9. Deliver me, O LORD, from mine enemies: I flee unto thee to hide me.
Deliver me, O LORD, from my enemies!
I have fled to thee for refuge! — RSV

10. Teach me to do thy will; for thou art my God:
Teach me how to do Your will, for You are my God — Har
Teach me to carry out Thy good pleasure,
for Thou art my God — Ber
teach me to obey you,
since you are my God — Jerus
thy spirit is good; lead me into the land of uprightness.
Let thy good spirit lead me
on a level path! — RSV
Let Thy good spirit
Lead me in an even land — JPS
guide me by thy good Spirit on a straight road — Mof
in thy gracious kindness, show me the level road — NEB

11. Quicken me, O LORD, for thy name's sake:
For thy name's sake, O LORD, preserve my life! — RSV
Keep me safe, O LORD, for the honour of thy name — NEB
Save my life, Lord, for the sake of Your reputation — Har
for thy righteousness' sake bring my soul out of trouble.
In Thy righteousness, bring my soul out of distress — DeW
in your justice free me from distress — NAB

12. And of thy mercy cut off mine enemies, and destroy all them that afflict my soul:
And in thy lovingkindness cut off all mine enemies,
And destroy all them that afflict my soul — ASV
Annihilate my enemies out of love for me,
and destroy all my rivals — Har
for I am thy servant.

PSALM 144

A Psalm of David.

1. Blessed be the LORD my strength, which teacheth my hands to war, and my fingers to fight:

2. My goodness, and my fortress; my high tower, and my deliverer; my shield, and he in whom I trust; who subdueth my people under me.
Blessed be the LORD my strength, who teacheth my hands to war, and my fingers to fight:
My hope and my fortress, my castle and deliverer, my defender in whom I trust; who subdueth my people that is under me — PBV
Blessed be Jehovah my rock,
Who teacheth my hands to war,
And my fingers to fight:
My lovingkindness, and my fortress,
My high tower, and my deliverer;
My shield, and he in whom I take refuge;
Who subdueth my people under me — ASV
Blessed be Yahweh, my rock,
who trains my hands for war
and my fingers for battle,
my love, my bastion,
my citadel, my saviour,
I shelter behind him, my shield,
he makes the nations submit to me — Jerus
May the Lord, my sure foundation, be praised:
He trains my hands for war, and my fingers for fighting.
He is my strong fortress, my shelter and my rescuer;

my protector, the one in whom I take refuge,
who brings peoples into submission to Himself — Har

3. **LORD, what is man, that thou takest knowledge of him! of the son of man, that thou makest account of him!**

Lord, what is Adam's race, that thou givest heed to it, what is man, that thou carest for him? — Knox

What is man, Lord, that You take notice of him,
or human offspring, that You should show concern? — Har

O Lord, what is man that you even notice him? Why bother at all with the human race? — Tay

4. **Man is like to vanity: his days are as a shadow that passeth away.**

The earthborn resembleth a vapour,
His days are like a passing shadow — Rhm

Man is like a breath: his life is like a shade which is quickly gone — Bas

Man is like a puff of wind;
his days are like a flitting shadow — Har

Like the wind he goes, like a shadow his days pass — Knox

5. **Bow thy heavens, O LORD, and come down: touch the mountains, and they shall smoke.**

Lower the cloud ceiling, Lord, and come down:
strike the mountains, so that they belch out smoke — Har

If thou, LORD, but tilt the heavens, down they come;
touch the mountains, and they smoke — NEB

6. **Cast forth lightning, and scatter them: shoot out thine arrows, and destroy them.**

Hurl down Your lightning and disperse them;
shoot out Your thunderbolts and rout them — Har

Shoot forth thy lightning flashes, far and wide,
and send thy arrows whistling — NEB

7. **Send thine hand from above; rid me, and deliver me out of great waters, from the hand of strange children;**

Stretch forth thy hand from on high, rescue me and deliver me from the many waters,
from the hand of aliens — RSV

8. **Whose mouth speaketh vanity, and their right hand is a right hand of falsehood.**

whose mouths speak lies,
and whose hands transact treachery — Har

Whose mouths swear false promises while their right hands are raised in perjury — NAB

9. **I will sing a new song unto thee, O God: upon a psaltery and an instrument of ten strings will I sing praises unto thee.**

O God! a new song will I sing unto thee,
On a harp of ten strings will I make music to thee — Rhm

10. **It is he that giveth salvation unto kings: who delivereth David his servant from the hurtful sword.**

Who givest victory unto kings, —
Who snatcheth away David his servant from the calamitous sword — Rhm

who givest victory to kings,
who rescuest David thy servant — RSV

the God to whom kings must look for victory, the God who has brought his servant David rescue — Knox

11. **Rid me, and deliver me from the hand of strange children, whose mouth speaketh vanity, and their right hand is a right hand of falsehood:**

Snatch me away and rescue me
out of the hands of the sons of the alien, —
Whose mouth hath spoken deceit,
and whose right hand is a right hand of falsehood — Rhm

Rescue me from the cruel sword,
and deliver me from the hand of aliens,
whose mouths speak lies,
and whose right hand is a right hand of falsehood — RSV

Free me and rescue me from the clutches of strangers
whose mouths speak lies,
and whose hands transact treachery — Har

12. **That our sons may be as plants grown up in their youth; that our daughters may be as corner stones, polished after the similitude of a palace:**

May our sons in their youth
be like plants full grown,

our daughters like corner pillars
cut for the structure of a palace — RSV

May our sons be like plants
well-nurtured in their youth,
Our daughters like wrought columns
such as stand at the corners of the temple — NAB

So that our sons may be as plants
Full grown in their youth;
Our daughters as corner pillars
Carved after the pattern of a palace — DeW

So may our sons grow to manhood, tall as the saplings, our daughters shapely as some column at the turn of a building, it may be, the temple itself — Knox

May our sons be like plants
growing strong from their earliest days,
our daughters like corner-statutes,
carvings fit for a palace — Jerus

13. **That our garners may be full, affording all manner of store:**

May our barns be full to overflowing
with every variety of produce — Har

may our barns overflow
with every possible crop — Jerus

that our sheep may bring forth thousands and ten thousands in our streets:

may our sheep bear in our pastures
by thousands and ten thousands — Har

may the sheep in our fields be counted
in their thousands and tens of thousands — Jerus

14. **That our oxen may be strong to labour; that there be no breaking in, nor going out; that there be no complaining in our streets.**

may our cattle be stout and strong;
and may there be an end of raids and exile,
and of panic in our streets — Jerus

may our oxen be well laden.
May there be no breach in the walls, no exile,
no outcry in our streets — NAB

May our oxen be heavy with young,
experiencing neither abortion nor miscarriage.
May there be no disturbances in our city streets — Har

may our cattle be heavy with young,
suffering no mischance or failure in bearing;
may there be no cry of distress in our streets! — RSV

15. **Happy is that people, that is in such a case:**

O the blessedness of the people with whom it is thus — DeW

The people in such a condition are fortunate indeed — Har

Happy the people to whom such blessings fall! — RSV

Yea, happy is that people, whose God is the LORD.

Yea, happy is the people whose God is Jehovah — ASV

How happy the people that hath Yahweh for its God! — Rhm

PSALM 145

David's Psalm of praise.

1. **I will extol thee, my God, O king;**

I will exalt Thee, My God and King — Ber

I sing your praises, God my King — Jerus

and I will bless thy name for ever and ever.

2. **Every day will I bless thee; and I will praise thy name for ever and ever.**

3. **Great is the LORD, and greatly to be praised; and his greatness is unsearchable.**

Great is the LORD, and marvellous worthy to be praised; there is no end of his greatness — PBV

Great is Yahweh — and worthy to be heartily praised,
And his greatness is unsearchable — Rhm

Great is the LORD and worthy of all praise;
his greatness is unfathomable — NEB

The Lord is great, and merits the highest praise;
His grandeur is limitless — Har

Can anyone measure the magnificence of Yahweh the great, and his inexpressible grandeur? — Jerus

4. **One generation shall praise thy works to another, and shall declare thy mighty acts.**

Generation unto generation shall celebrate thy works,
And thy mighty deeds shall they tell — Rhm

They will praise Your works generation after generation,
and narrate Your mighty doings — Har

One generation shall commend thy works to another
and set forth thy mighty deeds — NEB

5. I will speak of the glorious honour of thy majesty, and of thy wondrous works.

As for me, I will be talking of thy worship, thy glory, thy praise, and wondrous works — PBV

I will meditate on the glorious splendor of Your majesty,
and on Your wonderful deeds — Har

They speak of the splendor of your glorious majesty
and tell of your wondrous works — NAB

6. And men shall speak of the might of thy terrible acts: and I will declare thy greatness.

And men shall speak of the might of Thy tremendous acts;
And I will tell of Thy greatness — JPS

Men shall speak of the might of Thy awe-inspiring deeds,
and as for Thy greatness, I will recount it — Ber

They will discuss the power which underlies Your miracles:
I will proclaim Your greatness — Har

They discourse of the power of your terrible deeds
and declare your greatness — NAB

7. They shall abundantly utter the memory of thy great goodness, and shall sing of thy righteousness.

The memory of thy great goodness shall men pour forth,
And thy righteousness shall they shout aloud — Rhm

They publish the fame of your abundant goodness
and joyfully sing of your justice — NAB

they will celebrate your generous kindness
and joyfully acclaim your righteousness — Jerus

They shall recite the story of thy abounding goodness
and sing of thy righteousness with joy — NEB

8. The LORD is gracious, and full of compassion; slow to anger, and of great mercy.

Gracious and compassionate is Yahweh,
Slow to anger and of great lovingkindness — Rhm

He, Yahweh, is merciful, tenderhearted,
slow to anger, very loving — Jerus

9. The LORD is good to all: and his tender mercies are over all his works.

. . . universally kind; Yahweh's tenderness,
embraces all his creatures — Jerus

Good is Yahweh to all,
And his tender compassions are over all his works — Rhm

The LORD is loving unto every man;
and his mercy is over all his works — PBV

the Eternal is good to all who look to him,
and his compassion covers all that he has made — Mof

The LORD is good to all men,
and his tender care rests upon all his creatures — NEB

10. All thy works shall praise thee, O LORD; and thy saints shall bless thee.

Let all thy works praise thee, O Jehovah,
And thy saints bless thee — ABPS

All thy creatures praise thee, LORD,
and thy servants bless thee — NEB

11. They shall speak of the glory of thy kingdom, and talk of thy power;

12. To make known to the sons of men his mighty acts, and the glorious majesty of his kingdom.

They show the glory of thy kingdom, and talk of thy power;
That thy power, thy glory, and the mightiness of thy kingdom, might be known unto men — PBV

They shall speak of the glory of thy kingdom,
and tell of thy power,
to make known to the sons of men thy mighty deeds,
and the glorious splendor of thy kingdom — RSV

They shall speak of the glory of Thy kingdom
and tell of Thy might,

that they may make known to the children of men His feats of power, and the majestic glory of His kingdom — Ber

Kingly and glorious they proclaim you, they affirm your might.
Let mankind learn your acts of power,
and the majestic glory of your sovereignty! — Jerus

13. Thy kingdom is an everlasting kingdom, and thy domination endureth throughout all generations.[49]

. . . and thy dominion endures throughout all generations.
The LORD is faithful in all his words, and gracious in all his deeds — RSV

Your sovereignty is an eternal sovereignty,
your empire lasts from age to age.
Always true to his promises,
Yahweh shows love in all he does — Jerus

Your kingdom is of an eternal order;
Your rule extends across the ages — Har

14. The LORD upholdeth all that fall, and raiseth up all those that be bowed down.

Yahweh is ready to uphold all who are falling, And to raise all who are laid prostrate — Rhm

The Lord sustains all those who fall;
He lifts up those who are prostrate with grief — Har

15. The eyes of all wait upon thee; and thou givest them their meat in due season.

Everyone looks to you with expectation:
You give them their food at the appropriate time — Har

Patiently all creatures look to you
to feed them throughout the year — Jerus

The eyes of all are lifted to thee in hope,
and thou givest them their food when it is due — NEB

16. Thou openest thine hand, and satisfiest the desire of every living thing.

quick to satisfy every need,
you feed them all with a generous hand — Jerus

17. The LORD is righteous in all his ways, and holy in all his works.

Righteous is Yahweh in all his ways,
And kind in all his works — Rhm

Jehovah is righteous in all his ways,
And gracious in all his works — ASV

The Lord is just in all His behavior,
and beneficent in all His dealings — Har

Righteous in all that he does,
Yahweh acts only out of love — Jerus

18. The LORD is nigh unto all them that call upon him, to all that call upon him in truth.

the Eternal is near all who call on him,
who call on him sincerely — Mof

19. He will fulfil the desire of them that fear him: he also will hear their cry, and will save them.

He fulfilleth the desire of those that fear Him;
He heareth their cry for help, and saveth them — DeW

He will fulfil the wishes of those who revere Him:
He will hear their appealing cry, and will help them — Har

Those who fear him need only to ask to be answered;
he hears their cry for help and saves them — Jerus

20. The LORD preserveth all them that love him: but all the wicked will he destroy.

Under his protection the pious are safe,
but Yahweh is destruction to the wicked — Jerus

21. My mouth shall speak the praise of the LORD: and let all flesh bless his holy name for ever and ever.

Yahweh's praise be ever in my mouth,
and let every creature bless his holy name
for ever and ever! — Jerus

PSALM 146

1. Praise ye the LORD. Praise the LORD, O my soul.

Praise ye Jah.
Praise Jehovah, O my soul — ABPS

Hallelujah! Praise the LORD, O my soul! — Ber

[49]Observe that RSV and some other modern translations add a sentence to this verse for which KJV has no equivalent.

May God be praised.
Let my entire being praise the Lord — Har

2. While I live will I praise the LORD: I will sing praises unto my God while I have any being.

I will praise Yahweh while I live!
I will make melody to my God while I continue! — Rhm

I mean to praise Yahweh all my life,
I mean to sing to my God as long as I live — Jerus

3. Put not your trust in princes, nor in the son of man, in whom there is no help.

Rely not upon great men —
mere mortals who can give no help — Mof

Do not put your trust in princes; they are but men, they have no power to save — Knox

4. His breath goeth forth, he returneth to his earth; in that very day his thoughts perish.

For when the breath of man goeth forth, he shall turn again to his earth, and then all his thoughts perish — PBV

He breathes his last breath,
he returns to the dust;
and in that same hour all his thinking ends — NEB

His breath goeth out and he shall return to his earth; on that day all his projects shall perish — Sept

When his breath departs he returns to his earth;
On that very day his plans perish — AAT

As soon as the breath leaves his body, man goes back to the dust he belongs to; with that, all his designs will come to nothing — Knox

5. Happy is he that hath the God of Jacob for his help, whose hope is in the LORD his God:

How happy is he that hath the GOD of Jacob as his help,
Whose hope is on Yahweh his God — Rhm

O the blessedness of him
Whose help is in the Mighty One of Jacob,
Whose hope is in Jehovah, his God — DeW

Happy the man who has the God of Jacob to help him, whose hope is fixed on Yahweh his God — Jerus

6. Which made heaven, and earth, the sea, and all that therein is: which keepeth truth for ever:

who made heaven and earth,
the sea, and all that is in them;
who keeps faith for ever — RSV

7. Which executeth judgment for the oppressed: which giveth food to the hungry.

who executes justice for the oppressed;
who gives food to the hungry — RSV

The LORD looseth the prisoners:

8. The LORD openeth the eyes of the blind: the LORD raiseth them that are bowed down: the LORD loveth the righteous:

9. The LORD preserveth the strangers: he relieveth the fatherless and widow: but the way of the wicked he turneth upside down.

The Lord releases the prisoners;
the Lord gives sight to the blind.
The Lord raises those who are prostrate;
the Lord cherishes the upright.
The Lord protects the stranger,
and sustains the orphan and widow;
but He frustrates the designs of the wicked — Har

The Lord, who brings release to the prisoner, the Lord, who gives sight to the blind, the Lord, who comforts the burdened, the Lord, who befriends the innocent! The Lord, who protects the stranger, who defends orphan and widow, who overturns the counsel of the wicked! — Knox

10. The LORD shall reign for ever, even thy God, O Zion, unto all generations. Praise ye the LORD.

. . . Praise ye Yah! — Rhm
. . . Praise ye Jah! — YLT
. . . Hallelujah! — Ber

PSALM 147

1. Praise ye the LORD:

Praise ye Yah — Rhm
Praise ye Jah! — YLT
Hallelujah — JPS

for it is good to sing praises unto our God; for it is pleasant; and praise is comely.

for it is a good thing to sing praises

unto our God; yea, a joyful and pleasant thing it is to be thankful — PBV

For it is good to make melody to our God:
Yea, it is pleasant; a hymn of praise is seemly — DeW

For it is good to sing praises to our God;
for he is gracious, and a song of praise is seemly — RSV

it is good to sing
in honour of our God — sweet is his praise — Jerus

2. The LORD doth build up Jerusalem: he gathereth together the outcasts of Israel.

The Lord has rebuilt Jerusalem,
and assembled exiled Israel — Har

Yahweh, Restorer of Jerusalem!
He brought back Israel's exiles — Jerus

3. He healeth the broken in heart, and bindeth up their wounds.

The physician for the broken in heart;
And he binds up their pains — ABPS

He that healeth the broken in heart,
And that relieveth their sorrows — DeW

healing their broken hearts,
and binding up their wounds — Jerus

4. He telleth the number of the stars; he calleth them all by their names.

Counting the number of the stars,
To all of them — names he giveth — Rhm

He fixes the number of the stars,
and gives a name to each — Mof

5. Great is our Lord, and of great power: his understanding is infinite.

Great is our LORD, and abundant in power;
his understanding is beyond measure — RSV

our Lord is great, all-powerful,
of infinite understanding — Jerus

6. The LORD lifteth up the meek: he casteth the wicked down to the ground.

The LORD lifts up the downtrodden,
he casts the wicked to the ground — RSV

Jehovah raises up the lowly
He humbles the wicked even to the earth — ABPS

The LORD sustains the lowly;
the wicked he casts to the ground — NAB

The Eternal has relief for the afflicted,
he brings the ungodly to the ground — Mof

The Lord is the defender of the oppressed, and lays the wicked low in the dust — Knox

7. Sing unto the LORD with thanksgiving; sing praise upon the harp unto our God:

Respond to Yahweh with thanksgiving,
Make melody to our God with the lyre — Rhm

Answer Jehovah with thanksgiving,
Sing praise to our God with the harp — ABPS

Strike up to Jehovah with thanksgiving;
Make melody to our God with the harp — DeW

8. Who covereth the heaven with clouds, who prepareth rain for the earth, who maketh grass to grow upon the mountains.

He covers the skies with clouds,
and prepares rain for the earth.
He causes the grass to sprout on the hillsides — Har

9. He giveth to the beast his food, and to the young ravens which cry.

He provides food for the animals,
and for the young ravens when they caw — Har

He gives the cattle their food
and the young ravens all that they gather — NEB

10. He delighteth not in the strength of the horse: he taketh not pleasure in the legs of a man.

Not the well-mounted warrior is his choice, not the swift runner wins his favour — Knox

He does not delight in sheer animal strength,
and finds no pleasure in human sinews — Har

The strength of the war horse means nothing to him,
it is not infantry that interests him — Jerus

In the strength of the steed he delights not,
nor is he pleased with the fleetness of men — NAB

11. The LORD taketh pleasure in them that fear him, in those that hope in his mercy.

Jehovah taketh pleasure in them that fear him,

In those that hope in his lovingkindness — ASV

Yahweh is interested only in those who fear him,
in those who rely on his love — Jerus

For the Lord is gratified by those who revere Him,
and who trust in His loving mercy — Har

the Lord's favour is for those who fear him, and put their trust in his divine mercy — Knox

12. Praise the LORD, O Jerusalem; praise thy God, O Zion.

Praise Jehovah, O Jerusalem;
Praise thy God, O Zion — ABPS

Glorify the LORD, O Jerusalem;
Praise thy God, O Zion — JPS

13. For he hath strengthened the bars of thy gates; he hath blessed thy children within thee.

For He has strengthened the bars of your gates,
and has blessed your sons in your midst — Ber

For he has fortified your gates against all enemies, and blessed your children — Tay

14. He maketh peace in thy borders, and filleth thee with the finest of the wheat.

He has brought peace to your realm and given you fine wheat in plenty — NEB

15. He sendeth forth his commandment upon earth: his word runneth very swiftly.

16. He giveth snow like wool: he scattereth the hoarfrost like ashes.

17. He casteth forth his ice like morsels: who can stand before his cold?

18. He sendeth out his word, and melteth them: he causeth his wind to blow, and the waters flow.

He sends forth his command to the earth;
swiftly runs his word!
He spreads snow like wool;
frost he strews like ashes.
He scatters his hail like crumbs;
before his cold the waters freeze.
He sends his word and melts them;
he lets his breeze blow and the waters run — NAB

He gives an order;
his word flashes to earth:
to spread snow like a blanket,
to strew hoarfrost like ashes,
to drop ice like breadcrumbs,
and when the cold is unbearable,
he sends his word to bring the thaw
and warm wind to melt the snow — Jerus

He dispatches His decree to the earth:
His command speeds along quickly.
He sends snowflakes, light as fluff;
He sprinkles hoar frost like fine dust.
He showers down icicles in fragments;
who can withstand His cold?
When He gives the command, they melt;
when He whips up the wind, the waters flow — Har

See how he issues his command to the earth, how swift his word runs! Now he spreads a pall of snow, covers earth with an ashy veil of rime, doles out the scattered crusts of ice, binds the waters at the onset of his frost. Then, at his word, all melts away; a breath from him, and the waters flow! — Knox

19. He sheweth his word unto Jacob, his statutes and his judgments unto Israel.

He declares his word to Jacob,
his statutes and ordinances to Israel — RSV

He makes his word clear to Jacob, teaching Israel his laws and his decisions — Bas

20. He hath not dealt so with any nation: and as for his judgments, they have not known them.

He has not dealt thus with any other nation;
they do not know his ordinances — RSV

He has not done these things for any other nation: and as for his laws, they have no knowledge of them — Bas

Praise ye the LORD.

Praise ye Jah! — YLT

Hallelujah — JPS

PSALM 148

1. Praise ye the LORD. Praise ye the LORD from the heavens: praise him in the heights.
Praise ye Jah.
Praise Jehovah from the heavens;
Praise him in the heights — ABPS
Hallelujah.
Praise ye the LORD from the heavens;
Praise Him in the heights — JPS
May God be praised.
Praise the Lord from the skies;
glorify Him in the regions above — Har

2. Praise ye him, all his angels: praise ye him, all his hosts.
Let all His angels praise him;
commend Him, you who are His company — Har
praise him, all his angels,
praise him, all his armies! — Jerus

3. Praise ye him, sun and moon: praise him, all ye stars of light.
Praise him, sun and moon; praise him,
every star that shines — Knox
Praise him, sun and moon,
praise him, all you shining stars! — RSV

4. Praise him, ye heavens of heavens, and ye waters that be above the heavens.
Praise him, you highest heavens,
and you waters above the heavens! — RSV
Let the highest heavens give Him praise;
and the rain clouds which are in the skies — Har
Praise him, skies above. Praise him,
vapors high above the clouds — Tay

5. Let them praise the name of the LORD: for he commanded, and they were created.

6. He hath also stablished them for ever and ever: he hath made a decree which shall not pass.
And he established them for ever and ever;
he fixed their bounds which cannot be passed — RSV
He hath also established them for ever and ever:
He hath made a decree which shall not pass away — ASV
and He established them permanently.
He formulated a law which they were to obey — Har
he has fixed them in their place for ever,
by an unalterable statute — Jerus

7. Praise the LORD from the earth, ye dragons, and all deeps:

8. Fire, and hail; snow, and vapours; stormy wind fulfilling his word:
Praise the LORD from the earth,
you sea monsters and all deeps,
fire and hail, snow and frost,
stormy wind fulfilling his command! — RSV
Praise the Lord from the earth,
you denizens of the deep, and all oceans;
fire and hail, snow and fog,
boisterous wind, fulfilling His command — Har

9. Mountains, and all hills; fruitful trees, and all cedars:

10. Beasts, and all cattle; creeping things, and flying fowl:
Mountains and all hills,
fruit trees and all cedars!
Beasts and all cattle,
creeping things and flying birds! — RSV

11. Kings of the earth, and all people; princes, and all judges of the earth:

12. Both young men, and maidens; old men, and children:
Kings of the earth and all peoples,
princes and all rulers of the earth!
Young men and maidens together,
old men and children! — RSV

13. Let them praise the name of the LORD: for his name alone is excellent; his glory is above the earth and heaven.
Let them praise the name of Jehovah;
For his name alone is exalted;
His glory is above the earth and the heavens — ASV
Let them all praise the name of Yahweh,
for his name and no other is sublime,
transcending earth and heaven in majesty — Jerus

14. He also exalteth the horn of his people, the praise of all his saints; even of the children of Israel, a people near unto him.
and he has raised his people to high honour.
To praise him is for all his faithful,
for Israel, a folk pleasing to him — Mof

He has increased the authority of His people:
all His saints glorify Him —
the people of Israel, His protected race — Har
and now he has given fresh strength to his people. Shall not his faithful servants praise him, the sons of Israel, the people that draw near to him? — Knox

Praise ye the LORD.
Praise ye Jah! — YLT
Hallelujah! — Ber

PSALM 149

1. **Praise ye the LORD. Sing unto the LORD a new song, and his praise in the congregation of saints.**
Praise ye Jah.
Sing to Jehovah a new song,
His praise in the congregation of saints — ABPS
Hallelujah! Sing to the LORD a new song,
His praise in the congregation of the godly! — Ber
PRAISE YE JEHOVAH!
Sing to Jehovah a new song;
A hymn of praise in the assembly of His beloved! — DeW
2. **Let Israel rejoice in him that made him: let the children of Zion be joyful in their King.**
Let Israel be glad in his Maker,
let the sons of Zion rejoice in their King! — RSV
3. **Let them praise his name in the dance: let them sing praises unto him with the timbrel and harp.**
let them dance in praise of him,
make melody to him with drum and lyre — Mof
Let them praise his name with dancing;
Let them play to him on drum and lute — AAT
4. **For the LORD taketh pleasure in his people: he will beautify the meek with salvation.**
For the LORD takes pleasure in his people;
he adorns the humble with victory — RSV
For the LORD loves his people,
and he adorns the lowly with victory — NAB
For Yahweh has been kind to his people,
conferring victory on us who are weak — Jerus
5. **Let the saints be joyful in glory: let them sing aloud upon their beds.**
Let His beloved exult in glory;
Let them sing for joy upon their beds — DeW
Let the saints rejoice gloriously;
let them shout for joy upon their couches — Har
Let the godly rejoice in this honor;
let them shout for joy on their beds — Ber
6. **Let the high praises of God be in their mouth, and a two-edged sword in their hand;**
7. **To execute vengeance upon the heathen, and punishments upon the people;**
8. **To bind their kings with chains, and their nobles with fetters of iron;**
9. **To execute upon them the judgment written: this honour have all his saints.**
Let the high praises of God be in their throats
and two-edged swords in their hands,
to wreak vengeance on the nations
and chastisement on the peoples,
to bind their kings with chains
and their nobles with fetters of iron,
to execute on them the judgment written!
This is glory for all his faithful ones — RSV

Praise ye the LORD.
Praise ye Jah! — YLT
Hallelujah! — Ber

PSALM 150

1. **Praise ye the LORD. Praise God in his sanctuary: praise him in the firmament of his power.**
Praise ye Jah.
Praise God in his sanctuary;
Praise him in the expanse of his power — ABPS

Hallelujah!
Praise God in his sanctuary!

Praise him in his mighty firmament! — AAT

May God be praised.
Give praise to God in His shrine:
glorify Him in his majestic heaven — Har

Alleluia!
Praise God in his Temple on earth,
praise him in his temple in heaven — Jerus

2. Praise him for his mighty acts: praise him according to his excellent greatness.

Praise him for his mighty deeds,
praise him for his sovereign majesty — NAB

Praise him for his mighty achievements,
praise him for his transcendent greatness — Jerus

3. Praise him with the sound of the trumpet: praise him with the psaltery and harp.

Praise him with the sound of trumpet;
Praise him with lute and harp — ABPS

Praise him with the blast of a horn,
Praise him with the harp and lyre — Rhm

4. Praise him with the timbrel and dance: praise him with stringed instruments and organs.

Praise him with timbrel and dance,
Praise him with stringed instrument and flute — Rhm

Praise Him with the timbrel and dance;
Praise Him upon strings and pipe — DeW

Praise him with tambourines and dancing,
praise him with flute and strings — NEB

praise him with drums and dancing,
praise him with strings and reeds — Jerus

5. Praise him upon the loud cymbals: praise him upon the high sounding cymbals.

Praise him with the clang of the cymbals, the cymbals that ring merrily — Knox

Praise him with sounding cymbals;
praise him with loud clashing cymbals! — RSV

Praise Him with quivering cymbals;
praise Him with clashing cymbals — Har

Praise him with cymbals of clear note,
Praise him with cymbals of loud clang — Rhm

6. Let every thing that hath breath praise the LORD.

Let every breathing thing praise Yah — Rhm

Let everything that breathes praise the LORD! — AAT

Let all breath praise Jah — ABPS

Praise ye the LORD.

Praise ye Jah! — YLT

Hallelujah! — AAT

THE PROVERBS

CHAPTER 1

1. The Proverbs of Solomon the son of David, king of Israel;

The Proverbs of David's son Solomon, who reigned over Israel — Sept

Parables of Solomon the son of David, who was the king of Israel — Sprl

The wise sayings of Solomon, the son of David, king of Israel — Bas

Maxims of Solomon king of Israel, the son of David — Mof

These are the proverbs of King Solomon of Israel, David's son — Tay

2. To know wisdom and instruction; to perceive the words of understanding;

For the knowledge of wisdom and correction,
For receiving the correction of prudence — Rhm

To know wisdom and instruction;
To discern the words of understanding — ASV

For knowing wisdom and instruction,
For understanding sagacious words — ABPS

for gaining sagacity and intelligence, for a grasp of wise teaching — Mof

for learning what wisdom and discipline are,
for understanding words of deep meaning — Jerus

That men may appreciate wisdom and discipline,
may understand words of intelligence — NAB

He wrote them to teach his people how to live — how to act in every circumstance — Tay

3. To receive the instruction of wisdom, justice, judgment, and equity:

To receive instruction in wise dealing,
In righteousness and justice and equity — ASV

To receive the discipline of wisdom,
Justice, and right, and equity — JPS

For receiving the correction of prudence,
Righteousness and justice, and equity — Rhm

That they may receive instruction in wise conduct,
In rectitude, justice, and honesty — AAT

for training in right conduct,
in duty, goodness, and integrity — Mof

and by which they will gain a well-instructed intelligence,
righteousness, justice, and probity — NEB

4. To give subtilty to the simple, to the young man knowledge and discretion.

In order to impart prudence to the teachable,
To the young man knowledge and discretion — Sprl

that he might give sagacity to the innocent; and to the youth knowledge and discretion — Sept

for imparting insight to the ignorant, knowledge and sense to the young — Mof

To make the simple-minded sharp, and to give the young man knowledge, and serious purpose — Bas

That resourcefulness may be imparted to the simple,
to the young man knowledge and discretion — NAB

Here simplicity is put on its guard; here youth may find instruction and advice both together — Knox

5. A wise man will hear, and will increase learning; and a man of understanding shall attain unto wise counsels:

The wise will hear, and shall increase knowledge,
And guidance the discerning will obtain — ABPS

That the wise man may hear, and increase in learning;
And that the man of understanding may attain unto sound counsels — ASV

the wise man also may hear and increase in learning,
and the man of understanding acquire skill — RSV

Let the wise listen and he will learn yet more,
and the man of discernment will acquire the art of guidance — Jerus

If the wise man listens, he will increase his learning,
and the man of understanding will acquire skill — NEB

The wise man also may hear and increase his learning,
The man of intelligence acquire sound principles — AAT

6. To understand a proverb, and the interpretation; the words of the wise, and their dark sayings.
To understand a proverb, and a figure; the words of the wise, and their dark sayings — RV
To understand proverbs and figures of speech; the words of the wise and their dark sayings — Lam
to understand a proverb and a figure, the words of the wise and their riddles — RSV
To comprehend a proverb, even in its exquisiteness;
The words of the wise, and their enigmatical meanings — Sprl
for perceiving the meaning of proverbs and obscure sayings,
the sayings of the sages and their riddles — Jerus
he will read both parables and the interpretation of parables, both wise words and the hidden thoughts they signify — Knox
for understanding maxims and parables,
the sentences of sages and their aphorisms — Mof

7. The fear of the LORD is the beginning of knowledge: but fools despise wisdom and instruction.
The fear of the LORD is the beginning of knowledge;
But the foolish despise wisdom and discipline — JPS
The reverence of Yahweh is the beginning of knowledge,
Wisdom and correction the foolish have despised — Rhm
The fear of JEHOVAH is the summit of wisdom:
But wisdom and counsel fools despise — Sprl
Reverence for the Eternal is the first thing in knowledge,
but the impious scorn sagacity and intelligence — Mof
The fear of the Lord is the start of knowledge: but the foolish have no use for wisdom and teaching — Bas

8. My son, hear the instruction of thy father, and forsake not the law of thy mother:
Hear, my son, your father's instruction,
and reject not your mother's teaching — RSV
My son, hear the instruction of thy father and reject not the maxims of thy mother — Sept
Attend, my son, unto the counsels of thy father,
And forsake not the advice of thy mother — Sprl
Heed well, my son, thy father's warnings, nor make light of thy mother's teaching — Knox

9. For they shall be an ornament of grace unto thy head, and chains about thy neck.
For they shall be a chaplet of grace unto thy head,
And chains about thy neck — ASV
For a graceful garland will they be for your head,
And a chain for your neck — AAT
For they will be a crown of grace for your head, and chain-ornaments about your neck — Bas
for they are a fair garland for your head,
and pendants for your neck — RSV

10. My son, if sinners entice thee, consent thou not.
My son, if sinners entice thee be not willing — YLT
My son, if sinners try to seduce you,
do not give way — Jerus
My son, if sinners would take you out of the right way, do not go with them — Bas
My son, if scoundrels would lead you astray,
never agree to it — Mof

11. If they say, Come with us, let us lay wait for blood, let us lurk privily for the innocent without cause:
If they say to you, Come with us, let us lie in wait to shed blood, let us lie in wait for the innocent, wrongfully — Lam
Should they say: Come with us, we will lie in wait for blood;
We will plot against the innocent without cause — Sprl
If they say, "Come with us, let us lie in wait for the honest,

Let us wantonly ambush the innocent — AAT

If they say, Come with us; let us make designs against the good, waiting secretly for the upright, without cause — Bas

If they say, 'Come with us:
there is blood to be had if we lie in wait for it,
if we plan an ambush for the innocent — Jerus

12. Let us swallow them up alive as the grave; and whole, as those that go down to the pit:

Let us engulf them like hades alive,
While in health like them who are going down to the pit — Rhm

let us swallow them up like death,
swallow them whole, as men die in their prime — Mof

like Sheol let us swallow them alive
and whole, like those who go down to the Pit — RSV

Let us swallow them up, as the nether world does, alive,
in the prime of life, like those who go down to the pit — NAB

Let us overcome them living, like the underworld, and in their strength, as those who go down to death — Bas

13. We shall find all precious substance, we shall fill our houses with spoil:

We shall find much valuable treasure;
We shall fill our houses with spoil — Sprl

All kinds of precious wealth shall we find,
We shall fill our houses with spoil — AAT

we shall get all sorts of rare stuff,
and cram our houses with booty — Mof

No lack of treasures here, they say, rich plunder that shall find its way into our houses — Knox

We shall find treasures of every sort,
we shall fill our houses with plunder — Jerus

14. Cast in thy lot among us; let us all have one purse:

throw in your lot among us,
we will all have one purse — RSV

Take your chance with us, and we will all have one money-bag — Bas

throw in your lot with us,
and we will have a common purse — NEB

Come on, throw in your lot with us;
we'll split with you in equal shares — Tay

thou hast but to throw in thy lot with us; every man shares alike — Knox

15. My son, walk not thou in the way with them; refrain thy foot from their path:

My son! go not in the way with them,
Withhold thy foot from their path — YLT

Go not thou in the way with them; but turn thy foot from their paths — Sept

My son, do not go along with them,
keep clear of their ways — NEB

my son, never join them,
keep clear of their courses — Mof

My son, do not follow them in their way,
keep your steps out of their path — Jerus

Such errands, my son, are not for thee; never stir a foot in their company — Knox

16. For their feet run to evil, and make haste to shed blood.

For their feet to mischief do run,
And haste to the shedding of blood — Rhm

Because their feet hasten towards evil,
And they speed to shed blood — Sprl

they hasten hot-foot into crime,
impatient to shed blood — NEB

For their feet are running after evil, and they are quick to take a man's life — Bas

For crime is their way of life, and murder is their specialty — Tay

17. Surely in vain the net is spread in the sight of any bird.

Surely in vain is the net spread out before the eyes of any bird — YLT

and the snare is laid to no purpose if the bird is watching — Knox

the net is always spread in vain
if the bird is watching — Jerus

18. And they lay wait for their own blood; they lurk privily for their own lives.

but these men lie in wait for their own blood,
they set an ambush for their own lives — RSV

And they for their own blood lay wait,

They watch secretly for their own lives — YLT

These men lie in wait for their own blood,
they set a trap for their own lives — NAB

And they are secretly waiting for their blood and making ready destruction for themselves — Bas

and these men trap themselves in death,
'tis their own lives they ambush — Mof

What do they, but compass their own ruin, plot against their own lives — Knox

19. So are the ways of every one that is greedy of gain; which taketh away the life of the owners thereof.

Such are the paths of each glutton after lucre;
It seduceth the soul enslaved by it — Sprl

Such are the ways of everyone that graspeth with greed,
The life of the owners thereof it taketh away — Rhm

To this come all men who are after dishonest gain,
which robs of their lives all those who take it for their own — Jerus

This is the fate of men eager for ill-gotten gain:
it robs those who get it of their lives — NEB

So is the way of each one destroying for plunder;
it takes away the life of its followers — Ber

This is the fate of everyone greedy of loot:
unlawful gain takes away the life of him who acquires it — NAB

Such is the fate of all who live by violence and murder. They will die a violent death — Tay

20. Wisdom crieth without; she uttereth her voice in the streets:

Wisdom crieth aloud in the street;
She uttereth her voice in the broad places — ASV

Wisdom uttereth her song at the gates and in the streets speaketh boldly — Sept

Wisdom in the open place soundeth forth,
In the broadways she raiseth her voice — Rhm

Wisdom is crying out in the street; her voice is loud in the open places — Bas

And all the while Wisdom is publishing her message, crying it aloud in the open streets — Knox

Wisdom cries aloud in the street;
in the markets she raises her voice — RSV

21. She crieth in the chief places of concourse, in the openings of the gates: in the city she uttereth her words, saying,

She calleth at the head of the noisy streets,
At the entrances of the gates, in the city, she uttereth her words — JPS

At the head of the thronged ways she calls,
At the opening of the gates;
In the city she utters her words — ABPS

at the noisy intersections she calls;
in the entrances of the city gates she speaks her words — Ber

Down the crowded ways she calls out,
at the city gates she utters her words — NAB

22. How long, ye simple ones, will ye love simplicity? and the scorners delight in their scorning, and fools hate knowledge?

How long, ye thoughtless, will ye love thoughtlessness?
And how long will scorners delight them in scorning,
And fools hate knowledge — JPS

How long, O simple ones, will you love being simple?
How long will scoffers delight in their mocking
and fools despise knowledge — Ber

O heedless ones, how long will you choose to be heedless,
and scoffers delight in scoffing,
and senseless folk hate knowledge — Mof

You ignorant people, how much longer will you cling to your ignorance?
How much longer will mockers revel in their mocking
and fools hold knowledge contemptible — Jerus

23. Turn you at my reproof: behold, I will

pour out my spirit unto you, I will make known my words unto you.
Repent ye at My reproof!
Behold! I will pour out My Spirit upon you;
I will make known My words unto you — Sprl
Give heed to my reproof;
behold, I will pour out my thoughts to you;
I will make my words known to you — RSV
If only you would respond to my reproof,
I would give you my counsel
and teach you my precepts — NEB
If you but turn and pay heed to my admonition,
Lo! I will open my mind to you,
I will acquaint you with my thoughts — AAT
Pay heed, then, to my protest; listen while I speak out my mind to you, give you open warning — Knox

24. **Because I have called, and ye refused; I have stretched out my hand, and no man regarded;**
seeing I have called and you have not answered: and though I continued my speech, you did not attend — Sept
Because I besought and you refused,
I stretched out my hand and no one responded — Ber
Because I have called and you refused to listen,
have stretched out my hand and no one has heeded — RSV
Since I have called and you have refused me,
since I have beckoned and no one has taken notice — Jerus
Because your ears were shut to my voice; no one gave attention to my outstretched hand — Bas

25. **But ye have set at nought all my counsel, and would none of my reproof:**
And ye have refused all my counsel,
Nor would receive my reproof — ABPS
But ye dismissed all my counsel,
And to my rebuke would not yield — Rhm
But you have despised all my counsels, and you were not pleased with my reproof — Lam
You ignored all my counsel,
And would not have my admonition — AAT
because you spurned all my advice
and would have nothing to do with my reproof — NEB

26. **I also will laugh at your calamity; I will mock when your fear cometh;**
I also will laugh in the day of your calamity;
I will mock when your fear cometh — ASV
therefore I will laugh at your calamity;
and mock when your destruction cometh — Sept
I also, in your calamity, will laugh,
I will mock when your dread cometh — JPS
I, for my part, will laugh at your distress,
I will jeer at you when calamity comes — Jerus
So in the day of your trouble I will be laughing; I will make sport of your fear — Bas

27. **When your fear cometh as desolation, and your destruction cometh as a whirlwind; when distress and anguish cometh upon you.**
When your fear cometh as a storm,
and your calamity cometh on as a whirlwind; when distress and anguish come upon you — RV
When your fear comes as a tempest,
And your calamity shall come as a whirlwind;
When distress and anguish come upon you — ABPS
When your dread cometh as a storm,
And your calamity cometh on as a whirlwind;
When trouble and distress come upon you — JPS
When your terror comes like a storm,
And your doom descends like a whirlwind,
When distress and anguish befall you — AAT
When your fear cometh as destruction,
And your calamity as a hurricane doth come,
When on you come adversity and distress — YLT

28. **Then shall they call upon me, but I will not answer; they shall seek me early, but they shall not find me:**

Then they call me, and I do not answer,
They seek me earnestly, and find me not — YLT

Then will they cry unto Me, but I will not answer;
They shall seek Me diligently, but they shall not find Me — Sprl

Then they shall call to me, but I will not answer,
they shall seek me eagerly and shall not find me — Jerus

Then they will beseech me, but I will not answer;
they will seek me diligently, but will not find me — Ber

It will be their turn, then, to call aloud; my turn, then, to refuse an answer — Knox

Then I will not answer your cry for help. It will be too late though you search for me ever so anxiously — Tay

29. For that they hated knowledge, and did not choose the fear of the LORD:

For they were haters of knowledge, and did not give their hearts to the fear of the Lord — Bas

Because they despised knowledge,
and did not choose reverence for the LORD — Ber

They despised knowledge,
they had no love for the fear of Yahweh — Jerus

For you closed your eyes to the facts and did not choose to reverence and trust the Lord — Tay

30. They would none of my counsel: they despised all my reproof.

nor would they attend to my counsels, but contemned my reproofs — Sept

They were not pleased with my counsels; they rejected all of my reproof — Lam

They would not have my counsel,
They spurned all my admonition — AAT

They would have none of my counsel, but despised every warning of mine — Mof

Consented not to my counsel,
Disdained all my rebuke — Rhm

31. Therefore shall they eat of the fruit of their own way, and be filled with their own devices.

Now they must eat the fruit of their own way,
and with their own devices be glutted — NAB

so now they must eat the fruit of their own doings,
and have their fill of all that they devised — Mof

they shall eat the fruits of their behaviour
and have a surfeit of their own devices — NEB

so they must eat the fruits of their own courses,
and choke themselves with their own scheming — Jerus

therefore they will eat of the fruit of their way,
will be sated with their own counsel — Ber

32. For the turning away of the simple shall slay them, and the prosperity of fools shall destroy them.

For the backsliding of the simple shall slay them,
And the careless ease of fools shall destroy them — ASV

For the waywardness of the thoughtless shall slay them,
And the confidence of fools shall destroy them — JPS

For the defection of fools shall slay them,
And the security of the stupid shall destroy them — Sprl

For the simple are killed by their turning away,
and the complacence of fools destroys them — RSV

For the self-will of the simple kills them,
the smugness of fools destroys them — NAB

For the waywardness of the simple brings their death,
and the self-assurance of fools their destruction — Ber

33. But whoso hearkeneth unto me shall dwell safely, and shall be quiet from fear of evil.

But whoso hearkeneth unto me shall dwell securely, and shall be quiet without fear of evil — RV

But whoever gives ear to me will take his rest safely, living in peace without fear of evil — Bas

but he who listens to me will dwell secure
and will be at ease, without dread of evil — RSV
While he who listens to me shall live in security,
And shall enjoy peace of mind without dread of evil — AAT
Whereas he that hearkeneth unto me shall dwell safely,
And be at rest without dread of misfortune — Rhm
But he who obeys me dwells in security,
in peace, without fear of harm — NAB

CHAPTER 2

1. My son, if thou wilt receive my words, and hide my commandments with thee;
My son, if thou wilt receive my sayings,
And my commandments wilt treasure up by thee — Rhm
My son, if thou wilt accept my words,
And treasure my commandments within thy breast — Sprl
My son, if thou wilt receive my words,
And lay up my commandments with thee — ASV
My son, if you take to heart what I say,
and set store by my commands — Mof
My son, if you will take my words to your heart, storing up my laws in your mind — Bas

2. So that thou incline thine ear unto wisdom, and apply thine heart to understanding;
So as to direct thine ear to wisdom,
Incline thy heart to understanding — ABPS
So that thou make thine ear attend unto wisdom,
And thy heart incline to discernment — JPS
Inclining your ear to wisdom,
And applying your mind to reason — AAT
tuning your ear to wisdom,
and applying your heart to truth — Jerus
ever be thy ear attentive to wisdom,
thy mind eager to attain discernment — Knox

3. Yea, if thou criest after knowledge, and liftest up thy voice for understanding;
Yea, if thou cry after discernment,
And lift up thy voice for understanding — ASV
Yea, if thou call for understanding,
And lift up thy voice for discernment — JPS
yes, if you cry out for insight
and raise your voice for understanding — RSV
Truly, if you are crying out for good sense, and your request is for knowledge — Bas
if you cry to intelligence
and call for knowledge — Mof
yes, if you beseech understanding,
and lift your voice for discernment — Ber

4. If thou seekest her as silver, and searchest for her as for hid treasures;
If thou search for her as silver,
And as hidden treasures dig for her — ABPS
If you are looking for her as for silver, and searching for her as for stored-up wealth — Bas
if you seek her out like silver
and dig for her like buried treasure — NEB
if you look for it as if it were silver,
and search for it as for buried treasure — Jerus

5. Then shalt thou understand the fear of the LORD, and find the knowledge of God.
Then shalt thou comprehend the fear of JEHOVAH,
And shalt attain the knowledge of God — Sprl
Then shalt thou understand the reverence of Yahweh,
And the knowledge of God shalt thou find — Rhm
then you shall see what reverence for the Eternal is,
and find out what the knowledge of God means — Mof
Then you will understand how to worship the LORD and find the knowledge of God — Lam

Then you will understand reverence for the LORD,
And will discover the knowledge of God — AAT
Then the fear of the Lord will be clear to you, and knowledge of God will be yours — Bas

6. For the LORD giveth wisdom: out of his mouth cometh knowledge and understanding.
For the LORD giveth wisdom,
Out of His mouth cometh knowledge and discernment — JPS
for the LORD bestows wisdom
and teaches knowledge and understanding — NEB
For the LORD gives wisdom,
Out of his mouth come knowledge and reason — AAT
for it is the Eternal who supplies wisdom,
from him come insight and knowledge — Mof
For the Lord grants wisdom! His every word is a treasure of knowledge and understanding — Tay

7. He layeth up sound wisdom for the righteous: he is a buckler to them that walk uprightly.
He layeth up sound wisdom for the upright;
He is a shield to them that walk in integrity — ASV
And has help in store for the upright,
A shield for those who walk in integrity — ABPS
He has help in store for the upright,
He is a shield to those who walk honestly — AAT
He has counsel in store for the upright,
he is the shield of those who walk honestly — NAB
He keeps his help for honest men,
he is the shield of those whose ways are honourable — Jerus
Yea, he treasureth for the upright safety,
A shield is he to them who walk in integrity — Rhm

8. He keepeth the paths of judgment, and preserveth the way of his saints.
That He may guard the paths of justice,
And preserve the way of His godly ones — JPS
To protect them in the paths of judgment;
For He guardeth the way of His saints — Sprl
To keep the paths of rectitude,
And the way of his pious ones he guards — ABPS
he stands guard over the paths of justice,
he keeps watch on the way of his devoted ones — Jerus
for he guards the course of justice
and keeps watch over the way of his loyal servants — NEB

9. Then shalt thou understand righteousness, and judgment, and equity; yea, every good path.
Then shalt thou understand righteousness and justice,
And equity — every noble course — Rhm
Then you will understand right, justice and uprightness, every good road — Ber
Then you will understand righteousness and justice and the uprightness of all good ways — Lam
then you shall understand duty and goodness,
and keep to every honest course — Mof
Duty and right and honour thou shalt discern, and see ever where the best course lies — Knox

10. When wisdom entereth into thine heart, and knowledge is pleasant unto thy soul;

11. Discretion shall preserve thee, understanding shall keep thee:
For when wisdom entereth into thine understanding: and knowledge appeareth pleasant to thy soul: good counsel will keep thee, and holy prudence will guard thee — Sept
For wisdom shall enter into thy heart,
And knowledge shall be pleasant unto thy soul;
Discretion shall watch over thee;
Understanding shall keep thee — ASV
For wisdom cometh into thy heart,
And knowledge to thy soul is pleasant,
Thoughtfulness doth watch over thee,
Understanding doth keep thee — YLT

For when wisdom finds a welcome within you,
And knowledge becomes a pleasure to you,
Discretion will watch over you,
Reason will guard you — AAT

for wisdom will sink into your mind,
and knowledge will be your heart's delight.
Prudence will keep watch over you,
understanding will guard you — NEB

For wisdom will be welcome to your mind,
knowledge will be a joy to you,
good sense will take charge of you,
sound judgment will keep you right — Mof

12. To deliver thee from the way of the evil man, from the man that speaketh froward things;

To deliver thee from the way of evil,
from the men that speak froward things — RV

To preserve thee from the evil way,
From the man that speaks perverseness — ABPS

To rescue thee from the way of the wrongful,
From the man that speaketh perverse things — Rhm

Saving you from the way of evil men,
from men of perverse speech — NAB

Giving you salvation from the evil man, from those whose words are false — Bas

13. Who leave the paths of uprightness, to walk in the ways of darkness;

Who forsake the paths of uprightness,
To walk in the ways of darkness — ASV

From them who forsake the paths of rectitude,
To walk in the ways of darkness — Rhm

who forsake the honest course
to walk in ways of darkness — NEB

who leave the paths of right
to follow some dark course — Mof

from those who leave the paths of honesty
to walk the roads of darkness — Jerus

14. Who rejoice to do evil, and delight in the frowardness of the wicked;

15. Whose ways are crooked, and they froward in their paths:

Who rejoice to do evil;
Who delight in the perversity of the wicked,
Whose paths are perverted,
And they themselves froward in their ways — Sprl

Who rejoice to do evil,
And delight in the perverseness of evil;
Who are crooked in their ways,
And wayward in their paths — ASV

Who delight in doing evil,
rejoice in perversity;
Whose ways are crooked,
and devious their paths — NAB

Who delight in doing evil,
Exult in wanton wickedness;
Who are crooked in their ways,
And tortuous in their paths — AAT

And exult in doing wrong, for they thoroughly enjoy their sins. Everything they do is crooked and wrong — Tay

16. To deliver thee from the strange woman, even from the stranger which flattereth with her words;

To rescue thee from the woman that is a stranger,
From the female unknown who with her speeches seduceth — Rhm

to deliver you from the alien woman,
from the outsider with her flattering words — Amp

saving you also from the loose woman,
the harlot with her words so smooth — Mof

You will be saved from the loose woman,
from the adventuress with her smooth words — RSV

It will save you from the adulteress,
from the loose woman with her seductive words — NEB

Keeping you also from the alien woman,
from the stranger, with her wheedling words — Jerus

17. Which forsaketh the guide of her youth, and forgetteth the covenant of her God.

Who forsakes the partner of her youth,
And forgets the covenant of her God — ABPS

Who forsakes the companion of her youth,

And forgets her pledge to her God — AAT
Who forsaketh the husband of her youth,
And forsaketh the covenant of her God — Sprl
Who is false to the husband of her early years, and does not keep the agreement of her God in mind — Bas
Who forsakes the companion of her youth
and forgets the pact with her God — NAB
who leaves her own husband,
forgetting her married troth before God — Mof

18. For her house inclineth unto death, and her paths unto the dead.
Verily, her house leadeth down to death,
And her paths unto Hades — Sprl
for her house sinks down to death,
and her paths to the shades — RSV
For she hath appointed unto death her house,
And unto the shades her courses — Rhm
The house she dwells in is death's antechamber, the road by which she beckons leads to the grave — Knox

19. None that go unto her return again, neither take they hold of the paths of life.
None that go unto her return again,
Neither do they attain unto the paths of life — ASV
None who walk by her direction can ever return; nor ever recover the right paths — Sept
none going to her return,
nor reach the ways of life — Ber
None who enter thereon come back again,
or gain the paths of life — NAB
Of those who go to her not one returns,
they never regain the paths of life — Jerus
None who go to her return again, neither do they remember the path of life — Lam

20. That thou mayest walk in the way of good men, and keep the paths of the righteous.
That thou dost go in the way of the good,
And the paths of the righteous dost keep — YLT
So that you may go in the way of good men, and keep in the footsteps of the upright — Bas
Helping you to walk in the way of good men,
And to keep to the paths of the righteous — AAT
living the life of honest men
and keeping to the good man's road — Mof
Thus you may walk in the way of good men,
and keep to the paths of the just — NAB
Follow the steps of the godly instead,
and stay on the right path — Tay

21. For the upright shall dwell in the land, and the perfect shall remain in it.
For the upright will inhabit the land
and men of integrity remain in it — Ber
For the upright shall abide on the earth,
And the men of integrity shall remain therein — Rhm
For the upright shall abide in the earth,
And the just shall continue therein — Sprl
For the upright will live in the land,
And the honest will remain in it — AAT
For the land will be for honest men to live in,
the innocent will have it for their home — Jerus
For the upright will be living in the land, and the good will have it for their heritage — Bas

22. But the wicked shall be cut off from the earth, and the transgressors shall be rooted out of it.
But the wicked shall be cut off from the land,
And the treacherous shall be rooted out of it — ASV
But the wicked shall be cut off from the land, and they that deal treacherously shall be rooted out of it — RV
But the lawless out of the earth shall be cut off,

And traitors shall they tear away therefrom — Rhm
But the wicked shall be cut off from the land,
And the faithless shall be plucked up out of it — JPS
the ways of the wicked shall be destroyed from the land; and the transgressors shall be driven out of it — Sept
But sinners will be cut off from the land, and those whose acts are false will be uprooted — Bas
But the wicked shall be cut off from the earth,
And the hypocrites shall be taken out of it — Sprl

CHAPTER 3

1. My son, forget not my law; but let thine heart keep my commandments;
My son, mine instruction do not thou forget,
And my commandment let thy heart observe — Rhm
My son, do not forget my teaching, but guard my commands in your heart — NEB
My son, do not forget my teaching, let your heart keep my principles — Jerus
My son, forget not my directions, keep in mind what I command — Mof
Forget not then, my son, the teaching I give thee; lock these words of mine close in thy bosom — Knox
My son, keep my teaching in your memory, and my rules in your heart — Bas

2. For length of days, and long life, and peace, shall they add to thee.
For length of days, and years of life,
And peace, will they add to thee — ASV
For length of days and years,
Life and peace, shall they add unto thee — Sprl
for length of days and years of life and abundant welfare will they give you — RSV
For a long and happy life,
With abundant prosperity, will they bring to you — AAT
for these will give you lengthier days, longer years of life, and greater happiness — Jerus
for long life and years in plenty
will they bring you, and prosperity as well — NEB

3. Let not mercy and truth forsake thee: bind them about thy neck; write them upon the table of thine heart:
Let not kindness and truth forsake thee:
Bind them about thy neck;
Write them upon the tablet of thy heart — ASV
Let not kindness and good faith leave you;
Fasten them round your neck,
Write them on the tablet of your mind — AAT
Let not loyalty and faithfulness forsake you;
bind them about your neck,
write them on the tablet of your heart — RSV
Let not mercy and good faith go from you; let them be hanging round your neck, recorded on your heart — Bas
Never forget to be truthful and kind. Hold these virtues tightly. Write them deep within your heart — Tay

4. So shalt thou find favour and good understanding in the sight of God and man.
So find thou favour and good repute,
In the eyes of God and man — Rhm
So shalt thou find grace and good favour
In the sight of God and man — JPS
So shalt thou obtain love and gracious favour
In the sight of God and of man — Sprl
so you shall have goodwill and good repute
with God and man alike — Mof
Then will you win favor and good esteem
before God and man — NAB
thus finding favor and ideal understanding
in the sight of God and of man — Ber

5. Trust in the LORD with all thine heart; and lean not unto thine own understanding.

6. In all thy ways acknowledge him, and he shall direct thy paths.

Confide in JEHOVAH with all thine heart,
And depend not upon thine own understanding.
In all thy doings acknowledge Him;
And He will direct thy paths — Sprl

Trust in the LORD with all your heart,
and do not rely on your own insight.
In all your ways acknowledge him,
and he will make straight your paths — RSV

Rely with all your heart on the Eternal,
and never lean on your own insight;
have mind of him wherever you may go,
and he will clear the road for you — Mof

Trust in the LORD with all your heart,
on your own intelligence rely not;
In all your ways be mindful of him,
and he will make straight your paths — NAB

Trust wholeheartedly in Yahweh,
put no faith in your own perception;
in every course you take, have him in mind:
he will see that your paths are smooth — Jerus

Put all your hope in God, not looking to your reason for support.
In all your ways give ear to him, and he will make straight your footsteps — Bas

7. Be not wise in thine own eyes: fear the LORD, and depart from evil.

Be not wise in thine own conceit; but fear God and depart from all evil — Sept

Do not become wise in thine own eyes,
Revere Yahweh and avoid evil — Rhm

Never pride yourself on your own wisdom,
revere the Eternal and draw back from sin — Mof

Do not think how wise you are,
but fear the LORD and turn from evil — NEB

Do not give thyself airs of wisdom; enough that thou shouldst fear God and shun ill-doing — Knox

Do not think of yourself as wise,
fear Yahweh and turn your back on evil — Jerus

8. It shall be health to thy navel, and marrow to thy bones.

it will be healing to your body and nourishment to your bones — Ber

It shall be healing to your flesh and marrow to your bones — Lam

This will mean health for your flesh
and vigor for your bones — NAB

then shall thy body have health and thy bones a cure — Sept

This will give strength to your flesh,
and new life to your bones — Bas

9. Honour the LORD with thy substance, and with the first fruits of all thine increase:

Honour Jehovah from thy substance,
And from the beginning of all thine increase — YLT

Glorify JEHOVAH with thy wealth,
And with the best of all thine increase — Sprl

Honor the LORD with your substance and with the first fruits of all your crops — Lam

Honor the LORD with your wealth,
with first fruits of all your produce — NAB

Honor the Lord by giving him the first part of all your income — Tay

10. So shall thy barns be filled with plenty, and thy presses shall burst out with new wine.

So shall thy barns be filled with plenty,
And thy vats shall overflow with new wine — ASV

So shall thy storehouses be filled with plenty,
And with new wine shall thy vats overflow — Rhm

So will your barns be filled with grain,
And your vats will be bursting with wine — AAT

So your store-houses will be full of grain, and your vessels overflowing with new wine — Bas

11. My son, despise not the chastening of the LORD; neither be weary of his correction:

My son, do not despise the LORD's discipline
or be weary of his reproof — RSV

My son, slight not the correction of

the Lord; nor faint when reproved by him — Sept

My son, despise not the discipline of the LORD,
And resent not his correction — AAT

My son, spurn not the Eternal's schooling,
never be weary of the discipline — Mof

The chastening of Yahweh, my son, do not reject,
Nor loathe his rebuke — Rhm

Chastisement of Jehovah, my son, despise not,
And be not vexed with His reproof — YLT

12. For whom the LORD loveth he correcteth; even as a father the son in whom he delighteth.

For whom JEHOVAH loveth He chasteneth,
Even like unto a father the son he delighteth in — Sprl

For whom Jehovah loveth He reproveth,
Even as a father the son He is pleased with — YLT

his discipline is for the man he loves,
he chastens any son whom he delights in — Mof

It is where he loves that he bestows correction, like a father whose son is dear to him — Knox

for Yahweh reproves the man he loves, as a father checks a well-loved son — Jerus

13. Happy is the man that findeth wisdom, and the man that getteth understanding:

How happy the man who hath found wisdom,
And the man who draweth forth understanding — Rhm

Blessed is the man who has found wisdom,
the man who obtains understanding — Ber

Happy is the man who makes discovery of wisdom, and he who gets knowledge — Bas

Happy is the man who gathers wisdom,
the man who gains knowledge — Mof

Happy the man whose treasure-trove is wisdom, who is rich in discernment — Knox

14. For the merchandise of it is better than the merchandise of silver, and the gain thereof than fine gold.

For the gaining of it is better than the gaining of silver,
And the profit thereof than fine gold — ASV

For her gain is better than the gain of silver,
And her increase than gold — ABPS

for the gain from it is better than gain from silver
and its profit better than gold — RSV

For her profit is better than profit in silver,
and better than gold is her revenue — NAB

15. She is more precious than rubies: and all the things thou canst desire are not to be compared to her.

She is more precious than rubies: and none of the things thou canst desire are to be compared unto her — ASV

She is more precious than pearls,
And all thy valuables compare not with her — Sprl

More precious is she than corals,
Yea none of thy delightful things doth equal her — Rhm

She is more precious than jewels,
and nothing you desire can compare with her — RSV

She is beyond the price of pearls,
nothing you could covet is her equal — Jerus

16. Length of days is in her right hand; and in her left hand riches and honour.

Length of days is in her right hand,
In her left are wealth and honour — YLT

long days lie in her right hand,
wealth and honour in her left — Mof

Long life wisdom holds out to thee in one hand, riches and glory in the other — Knox

17. Her ways are ways of pleasantness, and all her paths are peace.

18. She is a tree of life to them that lay hold upon her: and happy is everyone that retaineth her.

her ways are ways of tranquil ease,
and all her paths are bliss: to those

who grasp her, she is vital strength—
happy are all who hold her fast — Mof

Her ways are ways of delight, and all her goings are peace.
She is a tree of life to all who take her in their hands, and happy is everyone who keeps her — Bas

Her ways are pleasant ways
and all her paths lead to prosperity.
She is a staff of life to all who grasp her,
and those who hold her fast are safe — NEB

Her ways are delightful ways,
her paths all lead to contentment.
She is a tree of life for those who hold her fast,
those who cling to her live happy lives — Jerus

her ways are pleasant ones, peaceful all her paths.
She is a tree of life to those laying hold of her,
making happy each one holding her fast — Ber

19. The LORD by wisdom hath founded the earth; by understanding hath he established the heavens.

By wisdom God founded the earth; and by understanding he furnished the heavens — Sept

The Lord by wisdom put in position the bases of the earth; by reason he put the heavens in their place — Bas

By wisdom, Yahweh set the earth on its foundations,
by discernment, he fixed the heavens firm — Jerus

The Lord's wisdom founded the earth; his understanding established all the universe and space — Tay

20. By his knowledge the depths are broken up, and the clouds drop down the dew.

By His knowledge depths have been rent,
And clouds do drop dew — YLT

By his knowledge the resounding deeps were burst open,
And the skies drop down dew — Rhm

By his knowledge the deeps were broken open,
And vapors distil the dew — ABPS

'twas with intelligence he broke up the abyss
and made the clouds drop dew — Mof

By His knowledge the deeps pour forth,
and the skies distil the dew — Ber

Through his knowledge the depths were carved out,
and the clouds rain down the dew — Jerus

21. My son, let not them depart from thine eyes: keep sound wisdom and discretion:

My son! let them not turn from thine eyes,
Keep thou wisdom and thoughtfulness — YLT

My son, let them not depart from thine eyes,
Guard thou counsel and purpose — Rhm

My son, let not these slip out of your sight:
keep advice and counsel in view — NAB

My son, let not my commandments depart from your eyes; keep my doctrine, and my counsels — Lam

My son, keep good sense, and do not let wise purpose go from your eyes — Bas

My son, keep watch over your ability and prudence,
do not let them slip from sight — NEB

22. So shall they be life unto thy soul, and grace to thy neck.

they will make your life long,
and add charm to it — Mof

that thy soul may live and that grace may be around thy neck — Sept

And they will be life to your inner self, and a gracious ornament to your neck [your outer self] — Amp

and they will be life for your soul and adornment for your neck — RSV

They will be life to you,
And an ornament round your neck — AAT

For they fill you with living energy,
and are a feather in your cap — Tay

23. Then shalt thou walk in thy way safely, and thy foot shall not stumble.

Then shalt thou walk in thy way securely,
And thy foot shall not stumble — ASV

Then wilt thou proceed on thy way safely,
And thy foot shall not stumble — Sprl

Then shalt thou walk in thy way securely,
And thou shalt not dash thy foot — JPS

Then you may go on your way in security,
Without striking your foot on a stone — AAT

Then you will walk your way confidently
and will not stumble — Ber

Then you shall walk in your way with hope and your foot shall not stumble — Lam

24. When thou liest down, thou shalt not be afraid: yea, thou shalt lie down, and thy sleep shall be sweet.

For when thou liest down, thou shalt be free from fear: and when thou sleepest, thou shalt sleep sweetly — Sept

When thou reclinest, thou shalt not be afraid,
And reclining, then thy sleep shall be refreshing — Sprl

When you take your rest you will have no fear, and on your bed sleep will be sweet to you — Bas

when you lie down it will not be in dread;
for when you lie down your sleep will be sweet — Ber

When you lie down, you need not be afraid,
when you rest, your sleep will be sweet — NAB

you can rest unafraid,
you can lie down to a sweet sleep — Mof

25. Be not afraid of sudden fear, neither of the desolation of the wicked, when it cometh.

Be not thou afraid of sudden dread,
Nor of the desolation of the lawless, when it cometh — Rhm

Be not afraid of sudden terror,
Neither of the destruction of the wicked, when it cometh — JPS

Do not be afraid of sudden panic,
or of the ruin of the wicked, when it comes — RSV

Be not dismayed at sudden fear,
Nor at the destruction of the wicked when it comes — ABPS

You will fear no sudden terror,
Nor the storm that falls on the wicked — AAT

never need you fear sudden blows
or the storm that strikes the wicked — Mof

26. For the LORD shall be thy confidence, and shall keep thy foot from being taken.

For Jehovah is at thy side,
And He hath kept thy foot from capture — YLT

For Yahweh will be in all thy ways,
And will keep thy foot from the snare — Rhm

For the Lord will be over all thy ways,
and will support thy foot that thou mayest not be shaken — Sept

For the LORD will be thy confidence,
And will keep thy foot from being caught — JPS

for the Eternal will be your protection,
and preserve you from all danger — Mof

27. Withhold not good from them to whom it is due, when it is in the power of thy hand to do it.

Withhold not help from the needy,
When it is in your power to render it — AAT

Hold back no benefit from those entitled to it,
when it is in the power of your hand to perform — Ber

Do not refuse to do that which is good,
when it is in the power of your hand to do it — Lam

Refuse no man any favour that you owe him
when it lies in your power to pay it — NEB

Do not refuse a kindness to anyone who begs it,
if it is in your power to perform it — Jerus

Do not keep back good from those who have a right to it, when it is in the power of your hand to do it — Bas

Refuse no one the good on which he has a claim
when it is in your power to do it for him — NAB

28. Say not unto thy neighbour, Go and come again, and tomorrow I will give; when thou hast it by thee.

Do not say to your neighbor, "Go, and come again,
tomorrow I will give it" — when you have it with you — RSV

Say not to your neighbor, "Go and come back
and tomorrow I will give"; when you already have it — Ber

never say to him, "Go, and come again,
I will have it to-morrow for you" — when you have it beside you — Mof

Say not to your neighbor, "Go, and come again,
tomorrow I will give," when you can give at once — NAB

29. Devise not evil against thy neighbour, seeing he dwelleth securely by thee.

Contrive not evil against thy neighbour
When he dwelleth in confidence beside thee — Sprl

Do not devise evil against your neighbor, seeing he dwells in peace beside you — Lam

Do not plot harm against your neighbour
as he lives unsuspecting next door — Jerus

Do not plan evil against your neighbor who dwells trustingly beside you — RSV

Plot no mischief against your neighbor,
When he lives in confidence beside you — AAT

Never plot harm against the friend that suspects no harm of thee — Knox

30. Strive not with a man without cause, if he have done thee no harm.

31. Envy thou not the oppressor, and choose none of his ways.

Strive not with a man without cause,
If he have done thee no harm.
Envy thou not the man of violence,
And choose none of his ways — ASV

Do not idly quarrel with a man,
If he have done you no harm.
Envy not the lawless man,
And choose none of his ways — AAT

Never quarrel with a man for no reason,
when he has never done you any harm.
Never envy a high-handed man,
or choose his methods — Mof

Do not take up a cause at law against a man for nothing, if he has done you no wrong.
Have no envy of the violent man, or take any of his ways as an example — Bas

Do not pick a quarrel with a man for no reason,
if he has not done you a bad turn.
Do not emulate a lawless man,
do not choose to follow his footsteps — NEB

Don't get into needless fights. Don't envy violent men. Don't copy their ways — Tay

32. For the froward is abomination to the LORD: but his secret is with the righteous.

For the perverse is an abomination to the LORD: but his secret is with the upright — RV

For the perverse is an abomination to Jehovah;
But his friendship is with the upright — ASV

for the perverse man is an abomination to the LORD,
but the upright are in his confidence — RSV

for an abomination to the LORD is the perverse,
but His intimate counsel is with the upright — Ber

For an abomination to Jehovah is the perverted,
And with the upright is His secret counsel — YLT

for the wilful wrong-doer is abhorrent to Yahweh,
who confides only in honest men — Jerus

33. The curse of the LORD is in the house of the wicked: but he blesseth the habitation of the just.

The curse of Yahweh is in the house of the lawless one,
But the home of the righteous he blesseth — Rhm

the Eternal's curse lies on the house of the wicked,
but he blesses the good man's dwelling — Mof

The curse of the LORD is on the house of the wicked,
But the home of the righteous he blesses — AAT

The curse of the LORD is on the house of the wicked,
but the dwelling of the just he blesses — NAB

34. Surely he scorneth the scorners: but he giveth grace unto the lowly.

Surely he scoffeth at the scoffers;
But he giveth grace unto the lowly — ASV

The Lord mocks at mockers, but helps the humble — Tay

He makes sport of the men of pride, but he gives grace to the gentle-hearted — Bas

As for scorners, He scorns them, but to the humble He gives grace — Ber

When he is dealing with the arrogant, he is stern,
but to the humble he shows kindness — NAB

Though he mocks at those who mock,
Yet gives he favor to the lowly — ABPS

Though God himself meets the arrogant with arrogance,
yet he bestows his favour on the meek — NEB

35. The wise shall inherit glory: but shame shall be the promotion of fools.

The wise shall inherit honor;
But fools he exalts to shame — ABPS

and the wise shall win renown; only to their shame are fools exalted — Knox

The wise shall inherit honour;
But as for the fools, they carry away shame — JPS

The wise will inherit honor,
but fools get disgrace — RSV

Honour is the portion of the wise,
all that fools inherit is disgrace — Jerus

The wise shall inherit honour;
But ignominy shall be the fame of fools — Sprl

CHAPTER 4

1. Hear, ye children, the instruction of a father, and attend to know understanding.

2. For I give you good doctrine, forsake ye not my law.

Hear, ye children, the instruction of a father,
And attend to know understanding.
For I give you good doctrine;
Forsake ye not my teaching — JPS

Hear, O sons, a father's instruction,
and be attentive, that you may gain insight;
for I give you good precepts:
do not forsake my teaching — RSV

Listen, my children, to a father's instruction,
attend and learn intelligence:
I give you good counsel,
turn not from my teaching — Mof

Hear, O sons, the instruction of a father;
listen carefully to gain insight.
Since I give you good doctrine do not forsake my teaching — Ber

Hear, O children, a father's instruction,
be attentive, that you may gain understanding!
Yes, excellent advice I give you;
my teaching do not forsake — NAB

3. For I was my father's son, tender and only beloved in the sight of my mother.

For a son became I to my father,
Tender and most precious in the sight of my mother — Rhm

For I was also a son to my father, tender and the only begotten in the sight of my mother — Lam

for I was a son obedient to a father; and beloved in the sight of a mother — Sept

For a son was I to my father;
Tender, and an only child, in the sight of my mother — ABPS

I too have been a father's son,
tender in years, my mother's only child — NEB

When as a boy I was tender in my father's sight,
And dearly beloved in the eyes of my mother — AAT

4. He taught me also, and said unto me,

Let thine heart retain my words: keep my commandments, and live.

And he instructed me, and he said unto me:
Let thine heart take fast hold of my words;
Keep my commandments, and live — Sprl

he taught me and told me this:
"Keep in mind what I say,
do what I bid you, and you shall live — Mof

He taught me, and said to me: "Hold fast my words in your mind,
Keep my commandments, and live — AAT

This was what he used to teach me,
'Let your heart treasure what I have to say,
keep my principles and you shall live — Jerus

And he gave me teaching, saying to me, Keep my words in your heart; keep my rules so that you may have life — Bas

He told me never to forget his words. "If you follow them," he said, "you will have a long and happy life — Tay

5. **Get wisdom, get understanding: forget it not; neither decline from the words of my mouth.**

Get wisdom, get understanding,
Do not forget, nor turn away
From the sayings of my mouth — YLT

acquire wisdom, acquire perception,
never forget her, never deviate from my words — Jerus

do not forget, and do not turn away from the words of my mouth.
Get wisdom; get insight — RSV

Forget not, and swerve not from the words of my mouth —
Get wisdom, get understanding — AAT

Get wisdom, get true knowledge; keep it in memory, do not be turned away from the words of my mouth — Bas

Get wisdom, get understanding!
Do not forget or turn aside from the words I utter — NAB

6. **Forsake her not, and she shall preserve thee: love her, and she shall keep thee:**

forsake it not, and it will defend thee:
love it and it will preserve thee — Sept

Forsake her not, and she will guard thee;
Love her, and she will preserve thee — Sprl

Do not forsake her, and she will preserve you; love her, and she will save you — Lam

Do not forsake her and she will protect you;
love her, and she will guard you — Ber

never leave her, and she will guard you,
love her, and she will take care of you — Mof

Do not give her up, and she will keep you; give her your love, and she will make you safe — Bas

7. **Wisdom is the principal thing; therefore get wisdom: and with all thy getting, get understanding.**

The first thing is wisdom; get wisdom,
And with all thy getting, get understanding — ABPS

The principal thing is wisdom; acquire thou wisdom,
With all thine acqusition acquire thou understanding — Rhm

The summit of all things is wisdom; therefore acquire wisdom:
And before all thy acquisitions acquire understanding — Sprl

The beginning of wisdom is this: Get wisdom,
and whatever you get, get insight — RSV

Above all things get wisdom;
Whatever else you get, get understanding — AAT

The first thing is to acquire wisdom;
gain understanding though it cost you all you have — NEB

8. **Exalt her, and she shall promote thee: she shall bring thee to honour, when thou dost embrace her.**

Esteem her very highly, and she will exalt thee;
She will honour thee if thou wilt embrace her — Sprl

Extol her, and she will exalt thee;
She will bring thee to honour
when thou dost embrace her — JPS

Prize her highly, and she will exalt you;
she will honor you if you embrace her — RSV
Exalt her and she will lift you up;
she will bring you honor when you embrace her — Ber
Love her, and she shall exalt you; embrace her, and she shall honor you — Lam
Hold her close, and she will make you great;
embrace her, and she will be your pride — Jerus

9. She shall give to thine head an ornament of grace: a crown of glory shall she deliver to thee.

She will give a garland of grace for thy head;
A crown of beauty will she deliver to thee — ABPS
She will give to thy head a chaplet of grace;
A crown of beauty will she deliver to thee — ASV
She giveth to thy head a wreath of grace,
A crown of beauty she doth give thee freely — YLT
She will give for thy head a wreath of beauty,
A crown of adorning will she bestow upon thee — Rhm
She will put on your head a graceful diadem;
a glorious crown will she bestow on you — NAB
She will put a crown of grace on your head, giving you a head-dress of glory — Bas

10. Hear, O my son, and receive my sayings; and the years of thy life shall be many.

Hear, my son, and accept my words, that the years of your life may be many — RSV
Listen, my son, take to heart what I say,
and the years of your life shall be many — Mof
Hear, my son, accept what I say,
and the years of your life will be many — Ber
Listen, my son, take my words to heart,
and the years of your life shall be multiplied — NEB
Listen, then, my son, and master the charge I give thee, as thou wouldst have long life — Knox

11. I have taught thee in the way of wisdom; I have led thee in right paths.

12. When thou goest, thy steps shall not be straitened; and when thou runnest, thou shalt not stumble.

for I am teaching thee ways of wisdom; and confirming thee in right paths. For when thou goest, thy steps will not be straitened: and when thou runnest thou shalt not be tired — Sept
In a way of wisdom I have directed thee,
I have caused thee to tread in paths of uprightness.
In thy walking thy step is not straitened,
And if thou runnest, thou stumblest not — YLT
In the wise way I have directed you;
I have led you on straight roads.
When you walk, your step will not be hindered;
and if you run, you will not stumble — Ber
I have taught you in the ways of wisdom; I have led you in right paths. When you walk, your steps will not be unsteady; and when you run, you will not stumble — Lam
I am giving you wise directions
and leading you aright;
when you walk, you will never be hindered,
when you run, you will not slip — Mof
On the way of wisdom I direct you,
I lead you on straightforward paths.
When you walk, your step will not be impeded,
and should you run, you will not stumble — NAB

13. Take fast hold of instruction; let her not go: keep her; for she is thy life.

Lay hold on instruction, let not go;
Keep her, for she is thy life — ABPS
Take fast hold of correction, let her not go, —
Keep her, for she is thy life — Rhm
Keep fast hold of instruction, let her not go;
Guard her, for she is your life — AAT

Hold fast to discipline, never let her go,
keep your eyes on her, she is your life — Jerus

Hold fast by the instruction thou hast received, and never let it go; guard it as thou wouldst guard thy life — Knox

14. Enter not into the path of the wicked, and go not in the way of evil men.

15. Avoid it, pass not by it, turn from it, and pass away.

Upon the path of the lawless do not thou enter,
And do not advance in the way of the wicked:
Avoid it, do not pass thereon —
Turn from it and depart — Rhm

Do not go in the road of sinners, or be walking in the way of evil men.
Keep far from it, do not go near; be turned from it, and go on your way — Bas

Enter not into the path of the wicked,
Nor go onward in the way of the evil.
Avoid it, pass not over it;
Turn off from it, and pass on — ABPS

Do not take to the course of the wicked
or follow the way of evil men;
do not set foot on it, but avoid it;
turn aside and go on your way — NEB

Never set foot upon a bad man's path,
and take not the road of evil men;
avoid it, never follow it,
shun it, and pass on — Mof

16. For they sleep not, except they have done mischief; and their sleep is taken away, unless they cause some to fall.

17. For they eat the bread of wickedness, and drink the wine of violence.

For they sleep not unless they have done wickedness;
And their sleep is removed if they have not caused delinquency.
For they eat the bread of injustice,
And they drink the wine of violence — Sprl

For they do not sleep until they have done mischief; and their sleep is taken away until their evil devices are carried out.
For they eat the bread of wickedness and drink the wine of violence — Lam

For they cannot sleep till they have done some wrong,
till they have tripped up someone, they are sleepless;
they eat ill-gotten food
and drink wine won by cruelty — Mof

For they cannot sleep unless they have done some wrong;
unless they have been someone's downfall they lose their sleep.
The bread they eat is the fruit of crime
and they drink wine got by violence — NEB

For evil men don't sleep until they've done their evil deed for the day. They can't rest unless they cause someone to stumble and fall. They eat and drink wickedness and violence — Tay

For they cannot sleep unless they have first done wrong,
they miss their sleep if they have not brought someone down;
wickedness is the bread they eat, and violence the wine they drink — Jerus

18. But the path of the just is as the shining light, that shineth more and more unto the perfect day.

But the path of the righteous is as the shining light,
That shineth more and more unto the perfect day — ASV

But the path of the righteous is as the light of dawn, —
Going on and brightening, unto meridian day — Rhm

But the way of the righteous is as the clear light,
Shining more and more, to the noonday — ABPS

But the path of the righteous is like the light of dawn,
which shines brighter and brighter until full day — RSV

But the path of the just is like shining light,
that grows in brilliance till perfect day — NAB

the course of good men, like a ray of dawn,

shines on and on to the full light of day — Mof

19. The way of the wicked is as darkness: they know not at what they stumble.

The way of the wicked is as thick darkness;
They know not at what they stumble — ABPS

The way of the wicked is like deep darkness;
they do not know over what they stumble — RSV

The way of the wicked is dark as pitch;
They know not at what they stumble — AAT

but the ways of the wicked are like darkness at night,
and they do not know what has been their downfall — NEB

The way of sinners is dark; they see not the cause of their fall — Bas

20. My son, attend to my words; incline thine ear unto my sayings.

21. Let them not depart from thine eyes; keep them in the midst of thine heart.

22. For they are life unto those that find them, and health to all their flesh.

Let them not slip out of your sight,
keep them within your heart;
For they are life to those who find them,
to man's whole being they are health — NAB

never lose sight of them,
but fix them in your mind;
to those who find them, they are life,
and health to all their being — Mof

do not let them out of your sight,
keep them deep in your heart.
They are life to those who grasp them,
health for the entire body — Jerus

Keep these thoughts ever in mind; let them penetrate deep within your heart, for they will mean real life for you, and radiant health — Tay

23. Keep thy heart with all diligence; for out of it are the issues of life.

Keep your heart with all vigilance;
for from it flow the springs of life — RSV

Above every charge keep thy heart,
For out of it are the outgoings of life — YLT

With all watchfulness guard thine heart;
For out of it flow the actions of life — Sprl

Above all that thou guardest keep thy heart;
For out of it are the issues of life — JPS

Use all thy watchfulness to keep thy heart true; that is the fountain whence life springs — Knox

Guard your heart more than any treasure,
for it is the source of all life — NEB

24. Put away from thee a froward mouth, and perverse lips put far from thee.

Put away from thee a wayward mouth,
And perverse lips put far from thee — ASV

Put away from you an evil tongue, and let false lips be far from you — Bas

Put away from you crooked speech,
and put devious talk far from you — RSV

Remove from thee perverseness of mouth,
And craftiness of lips put far from thee — Rhm

Turn your back on the mouth that misleads,
keep your distance from lips that deceive — Jerus

Put away from you dishonest talk,
deceitful speech put far from you — NAB

25. Let thine eyes look right on, and let thine eyelids look straight before thee.

Let thine eyes right onward look, —
And thine eyelashes point straight before thee — Rhm

Let your eyes look right in front,
And your eyelids be directed straight ahead of you — AAT

Let your eyes look forward
and your gaze straight ahead of you — Ber

let thy eyes see straight, thy gaze ever scan the path that lies before thee — Knox

Let your eyes look straight before you,
fix your gaze upon what lies ahead — NEB

Keep your eyes on what is in front of you, looking straight before you — Bas

26. Ponder the path of thy feet, and let all thy ways be established.

27. Turn not to the right hand nor to the left: remove thy foot from evil.
Make level the path of thy feet,
And let all thy ways be established.
Turn not to the right hand nor to the left:
Remove thy foot from evil — ASV
Take heed to the path of your feet,
then all your ways will be sure.
Do not swerve to the right or to the left;
turn your foot away from evil — RSV
Consider well the path for your feet
and all your ways will be sure.
Turn not to the right or to the left;
keep your foot away from evil — Ber
Survey the path for your feet,
and let all your ways be sure.
Turn neither to right nor to left,
keep your foot far from evil — NAB
keep a clear path before you,
and ever make your footing firm;
never turn to right or left,
draw back from a wrong step — Mof
Watch your step. Stick to the path and be safe. Don't sidetrack; pull back your foot from danger — Tay

CHAPTER 5

1. My son, attend unto my wisdom, and bow thine ear to my understanding:

2. That thou mayest regard discretion, and that thy lips may keep knowledge.
My son, listen attentively to my wisdom,
To my understanding incline thine ear:
So that thou maintain discretion,
And thy lips preserve knowledge — Sprl
My son to my wisdom attend,
And to mine understanding incline thou thine ear:
That thou mayest preserve discretion, —
And as for knowledge that thy lips may guard it — Rhm
My son, listen to my wisdom;
incline your ear to my discernment;
that you may protect discretion; that your lips may guard knowledge — Ber
My son, attend to wisdom,
bend your ear to knowledge,
that caution may be your safeguard,
and prudence may take care of you;
keep hold of caution and sound sense — Mof
My son, pay attention to my wisdom,
listen carefully to what I know,
and so have prudence and knowledge to protect you;
these will keep a guard on your lips — Jerus
My son, attend to my wisdom
and listen to my good counsel,
so that you may observe proper prudence
and your speech be informed with knowledge — NEB

3. For the lips of a strange woman drop as an honeycomb, and her mouth is smoother than oil:
For the lips of a strange woman drop honey,
And her mouth is smoother than oil — ASV
For the lips of a loose woman drop honeyed words
and her palate is smoother than oil — Ber
For the lips of the adulterous woman drop honey,
And her mouth is smoother than oil — AAT
For the lips of a strange woman drop as a honeycomb, and her words are smoother than oil — Lam
For the lips of a loose woman drip honey,
and her speech is smoother than oil — RSV
For the lips of a prostitute are as sweet as honey, and smooth flattery is her stock in trade — Tay

4. But her end is bitter as wormwood, sharp as a two-edged sword.

5. Her feet go down to death; her steps take hold on hell.
Yet at the last she is bitter as wormwood,
Keen as a many-edged sword:
Her feet descend to death,
And her steps invade hell — Sprl

But in the end she is bitter as wormwood,
Sharp as a two-edged sword.
Her feet go down to death;
Her steps take hold on Sheol — ASV
but the end with her is bitter as poison,
sharp as a sword with double edge;
her feet go down to Death,
her steps lead straight to the grave — Mof
but their outcome is bitter as wormwood,
sharp as a two-edged sword.
Her feet go down to death,
her steps lead down to Sheol — Jerus

6. Lest thou shouldst ponder the path of life, her ways are moveable, that thou canst not know them.
So that she findeth not the level path of life: her ways are unstable and she knoweth it not — RV
The path of life she does not consider; her paths meander, but she knows it not — Ber
she does not take heed to the path of life;
her ways wander, and she does not know it — RSV
Lest she should walk the even path of life,
Her ways wander, but she knoweth it not — JPS
far from following the path of life,
her ways are undirected, irresponsible — Jerus
Lest you see before you the road to life,
her paths will ramble, you know not where — NAB

7. Hear me now therefore, O ye children, and depart not from the words of my mouth.

8. Remove thy way far from her, and come not nigh the door of her house:
Now therefore, my son, hearken to me and slight not my words. Remove thy way far from her, go not near the doors of her house — Sept
So now, my son, listen to me,
And swerve not from the words of my mouth.
Keep far away from her,
And approach not the door of her house — AAT
Now listen to me, my son,
hold fast to what I say:
keep clear of her,
never go near her door — Mof
Give ear to me then, my sons, and do not put away my words from you. Go far away from her, do not come near the door of her house — Bas
Now, my son, listen to me
and do not ignore what I say:
keep well away from her
and do not go near the door of her house — NEB
Young men, listen to me, and never forget what I'm about to say: Run from her! Don't go near her house — Tay

9. Lest thou give thine honour unto others, and thy years unto the cruel:
Lest thou give thy glory to aliens,
And thy years to the profligate — Sprl
That thou mayest not give thy life to others, and thy substance to the cruel — Sept
Lest thou give thy vigour unto others,
And thy years unto the cruel — JPS
Lest you give up your wealth to others,
The earnings of your life to aliens — AAT
lest you give your honor to others,
and your years to the merciless — Ber
or you will surrender your honour to others,
your years to one who has no pity — Jerus

10. Lest strangers be filled with thy wealth; and thy labours be in the house of a stranger;
Lest strangers be filled with thy strength,
And thy labors be in the house of an alien — ASV
lest strangers take their fill of your strength,
and your labors go to the house of an alien — RSV
that strangers may not be filled with thy wealth, and thy labours go into the houses of strangers — Sept
Lest strangers have their fill of your substance,
And the produce of your labors go to an alien's house — AAT
strangers will batten on your wealth,

and your hard-won gains pass to another man's family — NEB
Lest strangers obtain your wealth, and you become the slave of foreigners — Tay

11. And thou mourn at the last, when thy flesh and thy body are consumed,

And thou moan, when thine end cometh,
When thy flesh and thy body are consumed — JPS
And you have remorse in your old age, when the flesh of your body is consumed — Lam
and at the end of your life you groan, when your flesh and body are consumed — RSV
And you will be full of grief at the end of your life, when your flesh and your body are wasted — Bas
till you are left at last to moan, when all you have is wasted — Mof
So shalt thou grieve in thy latter end, In the failing of thy flesh and of thy healthy condition — Rhm

12. And say, How have I hated instruction, and my heart despised reproof;

13. And have not obeyed the voice of my teachers, nor inclined mine ear to them that instructed me!

And thou shalt say —
How I hated correction!
And reproof my heart disdained;
Neither hearkened I to the voice of my teachers,
Nor to my instructors inclined I the ear — Rhm
Then wilt thou say: Wherefore have I hated instruction?
Wherefore hath my heart despised reproof?
Truly I hearkened not unto the voice of my teachers,
Nor inclined mine ear to those who instructed me — Sprl
and you say, "How I hated discipline, and my heart despised reproof!
I did not listen to the voice of my teachers
or incline my ear to my instructors — RSV
Ah! why did I hate guidance,
why did I despise all warning?
Why did not I listen to those who trained me
and bend my ear to those who were my guides? — Mof
and exclaim, Alas, I hated discipline, my heart spurned all correction;
I would not hear the voice of my masters,
I would not listen to those who tried to teach me — Jerus
Then thou wilt complain bitterly, Alas, why did I spurn every precept, reject every warning, unheard, unheeded, every lesson I was taught? — Knox

14. I was almost in all evil in the midst of the congregation and assembly.

In a short time I was in all manner of distress
Amidst the assembly and the congregation — Sprl
I was almost in utter ruin
in the midst of the congregation and assembly — Ber
I have all but come to utter ruin, condemned by the public assembly — NAB
I had well-nigh come to utter evil
In the midst of the assembled community — AAT
I soon earned a bad name
and was despised in the public assembly — NEB
Now I am all but reduced to the depths of misery,
in the presence of the whole community — Jerus

15. Drink waters out of thine own cistern, and running waters out of thine own well.

16. Let thy fountains be dispersed abroad, and rivers of waters in the streets.

Drink waters out of thine own cistern,
Even flowing ones out of thine own well.
Let thy fountains be scattered abroad,
In broad places rivulets of water — YLT
Drink water from your own cistern
and running water from your own spring;
do not let your well overflow into the road, your runnels of water pour into the street — NEB
Let water from your store and not that of others be your drink, and running water from your fountain.

Let not your springs be flowing in the streets, or your streams of water in the open places — Bas

Drink waters out of thine own cistern,
And running waters out of thine own well.
Should thy springs be dispersed abroad,
And streams of water in the streets? — ASV

Drink from your own cistern,
drink fresh water out of your own well.
Are you to seek your pleasures here and there,
and drink them in the streets — Mof

Nay, drink, and drink deep, at thy own well, thy own cistern; thence let thy offspring abound, like waters from thy own fountain flowing through the public streets — Knox

Drink the water from your own cistern,
fresh water from your own well.
Do not let your fountain flow to waste elsewhere,
nor your streams in the public streets — Jerus

Drink from your own well, my son — be faithful and true to your wife. Why should you beget children with women of the street? — Tay[1]

17. Let them be only thine own, and not strangers' with thee.

18. Let thy fountain be blessed: and rejoice with the wife of thy youth.

Let them be for thyself alone, —
And not for strangers with thee.
Let thy well-spring be blessed, —
And get thy joy from the wife of thy youth — Rhm

Let them be for thee, by thyself,
And not for strangers with thee.
Let thy fountain be blest;
And have joy of the wife of thy youth — ABPS

Let them be for yourself only, not for other men with you.
Let blessing be on your fountain; have joy in the wife of your early years — Bas

But let them be only your own,
and not those of aliens, too.
Let your own fountain be blessed;
derive delight from the wife of your youth — Ber

let them be yours alone, not shared with strangers.
Let your fountain, the wife of your youth,
be blessed, rejoice in her — NEB

. . . let your children be for you alone, and not the children of strangers with you.
Let your fountain — of human life — be blessed . . . and rejoice with the wife of your youth — Amp

19. Let her be as the loving hind and pleasant roe; let her breasts satisfy thee at all times; and be thou ravished always with her love.

As a loving hind and a pleasant doe,
Let her breasts satisfy thee at all times;
And be thou ravished always with her love — ASV

Loving as the hind, and affectionate as the gazelle,
Let her bosom ever satisfy thee;
And with her love be thou ever transported — Sprl

a lovely hind, a graceful doe.
Let her affection fill you at all times with delight,
be infatuated always with her love — RSV

A lovely hind, a graceful doe —
Let her breasts intoxicate you always,
With her love be continually ravished — AAT

a lovely hind, a charming doe is she;
let her breasts give you rapture,
let her love ever ravish you — Mof

fair as a hind, graceful as a fawn . . .
hers the breasts that ever fill you with delight,
hers the love that ever holds you captive — Jerus

Thy own bride, gentle as a hind, graceful as a doe; be it her bosom that steals away thy senses with the delight of a lover that loves still — Knox

20. And why wilt thou, my son, be ravished with a strange woman, and embrace the bosom of a stranger?

---

[1]The context clearly indicates that the imagery of this section has the meaning expressed by Tay. Some read vs. 16 as a question implying a negative answer (ASV, *et al.*), some as a prohibition.

For why shouldest thou, my son, be ravished with a strange woman,
And embrace the bosom of a foreigner — ASV

Why should you be infatuated, my son, with a loose woman
and embrace the bosom of an adventuress — RSV

Why be seduced, my son, by an alien woman,
and fondle the breast of a woman who is a stranger — Jerus

Why therefore, my son, shouldest thou be ravished with a stranger?
And embrace the bosom of a wanton woman — Sprl

Why, my son, should you be ravished with the wife of another,
And embrace the bosom of an adulteress — AAT

Why then, my son, should you go astray for another's wife
and accept the embraces of an adulteress — NAB

21. For the ways of man are before the eyes of the LORD, and he pondereth all his goings.

For over-against the eyes of Jehovah are the ways of each,
And all his paths He is pondering — YLT

For the ways of man are before the eyes of the LORD, and all his paths lie open in his presence — Lam

For each man's ways are plain to the LORD's sight;
all their paths he surveys — NAB

Man's goings are observed by the Eternal,
he takes account of all his ways — Mof

For directly before the eyes of the LORD are a man's ways,
and all his paths are well considered — Ber

For the ways of a husband are before the eyes of God, and he examineth narrowly all his paths — Sept

22. His own iniquities shall take the wicked himself, and he shall be holden with the cords of his sins.

His own iniquities shall ensnare the wicked,
And he shall be holden with the cords of his sin — JPS

His own iniquities do capture the wicked,
And with the ropes of his sin he is holden — YLT

The wicked man shall be taken by his iniquities,
And he shall be bound fast with the cords of his transgressions — Sprl

The evil-doer will be taken in the net of his crimes, and prisoned in the cords of his sin — Bas

By his own iniquities the wicked man will be caught,
in the meshes of his own sin he will be held fast — NAB

The wicked shall be caught by his own iniquities, and he will be bound with the cords of his sins — Lam

23. He shall die without instruction; and in the greatness of his folly he shall go astray.

He shall die for lack of instruction;
And in the greatness of his folly he shall go astray — ASV

He perishes for want of receiving correction;
And by the multitude of his follies he shall go astray — Sprl

He shall die for lack of discipline,
And by the abounding of his perversity shall he be lost — Rhm

He will die for want of instruction,
He will stagger to ruin through the greatness of his folly — AAT

for lack of sense he dies,
his utter folly ruins him — Mof

He shall die because he will not listen to the truth; he has let himself be led away into incredible folly — Tay

CHAPTER 6

1. My son, if thou be surety for thy friend, if thou hast stricken thy hand with a stranger,

2. Thou art snared with the words of thy mouth, thou art taken with the words of thy mouth.

My son, if thou hast become surety for thy neighbour,
If thou hast stricken thine hand with a stranger,

Thou art entangled with the words of thy mouth,
Thou art ensnared with the words of thy mouth — Sprl

My son, if you have made yourself responsible for your neighbour, or given your word for another,
You are taken as in a net by the words of your mouth, the sayings of your lips have overcome you — Bas

My son, if you have become surety for your friend, if you have obligated yourself to a stranger,
Then you are snared with the words of your mouth, you are caught with the words of your lips — Lam

My son, if you have become surety for your neighbor,
have given your pledge for a stranger;
if you are snared in the utterance of your lips,
caught in the words of your mouth — RSV

My son, if you have gone surety for your neighbour,
if you have guaranteed the bond of a stranger,
if you have committed yourself with your own lips,
if through words of yours you have been entrapped — Jerus

My son, if you pledge yourself to another man
and stand surety for a stranger,
if you are caught by your promise,
trapped by some promise you have made — NEB

3. Do this, now, my son, and deliver thyself, when thou art come into the hand of thy friend; go, humble thyself, and make sure thy friend.

Do this now, my son, and deliver thyself, seeing thou art come into the hand of thy neighbour; go, humble thyself, and importune thy neighbour — RV

Do this now, my son, and deliver thyself,
For thou art come into the power of thy friend;
Go humble thyself, and be urgent with thy friend — ABPS

Do this now, my son, and free yourself —
Since you have fallen into your neighbor's power —
Go in hot haste, and lay siege to your neighbor — AAT

Do this now, my son, and get clear,
Though thou art come under the hand of thy neighbour;
Go, humble thyself, and importune thy neighbour — Sprl

So do this, my son, to free yourself,
since you have fallen into your neighbor's power:
Go, hurry, stir up your neighbor — NAB

do this, my son, to extricate yourself —
since you have put yourself in the power of your neighbour:
go, go quickly, and plead with your neighbour — Jerus

then do this, my son — release yourself,
for you are in your fellow's power;
be quick, beseech your fellow — Mof

4. Give not sleep to thine eyes, nor slumber to thine eyelids.

5. Deliver thyself as a roe from the hand of the hunter, and as a bird from the hand of the fowler.

Give no sleep to your eyes,
Nor slumber to your eyelids;
Free yourself like a gazelle from the snare,
Like a bird from the hand of the fowler — AAT

permit no sleep to your eyes nor slumber to your eyelids;
deliver yourself as a captured gazelle, as a bird from the hand of the fowler — Ber

Give not sleep to thine eyes,
Nor rest to thine eyelids:
Escape like an antelope from the toils,
And like a bird from the fowler's snare — Sprl

give yourself no rest,
allow yourself no sleep.
Save yourself like a gazelle from the toils,
like a bird from the grasp of the fowler — NEB

Don't put it off. Do it now. Don't rest until you do. If you can get out of this trap you have saved yourself like a deer that escapes from a hunter, or a bird from the net — Tay

6. Go to the ant, thou sluggard; consider her ways, and be wise:

Go unto the ant, O slothful one,
See her ways and be wise — YLT

Go to the ant, you hater of work; give thought to her ways and be wise — Bas

Up with thee, idleness, go to school with the ant, and learn the lesson of her ways — Knox

Go to the ant, you sluggard,
look at her ways, learn sense — Mof

Go to the ant, O sluggard,
study her ways and learn wisdom — NAB

Take a lesson from the ants, you lazy fellow. Learn from their ways and be wise — Tay

7. Which having no guide, overseer, or ruler,

8. Provideth her meat in the summer, and gathereth her food in the harvest.

Which having no chief,
Overseer, or ruler,
Provideth her bread in the summer,
And gathereth her food in the harvest — ASV

Without having any chief,
officer or ruler,
she prepares her food in summer,
and gathers her sustenance in harvest — RSV

She has no overseer,
no governor or ruler;
but in summer she prepares her store of food
and lays in her supplies at harvest — NEB

For though she has no chief,
No officer, no ruler,
She secures her food in the summer,
She gathers her provisions in the harvest — AAT

For having no cultivated field, no driver, nor master, it provideth its food in summer, and layeth up a plentiful supply in harvest — Sept

no one gives her orders,
no overseer, no master,
yet all through the summer she makes sure of her food,
and gathers her supplies at harvest time — Jerus

9. How long wilt thou sleep, O sluggard? when wilt thou arise out of thy sleep?

Till when, O slothful one, dost thou lie?
When dost thou arise from thy sleep — YLT

Wilt thou for ever sleep, O sluggard?
When wilt thou arise from thy sleep — Sprl

How long will you be sleeping, O hater of work? when will you get up from your sleep — Bas

How long, you sluggard, will you lie abed?
When will you rouse yourself from sleep — NEB

And thou, idleness, art still a-bed; wilt thou never wake — Knox

10. Yet a little sleep, a little slumber, a little folding of the hands to sleep:

11. So shall thy poverty come as one that travelleth, and thy want as an armed man.

A little more sleep — a little more slumber —
A little more folding of the hands in sleep —
Behold, thy poverty advances like a traveller,
And thy want as a swift messenger — Sprl

A little sleep, a little slumber,
A little folding of the hands to rest: —
So shall come in as a highwayman thy poverty,
And thy want as one armed with a shield — Rhm

"Yet a little sleep, a little slumber,
a little folding of the hands to rest" —
and your poverty will come upon you as a bandit,
your want like an unyielding warrior — Ber

A little sleep, a little drowsiness,
a little folding of the arms to take life easier,
and like a vagrant, poverty is at your elbow and, like a beggar, want — Jerus

'Let me sleep for a little, a little!
let me fold my hands for a little, to rest?' —
yes, and poverty will pounce on you,
want will overpower you — Mof

"Let me sleep a little longer!"

Sure, just a little more! And as you sleep, poverty creeps upon you like a robber and destroys you; want attacks you in full armor — Tay

12. A naughty person, a wicked man, walketh with a froward mouth.

A man of worthlessness, a man of iniquity,
Walking with perverseness of mouth — YLT

A worthless person, a man of iniquity,
Is he that walketh with a perverse mouth — ASV

A vile man, a base man,
Is he who walks in falsehood — ABPS

A knave, a villain,
Is he who deals in crooked speech — AAT

A worthless person, a wicked man,
goes about with crooked speech — RSV

A good-for-nothing man is an evil-doer; he goes on his way causing trouble with false words — Bas

A scoundrel, a vicious man,
he goes with a leer on his lips — Jerus

13. He winketh with his eyes, he speaketh with his feet, he teacheth with his fingers;

He winketh with his eyes, he speaketh with his feet, he maketh signs with his fingers — RV

That winketh with his eyes, that scrapeth with his feet,
That pointeth with his fingers — JPS

But he winketh with his eye and maketh a sign with his foot; and teacheth, by pointing his fingers — Sept

Making signs with his eyes, rubbing with his feet, and giving news with his fingers — Bas

He winks with his eyes, he signals with his feet, he makes signs with his fingers — Lam

He winks his eyes,
shuffles his feet,
makes signs with his fingers — NAB

14. Frowardness is in his heart, he deviseth mischief continually; he soweth discord.

In whose heart is perverseness,
Who deviseth evil continually,
Who soweth discord — ASV

In whose heart is perverseness;
Devising evil at all times;
Who scatters discords — ABPS

Perverseness is in his heart,
He deviseth evil continually;
He stirreth up contention — Sprl

Subversion is the evil that he is plotting,
he stirs up quarrels all the time — NEB

In whose mind is perversity,
Who plots mischief all the time,
Who sows discord — AAT

with perverted heart devises evil,
continually sowing discord — RSV

15. Therefore shall his calamity come suddenly; suddenly shall he be broken without remedy.

For this cause suddenly cometh his doom,
In a moment shall he be torn in pieces and
there be no mending — Rhm

Therefore suddenly cometh his calamity,
Instantly he is broken — and no healing — YLT

therefore calamity will come upon him suddenly;
in a moment he will be broken beyond healing — RSV

Therefore his doom will come suddenly,
In an instant he will be crushed beyond recovery — AAT

Disaster will overtake him sharply for this,
suddenly, irretrievably, his fall will come — Jerus

For this cause his downfall will be sudden; quickly he will be broken, and there will be no help for him — Bas

16. These six things doth the LORD hate; yea, seven are an abomination unto him:

These six things JEHOVAH hateth;
Yea, seven an abomination to His soul — Sprl

Six things the LORD hates,
Seven are an abomination to him — AAT

Six things the Eternal hates,
ay, seven he loathes — Mof

Six things the LORD hates,
seven things are detestable to him — NEB

Six things are hated by the Lord; seven things are disgusting to him — Bas
There are six things that Yahweh hates, seven that his soul abhors — Jerus

17. A proud look, a lying tongue, and hands that shed innocent blood,
Eyes high — tongues false —
And hands shedding innocent blood — YLT
Haughty appearance, a lying tongue,
And hands that shed innocent blood — Sprl
the haughty look, the lying tongue, the hands that take innocent life — Knox
Eyes of pride, a false tongue, hands which take life without cause — Bas
Haughtiness
Lying
Murdering — Tay

18. A heart that deviseth wicked imaginations, feet that be swift in running to mischief,

19. A false witness that speaketh lies, and he that soweth discord among brethren.
A heart devising thoughts of vanity —
Feet hasting to run to evil —
A false witness who doth breathe out lies —
And one sending forth contentions between brethren — YLT
A heart that deviseth wicked thoughts,
Feet that are swift in running to evil;
A false witness that breatheth out lies,
And he that soweth discord among brethren — JPS
A mind that plots mischievous schemes,
Feet that are quick to run after evil;
A false witness who utters lies,
And he who sows discord among brothers — AAT
a mind with crafty plans,
feet eager to go mischief-making,
a false witness who tells lies,
and him who sows discord within his group — Mof
a heart that weaves wicked plots,
feet that hurry to do evil,
a false witness who lies with every breath,
a man who sows dissension among brothers — Jerus
A heart contriving iniquitous devices,
Feet hasting to run into mischief;
One that uttereth lies — a false witness,
And one sending forth strifes between brethren — Rhm

20. My son, keep thy father's commandment, and forsake not the law of thy mother:

21. Bind them continually upon thine heart, and tie them about thy neck.
Observe thou, my son, the commandment of thy father,
And do not decline from the instruction of thy mother:
Bind them upon thy heart continually,
Fasten them upon thy neck — Rhm
Observe, my son, your father's bidding, and reject not your mother's teaching;
Keep them fastened over your heart always,
put them around your neck — NAB
Keep, my son, your father's charge,
And reject not your mother's instruction;
Fasten them forever on your mind,
Hang them round your neck — AAT
Keep true, my son, to the charge thy father gives thee, nor make light of thy mother's teaching; wear them ever close to thy heart, hang them like a locket upon thy breast — Knox
My son, keep the laws of thy father, and reject not the maxims of thy mother. Bind them continually on thy mind: and tie them as a chain around thy neck — Sept
My son, do your father's bidding,
and reject not your mother's directions;
fix them ever in your mind,
tie them fast round your neck — Mof

22. When thou goest, it shall lead thee; when thou sleepest, it shall keep thee; and when thou wakest, it shall talk with thee.
When thou walkest, they shall guide thee;
When thou liest down, they shall guard thee;
When thou awakest, they shall talk with thee — Sprl
In thy going up and down, it leadeth thee,

In thy lying down, it watcheth over thee,
And thou hast awaked — it talketh with thee — YLT

When you are walking about, it will lead you;
when you are lying down, it will watch over you;
and when you awake, it will speak to you — Ber

When thou walkest, take this along and let it be with thee: and when thou sleepest, let it guard thee; that when thou awakest, it may talk with thee — Sept

When you walk, let them follow you; let them be with you, keep them that they may keep you; and when you awake, meditate on them — Lam

Wisdom, when you walk, will guide you,
when you rest, she will take care of you,
when you wake up, she will talk to you — Mof

23. For the commandment is a lamp; and the law is light; and reproofs of instruction are the way of life:

for a command is a lamp, and teaching a light,
reproof and correction point the way of life — NEB

For the charge is a lamp, and the instruction a light;
The admonitions of discipline are the way of life — AAT

For this principle is a lamp,
this teaching is a light;
correction and discipline are the way to life — Jerus

For the command is a lamp, and the law is a light;
And instructive reproofs are the way of life — ABPS

For the commandment is a lamp and the teaching a light,
and the reproofs of discipline are the way of life — RSV

For the bidding is a lamp, and the teaching a light,
and a way to life are the reproofs of discipline — NAB

For the command of a law is a lamp and light; and reproof and instruction is the way of life — Sept

24. To keep thee from the evil woman, from the flattery of the tongue of a strange woman.

Here is protection for thee against the temptress that would lure thee away with her seductions — Knox

To keep thee from the evil woman,
From the flattery of the foreigner's tongue — ASV

to preserve you from the evil woman,
from the smooth tongue of the adventuress — RSV

Keeping you safe from the evil woman,
From the smooth tongue of the adulteress — AAT

to keep you from the wife of another man,
from the seductive tongue of the loose woman — NEB

To keep thee from the wicked woman,
From the flattery of the tongue of her that is a stranger — Rhm

To preserve thee from the profligate woman,
From the flattering tongue of the strange woman — Sprl

25. Lust not after her beauty in thine heart; neither let her take thee with her eyelids.

Covet not her beauty in thy heart,
Nor let her take thee with her eyelids — ABPS

Do not covet her beauty in thy heart,
Neither let her take thee by her eyelashes — Rhm

Lust not in thine heart after her beauty,
Neither be seduced with her wanton eyelids — Sprl

Let not your heart's desire go after her fair body; let not her eyes take you prisoner — Bas

let not your heart long for her beauty,
let not her glances captivate you — Mof

Do not covet her beauty in your heart
or let her captivate you with the play of her eyes — Jerus

26. For by means of a whorish woman a man is brought to a piece of bread: and the adulteress will hunt for the precious life.

For the price of a harlot is scarce that of a single loaf; but an adulteress hunteth for the precious lives of men — Sept

for a harlot may be hired for a loaf of bread,

but an adulteress stalks a man's very life — RSV
for the harlot is only out to earn a meal, but the adulteress preys upon your very life — Mof
For a loose woman is looking for a cake of bread, but another man's wife goes after one's very life — Bas
For a prostitute will bring a man to poverty, and an adulteress may cost him his very life — Tay
For the price of a loose woman
may be scarcely a loaf of bread,
But if she is married,
she is a trap for your precious life — NAB

27. Can a man take fire in his bosom, and his clothes not be burned?

28. Can one go upon hot coals, and his feet not be burned?

Doth a man take fire into his bosom,
And are his garments not burnt?
Doth a man walk on the hot coals,
And are his feet not scorched — YLT
May a man take fire to his breast without burning his clothing?
Or may one go on lighted coals, and his feet not be burned — Bas
Can a man kindle fire in his bosom
without burning his clothes?
If a man walks on hot coals,
will his feet not be scorched — NEB
Can a man hold fire against his chest and not be burned?
Can he walk on hot coals and not blister his feet — Tay
Who can carry fire in his bosom, without singeing the clothes he wears, or walk on hot coals without burning his feet — Knox

29. So he that goeth in to his neighbour's wife: whosoever toucheth her shall not be innocent.

So he who cohabits with his neighbor's wife . . . he who touches her shall not be innocent . . . — Amp
So he that goeth in to his neighbor's wife;
Whosoever toucheth her shall not be unpunished — ASV
So he who goeth in, to a married woman, cannot escape punishment — no, nor any one who toucheth her — Sept
So he that goeth in unto his neighbour's wife,
No man shall be guiltless who toucheth her — Rhm
So is he who sleeps with his neighbour's wife;
no one can touch such a woman and go free — NEB
So it is the man who consorts with his neighbour's wife:
no one who touches her will go unpunished — Jerus

30. Men do not despise a thief, if he steal to satisfy his soul when he is hungry;

No one wonders at a thief when he is caught stealing, for he steals to satisfy himself when he is hungry — Lam
Men attach small blame to the thief who in hunger steals to fill his belly — Jerus
Excuses might even be found for a thief, if he steals when he is starving — Tay
Small blame to the thief, when he steals to fill his hungry belly — Knox
A thief is not despised if he steals
to satisfy his vital need when he is hungry — Ber

31. But if he be found, he shall restore sevenfold; he shall give all the substance of his house.

Yet if he be caught he must pay back sevenfold;
all the wealth of his house he may yield up — NAB
though, once caught, he must pay back sevenfold,
and has to hand over all his family resources — Jerus
if he is caught, he has to pay for it seven times over,
to give all his house contains — Mof
And if he is caught, he will pay sevenfold;
he will give all the goods of his house — RSV
But even so, he is fined seven times as much as he stole, though it may mean selling everything in his house to pay it back — Tay

32. But whoso committeth adultery with a woman lacketh understanding: he that doeth it destroyeth his own soul.

He that committeth adultery with a woman is void of understanding:

He doeth it who would destroy his own soul — ASV
But he who commits adultery with a woman is devoid of sense,
Only he who would bring ruin on himself does such a thing — AAT
But an adulterer is devoid of sense,
he ruins himself by what he does — Mof
He who commits adultery has no sense;
he who does it destroys himself — RSV
But he who commits adultery is a fool;
he who would destroy himself does it — NAB
He who takes another man's wife is without all sense: he who does it is the cause of destruction to his soul — Bas

33. A wound and dishonor shall he get; and his reproach shall not be wiped away.
Stripes and disgrace shall he meet with,
And his reproach shall not be obliterated — Sprl
Blows and shame shall he get;
And his reproach shall not be wiped away — ABPS
Scathe and scorn he wins for himself, and shame there is no blotting out — Knox
A degrading beating will he get,
and his disgrace will not be wiped away — NAB
he will get nothing but blows and contumely
and will never live down the disgrace — NEB
He suffereth pangs and dishonour; and his reproach can never be wiped away — Sept

34. For jealousy is the rage of a man: therefore he will not spare in the day of vengeance.
For jealousy is the fury of a man,
And he doth not spare in a day of vengeance — YLT
For jealousy is the husband's rage;
And he will not spare in the day of vengeance — ABPS
Surely the jealousy of a husband is furious,
And he will not be compassionate in the day of vengeance — Sprl
For vindictive is the husband's wrath,
he will have no pity on the day of vengeance — NAB
for jealousy rouses a husband to fury,
he has no mercy when he takes revenge — Mof
For jealousy rouses a strong man's anger;
in the day of vengeance he will not spare — Ber

35. He will not regard any ransom; neither will he rest content, though thou givest many gifts.
nor will he abate his enmity for any ransom; nor be appeased by many gifts — Sept
He will not consider any restitution,
nor be satisfied with the greatest gifts — NAB
He will not make any payment; and he will not make peace with you though your money offerings are increased — Bas
He will not regard any ransom; nor will he listen, though you increase the bribe — Lam
compensation will not buy his forgiveness;
no bribe, however large, will purchase his connivance — NEB
no money buys him off,
he will not be satisfied, for all you offer — Mof
He will accept no compensation,
nor be appeased though you multiply gifts — RSV

CHAPTER 7

1. My son, keep my words, and lay up my commandments with thee.

2. Keep my commandments, and live; and my law as the apple of thine eye.
My son, keep my sayings,
And my commandments treasure by thee;
Keep my commandments and live,
And mine instruction as the pupil of thine eye — Rhm
My son, keep my words

and store up my precepts within you.
Keep my precepts and live
and my teaching as the pupil of your eye — Ber

My son, do what I tell you,
set store by my commands,
do as I bid you, and you shall live,
keep my directions as the very apple of your eye — Mof

My son, keep my words,
and treasure my principles,
keep my principles and you will live,
keep my teaching as the apple of your eye — Jerus

My son, keep my sayings, and let my rules be stored up with you. Keep my rules and you will have life; let my teaching be to you as the light of your eyes — Bas

Follow my advice, my son; always keep it in mind and stick to it. Obey me and live! Guard my words as your most precious possession — Tay

3. Bind them upon thy fingers, write them upon the table of thine heart.

Bind these to your fingers,
write them on the tablet of your heart — Jerus

Fasten them on your fingers,
Write them on the tablet of your mind — AAT

Bind it fast about thy fingers, write it, as upon a tablet, on thy heart — Knox

Let them be fixed to your fingers, and recorded in your heart — Bas

Wear them like a ring on your finger; write them on the tablet of your memory — NEB

4. Say unto wisdom, Thou art my sister; and call understanding thy kinswoman:

Say to Wisdom, 'You are my darling,'
call Knowledge your kinswoman — Mof

Say to wisdom, You are my sister; and to understanding, You are my counselor — Lam

give to wisdom a sister's welcome, and hail discernment as thy friend — Knox

Say to Wisdom, "You are my sister!"
call Understanding, "Friend!" — NAB

Say to wisdom, "You are my sister,"
and call insight your intimate friend — RSV

Call Wisdom your sister,
greet Understanding as a familiar friend — NEB

Love wisdom like a sweetheart; make her a beloved member of your family — Tay

5. That they may keep thee from the strange woman, from the stranger which flattereth with her words.

To preserve thee from a strange woman,
From a stranger who hath made smooth her sayings — YLT

That they may keep thee from the strange woman,
From the alien woman that maketh smooth her words — JPS

to preserve you from the loose woman,
from the adventuress with her smooth words — RSV

to keep you from the unknown woman,
from the female stranger with flattering words — Ber

That they may keep you from the wife of another,
From the adulteress who plies you with smooth words — AAT

to preserve you from the alien woman,
from the stranger, with her wheedling words — Jerus

6. For at the window of my house I looked through my casement,

7. And beheld among the simple ones, I discerned among the youths, a young man void of understanding,

For at the window of my house
I looked forth through my lattice;
And I beheld among the simple ones,
I discerned among the youths,
A young man void of understanding — ASV

For at the window of my house
I looked forth through my lattice;
And I beheld among the thoughtless ones,
I discerned among the youths,
A young man void of understanding — JPS

For in the window of my house,
Through my lattice I looked out;
And saw among the simple ones,
Discerned among the youths
A young man lacking sense — Rhm

For at the window of my house
I looked out through my lattice
and I saw among the simple,
I perceived among the youths a senseless young man — Ber
Looking out from my house, and watching through a window,
I saw among the young men one without sense — Bas

8. **Passing through the street near her corner; and he went the way to her house,**

9. **In the twilight, in the evening, in the black and dark night:**
Passing on in the street, near her corner,
And the way to her house he doth step,
In the twilight — in the evening of day,
In the darkness of night and blackness — YLT
Passing through the street near her corner,
And on the way to her house he sauntered along;
In the twilight, in the evening of the day,
In the midst of the night and the gloom — Rhm
passing along the street near her corner,
taking the road to her house
in the twilight, in the evening,
at the time of night and darkness — RSV
Passing through a street near her corner,
And pacing about the way to her house
In the dusk, at the close of day,
In the evening gloom, yea, in darkness — Sprl
strolling along near the street-corner
in the direction of her house,
in the twilight of the evening
or at black midnight — Mof
passing along the street, at the corner,
stepping out in the direction of her house
at twilight, as the day faded,
at dusk as the night grew dark — NEB

10. **And, behold, there met him a woman with the attire of a harlot, and subtil of heart.**
And, behold, there met him a woman
With the attire of a harlot,
and wily of heart — ASV
And lo, a woman meeting him,
With harlot's attire, and deceitful in heart — ABPS
And lo! the woman comes to meet him,
In harlot's dress, and with treacherous mind — AAT
And lo! the woman comes to meet him,
robed like a harlot, with secret designs — NAB
And the woman came out to him, in the dress of a loose woman, with a designing heart — Bas

11. **(She is loud and stubborn; her feet abide not in her house:**

12. **Now is she without, now in the streets, and lieth in wait at every corner.)**
She is noisy and refractory;
Her feet will not abide in her home.
Sometimes in the street, sometimes in the market-place,
Yea, in every vacant corner she layeth in wait — Sprl
Boisterous is she and rebellious,
In her house abide not her feet;
Now outside, now in the broadways,
And near every corner she lieth in wait — Rhm
She is clamorous and wilful; her feet abide not in her house:
Now she is in the streets, now in the broad places, and lieth in wait at every corner — RV
She is loud and lewd;
her feet do not stay in her own house;
now in the street, now in the market places,
near every corner she sets her ambush — Ber
restless and restive, she must be out,
she cannot stay at home,
now in the streets and now in the squares,
haunting every corner — Mof
She is rebellious and gluttonous; her feet do not abide in her house;
But she roams around outside, now in the streets, and now lying in wait at the corners — Lam

13. **So she caught him, and kissed him, and with an impudent face said unto him,**

14. I have peace offerings with me; this day have I paid my vows.

And she laid hold on him,
and kissed him,
She hath hardened her face, and saith to him, "Sacrifices of peace-offerings are by me,
To-day I have completed my vows — YLT

She seizes him and kisses him
and with impudent face she says to him:
"I had to offer sacrifices,
and today I have paid my vows — RSV

So she catches him, and kisses him,
She puts on a bold face, and says to him:
"I was due to hold a thanksgiving feast,
And today I am paying my vows — AAT

Ha! she hath caught him and kissed him, and with an unblushing countenance, said to him:
"I have a peace offering; to-day I am paying my vows — Sept

So she took him by his hand, kissing him, and without a sign of shame she said to him:
I have a feast of peace-offerings, for today my oaths have been effected — Bas

And she laid hold upon him, and kissed him,
Emboldened her face, and said unto him:
I have an entertainment at my house,
This day have I redeemed my vows — Sprl

She caught hold of him and kissed him; brazenly she accosted him and said,
'I have had a sacrifice, an offering, to make
and I have paid my vows today — NEB

15. Therefore came I forth to meet thee, diligently to seek thy face, and I have found thee.

so I came out to find thee, longing for the sight of thee, and here thou art — Knox

Therefore I came out to meet you, for I have been waiting to see you, and now I have found you — Lam

So now I have come out to meet you,
to seek you eagerly,
and I have found you — RSV

So I came out in the hope of meeting you, looking for you with care, and now I have you — Bas

16. I have decked my bed with coverings of tapestry, with carved works, with fine linen of Egypt.

I have spread my couch with carpets of tapestry,
With striped cloths of the yarn of Egypt — ASV

With coverings I have spread my couch,
With embroideries of Egyptian thread — ABPS

I have decked my couch with coverlets,
With striped cloths of the yarn of Egypt — JPS

I have decked my couch with coverings,
colored sheets of Egyptian linen — Ber

I have made my bed gay with quilts,
spread the best Egyptian sheets — Jerus

With coverlets I have spread my couch,
with brocaded cloths of Egyptian linen — NAB

17. I have perfumed my bed with myrrh, aloes, and cinnamon.

18. Come, let us take our fill of love until morning: let us solace ourselves with loves.

Come! let us take our fill of endearments until morning,
Let us delight ourselves with caresses — Rhm

Come, let us intoxicate ourselves with love until the morning,
Let us solace ourselves with caresses — Sprl

Come, let us lose ourselves in dalliance, all the night through let us enjoy the long-desired embrace — Knox

Come, let us take our fill of love until morning; let us embrace each other with passion — Lam

Come, let us take our pleasure in love till the morning, having joy in love's delights — Bas

19. For the goodman is not at home, he is gone a long journey:

20. He hath taken a bag of money with him, and will come home at the day appointed.

For my husband is not at home, he is gone a long journey; he took in his hand a roll of silver, and will return to his house after many days — Sept

For the man is not at home;
He is gone a long journey:
He hath taken a bag of money with him;
He will come home at the full moon — ASV

For the goodman is not at home;
He has gone on a journey far away.
The purse of silver he has taken in his hand;
At the day of the full moon he will come home — ABPS

For my husband is not at home,
he has gone on a very long journey,
taking his moneybags with him;
he will not be back until the moon is full — Jerus

for the man of the house is away,
he has gone on a long journey,
he has taken a bag of silver with him;
until the moon is full he will not be home — NEB

For my husband is away on a long trip.
He has taken a wallet full of money with him, and won't return for several days — Tay

21. With her much fair speech she caused him to yield, with the flattering of her lips she forced him.

By the multitude of her allurements she beguiled him,
By the flattery of her lips she seduced him — Sprl

With her much fair speech she causeth him to yield,
With the blandishment of her lips she enticeth him away — JPS

With much seductive speech she persuades him;
with her smooth talk she compels him — RSV

With her coaxing pleas she persuades him,
with her smooth words she carries him away — Mof

She wins him over by her repeated urging,
with her smooth lips she leads him astray — NAB

By her sophistries she draws him away;
with the flattery of her lips she entices him — Ber

22. He goeth after her straightway, as an ox goeth to the slaughter, or as a fool to the correction of the stocks;

He goeth after her straightway,
As an ox goeth to the slaughter,
Or as one in fetters to the correction of the fool — ASV

He followeth her instantly,
As goeth the ox to the slaughter,
And as the manacled delinquent unto correction — Sprl

Suddenly he goes after her, as an ox goes to the slaughter, as in fetters a fool to his punishment — Ber

and he is enticed to follow her,
like an ox moving to the slaughter,
like a dog cajoled to the muzzle — Mof

All at once he follows her,
as an ox goes to the slaughter,
or as a stag is caught fast — RSV

Bemused, he follows her
like an ox being led to the slaughter,
like a stag caught in a noose—Jerus

23. Till a dart strike through his liver; as a bird hasteth to the snare, and knoweth not that it is for his life.

Till an arrow doth split his liver,
As a bird hasteth into a snare,
And hath not known that it is for its life — YLT

Until an arrow cleaveth his liver,
As a bird hasteth into a snare,
And knoweth not that for his life it is — Rhm

till an arrow pierces its entrails;
as a bird rushes into a snare;
he does not know that it will cost him his life — RSV

till an arrow pierces its liver;
Like a bird that rushes into a snare,
unaware that its life is at stake — NAB

Waiting to be killed with an arrow through its heart. He was as a bird flying into a snare, not knowing the fate awaiting it there —Tay

24. Hearken unto me now therefore, O ye

children, and attend to the words of my mouth.

25. **Let not thine heart decline to her ways, go not astray in her paths.**

And now, O ye children, hearken unto me,
And consider the words of my mouth.
Let not thine heart decline to her ways,
Stray not into her paths — Sprl

And now, ye sons, hearken to me,
And give attention to sayings of my mouth.
Let not thy heart turn into her ways,
Do not wander in her paths — YLT

Heed me well, my son; let not this warning be given in vain;
do not let her steal thy heart away,
do not be enticed by her beckoning — Knox

So now, my son, listen to me,
And attend to the words of my mouth;
Swerve not toward her ways, Stray not into her paths — AAT

So now, my sons, give ear to me; give attention to the sayings of my mouth;
Let not your heart be turned to her ways, do not go wandering in her footsteps — Bas

And now, my son, listen to me,
pay attention to the words I have to say:
do not let your heart stray into her ways,
or wander into her paths — Jerus

26. **For she hath cast down many wounded: yea, many strong men have been slain by her.**

for she hath wounded and brought down many; and innumerable are they whom she hath slain — Sept

For she hath cast down many wounded:
Yea, all her slain are a mighty host — ASV

For many are the wounded she caused to fall,
And mighty are all her slain ones — YLT

For many are the dead she has laid low,
A mighty host has she slain — AAT

for many victims she has brought down;
a great multitude are her slain — Ber

For many are those she has struck down dead,
numerous, those she has slain — NAB

27. **Her house is the way to hell, going down to the chambers of death.**

Her house is the way to Sheol, going down to the chambers of death — RV

Her house is the way to the netherworld,
Going down to the chambers of death — JPS

her house is the road to the grave,
it leads down to the chambers of death — Mof

Her house is the way to the underworld, going down to the rooms of death — Bas

Her house is the way to Sheol,
the descent to the courts of death — Jerus

truly her house is the grave's antechamber, opens the door into the secret closet of death — Knox

CHAPTER 8

1. **Doth not wisdom cry? and understanding put forth her voice?**

Doth not wisdom call?
And understanding give forth her voice — YLT

Doth not wisdom proclaim?
And understanding lift up her voice — Sprl

Doth not wisdom cry aloud?
And understanding send forth her voice — Rhm

Does not Wisdom call,
And Reason lift up her voice — AAT

Does Wisdom not call meanwhile?
Does Discernment not lift up her voice — Jerus

Is it not Wisdom calling,
Knowledge raising her voice — Mof

2. **She standeth in the top of high places, by the way in the places of the paths.**

On the top of high places by the way,

Where the paths meet, she standeth — ASV

On the top of the heights along the way,
at the crossroads she takes her stand — Ber

At the top of the highways, at the meeting of the roads, she takes her place — Bas

On the hilltop, on the road,
at the crossways, she takes her stand — Jerus

For wisdom is on the top of high places, she stands between the ways and by the paths — Lam

there she stands, on some high vantage-point by the public way, where the roads meet — Knox

3. She crieth at the gates, at the entry of the city, at the coming in at the doors.

Beside the gates, at the entry of the city, at the coming in at the doors, she crieth aloud — RV

by the gateways opening to the city,
at the entries, she is crying out — Mof

Where the roads go into town her cry goes out, at the doorways her voice is loud — Bas

beside the gates, in front of the town, from the portals' entrance she cries out — Ber

By the gates that enter the city,
At the doorways she cries aloud — AAT

beside the gate, at the entrance to the city
at the entry by the open gate she calls aloud — NEB

By the side of the gates, at the entrance of the city;
At the entrance of its doors she shouteth — Sprl

4. Unto you, O men, I call; and my voice is to the sons of man.

To you, O men, I call;
my voice is directed to the sons of men — Ber

Unto you, O men, do I proclaim;
And my call is unto the sons of men — Sprl

To you, O men, I call,
And my appeal is to the sons of men — AAT

To you, O men, I call, and utter my voice to the sons of men — Sept

O men, I am calling to you,
my appeal is to all men — Mof

5. O ye simple, understand wisdom: and, ye fools, be ye of an understanding heart.

O ye simple, understand prudence;
And, ye fools, be of an understanding heart — ASV

Learn shrewdness, ye simple,
And fools, be wise in heart — ABPS

Understand, ye simple ones, shrewdness,
And ye dullards understand sense — Rhm

Become expert in reason, O ye simple ones; you foolish ones, take training to heart — Bas

You ignorant ones! Study discretion; and you fools, come to your senses — Jerus

O heedless souls, learn insight,
O foolish folk, learn sense — Mof

understand, you simple fools, what it is to be shrewd;
you stupid people, understand what sense means — NEB

6. Hear; for I will speak of excellent things; and the opening of my lips shall be right things.

Hearken, for noble things I speak,
And the opening of my lips is uprightness — YLT

Hear, for princely things will I speak,
And the opening of my lips shall be of equity — Rhm

Hearken to me, for I will speak solemn things; and with my lips disclose things which are right — Sept

Hearken, for I will speak advisedly;
And the announcement of my lips shall be of right things — Sprl

Hear, for I will speak truth; and the opening of my mouth shall bring forth uprightness — Lam

Give heed! for noble things I speak;
honesty opens my lips — NAB

7. For my mouth shall speak truth; and wickedness is an abomination to my lips.

8. All the words of my mouth are in righteousness; there is nothing froward or perverse in them.

Sincere are all the words of my mouth,
There is nothing tortuous or perverse in them — AAT

All the words of my mouth are righteous;
there is nothing twisted or crooked in them — RSV
In righteousness shall be all the sayings of my mouth,
Nothing therein shall be crafty or perverse — Rhm
all I say is honest,
with nothing in it false or wrong — Mof
All that I say is right,
not a word is twisted or crooked — NEB
Sincere are all the words of my mouth,
no one of them is wily or crooked — NAB

9. They are all plain to him that understandeth, and right to them that find knowledge.
All of them are plain to the intelligent,
And upright to those finding knowledge — YLT
They are all straightforward to those of understanding,
And right to those who have discovered knowledge — Sprl
they are all clear to him who is discerning
and right to those finding knowledge — Ber
They are all plain to him who understands them, and right to those who are willing to find knowledge — Lam
'tis all plain to a man of sense,
and true for those who are intelligent — Mof
They are all true to him whose mind is awake, and straightforward to those who get knowledge — Bas

10. Receive my instruction, and not silver; and knowledge rather than choice gold.

11. For wisdom is better than rubies; and all the things that may be desired are not to be compared to it.
For better is wisdom than rubies,
Yea, all delights are not comparable with it — YLT
For better is wisdom than ornaments of coral,
And no delightful things can equal her — Rhm
For wisdom is more precious than pearls;
And no precious things can be comparable with her — Sprl
For wisdom is better than precious stones: and no costly thing is equal to it in value — Sept
For wisdom is better than pearls;
And all objects of delight will not compare with it — ABPS
For wisdom is more precious than pearls,
and nothing else is so worthy of desire — Jerus
For Wisdom is better than corals,
and no choice possessions can compare with her — NAB
for wisdom is better than rubies,
no treasure is equal to her — Mof

12. I wisdom dwell with prudence, and find out knowledge of witty inventions.
I wisdom have made prudence my dwelling,
And find out knowledge and discretion — ASV
I, wisdom, dwell in prudence,
And find out the knowledge of wise counsels — ABPS
I wisdom inhabit shrewdness, —
And the knowledge of sagacious things I gain — Rhm
I, wisdom, dwell with insight,
I find out knowledge through deliberating — Ber
I, Wisdom, dwell with experience,
and judicious knowledge I attain — NAB
What am I, the wisdom that speaks to you? To shrewdness I am a near neighbour, and I occupy myself with deep designs — Knox

13. The fear of the LORD is to hate evil: pride, and arrogancy, and the evil way, and the froward mouth, do I hate.
Reverence of the LORD despises evil;
pride, arrogance, evil ways, and perverse speech do I hate — Lam
Reverence of the LORD is hatred of evil.
Pride, arrogance, an evil way
and a perverse mouth I hate — Ber
The reverence of Yahweh is to hate wickedness:
Pride, arrogance, and the way of wickedness;
And a mouth of perverse things do I hate — Rhm
I fear JEHOVAH, I hate wickedness:

Pride and haughtiness, and the way of evil,
And a perverted mouth do I hate — Sprl
(To fear Yahweh is to hate evil.)
I hate pride and arrogance,
wicked behaviour and a lying mouth — Jerus

14. Counsel is mine, and sound wisdom: I am understanding; I have strength.
Counsel is mine, and sound knowledge: I am understanding; I have might — RV
I have counsel and sound wisdom,
I have insight, I have strength — RSV
Mine are counsel and effective working,
I am understanding, mine is valour — Rhm
Mine are counsel and skill,
Mine are reason and might — AAT
Wise design and good sense are mine;
reason and strength are mine — Bas
counsel and skill are mine,
I possess mind and might — Mof

15. By me kings reign, and princes decree justice.
By me kings reign, and princes decree righteousness — YLT
Through me kings reign,
And counsellors judge rightly — Sprl
By me kings reign,
and rulers decree what is just — RSV
By me kings reign,
and lawgivers establish justice — NAB
By me kings reign,
And rulers administer justice — AAT

16. By me princes rule, and nobles, even all the judges of the earth.

17. I love them that love me; and those that seek me early shall find me.
I love them that love me;
And those that seek me diligently shall find me — ASV
I love them that love me,
And those that seek me earnestly shall find me — JPS
Them that love me I love;
And they that earnestly seek me shall find me — ABPS
I love those who love me;
those who seek me eagerly shall find me — Jerus

18. Riches and honour are with me; yea, durable riches and righteousness.

19. My fruit is better than gold, yea, than fine gold; and my revenue than choice silver.
With me are riches and glory; even great possessions and righteousness. My fruit is better than gold and precious stones: and my productions are better than choice silver — Sept
Wealth and honour are with me,
Lasting substance and righteousness.
Better is my fruit than gold, even fine gold,
And mine increase than choice silver — YLT
Riches and honour are with me,
Lordly wealth, and righteousness;
Better is my fruit than gold — yea fine gold,
And mine increase than choice silver — Rhm
Riches and honour are with me;
Yea, enduring riches and righteousness.
My fruit is better than gold, yea, than fine gold;
And my produce than choice silver — JPS
Riches and honor are with me,
enduring wealth and prosperity.
My fruit is better than gold, even fine gold,
and my yield than choice silver — RSV
I hold wealth and honour,
position and good fortune;
what I yield is better than the best of gold,
what I bring in is better than rare silver — Mof
With me are riches and honour,
lasting wealth and justice.
The fruit I give is better than gold, even the finest,
the return I make is better than pure silver — Jerus

20. I lead in the way of righteousness, in the midst of the paths of judgment:

21. That I may cause those that love me to inherit substance; and I will fill their treasures.
I walk in the way of righteousness,
In the midst of the paths of justice;

That I may cause those that love me to inherit substance,
And that I may fill their treasuries — ASV

I walk in the way of rectitude,
In the midst of the paths of justice,
Endowing my friends with wealth,
And filling their treasuries — AAT

I walk in the way of righteousness,
Within the paths of rectitude;
To make those who love me inherit substance,
And the storehouses I will fill — ABPS

On the way of duty I walk,
along the paths of justice,
Granting wealth to those who love me,
and filling their treasuries — NAB

In the way of righteousness I walk
firmly in the midst of the paths of justice,
in order to bestow real substance
upon those loving me, and I will fill their treasuries — Ber

I follow the course of virtue,
my path is the path of justice;
I endow with riches those who love me
and I will fill their treasuries — NEB

22. The LORD possessed me in the beginning of his way, before his works of old.

The LORD made me as the beginning of His way,
The first of His works of old — JPS

JEHOVAH possessed Me in the beginning of His goings forth,
Before His works of antiquity — Sprl

The LORD created me at the beginning of his work,
the first of his acts of old — RSV

The LORD begot me, the firstborn of his ways,
the forerunner of his prodigies of long ago — NAB

The Lord made me as the start of his way, the first of his works in the past — Bas

The Lord formed me in the beginning, before he created anything else — Tay

The LORD made me in the beginning of His way, before His works of old — Ber

23. I was set up from everlasting, from the beginning, or ever the earth was.[2]

At the outset of the ages had I been established,
In advance of the antiquities of the earth — Rhm

In the earliest ages was I fashioned,
At the first, when the earth began — AAT

Before this age he founded me; in the beginning; before he made the earth — Sept

From everlasting was I anointed, from the beginning,
From times before the earth — ABPS

I was poured out from ages past, from the beginning, before the earth was — Ber

Ages ago I was set up,
at the first, before the beginning of the earth — RSV

Alone, I was fashioned in times long past,
at the beginning, long before earth itself — NEB

24. When there were no depths, I was brought forth; when there were no fountains abounding with water.

When no chaos, I was brought forth,
When there were no fountains pregnant with water — Sprl

I was born when there were no abysses, when there were no fountains full of water — Mof

The deep was not, when I was born, there were no springs to gush with water — Jerus

When there was no deep I was given birth, when there were no fountains flowing with water — Bas

I lived before the oceans were created, before the springs bubbled forth their waters onto the earth — Tay

25. Before the mountains were settled, before the hills was I brought forth:

Before mountains were sunk,
Before heights, I was brought forth — YLT

---

[2]The variants for the KJV "set up" come from the two uses of the Heb. verb, "pour out" (of oil = "anoint"; of molten metal, into a mold = "cast", "fashion", hence "set up"), and not from textual differences. The same is true of the verb for "possessed" in vs. 22: the Heb. = "acquire" (by procreation, purchase, or making).

Before the mountains were settled, before the hills were formed was I conceived — Lam

Before the mountains had been shaped, before the hills, I was brought forth — RSV

ere he sunk the bases of the mountains, ere the hills existed, I was born — Mof

Before the mountains were put in their places, before the hills was my birth — Bas

when I was born, the mountains had not yet sunk on their firm foundations, and there were no hills — Knox

26. While as yet he had not made the earth, nor the fields, nor the highest part of the dust of the world.

Not yet had He created the earth with its surroundings,
Or the primitive atoms of the globe — Sprl

While yet he had not made the earth nor the fields,
Nor the first clods of the habitable world — ABPS

While as yet he had not made the earth, nor the fields,
Nor the beginning of the dust of the world — ASV

when the earth and the field were yet unmade as well as the first dust particles of the world — Ber

before he made the earth, the countryside,
or the first grains of the world's dust — Jerus

While as yet he had not made the earth nor the valleys nor the best soil of the world — Lam

27. When he prepared the heavens, I was there: when he set a compass upon the face of the depth:

When he established the heavens, I was there: when he set a circle upon the face of the deep — RV

When he prepared the heavens there was I!
When he decreed a vault upon the face of the resounding deep — Rhm

When He prepared the heavens, there was I;
When He described a sphere upon the face of the deep — Sprl

When he made ready the heavens I was there: when he put an arch over the face of the deep — Bas

When he set the heavens in their place I was there,
when he girdled the ocean with the horizon — NEB

28. When he established the clouds above: when he strengthened the fountains of the deep:

29. When he gave to the sea his decree, that the waters should not pass his commandment: when he appointed the foundations of the earth:

When he made firm the skies above,
When the fountains of the deep became strong,
When he gave to the sea its bound,
That the waters should not transgress his commandment,
When he marked out the foundations of the earth — ASV

when he thickened the clouds above,
when he fixed fast the springs of the deep,
when he assigned the sea its boundaries
— and the waters will not invade the shore —
when he laid down the foundations of the earth — Jerus

In His strengthening clouds above,
In His making strong fountains of the deep,
In His setting for the sea its limit,
And the waters transgress His command,
In His decreeing the foundations of earth — YLT

when he fixed the sky overhead, and levelled the fountain-springs of the deep. I was there when he enclosed the sea within its confines, forbidding the waters to transgress their assigned limits, when he poised the foundations of the world — Knox

when he fixed the canopy of clouds overhead
and set the springs of ocean firm in their place,
when he prescribed its limits for the sea
and knit together earth's foundations — NEB

30. Then I was by him, as one brought

up with him: and I was daily his delight, rejoicing always before him;[3]

Then I was by Him, as a nursling;
And I was daily all delight,
Playing always before Him — JPS

I was with him then, his foster-child,
I was his delight day after day,
playing in his presence constantly — Mof

Then was I at His side — the faithful One.
And I was day by day His delights,
Rejoicing in His presence at all time — Sprl

Then I was by him, as a master workman;
And I was daily his delight,
Rejoicing always before him — ASV

I was by his side, a master craftsman,
delighting him day after day,
ever at play in his presence — Jerus

Then became I beside him a firm and sure worker,
Then became I filled with delight day by day,
Exulting before him on every occasion — Rhm

31. **Rejoicing in the habitable part of his earth; and my delights were with the sons of men.**

Rejoicing in his habitable earth; and my delight was with the sons of men — RV

Sporting in his habitable earth,
And my delight was with the sons of men — ABPS

rejoicing in his inhabited world
and delighting in the sons of men — RSV

playing here and there over his world,
finding my delight in humankind — Mof

playing on the earth, when he had finished it,
while my delight was in mankind — NEB

Sported in this world of his,
And found my delight in the sons of men — AAT

32. **Now therefore hearken unto me, O ye children: for blessed are they that keep my ways.**

33. **Hear instruction, and be wise, and refuse it not.**

And now, my sons, listen to me:
happy are those who keep my ways.
Hear instruction and be wise,
and do not neglect it — RSV

Give ear to me then, my sons: for happy are those who keep my ways. Take my teaching and be wise; do not let it go — Bas

And now, ye children, hearken unto Me:
For blessed are they who keep My ways.
Attend to instruction, and be ye wise;
And reject it not — Sprl

Therefore now, O sons, listen to me; for happy are those who keep my ways. Hear instruction, be wise, and do not refuse it — Ber

34. **Blessed is the man that heareth me, watching daily at my gates, waiting at the posts of my doors.**

Happy is the man that hearkeneth to me,
Watching daily at my gates,
Waiting at the posts of my doors — JPS

Blessed is the man who heeds me, watching daily at my gates, waiting at my threshold — Lam

Happy is the man listening to me, watching daily at my gates, keeping watch at my doorposts — Ber

happy the man who listens to me,
daily at my gate on the watch,
waiting at my doorway — Mof

Blessed are they who listen to me, keep vigil, day by day, at my threshold, watching till I open my doors — Knox

happy the man who listens to me,
watching daily at my threshold
with his eyes on the doorway — NEB

35. **For whoso findeth me findeth life, and shall obtain favour of the LORD.**

36. **But he that sinneth against me wrongeth his own soul: all they that hate me love death.**

Surely whoso findeth Me findeth life,
And obtaineth acceptance with JEHOVAH.
But whoso sinneth against Me wrongeth his own soul;

---

[3]The variants on the KJV "nursling" stem from attempts to decide which of two very similar words was intended in the Heb.; ASV, Jerus, and Rhm follow the LXX interpretation.

All those who hate Me love death — Sprl
For the one finding me finds life, and wins approval from the LORD. But the one missing me does violence to his own soul; all those hating me love death — Ber
For whoever gets me gets life, and grace from the Lord will come to him.
But he who does evil to me, does wrong to his soul: all my haters are in love with death — Bas
For he who finds me finds life,
and wins favor from the LORD;
But he who misses me harms himself;
all who hate me love death — NAB
He who finds me finds life,
and he wins favour from the Eternal;
he who ignores me is injuring himself,
for all who hate me are in love with death — Mof

CHAPTER 9

1. Wisdom hath builded her house, she hath hewn out her seven pillars:
2. She hath killed her beasts; she hath mingled her wine; she hath also furnished her table.
Wisdom hath built herself a house, and fixed underneath it seven pillars. She hath slain her victims. She hath mixed her wine for the cup and furnished her table — Sept
Wisdom has made her house, putting up her seven pillars.
She has put her fat beasts to death; her wine is mixed, her table is ready — Bas
Wisdom has built her house; she has set up in it seven pillars;
She has slaughtered her beasts; she has mingled her wine; she has also prepared her table — Lam
Wisdom has built her house,
she has hewn her seven pillars;
she has killed a beast and spiced her wine,
and she has spread her table — NEB
Wisdom has built her house,
she has set up her seven columns;
She has dressed her meat, mixed her wine,
yes, she has spread her table — NAB
Wisdom has built her mansion,
and set up her seven pillars;
her beasts are slain, her wines are blended,
her table is prepared — Mof
3. She hath sent forth her maidens: she crieth upon the highest places of the city,
She has despatched her maidservants and proclaimed from the city's heights — Jerus
She has sent out her maids to call
from the highest places in the town — RSV
she has sent forth her maidens; she calls upon the top of the high places of the city — Ber
She has sent out her maidens, and calls
On the heights of the city highways — AAT
She has sent out her maidens;
On the heights of the city she calls — ABPS
She has sent forth her servants to cry out upon the highest places and say — Lam

4. Whoso is simple, let him turn in hither: as for him that wanteth understanding, she saith to him,
'Whoso is thoughtless, let him turn in hither';
As for him that lacketh understanding, she saith to him — JPS
Simple hearts, she says, draw near to me; and to all that lack learning this is her cry — Knox
Whoever is simple, let him come in here; and to him who has no sense, she says — Bas
'Who is ignorant? Let him step this way.'
To the fool she says — Jerus

5. Come, eat of my bread, and drink of the wine which I have mingled.
6. Forsake the foolish, and live; and go in the way of understanding.
Come feed on my food,
And drink of the wine I have mingled; Forsake the simple ones and live,

And advance in the way of understanding — Rhm

Come, eat of my food,
And drink of the wine I have mixed.
Forsake follies, and live;
And go forward in the way of understanding — ABPS

Come, eat of my bread,
And drink of the wine I have mingled;
Forsake your folly, and live,
And keep straight on the path of reason — AAT

Come, eat my bread,
drink wines that I have blended;
leave your foolish ways and live,
follow the ways of thoughtful sense — Mof

Come, eat of my bread
and drink of the wine I have mixed.
Leave simpleness, and live,
and walk in the way of insight — RSV

Come, eat of my bread, and drink of the wine that I have mixed. Quit the company of the simple and live; walk in the way of understanding — Ber

7. He that reproveth a scorner getteth to himself shame: and he that rebuketh a wicked man getteth himself a blot.

He that correcteth a scoffer getteth to himself reviling;
And he that reproveth a wicked man getteth himself a blot — ASV

He that rebuketh a scoffer getteth to himself contempt,
And he that reproveth a lawless man getteth to himself his shame — Rhm

He who corrects a scoffer gets himself abuse,
and he who reproves a wicked man incurs injury — RSV

He who instructeth the wicked shall receive for himself dishonour; and he who reproveth the ungodly will blemish himself — Sept

He who corrects an arrogant man earns insult;
and he who reproves a wicked man incurs opprobrium — NAB

Correct a mocker and you make an enemy;
rebuke a wicked man, you get insult in return — Jerus

8. Reprove not a scorner, lest he hate thee:

Rebuke not a scoffer, lest he hate thee — ABPS

Reprove not a bad man, lest he hate you — Lam

Do not say sharp words to a man of pride, or he will have hate for you — Bas

Rebuke not the wicked, lest they hate thee — Sept

Do not rebuke the mocker, he will only hate you — Jerus

With a rash fool never remonstrate; it will make him thy enemy — Knox

rebuke a wise man, and he will love thee.

9. Give instruction to a wise man, and he will be yet wiser: teach a just man, and he will increase in learning.

Give to a wise man and he will be wiser still,
Inform a righteous man and he will increase learning — Rhm

Give an opportunity to a wise man, and he will be yet wiser; teach a just man, and he will increase in learning — Lam

Give teaching to a wise man, and he will become wiser; give training to an upright man, and his learning will be increased — Bas

Inform a wise man and he will become yet wiser; teach a righteous man and he will add to his grasp of things — Ber

Instruct a man of sense, and he will gain more sense;
teach a good man, and he will learn the more — Mof

Impart unto the wise, and they will be wiser yet;
Instruct the upright, and he acquireth more — Sprl

10. The fear of the LORD is the beginning of wisdom: and the knowledge of the holy is understanding.

The commencement of wisdom is the fear of Jehovah,
And a knowledge of the Holy Ones is understanding — YLT

The beginning of wisdom is reverence for the LORD,
And the knowledge of the Holy One is understanding — AAT

The first thing in knowledge is reverence for the Eternal,
to know the Deity is what knowledge means — Mof

The fear of the LORD is the beginning of wisdom,
and the knowledge of the Holy One is insight — RSV

True wisdom begins with fear of the Lord; he best discerns, who has knowledge of holy things — Knox

The fear of the Lord is the beginning of wisdom; and knowledge is the counsel of the holy — Sept

11. For by me thy days shall be multiplied, and the years of thy life shall be increased.

12. If thou be wise, thou shalt be wise for thyself: but if thou scornest, thou alone shalt bear it.

If thou art wise, thou art wise unto thyself;
And shouldst thou scorn, thyself alone shall suffer for it — Sprl

If you are wise, it is to your own advantage;
and if you are arrogant, you alone shall bear it — NAB

If you are wise, your wisdom will turn to your profit;
But if you are a scoffer, you must bear the consequences alone — AAT

If you are wise, it will be to your own advantage;
if you are haughty, you alone are to blame — NEB

If you are wise, you benefit yourself, and if you scorn, you alone will bear it — Ber

13. A foolish woman is clamorous: she is simple, and knoweth nothing.

The woman Stupidity is boisterous,
So simple that she knoweth not what she would do — Rhm

Dame Folly acts on impulse,
is childish and knows nothing — Jerus

The woman Folly is riotous;
She is thoughtlessness, and knoweth nothing — JPS

Folly is loud and alluring,
she knows no sense of shame — Mof

A foolish woman is noisy;
she is wanton and knows no shame — RSV

The foolish woman is full of noise;
she has no sense at all — Bas

14. For she sitteth at the door of her house, on a seat in the high places of the city,

15. To call passengers who go right on their ways:

She sits at the door of her house,
On a seat by the city highways,
Calling to those who pass by,
Who are keeping straight on their ways — AAT

She sits at the door of her house, on the seat in the high places of the city, to call to those passing by her way, to those going straight on their paths — Ber

Verily she sitteth at the door of her house,
Upon a seat on the heights in the city,
To call to the passengers by the way,
Who are going straight forwards — Sprl

She sits at the door of her house
upon a seat on the city heights,
Calling to passers-by
as they go on their straight way — NAB

She sits at the door of her house or stands at the street corners of the city, whispering to men going by, and to those minding their own business — Tay

16. Whoso is simple, let him turn in hither: and as for him that wanteth understanding, she saith to him,

17. Stolen waters are sweet, and bread eaten in secret is pleasant.

'Who is simple? let him turn aside hither.'
And whoso lacketh heart — she said to him,
'Stolen waters are sweet,
And hidden bread is pleasant'—YLT

Let him who is the simplest of you turn aside to me; and them who want prudence I exhort saying, Taste sweetly bread in secret and water sweeter for being stolen — Sept

Whoever is simple, let him come in here: and to him who is without sense, she says:
Drink taken without right is sweet,

and food in secret is pleasing — Bas

"Let all who are heedless turn in here!"
She calls to him who is devoid of sense,
"Sweet are stolen waters,
bread in secret is delicious!" — Mof

'Come in, you simpletons', she says. She says also to the fool, 'Stolen water is sweet
and bread got by stealth tastes good' — NEB

18. **But he knoweth not that the dead are there; and that her guests are in the depths of hell.**

But he knoweth not that the dead are there;
In the valley of death-shade are her guests — Sprl

But he knoweth not that the shades are there;
In the depths of hades are her guests — Rhm

But he does not know that ghosts are there; her guests are in the depths of Sheol — Ber

But he knoweth not that the shades are there;
That her guests are in the depths of the nether-world — JPS

Who shall warn them that dead men are her company, no guest of hers but is guest of the dark world beneath — Knox

The fellow does not realize that here the Shades are gathered,
that her guests are heading for the valleys of Sheol — Jerus

CHAPTER 10

1. **The Proverbs of Solomon.**
A wise son maketh a glad father: but a foolish son is the heaviness of his mother.

A wise son causeth a father to rejoice,
And a foolish son is an affliction to his mother — YLT

A wise son giveth joy unto his father,
But a foolish son causeth grief unto his mother — Sprl

A wise son makes his father glad, but a foolish son is the grief of his mother — Ber

A sensible son is a joy to his father,
but a senseless son is a grief to his mother — Mof

A wise son makes a glad father,
but a foolish son is a sorrow to his mother — RSV

A wise son makes his father glad, but a foolish son brings shame to his mother — Lam

2. **Treasures of wickedness profit nothing: but righteousness delivereth from death.**

Treasures unjustly acquired are of no avail;
But honesty saves from death — AAT

Wealth which comes from sin is of no profit, but righteousness gives salvation from death — Bas

Treasures wickedly come by give no benefit,
but right conduct brings delivery from death — Jerus

Ill-gotten wealth brings no profit;
uprightness is a safeguard against death — NEB

Ill-gotten gain brings no lasting happiness; right living does — Tay

3. **The LORD will not suffer the soul of the righteous to famish: but he casteth away the substance of the wicked.**

Jehovah will not suffer the soul of the righteous to famish;
But he thrusteth away the desire of the wicked — ASV

The Lord will not kill with hunger a righteous soul; but he will overthrow the life of the wicked — Sept

Jehovah will not let the spirit of the righteous famish;
But he repels the longing of the wicked — ABPS

The LORD does not let the soul of the righteous go hungry, but He frustrates the desire of the wicked — Ber

The LORD does not let the righteous go hungry,
but he thwarts the craving of the wicked — RSV

The LORD permits not the just to hunger,
but the craving of the wicked he thwarts — NAB

4. **He becometh poor that dealeth with a**

slack hand: but the hand of the diligent maketh rich.

He who is slow in his work becomes poor, but the hand of the ready worker gets in wealth — Bas

The negligent hand becometh poor;
But the hand of diligence maketh wealthy — Sprl

A slack hand brings poverty;
But the hand of the diligent brings wealth — AAT

A slack hand makes men poor:
a busy hand makes men rich — Mof

Idle hands make a man poor;
busy hands grow rich — NEB

Lazy men are soon poor; hard workers get rich — Tay

5. **He that gathereth in summer is a wise son: but he that sleepeth in harvest is a son that causeth shame.**

He who in summer gets together his store is a son who does wisely; but he who takes his rest when the grain is being cut is a son causing shame — Bas

A wise son gathereth in summer;
But a son that doeth shamefully sleepeth in harvest — JPS

A son who gathers in summer is prudent,
but a son who sleeps in harvest brings shame — RSV

A son who fills the granaries in summer is a credit;
a son who slumbers during harvest, a disgrace — NAB

He who works in summer is a wise man; but he who sleeps in harvest is a son that causes shame — Lam

He who reaps in summer acts wisely;
He who sleeps in harvest acts shamefully — AAT

6. **Blessings are upon the head of the just: but violence covereth the mouth of the wicked.**

7. **The memory of the just is blessed: but the name of the wicked shall rot.**

Blessings are for the head of the righteous man,
But the mouth of the lawless covereth up wrong.
The memory of the righteous yieldeth blessing,
But the name of the lawless dieth out — Rhm

Blessings are upon the head of the righteous, but the mouth of the wicked conceals violence.
The memory of the righteous continues a blessing, but the name of the wicked shall rot — Ber

Blessings are upon the head of the just;
But insult shall cover the face of the wicked.
The memory of the just is blessed;
But the name of the wicked shall be putrid — Sprl

The blessings of Yahweh are on the head of the virtuous man,
premature mourning stops the mouths of the wicked.
The virtuous man is remembered with blessings,
the wicked man's name rots away — Jerus

The blessing of the Lord is on the head of the righteous; but untimely grief shall stop the mouth of the wicked.
The just are remembered with praises; but the name of the wicked is extinguished — Sept

God's blessing is upon the good man's head,
but the bad man's face shall be darkened with disaster.
The memory of the upright is blessed,
but cursed shall be the name of wicked men — Mof

Blessings are showered on the righteous;
the wicked are choked by their own violence.
The righteous are remembered in blessings;
the name of the wicked turns rotten — NEB

8. **The wise in heart will receive commandments: but a prating fool shall fall.**

The wise-hearted will accept advice;
But a prating fool will continue stumbling — Sprl

A wise man heeds commands,
but a prating fool will be overthrown — NAB

The wise of heart will heed commandments,
but a prating fool will come to ruin — RSV

A man of sense defers to authority:
a silly chatterer comes to grief — Mof

The heart that is wise is obedient to instruction,
the gabbling fool is heading for ruin — Jerus

The wise man is glad to be instructed, but a self-sufficient fool falls flat on his face — Tay

9. He that walketh uprightly walketh surely: but he that perverteth his ways shall be known.

Whoso is walking in integrity walketh confidently,
And whoso is perverting his ways is known — YLT

He that walks in integrity will walk securely;
But he that perverts his ways will be known — ABPS

Whoso walketh uprightly, walketh securely;
But whoso perverteth his way shall be detected — Sprl

He who walks honestly walks safely;
But he who walks crookedly will be found out — AAT

A blameless life makes for security;
crooked ways bring a man down — NEB

He whose ways are upright will go safely, but he whose ways are twisted will be made low — Bas

He walks secure, who walks pure; cunning will yet be found out — Knox

10. He who winketh with the eye causeth sorrow: but a prating fool shall fall.

Whoso is winking the eye giveth grief,
And a talkative fool kicketh — YLT

Whoso winketh with the eye giveth offence;
And a prating fool shall stumble — Sprl

He that winketh with the eye causeth sorrow,
And he that is foolish with his lips shall be thrust aside — Rhm

He who winks with his eye causes heartache, and a prating fool will fall headlong — Ber

He who winketh deceitfully with his eyes, collecteth sorrows for men; but he who reproveth freely maketh peace — Sept

He who winks with the eye makes trouble;
He who frankly reproves makes peace — AAT

He who winks at a fault causes trouble, but he who frankly reproves promotes peace — NAB

11. The mouth of a righteous man is a well of life: but violence covereth the mouth of the wicked.

The mouth of the righteous is a fountain of life;
But the mouth of the wicked concealeth violence — JPS

A well-spring of life is the mouth of the righteous,
But the mouth of the lawless covereth wrong — Rhm

The mouth of the upright man is a fountain of life, but the mouth of the evil-doer is a bitter cup — Bas

The talk of good men is a life-giving fountain:
the talk of bad men overflows with harm — Mof

The mouth of the virtuous man is a life-giving fountain,
violence lurks in the mouth of the wicked — Jerus

The words of good men are a fountain of life;
the wicked are choked by their own violence — NEB

12. Hatred stirreth up strifes: but love covereth all sins.

Hatred exciteth strifes,
But love covereth over every transgression — Sprl

Hatred stirreth up strifes,
But over all transgressions love throweth a covering — Rhm

Hatred stirs up strife;
But love covers all offenses — ABPS

Hatred stirs up disputes,
but love covers all offenses — NAB

Hatred stirs old quarrels, but love overlooks insults — Tay

Hatred stirs up strife;
But love draws a veil over all transgressions — AAT

Hatred stirs up contentions, but love covers all transgressions — Ber

Hatred is ever ready to pick a quarrel; love passes over all kinds of offence — Knox

13. In the lips of him that hath understanding wisdom is found: but a rod is for the back of him that is void of understanding.

In the lips of him that hath discernment wisdom is found;
But a rod is for the back of him that is void of understanding — ASV

In the lips of the intelligent is wisdom found,
And a rod is for the back of him who is lacking understanding — YLT

The man of understanding has wisdom on his lips;
a rod is in store for the back of the fool — NEB

Good sense is on the lips of the intelligent, but folly lies in the talk of senseless men — Mof

On the lips of the discerning one wisdom is found, but a rod is for the back of one devoid of understanding — Ber

Men with common sense are admired as counselors; those without it are beaten as servants — Tay

14. Wise men lay up knowledge: but the mouth of the foolish is near destruction.

The wise treasure up knowledge;
But the fool's mouth is a near downfall — ABPS

Wise men lay up knowledge: but the mouth of the foolish is a present destruction — RV

Wise men store up knowledge, but the mouth of the foolish hastens ruin — Ber

Wise men produce knowledge;
But the mouth of a fool an approaching destruction — Sprl

Wise men lay up knowledge;
But the mouth of the foolish is an imminent ruin — JPS

Wise men store up knowledge;
But the mouth of a fool precipitates ruin — AAT

15. The rich man's wealth is his strong city: the destruction of the poor is their poverty.

The wealth of the rich man is his fortress; the ruin of the poor is their poverty — Ber

The substance of the rich is his strong city,
The terror of the poor is their poverty — Rhm

The rich man's wealth is his stronghold,
poverty is the poor man's undoing — Jerus

A rich man's wealth is his protection, but poverty is the ruin of the poor — Mof

A rich man's wealth is his strong city, but poverty is the undoing of the helpless — NEB

The rich man's wealth is his only strength. The poor man's poverty is his only curse — Tay

16. The labour of the righteous tendeth to life: the fruit of the wicked to sin.

The works of the righteous produce life; but the hands of the wicked produce sins — Sept

The work of the upright gives life: the increase of the evil-doer is a cause of sin — Bas

The labor of the righteous tendeth to life;
The increase of the wicked, to sin — ASV

The wages of the righteous is life;
The increase of the wicked is sin — JPS

The earnings of the righteous conduce to life;
The income of the wicked to death — AAT

The wage of the righteous leads to life,
the gain of the wicked to sin — RSV

The just man's recompense leads to life,
the gains of the wicked, to sin — NAB

17. He is in the way of life that keepeth instruction: but he that refuseth reproof erreth.

He is in the way of life that heedeth correction;
But he that forsaketh reproof erreth — ASV

A traveller to life is he who is keeping instruction,
And whoso is forsaking rebuke is erring — YLT

A way of life is he who heeds correction;
But he who forsakes reproof leads astray — ABPS

On the way to life is he that heedeth correction,

But he that hateth reproof is going astray — Rhm
He who heeds instruction is on the path to life,
but he who rejects reproof goes astray — RSV
Correction is the high road to life;
neglect reproof and you miss the way — NEB

18. He that hideth hatred with lying lips, and he that uttereth a slander, is a fool.
Whoso cloaketh hatred with lying lips,
And whoso uttereth a slander, is a fool — Sprl
He that covers hatred with lying lips,
And he that publishes an ill report, the same is a fool — ABPS
He that concealeth hatred hath false lips,
And he that sendeth forth slander the same is a dullard — Rhm
He that hideth hatred is of lying lips;
and he that uttereth a slander is a fool — RV
He who hides hatred has lying lips and he who spouts forth slander is a fool — Ber
It is the lips of the liar that conceal hostility;
but he who spreads accusations is a fool — NAB

19. In the multitude of words there wanteth not sin: but he that refraineth his lips is wise.
In the abundance of words transgression ceaseth not,
And whoso is restraining his lips is wise — YLT
In the multitude of words there wanteth not transgression;
But he that refraineth his lips doeth wisely — ASV
In speaking much thou canst not avoid sin; but if thou art sparing of thy lips, thou wilt be wise — Sept
Where there is much talk there will be no end to sin, but he who keeps his mouth shut does wisely — Bas
Where words abound, sin will not be wanting;
But he who holds his tongue acts wisely — AAT
When words are many, transgression is not lacking,
but he who restrains his lips is prudent — RSV

20. The tongue of the just is as choice silver: the heart of the wicked is little worth.

21. The lips of the righteous feed many: but fools die for want of wisdom.
Choice silver is the tongue of the righteous,
But the sense of the lawless is very small.
The lips of the righteous feed multitudes,
But the foolish for lack of sense shall die — Rhm
Silver refined is the just man's every word, and trash the sinner's every thought. The just man's talk plays the shepherd to many, while the fool dies of his own starved heart — Knox
Good men's talk is like rare silver:
a bad man's views are little worth.
The words of good men will make many wise,
but a fool's lack of sense is death to himself — Mof
The tongue of the righteous is as choice silver, but the heart of the wicked is of little value.
The lips of the righteous nourish many, but the foolish perish from lack of understanding — Ber
A good man's tongue is pure silver;
the heart of the wicked is trash.
The lips of a good man teach many,
but fools perish for want of sense — NEB
The tongue of the righteous is as choice silver;
But the heart of the wicked is as a thing of nought.
The lips of the righteous nourish many;
But fools die off for lack of knowledge — Sprl

22. The blessing of the LORD, it maketh rich, and he addeth no sorrow with it.
The blessing of Jehovah — it maketh rich,
And He addeth no grief with it — YLT
The blessing of the Lord is on the head of the righteous; it maketh rich, and to it no sorrow of heart shall be joined — Sept
The blessings of the LORD bring riches,

and there shall be no sorrow in them — Lam
The blessing of the LORD, it maketh rich,
And toil addeth nothing thereto — JPS
The blessing of Yahweh is what brings riches,
to this hard toil has nothing to add — Jerus
It is the LORD's blessing that brings wealth,
and no effort can substitute for it — NAB
The blessing of the LORD makes rich;
Toil yields no increase like it — AAT
'Tis the Eternal's blessing that brings wealth,
and never does it bring trouble as well — Mof
Of the Lord's gift comes wealth without drudgery — Knox

23. It is as sport to a fool to do mischief: but a man of understanding hath wisdom.

It is enjoyment to a fool to do wickedly;
But to a wise man to do wisely — Sprl
It is as sport to a fool to do wickedness;
And so is wisdom to a man of understanding — ASV
It is like sport to a fool to do wrong,
but wise conduct is pleasure to a man of understanding — RSV
It is sport to the foolish man to do evil,
but the man of good sense takes delight in wisdom — Bas
To a fool doing wickedness is sport,
just as wisdom is to a man of understanding — Ber
Crime is the entertainment of the fool;
so is wisdom for the man of sense — NAB

24. The fear of the wicked, it shall come upon him: but the desire of the righteous shall be granted.

25. As the whirlwind passeth, so is the wicked no more: but the righteous is an everlasting foundation.

The dread of the lawless one the same shall overtake him,
But the desire of the righteous shall be granted.
Like the passing away of a tempest so the lawless one is not,
But the righteous hath an age-abiding foundation — Rhm
The feared thing of the wicked it meeteth him,
And the desire of the righteous is given.
As the passing by of a hurricane,
So the wicked is not,
And the righteous is a foundation age-during — YLT
What the wicked man dreads will befall him;
But the desire of the righteous will be granted.
As the whirlwind passes, so the wicked man vanishes;
But the righteous is rooted forever — AAT
What the wicked dreads will come upon him,
but the desire of the righteous will be granted.
When the tempest passes, the wicked is no more,
but the righteous is established for ever — RSV
Whatever a bad man fears will befall him, but a good man's repose will last for ever.
When the storm sweeps by, the wicked are gone,
but the just are rooted forever — Mof
What the wicked man fears overtakes him,
what the virtuous desires comes to him as a present.
When the storm is over, the wicked man is no more,
but the virtuous stands firm for ever — Jerus

26. As vinegar to the teeth, and as smoke to the eyes, so is the sluggard to them that send him.

As vinegar to the teeth,
And as smoke to the eyes,
So is the slothful to those sending him — YLT
As vinegar to the teeth, and as smoke to the eyes,
So is the sluggard to those who send him on an errand — AAT
As vinegar to the teeth and as smoke

to the eyes, so is the lazy one to those who send him — Ber

As vinegar to the teeth, and smoke to the eyes,
is the sluggard to those who use him as a messenger — NAB

A lazy fellow is a pain to his employers — like smoke in their eyes or vinegar that sets the teeth on edge — Tay

27. The fear of the LORD prolongeth days: but the years of the wicked shall be shortened.

28. The hope of the righteous shall be gladness: but the expectation of the wicked shall perish.

The reverence of Yahweh addeth days,
But the years of the lawless shall be shortened.
The hope of the righteous shall be gladness,
But the expectation of the lawless shall vanish — Rhm

The fear of the LORD prolongs life,
but the years of the wicked will be short.
The hope of the righteous ends in gladness,
but the expectation of the wicked comes to nought — RSV

The fear of the Lord gives long life,
but the years of the evil-doer will be cut short.
The hope of the upright man will give joy, but the waiting of the evil-doer will have its end in sorrow — Bas

The fear of Yahweh adds length to life,
the years of the wicked will be cut short.
The hope of virtuous men is all joy,
the expectations of the wicked are frustrated — Jerus

The fear of the LORD brings length of days;
the years of the wicked are few.
The hope of the righteous blossoms;
the expectation of the wicked withers away — NEB

Reverence for the Eternal is the prolonging of life,
but the years of evil men are shortened.
The hopes of good men end in bliss;
bad men lose what they look for — Mof

29. The way of the LORD is strength to the upright: but destruction shall be to the workers of iniquity.

30. The righteous shall never be removed: but the wicked shall not inhabit the earth.

The way of Jehovah is a stronghold to the upright;
But it is a destruction to the workers of iniquity.
The righteous shall never be removed;
But the wicked shall not dwell in the land — ASV

The way of JEHOVAH is a fortress to the upright;
But destruction to the workers of iniquity.
The righteous shall never be removed;
But the wicked shall not abide in the land — Sprl

The LORD is a stronghold to him who walks honestly;
But ruin to those who do evil.
The righteous will never be moved;
But the wicked will have no foothold in the land — AAT

A stronghold for uprightness is the way of Jehovah;
But destruction to the workers of iniquity.
Forever, the righteous shall not be moved;
But the wicked shall not inhabit the land — ABPS

The LORD is a stronghold to him who walks honestly,
but to evil-doers, their downfall.
The just man will never be disturbed,
but the wicked will not abide in the land — NAB

A refuge for the blameless is the path of Yahweh,
But destruction awaiteth the workers of iniquity.
The righteous to times age-abiding shall remain unshaken,
But the lawless shall not inhabit the earth — Rhm

31. The mouth of the just bringeth forth wisdom: but the froward tongue shall be cut out.

32. The lips of the righteous know what is acceptable: but the mouth of the wicked speaketh frowardness.

The mouth of the righteous uttereth wisdom,
And the tongue of frowardness is cut out.
The lips of the righteous know a pleasing thing,
And the mouth of the wicked perverseness — YLT

The mouth of the righteous distilleth wisdom; but the tongue of the wicked shall be destroyed.
The lips of righteous men distil graces; but the mouth of the wicked is perverse — Sept

The mouth of the upright man is budding with wisdom, but the twisted tongue will be cut off.
The lips of the upright man have knowledge of what is pleasing, but twisted are the mouths of evil-doers — Bas

The mouth of the righteous brings forth wisdom; but a perverse tongue shall be silenced.
The lips of the righteous know what is good; but the mouth of the wicked speaks perverse things — Lam

The mouth of the righteous blossoms forth with wisdom, but the perverse tongue will be eliminated.
The lips of the righteous know what delights others, but the mouth of the wicked is perverse — Ber

Wisdom flows from the mouth of the righteous;
the subversive tongue will be rooted out.
The righteous man can suit his words to the occasion;
the wicked know only subversive talk — NEB

CHAPTER 11

1. A false balance is abomination to the LORD: but a just weight is his delight.

Balances of deceit are an abomination to Jehovah,
And a perfect weight is His delight — YLT

A false balance is the abomination of Jehovah;
But a full weight is his delight — ABPS

Scales of deceit are hated by the Lord, but a true weight is his delight — Bas

Deceitful scales are an abomination to the LORD, but an accurate weight is His delight — Ber

A false balance is abhorrent to Yahweh,
a just weight is pleasing to him — Jerus

A false balance the Lord hates; nothing but full weight will content him — Knox

2. When pride cometh, then cometh shame; but with the lowly is wisdom.

3. The integrity of the upright shall guide them: but the perverseness of transgressors shall destroy them.

When pride cometh then cometh contempt,
But with the modest is wisdom.
The integrity of the upright shall guide them,
But the crookedness of the treacherous shall be their ruin — Rhm

When pride comes, scorn comes;
But with the modest is wisdom.
Upright men are guided by their honesty;
But faithless men are ruined by their crookedness — AAT

When pride comes, then comes disgrace;
but with the humble is wisdom.
The integrity of the upright guides them,
but the crookedness of the treacherous destroys them — RSV

When pride comes, disgrace comes too:
modest men show good sense.
The upright are kept straight by their own honesty:
dishonest men are ruined by their vice — Mof

When presumption comes in, in comes contempt,
but wisdom goes with sagacity.
Honesty is a guide to the upright,
but rogues are balked by their own perversity — NEB

When pride comes, disgrace comes;
but with the humble is wisdom.

The honesty of the upright guides them;
the faithless are ruined by their duplicity — NAB

Proud men end in shame, but the meek become wise.
A good man is guided by his honesty; the evil man is destroyed by his dishonesty — Tay

4. Riches profit not in the day of wrath: but righteousness delivereth from death.

Wealth is of no profit in the day of wrath, but righteousness keeps a man safe from death — Bas

When the time for reckoning comes, little shall wealth avail; right living is death's avoidance — Knox

On the day of God's anger wealth is of no avail:
goodness alone saves man from death — Mof

Wealth is worth nothing in the day of wrath,
but uprightness is a safeguard against death — NEB

In the day of wrath riches will be of no advantage,
but virtuous conduct delivers from death — Jerus

Wealth is useless on the day of wrath, but virtue saves from death — NAB

5. The righteousness of the perfect shall direct his way: but the wicked shall fall by his own wickedness.

6. The righteousness of the upright shall deliver them: but transgressors shall be taken in their own naughtiness.

The righteousness of the upright shall direct his way;
But the wicked stumbleth through his wickedness.
The integrity of the righteous delivereth them;
But deceivers shall be taken in their own naughtiness — Sprl

The righteousness of the sincere shall make straight his way;
But the wicked shall fall by his own wickedness.
The righteousness of the upright shall deliver them;
But the faithless shall be trapped in their own crafty device — JPS

The righteousness of the blameless keeps his way straight,
but the wicked falls by his own wickedness.
The righteousness of the upright delivers them,
but the treacherous are taken captive by their lust — RSV

The righteousness of the blameless makes straight his way, but by his own wickedness the wicked falls.
The righteousness of the upright delivers them, but the treacherous are trapped by their own greediness — Ber

The righteousness of the blameless shall smooth his way,
But by his own lawlessness shall the lawless one fall.
The righteousness of the upright shall deliver them,
But by their own craving shall the treacherous be captured — Rhm

The upright are directed by their honesty; the wicked shall fall beneath their load of sins.
The good man's goodness delivers him; the evil man's treachery is his undoing — Tay

7. When a wicked man dieth, his expectation shall perish: and the hope of unjust men perisheth.

8. The righteous is delivered out of trouble, and the wicked cometh in his stead.

In the death of a wicked man, hope perisheth,
And the expectation of the iniquitous hath been lost.
The righteous from distress is drawn out,
And the wicked goeth in instead of him — YLT

When a wicked man dies, his expectation perishes;
All hope of success is lost.
The innocent man is rescued from trouble;
And the guilty takes his place — AAT

The hope of the wicked perishes with death,
the expectation of the godless is frustrated.
The virtuous man escapes misfortune,
the wicked man incurs it instead — Jerus

When a wicked man dies his hope perishes,
and what is expected from strength comes to nought.
The just man escapes trouble,
and the wicked man falls into it in his stead — NAB

When the wicked man dies, so does expectation perish; yes, the hope of his strength dies out. The righteous is delivered from trouble, and the wicked takes his place — Ber

When the wicked dies, his hope perishes,
and the expectation of the godless comes to nought.
The righteous is delivered from trouble,
and the wicked gets into it instead — RSV

9. An hypocrite with his mouth destroyeth his neighbour: but through knowledge shall the just be delivered.

With his mouth the godless man destroyeth his neighbor;
But through knowledge shall the righteous be delivered — ASV

With the mouth a profane man destroyeth his neighbour,
But through knowledge shall righteous men be delivered — Rhm

By the mouth the impure destroys his fellow;
But by knowledge the righteous are delivered — ABPS

By his mouth the hypocrite destroyeth his neighbours;
But by the knowledge of the just shall they be delivered — Sprl

Through his mouth the godless man is the ruin of his neighbour,
but by knowledge the virtuous are safeguarded — Jerus

False speech the hypocrite will use to ruin his neighbour; true knowledge is the saving of the just — Knox

With his mouth the impious man would ruin his neighbor,
but through their knowledge the just make their escape — NAB

10. When it goeth well with the righteous, the city rejoiceth: and when the wicked perish, there is shouting.

11. By the blessing of the upright the city is exalted: but it is overthrown by the mouth of the wicked.

When it is well with the righteous the city exulteth,
When the lawless perish there is a shout of triumph.
When the upright are blessed exalted is the city,
But by the mouth of the lawless it is overthrown — Rhm

In the good of the righteous a city exulteth,
And in the destruction of the wicked is singing.
By the blessing of the upright is a city exalted,
And by the mouth of the wicked thrown down — YLT

When it is well with the righteous, the city rejoices;
And when the wicked perish, there is a shout of joy.
By the blessing of the upright the city is raised up;
But by the mouth of the wicked it is torn down — ABPS

When virtuous men prosper the city rejoices,
there are glad cries, too, when the wicked are ruined.
A city is raised on the blessing of honest men,
and demolished by the mouth of the wicked — Jerus

When righteous men prosper, the city exults;
And when wicked men perish, there is jubilation.
Through the blessing of the upright the city is exalted;
But through the mouth of the wicked it is overthrown — AAT

When good men prosper, the city rejoices: when bad men perish, there are shouts of joy.
A city is exalted by the success of the upright, and overthrown by the policy of knaves — Mof

12. He that is void of wisdom despiseth his neighbour: but a man of understanding holdeth his peace.

He that despiseth his neighbor is void of wisdom;
But a man of understanding holdeth his peace — ASV

Whoso detracts from his neighbour lacketh heart;

But a man of understanding shall keep silence — Sprl

He that despises his neighbor is lacking in understanding;
But a man of intelligence holds his peace — ABPS

He that despiseth his neighbour lacketh understanding;
But a man of discernment holdeth his peace — JPS

He who belittles his neighbor lacks sense,
but a man of understanding remains silent — RSV

The senseless man pours contempt on his neighbor;
But the intelligent man keeps silent — AAT

13. A talebearer revealeth secrets: but he that is of a faithful spirit concealeth the matter.

He that goeth about as a talebearer revealeth secrets: but he that is of a faithful spirit concealeth the matter — RV

A busybody is revealing secret counsel,
And the faithful of spirit is covering the matter — YLT

He who is a habitual talebearer betrays confidence, but he who is trustworthy keeps a matter hidden — Ber

A double tongued man revealeth cabinet counsels: but one of a faithful spirit concealeth matters — Sept

He who goes about talking of others makes secrets public, but the true-hearted man keeps things covered — Bas

A tittle-tattler lets secrets out,
a trustworthy man keeps things hidden — Jerus

A gossip gives away secrets,
but a trusty man keeps his own counsel — NEB

14. Where no counsel is, the people fall: but in the multitude of counsellors there is safety.

Where no wise guidance is, the people falleth;
But in the multitude of counsellors there is safety — ASV

Where no wise direction is, a people falleth;
But in the multitude of counsellors there is safety — JPS

With no guidance a people will fall,
But safety lieth in the greatness of the counsellor — Rhm

For want of guidance a people will fall;
But safety lies in a wealth of counselors — AAT

For lack of guidance a people falls;
security lies in many counselors — NAB

For lack of statesmanship, a nation sinks:
the saving of it is a wealth of counsellors — Mof

15. He that is surety for a stranger shall smart for it: and he that hateth suretyship is sure.

Evil one suffereth when he hath been surety for a stranger,
And whoso is hating suretyship is confident — YLT

He shall be sore distressed who is surety for a stranger;
But whoso hateth suretiships hath security — Sprl

Ill fares one when he is surety for a stranger;
But he that hates sureties is secure — ABPS

He who makes himself responsible for a strange man will undergo much loss; but the hater of such undertakings will be safe — Bas

He who goes bail for a stranger will rue it,
the man who hates going surety is safe — Jerus

Be sure you know a person well before you vouch for his credit! Better refuse than suffer later — Tay

16. A gracious woman retaineth honour: and strong men retain riches.

A gracious woman obtaineth honor;
And violent men obtain riches — ASV

A gracious wife obtaineth honour,
But the diligent shall obtain wealth — Rhm

A lovely woman obtains honor;
Even as the violent obtain riches — ABPS

A gracious woman wins respect;
And diligent men win riches — AAT

A charming woman wins respect:
high-handed men win only wealth — Mof

Gracious ways may win a woman renown; man never grew rich but by hardiness — Knox

17. The merciful man doeth good to his own soul: but he that is cruel troubleth his own flesh.

18. The wicked worketh a deceitful work: but to him that soweth righteousness shall be a sure reward.

The man of lovingkindness dealeth well with his own soul,
But the cruel man troubleth his own flesh.
The lawless man earneth the wages of falsehood,
But he that soweth righteousness hath the reward of fidelity — Rhm

A kind man is rewarding his own soul,
And the fierce is troubling his own flesh.
The wicked is getting a lying wage,
And whoso is sowing righteousness — a true reward — YLT

A benevolent man is recompensed in his own soul;
But the outrageous troubleth his own flesh.
The wicked achieve a deceitful recompense;
But whoso soweth righteousness, a sure reward — Sprl

A kindly man benefits himself,
but a merciless man harms himself.
The wicked man makes empty profits,
but he who sows virtue has a sure reward — NAB

A kindly man does himself good, but a troublemaker hurts himself.
The wicked gets deceptive wages,
but he who sows righteousness gets a sure reward — Ber

The generous man is his own benefactor,
a cruel man injures his own flesh.
The livelihood won by the wicked is illusory,
he who sows virtue reaps a solid reward — Jerus

19. As righteousness tendeth to life: so he that pursueth evil pursueth it to his own death.

As righteousness tendeth to life,
So the pursuit of wickedness to death — Sprl

Stedfast righteousness tendeth to life;
But he that pursueth evil pursueth it to his own death — JPS

He that is stedfast in righteousness shall attain unto life;
And he that pursueth evil doeth it to his own death — ASV

He who is steadfast in righteousness will live,
but he who pursues evil will die — RSV

Surely righteousness brings life, but he who pursues evil brings about his own death — Ber

A man set on righteousness finds life,
but the pursuit of evil leads to death — NEB

It makes for life, to set one's heart on goodness: the fatal thing is to be bent on evil — Mof

20. They that are of a froward heart are abomination to the LORD: but such as are upright in their way are his delight.

They that are perverse in heart are an abomination to the LORD: but such as are perfect in their way are his delight — RV

Men of perverse mind are an abomination to the LORD,
but those of blameless ways are his delight — RSV

Evil-minded men are loathesome to the Eternal,
but a blameless life is his delight — Mof

The depraved in heart are an abomination to the LORD,
but those who walk blamelessly are his delight — NAB

Men of depraved heart are abhorrent to Yahweh,
dear to him, those whose ways are blameless — Jerus

The LORD detests the crooked heart,
but honesty is dear to him — NEB

A false heart the Lord cannot endure; nothing but honest dealing will content him — Knox

21. Though hand join in hand, the wicked shall not be unpunished: but the seed of the righteous shall be delivered.

My hand upon it! the evil man shall not be unpunished;
But the seed of the righteous shall escape — JPS

Although hand join to hand the wicked shall not be acquitted;

But the seed of the righteous shall escape — Sprl

Be assured, the evil man will not go unpunished, but the offspring of the righteous will escape — Ber

Certainly the evil-doer will not go free from punishment, but the seed of the upright man will be safe — Bas

Truly the evil man shall not go unpunished,
but those who are just shall escape — NAB

Depend upon it, the sinner shall never be held guiltless; the race of the just shall find acquittal — Knox

22. As a jewel of gold in a swine's snout, so is a fair woman which is without discretion.

A golden ring in the snout of a sow, and a pretty woman without sense! — Mof

As a jewel in the snout of a swine; so is beauty in a woman void of discretion — Sept

As a ring of gold in the snout of a swine
Is a woman of beauty who hath abandoned discretion — Rhm

A nose-ring of gold in a swine's snout,
Is a woman fair and without discretion — ABPS

As a ring of gold in a swine's snout,
So is a fair woman that turneth aside from discretion — JPS

Like a golden ring in a swine's snout is a beautiful woman with a rebellious disposition — NAB

A beautiful woman lacking discretion and modesty is like a fine gold ring in a pig's snout — Tay

23. The desire of the righteous is only good: but the expectation of the wicked is wrath.

The desire of the righteous is only for right;
But the desire of the wicked, wrath — Sprl

The desire of the righteous is only good,
The hope of the wicked is transgression — YLT

The desire of the righteous ends only in good;
the expectation of the wicked in wrath — RSV

The desire of the upright man is only for good, but wrath is waiting for the evil-doer — Bas

The desire of the righteous is altogether good; but the hope of the wicked shall perish — Sept

In the desires of the just only good dwells; the hopes of the wicked only lead to ruin — Knox

The desire of the virtuous ends in happiness,
the hope of the wicked is in vain — Jerus

24. There is that scattereth, and yet increaseth; and there is that withholdeth more than is meet, but it tendeth to poverty.

25. The liberal soul shall be made fat: and he that watereth shall be watered also himself.

One gives away, and still he grows the richer:
another keeps what he should give, and is the poorer.
A liberal soul will be enriched, and he who waters will himself be watered — Mof

It is possible to give away and become richer! It is also possible to hold on too tightly and lose everything. Yes, the liberal man shall be rich! By watering others, he waters himself — Tay

There is that scattereth, and yet increaseth;
And there is that withholdeth more than is meet, but it tendeth only to want.
The beneficent soul shall be made rich,
And he that satisfieth abundantly shall be satisfied also himself — JPS

One man gives freely, yet grows all the richer;
another withholds what he should give, and only suffers want.
A liberal man will be enriched,
and one who waters will himself be watered — RSV

One man is lavish yet grows still richer;
another is too sparing, yet is the poorer.
He who confers benefits will be amply enriched,
and he who refreshes others will himself be refreshed — NAB

One man spends, and grows still richer;
Another holds back his due share, only to bring himself to want.
The generous man will be enriched;
And he who waters will himself be watered — AAT

26. He that withholdeth corn, the people shall curse him: but blessing shall be upon the head of him that selleth it.

He that withholdeth grain, the people shall curse him;
But blessing shall be upon the head of him that selleth it — ASV

Whoso is withholding corn, the people execrate him,
And a blessing is for the head of him who is selling — YLT

The people will curse the man who holds back the grain, but a blessing will be on the head of the one selling it — Ber

Him who monopolizes grain, the people curse —
but blessings upon the head of him who distributes it! — NAB

Corn hoarded shall win thee a curse, corn sold freely a blessing, from the lips of the whole people — Knox

27. He that diligently seeketh good procureth favour: but he that seeketh mischief, it shall come unto him.

He that diligently seeketh good aimeth at favour,
But he that studieth mischief it shall come on himself — Rhm

He that diligently seeketh good seeketh favour: but he that searcheth after mischief, it shall come unto him — RV

He who eagerly seeks what is good finds much favour,
but if a man pursues evil it turns upon him — NEB

He who seeks what is good will win favor;
But he who aims at what is harmful will bring it upon himself — AAT

He who strives after good is striving after favour,
he who looks for evil will have evil come to him — Jerus

He who diligently seeks good seeks favor,
but evil comes to him who searches for it — RSV

28. He that trusteth in his riches shall fall: but the righteous shall flourish as a branch.

Whoso is confident in his wealth he falleth,
And as a leaf, the righteous flourish — YLT

He that trusteth in his riches shall fall;
But the righteous shall flourish as the green leaf — ASV

He that trusteth in his riches shall fall;
But the righteous shall flourish as foliage — JPS

Fall he must, that relies on riches; never shall the just fade or fail — Knox

He who relies on his wealth shall wither,
but a good man blooms like a green leaf — Mof

He who puts his faith in wealth will come to nothing; but the upright man will be full of growth like the green leaf — Bas

29. He that troubleth his own house shall inherit the wind: and the fool shall be servant to the wise of heart.

He shall feed on air, that misrules his own household; the fool will be slave and the wise man master in the end — Knox

He who stints his household will reap nothing but wind;
A wise man's slave will such a fool become — AAT

He who misgoverns his house inherits the wind,
and the fool becomes slave to the wise — Jerus

He who upsets his household has empty air for a heritage;
and the fool will become slave to the wise man — NAB

The fool who provokes his family to anger and resentment will finally have nothing worthwhile left. He shall be the servant of a wiser man — Tay

30. The fruit of the righteous is a tree of life; and he that winneth souls is wise.

The fruit of the righteous is a tree of life,
And he that rescueth souls is wise — Rhm

The fruit of the righteous is a tree of life;

And he that is wise winneth souls — ASV

The fruit of the righteous is a tree of life, and a wise man wins friends — Ber

Where right living bears its fruit, a tree of life grows up; the wise man's reward is living souls — Knox

31. **Behold, the righteous shall be recompensed in the earth: much more the wicked and the sinner.**

Behold, the righteous shall be requited in the earth;
How much more the wicked and the sinner! — JPS

If the upright man is rewarded on earth, how much more the evil-doer and the sinner — Bas

If here on earth the virtuous man gets his due,
how much more the wicked, how much more the sinner — Jerus

If the righteous in the land get their deserts,
how much more the wicked man and the sinner — NEB

If the most righteous in the land are punished,
How much more the wicked and the sinner — AAT

Even the godly shall be rewarded here on earth; how much more the wicked — Tay

CHAPTER 12

1. **Whoso loveth instruction loveth knowledge: but he that hateth reproof is brutish.**

Whoso loveth correction loveth knowledge;
But he that hateth reproof is brutish — ASV

He who loves discipline loves knowledge; but he who hates reproof is a fool — Lam

Whoever loves discipline loves knowledge, but he who hates reproof is like a cow — Ber

A lover of training is a lover of knowledge; but a hater of teaching is like a beast — Bas

He who cares to know cares to be set right,
but he who hates to be admonished is a stupid creature — Mof

He who loves instruction loves knowledge;
But he who hates admonition is stupid — AAT

2. **A good man obtaineth favour of the LORD: but a man of wicked devices will he condemn.**

3. **A man shall not be established by wickedness: but the root of the righteous shall not be moved.**

The good will obtain favor from Jehovah;
But the man of evil devices he will hold guilty.
A man shall not be established by wickedness;
But the root of the righteous shall not be moved — ABPS

A good man has grace in the eyes of the Lord; but the man of evil designs gets punishment from him.
No man will make himself safe through evil-doing; but the root of upright men will never be moved — Bas

A kindly man wins the Lord's favour, a schemer is his enemy.
Wickedness shall never thrive; the just have roots immovable — Knox

A good man earns favour from the LORD;
the schemer is condemned.
No man can establish himself by wickedness,
but good men have roots that cannot be dislodged — NEB

The good man wins the favour of Yahweh,
but he condemns the man who is a schemer.
No man is made secure by wickedness,
but nothing shakes the roots of virtuous men — Jerus

A good-natured man has the goodwill of the Eternal,
but He passes sentence on malicious men.
No man can hold his own by doing wrong,
but never shall the good man be uprooted — Mof

4. A virtuous woman is a crown to her husband: but she that maketh ashamed is as rottenness in his bones.

A worthy woman is the crown of her husband;
But she that maketh ashamed is as rottenness in his bones — ASV

A virtuous woman is a crown to her husband;
But she that doeth shamefully is as rottenness in his bones — JPS

A wife with strength of character is a crown to her husband, but she who acts disgracefully is rottenness in his bones — Ber

A good wife is the crown of her husband,
but she who brings shame is like rottenness in his bones — RSV

A worthy wife is the crown of her husband,
but a disgraceful one is like rot in his bones — NAB

5. The thoughts of the righteous are right: but the counsels of the wicked are deceit.

6. The words of the wicked are to lie in wait for blood: but the mouth of the upright shall deliver them.

The thoughts of the righteous are justice,
The counsels of the wicked—deceit.
The words of the wicked are: 'Lay wait for blood,'
And the mouth of the upright delivereth them — YLT

The thoughts of the righteous are just: but the counsels of the wicked are deceit.
The words of the wicked are of lying in wait for blood: but the mouth of the upright shall deliver them — RV

The thoughts of the righteous are upright; but the counsels of the wicked are deceit.
The counsel of the wicked is to lie in wait for the shedding of blood; but the mouth of the upright shall deliver them — Lam

The purposes of upright men are right, but the designs of evil-doers are deceit.
The words of sinners are destruction for the upright; but the mouth of upright men is their salvation — Bas

The thoughts of the righteous are reliable, but the suggestions of the wicked are deceptive.
The words of the wicked lie in wait for blood, but the mouth of the upright delivers them — Ber

The aims of a good man are honourable:
the plans of a bad man are underhand.
Knaves speak of secret bloodshed, but men are helped by plans of honest men — Mof

The plans of the just are legitimate; the designs of the wicked are deceitful.
The words of the wicked are a deadly ambush,
but the speech of the upright saves them — NAB

7. The wicked are overthrown, and are not: but the house of the righteous shall stand.

The wicked are overthrown, and they are no more;
But the house of the righteous shall stand — ABPS

The wicked subvert themselves, and are no more;
But the house of the righteous shall stand — Sprl

When the wicked is overthrown, he vanisheth: but the houses of the righteous shall remain — Sept

Once thrown down, the wicked are no more,
but the house of virtuous men stands firm — Jerus

Once the wicked are down, that is the end of them,
but the good man's line continues — NEB

A turn in their fortunes, and no more is heard of the wicked; only the just have abiding prosperity — Knox

8. A man shall be commended according to his wisdom: but he that is of a perverse heart shall be despised.

A man shall be commended according to his intelligence;
But he that is of distorted understanding shall be despised — JPS

In proportion to his prudence is a man to be praised,

But the perverse in heart shall be an object of contempt — Rhm

The praise of a man is in proportion to his prudence,
men of depraved heart are held in contempt — Jerus

A man is commended according to his good sense,
but one of perverse mind is despised — RSV

A man will be praised in the measure of his wisdom, but a wrong-minded man will be looked down on — Bas

According to his good sense a man is praised,
but one with a warped mind is despised — NAB

9. He that is despised, and hath a servant, is better than he that honoureth himself, and lacketh bread.

Better is he that is lightly esteemed, and hath a servant,
Than he that honoreth himself, and lacketh bread — ASV

Better is the lightly esteemed who hath a servant,
Than the self-honoured who lacketh bread — YLT

Better is he of no account who has a servant of his own,
Than he who boasteth and lacketh bread — Sprl

Better a man of low rank, with a servant,
than one who makes a show and has to do his own work — Mof

Better is the man, who unhonoured serveth himself: than he who honoureth himself and wanteth bread — Sept

Better a man of low rank, who works for himself,
Than he who assumes honor, yet has nothing to eat — AAT

It is better to be modest and earn one's living
than to be conceited and go hungry — NEB

10. A righteous man regardeth the life of his beast: but the tender mercies of the wicked are cruel.

A righteous man regardeth the desire of his beast,
But the compassions of the lawless are cruel — Rhm

A righteous man understands the needs of his livestock, but even the mercy of the wicked is cruel — Ber

An upright man has thought for the life of his beast, but the hearts of evil-doers are cruel — Bas

The righteous cares for the life of his beast;
But the bowels of the wicked are cruel — ABPS

A just man cares for the safety of the beasts he owns; the wicked are heartless through and through — Knox

11. He that tilleth his land shall be satisfied with bread: but he that followeth vain persons is void of understanding.

He who tills his ground will have his fill of bread, but he who follows vain pursuits is lacking in sense — Ber

He that tilleth his ground shall have plenty of bread;
But he that followeth after vain things is void of understanding — JPS

He who tills his own land has food in plenty,
but he who follows idle pursuits is a fool — NAB

He who tills his land will have plenty of bread,
but he who follows worthless pursuits has no sense — RSV

He who tills his land shall have bread and to spare,
he who chases fantasies has no sense — Jerus

The man who works his farm has plenty of food:
a man of useless interests has no sense — Mof

12. The wicked desireth the net of evil men: but the root of the righteous yieldeth fruit.

The wicked delights in the net of the evil;
But the root of the righteous will bring forth — ABPS

The wicked coveteth the prey of the evil doers;
But the root of the righteous yieldeth fruit — Sprl

The wicked man desires the booty of evil men, but the root of the righteous bears fruit — Ber

The wicked desire to do evil; but the

root of the righteous shall sprout — Lam

13. The wicked is snared by the transgression of his lips: but the just shall come out of trouble.

The ungodly is caught by the wickedness of his lips; but the righteous shall come out of trouble — Lam

An evil man is ensnared by the transgression of his lips,
but the righteous escapes from trouble — RSV

By the sin of his lips is the guilty man ensnared;
While the innocent escapes from trouble — AAT

In the transgression of the lips is a snare to the evil man;
But the righteous shall come out of trouble — ASV

In the sin of his lips the evil man is ensnared,
but the just comes free of trouble — NAB

By sins of the lips bad men get into trouble:
good men get out of trouble — Mof

In the sin of the lips is a net which takes the sinner, but the upright man will come out of trouble — Bas

14. A man shall be satisfied with good by the fruit of his mouth: and the recompence of a man's hands shall be rendered unto him.

A man shall be satisfied with good by the fruit of his mouth; and the doings of a man's hands shall be rendered unto him — RV

Of the fruit of a man's mouth shall he be satisfied with good,
And the dealing of the hands of a son of earth shall be paid back to him — Rhm

Of the fruit of the mouth shall a man be satisfied with good;
And the desert of one's hands shall return to him — ABPS

From the fruit of his words a man is well satisfied, and the work of a man's hands will come back to him — Ber

A man reaps the result of all his words, and he must answer for his deeds — Mof

Telling the truth gives a man great satisfaction, and hard work returns many blessings to him — Tay

15. The way of a fool is right in his own eyes: but he that hearkeneth unto counsel is wise.

A fool is ever right in his own thinking; the wise listen to advice — Knox

The way of a fool is right in his own eyes;
But he that is wise hearkeneth unto counsel — ASV

The way of a fool is straight in his own eyes;
But he that is wise hearkeneth unto counsel — JPS

In the eyes of a fool the way he goes is right,
the wise man listens to advice — Jerus

A fool thinks that he is always right;
wise is the man who listens to advice — NEB

The way of the fool seems right in his own eyes,
but he who listens to advice is wise — NAB

16. A fool's wrath is presently known: but a prudent man covereth shame.

A fool's vexation is presently known:
but a prudent man concealeth shame — RV

The vexation of a fool is known at once,
but the prudent man ignores an insult — RSV

A fool's anger is shown at once;
But a sensible man ignores an affront — AAT

A fool shows his ill humour at once;
a clever man slighted conceals his feelings — NEB

The fool's anger is known the same day;
But a shrewd man conceals an affront — ABPS

The fool immediately shows his anger,
but the shrewd man passes over an insult — NAB

A fool shows instantly that he is angry:
a prudent man ignores an insult — Mof

17. He that speaketh truth sheweth forth righteousness: but a false witness deceit.

18. There is that speaketh like the pierc-

ings of a sword: but the tongue of the wise is health.

He that whispereth faithfulness declareth righteousness,
But a false witness is a fraud.
There is who babbleth as with thrusts of a sword,
But the tongue of the wise hath healing — Rhm

He who breathes truth shows the right,
But a false witness fraud.
There is that prates as with thrusts of the sword;
But the tongue of the wise is a healing — ABPS

He who speaks the truth gives honest evidence,
but a false witness utters deceit.
There is one whose rash words are like sword thrusts,
but the tongue of the wise brings healing — RSV

He who speaks truth gives correct evidence, but a false witness practices deception.
Some speak rashly like the piercing of a sword, but the tongue of the wise heals — Ber

A righteous man speaks truth as it is evident; but a false witness is deceptive.
There are those whose speech is like the piercing of a sword; but the tongue of the wise heals — Lam

He who utters the truth affirms that which will stand;
But a lying witness that which will bring disappointment.
There are those whose prating is like the thrusts of a sword;
But the tongue of the wise brings healing — AAT

19. **The lip of truth shall be established for ever: but a lying tongue is but for a moment.**

20. **Deceit is in the heart of them that imagine evil: but to the counsellors of peace is joy.**

The truthful lip is established forever,
And the lying tongue but for a moment.
Deceit is in the heart of them that devise evil;
But to them that counsel peace there is joy — ABPS

The truthful lip will endure forever;
But the lying tongue is only for a moment.
Disappointment comes to those who plot evil;
But happiness to those who plan good — AAT

A lip that is faithful shall be firm to futurity,
But only for a twinkling is the tongue that is false.
Deceit is in the heart of contrivers of mischief,
But to the counsellors of peace shall be joy — Rhm

True lips are certain for ever, but a false tongue is only for a minute.
Deceit is in the heart of those whose designs are evil, but for those purposing peace there is joy — Bas

Truth told endures:
a lie lasts only for a little while.
Fraud is the aim of evil-minded men,
but those who plan the good of others prosper — Mof

Truthful lips endure forever,
the lying tongue, for only a moment.
Deceit is in the hands of those who plot evil,
but those who counsel peace have joy — NAB

21. **There shall no evil happen to the just: but the wicked shall be filled with mischief.**

There shall no mischief happen to the righteous;
But the wicked shall be filled with evil — ASV

No ill befalls the righteous,
but the wicked are filled with trouble — RSV

No evil shall happen to the righteous;
But the wicked are full of calamity — Sprl

There shall no harm befall the just;
But the wicked are filled with evil — ABPS

No harm befalls the righteous, but the wicked are filled up with trouble — Ber

No mischief will befall the righteous,
but wicked men get their fill of adversity — NEB

No real harm befalls the good, but there is constant trouble for the wicked — Tay

22. **Lying lips are abomination to the**

LORD: but they that deal truly are his delight.
An abomination to Yahweh are lips that are false,
But he that dealeth faithfully is his delight — Rhm
Lips that lie are abhorrent to Yahweh; dear to him are those who speak the truth — Jerus
Lying lips are an abomination to the LORD,
but those who act faithfully are his delight — RSV
Liars are loathsome to the Eternal, but the sincere are a delight to him — Mof
False lips are hated by the Lord, but those whose acts are true are his delight — Bas
The LORD detests a liar
but delights in the honest man — NEB

23. A prudent man concealeth knowledge: but the heart of fools proclaimeth foolishness.
A prudent man concealeth his learning;
But the heart of fools proclaimeth its folly — Sprl
A shrewd man covers knowledge;
But the heart of fools proclaims folly — ABPS
A man of insight conceals his knowledge, but the heart of fools proclaims foolishness — Ber
A man of sense conceals what he knows;
But fools proclaim their folly — AAT
A clever man conceals his knowledge, but a stupid man broadcasts his folly — NEB
A wise man doesn't display his knowledge, but a fool displays his foolishness — Tay

24. The hand of the diligent shall bear rule: but the slothful shall be under tribute.
The hand of the diligent shall bear rule;
But the slothful shall be put under taskwork — ASV
The hand of the diligent shall govern;
But the slothful shall be appointed to servile work — Sprl
The hand of the diligent will rule, while the slothful will be put to forced labor — RSV
The diligent will get the upper hand, but slothful men will end as serfs — Mof
The diligent hand will govern,
but the slothful will be enslaved — NAB

25. Heaviness in the heart of man maketh it stoop: but a good word maketh it glad.
Care in the heart of a man boweth it down;
But a good word maketh it glad — JPS
Sorrow in the heart of a man boweth down,
And a good word maketh him glad — YLT
Anxiety in a man's heart weighs it down, but a kind word makes it glad — Ber
Anxiety in a man's heart makes it sink;
But a kindly word will turn it into gladness — AAT
Worry makes a man's heart heavy,
a kindly word makes it glad — Jerus
A heart bowed down with anxiety,
how a kind word can refresh it! — Knox

26. The righteous is more excellent than his neighbour: but the way of the wicked seduceth them.[4]
The righteous excels his neighbour;
But the effort of the wicked is to lead him astray — Sprl
The just man surpasses his neighbor,
but the way of the wicked leads them astray — NAB
The righteous is a guide to his neighbor;
But the way of the wicked causeth them to err — ASV
The righteous will guide his fellow;
But the way of the wicked leads them astray — ABPS
The upright man is a guide to his neighbour, but the way of evil-doers is a cause of error to them — Bas
The good man gives a lead to his neighbour,

[4]Only Sprl and NAB agree with KJV in the first half. Others resemble ASV and RV, or adopt an altogether different reading.

a bad man's life will lead himself astray — Mof

27. The slothful man roasteth not that which he took in hunting: but the substance of a diligent man is precious.

Indolence roasteth not his own game,
But the substance of a man is precious when he is diligent — Rhm

The slothful man roasteth not that which he took in hunting: but the precious substance of men is to be diligent — RV

A slothful man will not catch his prey,
but the diligent man will get precious wealth — RSV

The slothful catcheth not his prey;
But to the diligent man belongeth precious substance — Sprl

The slothful man shall not hunt his prey;
But the precious substance of men is to be diligent — JPS

The lazy hunter puts up no game,
but the industrious man reaps a rich harvest — NEB

28. In the way of righteousness is life; and in the pathway thereof there is no death.[5]

In the path of righteousness is life,
And in the way of that path is no death — YLT

In the way of righteousness is life,
And in the path thereof immortality — Rhm

In the path of righteousness is life,
Even a beaten way, where is no death — ABPS

In the pathway of righteousness is life;
And in her well-worn track no death — Sprl

Life is in the way of the righteous, a pathway where there is no death — Ber

CHAPTER 13

1. A wise son heareth his father's instruction: but a scorner heareth not rebuke.

A wise son is instructed of his father;
But a scorner heareth not rebuke — JPS

A wise son is one chastened of the father;
But a scoffer hears not rebuke — ABPS

A wise son pays heed to his father's instruction;
But a scoffer listens to no rebuke — AAT

A wise son loves discipline,
a mocker will not listen to reproof — Jerus

A wise man sees the reason for his father's correction;
an arrogant man will not listen to rebuke — NEB

A wise youth accepts his father's rebuke; a young mocker doesn't — Tay

2. A man shall eat good by the fruit of his mouth: but the soul of the transgressors shall eat violence.

3. He that keepeth his mouth keepeth his life: but he that openeth wide his lips shall have destruction.

A man shall eat good by the fruit of his mouth;
But the soul of the treacherous shall eat violence.
He that guardeth his mouth keepeth his life;
But he that openeth wide his lips shall have destruction — ASV

A man from the fruit of his mouth shall eat pleasant things;
But the soul of the transgressors shall be filled with violence.
He that guardeth his mouth preserveth his life;
But whoso openeth wide his lips, destruction unto him — Sprl

From the fruit of his mouth a man will eat bountifully, but the desire of the treacherous is for violence.
He who guards his mouth controls himself, but he who opens wide his lips comes to ruin — Ber

A man will get good from the fruit of his lips, but the desire of the false is for violent acts.
He who keeps a watch on his mouth

[5]Most others have an antithetic second member, e.g.; RSV: "but the way of error leads to death."

keeps his life; but he whose lips are open wide will have destruction — Bas

Fair words yield a crop to content a man's heart; but not for the treacherous; they have no stomach but for wrong-doing. Guard thy tongue, guard thy soul; thoughtless speech may bring ruin — Knox

When a man has good things to eat, it is the fruit of his own words,
but the appetite of the treacherous feeds on violence.
He keeps his life who guards his mouth,
he who talks too much is lost — Jerus

The good man wins his case by careful argument; the evil-minded only wants to fight.
Self-control means controlling the tongue! A quick retort can ruin everything — Tay

4. The soul of the sluggard desireth, and hath nothing: but the soul of the diligent shall be made fat.

The soul of the slothful is desiring, and hath not,
And the soul of the diligent is made fat — YLT

The soul of the sluggard desireth, and hath nothing;
But the soul of the diligent shall be abundantly gratified — JPS

The soul of the lazy one craves and gets nothing, but the soul of the diligent is well supplied — Ber

The lazy man has longings, but gets nothing:
the diligent man is amply supplied — Mof

A lazy man is torn by appetite unsatisfied,
but the diligent grow fat and prosperous — NEB

The sluggard craves, but gets nothing;
The desire of the diligent is richly supplied — AAT

5. A righteous man hateth lying: but a wicked man is loathsome, and cometh to shame.

A word of falsehood the righteous man hateth,
But the lawless causeth shame and disgrace — Rhm

The righteous hate the lying word;
For the liar is odious and causeth shame — Sprl

Lying speech the righteous hates;
But base and shameful is the conduct of the wicked — ABPS

A righteous man hateth lying;
But a wicked man behaveth vilely and shamefully — JPS

A righteous man hates falsehood,
but a wicked man acts shamefully and disgracefully — RSV

Anything deceitful the just man hates,
but the wicked brings shame and disgrace — NAB

The virtuous man hates lying words,
but the wicked man slanders and defames — Jerus

6. Righteousness keepeth him that is upright in the way: but wickedness overthroweth the sinner.

Righteousness will keep the blameless way;
But wickedness will pervert to sin — ABPS

Righteousness guards him whose way is upright,
but sin overthrows the wicked — RSV

Righteousness guards him who is blameless in the way, but wickedness overthrows the sinner — Ber

Righteousness keeps safe him whose way is without error, but evil-doers are overturned by sin — Bas

To do right is the protection of an honest man,
but wickedness brings sinners to grief — NEB

The upright heart is protected by its own innocence; guilt trips the heel of the wrong-doer — Knox

7. There is that maketh himself rich, yet hath nothing: there is that maketh himself poor, yet hath great riches.

There is that pretendeth himself rich, yet hath nothing;
There is that pretendeth himself poor, yet hath great wealth — JPS

There are some who pretend to be rich, yet have nothing; there are others who pretend to be poor, yet have great riches — Lam

There is one who considers himself rich, yet has nothing; and one who considers himself poor, yet possesses great wealth — Ber

One man pretends to be rich, yet has nothing;
Another man pretends to be poor, yet has great wealth — AAT

8. The ransom of a man's life are his riches: but the poor heareth not rebuke.

A man will give his wealth in exchange for his life; but the poor will not give ear to sharp words — Bas

The ransom of a man's life is his wealth; but a poor man is not subject to threats — Sept

The ransom of a man's life is his riches;
But the poor heareth no threatening — ASV

A man's wealth may ransom his life, but the poor man sees no threat — Jerus

A rich man must buy himself off, but a poor man is immune from threats — NEB

9. The light of the righteous rejoiceth: but the lamp of the wicked shall be put out.

The light of the righteous shall be joyous;
But the lamp of the wicked shall go out — ABPS

The light of the righteous shall shine with splendour;
But the lamp of the wicked shall burn out — Sprl

The light of the righteous will burn brightly;
But the lamp of the wicked will be put out — AAT

The light of the just shines gaily, but the lamp of the wicked goes out — NAB

The light of good men shines out bright:
the lamp of bad men will go out — Mof

10. Only by pride cometh contention: but with the well advised is wisdom.

By pride cometh only contention;
But with the well-advised is wisdom — ASV

By insolence the heedless make strife, but with those who take advice is wisdom — RSV

A vain man through pride causeth debate,
And with the counselled is wisdom — YLT

The only effect of pride is fighting; but wisdom is with the quiet in spirit — Bas

A brainless fool causes strife by his presumption;
wisdom is found among friends in council — NEB

Ever there is wrangling among the proud; wisdom's part is to be guided by other men's counsel — Knox

Pride leads to arguments; be humble, take advice and become wise — Tay

11. Wealth gotten by vanity shall be diminished: but he that gathereth by labour shall increase.

Wealth dishonestly obtained shall waste away;
But that acquired by diligence shall multiply — Sprl

Wealth got by scheming will diminish;
But he who gathers little by little will increase his store — AAT

Wealth won in haste will dwindle,
but, gathered gradually it will grow — Mof

Riches soon won are soon spent; the patient hoard breeds best — Knox

A sudden fortune will dwindle away,
he grows rich who accumulates little by little — Jerus

Wealth from gambling quickly disappears; wealth from hard work grows — Tay

12. Hope deferred maketh the heart sick: but when the desire cometh, it is a tree of life.

Hope deferred sickeneth the heart, —
But a tree of life is desire fulfilled — Rhm

Hope protracted maketh the heart languish;
But the desire accomplished is a tree of life — Sprl

Hope put off is a weariness to the heart; but when what is desired comes, it is a tree of life — Bas

Hope drawn out makes the heart sick, but a longing come true is a tree of life — Ber

Hope deferred is sickening:
it is new life to have desire fulfilled — Mof

Hope deferred, how it crushes a man's spirits! The granted wish, a tree of life-giving fruit — Knox

13. Whoso despiseth the word shall be de-

stroyed: but he that feareth the commandment shall be rewarded.

Whoso despiseth the word shall suffer thereby;
But he that feareth the commandment shall be rewarded — JPS

Whoso despiseth the word bringeth destruction on himself;
But he that feareth the commandment shall be rewarded — ASV

He who despises the word will pay for it;
But he who reveres the command will be rewarded — AAT

He that despises the word shall be held accountable to it;
But whoso fears the command, he shall be rewarded — ABPS

He who makes sport of the word will come to destruction, but the respecter of the law will be rewarded — Bas

To despise a word of advice is to ask for trouble;
mind what you are told, and you will be rewarded — NEB

Despise God's word and find yourself in trouble. Obey it and succeed — Tay

14. The law of the wise is a fountain of life, to depart from the snares of death.

The instruction of the wise is a wellspring of life,
By departing from the snares of death — Rhm

The law of the wise is a fountain of life,
That one may depart from the snares of death — ASV

The teaching of the wise is a fountain of life,
that one may avoid the snares of death — RSV

The wise man's teaching is a life-giving fountain,
for eluding the snares of death — Jerus

A sage's teaching is a fount of life,
it shows how to evade the nets of Death — Mof

Unto the wise man the law is a fountain of life,
By turning him from the snares of death — Sprl

15. Good understanding giveth favour: but the way of transgressors is hard.

Good understanding giveth grace,
And the way of the treacherous is hard — YLT

Good understanding giveth favour: but the way of the treacherous is rugged — RV

Kindly wisdom procureth favour;
But the conduct of the ungodly, violence — Sprl

Good understanding giveth grace;
But the way of the faithless is harsh — JPS

Good sense wins favor,
but the way of the faithless is their ruin — RSV

Good intelligence wins favour,
but treachery leads to disaster — NEB

16. Every prudent man dealeth with knowledge: but a fool layeth open his folly.

Every prudent man worketh with knowledge;
But a fool flaunteth his folly — ASV

Every prudent man dealeth with forethought;
But a fool unfoldeth folly — JPS

Every shrewd man acts with knowledge;
But a fool displays folly — ABPS

Every prudent man deals wisely; but a fool speaks foolishness — Lam

Every man of discretion acts by the light of knowledge,
the fool parades his folly — Jerus

The shrewd man does everything with prudence,
but the fool peddles folly — NAB

17. A wicked messenger falleth into mischief: but a faithful ambassador is health.

A lawless messenger falleth into mischief,
But a faithful herald bringeth healing — Rhm

A bad messenger plunges men into trouble,
but a faithful envoy brings healing — RSV

An unreliable messenger precipitates trouble, but a faithful envoy brings healing — Ber

A wicked messenger brings on disaster,
but a trustworthy envoy is a healing remedy — NAB

A careless messenger is a calamity:

with a reliable envoy, all is well — Mof

A faithless messenger falls into trouble;
But a trustworthy envoy insures success — AAT

18. Poverty and shame shall be to him that refuseth instruction: but he that regardeth reproof shall be honoured.

Poverty and shame shall be to him who rejecteth correction;
But whoso regardeth reproof, shall be honoured — Sprl

Poverty and disgrace come to him who ignores instruction,
but he who heeds reproof is honored — RSV

Need and shame will be the fate of him who is uncontrolled by training; but he who takes note of teaching will be honoured — Bas

For the man who rejects discipline: poverty and disgrace;
for the man who accepts correction: honour — Jerus

If you refuse criticism you will end in poverty and disgrace; if you accept criticism you are on the road to fame — Tay

19. The desire accomplished is sweet to the soul: but it is abomination to fools to depart from evil.

Desire attained is sweet to the soul;
And it is the abomination of fools to depart from evil — ABPS

A desire fulfilled is sweet to the soul,
But it is an abomination to the lawless to depart from evil — Rhm

Longing fulfilled is sweet to the soul, thus it is an abomination to fools to give up evil — Ber

Satisfied desire is sweet to a person; therefore it is hateful and exceedingly offensive to . . . fools to give up evil . . . — Amp

Desire fulfilled is sweet;
But fools hate to turn from evil — AAT

Each man loves his own way best, and to a fool, there is no shame like sin's avoiding — Knox

20. He that walketh with wise men shall be wise: but a companion of fools shall be destroyed.

Walk with wise men, and thou shalt be wise;
But the companion of fools shall smart for it — ASV

By walking with the wise thou wilt be wise; but he who walketh with fools will be known — Sept

Walk with the wise, and become wise;
But a companion of fools shall come to harm — ABPS

Whoso walketh with wise men shall be wise;
But the companion of fools shall become corrupted — Sprl

Walk with wise men and you will become wise,
but the companion of fools will fare badly — NAB

Make the wise your companions and you grow wise yourself;
make fools your friends and suffer for it — Jerus

21. Evil pursueth sinners: but to the righteous good shall be repayed.

Evil pursueth sinners: but the righteous shall be recompensed with good — RV

Ill fortune will dog sinners;
But good fortune will overtake the righteous — AAT

Misfortune pursues sinners,
but prosperity rewards the righteous — RSV

Misfortune follows up the sinful,
but prosperity will overtake the pious — Mof

Evil will overtake sinners, but the upright will be rewarded with good — Bas

22. A good man leaveth an inheritance to his children's children: and the wealth of the sinner is laid up for the just.

The good will leave a heritage to children's children;
But the sinner's wealth is laid up for the righteous — ABPS

A good man shall leave an inheritance to his children; but the wealth of the wicked is treasured up for the righteous — Sept

A good man causeth sons' sons to inherit,
And laid up for the righteous is the sinner's wealth — YLT

A good man leaves an inheritance to his descendants,
but the sinner's hoard passes to the righteous — NEB

Son and grandson shall be the good man's heirs; the sinner lays up wealth for nobler men — Knox

23. Much food is in the tillage of the poor: but there is that is destroyed for want of judgment.

Much food is in the tillage of the poor;
But there is that is destroyed by reason of injustice — ASV

Much food is in the tillage of the poor;
But there is that is swept away by want of righteousness — JPS

Much food is in the fallowground of the poor,
But there is that is swept away for want of justice — Rhm

There is much food in the ploughed land of the poor; but it is taken away by wrong-doing — Bas

A poor man's farm may have good soil, but injustice robs him of its riches — Tay

24. He that spareth his rod hateth his son: but he that loveth him chasteneth him betimes.

He that withholdeth his rod hateth his son, —
But he that loveth him carefully correcteth him — Rhm

Whoso restraineth his rod hateth his son;
But he who loveth him, correcteth him in time — Sprl

He who spares the rod hates his son,
but he who loves him is diligent to discipline him — RSV

He who spares his rod hates his son,
but he who loves him takes care to chastise him — NAB

The man who fails to use the stick hates his son;
the man who is free with his correction loves him — Jerus

25. The righteous eateth to the satisfying of his soul: but the belly of the wicked shall want.

A righteous man eateth and satisfieth his soul; but the souls of the wicked are insatiate — Sept

The righteous eateth to satisfy his appetite,
But the belly of the lawless shall want — Rhm

The righteous eats to satisfy his need,
but the wicked's stomach never has enough — Ber

A righteous man eats his fill,
but the wicked go hungry — NEB

The righteous has enough to satisfy his appetite,
but the belly of the wicked suffers want — RSV

The righteous man eats to his heart's content;
But the appetite of the wicked is never satisfied — AAT

The just man eats his fill; the godless craves and never has enough — Knox

CHAPTER 14

1. Every wise woman buildeth her house: but the foolish plucketh it down with her hands.

Every wise woman hath builded her house,
And the foolish with her hands breaketh it down — YLT

Every wise woman buildeth up her house,
But a foolish one with her own hands would break it down — Rhm

Wise women have built houses; but the foolish hath pulled them down with her hands — Sept

The wisest women build up their homes;
the foolish pull them down with their own hands — NEB

Wisdom builds the house of life:
frivolity pulls it down — Mof

Wisdom builds her house,
but folly with her own hands tears it down — RSV

Wisdom builds herself a house;
with her own hands Folly pulls it down — Jerus

2. He that walketh in his uprightness feareth the LORD: but he that is perverse in his ways despiseth him.

He who walks in uprightness fears the LORD,
but he who is devious in his ways despises him — RSV

He whose course is honest fears Yahweh,

he whose paths are crooked scorns him — Jerus
An honest life shows reverence for the Eternal:
a wayward life despises him — Mof
A straightforward man fears the LORD;
the double-dealer scorns him — NEB
To do right honors God; to sin is to despise him — Tay

3. In the mouth of the foolish is a rod of pride: but the lips of the wise shall preserve them.
In the mouth of the foolish is a rod for his pride;
But the lips of the wise shall preserve them — ASV
In the fool's own mouth is a rod to shame his pride, but the wise men's lips shall preserve them — Amp
In the mouth of the foolish is a rod for his back;
But the lips of the wise will preserve them — AAT
In the mouth of the foolish man is a rod for his back, but the lips of the wise will keep them safe — Bas
Pride burgeons from the lips of fools; in modesty of speech the wise find safety — Knox
The speech of a fool is a rod for his back;
a wise man's words are his safeguard — NEB

4. Where no oxen are, the crib is clean: but much increase is by the strength of the ox.
Without cattle the crib is clean,
But much increase is in the strength of the ox — Rhm
Where there are no oxen, there is no grain;
But abundance of produce comes through the strength of the ox — AAT
Where there are no oxen, the cribs are clean; but abundant crops come by the strength of the ox — Lam
No oxen, no corn: good crops come from work done by the ox — Mof
No oxen, no cattle-feed;
stout ox, rich crop — Jerus

5. A faithful witness will not lie: but a false witness will utter lies.

6. A scorner seeketh wisdom, and findeth it not: but knowledge is easy unto him that understandeth.
A scoffer seeketh wisdom, and findeth it not;
But knowledge is easy unto him that hath understanding — ASV
The scorner searcheth for wisdom where it is not;
But knowledge is easy to the man of understanding — Sprl
The scoffer sought wisdom, but it came not;
But knowledge to the discerning is easy — ABPS
A scoffer seeks wisdom in vain,
but knowledge is easy for a man of understanding — RSV
A scorner hath sought wisdom, and it is not,
And knowledge to the intelligent is easy — YLT
The hater of authority, searching for wisdom, does not get it; but knowledge comes readily to the open-minded man — Bas

7. Go from the presence of a foolish man, when thou perceiveth not in him the lips of knowledge.
Leave the presence of a man who is a fool, for you will not discern words of knowledge there — Ber
Keep well clear of the fool,
you will not find wise lips there — Jerus
Leave the presence of a fool;
You will gain no knowledge from his talk — AAT
Avoid a stupid man,
you will hear not a word of sense from him — NEB
Go thy way, and let the fool go his; good sense is a strange language to him — Knox

8. The wisdom of the prudent is to understand his way: but the folly of fools is deceit.
The wisdom of the prudent will give them a knowledge of their ways; but the folly of fools is in error — Sept
The wisdom of the prudent is to look well to his way;
But the folly of fools is deceit — JPS
The wisdom of the man of insight is in his anticipating his way, but the folly of fools is deceiving — Ber
The wisdom of the prudent is to understand his goings;

But the folly of fools, injurious deception — Sprl
The wisdom of a man of sense enables him to understand his way;
But the folly of fools misleads them — AAT
The shrewd man's wisdom gives him knowledge of his way,
but the folly of fools is their deception — NAB
Shrewd men are wise in grasping their affairs,
but the folly of a fool leads him astray — Mof

9. Fools make a mock at sin: but among the righteous there is favour.[6]
The foolish scoff at guilt,
But between the upright is good pleasure — Rhm
The foolish make a mock of guilt: but among the upright there is good will — RV
Fools make light of the guilt that needs atonement, and leave honest men to enjoy the Lord's favour — Knox
A trespass-offering mocketh fools;
But among the upright there is good-will — ASV
Guilt has its home among fools;
Good will among the upright — AAT

10. The heart knoweth his own bitterness; and a stranger doth not intermeddle with his joy.
The heart knoweth its own bitterness,
And in its joy no stranger shareth — Rhm
The heart knows its own bitter misery, and no outsider shares its joy — Mof
The heart knows its own grief best, nor can a stranger share its joy — Jerus
No one has knowledge of a man's grief but himself; and a strange person has no part in his joy — Bas

11. The house of the wicked shall be overthrown: but the tabernacle of the upright shall flourish.
The houses of the wicked shall vanish; but the tents of the upright shall stand — Sept
The house of the wicked is destroyed,
And the tent of the upright flourisheth — YLT
The house of the wicked shall be demolished;
But the tent of the upright shall expand — Sprl
The house of the wicked shall be destroyed;
But the dwelling of the upright shall prosper — ABPS
Fall it must, the house of the wicked; where the upright dwell, all is increase — Knox

12. There is a way which seemeth right unto a man, but the end thereof are the ways of death.
There is a way right in the sight of a man;
But the end thereof — they are the ways of death — ABPS
There is a way that seems straight to a man;
But the end of it leads to death — AAT
A road may seem straightforward to a man,
yet may end as the way to death — NEB
There is a way which seemeth right to a man; but the end of it is at the bottom of Hades — Sept
There is a way that enticeth a man,
But at the latter end thereof are the ways of death — Rhm
There is a way that some think right,
but it leads in the end to death — Jerus

13. Even in laughter the heart is sorrowful; and the end of that mirth is heaviness.
Even in laughter is the heart pained,
And the latter end of joy is affliction — YLT
Even in laughter the heart may be sad,
And after joy comes grief — Sprl
Even in laughter the heart may be aching,
and joy may end in sorrow — Mof
Even in laughter the heart may grieve,
and mirth may end in sorrow — NEB
Laughter cannot mask a heavy heart.
When the laughter ends, grief remains — Tay

14. The backslider in heart shall be filled with his own ways: and a good man shall be satisfied from himself.
The dissembler in heart shall have his

[6]This vs. is problematic. Rhm and RV translate the Heb. in the most natural way. Others, including ASV, diverge more and more widely.

fill from his own ways;
And a good man shall be satisfied from himself — JPS

The unstable heart is satisfied with its own ways,
the good man with his own hard work — Jerus

The perverse man will reap the full fruit of his ways;
And the good man the full fruit of his deeds — AAT

The insolent in heart shall be filled with the fruit of his ways; and a good man shall be satisfied with the respect he receives — Lam

The incorrigible shall have a taste of his own ill-doings, and honest men shall have the better of him — Knox

The perverse man will get filled up on his own ways, and the good man gets satisfaction from his — Ber

15. The simple believeth every word: but the prudent man looketh well to his going.

The simple believes every thing;
But the shrewd gives heed to his going — ABPS

The thoughtless believeth every word;
But the prudent man looketh well to his going — JPS

The simple believes everything,
but the prudent looks where he is going — RSV

The simpleton believes what he is told:
the shrewd man watches where he goes — Mof

A simple man believes every word he hears;
a clever man understands the need for proof — NEB

16. A wise man feareth, and departeth from evil: but the fool rageth, and is confident.

A wise man feareth, and departeth from evil;
But the fool beareth himself insolently, and is confident — ASV

A wise man feareth and avoideth evil,
But a dullard is haughty and confident — Rhm

A wise man is cautious, and departs from evil; but the fool tampers with it confidently — Lam

The wise fear and depart from evil;
But the fool rushes on and is confident — Sprl

The wise man is cautious, and keeps away from trouble;
But the fool is blustering and confident in himself — AAT

The wise man sees evil coming and avoids it,
the fool is rash and presumptuous — Jerus

17. He that is soon angry dealeth foolishly: and a man of wicked devices is hated.[7]

Whoso is short of temper doth folly,
And a man of wicked devices is hated — YLT

He that is soon angry will deal foolishly: and a man of wicked devices is hated — RV

He who is quick-tempered acts foolishly, and a man who plans wickedness is hated — Ber

The impatient man blunders, as surely as the schemer makes enemies — Knox

18. The simple inherit folly: but the prudent are crowned with knowledge.

The simple inherit folly,
But the shrewd crowneth himself with knowledge — Rhm

The foolish inherit folly;
But the prudent shall be diademed with knowledge — Sprl

The thoughtless come into possession of folly;
But the prudent are crowned with knowledge — JPS

What simpletons acquire is folly:
shrewd men will pick up knowledge — Mof

The adornment of simpletons is folly,
but shrewd men gain the crown of knowledge — NAB

Foolish behaviour is the heritage of the simple, but men of good sense are crowned with knowledge — Bas

The simple acquire folly,
but the prudent are crowned with knowledge — RSV

19. The evil bow before the good; and the wicked at the gates of the righteous.

Let the bad fall before the good; and the wicked attend at the gates of the righteous — Sept

[7]Many others, in the last half-verse, read with LXX: "but a prudent man beareth many things."

The wicked have to bend low before the good,
And sinners before the gates of the righteous — Sprl

Evil men shall prostrate themselves before good men; and the wicked shall come to beg at the gates of the righteous — Lam

The knees of the evil are bent before the good; and sinners go down in the dust at the doors of the upright — Bas

Bad men must bow before the good, and wicked men must supplicate the just — Mof

20. The poor man is hated even of his own neighbour: but the rich hath many friends.

Even of his fellow is the poor man hated;
But the lovers of the rich are many — ABPS

Even by his neighbor the poor is spurned, but the friends of the rich man are many — Ber

The poor is disliked even by his neighbor,
but the rich has many friends — RSV

The poor man is detestable even to his neighbour,
but the rich man has friends and to spare — Jerus

A poor man is odious even to his friend;
the rich have friends in plenty — NEB

Of the beggar, his own neighbours grow weary; wealth never lacks friends — Knox

21. He that despiseth his neighbour sinneth: but he that hath mercy on the poor, happy is he.

He that despiseth his neighbour sinneth;
But he that hath pity on the poor, happy is he — ASV

He that despiseth his neighbour sinneth;
But he that is gracious unto the humble, happy is he — JPS

Whoso despiseth his neighbour sinneth;
But he who hath compassion upon the poor — blessings unto him — Sprl

He that sheweth contempt for his neighbour sinneth,
But he that sheweth favour to the afflicted how happy is he — Rhm

He who has no respect for his neighbour is a sinner, but he who has pity for the poor is happy — Bas

He sins who despises the hungry; but happy is he who is kind to the poor — NAB

22. Do they not err that devise evil? but mercy and truth shall be to them that devise good.

Shall they not go astray that devise evil?
But mercy and truth shall be for them that devise good — JPS

Do they not go astray who plot mischief? Loyal love and stability are for those who plan good — Ber

Do not those go astray who plan evil,
While those who plan good meet with kindness and good faith? — AAT

To be a schemer, is this not evil? Lay worthy plans, and kindliness and loyalty await you — Jerus

Do not evil-minded men fare miserably?
Good-natured men find people kind and true — Mof

Do they not err that devise evil?
Those who devise good meet loyalty and faithfulness — RSV

23. In all labour there is profit: but the talk of the lips tendeth only to penury.

By all labour there will be abundance,
But the talk of the lips tendeth only to want — Rhm

In all hard work there is profit, but talk only makes a man poor — Bas

In all labor there is profit, but idle talk leads only to poverty — Amp

In all toil there is profit,
but mere talk tends only to want — RSV

Hard work always yields its profit,
idle talk brings only want — Jerus

Hard work is sure wealth; of chattering comes only poverty — Knox

24. The crown of the wise is their riches: but the foolishness of fools is folly.[8]

[8]The later versions differ in their interpretations of the first half-verse, particularly, as e.g., Mof and RSV.

The crown of the wise is their riches;
But the folly of fools is only folly — ASV
The crown of the wise is their wealth;
The folly of fools — is folly — ABPS
The crown of the wise is their riches;
But the folly of fools remaineth folly — JPS
The crown of the wise is their riches;
but the perverseness of fools is their folly — Lam
The crown of wise men is their wisdom:
the coronet of fools is their own folly — Mof
The crown of the wise is their wisdom,
but folly is the garland of fools — RSV

25. A true witness delivereth souls: but a deceitful witness speaketh lies.
A true witness delivereth souls: but he that uttereth lies causeth deceit — RV
A deliverer of souls is a faithful witness,
But he that uttereth falsehoods is a fraud — Rhm
A faithful witness delivereth souls;
But whoso uttereth lies is a deceiver — Sprl
A truthful witness saves lives;
But he who utters lies destroys them — AAT
The truthful witness saves lives,
but he who utters lies is a betrayer — NAB
A truthful witness is a saver of lives,
he who utters lies is an imposter — Jerus

26. In the fear of the LORD is strong confidence: and his children shall have a place of refuge.

27. The fear of the LORD is a fountain of life, to depart from the snares of death.
In the fear of JEHOVAH is strong confidence;
And He will be a refuge unto His children.
The fear of JEHOVAH is a fountain of life,
To escape from the snares of death — Sprl
In the fear of Jehovah there is strong trust;
And his children shall have a refuge.
The fear of Jehovah is a well of life,
To turn from the snares of death — ABPS
In the reverence of Yahweh is strong security.
And his children shall have a place of refuge.
The reverence of Yahweh is a wellspring of life,
That a man may avoid the snares of death — Rhm
He who reveres the LORD has a strong ground of confidence,
In which his children also will find a refuge.
Reverence for the LORD is a fountain of life,
By which to avoid the snares of death — AAT
Fear of Yahweh gives good grounds for confidence,
in him his children find a refuge.
The fear of Yahweh is a life-giving spring,
for eluding the snares of death — Jerus
He who reverences the Eternal has strong ground for confidence;
his very children win security.
Reverence for the Eternal is a fount of life,
it shows how to evade the nets of Death — Mof
In the fear of the LORD is a strong defense;
even for one's children he will be a refuge.
The fear of the LORD is a fountain of life,
that a man may avoid the snares of death — NAB

28. In the multitude of people is the king's honour: but in the want of people is the destruction of the prince.
In the multitude of a people is the honour of a king,
And in the lack of people the ruin of a prince — YLT
In the multitude of a nation is the glory of a king; but in the failure of a people is the destruction of a prince — Sept
In the abundance of population is the king's honor; but in the destruction

of the people is the ruin of the king — Lam

In a multitude of people is the glory of a king,
but without people a prince is ruined — RSV

Many subjects make a famous king;
with none to rule, a prince is ruined — NEB

29. He that is slow to wrath is of great understanding: but he that is hasty of spirit exalteth folly.

He who is slow to be angry has great good sense; but he whose spirit is overquick gives support to what is foolish — Bas

To be forbearing is to show great sense;
the height of folly is to be quick-tempered — Mof

A forbearing man shows much intelligence;
A quick-tempered man shows great folly — AAT

The patient man shows much good sense,
but the quick-tempered man displays folly at its height — NAB

30. A sound heart is the life of the flesh: but envy the rottenness of the bones.

A tranquil heart is the life of the flesh;
But envy is the rottenness of the bones — ASV

The benevolent heart healeth the spirit;
But envy corrupts the bones — Sprl

The life of the whole body is a tranquil mind,
But a decay of the bones is jealousy — Rhm

A tranquil mind gives life to the flesh,
but passion makes the bones rot — RSV

A relaxed mind makes for physical health; but passion is rottenness to the bone — Ber

The life of the body is a tranquil heart,
but envy is a cancer in the bones — Jerus

31. He that oppresseth the poor reproacheth his Maker: but he that honoureth him hath mercy on the poor.

He that oppresseth the poor reproacheth his Maker: but he that hath mercy on the needy honoureth him — RV

He that oppresses the weak scorns his Maker;
But he that honors him has compassion on the needy — ABPS

He who oppresses the poor provokes his Maker; but he who honors the LORD has mercy on the needy — Lam

He who is hard on the forlorn reviles his Maker:
he honours his Maker who is kindly to the poor — Mof

He who oppresses the poor blasphemes his Maker,
but he who is kind to the needy glorifies him — NAB

He who oppresses the poor insults his Maker; he who is generous to the needy honours him — NEB

He that oppresseth the poor blasphemeth his Maker;
But he that is gracious unto the needy honoureth Him — JPS

32. The wicked is driven away in his wickedness: but the righteous hath hope in his death.[9]

The wicked is thrust down in his evil-doing;
But the righteous hath a refuge in his death — ASV

The wicked is thrust down in his misfortune;
But the righteous, even when he is brought to death, hath hope — JPS

The wicked is cast down by his wickedness;
But the righteous hath hope in his death — Sprl

In his wickedness is the wicked driven away,
And trustful in his death is the righteous — YLT

A wicked man shall be driven away by his wickedness; but in his sanctity the righteous is secure — Sept

The wicked is overthrown through his evil-doing,
but the righteous finds refuge through his integrity — RSV

33. Wisdom resteth in the heart of him that hath understanding: but that which

[9]Most others, as RSV, follow Sept., assuming a form of *tom*, 'integrity, uprightness,' rather than *mut*, 'death', in the second half-verse.

is in the midst of fools is made known.[10]

Wisdom resteth in the heart of him that hath understanding: but that which is in the inward part of fools is made known — RV

In the heart of the intelligent reposeth wisdom,
But in the midst of dullards it maketh itself known — Rhm

In the discerning heart, wisdom finds a resting-place; even among fools it can impart learning — Knox

Wisdom is enshrined in the hearts of men of common sense, but it must shout loudly before fools will hear it — Tay

In the good heart of a man there is wisdom; but in the heart of fools it is not discernable — Sept

Wisdom is at home in a discerning mind,
but is ill at ease in the heart of a fool — NEB

34. **Righteousness exalteth a nation: but sin is a reproach to any people.**

Righteousness exalteth a nation;
But sin diminisheth a people — Sprl

Integrity exalts a nation: evil brings any people low — Mof

By righteousness a nation is lifted up,
but sin is a cause of shame to the peoples — Bas

Virtue exalts a nation,
but sin is a people's disgrace — NAB

Godliness exalts a nation, but sin is a reproach to any people — Tay

Righteousness exalts a nation;
But sin is a people's ruin — Smith

35. **The king's favour is toward a wise servant: but his wrath is against him that causeth shame.**

The king's favor is toward a servant that dealeth wisely;
But his wrath will be against him that causeth shame — ASV

The king's favour is toward a servant that dealeth wisely;
But his wrath striketh him that dealeth shamefully — JPS

The good-pleasure of a king is due to a servant who is discreet,
But his indignation shall be against him that bringeth shame — Rhm

A wise servant has the king's favor;
But a base one has his wrath — ABPS

The king favors the intelligent servant,
but the worthless one incurs his wrath — NAB

The king favours an able minister:
his anger is for the incompetent — Mof

CHAPTER 15

1. **A soft answer turneth away wrath: but grievous words stir up anger.**

A soft answer turneth back fury,
And a grievous word raiseth up anger — YLT

A gentle answer turns away wrath;
But harsh words stir up anger — AAT

A pleasant answer turns away wrath, but a harsh word arouses anger — Ber

A mild reply turns wrath aside,
but a sharp word will stir up anger — Mof

A gentle answer is a quarrel averted; a word that gives pain does but fan the flame of resentment — Knox

A soft answer turns away wrath, but harsh words cause quarrels — Tay

2. **The tongue of the wise useth knowledge aright: but the mouth of fools poureth out foolishness.**

The tongue of the wise uttereth knowledge aright;
But the mouth of fools poureth out folly — ASV

The tongue of the wise utters useful knowledge;
But the mouth of fools pours forth folly — ABPS

The tongue of the wise dispenses knowledge,
but the mouths of fools pour out folly — RSV

The tongue of the wise adorneth knowledge, —
But the mouth of dullards belcheth out folly — Rhm

---

[10]Sept and one Heb. ms. read "not" before "made known," in the second half, which seems to yield better sense from this line. Several other translations follow this reading.

The tongue of the wise distils knowledge,
the mouth of fools spews folly — Jerus

A wise man's tongue spreads knowledge;
stupid men talk nonsense — NEB

3. The eyes of the LORD are in every place, beholding the evil and the good.

The eyes of the LORD are in every place, keeping watch upon the evil and the good — RV

The eyes of JEHOVAH are in all places; Watching over the evil and the good — Sprl

The eyes of the LORD are in every place, beholding the good men and the bad — Lam

The eyes of the LORD are everywhere, surveying evil and good men alike — NEB

4. A wholesome tongue is a tree of life: but perverseness therein is a breach in the spirit.

A gentle tongue is a tree of life;
But perverseness therein is a breaking of the spirit — ASV

A soothing tongue is a tree of life;
But perverseness therein is a wound to the spirit — JPS

A soothing tongue is a tree of life,
but a perverse one crushes the spirit — NAB

A soothing tongue is a tree of life;
But wild words break the spirit — AAT

Gentle words cause life and health; griping brings discouragement — Tay

Tongue that speaks peaceably is a tree whose fruit gives life; tongue undisciplined can break hearts — Knox

5. A fool despiseth his father's instruction: but he that regardeth reproof is prudent.

A foolish son spurneth the correction of his father,
But he that heedeth a reproof sheweth prudence — Rhm

The foolish rejects his father's correction, but he who remembers reproof is prudent — Ber

A fool despiseth his father's correction: but he that regardeth reproof getteth prudence — RV

A fool spurns his father's correction;
But he that regards reproof deals wisely — ABPS

A fool despises his father's instruction,
but he who heeds admonition is prudent — RSV

A senseless fellow scorns his father's counsel,
but he who listens to reproof shows his good sense — Mof

6. In the house of the righteous is much treasure: but in the revenues of the wicked is trouble.

In the house of the righteous is abundant treasure;
But in the revenues of the wicked is disturbance — Sprl

In the house of the righteous there is ample wealth;
But the revenue of the wicked will be cut off — AAT

In the house of the righteous is abundant strength,
And in the increase of the wicked — trouble — YLT

In the houses of the righteous there is much power; but the fruits of the wicked shall perish — Sept

In the house of the virtuous there is no lack of treasure,
the earnings of the wicked are fraught with anxiety — Jerus

In the righteous man's house there is ample wealth;
the gains of the wicked bring trouble — NEB

7. The lips of the wise disperse knowledge: but the heart of the foolish doeth not so.

The lips of the wise scatter abroad knowledge,
But the heart of dullards is not right — Rhm

The lips of the wise disperse knowledge;
But the heart of the foolish is not stedfast — JPS

The lips of the wise spread knowledge;
not so the mind of fools — RSV

The lips of the wise disseminate knowledge,
but the heart of fools is perverted — NAB

The talk of the wise is a seed-ground of learning; the thoughts of fools are ill matched with it — Knox

8. The sacrifice of the wicked is an abom-

ination to the LORD: but the prayer of the upright is his delight.

9. The way of the wicked is an abomination unto the LORD: but he loveth him that followeth after righteousness.

The offering of the evil-doer is disgusting to the Lord, but the prayer of the upright man is his delight.
The way of the evil-doer is disgusting to the Lord, but he who goes after righteousness is dear to him — Bas

Sacrifice from evil men is loathsome to the Eternal,
but the prayers of upright men are his delight.
A wicked life is loathsome to the Eternal:
he loves the man bent upon honesty — Mof

The sacrifice of the wicked is abhorrent to Yahweh,
dear to him is the prayer of honest men.
The conduct of the wicked is abhorrent to Yahweh,
but he loves the man who makes virtue his goal — Jerus

The wicked man's sacrifice is abominable to the LORD; the good man's prayer is his delight.
The conduct of the wicked is abominable to the LORD,
but he loves the seeker after righteousness — NEB

The Lord hates the gifts of the wicked, but delights in the prayers of his people.
The Lord despises the deeds of the wicked, but loves those who try to be good — Tay

10. Correction is grievous unto him that forsaketh the way: and he that hateth reproof shall die.

Chastisement is grievous to him who is forsaking the path,
Whoso is hating reproof dieth — YLT

There is grievous correction for him that forsaketh the way;
And he that hateth reproof shall die — ASV

A sore correction has he that forsakes the way;
He that hates reproof shall die — ABPS

Stern discipline awaits the man who leaves the right way;
He who hates admonition will die — AAT

Severe punishment is in store for the man who goes astray;
he who hates reproof will die — NAB

Correction is severe for him who leaves the way;
he who hates being reprimanded will die — Jerus

11. Hell and destruction are before the LORD: how much more then the hearts of the children of men?

Sheol and Abaddon are before Jehovah;
How much more then the hearts of the children of men — ASV

The nether-world and Destruction are before the LORD;
How much more then the hearts of the children of men — JPS

Death and the world of the dead lie open to the Eternal;
how much more the hearts of men — Mof

The mansion of the dead, and destruction, are open to the view of the Lord; how much more then the hearts of men — Sept

12. A scorner loveth not one that reproveth him: neither will he go unto the wise.

A scoffer loveth not to be reproved;
He will not go unto the wise — ASV

The scoffer loves not one that reproves him;
He will not go to the wise — ABPS

A scoffer loves not to be admonished;
To wise men he will not go — AAT

The hater of authority has no love for teaching: he will not go to the wise — Bas

A mocker stays away from wise men because he hates to be scolded — Tay

13. A merry heart maketh a cheerful countenance: but by sorrow of heart the spirit is broken.

A joyous heart maketh a cheerful countenance;
But from sorrow of heart the spirit is broken — Sprl

A joyful heart maketh glad the face,

And by grief of heart is the spirit smitten — YLT

A joyful heart maketh a pleasing countenance, —
But in sorrow of heart is a stricken spirit — Rhm

A glad heart lights up the face,
but by mental anguish the spirit is broken — NAB

14. **The heart of him that hath understanding seeketh knowledge: but the mouth of fools feedeth on foolishness.**

The heart of him that hath discernment seeketh knowledge;
But the mouth of fools feedeth on folly — JPS

The mind of him who has understanding seeks knowledge,
but the mouths of fools feed on folly — RSV

The heart of the just seeks knowledge; but the mouth of the wicked utters evil — Lam

The heart of the discerning makes knowledge its search,
the mouth of fools feeds on folly — Jerus

A wise man is hungry for truth, while the mocker feeds on trash — Tay

Truth is the quest of discerning minds, trifling the pasture-ground of the foolish — Knox

15. **All the days of the afflicted are evil: but he that is of a merry heart hath a continual feast.**

All the days of the afflicted are sorrowful,
But a cheerful heart is a continual banquet — Rhm

All the days of the poor are evil;
But a cheerful heart is a continual feast — ABPS

Afflicted are all the days of the dejected;
But the cheerful of heart hath a continual feast — Sprl

All the days of the troubled are evil;
but he whose heart is glad has an unending feast — Bas

For the miserable man every day is unhappy;
But the cheerful man enjoys a perpetual feast — AAT

All the days of the poor are filled with hardships; but those who are of a merry heart have a continual tranquillity — Lam

16. **Better is little with the fear of the LORD than great treasure and trouble therewith.**

17. **Better is a dinner of herbs where love is, than a stalled ox and hatred therewith.**

Better is a little with the fear of Jehovah,
Than much treasure, and tumult with it.
Better is an allowance of green herbs and love there,
Than a fatted ox, and hatred with it — YLT

Better a little with reverence for the LORD than great treasure and lamentation with it.
Better a vegetable meal where love is, than a fattened ox and hate with it — Ber

Better is a little with the fear of the Lord, than great wealth together with trouble.
Better is a simple meal where love is, than a fat ox and hate with it — Bas

Better a little, with reverence for the Eternal,
than large wealth with worry.
Better a dish of vegetables, with love,
than the best beef served with hatred — Mof

Better a pittance with the fear of the LORD
than great treasure and trouble in its train.
Better a dish of vegetables if love go with it
than a fat ox eaten in hatred — NEB

Better a little, with reverence for the LORD,
Than much treasure, and anxiety with it.
Better a dish of herbs, where love is,
Than a fatted ox, and hatred with it — AAT

18. **A wrathful man stirreth up strife: but he that is slow to anger appeaseth strife.**

A wrathful man stirreth up contention;

But he that is slow to anger appeaseth strife — ASV

A wrathful man stirreth up discord;
But he that is slow to anger appeaseth strife — JPS

A hot-tempered man stirs up strife,
but he who is slow to anger quiets contention — RSV

An ill-tempered man stirs up strife,
but a patient man allays discord — NAB

A quick-tempered man starts fights; a cool-tempered man tries to stop them — Tay

19. The way of the slothful man is as a hedge of thorns: but the way of the righteous is made plain.

The way of the sluggard is like a thorn hedge,
But the path of the upright is a raised road — Rhm

The way of the sluggard is as though hedged by thorns;
But the path of the upright is even — JPS

The way of the sluggard is as an hedge of thorns: but the path of the upright is made an high way — RV

The way of the wicked is hedged with thorns;
But the path of the upright is paved like a highway — AAT

The way of the lazy is strewn with thorns,
the path of the industrious is a broad highway — Jerus

The way of a sluggard is overgrown with thorns,
but the path of the upright is a level highway — RSV

20. A wise son maketh a glad father: but a foolish son despiseth his mother.

A wise son maketh a glad father; but a foolish son mocketh his mother — Sept

A wise son makes his father happy; but a foolish son is a disgrace to his mother — Lam

A wise son rejoiceth his father;
But a foolish son is a reproach to his mother — Sprl

A wise son makes a glad father, but a foolish man has no respect for his mother — Bas

A wise son brings joy to his father;
a young fool despises his mother — NEB

21. Folly is joy to him that is destitute of wisdom: but the man of understanding walketh uprightly.

Folly is joy to him that is void of wisdom;
But a man of understanding maketh straight his going — ASV

Folly is joy to him that lacketh understanding;
But a man of discernment walketh straightforwards — JPS

Folly is a joy to him who has no sense,
but a man of understanding walks aright — RSV

Folly is joy to one who lacks sense,
but a discerning man takes a straight course — Ber

Folly is joy to a man without sense;
But a man of intelligence keeps a straightforward course — AAT

Folly is a delight to senseless men,
but a man of sense leads a straightforward life — Mof

22. Without counsel purposes are disappointed: but in the multitude of counsellors they are established.

A purpose is disappointed for want of deliberation;
But by the counsel of many they come to pass — Sprl

Plans are frustrated for lack of consultation,
But by the multitude of counsellors shall counsel be established — Rhm

Where there are no wise suggestions, purposes come to nothing; but by a number of wise guides they are made certain — Bas

Without counsel plans are frustrated;
But by the multitude of counselors they are established — ABPS

When no counsel is taken, plans miscarry;
But when there are many advisers, they succeed — AAT

Plans fail when there is no counsel,
but they succeed when counselors are many — NAB

23. A man hath joy by the answer of his mouth: and a word spoken in due season, how good is it!

To make an apt answer is a joy to a man,

and a word in season, how good it is! — RSV

An apt utterance is a joy to a man;
And a word in season — how good it is! — AAT

Apt answers are a joy to men;
a word in season, what a help it is! — Mof

When a man has a ready answer he has joy too:
how satisfying is the apt reply! — Jerus

Everyone enjoys giving good advice, and how wonderful it is to be able to say the right thing at the right time! — Tay

24. The way of life is above to the wise, that he may depart from hell beneath.

A path of life is on high for the wise,
To turn aside from Sheol beneath — YLT

To the wise the way of life goeth upward,
That he may depart from Sheol beneath — ASV

The way of life leads upward for the wise, that he may depart from the depths of Sheol — Lam

The path of life is upward for the wise,
That he may turn from the underworld beneath — ABPS

The path of life leads the prudent man upward,
that he may avoid the nether world below — NAB

25. The LORD will destroy the house of the proud: but he will establish the border of the widow.

The LORD will root up the house of the proud: but he will establish the border of the widow — RV

The LORD will pluck up the house of the proud;
But He will establish the border of the widow — Sprl

The house of the haughty JEHOVAH will pull down;
But He will establish the border of the widow — Sprl

The house of proud men will Yahweh tear down,
But he will maintain the boundary of the widow — Rhm

The Eternal overthrows the proud man's house,
but he preserves the widow's field intact — Mof

The LORD overturns the house of the proud,
but he preserves intact the widow's landmark — NAB

26. The thoughts of the wicked are an abomination to the LORD: but the words of the pure are pleasant words.[11]

An evil thought is an abomination to the Lord: but the speeches of the chaste are grace — Sept

An abomination to Yahweh are the plottings of the wicked,
But with the pure are sayings of sweetness — Rhm

Evil designs are disgusting to the Lord,
but the words of the clean-hearted are pleasing — Bas

Evil devices are an abomination to Jehovah;
But pleasant words are pure — ASV

Wicked thoughts are an abomination to the LORD, but kindly words are pure — Ber

A bad man's thoughts are the LORD's abomination,
but the words of the pure are a delight — NEB

27. He that is greedy of gain troubleth his own house; but he that hateth gifts shall live.

He that is greedy of gain troubleth his own house;
But he that hateth bribes shall live — ASV

He who is greedy for unjust gain makes trouble for his household,
but he who hates bribes will live — RSV

He who seeks dishonest gain brings trouble on his house,
he who hates bribes shall have life — Jerus

He who traffics in ill-gotten gain wrecks his own household;
But he who hates a bribe will prosper — AAT

Let avarice lead thee away, thy home shall be ruined; long life is his, who scorns the bribe — Knox

28. The heart of the righteous studieth to

---

[11]The Heb. of the second half-verse offers two possible interpretations. KJV is one; ASV is an example of the other.

answer; but the mouth of the wicked poureth out evil things.

The heart of the righteous meditates for an answer;
But the mouth of the wicked pours out mischiefs — ABPS

The heart of the upright gives thought to his answer; but from the mouth of the evil-doer comes a stream of evil things — Bas

The mind of the righteous ponders before answering, but the mouth of the wicked pours forth evil things — Ber

The just man weighs well his utterance, but the mouth of the wicked pours out evil — NAB

A good man ponders what to say: bad men let out a flood of evil talk Mof

29. The LORD is far from the wicked: but he heareth the prayer of the righteous.

God is far removed from the wicked: but he hearkeneth to the prayers of the righteous — Sept

Yahweh stands far from the wicked, but he listens to the prayers of the virtuous — Jerus

The LORD stands aloof from the wicked,
he listens to the righteous man's prayer — NEB

Far off is Yahweh from the lawless,
But the prayer of the righteous will he hear — Rhm

30. The light of the eyes rejoiceth the heart: and a good report maketh the bones fat.

Bright eyes gladden the heart;
Good news fattens the bones — AAT

The sparkling of bright eyes rejoiceth the heart,
Good news gives marrow to the bones — Rhm

The light of the eyes rejoices the heart,
and good news refreshes the bones — RSV

A cheerful glance brings joy to the heart;
good news invigorates the bones — NAB

A kindly glance gives joy to the heart,
good news lends strength to the bones — Jerus

The eye that smiles, how it cheers the heart! Good news, how it lends vigour to a man's frame! — Knox

31. The ear that heareth the reproof of life abideth among the wise.

32. He that refuseth instruction despiseth his own soul: but he that heareth reproof getteth understanding.

The ear that hearkeneth to the reproof of life
Shall abide among the wise.
He that refuseth correction despiseth his own soul;
But he that hearkeneth to reproof getteth understanding — ASV

The ear that heareth reproof hath life,
And among the wise shall he abide.
Whoso refuseth instruction despiseth his own soul;
But he who hearkeneth unto reproof obtaineth understanding — Sprl

The man whose ear is open to the teaching of life will have his place among the wise.
He who will not be controlled by training has no respect for his soul, but he who gives ear to teaching will get wisdom — Bas

He who listens to wholesome admonition
Will dwell among the wise.
He who rejects instruction despises himself;
But he who listens to admonition gains understanding — AAT

The ear that listens to the reproof of life will stay among wise men.
He who ignores correction despises himself, and he who listens to reproof acquires intelligence — Ber

The ear attentive to wholesome correction
finds itself at home in the company of the wise.
He who rejects discipline despises his own self;
he who listens to correction wins discernment — Jerus

33. The fear of the LORD is the instruction of wisdom; and before honour is humility.

The fear of Jehovah is instruction in wisdom;
And humility is before honor — ABPS

Reverence for the Eternal trains men to be wise,

and to be humble is the way to honour — Mof

The fear of the LORD is training for wisdom,
and humility goes before honors — NAB

The fear of Yahweh is a school of wisdom,
humility goes before honour—Jerus

The fear of the LORD is a training in wisdom,
and the way to honour is humility — NEB

It is the fear of the Lord teaches the lessons of wisdom; humility goes first, and honour comes in her train — Knox

CHAPTER 16

1. The preparations of the heart in man, and the answer of the tongue is from the LORD.

To man belong the preparations of the heart,
But from Yahweh cometh the answer of the tongue — Rhm

The preparations of the heart are man's,
But the answer of the tongue is from the LORD — JPS

The plans of the heart belong to man;
But the answer of the tongue is from Jehovah — ASV

The reasoning of the mind is from man; but the answer of the tongue is from the LORD — Lam

The designs of the heart are man's, but the answer of the tongue comes from the Lord — Bas

A man may order his thoughts,
but the LORD inspires the words he utters — NEB

2. All the ways of a man are clean in his own eyes; but the LORD weigheth the spirits.

All the ways of a man are pure in his own sight,
But JEHOVAH weigheth their inspirations — Sprl

A man's conduct may strike him as pure,
Yahweh, however, weighs the motives — Jerus

A man's ways seem all right to him, but the Eternal has the verdict on his life — Mof

All the ways of a man may be pure in his own eyes,
but it is the LORD who proves the spirit — NAB

His own path man scans, and nothing sees amiss, but the divine balance weighs our thoughts — Knox

3. Commit thy works unto the LORD, and thy thoughts shall be established.

Commit thy works unto Jehovah,
And thy purposes shall be established — ASV

Commit your business to the LORD;
And your plans will prosper — AAT

Roll your work onto the LORD and your plans will be achieved — Ber

Commit to the LORD all that you do,
and your plans will be fulfilled — NEB

4. The LORD hath made all things for himself: yea, even the wicked for the day of evil.

All things hath Jehovah wrought for Himself,
And also the wicked worketh for a day of evil — YLT

Everything hath Yahweh made for its own purpose,
Yea even the lawless one for the day of calamity — Rhm

Every work of JEHOVAH answers His design,
Yea, even the wicked for the calamitous day — Sprl

The LORD hath made everything for its own end: yea, even the wicked for the day of evil — RV

Yahweh made everything for its own purpose,
yes, even the wicked for the day of disaster — Jerus

The Eternal has made everything for an end of its own —
yes, and the wicked for their day of doom — Mof

5. Every one that is proud in heart is an abomination to the LORD: though hand join in hand, he shall not be unpunished.

Every one that is proud in heart is an abomination to the LORD;

My hand upon it! he shall not be unpunished — JPS

Every proud-minded man is an abomination to the LORD;
My hand upon it! he will not go unpunished — AAT

Every one proud of heart is an abomination to the LORD; be assured he will not go unpunished — Ber

Every proud man is an abomination to the LORD;
I assure you that he will not go unpunished — NAB

A proud man the Lord holds in abhorrence; depend upon it, no acquittal shall he find — Knox

6. By mercy and truth iniquity is purged: and by the fear of the LORD men depart from evil.

By lovingkindness and fidelity shall iniquity be covered,
And in the revering of Yahweh is a turning away from wrong — Rhm

By mercy and truth iniquity is atoned for;
And by the fear of Jehovah men depart from evil — ASV

By mercy and truth iniquity is expiated;
And by the fear of the LORD men depart from evil — JPS

Through mercy and truth is iniquity pardoned;
And through fear of JEHOVAH evil is shunned — Sprl

By kindness and good faith guilt is atoned for;
And by reverence for the LORD one avoids calamity — AAT

Guilt is wiped out by faith and loyalty, and the fear of the LORD makes men turn from evil — NEB

7. When a man's ways please the LORD, he maketh even his enemies to be at peace with him.

When Jehovah delights in one's ways,
He causes even his enemies to be at peace with him — ABPS

When the LORD is pleased with a man's ways,
he makes even his enemies to be at peace with him — NAB

When the ways of man please the Eternal,
He makes even his foes friends with him — Mof

Live as the Lord would have thee live, and he will make even thy enemies into well-wishers — Knox

8. Better is a little with righteousness, than great revenues without right.

Better is a little, with righteousness,
Than great revenues with injustice — ASV

Better is a little with righteousness,
Than abundant resources without right — Sprl

Better is a little with righteousness by fair means than a large income without justice — Ber

Better a pittance honestly earned than great gains ill gotten — NEB

A little, gained honestly, is better than great wealth gotten by dishonest means — Tay

9. A man's heart deviseth his way: but the LORD directeth his steps.

A man may plan his course;
But the LORD directs his steps — AAT

A man's mind plans his way,
but the LORD directs his steps — RSV

A man thinks out his plans,
but the Eternal controls his course — Mof

A man may make designs for his way,
but the Lord is the guide for his steps — Bas

A man's heart plans out his way
but it is Yahweh who makes his steps secure — Jerus

10. A divine sentence is in the lips of the king: his mouth transgresseth not in judgment.

An oracle is on the lips of a king,
In giving sentence his mouth must not be unfaithful — Rhm

Sagacity should be upon the lips of the king,
Lest his mouth transgress in judgment — Sprl

Oracles are on the lips of the king;
his mouth does not err in judgment — Lam

An oracle is on the lips of the king;
In judgment his mouth shall not deal treacherously — ABPS

The king's mouth is an oracle,
he cannot err when he passes sentence — NEB

Inspired decisions are on the lips of a king;
his mouth does not sin in judgment — RSV

11. A just weight and balance are the LORD'S: all the weights of the bag are his work.

A just beam and balances are Jehovah's,
His work are all the stones of the bag — YLT

A just balance and scales are Jehovah's;
All the weights of the bag are his work — ASV

True measures and scales are the Lord's:
all the weights of the bag are his work — Bas

Balance and scales are set by the LORD;
All the weights in the bag are his concern — AAT

Balance and scales belong to the LORD;
all the weights used with them are his concern — NAB

12. It is an abomination to kings to commit wickedness: for the throne is established by righteousness.

It is an abomination when kings commit wickedness;
But by justice is the throne established — Sprl

It is an abomination to kings to do evil,
for the throne is established by righteousness — RSV

Evil-doing is disgusting to kings: for the seat of the ruler is based on righteousness — Bas

Kings have a horror of wrong-doing,
for the throne is maintained by justice — Mof

Wickedness is abhorrent to kings,
for a throne rests firm on righteousness — NEB

It is a horrible thing for a king to do evil. His right to rule depends upon his fairness — Tay

13. Righteous lips are the delight of kings; and they love him that speaketh right.

Righteous lips are acceptable to a king;
and he loveth right words — Sept

The delight of kings are righteous lips,
And whoso is speaking uprightly he loveth — YLT

Righteous lips are the delight of a king,
and he loves him who speaks what is right — RSV

The lips of a righteous man are the delight of a king; and he loves the word of the upright — Lam

Virtuous lips are welcome to a king,
he loves a man of honest words — Jerus

Honest talk is the delight of kings;
they love a man who tells the truth — Mof

14. The wrath of a king is as messengers of death: but a wise man will pacify it.

15. In the light of the king's countenance is life; and his favour is as a cloud of the latter rain.

The fury of a king is messengers of death,
And a wise man pacifieth it.
In the light of a king's face is life,
And his good-will is as a cloud of the latter rain — YLT

The wrath of a king is as a messenger of death;
But a wise man appeaseth it.
In the smile of the king's face is life;
And his favour like the cloud of the harvest rain — Sprl

The king's wrath is a forerunner of death;
But a wise man can appease it.
In the light of the king's countenance is life;
And his favor is like a spring rain-cloud — AAT

The king's wrath is the herald of death,
but a wise man will appease it.
When the king's face brightens it spells life,
his favour is like the rain in spring — Jerus

A deadly thing is the king's anger;
a sensible man will try to pacify it.
When the king's face is friendly, all goes well;
his favour is like rain-clouds in the spring — Mof

16. How much better is it to get wisdom than gold! and to get understanding rather to be chosen than silver!

To acquire wisdom how much better than gold!

And to get hold of understanding more choice than silver! — Rhm

To get wisdom is much better than gold; and to get understanding is better than silver — Lam

How much better to get wisdom than gold, as understanding is rather to be chosen than silver — Ber

How much better to acquire wisdom than gold!
To acquire understanding is more desirable than silver — NAB

To get wisdom is better than gold;
to get understanding is to be chosen rather than silver — RSV

Better gain wisdom than gold,
choose discernment rather than silver — Jerus

17. The highway of the upright is to depart from evil: he that keepeth his way preserveth his soul.

The highway of the upright is a turning from evil;
He that keeps his way preserves his soul — ABPS

The highway of the upright turneth away from iniquity;
Whoso giveth heed to his way preserveth his soul — Sprl

The highway of the upright is to be turned away from evil: he who takes care of his way will keep his soul — Bas

The path of the upright avoids calamity;
He who pays heed to his way safeguards his life — AAT

The path of the upright avoids misfortune;
he safeguards life who watches where he goes — Mof

18. Pride goeth before destruction, and a haughty spirit before a fall.

19. Better it is to be of an humble spirit with the lowly, than to divide the spoil with the proud.

Before destruction is pride,
And before stumbling — a haughty spirit.
Better is humility of spirit with the poor,
Than to apportion spoil with the proud — YLT

Before grievous injury pride!
And before a fall haughtiness of spirit!
Better is lowliness of spirit with the patient,
Than a portion of the spoil with the proud — Rhm

Pride is before destruction,
And a haughty spirit before a fall.
Better is the humble in spirit with the lowly,
Than to divide the spoil with the proud — ABPS

Before destruction comes pride, and before a fall a proud spirit.
It is better to be humble in spirit among the poor, than to divide the plunder with the proud — Ber

Pride comes before disaster,
and arrogance before a fall.
Better sit humbly with those in need than divide the spoil with the proud — NEB

Pride goes before disaster,
and a haughty spirit before a fall.
It is better to be humble with the meek
than to share plunder with the proud — NAB

20. He that handleth a matter wisely shall find good: and whoso trusteth in the LORD, happy is he.[12]

He that showeth discretion concerning a matter shall find good,
And he that trusteth in Yahweh how happy is he! — Rhm

He who plans a thing will be successful;
happy is he who trusts in the LORD — NAB

The shrewd man of business will succeed well,
but the happy man is he who trusts in the LORD — NEB

Whoso directeth himself according to the word, findeth favour;
And whoso trusteth in JEHOVAH, happy is he — Sprl

He that giveth heed unto the word shall find good;
And whoso trusteth in Jehovah, happy is he — ASV

He who pays heed to the word will prosper;

[12]The variations in the first half derive from the two possible uses of the Heb. *dabar*: (a) 'matter, affair'; (b) 'word, saying'. Most agree with ASV/RV.

And happy is he who trusts in the LORD — AAT

21. The wise in heart shall be called prudent: and the sweetness of the lips increaseth learning.

The wise in heart is called a man of discernment;
And the sweetness of the lips increaseth learning — JPS

The wise-hearted will be named men of good sense: and by pleasing words learning is increased — Bas

The wise in heart is a man of discernment; and he whose speech is sweet increases learning — Lam

The wise in heart will be called a discerning man, and pleasant speech will increase learning — Ber

The wise of heart is called a man of discernment,
and pleasant speech increases persuasiveness — RSV

A wise man is esteemed for being pleasant;
his friendly words add to his influence — Mof

22. Understanding is a wellspring of life unto him that hath it: but the instruction of fools is folly.

Understanding is a fountain of life to them who possess it: but the instruction of fools is evil — Sept

A well-spring of life is discretion to its owner,
But the correction of the foolish is folly — Rhm

Understanding is a wellspring of life unto him that hath it:
But the correction of fools is their folly — ASV

Understanding is a fountain of life unto him that hath it;
But folly is the chastisement of fools — JPS

Shrewdness is a fountain of life for its possessor,
the folly of fools is their own punishment — Jerus

Good sense is a fountain of life to its possessor,
but folly brings chastisement on fools — NAB

23. The heart of the wise teacheth his mouth, and addeth learning to his lips.

24. Pleasant words are as an honeycomb, sweet to the soul, and health to the bones.

The heart of the wise instructeth his mouth,
And addeth persuasion unto his lips.
Amiable words are like drops of honey,
Sweet to the soul, and healing to the bones — Sprl

The mind of the wise teaches his mouth, and adds learning to his lips.
Pleasant words are as a honeycomb, sweet to the soul and healing to the bones — Ber

The mind of man imparts intelligence to his speech,
And adds persuasiveness to the teaching of his lips.
Pleasant words are a honeycomb,
Sweet to the spirit, and healthful to the body — AAT

The mind of the wise makes his speech judicious,
and adds persuasiveness to his lips.
Pleasant words are like a honeycomb, sweetness to the soul and health to the body—RSV

The wise man's mind guides his speech, and what his lips impart increases learning.
Kind words are like dripping honey, sweetness on the tongue and health for the body — NEB

Good sense makes men judicious in their talk;
it adds persuasiveness to what they say.
Kindly words are like a honeycomb, both sweet and healthful — Mof

25. There is a way that seemeth right unto a man; but the end thereof are the ways of death.

There are ways which seem right to a man: but the latter ends of them look to the bottom of Hades — Sept

There is a way that enticeth a man,
But at the latter end thereof are the ways of death — Rhm

There is a way right in the sight of a man;
But the end thereof — they are ways of death — ABPS

There is a way that seems right in the eyes of men, but the paths thereof are the paths of death — Lam

Sometimes a way seems right to a man,

but the end of it leads to death — NAB
There is a way that some think right, but it leads in the end to death — Jerus

26. He that laboureth laboureth for himself; for his mouth craveth it of him.
The appetite of the laboring man laboreth for him;
For his mouth urgeth him thereto — ASV
The laborer's appetite labors for him;
For his mouth has laid a burden on him — ABPS
The hunger of the labouring man laboureth for him;
For his mouth compelleth him — JPS
The labourer's appetite is always plaguing him,
his hunger spurs him on — NEB
A labourer's appetite labours for him;
his hunger drives him to work — Mof

27. An ungodly man diggeth up evil: and in his lips there is as a burning fire.

28. A froward man soweth strife: and a whisperer separateth chief friends.
A worthless man raketh up evil,
And like a burning fire is upon his lips.
A perverse man disseminates strife;
And a whisperer disunites confidential friends — Sprl
A worthless man deviseth mischief;
And in his lips there is as a scorching fire.
A perverse man scattereth abroad strife;
And a whisperer separateth chief friends — ASV
A depraved man digs up evil;
While the words on his lips are like a scorching fire.
A fickle man sows discord;
And a whisperer separates friends — AAT
A worthless man plots harm, and his speech is like a searing flame.
A perverse man sows strife, and a whisperer separates familiar friends — Ber
A scoundrel digs deep for mischief-making,
on his lips is a fire that scorches.
A troublemaker sows strife,
a talebearer divides friend from friend — Jerus
A scoundrel is a furnace of evil,
and on his lips there is a scorching fire.
An intriguer sows discord,
and a talebearer separates bosom friends — NAB

29. A violent man enticeth his neighbour, and leadeth him into a way that is not good.

30. He shutteth his eyes to devise froward things: moving his lips he bringeth evil to pass.
A man of violence enticeth his neighbor,
And leadeth him in a way that is not good.
He that shutteth his eyes, it is to devise perverse things:
He that compresseth his lips bringeth evil to pass — ASV
A man of violence seduces his friend,
And leads him in a way that is not good.
When he shuts his eyes, he is devising perverseness;
When he bites his lips, he has perfected mischief — ABPS
A ruthless man enticeth his neighbour,
And leadeth him in a way not good.
Closing his eyes to devise perverse things,
Biting his lips he hath plotted mischief — Rhm
The knave misleads his neighbour,
and draws him into evil courses.
The slanderer concocts a lie,
the detractor has designs of mischief — Mof
A lawless man entices his neighbor,
And leads him into a way that is not good.
He who shuts his eyes is hatching some crooked scheme;
He who tightens his lips concocts some mischief — AAT
A man of violence draws others on
and leads them into lawless ways.
The man who narrows his eyes is disaffected at heart,
and a close-lipped man is bent on mischief — NEB

31. The hoary head is a crown of glory, if it be found in the way of righteousness.

Old age is a crown of glory, when found in the ways of righteousness — Sept

Hoariness is a diadem of glory,
When found in the way of righteousness — Sprl

A crown of beauty are grey hairs,
In the way of righteousness it is found — YLT

A hoary head is a crown of glory;
it is gained in a righteous life — RSV

The grey head is a crown of glory, if it is seen in the way of righteousness — Bas

32. **He that is slow to anger is better than the mighty; and he that ruleth his spirit than he that taketh a city.**

Better is he that is slow to anger than a hero,
And he that ruleth his spirit than he that captureth a city — Rhm

A forbearing man is better than a warrior;
He who rules his temper than he who takes a city — AAT

Whoso is tardy to anger is better than the mighty;
And whoso governeth his spirit than he who taketh a city — Sprl

A man who is slow to wrath is better than the mighty; and he who subdueth anger is better than he who taketh a city — Sept

A patient man is better than a warrior, and he who rules his temper, than he who takes a city — NAB

Patience is worth more than valour; better a disciplined heart than a stormed city — Knox

33. **The lot is cast into the lap; but the whole disposing thereof is of the LORD.**

Into the centre is the lot cast,
And from Jehovah is all its judgment — YLT

The lot is cast into the lap;
But its decision is all of Jehovah — ABPS

The lots may be cast into the lap,
but the issue depends wholly on the LORD — NEB

A thing may be put to the decision of chance, but it comes about through the Lord — Bas

We toss the coin, but it is the Lord who controls its decision — Tay

CHAPTER 17

1. **Better is a dry morsel, and quietness therewith, than a house full of sacrifices with strife.**

Better is a dry morsel, and quietness therewith,
Than a house full of slaughtered beasts, with strife — ABPS

Better is a dry crust and tranquillity therewith,
Than a house full of feastings with contention — Sprl

Better a dry crust and with it peace than a house where feast and dispute go together — Jerus

Better a morsel of dry bread and peace than a house full of banqueting and quarrels — Mof

2. **A wise servant shall have rule over a son that causeth shame, and shall have part of the inheritance among the brethren.**

A prudent servant shall rule over a son who causeth shame,
And in the midst of brothers shall he share the inheritance — Rhm

A capable servant will rule over a dissolute son,
And will share the inheritance among the brothers — AAT

A servant that dealeth wisely shall have rule over a son that causeth shame,
And shall have part in the inheritance among the brethren — ASV

A servant that dealeth wisely shall have rule over a son that dealeth shamefully,
And shall have part of the inheritance among the brethren — JPS

A slave who deals wisely will rule over a son who acts shamefully,
and will share the inheritance as one of the brothers — RSV

3. **The fining pot is for silver, and the furnace for gold: but the LORD trieth the hearts.**

As silver and gold are tried in a furnace; so are chosen hearts, by the Lord — Sept

A crucible is for silver, and the furnace is for gold,
and the LORD tries hearts — RSV

The crucible is for silver and the furnace for gold, but the LORD tests hearts — Ber

The melting-pot is for silver and the crucible for gold,
but it is the LORD who assays the hearts of men — NEB

For silver and gold, furnace and crucible; men's hearts are for the Lord's assaying — Knox

4. A wicked doer giveth heed to false lips; and a liar giveth ear to a naughty tongue.

An evil doer is attentive to lips of vanity,
Falsehood is giving ear to a mischievous tongue — YLT

An evil-doer giveth heed to wicked lips;
And a liar giveth ear to a mischievous tongue — ASV

An evil man pays heed to wicked words;
A false man gives ear to mischievous speech — AAT

Only a base man listens to malicious words;
only the false attend to mischievous talk — Mof

An evildoer listens to wicked lips, and a liar pays attention to a vicious tongue — Ber

5. Whoso mocketh the poor reproacheth his Maker: and he that is glad at calamities shall not be unpunished.

He who derideth a man in distress provoketh his maker; and he who rejoiceth at another's ruin shall not go unpunished — Sept

He that mocks at the poor scorns his Maker;
He that rejoices at calamity shall not be acquitted — ABPS

Whoso scorneth the poor reproacheth his Maker;
And whoso rejoiceth at distress shall not be innocent — Sprl

Whoever makes sport of the poor puts shame on his Maker; and he who is glad because of trouble will not go free from punishment — Bas

He who mocks the poor provokes his Maker; and he who is glad at calamity shall not be forgiven — Lam

A man who sneers at the poor insults his Maker,
and he who gloats over another's ruin will answer for it — NEB

6. Children's children are the crown of old men; and the glory of children are their fathers.

Sons' sons are the crown of old men,
And the glory of sons are their fathers — YLT

The crown of old men consists of childrens' children,
And the adornment of children is their fathers — Rhm

Grandchildren are the crown of the aged,
and the glory of sons is their fathers — RSV

An old man's grandchildren are his crowning glory. A child's glory is his father — Tay

Grandchildren are the crown of old men,
and the glory of children is their parentage — NAB

7. Excellent speech becometh not a fool: much less do lying lips a prince.

Fine speech is not becoming to a fool;
still less is false speech to a prince — RSV

Fine words are out of place in a fool;
how much more, lying words in a noble — NAB

Excellent speech is not suitable for a fool;
Much less is a lying lip for a noble — ABPS

Excellent speech is not suitable in a fool, much less deceitful speech in a prince — Ber

Overbearing speech becometh not a churl;
Much less do lying lips a prince — JPS

Fair words are not to be looked for from a foolish man, much less are false lips in a ruler — Bas

8. A gift is as a precious stone in the eyes of him that hath it: whithersoever it turneth, it prospereth.[13]

[13]The key word 'gift, gratuity' often has the connotation of 'bribe'; and many have so construed it here.

A gift in the eyes of its owner is a stone of beauty,
Whithersoever it turneth it bringeth prosperity — Rhm

A gift is a precious stone in the eyes of its possessor;
To whomsoever it turns, it prospers — ABPS

A gift works like a talisman for him who gives it:
he prospers whichever way he turns — Jerus

A bribe is a precious stone in the eyes of him that hath it;
Whithersoever it turneth, it prospereth — ASV

A stone of grace is the bribe in the eyes of its possessors,
Whithersoever it turneth, it prospereth — YLT

A bribe is a precious gem in the eyes of him who has it;
Wherever he turns, he prospers — AAT

9. He that covereth a transgression seeketh love; but he that repeateth a matter separateth very friends.

Whoso hideth a transgression seeketh after love;
But whoso repeateth a matter disuniteth confidential friends — Sprl

He that covereth a transgression seeketh love: but he that harpeth on a matter separateth chief friends — RV

He that covereth a transgression seeketh love;
But he that harpeth on a matter estrangeth a familiar friend — JPS

He who forgives an offense seeks love, but he who repeats a matter alienates a friend — RSV

He who covers up a misdeed fosters friendship,
but he who gossips about it separates friends — NAB

Love forgets mistakes; nagging about them parts the best of friends — Tay

10. A reproof entereth more into a wise man than an hundred stripes into a fool.

A rebuke entereth deeper into one that hath understanding
Than a hundred stripes into a fool — ASV

A reproof sinketh more deeply into an intelligent man
Than a hundred stripes into a dullard — Rhm

A reproof sinks deeper in a man of understanding,
Than beating a fool a hundred times — ABPS

A rebuke sinks deeper into a man of intelligence
Than a hundred lashes into a fool — AAT

11. An evil man seeketh only rebellion: therefore a cruel messenger shall be sent against him.

Every wicked man stirreth up contention: but the Lord will send him a cruel messenger — Sept

An uncontrolled man is only looking for trouble, so a cruel servant will be sent against him — Bas

A seditious man seeketh only rebellion;
But a messenger of vengeance shall be sent against him — Sprl

A wicked man seeks only rebellion; but a stern messenger will be sent against him — Ber

On rebellion alone is the wicked man bent,
but a merciless messenger will be sent against him — NAB

12. Let a bear robbed of her whelps meet a man, rather than a fool in his folly.

Let a bereaved bear encounter a man,
Rather than a dullard with his folly — Rhm

Let a bear robbed of her young meet a man,
And not a fool in his folly — ABPS

Let a man meet a she-bear robbed of her cubs,
rather than a fool in his folly — RSV

Better face a she-bear robbed of her cubs
than a stupid man in his folly — NEB

13. Whoso rewardeth evil for good, evil shall not depart from his house.

Whoso is returning evil for good,
Evil moveth not from his house — YLT

If anyone gives back evil for good, evil will never go away from his house — Bas

Whoever returns evil for good, calam-

ity will not leave his house — Ber
Evil shall still haunt his dwelling, that repays kindness with injury — Knox

14. The beginning of strife is as when one letteth out water: therefore leave off contention, before it be meddled with.
The commencement of strife is like the breaking forth of waters;
Therefore cease from a dispute before it degenerates into rage — Sprl
The beginning of contention is the breaking forth of water;
Desist then, before the strife is embittered — ABPS
The beginning of strife is as when one letteth out water;
Therefore leave off contention, before there is quarrelling — ASV
The start of fighting is like the letting out of water: so give up before it comes to blows — Bas
As well loose a flood as initiate legal proceedings;
break off before the dispute begins — Jerus
The start of strife is like the opening of a dam;
therefore, check a quarrel before it begins! — NAB

15. He that justifieth the wicked, and he that condemneth the just, even they both are abomination to the LORD.
He who acquitteth the wicked and condemneth the just, is unclean and abominable in the sight of God — Sept
He that justifieth the lawless and he that condemneth the righteous
An abomination to Yahweh are they both — Rhm
He who acquits the guilty, and he who condemns the innocent —
Both of them are an abomination to the LORD — AAT
To acquit the wicked and condemn the righteous,
both are abominable in the LORD's sight — NEB

16. Wherefore is there a price in the hand of a fool to get wisdom, seeing he hath no heart to it?
Wherefore this — a price in the hand of a fool
To purchase wisdom, when he hath no desire after it? — Sprl
What good is wealth in the possession of a fool who has no desire to acquire wisdom? — Lam
Why does a fool offer the sage a fee, when he has no mind to learn? — Mof
Wherefore is there a price in the hand of a fool to buy wisdom,
Seeing he hath no understanding? — ASV
Why is this — a price in the hand of a fool to buy wisdom, when he has no capacity? — Ber
Of what use is money in the hand of a fool
To buy wisdom, when he has no sense? — AAT
Of what use in the fool's hand are the means
to buy wisdom, since he has no mind for it? — NAB

17. A friend loveth at all times, and a brother is born for adversity.
A friend is loving at all times, and becomes a brother in times of trouble — Bas
A friend is always a friend,
he is a born brother for adversity — Mof
A friend is a friend at all times,
it is for adversity that a brother is born — Jerus
A friend is a loving companion at all times,
and a brother is born to share troubles — NEB
A true friend is always loyal, and a brother is born to help in time of need — Tay

18. A man void of understanding striketh hands, and becometh surety in the presence of his friend.
A man lacking sense is one who striketh hands,
Giving security before his neighbour — Rhm
A man without sense gives a pledge,
and becomes surety in the presence of his neighbor— RSV
A man without sense gives his hand in an agreement, and makes himself responsible before his neighbour — Bas
Senseless is the man who gives his hand in pledge,
who becomes surety for his neighbor — NAB

It is poor judgment to countersign another's note, to become responsible for his debts — Tay

19. He loveth transgression that loveth strife: and he that exalteth his gate seeketh destruction.

He loveth transgression who loveth strife;
And whoso is of haughty demeanour seeketh destruction — Sprl

He loves sin that loves contention;
He that makes high his gate seeks ruin — ABPS

He loves punishment who loves strife;
He courts destruction who builds his gate high — AAT

He who is fond of strife is fond of getting wounded;
he who talks arrogantly courts disaster — Mof

He who loves transgression loves strife, and he who opens wide his mouth seeks destruction — Ber

He loves a feud, that loves contention; build high, and court thy ruin — Knox

20. He that hath a froward heart findeth no good: and he that hath a perverse tongue falleth into mischief.

He that hath a wayward heart findeth no good;
And he that hath a perverse tongue falleth into mischief — ASV

The crooked in heart shall not find good,
And he that is perverse with his tongue shall fall into wickedness — Rhm

A man of crooked mind does not prosper,
and one with a perverse tongue falls into calamity — RSV

Nothing good comes to him whose heart is fixed on evil purposes: and he who has an evil tongue will come to trouble — Bas

The contrary heart does not find happiness,
the deceitful tongue falls into distress — Jerus

21. He that begetteth a fool doeth it to his sorrow: and the father of a fool hath no joy.

Whoso is begetting a fool hath affliction for it,
Yea, the father of a fool rejoiceth not — YLT

One begets a fool to his own sorrow;
And the father of the foolish shall not have joy — ABPS

He who begets a fool does it to his own shame; his father will have no joy in him — Lam

He that begetteth a fool doeth it to his sorrow;
And the father of a churl hath no joy — JPS

He who begets a fool does it to his sorrow;
And the father of a dolt will have no joy of him — AAT

To be a fool's parent is grief for a man; the father of a numskull has no joy — NAB

22. A merry heart doeth good like a medicine: but a broken spirit drieth the bones.

A cheerful heart is a good medicine;
But a broken spirit drieth up the bones — ASV

A cheerful heart is a good medicine,
but a downcast spirit dries up the bones — RSV

A rejoicing heart doth good to the body,
And a smitten spirit drieth the bone — YLT

A joyful heart worketh an excellent cure, —
But a stricken spirit drieth up the bone — Rhm

A cheerful heart makes a quick recovery, it is crushed spirits that waste a man's frame — Knox

A merry heart makes a cheerful countenance,
but low spirits sap a man's strength — NEB

23. A wicked man taketh a gift out of the bosom to pervert the ways of judgment.

A wicked man receiveth a bribe into his bosom;
Thus to pervert the ways of judgment — Sprl

A wicked man receiveth a bribe out of the bosom,
To pervert the ways of justice — ASV

A wicked man will accept a bribe from the bosom
To divert the course of justice — AAT

Bad men accept a secret bribe,
to twist the course of justice — Mof
Under cover of the cloak a venal man takes a gift
to pervert the course of justice — Jerus

24. Wisdom is before him that hath understanding; but the eyes of a fool are in the ends of the earth.
Before the face of the discerning is wisdom,
But the eyes of the dullard are in the ends of the earth — Rhm
Surely wisdom is present to the man of understanding;
But the eyes of the fool rove unto the ends of the world — Sprl
The face of a man of understanding is set toward wisdom; but the eyes of a fool are in the depths of the earth — Lam
A man of understanding sets his face toward wisdom,
but the eyes of a fool are on the ends of the earth — RSV
Wisdom is never out of sight of a discerning man,
but a stupid man's eyes are roving everywhere — NEB
The thoughtful are absorbed in wisdom,
but a fool's eyes go roaming far and wide — Mof

25. A foolish son is a grief to his father, and bitterness to her that bare him.
A foolish son is a vexation to a father; and sorrow to her who bore him — Sept
A foolish son is a grief to his father, and bitter pain to her who gave him birth — Bas
A foolish son is his father's sorrow, and the grief of her who gave him birth — Jerus
A rebellious son is a grief to his father and a bitter blow to his mother — Tay
A provocation to his father is a foolish son,
And bitterness to her that bare him — YLT

26. Also to punish the just is not good, nor to strike princes for equity.
Also to punish the righteous is not good,
Nor to smite the noble for their uprightness — ASV
Surely to fine the just is not right;
And to smite the liberal, not justice — Sprl
Also it is not good to lay a fine on the righteous,
To smite the noble for uprightness — ABPS
It is not fair to fine the innocent,
and most unfair to scourge a noble soul — Mof
To impose a fine on a righteous man is not good;
to flog noble men is wrong — RSV
it is wrong to fine an innocent man,
but beyond reason to scourge princes — NAB

27. He that hath knowledge spareth his words: and a man of understanding is of an excellent spirit.

28. Even a fool, when he holdeth his peace, is counted wise: and he that shutteth his lips is esteemed a man of understanding.
One acquainted with knowledge is sparing his words,
And the cool of temper is a man of understanding.
Even a fool keeping silence is reckoned wise,
He who is shutting his lips intelligent — YLT
He that spareth his words hath knowledge: and he that is of a cool spirit is a man of understanding.
Even a fool, when he holdeth his peace, is counted wise: when he shutteth his lips, he is esteemed as prudent — RV
Sparing of his words is one who valueth knowledge,
And of a thoughtful spirit is a man of intelligence.
Even a fool holding his peace is accounted wise, —
He that closeth his lips is thought to have understanding — Rhm
He who restrains his words has knowledge, and he who is calm of spirit is a man of understanding.
Even a fool when he is silent is thought to be wise, and he who keeps his lips closed is considered intelligent — Ber

A man who can control his tongue has knowledge,
a man of discernment keeps his temper cool.
If a fool can hold his tongue, even he can pass for wise,
and pass for clever if he keeps his lips shut — Jerus

Experience uses few words;
discernment keeps a cool head.
Even a fool, if he holds his peace, is thought wise;
keep your mouth shut and show your good sense — NEB

A man of sense is sparing of his words;
the prudent will keep cool.
Even a fool may pass for wise, if he says nothing;
with closed lips he may be counted sensible — Mof

CHAPTER 18

1. Through desire a man, having separated himself, seeketh and inter-meddleth with all wisdom.

A man seeketh for satisfaction going his own way,
Through all safe counsel he breaketh —Rhm

He that separateth himself seeketh his own desire,
And rageth against all sound wisdom — ASV

He that separates himself seeks his own pleasure;
Against all good counsel he is embittered — ABPS

He that separateth himself seeketh his own desire,
And snarlest against all sound wisdom — JPS

The recluse seeks his own selfish interests;
He quarrels with every sound principle — AAT

He who is estranged seeks pretexts
to break out against all sound judgment — RSV

2. A fool hath no delight in understanding, but that his heart may discover itself.

The fool hath no pleasure in knowledge,
Save only in displaying his own understanding — Sprl

A fool delighteth not in understanding,
But — in uncovering his heart — YLT

A foolish man has no pleasure in good sense,
but only to let what is in his heart come to light — Bas

A fool has no delight in learning,
but only in displaying what he is — Mof

The fool takes no delight in understanding,
but rather in displaying what he thinks — NAB

3. When the wicked cometh, then cometh also contempt, and with ignominy reproach.

When the lawless man cometh in then cometh also contempt,
And with shame reproach — Rhm

When the wicked comes, then comes also contempt,
And reproach along with shame — ABPS

With wickedness comes contempt;
And with dishonor comes disgrace — AAT

When wickedness comes, contempt comes too,
and, with disgrace, dishonour — Jerus

When wickedness comes in, in comes contempt;
with loss of honour comes reproach — NEB

4. The words of a man's mouth are as deep waters, and the wellspring of wisdom as a flowing brook.

The words of a man's mouth are like deep waters;
But the fountain of wisdom as a flowing brook — Sprl

The words of a man's mouth are as deep waters;
A flowing brook, a fountain of wisdom — JPS

The words of wise men are a deep pool,
a flowing stream, a fountain of life — Mof

The words from a man's mouth are deep waters,

but the source of wisdom is a flowing brook — NAB

Man's utterance has currents like the waters that run deep; from wisdom's well flows a stream in full flood — Knox

5. It is not good to accept the person of the wicked, to overthrow the righteous in judgment.

To prefer a lawless man is not good,
Thrusting away the righteous in judgment — Rhm

To respect the person of the wicked is not good,
Nor to turn aside the righteous in judgment — ASV

It is not good to show partiality to the wicked, to deprive a righteous man of justice — Ber

It is not good to be partial to a wicked man,
or to deprive a righteous man of justice — RSV

It is wrong for a judge to favor the wicked and condemn the innocent — Tay

6. A fool's lips enter into contention, and his mouth calleth for strokes.

7. A fool's mouth is his destruction, and his lips are the snare of his soul.

The lips of the depraved cause strife;
And his mouth proclaimeth, "Unto the battle!"
The fool's mouth is his destruction,
And his lips ensnare his soul — Sprl

The lips of a fool lead him into trouble; and his mouth when bold provoketh death.
The mouth of a fool is his destruction, and his lips are a snare for his soul — Sept

A fool's talk gets him into trouble,
his tongue brings him a beating.
A fool's tongue is the ruin of him,
his talk is a snare to himself — Mof

A fool's lips bring strife,
and his mouth invites a flogging.
A fool's mouth is his ruin,
and his lips are a snare to himself — RSV

The lips of the fool draw him into arguments
and his mouth pleads for a beating.
The mouth of the fool works his own ruin,
his lips are a snare for his own life — Jerus

8. The words of a talebearer are as wounds, and they go down into the innermost parts of the belly.[14]

The words of a tale-bearer are as self-inflicted wounds,
And they have gone down to the inner parts of the heart — YLT

The words of a tale-bearer are greedily swallowed down,
And they descend into the interior of the body — Sprl

The words of a whisperer are as dainty morsels,
And they go down into the innermost parts — ASV

The words of a gossip are tempting morsels, and they go down into the inner parts of the body — Ber

The words of a talebearer are like dainty morsels
that sink into one's inmost being — NAB

What dainty morsels rumors are. They are eaten with great relish! — Tay

9. He also that is slothful in his work is brother to him that is a great waster.

He also that is slack in his work is brother to him that is a destroyer — RV

Also he that shows himself slack in his service,
The same is a brother to the wasteful — ABPS

He who does not give his mind to his work is brother to him who makes destruction — Bas

Again, the lazy worker is own brother to the man who enjoys destruction — NEB

A lazy man is brother to the saboteur — Tay

10. The name of the LORD is a strong tower: the righteous runneth into it, and is safe.

A tower of strength is the name of Jehovah,
Into it the righteous runneth, and is set on high — YLT

The name of the LORD is a strong tower; into it runs the righteous and cannot be touched — Ber

[14]Nearly all others agree with the ASV rendering.

The Name of JEHOVAH is a strong tower;
The righteous runneth into it, and is secure — Sprl

No stronghold like the Lord's name; there the just take refuge, high above reach — Knox

11. The rich man's wealth is his strong city, and as a high wall in his own conceit.

The substance of a rich man is his strong city,
And like a high wall in his imagination — Rhm

A rich man's wealth is his stronghold, like a bulwark — so he thinks — Mof

A rich man's wealth is his fortress;
And like a high wall are his riches — AAT

A rich man's wealth is his strong city, a towering wall, so he supposes — NEB

12. Before destruction the heart of man is haughty; and before honour is humility.

Before destruction the heart of man is full of pride, and before honour goes a gentle spirit — Bas

The human heart is haughty until destruction comes,
humility goes before honour — Jerus

Before his downfall a man's heart is haughty,
but humility goes before honors — NAB

yet hearts are proudest when ruin is nearest; humility is the antechamber of renown — Knox

Haughtiness ends in disaster: to be humble is the way to honour — Mof

13. He that answereth a matter before he heareth it, it is folly and shame unto him.

He that giveth answer before he heareth,
It is folly and shame unto him — ASV

He that giveth answer before he heareth,
It is folly and confusion unto him — JPS

He who answereth a matter before he heareth it, exposeth his folly and incurreth contempt — Sept

He who answers a matter before he hears the facts, it is folly and shame to him — Amp

To answer a question before you have heard it out
is both stupid and insulting — NEB

14. The spirit of a man will sustain his infirmity; but a wounded spirit who can bear?

The spirit of a man will sustain his infirmity; but a broken spirit who can bear — RV

The spirit of a man will sustain his sickness;
But a broken spirit, who can bear it — ABPS

A man's spirit will endure sickness;
but a broken spirit who can bear — RSV

The spirit of a man will endure his suffering; but a distressing spirit who can bear — Lam

The spirit of a man sustaineth his sickness,
But a dejected spirit who can bear it — Rhm

A man's courage can sustain his broken body, but when courage dies, what hope is left — Tay

15. The heart of the prudent getteth knowledge; and the ear of the wise seeketh knowledge.

The heart of the intelligent getteth knowledge,
And the ear of the wise seeketh knowledge — YLT

The heart of a prudent man getteth knowledge; and the ears of the wise seek understanding — Sept

The heart of the discerning will get knowledge;
And for knowledge the ear of the wise will seek — ABPS

An intelligent mind acquires knowledge,
and the ear of the wise seeks knowledge — RSV

The mind of the intelligent gains knowledge,
and the ear of the wise seeks knowledge — NAB

16. A man's gift maketh room for him, and bringeth him before great men.

A man's gift will open up the way for him,

And will conduct him into the presence of the great — Sprl

A present opens every door for you and wins you access to the great — Jerus

A man's gift clears the way for him, and gains him access to great men — NAB

A present paves the way for any suitor, it wins him access to authorities — Mof

A bribe does wonders: it will bring you before men of importance — Tay

17. He that is first in his own cause seemeth just; but his neighbour cometh and searcheth him.

18. The lot causeth contentions to cease, and parteth between the mighty.

He that pleadeth his cause first seemeth just;
But his neighbor cometh and searcheth him out.
The lot causeth contentions to cease, and parteth between the mighty — ASV

He who states his case first seems right, until the other comes and examines him.
The lot puts an end to disputes and decides between powerful contenders — RSV

He who pleads first in a case appears to be in the right;
Then his rival comes and tests him.
The lot puts an end to disputes,
And decides between powerful rivals — AAT

He who puts his case first seems right, until his rival comes and cross-examines him.
To cast lots puts an end to disputes, and decides between powerful contenders — Amp

In a lawsuit the first speaker seems right,
until another steps forward and cross-questions him.
Cast lots, and settle a quarrel,
and so keep litigants apart — NEB

The man who first puts his cause before the judge seems to be in the right; but then his neighbour comes and puts his cause in its true light. The decision of chance puts an end to argument, parting the strong — Bas

19. A brother offended is harder to be won than a strong city: and their contentions are like the bars of a castle.

A brother transgressed against is as a strong city,
And contentions as the bar of a palace — YLT

A brother estranged is harder to win than a strong city;
And contentions are as the bar of a fortress — ABPS

An offended brother is like a strong city;
And his contentions are as the bars of a lofty tower — Sprl

A reluctant brother is more unyielding than a fortress,
and quarrels are stubborn as the bars of a castle — NEB

It is harder to win back the friendship of an offended brother than to capture a fortified city. His anger shuts you out like iron bars — Tay

20. A man's belly shall be satisfied with the fruit of his mouth; and with the increase of his lips shall he be filled.

A man's belly shall be filled with the fruit of his mouth;
With the increase of his lips shall he be satisfied — ASV

A man's body shall be satisfied with the fruit of his mouth;
With the produce of his lips shall he be filled — Sprl

Of the fruit of a man's mouth shall his inmost mind be satisfied,
With the product of his lips shall he be satisfied — Rhm

A man's moral self shall be filled with the fruit of his mouth, and with the consequences of his words he must be satisfied . . . — Amp

As mouth speaks, belly shall find its fare; a man's own words bear the fruit that must needs content him — Knox

A man may live by the fruit of his tongue,
his lips may earn him a livelihood — NEB

21. Death and life are in the power of the tongue: and they that love it shall eat the fruit thereof.

Death and life are in the power of the tongue;

And they that indulge it shall eat the fruit thereof — JPS

Death and life are determined by the tongue: the talkative must take the consequences — Mof

Death and life are in the power of the tongue;
those who make it a friend shall eat its fruit — NAB

Of life and death, tongue holds the keys; use it lovingly, and it will requite thee — Knox

Those who love to talk will suffer the consequences. Men have died for saying the wrong thing — Tay

22. Whoso findeth a wife findeth a good thing, and obtaineth favour of the LORD.

Who hath found a wife hath found a blessing,
And hath obtained favour from Yahweh — Rhm

Whoso findeth a wife findeth a great good,
And obtaineth favour of the LORD — JPS

He who finds a wife finds good fortune;
He wins favor from the LORD — AAT

He who has found a wife has gained a goodly portion. and obtains favor from the LORD — Ber

Whoever get a wife gets a good thing, and has the approval of the Lord — Bas

He who finds a wife finds happiness;
it is a favor he receives from the LORD — NAB

23. The poor useth entreaties; but the rich answereth roughly.

With supplications doth the poor speak,
And the rich answereth fierce things — YLT

The poor speak humbly; but the rich talk of great things — Lam

The poor man's language is entreaty, the rich man's answer harshness — Jerus

The poor useth entreaties;
But the rich answereth impudently — JPS

The poor man pleads and the rich man answers with insults — Tay

The poor man implores,
but the rich man answers harshly — NAB

24. A man that hath friends must shew himself friendly: and there is a friend that sticketh closer than a brother.[15]

A man with friends is to show himself friendly,
And there is a lover adhering more than a brother — YLT

A man of friendliness shall have many friends,
And there is a friend who sticketh closer than a brother — Sprl

He that maketh many friends doeth it to his own destruction;
But there is a friend that sticketh closer than a brother — ASV

A man having many friends shall come to ruin,
But there is a loving one who sticketh closer than a brother — Rhm

There are friends who pretend to be friends,
but there is a friend who sticks closer than a brother — RSV

Some friends bring ruin on us,
but a true friend is more loyal than a brother — NAB

There are friends who only bring you loss:
there is a friend more loyal than a brother — Mof

CHAPTER 19

1. Better is the poor that walketh in his integrity, than he that is perverse in his lips, and is a fool.

Better is a poor man walking in his integrity,
Than one of perverse lips and he a dullard — Rhm

Better a poor man living an honest life than the adept at doubletalk who is a fool — Jerus

Better is the poor that walketh in his integrity,
Than he that is perverse in his lips and a fool at the same time — JPS

Better is the poor who walketh in his integrity,

[15]Only YLT and Sprl are in some agreement with KJV. The majority, however, agree in sense with ASV, RSV, et al., above.

Than he who is perverse in his way though he be rich — Sprl

Better a poor man, who walks in his integrity,
Than one who is crooked in his ways, although he be rich — AAT

Better is the poor man whose ways are upright, than the man of wealth whose ways are twisted — Bas

Better be poor and honest than rich and dishonest — Tay

2. Also, that the soul be without knowledge, it is not good; and he that hasteth with his feet sinneth.

Surely it is not well for the soul to be without knowledge;
For whoso hasteth with his feet transgresseth — Sprl

It is not good for a man to be without knowledge,
and he who makes haste with his feet misses his way — RSV

Even as it is not good to be ignorant, so he who hurries his feet misses the mark — Ber

Also that the soul be without knowledge is not good;
And he that is hasty with the feet mis-steps — ABPS

It is no use to act before you think: to be hasty is to miss the mark — Mof

Without knowledge even zeal is not good;
and he who acts hastily, blunders — NAB

3. The foolishness of man perverteth his way: and his heart fretteth against the LORD.

The foolishness of man subverteth his way;
And his heart fretteth against Jehovah — ASV

By his foolish behaviour a man's ways are turned upside down, and his heart is bitter against the Lord — Bas

When a man's folly brings his way to ruin,
his heart rages against the LORD — RSV

The foolishness of man ruins his affairs, but his heart is resentful toward the LORD — Ber

A man's own folly wrecks his life,
and then he bears a grudge against the LORD — NEB

It is man's folly that spoils his fortunes,
yet it is against Yahweh that his heart rages — Jerus

4. Wealth makes many friends; but the poor is separated from his neighbour.

Wealth addeth many friends: but the poor is separated from his friend — RV

Wealth gathereth together many friends;
But the poor is unnoticed by his own neighbour — Sprl

Wealth makes many friends; but a poor man is deserted by his friends — Lam

Wealth makes many friends, but the poor is avoided by his neighbor — Amp

Wealth brings many a friend,
but a poor man's only friend will leave him — Mof

5. A false witness shall not be unpunished; and he that speaketh lies shall not escape.

A false witness shall not be held innocent,
And he that uttereth lies shall not escape — Rhm

A false witness shall not be acquitted;
And he that breathes lies shall not escape — ABPS

A false witness shall not go unpunished; and he who accuseth unjustly shall not escape — Sept

Perjury will bring its own punishment; never was liar yet that escaped his doom — Knox

6. Many will entreat the favour of the prince: and every man is a friend to him that giveth gifts.

Many will entreat the favor of the liberal man;
And every man is a friend to him that giveth gifts — ASV

Many importune the favour of the noble;
And each one is a friend to the man of gifts — Sprl

Many make court to a noble;
And every one is friend to a liberal man — ABPS

Many seek the favor of a generous man,

and every one is a friend to a man who gives gifts — RSV

Many pay court to a bountiful man: all are friends of a man who gives presents — Mof

7. All the brethren of the poor do hate him: how much more do his friends go far from him? he pursueth them with words, yet they are wanting to him.

The poor man's brothers hate him, every one;
his friends — how much the more do these desert him!
He goes in search of words, but there are none to be had — Jerus

The poor man, he is shunned of all his brethren;
How much more do his neighbours stand aloof from him?
He pursueth after them with entreaties — but in vain — Sprl

A poor man's brothers all hate him;
How much more do his friends stand aloof from him!
When he pursues them with words, they are gone — AAT

A poor man's own brothers turn away from him in embarrassment; how much more his friends! He calls after them, but they are gone — Tay

8. He that getteth wisdom loveth his own soul: he that keepeth understanding shall find good.

He who procureth wisdom loveth himself; and he who keepeth it shall find good things — Sept

He that acquireth sense loveth his own soul,
He that guardeth understanding shall find blessing — Rhm

He who gets wisdom loves himself; he who keeps understanding will prosper — RSV

He who gains intelligence is his own best friend;
he who keeps understanding will be successful — NAB

9. A false witness shall not be unpunished; and he that speaketh lies shall perish.[16]

10. Delight is not seemly for a fool; much less for a servant to have rule over princes.

Delicate living is not seemly for a fool;
Much less for a servant to have rule over princes — ASV

Luxury is not seemly for a fool;
Much less for a servant to have rule over princes — JPS

Luxury is not fitting for a fool,
much less for a slave to lord it over nobles — Mof

Ill days, when fools live in comfort; worse yet, when servants sway their own masters — Knox

It doesn't seem right for a fool to succeed or for a slave to rule over princes — Tay

11. The discretion of a man deferreth his anger; and it is his glory to pass over a transgression.

A man's discretion deferreth his wrath;
And it is his honour to pass by a transgression — Sprl

The discretion of a man maketh him slow to anger; and it is his glory to pass over a transgression — RV

It is good sense in a man to be forbearing,
And it is his glory to pass over an offense — AAT

A man's wisdom makes him slow to anger;
And it is his glory to pass over a fault — ABPS

It is prudent for a man to restrain his anger; it is his glory to overlook an offense — Ber

12. The king's wrath is as the roaring of a lion; but his favour is as dew upon the grass.

The wrath of a king is a growl as of a young lion,
And as dew on the herb is his good-will — YLT

The growl as of a young lion is the rage of a king,
But like dew upon the grass is his good pleasure — Rhm

A king's wrath is like a lion's roar;
But his favor is like dew on the grass — AAT

The king's anger is as dangerous as a lion's.
But his approval is as refreshing as the dew on the grass — Tay

---

[16]Compare vs. 5, above.

13. A foolish son is the calamity of his father:
A foolish son is a grievous affliction to his father — Sprl
A foolish son is ruin to his father — RSV
Great hurt it is to be a fool's father — Knox
A foolish son is the destruction of his father — Bas
A stupid son is a calamity to his father — NEB
and the contentions of a wife are a continual dropping.
And the bickerings of a wife are a continual dripping — ABPS
and the quarreling of a wife is as a constant dripping of water — Ber
and the nagging of a wife is an endless dripping — Mof
a woman's scolding is like a dripping gutter — Jerus

14. House and riches are the inheritance of fathers: and a prudent wife is from the LORD.
House and substance are an inheritance from one's fathers,
But from Yahweh cometh a wife who is prudent — Rhm
Fathers bequeath houses and wealth to children; but the Lord accommodateth a wife to a husband — Sept
House and wealth are an inheritance from fathers;
But a sensible wife is a gift from the LORD — AAT
House and wealth are a heritage from fathers, but a wife with good sense is from the Lord — Bas
A father can give his sons homes and riches, but only the Lord can give them understanding wives — Tay

15. Slothfulness casteth into a deep sleep; and an idle soul shall suffer hunger.
Sloth causeth deep sleep to fall,
And an indolent soul doth hunger — YLT
Sloth falleth into a deep sleep,
And a soul that is indolent shall famish — Rhm
Laziness makes one sleep heavily; an idle person will suffer hunger — Ber
Laziness plunges a man into deep sleep,
and the sluggard must go hungry — NAB
Sloth brings the sleep that has no awaking; idle hands, empty belly — Knox

16. He that guardeth the commandment keepeth his own soul; but he that despiseth his ways shall die.
He who keepeth the commandment preserveth his soul;
But he who despiseth His directions shall die — Sprl
He that keepeth the commandment keepeth his soul;
But he that is careless of his ways shall die — ASV
He who keeps the law keeps his own soul; but he who despises right ways shall die — Lam
To keep the commandments keeps a man safe,
but scorning the way of the LORD brings death — NEB
Keep the commandments and keep your life; despising them means death — Tay

17. He that hath pity upon the poor lendeth unto the LORD; and that which he hath given will he pay him again.
He who is kind to the poor lendeth to God; and according to his gift he will repay him — Sept
He that hath pity upon the poor lendeth unto the LORD, and his good deed will he pay him again — RV
He that is gracious unto the poor lendeth unto the LORD,
And his good deed will He repay unto him — JPS
He who is gracious to the poor is lending to the LORD; He will repay him for his benevolent action — Ber
He who cares for the poor is lending to the Eternal,
and for his kindness he shall be repaid — Mof
Befriend the poor, and lend to the Lord; he will repay faithfully — Knox

18. Chasten thy son while there is hope, and let not thy soul spare for his crying.[17]

---

[17]Only Sprl agrees with KJV. Most others basically agree with ASV/RV; but perhaps Mof and Tay catch the real meaning?

Correct thy son whilst there is hope;
And let not thy soul compassionate when he crieth aloud — Sprl

Chasten thy son, seeing there is hope;
And set not thy heart on his destruction — ASV

Chasten thy son, for there is hope;
But set not thy heart on his destruction — JPS

Correct thy son because there is hope,
Yet not so as to slay him let thy passion be excited — Rhm

Chastise your son while there is hope for him,
but be careful not to flog him to death — NEB

Chastise your son, while there is still hope of him,
and do not let him run to ruin — Mof

Discipline your son in his early years while there is hope. If you don't you will ruin his life — Tay

19. A man of great wrath shall suffer punishment: for if thou deliver him, yet thou must do it again.

The man of impatient wrath shall endure punishment;
For if thou deliverest him, yet will he again offend — Sprl

He that is rough in anger suffers punishment;
For if thou deliver, then thou must do it again — ABPS

A man of great wrath shall bear the penalty;
For if thou deliver him, thou must do it yet again — ASV

A man who gives way to anger must pay for it;
And if you come to his rescue, you will only add to his anger — AAT

A man of great wrath will have to take his punishment: for if you get him out of trouble you will have to do it again — Bas

20. Hear counsel, and receive instruction, that thou mayest be wise in thy latter end.

Hear counsel and receive correction;
That thou mayest be wise in thy after years — ABPS

Hear counsel, and accept instruction,
That you may be wise in the days to come — AAT

Listen to advice and accept instruction,
that you may gain wisdom for the future — RSV

Listen to counsel and receive instruction,
that you may eventually become wise — NAB

21. There are many devices in a man's heart; nevertheless the counsel of the LORD, that shall stand.

Changeable are the devices in the heart of a man;
But JEHOVAH's counsel, that shall endure — Sprl

There are many devices in a man's heart; nevertheless the counsel of the LORD shall stand firm — Lam

Many schemes are in a man's mind, but the counsel of the LORD will stand — Ber

Many are the plans in the mind of a man,
but it is the purpose of the LORD that will be established — RSV

A man's heart may be full of schemes, but the LORD's purpose will prevail — NEB

22. The desire of a man is his kindness: and a poor man is better than a liar.

The charm of a man is his lovingkindness, —
And better a poor man than one who deceiveth — Rhm

That which maketh a man to be desired is his kindness;
And a poor man is better than a liar — ASV

The charm of a man is his kindness;
And better is the poor than a man of falsehood — ABPS

Friendliness bears fruit for a man:
better be poor and good than false — Mof

A man's attraction lies in his kindness,
better a poor man than a liar — Jerus

Kindness makes a man attractive. And it is better to be poor than dishonest — Tay

23. The fear of the LORD tendeth to life: and he that hath it shall abide satisfied; he shall not be visited with evil.

The fear of JEHOVAH tendeth to life;
And whoso is filled with it shall abide, neither be visited with evil — Sprl

The reverence of Yahweh leadeth to life,
Satisfied then let a man remain — let him not be visited by calamity — Rhm

Reverence for the LORD conduces to life;
He who is satisfied with that will abide unvisited by misfortune — AAT

Reverence for the LORD leads to life; he who remains satisfied with that will not be visited by harm — Ber

The fear of the Lord gives life: and he who has it will have need of nothing; no evil will come his way — Bas

The fear of the LORD is life;
he who is full of it will rest untouched by evil — NEB

24. A slothful man hideth his hand in his bosom, and will not so much as bring it to his mouth again.

The sluggard burieth his hand in the dish,
And will not so much as bring it to his mouth again — ASV

The lazy man drops his hand deep in the dish;
he will not so much as lift it to his lips — Mof

The hater of work puts his hand deep into the basin, and will not even take it to his mouth again — Bas

The sluggard loses his hand in the dish;
he will not even lift it to his mouth — NAB

25. Smite the scorner, and the simple will beware: and reprove one that hath understanding, and he will understand knowledge.

Smite a scoffer, and the simple will learn prudence;
And reprove one that hath understanding, and he will understand knowledge — ASV

When thou smitest a scorner, the simple will become prudent;
And when one that hath understanding is reproved, he will understand knowledge — JPS

If thou smite a scoffer, even the simple will deal wisely;
And admonish the discerning, he will learn knowledge — ABPS

Smite the scoffer, that, though simple, he may become wise;
And admonish the prudent, and he will acquire knowledge — Sprl

Strike a mocker and the ignorant will be more wary,
correct a man of discernment and he will listen to reason — Jerus

26. He that wasteth his father, and chaseth away his mother, is a son that causeth shame, and bringeth reproach.

He that doeth violence to his father, and chaseth away his mother,
Is a son that causeth shame and bringeth reproach — ASV

He who ill-treats his father and expels his mother
is a vile, despicable son — Mof

He that bringeth dishonour on a father and causeth his mother to flee; shall be exposed to shame and shall be reproached — Sept

A son who slanders his father and drives out his mother acts shamefully and disgracefully — Ber

A son who mistreats his father or mother is a public disgrace — Tay

He who mistreats his father, or drives away his mother,
is a worthless and disgraceful son — NAB

27. Cease, my son, to hear the instruction that causeth to err from the words of knowledge.

Cease, my son, to hear instruction only to err from the words of knowledge — RV

Cease, my son, to hear instruction only to stray from the words of knowledge — RSV

Give up listening to instruction, my son,
and ignoring what knowledge has to say — Jerus

If you cease, my son, to hear instruction,
You will wander from the words of knowledge — AAT

A son who ceases to accept correction is sure to turn his back on the teachings of knowledge — NEB

28. An ungodly witness scorneth judgment: and the mouth of the wicked devoureth iniquity.

A faithless witness derideth at justice;
And the mouth of the wicked swalloweth iniquity — Sprl

An ungodly witness mocketh at right;
And the mouth of the wicked devoureth iniquity — JPS

A worthless witness mocketh at justice;
And the mouth of the wicked swalloweth iniquity — ASV

A rascal of a witness scoffs at justice,
and perjury pours from a scoundrel's lips — Mof

An unprincipled witness perverts justice,
and the mouth of the wicked pours out iniquity — NAB

A rascally witness perverts justice,
and the talk of the wicked fosters mischief — NEB

29. Judgments are prepared for scorners, and stripes for the back of fools.

Prepared for scoffers are punishments,
And stripes for the back of dullards — Rhm

Punishments are prepared for scoffers;
And blows for the back of fools — AAT

Condemnation is ready for scoffers,
and flogging for the backs of fools — RSV

The stick was created for mockers,
and beating for the backs of fools — Jerus

There is a doom awaiting the reckless;
there are thick cudgels ready for the fool's back — Knox

Rods are prepared for the profligate:
and punishments in like manner for fools — Sept

CHAPTER 20

1. Wine is a mocker, strong drink is raging: and whosoever is deceived thereby is not wise.

Wine is a scoffer and strong drink a brawler,
Every one therefore who erreth therein is unwise — Rhm

Wine is a mocker, strong drink a brawler;
And whosoever erreth thereby is not wise — ASV

Wine is a mocker, strong drink is riotous;
And whosoever reeleth thereby is not wise — JPS

Wine mocketh, strong drink maketh an uproar,
And all they who indulge therein are not wise — Sprl

Wine is reckless, strong drink quarrelsome;
unwise is he whom it seduces — Jerus

Wine is an insolent fellow, and strong drink makes an uproar;
no one addicted to their company grows wise — NEB

2. The fear of a king is as the roaring of a lion: whoso provoketh him to anger sinneth against his own soul.

The fear of a king is a growl as of a young lion,
He who is causing him to be wroth is wronging his soul — YLT

The terror of a king is as the roaring of a lion: he that provoketh him to anger sinneth against his own life — RV

A king's rage is like a lion's roar;
He who provokes him to anger forfeits his life — AAT

The wrath of a king is like the loud cry of a lion: he who makes him angry does wrong against himself — Bas

Beware of the king's power, as of lion roaring; challenge it, and thy life is forfeit — Knox

3. It is an honour for a man to cease from strife: but every fool will be meddling.

Honour hath a man who sitteth away from strife,
But any fool may break through — Rhm

It is an honor to a man to dwell apart from strife;
But every fool will get angry — ABPS

It is an honor for a man to keep aloof from strife;
But every fool will be quarrelling — ASV

It is an honour for a man to abstain from railing; but with such things every fool is entangled — Sept

It is an honor for a man to stay out of a fight. Only fools insist on quarreling — Tay

4. The sluggard will not plow by reason of the cold; therefore shall he beg in harvest, and have nothing.

The slothful will not plow by reason of the winter; therefore he shall beg in harvest, and have nothing — RV

The sluggard will not plow, then winter setteth in;
Therefore he shall beg in harvest, and have nothing — JPS

The sluggard will not plow in autumn;
So in harvest he looks for a crop in vain — AAT

Autumn is over but the idler does not plough,
at harvest time he looks — nothing there! — Jerus

5. Counsel in the heart of man is like deep water; but a man of understanding will draw it out.

Counsel in the heart of man is like deep wells;
And a wise man draweth therefrom — Sprl

The purpose in a man's mind is like deep water,
but a man of understanding will draw it out — RSV

The intention in the human heart is like water far below the surface,
but a man of intelligence draws it forth — NAB

A man's mind may lie deep as water in a well,
but a clever man will draw it from him — Mof

Prudent counsel is a well buried deep in man's heart; but the wise know how to draw from it — Knox

6. Most men will proclaim every one his own goodness: but a faithful man who can find?

Most men will proclaim every one his own kindness;
But a faithful man who can find? — ASV

Many a man will proclaim his goodwill;
But a faithful man who shall find? — ABPS

Many a man proclaims his own steadfast love, but who can find a faithful man? — Ber

Many a man proclaims his own loyalty,
but a faithful man who can find? — RSV

Many a person is called kind,
but a trustworthy man is a rare find — Mof

Many a man protests his loyalty,
but where will you find one to keep faith? — NEB

7. The just man walketh in his integrity: his children are blessed after him.

A righteous man that walketh in his integrity,
Blessed are his children after him — ASV

He that walketh in his integrity as a just man,
Happy are his children after him — JPS

The righteous is walking habitually in his integrity,
O the happiness of his sons after him! — YLT

He who walks righteously in his integrity — how happy his children after him! — Ber

When a man walks in integrity and justice,
happy are his children after him! — NAB

8. A king that sitteth in the throne of judgment scattereth away all evil with his eyes.

A king, sitting on the throne of judgment,
Searches out all evil with his eyes — ABPS

A king who sits on the throne of judgment
winnows all evil with his eyes — RSV

A king seated on the throne of judgment
dispels all evil with his glance — NAB

A king seated on the judgment throne
Sifts every evil man with his eyes — AAT

A king seated on the judgement-throne
has an eye to sift all that is evil — NEB

When a righteous king sitteth on a throne, nothing that is evil can stand before his eyes — Sept

9. Who can say, I have made my heart clean, I am pure from my sin?

10. Divers weights, and divers measures,

both of them are alike abomination to the LORD.

Diverse weights and diverse measures, Both of them alike are an abomination to Jehovah — ASV

Diverse weights and diverse measures are impure in the sight of the Lord — Sept

Different weights and different measures, the Eternal loathes them alike — Mof

Unequal weights and unequal measures, they are all disgusting to the Lord — Bas

A double standard in weights and measures is an abomination to the LORD — NEB

11. Even a child is known by his doings, whether his work be pure, and whether it be right.

Even a child shall be known by his deeds, Whether his act be pure and whether it be right — Sprl

Even a child maketh himself known by his doings, whether his work be pure, and whether it be right — RV

Even by his actions a youth maketh himself known, Whether his work be pure or upright — YLT

Even a child is known by his deeds, According as his conduct is crooked or straight — AAT

Even by his manners the child betrays whether his conduct is innocent and right — NAB

12. The hearing ear, and the seeing eye, the LORD hath made even both of them.

The ear heareth and the eye seeth; and both are the work of the Lord — Sept

The hearing ear and the seeing eye are equally the Lord's work — Bas

Ear that hears, eye that sees, Yahweh has made both of these — Jerus

The ear that listens, the watchful eye, are both of the Lord's fashioning — Knox

If you have good eyesight and good hearing, thank God who gave them to you — Tay

13. Love not sleep, lest thou come to poverty; open thine eyes, and thou shalt be satisfied with bread.

Love not sleep, lest thou become poor, Open thine eyes — be satisfied with bread — YLT

Love not sleep, lest thou come to poverty; Open thine eyes, and thou shalt have bread in plenty — JPS

Love not sleep, lest you fall into poverty: waken, and you will have ample food — Mof

Do not love sleep or you will know poverty; keep your eyes open and have bread and to spare — Jerus

Love not sleep, lest you be reduced to poverty; eyes wide open mean abundant food — NAB

14. It is nought, it is nought, saith the buyer: but when he is gone his way, then he boasteth.

It is bad, it is bad, saith the buyer; But when he is gone his way, then he boasteth — ASV

A poor thing, says the buyer, a poor thing! Then off he goes, and boasts of it — Knox

"Poor stuff! poor stuff!" a man says, as he buys; but when he leaves, he boasts about his bargain — Mof

'A bad bargain!' says the buyer to the seller, but off he goes to brag about it — NEB

'No good, no good!' says the buyer, but he goes off congratulating himself — Jerus

15. There is gold, and a multitude of rubies: but the lips of knowledge are a precious jewel.

Precious is gold with a cluster of pearls; But jewels more rare are the lips of knowledge — Sprl

There is gold, and abundance of costly stones; but the lips of knowledge are a precious jewel — RSV

There is gold and a store of corals: but the lips of knowledge are a jewel of great price — Bas

Gold thou mayst have in abundance, and jewels a many, but the finest ware of all is wise speech — Knox

There is gold in plenty and coral too, but a wise word is a rare jewel — NEB

Gold, wealth of rubies, jewels rare — such are wise words — Mof

16. Take his garment that is surety for a stranger: and take a pledge of him for a strange woman.

Take his garment that is surety for a stranger;
And hold him in pledge that is surety for foreigners — ASV

Take away his garment, when he is surety for an alien;
And for strangers, take a pledge of him — ABPS

Take a man's garment if he becomes surety for a stranger;
Hold him to account for the other — AAT

Take the garment of him who is surety for a stranger; and take his pledge for the sake of a stranger — Lam

Take the man's clothes! He has gone surety for a stranger.
Seize him to the profit of persons unknown! — Jerus

17. Bread of deceit is sweet to a man;

Bread gained by deceit is sweet to a man — RSV

Sweet to a man is food gained by deceit — Ber

Food won by fraud has a sweet taste — Mof

Bread won by fraud tastes sweet to a man — AAT

Ill-gotten wealth is bread most appetizing — Knox

but afterward his mouth shall be filled with gravel.

18. Every purpose is established by counsel: and with good advice make war.

Plans by counsel shalt thou establish,
And with concerted measures make thou war — Rhm

Take counsel when you form a plan, and have some policy when you make war — Mof

Form plans under advice;
And under wise guidance make war — AAT

Care is the secret of good planning; wars are won by skilful strategy — NEB

Every plan is confirmed by counsel, and thus by wise guidance you carry on war — Ber

Weigh your plans in consultation, with sound guidance wage your war — Jerus

19. He that goeth about as a talebearer revealeth secrets: therefore meddle not with him that flattereth with his lips.

A revealer of secret counsels is the busybody,
And for a deceiver with his lips make not thyself surety — YLT

He that goes talebearing is a revealer of secrets;
Then meddle not with one of open lips — ABPS

He who goes about gossiping reveals secrets;
therefore do not associate with one who speaks foolishly — RSV

A newsmonger reveals secrets,
so have nothing to do with a babbler — NAB

He who goes about talking of the business of others gives away secrets: so have nothing to do with him whose lips are wide open — Bas

Don't tell your secrets to a gossip unless you want them broadcast to the world — Tay

20. Whoso curseth his father or his mother, his lamp shall be put out in obscure darkness.

Whoso curseth his father or his mother,
His lamp shall be put out in blackness of darkness — ASV

Whoso curseth his father or his mother,
His lamp shall be put out in the blackest darkness — JPS

He who curses his father or mother —
His light will go out in utter darkness — AAT

Whoever curses father or mother
in blackest darkness shall have his lamp snuffed out — Jerus

He who curses his father or his mother, his lamp of life will go out in black darkness — Mof

21. An inheritance may be gotten hastily at the beginning; but the end thereof shall not be blessed.

An estate may be gotten hastily at the beginning;

But the end thereof shall not be blessed — JPS

An inheritance hastily obtained in the beginning,
Verily shall not be blessed in the end — Sprl

An inheritance gotten wrongly at first,
Even its latter end is not blessed — YLT

The inheritance too soon come by, too late thou shalt find unblessed — Knox

If you begin by piling up property in haste,
it will bring you no blessing in the end — NEB

22. Say not thou, I will recompense evil; but wait on the LORD, and he shall save thee.

Do not say, I will requite wrong!
Wait thou for Yahweh that he may save thee — Rhm

Say not, I will avenge the wrong!
Trust in JEHOVAH, and He will deliver thee — Sprl

Say not, I will repay evil;
Wait on Jehovah, and he shall help thee — ABPS

Say not, "I will pay back evil!"
Wait for the LORD to help you — AAT

Never say, "I will revenge my wrongs";
wait for the Eternal to help you — Mof

Don't repay evil for evil. Wait for the Lord to handle the matter — Tay

23. Divers weights are an abomination unto the LORD; and a false balance is not good.[18]

Differing weights are an abomination unto JEHOVAH;
And a deceptive balance is not right — Sprl

Unequal weights are disgusting to the Lord, and false scales are not good — Bas

Varying weights are an abomination to the LORD,
and false scales are not good — NAB

A double standard in weights is an abomination to the LORD,
and false scales are not good in his sight — NEB

24. Man's goings are of the LORD; how can a man then understand his own way?[19]

The steps for a man are plainly set forth by the Lord: how then should a mortal man consider his ways! — Sept

A man's steps are directed by the LORD; who is the man, then, who can direct his own way — Lam

A man's steps are ordered by the LORD; how then can man understand his way — RSV

Man's movements are controlled by the Eternal;
then how can any understand his life — Mof

Every step man takes is of the Lord's choosing; and thou, poor mortal, wouldst thou plot out thy path — Knox

25. It is a snare to the man who devoureth that which is holy, and after vows to make inquiry.

The hasty dedication of his property is a snare to a man: for after the vow a change of mind happeneth — Sept

It is a snare to a man rashly to say, It is holy,
And after vows to make inquiry — ASV

It is a snare for a man rashly to say, "This is sacred!"
And after his vows to make inquiry — AAT

It is a snare to a man that he should rashly cry Holy!
And after making vows to reflect — Rhm

It is a danger to a man to say without thought, It is holy, and, after taking his oaths, to be questioning if it is necessary to keep them — Bas

It is a snare for a man who vows to give something to a holy place, and regrets after he has vowed — Lam

26. A wise king scattereth the wicked, and bringeth the wheel over them.

A wise king sifteth the wicked,
And turneth the wheel over them — JPS

A wise king winnoweth the wicked, and bringeth the threshing wheel over them — RV

A wise king disperseth the wicked,

[18]Compare vs. 10, above.
[19]Compare Prov. 16:9.

When he bringeth the wheel of the waggon over them — Sprl

A wise king winnows the wicked, and threshes them under the cartwheel — NAB

A wise king sifts the wicked, And requites them for their guilt — AAT

27. **The spirit of man is the candle of the LORD, searching all the inward parts of the belly.**

The spirit of man is the lamp of Jehovah, Searching all his innermost parts — ASV

The spirit of man is a light of the Lord, who searcheth the inward recesses of the body — Sept

The soul of a man is the lamp of the LORD, searching all the inward parts of the heart — Lam

Man's spirit is the lamp of Yahweh, searching his deepest self — Jerus

Man's conscience is the lamp of the Eternal, flashing into his inmost soul — Mof

A man's conscience is the Lord's searchlight exposing his hidden motives — Tay

28. **Mercy and truth preserve the king: and his throne is upholden by mercy.**

Grace and truth should fashion the king; And his throne is sustained by mercy — Sprl

Kindness and truth preserve the king; And his throne is upholden by kindness — ASV

Loyalty and faithfulness preserve the king, and his throne is upheld by righteousness — RSV

Kindness and good faith are the safeguards of a king; And by justice his throne is established — AAT

Kindness and loyalty mount guard over the king, his throne is founded on kindness — Jerus

Mercy and good faith keep the king safe, and the seat of his power is based on upright acts — Bas

29. **The glory of young men is their strength: and the beauty of old men is the grey head.**

The beauty of young men is their strength, And the ornament of old men a hoary head — Rhm

The glory of young men is their strength, and the attractiveness of old men is their gray head — Ber

The glory of young men is their strength; And the honor of old men is the gray head — ABPS

The glory of young men is their strength, and the dignity of old men is gray hair — NAB

30. **The blueness of a wound cleanseth away evil: so do stripes the inward parts of the belly.**

The probing of a wound cleanseth away evil; So wholesome strokes the recesses of the body — Sprl

Stripes that wound cleanse away evil; And strokes reach the innermost parts — ASV

Sharp wounds cleanse away evil; So do stripes that reach the inward parts — JPS

A good beating purges the mind, and blows chasten the inmost being — NEB

Punishment that hurts chases evil from the heart — Tay

Hurts that bruise cruelly, chastisement felt deep within, are sin's best remedy — Knox

CHAPTER 21

1. **The king's heart is in the hand of the LORD, as the rivers of water: he turneth it whithersoever he will.**

Rivulets of water is the heart of a king in the hand of Jehovah, Wherever He pleaseth He inclineth it — YLT

Like channels of water is the heart of a king in the hand of Yahweh, — Whithersoever he will he turneth it — Rhm

The king's heart is in the hand of Jehovah as the watercourses: He turneth it whithersoever he will — ASV

The king's heart is a stream of water

in the hand of the LORD;
he turns it wherever he will — RSV

Like a stream is the king's heart in the hand of the LORD;
wherever it pleases him, he directs it — NAB

2. Every way of a man is right in his own eyes: but the LORD pondereth the hearts.

Every way of man is right in his own eyes;
But JEHOVAH weigheth the heart's desires — Sprl

Every man appeareth righteous in his own eyes: but the Lord directeth hearts — Sept

Every way of a man seems right to himself, but the Lord is the tester of hearts — Bas

Every way of a man is right in his own eyes;
But the LORD weighs the motives — AAT

Man's ways are always right in his own eyes,
but the Eternal has the verdict on his life — Mof

3. To do justice and judgment is more acceptable to the LORD than sacrifice.

To do righteousness and justice
Is more acceptable to Jehovah than sacrifice — ASV

To do righteousness and justice
Is more choice to Yahweh than sacrifice — Rhm

To do what is right and just
is more acceptable to the LORD than sacrifice — NAB

Mercy shown and justice done win the Lord's favour beyond any sacrifice — Knox

4. A high look, and a proud heart, and the plowing of the wicked, is sin.

Loftiness of eyes and ambition of heart —
The lamp of the lawless are sin — Rhm

A haughty look, and a proud heart —
The tillage of the wicked is sin — JPS

An high look, and a proud heart, even the lamp of the wicked, is sin — RV

Haughty looks, a proud heart,
showy splendour — it is all sin — Mof

5. The thoughts of the diligent tend only to plenteousness; but of every one who is hasty only to want.

The purposes of the diligent are only to advantage,
And of every hasty one, only to want — YLT

The thoughts of the diligent tend only to plenteousness;
But every one that is hasty hasteth only to want — ASV

The plans of the diligent lead surely to abundance,
but every one who is hasty comes only to want — RSV

Forethought and diligence are sure of profit;
the man in a hurry is as sure of poverty — NEB

6. The getting of treasures by a lying tongue is a vanity tossed to and fro of them that seek death.

The getting of treasures by a lying tongue is a vapour driven to and fro; they that seek them seek death — RV

He who gains treasures by a lying tongue
Is chasing a vapor to snares of death — AAT

He who getteth treasures by a lying tongue, pursueth vanity to the snares of death — Sept

The getting of riches by a lying tongue is a fleeting vapor, a pursuit of death — Ber

A man making money by fraud
chases a bubble to his own doom — Mof

7. The robbery of the wicked shall destroy them; because they refuse to do judgment.

The violence of the wicked shall sweep them away,
Because they refuse to do justice — ASV

The violence of the wicked shall drag them away;
Because they refuse to do justly — JPS

The destruction of the wicked shall come upon them because they refused to do justice — Lam

The oppression of the wicked will sweep them away,
because they refuse to do what is right — NAB

The wicked are caught up in their own violence,
because they refuse to do what is just — NEB

8. The way of man is froward and strange: but as for the pure, his work is right.

The conduct of a guilty man is full of turnings;
But the pure is straightforward in his work — Sprl

The way of him that is laden with guilt is exceeding crooked;
But as for the pure, his work is right — ASV

A man of crooked way turns aside;
But the pure, his work is straight — ABPS

Crooked is the way of a guilty man,
But as for the pure straight is his dealing — Rhm

The way of the felon is devious,
the conduct of the innocent straightforward — Jerus

The way of the guilty is crooked,
but the conduct of the pure is right — RSV

9. It is better to dwell in a corner of the housetop, than with a brawling woman in a wide house.

It is better to dwell in a corner of the house-top,
Than with a brawling woman and a house in common — ABPS

It is better to dwell in a corner of the housetop
Than with a contentious woman in a many-roomed house — Sprl

It is better to dwell alone in a corner of the housetop than to live with a quarrelsome woman in a large house — Lam

It is better to dwell in a corner of the housetop
than in a roomy house with a quarrelsome woman — NAB

It is better to live in the corner of an attic than with a crabby woman in a lovely home — Tay

10. The soul of the wicked desireth evil: his neighbour findeth no favour in his eyes.

The desire of the evil-doer is fixed on evil: he has no kind feeling for his neighbour — Bas

The soul of the wicked desires evil;
his neighbor finds no mercy in his eyes — RSV

The wicked man is bent on doing harm;
His neighbor finds no pity in his eyes — AAT

The wicked man's soul is intent on evil,
he looks on his neighbour with dislike — Jerus

Bad men are bent on doing harm;
none wins a kindly thought from them — Mof

The wicked man is set on evil;
he has no pity to spare for his friend — NEB

11. When the scorner is punished, the simple is made wise: and when the wise is instructed, he receiveth knowledge.[20]

When the scoffer is punished, the simple is made wise;
And when the wise is instructed, he receiveth knowledge — ASV

When a profligate is punished the innocent become more cautious; and the intelligent wise man will gain knowledge — Sept

When a scoffer is punished, the simple learns wisdom;
When a wise man receives a lesson, he gains knowledge — AAT

When the scoffer is fined, the foolish is made wise;
And by instruction the wise shall attain knowledge — Sprl

When the arrogant man is punished, the simple are the wiser;
when the wise man is instructed, he gains knowledge — NAB

12. The righteous man wisely considereth the house of the wicked: but God overthroweth the wicked for their wickedness.

The righteous man considereth the house of the wicked; how the wicked are overthrown to their ruin — RV

The righteous observes the house of the wicked;
the wicked are cast down to ruin — RSV

The righteous man deals considerately with the house of the wicked; the wicked are tumbled into ruin — Ber

[20]Compare Prov. 19:25.

The Righteous One considereth the house of the wicked,
Overthrowing the wicked to their ruin — JPS

The Righteous One observeth the house of the lawless, —
He is ready to cast down lawless men into misfortune — Rhm

The just man appraises the house of the wicked:
there is one who brings down the wicked to ruin — NAB

A just God cares for the good,
but he brings down the wicked with a crash — Mof

13. Whoso stoppeth his ears at the cry of the poor, he also shall cry himself, but shall not be heard.

Whoso is shutting his ear from the cry of the poor,
He also doth cry and is not answered — YLT

He that shutteth his ear from the cry of the poor
Even he shall call and not be answered — Rhm

He who closes his ear against the cry of the poor
Will himself also call and not be answered — AAT

He who shuts his ear to the poor man's cry
shall himself plead and not be heard — Jerus

If a man shuts his ears to the cry of the helpless,
he will cry for help himself and not be heard — NEB

He who shuts his ears to the cries of the poor will be ignored in his own time of need — Tay

14. A gift in secret pacifieth anger: and a reward in the bosom, strong wrath.

A gift in secret shall allay anger;
And a gift in the bosom strong wrath — Sprl

A gift in secret pacifies anger,
And a bribe in the bosom, violent wrath — AAT

A gift in secret quiets anger, and a present in the bosom calms fury — Ber

A gift in secret averts anger;
and a bribe in the bosom, strong wrath — RSV

A secret bribe appeases anger,
a present slipped into the hand will allay fury — Mof

A secret gift allays anger,
and a concealed present, violent wrath — NAB

15. It is a joy to the just to do judgment: but destruction shall be to the workers of iniquity.

It is joy to the righteous to do justice;
But it is a destruction to the workers of iniquity — ASV

To do justly is joy to the righteous,
But ruin to the workers of iniquity — JPS

When justice is done, it is a joy to the righteous,
but dismay to evildoers — RSV

The doing of justice is a joy to the righteous, but to the workers of iniquity it is a calamity — Ber

To practice justice is a joy for the just,
but terror for evildoers — NAB

16. The man that wandereth out of the way of understanding shall remain in the congregation of the dead.

The man who wandereth from the way of discretion
In the gathered hosts of the shades shall settle down — Rhm

The man that wandereth out of the way of understanding
Shall rest in the assembly of the dead — ASV

The man who wanders from the way of wisdom,
Shall abide in the congregation of the shades — ABPS

A man who wanders out of the right road
will find his rest among the dead below — Mof

A man who takes leave of common sense
comes to rest in the company of the dead — NEB

17. He that loveth pleasure shall be a poor man: he that loveth wine and oil shall not be rich.

The lover of pleasure will be a poor man: the lover of wine and oil will not get wealth — Bas

Pleasure-lovers stay poor,
he will not grow rich who loves wine and good living — Jerus

He who loves pleasure will suffer want;

he who loves wine and perfume will not be rich — NAB

A man who loves pleasure becomes poor; wine and luxury are not the way to riches — Tay

Of greed comes want; he grows not rich that loves wine and oil — Knox

18. The wicked shall be a ransom for the righteous, and the transgressor for the upright.

. . . And the faithless cometh in the stead of the upright — JPS

. . . And the treacherous cometh in the stead of the upright — ASV

. . . And instead of upright men the traitor — Rhm

. . . and the deceitful for the upright — Lam

. . . so does a traitor for the upright — NEB

19. It is better to dwell in the wilderness, than with a contentious and an angry woman.

It is better to dwell in a desert land, than with a contentious and fretful woman — RV

It is better to be living in a waste land, than with a bitter-tongued and angry woman — Bas

Better is it to dwell in a desert land,
Than with a brawling and fretful woman — ABPS

It is better to dwell in a desert
Than with a quarrelsome and nagging wife — AAT

Better to live in a desert land
than with a scolding and irritable woman — Jerus

20. There is treasure to be desired and oil in the dwelling of the wise; but a foolish man spendeth it up.

There is precious treasure and oil in the dwelling of the wise;
But a foolish man swalloweth it up — ASV

There is desirable treasure and oil in the dwelling of the wise;
But a foolish man swalloweth it up — JPS

A desirable treasure abideth in the home of the wise;
But the foolish man swalloweth his up — Sprl

Precious treasure remains in a wise man's dwelling,
but a foolish man devours it — RSV

The wise man has his home full of fine and costly treasures;
the stupid man is a mere spendthrift — NEB

21. He that followeth after righteousness and mercy findeth life, righteousness and honour.

Whoso is pursuing righteousness and kindness,
Findeth life, righteousness, and honour — YLT

He that pursueth righteousness and lovingkindness
Shall find life, righteousness and honour — Rhm

He who follows after justice and kindness
Will find life, prosperity, and honor — AAT

The man who tries to be good, loving and kind finds life, righteousness and honor — Tay

22. A wise man scaleth the city of the mighty, and casteth down the strength of the confidence thereof.

A wise man hath scaled strong cities and demolished fortifications in which the wicked trusted — Sept

A wise man scales the defenses of the city of mighty men and conquers the stronghold in which they trusted — Lam

A wise man scales the city of the mighty
and brings down the stronghold in which they trust — RSV

A wise man goes up into the town of the strong ones, and overcomes its strength in which they put their faith — Bas

A wise man climbs into a city full of armed men
and undermines its strength and its confidence — NEB

23. Whoso keepeth his mouth and his tongue keepeth his soul from troubles.

Whoso guardeth his mouth and his tongue
Protecteth his soul from troubles — Sprl

He who is careful of his lips and tongue
will manage to keep clear of trouble — Mof

He who keeps watch over his mouth and his tongue

preserves himself from disaster — Jerus

Guard lips and tongue, as thou wouldst guard thy life from peril — Knox

24. Proud and haughty scorner is his name, who dealeth in proud wrath.

The proud and haughty man, scoffer is his name;
He worketh in the arrogance of pride — ASV

Scoffer is he called who is haughty and arrogant,
Who acts with insolent pride — AAT

A haughty insolent one — Scoffer is his name
Is he that acteth in a transport of pride — Rhm

"Scoffer" is the name of the proud, haughty man
who acts with arrogant pride — RSV

25. The desire of the slothful killeth him; for his hands refuse to labour.

The restraint of the slothful killeth him,
For his hands refuse to work — Sprl

A lazy man's ease is his undoing, for his hands will not labour — Mof

The idler's desires are the death of him, since his hands will not do work — Jerus

The sluggard's propensity slays him, for his hands refuse to work — NAB

26. He coveteth greedily all the day long: but the righteous giveth and spareth not.

All day long he has longing desire;
But the righteous shall give, and not spare — ABPS

All the day he greatly craveth,
Whereas the righteous giveth and doth not spare — Rhm

The wicked man is greedy all day long;
But the righteous man gives without stint — AAT

The godless is forever coveting,
the virtuous man gives without ever refusing — Jerus

He is greedy to get, while the godly love to give — Tay

27. The sacrifice of the wicked is abomination: how much more, when he bringeth it with a wicked mind?

The sacrifice of the wicked is an abomination;
How much more, when he bringeth it with the proceeds of wickedness — JPS

The sacrifice of the wicked is an abomination; how much more when he brings it with evil intent — Ber

Sacrifice from evil men God loathes — much more, when it is offered to atone for crime — Mof

The sacrifice of wicked men is abhorrent,
above all when they offer for bad motives — Jerus

28. A false witness shall perish: but the man that heareth speaketh constantly.

A false witness shall perish,
but the man who hearkeneth with abiding effect shall speak — Rhm

A false witness shall perish;
But the man that heareth shall speak so as to endure — ASV

A false witness will perish,
but the word of a man who hears will endure — RSV

A false witness will perish, but a man who listens faithfully will be at liberty to speak — Ber

A lying witness will perish;
But a truthful witness will speak on to the end — AAT

29. A wicked man hardeneth his face: but as for the upright, he directeth his way.

A wicked man hardeneth his face: but as for the upright, he ordereth his ways — RV

A wicked man impudently hardeneth his face: but the upright will himself consider his ways — Sept

The evil-doer makes his face hard; but as for the upright, he gives thought to his way — Bas

The face of a wicked man is shameless; but he who is upright amends his ways — Lam

An evil man is stubborn, but a godly man will reconsider — Tay

30. There is no wisdom nor understanding nor counsel against the LORD.

No wisdom and no discernment,
And no counsel can succeed in opposition to JEHOVAH — Sprl

There is no wisdom nor understanding,
Nor counsel to confront Yahweh — Rhm

No wisdom, no intelligence,
No counsel can avail against the LORD — AAT

Intelligence, skill, strategy —
none can avail against the Eternal — Mof

Wisdom is none, prudence is none,
counsel is none that can be matched against the Lord's will — Knox

31. **The horse is prepared against the day of battle: but safety is of the LORD.**

A horse is provided for the day of battle: but help cometh from the Lord — Sept

The horse is equipped for the day of battle,
but victory is the LORD's — NAB

The horse is made ready for the day of battle,
but the victory belongs to the LORD — RSV

Chargers are harnessed for the battle,
but saving victory comes from the Eternal — Mof

The horse may be prepared for the day of battle; but salvation is of the LORD — Lam

Go ahead and prepare for the conflict,
but victory comes from God — Tay

CHAPTER 22

1. **A good name is rather to be chosen than great riches, and loving favour rather than silver and gold.**

A good name is preferable to great riches,
And esteem preferable to silver or gold — Sprl

Reputation is a better choice than riches;
esteem is more than money — Mof

A good name is more desirable than great riches,
A good reputation than silver and gold — AAT

A good name is more to be desired than great wealth, and to be respected is better than silver and gold — Bas

Precious beyond all treasure is good repute; not gold or silver is so worth winning, as to be loved — Knox

2. **The rich and poor meet together: the LORD is the maker of them all.**

Rich and poor stand side by side:
it was the Eternal who made them all — Mof

Rich and poor are found together,
Yahweh has made them all — Jerus

Rich and poor have a common bond:
The LORD is the maker of them all — NAB

The rich and the poor are alike before the Lord who made them all — Tay

3. **A prudent man foreseeth the evil, and hideth himself: but the simple pass on, and are punished.**

A prudent man seeth calamity and hideth himself,
But the simple pass on and suffer — Rhm

A prudent man seeth the evil, and hideth himself;
But the simple pass on, and suffer for it — ASV

A prudent man seeth the evil, and hideth himself;
But the thoughtless pass on, and are punished — JPS

The prudent espieth the calamity and will shelter himself;
But the foolish go forward and they will suffer — Sprl

The sharp man sees the evil and takes cover: the simple go straight on and get into trouble — Bas

A shrewd man sees trouble coming and lies low;
the simple walk into it and pay the penalty — NEB

4. **By humility and fear of the LORD are riches, and honour, and life.**

The reward of humility and the fear of the LORD is riches, and honour, and life — RV

The reward of humility, of the fear of Jehovah,
Is wealth, and honor, and life — ABPS

The consequence of humility with the fear of JEHOVAH
Are riches, and honour, and life — Sprl

The humble and the reverent are rewarded
with wealth and honour and long life — Mof

5. Thorns and snares are in the way of the froward: he that doth keep his soul shall be far from them.

Thorns and snares are in the way of the perverse:
He that keepeth his soul shall be far from them — ASV

Thorns and snares are on the path of the crooked;
he who would safeguard his life will shun them — NAB

Snares and traps are found on a crooked way; he who keeps his soul shall be far from them — Lam

Thorns and snares are in crooked paths: but he who watcheth his soul shall avoid them — Sept

The crooked man's path is set with snares and pitfalls;
the cautious man will steer clear of them — NEB

6. Train up a child in the way he should go: and when he is old, he will not depart from it.

Train up a youth in the direction of his duty,
Even when he becometh old he will not depart from it — Rhm

Give instruction to a youth about his way,
Even when he is old he turneth not from it — YLT

Educate a child according to his life requirements; even when he is old he will not veer from it — Ber

Train a boy in the way he should go; even when he is old, he will not swerve from it — NAB

Train a child for his proper trade, and he will never leave it, even when he is old — Mof

7. The rich ruleth over the poor, and the borrower is servant to the lender.

The rich rules over the poor, and the borrower is the slave of the lender — RSV

The man of wealth has rule over the poor, and he who gets into debt is a servant to his creditor — Bas

The rich man lords it over the poor, the borrower is the lender's slave — Jerus

Just as the rich rule the poor, so the borrower is servant to the lender — Tay

Rich rules poor, debtor must wait on creditor — Knox

8. He that soweth iniquity shall reap vanity: and the rod of his anger shall fail.

He that soweth iniquity shall reap calamity;
And the rod of his wrath shall fail — ASV

He who soweth iniquity shall reap vexation;
And the sceptre of his haughtiness shall be brought to nought — Sprl

He that sows iniquity shall reap mischief;
And the rod for his pride shall be ready — ABPS

He who sows iniquity shall reap deceit; and the staff of his anger shall be broken — Lam

He who sows crime will reap calamity;
The result of his work will be ruin — AAT

The man who sows injustice reaps trouble,
and the end of his work will be the rod — NEB

9. He that hath a bountiful eye shall be blessed; for he giveth of his bread to the poor.

A benevolent eye the same shall be blessed, —
Because he hath given of his bread to the poor — Rhm

He whose eye is generous will be blessed, for he gives food to the poor — Ber

A generous man will have God's blessing,
because he shares his food with poor folk — Mof

The kindly man will be blessed,
for he gives of his sustenance to the poor — NAB

Happy is the generous man, the one who feeds the poor — Tay

10. Cast out the scorner, and contention shall go out; yea, strife and reproach shall cease.

Cast out the scoffer, and contention will go out;
Yea, strife and ignominy will cease — ASV

Expel the scorner and contention shall depart;

And strife and reproach will cease — Sprl
Drive out the scoffer, and contention will go forth;
And litigation and reproach will cease — ABPS
Drive out a scoffer, and strife will go out,
and quarreling and abuse will cease — RSV
Send away the man of pride, and argument will go out; truly fighting and shame will come to an end — Bas
Banish the reckless spirit, and strife goes out with him; thou art rid of quarreling and disgrace — Knox

11. He that loveth pureness of heart, for the grace of his lips the king shall be his friend.

Whoso is loving cleanness of heart,
Grace are his lips, a king is his friend — YLT
He that loveth pureness of heart,
That hath grace in his lips, the king shall be his friend — JPS
He who loves purity of heart and whose speech is pleasant will have the king as his friend — Ber
He who loves purity of heart,
and whose speech is gracious, will have the king as his friend — RSV
The LORD loves the pure in heart;
And he who is gracious in speech — the king is his friend — AAT
Whoso loveth with pure affection,
His speech is acceptable, the king is his friend — Sprl

12. The eyes of the LORD preserve knowledge, and he overthroweth the words of the transgressor.

The eyes of Yahweh watch over knowledge,
Therefore hath he overturned the words of the treacherous — Rhm
The eyes of the LORD protect knowledge, and He turns aside the words of the treacherous — Ber
The eyes of Yahweh see knowledge safe preserved,
but he confounds the words of liars — Jerus
The eyes of Jehovah preserve him that hath knowledge;
But he overthroweth the words of the treacherous man — ASV
The eyes of the LORD preserve him that hath knowledge,
But He overthroweth the words of the faithless man — JPS
The eyes of the LORD keep watch on him who has knowledge,
But he upsets the plans of the faithless — AAT
The eyes of the LORD preserve knowledge and destroy the words of deceit — Lam

13. The slothful man saith, There is a lion without, I shall be slain in the streets.

The slothful exclaims: A lion is in the streets!
In the midst of the streets shall I be murdered! — Sprl
'There is a lion outside,' says the idler 'I shall be killed in the street!' — Jerus
The hater of work says, There is a lion outside: I will be put to death in the streets — Bas
A slothful man maketh excuse and saith, There is a lion in the highways and murderers in the streets — Sept

14. The mouth of strange women is a deep pit: he that is abhorred of the LORD shall fall therein.

A deep chasm is the mouth of strange women,
He with whom Yahweh is indignant falleth there — Rhm
The mouth of a profligate woman is a deep pitfall;
Whoso is abhorred of JEHOVAH shall fall therein — Sprl
The mouth of a strange woman is a deep pit; he with whom the LORD is angry shall fall into it — Lam
The mouth of strange women is a deep pit;
He that is hated of Jehovah shall fall therein — ABPS
The mouth of an alien woman is a deep pit,
into it falls the man whom Yahweh detests — Jerus
The words of an adulteress are like a deep pit;
those whom the LORD has cursed will fall into it — NEB

15. Foolishness is bound in the heart of a child; but the rod of correction shall drive it far from him.

Folly is bound up in the heart of a youth,
The rod of chastisement putteth it far from him — YLT

Folly is bound up in the heart of a child: but a rod and instruction will drive it from him — Sept

Foolish ways are deep-seated in the heart of a child, but the rod of punishment will send them far from him — Bas

Foolishness is bound up in the heart of a child, but the rod of discipline will drive it far from him — Ber

Innate in the heart of a child is folly, judicious beating will rid him of it — Jerus

16. He that oppresseth the poor to increase his riches, and he that giveth to the rich, shall surely come to want.

He that oppresseth the poor to increase his gain,
And he that giveth to the rich, shall come only to want — ASV

He that oppresseth the poor to make increase for himself,
Giving to the rich shall surely come to want — Rhm

He that oppresses the weak, to make increase for himself,
Is one that gives to the rich, only to want — ABPS

He who oppresses the poor to enrich himself
will yield up his gains to the rich as sheer loss — NAB

A man may crush the poor and so be rich,
but presents to the rich will only make him poor — Mof

He who gains by oppressing the poor or by bribing the rich shall end in poverty — Tay

17. Bow down thine ear, and hear the words of the wise, and apply thine heart unto my knowledge.

Incline thine ear, and hear the words of the wise, and apply thine heart unto my knowledge — RV

Bend thine ear and hearken unto the words of the wise,
And apply thine heart unto my knowledge — Sprl

Incline your ear, and hear the words of the wise,
And apply your mind to know them — AAT

The sayings of the wise:
Incline your ear; and hear my words,
and apply your heart to my doctrine — NAB

The sayings of the wise:
Pay heed and listen to my words,
open your mind to the knowledge I impart — NEB

18. For it is a pleasant thing if thou keep them within thee; they shall withal be fitted in thy lips.

19. That thy trust may be in the LORD, I have made known to thee this day, even to thee.

For it is a pleasant thing if thou keep them within thee,
If they be established together upon thy lips.
That thy trust may be in Jehovah,
I have made them known to thee this day, even to thee — ASV

For sweet shall they be when thou shalt keep them in thine inmost mind,
They shall fit well together upon thy lips.
That in Yahweh may be thy trust
I have made them known to thee to-day even to thee — Rhm

For they are pleasant when thou dost keep them in thy heart,
They are prepared together for thy lips.
That thy trust may be in Jehovah,
I caused thee to know to-day, even thou — YLT

for it will be pleasant if you keep them within you,
if all of them are ready on your lips.
That your trust may be in the LORD,
I have made them known to you today, even to you — RSV

For it is pleasant, if thou keep them in thy breast;
If they are ready all of them on thy lips.
That thy trust may be in Jehovah,
I have taught thee this day, yea thee — ABPS

to keep them in your heart will be a pleasure,
and then you will always have them ready on your lips.

I would have you trust in the LORD and so I tell you these things this day for your own good — NEB

20. Have not I written to thee excellent things in counsels and knowledge,[21]

21. That I might make thee know the certainty of the words of truth; that thou mightest answer the words of truth to them that send unto thee?

Have I not written unto thee these rules
Concerning counsels and knowledge,
To acquaint thee of the certainty of the words of truth,
That thou mightest answer the words of truth to those I send unto thee? — Sprl

Have not I written unto thee excellent things of counsels and knowledge;
To make thee know the certainty of the words of truth, that thou mayest carry back words of truth to them that send thee? — RV

Have not I written for you previously of counsels and knowledge, so that I might make you know certainty, even the words of truth, that you might return words of truth to those who send you? — Ber

Have I not written to thee heretofore,
With counsels and knowledge;
To teach thee the rightness of words of truth,
That thou mayest answer truth to them that send thee? — ABPS

Have I not written for you these thirty sayings,
Respecting counsel and knowledge,
To acquaint you with the reality of true words,
That you may bring back a true report to him who sends you? — AAT

Here I have written out for you thirty sayings,
full of knowledge and wise advice,
to impart to you a knowledge of the truth,
that you may take back a true report to him who sent you — NEB

22. Rob not the poor, because he is poor: neither oppress the afflicted in the gate.

23. For the LORD will plead their cause, and spoil the soul of those that spoiled them.

Rob not the weak, because he is weak,
Neither crush the poor in the gate;
For the LORD will plead their cause,
And despoil of life those that despoil them — JPS

Do not take away the property of the poor man because he is poor, or be cruel to the crushed ones when they come before the judge:
For the Lord will give support to their cause, and take the life of those who take their goods — Bas

Rob not the poor because he is poor,
waste not the weak with lawsuits;
for the Eternal will take their part,
he will rob robbers of their life — Mof

Do not oppress the poor because he is poor; neither afflict the needy in the gate.
For the LORD will plead their cause and avenge the injustice which is done to them — Lam

Because a man is poor, do not therefore cheat him,
nor, at the city gate, oppress anybody in affliction;
for Yahweh takes up their cause,
and extorts the life of their extortioners — Jerus

Never oppress the poor; his poverty protects him; never bear hard on the friendless at law; be sure the Lord will grant redress, and claim life for life — Knox

24. Make no friendship with an angry man; and with a furious man thou shalt not go;

25. Lest thou learn his ways, and get a snare to thy soul.

Make no friendship with a man that is given to anger;
And with a wrathful man thou shalt not go:
Lest thou learn his ways,
And get a snare to thy soul — ASV

Have no fellowship with a man addicted to wrath; nor lodge with a friend who is passionate: lest thou learn his ways and lay a snare for thine own life — Sept

[21]The word underlying the variants is ambiguous in the text, to be read either as 'previously' or 'thirty'. Other renderings are guesses. 'Thirty' is the more likely intent.

Shew not thyself friendly with an angry man,
And with a man of fury go not in,
Lest thou learn his paths,
And have received a snare to thy soul — YLT
Form no friendship with a hot-tempered man,
And with a passionate man go not;
Lest you learn his ways,
And get yourself into a snare — AAT
Be not friendly with a hotheaded man,
nor the companion of a wrathful man,
Lest you learn his ways,
and get yourself into a snare — NAB
Keep away from angry, short-tempered men, lest you learn to be like them and endanger your soul — Tay

26. Be not thou one of them that strike hands, or of them that are sureties for debts.

27. If thou hast nothing to pay, why should he take away thy bed from under thee?

Be not one of those who give their hands in an agreement, or of those who make themselves responsible for debts;
If you have nothing with which to make payment, he will take away your bed from under you — Bas
Be not among those who give pledges, who are securities for debts; if you do not have the means to pay, why should your bed be taken from under you? — Ber
Be not one of those who give pledges, who become surety for debts.
If you have nothing with which to pay,
why should your bed be taken from under you? — RSV
Be not one of those who give their hand in pledge,
of those who become surety for debts;
For if you have not the means to pay,
your bed will be taken from under you — NAB
Never be one to give guarantees,
or to pledge yourself as surety for another;
for if you cannot pay, beware:
your bed will be taken from under you — NEB

28. Remove not the ancient landmark, which thy fathers have set.

Remove not ancient boundaries which thy fathers have set — Sept
Displace not the ancient landmark
Which thy fathers have erected — Sprl
Do not displace the ancient landmark,
set by your ancestors — Jerus
Remove not a border of olden times,
That thy fathers have made — YLT

29. Seest thou a man diligent in his business? he shall stand before kings; he shall not stand before mean men.

Seest thou a man prompt in his business:
Before kings shall he stand,
He shall not stand before men who are obscure — Rhm
Seest thou a man diligent in his business?
He shall stand in the presence of kings;
He shall not stand before men of no mark — Sprl
Have you seen a man who is expert in his business? he will take his place before kings; his place will not be among low persons — Bas
Do you see a man skilful in his work?
Before kings he will stand; he shall not stand before the undistinguished — Ber
You see a man skilful at his craft:
he will serve kings, he will not serve common men — NEB
You see some man sharp at business?
He will come to serve kings.
Not for him the service of obscure people — Jerus

CHAPTER 23

1. When thou sittest to eat with a ruler, consider diligently what is before thee:

2. And put a knife to thy throat, if thou be a man given to appetite.

When thou sittest to eat with a ruler
Thou shalt consider well what is before thee;
And shalt put a knife to thy throat,
If of great appetite thou art — Rhm
When thou sittest down to eat bread with a ruler,

Discreetly discern what is placed before thee;
And put restraint upon thine appetite,
If thou be inclined to indulgence — Sprl

When thou sittest to eat with a ruler,
Mark well what is before thee;
And put a knife to thy throat,
If thou art given to appetite — ABPS

When thou sittest to eat with a ruler,
Consider diligently him that is before thee;
And put a knife to thy throat,
If thou be a man given to appetite — ASV

When you sit down to dine with a ruler,
Bear in mind who is before you;
And put a knife to your throat,
If you be a man of keen appetite — AAT

When you sit down to dine with a ruler,
keep in mind who is before you;
And put a knife to your throat
if you have a ravenous appetite — NAB

When you are sitting at a ruler's table,
be careful how you eat;
control yourself,
if you have a large appetite — Mof

3. **Be not desirous of his dainties: for they are deceitful meat.**

Long not for his dainties;
For it is treacherous food — ABPS

Do not desire his delicacies,
for they are deceptive food — RSV

Do not crave his choice food,
for it is doubtful nourishment — Jerus

Have no desire for his delicate food,
for it is the bread of deceit — Bas

Lust not after his dainties,
For they are larded with deceit — AAT

4. **Labour not to be rich: cease from thine own wisdom.**

5. **Wilt thou set thine eyes upon that which is not? for riches certainly make themselves wings; they fly away as an eagle toward heaven.**

Labour not to make wealth,
From thine own understanding cease,
Dost thou cause thine eyes to fly upon it?
Then it is not.
For wealth maketh to itself wings,
As an eagle it flieth to the heavens — YLT

Weary not thyself to be rich;
Cease from thine own wisdom.
Wilt thou set thine eyes upon that which is not?
For riches certainly make themselves wings,
Like an eagle that flieth toward heaven — ASV

Do not toil to get wealth,
Of thine own understanding forbear;
Wilt thou let thine eye fly thereupon when it is nothing?
For it will surely make itself wings,
Like an eagle will it wing its way across the heavens — Rhm

Do not toil to get wealth; surrender that personal ambition.
Do your eyes light on it? But it is gone; for riches surely take wings like an eagle that flies heavenward — Ber

Do not slave to get wealth;
be a sensible man, and give up.
Before you can look around, it will be gone;
it will surely grow wings
like an eagle, like a bird in the sky — NEB

Toil not to gain wealth,
cease to be concerned about it;
While your glance flits to it, it is gone!
for assuredly it grows wings,
like the eagle that flies toward heaven — NAB

6. **Eat thou not the bread of him that hath an evil eye, neither desire thou his dainty meats:**

7. **For as he thinketh in his heart, so is he: Eat and drink, saith he to thee; but his heart is not with thee.**

Eat thou not the bread of him that hath an evil eye, neither desire thou his dainties:
For as he reckoneth within himself, so is he: Eat and drink, saith he to thee; but his heart is not with thee — RV

Eat not the bread of the evil-eyed;
And long not for his dainties.

For as he thinks in his soul, so is he;
Eat and drink, will he say to thee,
But his heart is not with thee — ABPS

Never dine with a niggardly man,
never fancy his dainties;
he counts his dishes,
even as he bids you "Eat and drink" —
he has no mind to you — Mof

Do not eat the bread of the man who is stingy;
do not desire his delicacies;
for he is like one who is inwardly reckoning.
"Eat and drink!" he says to you;
but his heart is not with you — RSV

Eat not the bread of him whose eye is selfish, neither desire his delicacies; for as one who inwardly figures the cost, so is he; "Eat and drink," he says to you, but his heart is not with you — Ber

8. The morsel which thou hast eaten shalt thou vomit up, and lose thy sweet words.

Thou shalt expel the morsel thou hast eaten,
And mar thy complimentary speeches —Sprl

The food which you have taken will come up again, and your pleasing words will be wasted — Bas

You will vomit up the morsels which you have eaten,
and waste your pleasant words — RSV

The little you have eaten you will vomit up,
and you will have wasted your agreeable words — NAB

You will spit out what little you have eaten
and find your compliments wasted — Jerus

9. Speak not in the ears of a fool: for he will despise the wisdom of thy words.

In the ears of a fool speak not,
For he treadeth on the wisdom of thy words — YLT

In the ears of a dullard do not speak,
For he will despise the good sense of thy words — Rhm

Never talk to a fool,
for he will despise your words of wisdom — Mof

Hold your tongue in the hearing of a stupid man;
for he will despise your words of wisdom — NEB

Do not waste words on a fool,
he will not appreciate the shrewdness of your remarks — Jerus

Make no addresses to a man void of understanding: lest he peradventure mock thy judicious discourse — Sept

10. Remove not the old landmark; and enter not into the fields of the fatherless:

11. For their redeemer is mighty; he shall plead their cause with thee.

Remove not a border of olden times,
And into fields of the fatherless enter not,
For their Redeemer is strong,
He doth plead their cause with thee — YLT

Do not move back the ancient boundary,
And into the fields of the fatherless do not enter;
For their near of kin is strong,
He will plead their cause with thee — Rhm

Remove not the widow's landmark,
Nor enter the fields of orphans; for their Champion is strong,
And he will defend their cause against you — AAT

Do not let the landmark of the widow be moved, and do not go into the fields of those who have no father;
For their saviour is strong, and he will take up their cause against you — Bas

Remove not an old landmark;
And enter not into the orphans' fields.
For their Deliverer is strong;
He will plead their cause with thee — ABPS

Do not move the ancient boundary-stone
or encroach on the land of orphans:
they have a powerful guardian
who will take up their cause against you — NEB

12. Apply thine heart unto instruction, and thine ears to the words of knowledge.

Apply thine heart to understanding,
And thine ears to the words of knowledge — Sprl

Bring thy heart to instruction,
And thy ears to words of knowledge — ABPS

Apply your mind to instruction,
And your ears to words of knowledge — AAT

Apply your mind to instruction,
attend to words of knowledge — Mof

Still let thy heart be attentive to warnings, open be thy ear to words of instruction — Knox

Apply your heart to discipline,
and your ears to words that are wise — Jerus

13. Withhold not correction from the child: for if thou beatest him with the rod, he shall not die.

14. Thou shalt beat him with the rod, and shalt deliver his soul from hell.

Withhold not correction from the child,
But chastise him with the rod; he shall not die:
Chastise him with the rod,
And thou shalt deliver his soul from death-shade — Sprl

Withhold not correction from a child;
For if thou smite him with the rod, he shall not die.
Thou with the rod wilt smite him;
But his soul thou shalt deliver from the underworld — ABPS

Do not withhold chastisement from a child; for if you beat him, he will not die.
For when you beat him with the rod, you will deliver his soul from Sheol — Lam

Do not withhold discipline from a child;
if you beat him with a rod, he will not die.
If you beat him with the rod
you will save his life from Sheol — RSV

Do not withhold discipline from a boy;
take the stick to him, and save him from death.
If you take the stick to him yourself,
you will preserve him from the jaws of death — NEB

15. My son, if thine heart be wise, my heart shall rejoice, even mine.

16. Yea, my reins shall rejoice, when thy lips speak right things.

My son, if thy heart be wise,
My heart will be glad, even mine:
Yea, my heart will rejoice,
When thy lips speak right things — ASV

My son, if thine heart be wise,
Mine heart, even mine, shall rejoice:
And my inner man shall exult,
When thy lips utter right things — Sprl

My son, if you are wise,
I shall indeed be joyful;
my heart will be glad
to hear wise words from you — Mof

My son, if your heart is wise,
then my own heart is glad,
and my innermost self rejoices
when from your lips come honest words — Jerus

My son, if your heart becomes wise, I, even I, will be glad in heart;
And my thoughts in me will be full of joy when your lips say right things — Bas

17. Let not thine heart envy sinners; but be thou in the fear of the LORD all the day long.

18. For surely there is an end; and thine expectation shall not be cut off.

Let not thy heart be envious of sinners,
Only of the reverence of Yahweh all day long;
For surely there is a future,
And thine expectation shall not be cut off — Rhm

Let not your heart envy sinners,
but continue in the fear of the LORD all the day.
Surely there is a future,
and your hope will not be cut off — RSV

Let not your heart envy sinners; but revere the LORD all the day long.
For surely you will have a future; and your hope will not be cut off — Lam

Let not thy heart be envious at sinners,
But — in the fear of Jehovah all the day.
For, is there a posterity?
Then thy hope is not cut off — YLT

Never envy evil men,
but always reverence the Eternal;
for something will yet come to you,
your hope will not be lost — Mof

Do not let your heart be envious of sinners
but be steady every day in the fear of Yahweh;
for there is a morrow,
and your hope will not be nullified — Jerus

Let not thy heart be envious at sinners,
But be ever in Jehovah's fear.
For if there is an end,
Then thy expectation shall not be cut off — ABPS

19. Hear thou, my son, and be wise, and guide thine heart in the way.

20. Be not among winebibbers; among riotous eaters of flesh:

Hearken thou, my son, and be wise;
And direct thine heart in the right way.
Be not amongst the drunkards,
Who associate together in gluttonous prodigality — Sprl

Hear thou my son and be wise,
And lead forward in duty thy heart.
Do not be among them who tipple with wine, —
Among them who are gluttons — Rhm

Hear thou, my son, and be wise;
And guide thy heart aright in the way.
Be not among wine-drinkers,
Among those who are prodigal of their own flesh — ABPS

Listen, my son, and learn to be wise,
and guide your heart in the way . . .
Do not be one of those forever tippling wine
nor one of those who gorge themselves with meat — Jerus

Hear, my son, and be wise,
and guide your heart in the right way.
Consort not with winebibbers,
nor with those who eat meat to excess — NAB

Hear, my son, and be wise,
and direct your mind in the way.
Be not among winebibbers,
or among gluttonous eaters of meat — RSV

21. For the drunkard and the glutton shall come to poverty: and drowsiness shall clothe a man with rags.

22. Hearken unto thy father that begat thee, and despise not thy mother when she is old.

Give ear to your father whose child you are, and do not keep honour from your mother when she is old — Bas

Heed your father who begot you and despise not your mother when she is old — Ber

Listen to your father, who gave you life,
and do not despise your mother when she is old — NEB

Listen to your father's advice and don't despise an old mother's experience — Tay

23. Buy the truth, and sell it not; also wisdom, and instruction, and understanding.

Truth buy thou but do not sell,
Wisdom and correction and understanding — Rhm

Buy the truth, and do not sell wisdom; also buy understanding and instruction — Lam

Truth you must purchase, never sell; this is wisdom, discipline, and discernment — Jerus

Get for yourself that which is true, and do not let it go for money; get wisdom and teaching and good sense — Bas

24. The father of the righteous shall greatly rejoice: and he that begetteth a wise child shall have joy of him.

The father of the righteous rejoiceth greatly,
The begetter of the righteous rejoiceth in him — YLT

The father of a righteous man shall greatly rejoice; and he who begets a wise child shall be glad — Lam

The father of a just man will exult with glee;
he who begets a wise son will have joy in him — NAB

A good man's father will rejoice
and he who has a wise son will delight in him — NEB

The father of a godly man has cause for joy — what pleasure a wise son is! — Tay

25. Thy father and thy mother shall be glad, and she that bare thee shall rejoice.

Let thy father and thy mother be glad,
And let her that bare thee rejoice — ASV
Let thy father and thy mother have joy in thee; and let her who bare thee rejoice — Sept
Therefore let your father and your mother be glad,
Let her who bore you rejoice — AAT
such joy let thy father have, such pride be hers, the mother who bore thee! — Knox

26. My son, give me thine heart, and let thine eyes observe my ways.
My son, give me thy heart;
And let thine eyes delight in my ways — ASV
Oh give, my son, thy mind unto me,
And let thine eyes observe my ways — Rhm
Give, my son, thy heart to me,
And let thine eyes watch my ways — YLT
My son, give heed to me,
And let your eyes take note of my ways — AAT
Attend to me, my son,
mark my injunctions — Mof
My son, mark my words,
and accept my guidance with a will — NEB

27. For a whore is a deep ditch; and a strange woman is a narrow pit.
For a harlot is a deep ditch;
And a foreign woman is a narrow pit — ASV
Surely a harlot is a deep ditch;
And a profligate woman a narrow pit — Sprl
For a harlot is a deep ditch;
And an alien woman is a narrow pit — JPS
For a harlot is a deep pit;
an adventuress is a narrow well — RSV
For a loose woman is a deep hollow, and a strange woman is a narrow waterhole — Bas

28. She also lieth in wait as for a prey, and increaseth the transgressors among men.
She also, as catching prey, lieth in wait,
And the treacherous among men she increaseth — YLT
Yea, she lieth in wait as a robber, and increaseth the treacherous among men — RV
Yea, as for prey, she lies in wait;
And multiplies them that deal perfidiously with men — ABPS
She also lieth in wait as a robber,
And increaseth the faithless among men — JPS
yes, and she lies in wait like a robber, and many a man she plunders — Mof

29. Who hath woe? who hath sorrow? who hath contentions? who hath babbling? who hath wounds without cause? who hath redness of eyes?
Who has wailing? who has want?
Who has contentions? who has complaining?
Who has wounds without cause?
Who has dimness of the eyes? — ABPS
Who hath woes? Who hath trouble? Who hath law suits? Who hath vexations and squabbles? Who hath wounds without cause? Whose are the eyes suffused with blood — Sept
Who crieth: 'Woe'? who: 'Alas'?
Who hath contentions? who hath raving?
Who hath wounds without cause?
Who hath redness of eyes — JPS
Whose is the misery? whose the remorse?
Whose are the quarrels and the anxiety?
Who gets the bruises without knowing why?
Whose eyes are bloodshot — NEB
Who scream? Who shriek?
Who have strife? Who have anxiety?
Who have wounds for nothing?
Who have black eyes — NAB

30. They that tarry long at the wine; they that go to seek mixed wine.
Those who are seated late over the wine: those who go looking for mixed wine — Bas
They who tarry long over wine, they who go to sample mixed wine — Ber
For those who linger over wine too long,
ever on the look-out for the well-blended wine — Jerus
Those who stay long over wine,

Who go often to test the mixture — AAT

It is the one who spends long hours in the taverns, trying out new mixtures — Tay

31. Look not thou upon the wine when it is red, when it giveth his colour in the cup, when it moveth itself aright.

Look not thou upon the wine when it is red,
When it giveth its colour in the cup.
When it glideth down smoothly — JPS

Look not thou upon the wine when it is red,
When it sparkleth in the cup,
When it goeth down smoothly — ASV

Look not on the wine when it is red,
when it sparkles in the glass.
It goes down smoothly — NAB

Never relish how red it is, this wine,
how sparkling in the cup,
how smooth its flow — Jerus

32. At the last it biteth like a serpent, and stingeth like an adder.

33. Thine eyes shall behold strange women, and thine heart shall utter perverse things.

Its after effect is that like a serpent it biteth,
And like a viper it doth sting.
Thine eyes will see strange women,
And thy heart will speak perverse things — Rhm

At the last it biteth like a serpent,
And stingeth like an adder.
Thine eyes shall behold strange things,
And thy heart shall utter perverse things — ASV

Afterwards it biteth like a serpent,
And stingeth like the basilisk.
Thine eye shall see with indistinctness,
And thine heart shall utter distortions — Sprl

in the end it will bite like a snake
and sting like a cobra.
Then your eyes see strange sights,
your wits and your speech are confused — NEB

In the end its bite is like a serpent's,
its sting as sharp as an adder's.
Your eyes will see strange things,
distorted words will come from your heart — Jerus

but in the end it bites like any snake,
it stings you like an adder.
You will be seeing odd things,
you will be saying queer things — Mof

34. Yea, thou shalt be as he that lieth down in the midst of the sea, or as he that lieth upon the top of a mast.

And thou shalt be like one reclining in the midst of the sea;
Or like one lying down on top of a mast — Sprl

Yes, you will be like him who takes his rest on the sea, or on the top of a sail-support — Bas

You will be like a man asleep at sea,
Asleep in the midst of a violent storm — AAT

you will be like a man asleep at sea,
asleep in the midst of a storm — Mof

you become like a man tossing out at sea,
like one who clings to the top of the rigging — NEB

Yea, you shall be as he who lies down in the midst of the sea, or as a sailor in a tempest — Lam

35. They have stricken me, shalt thou say, and I was not sick; they have beaten me, and I felt it not: when shall I awake? I will seek it yet again.

They have struck me, and I felt it not,
They have beaten me, and I knew it not;
When shall I awake? I will seek it yet again — JPS

They struck me; I did not feel it! They beat me; I did not know it! When shall I awake? I will seek it yet again — Ber

They may strike me, but I feel no pain;
They may beat me, but I know it not.
When shall I awake from my wine,
That I may seek it again? — AAT

Struck me, have they? But I'm not hurt.
Beaten me? I don't feel anything.
When shall I wake up? . . .
I'll ask for more of it — Jerus

CHAPTER 24

1. Be not thou envious against evil men, neither desire to be with them:

2. For their heart studieth destruction, and their lips talk of mischief.

Be not thou envious of wicked men,
Neither crave to be with them;
For violence their heart muttereth,
And mischief their lips do speak — Rhm

Be not envious of evil men,
And desire not to be with them,
For destruction doth their heart meditate,
And perverseness do their lips speak — YLT

My son, envy not bad men, nor desire to be with them: for their hearts study falsehood; and their lips utter mischief — Sept

Be not envious of evil men;
And long not to be with them.
For their heart meditates violence,
And their lips talk of mischief — ABPS

Be not thou envious against evil men;
Neither desire to be with them:
For their heart studieth oppression,
And their lips talk of mischief — ASV

Never envy evil men,
never seek their company;
for their one thought is plunder,
and mischief is their theme — Mof

3. Through wisdom is a house builded; and by understanding it is established:

4. And by knowledge shall the chambers be filled with all precious and pleasant riches.

By wisdom is a house builded;
And by understanding is it established,
And by knowledge shall the chambers be replenished
With every treasure that is precious and pleasant — Sprl

The building of a house is by wisdom,
and by reason it is made strong:
And by knowledge its rooms are full of all dear and pleasant things — Bas

What builds a house is skill,
it is erected by intelligence;
and knowledge furnishes the rooms
with all that is rare and pleasant — Mof

By wisdom a house is built,
by discernment the foundation is laid;
by knowledge its storerooms filled
with riches of every kind, rare and desirable — Jerus

Wisdom builds the house,
good judgement makes it secure,
knowledge furnishes the rooms
with all the precious and pleasing things that wealth can buy — NEB

By wisdom is a house built,
by understanding is it made firm;
And by knowledge are its rooms filled
with every precious and pleasing possession — NAB

5. A wise man is strong; yea, a man of knowledge increaseth strength.

6. For by wise counsel thou shalt make thy war: and in multitude of counsellors there is safety.

A wise man is strong;
Yea, a man of knowledge increaseth might.
For by wise guidance thou shalt make thy war;
And in the multitude of counsellors there is safety — ASV

A wise man is mighty,
And a man of knowledge becometh alert in vigour.
Surely with concerted measures shalt thou make for thyself war,
And success lieth in the greatness of the counsellor — Rhm

A wise man is strong, and a man of knowledge adds to his strength;
for by wise guidance you will wage your war, and there is victory in a multitude of counsellors — Ber

A wise man prevaileth over the powerful;
And a man of knowledge over the mighty in strength.
Therefore with well-matured counsels shalt thou make war;
Because in the multitude of counsellors is safety — Sprl

A wise man is better than a strong man,

And a man of knowledge than a man of might;
For by wise guidance you wage war,
And victory lies in a wealth of counselors — AAT

A wise man is mightier than a strong man,
and a man of knowledge than he who has strength;
for by wise guidance you can wage your war,
and in abundance of counselors there is victory — RSV

7. Wisdom is too high for a fool: he openeth not his mouth in the gate.

Wisdom is as unattainable to a fool as corals;
He openeth not his mouth in the gate — JPS

Unattainable to a foolish man are the dictates of wisdom,
In the gate he openeth not his mouth — Rhm

Wisdom is unattainable for a fool;
So he opens not his mouth in the gate — AAT

Wisdom is beyond a fool's reach;
so he can say nothing in a council — Mof

Wisdom is too high for a fool;
he dare not open his mouth in court — NEB

8. He that deviseth to do evil shall be called a mischievous person.

9. The thought of foolishness is sin: and the scorner is an abomination to men.

He that deviseth to do evil,
Men shall call him a mischief-maker.
The thought of foolishness is sin;
And the scoffer is an abomination to men — ASV

Whoso is devising to do evil,
Him they call a master of wicked thoughts.
The thought of folly is sin,
And an abomination to man is a scorner — YLT

He who premeditates to do wrong,
He shall be called a designing fellow.
To premeditate folly is sin;
And the scorner is an abomination unto men — Sprl

He whose purposes are bad will be named a man of evil designs.
The purpose of the foolish is sin:
and the hater of authority is disgusting to others — Bas

He who plots evil doing —
men call him an intriguer.
Beyond intrigue and folly and sin,
it is arrogance that men find abominable — NAB

To plan evil is as wrong as doing it.
The rebel's schemes are sinful, and the mocker is the scourge of all mankind — Tay

10. If thou faint in the day of adversity, thy strength is small.

11. If thou forbear to deliver them that are drawn unto death, and those that are ready to be slain;

If thou give way in the day of adversity,
Thy strength is small. Deliver those who are seized with mortal sickness,
And those who slip aside on the brink of destruction — oh rescue them — Sprl

If thou faint in the day of adversity,
thy strength is small.
Deliver them that are carried away to death, and those that are ready to be slain see that thou hold back — RV

If you give way in the time of trouble,
your strength is small.
Be the saviour of those who are given up to death, and do not keep back help from those who are slipping to destruction — Bas

If you faint in the day of adversity,
your strength is small.
Deliver those who are being taken to their death; and from those staggering toward slaughter will you withhold yourself? — Ber

If you remain indifferent in time of adversity,
your strength will depart from you.
Rescue those who are being dragged to death,
and from those tottering to execution withdraw not — NAB

12. If thou sayest, Behold, we knew it not; doth not he that pondereth the heart consider it? and he that keepeth thy soul, doth not he know it? and shall not he render to every man according to his works?

Though thou say,

Lo! we knew not this,
Shall not he that proveth hearts himself discern?
And he that formeth thy soul himself know?
And bring back to a son of earth according to his deed — Rhm

For if thou say, Lo, we knew not this;
Shall not he, the trier of hearts, perceive,
And the keeper of thy soul, shall not he know?
And he renders back to man according to his deed — ABPS

When thou sayest, 'Lo, we knew not this.'
Is not the Ponderer of hearts He who understandeth?
And the Keeper of thy soul He who knoweth?
And He hath rendered to man according to his work — YLT

If you say, "We knew nothing of this,"
Does not he who weighs the thoughts perceive it,
And is not he who guards your life aware of it,
And will he not requite each man according to his work? — AAT

Will you object, 'But look, we did not know'?
Has he who weighs the heart no understanding,
he who scans your soul no knowledge?
He himself will repay a man as his deeds deserve — Jerus

You say, "But I knew nothing of it"?
Yet he who reads the heart sees through you,
he knows, he who watches you —
will he not requite each man for what he did? — Mof

13. My son, eat thou honey, because it is good; and the honeycomb, which is sweet to thy taste:

14. So shall the knowledge of wisdom be unto thy soul: when thou hast found it, then there shall be a reward, and thy expectation shall not be cut off.

My son, eat thou honey, for it is good;
And the droppings of the honeycomb, which are sweet to thy taste:
So shalt thou know wisdom to be unto thy soul;
If thou hast found it, then shall there be a reward,
And thy hope shall not be cut off — ASV

My son, eat honey (for a honey comb is good) that thy palate may be sweetened. In like manner let thy soul taste wisdom; for if thou find it, thy end will be good and hope will not forsake thee — Sept

My son, eat honey because it is wholesome,
And the honeycomb, which is sweet unto thy taste.
So shall the acquirement of wisdom be to thy soul;
When thou hast discovered that there is a future state,
And that thy hope shall not be cut off — Sprl

My son, eat honey because it is good, and the honeycomb, which is sweet to your taste.
Thus shall wisdom find your soul; and you will have good prospects, and your hope shall not be cut off — Lam

My son, eat honey, for it is good,
and the drippings of the honeycomb are sweet to your taste.
Know that wisdom is such to your soul; if you find it, there will be a future,
and your hope will not be cut off — RSV

Eat honey, my son, since it is good;
honey that drips from the comb is sweet to the taste;
and such is knowledge of wisdom for your soul:
find it, and there will be a morrow,
and your hope will not be in vain — Jerus

15. Lay not wait, O wicked man, against the dwelling of the righteous; spoil not his resting place:

16. For a just man falleth seven times, and riseth up again: but the wicked shall fall into mischief.

Lay not wait, O wicked man, against the habitation of the righteous;
Destroy not his resting-place:
For a righteous man falleth seven times, and riseth up again;
But the wicked are overthrown by calamity — ASV

Lie not in wait, O wicked man, against the dwelling of the righteous,
Spoil not his resting-place;
For a righteous man falleth seven times, and riseth up again,
But the wicked stumble under adversity — JPS

Do not lie in wait, thou lawless man, against the home of the righteous,—
Neither destroy thou his place of rest;
For seven times may the righteous fall and yet arise,
But lawless men shall stumble into calamity — Rhm

Lie not in wait, O wicked man, against the dwelling of the righteous; do no violence to his home; for the righteous may fall seven times and yet arise, but the wicked stumbles headlong in adversity — Ber

Do not lie in wait like a felon at the good man's house,
or raid his farm.
Though the good man may fall seven times, he is soon up again,
but the rascal is brought down by misfortune — NEB

Lie not in wait, wicked man, at the dwelling of the righteous;
Despoil not his resting-place.
For seven times shall the righteous fall, and arise;
But the wicked stumble into ruin — ABPS

17. Rejoice not when thine enemy falleth, and let not thine heart be glad when he stumbleth:

18. Lest the LORD see it, and it displease him, and he turn away his wrath from him.

If thine enemy fall rejoice not over him; nor be elated at his stumbling: for the Lord will see and it will displease him, and he will turn away his wrath — Sept

Do not be glad at the fall of your hater, and let not your heart have joy at his downfall:
For fear that the Lord may see it, and it may be evil in his eyes, and his wrath may be turned away from him — Bas

Rejoice not when thine enemy falleth;
And let not thine heart exult when he stumbleth:
Lest Jehovah regard it, and it be wrong in his eyes,
And He transfer His anger from him to thee — Sprl

Rejoice not when your enemy falls,
Nor exult when he stumbles;
Lest the LORD see it, and be displeased,
And turn back his anger from him — AAT

Rejoice not when your enemy falls,
and when he stumbles, let not your heart exult,
Lest the LORD see it, be displeased with you
and withdraw his wrath from your enemy — NAB

Rejoice not when your enemy falls,
never exult when he is overthrown;
lest the Eternal see it and in displeasure
divert his wrath from him to you — Mof

19. Fret not thyself because of evil men, neither be thou envious at the wicked;

20. For there shall be no reward to the evil man; the candle of the wicked shall be put out.

Fret not thyself because of evil-doers;
Neither be thou envious at the wicked:
For there shall be no reward to the evil man;
The lamp of the wicked shall be put out — ASV

Be not angry against evil-doers;
Be not envious at the wicked.
For there shall not be an end and after-time for the evil;
The light of the wicked shall go out — ABPS

Burn not with vexation against evil-doers,
Be not envious of lawless men;
For there shall be no future for the wicked,
The lamp of the lawless shall go out — Rhm

Do not envy evildoers nor be jealous of the wicked;
For there shall be no future for evil men, and the lamp of the wicked shall be put out — Lam

Do not be indignant about the wicked,
do not be envious of evil men,
since there is no morrow for the wicked man;
the lamp of the wicked will be snuffed out — Jerus

Do not be impatient when the wicked thrive, do not envy the lot of evil-doers; villainy has no hope in store, its light flickers and is gone — Knox

21. My son, fear thou the LORD and the king; and meddle not with them that are given to change:

22. For their calamity shall rise suddenly; and who knoweth the ruin of them both?

Fear Jehovah, my son, and the king,
With changers mix not up thyself,
For suddenly doth their calamity rise,
And the ruin of them both — who knoweth? — YLT

My son, fear thou Jehovah and the king;
And company not with them that are given to change:
For their calamity shall rise suddenly;
And the destruction from them both, who knoweth it? — ASV

My son, fear the LORD and the king,
and do not disobey either of them,
for disaster from them will rise suddenly,
and who knows the ruin that will come from them both? — RSV

My son, reverence the LORD and the king,
And meddle not with those of high rank;
For suddenly comes ruin at their hands,
And who knows the doom that both of them bring? — AAT

My son, fear the LORD and the king;
have nothing to do with those who rebel against them;
For suddenly arises the destruction they send, and the ruin from either one, who can measure? — NAB

My son, watch your step before the Lord and the king, and don't associate with radicals. For you will go down with them to sudden disaster,
and who knows where it all will end? — Tay

23. These things also belong to the wise. It is not good to have respect of persons in judgment.

These also are sayings of the wise. To have respect of persons in judgement is not good — RV

Also these sayings from the wise:
To have respect to persons in judgment is not good — Sprl

These also are sayings of the wise.
Partiality in judging is not good — RSV

More maxims of the wise. It is ill done, to let partiality sway thy judgement — Knox

Further sayings of the sages.
It is not fair to favour one side in a suit — Mof

24. He that saith unto the wicked, Thou art righteous; him shall the people curse, nations shall abhor him:

25. But to them that rebuke him shall be delight, and a good blessing shall come upon them.

He that saith unto the wicked: 'Thou art righteous,'
Peoples shall curse him, nations shall execrate him;
But to them that decide justly shall be delight,
And a good blessing shall come upon them — JPS

He who saith of the wicked, "He is not guilty," shall be cursed by the tribes and hateful to the nations: but they who reprove shall appear better; and upon them a blessing shall come — Sept

He who says to the guilty man, "You are in the right" —
Men will curse him, people will execrate him;
But those who judge honestly will fare pleasantly,
On them will rest the blessing of prosperity — AAT

He that saith to the lawless man,
Righteous thou art,
Peoples shall denounce him,
Populations shall curse him;
But to reprovers one should be pleasant,

And upon them should come an excellent blessing — Rhm
He who says to the wicked man, "You are just" —
men will curse him, people will denounce him;
But those who convict the evildoer will fare well,
and on them will come the blessing of prosperity — NAB

26. Every man shall kiss his lips that giveth a right answer.
Kiss his lips
Who returneth an apposite answer — Sprl
He kisses the lips,
Who answers with right words — ABPS
He who gives a right answer kisses the lips — RSV
He who gives a straight answer
Is like one who kisses the lips — AAT
A straightforward answer
is as good as a kiss of friendship — NEB
He who returns an honest answer
plants a kiss on the lips — Jerus

27. Prepare thy work without, and make it fit for thyself in the field; and afterwards build thine house.
Prepare in the open thy work,
And make ready in the field for thyself,
Afterwards shalt thou build thy house — Rhm
Prepare thy work without,
And make it ready for thee in the field;
And afterwards build thy house — ASV
Set your business in order,
Arrange your work in the fields;
Afterward you may build up your house — AAT
First work your farm,
and till the soil —
then marry and set up house — Mof
First put all in order out of doors
and make everything ready on the land;
then establish your house and home — NEB

28. Be not a witness against thy neighbour without cause; and deceive not with thy lips.

29. Say not, I will do so to him as he hath done to me: I will render to the man according to his work.
Be not a witness against thy neighbour without cause;
Neither deceive with thy lips.
Say not: According as he hath done to me, so will I do to him;
I will recompense to the man according to his work — Sprl
Be not witness without cause against thy neighbor;
For wouldst thou deceive with thy lips?
Say not, As he has done to me, so will I do to him;
I will render to a man according to his deed — ABPS
Do not come forward as a witness against thy neighbour; wouldst thou spread lying tales? Nor be content to say, I am but serving him as he served me; I pay off old scores — Knox
Never give baseless evidence against your neighbour,
never mislead men by what you say.
Never think, "I will treat him as he treated me.
I will pay back the man for what he did" — Mof
Don't testify spitefully against an innocent neighbor. Why lie about him? Don't say, "Now I can pay him back for all his meanness to me!" — Tay

30. I went by the field of the slothful, and by the vineyard of the man void of understanding;

31. And, lo, it was all grown over with thorns, and nettles had covered the face thereof, and the stone wall thereof was broken down.
By the field of the sluggard I passed,
And by the vineyard of a man lacking sense;
And lo! There had come up all over it — thorns,
There had covered the face thereof — thistles,
And the stone fence thereof had been thrown down — Rhm
I passed by the field of a lazy man, by

the vineyard of a man who lacked understanding; and, see, it was completely overgrown with thorns; the ground was covered with nettles, and its stone wall was broken down — Ber

I went by the field of the hater of work, and by the vine-garden of the man without sense;
And it was full of thorns, and covered with waste plants, and its stone wall was broken down — Bas

I passed by the field of the sluggard, by the vineyard of the man without sense;
And behold! it was all overgrown with thistles;
its surface was covered with nettles, and its stone wall broken down — NAB

I passed by the field of an idle man, by the vineyard of a man with no sense.
I looked, and it was all dried up,
it was overgrown with thistles
and covered with weeds,
and the stones of its walls had been torn down — NEB

I walked by the field of a certain lazy fellow and saw that it was overgrown with thorns, and covered with weeds; and its walls were broken down — Tay

32. Then I saw, and considered it well: I looked upon it, and received instruction.

And as I gazed I considered in my heart,
I saw and I gathered up instruction — Sprl

Then I beheld, and considered well;
I saw, and received instruction — ASV

I looked, and reflected upon it;
I saw, and learned a lesson — AAT

Then looking at it, I gave thought: I saw, and I got teaching from it — Bas

And as I gazed I pondered,
I drew this lesson from the sight — Jerus

33. Yet a little sleep, a little slumber, a little folding of the hands to sleep:

34. So shall thy poverty come as one that travelleth; and thy want as an armed man.[22]

A little sleep,
A little slumber,
A little folding of the hands to rest:
So shall come in, as a highwayman, thy poverty,
And thy want as one armed with a shield — Rhm

A little sleep, a little slumber,
a little folding of the hands to rest,
and poverty will come upon you like a robber,
and want like an armed man — RSV

"Yet a little sleep, a little slumber, a little folding of the hands to rest" — and your poverty will come upon you as a bandit, your want like an unyielding warrior — Ber

Sleep on (thought I) a little longer, yawn a little longer, a little longer pillow head on hand; ay, but poverty will not wait, the day of distress will not wait; like an armed vagabond it will fall upon thee — Knox

A little sleep, a little drowsiness,
a little folding of the arms to take life more easily,
and like a vagrant, poverty is at your elbow
and, like a beggar, want — Jerus

CHAPTER 25

1. These are also proverbs of Solomon, which the men of Hezekiah king of Judah copied out.

These also are proverbs of Solomon, — which the men of Hezekiah king of Judah transcribed — Rhm

The following also are maxims of Solomon, copied out by scholars under Hezekiah king of Judah — Mof

These also are proverbs of Solomon.
The men of Hezekiah, king of Judah, transmitted them — NAB

These proverbs of Solomon were discovered and copied by the aides of King Hezekiah of Judah — Tay

These are more wise sayings of Solomon, copied out by the men of Hezekiah, king of Judah — Bas

2. It is the glory of God to conceal a

[22]See also Prov. 6:10-11.

thing: but the honour of kings is to search out a matter.

The honour of God is to hide a thing,
And the honour of kings to search out a matter — YLT

It is the glory of God to conceal a purpose,
But the honour of kings to discover a purpose — Sprl

It is the glory of God to keep a thing secret: but the glory of kings is to have it searched out — Bas

Mystery is God's glory,
but a king's glory is to search out secrets — Mof

To conceal a matter, this is the glory of God,
to sift it thoroughly, the glory of kings — Jerus

God has glory in what he conceals,
kings have glory in what they fathom — NAB

3. The heaven for height, and the earth for depth, and the heart of kings is unsearchable.

Heaven is high and the earth is deep: and the heart of a king is unsearchable — Sept

As the heavens for height, and the earth for depth,
So the heart of kings is unsearchable — ASV

Like the heavens for height, and the earth for depth,
The mind of kings is unfathomable — AAT

The heavens for height and the earth for depth and there is no searching out the mind of a king — Ber

4. Take away the dross from the silver, and there shall come forth a vessel for the finer.

5. Take away the wicked from before the king, and his throne shall be established in righteousness.

Remove the dross from the silver
And there cometh forth to the refiner a vessel:
Remove a lawless man from before the king
That his throne may be established in righteousness — Rhm

Remove the dross from the silver,
And there cometh forth pure metal for the refiner.
Remove the wicked from the presence of the king,
And his throne shall be established in righteousness — Sprl

Take dross from silver,
and the silver shines out pure;
remove scoundrels from a king,
and his throne will rest on justice — Mof

Rid silver of dross, and the cup shines bright; rid the court of knaves, and the throne stands firm — Knox

When you remove dross from silver, you have sterling ready for the silversmith. When you remove corrupt men from the king's court, his reign will be just and fair — Tay

6. Put not forth thyself in the presence of the king, and stand not in the place of great men:

7. For better it is that it be said unto thee, Come up hither; than that thou shouldest be put lower in the presence of the prince whom thine eyes have seen.[23]

Honour not thyself before a king,
And in the place of the great stand not.
For better that he hath said to thee, 'Come thou up hither,'
Than that he humble thee before a noble,
Whom thine eyes have seen — YLT

Glorify not thyself in the presence of the king,
And stand not in the place of great men;
For better it is that it be said unto thee: 'Come up hither,'
Than that thou shouldest be put lower in the presence of the prince,
Whom thine eyes have seen — JPS

Do not bear thyself proudly before the king;
And stand not in the place of the great.
For it is better that one say to thee, Come up hither,
Than that thou be put lower in the presence of the prince,
Whom thine eyes have seen — ABPS

Do not put yourself forward in the presence of the king and do not

[23]Several versions put the last clause of vs. 7 at the beginning of vs. 8, perhaps following the Sept.

stand in the place of great men; for it is better to be told, "Come up here," than that you should be put lower in the prince's presence, as your eyes have seen — Ber

Never play the great lord at court, and mingle with men of rank; who would not rather be beckoned to a higher place, than be put to the blush, and in the king's presence? — Knox

8. Go not forth hastily to strive, lest thou know not what to do in the end thereof, when thy neighbour hath put thee to shame.

Go not forth in haste to contention,
Lest peradventure thou do somewhat in the end thereof
Whereby thy neighbour may put thee to blush — Sprl

Do not go forth hastily to bring a suit, lest when you plead your cause, at the end your neighbor shall reproach you — Lam

Do not go out hastily to strive, else what will you do in the outcome when your neighbor puts you to shame? — Ber

What your eyes have seen
do not hastily bring into court;
for what will you do in the end,
when your neighbor puts you to shame? — RSV

What your eyes have seen
bring not forth hastily against an opponent;
For what will you do later on
when your neighbor puts you to shame? — NAB

Never be in a hurry to repeat
something you may have seen;
for what will you do, later on,
when you are taxed with it? — Mof

9. Debate thy cause with thy neighbour himself; and discover not a secret to another:

10. Lest he that heareth it put thee to shame, and thine infamy turn not away.

Thy contention urge thou with thy neighbour,
And the secret of another do not reveal:
Lest he that heareth expose thee,
And the report concerning thee turn not away — Rhm

Debate thy cause with thy neighbor himself,
And disclose not the secret of another;
Lest he that heareth it revile thee,
And thine infamy turn not away — ASV

Debate your cause with your neighbor himself; and do not disclose the secret to another,
Lest he who hears it reproach you and many people mock you — Lam

Have the quarrel out with your neighbour,
but do not disclose another's secret,
or someone, hearing, will reproach you with it,
and so you lose your reputation — Jerus

Argue your own case with your neighbour,
but do not reveal another man's secrets,
or he will reproach you when he hears of it
and your indiscretion will then be beyond recall — NEB

11. A word fitly spoken is like apples of gold in pictures of silver.

12. As an earring of gold, and an ornament of fine gold, so is a wise reprover upon an obedient ear.

Apples of gold in imagery of silver,
Is the word spoken at its fit times.
A ring of gold, and an ornament of pure gold,
Is the wise reprover to an attentive ear — YLT

Apples of gold in gravings of silver,
Is a word spoken in its season.
An ear-ring of gold, and a necklace of fine gold,
Is a wise reprover, to a listening ear — ABPS

Like apples of gold in a setting of carved silver
Is a word that is aptly spoken.
Like an earring of gold, or a necklace of fine gold,
Is a wise man's reproof on a listening ear — AAT

Like apples of gold in settings of silver,
so is a word spoken at the right moment.

Like a gold ring and an ornament of gold, so is a wise reprover for a listening ear — Ber

A word spoken at the right time, Is like citrons of gold in curiously engraved work of silver.
A wise reprover to an ear attent, Is like a ring of gold and an ornament of standard gold — Sprl

Golden fruit in figured silver baskets Is a word spoken on fitting occasion.
A ring of gold and a vessel of precious metal
Is a wise reprover on a hearing ear — Rhm

13. As the cold of snow in the time of harvest, so is a faithful messenger to them that send him: for he refresheth the soul of his masters.

As the coolness of snow in time of harvest,
Is a trusty messenger to them that send him;
For he restores the spirit of his masters — ABPS

The coolness of snow in harvest time, such is the trusty messenger to those who send him:
he revives the soul of his master — Jerus

Like snow that cools a harvest drink, so is a messenger who can be trusted;
he is a treat to those who send him — Mof

Like the coolness of snow in the heat of the harvest
is a faithful messenger for the one who sends him. He refreshes the soul of his master — NAB

14. Whoso boasteth himself of a false gift is like clouds and wind without rain.

Whoso falsely boasteth of liberality, Is like clouds and wind without rain — Sprl

As clouds and wind without rain, So is he that boasteth himself of his gifts falsely — ASV

As vapours and wind without rain, So is he that boasteth himself of a false gift — JPS

Like clouds with wind that bring no rain
Is the man who boasts of gifts not given — AAT

Like clouds and wind that bring no rain
is the man who boasts of gifts he never gives — NEB

15. By long forbearing is a prince persuaded, and a soft tongue breaketh the bone.

By long patience is a judge persuaded, And a soft tongue breaketh the bone — Rhm

By long forbearing is a ruler persuaded,
And a soft tongue breaketh the bone — ASV

By long forbearing is a governor persuaded,
And a gentle tongue breaketh the bones — Sprl

When one is slow to anger a ruler is persuaded, and soft speech will break a bone — Ber

With patience a ruler may be persuaded,
and a soft tongue will break a bone — RSV

With patience a judge may be cajoled: a soft tongue breaks bones — Jerus

16. Hast thou found honey? eat so much as is sufficient for thee, lest thou be filled therewith, and vomit it.

Hast thou found honey? eat only to suffice thee,
Lest thou be surfeited therewith, and emit it — Sprl

Hast thou found honey, eat what suffices thee;
Lest thou be sated with it, and vomit it up — ABPS

Having found honey eat just what is sufficient: lest being glutted thou vomit it up — Sept

If you find honey, eat only what you need,
lest you become glutted with it and vomit it up — NAB

If you find honey, eat no more than you need;
you may surfeit yourself and vomit — Mof

If you find honey, eat only what you need,
too much of it will make you sick — NEB

17. Withdraw thy foot from thy neighbour's house; lest he be weary of thee, and so hate thee.

Restrain thy foot from the house of thy friend;
Lest he become weary of thee and hate thee — ABPS

Let thy foot be seldom in thy neighbor's house,
Lest he be weary of thee, and hate thee — ASV

Do not visit your neighbor's house too frequently, lest he become weary of you and so hate you — Lam

Let not your foot be frequently in your neighbour's house, or he may get tired of you, and his feeling be turned to hate — Bas

Rare be thy visits to a neighbour; he will soon have enough, and weary of thee — Knox

18. A man that beareth false witness against his neighbour is a maul, and a sword, and a sharp arrow.

A man who answereth as a false witness against his neighbour,
Is like a club, and a sword, and a sharpened arrow — Sprl

A man who bears false witness against his neighbor,
is like a war club, or a sword, or a sharp arrow — RSV

Sharp is a nail and a sword and an arrow: so is a man who beareth false witness against his friend — Sept

Like a club, a sword, or a sharp-pointed arrow,
Is a man who bears false witness against his neighbor — AAT

A mace, a sword, a keen arrow, such is the man who bears false witness against his neighbour — Jerus

19. Confidence in an unfaithful man in time of trouble is like a broken tooth, and a foot out of joint.

A broken tooth and a faltering foot
Is confidence in the treacherous in the day of danger — Rhm

A broken tooth, and an unsteady foot,
Is trust in the faithless in time of trouble — ABPS

Like a tooth decayed or a foot limping is a traitor relied on in the day of trouble — NEB

Like a broken tooth or a foot out of joint, so is trust in a faithless man in a time of adversity — Ber

Like an infected tooth or an unsteady foot
is dependence on a faithless man in time of trouble — NAB

20. As he that taketh away a garment in cold weather, and as vinegar upon nitre, so is he that singeth songs to a heavy heart.[24]

As one that taketh off a garment in cold weather, and as vinegar upon soda,
So is he that singeth songs to a heavy heart — ASV

Like one who takes off a garment on a cold day, or like vinegar upon soda, so is a singer of songs to a heavy heart — Ber

He who sings songs to a heavy heart is like one who takes off a garment on a cold day,
and like vinegar on a wound — RSV

Like one who takes off clothing in cold weather and like acid on a wound, is he who makes melody to a sad heart — Bas

Being happy-go-lucky around a person whose heart is heavy is as bad as stealing his jacket in cold weather, or rubbing salt in his wounds — Tay

21. If thine enemy be hungry, give him bread to eat; and if he be thirsty, give him water to drink:

22. For thou shalt heap coals of fire upon his head, and the LORD shall reward thee.

If thy enemy hungers give him bread to eat;
And if he thirsts, give him water to drink.
For thou heapest burning coals on his head;
And Jehovah will requite thee — ABPS

If your enemy be hungry, give him food to eat,
if he be thirsty, give him to drink;
For live coals you will heap on his head,
and the LORD will vindicate you — NAB

If he that hateth thee hunger give him bread to eat,
And if he be thirsty give him water to drink;

[24]Vinegar on "nitre/soda" or on "a wound" is the major variant; although some omit the first line. Tay seems the best interpretation.

For burning coals shalt thou be heaping upon his head, —
And Yahweh will repay thee — Rhm

If thine enemy hunger feed him; if he be thirsty give him drink: for by doing this thou wilt use the means to melt him; and the Lord will reward thee with good — Sept

If your enemy is hungry give him food, and give him water if he thirsts;
for so you shall quench blazing passions,
and the Eternal will reward you — Mof

If your enemy be hungry, give him bread to eat; and if he be thirsty, give him water to drink;
For when you shall do these things for him, you will heap coals of fire upon his head, and the LORD will reward you — Lam

23. The north wind driveth away rain: so doth an angry countenance a backbiting tongue.[25]

The north wind driveth away rain,
So doth an indignant countenance the slanderous tongue — Sprl

As the north wind holds back the rain,
so an angry glance holds back slander — NEB

The north wind stops rain, and a frown the backbiter — Knox

The north wind bringeth forth rain;
So doth a backbiting tongue an angry countenance — ASV

The north wind brings forth rain;
and a backbiting tongue, angry looks — RSV

As the north wind gives birth to rain, so is an angry face caused by a tongue saying evil secretly — Bas

24. It is better to dwell in the corner of the housetop, than with a brawling woman and in a wide house.[26]

25. As cold waters to a thirsty soul, so is good news from a far country.

As cold waters to a faint soul,
So is good news from a far country — JPS

As cold waters for a weary soul,
So is a good report from a far country — YLT

Cold water to the fainting spirit;
So is good news from a far country — ABPS

As cold water is grateful to a thirsty soul; so is good news from a distant country — Sept

Like cold water to the thirsty,
so good news from a far land is refreshing — Mof

26. A righteous man falling down before the wicked is as a troubled fountain, and a corrupt spring.

As a troubled fountain, and a corrupted spring,
So is a righteous man that giveth way before the wicked — ASV

A churned up spring, a fountain fouled: such is the virtuous man trembling before the wicked — Jerus

Like a troubled fountain and a dirty spring, is an upright man who has to give way before evil-doers — Bas

Like a muddied spring or a tainted well
is a righteous man who gives way to a wicked one — NEB

If a godly man compromises with the wicked, it is like polluting a fountain or muddying a spring — Tay

27. It is not good to eat much honey: so for men to search their own glory is not glory.

It is not good to eat much honey;
So for men to search out their own glory is grievous — ASV

To eat honey in abundance is not good,
Nor is searching out their own honour an honourable thing — Rhm

To eat honey in excess is not good;
And their searching after honor is not honor — ABPS

It is not good to eat much honey, nor to search for high praises for oneself — Lam

To eat too much honey is not good;
nor to seek honor after honor — NAB

28. He that hath no rule over his own spirit is like a city that is broken down, and without walls.

[25]The majority agree with ASV: the interpretation of the verb is the question.

[26]See Prov. 21:9.

He whose spirit is without restraint is like a city that is broken down and hath no wall — RV
Like a city broken down and without a wall,
So is he whose spirit is without restraint — JPS
A man without self-control
is like a city broken into and left without walls — RSV
Like a city breached and defenseless
Is a man who has no control of his temper — AAT
An open town, and without defenses: such is a man lacking self-control — Jerus

CHAPTER 26

1. As snow in summer, and as rain in harvest, so honour is not seemly for a fool.
Like snow in summer or rain in harvest,
so honor is not fitting for a fool — RSV
Like snow in summer, or rain in harvest,
Honor is unseasonable for a fool — AAT
As well snow in summer or rain in harvest, as honour paid to a fool — Knox
Like snow in summer and rain when the grain is being cut, so honour is not natural for the foolish — Bas
Honor doesn't go with fools any more than snow with summertime or rain with harvest time — Tay

2. As the bird by wandering, as the swallow by flying, so the curse causeless shall not come.
As a bird by wandering, as a swallow by flying,
So reviling without cause doth not come — YLT
As the sparrow in her wandering, as the swallow in her flying,
So the curse that is causeless alighteth not — ASV
Like sparrows wandering and like birds flying in the air, so the curse that is causeless shall be driven away — Lam
As a sparrow wanders and a swallow flies about, so an unjustified curse does not alight — Ber
Like the sparrow in its flitting, like the swallow in its flight,
a curse uncalled-for arrives nowhere — NAB
As the sparrow escapes, and the swallow flies away,
so the undeserved curse will never hit its mark — Jerus

3. A whip for the horse, a bridle for the ass, and a rod for the fool's back.
A whip is for a horse, a bridle for an ass,
And a rod for the back of fools — YLT
A whip for the horse, a goad for the ass, and a rod for the back of a fool — Lam
A whip for the horse, a mouth-bit for the ass, and a rod for the back of the foolish — Bas
Guide a horse with a whip, a donkey with a bridle, and a rebel with a rod to his back — Tay

4. Answer not a fool according to his folly, lest thou also be like unto him.

5. Answer a fool according to his folly, lest he be wise in his own conceit.
Do not answer a dullard according to his folly,
Lest even thou thyself become like him;
Answer a dullard according to his folly,
Lest he become wise in his own eyes — Rhm
Answer not a fool conformably to his folly; lest thou become like him. But answer a fool according to his folly; that he may not think himself wise — Sept
Never answer a fool according to his folly, lest you become like him:
answer a fool according to his folly, lest he imagines he is wise — Mof
Do not answer a fool in the terms of his folly
for fear you grow like him yourself.
Answer a fool in terms of his folly
for fear he imagines himself wise — Jerus

Do not answer a stupid man in the language of his folly,
or you will grow like him;
answer a stupid man as his folly deserves,
or he will think himself a wise man — NEB

6. He that sendeth a message by the hand of a fool cutteth off the feet, and drinketh damage.

7. The legs of the lame are not equal: so is a parable in the mouth of fools.

He that sendeth a message by the hand of a fool
Cutteth off his own feet, and drinketh in damage.
The legs of the lame hang loose;
So is a parable in the mouth of fools — ASV

One who cutteth off feet, one who drinketh down wrong,
Is he who sendeth a message by the hand of a dullard.
Useless are the legs of the lame
And a proverb in the mouth of a dullard — Rhm

He who sends a message by the hand of a fool
cuts off his own feet and drinks violence.
Like a lame man's legs, which hang useless,
is a proverb in the mouth of fools — RSV

He cuts off his feet, drinks in disaster,
Who sends a message by a fool.
Like legs hanging helpless from the lame
Is a parable in the mouth of fools — AAT

He cuts off his feet,
he drinks down violence,
who sends messages by a fool.
A proverb in the mouth of a fool hangs limp, like crippled legs — NAB

8. As he that bindeth a stone in a sling, so is he that giveth honour to a fool.

As one who is binding a stone in a sling,
So is he who is giving honour to a fool — YLT

He who bindeth a stone in a sling is like him who giveth honour to a fool — Sept

Like fixing a stone tight in the sling,
so is giving honours to a fool — Jerus

Like one who gets the stone caught in his sling
is he who bestows honour on a fool — NEB

Honoring a rebel will backfire like a stone tied to a slingshot — Tay

9. As a thorn goeth up into the hand of a drunkard, so is a parable in the mouth of fools.

As a hooked thorn which goeth up into the hand of a drunkard,
So is a parable in the mouth of fools — Sprl

As a thorn that cometh into the hand of a drunkard,
So is a parable in the mouth of fools — JPS

like thorny branches brandished by a drunkard,
so are maxims on the lips of a fool — Mof

Speech fits as well in a fool's mouth as branch of bramble in the hand of a drunkard — Knox

Like a thorn stick brandished by the hand of a drunkard
is a proverb in the mouth of a fool — NAB

10. The great God that formed all things both rewarded the fool, and rewardeth transgressors.[27]

A master-workman forms all things;
But he that hires a fool,
Is as he that hires passers-by — ABPS

The master workman does everything himself;
But the fool hires a passer-by — AAT

An able man does everything himself:
a fool hires the first passer-by — Mof

As an archer that woundeth all,
So is he that hireth a fool and he that hireth them that pass by —ASV

Like an archer who wounds everybody
is he who hires a passing fool or drunkard — RSV

Like an archer who shoots at any passer-by
is one who hires a stupid man or a drunkard — NEB

[27]Only YLT reads with KJV here. The above are samples of the two main trends in the versions.

11. As a dog returneth to his vomit, so a fool returneth to his folly.

12. Seest thou a man wise in his own conceit? there is more hope of a fool than of him.

As a dog that returneth to his vomit, So is a fool that repeateth his folly. Seest thou a man wise in his own eyes? There is more hope of a fool than of him — JPS

Like a dog at his vomit, the fool goes back ever to his own folly. Who is in more perilous case than the fool himself? The man who lays claim to wisdom — Knox

As a dog that returns to his vomit, so is a fool that misbehaves in his folly. If you should see a man wise in his own eyes, a fool is much better than he — Lam

A dog goes back to his vomit, and a fool repeats his folly. You see a man of self-conceit? More hope for a fool than for him — Mof

As a dog returns to its vomit, so a fool reverts to his folly. You see some man who thinks himself wise? More hope for a fool than for him — Jerus

13. The slothful man saith, There is a lion in the way; a lion is in the streets.[28]

14. As the door turneth upon his hinges, so doth the slothful upon his bed.

The door turneth round on its hinge, And the slothful on his bed — YLT

The door turns on its hinge, And the sluggard on his couch — ABPS

The door is turning upon its hinges, And the sluggard is still upon his bed — JPS

The door turns on its hinges, and the lazy man upon his back — Mof

The door turns on its hinges, the idler, on his bed — Jerus

15. The slothful hideth his hand in his bosom; it grieveth him to bring it again to his mouth.[29]

16. The sluggard is wiser in his own conceit than seven men that can render a reason.

The sluggard is wiser in his own eyes Than seven man that give wise answer — JPS

Wiser is the sluggard in his own eyes, Than seven persons who can answer with judgment — Rhm

The sluggard is wiser in his own eyes Than seven men who can return a judicious answer — Sprl

The sluggard is wiser in his own eyes than seven men who can answer discreetly — RSV

The lazy man imagines he is wiser than a dozen men who argue ably — Mof

17. He that passeth by, and meddleth with strife belonging not to him, is like one that taketh a dog by the ears.

He that passeth by, and vexeth himself with strife belonging not to him, Is like one that taketh a dog by the ears — ASV

He lays hold of a dog by the ears, Who, passing by, gets angry in a quarrel that is not his — ABPS

He who gets mixed up in a fight which is not his business, is like one who takes a dog by the ears while it is going by — Bas

Like a man who seizes a passing cur by the ears is he who meddles in another's quarrel — NEB

18. As a mad man who casteth firebrands, arrows, and death,

19. So is the man that deceiveth his neighbour, and saith, Am not I in sport?

Like a madman who hurls Deadly firebrands and arrows Is he who deceives his neighbor And says, "Was I not joking?" — AAT

Like a madman who throws firebrands, arrows, and death, is the man who deceives his neighbor and says, "I am only joking!" — RSV

Like a lunatic who lets fly deadly brands and arrows, so is he who deceives his neighbour, and then says it was in fun — Mof

Like a crazed archer

[28]See Prov. 22:13.
[29]See Prov. 19:24.

scattering firebrands and deadly arrows
Is the man who deceives his neighbor,
and then says, "I was only joking" — NAB

A man who is caught lying to his neighbor and says, "I was just fooling," is like a madman throwing around firebrands, arrows and death — Tay

20. Where no wood is, there the fire goeth out: so where there is no talebearer, the strife ceaseth.

For lack of wood the fire goeth out;
And where there is no whisperer, contention ceaseth — ASV

Without wood a fire is quenched
And where there is no tattler strife is hushed — Rhm

Where there is no more wood, the fires goes out;
And where there is no talebearer, contention ceases — ABPS

Without wood, the fire goes out; and where there is no secret talk, argument is ended — Bas

For lack of fuel a fire dies down
and for want of a tale-bearer a quarrel subsides — NEB

No fuel, no fire; no tell-tale, no quarrel — Knox

21. As coals are to burning coals, and wood to fire; so is a contentious man to kindle strife.

As coals are to hot embers, and wood to fire; so is a contentious man to inflame strife — RV

As blasts of fire to burning coals, and wood to fire,
so is a contentious man to enkindle strife — Sprl

As charcoal to hot embers and wood to fire,
so is a quarrelsome man for kindling strife — RSV

Charcoal for live embers, wood for fire,
for kindling strife a quarrelsome man — Jerus

What a bellows is to live coals, what wood is to fire,
such is a contentious man in enkindling strife — NAB

22. The words of a talebearer are as wounds, and they go down into the innermost parts of the belly.[30]

23. Burning lips and a wicked heart are like a potsherd covered with silver dross.

Flattering lips with a wicked heart,
Are like a potsherd overlaid with silver dross — Sprl

Fervent lips and a wicked heart
Are like an earthen vessel overlaid with silver dross — ASV

Smooth lips and an evil heart are like a vessel of earth plated with silver waste — Bas

Like silver dross which sticks to an earthen pot, so are enraged lips and an evil heart — Lam

Like the glaze covering an earthen vessel
are smooth lips with an evil heart — RSV

24. He that hateth dissembleth with his lips, and layeth up deceit within him;

25. When he speaketh fair, believe him not: for there are seven abominations in his heart.

With his lips the hater dissembleth,
But within himself he layeth up deceit:
Though he make gracious his voice do not trust him,
For seven abominations are in his heart — Rhm

He who hateth dissembleth with his lips,
And storeth up deceit within him:
Although his voice be kindly, believe him not,
For his heart is full of abominations — Sprl

He that hates dissembles with his lips;
But in his breast he lays up deceit.
When he makes his voice gracious, believe him not;
For seven abominations are in his heart — ABPS

Your enemy may dissemble with his lips,
But in his mind he harbors deceit;
When he speaks fair, believe him not,
For seven abominations are in his mind — AAT

He who hates, pretends with his lips,

[30]See Prov. 18:8.

but he harbors deceit within; when he speaks pleasantly, do not trust him, for there are seven abominations in his heart — Ber

With his lips an enemy pretends,
but in his inmost being he maintains deceit;
When he speaks graciously, trust him not,
for seven abominations are in his heart — NAB

26. Whose hatred is covered by deceit, his wickedness shall be shewed before the whole congregation.

Though his hatred cover itself with guile,
His wickedness shall be openly showed before the assembly — ASV

Though his hatred be concealed with deceit,
His wickedness shall be revealed before the congregation — JPS

yet, though he hid his hatred craftily,
his malice shall be publicly exposed — Mof

he may cloak his enmity with dissimulation,
but his wickedness is shown up before the assembly — NEB

Hatred may well dsguise itself with guile,
only to unmask its spite before the community — Jerus

Vain the pretences that cloak his malice; before the whole assembly it shall be made known — Knox

27. Whoso diggeth a pit shall fall therein: and he that rolleth a stone, it will return upon him.

Whoso is digging a pit falleth into it,
And the roller of a stone, to him it turneth — YLT

Whoever digs a pit shall fall into it;
the stone a man sets rolling recoils upon himself — Mof

He who digs a pit will fall into it;
And he who rolls a stone — it will come back upon him — AAT

He who digs a pit will fall into it, and a stone will come back upon him who starts it rolling — RSV

May he who diggeth a pit for his neighbour fall into it; and he who rolleth a stone, roll it on himself — Sept

28. A lying tongue hateth those that are afflicted by it; and a flattering mouth worketh ruin.

A false tongue hateth them who are crushed by it,
And a flattering mouth worketh occasion of stumbling — Rhm

A lying tongue hateth those whom it hath wounded;
And a flattering mouth worketh ruin — ASV

A false tongue hates its victims;
And a smooth mouth will work ruin — ABPS

A lying tongue hateth truth; and a flattering mouth worketh ruin — Sept

A false tongue has hate for those who have clean hearts, and a smooth mouth is a cause of falling — Bas

A lying tongue brings destruction to itself;
And a flattering mouth works its own ruin — AAT

CHAPTER 27

1. Boast not thyself of to-morrow; for thou knowest not what a day may bring forth.

Boast not of things of to-morrow; for thou knowest not what the coming day will bring forth — Sept

Do not flatter thyself with hopes of to-morrow; what lies in the womb of the future thou canst not tell — Knox

Do not flatter yourself about tomorrow,
for you never know what a day will bring forth — NEB

Don't brag about your plans for tomorrow — wait and see what happens — Tay

2. Let another man praise thee, and not thine own mouth; a stranger, and not thine own lips.

3. A stone is heavy, and the sand weighty; but a fool's wrath is heavier than them both.

Heavy is a stone and weighty is sand, —
But the vexation of a fool is heavier than both — Rhm

A stone is heavy, and sand is weighty, but a fool's provocation is heavier than both — RSV

A stone is heavy, sand is weighty; but a vexatious fool is worse to bear than both — Mof

Stone is a burden and sand a dead weight,
but to be vexed by a fool is more burdensome than either — NEB

4. Wrath is cruel, and anger is outrageous; but who is able to stand before envy?

Wrath is cruel, and anger is overwhelming;
But who is able to stand before jealousy — ASV

Fury is fierce, and anger is overflowing,
And who standeth before jealousy — YLT

Anger is violent; and like an inundation is wrath;
But who can abide in the presence of jealousy — Sprl

Wrath is cruel, and anger is impetuous;
But who can stand before jealousy — ABPS

Anger is relentless, and wrath overwhelming —
but before jealousy who can stand — NAB

Wrath is cruel, and angry feeling an overflowing stream; but who does not give way before envy — Bas

5. Open rebuke is better than secret love.

6. Faithful are the wounds of a friend; but the kisses of an enemy are deceitful.

Better is open rebuke than love that is hidden.
Faithful are the wounds of a friend: but the kisses of an enemy are profuse — RV

Better is open reproof than hidden love.
Faithful are the wounds of a lover,
And abundant the kisses of an enemy — YLT

Open rebukes are better than concealed love.
More faithful are the wounds of a friend; than the feigned kisses of an enemy — Sept

Better is open rebuke
Than hidden love.
Sincere are the wounds of a friend;
But deceitful are the kisses of an enemy — AAT

Better a rebuke revealed than love concealed. Faithful are the wounds of a friend; profuse are the kisses of an enemy — Ber

Better open reproof
than voiceless love.
From one who loves, wounds are well-intentioned;
from one who hates, kisses are ominous — Jerus

Better a frank word of reproof
than the love that will not speak.
Wounds from a friend are honest,
but an enemy's kisses are false — Mof

7. The full soul loatheth an honeycomb; but to the hungry soul every bitter thing is sweet.

The repleted appetite loatheth virgin honey,
And to a famishing soul every bitter thing is sweet — Sprl

A sated spirit tramples the dripping honey;
But a famished spirit — every bitter thing is sweet — ABPS

He who is sated loathes honey,
but to one who is hungry everything bitter is sweet — RSV

The full man has no use for honey, but to the man in need of food every bitter thing is sweet — Bas

A man full-fed refuses honey,
but even bitter food tastes sweet to a hungry man — NEB

8. As a bird that wandereth from her nest, so is a man that wandereth from his place.

Like a bird that strays from her nest
Is a man that strays from his home — AAT

Like a bird that wanders from her nest,
so is a man who wanders far from home — Mof

Like a bird that wanders from its nest,
so is a man who is moved from his place — Lam

Like a bird that strays from its nest, so is the man who strays from where he belongs — Jerus

9. Ointment and perfume rejoice the heart: so doth the sweetness of a man's friend by hearty counsel.

Oil and perfume rejoice the heart;
So doth the sweetness of a man's friend that cometh of hearty counsel — ASV

Oil and perfume make the heart rejoice, as does the pleasantness of a friend's suggestions from the heart — Ber

Oil and perfume rejoice the heart; so does the sweetness of a friend's counsel that comes from the heart — Amp

Oil and perfume make glad the heart, and the wise suggestion of a friend is sweet to the soul — Bas

Fragrant oil gladdens the heart,
friendship's sweetness comforts the soul — Jerus

10. Thine own friend, and thy father's friend, forsake not; neither go into thy brother's house in the day of thy calamity: for better is a neighbour that is near than a brother far off.

Thine own friend and thy father's friend cast not off,
Then shalt thou not need to go to thy brother's house in the day of thy calamity;
For better is a neighbour dwelling near than a brother afar off — Sprl

Friend of thine, and friend that was thy father's, never forsake; so, in thy sore need, no kinsman's door thou shalt need to enter.
Neighbour over the way is better than kinsman at a distance — Knox

Your own friend and your father's friend forsake not;
but if ruin befalls you, enter not a kinsman's house.
Better is a neighbour near at hand than a brother far away — NAB

Do not abandon friend, or father's friend;
when trouble comes, do not go running to your brother's house.
Better a friend near than a brother far away — Jerus

Never abandon a friend — either yours or your father's. Then you won't need to go to a distant relative for help in your time of need — Tay

11. My son, be wise, and make my heart glad, that I may answer him that reproacheth me.

My son, wouldst thou be thy father's pride?
Court wisdom, and silence thy detractors — Knox

My son, be wise, and make my heart glad,
That I may answer him that taunteth me — JPS

Be wise, my son, and gladden my heart,
That I may answer the man who would taunt me — AAT

Learn to be wise, my son, and gladden my heart,
that I may have an answer for the man who insults me — Jerus

Be wise, my son, then you will bring joy to my heart,
and I shall be able to forestall my critics — NEB

Delight my heart by being wise, my son,
that I may answer anyone who taunts me — Mof

12. A prudent man foreseeth the evil, and hideth himself; but the simple pass on, and are punished.

A prudent man seeth the evil, and hideth himself;
But the simple pass on, and suffer for it — ASV

A prudent man seeth the evil, and hideth himself;
But the thoughtless pass on, and are punished — JPS

When ills approach, a prudent man is hidden: but the simple pass on to their sorrow — Sept

A prudent man sees danger and hides himself;
but the simple go on, and suffer for it — RSV

A prudent man foresees the evil and hides himself; but the fools pass on, and suffer loss — Lam

The shrewd man perceives evil and hides;
simpletons continue on and suffer the penalty — NAB

13. Take his garment that is surety for a

stranger, and take a pledge of him for a strange woman.[31]

14. He that blesseth his friend with a loud voice, rising early in the morning, it shall be counted a curse to him.

He who blesseth a friend with a loud voice, rising early, will appear not unlike one who curseth him — Sept

He that blesseth his friend with a loud voice in the morning early
A reproach shall it be reckoned to him — Rhm

He that blesses his neighbor with loud voice,
Rising early in the morning,
It shall be accounted to him as cursing — ABPS

He who blesses his neighbor with a loud voice,
rising early in the morning,
will be counted as cursing — RSV

He who at dawn loudly blesses his neighbour
is accounted to curse — Jerus

15. A continual dropping in a very rainy day and a contentious woman are alike.

16. Whosoever hideth her hideth the wind, and the ointment of his right hand, which bewrayeth itself.

A continual dropping in a very rainy day
And a contentious woman are alike:
He that would restrain her restraineth the wind;
And his right hand encountereth oil — ASV

A continual dropping in a day of rain,
And a woman of contentions are alike,
Whoso is hiding her hath hidden the wind,
And the ointment of his right hand calleth out — YLT

A constant drip on a rainy day
And a quarrelsome wife are alike;
He who would restrain her would restrain the wind,
Or grasp oil with his right hand — AAT

Endless dripping on a rainy day —
that is what a nagging wife is like.
As well try to control the wind as to control her!
As well try to pick up oil in one's fingers — NEB

A constant dripping on a rainy day and a cranky woman are much alike! You can no more stop her complaints than you can stop the wind or hold onto anything with oil-slick hands — Tay

17. Iron sharpeneth iron; so a man sharpeneth the countenance of his friend.

Iron sharpens iron,
and one man sharpens another — RSV

As iron whets iron,
so one man whets another — Mof

Iron sharpens iron; so a man enlightens the face of his friend — Lam

Iron is made the finer by iron,
a man is refined by contact with his neighbour — Jerus

As iron sharpens iron, so one man sharpens the wits of another — NEB

Iron whets iron, friend shapes friend — Knox

18. Whoso keepeth the fig tree shall eat the fruit thereof: so he that waiteth on his master shall be honoured.

He who planteth a fig tree shall eat of its fruit; and he who guardeth his master shall be honoured — Sept

The keeper of a fig-tree eateth its fruit,
And the preserver of his master is honoured — YLT

Whoso cultivates the fig-tree shall eat of its fruit;
And whoso waiteth on his master shall be honoured — Sprl

He who takes care of his fig tree will eat the fruit of it;
And he who attends to his master will be honored — AAT

He who tends a fig tree eats its fruit,
and he who is attentive to his master will be enriched — NAB

19. As in water face answereth to face, so the heart of man to man.

Like face looking at face in water, so are the hearts of men to one another — Bas

As face reflects face in water,
So the mind of man reflects man — AAT

[31]See Prov. 20:16.

As one face is like another,
so is one mind like another — Mof
As in water face answers to face,
so the mind of man reflects the man — RSV
As face answers face reflected in the water,
so one man's heart answers another's — NEB

20. Hell and destruction are never full; so the eyes of man are never satisfied.
Sheol and Abaddon are never satisfied;
And the eyes of man are never satisfied — ASV
The grave and destruction are never satisfied: in like manner the eyes of men are insatiable — Sept
The nether-world and Destruction are never satiated;
So the eyes of man are never satiated — JPS
The nether world and the abyss are never satisfied;
so too the eyes of men — NAB
The underworld and Abaddon are never full, and the eyes of man have never enough — Bas

21. As the fining pot for silver, and the furnace for gold; so is a man to his praise.
A refining pot for silver, and a furnace for gold;
So is a man to the mouth that praises him — ABPS
As the fining pot is for silver, and the furnace for gold;
So is a man tested by the mouth of those who flatter him — Sprl
The refining pot is for silver, and the furnace for gold;
And a man is tried by his praise — ASV
The crucible is for silver, and the furnace for gold, and a man is tested by what he praises — Ber
The melting-pot is for silver and the crucible for gold,
but praise is the test of character — NEB

22. Though thou shouldest bray a fool in a mortar among wheat with a pestle, yet will not his foolishness depart from him.
Though thou pound a fool in a mortar amidst grain with a pestle
His folly will not depart from him — Rhm
Though you crush the fool in a mortar with a pestle among the crushed grain, yet his foolishness will not leave him — Ber
Crush a fool in a mortar with a pestle along with crushed grain, yet his folly will not depart from him — RSV
Though you should pound the fool to bits
with the pestle, amid the grits in a mortar,
his folly would not go out of him — NAB
Pound the fool in a mortar as you may,
you will not separate him from his folly — Jerus

23. Be thou diligent to know the state of thy flocks, and look well to thy herds:

24. For riches are not for ever: and doth the crown endure to every generation?
Be careful to know the state of thy flock; and pay close attention to thy herd: for wealth and power do not continue with a man forever; nor can he transmit them from one generation to another — Sept
Look well to the appearance of thy flock;
Give heed to the herds.
For wealth is not forever,
Nor is a crown to generation to generation — ABPS
Look well to the state of your flocks,
and be careful of your herds;
for riches do not last for ever,
nor wealth from age to age — Mof
Know thoroughly the condition of your flocks; keep your mind on your herds; for riches are not forever — and is a crown from generation to generation? — Ber
Be careful to know your own sheep and take good care of your flocks;
for possessions do not last for ever,
nor will a crown endure to endless generations — NEB

25. The hay appeareth, and the tender grass sheweth itself, and herbs of the mountains are gathered.

26. The lambs are for thy clothing, and the goats are the price of the field.

The grass is taken away and the young shoot showeth itself,
And the herbage of the mountains is gathered;
There are lambs for thy clothing
And for the price of thy field there are he-goats — Rhm

When the grass shoots forth, and the tender herb is seen,
Then let the herbage of the mountain be gathered.
The lambs are for thy clothing,
And the goats to pay the price of the field — Sprl

The hay is carried, and the tender grass showeth itself,
And the herbs of the mountains are gathered in.
The lambs are for thy clothing,
And the goats are the price of the field — ASV

When the hay is cut, and the aftermath appears,
And the grass of the mountains is gathered in,
Lambs will supply you with clothing,
And goats with the price of a field — AAT

When the grass is taken away and the aftergrowth appears,
and the mountain greens are gathered in,
The lambs will provide you with clothing,
and the goats will bring the price of a field — NAB

27. And thou shalt have goats' milk enough for thy food, for the food of thy household, and for the maintenance for thy maidens.

there will be enough goats' milk for your food,
for the food of your household
and maintenance for your maidens — RSV

There will be goats' milk enough for your food, and for the support of your servant-girls — Bas

with ample milk to feed you,
and to maintain your maids — Mof

goats' milk sufficient to feed you,
and to provide for your serving girls — Jerus

while the goats' milk is enough for your food
and nourishment for your maidens — NEB

CHAPTER 28

1. The wicked flee when no man pursueth: but the righteous are bold as a lion.

The wicked flee, when no one pursues;
But the righteous are bold as the young lion — ABPS

The wicked flee when there is no one pursuing, but the righteous are as fearless as a young lion — Ber

The lawless fleeth when no man pursueth,
But the righteous like a lion are confident — Rhm

The wicked flee when no man pursueth;
But the righteous are secure as a young lion — JPS

The evil man goes running away when no man is after him, but the upright are without fear, like the lion — Bas

2. For the transgression of a land many are the princes thereof: but by a man of understanding and knowledge the state thereof shall be prolonged.

When a land transgresses it has many rulers;
but with men of understanding and knowledge
its stability will long continue — RSV

Through the rebellion of a land many are its princes;
But through the prudence of men government shall be prolonged — Sprl

When a land revolts, its princes are many;
But, with discerning and knowing men, there may be permanence — ABPS

When rebellion breaks out in a land, there arise many rulers;
But through men of wisdom and intelligence, order will long prevail — AAT

If a land is rebellious, its princes will be many;
but with a prudent man it knows security — NAB

3. A poor man that oppresseth the poor is like a sweeping rain which leaveth no food.

A needy man that oppresseth the poor
Is like a sweeping rain which leaveth no food— ASV

A poor man that oppresseth the weak
Is like a sweeping rain which leaveth no food — JPS

A poor man who oppresseth the helpless
Is like a rain beating down, leaving no food — Rhm

A poor man who oppresses the weak is like a cloudburst that leaves no nourishment — Ber

When a poor man oppresses those even poorer, he is like an unexpected flood sweeping away their last hope — Tay

4. They that forsake the law praise the wicked: but such as keep the law contend with them.

Those forsaking the law praise the wicked,
Those keeping the law plead against them — YLT

Lawbreakers praise the wicked;
But the law-biding are zealous against them — AAT

Those who abandon the law praise the wicked man,
but those who keep the law war against him — NAB

Those who forsake the law have a good word for the wicked,
those who observe the law have not time for such — Jerus

The lawless praise wicked men;
the law-abiding contend with them — NEB

5. Evil men understand not judgment; but they that seek the LORD understand all things.

Evil men understand not justice:
But they that seek Jehovah understand all things — ASV

Wicked men consider not justice,
But they who seek Yahweh consider everything — Rhm

Wicked men do not regard justice;
But those who seek Jehovah, regard it in all things — Sprl

Bad men will not understand judgment: but they who seek the Lord will be wise in everything — Sept

Evil men do not understand justice,
but those who seek the LORD understand it completely — RSV

6. Better is the poor that walketh in his uprightness, than he that is perverse in his ways, though he be rich.

Better is the poor that walketh in his integrity, than he that is perverse in his ways, though he be rich — RV

Better is a poor man who walks in his integrity
Than he who is crooked in his ways, although he be rich — AAT

Better a poor man of honest life than a false creature, for all his wealth — Mof

Better is a poor man who walketh in truth than a rich liar — Sept

Better be poor and above reproach than rich and crooked — NEB

7. Whoso keepeth the law is a wise son: but he that is a companion of riotous men shameth his father.

Whoso keepeth the law is a wise son;
But he that is a companion of gluttons shameth his father — ASV

A wise son observeth the teaching;
But he that is a companion of gluttonous men shameth his father — JPS

He that keepeth instruction is a son with discernment,
But a companion of squanderers bringeth shame to his father — Rhm

He is a discerning son who keeps the law, but a companion of gluttons puts his father to shame — Ber

A discerning son is he who keeps the Law;
an associate of profligates brings shame on his father — Jerus

A son's wisdom is to obey his father's teaching, not to shame him by keeping riotous company — Knox

8. He that by usury and unjust gain increaseth his substance, he shall gather it for him that will pity the poor.

He that augmenteth his substance by interest and increase,
Gathereth it for him that hath pity on the poor — ASV

Whoso increaseth his wealth by usury and by interest,
He shall gather it for him who shall pity the poor — Sprl

He who increases his wealth by usury

and unjust means shall leave it for him who is kind to the poor — Lam

He who increases his wealth by interest and overcharge
gathers it for him who is kind to the poor — NAB

He who increases his wealth by usury and interest
amasses it for someone else who will bestow it on the poor — Jerus

9. He that turneth away his ear from hearing the law, even his prayer shall be abomination.

He that turneth away his ear from hearing instruction
Even his prayer is an abomination — Rhm

As for him who turneth away his ear from hearkening to the law; even his prayer is an abomination — Sept

He who turns a deaf ear to instruction —
His very prayer is an abomination — AAT

As for the man whose ear is turned away from hearing the law, even his prayer is disgusting — Bas

If a man is deaf to the orders of religion,
his very prayer is loathsome to the Eternal — Mof

10. Whoso causeth the righteous to go astray in an evil way, he shall fall himself into his own pit: but the upright shall have good things in possession.

Whoso leadeth the righteous astray in an evil way,
He shall fall into his own pit;
But the upright shall inherit blessing — Sprl

Whoso causeth the upright to go astray in an evil way,
He shall fall himself into his own pit;
But the whole-hearted shall inherit good — JPS

He who misleads the upright into an evil way
will fall into his own pit;
but the blameless will have a goodly inheritance — RSV

Ruin he brings on himself, that leads the innocent into ill ways, and honest men shall be the heirs of him — Knox

A curse on those who lead astray the godly. But men who encourage the upright to do good shall be given a worthwhile reward — Tay

11. The rich man is wise in his own conceit; but the poor that hath understanding searcheth him out.

Wise in his own eyes is the man that is rich,
But a poor man of discernment searcheth him out — Rhm

A rich man is wise in his own conceit.
But a poor man who hath understanding will find him out — Sept

Wise in his own eyes is a rich man, but a discerning poor man sees through him — Ber

Rich men may think that they are wise,
but the poor have wit to see through him — Mof

The rich man is wise in his own eyes, but a poor man who is intelligent sees through him — NAB

The rich man may think himself wise, but a poor man with sense will unmask him — Jerus

12. When righteous men do rejoice, there is great glory: but when the wicked rise, a man is hidden.

In the exulting of the righteous the glory is abundant,
And in the rising of the wicked, man is apprehensive — YLT

When the righteous triumph, there is great glory;
But when the wicked rise, men hide themselves — ASV

When the righteous exult, there is great glory;
But when the wicked rise, men must be sought for — JPS

When the righteous triumph, there is a great celebration;
But when the wicked rise to power, men hide themselves — AAT

When the just are triumphant, there is great jubilation;
but when the wicked gain preeminence, people hide — NAB

13. He that covereth his sins shall not prosper: but whoso confesseth and forsaketh them shall have mercy.

He that covereth his transgressions shall not prosper; but whoso confesseth and forsaketh them shall obtain mercy — RV

Whoso excuseth his transgressions shall not prosper;
But whoso confesseth and forsaketh them shall find mercy — Sprl

He who covereth his wickedness shall not prosper; but he who confesseth and forsaketh will be beloved — Sept

He who hides his transgression shall not prosper; but he who confesses his sins and forsakes them, God will have mercy upon him — Lam

Conceal your faults, and you will not prosper;
confess and give them up, and you will find mercy — NEB

14. Happy is the man that feareth alway: but he that hardeneth his heart shall fall into mischief.

How happy is the man who is ever circumspect,
Whereas he that hardeneth his heart shall fall into calamity — Rhm

Blessed is the man who fears the LORD always;
but he who hardens his heart will fall into calamity — RSV

Happy is the man who lives always in awe;
But he who hardens his conscience will fall into misfortune — AAT

Blessed is the man who is always reverent; but he who hardens his heart will fall into calamity — Ber

Happy the man who lives in fear of sin: reckless men come to grief — Mof

Blessed is the man who reveres God, but the man who doesn't care is headed for serious trouble — Tay

15. As a roaring lion, and a ranging bear; so is a wicked ruler over the poor people.

As a roaring lion, and a ravenous bear;
So is a wicked ruler over a poor people — JPS

A growling lion, and a ranging bear,
Is a wicked ruler over a feeble people — ABPS

Like a loud-voiced lion and a wandering bear, is an evil ruler over a poor people — Bas

A roaring lion, a bear on the prowl — such is a tyrant over a poor people — Mof

A roaring lion, a hungry bear,
such is the bad ruler of a poor people — Jerus

16. The prince that wanteth understanding is also a great oppressor: but he that hateth covetousness shall prolong his days.

A leader lacking understanding multiplieth oppressions,
Whoso is hating dishonest gain prolongeth days — YLT

A ruler who lacks understanding is a cruel oppressor;
but he who hates unjust gain will prolong his days — RSV

A prince who is an oppressor is devoid of intelligence;
But he who hates ill-gotten gain will prolong his life — AAT

The less prudent the prince, the more his deeds oppress.
He who hates ill-gotten gain prolongs his days — NAB

A prince lacking sense is rich in rapacity,
he who hates avarice will lengthen his days — Jerus

17. A man that doeth violence to the blood of any person shall flee to the pit; let no man stay him.

A man that is laden with the blood of any person
Shall flee unto the pit; let no man stay him — ASV

A man that is laden with the blood of any person
Shall hasten his steps unto the pit; none will support him — JPS

A man oppressed by the commission of manslaughter,
Fleeth to the pit lest they should catch him:
Let no one detain him — Sprl

A man oppressed with life-blood,
Will flee even to the pit, that they may not lay hold on him — ABPS

If a man is burdened with the blood of another,
let him be a fugitive until death;
let no one help him — RSV

Though a man burdened with human blood
were to flee to the grave, none should support him — NAB

18. Whoso walketh uprightly shall be

saved: but he that is perverse in his ways shall fall at once.

He that walketh with integrity shall be saved,
But he that is crooked, turning two ways, shall fall in one — Rhm

He who walketh righteously will be helped; but he who walketh in crooked ways will be entangled — Sept

He whose ways are upright will be safe, but sudden will be the fall of him whose ways are twisted — Bas

He who walks uprightly shall be saved; but he who is perverse in his ways shall fall into a pit — Lam

Whoever walks wholeheartedly will be saved, but the perverse in his double-dealing will fall in a moment — Ber

19. He that tilleth his land shall have plenty of bread: but he that followeth after vain persons shall have poverty enough.[32]

Whoso is tilling his ground is satisfied with bread,
And whoso is pursuing vanity,
Is filled with poverty — YLT

Whoso tilleth his land shall be satisfied with bread;
And whoso pursueth worthless things shall have poverty enough — Sprl

He who tilleth his own ground shall have plenty of bread; but he who followeth idleness, shall have plenty of poverty — Sept

He who tills his ground will have plenty of food;
But he who follows empty pursuits will have plenty of poverty — AAT

One who cultivates his land has plenty to eat;
idle pursuits lead to poverty — NEB

20. A faithful man shall abound with blessings: but he that maketh haste to be rich shall not be innocent.

A faithful man shall abound with blessings;
But he that maketh haste to be rich shall not be unpunished — ASV

A man of fidelity aboundeth in blessings,
But one hasting to be rich shall not be held innocent — Rhm

A man of good faith will have great blessing, but one attempting to get wealth quickly will not go free from punishment — Bas

Trustworthy men are richly blessed: men in a hurry to get rich incur guilt — Mof

The man who wants to do right will get a rich reward. But the man who wants to get rich quick will quickly fail — Tay

21. To have respect of persons is not good: for for a piece of bread that man will transgress.

To have respect of persons is not good;
For a man will transgress for a piece of bread — JPS

To be partial in judgment is not good;
Even for a morsel of bread a man may fall into sin — AAT

To show partiality is never good: for even a morsel of bread a man may do wrong — NAB

To have respect of persons is not good: neither that a man should transgress for a piece of bread — RV

To favour one side is not fair —
to sin, bribed by a bit of bread — Mof

22. He that hasteth to be rich hath an evil eye, and considereth not that poverty shall come upon him.

He that is eager for wealth is a man of evil eye,
And knows not when want shall come upon him — ABPS

He chases after wealth, the man of greedy eye,
not knowing that want is overtaking him — Jerus

He that hath an evil eye hasteth after riches,
And knoweth not that want shall come upon him — ASV

A man who hath a covetous eye hasteneth after riches,
And considereth not that want may come upon him — Sprl

The selfish man is eager to get rich;
he never dreams he may be in distress — Mof

The avaricious man rushes after wealth,
Not knowing that want will befall him — AAT

[32]Compare with Prov. 12:11.

23. He that rebuketh a man afterwards shall find more favour than he that flattereth with the tongue.

Whoso is reproving a man afterwards findeth grace,
More than a flatterer with the tongue — YLT

He who reproveth a man's ways shall have more thanks than he who hath a flattering tongue — Sept

He who says words of protest to a man will later have more approval than one who says smooth words with his tongue — Bas

Take a man to task and in the end win more thanks
than the man with a flattering tongue — NEB

More thanks thou wilt have, in the end, for honest reproof than for designing flattery — Knox

24. Whoso robbeth his father or his mother, and saith, It is no transgression; the same is the companion of a destroyer.

He that robbeth his father or his mother, and saith
It is no transgression
Companion is he to one who wasteth — Rhm

He that robs his father and his mother,
And says, It is no trespass;
The same is a companion for a destroyer — ABPS

He who robs his father or his mother and says, It is no transgression, the same is the companion of a wicked man — Lam

He who defrauds father or mother and calls it no sin,
is a partner of the brigand — NAB

He who takes from his father or his mother what is theirs by right, and says, It is no sin; is the same as a taker of life — Bas

A man who robs his parents and says, "What's wrong with that?" is no better than a murderer — Tay

25. He that is of a proud heart stirreth up strife: but he that putteth his trust in the LORD shall be made fat.

He that is of a greedy spirit stirreth up strife;
But he that putteth his trust in Jehovah shall be made fat — ASV

He that is of a greedy spirit stirreth up strife;
But he that putteth his trust in the LORD shall be abundantly gratified — JPS

Whoso is covetous stirreth up strife;
But whoso trusteth in JEHOVAH shall be made prosperous — Sprl

A grasping nature stirs up enmity,
but he who trusts in the Eternal thrives — Mof

A self-important man provokes quarrels,
but he who trusts in the LORD grows fat and prosperous — NEB

26. He that trusteth in his own heart is a fool: but whoso walketh wisely, he shall be delivered.

He who putteth confidence in the boldness of his heart is a fool: but he who walketh wisely shall be saved — Sept

He whose faith is in himself is foolish; but everyone walking wisely will be kept safe — Bas

He who trusts in his own mind is a fool;
but he who walks in wisdom will be delivered — RSV

He is a fool that trusts his own wit; follow the rule of wise men, if thou wouldst reach safety — Knox

He who trusts his own promptings is a fool,
he whose ways are wise will be safe — Jerus

A man is a fool to trust himself! But those who use God's wisdom are safe — Tay

27. He that giveth unto the poor shall not lack: but he that hideth his eyes shall have many a curse.

He who gives to the poor shall not come to want;
But he who shuts his eyes against them will have many a curse — AAT

He who gives to the poor shall not lack; but he who turns his eyes away from the needy shall have many a curse — Lam

A man who helps the poor will never want;
he who ignores them will get many a curse — Mof

He who gives to the poor will never be in need, but great curses will be on him who gives no attention to them — Bas

28. When the wicked rise, men hide themselves: but when they perish, the righteous increase.

When lawless men arise a common man will hide himself,
But when they perish righteous men multiply — Rhm

When wicked men are exalted, men hide themselves;
But when they perish, the righteous multiply — Sprl

When the wicked rise to power, men hide themselves;
But when they perish, the righteous flourish — AAT

When the wicked gain pre-eminence, other men hide;
but at their fall the just flourish — NAB

When the wicked are in the ascendant, men take cover,
but when they perish, virtuous men multiply — Jerus

When the wicked prosper, good men go away; when the wicked meet disaster, good men return — Tay

CHAPTER 29

1. He, that being often reproved hardeneth his neck, shall suddenly be destroyed, and that without remedy.

A man often reproved, who hardens his neck,
Shall suddenly be destroyed, and without remedy — ABPS

He who is often reproved, yet stiffens his neck
will suddenly be broken beyond healing — RSV

He that being often reproved stiffeneth his neck
Suddenly shall be hurt and there be no healing — Rhm

He who stiffens his neck against many reproofs
Will suddenly be broken beyond repair — AAT

He who is obstinate, in spite of many a warning,
will suddenly be done for — Mof

A man who is still stubborn after much reproof
will suddenly be broken past mending — NEB

2. When the righteous are in authority, the people rejoice: but when the wicked beareth rule, the people mourn.

When the righteous are exalted the people rejoice;
But when the wicked rule, the people lament — Sprl

When the righteous are increased, the people rejoice;
But when a wicked man beareth rule, the people sigh — ASV

When the righteous are many, the people increase; but when the wicked are in authority, the people groan — Lam

When the upright have power, the people are glad; when an evil man is ruler, grief comes on the people — Bas

When the just prevail, the people rejoice;
but when the wicked rule, the people groan — NAB

With good men in authority, the people rejoice; but with the wicked in power, they groan — Tay

3. Whoso loveth wisdom rejoiceth his father: but he that keepeth company with harlots spendeth his substance.

A man who loveth wisdom gladdeneth his father,
But a companion of harlots destroyeth wealth — Rhm

One that loves wisdom rejoices his father;
But a companion of harlots squanders wealth — ABPS

A lover of wisdom brings joy to his father,
but one who keeps company with harlots squanders his wealth — NEB

The lover of Wisdom makes his father glad,
but the patron of harlots fritters his wealth away — Jerus

4. The king by judgment establisheth the land: but he that receiveth gifts overthroweth it.

The king by justice establisheth the land;

But he that exacteth gifts overthroweth it — ASV

The king establisheth a land by justice; But a man who taketh bribes destroyeth it — Sprl

A king by justice gives stability to a land; But he who makes heavy exactions brings it to ruin — AAT

By justice a king gives stability to the land, but one who exacts gifts ruins it — RSV

A just king gives stability to his nation, but one who demands bribes destroys it — Tay

5. A man that flattereth his neighbour spreadeth a net for his feet.

6. In the transgression of an evil man there is a snare: but the righteous doth sing and rejoice.

A man who flattereth his neighbour Spreadeth a net over his steps. In the transgression of a wicked man is a snare, But the righteous doth shout in triumph and rejoice — Rhm

A man who says smooth things to his neighbour is stretching out a net for his steps. In the steps of an evil man there is a net for him, but the upright man gets away quickly and is glad — Bas

A man who flatters his neighbor spreads a net for his feet. An evil man shall be ensnared in his wickedness; but the righteous shall sing and rejoice — Lam

The man who flatters his neighbor is spreading a net under his feet. The wicked man steps into a snare, but the just man runs on joyfully — NAB

A man who flatters his fellow is spreading a net to trip him up. A bad man is snared by his own sin, but good men can go forward happily — Mof

By empty flattery thou mayst lay a snare for thy friend's feet. By his own false steps the sinner is entangled; innocence goes singing and rejoicing on its way — Knox

7. The righteous considereth the cause of the poor: but the wicked regardeth not to know it.

The righteous regards the cause of the weak; The wicked will not discern knowledge — ABPS

The righteous taketh knowledge of the cause of the poor; The wicked hath not understanding to know it — ASV

The righteous man knows the rights of the weak; the wicked man does not understand such knowledge — Ber

The upright man gives attention to the cause of the poor: the evildoer gives no thought to it — Bas

A good man respects the rights of the poor; A wicked man knows no respect — AAT

The just man has a care for the rights of the poor; the wicked man has no such concern — NAB

8. Scornful men bring a city into a snare: but wise men turn away wrath.

Scoffers set a city in a flame; But wise men turn away wrath — ASV

Men given to mockery inflame a city, — But wise men turn away anger — Rhm

Scorning men kindle discord in a city, But wise men suppress the indignation — Sprl

Scoffers set cities in a ferment, but wise men moderate anger — Jerus

Unscrupulous men kindle strife in a city: the sensible discourage party-spirit — Mof

Arrogance can inflame a city, but wisdom averts the people's anger — NEB

9. If a wise man contendeth with a foolish man, whether he rage or laugh, there is no rest.

If a wise man hath a controversy with a foolish man, whether he be angry or laugh, there will be no rest — RV

When a wise man goes to law with a foolish man, Whether he be angry or laugh, there is no rest — ABPS

If a wise man goes to law with a fool,

he will meet abuse or derision, but get no remedy — NEB
If a wise man has an argument with a fool,
the fool only rages and laughs, and there is no quiet — RSV
Let a wise man argue with a fool,
be he angry or good-humoured he will not gain his end — Jerus

10. The bloodthirsty hate the upright: but the just seek his soul.[33]
Bloodthirsty men hate the man of integrity, but the upright seek his life — Ber
Bloodthirsty men hate the honest man, but the upright show concern for his life — NAB
Blood-thirsty creatures hate a blameless man;
the upright plan how to protect him — Mof
The bloodthirsty hate him that is perfect;
And as for the upright, they seek his life — ASV
Bloodthirsty men hate one who is blameless,
and the wicked seek his life — RSV
Bloodthirsty men hate the innocent,
And seek the life of the upright — AAT

11. A fool uttereth all his mind: but a wise man keepeth it in till afterwards.
A fool spendeth all his spirit,
But a wise man stilleth it within him — JPS
All his anger doth a dullard let go,
But a wise man by keeping it back stilleth it — Rhm
A fool uttereth all his anger: but a wise man keepeth it back and stilleth it — RV
A foolish man lets out all his wrath, but a wise man keeps it back quietly — Bas
The fool comes out with all his angry feelings,
but the wise man subdues and restrains them — Jerus
A stupid man gives free rein to his anger;
a wise man waits and lets it grow cool — NEB

12. If a ruler hearken to lies, all his servants are wicked.
A ruler who payeth attention to lying words,
All his servants will be wicked men — Sprl
When a king hearkeneth to falsehood, all under him are transgressors — Sept
When a ruler listens to false accusations,
his servants become scoundrels — Mof
If a ruler listen to lies,
All his servants become depraved — AAT
If a ruler listens to false suggestions all his officials will be wicked — Ber

13. The poor and the deceitful men meet together: the LORD lighteneth their eyes.
The poor man and the man of usury meet together,
He that enlighteneth the eyes of them both is Yahweh — Rhm
The poor man and the oppressor meet together;
Jehovah hath given eyesight unto both — ASV
The poor and the oppressor meet together;
JEHOVAH hath given eyesight unto them both — Sprl
The poor and the oppressor have a common bond:
the LORD gives light to the eyes of both — NAB
Rich and poor are alike in this: each depends on God for light — Tay
Poor man and oppressor have this in common:
what happiness each has comes from the LORD — NEB

14. The king that faithfully judgeth the poor, his throne shall be established forever.
A king that is judging truly the poor,
His throne for ever is established — YLT
A king that truthfully judges the weak, —
His throne shall stand forever firm — ABPS
When a king judgeth the poor faithfully; his throne will be established for a memorial — Sept

[33]Two interpretations of the last half-verse seem possible, as illustrated in the last three variants.

If a king judges the poor with equity his throne will be established for ever — RSV

King that gives due redress to the poor has a throne unshakeable — Knox

15. The rod and reproof give wisdom: but a child left to himself bringeth his mother to shame.

A rod with rebuke giveth wisdom,
But a youth unrestrained bringeth shame to his mother — Rhm

The rod and reproof impart wisdom;
But a child neglected bringeth his mother to shame — Sprl

The rod of correction gives wisdom;
But a child who is left to himself brings disgrace on his mother — AAT

The rod and reproof give wisdom, but an undisciplined child causes his mother shame — Ber

The rod and sharps words give wisdom: but a child who is not guided is a cause of shame to his mother — Bas

16. When the wicked are multiplied, transgression increaseth: but the righteous shall see their fall.

When the wicked abound, transgressions are multiplied: but when they fall, the righteous are awed — Sept

When the wicked are increased, transgression increaseth;
But the righteous shall gaze upon their fall — JPS

When the lawless become great transgression increaseth,
But the righteous shall behold their ruin — Rhm

When the wicked prevail, crime increases;
but their downfall the just will behold — NAB

When rulers are wicked, their people are too; but good men will live to see the tyrant's downfall — Tay

17. Correct thy son, and he shall give thee rest; yea, he shall give delight unto thy soul.

Chastise thy son, and he giveth thee comfort,
Yea, he giveth delights to thy soul — YLT

Discipline your son, and he will give you rest;
he will give delight to your heart — RSV

Correct your son, that he may give you peace of mind,
And bring delight to your heart — AAT

Give your son training, and he will give you rest; he will give delight to your soul — Bas

Chastise your son, and have an easy mind:
he will delight your soul — Mof

18. Where there is no vision, the people perish: but he that keepeth the law, happy is he.

Where there is no vision, the people cast off restraint;
But he that keepeth the law, happy is he — ASV

Where there is no vision, the people are unrestrained;
But he that keeps the law, — happy is he — ABPS

Where there is no vision the people run wild; but happy is he who keeps the law — Ber

Where there is no prophecy the people cast off restraint,
but blessed is he who keeps the law — RSV

Without prophecy the people become demoralized;
but happy is he who keeps the law — NAB

19. A servant will not be corrected by words: for though he understand he will not answer.

A servant will not be corrected by words,
Who, when he understands, will not even reply — Sprl

A stubborn servant will not be instructed by words: for though he may understand he will not obey — Sept

A servant will not be trained by words; for though the sense of the words is clear to him, he will not give attention — Bas

Mere words will never train a slave;
he understands, but he will not obey — Mof

Not by words is a slave corrected:
even if he understands, he will take no notice — Jerus

20. Seest thou a man that is hasty in his

words? there is more hope of a fool than of him.[34]

21. He that delicately bringeth up his servant from a child shall have him become his son at the length.

One brings up his servant tenderly from childhood,
And in the end he will be as a son — ABPS

He that delicately bringeth up his servant from a child
Shall have him become a son at the last — ASV

He that dealeth tenderly with his servant from childhood,
In his after life shall have him for a son — Rhm

He who pampers his servant from childhood,
will in the end find him his heir — RSV

He that delicately bringeth up his servant from a child
Shall have him become master at last — JPS

22. An angry man stirreth up strife, and a furious man aboundeth in transgression.

An angry man stirreth up contention,
And a furious man is multiplying transgression — YLT

A wrathful man stirreth up contention,
And a passionate man aboundeth in transgression — Sprl

A man of passion stirs up discord;
And a hot-tempered man is the cause of much mischief — AAT

A quick-tempered man stirs up strife,
and a wrathful man abounds in wrong — Ber

A man prone to anger provokes a quarrel
and a hot-head is always doing wrong — NEB

23. A man's pride shall bring him low: but honour shall uphold the humble in spirit.

A man's pride shall bring him low;
But he that is of a lowly spirit shall obtain honor — ASV

A man's pride shall bring him low; but his meekness shall add to his honor — Lam

Pride will come low; honour awaits the humble — Knox

Man's pride will lay him low:
lowly souls rise to honour — Mof

Man's pride causes his humiliation,
but he who is humble of spirit obtains honor — NAB

24. Whoso is partner with a thief hateth his own soul: he heareth cursing, and bewrayeth it not.

Whoso is sharing with a thief is hating his own soul,
Execration he heareth, and telleth not — YLT

He that divides with a thief hates his own soul;
He hears the curse, but does not inform — ABPS

Whoso is partner with a thief hateth his own soul: he heareth the adjuration and uttereth nothing — RV

He who is partner with a thief hates his own soul; they put him under oaths, but he does not confess — Lam

He who goes shares with a thief is his own enemy:
he hears himself put on oath and dare not give evidence — NEB

25. The fear of man bringeth a snare: but whoso putteth his trust in the LORD shall be safe.

The fear of man setteth a snare,
But he that trusteth in Yahweh shall be placed on high — Rhm

The fear of man bringeth a snare;
But whoso trusteth in JEHOVAH shall be preserved — Sprl

The fear of man leads one into a snare;
But he who trusts in the LORD will be placed in safety — AAT

To be afraid of men is a snare,
he who puts his trust in Yahweh is secure — Jerus

Fear of man is a dangerous trap, but to trust in God means safety — Tay

26. Many seek the ruler's favour; but every man's judgment cometh from the LORD.

Many seek the face of the ruler;
But from Jehovah is man's judgment — ABPS

Many seek the ruler's favor, but justice due a man comes from the LORD — Ber

Many court the ruler's favor;
But a man's case is decided by the LORD — AAT

[34]Compare Prov. 26:12.

Many seek the favor of a ruler,
but from the LORD a man gets justice — RSV
Many seek audience of a prince,
but in every case the LORD decides — NEB

27. **An unjust man is an abomination to the just: and he that is upright in the way is abomination to the wicked.**
An abomination to the righteous is the perverse man,
And an abomination to the wicked is the upright in the way — YLT
An unjust man is an abomination to the righteous,
but he whose way is straight is an abomination to the wicked — RSV
The good man loathes the villain;
the villain loathes the upright — Mof
The righteous cannot abide an unjust man,
nor the wicked a man whose conduct is upright — NEB
The good hate the badness of the wicked. The wicked hate the goodness of the good — Tay

CHAPTER 30

1. **The words of Agur the son of Jakeh, even the prophecy:**[35]
Words of Agur, son of Jakeh; the oracle — ABPS
The words of Agur the son of Jakeh; the oracle — ASV
The words of Agur the son of Jakeh; the burden — JPS
The words of Agur, the son of Jakeh, from Massa — Bas
Sayings of Agur the son of Yakeh, from Massa — Mof
the man spake unto Ithiel, even unto Ithiel and Ucal,
The man saith unto Ithiel, unto Ithiel and Ucal — RV
Oracle of this man for Ithiel, for Ithiel and for Ucal — Jerus
the sententious sayings which he made to Ithiel and Ucal — Sprl
The oracle of the man: "I am wearied, O God,
I am wearied, O God, and spent — AAT
The pronouncement of mortal man: "I am not God;
I am not God, that I should prevail — NAB
This is the great man's very word: I am weary, O God,
I am weary and worn out — NEB

2. **Surely I am more brutish than any man, and have not the understanding of a man.**

3. **I neither learned wisdom, nor have the knowledge of the holy.**
Surely more brutish am I than any man,
Nor doth the understanding of a son of earth pertain to me;
Neither have I learned wisdom,
Nor the knowledge of the Holy Ones can I acquire — Rhm
Surely I am brutish, unlike a man,
And have not the understanding of a man;
And I have not learned wisdom,
That I should have the knowledge of the Holy One — JPS
For I am more brutish than anyone,
And have not the understanding of a man.
Nor have I learned wisdom,
Yet the knowledge of the Holy Ones I know — YLT
For I am a brute beast, and no man,
I have nought of human intelligence;
No wisdom have I learned,
No knowledge have I of the Holy One — AAT
For I am more like a beast than any man, I have no power of reasoning like a man:
I have not got wisdom by teaching, so that I might have the knowledge of the Holy One — Bas
I am a dumb brute, scarcely a man, without a man's powers of understanding;
I have not learnt wisdom
nor have I received knowledge from the Holy One — NEB

4. **Who hath ascended up into heaven, or descended? who hath gathered the**

[35] This verse, particularly the second half, is difficult: commentaries should be consulted. Several try to translate the words which KJV, ASV, et al., have treated as proper names.

wind in his fists? who hath bound the waters in a garment? who hath established all the ends of the earth? what is his name, and what is his son's name, if thou canst tell?

Who hath ascended the heavens and then descended?
Who hath gathered the wind into his two hands?
Who hath wrapped up the waters in a mantle?
Who hath set up all the ends of the earth?
What is his name and what the name of his son, when thou knowest? — Rhm

Who ever climbed to heaven and then came down?
who ever gathered the wind in his fingers,
or wrapped the waters in a robe of clouds,
or fixed the bounds of earth?
What is his name, or his son's name?
You do not know it? — Mof

Tell me, Who has ascended up into heaven and come down? Who has gathered the wind in his fists? Who has bound the waters in a handkerchief? Who has established all the borders of the earth? What is his name, and what is his son's name, if you can tell? — Lam

Who has mounted to the heavens, then descended?
Who has gathered the wind in the clasp of his hand?
Who has wrapped the waters in his cloak?
Who has set all the ends of the earth firm?
What is his name, or the name of his son, if you know it? — Jerus

Who has scaled the heavens and come down?
Who has gathered the wind in his fists?
Who has wrapped the waters in a garment?
Who has established the bounds of the earth?
What is his name, and what is his son's name?
For surely you know! — AAT

5. Every word of God is pure: he is a shield unto them that put their trust in him.

6. Add thou not unto his words, lest he reprove thee, and thou be found a liar.

Every saying of God is tried,
A shield is He to those trusting in Him.
Add not to His words, lest He reason with thee,
And thou hast been found false — YLT

Every word of God is tried;
He is a shield unto them that take refuge in him.
Add thou not unto his words,
Lest he reprove thee, and thou be found a liar — ASV

All God's promises are like metal tested in the fire; he is the sure defence of all who trust in him. Add to his word no word of thine; speedily thy practices shall come to light — Knox

Every word of God is tested: he is a breast-plate to those who put their faith in him.
Make no addition to his words, or he will make clear your error, and you will be seen to be false — Bas

God's every promise has stood the test: he is a shield to all who seek refuge with him.
Add nothing to his words,
or he will expose you for a liar — NEB

7. Two things have I required of thee; deny me them not before I die:

8. Remove far from me vanity and lies; give me neither poverty nor riches; feed me with food convenient for me:

Two things have I asked of thee;
Deny me them not before I die:
Remove far from me falsehood and lies;
Give me neither poverty nor riches;
Feed me with the food that is needful for me — ASV

Two things have I asked of Thee;
Deny me them not before I die:
Remove far from me falsehood and lies;
Give me neither poverty nor riches;
Feed me with mine allotted bread — JPS

Two things have I asked of thee;

Withold them not from me before I die.
Put far from me vanity and lies;
Give me not poverty, nor riches;
Feed me with food sufficient for me — ABPS

For two boons from thy hand I cry
(deny me not, before I die):
put lies and falsehood far from me,
give neither wealth nor poverty,
but feed me with the food I need —Mof

Two things I beg of you,
do not grudge me them before I die:
keep falsehood and lies far from me,
give me neither poverty nor riches,
grant me only my share of bread to eat — Jerus

O God, I beg two favors from you before I die:
First, help me never to tell a lie.
Second, give me neither poverty nor riches! Give me just enough to satisfy my needs — Tay

9. Lest I be full, and deny thee, and say, Who is the LORD? or lest I be poor, and steal, and take the name of my God in vain.

Lest I be full, and deny thee, and say, Who is the LORD? or lest I be poor, and steal, and use profanely the name of my God — RV

Lest I be full and deny
And say — Who is Yahweh?
Or lest I be impoverished and steal,
And do violence to the Name of my GOD — Rhm

Lest I be full, and disown thee,
Saying, "Who is the LORD?"
Or lest I be in want, and steal,
And profane the name of my God — AAT

lest I be full and deny thee and say, "Who is the LORD?" or lest I be poor, and steal, and violate God's name — Ber

If I have too much, I shall deny thee and say, 'Who is the LORD?'
If I am reduced to poverty, I shall steal
and blacken the name of my God — NEB

10. Accuse not a servant unto his master, lest he curse thee, and thou be found guilty.

Slander not a servant unto his master,
Lest he curse thee, and thou be held guilty — ASV

Accuse not a servant unto his lord,
Lest he disesteem thee, and thou be found guilty — YLT

Do not say evil of a servant to his master, or he will put a curse on you, and you will get into trouble — Bas

Slander not a servant to his master,
Lest he curse you, and you have to pay for it — AAT

Never disparage a slave to his master, or he will speak ill of you, and you will pay for it — NEB

11. There is a generation that curseth their father, and doth not bless their mother.

12. There is a generation that are pure in their own eyes, and yet is not washed from their filthiness.

A generation! Its father it revileth,
And its mother it doth not bless.
A generation! Pure in its own eyes,
Yet from its filth hath it not been bathed — Rhm

There be a generation who curseth their father,
And blesseth not their mother;
A generation, pure in their own eyes,
Which hath not been washed from their filthiness — Sprl

There are those who curse their father and do not bless their mother. There are those who are pure in their own eyes and yet are not washed from their own filth — Ber

Some curse their father,
and bless not their mother.
Some think that they are pure —
with stains still on them! — Mof

A bad breed it is, that curse their fathers and for their mothers have no good word. A bad breed, that owns no blot, yet is all unpurged from its defilement — Knox

There are those who curse their father and mother, and feel themselves faultless despite their many sins — Tay

13. There is a generation, O how lofty are their eyes! and their eyelids are lifted up.

14. There is a generation, whose teeth are as swords, and their jaw teeth as knives,

to devour the poor from off the earth, and the needy from among men.

A generation — how high are their eyes,
Yea, their eyelids are lifted up.
A generation — swords are their teeth,
And knives — their jaw-teeth,
To consume the poor from the earth,
And the needy from among men — YLT

There is a class of people with O! such haughty eyes,
And such uplifted eyelids.
There is a class of people whose teeth are swords,
And whose fangs are knives,
To devour the poor from the earth,
And the needy from among men — AAT

There is a generation, O how full of pride are their eyes! O how their brows are lifted up!
There is a generation whose teeth are like swords, their strong teeth like knives, for the destruction of the poor from the earth, and of those who are in need from among men — Bas

There is a group — how haughty their eyes!
how overbearing their glance!
There is a group whose incisors are swords,
whose teeth are knives,
Devouring the needy from the earth,
and the poor from among men — NAB

a breed haughty of eye,
with disdain in every glance;
a breed with swords for teeth,
with knives for jaws,
with which to devour the poor and rid the earth of them,
to devour the needy and rid mankind of them — Jerus

15. **The horseleach hath two daughters, crying, Give, give. There are three things that are never satisfied, yea, four things say not, It is enough:**

16. **The grave; and the barren womb; the earth that is not filled with water; and the fire that saith not, It is enough.**

To the leech are two daughters, 'Give, give,'
Lo, three things are not satisfied,
Four have not said 'Sufficiency;'
Sheol, and a restrained womb,
Earth — it is not satisfied with water,
And fire — it hath not said, 'Sufficiency' — YLT

The vampire hath two daughters, Give! Give!
Three there are will not be satisfied,
Four have not said, Enough!
Hades,
And barrenness, —
A land not satisfied with water,
And fire that saith not, Enough! — Rhm

The leech has two daughters, Give, Give.
Three things there are that are not satisfied;
Four say not, — Enough!
The underworld and the barren womb;
The earth that is not satisfied with water,
And fire, that says not, Enough! — ABPS

The leech has two daughters;
"Give, give," they cry.
Three things are never satisfied;
four never say, "Enough":
Sheol, the barren womb,
the earth ever thirsty for water,
and the fire which never says, "Enough" — RSV

The two daughters of the leech are, "Give, Give."
Three things are never satisfied,
four never say, "Enough!"
The nether world, and the barren womb;
the earth, that is never saturated with water,
and fire, that never says, "Enough!" — NAB

17. **The eye that mocketh at his father, and despiseth to obey his mother, the ravens of the valley shall pick it out, and the young eagles shall eat it.**

An eye that mocketh at his father,
And despiseth the teaching of his mother,
The ravens of the valley shall pluck it out,
And the sons of the eagle shall devour it — Sprl

The eye that mocks a father and scorns to obey a mother will be picked out by the ravens of the valley and eaten by young vultures — Ber

The eye which looks jeeringly on a father,
and scornfully on an ageing mother,
shall be pecked out by the ravens of the valley, and eaten by the vultures — Jerus

The man who mocks his father
and scorns his aged mother,
ravens shall pick the eyes out of his corpse, and vultures shall devour him — Mof

18. There be three things which are too wonderful for me, yea, four which I know not:

19. The way of an eagle in the air; the way of a serpent upon a rock; the way of a ship in the midst of the sea; and the way of a man with a maid.

Three things there are too wonderful for me,
Yea, four which I cannot understand:
The flight of an eagle through the air,
The track of a sea-serpent upon the rock,
The track of a ship in the heart of the sea,
And the way of a man with a maid — Sprl

Three things there are, too difficult for me;
And four, which I understand not.
The way of the eagle in the heavens;
The way of the serpent on a rock;
The way of a ship in the midst of the sea;
And the way of a man with a maid — ABPS

There are three things, the wonder of which overcomes me, even four things outside my knowledge:
The way of an eagle in the air; the way of a snake on a rock; the way of a ship in the heart of the sea; and the way of a man with a girl —Bas

There are three things beyond my comprehension,
four, indeed, that I do not understand:
the way of an eagle through the skies,
the way of a snake over the rock,
the way of a ship in mid-ocean,
the way of a man with a girl — Jerus

There are three things too wonderful for me to understand — no, four!
How an eagle glides through the sky.
How a serpent crawls upon a rock.
How a ship finds its way across the heaving ocean.
The growth of love between a man and a girl — Tay

Three mysteries there are too high for me, and a fourth is beyond my ken; eagle that flies in air, viper that crawls on rock, ship that sails the sea, and man that goes courting maid — Knox

20. Such is the way of an adulterous woman; she eateth, and wipeth her mouth, and saith, I have done no wickedness.

So is the way of a woman committing adultery,—
She eateth and wipeth her mouth,
And saith, I have done no iniquity! — Rhm

This is the way of a false wife; she takes food, and, cleaning her mouth, says, I have done no wrong — Bas

The way of an unfaithful wife is this: she eats, then she wipes her mouth and says, 'I have done no harm' — NEB

This is how the adulteress behaves:
when she has eaten,
she wipes her mouth clean and says,
'I have done nothing wrong' — Jerus

21. For three things the earth is disquieted, and for four which it cannot bear:

22. For a servant when he reigneth; and a fool when he is filled with meat;

23. For an odious woman when she is married; and a handmaid that is heir to her mistress.

For three things the earth doth tremble,
And for four, which it cannot bear:
For a servant when he is king;
And a fool when he is filled with food;
For an odious woman when she is married;
And a handmaid that is heir to her mistress — ASV

On account of three things doth the earth tremble;

Yea, on account of four it cannot bear up:
On account of a servant when he beareth rule,
And a fool when he is replenished with food:
On account of a hateful woman when she is married,
And a handmaid when she is heir to her mistress — Sprl

Under three things the earth trembles;
under four it cannot bear up:
a slave when he becomes king,
and a fool when he is filled with food;
an unloved woman when she gets a husband,
and a maid when she succeeds her mistress — RSV

Under three things the earth quakes,
and under four it cannot endure:
Under a servant when he reigns; and under a fool when he is filled with bread;
Under an odious woman when she is married; and under a maidservant who ousts her mistress — Lam

Under three things the earth trembles,
yes, under four it cannot bear up:
Under a slave when he becomes king,
and a fool when he is glutted with food;
Under an odious woman when she is wed,
and a maidservant when she displaces her mistress — NAB

At three things the earth shakes,
four things it cannot bear:
a slave turned king,
a churl gorging himself,
a woman unloved when she is married,
and a slave-girl displacing her mistress — NEB

24. There are four things which are little upon the earth, but they are exceeding wise:

There are four things little upon earth,
Yet are they wiser than the wise — Sprl

There are four things that are small upon the earth, but they are wiser than wise men — Lam

Four things are small on earth,
small but extremely shrewd — Mof

Four things there are, the smallest of the earth,
And they wise, instructed in wisdom — ABPS

25. The ants are a people not strong, yet they prepare their meat in the summer;
26. The conies are but a feeble folk, yet make they their houses in the rocks;

The ants are a people not strong,
Yet they provide their food in the summer;
The rock-badgers are but a feeble folk,
Yet they make their houses in the crags — JPS

The ants — they are no strong folk,
Yet they lay up their food in the summer;
The marmots — they are no mighty folk,
Yet they make their home in the crags — AAT

Ants — a species not strong,
yet they store up their food in the summer;
Rock-badgers — a species not mighty,
yet they make their home in the crags — NAB

Ants: they aren't strong, but store up food for the winter.
Cliff-badgers: delicate little animals who protect themselves by living among the rocks — Tay

the ants, a race with no strength,
yet in the summer they make sure of their food;
the rock rabbits, a race with no defences,
yet they make their home in the rocks — Jerus

27. The locusts have no king, yet go they forth all of them by bands;
28. The spider taketh hold with her hands, and is in king's palaces.

The locusts have no king,
Yet go they forth all of them by bands;
The spider thou canst take with the hands,
Yet is she in kings' palaces — JPS

The locusts have no king,
Yet go they forth all of them by bands;
The lizard taketh hold with her hands,

Yet is she in kings' palaces — ASV
The locusts — they have no king,
Yet they march all in ranks;
The lizard — she holds on by her forefeet,
Yet she finds her way into the king's palace — AAT
the locusts have no king to lead them,
but they advance in order; the lizard — you may lift it in your hand,
but it will push into a palace — Mof
The locusts who have no king, and yet they all gather together.
The chameleon which takes hold with her hands, but is found in kings' palaces — Lam
locusts, which have no king,
yet they all sally forth in detachments;
the lizard, which can be grasped in the hand,
yet is found in the palaces of kings — NEB

29. There are three things which go well, yea, four are comely in going:

30. A lion which is strongest among beasts, and turneth not away for any;

31. A greyhound; a he goat also; and a king, against whom there is no rising up.

There are three things which step becomingly,
Yea, four which proceed with grace:
The lion, the mightiest amongst the beasts,
Who retreateth not from the presence of any:
The greyhound, also the he-goat,
And the king, against whom there is no resistance offered — Sprl
There be three things which are stately in their march, yea, four which are stately in their going:
The lion, which is mightiest among the beasts, and turneth not away for any;
The greyhound; the he-goat also; and the king, against whom there is no rising up — RV
Three things there are, graceful in step,
And four are graceful in going:
A lion, mighty among beasts,
And he turns not back before any;
A greyhound, or a he-goat,
And a king, with whom are the people — ABPS
Three things have a stately stride,
four things have a stately tread;
a lion, mightiest of beasts,
that never runs away;
a strutting cock, and a he-goat,
and a king at the head of a host — Mof
There are three stately monarchs in the earth — no, four:
The lion, king of the animals. He won't turn aside for anyone.
The peacock.
The he-goat.
A king as he leads his army — Tay

32. If thou hast done foolishly in lifting up thyself, or if thou hast thought evil, lay thine hand upon thy mouth.

If thou has been foolish in exalting thyself,
And if thou hast thought evil, — the hand to the mouth! — ABPS
If thou hast done foolishly in lifting up thyself,
Or if thou hast planned devices,
lay thy hand upon thy mouth — JPS
If you have been foolish in exalting yourself,
Or if you have hatched a scheme,
Lay your hand upon your mouth — AAT
If you have played the fool in exalting yourself, or if you have devised evil,
put your hand to your mouth — Ber
If you have foolishly been proud or presumptious — put your hand on your mouth — NAB

33. Surely the churning of milk bringeth forth butter, and the wringing of the nose bringeth forth blood: so the forcing of wrath bringeth forth strife.

Surely the churning of milk bringeth forth curd,
And the pressing of the nose bringeth forth blood,
And the pressing of wrath bringeth forth strife — Rhm
Surely the churning of milk bringeth forth butter,
So the inciting to wrath causeth bloodshed:
And he who provoketh passion, produceth contention — Sprl
For pressing milk produces curds,

pressing the nose produces blood,
and pressing anger produces strife — RSV
for wringing out the milk produces curd
and wringing the nose produces blood,
so provocation leads to strife — NEB
For by churning the milk you produce butter,
by wringing the nose you produce blood,
and by whipping up anger you produce strife — Jerus

CHAPTER 31

1. The words of king Lemuel, the prophecy that his mother taught him.[36]
The words of king Lemuel; the oracle which his mother taught him — ASV
The words of king Lemuel; the burden wherewith his mother corrected him — JPS
Words of Lemuel a king, a declaration that his mother taught him — YLT
Sayings that Lemuel king of Massa learned from his mother — Mof
The words of Lemuel, king of Massa: the teaching which he had from his mother — Bas
The words of Lemuel, king of Massa. The advice which his mother gave him — NAB
2. What, my son? and what, the son of my womb? and what, the son of my vows?
3. Give not thy strength unto women, nor thy ways to that which destroyeth kings.
What my son?
And what, the son of my womb?
Aye what, the son of my vows?
Do not give to women thy strength,
Nor thy ways to them who ruin kings — Rhm
Oh my son! Oh the son of my womb!
Oh the son of my vows!
Give not your strength to women,
nor your ways to the extravagance of kings — Lam
What, my son? And what, O son of my womb? What, O son of my vows? do not give your strength to women, nor your ways to what destroys kings — Ber
Son of mine, heed what I say,
listen, O son of my prayers, and obey.
Waste not your strength on women,
your love on these destroyers of a king — Mof
What, my son, my first-born!
What, O son of my womb;
what, O son of my vows!
Give not your vigor to women,
nor your strength to those who ruin kings — NAB
4. It is not for kings, O Lemuel, it is not for kings to drink wine; nor for princes strong drink:
5. Lest they drink, and forget the law, and pervert the judgment of any of the afflicted.
It is not for kings, O Lemuel,
it is not for kings to drink wine;
Nor for princes to say, Where is strong drink?
Lest they drink, and forget the law,
And pervert the justice due to any that is afflicted — ASV
Not for kings, O Lemuel,
Not for kings, to drink wine,
And for princes a desire of strong drink.
Lest he drink, and forget the decree,
And change the judgment of any of the sons of affliction — YLT
It is not for kings, O Lemuel,
it is not for kings to drink wine,
or for rulers to desire strong drink;
lest they drink and forget what has been decreed,
and pervert the rights of all the afflicted — RSV
Nor be it for kings, O Lemuel,
For kings to drink wine,
For princes to quaff strong drink;
Lest, as they drink, they forget the law,
And violate the rights of any in trouble — AAT
It is not for kings, O Lemuel, not for kings to drink wine

[36]As in 30:1, the word *massa'* occurs. As a Heb. word, it would mean 'burden, oracle'; but others believe it is the proper name of one of the Ishaelite tribes listed in Gen. 25:14 and 1 Chron. 1:30.

nor for princes to crave strong drink;
if they drink, they will forget rights and customs
and twist the law against their wretched victims — NEB

6. Give strong drink unto him that is ready to perish, and wine unto those that be of heavy hearts.

7. Let him drink, and forget his poverty, and remember his misery no more.

Give the intoxicating draft to the dying,
And wine to the afflicted soul;
Let him drink and forget his distress,
And no more remember his misery — Sprl

Let strong drink be given to those who mourn, and wine to those who are of heavy heart,
That they may drink, and forget their sorrows, and remember their miseries no more — Lam

Give strong drink to him who is near to destruction, and wine to him whose soul is bitter;
Let him have drink, and his need will go from his mind, and the memory of his trouble will be gone — Bas

Procure strong drink for a man about to perish,
wine for the heart that is full of bitterness:
let him drink and forget his misfortune,
and remember his misery no more — Jerus

Give strong drink to one who is perishing,
and wine to the sorely depressed;
When they drink, they will forget their misery,
and think no more of their burdens — NAB

8. Open thy mouth for the dumb in the cause of all such as are appointed to destruction.

9. Open thy mouth, judge righteously, and plead the cause of the poor and needy.

Open thy mouth for the dumb,
In the cause of all such as are left desolate.
Open thy mouth, judge righteously,
And minister justice to the poor and needy — ASV

Open thy mouth for the dumb,
For the cause of all the children of the departed.
Open thy mouth — judge righteously, —
And administer justice for the poor and the needy — Rhm

Open your mouth on behalf of the dumb,
In defense of the rights of all who are suffering;
Open your mouth on the side of justice,
And defend the rights of the poor and the needy — AAT

Do justice to a widow,
and let orphans have their rights;
decide your cases fairly,
champion the weak and wretched — Mof

You should defend those who cannot help themselves.
Yes, speak up for the poor and needy and see that they get justice — Tay

10. Who can find a virtuous woman? for her price is far above rubies.[37]

11. The heart of her husband doth safely trust in her, so that he shall have no need of spoil.

A worthy woman who can find?
For her price is far above rubies.
The heart of her husband trusteth in her,
And he shall have no lack of gain — ASV

Who can find a virtuous woman?
For her price is far beyond pearls.
Her husband may trust his heart with her;
She will not deprive him of the spoil — Sprl

A virtuous woman who can find?
For far beyond corals is her worth.
The heart of her husband trusteth her,
And gain he shall not lack — Rhm

Who may make discovery of a woman of virtue? For her price is much higher than jewels.
The heart of her husband has faith

[37]Here begins an alphabetic acrostic poem: in the original, each verse begins with a different Hebrew letter in the sequence of the Hebrew alphabet.

in her, and he will have profit in full measure — Bas

Who can find a wife with strength of character? She is far more precious than jewels. The heart of her husband trusts in her, and he will never lack profit — Ber

When one finds a worthy wife,
her value is far beyond pearls.
Her husband, entrusting his heart to her,
has an unfailing prize — NAB

12. She will do him good and not evil all the days of her life.

13. She seeketh wool, and flax, and worketh willingly with her hands.

She will render to him good, and not evil,
All the days of her life.
She seeks for wool and flax;
And works with her willing hands — ABPS

She will requite him with good and not evil
All the days of her life.
She seeketh wool and flax,
And worketh with diligent hands — Sprl

Content, not sorrow, she will bring him as long as life lasts. Does she not busy herself with wool and thread, plying her hands with ready skill — Knox

She brings him good, and not harm,
All the days of his life.
She sorts out wool and flax,
And works it up as she wills — AAT

She repays him with good, not evil,
all her life long.
She chooses wool and flax
and toils at her work — NEB

14. She is like the merchants' ships; she bringeth her food from afar.

15. She riseth also while it is yet night, and giveth meat to her household, and a portion to her maidens.

She is like the trading-ships, getting food from far away.
She gets up while it is still night, and gives meat to her family, and their food to her servant-girls — Bas

She is like the merchant-ships;
She bringeth her bread from afar.
She riseth also while it is yet night,
And giveth food to her household,
And their task to her maidens — ASV

She is like the merchant's ship, she brings her merchandise from afar. She rises also while it is yet night, and gives food to her household and work to her maids — Lam

She is like a merchant vessel
bringing her food from far away.
She gets up while it is still dark
giving her household their food,
giving orders to her serving girls — Jerus

She buys imported foods, brought by ship from distant ports.
She gets up before dawn to prepare breakfast for her household, and plans the day's work for her servant girls — Tay

16. She considereth a field, and buyeth it: with the fruit of her hands she planteth a vineyard.

17. She girdeth her loins with strength, and strengtheneth her arms.

She considereth a field and procureth it,
Out of the fruit of her hands she planteth a vineyard:
She girdeth with strength her loins,
And putteth vigour into her arms — Rhm

She examines a field, and buys it;
With her earnings she plants a vineyard.
She girds her loins with strength,
And she makes her arms strong — AAT

She purchases land prudently;
with her earnings she plants a vineyard.
She girds herself to work,
and plies her arms with vigour — Mof

Ground must be examined, and bought, and planted out as a vineyard, with the earnings of her toil. How briskly she girds herself to the task, how tireless are her arms — Knox

She picks out a field to purchase;
out of her earnings she plants a vineyard.
She is girt about with strength,
and sturdy are her arms — NAB

18. She perceiveth that her merchandise is good: her candle goeth not out by night.

19. She layeth her hands to the spindle, and her hands hold the distaff.

She perceiveth that her merchandise is profitable;
Her lamp goeth not out by night.
She layeth her hands to the distaff,
And her hands hold the spindle — ASV

She perceiveth that her traffic is successful;
Even in the night her lamp is not extinguished.
She putteth her hands to the spindle,
And her fingers lay hold of the distaff — Sprl

She perceives that her gains are good;
Her lamp goes not out by night.
She puts forth her hands to the distaff,
And her hands lay hold on the spindle — ABPS

She sees that her marketing is of profit to her: her light does not go out by night.
She puts her hands to the cloth-working rod, and her fingers take the wheel — Bas

She sees that her business goes well,
and never puts out her lamp at night.
She holds the distaff in her hand,
and her fingers grasp the spindle — NEB

20. She stretcheth out her hand to the poor; yea, she reacheth forth her hands to the needy.

Her palm she spreadeth out to the oppressed,
And her hands she extendeth to the needy — Rhm

She spreadeth out her hand to the poor; yea, she reacheth forth her hands to the needy — RV

She opens her hand to the poor,
and reaches out her hands to the needy — RSV

She is open-handed to the wretched
and generous to the poor — NEB

Kindly is her welcome to the poor, her purse ever open to those in need — Knox

21. She is not afraid of the snow for her household: for all her household are clothed with scarlet.

22. She maketh herself coverings of tapestry; her clothing is silk and purple.

She is not afraid of the snow for her household;
For all her household are clothed with scarlet.
She maketh for herself carpets of tapestry;
Her clothing is fine linen and purple — ASV

She is not alarmed for her household because of the snow,
Because all her household are clothed in double vestments.
She maketh herself woven coverlets;
Cotton and purple are her clothing — Sprl

Snow may come, she has no fears for her household,
with all her servants warmly clothed.
She makes her own quilts,
she is dressed in fine linen and purple — Jerus

She has no fear for her household when it snows,
for they are wrapped in two cloaks.
She makes her own coverings,
and clothing of fine linen and purple — NEB

She has no fear of winter for her household, for she has made warm clothes for all of them.
She also upholsters with finest tapestry; her own clothing is beautifully made — a purple gown of pure linen — Tay

23. Her husband is known in the gates, when he sitteth among the elders of the land.

And her husband is distinguished in the gates; when he sitteth in council with the elders of the land — Sept

Her husband is a man of note,
he sits with the sheikhs in council — Mof

Her husband is prominent at the city gates,
as he sits with the elders of the land — NAB

Her husband is a man of note in the public place, when he takes his seat among the responsible men of the land — Bas

Her husband is respected at the city gates,
taking his seat among the elders of the land — Jerus

24. She maketh fine linen, and selleth it; and delivereth girdles unto the merchant.

25. Strength and honour are her clothing; and she shall rejoice in time to come.

She maketh linen garments and selleth them,
And delivereth girdles unto the merchant.
Strength and dignity are her clothing;
And she laugheth at the time to come — ASV

Fine linen wraps she maketh and selleth,
And girdles doth she deliver to the trader:
Strength and dignity are her clothing,
And she laugheth at the time to come — Rhm

Fine undergarments she makes and sells,
And delivers girdles to the merchant.
Dignity and honor are her clothing;
And she laughs at the time to come — ABPS

She makes linen garments and sells them, and delivers sashes to the merchants.
Strength and dignity clothe her and she laughs at the future — Ber

She makes linen vests, and sells them,
She supplies the merchants with girdles.
She is clothed with strength and dignity,
And she laughs at the days to come — AAT

26. She openeth her mouth with wisdom; and in her tongue is the law of kindness.

27. She looketh well to the ways of her household, and eateth not the bread of idleness.

Her mouth she hath opened in wisdom,
And the law of kindness is on her tongue.
She is watching the ways of her household,
And bread of sloth she eateth not — YLT

She openeth her mouth in wisdom;
And the law of kindness is upon her tongue.
She surveyeth the ways of her household;
And the bread of slothfulness she eateth not — Sprl

She opens her mouth with wisdom; and upon her tongue is the law of kindness.
The ways of her household are above reproach, and she does not eat the bread of idleness — Lam

Ripe wisdom governs her speech, but it is kindly instruction she gives.
She keeps watch over all that goes on in her house, not content to go through life eating and sleeping — Knox

She talks shrewd sense,
and offers kindly counsel.
She keeps an eye upon her household;
she never eats the bread of idleness — Mof

When she speaks, her words are wise, and kindness is the rule for everything she says.
She watches carefully all that goes on throughout her household, and is never lazy — Tay

28. Her children rise up, and call her blessed; her husband also, and he praiseth her.

29. Many daughters have done virtuously, but thou excellest them all.

Her children rise up and call her happy!
Her husband, and he praiseth her:—
Many daughters have done virtuously,
But thou excellest them all — Rhm

Her children get up and give her honour, and her husband gives her praise, saying,
Unnumbered women have done well,
but you are better than all of them — Bas

Her children rise up and call her blessed;
her husband also, and he praises her:
"Many women have done excellently,
but you surpass them all" — RSV

Her children rise up and call her

blessed; her husband, too, and he praises her: "Many daughters have done nobly, but you transcend them all" — Ber

Her children rise up and praise her; her husband, too, extols her: "Many are the women of proven worth, but you have excelled them all" — NAB

Her sons congratulate her,
and thus her husband praises her:
"Many a woman does nobly,
but you far outdo them all!" — Mof

30. Favour is deceitful, and beauty is vain: but a woman that feareth the LORD, she shall be praised.

31. Give her of the fruit of her hands; and let her own works praise her in the gates.

Comeliness is a deception, and beauty is a vain thing;
A woman that fears Jehovah, she shall be praised.
Give to her of the fruit of her hands;
And let her works praise her in the gates — ABPS

Charms are deceptive, and beauty is a breath;
But a woman who reveres the LORD — she will be praised.
Give her the due reward of her work;
And let her deeds bring her praise at the gates — AAT

Charm is deceitful and beauty is passing, but a woman who reveres the LORD will be praised.
Acknowledge the product of her hands; let her works praise her in the gates — Ber

Charms may wane and beauty wither, keep your praise for a wife with brains;
give her due credit for her deeds, praise her in public for her services — Mof

Charm is a delusion and beauty fleeting;
it is the God-fearing woman who is honoured.
Extol her for the fruit of all her toil, and let her labours bring her honour in the city gate — NEB

ECCLESIASTES

CHAPTER 1

1. The words of the Preacher, the son of David, king in Jerusalem.

The words of Koheleth, the son of David, king in Jerusalem — JPS

The words of the Proclaimer, son of David, king in Jerusalem — Rhm

Sayings of the Speaker, David's son, king in Jerusalem — Mof

Words of the Spokesman, king David's son, that reigned once at Jerusalem — Knox

The author: Solomon of Jerusalem, King David's son, "The Preacher" — Tay

2. Vanity of vanities, saith the Preacher, vanity of vanities; all is vanity.

3. What profit hath a man of all his labour which he taketh under the sun?

Vanity of vanities, saith the Preacher; vanity of vanities, all is vanity. What profit hath man of all his labor wherein he laboreth under the sun? — ASV

Vanity of vanities! saith the Proclaimer, vanity of vanities! all is vanity.
What profit hath Man, — in all his toil wherewith he toileth under the sun? — Rhm

Vanity of vanities, said the preacher.
Vanity of vanities. All is vanity.
What lasting advantage hath a man by all the labour with which he toileth under the sun? — Sept

Utterly vain, utterly vain,
everything is vain!
Man labours at his toil under the sun;
what does he gain? — Mof

Futility of futilities, say the Preacher, futility of futilities, all is futile.
What is the advantage to man in all his labor at which he toils under the sun? — Ber

Emptiness, emptiness, says the Speaker, emptiness, all is empty. What does man gain from all his labour and his toil here under the sun? — NEB

4. One generation passeth away, and another generation cometh: but the earth abideth forever.

5. The sun also ariseth, and the sun goeth down, and hasteth to his place where he arose.

Generation goes, and generation comes; but the earth stands forever. The sun also rises, and the sun goes down, and hastens to his place where he rises — ABPS

One generation goes and another comes; but the earth is for ever. The sun comes up and the sun goes down, and goes quickly back to the place where he came up — Bas

One generation goes, and another comes,
While the earth endures forever.
The sun rises and the sun sets,
And hastens to the place where he rose — AAT

One generation passes and another comes,
but the world forever stays.
The sun rises and the sun goes down;
then it presses on to the place where it rises — NAB

A generation goes, a generation comes, yet the earth stands firm for ever. The sun rises, the sun sets; then to its place it speeds and there it rises — Jerus

6. The wind goeth toward the south, and turneth about unto the north; it whirleth about continually, and the wind returneth again according to his circuits.

7. All the rivers run into the sea; yet the sea is not full: unto the place from whence the rivers come, thither they return again.

Going unto the south, and turning round unto the north, turning round, turning round, the wind is going, and by its circuits the wind hath returned. All the streams are going unto the sea, and the sea is not full; unto a place whither the streams are going, thither they are turning back to go — YLT

The wind goeth toward the south and veereth round to the north,
Around, around whirleth the wind,
revolveth according to its circuits.
All the rivers flow into the sea, yet the sea is not full;
Into the place from whence the

rivers come, thither they return — Sprl

The wind blows to the south,
and goes round to the north;
round and round goes the wind,
and on its circuits the wind returns.
All streams run to the sea,
but the sea is not full;
to the place where the streams flow,
there they flow again — RSV

The wind blows south, the wind blows north, round and round it goes and returns full circle. All streams run into the sea, yet the sea never overflows; back to the place from which the streams ran they return to run again — NEB

From south to north the wind blows round,
the wind turns as it blows, turning and then returning on its track.
The streams all flow into the sea,
but the sea they never fill,
though the streams are flowing still — Mof

8. All things are full of labour; man cannot utter it: the eye is not satisfied with seeing, nor the ear filled with hearing.

9. The thing that hath been, it is that which shall be; and that which is done is that which shall be done: and there is no new thing under the sun.

All these considerations are wearisome. Man cannot recount them: nor can the eye be satisfied with seeing; nor the ear filled with hearing.
What is that which hath been? The very same which shall be. And what is that which hath been done? The very same which shall be done: for there is nothing entirely new under the sun — Sept

All things are full of weariness; man cannot utter it: the eye is not satisfied with seeing, nor the ear filled with hearing. That which hath been is that which shall be; and that which hath been done is that which shall be done: and there is no new thing under the sun — ASV

All things are unspeakably tiresome; the eye is not satisfied with seeing, nor does the ear get enough hearing. Whatever has been, that will be, and whatever has been done that will be done; and there is nothing new under the sun — Ber

All things are wearisome: a man is not satisfied with utterance, his eye is not satisfied with seeing, nor his ear satisfied with hearing.
The thing that has been is that which shall be; and that which has been done is that which shall be done; and there is nothing new under the sun — Lam

Weariness, all weariness; who shall tell the tale? Eye looks on unsatisfied; ear listens, ill content. Ever that shall be that ever has been, that which has happened once shall happen again; there can be nothing new, here under the sun — Knox

A man cannot mention all those things in which there is travail;
The eye is not satisfied with seeing, and the ear is never satisfied with hearing.
What hath been is that which shall be,
And that which is accomplished is that which shall be accomplished,
And there is no new thing under the sun — Sprl

10. Is there any thing whereof it may be said, See, this is new? it hath been already of old time, which was before us.

11. There is no remembrance of former things; neither shall there be any remembrance of things that are to come with those that shall come after.

Is there a thing whereof men say, See, this is new? it hath been already, in the ages which were before us.
There is no remembrance of the former generations; neither shall there be any remembrance of the latter generations that are to come, among those that shall come after — RV

Is there a thing whereof it is said: 'See, this is new'? — it hath been already, in the ages which were before us. There is no remembrance of them of former times; neither shall there be any remembrance of them of latter times that are to come, among those that shall come after — JPS

Is there a thing of which it is said, 'Lo, this is new'?
It was already in existence in the ages
Which were before us.
There is no memory of earlier people;
And likewise of later people who shall be,
There will be no memory with those who are later still — AAT

Whoever speaks and says, Look, this is new, should know that it already has been in the ages which were before us.
There is no remembrance of former generations; neither shall there be any remembrance of generations that are to come with those that will come after — Lam

Even the thing of which we say, "See, this is new!" has already existed in the ages that preceded us. There is no remembrance of the men of old; nor of those to come will there be any remembrance among those who come after them — NAB

Is there anything of which men say, See, this is new? It has been in the old time which was before us. There is no memory of those who have gone before, and of those who come after there will be no memory for those who are still to come after them — Bas

12. I the Preacher was king over Israel in Jerusalem.

13. And I gave my heart to seek and search out by wisdom concerning all things that are done under heaven: this sore travail hath God given to the sons of man to be exercised therewith.

I the Proclaimer was king over Israel in Jerusalem. And I gave my heart to seek and to search out wisely, concerning all things which are done under the heavens, — the same is the vexatious employment God hath given to the sons of men to work toilsomely therein — Rhm

The Preacher was king over Israel in Jerusalem. And I applied my heart to seek and to search out by wisdom concerning all that is done under the heavens: it is an evil exercise that God has given to the sons of men with which to exercise themselves — ABPS

I, Koheleth, was king over Israel in Jerusalem; and I set my mind to search and to investigate through wisdom everything that is done beneath the heavens. It is an evil task that God has given the sons of men with which to occupy themselves — AAT

I the Preacher have been king over Israel in Jerusalem. And I applied my mind to seek and to search out by wisdom all that is done under heaven; it is an unhappy business that God has given to the sons of men to be busy with — RSV

I, the Speaker, ruled as king over Israel in Jerusalem; and in wisdom I applied my mind to study and explore all that is done under heaven. It is a sorry business that God has given men to busy themselves with — NEB

I, Qoheleth, have reigned in Jerusalem over Israel. With the help of wisdom I have been at pains to study all that is done under heaven; oh, what a weary task God has given mankind to labour at! — Jerus

14. I have seen all the works that are done under the sun; and, behold, all is vanity and vexation of spirit.

15. That which is crooked cannot be made straight: and that which is wanting cannot be numbered.

I have contemplated every work performed under the sun: and behold, vanity of vanity and vexation of spirit! That which is crooked cannot be made straight; and that which is defective cannot be made complete — Sprl

I took a view of all the different sorts of work which are done under the sun. And behold they are all vanity and vexation of spirit. That which is crooked cannot be made straight, nor can wants be numbered — Sept

I saw all the things which were done under the sun and truly, all is worthlessness and chasing of wind. What is crooked cannot be straightened, and what is lacking cannot be counted — Ber

I have seen all that goes on in this

world; it is a vain, futile business.
You cannot straighten what is twisted,
nor can you count up the defects in life — Mof

All that men do beneath the sun I marked, and found it was but frustration and lost labour, all of it; there was no curing men's cross-grained nature, no reckoning up their follies — Knox

16. **I communed with mine own heart, saying, Lo, I am come to great estate, and have gotten more wisdom than all they that have been before me in Jerusalem: yea, my heart had great experience of wisdom and knowledge.**

I communed with mine own heart, saying, Lo, I have gotten me great wisdom above all that were before me in Jerusalem; yea, my heart hath had great experience of wisdom and knowledge — ASV

I said to myself, "I have acquired great wisdom, surpassing all who were over Jerusalem before me; and my mind has had great experience of wisdom and knowledge — RSV

I spoke with my own heart, saying, 'Lo, I have gotten great wisdom, more also than all that were before me over Jerusalem'; yea, my heart hath had great experience of wisdom and knowledge — JPS

Then I said to myself, "Behold, I have become great and stored up wisdom beyond all who were before me in Jerusalem, and my mind has broad experience of wisdom and knowledge — NAB

I thought to myself, 'I have acquired a greater stock of wisdom than any of my predecessors in Jerusalem. I have great experience of wisdom and learning — Jerus

17. **And I gave my heart to know wisdom, and to know madness and folly: I perceived that this also is vexation of spirit.**

And I applied my heart to know wisdom, and to know madness and folly: I perceived that this also was a striving after wind — RV

yea I have given my heart to know wisdom, and to know madness and folly, — I know that even this is a feeding on wind — Rhm

And I gave my heart to getting knowledge of wisdom, and of the ways of the foolish. And I saw that this again was desire for wind — Bas

So I set my mind to knowing wisdom and to knowing madness and folly. I am convinced that this too is striving for the wind — AAT

I have applied myself to wisdom and knowledge as well as to mad folly, and I find it futile — Mof

18. **For in much wisdom is much grief: and he that increaseth knowledge increaseth sorrow.**

For in much wisdom is much vexation;
And he that increaseth knowledge increaseth sorrow — JPS

for in much wisdom is much weariness, and whoso acquireth knowledge, acquireth care — Sprl

For in much wisdom is much vexation, and he that increases knowledge increases pain — ABPS

For in more wisdom is more vexation, and increasing one's knowledge increases one's distress — Ber

For in much wisdom there is much sorrow,
and he who stores up knowledge stores up grief — NAB

Much wisdom, much grief,
the more knowledge, the more sorrow — Jerus

CHAPTER 2

1. **I said in mine heart, Go to now, I will prove thee with mirth; therefore enjoy pleasure: and, behold, this also is vanity.**
2. **I said of laughter, It is mad: and of mirth, What doeth it?**

I said in my heart, 'Pray, come, I try thee with mirth, and look thou on gladness;' and lo, even it is vanity. Of laughter I said, 'Foolish!' and of mirth, 'What is this it is doing?' — YLT

I said in my heart: 'Come now, I will try thee with mirth, and enjoy pleasure'; and, behold, this also was vanity. I said of laughter: 'It is mad';

and of mirth: 'What doth it accomplish?' — JPS

I said in my heart, I will give you joy for a test; so take your pleasure — but it was to no purpose. Of laughing I said, It is foolish; and of joy — What use is it? — Bas

I said to myself, "Come now and I will test you in gladness; have a good time." But this also is worthless. Of laughter I said, "It is madness," and of amusement, "What does it accomplish?" — Ber

Said I to myself, "Come, try pleasure and enjoy yourself." But this too was in vain. Mirth is madness, I reflected, and what is the good of pleasure? — Mof

I thought to myself, 'Very well, I will try pleasure and see what enjoyment has to offer.' And there it was: vanity again! This laughter, I reflected, is a madness, this pleasure no use at all — Jerus

3. I sought in mine heart to give myself unto wine, yet acquainting mine heart with wisdom; and to lay hold on folly, till I might see what was that good for the sons of men, which they should do under the heaven all the days of their life.

I searched in my heart how to cheer my flesh with wine, my heart yet guiding me with wisdom, and how to lay hold on folly, till I might see what it was good for the sons of men that they should do under heaven all the days of their life — ASV

I enquired within my heart
Whether I should give myself to wine, and to viands:
Or my heart to select wisdom, or embrace folly,
Until that I might discern which was the better for the sons of men,
That they should pursue under the heavens,
Throughout the number of their days — Sprl

I searched with my mind how to cheer my body with wine — my mind still guiding me with wisdom — and how to lay hold on folly, till I might see what was good for the sons of men to do under heaven during the few days of their life — RSV

I thought in my heart to give myself to wine, but my heart reasoned with wisdom; and I laid hold upon understanding, till I might see what was good for the sons of men, which they should do under the sun all the days of their lives — Lam

I searched in my mind how to stimulate my flesh with wine, and, while my mind conducted itself with wisdom, how to lay hold upon folly, until I might see which is better for the sons of men to practice under the heavens all the days of their life — AAT

So, after a lot of thinking, I decided to try the road of drink, while still holding steadily to my course of seeking wisdom.
Next I changed my course again and followed the path of folly, so that I could experience the only happiness most men have throughout their lives — Tay

4. I made me great works; I builded me houses; I planted me vineyards:

5. I made me gardens and orchards, and I planted trees in them of all kinds of fruit:

6. I made me pools of water, to water therewith the wood that bringeth forth trees:

I made me gardens and parks, and I planted trees in them of all kinds of fruit:
I made me pools of water, to water therefrom the forest where trees were reared — RV

I would have park and orchard, planted with every kind of tree; and to water all this greenery there must be pools of water besides — Knox

I . . . laid out gardens and parks in which I planted all manner of fruit-trees, making pools to water the trees in my plantations — Mof

I made gardens and parks, and set out in them fruit trees of all sorts. And I constructed for myself reservoirs to water a flourishing woodland — NAB

7. I got me servants and maidens, and had servants born in my house; also I had great possessions of great and small cattle above all that were in Jerusalem before me:

I acquired men-servants and maid-servants, and had servants born in my house; also I had great possessions of herds and flocks, above all that were before me in Jerusalem — JPS

I bought men-servants and maid-servants, and had servants born in my house; also I had great possessions of herds and flocks, above all that were before me in Jerusalem — ASV

I purchased men servants and maid servants; and had servants born in my family. And my stock of herds and flocks was great above all who were before me in Jerusalem — Sept

I bought slaves, both men and women, and had slaves born within my household; I had large herds and flocks, larger than any before me in Jerusalem — Mof

8. **I gathered me also silver and gold, and the peculiar treasure of kings and of the provinces: I gat me men singers and women singers, and the delights of the sons of men, as musical instruments, and that of all sorts.**

I heaped up unto myself also silver and gold,
And the peculiar treasure of kings, and of the provinces.
I obtained myself men-singers, and women-singers,
Even the luxuries of the children of men;
Also men and women cupbearers — Sprl

I gathered for myself silver and gold and the possessions of kings and cities; I got me men singers and women singers and the delights of the sons of men, and I appointed for myself butlers and waitresses — Lam

I gathered me also silver and gold, and the peculiar treasure of kings and of the provinces: I gat me men singers and women singers, and the delights of the sons of men, concubines very many — RV

I also gathered for myself silver and gold and the treasure of kings and provinces; I got singers, both men and women, and many concubines, man's delight — RSV

I amassed silver and gold also, the treasure of kings and provinces; I acquired singers, men and women, and all that man delights in — NEB

9. **So I was great, and increased more than all that were before me in Jerusalem: also my wisdom remained with me.**

10. **And whatsoever mine eyes desired I kept not from them, I withheld not my heart from any joy; for my heart rejoiced in all my labour: and this was my portion of all my labour.**

and nothing that mine eyes asked withheld I from them, — I did not keep back my heart from any gladness for my heart obtained gladness out of all my toil, and so this was my portion out of all my toil — Rhm

And whatsoever mine eyes coveted I kept not from them,
I restrained not my heart from any joy;
And this was the reward of all my labour, that my heart delighted in all my pursuits — Sprl

Eyes denied nothing that eyes could covet, a heart stinted of no enjoyment, free of all the pleasures I had devised for myself, this was to be my reward, this the fruit of all my labours — Knox

And nothing which was desired by my eyes did I keep from them; I did not keep any joy from my heart, because my heart took pleasure in all my work, and this was my reward — Bas

Nothing I coveted did I refuse myself; I denied my heart no joy — for my heart did feel joy in all this toil; so much did I get from all my efforts — Mof

11. **Then I looked on all the works that my hands had wrought, and on the labour that I had laboured to do: and, behold, all was vanity and vexation of spirit, and there was no profit under the sun.**

Then I looked on all the works that my hands had wrought, and on the labor that I had labored to do; and behold, all was vanity and a striving after wind, and there was no profit under the sun — ASV

therefore I looked back on all the works which my hands had done, and on the labour with which I had toiled to execute them; and behold all was vanity and vexation of spirit and there is no lasting advantage under the sun — Sept

Then I considered all that my hands had done and the toil I had spent in doing it, and behold, all was vanity and a striving after wind, and there was nothing to be gained under the sun — RSV

But when I turned to all the works that my hands had wrought, and to the toil at which I had taken such pains, behold! all was vanity and a chase after wind, with nothing gained under the sun — NAB

But as I looked at everything I had tried, it was all so useless, a chasing of the wind, and there was nothing really worthwhile anywhere — Tay

12. And I turned myself to behold wisdom, and madness, and folly: for what can the man do that cometh after the king? even that which hath been already done.

Thus turned I to look at wisdom, and madness and folly, — for what can the man do more who cometh after the king? save that which already men have done — Rhm

Then I turned myself to discriminate wisdom from madness and folly:
For what will the man do who succeedeth after the king,
Than that which hath been already done? — Sprl

So I turned again to look upon wisdom, madness, and folly; for what can the man do who comes after the king? That which has already been done — AAT

My reflections then turned to wisdom, stupidity, folly. For instance, what can the successor of a king do? What has been done already — Jerus

And I went again in search of wisdom and of foolish ways. What may the man do who comes after the king? The thing which he has done before — Bas

13. Then I saw that wisdom excelleth folly, as far as light excelleth darkness.

14. The wise man's eyes are in his head; but the fool walketh in darkness: and I myself perceived also that one event happeneth to them all.

And I saw that there is an advantage to wisdom above folly, like the advantage of the light above the darkness. The wise! — his eyes are in his head, and the fool in darkness is walking, and I also knew that one event happeneth with them all — YLT

I saw indeed that there is an advantage in wisdom above folly, like the advantage of light above darkness. The wise man's eyes are in his head; but the fool walketh in darkness. Nevertheless I knew that one event will happen to them all — Sept

I saw, indeed, that wisdom differed from folly as light from darkness; the wise man had eyes in his head, while the fool went his way benighted; but the ending of them? In their ending both were alike — Knox

More is to be had from wisdom than from folly, as from light than from darkness; this, of course, I see:
The wise man sees ahead,
the fool walks in the dark.
No doubt! But I know, too, that one fate awaits them both — Jerus

And I saw that wisdom has the advantage over folly as much as light has the advantage over darkness.
The wise man has eyes in his head, but the fool walks in darkness.
Yet I knew that one lot befalls both of them — NAB

15. Then said I in my heart, As it happeneth to the fool, so it happeneth even to me; and why was I then more wise? Then I said in my heart, that this also is vanity.

So I said to myself, 'As it befalls the fool, so will it befall me; why, then, should I be otherwise?' So I said to myself, 'This too is vanity!' — AAT

So I said to myself, "If the fool's fate is to be my fate, what is the use of all my wisdom? This too is vain," said I to myself — Mof

Then said I in my heart: As it comes to the foolish man, so it will come to me; so why have I been wise overmuch? Then I said in my heart: This again is to no purpose — Bas

Then I said to myself, "What happens to the fool will also happen to me;

why then have I acted so extremely wise?" And I said to myself, "This too is futile" — Ber

16. **For there is no remembrance of the wise more than of the fool for ever; seeing that which now is in the days to come shall all be forgotten. And how dieth the wise man? as the fool.**

For of the wise man, even as of the fool, there is no remembrance for ever; seeing that in the days to come all will have been long forgotten. And how doth the wise man die even as the fool! — ASV

Surely the wise together with the fool are not remembered for ever,
For verily the days will arrive when all will be forgotten:
And assuredly the wise die together with the fool — Sprl

Endlessly forgotten, wise man and fool alike, since to-morrow's memory will be no longer yesterday's; wise man and fool alike doomed to death — Knox

For of the wise man as of the fool there is no enduring remembrance, seeing that in the days to come all will have been long forgotten. How the wise man dies just like the fool! — RSV

The wise man is remembered no longer than the fool, for, as the passing days multiply, all will be forgotten. Alas, wise man and fool die the same death! — NEB

17. **Therefore I hated life; because the work that is wrought under the sun is grievous unto me: for all is vanity and vexation of spirit.**

Therefore I hated life, for a vexation unto me was the work which was done under the sun, — for all was vanity and a feeding on wind — Rhm

So I hated life; because the work that is wrought under the sun was grievous unto me: for all is vanity and a striving after wind — RV

So I hated life; for all that goes on under the sun seemed evil to me, all of it vain and futile — Mof

So now I hate life because it is all so irrational; all is foolishness, chasing the wind — Tay

Life I have come to hate, for what is done under the sun disgusts me, since all is vanity and chasing of the wind — Jerus

18. **Yea, I hated all my labour which I had taken under the sun: because I should leave it unto the man that shall be after me.**

19. **And who knoweth whether he shall be a wise man or a fool? yet shall he have rule over all my labour wherein I have laboured, and wherein I have shewed myself wise under the sun. This is also vanity.**

I hated all my toil at which I had laboured under the sun, seeing that I must leave it to the man coming after me; and who knows whether he will be a wise or a foolish man? Yet he will be master over all my possessions for which I laboured and used my wisdom under the sun; this, too, is worthlessness — Ber

Hate had I for all my work which I had done, because the man who comes after me will have its fruits. And who is to say if that man will be wise or foolish? But he will have power over all my work which I have done in which I have been wise under the sun. This again is to no purpose — Bas

I hated all my toil at which I had toiled under the sun, seeing that I must leave it to the man who should follow me. And who knows whether he will be a wise man or a fool? Yet he will have control of all the product of my toil at which I have toiled and of the wisdom which I have won under the sun. This too is vanity — AAT

And I detested all the fruits of my labor under the sun, because I must leave them to a man who is to come after me. And who knows whether he will be a wise man or a fool? Yet he will have control over all the fruits of my wise labor under the sun. This also is vanity — NAB

I hated all my toil in which I had toiled under the sun, seeing that I must leave it to the man who will come after me; and who knows whether he will be a wise man or a fool? Yet he will be master of all for which I toiled and used my wisdom under the sun — RSV

20. Therefore I went about to cause my heart to despair of all the labour which I took under the sun.

And I turned round to cause my heart to despair concerning all the labour that I laboured at under the sun — YLT

Therefore I turned about to give my heart up to despair concerning all the toil with which I had toiled under the sun — ABPS

So again I gave myself up to despair concerning all the toil at which I had toiled under the sun — AAT

And hence I have come to despair of all the efforts I have expended under the sun — Jerus

So I turned in despair from hard work as the answer to my search for satisfaction — Tay

21. For there is a man whose labour is in wisdom, and in knowledge, and in equity; yet to a man that hath not laboured therein shall he leave it for his portion. This also is vanity and a great evil.

For there is a man whose labor is with wisdom, and with knowledge, and with skilfulness; yet to a man that hath not labored therein shall he leave it for his portion. This also is vanity and a great evil — ASV

For here is a man whose toil hath been with wisdom and with knowledge and with skill, — yet to a man who hath not toiled therein shall he leave it as his portion, even this was vanity and a great vexation — Rhm

There is a man who labors with wisdom and knowledge and success; and yet he leaves his portion to a man who has not labored for it. This also is vanity and a great misfortune — Lam

for a man who has toiled skilfully and thoughtfully and ably has to leave all his gains to one who has never worked for them. This too is vain, it is a great evil — Mof

For anyone who toils with wisdom, knowledge, and skill must leave it all to a man who has spent no labour on it. This too is emptiness and utterly wrong — NEB

22. For what hath man of all his labour, and of the vexation of his heart, wherein he hath laboured under the sun?

23. For all his days are sorrows, and his travail grief; yea, his heart taketh not rest in the night. This is also vanity.

For what hath a man of all his labour, and of the striving of his heart, wherein he laboureth under the sun? For all his days are but sorrows, and his travail is grief; yea, even in the night his heart taketh no rest. This also is vanity — RV

For what hath man of all his labour, and of the vexation of his heart, Wherein he hath wearied under the sun?
For all his days are marred because fretted with sorrow.
Also at night his heart taketh no repose;
This is also vanity! — Sprl

What does a man get for all his work, and for the weight of care with which he has done his work under the sun?
All his days are sorrow, and his work is full of grief. Even in the night his heart has no rest. This again is to no purpose — Bas

For what does a man get for all his toil and for all his heart's striving with which he wearies himself under the sun? For all his days are full of pain and his task vexatious; even at night his mind has no rest. This also is emptiness — Ber

For what does a man get for all his toil and the striving of his mind with which he has toiled under the sun? For all his days are sorrowful and his task is melancholy, and at night his mind finds no rest. This too is vanity — AAT

24. There is nothing better for a man, than that he should eat and drink, and that he should make his soul enjoy good in his labour. This also I saw, that it was from the hand of God.

25. For who can eat, or who else can hasten hereunto, more than I?

There was nothing more blessed for Man than that he should eat and drink, and see his desire for blessedness in his toil, — even this saw I myself, that from the hand of God it was. For who could eat and who could enjoy so well as I — Rhm

There is nothing better for a man than that he should eat and drink, and make his soul enjoy good in his toil. This also I saw, that it is from the hand of God. For who can eat, or who can have enjoyment, apart from him — ABPS

There is nothing better for a man than that he should eat and drink, and find enjoyment in his toil. This also, I saw, is from the hand of God; for apart from him who can eat or who can have enjoyment — RSV

There is nothing better for a man than to eat and drink and enjoy himself, as he does his work. And this, I find, is what God grants; for who can eat, who can enjoy himself, apart from God — Mof

There is nothing better for man than to eat and drink and provide himself with good things by his labors. Even this, I realized, is from the hand of God. For who can eat or drink apart from him — NAB

26. For God giveth to a man that is good in his sight wisdom, and knowledge, and joy: but to the sinner he giveth travail, to gather and to heap up, that he may give to him that is good before God. This also is vanity and vexation of spirit.

For to the man that pleaseth him God giveth wisdom, and knowledge, and joy; but to the sinner he giveth travail, to gather and to heap up, that he may give to him that pleaseth God. This also is vanity and a striving after wind — ASV

But He giveth to man that which is right in His sight,
Wisdom, and knowledge, and joy:
But unto the sinner He giveth trouble in gathering and heaping up,
That he may provide for him that is worthier in God's sight.
This also is vanity and vexation of spirit — Sprl

For to the man who is good in his sight he hath given wisdom and knowledge and joy; and to the sinner he hath given the trouble of gathering and heaping up to give to him who is good in the sight of God. So that this also is vanity and vexation of spirit — Sept

God gives wisdom and knowledge and joy to the man who pleases him, while to the sinner is given the trouble of gathering and amassing wealth only to hand it over to someone else who pleases God. This too is emptiness and chasing the wind — NEB

For God gives to those who please him wisdom, knowledge, and joy; but if a sinner becomes wealthy, God takes the wealth away from him and gives it to those who please him. So here, too, we see an example of foolishly chasing the wind — Tay

CHAPTER 3

1. To every thing there is a season, and a time to every purpose under the heaven:

For every thing there is a season, —
And a time for every pursuit under the heavens — Rhm

Time is for all things: but there is a particular portion of time for every particular affair under heaven — Sept

For everything there is a fixed time, and a time for every business under the sun — Bas

For everything there is an appointed season, and there is a proper time for every project under heaven — Ber

Everything has its appointed hour, there is a time for all things under heaven — Mof

There is a season for everything, a time for every occupation under the sun — Jerus

2. A time to be born, and a time to die; a time to plant, and a time to pluck up that which is planted;

A time to be born, and a time to die;
A time for planting, and a time for uprooting — AAT

A time for birth, a time for death,

a time to plant and a time to uproot — Mof

A time to be born,
A time to die;
A time to plant;
A time to harvest — Tay

3. A time to kill, and a time to heal; a time to break down, and a time to build up;

4. A time to weep, and a time to laugh; a time to mourn, and a time to dance;

5. A time to cast away stones, and a time to gather stones together; a time to embrace, and a time to refrain from embracing;

. . . A time to unite together, a time to remove afar off — Sprl

. . . a time for kissing and a time to keep from kissing — Bas

. . . A time to hug;
A time not to hug — Tay

6. A time to get, and a time to lose; a time to keep, and a time to cast away.

7. A time to rend, and a time to sew; a time to keep silence, and a time to speak;

a time to tear and a time to mend;
a time for silence and a time for speech — NEB

A time for tearing,
a time for sewing;
a time for keeping silent, a time for speaking — Jerus

A time for undoing and a time for stitching; a time for keeping quiet and a time for talk — Bas

8. A time to love, and a time to hate; a time of war, and a time of peace.

9. What profit hath he that worketh in that wherein he laboureth?

10. I have seen the travail, which God hath given to the sons of men to be exercised in it.

What advantage hath the doer in that which he is labouring at? I have seen the travail that God hath given to the sons of man to be humbled by it — YLT

What benefit does the workman get from that for which he wears himself out? I have observed the employments in which God has granted men to be engaged — Ber

What gain has the worker from his toil? I have seen the business that God has given to the sons of men to be busy with — RSV

What advantage has the worker from his toil? I have considered the task which God has appointed for men to be busied about — NAB

11. He hath made every thing beautiful in his time: also he hath set the world in their heart, so that no man can find out the work that God maketh from the beginning to the end.

He hath made everything beautiful in its time: also he hath set eternity in their heart, yet so that man cannot find out the work that God hath done from the beginning even to the end — ASV

he assigned each to its proper time, but for the mind of man he has appointed mystery, that man may never fathom God's own purpose from beginning to end — Mof

He has made everything right in its time; but he has made their hearts without knowledge, so that man is unable to see the works of God, from the first to the last — Bas

He has made everything to suit its time; moreover he has given men a sense of time past and future, but no comprehension of God's work from beginning to end — NEB

All that he does is apt for its time; but though he has permitted men to consider time in its wholeness, man cannot comprehend the work of God from beginning to end — Jerus

12. I know that there is no good in them, but for a man to rejoice, and to do good in his life.

13. And also that every man should eat and drink, and enjoy the good of all his labour, it is the gift of God.

I know that there is nothing better for them, than to rejoice, and to do good so long as they live.
And also that every man should eat and drink, and enjoy good in all his labour, is the gift of God — RV

I have known that there is no good for them except to rejoice and to do good during their life, yea, even every man who eateth and hath drunk and seen good by all his labour, it is a gift of God — YLT

I perceive that there is no advantage in them,
Unless to rejoice in them, and to do good throughout his life.
And also that every man should eat and drink and behold the benefit
Of all his labour which God hath appointed him — Sprl

I know that there is nothing better for them, than to rejoice, and to get pleasure so long as they live. But also that every man should eat and drink, and enjoy pleasure for all his labour, is the gift of God — JPS

I recognized that there is nothing better than to be glad and to do well during life. For every man, moreover, to eat and drink and enjoy the fruit of all his labor is a gift of God — NAB

14. I know that, whatsoever God doeth, it shall be for ever: nothing can be put to it, nor any thing taken from it: and God doeth it, that men should fear before him.

I know that whatsoever God does will be forever; nothing may be added to it and nothing may be withdrawn from it; God has ordained it that they shall be in awe before him — AAT

I know that everything that God does shall remain forever; nothing can be added to it nor can anything be taken from it. God did it, so that they should be reverent in His presence — Ber

I know that whatever God does endures for ever; nothing can be added to it, nor anything taken from it; God has made it so, in order that men should fear before him — RSV

Also, I find, whatever God may do shall stand unchanged; nothing can be added to it, nothing can be taken from it. So God orders things, that men may stand in awe of him — Mof

And I know this, that whatever God does is final — nothing can be added or taken from it; God's purpose in this is that man should fear the all-powerful God — Tay

15. That which hath been is now; and that which is to be hath already been; and God requireth that which is past.

That which was already had been, and that which shall be already shall have been, — but God seeketh that which hath been chased away—Rhm

That which is hath been long ago; and that which is to be hath long ago been: and God seeketh again that which is passed away — ASV

Whatever is has been before, and what is to be is now; because God makes search for the things which are past — Bas

Nothing that has been, but lasts on still; nothing that will be, but has been already; he is ever repeating the history of the past — Knox

Whatever is has been already, and whatever is to come has been already, and God summons each event back in its turn — NEB

16. And moreover I saw under the sun the place of judgment, that wickedness was there; and the place of righteousness, that iniquity was there.

And again, I have seen under the sun the place of judgment — there is the wicked; and the place of righteousness — there is the wicked — YLT

And again I perceived under the sun the place of judgment,
That wickedness was there;
And the place of justice, that wickedness was there — Sprl

Moreover I saw under the sun that in the place of justice, even there was wickedness, and in the place of righteousness, even there was wickedness — RSV

And still under the sun in the judgment place I saw wickedness, and in the seat of justice, iniquity — NAB

But I still observe that under the sun crime is where law should be, the criminal where the good should be — Jerus

17. I said in mine heart, God shall judge the righteous and the wicked: for there is a time there for every purpose and for every work.

Then I said in my heart God will judge the whole class of the righteous, and the whole class of the wicked. For there is a time for everything; and he is there over all the work — Sept

Said I in my heart, Both the righteous and the lawless will God judge, — for there will be a time for every pursuit, and concerning every work — there — Rhm

I said in my heart, God will be judge of the good and of the bad; because a time for every purpose and for every work has been fixed by him — Bas

and I told myself that God would give judgement one day between the just and the sinners, and all things would reach their appointed end then — Knox

I said to myself, "In due season God will judge everything man does, both good and bad" — Tay

18. I said in mine heart concerning the estate of the sons of men, that God might manifest them, and that they might see that they themselves are beasts.

I said in my heart, It is because of the sons of men, that God may prove them, and that they may see that they themselves are but as beasts — ASV

I said to myself, "For the sake of men God is testing them and causes them to see that in themselves they are but animals" — Ber

I said to myself regarding the sons of men, 'It is that God may test them and see that they are beasts'—Smith

And I said to myself: As for the children of men, it is God's way of testing them and of showing that they are in themselves like beasts — NAB

This, I reflected, is God showing what men are, to let them see they are no better than the beasts — Mof

19. For that which befalleth the sons of men befalleth beasts; even one thing befalleth them: as the one dieth, so dieth the other; yea, they have all one breath; so that a man hath no preeminence above a beast: for all is vanity.

For an event is to the sons of man, and an event is to the beasts, even one event is to them; as the death of this, so is the death of that; and one spirit is to all, and the advantage of men above the beast is nothing, for the whole is vanity — YLT

For as regardeth the destiny of the sons of men and the destiny of beasts one fate have they, as dieth the one so dieth the other, and one spirit have they all, — and the preeminence of man over beast is nothing, for all were vanity — Rhm

Surely that which befalleth the sons of men, say they,
Befalleth the beasts; even one thing happeneth to them both.
As the one dieth, so dieth the other; yea, they all have one breath;
So that man hath no rank above a beast.
Surely vanity of vanity! — Sprl

For the fate of the sons of men and the fate of beasts is the same; as one dies, so dies the other. They all have the same breath, and man has no advantage over the beasts; for all is vanity — RSV

For the same misfortune which befalls the sons of men befalls the beasts; even one misfortune befalls them: as the one dies, so dies the other; yea, they have all one breath; so that man has no pre-eminence over the beast; for all is vanity — Lam

For man is a creature of chance and the beasts are creatures of chance, and one mischance awaits them all: death comes to both alike. They all draw the same breath. Men have no advantage over beasts; for everything is emptiness — NEB

20. All go unto one place; all are of the dust, and all turn to dust again.

21. Who knoweth the spirit of man that goeth upward, and the spirit of the beast that goeth downward to the earth?

They are all for one place. They were all from dust: and to dust they shall return. And who hath seen the breath of the sons of men whether it ascendeth upwards; and the breath of the beast, whether it descendeth downwards into the earth? — Sept

What! do all go to one place, though all are of dust,
And though all return unto dust?
Who discriminateth the spirit of the sons of man,
Which ascending it ascendeth,
From the spirit of the beast which descending, resolveth itself into the earth? — Sprl

All go unto one place; all are of the dust, and all turn to dust again. Who knoweth the spirit of man, whether it goeth upward, and the spirit of the beast, whether it goeth downward to the earth? — ASV

All go to one place, all are of the dust, and all will be turned to dust again. Who is certain that the spirit of the sons of men goes up to heaven, or that the spirit of the beasts goes down to the earth? — Bas

All go to one place — the dust from which they came and to which they must return. For who can prove that the spirit of man goes upward and the spirit of animals goes downward into dust? — Tay

22. Wherefore I perceive that there is nothing better, than that a man should rejoice in his own works; for that is his portion: for who shall bring him to see what shall be after him?

Wherefore I saw that there is nothing better, than that a man should rejoice in his works; for that is his portion: for who shall bring him back to see what shall be after him? — RV

So I saw that there is nothing better than that a man should rejoice in his works, for that is his portion. Who can bring him to consider what shall be after him? — Ber

So I saw the best thing for man was to be happy in his work; that is what he gets out of life — for who can show him what is to happen afterwards? — Mof

So I became aware that it is best for man to busy himself here to his own content; this and nothing else is his allotted portion; who can show him what the future will bring? — Knox

I see there is no happiness for man but to be happy in his work, for this is the lot assigned him. Who then can bring him to what is to happen after his time? — Jerus

CHAPTER 4

1. So I returned, and considered all the oppressions that are done under the sun: and behold the tears of such as were oppressed, and they had no comforter; and on the side of their oppressors there was power; but they had no comforter.

Then again I considered all the oppressive deeds which were done under the sun, — and lo! the tears of the oppressed, and they have no comforter, and on the side of their oppressors is power, and they have no comforter — Rhm

Again I saw the oppressions that are practiced under the sun. And behold, the tears of the oppressed, and they had no one to comfort them! On the side of their oppressors there was power, and there was no one to comfort them — RSV

So I turned and considered all the oppressions that are done under the sun; and behold, the tears of the oppressed, and they had no comforter to deliver them from the hand of their oppressors, having neither strength nor helper — Lam

And then my thoughts would turn back to all the wrongs that are done under the sun's eye. Innocent folk in tears, and who is to comfort them? Who is to comfort them, powerless against their oppressors? — Knox

Next I observed all the oppression and sadness throughout the earth — the tears of the oppressed, and no one helping them, while on the side of their oppressors were powerful allies — Tay

2. Wherefore I praised the dead which are already dead, more than the living which are yet alive.

3. Yea, better is he than both they, which hath not yet been, who hath not seen the evil work that is done under the sun.

Wherefore I praised the dead that have been long dead more than the living that are yet alive; yea, better than them both did I esteem him that hath not yet been, who hath not seen the evil work that is done under the sun — ASV

Therefore I congratulated the dead which are already dead,
More than the living which are yet alive:
But better is he than they both, who hath not yet existed;
Neither beheld the evil work which is done under the sun — Sprl

Wherefore I esteemed happy the dead who are already dead more than the living who are yet alive; but better than them both did I esteem him who has not yet been, who has not seen the evil work that is done under the sun — ABPS

So my praise was for the dead who have gone to their death, more than for the living who still have life.
Yes, happier than the dead or the living seemed he who has not ever been, who has not seen the evil which is done under the sun — Bas

So, rather than the living who still have lives to live, I salute the dead who have already met death; happier than both of these is he who is yet unborn and has not seen the evil things that are done under the sun — Jerus

4. Again, I considered all travail, and every right work, that for this a man is envied of his neighbour. This is also vanity and vexation of spirit.

Then I saw all labour and every skilful work, that for this a man is envied of his neighbour. This also is vanity and a striving after wind — RV

Again, I considered all labour and all excelling in work, that it is a man's rivalry with his neighbour. This also is vanity and a striving after wind — JPS

Also I saw that human toil and skill mean jealousy between man and man. (This too is vain and futile!) — Mof

Then I saw that all toil and skillful work is the rivalry of one man for another. This also is vanity and a chase after wind — NAB

Then I observed that the basic motive for success is the driving force of envy and jealousy! But this, too, is foolishness, chasing the wind — Tay

5. The fool foldeth his hands together, and eateth his own flesh.

6. Better is a handful with quietness, than both the hands full with travail and vexation of spirit.

The fool foldeth his hands together, and eateth his own flesh. Better is a handful, with quietness, than two handfuls with labor and striving after wind — ASV

The fool is clasping his hands, and eating his own flesh: 'Better is a handful with quietness, than two handfuls with labour and vexation of spirit' — YLT

The fool folds his hands together and consumes his own flesh. Better is a handful with rest, than both fists full of toil and chasing after wind — Ber

The fool folds his arms
and eats his own flesh away.
— Better one handful of repose
than two hands full of effort
in chasing the wind — Jerus

7. Then I returned, and saw vanity under the sun.

8. There is one alone, and there is not a second; yea, he hath neither child nor brother: yet there is no end of all his labour;

Then I turned and took a view of a vanity under the sun — Here is a single individual who hath no second; at least he hath neither son nor brother, yet there is no end to all his labour — Sept

And I have turned, and I see a vain thing under the sun: There is one, and there is not a second; even son or brother he hath not and there is no end to all his labour! — YLT

Then again I looked at a vain thing under the sun: — Here is one without a second, even son or brother he hath none, yet is there no end to his toil — Rhm

Then I turned, and I saw vanity under the sun.
When there is but one man, and not a second, and he has neither son nor brother, there is no end to all his labor — Lam

Then I came back, and I saw an example of what is to no purpose under the sun.

It is one by himself, without a second, and without son or brother; but there is no end to all his work — Bas

neither is his eye satisfied with riches; neither saith he, For whom do I labour, and bereave my soul of good? This is also vanity, yea, it is a sore travail.

neither are his eyes satisfied with riches. For whom then, saith he, do I labor, and deprive my soul of good? This also is vanity, yea, it is a sore travail — ASV

and his eyes are never satisfied with riches, so that he never asks, "For whom am I toiling and depriving myself of pleasure?" This also is vanity and an unhappy business — RSV

His eyes are not satisfied with wealth and (he never reflects), "For whom am I working and denying myself enjoyment?" This, too, is worthlessness and a sorry situation — Ber

he cannot satisfy himself with what he gains, and he never asks for whose sake he is toiling and stinting himself of pleasure. This too is vain, a sorry business — Mof

9. Two are better than one; because they have a good reward for their labour.

10. For if they fall, the one will lift up his fellow; but woe to him that is alone when he falleth; for he hath not another to help him up.

Two are better than one. They have a better reward for their labour. For if they chance to fall the one can raise up his fellow. But alas for him who is alone, when he falleth and hath not another to raise him up — Sept

The two are better than the one, in that they have a good reward by their labour. For if they fall, the one raiseth up his companion, but wo [*sic*] to the one who falleth, and there is not a second to raise him up — YLT

Two are better than one: they get a good wage for their labor. If the one falls, the other will lift up his companion. Woe to the solitary man! For if he should fall, he has no one to lift him up — NAB

Two are better than one, for they get a good wage for their toil; and if they fall, the one can lift up his companion, but if a solitary person falls there is no partner to lift him up — AAT

Better be in partnership with another, than alone; partnership brings advantage to both. If one falls, the other will give support; with the lonely it goes hard; when he falls, there is none to raise him — Knox

Better two than one by himself, since thus their work is really profitable. If one should fall, the other helps him up; but woe to the man by himself with no one to help him up when he falls down — Jerus

11. Again, if two lie together, then they have heat: but how can one be warm alone?

12. And if one prevail against him, two shall withstand him; and a threefold cord is not quickly broken.

Moreover if two lie together then have they warmth, — but how can one have warmth? And though an enemy should prevail against one, two might make a stand before him, — and a threefold cord cannot soon be broken — Rhm

Again, if two lie together, they are warm; but how can one be warm alone? And though a man might prevail against one who is alone, two will withstand him. A threefold cord is not quickly broken — RSV

So again, if two are sleeping together they are warm, but how may one be warm by himself?
And two attacked by one would be safe, and three cords twisted together are not quickly broken — Bas

Again, if two men lie together, they keep warm; but how can any man keep warm alone? Also, two men can stand up to a robber, when a single man would be overpowered. And a threefold cord is not easily broken — Mof

And, if two lie side by side, they keep each other warm; but how can one keep warm by himself? If a man is alone, an assailant may overpower him, but two can resist; and a cord of three strands is not quickly snapped — NEB

13. Better is a poor and wise child, than an old and foolish king, who will no more be admonished.

14. For out of prison he cometh to reign; whereas also he that is born in his kingdom becometh poor.

Better is a frugal and wise child
Than an old and foolish king,
Who will not understand to be further admonished.
For from the house of imprisonment he went forth to reign;
Yea, even in his own kingdom was he born poor — Sprl

Better is a poor and wise child than an old and foolish king, who knoweth not how to receive admonition any more. For out of prison he came forth to be king; although in his kingdom he was born poor — JPS

Better is a youth who is poor and wise than a king who is old and foolish, and does not know how to receive admonition.
Out of prison he has come to reign, because also in his own kingdom he had been born miserable — Lam

Better is a youth poor and wise, than a king old and foolish, who no longer knows how to take advice; for the former comes from prison to be king, although in the other's kingdom he was born poor — Ber

It is better to be a poor but wise youth than to be an old and foolish king who refuses all advice. Such a lad could come from prison and succeed. He might even become king, though born in poverty — Tay

15. I considered all the living which walk under the sun, with the second child that shall stand up in his stead.

I saw all the living, who were going hither and thither under the sun, — that they were with the boy who was to be the second, who was to stand in the other's place — Rhm

I saw all the living that walk under the sun, that they were with the youth, the second, that stood up in his stead — ASV

I saw all the living under the sun running with the youth who was to stand in his place — AAT

I have seen all the living on earth side with such a youth, who was destined to reign instead of the old king — Mof

I have seen the whole world, from east to west, take part with the young man, the usurper that rises in the old king's stead — Knox

16. There is no end of all the people, even of all that have been before them: they also that come after shall not rejoice in him. Surely this also is vanity and vexation of spirit.

There was no end of all the people, even of all them over whom he was: yet they that come after shall not rejoice in him. Surely this also is vanity and a striving after wind — ASV

There is no end of all the people — of all who resorted to them. Yet they who come last will have no joy in him. Surely this also is vanity and vexation of spirit — Sept

There was no end of all the people, even of all them whom he did lead; yet they that come after shall not rejoice in him. Surely this also is vanity and a striving after wind—JPS

there was no end of all the people; he was over all of them. Yet those who come later will not rejoice in him. Surely this also is vanity and a striving after wind — RSV

He takes his place at the head of innumerable subjects; sad, if later no one has cause to be glad of him. This too, most certainly, is vanity and chasing of the wind — Jerus

CHAPTER 5

1. Keep thy foot when thou goest to the house of God, and be more ready to hear, than to give the sacrifice of fools: for they consider not that they do evil.

Keep thy foot when thou goest unto the house of God, and be more ready to hear, than dullards to offer sacrifice, — for they make no acknowledgement of doing wrong — Rhm

Keep thy foot when thou goest to the house of God; for to draw nigh to hear is better than to give the sacrifice of fools: for they know not that they do evil — ASV

Guard your steps when you go to the house of God; and to draw near to obey is better than that fools should offer sacrifice, for they know nothing but to do wrong — AAT

Guard your feet when you go to the house of God; to be ready to listen is better than to give sacrifice like the fools, who do not know when they do wrong — Ber

Never enter God's house carelessly; draw near him to listen, and then your service is better than what fools offer — for all a fool knows is how to do wrong — Mof

2. Be not rash with thy mouth, and let not thine heart be hasty to utter anything before God: for God is in heaven, and thou upon earth: therefore let thy words be few.

3. For a dream cometh through the multitude of business; and a fool's voice is known by multitude of words.

Be not rash with thy mouth, and let not thy heart be hasty to utter a word before God, for God is in heaven, and thou upon earth; therefore let thy words be few. For a dream comes through a multitude of travail, and a fool's voice through a multitude of words — ABPS

Be not precipitate with thy mouth,
And let not thine heart be hasty,
To utter speech before God:
For God is in heaven, and thou upon earth:
Therefore let thy words be few.
Surely a dream cometh from multiplicity of business;
So is a fool's voice known by a multiplicity of words — Sprl

Be not hasty in your utterance and let not your heart be quick to make a promise in God's presence. God is in heaven and you are on earth; therefore let your words be few.
For nightmares come with many cares,
and a fool's utterance with many words — NAB

Be in no hurry to speak; do not hastily declare yourself before God; for God is in heaven, you on earth. Be sparing, then, of speech:
Dreaming comes from much worrying,
foolish talk from a multiplicity of words — Jerus

Do not rush into speech, let there be no hasty utterance in God's presence. God is in heaven, you are on earth; so let your words be few. The sensible man has much business on his hands; the fool talks and it is so much chatter — NEB

4. When thou vowest a vow unto God, defer not to pay it; for he hath no pleasure in fools: pay that which thou hast vowed.

5. Better is it that thou shouldest not vow, than that thou shouldest vow and not pay.

When thou vowest a vow to God, delay not to complete it, for there is no pleasure in fools; that which thou vowest — complete. Better that thou do not vow, than that thou dost vow and dost not complete — YLT

Vow to God if thou utterest, without delay perform it, he will have no light and rash promises; vow made must be vow paid. Far better undertake nothing than undertake what thou dost not fulfil — Knox

When you vow a vow to God, do not delay fulfilling it; for he has no pleasure in fools; but as for you, pay that which you have vowed. It is much better that you should not vow than that you should vow and not fulfill it — Lam

When you take an oath before God, put it quickly into effect, because he has no pleasure in the foolish; keep the oath you have taken.
It is better not to take an oath than to take an oath and not keep it — Bas

When you vow a vow to God, pay it without delay (for the vows of the foolish displease him). Pay your vow; better not vow at all than vow and fail to pay — Mof

6. Suffer not thy mouth to cause thy flesh to sin; neither say thou before the angel, that it was an error: wherefore should God be angry at thy voice, and

destroy the work of thine hands?

7. For in the multitude of dreams and many words there are also divers vanities: but fear thou God.

Suffer not thy mouth to bring thy flesh into guilt, neither say thou before the messenger, that it was an error; wherefore should God be angry at thy voice, and destroy the work of thy hands? For through the multitude of dreams and vanities there are also many words; but fear thou God — JPS

Do not let thy mouth cause thy flesh to sin, — neither say thou before the messenger, that it was a mistake, — wherefore should God be indignant at thy voice, and destroy the work of thy hands? For it was done amidst a multitude of dreams and vanities and many words, — but towards God be thou reverent — Rhm

Let not your mouth bring you into sin, and say not before the messenger, 'It was a mistake.' Why should God be angered at your voice and destroy the work of your hands? For through many empty dreams come many vows. But do you fear God! — AAT

Do not allow your mouth to cause you to sin, and do not say before His messenger that it is a mistake. Why should God be angry at your voice and destroy the work of your hand? For in many dreams and follies and many words — this remains: You shall revere God — Ber

Let not your mouth lead you into sin, and do not say before the messenger that it was a mistake; why should God be angry at your voice, and destroy the work of your hands?
For when dreams increase, empty words grow many: but do you fear God — RSV

8. If thou seest the oppression of the poor, and violent perverting of judgment and justice in a province, marvel not at the matter: for he that is higher than the highest regardeth; and there be higher than they.

9. Moreover the profit of the earth is for all: the king himself is served by the field.

If oppression of the poor, and violent taking away of judgment and righteousness thou seest in a province, do not marvel at the matter, for a higher than the high is observing, and high ones are over them. And the abundance of a land is for all. A king for a field is served — YLT

If you see the poor under a cruel yoke, and law and right being violently overturned in a country, be not surprised, because one authority is keeping watch on another and there are higher than they.
It is good generally for a country where the land is worked to have a king — Bas

When you see the poor being oppressed, or right and justice tampered with in the State, be not surprised; it is one official preying on another. But over both there is a supreme authority; after all, a country prospers with a king who has control — Mof

If you witness in some province the oppression of the poor and the denial of right and justice, do not be surprised at what goes on, for every official has a higher one set over him, and the highest keeps watch over them all. The best thing for a country is a king whose own lands are well tilled — NEB

If in a province you see the poor oppressed, right and justice violated, do not be surprised. You will be told that officials are under the supervision of superiors, who are supervised in turn; you will hear talk of 'the common good' and 'the service of the king' — Jerus

10. He that loveth silver shall not be satisfied with silver; nor he that loveth abundance with increase: this is also vanity.

11. When goods increase, they are increased that eat them: and what good is there to the owners thereof, saving the beholding of them with their eyes?

He that loveth silver shall not be satisfied with silver nor he that loveth abundance with revenue, — even this was vanity.
When blessings are increased, increased are the eaters thereof, — what profit then to the owner of them saving the sight of his eyes

— Rhm

He who loves money will not be satisfied with money; nor he who loves wealth, with gain: this also is vanity. When goods increase, they increase who eat them; and what gain has their owner but to see them with his eyes — RSV

The lover of money shall not be satisfied with money, nor the lover of wealth with his gain; this, too, is futility. With the increase of goods there is an increase of those consuming them, and what advantage is there to the owner, except that he sees it with his eyes — Ber

A lover of silver cannot be satisfied with silver; but did any one ever love what the abundance of this produceth? Surely this is vanity. By an abundance of wealth they who consume it are multiplied. And what is the mighty advantage of the owner from it? That he hath the first sight of it with his eyes — Sept

The covetous man is never satisfied with money, and the lover of wealth reaps no fruit from it; so this too is vanity. Where there are great riches, there are also many to devour them. Of what use are they to the owner except to feast his eyes upon — NAB

12. The sleep of the labouring man is sweet, whether he eat little or much: but the abundance of the rich will not suffer him to sleep.

Sweet is the sleep of the labourer whether he eat little or much; and the sufficiency of the wealthy is not suffering him to sleep — YLT

Sweet is the sleep of a labouring man, whether he eat little or much; but the satiety of the rich will not suffer him to sleep — JPS

Sweet is the sleep of the laborer, whether he eat little or much;
But the surfeit of the rich allows him no sleep — AAT

The man who works hard sleeps well whether he eats little or much, but the rich must worry and suffer insomnia — Tay

13. There is a sore evil which I have seen under the sun, namely, riches kept for the owners thereof to their hurt.

14. But those riches perish by evil travail: and he begetteth a son, and there is nothing in his hand.

There is a grievous evil which I have seen under the sun, namely, riches kept by the owner thereof to his hurt: and those riches perish by evil adventure; and if he hath begotten a son, there is nothing in his hand — ASV

Here was an incurable evil, I had seen under the sun, — riches kept by the owner thereof to his hurt; and those riches perish by being ill employed, — and though he begetteth a son, yet is there in his hand nothing at all — Rhm

There is a great evil which I have seen under the sun — wealth kept by the owner to be his downfall.
And I saw the destruction of his wealth by an evil chance; and when he became the father of a son he had nothing in his hand — Bas

A sore evil have I seen in the world, wealth hoarded to the owner's loss: in some unlucky venture it is lost, and the man has nothing to leave to his son — Mof

There is a great injustice that I observe under the sun: riches stored and turning to loss for their owner. One unlucky venture, and those riches are lost; a son is born to him, and he has nothing to leave him — Jerus

15. As he came forth of his mother's womb, naked shall he return to go as he came, and shall take nothing of his labour, which he may carry away in his hand.

As he came forth of his mother's womb, naked shall he go again as he came, and shall take nothing for his labour, which he may carry away in his hand — RV

As he proceeded from his mother's womb,
naked shall he return to go as he came.
Neither shall he bear away anything of his labour, which he may carry in his hand — Sprl

As he came naked out of his mother's womb, he shall turn about and go as he came. He shall take nothing by his labour to go with him in his hand — Sept

Just as he emerged from his mother's womb,
Naked does he return, going even as he came;
And he carries away nothing of his toil which he can carry in his hand — AAT

Naked he came forth from his mother's womb, and naked he must return; for all his toil, he has nothing to take with him — Mof

16. And this also is a sore evil, that in all points as he came, so shall he go: and what profit hath he that hath labored for the wind?

17. All his days also he eateth in darkness, and he hath much sorrow and wrath with his sickness.

And surely this is a sore evil, that just as he came so he departs;
For what advantage is there to him who hath laboured for the wind?
Moreover, all his days he eateth in seclusion, with much sorrow,
And weariness, and sad anger — Sprl

This, indeed, is a sore evil: just as he came, so will he go;
And what profit has he in that he toileth for the wind,
And spent all his days in darkness and mourning,
And in much trouble, sickness, and anger — AAT

This, too, is a grievous misfortune; in all points as he came so shall he go, and what profit did he get from wearing himself out for wind, all his days eating in darkness with plenty of grief, sickness and wrath — Ber

This too is a grievous evil, that he goes just as he came. What then does it profit him to toil for wind? All the days of his life are passed in gloom and sorrow, under great vexation, sickness and wrath — NAB

This, as I said, is a very serious problem, for all his hard work has been for nothing; he has been working for the wind. It is all swept away. All the rest of his life he is under a cloud — gloomy, discouraged, frustrated, and angry — Tay

18. Behold that which I have seen: it is good and comely for one to eat and to drink, and to enjoy the good of all his labour that he taketh under the sun all the days of his life, which God giveth him: for it is his portion.

Lo, that which I have seen: It is good, because beautiful, to eat, and to drink, and to see good in all one's labour that he laboureth at under the sun, the number of days of his life that God hath given to him, for it is his portion — YLT

Lo! what I myself have seen — Better that it should be excellent to eat and to drink and to see blessedness in all one's toil wherein one toileth under the sun for the number of days of his life in that God hath given it him, for that is his portion — Rhm

Behold I have seen a good which is comely, namely to eat and drink, and to have a good enjoyment in all the labour with which one toileth under the sun, the number of the days of his life which God hath given him; for this is his portion — Sept

Behold, that which I have seen to be good and to be comely is for one to eat and to drink, and to enjoy good in all his labor, wherein he laboreth under the sun, all the days of his life which God hath given him: for this is his portion — ASV

What I have seen is this: that it is good and proper for a man to eat and drink and enjoy himself in return for his labours here under the sun, throughout the brief span of life which God has allotted him — NEB

Behold, what I have seen to be good and to be fitting is to eat and drink and find enjoyment in all the toil with which one toils under the sun, the few days of his life which God has given him, for this is his lot — RSV

19. Every man also to whom God hath given riches and wealth, and hath given him power to eat thereof, and to take his portion, and to rejoice in his labour; this is the gift of God.

20. For he shall not much remember the days of his life; because God answereth him in the joy of his heart.

Also to every man unto whom God hath bestowed riches and wealth,
And hath given him permission to enjoy them, and to delight in his portion,
And to rejoice in his labour — it is God's gift to him:
For he will not care for the multitude of the days of his life;
Because God satisfieth him in the rejoicing of his heart — Sprl

And every man indeed to whom God hath given riches and wealth, and granted him power to eat thereof, and to take his portion, hath by means of his being made glad in his labour, this further gift of God, that he will not much remember the days of his life, because God occupieth him with the joy of his heart — Sept

Further, every man to whom God has given riches and wealth and whom He has given power to enjoy them, to take his portion and to find enjoyment in his labor — that is the gift of God. For he shall not often think of the brevity of his life, because God keeps his heart occupied with gladness — Ber

yes, it is God's own gift when a man is made rich and wealthy and able to enjoy it all, to partake of what may be allotted him and to enjoy himself as he toils. Then he will never brood over the fewness of his days, for God is giving him his heart's delight — Mof

Any man to whom God gives riches and property, and grants power to partake of them, so that he receives his lot and finds joy in the fruits of his toil, has a gift from God. For he will hardly dwell on the shortness of his life, because God lets him busy himself with the joy of his heart — NAB

CHAPTER 6

1. **There is an evil which I have seen under the sun, and it is common among men:**

There is an evil which I have seen under the sun, and it is heavy upon men — ASV

There is an evil which I have seen under the sun, and it is heavy upon mankind — AAT

With another hardship I have seen men visited here beneath the sun, and commonly — Knox

There is an evil I observed under the sun, that weighs men down — Jerus

2. **A man to whom God hath given riches, wealth, and honour, so that he wanteth nothing for his soul of all that he desireth, yet God giveth him not power to eat thereof, but a stranger eateth it: this is vanity, and it is an evil disease.**

A man to whom God giveth riches and gains and honour so that nothing doth he lack for his soul — of all that he craveth and yet God doth not give him power to eat thereof, but a man unknown eateth it, — this was vanity and an incurable evil it was — Rhm

A man to whom God has given riches, and wealth, and honour,
So that his soul needeth nothing of all that he desireth;
Yet God giveth him not the power to partake thereof,
But a stranger partaketh of it:
This is vanity, and it is a distressing evil — Sprl

God making a man rich, wealthy, and honoured, till he has everything his heart desires, and yet he is unable to enjoy it; an outsider gets the good of it. This is vain, a sore misfortune — Mof

there is the man to whom God gives riches and property and honor, so that he lacks none of all the things he craves; yet God does not grant him power to partake of them, but a stranger devours them. This is vanity and a dire plague — NAB

3. **If a man beget a hundred children, and live many years, so that the days of his years be many, and his soul be not filled with good, and also that he have no burial; I say, that an untimely birth is better than he.**

If a man doth beget a hundred, and

live many years, and is great, because they are the days of his years, and his soul is not satisfied from the goodness, and also he hath not had a grave, I have said, 'Better than he is the untimely birth' — YLT

If a man becomes father of a hundred children and lives many years and many are the days of his years, but he is not satisfied with good, nor does he obtain burial, I say that a premature birth is better than he — AAT

A man may have a hundred children and live a long life; but however many his days may be, if he does not get satisfaction from the good things of life and in the end receives no burial, then I maintain that the still-born child is in better case than he — NEB

Even if a man has a hundred sons and as many daughters and lives to be very old, but leaves so little money at his death that his children can't even give him a decent burial — I say that he would be better off born dead — Tay

4. For he cometh in with vanity, and departeth in darkness, and his name shall be covered with darkness.

5. Moreover he hath not seen the sun, nor known any thing: this hath more rest than the other.

For it entereth a worthless thing and departeth in obscurity;
And its name is concealed in oblivion.
Also it hath not seen the sun, neither perceived anything:
This hath more rest than the other — Sprl

For that comes in vain; in darkness it departs and in darkness its name is covered, it has neither seen nor known the sun; it has more rest than he — Ber

Though it came in vain and goes into darkness and its name is enveloped in darkness; though it has not seen or known the sun, yet the dead child is at rest rather than such a man — NAB

6. Yea, though he live a thousand years twice told, yet hath he seen no good: do not all go to one place?

yea, though he live a thousand years twice told, and yet enjoy no good, do not all go to one place — ASV

Even though he lives a thousand years twice over and gets no enjoyment — do not all go to one place — AAT

Even if the man lived a thousand years twice over, without deriving profit from his estate, do not both alike go to the same place — Jerus

Though a man lives a thousand years twice over, but doesn't find contentment — well, what's the use — Tay

7. All the labour of man is for his mouth, and yet the appetite is not filled.

8. For what hath the wise more than the fool? what hath the poor, that knoweth to walk before the living?

9. Better is the sight of the eyes than the wandering of the desire: this is also vanity and vexation of spirit.

here then a wise man hath the advantage over a fool; since the poor man knoweth that to pass through life, what he sees with the eyes is better for him than to be wandering after appetite, which is indeed vanity and vexation of spirit — Sept

Is [the] wise man more to be envied than [the] fool? Where should a man go when he is poor, save where he can find a livelihood?
Better aim at what lies in view than hanker after dreams. But indeed all is frustration, and labour lost — Knox

A wise man fares no better than a fool; nor does a poor man, with sense to live aright.
Better a joy at hand
than wants that roam abroad — Mof

What advantage then in facing life has the wise man over the fool, or the poor man for all his experience? It is better to be satisfied with what is before your eyes than give rein to desire; this too is emptiness and chasing the wind — NEB

10. That which hath been is named already, and it is known that it is man: neither may he contend with him that is mightier than he.

Whatsoever hath been, the name

thereof was given long ago; and it is known what man is; neither can he contend with him that is mightier than he — ASV

Whatsoever cometh into being, the name thereof was given long ago, and it is foreknown what man is; neither can he contend with him that is mightier than he — JPS

Whatever has been, his name was called long ago, and it is known that it is Adam; neither can he contend with him that is mightier than he — ABPS

Whatever has come to be has already been named, and it is known what man is, and that he is not able to dispute with one stronger than he — RSV

Whatever is, was long ago given its name, and the nature of man is known, and that he cannot contend in judgment with one who is stronger than he — NAB

11. **Seeing there be many things that increase vanity, what is man the better?**

12. **For who knoweth what is good for man in this life, all the days of his vain life which he spendeth as a shadow? for who can tell a man what shall be after him under the sun?**

Though verily his greatest performances magnify vanity,
What is comparable with man?
Yet who knoweth what is best for man in this life,
During the number of the days of his vain life,
Which he expendeth like a shadow?
For who can relate unto man what shall succeed after him,
Under the sun — Sprl

Since there are many arguments to prove the abundance of vanity; is there any one thing better than another for man? Doth any one know what is good for man in this life? All the days of his life of vanity he hath indeed done these things under a shade; is there any one who can tell him what will be after him under the sun — Sept

The more words, the more worthlessness; what advantage does man gain from them? For who knows what is good for man in the numbered days of his empty life which he spends as a shadow? For who can declare to man what shall be after him under the sun — Ber

The more words, the greater the vanity of it all; and what does man get from it?
Who knows what is good for man in his lifetime, in those few days he lives so vainly, days that like a shadow he spends? Who can tell a man what will happen under the sun after his time — Jerus

CHAPTER 7

1. **A good name is better than precious ointment; and the day of death than the day of one's birth.**
2. **It is better to go to the house of mourning, than to go to the house of feasting: for that is the end of all men; and the living will lay it to his heart.**
3. **Sorrow is better than laughter: for by the sadness of the countenance the heart is made better.**

It is better to go to a house of mourning than to a house of feasting. As that is the end of every man therefore the living will improve his understanding. Grief is better than laughter; for by a sadness of countenance a heart may be made better — Sept

Better to go to the house of mourning than to the house of feasting; for this is the destiny of all men, and the living should take it to heart.
Better is sorrow than laughter;
for by the facial sadness the heart is made glad — Ber

Better go to the house of mourning
than to the house of feasting;
for death is the end of all men,
and the living should keep that in mind.
Grief is better than gaiety, for sadness does the soul good — Mof

It is better to spend your time at funerals than at festivals. For you are going to die and it is a good

thing to think about it while there is still time.
Sorrow is better than laughter, for sadness has a refining influence on us — Tay

4. The heart of the wise is in the house of mourning; but the heart of fools is in the house of mirth.

5. It is better to hear the rebuke of the wise, than for a man to hear the song of fools.

6. For as the crackling of thorns under a pot, so is the laughter of the fool: this also is vanity.

The hearts of the wise are in the house of weeping; but the hearts of the foolish are in the house of joy.
It is better to take note of the protest of the wise, than for a man to give ear to the song of the foolish.
Like the cracking of thorns under a pot, so is the laugh of a foolish man; and this again is to no purpose — Bas

The mind of the wise is in the house of mourning,
But the mind of fools is in the house of mirth.
It is better that a man should hear the rebuke of the wise,
Than that he should hear the song of fools.
For like the sound of thorns under the pot,
So is the laughter of the fool. This too is vanity — AAT

Sadness, a home for the wise man's thoughts, mirth for the fool's.
Better receive a wise man's rebuke, than hear thy praises sung by fools.
Loud but not long the thorns crackle under the pot, and fools make merry; for them, too, frustration — Knox

The heart of the wise is in the house of mourning,
the heart of fools in the house of gaiety.
Better attend to a wise man's reprimand
than listen to a song sung by a fool.
For like the crackling of thorns under the cauldron
is the laughter of fools: this is vanity, too — Jerus

7. Surely oppression maketh a wise man mad; and a gift destroyeth the heart.

Surely extortion maketh the wise man foolish; and a bribe destroyeth the understanding — ASV

The wise are troubled by the ways of the cruel, and the giving of money is the destruction of the heart — Bas

Surely, extortion maddens the wise man, and a bribe corrupts the heart — Ber

Surely oppression turneth a wise man into a fool;
And a gift destroyeth the understanding — JPS

Oppression bewilders even a wise man's wits, and undermines his courage — Knox

8. Better is the end of a thing than the beginning thereof: and the patient in spirit is better than the proud in spirit.

9. Be not hasty in thy spirit to be angry: for anger resteth in the bosom of fools.

Better is the end of a thing than its beginning;
Better the patient in spirit than the proud in spirit.
Be not hasty in thy spirit to be vexed;
For vexation rests in the bosom of fools — ABPS

Better is the end of a thing than its beginning; and the patient man in humbleness is better than the proud in spirit.
Be not hastily angry, for anger rests in the bosom of the fools — Lam

Better is the end of a thing than its beginning;
and the patient in spirit is better than the proud in spirit.
Be not quick to anger, for anger lodges in the bosom of fools — RSV

Better the end of anything than its beginning; better patience than pride.
Do not be quick to show resentment; for resentment is nursed by fools — NEB

10. Say not thou, What is the cause that the former days were better than these? for thou dost not inquire wisely concerning this.

Do not say,
What hath happened, that the former days were better than these?

For not wisely askest thou concerning this — Rhm

Say not thou: Wherefore is it that the former days were better than these? Surely thou dost not enquire wisely concerning this — Sprl

Do not say: How is it that former times were better than these? For it is not in wisdom that you ask about this — NAB

Do not ask why earlier days were better than these, for that is not a question prompted by wisdom — Jerus

11. Wisdom is good with an inheritance: and by it there is profit to them that see the sun.

12. For wisdom is a defence, and money is a defence: but the excellency of knowledge is, that wisdom giveth life to them that have it.

Wisdom is good with an inheritance,
And an advantage it is to those beholding the sun.
For wisdom is a defence, money is a defence,
And the advantage of the knowledge of wisdom is,
She reviveth her possessors — YLT

Wisdom is as good as an inheritance; yea, more excellent is it for them that see the sun. For wisdom is a defence, even as money is a defence; but the excellency of knowledge is, that wisdom preserveth the life of him that hath it — ASV

Wisdom with an inheritance is good,
And an advantage to those who see the sun;
For in the protection of wisdom is the protection of money;
And the advantage of knowledge is that wisdom preserves the life of its owner — AAT

Wisdom is as beneficial as a legacy; an advantage to those who see the sun. For wisdom protects as wealth protects; but the advantage lies with knowledge. Wisdom preserves the lives of those who possess it — Ber

Wisdom is better than possessions and an advantage to all who see the sun. Better have wisdom behind you than money; wisdom profits men by giving life to those who know her — NEB

13. Consider the work of God: for who can make that straight, which he hath made crooked?

14. In the day of prosperity be joyful, but in the day of adversity consider: God also hath set the one over against the other, to the end that man should find nothing after him.

Consider the work of God: for who can make that straight, which he hath made crooked?
In the day of prosperity be joyful, and in the day of adversity consider: God hath even made the one side by side with the other, to the end that man should not find out any thing that shall be after him — RV

Consider the work of God:
who can make straight what he has made crooked?
In the day of prosperity be joyful, and in the day of adversity consider; God has made the one as well as the other, so that man may not find out anything that will be after him — RSV

Consider the work of God. Who can make straight what he has made crooked? On a good day enjoy good things, and on an evil day consider: Both the one and the other God has made, so that man cannot find fault with him in anything — NAB

15. All things have I seen in the days of my vanity: there is a just man that perisheth in his righteousness, and there is a wicked man that prolongeth his life in his wickedness.

All this have I seen in my days of vanity: there is a righteous man that perisheth in his righteousness, and there is a wicked man that prolongeth his life in his evil-doing — ASV

In the days of my vanity I took a view of all classes. Here is a righteous man perishing for his righteous act: there a wicked man continuing in his wickedness — Sept

In my vain life I have seen everything; there is a righteous man who perishes in his righteousness, and there is a wicked man who prolongs his life in his evil-doing — RSV

I have seen all sorts of things in my empty life:

For example, the righteous man perishing in his righteousness,
And the wicked prolonging his life in his wickedness — AAT

16. Be not righteous over much; neither make thyself over wise: why shouldest thou destroy thyself?

17. Be not over much wicked, neither be thou foolish: why shouldest thou die before thy time?

Do not become so very righteous, neither count thyself wise beyond measure, — wherefore shouldest thou destroy thyself?
Do not be so very lawless neither become thou foolish, — wherefore shouldst thou die before thy time — Rhm

Be not thou over-righteous amongst the multitude;
Neither boast thou of over-much wisdom;
Wherefore shouldest thou be singular?
Neither be thou over-faulty amongst the multitude;
Neither play the fool;
Wherefore shouldest thou die before thy time — Sprl

Be not over-good, be not over-wise; why expose yourself to trouble? And be not over-evil either, never play the fool; why die before your time — Mof

Be not given overmuch to righteousness and be not over-wise. Why let destruction come on you?
Be not evil overmuch, and be not foolish. Why come to your end before your time — Bas

Do not be over-righteous and do not be over-wise. Why make yourself a laughing-stock? Do not be over-wicked and do not be a fool. Why should you die before your time — NEB

18. It is good that thou shouldest take hold of this; yea, also from this withdraw not thine hand: for he that feareth God shall come forth of them all.

It is good that thou shouldest take hold of the one; yea, also from the other withdraw not thy hand; for he that feareth God shall discharge himself of them all — JPS

It is well that you get hold of this, and from that do not withdraw your hand, or he who reveres God comes clear with both — Ber

The best thing is to hold the one and not let go the other, for both of these will happen to the God-fearing man — Jerus

It is good to hold to this rule, and not to let that one go; but he who fears God will win through at all events — NAB

19. Wisdom strengtheneth the wise more than ten mighty men which are in the city.

20. For there is not a just man upon earth, that doeth good, and sinneth not.

Wisdom is a strength to the wise man more than ten rulers that are in a city. Surely there is not a righteous man upon earth, that doeth good, and sinneth not — ASV

Wisdom strengthens the wise more than ten princes that are in the city. For there is no just man upon the earth, that does good, and sins not — Lam

Wisdom makes a wise man stronger
Than the ten rulers who are in the city.
For there is no man on earth so righteous
That he does good and never fails — AAT

Wisdom is a surer ally than ten city magistrates; there is no man on earth so exact over his duties that he does ever the right, never commits a fault — Knox

Wisdom makes the wise man stronger than the ten rulers of a city. The world contains no man so righteous that he can do right always and never do wrong — NEB

21. Also take no heed unto all words that are spoken; lest thou hear thy servant curse thee:

22. For oftentimes also thine own heart knoweth that thou thyself hast cursed others.

Also to all the words that they speak give not thy heart, that thou hear not thy servant reviling thee. For many times so hath thy heart known that thou thyself also hast reviled others — YLT

therefore thou shouldst not pay too

close attention to all the words which the wicked shall utter, that thou mayst not hear thy servant cursing thee. For many a time he may revile thee and in many ways vex thy heart, because thou perhaps in like manner didst curse others — Sept

Moreover not to all the words which men speak do thou apply thy heart, — lest thou hear thine own servant reviling thee! For truly many times thy heart knoweth, — that even thou thyself hast reviled others — Rhm

One thing more. Never listen to all that people say; you may hear your own slave cursing you. As many a time, you must confess, you yourself have cursed other people — Mof

Do not give heed to every word that is spoken lest you hear your servant speaking ill of you, for you know in your heart that you have many times spoken ill of others — NEB

23. All this I have proved by wisdom: I said, I will be wise; but it was far from me.

24. That which is far off, and exceeding deep, who can find it out?

I have tried all these things by wisdom; I said, I will be wise; but wisdom was far from me.
Yea, wisdom was far off; it also had depth beyond depth; who can find it out — Lam

All this I have put to the test by wisdom: I said, I will be wise, but it was far from me.
Far off is true existence, and very deep; who may have knowledge of it — Bas

All this I have tested from the viewpoint of wisdom; I said, "I will be wise," and it was far beyond me. What exists is beyond reach and unfathomable; who can master it — Ber

25. I applied mine heart to know, and to search, and to seek out wisdom, and the reason of things, and to know the wickedness of folly, even of foolishness and madness:

I turned about, and my heart was set to know and to search out, and to seek wisdom and the reason of things, and to know that wickedness is folly, and that foolishness is madness — ASV

I turned my mind to know and to search out and to seek wisdom and the sum of things, and to know the wickedness of folly and the foolishness which is madness — RSV

I turned my mind to knowledge and to searching and seeking wisdom and substance, and to the knowledge that wickedness is folly and foolishness is madness — AAT

I cast about in my mind to know and survey and discover wisdom and the reason of things, finding that wickedness is folly and folly madness — Mof

I went on to reflect, I set my mind to inquire and search for wisdom and for the reason in things, only to discover that it is folly to be wicked and madness to act like a fool — NEB

26. And I find more bitter than death the woman, whose heart is snares and nets, and her hands as bands: whoso pleaseth God shall escape from her; but the sinner shall be taken by her.

And I saw a thing more bitter than death, even the woman whose heart is full of tricks and nets, and whose hands are as bands. He with whom God is pleased will get free from her, but the sinner will be taken by her — Bas

I found more bitter than death the woman who is snares and nets at heart and whose hands are chains. Whoever pleases God, will escape her; but the sinner will be ensnared by her — Ber

I find woman more bitter than death; she is a snare, her heart a net, her arms are chains;
He who is pleasing to God eludes her,
but the sinner is her captive — Jerus

And this I have ascertained; death itself is not so cruel as woman's heart that wheedles and beguiles, as woman's clutches that release their captive never. God's friends escape her; of sinners she makes an easy prey — Knox

More bitter than death I find the

woman who is a hunter's trap, whose heart is a snare and whose hands are prison bonds. He who is pleasing to God will escape her, but the sinner will be entrapped by her — NAB

27. Behold, this have I found, saith the preacher, counting one by one, to find out the account:

28. Which yet my soul seeketh, but I find it not: one man among a thousand have I found; but a woman among all those have I not found.

See! This have I found, saith the Proclaimer counting one by one to find a conclusion; what my soul still sought yet I found not, — one man out of a thousand have I found, but a woman among all these have I not found — Rhm

Behold, this have I discovered, saith the preacher,
Making up the computation one by one,
Which yet my soul desireth, yet I cannot find:
One righteous man amongst a thousand I have found;
But a righteous woman amongst all these have I not found — Sprl

Behold, this have I found, saith the Preacher, laying one thing to another, to find out the account; which my soul still seeketh, but I have not found: one man among a thousand have I found; but a woman among all these have I not found — ASV

Behold, this is what I found, says the Preacher, adding one thing to another to find the sum, which my mind has sought repeatedly, but I have not found. One man among a thousand I found, but a woman among all these I have not found — RSV

'See,' says the Speaker, 'this is what I have found, reasoning things out one by one, after searching long without success: I have found one man in a thousand worth the name, but I have not found one woman among them all — NEB

29. Lo, this only have I found, that God hath made man upright; but they have sought out many inventions.

See, this alone I have found, that God made man upright, and they — they have sought out many devices — YLT

Only see this which I have found, that God made man upright, but they have sought out many contrivances — AAT

Here is all I have been able to discover: God made the race of men upright, but many a cunning wile have they contrived — Mof

Of this, beyond all else, I have satisfied myself; man's nature was simple enough when God made him, and these endless questions are of his own devising — Knox

This, however, you must know: I find that God made man simple; man's complex problems are of his own devising — Jerus

Behold, only this have I found out: God made mankind straight, but men have had recourse to many calculations — NAB

CHAPTER 8

1. Who is as the wise man? and who knoweth the interpretation of a thing? a man's wisdom maketh his face to shine, and the boldness of his face shall be changed.

Who is really a wise man,
And who knoweth the interpretation of a thing?
The wisdom of a man lighteth up his countenance,
But by defiance of countenance one is disfigured — Rhm

Who is as the wise? and who knoweth the interpretation of a thing? The wisdom of man causeth his face to shine, and the hardness of his face is changed — YLT

Who is like the wise man? and to whom is the sense of anything clear? A man's wisdom makes his face shining, and his hard face will be changed — Bas

Who is like the wise man and who knows the true meaning of things?

A man's wisdom brightens his face; the crudeness of his face becomes refined — Ber

How wonderful to be wise, to understand things, to be able to analyze them and interpret them. Wisdom lights up a man's face, softening its hardness — Tay

2. I counsel thee to keep the king's commandment, and that in regard of the oath of God.

3. Be not hasty to go out of his sight: stand not in an evil thing; for he doeth whatsoever pleaseth him.

I charge thee to keep the king's commandment,
Even because thou hast spoken the oath unto God.
Be not in a hurry to go from his presence;
But agree thou not in an evil cause;
Because he doeth all whatsoever pleaseth him — Sprl

I counsel thee, keep the king's command, and that in regard of the oath of God. Be not hasty to go out of his presence; persist not in an evil thing: for he doeth whatsoever pleaseth him — ASV

I obey the order of a king, because of the divine oath.
Do not be in a hurry to leave his presence;
Do not stand firm in a bad cause,
For he does whatsoever he will — AAT

Keep the king's command, and in regard of the oath of God be not hasty.
Go from his presence; and do not stand firm in an evil matter; for he does whatsoever pleases him—Lam

Keep the king's command, and because of your sacred oath be not dismayed; go from his presence, do not delay when the matter is unpleasant, for he does whatever he pleases — RSV

Obey the king, for you swore him loyalty before God. Rebel not rashly against him, never thwart him, for he does as he pleases — Mof

Observe the precept of the king, and in view of your oath to God, be not hasty to withdraw from the king; do not join in with a base plot, for he does whatever he pleases — NAB

4. Where the word of a king is, there is power: and who may say unto him, What doest thou?

5. Whoso keepeth the commandment shall feel no evil thing: and a wise man's heart discerneth both time and judgment.

Where the word of a king is there is power, — who then may say to him, What wouldst thou do? He that observeth the commandment will not notice a vexatious thing, — and of time and manner will the heart of the wise take note — Rhm

Since the king's word prevails, who can say to him, "What are you doing?" Whoever observes the royal orders will experience no harm.
The heart of the wise man knows time and procedure — Ber

For the king's word carries authority. Who can question what he does? Whoever obeys a command will come to no harm. A wise man knows in his heart the right time and method for action — NEB

the king's word is supreme, and none dare ask him what he means. He who obeys the royal command will never come to harm. Still, the wise heart knows there is a time of judgment coming — Mof

for the word of the king is paramount, and who dare say to him, 'Why do that?'
He who obeys the command will come to no harm,
and the wise man knows there will be a time of judgment — Jerus

The king's command is backed by great power, and no one can withstand it or question it. Those who obey him will not be punished. The wise man will find a time and a way to do what he says — Tay

6. Because to every purpose there is time and judgment, therefore the misery of man is great upon him.

7. For he knoweth not that which shall be: for who can tell him when it shall be?

for to every purpose there is a time and judgment; because the misery of man is great upon him: for he knoweth not that which shall be; for who can tell him how it shall be — ASV

For to every matter there is a time and judgment; for the evil of man is great upon him. For he knoweth not that which shall be; for even when it cometh to pass, who shall declare it unto him — JPS

for to every purpose there is a time and judgment, because the wickedness of man is great upon him; for he knows not that which shall be, for who can tell him how it shall be — ABPS

For every purpose there is a time and a decision, because the sorrow of man is great in him.
No one is certain what is to be, and who is able to say to him when it will be — Bas

for there is a time and a judgement for everything." — Yet it is a great affliction for man that he is ignorant of what is to come; for who will make known to him how it will be — NAB

8. There is no man that hath power over the spirit to retain the spirit; neither hath he power in the day of death: and there is no discharge in that war; neither shall wickedness deliver those that are given to it.

No man is absolute commander over wind to stop the current of it, and over the day of death he hath no authority; nor is there a discharge in the day of battle; nor can wickedness save him who is under its sway — Sept

There is no man ruling over the spirit to restrain the spirit, and there is no authority over the day of death, and there is no discharge in battle, and wickedness delivereth not its possessors — YLT

No man hath power over the spirit to retain the spirit, and none hath power over the day of death, and there is no furlough in war, — neither shall lawlessness deliver them who are given thereto — Rhm

There is nobody in authority over the wind to restrain the wind. Nor is there anybody in control of the day of death, nor is there release in war, nor can wickedness deliver its possessors — AAT

The breath of life man must resign at last; the day of his death he cannot determine; nor ever does war give release from service, nor sin discharge to the sinner — Knox

9. All this have I seen, and applied my heart unto every work that is done under the sun: there is a time wherein one man ruleth over another to his own hurt.

All this have I witnessed.
Then applied I mine heart to every work which is done under the sun,
Wherein a man ruleth over another to his own hurt — Sprl

Having taken a view of this as a whole, I applied my heart to every work which is done under the sun — to all those things in which man exercised authority over man to his hurt — Sept

All this have I seen, even applied my heart thereto, whatever the work that is done under the sun; what time one man had power over another to his hurt — JPS

All this I observed while applying my mind to all that is done under the sun, while man lords it over man to his hurt — RSV

I considered all this and paid attention to all the work which was done under the sun — a time when man has the mastery over another to harm him — Ber

All these things I considered and I applied my mind to every work that is done under the sun, while one man tyrannizes over another to his hurt — NAB

10. And so I saw the wicked buried, who had come and gone from the place of the holy, and they were forgotten in the city where they had so done: this is also vanity.*

So I saw the wicked buried, and they came to the grave; and they that had done right went away from the holy place, and were forgotten in the city: this also is vanity — ASV

*There are textual difficulties in the original. The revisions have recourse to the Sept and other early translations to help make sense of it.

And so I saw the wicked buried, and they entered into their rest; but they that had done right went away from the holy place, and were forgotten in the city; this also is vanity — JPS

I saw how the wicked were buried, who had gone in and out from the holy place, and they were forgotten in the city as having behaved like that; this also is ineffective — Ber

And then I see the wicked brought to burial and people come from the Temple to honour them in the city for having been the men they were. This, too, is vanity — Jerus

Then I saw bad men being borne to burial, carried to their rest, while the pious had to leave the sanctuary and were forgotten in the city (which also is vanity!) — Mof

And so I have seen wicked men carried to the tomb and praised from the holy place and lauded in the city where they had acted thus. This too is vanity — AAT

11. Because sentence against an evil work is not executed speedily, therefore the heart of the sons of men is fully set in them to do evil.

Because vengeance against the evil-doers is not executed speedily, therefore the heart of the sons of men is fully set in them to do evil — Lam

Because punishment for an evil work comes not quickly, the minds of the sons of men are fully given to doing evil — Bas

Because those who do evil are not speedily called to account, therefore the heart of the children of men is fully set in them to do evil — Sept

It is because sentence upon a wicked act is not promptly carried out that men do evil so boldly — NEB

Because sentence is not pronounced upon the evil-doers without more ado, men are emboldened to live sinfully — Knox

12. Though a sinner do evil a hundred times, and his days be prolonged, yet surely I know that it shall be well with them that fear God, which fear before him:

13. But it shall not be well with the wicked, neither shall he prolong his days, which are as a shadow; because he feareth not before God.

Though a sinner does evil a hundred times and prolongs his life, yet I know it will be well with those who fear God, because they fear before him; but it will not be well with the wicked, neither will he prolong his days like a shadow, because he does not fear before God — RSV

Though a sinner be committing wickedness a hundred times and continuing long in his own way yet I surely know that it shall be well to them who revere God, who stand in awe before him; but well shall it not be to the lawless man, neither shall he lengthen out his days like a shadow, — because he standeth not in awe before God — Rhm

but although a sinner may sin repeatedly and thrive, I know it is the reverent who are safe, as they revere God, while the bad man fares ill — he cannot thrive, for lives that lack all reverence for God pass like a shadow — Mof

Even though a sinner does wrong a hundred times and still continues living, yet I know that it shall be well with those who fear God, who are in awe before him; but it shall not be well with the wicked, nor shall he prolong his life like a shadow, since he is not awed in the presence of God — AAT

But though a man sins a hundred times and still lives, I know very well that those who fear God will be better off, unlike the wicked, who will not live long, good lives — their days shall pass away as quickly as shadows because they don't fear God — Tay

14. There is a vanity which is done upon the earth; that there be just men, unto whom it happeneth according to the work of the wicked; again, there be wicked men, to whom it happeneth according to the work of the righteous: I said that this also is vanity.

There is a vanity which is acted upon the earth,
That there exist just men unto whom it happeneth

According to the recompense of the wicked;
And there are wicked men unto whom it happeneth
According to the recompense of the righteous.
I declared that this also is vanity — Sprl

Here also is a futility that goes on upon the earth: there are righteous men who fare as though they were wicked, and wicked men who fare as though they were righteous. I said that this also is vanity — Amp

Another kind of frustration, too, earth sees; there are upright men that are plagued as though they lived the life sinners live, just as there are sinners who take no more harm than if they could plead innocence; I say this is frustration indeed — Knox

There is an empty thing found on earth: when the just man gets what is due to the unjust, and the unjust what is due to the just. I maintain that this too is emptiness — NEB

But there is a vanity found on earth; the good, I mean, receive the treatment the wicked deserve; and the wicked the treatment the good deserve. This, too, I say, is vanity — Jerus

15. Then I commended mirth, because a man hath no better thing under the sun, than to eat, and to drink, and to be merry: for that shall abide with him of his labour the days of his life, which God giveth him under the sun.

Then extolled I gladness, in that there was nothing better for a man under the sun, than to eat and to drink and to be glad, — since that should tarry with him in his toil for the days of his life which God had given him under the sun — Rhm

And I commended enjoyment, for man has no good thing under the sun but to eat, and drink, and enjoy himself, for this will go with him in his toil through the days of life which God gives him under the sun — RSV

and I praised pleasurable enjoyment, because there is nothing good for men under the sun — nothing save eating and drinking and being made glad; and this one may have conjoined with his labour all the days of his life which God giveth him under the sun — Sept

So I gave praise to joy, because there is nothing better for a man to do under the sun than to take meat and drink and be happy; for that will be with him in his work all the days of his life which God gives him under the sun — Bas

So I praise pleasure: the best thing under the sun for man is to eat and drink and enjoy himself, and to keep this up as he goes toiling through the life God gives him in this world — Mof

16. When I applied mine heart to know wisdom, and to see the business that is done upon the earth: (for also there is that neither day nor night seeth sleep with his eyes:)

According as I gave mine heart to understand wisdom,
And to perceive the travail that is done upon the earth,
Even that there are who see not sleep with their eyes day or night — Sprl

When I gave my heart to know wisdom, and to consider the business that was done upon the earth then surely by day and by night there was one who suffered not his eyes to sleep — Rhm

When I applied my heart to know wisdom, and to see the business that is done upon the earth — for neither day nor night do men see sleep with their eyes — JPS

When I applied my heart to acquire wisdom and to see the activity taking place on the earth, that one neither by day nor by night sees himself sleeping — Ber

Wisdom having been my careful study, I came to observe the business that goes on here on earth. And certainly the eyes of man never rest, day and night — Jerus

17. Then I beheld all the work of God, that a man cannot find out the work that is done under the sun: because though a man labour to seek it out,

yet he shall not find it; yea farther; though a wise man think to know it, yet shall he not be able to find it.

then I considered all the work of God, that man is not able to find out the work that hath been done under the sun, because though man labour to seek, yet he doth not find; and even though the wise man speak of knowing he is not able to find — YLT

then I saw all God's work, that man is unable to discover the work which is done under the sun, inasmuch as man may labor in its search, but he will not find it; and even if the wise man thinks that he is on the point of knowing it, he will be unable to find it — AAT

Then I saw all the work of God, and that man may not get knowledge of the work which is done under the sun; because, if a man gives hard work to the search he will not get knowledge, and even if the wise man seems to be coming to the end of his search, still he will be without knowledge — Bas

I found that man is unable to grasp the truth of all that God is doing in this world; he may labour in his efforts to attain it, in a sleepless quest for it by day and night, but he will never find it out; a wise man may think he is coming on the secret, but even he will never find it out — Mof

and always I perceived that God has so ordered it that man should not be able to discover what is happening here under the sun. However hard a man may try, he will not find out; the wise man may think that he knows, but he will be unable to find the truth of it — NEB

CHAPTER 9

1. **For all this I considered in my heart even to declare all this, that the righteous, and the wise, and their works, are in the hand of God: no man knoweth either love or hatred by all that is before them.**

But all this I have laid unto my heart, so as to clear up the whole of this, that the righteous and the wise, and their works, are in the hand of God, neither love nor hatred doth man know, the whole is before them — YLT

For all this I laid to my heart, even to explore all this: that the righteous, and the wise, and their works, are in the hand of God; whether it be love or hatred, man knoweth it not; all is before them — ASV

for this cause I laid this whole system before my heart, and my heart took a view of it. As the righteous and the wise and their works are in the hand of God, man indeed knoweth not what to love or what to hate: with regard to all things before him there is vanity in them all — Sept

Because of all this I gave my heart that I might clear up all this;
How that the righteous and the wise and their achievements
Are in the hand of God:
Also friendship or hatred no man can perceive
From any thing that has preceded them — Sprl

For all this I took to heart and clearly understood, that the righteous and the wise and their activities are in the hand of God — love as well as hate. Man knows nothing of what lies before him — Ber

All this I have kept in mind and recognized: the just, the wise, and their deeds are in the hand of God. Love from hatred man cannot tell; both appear equally vain — NAB

2. **All things come alike to all; there is one event to the righteous, and to the wicked; to the good and to the clean, and to the unclean; to him that sacrificeth, and to him that sacrificeth not: as is the good, so is the sinner; and he that sweareth, as he that feareth an oath.**

Every one was like every one else, one destiny had the righteous and the lawless, the good and the pure and the impure, and he that sacrificed and he that did not sacrifice, — as the good man so the sinner, he that took an oath as he who of an oath stood in fear — Rhm

All things happen alike to all; there is one chance for the righteous and for the wicked; to the good and to the bad, to the clean and to the unclean; to him who sacrifices and to him who does not sacrifice; as is the good man, so is the sinner; and he who swears is as he who fears an oath — Lam

Because to all there is one event, to the upright man and to the evil, to the clean and to the unclean, to him who makes an offering and to him who makes no offering; as is the good so is the sinner; he who takes an oath is as he who has fear of it — Bas

Everything in the past is vanity, inasmuch as there is one fate for all, for the righteous, for the wicked, and for the good; for the clean and the unclean, for him who offers sacrifice and for him who does not; as is the good, so is the sinner; he who takes an oath is as he who fears an oath — AAT

Just as one fate comes to all, to virtuous as to wicked, to clean and unclean, to him who sacrifices and to him who does not sacrifice, so it is with the good man and the sinner, with him who takes an oath and him who shrinks from it — Jerus

3. This is an evil among all things that are done under the sun, that there is one event unto all: yea, also the heart of the sons of men is full of evil, and madness is in their heart while they live, and after that they go to the dead.

There is this evil in every thing done under the sun, that one event happeneth to them all, so that the heart of the children of men being filled with evil there is an instability in their heart during their life, and it followeth them to the dead — Sept

Is this an evil concerning all things done under the sun,
That one event happeneth to all?
But also the hearts of the sons of men are full of wickedness,
And mad folly is in their hearts during their lives,
And afterwards they go to the dead — Sprl

Of all that goes amiss, here under the sun, nothing does more hurt than this equality of fortunes; what wonder if men's hearts, while yet they live, are full of malice and defiance? And so they journey on to the grave — Knox

There is no evil like this in the world, that all men have one fate; it makes men seethe with evil aims and mad desires during their life, and then they join the dead — not one is left — Mof

This is what is wrong in all that is done here under the sun: that one and the same fate befalls every man. The hearts of men are full of evil; madness fills their hearts all through their lives, and after that they go down to join the dead — NEB

4. For to him that is joined to all the living there is hope: for a living dog is better than a dead lion.

5. For the living know that they shall die: but the dead know not any thing, neither have they any more a reward; for the memory of them is forgotten.

But to him who is joined unto all the living there is confidence, for to a living dog it is better than to the dead lion. For the living know that they die, and the dead know not anything, and there is no more to them a reward, for their remembrance hath been forgotten — YLT

For whosoever was united to all the living for him there was hope, — inasmuch as a living dog fared better than a dead lion. For the living knew that they should die, — but the dead knew not anything, neither had they any longer a reward, because forgotten was their memory — Rhm

But he who is joined with all the living has hope, for a living dog is better than a dead lion. For the living know that they will die, but the dead know nothing, and they have no more reward; but the memory of them is lost — RSV

For anyone who is linked with all that live still has some hope, a live dog being better than a dead lion. The living know at least that they will die, the dead know nothing; no more reward for them, their memory has passed out of mind — Jerus

Indeed, for any among the living there is hope; a live dog is better off than a dead lion. For the living know that they are to die, but the dead no longer know anything. There is no further recompense for them, because all memory of them is lost — NAB

6. **Also their love, and their hatred, and their envy, is now perished; neither have they any more portion for ever in any thing that is done under the sun.**

As well their love, as their hatred and their envy, is perished long ago; neither have they any more a portion for ever in anything that is done under the sun — ASV

Not only the love of them, but the hatred of them, and the envy of them have already perished, and they no longer have any share in anything that is done under the sun — AAT

no love, no hatred, no envy can they feel; they have said good-bye to this world, and to all its busy doings, here under the sun — Knox

Whatever they did in their lifetimes — loving, hating, envying — is long gone, and they have no part in anything here on earth any more — Tay

7. **Go thy way, eat thy bread with joy, and drink thy wine with a merry heart; for God now accepteth thy works.**

8. **Let thy garments be always white; and let thy head lack no ointment.**

Go thy way, eat thy bread with joy, and drink thy wine with a merry heart; for God hath already accepted thy works.
Let thy garments be always white; and let not thy head lack ointment — RV

come eat thy bread with cheerfulness, and drink thy wine with a good heart: because God hath approved of thy works, let thy garments be always white; and let not oil be wanting on thy head — Sept

Come, eat your food with joy and drink your wine with a glad heart, for to do this has God's approval. Wear white robes always, and spare not oil for your head — Mof

Come, take your bread with joy, and your wine with a glad heart. God has taken pleasure in your works.
Let your clothing be white at all times, and let not your head be without oil — Bas

Go to it then, eat your food and enjoy it, and drink your wine with a cheerful heart; for already God has accepted what you have done. Always be dressed in white and never fail to anoint your head — NEB

9. **Live joyfully with the wife whom thou lovest all the days of the life of thy vanity, which he hath given thee under the sun, all the days of thy vanity: for that is thy portion in this life, and in thy labour which thou takest under the sun.**

Enjoy life with the wife whom thou lovest all the days of the life of thy vanity, which He hath given thee under the sun, all the days of thy vanity; for that is thy portion in life, and in thy labour wherein thou labourest under the sun — JPS

Enjoy with a wife whom thou lovest all the days of thy life of vanity, which he has given thee under the sun, all the days of thy vanity; for that is thy portion in life, and in thy toil which thou toilest under the sun — ABPS

Enjoy life with the wife whom you love
All the days of your empty life,
Which he has given you under the sun;
All your empty life.
For that is your lot in life and in your toil at which you toil under the sun — AAT

Enjoy life with the wife you love all the days of the passing life which He grants you under the sun, all your unprofitable days; for that is your portion among the living and your labor in which you weary yourself under the sun — Ber

Enjoy life with the wife whom you love, all the days of the fleeting life that is granted you under the sun. This is your lot in life, for the toil of your labors under the sun — NAB

10. **Whatsoever thy hand findeth to do, do it with thy might; for there is no**

work, nor device, nor knowledge, nor wisdom, in the grave, whither thou goest.

All that thy hand findeth to do, with thy power do, for there is no work, and device, and knowledge, and wisdom in Sheol whither thou art going — YLT

Whatever thy hand finds to do, do with thy might: for there is no work, nor reckoning, nor knowledge, nor wisdom in Sheol, whither thou goest — ABPS

Whatever thy hand findeth to do, do it with all thy might; since there is no work, nor device, nor knowledge, nor wisdom in the mansion of the dead to which thou must go — Sept

Whatever comes to your hand to do with all your power, do it because there is no work, or thought, or knowledge, or wisdom in the place of the dead to which you are going — Bas

Throw yourself into any pursuit that may appeal to you, for there is no pursuit, no plans, no knowledge or intelligence, within the grave where you are going — Mof

11. I returned, and saw under the sun, that the race is not to the swift, nor the battle to the strong, neither yet bread to the wise, nor yet riches to men of understanding, nor yet favour to men of skill; but time and chance happeneth to them all.

I turned and saw under the sun that the race is not to the swift nor the battle to the strong nor bread to the wise nor riches to the men of understanding nor glory to the learned men; because time and chance happen to them all — Lam

Again I saw that under the sun the race is not to the swift, nor the battle to the strong, nor bread to the wise, nor riches to the intelligent, nor favor to the men of skill; but time and chance happen to them all — RSV

Once more I observed under the sun that the race is not to the swift, nor the battle to the strong; nor is there bread for the wise, nor riches for the intelligent, nor favor for scholars; but time and chance happen to all of them — AAT

Again I saw under the sun that the race is not won by the swift, nor the battle by the valiant, nor a livelihood by the wise, nor riches by the shrewd, nor favor by the experts; for a time of calamity comes to all alike — NAB

Again I looked throughout the earth and saw that the swiftest person does not always win the race, nor the strongest man the battle, and that wise men are often poor, and skillful men are not necessarily famous; but it is all by chance, by happening to be at the right place at the right time — Tay

12. For man also knoweth not his time: as the fishes that are taken in an evil net, and as the birds that are caught in the snare; so are the sons of men snared in an evil time, when it falleth suddenly upon them.

Surely also man is unacquainted with his time:
As the fishes that are caught in an evil net,
And as birds that are taken in the snare,
So the sons of men shall be snared in an evil time,
When it falleth suddenly upon them — Sprl

That man indeed no more knoweth his time than the fishes which are enclosed in an evil dredge, or than birds which are caught in a net. Like them the sons of men are drawn into an evil time when it cometh upon them suddenly — Sept

Even man has no knowledge of his time; like fishes taken in an evil net, or like birds taken by deceit, are the sons of men taken in an evil time when it comes suddenly on them — Bas

For even man knows not his time; as fish caught in a treacherous net and as birds seized in a snare, even so are men trapped in a disastrous time, when it comes down on them suddenly — Ber

Man does not know his hour; like fish caught in the treacherous net, like birds taken in the snare, so is man overtaken by misfortune suddenly falling on him — Jerus

13. This wisdom have I seen also under the sun, and it seemed great unto me.

14. There was a little city, and few men within it; and there came a great king against it, and besieged it, and built great bulwarks against it:

Also this have I seen as an example of wisdom under the sun and it greatly impressed me. There was a small city, with few men in it, and there came against it a great king and surrounded it and built great siege-works against it — AAT

Here is another case of wisdom which I have seen on earth, and I was struck by it. A little town there was, with few men in it; and a great king attacked it, he invested it, and built great siege-works round it — Mof

This too is an example of wisdom as I have observed it here under the sun, and notable I find it. There was a small town with few inhabitants, and a great king came to attack it; he besieged it and constructed great siege-works against it — NEB

Here is another thing that has made a deep impression on me as I have watched human affairs: There was a small city with only a few people living in it, and a great king came with his army and besieged it — Tay

15. Now there was found in it a poor wise man, and he by his wisdom delivered the city; yet no man remembered that same poor man.

16. Then said I, Wisdom is better than strength: nevertheless the poor man's wisdom is despised, and his words are not heard.

17. The words of wise men are heard in quiet more than the cry of him that ruleth among fools.

Then I said: Wisdom is better than might.
Nevertheless the frugal man's wisdom is despised,
And his words are not heeded.
The quiet words of the wise ought to be heard
More than the clamour of him who ruleth among fools — Sprl

Now I have said, Wisdom is better than power, yet the wisdom of this poor man is despised and his words are not regarded. The words of wise men in a time of rest are more minded than the shout of men exercising authority in the bustles of folly — Sept

Then said I, Better is wisdom than strength, — although the wisdom of the poor man be despised, and his words not heard. The words of the wise in quietness are heard, beyond the outcry of one who ruleth over dullards — Rhm

But I say that wisdom is better than might, though the poor man's wisdom is despised, and his words are not heeded.
The words of the wise heard in quiet are better than the shouting of a ruler among fools — RSV

Though I had said, "Wisdom is better than force," yet the wisdom of the poor man is despised and his words go unheeded.
"The quiet words of the wise are better heeded
than the shout of a ruler of fools"—! — NAB

18. Wisdom is better than weapons of war: but one sinner destroyeth much good.

Wisdom is preferable to weapons of war,
But one error destroyeth much good — Sprl

Arms cannot match wisdom; by one slip what great advantage is lost — Knox

Wisdom is better than weapons of war; often a single error spoils good strategy — Mof

Better wisdom than warlike weapons, but one mistake undoes a deal of good — Jerus

CHAPTER 10

1. Dead flies cause the ointment of the apothecary to send forth a stinking savour: so doth a little folly him that is in reputation for wisdom and honour.

Dead flies cause the oil of the perfumer to send forth an evil odor; so doth a little folly outweigh wisdom and honor — ASV

Dead flies cause the ointment of the perfumer to stink and putrefy;
So does a little folly outweigh wisdom and honor — ABPS

Dead flies cause an unpleasant smell, and putrefy the apothecary's ointment:
So doth a little folly the man who excelleth in wisdom and fame — Sprl

Like dead flies which make the container of precious ointment stink, so does a great folly outweigh wisdom and honor — Lam

Dead flies make the perfumer's sweet ointment turn rancid and ferment; so can a little folly make wisdom lose its worth — NEB

2. A wise man's heart is at his right hand; but a fool's heart at his left.

3. Yea also, when he that is a fool walketh by the way, his wisdom faileth him, and he saith to every one that he is a fool.

A wise man's understanding is at his right hand;
But a fool's understanding at his left.
Yea also, when a fool walketh by the way, his understanding faileth him, and he saith to every one that he is a fool — JPS

The sense of the wise is on his right hand, —
But the sense of the dullard on his left:
Yea even by the way as the foolish man walketh along his sense faileth him — and he telleth everyone that foolish is he — Rhm

The heart of the wise man goes in the right direction; but the heart of a foolish man in the wrong.
And when the foolish man is walking in the way, he has no sense and lets everyone see that he is foolish — Bas

A wise man's heart turns to the right; a fool's heart turns to the left.
In whatever path a fool walks, he lacks sense;
he makes known to all that he is a fool — Ber

The wise man's heart leads him aright, the fool's heart leads him astray.
A fool has only to walk along the road and, having no sense, he makes plain to all what a fool he is — Jerus

4. If the spirit of the ruler rise up against thee, leave not thy place; for yielding pacifieth great offenses.

Should the spirit of the ruler rise up against thee,
Desert not thy place, for submission pacifieth great offences — Sprl

If the spirit of the ruler rise up against thee, leave not thy place; for gentleness allayeth great offences — ASV

If the spirit of a ruler rise up against thee, resign not thy place: for a reconciliation will mollify great offences — Sept

Though a prince's anger should mount against thee, do not desert thy post; great harm by thy healing touch may yet be assuaged — Knox

If a ruler's wrath flares up against you, never resign your post;
defer to him,
and you will pacify his rage — Mof

5. There is an evil which I have seen under the sun, as an error which proceedeth from the ruler:

6. Folly is set in great dignity, and the rich sit in low place.

7. I have seen servants upon horses, and princes walking as servants upon earth.

There is an evil which I have seen under the sun,
As it were an error which proceeds from the ruler:
Folly is set in great heights,
And the rich sit in a low place.
I have seen servants upon horses,
And princes walking as servants upon the earth — ABPS

There is an evil I have seen under the sun,
As an error that goeth out from the ruler,
He hath set the fool in many high places,
And the rich in a low place do sit.
I have seen servants on horses,
And princes walking as servants on the earth — YLT

Here was a misfortune I had seen under the sun, — a veritable mistake that was going forth from the pres-

ence of one who had power:
Folly placed in great dignity, —
While the rich in a low place took their seat:
I had seen servants upon horses, —
And rulers walking like servants on the ground — Rhm

There is an evil which I have seen under the sun, like an error which comes by chance from a ruler:
The foolish are placed in high positions, but men of wealth are kept low.
I have seen servants on horses, and rulers walking on the earth as servants — Bas

There is an evil which I have seen under the sun, like an accidental error which comes forth from before a ruler.
"The fool is often set in high positions;
While the nobles dwell in low estate.
I have seen slaves upon horses,
While princes walked on the ground like slaves — AAT

I have seen under the sun another evil, like a mistake that proceeds from the ruler: a fool put in lofty position while the rich sit in lowly places. I have seen slaves on horseback, while princes walked on the ground like slaves — NAB

8. He that diggeth a pit shall fall into it; and whoso breaketh a hedge, a serpent shall bite him.

9. Whoso removeth stones shall be hurt therewith; and he that cleaveth wood shall be endangered thereby.

He that diggeth a pit shall fall into it; and whoso breaketh through a wall, a serpent shall bite him. Whoso heweth out stones shall be hurt therewith; and he that cleaveth wood is endangered thereby — ASV

He that diggeth a pit shall fall into it;
And whoso breaketh through a fence, a serpent shall bite him.
Whoso quarrieth stones shall be hurt therewith;
And he that cleaveth wood is endangered thereby — JPS

He who digs a pit will fall into it; and a serpent will bite him who breaks through a wall.
He who quarries stones is hurt by them;
and he who splits logs is endangered by them — RSV

He who makes a hole for others will himself go into it, and for him who makes a hole through a wall the bite of a snake will be a punishment.
He who gets out stones from the earth will be damaged by them, and in the cutting of wood there is danger — Bas

Dig a well — and fall into it!
Demolish an old wall — and be bitten by a snake!
When working in a quarry, stones will fall and crush you! There is risk in each stroke of your axe — Tay

10. If the iron be blunt, and he do not whet the edge, then must he put to more strength: but wisdom is profitable to direct.

Should the iron be blunt and not sharpened on the grindstone,
Much strength must be applied; but wisdom is most excellent to direct — Sprl

If the ax be dull,
And he do not sharpen its edge,
Then he must exert greater strength;
But wisdom is advantageous for winning success — AAT

If the axe is blunt and its edge unwhetted,
more strength must be put into the blow;
successful skill comes from shrewd sense — Mof

If for want of sharpening the axe is blunt, you have to strike very hard, but the reward given by wisdom is success — Jerus

11. Surely the serpent will bite without enchantment; and a babbler is no better.

If the serpent bite before it is charmed, then there is no advantage in the charmer — ASV

If the serpent bites without being charmed; then in vain is a charmer — Lam

If the snake bites before the charming, then the charmer's skill does not benefit — Ber

If a snake bites before it is charmed,

the snake-charmer loses his fee — NEB

12. The words of a wise man's mouth are gracious; but the lips of a fool will swallow up himself.

13. The beginning of the words of his mouth is foolishness: and the end of his talk is mischievous madness.

Words from a wise mouth are gracious;
But the lips of a fool will destroy him.
The commencement of the words of his mouth are foolishness,
And the end of his conversation mischievous madness — Sprl

The words of a wise man's mouth are sweet to all, but the lips of a foolish man are his destruction.
The first words of his mouth are foolish, and the end of his talk is evil crime — Bas

The words of a wise man's mouth win him favor,
but the lips of a fool consume him.
The beginning of the words of his mouth is foolishness, and the end of his talk is wicked madness — RSV

Wise utterance wins favour; the fool that opens his mouth does but ruin himself, his preface idle talk, his conclusion madness — Knox

It is pleasant to listen to wise words, but a fool's speech brings him to ruin. Since he begins with a foolish premise, his conclusion is sheer madness — Tay

14. A fool also is full of words: a man cannot tell what shall be; and what shall be after him, who can tell him?

15. The labour of the foolish wearieth every one of them, because he knoweth not how to go to the city.

Though the fool multiplieth words, a man doth not know what the matter is; and what that shall be which will follow who can tell him. The labour of the foolish will tire them like that of one who knoweth not the way to a city — Sept

The fool multiplies words; man does not know what is to be;
who can tell him what will happen after his lifetime?
The efforts of a fool weary him, for he does not even know the way to the city — Ber

The fool talks on and on; but no man knows what is coming, and who can tell him what will come after that?
The fool wearies himself to death with all his labour, for he does not know the way to town — NEB

The fool multiplies words —
But man knows not what will be,
And who can tell him what will be after him?
When will the toil of the fool weary him
Who does not know enough to go to an interpreter? — AAT

A fool multiplies words; a man cannot tell what has been; and what shall be after him, who can tell him?
The labor of fools wears them out because they do not know how to buy and sell in the city — Lam

16. Woe to thee, O land, when thy king is a child, and thy princes eat in the morning!

17. Blessed art thou, O land, when thy king is the son of nobles, and thy princes eat in due season, for strength, and not for drunkenness!

Woe to thee, O land, when thy king is a boy,
And thy princes feast in the morning!
Happy art thou, O land, when thy king is a free man,
And thy princes eat in due season,
In strength and not in drunkenness — JPS

Woe unto thee, O land, when thy king is a youth,
And when thy princes feast in the morning!
Blessed art thou, O land, when thy king is of mature age,
And thy princes eat in moderation for support, and not unto repletion — Sprl

Woe betide you, O land, when your king is a mere boy,
and your princes revel in the morning!
Well for you when your king is nobly born,
and princes revel at right hours,
stalwart men, not sots — Mof

Woe to the land that has young blood

on the throne, whose court sits feasting till daybreak! And happy the land whose king is of true princely breed, whose courtiers feast when feast should be, to comfort their hearts, not all in revelry — Knox

Woe to the land whose king is a child and whose leaders are already drunk in the morning. Happy the land whose king is a nobleman, and whose leaders work hard before they feast and drink, and then only to strengthen themselves for the tasks ahead — Tay

18. **By much slothfulness the building decayeth; and through idleness of the hands the house droppeth through.**

By slothfulness the roof sinketh in; and through idleness of the hands the house leaketh — ASV

By slothfulness is the wall brought low,
And by idleness of the hands doth the house drop — YLT

Through continual neglect the ceiling sinks,
and because of slack hands the house leaks — Ber

Through sloth the roof sinks in,
and through indolence the house leaks — RSV

When hands are lazy the rafters sag; when hands are slack, the house leaks — NAB

19. **A feast is made for laughter, and wine maketh merry: but money answereth all things.**

A feast is made for laughter, and wine gladdens life;
And money answers all things — ABPS

A feast is appointed for merriment, and wine exhilarateth,
But money answereth to all purposes — Sprl

Men feast for merry-making,
and they drink for revelry —
and money does it all — Mof

Food will cheer thee, wine bring thee gladness, but money, it answers every need — Knox

But meals are made for laughter. Wine gives joy to life. Money is the answer to everything — Jerus

20. **Curse not the king, no not in thy thought; and curse not the rich in thy bedchamber: for a bird of the air shall carry the voice, and that which hath wings shall tell the matter.**

Revile not the king, no, not in thy thought; and revile not the rich in thy bed-chamber: for a bird of the heavens shall carry the voice, and that which hath wings shall tell the matter — ASV

Therefore curse not a king in thy mind, and in the inmost recesses of thy bed-chamber curse not a rich man: for a bird of the air will carry thy voice, and that which hath wings will tell thy saying — Sept

Even in thy thought do not revile the king,
Nor within thy bed-chambers revile thou the rich, —
For a bird of the heavens might carry your voice,
Yea an owner of wings might tell the matter — Rhm

Do not speak ill of the king in your ease, or of a rich man in your bedroom; for a bird may carry your voice, and a winged messenger may repeat what you say — NEB

Do not curse the king, even in thought; do not curse the rich, even in your bedroom,
for a bird of the air will carry the news;
indiscretion sprouts wings — Jerus

CHAPTER 11

1. **Cast thy bread upon the waters: for thou shalt find it after many days.**

2. **Give a portion to seven, and also to eight; for thou knowest not what evil shall be upon the earth.**

Send forth thy bread on the face of the waters,
For in the multitude of the days thou dost find it.
Give a portion to seven, and even to eight,
For thou knowest not what evil is on the earth — YLT

Cast thy bread upon the face of the waters,

For thou shalt find it after many days.
Give a portion to seven, yea, also to eight,
Though thou knowest not what calamity may be upon the earth — Sprl

Put out your bread on the face of the waters; for after a long time it will come back to you again.
Give a part to seven or even to eight, because you have no knowledge of the evil which will be on the earth — Bas

Trust your goods far and wide at sea, till you get good returns after a while.
Take shares in several ventures; you never know what will go wrong in this world — Mof

Send your grain across the seas, and in time you will get a return. Divide your merchandise among seven ventures, eight maybe, since you do not know what disasters may occur on earth — NEB

3. If the clouds be full of rain, they empty themselves upon the earth: and if the tree fall toward the south, or toward the north, in the place where the tree falleth, there it shall be.

4. He that observeth the wind shall not sow; and he that regardeth the clouds shall not reap.

5. As thou knowest not what is the way of the spirit, nor how the bones do grow in the womb of her that is with child: even so thou knowest not the works of God who maketh all.

He that observeth the wind will not sow, —
And he that watcheth the clouds will not reap.
Just as thou knowest not what is the way of the spirit, when the body is in the womb of her that is with child
Even so canst thou not know the work of God, who maketh all — Rhm

He who observes the wind shall not sow; and he who regards the clouds shall not reap.
As you do not know the path of the wind, and the manner of a woman who is with child; even so you do not know the works of the LORD who makes all — Lam

He who watches the wind shall not sow; he who studies the clouds shall not reap. Even as you do not know how the wind blows, or how the embryo develops in the womb of a pregnant woman, so you do not know the works of God, who makes everything — Ber

One who pays heed to the wind will not sow,
and one who watches the clouds will never reap.
Just as you know not how the breath of life
fashions the human frame in the mother's womb,
So you know not the work of God which he is accomplishing in the universe — NAB

Keep watching the wind and you will never sow,
stare at the clouds and you will never reap.
Just as you do not know the way of the wind or the mysteries of a woman with child, no more can you know the work of God who is behind it all — Jerus

6. In the morning sow thy seed, and in the evening withhold not thine hand: for thou knowest not whether shall prosper, either this or that, or whether they both shall be alike good.

In the morning sow thy seed,
And at even withdraw not thy hand,
For thou knowest not which is right, this or that,
Or whether both of them alike are good — YLT

In the morning sow thy seed; and in the evening let not thy hand forbear; for thou knowest not which will succeed, whether this or that; and should both prosper alike, they are good — Sept

Early abroad, to sow thy seed, and let evening find thee still at work; which sowing shall speed better, none knows, or whether both shall thrive to thy profit — Knox

Sow your seed in the morning of life, and stay not your hand till evening; you never know if this or that shall prosper, or whether both shall have success — Mof

In the morning sow your seed betimes, and do not stop work until evening, for you do not know whether this or that sowing will be successful, or whether both alike will do well — NEB

7. Truly the light is sweet, and a pleasant thing it is for the eyes to behold the sun:

8. But if a man live many years, and rejoice in them all; yet let him remember the days of darkness; for they shall be many. All that cometh is vanity.

Although a man live many years, and rejoice in them all,
Yet let him remember the days of tribulation, for they shall be many:
All that follow are vanity — Sprl

Therefore, if a man lives many years and rejoices in them all, let him consider the days of darkness, for they will be many. All that comes is nothingness — Ber

But even if a man's life is long and he has joy in all his years, let him keep in mind the dark days, because they will be great in number. Whatever may come is to no purpose — Bas

However great the number of the years a man may live, let him enjoy them all, and yet remember that dark days will be many. All that is to come is vanity — Jerus

However many years a man may live, let him, as he enjoys them all, remember that the days of darkness will be many. All that is to come is vanity — NAB

9. Rejoice, O young man, in thy youth; and let thy heart cheer thee in the days of thy youth, and walk in the ways of thine heart, and in the sight of thine eyes: but know thou, that for all these things God will bring thee into judgment.

Rejoice O young man in thy youth
And let thy heart gladden thee in the days of thine early manhood,
And walk thou —
In the ways of thine own heart,
And in that which is seen by thine own eyes, —
Yet know that for all these things
Will God bring thee into judgment — Rhm

Rejoice, O young man, in your youth,
And let your mind be glad in the days of your vigor,
And walk in the ways of your mind and in the sight of your eyes;
But know that for all these things
God will bring you into judgment — AAT

Rejoice, O young man, in your adolescence, and let your heart cheer you in the days of your full-grown youth, and walk in the ways of your heart, and in the sight of your eyes. But know that for all these things God will bring you into judgment — Amp

Delight in your boyhood, young man, make the most of the days of your youth; let your heart and your eyes show you the way; but remember that for all these things God will call you to account — NEB

Young man, it's wonderful to be young! Enjoy every minute of it! Do all you want to; take in everything, but realize that you must account to God for everything you do — Tay

10. Therefore remove sorrow from thy heart, and put away evil from thy flesh: for childhood and youth are vanity.

Therefore remove sorrow from thy heart, and put away evil from thy flesh; for youth and the dawn of life are vanity — ASV

Rid thy heart, then, of resentment, thy nature of ill humours; youth and pleasures, they are so quickly gone — Knox

Therefore remove anger from your heart, and put away evil from your flesh; for youth and ignorance are vanity — Lam

Banish grief from your mind and keep pain from your body, for youth and the dawn (of life) are transitory — Ber

Remove vexation from your mind, and put away pain from your body; for youth and the dawn of life are vanity — RSV

CHAPTER 12

1. Remember now thy Creator in the days of thy youth, while the evil days come not, nor the years draw nigh, when thou shalt say, I have no pleasure in them;

Yet remember thy Creator, in the days of thy vigour, —
Or ever come in the days of discomfort,
And the years arrive in which thou shalt say —
I have in them no pleasure — Rhm

Let your mind be turned to your Maker in the days of your strength, while the evil days come not, and the years are far away when you will say, I have no pleasure in them — Bas

Remember your Creator in the days of your vigor,
Before the evil days come,
And the years approach of which you will say,
'I have no pleasure in them' — AAT

Be mindful of your Creator in the days of your youth before the troubling days come and the years draw near when you will say, "I do not enjoy them" — Ber

Remember your Creator in the days of your youth, before the time of trouble comes and the years draw near when you will say, 'I see no purpose in them' — NEB

2. While the sun, or the light, or the moon, or the stars, be not darkened, nor the clouds return after the rain:

3. In the day when the keepers of the house shall tremble, and the strong men shall bow themselves, and the grinders cease because they are few, and those that look out of the windows be darkened,

4. And the doors shall be shut in the streets, when the sound of the grinding is low, and he shall rise up at the voice of the bird, and all the daughters of music shall be brought low;

In the day when the supporters of the house shall tremble,
And the valiant men totter;
And the grinding slaves cease their toil, because they are few;
And those who attentively regard from the windows, be obscured;
And the doors shall be shut in the streets;
And the sound of the mill be faintly heard;
When he shall be aroused at the crow of the cock;
Whilst all the daughters of song repose — Sprl

One day, palsy will shake those door-keepers, those stalwart guards will be bowed with age; rarer, now, the busy maidens at the mill, dimmer, now, those bright glances from the windows. The street-doors shut, muffled the hum of the mill, bird-song for waking-time, and all the echoes of music faint — Knox

In the day when the legs tremble and the arms weaken, and the teeth chew no more because they are few, and the eyes are dimmed.
And the ears shall be so dulled that the sound of women grinding at the mill is low, and a man shall rise up at the song of birds; and the sound of women singing shall be low — Lam

when the guards tremble in the house of Life,
when its upholders bow, when the maids that grind are few and fail, and ladies at the lattice lose their lustre,
when the doors to the street are shut, and the sound of the mill is low;
when the twitter of birds is faint, and dull the daughters of song — Mof

When the guardians of the house tremble,
and the strong men are bent,
And the grinders are idle because they are few,
and they who look through the windows grow blind;
When the doors to the street are shut,
and the sound of the mill is low;
When one waits for the chirp of a bird,
but all the daughters of song are suppressed — NAB

5. Also when they shall be afraid of that which is high, and fears shall be in the way, and the almond tree shall flourish, and the grasshopper shall be a burden, and desire shall fail: because man goeth to his long home, and the mourners go about the streets:

Yea, they shall be afraid of that which is high, and terrors shall be in the way; and the almond tree shall blossom, and the grasshopper shall be a burden, and the caper-berry shall fail: because man goeth to his long home, and the mourners go about the streets — RV

they are afraid also of what is high, and terrors are in the way; the almond tree blossoms, the grasshopper drags itself along and desire fails; because man goes to his eternal home, and the mourners go about in the streets — RSV

Also, he is afraid of a height,
And terrors are on the road;
And he rejects the almond,
And the locust is burdensome,
And the caperberry is ineffectual;
Because man is going to his eternal home,
And the mourners go about in the streets — AAT

when men are afraid of a steep place and the street is full of terrors, when the blossom whitens on the almond-tree and the locust's paunch is swollen and caper-buds have no more zest. For man goes to his everlasting home, and the mourners go about the streets — NEB

6. Or ever the silver cord be loosed, or the golden bowl be broken, or the pitcher be broken at the fountain, or the wheel broken at the cistern.

7. Then shall the dust return to the earth as it was: and the spirit shall return unto God who gave it.

before the silver cord is loosed, or the golden bowl is broken, or the pitcher is broken at the fountain, or the wheel broken at the cistern, and the dust returneth to the earth as it was, and the spirit returneth unto God who gave it — ASV

Before the silver cord is snapped asunder,
And the golden bowl is shattered,
And the pitcher is broken at the fountain,
And the wheel falleth shattered into the pit;
And the dust returneth to the earth as it was,
And the spirit returneth unto God who gave it — JPS

before the silver cord has snapped,
or the golden lamp been broken,
or the pitcher shattered at the spring,
or the pulley cracked at the well,
or before the dust returns to the earth as it once came from it, and the breath to God who gave it — Jerus

Before the silver cord is severed, the golden bowl shattered, the pitcher broken at the fountain and the wheel broken at the cistern. Then the dust returns to the earth as it was, and the spirit returns to God who gave it — Ber

Before the silver cord is snapped
and the golden bowl is broken,
And the pitcher is shattered at the spring,
and the broken pulley falls into the well,
And the dust returns to the earth as it once was,
and the life breath returns to God who gave it — NAB

8. Vanity of vanities, saith the preacher; all is vanity.

9. And moreover, because the preacher was wise, he still taught the people knowledge; yea, he gave good heed, and sought out, and set in order many proverbs.

10. The preacher sought to find out acceptable words: and that which was written was upright, even words of truth.

And further, because the Preacher was wise, he still taught the people knowledge; yea, he pondered, and sought out, and set in order many proverbs.
The Preacher sought to find out acceptable words, and that which was written uprightly, even words of truth — RV

And the preacher excelled in wisdom,
Even to instruct the people in knowledge;

And to balance, and accurately to search, and to compose many proverbs.
The preacher sought to discover acceptable words;
And to write accurately words of truth — Sprl

And because the Preacher was wise he still gave the people knowledge; searching out, testing, and putting in order a great number of wise sayings.
The Preacher made search for words which were pleasing, but his writing was in words upright and true — Bas

In addition to the fact that Koheleth was wise, he still taught the people knowledge, and he composed, and sought out, and arranged many proverbs. Koheleth sought to find pleasing words, and what is written correctly, namely, true things — AAT

Besides being a sage, Qoheleth also taught his knowledge to the people, having weighed, studied and amended a great many proverbs. Qoheleth tried to write in an attractive style and to set down truthful thoughts in a straightforward manner — Jerus

11. The words of the wise are as goads, and as nails fastened by the masters of assemblies, which are given from one shepherd.

Words of the wise are as goads, and as fences planted by the masters of collections, they have been given by one shepherd — YLT

The words of the wise are as goads; and as nails well fastened are the words of the masters of assemblies, which are given from one shepherd — ASV

The words of the wise are as goads,
Yea as driven nails their well-ordered sayings, —
Given from one shepherd — Rhm

Sharp goads they are to sting us, sharp nails driven deep home, these wise words left us by many masters, but all echoing one shepherd's voice — Knox

The sayings of the wise are like goads, and like nails firmly fixed are the collected sayings which are given by one Shepherd — RSV

12. And further, by these, my son, be admonished: of making many books there is no end; and much study is a weariness of the flesh.

13. Let us hear the conclusion of the whole matter: Fear God, and keep his commandments: for this is the whole duty of man.

14. For God shall bring every work into judgment, with every secret thing, whether it be good, or whether it be evil.

This is the end of the matter; all hath been heard: Fear God, and keep his commandments; for this is the whole duty of man.
For God will bring every work into judgment, with every hidden thing, whether it be good, or whether it be evil — ASV

Let us listen to the conclusion of the whole subject:
Fear God, and keep His commandments;
For this is all required of man:
Because God will bring every work into judgment,
With every secret thing, whether it be good or whether it be evil — Sprl

As a conclusion of the discourse, hear thou the whole sum and substance. — Fear God and keep his commandments: for this conclusion every man should draw, That God will bring the whole work into judgment in every case not taken notice of, whether it be good or whether it be evil — Sept

The end of the matter, all having been heard: fear God, and keep His commandments; for this is the whole man. For God shall bring every work into judgment concerning every hidden thing, whether it be good or whether it be evil — JPS

This is the end of the matter: you have heard it all. Fear God and obey his commands; there is no more to man than this. For God brings everything we do to judgment, and every secret, whether good or bad — NEB

THE SONG OF SOLOMON

CHAPTER 1

1. The song of songs, which is Solomon's.

The song of all songs, which is Solomon's — Mof

The song of songs — the most excellent of them all — which is Solomon's — Amp

The Song of Songs, which pertaineth to Solomon — Rhm

This song of songs, more wonderful than any other, was composed by King Solomon — Tay

2. Let him kiss me with the kisses of his mouth: for thy love is better than wine.

3. Because of the savour of thy good ointments thy name is as ointment poured forth, therefore do the virgins love thee.

Let him kiss me with the kisses of his mouth;
For thy love is better than wine.
Thine oils have a goodly fragrance;
Thy name is as oil poured forth;
Therefore do the virgins love thee — ASV

Let him kiss me with kisses of his mouth,
For better are thy loves than wine.
For fragrance are thy perfumes good.
Perfume emptied out — thy name,
Therefore have virgins loved thee! — YLT

Let Him kiss me with the kisses of His mouth!
Surely more delicious than wine are Thy love-favours.
Thy renown, like the fragrance of Thy Own exquisite perfumes,
Is a perfume diffused.
Therefore do the virgins love Thee — Sprl

Oh, that he would kiss me with the kisses of his lips,
for your love is sweeter than wine.
The savor of your ointments is fragrant;
your name is as perfume poured out;
therefore do the maidens love you — Ber

Oh for a kiss from your lips!
your caresses are dearer than wine.
rare is the fragrance of your perfumes,
the sound of your name is wafted like scent.
The girls are all in love with you — Mof

A kiss from those lips! Wine cannot ravish the senses like that embrace, nor the fragrance of rare perfumes match it for delight. Thy very name spoken soothes the heart like the flow of oil; what wonder the maids should love thee — Knox

4. Draw me, we will run after thee: the king hath brought me into his chambers: we will be glad and rejoice in thee, we will remember thy love more than wine: the upright love thee.

Draw me!
After thee will we run!
The king hath brought me into his chambers.
We will exult and rejoice in thee,
We will mention thy caresses beyond wine.
Sincerely they love thee — Rhm

Draw me, we will run after thee;
The king hath brought me into his chambers;
We will be glad and rejoice in thee,
We will find thy love more fragrant than wine!
Sincerely do they love thee — JPS

Draw me; we will run after thee: the king hath brought me into his chambers: we will be glad and rejoice in thee, we will make mention of thy love more than of wine: rightly do they love thee — RV

Take me along with you, let us hasten;
Bring me, O king, into your chamber,
That we may exult and rejoice in you,
That we may praise your love more than wine;
Rightly are you loved — AAT

Draw me! —
We will follow you eagerly!
Bring me, O king, to your chambers.
With you we rejoice and exult,
we extol your love; it is beyond wine:
how rightly you are loved — NAB

5. I am black, but comely, O ye daughters

of Jerusalem, as the tents of Kedar, as the curtains of Solomon.

6. Look not upon me, because I am black, because the sun hath looked upon me:

I am black, but comely,
O ye daughters of Jerusalem,
As the tents of Kedar,
As the curtains of Solomon.
Look not upon me, because I am swarthy,
Because the sun hath scorched me — ASV

Dark am I, and comely, daughters of Jerusalem,
As tents of Kedar, as curtains of Solomon.
Fear me not, because I am very dark,
Because the sun hath scorched me — YLT

I am brown but comely, O daughters of Jerusalem; like the tents of Kedar — like the curtains of Solomon. Look not on me, because I am of a dark complexion — Because the sun hath looked upon me — Sept

I am dark, but comely,
Daughters of Jerusalem,
As the tents of Kedar,
As the tent curtains of Solomon.
Look not upon me, because I am swarthy,
Because the sun has tanned me — ABPS

I am dark, but fair of form, O daughters of Jerusalem, as the tents of Kedar, as the curtains of Solomon. Let not your eyes be turned on me, because I am dark, because I was looked on by the sun — Bas

I am black but lovely, daughters of Jerusalem,
like the tents of Kedar,
like the pavilions of Salmah.
Take no notice of my swarthiness,
it is the sun that has burnt me — Jerus

Don't look down on me, you city girls, just because my complexion is so dark — the sun has tanned me — Tay

my mother's children were angry with me; they made me the keeper of the vineyards; but mine own vineyard have I not kept.

My mother's sons were incensed against me, they made me keeper of the vineyards; but mine own vineyard have I not kept — RV

My mother's children derided me,
They made me inspectress of the fruiteries;
But mine own fruitery have I not kept — Sprl

My stepbrothers were angry with me, and they made me keeper of the vineyards; but my own vineyard . . . I have not kept — Amp

My mother's sons were displeased with me,
they sent me to watch over the vineyards;
so I did not watch over my own vineyard — NEB

My brothers were angry with me and sent me out into the sun to tend the vineyards, but see what it has done to me — Tay

7. Tell me, O thou whom my soul loveth, where thou feedest, where thou makest thy flock to rest at noon: for why should I be as one that turneth aside by the flocks of thy companions?

Tell me, thou loved of my soul!
Where wilt thou pasture thy flock?
Where wilt thou let them recline at noon?
For why should I be as one that wrappeth a veil about her by the flocks of thy companions — Rhm

Tell me, O thou whom my soul loveth,
Where thou feedest thy flock,
Where thou makest it to rest at noon:
For why should I be as one that is veiled
Beside the flocks of thy companions — ASV

Tell me, you whom my soul loves,
where you pasture your flock,
where you make it lie down at noon;
for why should I be like one who wanders
beside the flocks of your companions — RSV

Tell me, love of my soul,
where do you rest your flock at noon;

for why should I go roaming
from flock to flock of your mates — Mof

Tell me, my true love, where is now thy pasture-ground, where now is thy resting-place under the noon's heat? Thou wouldst not have me wander to and fro where the flocks graze that are none of thine? — Knox

Tell me, you whom deep in my soul I love,
where you pasture your flock,
where you have it lie down at mid-day
for why should I be as a veiled woman,
wandering among the flocks of your companions — Ber

8. **If thou know not, O thou fairest among women, go thy way forth by the footsteps of the flock, and feed thy kids beside the shepherds' tents.**

If thou knowest not, O fair among women,
Get thee forth by the traces of the flock,
And feed thy kids by the shepherds' dwellings — YLT

If thou knowest not, O thou most elegant of women!
Go thee forth by the footsteps of the flock,
And tend thine own kids
Besides the shepherds' tents — Sprl

If you do not know, O most beautiful of women,
Follow in the tracks of the flock,
And pasture your kids, beside the tents of the shepherds — AAT

If you do not know this, O loveliest of women,
follow the tracks of the flock,
and take your kids to graze
close by the shepherds' tents — Jerus

If you do not know,
O most beautiful among women,
Follow the tracks of the flock
and pasture the young ones near the shepherds' camps — NAB

If you don't know, O most beautiful woman in all the world, follow the trail of my flock to the shepherds' tents, and there feed your sheep and their lambs — Tay

9. **I have compared thee, O my love, to a company of horses in Pharaoh's chariots.**

10. **Thy cheeks are comely with rows of jewels, thy neck with chains of gold.**

11. **We will make thee borders of gold with studs of silver.**

I have compared thee, O my love,
To a steed in Pharaoh's chariots.
Thy cheeks are comely with circlets,
Thy neck with beads.
We will make thee circlets of gold
With studs of silver — JPS

I have compared thee, O my love,
To a steed in Pharaoh's chariots.
Thy cheeks are comely with plaits of hair,
Thy neck with strings of jewels.
We will make thee plaits of gold
With studs of silver — ASV

To a mare of mine in the chariots of Pharaoh
Have I likened thee, my fair one!
Comely are Thy cheeks with bead-rows,
Thy neck with strings of gems.
Rows of golden ornaments will we make thee,
With studs of silver — Rhm

I have compared you, O my beloved,
to a mare in Pharaoh's chariot.
Your cheeks are comely with braided hair, and your neck with necklaces.
We will make for you golden chains
with studs of silver — Lam

I compare you, my love,
to a mare of Pharaoh's chariots.
Your cheeks are comely with ornaments,
your neck with strings of jewels.
We will make you ornaments of gold,
studded with silver — RSV

I would compare you, my dearest,
to Pharaoh's chariot-horses.
Your cheeks are lovely between plaited tresses,
your neck with its jewelled chains.
We will make you braided plaits of gold
set with beads of silver — NEB

What a lovely filly you are, my love!
How lovely your cheeks are, with your hair falling down upon them!

How stately your neck with that long string of jewels.
We shall make you golden earrings and silver beads — Tay

12. While the King sitteth at his table, my spikenard sendeth forth the smell thereof.

13. A bundle of myrrh is my wellbeloved unto me; he shall lie all night betwixt my breasts.

14. My beloved is unto me as a cluster of camphire in the vineyards of En-gedi.

While the king is in his circle,
My spikenard hath given its fragrance.
A bundle of myrrh is my beloved to me,
Between my breasts it lodgeth.
A cluster of cypress is my beloved to me,
In the vineyards of En-Gedi — YLT

While the king is seated at his table, my spices send out their perfume.
As a bag of myrrh is my well-loved one to me, when he is at rest all night between my breasts.
My love is to me as a branch of the cypress-tree in the vine-gardens of En-gedi — Bas

While the king sat at his table, my spikenard sent forth its fragrance.
My beloved is unto me as a bundle of myrrh, that lieth betwixt my breasts.
My beloved is unto me as a cluster of henna-flowers in the vineyards of En-gedi — RV

While the king was on his couch,
his nard gave forth its fragrance.
A bunch of myrrh is my beloved to me,
as he lies at night between my breasts;
A cluster of henna is my beloved to me,
from the gardens of Engedi — AAT

As long as the king was on his couch,
my spikenard gave forth its fragrance;
My loved one is to me a bundle of myrrh
lying between my breasts;
He is to me a cluster of henna
of the gardens of Engedi — Ber

— While the King rests in his own room
my nard yields its perfume.
My Beloved is a sachet of myrrh
lying between my breasts.
My Beloved is a cluster of henna flowers
among the vines of Engedi — Jerus

15. Behold, thou art fair, my love; behold, thou art fair; thou hast doves' eyes.

16. Behold, thou art fair, my beloved, yea, pleasant: also our bed is green.

17. The beams of our house are cedar, and our rafters of fir.

Behold, thou art beautiful, my friend;
behold, thou art beautiful;
Thine eyes are doves.
Behold, thou art beautiful, my beloved, yea, charming;
Also our couch is green.
The beams of our house are cedars,
And our rafters are firs — ABPS

Behold, thou art fair, my love;
Behold, thou art fair;
Thine eyes are as doves.
Behold, thou art fair, my beloved, yea, pleasant:
Also our couch is green.
The beams of our house are cedars,
And our rafters are firs — ASV

Lo! thou art beautiful, my fair one,
Lo! thou art beautiful,
Thine eyes are doves!
Lo! thou art beautiful my beloved,
Yea, delightful! Yea! our couch is covered with leaves:
The beams of our house are cedars,
Our fretted ceiling is cypress-trees — Rhm

See how fair is the maid I love! Soft eyes thou hast, like a dove's eyes.
And see how fair is the man I love, how stately! Green grows that bower, thine and mine, with its roof of cedars, with a covert of cypress for its walls — Knox

How fair you are, my dear,
how fair with dove-like eyes!
And how fair you are, my darling, oh how sweet!
Our bed of love is the green sward,
our roof-beams are yon cedar-boughs,
our rafters are the firs — Mof

CHAPTER 2

1. I am the rose of Sharon, and the lily of the valleys.

2. As the lily among thorns, so is my love among the daughters.

— I am the rose of Sharon,
the lily of the valleys.
— As a lily among the thistles,
so is my love among the maidens — Jerus

I am a rose of Sharon,
a lily of the valleys.
As a lily among brambles,
so is my love among maidens — RSV

I am only a blossom of the plain,
a mere lily of the dale,
"Like a lily among briars,
so is my dear among women!" — Mof

I am but a wild rose of Sharon,
A mere lily of the valleys.
As the lily distinguished above the brambles,
So is My Consort amongst the daughters — Sprl

"I am a saffron of the plain,
a hyacinth of the valleys."
"Like a hyacinth among thistles,
so is my loved one among the maidens" — AAT

Count me no more than wild rose on the lowland plain, wild lily on the mountain slopes.
A lily, matched with these other maidens, a lily among the brambles, she whom I love! — Knox

3. As the apple tree among the trees of the wood, so is my beloved among the sons. I sat down under his shadow with great delight, and his fruit was sweet to my taste.

Like an apple tree among the trees of the forest, so is my beloved among the young men. I sat down under his shadow with great delight, and his fruit was sweet to my taste — Lam

As a citron among trees of the forest,
So is my beloved among the sons,
In his shade I delighted, and sat down,
And his fruit was sweet to my palate — YLT

As the citron tree among the trees of the forest; so is my dear brother among the youths. In its shade I took great delight and sat, and its fruit was sweet to my taste — Sept

Like an apricot-tree among the trees of the wood,
so is my beloved among boys.
To sit in its shadow was my delight,
and its fruit was sweet to my taste — NEB

As an apple tree among the trees of the wood,
so is my lover among the sons.
In his shadow I delight to sit,
and his fruit is sweet to my taste — Ber

4. He brought me to the banqueting house, and his banner over me was love.

5. Stay me with flagons, comfort me with apples: for I am sick of love.

He brought me to the banqueting-house,
And his banner over me was love.
Stay ye me with raisins, refresh me with apples;
For I am sick from love — ASV

He conducted me to the banqueting-house,
And love was His banner that waved over me.
Invigorate me with cordials!
Strew citrons around me!
For I am fainting with love! — Sprl

He brought me to the banqueting house, and assigned as my portion love.
Sustain me with delicacies, surround me with apples; for I am sick for love —Lam

Bring me to the house of wine,
and look upon me with love.
Stay me with raisin-cakes,
refresh me with apples;
for I am sick with love — AAT

He has brought me to his chamber of joy,
hung over with love.
Sustain me with raisins,
revive me with apples,
for I swoon with love! — Mof

He brings me into the banquet hall
and his emblem over me is love.

Sustain me with raisin cakes,
refresh me with apples,
for I am faint with love — NAB

6. His left hand is under my head, and his right hand doth embrace me.

7. I charge you, O ye daughters of Jerusalem, by the roes, and by the hinds of the field, that ye stir not up, nor awake my love, till he please.[1]

Let his left hand be under my head,
And his right hand embrace me.
'I adjure you, O daughters of Jerusalem,
By the gazelles, and by the hinds of the field,
That ye awaken not, nor stir up love,
Until it please' — JPS

O that his left hand were under my head,
and that his right hand embraced me!
I adjure you, O daughters of Jerusalem,
by the gazelles or the hinds of the field,
that you stir not up nor awaken love
until it please — RSV

His left arm is under my head,
his right embraces me.
— I charge you,
daughters of Jerusalem,
by the gazelles, by the hinds of the field,
not to stir my love, nor rouse it,
until it please to awake — Jerus

Let his left hand caress my head,
let his right hand embrace me.
O maidens of Jerusalem, I charge you,
by the roe-deer and the hinds,
never rouse lovers, never stir them,
till they are satisfied — Mof

His left hand pillows my head; his right hand, even now, ready to embrace me.
An oath, maidens of Jerusalem! By the gazelles and the wild fawns I charge you, wake never from her sleep my heart's love, till wake she will — Knox

His left hand is under my head and with his right hand he embraces me.
O girls of Jerusalem, I adjure you by the gazelles and deer in the park, that you do not awaken my lover. Let him sleep! — Tay

8. The voice of my beloved! behold, he cometh leaping upon the mountains, skipping upon the hills.

9. My beloved is like a roe or a young hart: behold, he standeth behind our wall, he looketh forth at the windows, showing himself through the lattice.

The voice of my beloved! lo, there he comes,
Leaping upon the mountains, springing upon the hills.
My beloved is like a gazelle or a young hart,
Behold, there he stands behind our wall,
Looking in at the windows,
Glancing through the lattice — ABPS

The voice of my beloved!
Lo! here he cometh, —
Leaping over the mountains,
Skipping over the hills.
Resembleth my beloved a gazelle,
Or a young stag, —
Lo! here he is standing behind our wall,
Looking in at the windows,
Peeping in at the lattice — Rhm

Hark! my beloved!
ah, here he comes,
Leaping over the mountains,
skipping over the hills.
My beloved is like a gazelle,
or a young stag.
Ah, here he stands,
behind our wall,
Looking through the windows,
peering through the lattices — AAT

The voice of my loved one! See, he comes dancing on the mountains, stepping quickly on the hills.
My loved one is like a roe; see, he is on the other side of our wall, he is looking in at the windows, letting himself be seen through the spaces — Bas

Hark! My Beloved! Here he comes, bounding over the mountains, leaping over the hills.
My beloved is like a gazelle
or a young wild goat:
there he stands outside our wall,

[1]Compare 3:5.

peeping in at the windows, glancing through the lattice — NEB

10. My beloved spake, and said unto me, Rise up, my love, my fair one, and come away.

11. For lo, the winter is past, the rain is over and gone;

My dear brother addressing me saith, "Arise my love, my fair one, my dove! For lo! the winter is past — the rain is over: is gone — Sept

My beloved spoke, and said to me,
Rise up, my friend, my beauty, and come away.
For, lo, the winter is past,
The rain is over and gone — ABPS

My beloved sings, and he calls to me:
Arise, my love, my beauty, and come along with me;
For lo! the winter is past,
the season of rain is over and gone — Ber

I can hear my true love calling to me:
Rise up, rise up quickly, dear heart, so gentle, so beautiful, rise up and come with me. Winter is over now, the rain has passed by — Knox

My lover speaks; he says to me,
"Arise, my beloved, my beautiful one,
and come!
"For see, the winter is past,
the rains are over and gone — NAB

12. The flowers appear on the earth; the time of the singing of birds is come, and the voice of the turtle is heard in our land;

13. The fig tree putteth forth her green figs, and the vines with the tender grape give a good smell. Arise, my love, my fair one, and come away.

The flowers appear on the earth;
The time of the singing of birds is come,
And the voice of the turtle-dove is heard in our land;
The fig-tree ripeneth her green figs,
And the vines are in blossom;
They give forth their fragrance.
Arise, my love, my fair one, and come away — ASV

The flowers appear on the meads,
The harmonious season has arrived,
And the voice of the turtle-dove re-echoes in our land.
The fig tree sweeteneth her first young figs,
And the budding flowers of the vines yield fragrance.
Rise up, and haste thee away, O my consort!
Yea, my fair one, haste thee away — Sprl

The flowers have appeared on the earth,
the time of song has come;
And the call of the turtle dove
is heard in our land;
The fig tree is putting forth its figs,
and the blossoming grape vines give forth fragrance.
Rise, my love,
my beautiful one, come away — AAT

the country's a-flower,
'tis the season for pruning,
the ring-dove's note is heard,
the figs are ripening red,
the vines are all blossom and fragrance —
come, dear, come away, my beauty — Mof

the flowers appear in the country-side;
the time is coming when the birds will sing,
and the turtle-dove's cooing will be heard in our land;
when the green figs will ripen on the fig-trees
and the vines give forth their fragrance.
Rise up, my darling;
my fairest, come away — NEB

14. O my dove, that art in the clefts of the rock, in the secret places of the stairs, let me see thy countenance, let me hear thy voice; for sweet is thy voice, and thy countenance is comely.

My dove, in clefts of the rock,
In a secret place of the ascent,
Cause me to see thine appearance,
Cause me to hear thy voice,
For thy voice is sweet, and thy appearance comely — YLT

O my dove, that art in the clefts of the rock, in the covert of the steep place, let me see thy countenance, let me hear thy voice; for sweet is thy voice, and thy countenance is comely — RV

O my dove, that art in the clefts of the rock, in the covert of the cliff,
Let me see thy countenance, let me hear thy voice;
For sweet is thy voice, and thy countenance is comely — JPS

O my dove, who nests in the clefts of the rock and in the secret places of the hedge, let me see your countenance, let me hear your voice; for sweet is your voice, and your countenance is comely — Lam

O my dove in the clefts of the rock, in the secret recesses of the cliff,
Let me see you,
let me hear your voice,
For your voice is sweet,
and you are lovely — NAB

15. Take us the foxes, the little foxes, that spoil the vines: for our vines have tender grapes.

Take us the foxes, the little foxes,
That spoil the vineyards;
For our vineyards are in blossom — ASV

Catch for us the foxes,
the little foxes,
That are despoiling the vineyards,
since our vineyards are in bloom — AAT

Catch for us the jackals, the little jackals,
that spoil our vineyards, when the vines are in flower — NEB

16. My beloved is mine, and I am his: he feedeth among the lilies.

17. Until the day break, and the shadows flee away, turn, my beloved, and be thou like a roe or a young hart upon the mountains of Bether.

My beloved is mine, and I am his: he feedeth his flock among the lilies.
Until the day be cool, and the shadows flee away, turn, my beloved, and be thou like a roe or a young hart upon the mountains of Bether — RV

My beloved is mine, and I am his,
That feedeth among the lilies.
Until the day breathe, and the shadows flee away,
Turn, my beloved, and be thou like a gazelle or a young hart
Upon the mountains of spices — JPS

My Beloved is mine, and I am His:
He taketh care of the lilies.
Until the day breathe and the shadows flee away,
Turn, my Beloved, and be Thou like an antelope,
Or fawn of the deer, upon the mountains of separation — Sprl

My darling is mine, and I am his,
he feeds among my lilies.
Till the cool of the dawn,
till the shadows depart,
oh turn to me, darling,
and play like a roe or a hart
on my perfumed slopes — Mof

My beloved is mine and I am his. He is feeding among the lilies! Before the dawn comes and the shadows flee away, come to me, my beloved, and be like a gazelle or a young stag on the mountains of spices — Tay

CHAPTER 3

1. By night on my bed I sought him whom my soul loveth: I sought him, but I found him not.

Upon my couch in the night-time sought I the beloved of my soul, —
I sought him, but found him not — Rhm

In the night watches, as I lay abed, I searched for my heart's love, and searched in vain — Knox

Night after night on my bed
I have sought my true love;
I have sought him but not found him,
I have called him but he has not answered — NEB

Night after night in bed
I dreamed I sought my beloved,
and sought him in vain — Mof

"One night my lover was missing from my bed. I got up to look for him but couldn't find him — Tay

2. I will rise now, and go about the city in the streets, and in the broad ways I will seek him whom my soul loveth: I sought him, but I found him not.

3. The watchmen that go about the city

found me: to whom I said, Saw ye him whom my soul loveth?

— Pray, let me rise, and go round the city,
In the streets and in the broad places,
I seek him whom my soul hath loved!
— I sought him, and I found him not.
The watchmen have found me,
(Who are going round about the city),
'Him whom my soul hath loved saw ye?' — YLT

"I will rise now and go about the city,
in the streets and in the squares;
I will seek him whom my soul loves."
I sought him, but found him not.
The watchmen found me,
as they went about in the city.
"Have you seen him whom my soul loves?" — RSV

I will arise now and walk round about the city:
In the streets and highways thereof
Will I seek Him whom my soul loveth.
I sought him, but I found Him not.
The guards who surround the city met me:
I said: Oh have ye seen Him whom my soul loveth? — Sprl

I will get up now and go about the town, in the streets and in the wide ways I will go after him who is the love of my soul: I went after him, but I did not see him.
The watchmen who go about the town came by me; to them I said, Have you seen him who is my heart's desire? — BAS

I shall arise now and go round about the city
in the streets and the market places,
and I shall seek him whom my soul loves.
I sought him, and I found him not.
The watchmen that go about in the city found me;
I said to them, "Have you seen him whom my soul loves?" — Ber

4. It was but a little that I passed from them, but I found him whom my soul loveth: I held him, and would not let him go, until I had brought him into my mother's house, and into the chamber of her that conceived me.

Scarcely had I passed from them
When I found the beloved of my soul, —
I caught him and would not let him go,
Until that I had brought him into the house of my mother,
And into the chamber of her that conceived me — Rhm

'Twas but a little I had passed on from them
When I found Him whom my soul loveth.
I held Him fast, and would not release Him
Until I had brought Him unto the house of my mother;
Even into the apartment of her who conceived me — Sprl

Scarcely did I get by them,
when I found him whom I love.
I held him and would not let him go,
until I brought him to my mother's house,
to the chamber of her who bore me — AAT

I had hardly left them
when I found him whom my heart loves.
I took hold of him and would not let him go
till I should bring him to the home of my mother,
to the room of my parent — NAB

It was only a little while afterwards that I found him and held him and would not let him go until I had brought him into my childhood home, into my mother's old bedroom — Tay

5. I charge you, O ye daughters of Jerusalem, by the roes, and by the hinds of the field, that ye stir not up, nor awake my love, till he please.[2]

I adjure you, O daughters of Jerusalem,
By the roes, or by the hinds of the field,

[2]Compare 2:7.

That ye stir not up, nor awake my love,
Until he please — ASV

I adjure you, O ye daughters of Jerusalem,
By the gazelles or by the deer of the field,
That ye arouse me not; that ye disturb not this dream of love,
Until love herself so desire it — Sprl

I charge you,
daughters of Jerusalem,
by the gazelles, by the hinds of the field,
not to stir my love, nor rouse it,
until it please to awake — Jerus

I say to you, O daughters of Jerusalem, by the roes of the field, let not love be moved till it is ready — Bas

6. Who is this that cometh out of the wilderness like pillars of smoke, perfumed with myrrh and frankincense, with all powders of the merchant?

Who is this coming up out of the wilderness,
Like pillars of smoke, —
With perfume of myrrh and frankincense,
Besides all the aromatic powder of the merchant? — Rhm

Who is this coming up from the wilderness,
Like palm-trees of smoke,
Perfumed with myrrh and frankincense,
From every powder of the merchant? — YLT

What is this coming up from the country,
like columns of smoke,
perfumed with myrrh and frankincense,
with every scent to be bought? — Mof

Who is this coming up from the wilderness,
like columns of smoke,
Perfumed with myrrh and frankincense,
made from all kinds of merchants' spices? — AAT

Who is this that comes up from the wilderness like pillars of smoke, perfumed with myrrh and frankincense, compounded from all kinds of powdered sweet spices? — Lam

7. Behold his bed, which is Solomon's; threescore valiant men are about it, of the valiant of Israel.

8. They all hold swords, being expert in war: every man hath his sword upon his thigh because of fear in the night.

Behold, it is the litter of Solomon;
Threescore mighty men are about it,
Of the mighty men of Israel.
They all handle the sword, and are expert in war:
Each one hath his sword upon his thigh,
Because of fear in the night — ASV

Lo, this is the palanquin of Solomon:
Threescore mighty men surround it,
Of the valiant of Israel:
Each one grasping his sword,
Expert in warfare:
Each one hath his sword upon his thigh
Because of peril by night — Sprl

It is the palanquin of Solomon, three score chiefs of the chiefs of Israel are around it. All swordsmen expert in war. Every man with his sword on his thigh, for fear of danger by night — Sept

Lo! his couch, 'tis Solomon's own,
Threescore heroes around it, —
Of the heroes of Israel:
All of them grasping the sword,
Trained for war, —
Every man with his sword upon his thigh,
Because of dread in the night-time — Rhm

Ah, it is the litter of Solomon:
sixty valiant men surround it,
of the valiant men of Israel:
All of them expert with the sword,
skilled in battle,
Each with his sword at his side
against danger in the watches of the night — NAB

Look, it is the chariot of Solomon with sixty of the mightiest men of his army surrounding it. They are all skilled swordsmen and experienced bodyguards. Each one has his sword upon his thigh to defend his king against any onslaught in the night — Tay

9. King Solomon made himself a chariot of the wood of Lebanon.
10. He made the pillars thereof of silver, the bottom thereof of gold, the covering of it of purple, the midst thereof being paved with love, for the daughters of Jerusalem.

King Solomon made himself a palanquin of the wood of Lebanon.
He made the pillars thereof of silver, the bottom thereof of gold, the seat of it of purple, the midst thereof being paved with love, from the daughters of Jerusalem — RV

King Solomon made himself a palanquin
Of the wood of Lebanon.
He made the pillars thereof of silver,
The top thereof of gold,
The seat of it of purple,
The inside thereof being inlaid with love,
From the daughters of Jerusalem — JPS

King Solomon made himself a palanquin
from the wood of Lebanon.
He made its posts of silver,
its back of gold, its seat of purple;
it was lovingly wrought within
by the daughters of Jerusalem — RSV

My king has made him a sedan,
of wood from Lebanon,
silver the feet of it,
golden the back of it,
purple the seat of it,
inlaid with ebony — Mof

The palanquin which King Solomon had made for himself
was of wood from Lebanon.
Its poles he had made of silver,
its head-rest of gold;
its seat was of purple stuff;
and its lining was of leather — NEB

For King Solomon made himself a chariot from the wood of Lebanon.
Its posts are silver, its canopy gold, the seat is purple; and the back is inlaid with these words: 'With love from the girls of Jerusalem!' — Tay

11. Go forth, O ye daughters of Zion, and behold king Solomon with the crown wherewith his mother crowned him in the day of his espousals, and in the day of the gladness of his heart.

Go forth, O ye daughters of Zion,
and behold king Solomon,
With the crown with which his mother crowned him
In the day of his marriage,
And in the day of the gladness of his heart — ABPS

Go forth and gaze, ye daughters of Zion, upon King Solomon, —
Wearing the crown wherewith his mother crowned him
In the day of his marriage, and
In the day of his heart gladness — Rhm

Come out, maidens of Sion, and see king Solomon wearing the crown that was his mother's gift to him on his day of triumph, the day of his betrothal — Knox

O daughters of Jerusalem, go forth,
and gaze upon King Solomon,
On the crown with which his mother crowned him
on the day of his nuptials,
on the day of his gladness of heart — AAT

Daughters of Zion,
come and see
King Solomon,
wearing the diadem with which his mother crowned him
on his wedding day,
on the day of his heart's joy — Jerus

Go forth, O you daughters of Zion,
and gaze upon king Solomon, upon the crown
with which his mother crowned him
on his wedding day,
the day of his gladness of heart — Ber

CHAPTER 4

1. Behold, thou art fair, my love; behold thou art fair; thou hast doves' eyes within thy locks: thy hair is as a flock of goats, that appear from mount Gilead.

Lo! thou art beautiful, my fair one,
Lo! thou art beautiful,
Thine eyes are doves from behind thy veil, —
Thy hair is like a flock of goats,

which are reclining on the sides of Mount Gilead — Rhm

Behold, thou art fair, my love; behold, thou art fair;
Thine eyes are as doves behind thy veil.
Thy hair is as a flock of goats,
That lie along the side of mount Gilead — ASV

Behold, thou art fair, my love;
behold, thou art fair;
Thine eyes are as doves behind thy veil;
Thy hair is as a flock of goats,
That trail down from mount Gilead — JPS

Behold, you are beautiful, my love,
behold, you are beautiful!
Your eyes are doves
behind your veil.
Your hair is like a flock of goats,
moving down the slopes of Gilead — RSV

Ah, you are beautiful, my beloved,
ah, you are beautiful!
Your eyes are doves
behind your veil.
Your hair is like a flock of goats
streaming down the mountain of Gilead — NAB

2. Thy teeth are like a flock of sheep that are even shorn, which came up from the washing; whereof every one bear twins, and none is barren among them.

3. Thy lips are like a thread of scarlet, and thy speech is comely: thy temples are like a piece of a pomegranate within thy locks.

Thy teeth are like the shorn flock
As they come up out of the washing pool;
All of them by twins,
And none is bereaved among them.
Thy lips are like a line of scarlet,
And thy speech is delicious.
As the blushing blossom of the pomegranate,
So are thy cheeks from under thy locks — Sprl

Thy teeth are like a flock of ewes that are newly shorn, which are come up from the washing; whereof every one hath twins, and none is bereaved among them.
Thy lips are like a thread of scarlet, and thy mouth is comely:
thy temples are like a piece of pomegranate behind thy veil — RV

Your teeth are like a flock of ewes ready for shearing,
that have come up from the washing,
All of which bear twins,
and none of which loses its young.
Your lips are like a thread of scarlet,
and your mouth is comely.
Your temple is like a slice of pomegranate,
behind your veil — AAT

Your teeth are as a flock of ewes, ready for the shearing,
all fresh from their washing.
They are in pairs, not one of them is missing.
Your lips are as a scarlet thread,
and your mouth is very comely.
Your cheeks are as halves of a pomegranate
gleaming behind your veil — Ber

your teeth are like shorn ewes
fresh from the dipping,
paired together in rows,
not one a-wanting;
your lips like a scarlet thread,
your mouth so delicious;
your cheeks like slices of pomegranate
behind your veil — Mof

4. Thy neck is like the tower of David builded for an armoury, whereon there hang a thousand bucklers, all shields of mighty men.

5. Thy two breasts are like two young roes that are twins, which feed among the lilies.

Thy neck is like the tower of David, which was built for an armoury: on it are hung a thousand shields; all the javelins of the worthies. Thy two breasts are like two twin fawns of a roe; which are browzing among lilies — Sept

Like the tower of David is thy neck, built for war, —
A thousand shields hung thereon,
All the equipment of heroes:
Thy two breasts are like two young roes, twins of a gazelle, —
Which pasture among lilies — Rhm

Thy neck is like the tower of David
Builded with turrets,
Whereon there hang a thousand shields,

All the armour of the mighty men.
Thy two breasts are like two fawns
That are twins of a gazelle,
Which feed among the lilies — JPS

Your neck beneath your veil is like the tower of David, built for an armory, whereon there hang a thousand bucklers, all quivers of valiant men. Your two breasts are like two young roes, twins of a gazelle, which feed among the lilies — Lam

Your neck is like David's tower
girt with battlements;
A thousand bucklers hang upon it,
all the shields of valiant men.
Your breasts are like twin fawns,
the young of a gazelle
that browse among the lilies — NAB

Your neck is stately as the tower of David, jeweled with a thousand heroes' shields. Your breasts are like twin fawns of a gazelle, feeding among the lilies — Tay

6. Until the day break, and the shadows flee away, I will get me to the mountain of myrrh, and to the hill of frankincense.

7. Thou art all fair, my love; there is no spot in thee.

Until the day be cool, and the shadows flee away,
I will get me to the mountain of myrrh,
And to the hill of frankincense.
Thou art all fair, my love;
And there is no spot in thee — ASV

Until the day breathes and the shadows flee,
I will get Me unto the mountain of myrrh,
And unto the hill of frankincense.
Thou art altogether fair, My Consort,
And there is no blemish in thee — Sprl

Until the day blows,
and the shadows flee,
I will betake myself to the mountain of myrrh,
and to the hill of frankincense.
You are altogether beautiful, my love,
and there is no blemish in you — AAT

Before the dawn-wind rises,
before the shadows flee,
I will go to the mountain of myrrh,
to the hill of frankincense.
You are wholly beautiful, my love,
and without blemish — Jerus

Yes, till the cool of the dawn, till the shadows depart,
I will hie me to your scented slopes,
your fragrant charms.
You are all fair, my dear,
you are spotless — Mof

Until the morning dawns and the shadows flee away, I will go to the mountain of myrrh and to the hill of frankincense. You are so beautiful, my love, in every part of you — Tay

8. Come with me from Lebanon, my spouse, with me from Lebanon: look from the top of Amana, from the top of Shenir and Hermon, from the lions' dens, from the mountains of the leopards.

9. Thou hast ravished my heart, my sister, my spouse; thou hast ravished my heart with one of thine eyes, with one chain of thy neck.

Come from Libanus, my spouse; come from Libanus. Thou canst come, yes come safely from the top of Pistis — from the summit of Sanir and Hermon — from lions dens, from the leopards mountains. Thou hast ravished my heart, my sister spouse: thou hast ravished my heart with a glance of thine eyes — with an endearing turn of thy neck — Sept

Come from Lebanon, O spouse,
Come from Lebanon, come thou in.
Look from the top of Amana,
From the top of Shenir and Hermon,
From the habitations of lions,
From the mountains of leopards.
Thou hast emboldened me, my sister-spouse,
Emboldened me with one of thine eyes,
With one chain of thy neck — YLT

With me from Lebanon, O bride,
With me from Lebanon shalt thou enter, —
Thou shalt look round from the top of Amana,
From the top of Senir and Hermon,
From the dens of lions,
From the mountains of leopards.
Thou hast encouraged me, my sister bride, —

Thou hast encouraged me with one glance of thine eyes,
With one ornament of thy neck — Rhm

With me from Lebanon, my bride,
with me from Lebanon, come!
Gaze from the summit of Amana,
from the top of Senir,
that is Hermon, from the dens of lions,
from the mountains of the panthers.
You have ravished my heart, my sister, my bride,
you have ravished my heart with one glance of your eyes,
with a single bead of your necklace — Ber

Come with me from Lebanon, my bride;
come with me from Lebanon.
Depart from the peak of Amana,
from the peak of Senir and Hermon,
from the dens of lions,
from the mountains of leopards.
You have ravished my heart, my sister, my bride,
you have ravished my heart with a glance of your eyes,
with one jewel of your necklace — RSV

Come from Lebanon, by bride;
come with me from Lebanon.
Hurry down from the top of Amana,
from Senir's top and Hermon's,
from the lion's lairs, and the hills the leopards haunt.
You have stolen my heart, my sister,
you have stolen it, my bride,
with one of your eyes, with one jewel of your necklace — NEB

10. How fair is thy love, my sister, my spouse! how much better is thy love than wine! and the smell of thine ointments than all spices!

11. Thy lips, O my spouse, drop as the honeycomb: honey and milk are under thy tongue; and the smell of thy garments is like the smell of Lebanon.

How delightful thy love-tokens, My Sister Spouse!
More delicious than wine thy love-tokens,
And the fragrance of thine ointments than all sweet spices!
Thy lips, O Spouse! distil the honey-comb;
Honey and milk from under thy tongue;
And the perfume of thy garments is like the smell of Lebanon — Sprl

How beautiful is thy love, my sister, bride!
How much better is thy love than wine!
And the smell of thine oils than all matter of spices!
Thy lips, O bride, drop honey;
Honey and milk are under thy tongue,
And the smell of thy garments is like the smell of Lebanon — ABPS

How fair is thy love, my sister! How much better is your love than wine, and the smell of your oils than any perfume!
Your lips are dropping honey; honey and milk are under your tongue; and the smell of your clothing is like the smell of Lebanon — Bas

How beautiful is your love,
my sister, my bride!
How much better is your love than wine,
and the fragrance of your ointments than all kinds of perfume!
As for your lips, my bride,
they distil sweetness;
Honey and milk are under your tongue,
and the fragrance of your garments is like the fragrance of Lebanon — AAT

How sweet is your love, my sister, my bride!
how much better is your love than wine,
and the fragrance of your oils than any spice!
Your lips distil nectar, my bride;
honey and milk are under your tongue;
the scent of your garments is like the scent of Lebanon — RSV

12. A garden inclosed is my sister, my spouse; a spring shut up, a fountain sealed.

13. Thy plants are an orchard of pome-

granates, with pleasant fruits; camphire, with spikenard.

A garden shut up is my sister, my bride;
A spring shut up, a fountain sealed.
Thy shoots are an orchard of pomegranates, with precious fruits;
Henna with spikenard plants — ASV

A garden barred is my sister bride,—
A garden barred, A fountain sealed:
Thy buddings forth are a paradise of pomegranates,
With precious fruits, —
Henna bushes with nard blossoms — Rhm

A garden enclosed is my sister, my bride; yea, a garden guarded, a fountain sealed.
Your shoots are an orchard of pomegranates, with pleasant fruits; henna-flower with spikenard — Lam

A garden you are, my sister, my bride, a garden walled in, a fountain well sealed;
A pomegranate orchard with precious fruits,
a garden of henna with spikenard — Ber

My own, my bride, a garden enclosed, a spring of water sealed secure!
Your charms are a pomegranate paradise —
with henna and roses — Mof

My darling bride is like a private garden, a spring that no one else can have, a fountain of my own. You are like a lovely orchard bearing precious fruit, with the rarest of perfumes — Tay

14. Spikenard and saffron; calamus and cinnamon, with all trees of frankincense; myrrh and aloes, with all the chief spices:

15. A fountain of gardens, a well of living waters, and streams from Lebanon.

spikenard and saffron, sweet cane and cinnamon; with all kinds of trees of incense — myrrh, aloth with all the principal spices. A garden fountain and a well of living water, flowing with gentle murmurs from Libanus — Sept

nard and saffron,
calamus and cinnamon,
with all the incense-bearing trees;
myrrh and aloes,
with the subtlest odours.
Fountain that makes the gardens fertile,
well of living water,
streams flowing down from Lebanon —Jerus

Nard and saffron, calamus and cinnamon,
with all kinds of incense;
Myrrh and aloes,
with all the finest spices.
You are a garden fountain, a well of water
flowing fresh from Lebanon — NAB

nard and saffron, calamus and cinnamon, and perfume from every other incense tree; as well as myrrh and aloes, and every other lovely spice. You are a garden fountain, a well of living water, refreshing as the streams from the Lebanon mountains — Tay

no lack there whether of spikenard or saffron, of calamus, cinnamon, or incense tree, of myrrh, aloes or any rarest perfume. A stream bordered with garden; water so fresh never came tumbling down from Lebanon — Knox

16. Awake, O north wind; and come, thou south; blow upon my garden, that the spices thereof may flow out. Let my beloved come into his garden and eat his pleasant fruits.

Awake, O north wind, and come in, thou south,
Fan my garden — its balsams will flow out, —
Let my beloved enter his garden,
And eat his precious fruits — Rhm

Be awake, O north wind; and come, O south, blowing on my garden, so that its spices may come out. Let my loved one come into his garden, and take of his good fruits — Bas

Awake, O north wind, and come, you south wind,
blow you both upon my garden,
that its fragrance may be wafted abroad.
Let my beloved come into his garden,
and eat its choice fruits; they are his — Ber

O north wind, waken,
O south wind, blow,
and breathe on my garden,
to waft out the perfume!"
Let my darling come into his garden,
let him taste the choice fruits that are his! — Mof

Awake, north wind, and come, south wind;
blow upon my garden that its perfumes may pour forth,
that my beloved may come to his garden
and enjoy its rare fruits — NEB

CHAPTER 5

1. I am come into my garden, my sister, my spouse: I have gathered my myrrh with my spice; I have eaten my honeycomb with my honey; I have drunk my wine with my milk: eat, O friends; drink, yea, drink abundantly, O beloved.

I am come into my garden, my sister, my bride:
I have gathered my myrrh with my spice;
I have eaten my honeycomb with my honey;
I have drunk my wine with my milk.
Eat, O friends;
Drink, yea, drink abundantly, O beloved — ASV

I am in My garden, My Sister Spouse!
I gather My myrrh with My spice!
I eat My honey-comb with My honey!
I drink My wine with My milk!
Eat, O my Friend! drink,
Yea, drink abundantly, O my Beloved! — Sprl

I have come to my garden, my sister, my bride,
To gather my myrrh with my spice,
To eat my honeycomb with my honey,
To drink my wine and my milk."
"Eat, friends, drink, and be drunk with love" — AAT

I have come to my garden, my sister, my bride;
I gather my myrrh and my spices,
I eat my honey and my sweetmeats,
I drink my wine and my milk.
Eat, friend; drink! Drink freely of love! — NAB

"My own, my bride, I come into my garden,
to gather me balsam and myrrh,
to eat my honey in the comb,
to drink my wine and milk." (Eat away, dear ones,
drink your fill of love!) — Mof

2. I sleep, but my heart waketh: it is the voice of my beloved that knocketh, saying, Open to me, my sister, my love, my dove, my undefiled: for my head is filled with dew, and my locks with the drops of the night.

3. I have put off my coat; how shall I put it on? I have washed my feet; how shall I defile them?

I was sleeping, but my heart was awake, —
The voice of my beloved — knocking!
Open to me, my sister, my fair one, my dove, my perfect one,
For my head is filled with dew,
My locks with the moisture of the night.
I have put off my tunic, oh how shall I put it on?
I have bathed my feet, oh how shall I soil them? — Rhm

I sleep, but my heart waketh;
Hark! my beloved knocketh:
'Open to me, my sister, my love, my dove, my undefiled;
For my head is filled with dew,
My locks with the drops of the night.'
I have put off my coat;
How shall I put it on?
I have washed my feet;
How shall I defile them? — JPS

I was asleep, but my heart was awake;
Listen! A sound! My lover is knocking!
He pleads, "Open to me, my sister, my love, my dove, my perfect one;
for my head is wet with dew, and my hair is drenched with the dew of night."
"I have put off my coat; why should I put it on again;
I have washed my feet; why should I soil them again?" — Ber

"I was asleep, but my fancy was alert;
hark! my beloved is knocking:

'Open to me, my sister, my love, my dove, my perfect one;
For my head is filled with dew,
my locks with the mist of the night.'
'I have taken off my garments;
why should I put them on again?
I have washed my feet;
why should I soil them?' — AAT

"One night as I was sleeping, my heart awakened in a dream. I heard the voice of my beloved; he was knocking at my bedroom door. 'Open to me, my darling, my lover, my lovely dove,' he said, 'for I have been out in the night and am covered with dew.'
But I said, 'I have disrobed. Shall I get dressed again? I have washed my feet, and should I get them soiled?' — Tay

4. My beloved put in his hand by the hole of the door, and my bowels were moved for him.

5. I rose up to open to my beloved; and my hands dropped with myrrh, and my fingers with sweet smelling myrrh, upon the handles of the lock.

My beloved put in his hand by the hole of the door,
And my heart was moved for him.
I rose up to open to my beloved;
And my hands dropped with myrrh,
And my fingers with liquid myrrh,
Upon the handles of the bolt — ASV

My Beloved thrust His hand through the latch,
And my bowels were perturbed on account of Him.
I rose up, I opened the door unto my Beloved,
And my hands dropped with myrrh,
Yea, with fragrant myrrh my fingers trickled down
Upon the handles of the lock — Sprl

My beloved put in his hand by the opening of the door, and my heart was moved for him.
I rose up to open to my beloved; and my hands dropped myrrh, yea, and my fingers dropped myrrh upon the handles of the lock — Lam

My lover put his hand through the opening;
my heart trembled within me,
and I grew faint when he spoke.
I rose to open to my lover, with my hands dripping myrrh:
With my fingers dripping choice myrrh
upon the fittings of the lock — NAB

Then my true love thrust his hand through the lattice, and I trembled inwardly at his touch. I rose up to let him in; but my hands dripped ever with myrrh; still with the choicest myrrh my fingers were slippery, as I caught the latch — Knox

6. I opened to my beloved; but my beloved had withdrawn himself, and was gone: my soul failed when he spake: I sought him, but I could not find him; I called him, but he gave me no answer.

I opened to my beloved,
But my beloved withdrew — he passed on,
My soul went forth when he spake,
I sought him, and found him not.
I called him, and he answered me not — YLT

I opened to my beloved; but my beloved had withdrawn himself, and was gone. My soul had failed me when he spake: I sought him, but I could not find him; I called him, but he gave me no answer — RV

I opened to my beloved,
but my beloved had turned away, had passed by.
My heart sank when he turned his back;
I sought him, but could not find him;
I called him, but he did not answer me — AAT

I opened to my Beloved,
but he had turned his back and gone!
My soul failed at his flight.
I sought him but I did not find him,
I called to him but he did not answer — Jerus

I opened to my beloved, but he was gone. My heart stopped. I searched for him but couldn't find him anywhere. I called to him, but there was no reply — Tay

7. The watchmen that went about the city found me, they smote me, they wounded me; the keepers of the walls took away my veil from me.

8. I charge you, O daughters of Jerusalem, if ye find my beloved, that ye tell him, that I am sick of love.

The watchmen who go about the city discovered me;
They smote me, they wounded me:
The watchmen of the walls lifted up my veil from off me!
I adjure you, O ye daughters of Jerusalem,
If ye find my own Beloved,
That ye tell Him I am wounded with love! — Sprl

The watchmen, making the round of the city, found me;
they struck me, they wounded me,
they stripped me of my mantle,
those guardians of the city walls.
I adjure you, O daughters of Jerusalem,
if you find my lover, that you tell him I am lovesick — Ber

The keepers who go about the town overtook me; they gave me blows and wounds; the keepers of the walls took away my veil from me.
I say to you, O daughters of Jerusalem, if you see my loved one, what will you say to him? That I am overcome with love — Bas

The watchmen met me on their rounds,
struck me and wounded me;
they robbed me of my mantle,
these warders of the walls.
O maidens of Jerusalem, I charge you,
if you find my darling,
tell my darling this,
that I am lovesick — Mof

The watchmen, going the rounds of the city, met me;
they struck me and wounded me;
the watchmen on the walls took away my cloak.
I charge you, daughters of Jerusalem,
if you find my beloved, will you not tell him
that I am faint with love? — NEB

9. What is thy beloved more than another beloved, O thou fairest among women? what is thy beloved more than another beloved, that thou dost so charge us?

What is thy beloved more than any other beloved,
Thou most beautiful among women?
What is thy beloved more than any other beloved,
That thus thou hast adjured us — Rhm

What makes your Beloved better than other lovers,
O loveliest of women?
What makes your Beloved better than other lovers,
to give us a charge like this — Jerus

Nay, but tell us, fairest of women, how shall we know this sweetheart of thine from another's? Why is he loved beyond all else, that thou art so urgent with us — Knox

How does your lover differ from any other,
O most beautiful among women?
How does your lover differ from any other,
that you adjure us so — NAB

"O woman of rare beauty, what is it about your loved one that is better than any other, that you command us this" — Tay

10. My beloved is white and ruddy, the chiefest among ten thousand.

11. His head is as the most fine gold; his locks are bushy, and black as a raven.

12. His eyes are as the eyes of doves by the rivers of waters, washed with milk, and fitly set:

My dear brother is white and ruddy, he is the chiefest among tens of thousands. His head is gold of Kephas; his flowing locks black as a raven. His eyes are like doves by streams of water — milk white doves sitting by streams — Sept

My beloved is clear and ruddy,
Conspicuous above a myriad!
His head is pure gold — fine gold,
His locks flowing dark as a raven.
His eyes as doves by streams of water,
Washing in milk, sitting in fulness — YLT

My beloved is fair and ruddy,
distinguished among myriads.
His head is fine gold,
his locks palm branches,
as black as a raven.
His eyes are like doves,
by streams of water,
Bathing in milk,
sitting by a pool — AAT

My lover is fair and ruddy,
the choicest among ten thousand.
His head is finest gold,
his locks are wavy, black as a raven.
His eyes are like doves beside brooks of water,
washed with milk and fitly set — Ber

My beloved is all radiant and ruddy,
distinguished among ten thousand.
His head is the finest gold;
his locks are wavy,
black as a raven.
His eyes are like doves
beside springs of water,
bathed in milk,
fitly set — RSV

Fresh and ruddy is my darling,
the pick of ten thousand;
his head is a crown of gold,
his curls black as the raven,
his eyes like doves upon the water,
bathed in milk, limpid and swimming — Mof

13. His cheeks are as a bed of spices, as sweet flowers: his lips like lilies, dropping sweet smelling myrrh.

14. His hands are as gold rings set with the beryl: his belly is as bright ivory overlaid with sapphires.

His cheeks are as a bed of spices,
As banks of sweet herbs:
His lips are as lilies, dropping liquid myrrh.
His hands are as rings of gold set with beryl:
His body is as ivory work overlaid with sapphires — ASV

His cheeks are like a bed of spices,
towers of perfumes;
His lips are lilies, dropping liquid myrrh;
His hands are cylinders of gold set with topaz;
His body is ivory work overlaid [with] sapphires — ABPS

His face is as beds of spices, giving out perfumes of every sort; his lips like lilies, dropping liquid myrrh.
His hands are as rings of gold ornamented with beryl-stones; his body is as a smooth plate of ivory covered with sapphires — Bas

His cheeks are as a bed of spices,
As banks of sweet herbs;
His lips are as lilies,
Dropping with flowing myrrh.
His hands are as rods of gold
Set with beryl;
His body is as polished ivory
Overlaid with sapphires — JPS

His cheeks are like beds of spices or chests full of perfumes;
his lips are lilies, and drop liquid myrrh;
his hands are golden rods set in topaz; his belly a plaque of ivory overlaid with lapis lazuli — NEB

15. His legs are as pillars of marble, set upon sockets of fine gold: his countenance is as Lebanon, excellent as the cedars.

16. His mouth is most sweet: yea, he is altogether lovely. This is my beloved, and this is my friend, O daughters of Jerusalem.

his legs, pillars of marble fixed on pedestals of gold: his countenance like Libanus, majestic as the cedars: his mouth is sweetness itself. He is altogether lovely. Such is my dear brother, and such is my love, O daughters of Jerusalem — Sept

His legs pillars of white marble,
founded on sockets of gold, —
His form like Lebanon, choice as cedars:
His mouth most sweet,
Yea altogether he is delightful, —
This is my beloved,
Yea this is my dear one, ye daughters of Jerusalem — Rhm

His legs are like pillars of fine Parian marble,
Set upon bases of pure gold!
His aspect as Lebanon! majestic as the cedars!
His speech is the very perfection of sweetness!
And Himself — the concentration of loveliness!
This is my Beloved, and this is my Consort,
O ye daughters of Jerusalem — Sprl

legs straight as marble columns, that stand in sockets of gold. Erect his stature as Lebanon itself, noble as Lebanon cedar. Oh, that sweet utterance! Nothing of him but awakes desire. Such is my true love, maidens of Jerusalem; such is the companion I have lost — Knox

His legs are alabaster columns,
set upon bases of gold.
His appearance is like Lebanon,
choice as the cedars.
His speech is most sweet,
and he is altogether desirable.
This is my beloved and this is my friend,
O daughters of Jerusalem — RSV

His legs are columns of marble resting on golden bases.
His stature is like the trees on Lebanon,
imposing as the cedars.
His mouth is sweetness itself;
he is all delight.
Such is my lover, and such my friend,
O daughters of Jerusalem — NAB

CHAPTER 6

1. **Whither is thy beloved gone, O thou fairest among women? whither is thy beloved turned aside? that we may seek him with thee.**

Whither is thy Beloved gone, O thou most elegant of women?
Whither hath Thy Beloved turned aside, that we may seek Him with thee? — Sprl

Whither has your loved one gone, thou fairest among women?
Where has he hidden himself?
We would seek him with you — Ber

And where has your darling gone,
O fairest of women?
Where has your darling wandered,
that we may look for him too? — Mof

Where has your lover gone,
O most beautiful among women?
Where has your lover gone
that we may seek him with you? — NAB

O rarest of beautiful women, where has your loved one gone? We will help you find him — Tay

2. **My beloved is gone down into his garden, to the beds of spices, to feed in the gardens, and to gather lilies.**

3. **I am my beloved's, and my beloved is mine: he feedeth among the lilies.**

My beloved went down to his garden,
To the beds of the spice,
To delight himself in the gardens, and to gather lilies.
I am my beloved's, and my beloved is mine,
Who is delighting himself among the lilies — YLT

Where should he be, my true love, but among the spices; where but in his garden, gathering the lilies? All mine, my true love, and I all his; ever he would choose the lilies for his pasture-ground — Knox

My beloved is gone down to his garden,
To the beds of balsam, —
To pasture in the gardens,
And to gather lilies,
I am my beloved's
And my beloved is mine,
He that pastureth among lilies — Rhm

My beloved has gone down to his garden,
to the beds of spices,
to pasture his flock in the gardens,
and to gather lilies.
I am my beloved's and my beloved is mine;
he pastures his flock among the lilies — RSV

My beloved has gone down to his garden,
to the beds of spices,
To pasture his flock in the gardens,
and gather hyacinths.
I belong to my beloved, and my beloved to me,
who pastures his flock among the hyacinths — AAT

4. **Thou art beautiful, O my love, as Tirzah, comely as Jerusalem, terrible as an army with banners.**

5. **Turn away thine eyes from me, for they have overcome me: thy hair is as a flock of goats that appear from Gilead:**

Thou my consort, art beautiful as Terzah; comely as Jerusalem; dazzling as embattled hosts! Turn thine eyes aside from me for they have transported me. Thy hair is like a flock of goats which are seen on mount Galaad — Sept

Thou art fair, O my love, as Tirzah,
Comely as Jerusalem,
Terrible as an army with banners.
Turn away thine eyes from me,
For they have overcome me.
Thy hair is as a flock of goats,
That lie along the side of Gilead — ASV

O My consort, thou art lovely as Tirzah!
Beautiful as Jerusalem! Dazzling as bannered hosts!
Turn away thine eyes from Me,
For they have overpowered Me!
Thy tresses resemble a flock of goats,
Which glisten upon the Mount Gilead — Sprl

You are beautiful, my love, beautiful as Tirzah,
lovely as Jerusalem;
captivating as an army with banners.
Turn your eyes away from me, for they overcome me;
Your hair is like a flock of goats
moving down the trail of Gilead — Ber

You are beautiful, my dearest, as Tirzah,
lovely as Jerusalem.
Turn your eyes away from me;
they dazzle me.
Your hair is like a flock of goats
streaming down Mount Gilead — NEB

6. Thy teeth are as a flock of sheep which go up from the washing, whereof every one beareth twins, and there is not one barren among them.

7. As a piece of pomegranate are thy temples within thy locks.

Thy teeth are like a flock of ewes,
Which are come up from the washing;
Whereof all are paired,
And none faileth among them.
Thy temples are like a pomegranate split open
Behind thy veil — JPS

Thy teeth are like a flock of ewes,
which are come up from the washing;
whereof every one hath twins, and none is bereaved among them.
Thy temples are like a piece of pomegranate behind thy veil — RV

Your teeth are a flock of ewes,
that have come up from the washing,
All of which bear twins,
and none of which loses its young.
Your temple is like a slice of pomegranate, behind your veil — AAT

Your teeth are like a flock of sheep
as they come up from the washing.
Each one has its twin,
not one unpaired with another.
Your cheeks, behind your veil,
are halves of pomegranate — Jerus

8. There are threescore queens, and fourscore concubines, and virgins without number.

9. My dove, my undefiled is but one; she is the only one of her mother, she is the choice one of her that bare her. The daughters saw her, and blessed her; yea, the queens and the concubines, and they praised her.

There are sixty queens,
And eighty concubines,
And virgins without number.
My dove, my perfect one, is [but] one;
She is the only one of her mother;
She is the choice one of her that bore her.
The daughters saw her, and called her blessed,
The queens and the concubines, and they praised her — ABPS

There are sixty queens and eighty concubines, and virgins without number: one is my dove, my consecrated one. One is her mother's only child — the darling of her who bore her. Daughters viewed her — nay queens and even concubines will hail her happy and thus extoll her — Sept

In My pavilion there are threescore queens
And fourscore concubines, And virgins without number:
But My dove, my perfect one; an only one is she!
She is an only one of her mother;
She is the choice one of her that bare her!
The daughters saw her, and they blessed her!
The queens and the concubines, and they praised her — Sprl

Threescore are the queens,
And fourscore are the concubines,—

And virgins there are without number.
One alone is my dove, my perfect one,
One alone was she to her mother,
Pure was she to her that bare her, —
The daughters have seen her and pronounced her happy,
Queens and concubines and they have praised her — Rhm

Sixty queens there are and eighty concubines, and harem daughters beyond number;
My dove, my undefiled, stands out alone;
she was an only one to her mother,
first choice of her who bore her;
The daughters saw her and called her happy,
the queens and concubines, too,
and thus they praised her — Ber

There may be sixty princesses,
eighty concubines, and young women past counting,
but there is one alone, my dove, my perfect one,
her mother's only child,
devoted to the mother who bore her;
young girls see her and call her happy,
princesses and concubines praise her — NEB

10. Who is she that looketh forth as the morning, fair as the moon, clear as the sun, and terrible as an army with banners?

Who is this that is looking forth as morning,
Fair as the moon — clear as the sun,
Awe-inspiring as bannered hosts? — YLT

Who is this that looketh forth like the dawn,
Beautiful as the moon,
Pure as the sun,
Majestic as bannered hosts? — Rhm

Who is she, looking down as the morning light, fair as the moon, clear as the sun, who is to be feared like an army with flags? — Bas

Who is this, glowing like the dawn,
fair as the moon,
clear as the sun,
overawing like an army with banners? — Mof

Who is this that comes forth like the dawn,
as beautiful as the moon, as resplendent as the sun,
as awe-inspiring as bannered troops? — NAB

11. I went down into the garden of nuts to see the fruits of the valley, and to see whether the vine flourished, and the pomegranates budded.

12. Or ever I was aware, my soul made me like the chariots of Amminadib.[3]

I went down into the garden of nuts,
To see the green plants of the valley,
To see whether the vine budded,
And the pomegranates were in flower.
Before I was aware, my soul set me
Among the chariots of my princely people — ASV

I went down to see the nut garden
to see the green plants of the valley;
to see whether the vines already had budded,
and the pomegranates had put forth their bloom.
Ere I was aware, my soul's fancy seated me in a princely chariot of my people — Ber

I went down to the nut orchard,
to look at the blossoms of the valley,
to see whether the vines had budded,
whether the pomegranates were in bloom.
Before I was aware, my fancy set me
in a chariot beside my prince — RSV

I went down to the nut garden,
to look at the verdure of the valley,
To see whether the grapevine had budded,
whether the pomegranates had bloomed.
Before I knew it, my fancy set me
in the chariot of my ardent lover — AAT

I went down into the orchard of nuts
and out to the valley to see the springtime there, to see whether the grapevines were budding or the pomegranates were blossoming yet.
Before I realized it I was stricken

[3]The Hebrew of verse 12 is very difficult, and the versions and translations all struggle with it.

with terrible homesickness and wanted to be back among my own people — Tay

13. **Return, return, O Shulamite; return, return, that we may look upon thee. What will ye see in the Shulamite? As it were the company of two armies.**

Return, return, O Shulamite!
Return, return, that we may gaze upon thee!
What is there to gaze at in the Shulamite? Like the triumphant exultation of two armies! — Sprl

Return, return, O Shulammite; return, return, that we may look upon thee.
Why will ye look upon the Shulammite, as upon the dance of Mahanaim? — RV

"Maid of Shulem, turn, ah turn, turn, ah turn, that we may see you."
And what would you see in the maid of Shulem?
"We would see her in the sword-dance" — Mof

Return, return, O Shulammite;
Return, return, that we may look upon thee.
What will ye see in the Shulammite?
As it were a dance of two companies — JPS

Return, return, O maid of Shulam, return, return, that we may gaze on you!
Why do you gaze on the maid of Shulam
dancing as though between two rows of dancers? — Jerus

Come back, maid of Sulam, come back; let us feast our eyes on thee.
Maid of Sulam, come back, come back!
What can the woman of Sulam give you to feast your eyes on, if it be not the dance of the Two Camps — Knox

CHAPTER 7

1. **How beautiful are thy feet with shoes, O prince's daughter! the joints of thy thighs are like jewels, the work of the hands of a cunning workman.**
2. **Thy navel is like a round goblet, which wanteth not liquor: thy belly is like a heap of wheat set about with lilies.**

How beautiful are thy feet in sandals,
O prince's daughter!
Thy rounded thighs are like jewels,
The work of the hands of a skilful workman.
Thy body is like a round goblet,
Wherein no mingled wine is wanting:
Thy waist is like a heap of wheat
Set about with lilies — ASV

How beautiful are thy feet in sandals,
O daughter of a noble, —
The curvings of thy hips are like ornaments wrought by the hands of a skilled workman:
Thy navel is a round bowl, may it not lack spiced wine!
Thy body a heap of wheat fenced about with lilies— Rhm

How graceful are your feet in sandals,
O queenly maiden!
Your rounded thighs are like jewels,
the work of a master hand.
Your navel is a rounded bowl
that never lacks mixed wine.
Your belly is a heap of wheat,
encircled with lilies — RSV

How beautiful are your sandalled feet,
O prince's daughter!
The curves of your thighs are like jewels,
the work of a skilled craftsman.
Your navel is a rounded goblet
that never shall want for spiced wine.
Your belly is a heap of wheat
fenced in by lilies — NEB

How neatly you trip it,
O princess mine,
your thighs are swaying like links of a chain
that a master-hand has molded;
your waist is round as a goblet
(ever be it filled!);
your body a bundle of wheat encircled by lilies — Mof

3. **Thy two breasts are like two young roes that are twins.**
4. **Thy neck is as a tower of ivory; thine eyes like the fishpools in Heshbon, by the gate of Bath-rabbim: thy nose is as the tower of Lebanon which looketh toward Damascus.**

Thy two breasts are like two fawns
That are twins of a gazelle.
Thy neck is as a tower of ivory,
Thine eyes as the pools in Heshbon,
By the gate of Bath-rabbim;
Thy nose is like the tower of Lebanon
Which looketh toward Damascus — JPS

Your two breasts are like two young roes of the same birth.
Your neck is as a tower of ivory; your eyes like the waters in Heshbon, by the doorway of Bath-rabbim; your nose is as the tower on Lebanon looking over Damascus — Bas

Your breasts are as two fawns, the twins of a gazelle;
Your neck is as a tower of ivory, your eyes as pools in Heshbon by the gate Bath-rabbim.
Your nose is as a tower of Lebanon, looking down upon Damascus — Ber

Your two breasts are like two fawns, twin fawns of a gazelle.
Your neck is like a tower of ivory.
Your eyes are the pools in Heshbon, beside the gate of the crowded city.
Your nose is like towering Lebanon that looks towards Damascus — NEB

Graceful thy breasts as two fawns of the gazelle. Thy neck rising proudly like a tower, but all of ivory; deep, deep thy eyes, like those pools at Hesebon, under Beth-rabbim Gate; thy nose imperious as the keep that frowns on Damascus from the hill-side — Knox

5. Thine head upon thee is like Carmel, and the hair of thine head like purple; the king is held in the galleries.

6. How fair and how pleasant art thou, O love, for delights!

Thy head upon thee as Carmel,
And the locks of thy head as purple,
The king is bound with the flowings!
How fair and how pleasant hast thou been,
O love, in delights — YLT

Thy rising head-dress on thee, like Carmel,
With the tresses of thy head adorned with purple ribbands:
The King is held captive in these plaitings!
How beautiful and how sweet
Art thou, O love, for delights! — Sprl

Thy head upon thee is like Carmel,
And the hair of thy head like purple;
The king is held captive in the tresses thereof.
How fair and how pleasant art thou,
O love, for delights — ASV

Thy head erect as Carmel, bright as royal purple the braided ripples of thy hair. How graceful thou art, dear maiden, how fair, how dainty — Knox

Your head rises like Carmel;
your hair is like draperies of purple;
a king is held captive in its tresses.
How beautiful you are, how pleasing,
my love, my delight — NAB

As Mount Carmel crowns the mountains, so your hair is your crown.
The king is held captive in your queenly tresses.
Oh, how delightful you are; how pleasant, O love, for utter delight — Tay

7. This thy stature is like to a palm tree, and thy breasts to clusters of grapes.

8. I said, I will go up to the palm tree, I will take hold of the boughs thereof: now also thy breasts shall be as clusters of the vine, and the smell of thy nose like apples;

This thy stature is like to a palm-tree,
And thy breasts are like clusters:
I said,
I will ascend the palm-tree,
I will lay hold of its fruit stalks —
Oh then, let thy breasts, I pray thee, be like vine-clusters,
And the fragrance of thy nose like apples — Rhm

Your very stature is like a palm tree, and your breasts like clusters.
I said, 'Let me climb the palm tree, let me take hold of its clusters,
And let your breasts be like clusters of the vine,
and the breath of your nose like apples — AAT

This thy stature is like to a palm-tree,
And thy breasts to its clusters.

I said, I will climb up into the palm-tree,
I will take hold of the branches thereof:
Let thy breasts be as clusters of the vine,
And the smell of thy breath like apples — ASV

Your stature itself is a stately palm,
your breasts are as clusters of grapes.
I said, I will climb into my palm tree,
I will take hold of the branches of it.
Your breasts shall be as clusters of vines, the fragrance of your breath as of apples — Ber

You stand there straight as a palm,
with breasts like clusters of fruit;
methinks I will climb that palm,
taking hold of the boughs!
Oh may your breasts be clusters of fruit,
and your breath sweet as an apple — Mof

9. And the roof of thy mouth like the best wine for my beloved, that goeth down sweetly, causing the lips of those that are asleep to speak.

And thy mouth like the best wine, that goeth down smoothly for my beloved, gliding through the lips of those that are asleep — RV

Surely the speech of Thy mouth is like the best wine of my Beloved's,
Which travelleth sweetly.
It might make the very lips of the sleeping to speak — Sprl

And your palate is like the best wine for my beloved, that goes down in the mouth of my beloved and makes me move my lips and my teeth — Lam

And the roof of your mouth like good wine flowing down smoothly for my loved one, moving gently over my lips and my teeth — Bas

and your kisses like the best wine
that goes down smoothly,
gliding over lips and teeth — RSV

And your mouth like an excellent wine —
that flows smoothly for my lover,
spreading over the lips and the teeth — NAB

10. I am my beloved's, and his desire is toward me.

11. Come, my beloved, let us go forth into the field; let us lodge in the villages.

I am my beloved's,
And unto me is his longing.
Come, my beloved,
Let us go forth into the country,
Let us stay the night in the villages — Rhm

I belong to my lover
and for me he yearns.
Come, my lover, let us go forth to the fields
and spend the night among the villages — NAB

I am my Beloved's
and his desire is for me.
Come, my Beloved,
let us go to the fields.
We will spend the night in the villages — Jerus

I am my beloved's and I am the one he desires.
Come, my beloved, let us go out into the fields and stay in the villages — Tay

I belong to my beloved,
and his longing is for me.
Come, my beloved, let us go into the field,
let us rest among the henna flowers — AAT

I am my beloved's, his longing is all for me.
Come, my beloved, let us go out into the fields
to lie among the henna-bushes — NEB

12. Let us get up early to the vineyards; let us see if the vine flourish, whether the tender grape appear, and the pomegranates bud forth: there will I give thee my loves.

Let us rise early to the vineyards,
Let us see whether the vine flourish,
If the tender grape appears, and the pomegranates bud forth:
There will I give Thee my love-tokens — Sprl

Let us get up early to the vineyards,
Let us see whether the vine hath burst forth,
The blossom hath opened,
The pomegranates have bloomed, —
There will I give my caresses to thee — Rhm

Let us get up early to the vineyard; let us see if the vine has budded, whether the tender shoots appear, and the pomegranates are in bloom; there will I give you my breasts — Lam

Let us get up early to the vineyards;
Let us see whether the vine hath budded,
And its blossom is open,
And the pomegranates are in flower:
There will I give thee my love — ASV

Let us rise and go early to the vineyards;
let us see whether the vines have now budded,
whether the blossoms have already opened
and the pomegranates are come into flower;
there will I give you my love — Ber

Dawn shall find us in the vineyard, looking to see what flowers the vine has, and whether they are growing into fruit; whether pomegranates are in blossom. And there thou shalt be master of my love — Knox

13. The mandrakes give a smell, and at our gates are all manner of pleasant fruits, new and old, which I have laid up for thee, O my beloved.

The mandrakes have given fragrance,
And at our openings all pleasant things,
New, yea, old, my beloved, I laid up for thee — YLT

The mandrakes give forth fragrance, and at our doors are all manner of precious fruits, new and old, which I have laid up for thee, O my beloved — RV

The mandrakes give forth fragrance,
And over our doors are all manner of precious fruits, new and old,
Which I have laid up for thee, O my beloved — ABPS

The mandrakes have shed a fragrance: and in our hoards are all manner of delicious fruits, newly gathered as well as old. For thee, my dear brother I have kept them — Sept

The mandrakes give forth fragrance, and at our doors are all choice fruits;
Both fresh and mellowed fruits, my lover,
I have kept in store for you — NAB

There the mandrakes give forth their fragrance and the rarest fruits are at our doors, the new as well as old, for I have stored them up for my beloved — Tay

CHAPTER 8

1. O that thou wert as my brother, that sucked the breasts of my mother! when I should find thee without, I would kiss thee; yea, I should not be despised.

Oh that thou hadst been a very brother to me,
Who had sucked the breasts of my own mother, —
Had I found thee without I had kissed thee,
Yea folk would not have despised me — Rhm

Would that thou wert my brother, nursed at my own mother's breast! Then I could meet thee in the open street and kiss thee, and earn no contemptuous looks — Knox

O that you were really my brother,
who had sucked the breasts of my mother,
That I might find you in the street and kiss you,
and none then despise me — AAT

Oh, that you were as my brother,
who nursed at the breast of my mother!
Should I find you outside in the open,
I would kiss you, and no one would scorn me — Ber

Ah, why are you not my brother,
nursed at my mother's breast!
Then if I met you out of doors, I could kiss you
without people thinking ill of me — Jerus

Oh, if only you were my brother; then I could kiss you no matter who was watching, and no one would laugh at me — Tay

2. I would lead thee, and bring thee into my mother's house, who would instruct me: I would cause thee to drink of spiced wine of the juice of my pomegranate.

I lead thee, I bring thee in unto my mother's house,
She doth teach me,
I cause thee to drink of the perfumed wine,
Of the juice of my pomegranate — YLT

I would conduct Thee, I would bring Thee
Unto the house of my mother,
Who would instruct me.
I would give unto Thee aromatic wine,
Flavoured with the fresh juice of my pomegranate — Sprl

I should lead you and bring you to the house of my mother,
and she would instruct me;
I should give you some spiced wine to drink,
also the juice of my pomegranate — Ber

I would take you by the hand into my mother's house, and she would be my teacher. I would give you drink of spiced wine, drink of the pomegranate — Bas

To my mother's house I will lead thee, my captive; there thou shalt teach me my lessons, and I will give thee spiced wine to drink, fresh brewed from my pomegranates — Knox

I would lead you, bring you in to the home of my mother.
There you would teach me to give you
spiced wine to drink, and pomegranate juice — NAB

3. His left hand should be under my head, and his right hand should embrace me.

4. I charge you, O daughters of Jerusalem, that ye stir not up, nor awake my love, until he please.

His left hand should be under my head,
And his right hand should embrace me.
I adjure you, O daughters of Jerusalem,
Why do ye stir up, or awaken love,
Until it please — ABPS

His left hand under my head
Then his right hand embraced me.
I adjure you, O ye daughters of Jerusalem, —
Why will ye wake and why will ye arouse the dear love until she please — Rhm

His left hand would be under my head, and his right hand about me.
I say to you, O daughters of Jerusalem, do not let love be moved till it is ready — Bas

His left hand is under my head
and his right arm embraces me.
I adjure you, daughters of Jerusalem,
by the gazelles and hinds of the field,
Do not arouse, do not stir up love,
before its own time — NAB

His left arm is under my head
and his right embraces me.
I charge you,
daughters of Jerusalem,
not to stir my love, nor rouse it,
until it please to awake — Jerus

5. Who is this that cometh up from the wilderness, leaning upon her beloved? I raised thee up under the apple tree: there thy mother brought thee forth; there she brought thee forth that bare thee.

Who is this coming from the wilderness,
Hasting herself for her beloved?
Under the citron-tree I have waked thee,
There did thy mother pledge thee,
There she gave a pledge that bare thee — YLT

Who is this who cometh up out of the wilderness,
Leaning upon her Beloved?
Under the citron-tree I urged thee:
There thy mother delivered thee over to Me;
There she who bare thee delivered thee unto Me — Sprl

Who is this that cometh up from the wilderness,
Leaning upon her beloved?
Under the apple-tree I awakened thee:

There thy mother was in travail with thee,
There was she in travail that brought thee forth — ASV

(Who is this, coming up from the country,
leaning on her darling?)
I awoke you there, under the apple-tree,
just where you were swaddled,
a babe, just there, by your mother — Mof

Who is this coming up from the wilderness
leaning on her beloved?
Under the apricot-tree I roused you,
there where your mother was in labour with you,
there where she who bore you was in labour — NEB

Who is this coming up from the desert,
leaning on her beloved?
Under the apple tree where your mother gave birth to you in her travail, there I awakened your love — Tay

6. Set me as a seal upon thine heart, as a seal upon thine arm: for love is strong as death; jealousy is cruel as the grave: the coals thereof are coals of fire, which hath a most vehement flame.

Set me as a seal upon thine heart, as a seal upon thine arm: for love is strong as death; jealousy is cruel as the grave: the flashes thereof are flashes of fire, a very flame of the LORD — RV

Set me as a seal upon thy heart,
As a seal upon thine arm,
For mighty as death is love,
Exacting as hades is jealousy, —
The flames thereof are flames of fire,
The flash of Yah — Rhm

Set me as a seal upon your heart, as a seal upon your arm; for love is strong as death; desire is cruel as Sheol; its flashes are flashes of fire and flame — Lam

Place me like a seal upon your heart,
like a seal upon your arm;
For love is as mighty as death,
as strong as Sheol;
As for passion, its bolts are bolts of fire,
furious flames — AAT

Set me like a seal on your heart,
like a seal on your arm.
For love is strong as Death,
jealousy as relentless as Sheol.
The flash of it is a flash of fire,
a flame of Yahweh himself — Jerus

Wear me as a seal close to your heart,
wear me like a ring upon your hand;
for love is strong as death itself,
and passion masters like the grave,
its flashes burn like flame,
true lightning-flashes — Mof

7. Many waters cannot quench love, neither can the floods drown it: if a man would give all the substance of his house for love, it would utterly be contemned.

Much water cannot quench love; nor can floods drown it. Though a man give all his substance for love, he may be thoroughly despised — Sept

Many waters cannot quench love,
Nor rivers drown it.
If a man would give all the substance of his house for love,
He would be utterly despised — ABPS

Many waters cannot extinguish love,
nor can rivers drown it.
If a man should offer for love all the wealth of his house,
it would be scornfully refused — Ber

Much water may not put out love, or the deep waters overcome it: if a man would give all the substance of his house for love, it would be judged a price not great enough — Bas

Deep waters cannot quench love,
nor floods sweep it away.
Were one to offer all he owns to purchase love,
he would be roundly mocked — NAB

8. We have a little sister, and she hath no breasts: what shall we do for our sister in the day when she shall be spoken for?

9. If she be a wall, we will build upon her a palace of silver: and if she be a door, we will enclose her with boards of cedar.

We have a younger sister,
And her bosom is not matured:
What shall we do for our sister

In the day when she shall be demanded in marriage?
If she be a wall, we will build upon her turrets of silver,
And if she be a doorway, we will fortify her with boarding of cedar wood — Sprl

We have a little sister,
and she has no breasts.
What shall we do for our sister,
on the day when she is spoken for?
If she is a wall,
we will build upon her a battlement of silver;
but if she is a door,
we will enclose her with boards of cedar — RSV

We have a little sister whose breasts have not developed; what shall we do for our sister in the day when they shall seek her hand?
If she be a wall, we will build upon her an upper chamber of silver; and if she be a door, we will enclose her with boards of silver — Lam

Our sister is little
and she has no breasts as yet.
What shall we do for our sister
when her courtship begins?
If she is a wall,
we will build upon it a silver parapet;
If she is a door,
we will reinforce it with a cedar plank — NAB

"We have a young sister,
and she has no breasts yet; but what shall we do with our sister,
when her wooers come?
If she holds out like a wall,
we will adorn her with silver for dowry;
if she gives way to lovers like a door,
then we will plank her up — Mof

10. I am a wall, and my breasts like towers: then was I in his eyes as one that found favor.

I am a wall, and my breasts like the towers thereof: then was I in his eyes as one that found peace — RV

I was a wall, and my breasts like towers, —
Then became I in his eyes one who did indeed find good content — Rhm

If I were a wall,
and my breasts like towers,
Then would I be in his eyes,
like one who finds favor — AAT

I am a wall and my breasts are like towers;
so in his eyes I am as one who brings contentment — NEB

And I, I am a wall; impregnable this breast as a fortress; and the man who claimed me found in me a bringer of content — Knox

11. Solomon had a vineyard at Baal-hamon; he let out the vineyard unto keepers; every one for the fruit thereof was to bring a thousand pieces of silver.

12. My vineyard, which is mine, is before me: thou, O Solomon, must have a thousand, and those that keep the fruit thereof two hundred.

Solomon had a vineyard at Baal-hamon;
he let out the vineyard to keepers;
each one was to bring for its fruit a thousand pieces of silver.
My vineyard, my very own, is for myself;
you, O Solomon, may have the thousand,
and the keepers of the fruit two hundred — RSV

Solomon had a vineyard, and its fruits were abundant; he let out the vineyard to keepers; a man offered for its fruits a thousand pieces of silver.
My vineyard which is mine is before me; a thousand pieces of silver are yours, O Solomon, and two hundred for the keepers of the fruit — Lam

Solomon had a vineyard in Baal-hamon;
he entrusted the vineyard to keepers.
Each man was to bring for his share of the fruit
a thousand pieces of silver.
My vineyard, my own, lies before me.
The thousand is yours, O Solomon,
and two hundred each to those keeping the fruit — Ber

Solomon had a vineyard at Baal-hamon. He entrusted it to overseers, and each one was to pay him the value of its produce, a thousand shekels of silver. But I look after my own vineyard myself. You, Solomon, may have your thousand shekels, and those who oversee its produce their two hundred — Jerus

Solomon had a vineyard at Baal-Hamon; and when he gave the care of it to vine-dressers, each of these must pay a thousand silver pieces for the revenue of it.

A vineyard I have of my own, here at my side; keep thy thousand pieces, Solomon, and let each vine-dresser have his two hundred; not mine to grudge them — Knox

Solomon had a vineyard at Baal-hamon;
he gave over the vineyard to caretakers.
For its fruit one would have to pay a thousand silver pieces.
My own vineyard is at my own disposal;
the thousand pieces are for you, O Solomon,
and two hundred for the caretakers of its fruit — NAB

13. Thou that dwellest in the gardens, the companions hearken to thy voice: cause me to hear it.

14. Make haste, my beloved, and be thou like to a roe or to a young hart upon the mountains of spices.

Thou that dwellest in the gardens,
The companions hearken for thy voice:
'Cause me to hear it.'
Make haste, my beloved,
And be thou like to a gazelle or to a young hart,
Upon the mountains of spices — JPS

Thou that dwellest in the gardens,
The companions are listening for thy voice;
Let me hear it.
Flee, my beloved,
And be like a gazelle,
Or a young hart,
Upon the mountains of spices — ABPS

O thou who dwellest in the gardens!
The companions are attent unto thy call,
Let me also hear thy voice!
Make haste, my Beloved!
And resemble thou the antelope, or the fawn of the deer,
Upon the mountain clouds of heaven — Sprl

O garden-dweller,
my friends are listening for your voice,
let me hear it!
Be swift, my lover,
like a gazelle or a young stag
on the mountains of spices — NAB

O you who dwell in my gardens,
your companions listening to your voice,
make me hear it, too.
Come quickly, my lover, beloved,
and be like a gazelle,
or like a young hart upon mountains of spices — Ber

My comrades hear your voice,
girl in the garden haunt:
ah, let me hear it too! —
"Hasten, then, O my darling;
play like a roe or a hart
upon my scented slopes!" — Mof